W9-CNG-946

The Serrane Guide

Stamp Forgeries
of the World to 1926

by Fernand Serrane

Translated by Cortland Eyer

With a new bibliography
and introduction by Varro E. Tyler

An American Philatelic Society Handbook
Published by the
American Philatelic Society
P.O. Box 8000
State College, Pennsylvania 16803

Originally published as *I: Vade-Mecum du spécialiste en timbres-poste d'Europe*
©1927 L'Eclaireur de Nice Press, Nice, France
and
II: Vade-Mecum du spécialiste en timbres-poste hors d'Europe
©1929 Générale du Sud-ouest (J. Castanet), Bergerac, France

ISBN 0-933580-16-9
©1998 by the American Philatelic Society
All rights reserved.

Printed in the United States of America by
CONSOLIDATED GRAPHIC COMMUNICATIONS
A Division of CHAMPION INDUSTRIES, INC.
Blanchard, Pennsylvania

Table of Contents

About the Author and the Translator

Fernand Serrane

Fernand Serrane (1880–1932) — author of the classic masterworks *Vade-Mecum du spécialiste-expert en timbres-poste d'Europe* (Volume 1, 1927) and *Vade-Mecum du spécialiste-expert en timbres-poste hors d'Europe* (Volume 2, 1929) — was a native of Belgium. He gained his philatelic fame in France, where he was a prolific and popular author. A contemporary said of him, "He loved stamps with a passion and studied them with scrupulous attention. He was a formidable adversary for forgers."

Serrane joined the American Philatelic Society in 1925 at age 45, a year before the first volume of his classic *Vade-Mecum* was published in France. The references he listed on his application were two of the most prominent names in French philately: Theodore Champion and Louis Yvert. On that same application, Serrane, an avid fisherman, listed his occupation as "man of letters."

The translator of Serrane's *Vade-Mecum,* Dr. Cortland Eyer (1906–89), was professor emeritus of Romance languages at the Pennsylvania State University, State College, Pennsylvania. He retired in 1970 after a distinguished teaching career at that institution and at Northwestern, where he received his M.A. and Ph.D. degrees in 1929 and 1935, respectively. He earned his B.A. from the University of Delaware in 1927 and was elected to Phi Kappa Phi and Phi Beta Kappa.

His translation, commissioned by APS members Joseph D. Hahn and the late Lt. Col. Joseph M. Sousa and James H. Beal, not only reflects years of exacting training in the French language, but also his own longtime interest in philately. The project took four years (1971–74), during which time Dr. Eyer made several trips — to New York and Washington and even one to Paris to visit the Bibliothéque National in search of a book — meticulously checking every reference made by Serrane.

Dr. Cortland Eyer

Introduction to
The Serrane Guide

by Varro E. Tyler

Forgeries of desirable collectibles have been common for more than 2,000 years. Even before the time of Cicero (106–43 B.C.E.) fictitious masterpieces of painting and sculpture signed with the forged names of noted artists were found on the Roman market. Since that time almost all conceivable objects of value, including antiquities, ceramics, coins, documents, furniture, jewelry, paintings, scientific instruments, and, of course, postage stamps, have been imitated, primarily to deceive collectors.

For the uninitiated, the magnitude of illicit production is almost inconceivable. During his entire lifetime, Jean-Baptiste Camille Corot painted only a few hundred pictures, but during a recent twenty-year period, 103,000 productions attributed to him were imported into the United States. In 1995, the U.S. Postal Inspection Service auctioned off 12,000 fake Salvador Dali prints and sculptures seized ten years previously from the Center Art Galleries–Hawaii.

Literature dealing with forgeries is as varied as the counterfeits themselves. When the Minneapolis Institute of Arts mounted an extensive display of some artistic frauds from its collection in 1973, it published an extensive hardbound book, *Fakes and Forgeries,* describing the 310 exhibits in detail. A beautifully illustrated eighty-page book by Raymond Li devoted to *The Art of Imitation in Chinese Snuff Bottles* appeared in Hong Kong in 1985. A monthly journal, *Antique & Collectors Reproduction News,* describing methods of detection of forgeries of all types of antiques, began its seventh year of publication in 1998.

Just fourteen years after the appearance of the first postage stamp in 1840, counterfeits of stamps intended to defraud the government appeared in Spain. Then in 1856, an Antwerp merchant whose name is not recorded prepared the very first philatelic forgeries by imitating the Brazilian Goat's Eyes issue. Other counterfeiters quickly followed this example, and by 1862 so many forgeries existed that J.-B. Moens, the great Belgian pioneer dealer, found it necessary to publish a thirty-four-page

booklet titled *De la falsification des timbres-poste* [Concerning the forgery of postage stamps]. Although Moens is listed as the author, this booklet and all subsequent ones supposedly written by Moens were actually prepared by Louis Hanciau, the real philatelist in the Moens organization. A defective English translation of the work by E. Doble also appeared in 1862.

These volumes pointed to the urgent need for additional information on the subject, so a year later, in 1863, Edward L. Pemberton, an early-day British dealer, and Thornton Lewes, son of the author George Eliot, published a more satisfactory guide titled *Forged Stamps: How to Detect Them.* Both authors of this thirty-six-page study were then 19 years old. In 1865, a thirty-nine-page booklet, *How to Detect Forged Stamps,* was authored by Thomas Dalton. That same year, J.M. Stourton's sixty-page effort, *Postage Stamp Forgeries,* made its appearance. This was followed by a series of sixty-seven articles, "The Spud Papers," written in turn by W. Dudley Atlee, Edward L. Pemberton, and the Rev. Mr. Robert B. Earée, that appeared in various British philatelic publications between 1871 and 1881. The series, illustrated with actual copies of many of the various forgeries described, was reproduced in book form, *The Spud Papers: An Illustrated Descriptive Catalogue of Early Philatelic Forgeries,* with an introductory essay by Lowell Ragatz, in 1952.

Other general works on the detection of forgeries, written in both English and German, followed, but the first truly encyclopedic study was *Album Weeds,* authored by the Rev. Mr. Earée and published by Stanley Gibbons in 1882. That one-volume first edition of 560 pages was followed in 1892 by a 726-page second edition which remained the definitive reference source until the third and final edition appeared in two volumes (587 pages and 709 pages) in 1906–7. Unfortunately, *Album Weeds* is not illustrated except with cuts of the type used to illustrate the Gibbons albums, so users are forced to wade through lengthy descriptions of design details. Nevertheless, the third edition remains a useful reference on forgeries produced prior to 1905 and often is consulted by specialists.

The last of the comprehensive reference works is this volume, Fernand Serrane's *Vade-Mecum du spécialiste-expert* that was originally published in the French language in two volumes in 1927 and 1929. Although somewhat less comprehensive than *Album Weeds,* it does cover forgeries produced up to twenty years after the appearance of that work. It was during this period that some of the more prolific forgers operated, including François Fournier, N. Imperato, Angelo Panelli, Lucian Smeets, and many others. Consequently, *The Serrane Guide* is particularly useful because it describes the productions of some of these individuals. It is also useful because it is illustrated, not with photographs but with excellent sketches featuring key portions of designs. Forgery enthusiasts have long considered it an indispensable reference, and now its availability in English renders it accessible to more collectors than ever before.

During the two-thirds century that elapsed between the publication of the initial forgery study by Moens and the final comprehensive one by Serrane, those who wished to collect and study forgeries as well as those who wished to document their findings about them through publication encountered many difficulties. Some philatelists actually decried the efforts of others to publish information that would enable collectors to distinguish the good from the bad. These individuals apparently believed that philatelic knowledge regarding counterfeit detection should remain esoteric, the property of a chosen few (some of whom made their living expertizing stamps), not to be disseminated among the rank-and-file collectors. The stated reasons for this attitude were that such knowledge would assist the forgers in improving their products, or that collectors would be unable to understand the information and might make mistakes in evaluating a specimen. Some even went so far as to assert that the collection of forgeries was without value — as if any hobby had value other than the pleasure it provides the participant. Nevertheless, some of these specious, antiforgery literature arguments are interesting and worthy of examination.

The editor of *The Philatelic Record,* Maitland Burnett, reviewed the first edition of *Album Weeds* in the February 1882 issue of his journal and upheld the necessity of certain philatelic knowledge being accessible only to the privileged few with the following comment:

> We have always made it a rule, when asked for an opinion upon a stamp, to give our verdict, but no reasons; and when we find Mr. Earée dissecting all the old tests for Swiss stamps for the benefit of the forgers, we confess that we cherish sentiments other than gratitude towards him.

John N. Luff, pioneer American expert and editor of the *American Journal of Philately,* also reflected this opinion in the December 1, 1901, issue of that publication:

> Very few philatelists are either students or sufficiently interested and painstaking to follow articles in the papers and decide for themselves as to the merits of their stamps. The majority of collectors find it easier to refer such matters to their favorite dealer and accept his decision without question....
>
> The time has arrived when publishers should remember that "silence is golden."

More recently, Edwin Mueller, member of the Friedl Expert Committee, writing in the March 1953 issue of the *Mercury Stamp Journal,* went so far as to describe books devoted to the detection of forgeries as being "of no value to the expert." He continued to say that "literature of this kind is dangerous." In addition, both Mueller and his protégé, renowned expertizer Herbert J. Bloch, repeatedly denigrated the collection of forgeries. Mueller was a prolific and knowledgeable philatelic author, but he assiduously avoided the subject of forgeries and their detection; Bloch's comprehensive knowledge of stamps never was recorded in any substantive form.

Fortunately for collectors, the extreme views of these individuals who probably saw the publication of information about forgeries primarily as a threat to their income from expertizing fees have not prevailed. Writing in the January 13, 1902, issue of *Mekeel's Stamp Collector,* the editors of that publication wisely noted that:

> In fact it is not at all uncommon for forged and faked stamps to be sold by ignorant dealers who have themselves been imposed upon....
>
> As to counterfeits, we believe in the publication of information that will enable the intelligent collector to protect his interests."

With rare exceptions, the philatelic press has followed this advice, and much valuable information has accumulated in its pages thanks to such pioneer writers as A.R. Cowman, H.G.L. Fletcher, Robson Lowe, Donald Patton, Elliott Perry, Lowell Ragatz

(George van den Berg), Ben Reeves (Spying Eye), Herman Schloss, Otto Stiedl, L.N. and M. Williams, John F. Weigand, and many, many others.

If any one person may be said to be responsible for popularizing the collecting of forgeries and stimulating the dissemination of information about them in the United States, that individual would be Lowell Ragatz. Writing under the pen name of George van den Berg, he wrote a column that appeared in *Stamps* under various titles, especially "Philatelic Notes," for some forty-five years. In it, he continually offered his readers forgeries and forgery-related literature at very modest prices. Ragatz was responsible for collecting and publishing *The Spud Papers* in a single volume, for reprinting *Fournier's 1914 Price-List of Philatelic Forgeries* as well as *The Fournier Album of Philatelic Forgeries*. He also published reprint editions of *Phantom Philately* and *Album Weeds*. His seminal articles on François Fournier and the Spiro Brothers were published in *Stamps*. Ragatz also dealt in forgeries, fantasies, and related cinderella items under the name Janet van den Berg. Most mature collectors of forgeries in this country entered the field due to his widespread influence.

There will never be another comprehensive work on worldwide forgeries like *The Serrane Guide*. Remember, when it was published, all of the stamps of the world could be listed in a one-volume catalogue of about 1,600 pages in a minuscule 4-by-6-inch two-column format. Today, five volumes of some 1,100 pages each in 8-by-11-inch four-column format are required. In recent years, the number of stamps and miniature sheets issued annually has increased to nearly 12,000. The sheer number of items requiring coverage obviously precludes any such encyclopedic work. It also precludes any single author from possessing the knowledge necessary to prepare such a study. The age of the expert who is knowledgeable on all issues worldwide is now past.

However, the end of comprehensive studies does not mean that literature dealing with forgeries has been in the doldrums since the publication of Serrane more than sixty-five years ago. As a matter of fact, it has advanced steadily during that period and has never been better, both quantitatively and qualitatively, than it is at present. Part of the reason is the prolific nature of present-day specialized

philatelic literature. The literature devoted to stamp collecting always has been the most extensive of any hobby, and the scores of specialty journals devoted to single countries or topics provide a ready outlet for forgery articles. In addition, the improvement in the reproduction of photographs and the use of microphotography for minute details has allowed the visualization of discussed items in a manner far superior to the wordy descriptions of the past.

One problem has nevertheless remained. In spite of several abortive attempts, the vast philatelic literature is not indexed adequately, and many excellent studies on forgeries buried in its depths remain unknown, even to specialist collectors. Consequently, in republishing the Serrane translation in book form, it has been deemed desirable to "update it" by the addition of both book and periodical references that have appeared in the intervening years. These will enable the interested collector to supplement the original descriptions with additional information, and frequently illustrations as well, that will render forgery detection both easier and more certain. The availability of the references in several philatelic libraries throughout the nation, and in particular the American Philatelic Research Library housed in the American Philatelic Building at State College, Pennsylvania, will render most of them as accessible as the collector's telephone or computer.

It is hoped that a large number of collectors, generalists, specialists, and forgery enthusiasts alike will find this modernized version of the *Serrane Guide* to be of value. It must be remembered, however, that just because a particular stamp or issue is not covered in the philatelic literature does not mean that it has not been forged. Modern methods of photolithography and similar techniques produce forgeries that often are difficult to distinguish from the originals. Collectors are urged to study their stamps, not just to take them for granted. If even one reader discovers one new type of forgery as a result of the stimulation provided by the information in this book and shares that discovery with others by publication in the philatelic press, then the laborious task of updating *The Serrane Guide* by means of this comprehensive forgery bibliography (see page 367) will have been worthwhile.

Foreword

Et c'est une folie a nulle autre seconde
De vouloir se mêler de corriger le monde.
— Le Misanthrope (*Molière*)

In previous works, the rhetorical devices we used to emphasize and expose shady philatelic practices were sometimes criticized as being inappropriate, but the fact that we lashed out at fraud, speculation, and the reprehensible doctoring of stamps elicited great praise. Each of these reactions offers us a precious incentive to try again.

Old Collections, Old Dealers

In the olden days, the amateur stamp collector, who usually came in contact with the dealer only, ran the risks inherent in making hasty purchases.

Stamp quality was relatively unimportant; authenticity alone was the prime concern of generally honest dealers who had spent their entire lives in the business. From the outset, however, the lack of philatelic publications made it possible to defraud dealers and collectors by offering facsimile reproductions more or less openly for sale.

So, our forefathers' collections comprised a great many stamps that were in bad condition and forgeries that were knowingly acquired when authentic stamps were unavailable or too expensive.

Early Catalogues

Catalogues for the use of collectors supplied exact quotations reflecting the world market; they were guides, and their chief interest was the careful recording of actual prices.

Little by little, the proliferation of collectors and issues, the breadth and volume of transactions, the development of faking and of methods of falsification finally evolved new procedures, the advantages and disadvantages of which we shall see.

Approval Selections

The selection on display, with prices clearly indicated, is the first improvement in purchasing methods. This kind of purchase is made on ordinary demand by furnishing references and has the advantage of allowing for the study of each stamp and the maximum appraisal of its qualities.

If you are relatively inexperienced, make sure the dealer is honest and require the stamps to be identified with his name.

Philatelic Societies

The purpose of these societies is to facilitate the exchange of duplicates, thus bypassing costly, time-consuming intermediaries. With prices clearly marked, the stamps are assembled in booklets of approval selections. Dealers are admitted as society members, and they are entrusted with furnishing booklets; they must not receive any approvals, however, because that is contrary to the purpose envisaged.

In an efficient philatelic society, all stamps are marked on their backs; the approvals are indicated by specialty (Europe, France and Colonies, Great Britain and Colonies, former German States and Colonies, former Italian States and Colonies, outside of Europe, etc.), and are distributed in a systematic way, each society member taking his turn; the booklets are returned to their owners within a maximum period of ten months after three complete circulations and are immediately inventoried. Before making a contract for stamps, ascertain carefully whether all these conditions have been met.

Experts

Stamp forgery and counterfeiting have given rise to the service of "experts," who are entrusted with examining stamps for less competent amateurs. Many assume this title who recognize only the obvious forgeries and rely on conjecture to give advice as freely as heads or tails is played. Modern methods of counterfeiting often have shown that more serious investigation is indispensable.

The immensity of the numbers of stamps issued makes universal expertizing impossible, particularly for overprints. The material necessary for comparison — originals, reprints, essays, forgeries, fakes, overprints, and cancellations — is already immense, even in one specialty; one easily can understand why the wise expert often restricts himself to one specialty.

The most competent experts occasionally have gone astray; this happens when the workload is heavy, or when some very good new counterfeits on which their references are silent are being studied. Egg candlers, astronomers, or even mathematicians also are familiar with these errors of distraction, quite excusable in view of the services rendered.

Artistic repairing also increases their work; restoration is done today with such care that most amateurs are completely fooled by it.

There is good reason to point out that the seal or the signature of an expert is not always a guarantee: seal and signature may have been forged. When you want to be absolutely certain, you yourself must arrange for expertizing.

The cost of expertizing should not be more than 50 gold centimes, with a like amount for cancellation, if a cancellation is involved.

Public Sales

The high prices brought by extremely rare stamps of exceptional quality attract collectors to public sales with the hope of making a big profit. Let us see what the real situation is.

The dealer's expenses are 10 percent (the expert's commission), plus 1 franc 50 centimes (gold) per photograph, plus 50 centimes (gold) per lot advertised, a total of about 15 percent for large sales and 20 to 25 percent for the small ones. The sale price includes, moreover, the sales tax (10 to $19\frac{1}{2}$ percent, depending on the country); the buyer takes that into consideration when he makes offers.

If one adds the depreciation of slightly damaged major value stamps (there are always some in the best collections), the depreciation of issues in limited demand and of the sets of minor value stamps (tail end of the collection), it is evident that the total is often lower than half of the catalogued value.

The dealer imagines that all of his lots will be ordered, but, depending on the period, the importance of the collection, the honesty or the reputation of the auctioneer, half or sometimes even only a fourth of the lots will receive firm offers. It would be imprudent not to set limits; otherwise, the other lots will go for almost nothing, or will be bought cheap by the auctioneer. Exact payment is not made on the spot, but within a period of one or sometimes two months; if the money exchange goes down meanwhile, it is most unfortunate. So sell in countries where your money is relatively high in

value if you want to receive an exact cash payment for the product obtained from you.

On the other hand, buying at public sales is to be recommended, but only when single, detached stamps, which are described as "very beautiful," with a photograph for examination of margins, centering, and cancellation, are involved. Reject the stamp if its brightness does not measure up to the description given. Lots of several stamps are occasionally sold without expertizing; get information before buying.

Every auctioneer sends a catalogue on request and bids on the stamps acquired; it is useless therefore to pay an additional commission to other persons when you want to make a cash offer on lots.

Brokers in Rare Stamps

The big difference between selling and purchasing prices and the markup of public sale costs have brought the broker on the philatelic scene; he is a useful agent when collectors find themselves in disagreement. If he is fair, he will charge only 5 to 10 percent as commission, in addition to legal charges; quite a successful business is possible on this basis.

The General Collection

General collecting is dead, quite dead, despite the album publishers' attempts to revive it. Gradually rendered ineffectual by the overwhelming number of new issues and undermined by the enormous devaluation of money in modern times, speculation and counterfeiting — it is a natural prey for these — have really dealt a fatal body blow to general collecting. Just imagine the amount of time and money it would require today.

New Catalogues, New Dealers

The serious collector and particularly the specialist accept catalogue quotations only after studying and comparing them.

Today, the catalogues of large firms are price-list catalogues, not guides. Their concern is to sell what the firm has in plentiful supply at a good profit or what easily can be obtained from various sources, especially mass-produced new stamps and super-profit speculative issues.

We have asked a hundred times that quotations be listed in gold equivalent value and that the collectors' federation of each country publish the exact, undiscounted quotation of its country's stamps once a year. That would provide effective advertising, and its sale would bring in a lot of money. New stamps and certain overprints would no longer be valued at a fifth of the catalogue price-listing, nor would perforated bisects be sold at half-price, and early and rare stamps be underpriced. How many young amateurs can distinguish these different stamp classifications?

Again, quotations are meaningless when a few individuals corner the market for one or several new issues so that excessively high prices subsequently can be dictated; catalogues are duty-bound to record such a market situation and to inform readers. By doing so, their reliability as sources of information would be established. If they do not do this, collectors who wish to eliminate such philatelic corruption have only to refrain from using their services.

Rare Stamps

The intrinsic rarity of a stamp is determined only by the number of copies printed. Stamps may be classified according to their age in four categories:
1. New (1910 to the present).
2. Contemporary (1890 to 1910).
3. Modern (1870 to 1890).
4. Early (1847 to 1870).

In the first category, all copies, or almost all, are in good condition. As for contemporary stamps, a relatively low percentage have disappeared; after 1890, collectors were already numerous and only currently used stamps were thrown away.

The number of stamps that are extant diminishes as we go back into the past. With respect to modern stamps, the proportion is one to five; early ones, it is scarcely one to ten; and very early ones, up to about 1860, it decreases to 1 or 2 percent (a dozen "Post Office Mauritius" stamps from an original print order of 1,000 copies are still extant).

If we look into the number of extant stamps that are in perfect condition, the above proportions are radically reduced: imperforate stamps with wide margins are found once in ten times among stamps with narrow gutters (Tuscany, Thurn and Taxis), and scarcely once in three times among the stamps with wide gutters (Netherlands, Portugal); smudgy cancellations occasionally remove as many as four-fifths of the remaining portion (Belgium, 1849, "Epaulettes"); and various other factors like wear (thinning, cuts, lack of freshness, etc.) or lack of centering accentuate or increase still more the diminution in the numerical progression. Our conclusion, which has a significant bearing on the question of real rarity in stamps, is that the printing order figure of modern stamps should be divided by

10 to 100, according to situation, and that of early stamps, by 200 to 2,000 (one or two "Post Office" stamps in perfect condition out of 2,000, and 2,000 to 3,000 Belgian "Epaulettes" out of five million).

Flawless Stamps

The flawless stamp is fresh in color, neatly canceled, and minimally has four average margins, or, if it is perforated, perfect centering. From our explanation in the preceding paragraph, it can be understood that the flawless stamp, exempt from any defect whatsoever, is understandably of extremely rare quality. When one considers early stamps of this sort, catalogue prices are frequently ridiculous.

An apparently first-rate collection always provides great surprises when it is examined carefully: defects that have been overlooked, repairing, faking, forged overprints, counterfeit cancellations, and forgeries of all kinds. Amateurs who are willing to subject their albums to critical study, to look at their stamps with suspicion and caution or with the attentiveness and concentration of an expert, will agree that we are right.

We therefore must advise the amateur to take offers of early canceled stamps that are in perfect condition without any hesitation whenever the price is not excessive, and dissuade him from parting with such stamps at a price below their quality. Mercury is a triple-threat god, to be feared especially in our delightful period, because even the least important dealers will try to make a 100 percent profit. Stamps of fine appearance that are priced cheaply should be carefully examined: they always have some defects *Vulgus vult decipi*.

Mint Stamps

The mint stamp must have the same qualities as the used one, and, with few exceptions, it must possess its original gum. Recent stamps or remainders (last issues of Thurn and Taxis) usually have the original gum, which is found even on marginal or corner copies. (This is rare in early cancellations.)

Early mint stamps are rare, so faking is rife. Stamps from which cancellations have been removed, regummed stamps which have been camouflaged by repairing before regumming — all should be subjected to the quadruple testing of magnifying glass, benzine, water, and boiling water. That is one reason why young amateurs should be advised to forego early mint stamps; they will run risk enough with reprints and essays. The mint stamp is not even necessary for specialized study;

the canceled stamp is more useful in view of new expertizing techniques based on the official device used in cancellation (notably for overprinted stamps of the French and German colonies).

Bluntly speaking, is a collection built by obtaining at the post office stamps suitable for insertion in albums? With very rare exception, one should rather insert only stamps that have really been used and that possess other traces of viability than a time-worn administrative birth certificate. Just go and share these views with the partisans of the least effort who push for easy sales and reckon on a percentage not only from each new set, but also from the Bristol paper on which it will be pasted.

New Stamps

The obsession with forgery — which this work effectively combats — is one of the grounds for the alienation of beginners from classical early stamps. Naive in their ignorance, they listened to the bad shepherds who kept saying, "Dear collector: please accept these new stamps. With them, you will not have to worry about cancellations; look — they are *new* and there are no forgeries (How false that is!); they are not very dear (Really!), and they are available everywhere...especially at my place."

Evidently, attentive interest in a new set of stamps is understandable and quite natural, but it is ridiculous to buy only each country's most recently issued stamps. Have you ever seen a furniture collector (dealer) purchase only the most recent styles of Dufayel? The mass-produced collection, a post-war development, requires no mental effort; masses of stamps resembling each other are accumulated, producing an easy profit for those who have tendered the bait. That is the wrong kind of example to follow. One should rather give priority to the acquisition of rare items that are in great demand; as for the rest, believe me, you will have all the time you need.

Moreover, those who are willing to calculate the price of their purchases in gold — especially for the 1919 and 1920 issues — and in their present paper money value, will be astounded at their losses despite the few profitable deals that may have come their way. If they are out for a killing, let them look around them at the fortunes built on the shifting sands of these philatelic trifles. They have had plenty of warning.

Nevertheless — it is a sign of a change for the better — responsible collecting is winning out, and novices who have become fellow professionals now are beginning to look at their albums' pages with pride.

Specialization

The frequent contributions of specialized studies have rescued stamp collecting from the threat of oblivion. This exploratory research has produced detailed catalogues — the current official Italian catalogue is a perfect model — and at the same time has engendered an embryonic group of specialists who know where they are going and what they want.

Specialization is definitely on today's agenda. Only specialization, which becomes more and more exciting as research develops, makes it possible to build a harmonious collection. Only specialization can determine the exact value of thousands of varieties on which general catalogues are necessarily silent. Specialization shows with clear evidence that the world values of stamps are not determined by the stocks of a few firms, but rather by collectors' demands, exchanges, and sales, because collectors unquestionably possess the most extensive stocks in existence.

Let collectors become aware of their power; let them help one another by organizing national federations that are devoted exclusively to their interests. That is the indispensable counterweight needed to eliminate the practices that are so harmful to Philately.

Stamp Classification

In stamp study, chronological order is the only orderly system to follow. Rigorously logical, it traces the history and manufacture of issues step by step, and the succession of plates and printings is given chronological priority to all secondary matters such as shades, paper, perforations, etc.

With their frequently arbitrary listings (and their offshoots, albums with filing compartments), general catalogues unfortunately have done lasting harm with their illogical classification systems. Committed to artificial descriptive classifications, they have neglected the systematic natural order. Cuvier in zoology, Jussieu in botany, rejected the unsound methodological procedures of their predecessors. Just so, specialized studies, methodically organized on loose-leaf pages, with notation of indispensable scientific details, will resolutely reject the mistaken ideas of stamp classification of bygone days.

Exchanges

Since World War I, currency exchanges everywhere have experienced innumerable quotation fluctuations in relation to real values, obliging the collector to perform a maze of exchange calculations — another reason why specialization with an exact knowledge of values is so attractive.

In coping with the uncertainties of the exchange, one should calculate on the basis of gold and refer all price quotations to it. To find the value in the paper money of various countries, multiply the gold value quotation by the coefficient of monetary depreciation, proceeding by levels of fixed coefficients as long as the exchange shows no evidence of perceptible fluctuation.

Postscript

L'Art est long et le Temps est court.

The first volume was warmly received not only by collectors and dealers who wanted to avoid burdensome or unpleasant formal training in philately, but also by real connoisseurs who were concerned with getting the distinguishing marks of counterfeit stamps as quickly as possible, along with other philatelic information given by the author.

The work was justifiably criticized in certain respects and a few errors were pointed out: that is the lot of any human endeavor. What is really important is that it is daily rendering service and is helping to instruct the legion of experts so urgently needed in connection with the growth of Philately.

Numerous correspondents, who have since become friends, have called for a similar work for stamps of countries outside of Europe, in a still more condensed form to facilitate research.

This is the work we confidently offer to collectors today. — *F. Serrane*

Preface

Fraude Coeli sereni deceptus.
— Virgil

Establishments for the manufacture of facsimiles appeared in Germany, Italy, and Switzerland from the very beginning of Philately. Rare stamps were copied; the manufacture of a single cliché for a particular stamp was followed by the same operation for the entire set. These early counterfeits are almost always so crudely executed that the knowledgeable collector, and even more so, the specialist, can recognize them at a glance: design, format, shade, paper, everything clashes. The collecting of these naive counterfeits is of interest only to the beginner. It may serve as initiation into the great secret of professional expertizing: experienced scrutiny of the stamp.

The forgeries of this period that were made to defraud the postal services deserve special comment. Because they often are quite deceptive, they are in demand with an original cancellation, which gives them a kind of rarity. As mints, they may appear among reference stamps, next to reprints and essays; however, only a very minimal value should be accorded them. The attribution of excessive value encourages further reproduction and manufacture of issues that probably also would be copied in their turn. This has already happened.

The development of Philately and the studies published by our predecessors soon obliged forgers to fall back on more common sets of stamps. The number of forgers increased, and some of them strained their ingenuity to such an extent that the struggle soon resembled that of cannon and armor. Amateurs took refuge behind experts when making decisions on valuable stamps. Expertizing became indispensable after the appearance of stamps that were offered for sale by people who knew photolithography and the resources of typography, engraving, and chemical processes, and who used similar inks.

Now, a mere glance is insufficient, for the appearance of modern counterfeits is often very good; comparison with an authentic stamp has become normal procedure for all those with a limited knowledge of stamps. Fraud is uncovered by closely examining the distinctive characteristics of the original — paper, method of printing, perforation, shade, etc. — and by concentrating on the most significant aspects of the design. One must remember that the rarest stamps often have the same characteristics as the commonest one in the set.

The counterfeiting evil increases daily. Now the most ordinary sets are counterfeited, particularly those that have been issued recently: the lack of information on these facilitates acceptance without examination. Our ultramodern forgers have even tried to break all records by issuing forgeries and forged overprints (Alexandria, Batum, Poland, Memel, Syria, etc.) almost concurrently with the regular issue. The whole counterfeited stock is disposed of in that way before the distinctive characteristics of the forgeries are published.

These problems could have been avoided if there had been an energetic counterreaction from the outset; however, because of some strange aberration, this deceitful business was given more encouragement than collectors' studies of original stamps! For example, we see that firm "F" in Geneva obtained, for its adulterated goods that were exhibited advantageously, "six Crosses of Merit, eight Gold Medals, four Grand Prizes, and six Diplomas of Honor [*sic*] at the International Exhibitions of Saint Etienne (1895), Nice (1896), Marseilles (1897), Toulouse and Lyon (1898)"!

Consequently, it is no longer surprising to see sporadic growth become spontaneous and universal. The rare productions of forgeries that preserved a semblance of honesty by mentioning "facsimile" or "falsch" now join the apparent majority in their shameless raids on collections.

What has been done to remedy this situation? Nothing, or almost nothing. A few isolated trials with no probing follow-through. Stocks have been seized, but the clichés frequently have departed for other climes, and the stocks of branch firms continue to circulate.

Although in a good position to know what is going on, dealers' associations (chambers of commerce, etc.) have not proceeded with the authority and unanimity necessary for obtaining lasting restraining regulations. The fear of seeing their members compromised by receiving and concealing forged goods should not paralyze them, for chambers of commerce, stock exchanges, and bank associations do not hesitate to remove an unscrupulous member from their midst. It sets a good example and adds further proof of their good reputation.

Aided by dealers' associations, collectors' federations are strong enough to police themselves and to undertake a thorough housecleaning. Let them act energetically against the pirates. The laws of every country provide for severe punishment of fraudulent misrepresentation, swindle, and deception on the quality of the merchandise sold, and, in common law, provision is made for compensatory damages. Let them act together with their representatives in the Legislature and submit precisely worded bills. They have the advantage of numbers for electoral leverage, and the power of their interests is ten times greater than that of lobbies that successfully influence public authorities. The organization and publicity designed for this crusade should be the first item on the agenda of philatelic congresses. These congresses would then amount to something.

It is impossible for the isolated collector to keep an up-to-date record of forgers and fakers; these people change their names and addresses every time they make a mistake. However, it would be in the interest of the organizations mentioned to keep such lists and to use them as records of punishment for their own information and for the protection of their affiliates. Federations can also advise the press — a double-edged weapon, like Aesop's language — to show a bit more consideration for the general public interest by refusing to accept suspicious advertisements of reprints or of cheap lots, which too often are replete with defective stamps.

* * * *

This exordium should not frighten the collector, for *perfection in stamp reproduction is absolutely impossible.*

There is always some significant difference in a counterfeit's design; with rare exceptions, the paper is never the same, and an examination of the transparency, micrometric measurement, and the use of the microscope always reveal the difference; the design's dimensions vary; the perforations are rarely regular and show telltale defects, especially at corners, the forgers not having perforators of all the sizes needed for all combinations; finally, the shades are so rarely identical that the specialist who has access to numerous references can spot strange tints or colors right away.

We have little fear of revealing the distinctive characteristics of deceptive forgeries, because the forger cannot attain perfection in reproduction, even if he makes a hundred new clichés. Each time he makes a correction, new errors will appear, and all the resources of photography will never make the exact reproduction of a stamp or of a banknote possible. Moreover, the number of characteristics described is minimal in relation to the number of differences found in all counterfeit reproductions.

We must point out that most forgeries are lithographed, which eliminates immediately all those whose originals are intaglio-engraved and the typographed originals from matrices reproduced by embossing or electrotyping (white dots in colored background or blurred lines in bold prints). The lines of the lithographed forgeries are not very sharp (smudges), and the stone's texture shows through the design, but when the paper and the shades do not indicate forgeries — which is highly improbable — study of transfer-type characteristics will provide decisive evidence.

The amateur who is willing to compare a few of the best forgeries with the help of this manual quickly will see that none of them is too formidable, none too difficult, if he follows our explicit instructions for visual examination and, like the mariner, keeps a close eye on his compass when he returns to port. Then let him make converts; then it will be easy sailing for philatelic science's resolve to reduce and eliminate swindling.

In order to clarify this question further, the reader will kindly allow us to recount a personal experience.

A "Category XXVI (Division VI)" for forged stamps and studies dealing with forgeries was announced in the prospectus of the 1925 Paris Exhibition.

Having been properly registered and having paid the fee for an exhibition space of ten square meters, I was about to arrange my mountings when the management objected, saying that the forgeries category had just been canceled. Just who had given that annoying directive? Clearly within my rights, I protested and declared my intention to set up a private exhibit at Hotel Normandy. After that, I was authorized to exhibit my materials two and a half meters above the floor, right against the wall, without any protective glass partition.

This attempt to make the truth inaccessible produced the following protest in the Exhibition's visitors' book:

I wish to lodge a protest against the location assigned to a collection that I consider one of the most interesting in the Exhibition. I refer to the collection entitled "Forgery Studies" by Mr. F. Serrane. This collection is not placed on the ogee moulding, but near the cornice, more than two and a half meters from the floor, at such a height that one can hardly see it, or, if it is noticed, it is impossible to study it. Apparently there was some intention to make it difficult for unsuspecting easy marks — those victims of forgers and counterfeiters — to get information. I do not have the honor of knowing Mr. Serrane personally, but I have read some of his articles. I make this protest not only on my own behalf, but on behalf of other collectors who are desirous of improving their minds and their information.

Ch. P......
(Signature and address)

This curious manifestation of fear stems from an ostrich-like policy. Who can possibly believe today that it is better to hide the dangers of philatelic fraud and misrepresentation and to intimidate those who are sounding the tocsin in a disinterested, fraternal way than to pull down the false gods, lock up the forgers, and obtain laws that will effectively restrict and eliminate their fraudulent operations?

However, let us return to our subject.

Forged cancellations are dangerous only because the inexperienced amateur does not know them all. Most of them are poorly executed in different inks or in inks that are too new.

Forged overprints, which are not very numerous on early European stamps, are more difficult to expertize than forged stamps, because the surface to be examined is not so large and a certain number of reference stamps is indispensable for good judgment.

The shade, the degree of oiliness, and the thickness of the ink eliminate many counterfeits; the degree of indention (relief produced on the back of the stamp by heavy pressure typography) is a clear indication for others. The shape, arrangement, and measurement of the letters and other marks, as well as the exact measurement of the gutters, justify rejection of many, particularly early forgeries. Finally, details not known to forgers, such as the exact shade and perforation, the kind of paper, and the centering of officially overprinted stocks, help to expose a few more obvious forgeries. Clichés obtained by photography are better, but the ink shade, the measurements, and the fuzziness of the counterfeits made from them call for expertizing.

Nevertheless, we have to admit that there are perfectly counterfeited overprints. Because of this, certain people have said, with evident relish, "If they cannot be expertized, they are really good!" These individuals forget that some new development tomorrow or the day after tomorrow may eliminate such specimens from albums. That is another good reason why stamp purchases should be signed by the dealer.

For a long time, we have been asking specialists and experts to describe, each in his own area, the varieties and the minor peculiarities of overprints. It is true that this work requires the enlargement of the original sheets by several diameters; however, it often proves that there are no two rigorously identical overprints on a single sheet. We will have to accept the necessity of doing this if we want to be absolutely sure. An examining magistrate, in the end, finally obtains the exact number of the typewriter on which an incriminating page was written.

Another area where faking is all the rage is *stamp repairing.* (A single firm is known to have repaired two million gold francs' worth of stamps — catalogue values — in one year.) This originally was done for very rare stamps that lacked a corner or a few perforations, or to mask a tear, but unscrupulous operators all over the world have taken over this business and are expanding its activities.

Imperforate stamps have been given extremely wide margins; perforated ones have received new teeth; those that have been thinned down or that have holes in them are doctored up or remounted; cancellations are cleaned from stamps that are laminated on the back to prevent the gum from going through the original paper, now made absorbent by acids (sometimes it is necessary to remove the gum to verify the repairing); detached stamps are joined to form pairs, tête-bêche, and blocks of stamps; the value tablet is removed from a damaged rare stamp and transferred to a common one of the same shade; centers are easily inverted; etc.

Unfortunately, these stamps are maltreated by the addition of foreign materials, by successive repainting to mask joinings or to redraw the design. Their value is diminished proportionately; those stamps of which the back has been completely repaired are not worth more than one-twentieth of the catalogue value.

The best kind of repair job is not dangerous: occasionally it is visible to the naked eye; more often a magnifying glass is needed. Benzine or cold or hot water show the damage. A changed shade is a basic indication of a repaired stamp, and the use of a microscope is necessary only rarely. An early stamp on handmade paper found on a piece of machine-made paper with colored silk threads will produce a knowing, amused smile at times.

Always examine your purchases carefully with a magnifying glass, looking at the front and back, as well as at the transparency of the paper; repairing and repainting often are discovered this way. Many bad stamps will remain unsold at the dealer's place of business if prospective purchases are carefully examined.

And when you arrive home, give your acquisitions another good going-over; get rid of those that are probably faked.

How To Use This Guide

Our *Guide du Spécialiste* (1919) and the *Catalogue du Spécialiste d'Europe* (1922) did little more than point out the dangers inherent in purchasing forged stamps.

The chief purpose of this work is to give a clear, convincing description of the distinctive characteristics of forgeries and original stamps. The section usually entitled "Price List" may appear to have been sacrificed, but, in dealing with each issue, we shall state all the specific points that may be useful to the expert in reaching a sound decision concerning the value of the stamps submitted to him. In this, we shall emphasize the things that are not mentioned in general catalogues. One can also obtain adequate information in research and specialized catalogue publications.

The book is organized in the following way:

I. *Printing figures.* For early stamps when the figures are known and useful.

II. *Select stamps.* Indication of four-margin minimum measurements in imperforate stamps. (Stamps cut in the middle of the gutters.)

III. *Manufacturing details.* Layout of sheets and of transfers, papers used, and printing techniques. No clichés for different issues, because these are known well enough.

IV. *Rare shades.* Proportional value given according to the value of the usual shade using letters M (Mint) and U (Used, canceled), with multipliers or decimal additives. Rare shades quoted in general catalogues are not given.

V. *Varieties.* Proportional value using the same method.

VI. *Pairs, blocks.* Proportional value for select stamps. Without any other indication, mint and used pairs are worth 3M and 3U; blocks of four (mint): 6M.

VII. *Cancellations.* Illustrations of the most usual cancellations, with some indication of their proportional value. This information is sufficient to guide the average reader; it is impossible to enlarge upon this subject here, a substantial volume being necessary sometimes to describe all the cancellations of a single country.

VIII. *Reprints, essays, and fantasies.* A detailed description of their relationship to their original stamps.

IX. *Fakes.* A descriptive classification of the principal fakes.

X. *Forgeries and originals.* Illustration of the distinctive features of originals when there are several good sets of forgeries from different sources, or a mere listing of those features when that is sufficient. Illustration of characteristics or descriptions of the most deceptive forgeries.

XI. *Forged cancellations.* A descriptive classification of the best-known mass-produced forged cancellations. The only purpose of this is to stimulate reader interest, for there are many forged cancellations of single stamps and many authentic postmarks that no longer are in use — the mere mention of which would require volumes.

Note: The numbers indicated after issues are those of Yvert and Tellier, *Catalogue général de langue française.*

The prices shown are always in gold francs.

The names of forgers are not given because all of them are not known, and the names of fakers — a breed that is just as bad — would necessarily have to be omitted; moreover, this kind of publicity is unpleasant for honest people who happen to have the same name. The place of origin with the initials of the author's name will effectively eliminate the possibility of mistaken reference.

Regretfully, we think that this book is going to expose many undesirable stamps; the overconfident collector will assign them to profit or loss and swear that he will not be caught again. He will have the consolation, if indeed it is a consolation, of observing that those of his colleagues who deal in overprints and new stamps are ill-favored by fortune in other ways. *Claritatem oculis facere.*

We urge the reader to express his criticism of our work and his suggestions for improving it. They will be taken into consideration in subsequent editions. On the other hand, any money-making schemes will be promptly dismissed.

How To Look at a Stamp

Chaque îlot signalé par l'homme de vigie
Est un Eldorado promis par le destin!

L'Imagination qui dresse son orgie
Ne trouve qu'un récif aux clartés du matin.
— Le Poète

The Queen of Sheeba used to test Solomon's wisdom by proposing enigmas to him.

The modern stamp collector does little more than place a paper rectangle in your hand and, blandly indifferent to contingencies, asks for an immediate opinion or judgment. He thinks that a look should suffice when he shows you a very early rarity, some shade variety from a remote country, or a recent overprint for which there are twenty different types in a sheet. It is not always as easy as one imagines!

To be sure, if early counterfeits, crudely executed in gaudy colors, are involved, those who really know stamps will pass judgment after a quick glance. For the better-looking counterfeits in a similar shade, experience is needed; they offer no special difficulty for specialists and dealers with long years of experience.

The counterfeits made to deceive and to defraud, using modern stereotype or photolithograph processes, require more careful examination each time their shades are judged to be admissible. The so-called reprints, printed from original clichés, and the clandestine reprintings from the original plates, both lacking any official status, require close study of paper, shade, measurements, and even design, the latter possibly having been altered by oxidation, printing press impact, press clogging, different printing pressures, or more or less heavy inking.

There are also refined, subtle forgeries that, fortunately, are few in number. These are obtained by the forged printing of a rare value on the original paper (perforated or not) of a common-value stamp whose original impression has conveniently disappeared. These forgeries call for detailed design and shade study. Finally, official reprints and essays in the original shade further complicate the problem.

But I want to reassure the reader. It is absolutely impossible to create a perfect counterfeit of a stamp. If one occasionally succeeds in producing a perfect counterfeit of an overprint whose printing type or design occupies a surface of only ten to thirty square millimeters, it must be remembered that the stamp itself has a surface that is twenty times larger and is covered with lines of various thicknesses, sometimes with extremely delicate, fine lines. Add to this the difficulty of exactly counterfeiting paper, shade, perforation, and watermark, and you will understand why it is almost as impossible to make a perfect counterfeit as it is to square a circle.

No one can remember the distinctive features of every forgery. To do this would be superhuman. The purpose of this study is to indicate precisely the established, recurring differences so that comparative research and expertizing will be reduced to a necessary minimum.

Many journals and works rely upon side-by-side photographic reproductions of the genuine stamp and of its forged counterpart for comparative research. This is basically a good system, especially if enlargements are used; the dissector's work will be facilitated in proportion as design differences are enlarged. But the insufficiently experienced specialist and even more so incompetent collectors will perceive very little in the reproductions when there are minimal dissimilarities or when the clichés are poorly executed or printed. Half-tone engraving is better for normal examination at a certain distance; however, it has the great disadvantage of nonadaptability to the use of the magnifying glass.

This is why we have preferred the graphic method, despite the long, detailed pen-sketching work involved. Arrows indicate the only points to be examined. Two or several distinctive marks are shown whenever possible, certain ones possibly being concealed, intentionally or not, by a forged cancellation or overprint. We also have taken the trouble to sketch a few generic characteristics of the original design, especially of its most delicate parts, the ones that are counterfeited least easily, so that the amateur can get his bearings, even if he is confronted with new or unintentionally omitted falsification.

Examine carefully a few genuine stamps. You almost always will see, at least in early stamps, a regular design, inscriptions in alignment, well-spaced lettering of uniform thickness; curves and regular symmetrical lines; identical ornaments that touch or do not touch the other parts of the design, depending upon the designer's intention. In the portraits, the lines are regular and the shading is arranged naturally. We know the work we have been examining was executed by artists who were masters of their art. On the other hand, when you can point to relatively crude design defects, it is a safe bet that the copies under examination were made by more or less ingenuous counterfeiters. You should do this prognostic exercise often; frequently you will find more than fifty points of dissimilarity in the counterfeits. The whole secret of expertise is knowing how to look at a stamp.

After examining the stamp's design, the reader must consult the text, where additional necessary information will be found.

When measurements are shown or described, width is given first, height second. The same order prevails for perforations.

Except for explicit statement to the contrary, the forgeries described are lithographed.

In general, we attach little importance to the question of impression or paper shades because the frankly arbitrary shades quickly are spotted by specialists; because the possible shades must be compared, the point of comparison for the rare ones often not being available in albums; and finally because the clichés of modern forgeries are still extant and color shades thus may change tomorrow or the day after tomorrow.

The abundance of the materials being studied has obliged us to omit descriptions of original or forged cancellations. However, the latter will be described when they were applied to very widely circulated complete sets and when in this situation they can be used to attract immediate attention.

For the same reason, only brief notes concerning overprints will be given when the comparison is useful or indispensable. As a matter of fact, one would have to compose several books in any attempt to give a detailed description of original overprints with all their varieties, and their photographic reproduction, even in incorrect enlargements, would render a great service to counterfeiters.

As for forged overprints, it would be impossible to describe them all in detail, for in addition to types known to experts and applied on entire sets, there are others which have been executed in isolation here and there all over the world, and certain overprints were counterfeited in fifty different ways! Moreover, all this work would serve no useful purpose; every day more and more deceptive overprints are manufactured, and the amateur might justifiably believe, perhaps, that an overprint is original when it does not correspond to the descriptions given!

Here again, without an overprint model one visually can spot the poorly made early forgeries whose authors were scarcely ever concerned with measurements; they were satisfied with a vague resemblance. As for incorrectly designed overprints, which already are refined considerably, a sliding gauge will be useful. In difficult cases, comparison alone may be convincing. When it is done scientifically and logically, it often removes all doubt.

The use of a mica template, on which the original overprint's contour is traced with the engraver's stylus, is adequate nine times out of ten.

One should not overlook other means of investigation, among which the following may be mentioned: the exact ink shade (dullness or brilliance), its opacity, its "strike-through" on the back of the stamp, its degree of greasiness, and, in certain cases, its thickness and the slippage of hand-held cancellation devices, the degree of indention, or bite, in letter-press printed overprints, especially on mint stamps, or the absence of print-through in lithographed overprints. Certain details that often are unknown to counterfeiters may prove useful: the shade of the officially overprinted stock, its perforation, its paper, and even its poor centering for perforated stamps of certain values. In a few cases, a knowledge of the exact location of the overprint on all the stamps of a sheet, a knowledge of the tiniest flaws of the letterpress composition (smudges, skips, etc.) or on a postmark applied by hand — all of these things are enlightening. Finally, cancellation is an excellent means of control in most cases.

May this work be received with kindness and may it roam the world over with its message of prudence, may it effectively show the collector that with a little study he has nothing to fear, may it help develop serious philatelists' potential for observation and make experts of them. That will be our greatest reward. — *F. Serrane*

Note: Readers should be aware of the following points when using *The Serrane Guide*.

* The numbers used to identify stamps are those of the Yvert general catalogue of 1925–26, the French equivalent of the Scott catalogue.
* The Geneva notation means that forged overprints and cancellations can be compared in Fournier's *Album des fac-similes*, produced in 1928 by the Philatelic Union of Geneva. The information of the characteristic features of all Geneva facsimile stamps will help to pinpoint them quickly.
* Among the many sources referenced by Serrane are:

E.D. Bacon, *Reprints of Postal Adhesive Stamps and Their Characteristics*, London, Stanley Gibbons, 1899.

Henry Collin and Henry L. Calman, *A Catalogue for Advanced Collectors of Postage Stamps, Stamped Envelopes and Wrappers*, New York, Scott Stamp & Coin Co. Ltd., 1901.

Baron de Vinck de Winnezeele, *Colonies françaises et bureaux à l'étranger: étude des timbres sur* surcharges et des emissions d'impression locale 1852 à 1919, Brussels, Edition du "Philatéliste Belge," 1928.

Hugo Griebert, *The Stamps of Spain (1850–54)*, London, The Author, 1919.

F. Marconnet, *Les Vignettes postales de la France et de ses colonies: catalogue historique et raisonne de toutes les emissions métropolitaines et coloniales depuis 1er Janvier 1849 jusqu'au 1er Juillet 1897*, Nancy, France, Louis Kreis, 1897.

Paul Mirabaud and Baron Axel de Reuterskiöld, *Les Timbres-poste suisses, 1843–1862*, Paris, Librairies-Imprimeries Réunies, 1898.

Varro E. Tyler

The introduction and bibliography represent the longtime work of internationally recognized philatelist Varro E. Tyler. A specialist in the stamps of Japan, he served as chairman of the expertizing committee of the International Society for Japanese Philately for eight years. His work there led him to develop an interest in the forged postage stamps of all countries. In addition to collecting counterfeit stamps, Varro Tyler now lectures and writes extensively about them. His illustrated column, "Focus on Forgeries," appears fortnightly in *Linn's* and a second edition of his book, *Philatelic Forgers: Their Lives and Works* appeared in 1991. His contributions to the field were most recently recognized in 1998 with the John N. Luff Award for Distinguished Philatelic Research — the highest recognition accorded by the American Philatelic Society.

Afghanistan

Period of 1870–91. Nos. 1 to 192. The large number of different figures requires specialization.

1870–71. There are four plates in which the inner circle measures 12½ or 14 mm. The forged set of this issue was produced in various shades in the 6-shahi type of 1871–72 (No. 5) on white laid paper.

1871–72. Thin white wove paper. Two varieties of each value.

Forgeries are bright lilac instead of mauve and are not water-resistant.

1872–73. No. 7. Same paper, twelve varieties.

1872–74. Nos. 8 to 12. Two plates ([Muhammadan] year dates 1290 and 1291). White laid paper. Five or six varieties for each value.

1874–75. White laid paper. Ten varieties of Nos. 13–15. Five varieties of Nos. 14–16.

1875–76. Nos. 17 to 26. Year date 1293 (at bottom). White laid paper. Two varieties for each value designation and three additional varieties in Nos. 18–21 and 22–26. Twelve varieties in Nos. 17–22.

1875–76. Year date 1293 (in the inscriptions on white). White laid paper. In each shade, there are twenty-four varieties for the 1-shahi (one plate, 4 x 6); in the second plate, twelve varieties for the 1-sanar, six for the 1-abasi, and three for the other two values.

1876–77. Year date 1294. Same paper, larger wire marks, papers of various thicknesses. Sheets of forty stamps (5 x 8) comprising the five values. Each stamp is different, so there are forty varieties: three for the 1-abasi (Nos. 1, 6, and 10), two for the ½-rupee (Nos. 2 and 3), two for the 2-rupee (Nos. 4 and 5), and twenty-five for the 1-shahi (Nos. 16–40), all of this in each of the shades.

1878. Year date 1295. Two plates of forty stamps (5 x 8). One for the 1-shahi, for which there thus are forty varieties, and the other values: 1-abasi (Nos. 1 and 6–10) with six varieties, the ½-rupee, with two varieties (Nos. 2–3), and the 1-rupee, two varieties (Nos. 4–5), and 1-sanar, thirty varieties (Nos. 11–40) in each of the shades.

1878. Nos. 102 to 106. Thin white laid paper. Forty varieties (one plate) for each value. To the values described in Yvert should be added the 1-shahi black-brown, the 1-shahi emerald, and the 1-shahi black-brown on similar paper, but bistre shade.

The subsequent issues are hand-printed with aniline ink in single printer's type. See the catalogues for the papers that were used.

Forgeries: in addition to the counterfeits described under the first two issues, there are many others whose overall characteristic is thin wove paper. The 1871–72 issue requires comparative study. A few forgery types are found in Fournier's *Geneva Album,* in the part reserved for experts. Genuine stamps were canceled by having a portion of the stamp torn off. The forgeries show red cancellations. The value is indicated in the originals in the lower right position when the head is shown full-face, but in the 1877 issue the head is turned to the right. No reprints are known. There are Kabul stamp *fantasies* in the type of Nos. 107–9 that easily are identified because the broken line of the outer and inner circles is too thick.

1893–99. Nos. 196 to 200a. Originals are 35 x 24½ mm. There are *forgeries* made to defraud the revenue, with incorrect dimensions. No. 198 on rose-tinted paper (and probably on other shades as well) was counterfeited in Geneva: dimensions 36 x 25¾ mm, curved part of figure "3" in year date at top right is not very visible and seems to be horizontal; the zero (a white dot) is invisible.

Albania

This is a country of many overprints, which the average amateur should avoid collecting: there are ten times more forgeries than authentic stamps there. Only top-flight specialists, who examine each stamp, each overprint, without giving any consideration to cancellations on the backs of stamps, know their way around here.

This little country proves that it is better to issue an abundance of well-printed sets of stamps and to provide generous supplies of them in all post offices than to issue nondescript stamps that are easy to counterfeit. Such stamps channel collectors' money into the pockets of swindlers, not into the coffers of the state.

Before regular stamps were available, independent Albania used Turkish stamps with a circular, dated cancellation with Roman type, which may have been placed in use subsequently in five post offices.

These stamps, which are still rare, constitute the first part of this country's collection. They should be bought on cover, for there are forged cancellations, notably Vlone (Valona) in blue, with a break in the outer circle to the left of this word.

Italian Levant post office stamps overprinted "Albania," "Durazzo," "Scutari di Albania," and "Valona" also can be included in this specialized area.

The first issue (1913) has a black or gray-black overprint that becomes oily and blurred near the end of the printing. It can be found in red or blue on essays that have franked a few letters. There exists an unofficial reprint with ink that is oily and of a darker hue than that of the original, thus producing greater transparency (rare). The 5-para and 5-piaster stamps exist in tête-bêche pairs; the 25- and 50-piaster stamps are fantasies, like all the uncatalogued values in Yvert. No. 12c is a provisional stamp, used in service at Elbassan only a very short time.

Forgeries: numerous. They can be identified by comparing the eagle's plumage. Sometimes a Turkish cancellation is found under the overprint! A set made in Constantinople does not have the protuberance on the back of the right eagle's head; another, made in Geneva, can be identified by a foreshortened eagle's leg. Overprint measurement (wing spread, head, feet, total height, etc.) is necessary.

Second issue (1913). Nos. 13 to 19. No. 13, used before the others, does not have the little eagle control mark or the value figure; gray shade like that of No. 16; clean-cut print. Nos. 14 to 19 (October 25, 1913) have numerous errors in the value designation — 1-, 2-, 19-, 30-para: "pata," "parz," "ara," "aral," "praa," "npara," "paraa," "pqura," "pqra"; 10- and 55-grossion: "grohs," "vgrosh," "grpsh," "gros," "grsh," etc. The control mark is sometimes misplaced, double, upside down, etc. Shades vary with the printings.

Forgeries: numerous. Authenticating by comparison is necessary.

Third issue (end of December 1913). Nos. 20 to 24. Copper cliché, handmade overprint; value overprinted by handstamp. Horizontal or vertical laid paper. Color errors are rare; one finds values omitted and figure errors.

Naturally, the errors in these provisional issues are frequently intentional, like all those in the post-1900 trickery business; it is difficult to distinguish between real errors and those intended as a means of raiding the collector's purse. Conclusion: extreme caution is necessary.

Forgeries: numerous. Comparison is necessary.

Central Albania (Essad Pacha). 1. Use of a large triple-circle (4 cm) hand-canceling stamp in violet; may be considered an official postmark that was used occasionally as a postage stamp, with the regular cancellation on the envelope. A curiosity, nothing more, because of the irregular situation of Essad Pacha.

2. A set executed in Vienna, with inscription, "Albanie Centrale," ordered by Essad Pacha, but not issued, is a fantasy.

Scanderberg issue (1913). Nos. 25 to 30. No forgeries.

1914. Preceding issue overprinted (March 7). Nos. 31 to 36. Handmade overprints, struck twice; 5- and 25-para overprinted with "1461" inscription, etc., inverted.

Koritza stamps. No. 27. There are two values, 10- and 25-para (domestic and foreign postage). Handmade postmark, struck twice on envelopes, then printed on sheets used only on March 30 and 31. The new stamps of the rest of the stock are considered reprints.

Forgeries: very numerous. Compare inks and the design.

Subsequent issues. All of the subsequent issues were extensively forged. Comparison is necessary. All of the uncatalogued sets in Yvert, and Nos. 108–13 (official) and postage due stamps, Nos. 18–22 (1920) are fantasies of no value.

Algeria

1927. Nos. 58 to 70. Well-made forged overprints are known.

Allenstein

Not very interesting stamps. Numerous forged overprints.

1920. Plebiscite. Nos. 1 to 14. The overprint was well copied in excessively boldface type on the entire set. Several other forgery types from the 15-pfennig, No. 4, are in circulation. Comparison is necessary.

1920. Versailles Treaty. Nos. 15 to 28. Forged Chemnitz overprint; about 1 mm shorter and ¼ mm narrower. Several other types from the 15-pfennig lilac, No. 18, are in circulation.

Angola

1870–85. Crown type. Nos. 1 to 14. *Geneva forgeries* are very widespread. (See the illustrations under Portuguese Colonies for distinctive features.) The cross on the crown and the left side of the bandeau sometimes look alike, depending on the type of small counterfeited leaves or the impression. The unissued 40-reis stamp also was counterfeited. The lateral inner frames, which in the originals are thinner than the other frames, are of the same thickness here. Perf 12½.

Forged cancellations (Geneva): double circle with date, CORREIO DE LOANDA 15/10 1881; partial double oval: CORREIO 23 Nov⁰ 73. IASSANS. *Early forgeries* are so poorly executed that they do not deserve description.

Reprints: all values on pure white paper, without gum, and perf 13½ only. A second set (168th printing set) has SPECIMEN on most of the stamps, on chalky paper, with transparent gum, and perf 13½.

1886. The 5-, 20-, and 100-reis were *reprinted* on white paper.

1894. Stamps overprinted 25-reis, No. 37. *Geneva forged overprint:* inner circle is not perfect on left. The cross-hatch lines on the left of REIS are not parallel.

1902. Nos. 57 to 61. The stamps were *reprinted* and are identified by overprint comparison.

Angra

1892. Reprints exist of Nos. 1–8 on nonchalky paper. Perf 13½.

Anjouan

1892–1907. Peace and Commerce type. Nos. 1 to 19. For details on the *forgeries,* see the Peace and Commerce type under the French Colonies (Geneva). The Geneva forged *cancellation* is made of a double octagon with inscription ANJOUAN 19 JUIN 04 COL. FRANC.

1912. Overprinted stamps. Nos. 20 to 30. Comparison is necessary to identify the *forged (Geneva) overprints.*

Annam and Tonkin

A great many overprint varieties are known. We advise specialists to consult F. Marconnet's book (1897), pages 248–54, and Baron de Vinck de Winnezeele's text (1928). Forged overprints are very numerous. Detailed comparison is indispensable. Avoid these overprints unless you are specializing, for authentic handstamp devices subsequently were used to make counterfeits. Ink comparison is mandatory. The "5" on 2-centime brown is an unissued stamp.

Geneva counterfeits: overprints of No. 1 (two types); No. 2 (four types); Nos. 3 and 4 (seven types); Nos. 5 and 6 (one type); No. 7 (one type).

Forged Geneva cancellations: double circle HA-NOI 2ᵉ 21 JUIL. 92 TONKIN; double circle with broken line inner circle: NAM-DINH 1 OCT 92 TONKIN; HANOI 3ᵉ 27 FEVRIER 88 TONKIN, and HUE 6 JUIL 88 ANNAM. Interchangeable figures.

Antigua

First issues, 1- and 6-pence. *Early forgeries* have no watermark and usually are perf 13. These are very mediocre lithographs. A quick comparison with an original, that is, No. 6, which is rather common used, will justify rejection of the forgeries. The seventeen regular lozenges of the lateral cross-hatching in the genuine are arbitrarily shaped in the forgery.

Antioquia

See Colombia.

Arabia

See Saudi Arabia.

Argentina

1858. Nos. 1, 2, and 3. *Early forgeries:* a half-dozen forged sets with various forged postmarks. They may be identified by the following: dot after the "10" or "15"; the final letters of the upper inscription are equidistant from the lateral frames; letters "R G" are almost touching the upper frame; the large oval does not touch the lateral frames or touches only one of them; single line, not double, under abbreviation "on"; the "C" of CONFEᵒⁿ is touching the left frame; unnecessary outer framework, 1 and sometimes 2 mm away from stamp; paper tinted on back (10-centavo); etc. See the illustration also.

Photolithographed Geneva forgeries: more deceptive than the preceding ones; width, 19¼ instead of about 19½ mm. Shades: brownish red, yellowish green, and dark blue (the latter is rare in the originals). Paper is too thin (50 microns) and too transparent. The distinctive transfer marks are missing.

Forged Geneva cancellations: (1) oval containing the word FRANCA (inner oval is too thick); (2) oval with CORREOS NATIONAL FRANCA DE MENDOZA; (3) double oval: CORREOS NATIONAL FRANCA DEL ROSARIO (terminal lines embryonic or missing); (4) oval with date: MENSAGE. . . . 15 MZ MENDOZA; (5) left half of single oval with ADMᵒⁿ DE C DE CHIVILC; (6) word FRAN on one line. Ink is too gray in all of them. There are no reprints.

1861. No. 4. In this issue, the originals, including Nos. 4a and 4b (unissued), have a dividing frame line between the stamps. The large oval is about ¹/₂ mm away from the lateral frames. The figures are much too large; the upper inscription is more symmetrically arranged; the Greek ornament is more delicately executed; there is only one line under the abbreviations "on"; etc. The illustration will show the principal defects of the 5-centavo stamp, which was counterfeited in Geneva with the previously described cancellations. Red and red-brown shade; paper is too thin.

1862–63. Nos. 5, 6, and 7. *Originals:* the 5-centavo has two types. Type I: fourteen shade lines in the medallion and seventy-four pearls; the "V" of CENTAVOS is more open. Type II (1864): eleven horizontal lines and seventy-two pearls. The 10-centavo has fourteen horizontal lines, seventy-eight pearls; the 15-centavo, fifteen lines and seventy-two pearls. In the 10- and 15-centavo, the "A" letters, the extremities of the foliage on the right of the medallion, and the "C" of CENTAVOS are similar to the 5-centavo, Type I.

Early forgeries: various lithographed sets of the three values. Type I: eleven shade lines, horizontal arm lines; no accent after the figure; eighty-one pearls. Type II: ten lines, seventy-six pearls. Type III: practically no lines, seventy-nine pearls (counterfeits from the worn plate of the 6-centavo, 1863). Naturally, none of these forgeries nor the following ones show the transfer plate marks.

Geneva forgeries: first, the 5-centavo, Type II, was reproduced (eleven shade lines, seventy-two pearls) by using a so-called "reprint." Thin (60–65 microns), transparent and stippled paper; or thick (90–100 microns) wove paper. Almost congruent value inscription, but the accent after the "S" is too rectangular, and the white circle surrounding the pearls is too narrow above TIN (see the illustration also).

Next, from this first photolithographed cliché, they printed secondary reproductions, which are similar in every respect (seventy-two pearls), if one changes the value figures to "10" and "15." These figures are placed too high and the accent has disappeared completely. These forgeries are more widespread than the so-called "reprints." There are arbitrary shades: 15-centavo milky blue or dark blue-gray. Same forged cancellations as in the first issue.

So-called "reprints": these really good-looking counterfeits were reproduced from the original matrix of the 5-centavo, Type II. Thus, there are eleven shade lines; seventy-two pearls; the "C" is narrow and the "A" letters are pointed at the top. The Phrygian bonnet is white, except for a faint color dot in the middle, on top; its supporting attachment is rather wide and is terminated below by a very faint line. The 10- and 15-

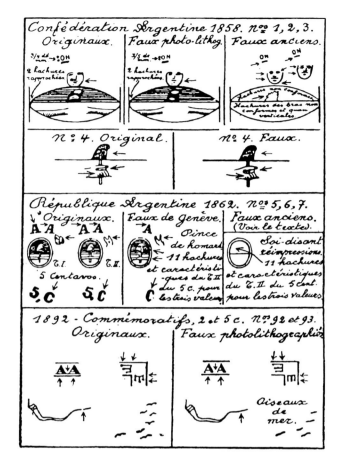

Top: Argentine Confederation, 1858. Nos. 1, 2, 3. Left: originals, ³/₄ mm, two closely set shade lines. Center: photolithographed forgeries, ³/₅ mm, two closely set shade lines. Right: early forgeries; noncongruent shading; noncongruent, almost vertical arm shade lines. Second row: left: No. 4 original. Right: No. 4 forgery. Third row: Argentine Republic, 1862. Nos. 5, 6, 7. Left: originals, Types I and II, 5-centavo. Center: Geneva forgeries, lobster claw, eleven shade lines and Type II characteristics of 5-centavo for the three values. Right: early forgeries, so-called "reprints," eleven shade lines and Type II characteristics of 5-centavo for the three values. Bottom: 1892. Commemorative stamps. 2- and 5-centavo, Nos. 92 and 93. Left: originals. Right: photolithographed forgeries, seagulls.

centavo stamps were reproduced from the same matrix by changing the figures, the other characteristics remaining the same. No reprints.

1864. Rivadavia. The recess print engraving of the originals allows one to spot the early counterfeits with the naked eye; they are poor lithographed images without a watermark. Nevertheless, we will indicate a few distinctive features: the "C" of CENTAVOS resembles an "S"; the circular ornament before QUINCE in the 15-centavo is broken at bottom and the thickest circle is touching the break; the ornament after CENTAVOS is touching the line on its left; etc.

1867–68. Nos. 18 to 20. The originals are recess print engraved and perf 12. Some of the early lithographed forgeries of this set are so bad that they do not merit description.

1877. Stamps overprinted "1," "2," and "8." Nos. 29 to 31. The original overprint of "2" measures $10^1/_2$ x 14 mm. Upright and inverted forged overprints: comparison is indispensable. All three values were counterfeited in Geneva.

1884. Stamps overprinted "1884$^1/_2$." No. 43. Forged overprints in black and red: comparison would be useful. In the overprint counterfeited in Geneva, the horizontal bar of the "4 " is thick and has no terminal line.

1890. Inverted "$^1/_2$" overprints. Nos. 91b and 91c. Forged inverted overprints in black and red (Geneva); comparison is necessary.

1892. Commemorative stamps. Nos. 92 and 93. The two values, which were engraved expertly by the South American Company, were nicely copied in Geneva. The upper corner designs differ; letters are well separated; also, look at the oriflamme and the seagulls in the illustration. In the 5-centavo forgery, the "S" of CENTAVOS is heavily notched, bottom right. Forged sun watermark; allowable perforation; arbitrary shades, especially the 5-centavo, which is too indigo. 2-centavo, width: $26^1/_4$ instead of $26^1/_6$ mm; 5-centavo, $25^1/_5$ instead of $26^1/_3$ mm. Forged round cancellation with date: BUENOS AIRES A OC 12 7.92.

1921. 5-centavo orange. No. 233. Used postal forgery. Perf $11^1/_2$ instead of $13^1/_2$ x $12^1/_2$ or $13^1/_2$; eighteen white hatch lines in the tunic instead of twenty-two, between its collar and the figure on the right.

Official stamps. 1884. Nos. 1 to 24. Numerous forged overprints; comparison is indispensable. The two overprint types were counterfeited in Geneva.

Buenos Aires. 1858. Vessel. *Originals:* typographed from a woodcut: 22 x $18^1/_2$ mm. (1) The second "O" of CORREOS is larger than the other letters. (2) There is a hyphen (usually a white dot) between BUENOS and AIRES. (3) Three of the white corner circles (worn type traces) are touching the outer frame. (4) There are seven rope lines between the bowsprit and the mainmast, which are usually broken. (5) The mainmast oriflamme is formed with two lines; the one on top is horizontal; the other is an oblique ascending line. (6) The stern colors are formed with two horizontal lines, which are pointed toward the "A" of FRANCO,

touching the oval. (7) The stamp margins are always very narrow: only $^1/_2$–$^3/_4$ mm between stamps.

Forgeries: lithographed. There are about twenty counterfeits of various values, several of which exist in sets. It would take too long to enumerate them in detail; however, all of them have one of the following distinctive marks: (1) letters of CORREOS, identical with those of BUENOS AIRES instead of larger. (2) Upper bar of the "E" of CORREOS is much too long. (3) Letters of the same word are too slender. (4) The second "O" of the word is just as large or smaller than the other letters. (5) No hyphen between BUENOS and AIRES. (6) Nine rope lines between the bowsprit and the mainmast (or five, or six). (7) None of the white circles is touching the outer frame (or a single one is touching). (8) The two oriflamme lines (mainmast) are horizontal, or they come together, or there is only one. (9) The stern colors are pointing toward the "N" of FRANCO or the bottom of the stamp; it does not touch the oval; it gets wider near the oval; it goes past the oval. (10) The sun is hardly visible; its rays are vertical instead of fan-shaped; etc.

A few distinctive features of the value indication can be mentioned: (1) "IN PS" printed "IR PS"; "UN PS" printed "1 PS"; "T PS" printed "IN PS " but the right downstroke of the "N" is missing and the foot of the "P" is almost touching the tablet; "UN-PS" (with hyphen). Most of the time no trace of the scraped off "C" is found. (2) "DOS PS," letters are too large and are almost touching the tablet edge; "2 PS"; "DOS-PS" (with hyphen). (3) "TRES PS" printed "3 PS." (4) "CUATRO PS" printed "4 P^s," "CUATR PS," "FOUR PS." (5) "CINCO PS" printed "5 PS," etc.

Paper and shades are arbitrary, especially in the complete Geneva set (yellowish or white paper, in blocks) in which the BUENOS AIRES lettering is very variable in height. Forged cancellations as on the forged set of the first Argentina issues. Note: Most of the counterfeits are not transparent, whereas the originals are always sufficiently so.

Reprints: the problem of reprints made with stolen clichés is an additional complication; specialization is advisable. No. 1 (2-peso) was executed in milky blue and dark dull blue; No. 2 (3-peso), on thin transparent paper; No. 7 ("IN PS"), in the shades of the No. 1 reprints. Other reprintings of Nos. 1 and 2 were made in 1893 on very thick, yellowish paper in blue and yellow-green (rare).

Buenos-Aires. 1860. Liberty type. *Originals:* (1) the inscriptions are equidistant from the four sides of the tablet. (2) The hyphen between BUENOS and AIRES is sometimes invisible in the heavy impressions. (3) Letters of CORREOS are thicker than those of the bottom inscription. (4) There are five shading lines in the tuck of the Phrygian bonnet and three short lines in the white section above the tuck. (5) On the right and left of the circle, there are four fine shade lines (not including the inner frame). (6) The outer frame is more than half as finely printed as the frame of the lateral tablets.

Forgeries: various sets offend in one of the following ways. (1) The inscriptions are misplaced in one or another direction. (2) No hyphen between BUENOS and AIRES. (3) There are three small lines in the bonnet tuck, or two, or a few lines pointing downwards. (4) Seven shade lines on the right of the circle and six on the left, or three thick ones on the right and two on the left, or (Geneva) four nonsymmetrical ones on the left and three on the right. (5) The "S" of BUENOS resembles an inverted "Z." (6) The first "O" of CORREOS is a "Q." (7) The outer frame line is as thick as the lateral tablet frame. (8) A dot after REALES in the 4-real stamp. (9) Letters "NOS" (Geneva) are twice as thick as "BUE." (10) The shade lines on the right of the cheek are practically horizontal instead of pointing toward the chin (Geneva set). Some so-called "essays" of the "TRES PS" were lithographically printed without gum, in dark green and other shades in conformity with a stolen cliché.

Reprints: Nos. 1, 2, 6, 7, and 8 were reprinted lithographically (not typographically), without gum, on very thick (160 microns) glossy paper, in slightly different shades.

Córdoba. 1858. Nos. 1 and 2. *Originals:* 5-centavo, horizontally laid paper; 10-centavo, vertically laid paper; both values can be found only partly laid. The 5-centavo has no dot after CEN except in a single stamp of the plate: thirty stamps (10 x 3); the gutters between stamps are $1/2$–$1 1/2$ mm wide, maximum; the 10-centavo is surrounded by a very fine rectangular frame which is only partly visible quite often. $16 3/4$ x about $22 1/2$ mm axis length; letters without terminal lines; figure "1," likewise; the top of the "5" is almost touching the oval. There is always a dot after figure "10." The center design is surrounded by a thin oval line, then by a heavy oval line, finally, by two thin oval lines; the last three of these are joined by heavy lines; this part of the design appears as a succession of double white lines surrounding the heavy oval line; in the originals (secret mark?), there is only one thick white line immediately on the right of the "N" of CEN. No reprints.

Forgeries: (1) typographed; wove paper; 5-centavo in blue-green; 10-centavo in gray-brown; in this last value, no dot after CEN; the "5" is quite far removed from the center oval. This set is easily identifiable by the lack of the vertical shading in the two tower foundations; two white lines on the right above the "N" of CEN. (2) Lithographed; wove paper; 5-centavo, always with dot; 10-centavo, always without dot after CEN; a set easy to

check, the two outer oval lines almost joining above letters "R D O." (3) Much better set; lithographed; paper vertically laid for the two values; both with dot after CEN; nearly 17 x $22 3/4$–$22 4/5$ mm, axis length; letters "D," "A," and "N" with terminal lines, as well as figure "1," which is provided with a heavy oblique line and a heavy horizontal line at its base; there are two thin white lines instead of a single thick one, on the right, above the "N" of CEN. The first pearl, top left, is too small and has inside it, in its lower part, a short colored line, instead of a wide curving line on the right of the pearl in the originals; the top right pearl is too elongated; in general, it is a set that is new, with fine margins. The 15-, 20-, 30-centavo and 1-peso stamps are fantasies. There is a forged Geneva cancellation of CORDOBA, but it is applied on original stamps or on Argentina forgeries: rectangular, with corners cut off, divided in three by two horizontal bars with inscriptions, CERTIFICADO 14 MAY. 99 CORDOBA.

Corrientes. 1856. Nos. 1 and 2. *Originals:* typographed; 19 x 22 mm; sixteen grapes; regular corner crosses, and no wider than the frame's white lines.

Forgeries: (1) lower inscription — "1 REALE N C" instead of "UN REAL M C"; five horizontal hatch lines under the nose; nine grapes that are unconvincingly arranged; corner crosses are nearly $1/2$ mm wide. (2) Bad face design; bunch of nine oblong grapes. The forgeries are lithographed on excessively thick paper; the inscriptions are too sharply etched.

1861–74. No value indication. Nos. 3 to 9. *Forgeries:* few distinguishing features of the counterfeited sets follow: (1) the two laurel leaves behind the head are undefinable. (2) The vertical lines of the inner corners are not straight. (3) The bottom of the vertical downstroke of the first "R" of CORRIENTES is broken by a black spot (Geneva). (4) The grapes are round or else lozenge-like (Geneva). (5) The back downstroke of the first "R" of CORRIENTES is touching the bottom of the tablet.

Reprints. No. 3 blue-gray instead of blue; No. 4 gray-green instead of green; No. 6 brownish orange instead of yellow or brownish yellow; No. 8 or 9 violet instead of rose or magenta. No. 4a was reprinted also in yellow-green, and No. 6 in yellow, shades that are not very different from the originals. Comparison is indicated.

Armenia

All overprinted sets must undergo close comparative examination.

Austria

The first issues are among the most interesting: varieties of types, papers, shades, cancellations, pairs, strips, blocks, and secondary varieties. The classification of about a hundred very different specimens of each of the values of the 1850 issue is possible. Research in cancellations, some of which are very rare, will add to this number.

Select imperforate stamps must have four margins, minimum 1 mm wide. For postage due stamps on newspapers, a 1 mm margin is sufficient. Newspaper stamps, Nos. 1 to 4, have vertical margins $1/2$ mm wide, horizontal margins, a little wider.

1850. First issue. Values in kreuzer. Nos. 1 to 5.
Sheets of 240 in four panes of sixty-four (8 x 8), each pane containing sixty stamps and, at the bottom, four St. Andrew's crosses. These crosses are rare when they form a pair with a normal stamp: 20–100 francs. Single crosses are not very interesting.

From 1850 to 1853, the paper, which was handmade, had the "K.K.H.M." watermark (the initials of the Imperial and Royal Ministry of Commerce). These English capital letters were placed vertically in the middle of the sheet and overlay only four stamps of each pane.

From 1854, the paper was machine-made, thin, glossy, and without watermark. Especially when it is thin, the handmade paper shows transparencies more extensively and irregularly than does machine-made paper, where the transparencies are more symmetrical. The greater number of transparencies may be attributed to irregularities in the rollers of the paper-making machine.

The thin paper reminds one of certain kinds of tissue paper. The thickness of the papers, which is variable, may approach that of card paper.

Types are recognized by the position of the figure in the tablet and by its distance from the "K." See the accompanying illustration. Types III and IV are found only in the 9-kreuzer stamp.

A few specimens of a 12-kreuzer unissued stamp are known canceled. The color error, 3-kreuzer blue instead of red, is exceedingly rare. The 2- and 6-kreuzer were used bisected. The 1-, 3-, 6-, and 9-kreuzer stamps were rouletted (unofficially) in Hungary (Tokay, Varonne, and Homonna). Buy them on cover only!

Transparent and very defective prints are in demand — for example, the printing errors "K E," "E K," or "K P" for "K K"; the letters "K K" connected at the top; STAMPEI; KREUZEP; the figure "2" without a loop; a white spot measuring 2 mm in the eagle on the right (plate defect of No. 3); the "T" of "K K POST" with a loop on the right (first composition).

The 1-kreuzer is found printed on both sides, with the impression upright, inverted, or un-inked (visible only as a plate impression).

For cancellation study, we recommend the work of M.H. Kropf, *Die Abstempelungen der Marken von Oesterreich-Ungarn und Lombardei-Venetien* (Prague, 1899, 161 pp.).

Type A dumb cancellations are in demand; the Vienna and Cracow specimens (ornamented circle) are worth from 3 to 5U; others, rarer, are worth up to 30U on Nos. 1 and 2, and up to 50 or 60 francs on Nos. 3–5. There are about twenty types.

One finds ornamented cancellations, with name of town or city, that are just as rare, and common cancellations, Types D, E, and F, may be very rare when they come from sparsely populated communities.

Type B is rare; Type C varies in rarity, but Vienna is common; Type D, circle with date, also is found with time indication, ornaments, or the names of provinces at the bottom. Type E is made with straight, slanted, or cursive capital letters; it is unframed or framed by a

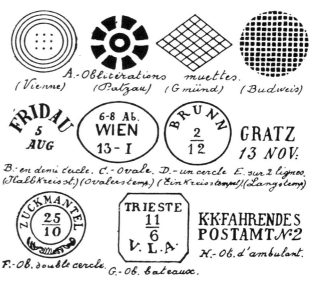

A. Dumb cancellations (Vienna, Patzau, Gmund, and Budweis). B. Half Circle. C. Oval. D. Circle. E. Two lines. F. Double circle. G. Ship. H. Mobile (railway post office).

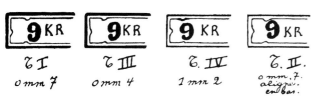

The distance between the figure "9" and the letters "KR." From left, the types are I, 0.7 mm; III, 0.4 mm; IV, 1.2 mm; II, 0.7 mm. Notice that the bottom of the "KR" and the "9" align.

rectangle or an octagon. Type F, like Type D, is found with or without ornaments at the bottom or with province name. The ship cancellations (Type G) are recognized by the letters VLA, except that RIVA VAPORE and the postmarks of Type E are of varying rarity.

Railway station postmarks bear the word "Bahnhof" or its abbreviation, "BF"; printed matter (books, magazines, etc.) has markings of the "Zeitungs" dispatch; military postal service, "Feldpost," etc.

In addition, there are printed matter, "Franco," and registered letter cancellations with or without city or town name. Red cancellations are rare, except Vienna. Levant cancellations are rare in general. Lombardy cancellations are in demand.

Pairs are worth 3U; strips of three: 6U for the 1- and 2-kreuzer stamps, 10U for the other values. Strips of four are worth 15U for the 1- and 2-kreuzer stamps, but 80U for the other values. Blocks of four are rare; No. 1: 500 francs; No. 2: 1,000 francs; No. 3: 125 francs; No. 4: 400 francs; No. 5: 250 francs.

Reprints: shades are generally too vivid, but the impression is good and clear.

1866. White glossy paper, thin yellowish gum. No. 1, sulfur color; No. 2, deep black; No. 3, old rose; No. 4, yellow-brown; No. 5, violet-blue. Rare.

1870. Thick glossy paper, thick yellowish gum. No. 1, sulfur color; No. 2, black; No. 3, red; No. 4, pale brown; No. 5, dark blue. Blurred printing, especially Nos. 1, 2, and 4.

1884. Orange, black, red, gray-brown, blue-gray.

1887. 1-kreuzer dull orange, golden yellow.

1892. 2-kreuzer black. For mint stamps, comparison is obligatory.

Forgeries: 1. a few early forgeries, badly done, deserve only brief mention.

2. The 3-, 6-, and 9-kreuzer were cleverly counterfeited in Geneva (F.), using forged plates from Lombardy. (See this region, which follows.)

3. The 2-kreuzer black is an Olmutz forgery. Modern paper, occasionally ribbed. Comparison of the escutcheon's stippling and of the small shield's design will suffice. This forgery was made in pairs, hence a St. Andrew's cross; presumably the whole set will be counterfeited this way.

1858. Embossed impression. Perf 15. Nos. 7 to 16.
Select: centered, with cancellation light enough to allow one to see the type.

Types: Type I has a slight bump at the top of the forehead, but in Type II, the end of a laurel leaf, which is separated from the forehead by a color dot, can be seen quite clearly. The laurel crown barely rises above the head in Type I, but in Type II, it has three very clear-cut, higher points. See the Lombardy illustration for the curl behind the neck.

The 15-kreuzer, Type I, has a dot after "K R"; in Type II, this dot has disappeared.

Nos. 11 to 16 were issued February 20, 1859; the 3-kreuzer, Type I, was used only from November 1858 to the end of July 1859.

Varieties: in demand: transparent and very defective prints; double prints of the 5- and 10-kreuzer stamps; double print of the portrait, one of which is inverted, in the 15-kreuzer. The 2-kreuzer stamp was bisected: very rare. The 3-kreuzer black stamps, Type I, with white shading of very visible ornaments are rare. The St. Andrew's cross stamps that form a pair with a normal stamp are very rare: 400 francs.

Cancellations: black, common; red, rather common; blue, 2U; Lombardy in blue, very rare.

Pairs: 3U; blocks of four: all rare; Nos. 14–16: 40U.

Reprints: Nos. 11–16. Same dates and paper as for the previous issue. All are Type II. Different shades and perforations.

1865. Perf 12. Rare.

1870. Perf 10½.

1884. Perf 13 and imperforate. Note: The 2-kreuzer orange of this set was not reprinted.

1887. Perf 13, and imperforate of the 2-kreuzer yellow and orange and of the 3-kreuzer black and green.

1889. 2-kreuzer orange, perf 12½.

Fakes: imperforate reprints fraudulently perf 15, and perforated stamps fraudulently reperforated.

Forged cancellations: numerous on the reprints. In the first two issues, we can mention the following: circular postmark Mira 26-5; double circle Massa; rectangular postmark without inscription other than "58"; a number of forged postmarks; and even forgeries of many authentic postmarks that were discarded by the postal service.

1861. Embossed portrait. Perf 14. Nos. 17 to 21.
Rare shades: 2-kreuzer, vivid yellow; 10-kreuzer, brown-black (very dark brown); 15-kreuzer, blue-black (very dark blue).

Varieties: 2-kreuzer, ribbed paper: rare; laid paper: 250 francs; the 10-kreuzer was used bisected: very rare; transparent prints, No. 18: 7.50 francs; Nos. 19–22: 5 francs; 5-kreuzer, double print: very rare.

Cancellations: oval or octagonal from Vienna in red: not very common; blue cancellations: rare; Trieste Col Vapore: 5 francs.

Reprints: 1866. Glossy paper; 2-kreuzer sulfur color; 3-kreuzer yellow-green; 5-kreuzer brick red; 10-kreuzer red-brown; 15-kreuzer dark blue. Perf 12. Rare.

1871. Thick white paper, yellowish gum. Perf 10½, 2-kreuzer orange; the other values as in 1866.

1884. Thin glossy paper, white gum. Perf 13 and imperforate. 2-kreuzer lemon color; 3-kreuzer pale olive green; 5-kreuzer pale orange; 10-kreuzer pale red-brown; 15-kreuzer pale blue.

1887. Same paper. Perf 12 and 12½. 2-kreuzer yellow and orange; 3-kreuzer green.

1863. Coat of arms. Perf 14. Nos. 22 to 26.
Shades: the very dark shaded 10- and 15-kreuzer stamps are not common.

Varieties: transparent prints: rare.

Cancellations: see the previous issue.

Reprints: 1884: glossy paper; perf 13 and imperforate. 2-kreuzer sulfur color; 3-kreuzer pale olive; 5-kreuzer rose red; 10-kreuzer dull blue; 15-kreuzer yellow-brown.

1887–92: thin paper; 2-kreuzer sulfur color and orange; 3-kreuzer yellow-green — both perf 10½ and imperforate; 5-kreuzer rose (aniline) and 10-kreuzer blue, perf 13¼; and 15-kreuzer yellowish brown, perf 11½.

1864. Coat of arms. Perf 9½. Nos. 27 to 31.
Watermark: watermarks in double line capitals reaching to the middle of the sheet.

Varieties: 2-kreuzer tête-bêche: very rare; 2- and 5-kreuzer, vertical laid paper: very rare; 15-kreuzer, printed both sides: very rare. With parts of watermark: 3U. The transparent prints of the 2- and 3-kreuzer stamps are rare; others: 5 francs.

Reprints: see the preceding issue. Envelope cutouts are known; they are rare on cover.

Subsequent issues. For a detailed description of subsequent issues, which are too numerous for our study and less interesting than the first ones, we refer the reader to the general and specialized catalogues.

1867. The 2-kreuzer yellow stamp, perf 10¼ x 13, is very rare. It is known to exist bisected diagonally. Of the 3-kreuzer red, color error, only three copies are known to be extant; the 2-, 10-, and 15-kreuzer stamps are known with double print, and all values with print transparency. A block of four of the 15-kreuzer is rare. The 25- and 50-kreuzer stamps on cover: rare.

Fakes: the rare perforations were produced by using common stamps that were repaired and given forged perforations. No. 38, an envelope cutout, was given a rare forged perforation; on grayer, more fleecy paper.

Forgeries to cheat the postal service: 10-kreuzer blue. Poor workmanship. Compare corners and beard design.

Vienna forgeries: only half of the necessary shading is under the "50"; beard and ornament design at variance with the original.

1883. Each value comprises two types, which are recognizable by the figures.

Faking of rare perforations as above, or perforation applied to common stamps that are too large in format.

Reprint: 1883. 5-kreuzer dull red, perf 10½.

1890–96. 1-kreuzer gray, figure definitely out of place: rare; 10-kreuzer blue, without figure in three corners: very rare.

Official forgeries: the set of 1- to 20-kreuzer stamps may have been counterfeited on thick paper like that of the 24- to 50-kreuzer and the 1- and 2-groschen stamps. We do not know whether the paper used was official, whether the forgeries were printed in the state's shops by an undisciplined foreman (H), or whether they were made elsewhere.

New Stamps

1918. Air mail. A forged set. Comparison with No. 157 or 158 will identify these forgeries, which are sometimes offered for sale on covers furnished with everything necessary to attract a buyer.

1919–21. Inverted center. *Fake* with a center that has been pasted on, visible through a magnifying glass or a microscope.

Fantasy sets: rather numerous. Consult reliable catalogues only.

Newspaper Stamps

1851–58. Mercury head. Imperforate. Nos. 1 to 4.
Select: vertical margins, ½ mm wide; horizontal margins, minimum ¾ mm.

Types: there are three types (see the accompanying illustration); all three are found in No. 1 (Type III, rare: 2U); Nos. 2 and 4 are Type I; No. 3 (1856) belongs to Type II.

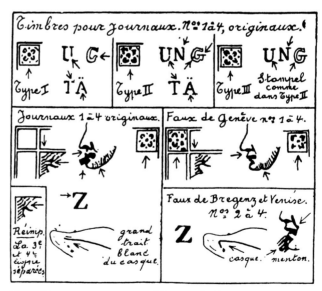

Top: Newspaper stamps. Nos. 1–4. Originals. "Stampel" as in Type II. Middle: Geneva forgeries. Bottom: Reprint; third and fourth lines broken; heavy white line in helmet. Forgeries of Bregenz and Venice, Nos. 2–4. Helmut; chin.

Paper: thick handmade, or thin machine-made; No. 1 exists also on ribbed paper with its usual dull greenish blue shade.

Cancellations: the Lombardy cancellations are in demand.

Pairs: No. 1: 5U; the other: very rare; blocks of four: very rare.

Reprints: all in Type I. Machine-made paper. The illustration shows distinguishing characteristics.

1866. Thick smooth paper; shades very close to the originals: rare.

1870. Rough thick paper; same shades, but darker; No. 4 in rose and carmine; yellowish gum.

1884. Thin yellowish paper, yellowish gum; different shades; No. 2, bright yellow; No. 3, red.

1885. Thin paper; dull white gum; No. 1, slate; No. 2, pale yellow; No. 3, vermilion red; No. 4, dark purplish rose. Not very common.

1887–1903. The three reprints of this set are somewhat different in shade: No. 1, dull blue, slate blue; No. 2, dull, lifeless yellow; No. 3, vermilion red; No. 4, dark rose. Smooth glossy paper; white gum.

Crude early forgeries: about ten different forgeries, poorly executed and sometimes in sets, can be recognized very easily by comparing the design with a reprinted copy or with a copy of the common No. 1 stamp.

An examination of the lettering, the rosettes, the background burelage, and the details of the head and winged helmet will justify immediate rejection of these forgeries: no need to examine paper, shades, and cancellations. For example, the letters "K K" are too narrow by half, or too wide; ZEITUNGS is only a little more than half as high as it should be; copies have a double frame; the "S" of STAMPEL is normal; the "P" of POST or the first "K" lacks a curvilinear line at the bottom, or the lines are too thick. They frequently are found canceled with date or with dotted lozenge.

Better early and modern forgeries: there are almost as many of these as of the early, crude ones just described. They look better: the design is better executed (occasionally photolithographed), and the shades are closer to those of the originals.

Here, too, the shape and height of the lettering (especially the "S" of STAMPEL), the shape of the corner rosettes, the arrangement of burelage lines and of shading of the helmet and face (eye, nostril, ear, shading of cheek or of neck), the absence of dots after STAMPEL or "K K" — these are enough to identify and eliminate the forgeries.

The Geneva forgeries (F.) can be classified in this category (see illustration). Naturally, the shades are not the same, but some of them are very close to the shades of the originals or of certain reprints. The cancellations, which are more competently counterfeited, are good enough to fool anyone who does not examine his purchases with care, or who is naive enough to rely on the good faith of a fellow human being.

Finally, two or three counterfeits — for example, the Bregenz and Venice sets, Nos. 2, 3, 4 — require further study. This is sometimes difficult with the yellow shade. It is suggested that stamp type be considered (see illustration); if a No. 3 stamp belongs to Type I, as is the case with the Geneva forgeries, the copy offered evidently is forged.

One must not forget that the originals are printed on white paper, on which yellow does not come out very well. One should note also that the printing is not first rate, and that the shades are fresh and bright. See the illustration for the best forgeries known: Bregenz and Venice.

Forged cancellations: innumerable on reprints and on forgeries of all sorts.

On Geneva forgeries: circular postmarks, 22 mm, woodcut — POLA 20/5; BREITEN 17/12 52; RADOTIN 6/12 50; WIEN 9-11 N 2 III. These postmarks also are found on reprints.

On Bregenz forgeries: inks too new, postmarks at variance with originals: double circle EXPEDIZIONE GAZETTE VENEZIA, letters too high, Bregenz in Roman capitals on two lines with date, its letters too high; Bregenz in slanted italics, the "G" too narrow in Bregenz 2 JUN. There are double circle postmarks, too: ZEITUNGS EXPED WIEN 10/4; and an octagonal postmark of Salzburg of which the cut-off corners are too long; etc.

Fakes: there are fakes made by chemical treatment, in particular of No. 1, to obtain yellow. Use a spectroscope.

1858–59–61. Embossed portrait. Nos. 5 to 8.
Select: four margins 1 mm wide, minimum.

No. 5 belongs to Type I of the 1858 stamps; No. 6 belongs to Type II. No. 5 is found on thick or thin paper.

Shades: No. 5 (1858), blue and dark blue; No. 6 (1859), various shades that can be subdivided into more or less dark lilac and gray: 50M. No. 7 (1861), of which Yvert's No. 8 is only a shade variety, has shades from brownish lilac to pale gray, with intermediate shades of purplish and greenish gray.

Cancellations: Lombardy cancellations are in demand (Udine, Venice, etc.). The ornamental cancellation of Cracow is not very common.

Pairs: 4U; blocks of four: very rare.

Reprints: 1866: very good impression; No. 5, bright blue; No. 6, lilac-gray; No. 7, lilac-gray: rare.

1870: slightly defective impression; No. 5, dull blue; No. 6, reddish violet; No. 7, lilac-gray and brownish lilac.

1884: good impression; No. 5, greenish blue; No. 6, brownish purple-red; No. 7, like 1870.

1885: No. 5, dark blue; No. 6, dark violet; No. 7, dark violet.

1887–92: Good impression; No. 5, dull blue; No. 6, pale violet; No. 7, lilac-gray and reddish lilac.

Forgeries: not numerous, the reprints having provided enough material for fraud, particularly forged cancellations.

A rather attractive forgery of No. 5, which is poorly executed, belongs to Type II; the white ornaments of the four tablets are adorned on the inside with a blue flourish; the bottoms of the letters of POST are touching the tablet's white line, and the opening of the horn in the upper left corner is facing right! (This was described in my 1922 *Catalogue du Spécialiste d'Europe*.)

1863. Coat of arms. Embossed impression. No. 9. *Select:* four margins 1 mm wide.

Shades: gray, gray-brown, lilac-gray.

Watermark: ZEITUNGS-MARKEN. Two specimens of tête-bêche stamps are known. With part of watermark: 2U.

Reprints: brownish lilac in 1870, 1884 (yellowish paper), and 1887–92. Dark lilac-gray in 1885.

Postage Due Stamps

1918–19. Nos. 64 to 74. The overprint was counterfeited for the whole set. Comparison is necessary.

Telegraph Stamps

1873. Lithographed. Perf 12. In the 5-kreuzer, Type I, the value is in bolder type, and the year date is in type that is shorter than that of Type II. The 20-, 40-, and 60-kreuzer stamps belong to Type II.

The lithographed stamps have duller shades than those engraved in 1874–76. In these, the value stands out against a cross-ruled background, in which press-clogging often produces an impression of fullness, and the "3" of 1873 appears to be an "8."

Fakes: the bisected 50-kreuzer of the lithographic sets has a forged perforation. Compare shade and format, and check perforation.

Postage Due Stamps for Newspapers

Types: I. Large crown. A sort of crest shaped like a Napoleonic hat appears on the head of the eagle on the left; the crest ends in a point directed toward the tip of the eagle's wing.

II. Large crown. The aforementioned ornament is detached from the head and forms a three-point oriflamme.

III. Small crown.

1853–78. Imperforate. *Select:* four margins 1 mm wide.

Type I, 1-kreuzer blue (1858): rare; Types II and III (1878), common. 2-kreuzer green (1853), Type I, yellow-green, blue-green, or dark green. 2-kreuzer brown (1858), Type II; (1878) Type III. 4-kreuzer brown (1858), Type I.

Watermark: the 1- and 2-kreuzer Type III stamps (1878) have the ZEITUNGSMARKEN watermark above the sheet.

Varieties: the bisected 2-kreuzer green and 2-kreuzer blue: rare. The 2- and 4-kreuzer are found with manuscript overprint. The 4-kreuzer is rare on cover: 2U. The 2-kreuzer, Type II, exists as tête-bêche with gutter.

Reprints: 1873, 2-kreuzer dark green good impression on yellowish stamp belonging to Type I, and 4-kreuzer brown on thin paper, Type II.

Early forgeries: fantastic counterfeits in various shades — for example, the 2-kreuzer in black. Compare the center shield with a common original; the bottom of the heraldic eagle must not touch the inner frame.

Modern forgeries: a good photolithographed counterfeit of the 4-kreuzer was made in Geneva; width, 21$^2/_5$ instead of 21$^1/_{10}$ mm. The tongue of the eagle on the left is not touching its head, and the arc in the circular ornament, bottom left, is half as long as it should be. The 1-kreuzer, same source, was forged on Type II with a two-point oriflamme ornament; it is found especially in black. (See Lombardy-Venetia.)

Same forged cancellations as for newspaper stamps.

Internal revenue forgeries (Roverto): 1-kreuzer blue, Type II; the two outer frames appear to be only one frame; the cross above the crown is slanted to the right and is not touching the inner frame; the lozenge-like ornaments touch the round ornaments; numerous design defects. Three types. Internal Revenue obliteration.

Military Mail Service

1915. Bosnian overprinted stamps. The overprint was counterfeited on the whole set. Make comparison. Overprints that are inverted, double, red, etc., are unofficial fantasies. Do not buy. Same advice for the imperforate stamps.

1915. Portrait. Same comment as above.

Forgeries: No. 47. Crude forgery. Comparison will be enough. The set of values in kreuzer will probably be forged too.

Danube Steam Navigation Co.

1866. 10-soldo lilac, dark lilac; 17-soldo scarlet, perf 9$^1/_2$ (also perf 12).

1868–71. 10-soldo green (shades); 10-soldo scarlet (1871), perf 9$^1/_2$. The imperforate stamps are remainders.

Originals: the burelage has secret expertizing marks in the form of broken lines, color dots, etc. — for example, the third and fourth lines are connected and the fifth is broken above the "DO" of DONAU.

Reprints: thick paper, perf 10 or imperforate. 10-soldo pale lilac; 10-soldo green; 10-soldo red-orange. Same identification marks.

Forgeries: two good sets: 1. Geneva (F.). The zero of "10" is too high, almost 3 mm instead of $2^1/_2$ mm; the horizontal bar of the "7" is too long at the top, $1^3/_4$ instead of $1^1/_2$ mm. The secret expertizing marks are missing. Stippling between the two burled lines going to the right between the double "F" of DAMPFSCHIFFAHRT.

2. Another type. The dot after the "10" is closer to the wavy burelage than to the zero. Absence of secret marks.

Lombardy-Venetia

I. Imperforate

1850 (June 1). Value in centesimi. Nos. 1 to 5.
Sheets of 240 stamps in four panes of sixty-four (8 x 8), the last four stamps of each pane replaced by St. Andrew's crosses (bottom rows, right and left). (See also Austria.)

Types: see illustration.
5-centesimi, Type II, is not common. 10-centesimi, Type I, is found with figure "0" open or closed. In Type II (thick paper), the closed zero numeral is rare.

Paper: handmade, from the pulp vat, was used first from 1850 to 1853. This handmade paper is rough and furrowed. When you look at it against a light, you can see more or less extensive thin spots resulting from stippled paper texture. The paper is pliable like the rag from which it was made; medium thickness, 60–100

microns. However, there are thicknesses of more than 100 microns, which are rare.

Machine-made paper, which was used from 1854, is more thoroughly worked and is of uniform thickness. Against a light, one can see only very small, light specks. It obviously is more woven, smoother. This can be seen especially on the back of the stamp. Thickness 50–150 microns, maximum. This kind of paper was not used in the 5-centesimi value.

Naturally, copies from which the gum has been removed in hot water should be measured.

An international agreement on paper thickness classification (see Belgium) would be advantageous in standardizing catalogue descriptions. The importance of this question can be appreciated if one considers that stamps on pelure, card, or cardboard paper sometimes are very rare in the issues of certain countries.

Watermark: letters "KKHM," in English capitals, on sixteen stamps (four from each pane) in the middle of the sheet. Stamps with pieces of the watermark are in demand: 2U. The watermark is found only in handmade paper, including ribbed and laid paper. It is upright, inverted, or reversed.

Select: four margins more than 1 mm wide. The first printing of each value had slightly narrower spacing than the following printings.

Shades: 5-centesimi orange-yellow and a light ochre-yellow that is always orange-tinted: common. Yellow without a trace of orange: rare. Light lemon yellow: extremely rare. 10-centesimi gray-black and black, deep black being less common. 15-centesimi, shades from pale rose red to bright vermilion-tinted red. 30-centesimi, from light red-brown to dark brown, with chocolate in between. 45-centesimi, from pale, sometimes milky, blue to dark blue.

The very numerous shades of all stamp values permit one to create attractive color scales in one's collection.

Varieties: the fine impressions of the first printing are in active demand. There are some defective impressions: 2U. 5-centesimi, very pale ochre-orange: 2U. Printed on both sides: 5M, 5U. Tête-bêche on back: extremely rare. Transparent impression: 2U. 10-centesimi, machine-made paper (1857): 50M, 50U. Transparent impression: 2U. 15-centesimi. Laid paper: extremely rare (vertical lines spaced about $1^1/_2$ mm apart, with a single horizontal line), transparent impression: 4U. Ribbed paper: rare. There are partly albino impressions. 30-centesimi, ribbed paper: rare. Transparent impression: 10U. The 30-centesimi was bisected at Tolmezzo: very rare. 45-centesimi, ribbed paper; transparent impression: 8U.

The stamps without value indication are essays. The 12-centesimi blue is an unissued stamp: rare.

St. Andrew's crosses: single: 5–20 francs. Attached: very rare when the crosses are intact.

Top: "0" open or closed. Bottom: head; nape of neck.

Pairs: 4U, except the 15-centesimi: 3U. Strips of three (horizontal strip or block of four with one stamp missing) are rare: 6–8U, except the 15-centesimi. Strip of five, 15-centesimi: rare. Blocks of four are exceedingly rare. Cancellations intended for the 1858 issue are rare when found on the imperforate stamps.

Cancellations: see the illustration for the principal types. Austrian and color cancellations, which are rare, are in demand.

In order to become familiar with the rarity of various postmarks, it is indispensable to consult the works that specialize in this matter. Here are some data on the cancellations of the first issue:

Type A, without date: very rare. With date: various degrees of rarity. Milan, Lodi, and Pavia are the most common cancellations of this type: 3U.

Type B, letters straight or slanted, same height, or slanted type with higher capitalized initial: various degrees of rarity.

Type C, two, three, four circles close together: not

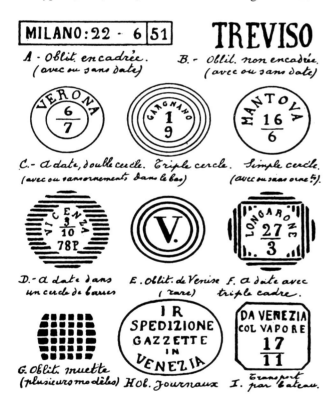

Top: A. Framed cancellation (with or without date). B. Unframed cancellation (with or without date). Second: C. Double circle with date (with or without ornaments at bottom); triple circle; single circle (with or without ornaments). Third: D. With date, in a barred circle. E. Venice cancellation (rare). F. With date and triple frame. Bottom: G. Dumb cancel (several styles). H. Newspaper cancellation. I. Maritime cancellation.

very common. One or two circles, common postmark with date: various degrees of rarity. Postmarks of this kind in a larger format (two circles, outer circle, 27 mm in diameter) are found: rare. Two circles close to each other with cogwheel circle outside (30 mm), Bergamo, Como, Venice: rare. Circular dated postmarks with military postal inscription (rural mail, etc.) are always very rare.

Types D and F: various rarity. Type E: 4U.

Type G, all dumb cancellations are very rare: 10–100U.

Type H, there are various styles.

Type I, various styles of different degrees of rarity.

Special cancellations (RACCOMANDATA, DISTRIBUZIONE, "D," etc.) are always rare.

On the following issues, the circular dated postmark and Type B are most common. All the others are more or less rare.

There is good reason to examine cancellations originating in Austrian post offices in Turkey between 1863 and 1869 — all are rare on Lombardy stamps.

Reprints: all values in 1866, 1870, and 1884, the 5-centesimi in 1887, and the 10-centesimi in 1892. Machine-made paper, different shades: 5-centesimi sulfur color, orange-yellow; 10-centesimi black; 15-centesimi vermilion or red; 30-centesimi yellow-brown, gray-brown; 45-centesimi purplish blue, dark blue, blue-gray. The 10-, 15-, 30-, and 45-centesimi belong to Type II. The printing is usually better than that of the originals. The 1866 reprints, which are rare, have white gum instead of yellow gum.

Fakes: reprints have been fraudulently canceled. The 30-centesimi was fraudulently printed on back. Pen cancellations have been cleaned to make "mint" stamps.

Used postal forgeries:

1. Verona (1853): very rare. Printed from a metal engraving on thick, machine-made paper. The 15-centesimi is red-brown, with "N" and "S" too squat and thickset. 30-centesimi, "E N T" is too wide.

2. Milan (1857): very rare. Typographed on paper similar to the foregoing, but the design is cruder. There are several types for each value. Shades don't match the originals. On the 15-centesimi, CENTES. is too wide. 30-centesimi, the banderole streamers on the shield are not bent downward. 45-centesimi, letter "S" of CENTES. is higher than the other letters. Comparison with the original marks in the illustrations will reveal other differences.

Modern forgeries: the illustration will give information on the best forgeries in this set.

1. Italian forgeries: 5- and 10-centesimi. Handmade paper that is rougher, more furrowed, than the original paper. The paper is a little less transparent, thickness 85–95 microns. The 5-centesimi is yellow or dark yellow. The 10-centesimi is 17$\frac{1}{2}$ mm wide instead of

13

$17^3/_4$ mm. Forged cancellations on this forgery: BUSTO ARSIZIO, straight line; single circle with date, GORZ $3^1/_5$; Type A postmark; etc.

2. Genoa forgeries (I.): 5- and 10-centesimi. Bad photoliths, jumbled impression. Shield details are hazy and the frames touch in numerous places. The 5-centesimi is light yellow.

3. Geneva forgeries (F.): 15-, 30-, and 40-centesimi, usually mint. Very deceptive counterfeits. The clichés were used to counterfeit the Austrian values of the same issue. Thin or very thick (Bristol), machine-made paper. The inner left frame of the 30- and 45-centesimi forgeries is not broken in two places; in the 30- and 45-centesimi. Type I originals, it is broken. Fraudulently ribbed paper is encountered. A forged cancellation in red, PAVIA 27 APR. (Type B, slanted letters), is found on a piece which was given a forged circular postmark with date in black, GENEVE 26 AVRI 59 4 S. The same thing will probably happen to all exceedingly rare cancellations. Expertizing is necessary.

There are other forgeries, in particular a set on laid paper. Comparative study will track them all down very easily. All letters and numerals should be examined with great care.

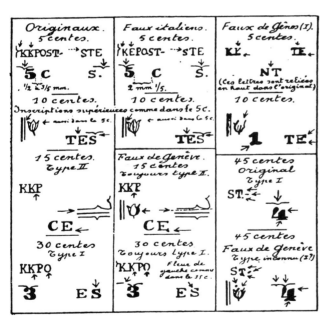

First column, originals; second column, Italian forgeries; third column, Geneva forgeries. Top: upper inscriptions as in the 5-centesimi; also in the 5-centesimi; these letters are connected on top in the original. Middle: still Type II. Bottom: flower on left as in 15-centesimi; type unknown (I?).

II. Perforated Stamps

1858 (November 1). Head of Franz Joseph. Perf 15. Type I, Nos. 6 and 9. (See the preceding illustration for the types and the corresponding Austrian issue for various details.)

Sheets: like the imperforate stamp sheets, but the St. Andrew's crosses are white. Select stamps must be centered.

Shades: not very distinctive. More-or-less-vivid color tones.

Varieties: fine impressions in which the hatching is quite visible are in demand. 15-soldo, printed on both sides: 100U. The 2-, 3-, 5-, 10-, and 15-soldo stamps have transparent impression: rare. The 15-soldo with embossed double print: rare. 3-soldo, perf 15 x 16, perforation in reverse order, or perf 16: rare.

Cancellations: see first issue. All Austrian cancellations are in active demand.

Pairs: 4U. Blocks: rare.

1859 (February 20). Type II. Nos. 10 to 15. See the illustration for the distinguishing characteristics of this type. It should be noted that the 3-soldo black and green stamps have a tiny white dot after and above the word SOLDI. This dot is not always visible, especially in the 3-soldo green original with its excessively fluid color. It is, however, quite visible in the reprints.

Sheets: as above. The 3-soldo green is an 1862 stamp.

Shades: as above.

Varieties: 3-soldo, worn plate: rare. With worn frame line: 50U. Transparent impression: rare.

Pairs and blocks: as above. The strip of three of the 2-soldo is very rare in the two types.

Fakes: fraudulently canceled reprints. Reprints with trimmed perforation followed by reperf 15.

Brunn forgeries (T.): 2-soldo, Type I. Crude, shade and perforation, noncongruent.

Reprints: still Type II. Thick paper. Gum not so thick.

1866. Six values, perf 12 ($11^3/_4$ x 12): rare.

1870. Six values, perf $10^1/_2$ ($10^1/_4$ x 11).

1884. Six values, perf 13 (also imperforate).

1887. 2-soldo yellow and orange. 3-soldo green and black, perf 12 ($11^3/_4$ x $12^1/_4$ or $12^1/_2$).

1892. 2-soldo bright yellow and orange, same perforation. There also are essays.

Forgeries: the 2- and 3-soldo stamps were counterfeited in Geneva. Make comparison.

1861–62. Embossed impression. Head facing right. Nos. 16 and 17. *Sheets* of 400 in four panes of 100. The 10-soldo was printed in 1862.

Varieties: both values are found with transparent impression.

Reprints: thick paper. Numerous reprints, Type 1861–62, with values of 2-, 3-, 5-, 10-, and 15-soldo. There is also an essay without values.

The 5- and 10-soldo stamps were reprinted in dissimilar shades in 1866, perf 12; 1870, perf 8¾–11; 1884, perf 14.

Unissued stamps: 2-, 3-, and 15-soldo.

Forgeries: lithographed 5- and 10-soldo. Noncongruent, nonembossed head. Imperforate or arbitrary perforation.

1863. Embossed coat of arms. Perf 15. Nos. 18 to 22. *Sheets:* as in the preceding issue.

Varieties: the 2-, 5-, and 10-soldo stamps are found with transparent impression: rare.

Cancellations: these stamps and the following ones, whose cancellations are often rare and in demand, were used in the Levant until 1869.

Pairs: 3U. Blocks: rare.

Reprints: see next issue.

Fakes: reprints fraudulently perf 14.

1864. Same type. Perf 9½. Nos. 23 to 27. *Sheets:* same, but with BRIEFMARKEN in large double capitals in the middle of the two left and right panes of 100.

Varieties: transparent impression of the 3-, 5-, and 10-soldo: rare.

Cancellations: same. Cancellations on No. 23 must always be expertized.

Pairs: 3U. Blocks: rare.

Reprints: thick paper.

1884. The five values, perf 13, and imperforate.

1887. The 2- and 3-soldo, perf 10½ (10¼–11).

III. Revenue Stamps

Fiscals were used in the postal service in a few Venetian post offices. They have value only on complete cover. Cancellations must be expertized. A few can be found on parcel post stickers; these have no philatelic value.

IV. Newspaper Tax Stamps

1853. 2-kreuzer green. (See Austria.)

1858. Coat of arms. 1-, 2-, and 4-kreuzer Nos. 1, 2, and 3. The types are described in the general catalogues. (See Austria.)

The 1- and 4-kreuzer stamps belong to Type I; the 2-kreuzer red to Type II; thick, relatively white paper.

The 2-kreuzer is found in vermilion and in dull red.

Cancellations: various types, but there are also common cancellations. These are circular with name of city and date, etc.

The cancellation of No. 1 must be expertized.

Reprints (1873): all of them, Type II. Tough, thin, yellowish paper. The 4-kreuzer is red. The 2-kreuzer is worth 50 percent of the value of a used stamp.

Geneva forgeries (F.): the 1- and 4-kreuzer were well counterfeited, but the paper, shades, and dimensions differ. Moreover, the outer circumference of the four circles in the four corners is poorly executed; the upper one on the left is not closed on top (one dot and one line); the one on the right (four small lines above it), and the ones below it are not closed.

Another forgery: a good watermarked 4-kreuzer forgery measures 21½ x 21 mm. Design comparison is sufficient.

Forged cancellations: No. 1 must always be checked for cancellation forgery. The forged Geneva cancellations have a circular postmark with ZEITUNGSMARKED and a two-line postmark, ...GEN.

Azerbaijan

Numerous forged overprints. Comparison is necessary.

Azores

Original cancellations "42"–"44," "48"–"50," or with date.

Reprints: very white paper.

1868. Nos. 1 to 6. *Original overprint:* Type I; narrow "E," "S" slanted to the right; 14 x 3 mm.

Reprints: Type IV; 13½ x 12½ mm; cedilla-shaped-like accent; wide "E"; normal "S."

Forged overprints: comparison is indispensable (Geneva, two types).

1868. Nos. 7 to 14, and 1870, No. 15. Perf 12½. *Original overprints:* Type I; 5-, 10-, 25-, 80-, and 240-reis, also Type II; medium-sized "E," "S" slanted to left; 12 x 3 mm; 25-reis, also Type III; 9½ x 2½ mm.

Reprints: Type IV, perf 13½.

Forged overprints: see first issue.

1877–79. Nos. 17 to 31. *Original overprint:* Type I.

Reprints: as above, perf 13½.

1880. Nos. 33 to 36. *Original overprint:* reprinted Type IV.

1882–85. Various values were reprinted without gum and occasionally with different perforations. Forged overprints on a few values; comparison is necessary (Geneva, two types).

1895. Saint Anthony. The whole set was counterfeited in Geneva (see Portugal) and given a forged overprint, 10½ x 1 mm, instead of 10 x 1½ mm, the letters having serifs, especially the "A."

Bahamas

1859–82. 1-pence. Nos. 1, 2, 5, 9, 12, and 14.
Originals: recess print engraved. Imperforate or various perforations (see the catalogues). Watermarked from 1863. The top of the pineapple does not touch the oval.

1861–82. 4- and 6-pence. Nos. 3, 4, 6, 7, 10, 13, and 15. *Originals:* the fine cross-hatching enables one to identify the two bad forged sets with the naked eye; Type a is often imperforate; Type b, a little better; both without watermark.

1863–82. 1-shilling green. Nos. 8, 11, and 16.
Originals: the shaded background lines are rather thick; where they stop determines the face "contour." Under the second "A" of BAHAMAS one finds two concentric circles. Watermarked "C C" or "C A."

Forgeries: a line defines the face and neck contours; the shade lines in the center background do not form a perfect oval and are too fine; the small circle under the second "A" of BAHAMAS contains a color dot. No watermark.

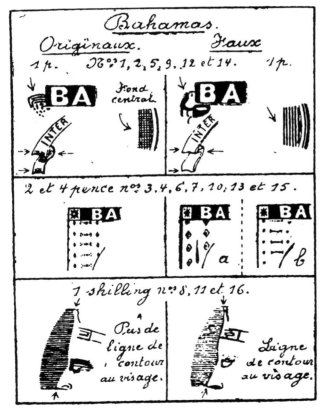

Top: Bahamas. Originals; forgeries. 1-penny; Nos. 1, 2, 5, 9, 12, and 14. Middle: 2- and 4-pence; Nos. 3, 4, 6, 7, 10, 13, and 15. Type a; Type b. Bottom: 1-shilling; Nos. 8, 11, and 16. No facial contour line; facial contour line.

Bangkok

Numerous forged overprints, which should be expertized by comparing with an original.

Barbados

1852, 1857, 1861. No value indication. Nos. 1 to 5 and 8 to 10. *Originals:* recess print engraved. There are eleven complete circle arcs at the top of the stamp. About $18^{1}/_{2}$ x 22 mm (see the illustration for other details).

Early forgeries: (1) the mainmast has no oriflamme; eight hatch lines in the shield; the spear point is lower than the helmet tuft; the helmet, which is amateurishly executed, seems like the continuation of the hair; $18^{1}/_{2}$ x $21^{1}/_{2}$ mm. (2) Only ten circle arcs at top; spear with no inner hatching; very unsuccessful ornamental design of top and sides; 18 x 21 mm. (3) The best set; see the distinctive features in the illustration; twelve hatch lines in the shield; $18^{1}/_{4}$ x $21^{1}/_{2}$ mm. The copies shown in the illustration can be identified more easily even than the originals of 1870 and 1871–73 (Nos. 14–16 and 19–22), for they have no watermark. No reprints.

1859 to 1871–73. 6-pence and 1-shilling. *Originals:* same distinctive marks as above; star watermark for Nos. 17 and 18, 23 and 24.

Forgeries: executed by reproducing the forged clichés described above and with the same defects, consequently. Forged Geneva cancellation, one circle (19 mm), BARBADOS I JY.. 59.

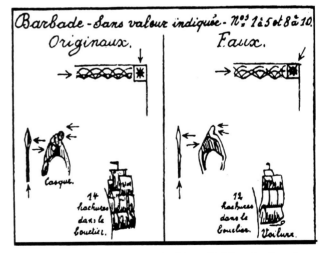

Top: Barbados. No value indicated. Nos. 1–5 and 8–10. Originals, helmet, fourteen shade lines in the shield. Forgeries, twelve shade lines in the shield, sails.

Batum

1919. Nos. 1 to 6. *Originals:* values in kopecks; six pearls above the figure on the right; No. 4, eight irregular pearls above the figure on the left; No. 5, letters "B A" do not touch; No. 6, letters "T Y" are touching. Height: about 25½ mm.

Forgeries: 26 mm high; Nos. 1–3: seven pearls above the figure on the right; No. 4, eight round pearls above the figure on the left; No. 5, letters "B A" are touching; No. 6, letters "T Y" are not touching; etc.

Subsequent issues. Beginning with No. 15, there is a multitude of forged overprints which must be compared.

Bechuanaland

Very numerous *forged overprints* of the issues of 1886–89, Nos. 1–9, and of 1888, Nos. 23–28, as well as of the 1888 issue that was overprinted PROTECTORATE; comparison is indispensable. [Geneva: two types, 1886–89, Nos. 1–9; one type, 1892, Nos. 31–35, and 1898–1902, Nos. 15–21, applied on various used originals of the Cape (Capetown) or of Great Britain.]

Belgian Congo

1886. Nos. 1 to 5. Were clandestine *reprintings* made on original plates in the possession of Germans during World War I? We have not been able to confirm or deny this.

Forgeries: the 5-franc in particular was counterfeited; an illustration of the 5-franc of Belgium, with the portrait of Leopold II, is reproduced under Belgium, the distinctive features being the same for the Congolese forgeries obtained by reproducing forged Belgian clichés. It was chiefly the improved cliché II with the inscriptions that was executed for the Congo. In it one finds the serious design defect behind the ear, and, equally serious, the very short hair parting (under the "G" of BELGIQUE; here, between the "A" and the "U"); imperforate or noncongruent perforation; paper, 50 microns instead of 55; the section of the design terminating the horns of plenty (bottom of the stamp, under letters "I" and "C") is like an "N" slanting to the right; height, about 21⅕ mm instead of 21 mm. Since this forgery is rather well known, I think it is a good idea to point out a few additional defects in the illustration. There is almost always a white dot between

"F" and "R" near the middle of the "R" and another on the right of the top of letter "A."

Some Fournier essays in the two shades show the ear's auditory canal and the inner edge of the lobe by means of the same single color line; other essays of Fournier with reduced dimensions (16½ x 20½ mm) have a white line above the four letters ("FR" and "Cˢ" of FRANCS).

Other 5-franc forgeries display similar defects: in one where the engraver's initials are replaced by indefinite white lines, the design is too large (17⅖ x 21½); in another (Genoa), whose primary cliché was executed for the Belgian stamp, the upper dividing frame line merges with the background; the inscription letters are cut with lines; the "D" (engraver's initial) is shapeless and twice as large as it should be; the rest of the design is formless. In a complete set, the upper inscription is not very clear cut; the "T" is poorly executed (compare with a common 5-centime original); the shades are arbitrary. Note: The acute angle above "E" (see Type IV in the illustration) is forged in the Belgian 5-franc and original in Congolese stamps.

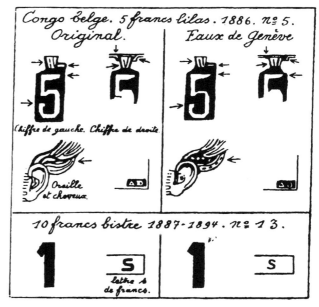

Top of box: Belgian Congo. 5-franc lilac. 1886. No. 5. Left: Original; left figure, ear and hair; right figure. Right: Geneva forgeries. Bottom section: 10-franc bistre 1887–94. No. 13. Middle: letter "S" of FRANCS.

1887–94. Nos. 6 to 13b. Clandestine *reprintings?* Same comment as for the first issue.

Forgeries: 5-franc, lithographed forgery; shade, more like lilac than violet; lettering in the lower tablet is not symmetrical; letters of CONGO in particular are too thick; letters of FRANCS are too thin; various defects in the hair and ear design. Another forgery is characterized by a bulge in the nose at eye level, but in the original the nasal line is straight and only slightly shaded. 10-franc, Geneva forgery (see the preceding illustration); paper, 70 microns, instead of about 55; ochre instead of bistre; allowable perf 15; the white line under "N D" of INDEPENDANT is almost horizontal; practically no shading on the nose or under the right eye; forehead shading is incomplete, the lines of the center forehead being too fine.

Forged cancellations, round with date, in blue or black, BANANA 2 MARS 8 M 1890, interchangeable figures; it was used for the first issue with "1886": BOMA 3 OCTO 8–M 1886; BOMA 11 AOUT 7–5 1886, all three, one circle, 23 mm in diameter. The 5-franc also was counterfeited in Geneva in violet and gray, same type as the 10-franc, but with a more successfully executed "S" of FRANCS. They easily are identified by two white spots in the center oval shading on the right of the forehead. Three other forgeries of this value have similar defects in the shading (compare with a common value, a 5-centime green); among them, one finds the buckled nose type, like the 10-franc forgery, No. 13. Counterfeited in sheets of ten; the lower frame has a concavity under the left zero, and the ornament under the "S" of FRANCS does not have the inverted "T" seen in the originals.

1894–1900. Nos. 14 and 17. *Fakes:* these values were obtained by altering the colors of Nos. 16 and 19.

1908. Nos. 30 to 49. Very numerous forged overprints; comparison is indispensable.

1923. 25-CENTIME local overprint. Nos. 104 and 105. Forged overprints, normal and inverted; also, double overprints for No. 104. A fraudulently overprinted set, 10 x 5 mm instead of 7 x 4^1/$_2$ mm, has the forged cancellation, BOMA 4 VI 23.

Postage due stamps. Numerous forged overprints, especially for the first three issues; certain models are found only on the major values. Comparison is necessary.

Parcel post stamps. Forged overprints, Nos. 1 to 5. Comparison is indispensable. The two types, framed and unframed, were counterfeited in Geneva with very faint dots.

Ruanda and Urundi. See German East Africa. Forged overprints on the 1.25-franc of the Belgian Congo. Make comparison.

Belgium

The stamps of the first Belgian issues have been given a decided preference by collectors. This can be attributed to the beauty of these masterpieces of the engraver's art.

I. Imperforate Stamps

1849. Epaulettes. Nos. 1 and 2. Three printings: May 1849 (official issue, July 1); September 1849; April 1850. Classification of the printings by shades is very difficult; red-brown stamps, for example, are found as early as 1849.

Sheets of 200 stamps in two panes of 100 (10 x 10), divided by a strip 12 mm wide containing the word BELGIQUE in double-lined capitals; on the sides, inscription: TIMBRES DES POSTES; top and bottom: MINISTERE DES TRAVAUX PUBLICS. Each stamp is watermarked "L L," a framed monogram, the top of the letters being turned toward the median strip. Handmade paper of different thicknesses. Note: In our opinion, the question of paper thicknesses should be regulated internationally by adopting the following proposal: pelure paper: 0–40 microns; thin: 41–60 microns; medium: 61–80 microns; thick: 81–100 microns; very thick: 101–130 microns; card on Bristol: 131–180 microns; cardboard: 181–?? microns. This recommendation was placed before the Philatelic Congress of Marseilles in 1926 by the Association Philatélique de la Côte d'Azur.

Belgium: The "L L" watermark, showing the tops of the letters turned toward the median.

The double-printed impressions (rare) were produced by double striking of the plate; when the impressions are partial or simply blurred, that is a result of play in the paper.

The "reentry," which might be called *rengrénee* or *treflee printing* [possible translations: *rengrénee* =

restippled; *treflee* = irregularly struck] because of its similarity to currency minting procedures, has many lines with a dual function; however, only one impression was received from the plate.

With respect to the reentry matter, at first it was believed that it was a question of traces of a first engraving remaining on a plate that had been poorly scraped. But the lucky find of essays bearing reentries discredited that explanation and advanced the following one:

The copper plates used for intaglio printing are impressed by a steel cylinder transfer roll carrying the die in relief, a transfer from the original hollow die. Following a bad adjustment or improper alignment, a trial application was made, to rock in the subject, after which the transfer roll was raised to adjust the alignment. This operation left more or less visible traces, which reappear in the printing each time they do not coincide with the impression from the final application of the roll. When the transfer roll misses twice in succession, we have double reentries or "tri-entries," if this *cordiale entente* neologism is admissible, or impressions that are double *rengrénees*.

The parts most in relief have evidently left the most visible traces: frames, whole figures, heavy shading of hair, collar, coat, etc. (See the accompanying illustration.)

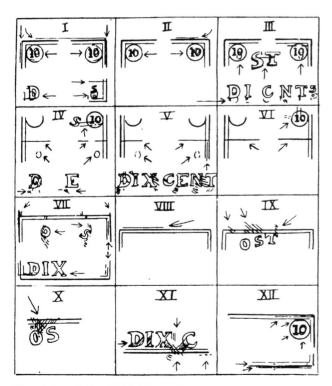

Reentries of the 1849 10-centime stamps.

Types I and VII are the most interesting double reentries: 4M, 6U. In Type I, the upper frame and the figures are duplicated, and the zeros are also marked at the bottom. In Type VII, the lower frame is duplicated with deviation toward the left, and is again lightly printed through the epaulette, the decoration, and the jabot as far as the lateral frames; at the same time, the hair is duplicated in correlation with this third lower frame.

Types II–VI are worth 3M, 5U. In Type II, the upper frame and the zeros are partly duplicated; in Type III, similarly, with duplication of the bottom letters; in Type IV, upper frame and zeros duplicated, wrong lines coming from the guilloche, the left epaulette, the coat lapel, and, on the chin, false eyebrow marks; Type V, same, false epaulette, coat, and lapel lines; Type VI, upper frame duplicated. The jabot of Type III is always blank. Types VIII–XII, and a few other similar ones, are worth 2M, 2–3U. Type IX, false left epaulette, coat, and lapel lines; Type X, false lines of the collar; Type XI, forged lines of the left epaulette, coat, and lapels.

There is a double print of the figures and of POSTES for the 20-centime stamp (a reentry?): 4M, 10U. The specimens in which this defect is only blurred are worth much less. (See the accompanying illustration). Types A, B, C are reentries: 2M, 6U; engraving defects D and F are worth 2M, 5U; Types E, G, H, and other similar minor defects: 50M, 4U.

Retouched stamps: the illustration of the 20-centime stamp types shows three examples of retouched stamps at the bottom; there are a few others. Most visible, 10- and 20-centime, Type I: 2M, 4–6U; 20-centime, Type II: 50M, 3U.

Gutters: ¹/₂ to 2 mm wide, depending on the plate and the position of the stamps on the sheet; the average gutter is 1 mm wide.

Select: four margins, minimum width ¹/₂ mm. Despite the large printing (5 million for each value), the number of stamps that have disappeared (ninety-eight percent?), the number too heavily canceled (eighty percent?), and finally the number that have inadequate margins or are defective for other reasons (thinning, cuts, etc.) (ninety percent?) — all of these factors reduce the number of select copies to such an extent that one can say that there are no more than 2,000 copies extant of each value. The copies that are off-center with wide margins and very light cancellation bring low prices: 3–10U. Corner copies: 2U.

Mint stamps are rare with gum; the remainders were bar canceled with red ink. Sometimes these are cleaned and offered for sale as mint stamps.

Shades: 10-centime brown, gray-brown, dark brown. The 10-centime brown on very thin paper and the red-brown on thin paper: 2M, 2U; the superbly printed

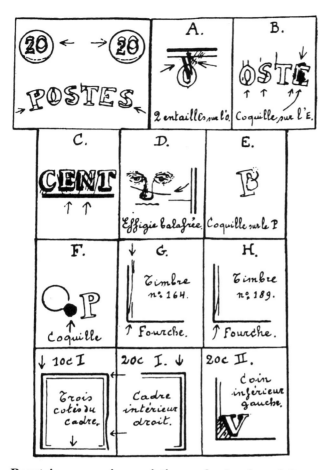

Reentries, engraving varieties, and retouches of the 20-centime value. (A.) Two slashes on the "O." (B.) Misprint on the "E." (D.) Slashed portrait. (E.) Misprint on the "P." (F.) Misprint. (G.) Stamp No. 164 — fork. (H.) Stamp No. 189 — fork. Bottom: 10-centime Type I; three sides of the frame. 20-centime Type I; inner right frame. 20-centime Type II; lower left corner.

copies (first printing), bistre-brown on thin paper: 3M, 3U. The 20-centime stamps, blue, dark blue, light blue, have the same value on ordinary or thin paper; milky blue, blue-black (deep blue): 2M, 2U; stamps of which the paper is heavily colored on the obverse side by the impression (visible in the margins), slate blue on ordinary paper and bright blue on thin paper: 2.5M, 4U. The ultramarine blue is *recherche;* it is often obtained by chemical treatment (paper too white, made spongy by the oxidizing acid, and bearing purplish traces of the aforesaid reagent).

Pairs: 10-centime: 3M, 4U; 20-centime: 3M, 8U. Blocks of four being exceedingly rare (10M, 150U), strips of four are in demand: 60U.

Cancellations: Type A: common (see illustration, numeral cancellation "120"). The "56" model was used

in distribution centers: less common; in red: rare (cancel error). Letters having a dated postmark in red or green are just as exceptional on the stamp. Type A has seventeen or eighteen bars (distribution centers, eighteen bars); the rural mailman's postmark, without a number, has fourteen bars (rare). Postmark C, railway or mobile mail service: rare.

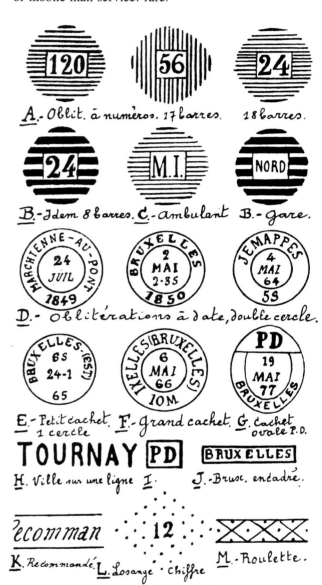

Cancellations found on the 1849 issue. First row: (A.) Numeral cancel — seventeen and eighteen bars. Second: (B.) Same, eight bars. (C.) Mobile (B.) Station. Third: (D.) cancels with date in double circle. Fourth: (E.) Small postmark, single circle. (F.) Large postmark. (G.) Oval postmark with "P.D." Fifth: (H.) Town, on one line. (J.) Brussels, framed. Bottom: (K.) Registered. (L.) Numeral lozenge. (M.) Roulette.

20

Stamps on cover: 2U.

Reprints: single stamps, from the matrix. No watermark. 1866: in brown, red-brown, and blue for the 20-centime stamp. On thick laid paper: 50 francs; on thick wove paper: 40 francs; on ordinary wove paper: 30 francs. Whether these are essays is debatable. 1895: on thin glossy paper, 10-centime, lilac-brown: 25 francs; 20-centime, blue: 10 francs; dark blue: 15 francs.

Genoa forgeries (V.): no watermark. Crude execution. One must be very trusting indeed to allow oneself to be fooled by these pretty pictures, the wide margins of which attract attention immediately.

1849–50. Watermark "L L" framed. Nos. 3 to 5.
Printing figures. 10-centime stamp: 498,000; 20-centime: 376,000; 40-centime: 292,000. These stamps are much rarer than those of the first issue.

Sheets: 200 stamps, as above. Intaglio engraved.

Paper: handmade, thin, ordinary, or thick. The very thin paper is in demand.

Select: four margins, $^1/_2$ mm wide. The well-margined copies are quite rare.

Cancellations: see first issue.

Shades: two per value.

Varieties: No. 3, bisected vertically: extremely rare. The mint stamps with red bar cancel are worth fifty percent.

Reentry: 10-centime with double figures: 4M, 30U.

Retouched stamps: in the foliage, above the "D" of DIX and to the right or left of VINGT-CINQ: 2–3M, 3–6U, depending on the desirability of the stamp.

Pairs: 4U; block of four: 4M, 60U, except the 40-centime stamp: 20U.

1851. Watermark "L L" unframed. Nos. 6 to 8.
Sheets: as above.

Printing figures: 10-centime stamp: 53,800,000; 20-centime: 39,200,000; 40-centime: 4,350,000. Thus, the 40-centime stamp is as rare as Nos. 1 and 2.

Ordinary paper: thick: less common; thin (10-centime: 400,000; 20-centime: 300,000; 40-centime: 240,000): 2M, 3U; ribbed horizontally (10-centime: 100,000; 20-centime: 60,000; 40-centime: 45,000): 2M, 6U, except the 40-centime stamp: 2U. The vertically ribbed paper is worth double.

Rare shades: 20-centime pale blue (thin paper): four times the canceled stamp of usual shade on thin paper; cobalt blue (ordinary paper): 6U.

Reentries: the "10" figures and POSTES double printed as in the previous issue: 10M, 150U. Inner frame doubled: 3M, 60U.

Retouched stamps: rather numerous — see examples in the accompanying illustration. Value: 25–30M, 3–20U, according to the stamp's desirability.

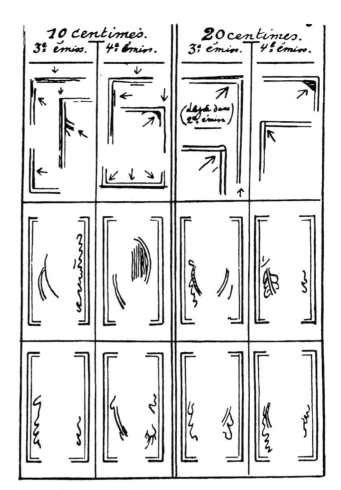

Retouched stamps. 10-centime, third and fourth issues; 20-centime, third and fourth issues. Already in second issue.

Pairs: 4U; blocks of four: 8M, 120U, but the 40-centime stamp: 30U.

Cancellations: as in the previous issues. But Type A postmark has fourteen bars: less common; the twenty-six barred postmark (No. 24): very rare; the large dot postmark: very rare.

1858 (July). 10-, 20-, and 40-centime. Some general catalogues do not describe this issue, not even as a variation of the previous issue; when one considers the time the issue has been known, that is strange. The omission can be explained only as a desire to avoid rearranging albums.

Format: 18 x 21 mm. The center medallion, more rounded than in the next issue, measures 15 mm wide by $17^1/_2$ mm high instead of $14^1/_2$ by 16 mm high.

No watermark: sheets of 200 stamps as above.

Printing figures: 10-centime: 28,800,000; 20-centime: 20,700,000; 40-centime: 2,300,000.

Thin paper, glossy, machine-made: common; value same as for the ordinary paper of the previous issue.

Thick, handmade paper (10-centime: 72,000; 20-centime: 54,000; 40-centime: 36,000). Loss and deterioration have contributed to the rarity of these varieties: 10- and 20-centime mint stamps: 150 francs; 40-centime: 500 francs; used, 10- and 20-centime: 20 francs; 40-centime: 75 francs.

Pairs: 4U; blocks of four: 80U; 40-centime: 20U (thin paper); thick paper: exceedingly rare.

Cancellations: as above. Type J: rare.

Retouched stamps: as in the previous issue.

1861. Without watermark. Nos. 9 to 12. *Format:* $17^2/_3$ x $21^3/_4$ mm. Oblong medallion, $14^1/_2$ mm wide by 18 mm high.

Sheets of 300 stamps.

Select: four margins $^1/_2$ mm minimum width. Copies with four wide margins are rare.

Printing figures: 1-centime: 16,000,000; 10-centime: 24,500,000; 20-centime: 16,900,000; 40-centime: 3,100,000.

The 1-centime stamp was intended to be affixed to printed matter and newspapers, not to letters, to lighten the burden of canceling them. The rarity of the 1-centime stamp in comparison with the 20-centime can be explained by the large number of printed matter items that are thrown away, and the number of letters that are kept.

Ordinary paper: thin, or slightly striated horizontally: 2U; vertically: 5U.

Varieties: there are double prints (rare on the 10-, 20-, and 40-centime stamps) and greasy prints.

Retouched stamps: see the accompanying illustration for a few examples. In addition, one can find much retouching of the foliage in the 10- and 20-centime stamps, and, in the 10-centime, an extensive retouching of the cross-hatched background (vertical lines to the right of the head): 6M, 50 francs used. 1-centime, retouched stamp, Type I: 2M, 2U; Type II: 5M, 5U; Types III–X: 25M, 25U. 10-centime, Types I–IV and foliage retouching: 2–5M, 2–10U, depending on the stamp's desirability; 20-centime: same; 40-centime: 50M, 2U.

Cancellations: the 1-centime stamp is almost always canceled with date; Types A and B: rare, this value having rarely been applied to letters; the other values are rarely date canceled for the opposite reason. Cancellations "P" and "L": rare. In addition to the barred and numeral postmarks already mentioned, B types (eight to ten bars) are found with numerals. Type B is also found with the name of the railway system (mobile, eight bars).

Forgeries: the 1-centime stamp, both imperforate and perforated, was crudely lithographed. Comparison with

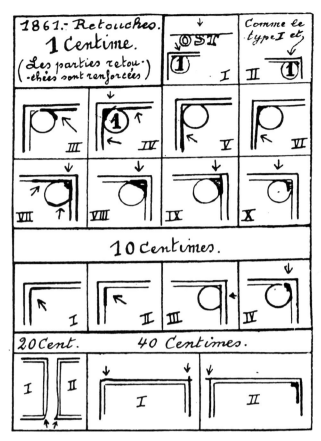

1861 retouches. (The retouched parts are reinforced.)

a 10- or 20-centime stamp will prove decisive. Check especially the center background.

Fakes: the perforated 1- and 40-centime stamps were made imperforate with close margins by removing the perforations and completely rebacking them. As for the used stamps, cancellations join in the margins.

Pairs: 3U; blocks of four: 6M; 1-centime stamp: 6U; 10- and 20-centime: 16M, 100U; 40-centime: 8M, 20U.

II. Perforated Stamps

The perforated stamps must be centered.

1863. Same type. Perforated. Nos. 13 to 16. *Plates* of 300 stamps. Medium and thin paper. Perf $12^1/_2$; $12^1/_2$ x $13^1/_2$; $14^1/_2$.

Varieties: double prints: rare. The 1-centime, worn plate: 3M, 2U. Greasy, transparent print, 1-centime: 2M, 2U; 10-centime: 3M, 20U; 1-centime blue-green, perf $12^1/_2$: 2M, 2U. The 10- and 20-centime, perf $14^1/_2$: same value.

Retouched stamps: 1-centime, upper or lower frame retraced with overlay on the letters and figures; letters "I M E" retraced, and lower left corner, redone: 5–

10M and U. Slight retouching of the stamp's value ovals.

Cancellations: on the 1-centime, Types D and E: common; Type F (large postmark): 50U; Type G: 2U; Type H: 50U; Type A: rare. On the other values, Type L: common; with letters and figures: less common; Type B: 50U; Type A: 2U; Type J: rare.

Pairs: 3U; No. 16: 4U; No. 13, strip of five: 8U; blocks of four, No. 13: 6U; Nos. 14 and 15: 25 francs; No. 16: 20U.

Reprints (1895): imperforate; thin, glossy paper; bright colors, 1-centime pale yellow-green, 40-centime bright red.

1865–66. Leopold I facing left. Nos. 17 to 21.
Sheets of 300 stamps typographed in six panes of fifty (5 x 10).

Printing figures: 30-centime: 5,700,000; 40-centime: 4,800,000; 1-franc: 465,000.

Select: stamps must be centered. Some copies have a small format, others are too large because of perforation spacing in both directions. Remember this when you buy imperforate stamps.

Rare shades: 20-centime cobalt; 30-centime chocolate, brown-black (deep brown); 1-franc, so-called "cabbage red": 2M, 2U.

Perforations: 14 x 14 (London), 1-franc only; 14½ x 14, first-class Belgian printing, 10- and 20-centime stamps: rare; other values: 3M, 2U; on glossy paper; the subsequent printings, on thin, ordinary paper are common; perf 15: common.

Varieties: the horizontally imperforate 30-centime stamp is known to exist. The 10-, 20-, 30-, and 40-centime stamps of the first-class London printing, which are known imperforate, can be regarded as essays; they also exist in ordinary printing.

Cancellations: "L": common; "L" with letters: 50U; with date on Nos. 17–20: rare; on No. 21: 25U; Type J: rare.

Pairs: 3U; blocks of four, Nos. 17 and 18, used: 15 francs; Nos. 19, 20, and 21: 6M, 20U; but the 40-centime: 8M; 1-franc: 12M.

Reprints (1895): imperforate; glossy paper; bright shades. The whole set: 50 francs. These private reprints made with plates stolen during the war require paper comparison.

Fakes: oversized perforated stamps bisected to make imperforates. This explains why imperforate pairs or copies with extra wide margins are in demand. It is easy to detect faked imperforates with forged margins.

Forgeries: good photolithographed forgeries with wide margins of the 30-centime, 50-centime, and 1-franc stamps are found single or on piece with Type L forged cancellations: Nos. 12, 60, 63, 64, 70, 141, 283, 298, etc. Sometimes they are imperforate or perf 14.

On the original, the lock of hair above the forehead is shaped like a scythe blade with unbroken upper line and horizontal lower line; on the forgeries, the upper line is broken, the lower line, wavy; the line that obliquely traverses the ear (northwest to southeast) is too thin; the line forming the bottom of the nostril is wavy (a simple curve on the originals); the white line of light in front of the chin and on the Adam's apple stands out clearly, whereas it is much less distinct on the originals, the ends of the shading curving around so as to come very close to the background lines; the same thing applies to the nose.

The shaded line limiting the neck on the right is thin but prominent, whereas on the London original and on the 14½ x 14 Brussels imprint, the impressions that are closest to these forgeries, the line is formed evidently by a reinforcement of the neck shading. Comparison of the hairlines, especially above the ear, of the ear lines, eyelashes, and eyebrows reveals numerous differences. The inscription, UN FRANC, is ⅙ mm too long.

Microscopic examination of paper texture would be helpful in making a much quicker decision. The early forgeries and a set of modern ones can be identified immediately by comparing them with Nos. 17 and 18.

1866–67. Small lion type. Nos. 22 to 25.
Sheets: as above. Printed matter stamps are typographed.

Select: the 1-centime imperforate stamp must have four margins ¾ mm wide. Despite the printing of almost 7 million copies, this stamp has become rare, because, as is the case with No. 9, most printed matter or newspapers on which it was used were immediately thrown away.

Perforations: 14½ x 14; 15.

Paper: different thicknesses; Nos. 23b (blue-tinted gray) and 25a (pale bistre–reddish brown) are on thick paper, the latter being rare (small printing: 180,000).

Varieties: Nos. 24 and 25, imperforate: 100 gold francs. Plate defects: 2-centime, oval broken on the right of the crown: 4M, 3U; 1-centime, with a dot between "T" and "E" of POSTES; 5-centime, a dot before the "T" of POSTES, etc. No. 24, double print: rare.

Cancellations: with date, Types D, E, F: common; Type G: 25U; Type L: 50U.

Pairs: 3U; blocks of four, No. 22: 5U; No. 23, same; Nos. 24 and 25: 6M, 10U.

Reprints (1895): imperforate; shades too bright; thin, glossy paper; first-class printing. Essays in the stamp shades are also found.

Originals: the 1-centime: format 18⅖ x 22½ mm; three horizontal lines under CENTIMES, the lowest one double the thickness of the others; eight quite visible pearls on each side of the crown, but do not confuse the lateral ornaments with these. (See also a few of the descriptive characteristics in the accompanying illustration.)

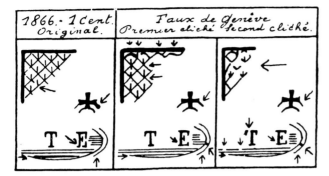

1866 1-centime original; Geneva forgeries, first and second clichés.

The 2- and 5-centime, format 18 x 21³/₄ mm or 22 mm for the 2-centime and 18²/₅ or 18¹/₂ x 22 mm for the 5-centime; two slightly curved lines of equal thickness under CENTIME; letters "I M E" of this word are almost always joined above and below; five pearls on each side of the crown; the ornaments of the crown are different from those of the 1-centime stamp.

In the three values, the letters of POSTES are equidistant from the edges of the tablet; the letters of CENTIMES, also well-aligned, are 1¹/₄ mm high.

These indications enable one to identify all of the forgeries made until now without even bothering about the paper, which is always so different.

Early and modern forgeries: the 1-centime stamp. Check the format, the inscriptions, and the distinguishing marks in the illustration; the reprints, faked by reverse backing, measure 18³/₅ x 22³/₄ mm.

In a tolerably good early (?) forgery, guilloche lines are missing on the left of the banderole of POSTES; the "P" of this word is open on top, the second "E" of CENTIME is not broken at the bottom; etc.

The 2- and 5-centime stamps. Check format, inscriptions, perforation, and lines under CENTIMES. In a photolithographic copy of these two values, the two "S" letters of POSTES are touching the bottom of the tablet; the "C," "E," and "S" of CENTIMES are touching the second of the three lines underscoring this word; two of these lines extend 1 mm beyond the word; the cachectic lion does not have the respectable dimensions of the "Leeuw van Vlaanderen" (Lion of Flanders), 18¹/₂ x 21²/₃ mm. The reprint format is too large.

Geneva forgeries (F.): the 1-centime, imperforate and perforated. This value was counterfeited photolithographically; the widely circulated product requires more extensive descriptive data.

Format: 18 x 22 mm. Paper of medium thickness (65–75 microns), yellowish or white shade, in two different clichés. Inordinate attention should not be given to the paper or its shade, because other papers have possibly been used for better deception.

On the original, a line of the guilloched background, indicated by an arrow in the illustration, and the base of the "E" of CENTIME are always broken, except in heavily inked printing with unbroken, thin lines. The imperforate stamp is the one that is most often counterfeited; however, the clichés must have been used to make perforated stamps!

The forged cancellation, DEYNZE 17 NOV 67 1-2, is found rather often. Note: See F. Serrane, "Faux de Belgique," *L'Écho de la Timbrologie,* No. 697 (January 15, 1925): 5–7.

Subsequent issues. The wealth of materials available obliges us to refer the reader to general or specialized catalogues for everything that does not fall within the scope of our work.

1869. Figure and recumbent lion. No. 29. *The 8-centime forgery:* rather deceptive, but the design, obtained by transfer, is less clear-cut than that of the originals; the perforation is arbitrary; the paper is too thin (50 microns), slightly transparent; the shade is lilac-gray. The original shades are pale lilac, lilac, and mauve (rare), all three on paper 70–80 microns thick; the violet is on nontransparent paper, 60 microns. Compare with the 1-, 2-, or 5-centime stamp.

1878. Portrait of Leopold II. 5-franc. Nos. 37 and 37a. *Originals:* first printing, February 1878 (33,000 copies), red-brown, printed by typography with excessively thick Belgian inks that produced small white spots in the background of the stamp, particularly under the neck. Second printing, made in June (14,700 copies), pale brown, good impression, executed with inks from the De La Rue firm in London. Third printing, August 1881 (11,400 copies), dark red-brown, printed with sufficiently fluid Belgian vegetable inks; good impression. Medium white paper, nontransparent, about 75 microns thick; format 17 x 21 mm; perf 15.

Modern forgeries: rather numerous, but all of them easy to spot by comparing them with the distinctive characteristics of the originals (see the accompanying illustration), by measuring, and by examining perforation and shades. The worst of these is the Genoa (I.) forgery, in which the nostril wing is drawn with two lines, the "5" on the left is broken in the middle, the inscriptions are cut by hairlines, and the lower part of the ear is missing. Format 27¹/₄ x 21 mm.

Geneva forgeries (F.): these forgeries are most widely circulated, especially outside of Europe. They were manufactured in great quantities in the three

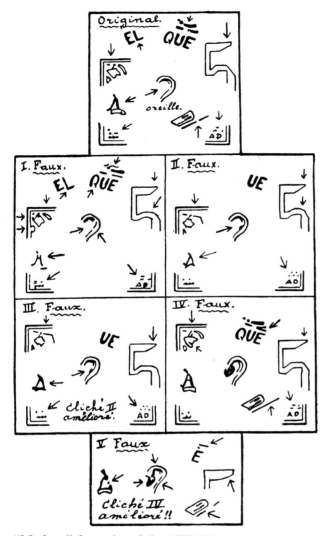

"Modern" forgeries of the 1878 5-franc are numerous, but easy to spot. Note that forgery III is an improved cliché of forgery II; forgery V is an improved cliché of forgery IV.

shades of the originals, and offer evidence of expert workmanship with improved, retouched clichés. In spite of that, many differences can be pointed out, the most obvious ones being reproduced in sections I–V in the illustration. Type III is an improved cliché of Type II, and Type V is a retouched cliché of Type IV — the acute angle above the "E" makes the letter recognizable to the naked eye. Types III and V give us proof, once more, that perfect stamp imitation is impossible.

Types I, II, III are often on yellow, stringy, transparent, almost pelure paper (45 microns), also on slightly transparent, medium white paper; forgery Types IV and V are on white paper of good thickness, but most frequently are on soft, easily controllable paper.

Measurements approximate those of the originals: 17 x 20²/₃ mm; 17 x 20³/₄ mm.

Forged cancellations on Geneva forgeries: Types I, II, III: LOUVAIN 1 SEPT 2-5 1881; GAND 2 AVRIL 1-5 1878; LIEGE 26 AOUT 8-M 1878.

Types IV and V: ROULERS 23 FEVR 1880 and savings bank cancellation (roulette).

These forged postmarks were sometimes applied to red-brown originals. Note: See F. Serrane, "Faux de Belgique," *L'Écho de la Timbrologie,* No. 697 (January 15, 1925): 6.

Naturally, there are other forged postmarks made at home by unscrupulous operators; one can also find "rouletted" cancellations that have been cleaned and replaced by a forged dated postmark.

1893–1900. Dominical headband. Nos. 53 to 67. The 25-centime very bright, dark blue stamp, a variation of No. 60, is worth 100 francs mint and 40 francs used; 1-franc carmine on green, No. 64, imperforate vertically: 50 francs mint, 25 francs used.

The 2-franc violet on white, No. 67, was printed in 140,000 copies, while the 2-franc lilac on rose was printed in 168,000.

Forgeries of the 2-franc violet on white, No. 67:
1. crude forgery, the entire design of which is different. Compare the vertical shading lines on the right of the "U" of BELGIQUE (three lines instead of five), the ornament in the lower left corner, above the headband (single instead of double line design), the ornaments in the bottom corners of the headband (dots instead of double line crosses). The cliché of this forgery was retouched, but comparison with design, hair, and beard is still quite adequate to identify it.

2. Another forgery is identified also by the beard and hair sketching; on the original, the loop of the figure "2" is moved away from the circle, but here there is only a gap; the upper bar of the "T" is too thick. Forgeries canceled LIEGE 25 JUIN 1892 are easily spotted: the issue did not come out before June 1, 1893!

1894. Antwerp exhibition. Nos. 68 to 70. *Forged cancellations:* numerous on No. 70. Expertizing is indicated. One forged postmark has "13 à 24 heures" as the time notation; this was not adopted until a few years later.

1905. Large portrait of Leopold II. Nos. 74 to 80. A 10-centime gooseberry-red stamp on white paper is rare: 25 francs M or U. Imperforate stamps are worth 20 francs; the 25-centime is more common: 10 francs.

Forgeries: 2-franc violet. Crude forgery. Comparison of beard, hair, epaulette, and tunic design will produce convincing evidence of forgery. Forged postmark: DINANT 15 AOUT 1910.

25

1911. Overprinted stamps of 1910. Nos. 92 to 107. There is an inverted overprint on the 1-centime stamp (No. 84), and double overprints, one of which is inverted, are found on the 5- and 10-centime (Nos. 86 and 87). Value: 125 francs.

Forged overprints: Nos. 92–94. Comparison of shade, impression, and printing type is indispensable for well-executed overprints. In one crude forgery, the two "1" figures are only about $2/3$ mm apart.

1914. Red Cross. Merode monument. Nos. 126 to 131. Terribly common, if we judge by the large number in circulation; however, their limited printing order has made them rare: 5-centime, 23,214; 10-centime, 14,650; 20-centime, 8,663.

Competent experts, notably Mr. P. de S..., have refused to go along with the unreasoning mob of dealers who kept declaring pontifically that all of these stamps were originals. One of them, Mr. V. G..., from Brussels, in an article in the June 1922 issue of *Le Trait d'Union des Collectionneurs* entitled *"Errare humanum est,"* referred scornfully to "improvised experts" and "obstinate, foolhardy polemists"; another, Mr. G. M..., also from Brussels, in an article in *La Revue Postale et l'Annonce Timbrologique Réunies,* entitled "Une Mise-au-point," accused Mr. P. de S... of blundering, and offered 5,000 francs to anyone who could prove that Types II and III, "Second and Third Printings," were "the product of private manufacture."

The mistaken views of these dealers, expressed in good faith for the most part, were based on statements made by the official printer. Obviously, a careful examination and a detailed study of the transfer block of the stamps in question would have had greater validity. Judgments since handed down by the Antwerp Civil and Appeal Courts have proved that the stamps were illegally manufactured by the printer himself on reconstructed plates, and we have been informed that the illicit trading in these stamps was tremendous. One surprised agent alone had 200,000 copies on hand!

The moral of all this is that a stamp must always be subjected to careful examination, irrespective of its origin, even though it may be a gift from one's own father, from a peer of the realm, or from the King of England.

There are numerous distinctive characteristics. One may possibly be content with the following:

Nos. 126–28. The "Q" of BELGIQUE forms an "O" (no terminal stroke) in the forgeries. The BELGIQUE inscription is regularly placed in the tablet of the 5-centime stamp and shifted toward the top in the 10- and 20-centime. On the forgeries, it is just the opposite.

Nos. 129–31. The 5- and 10-centime originals are $1/2$ mm higher than the forgeries; on the genuine 20-centime, BELGIQUE is elevated in its tablet, while on the forgeries, it is properly placed. The original paper of the 20-centime is pinkish white.

Naturally, there are many other differences, which comparison and the absence of those defects that characterize the original may help one to perceive.

1915. Red Cross. Nos. 132 to 134. Fake: the 20-centime imperforate was transformed into a perf 14 x 12 (rare). Expertizing is necessary.

1918. "Red Cross" overprint. Nos. 150 to 163. Occasionally offered for sale on entire cover with forged Belgian postmark of SAINTE-ADRESSE (France), or of military posts — which doubles the value of these stamps.

1921. 20-centime on 5-centime. Overprint. "Olympic Games." No. 184. There are forged clandestine overprints (expertizing is necessary) and forged overprints made for export trade.

1921. 50-centime. Portrait of King Albert. Nos. 187 and 201. The Brussels Exhibition stamp is dark indigo blue (No. 187) (sheets of twenty-five); the blue shade of the regular set (September) is much paler: blue-gray-slate.

III. Postage Due Stamps

1895–1912. Perf 14. Nos. 3 to 11. The 1-franc carmine-tinted rose (No. 10) and orange (No. 11) were faked.

Forgeries: the 1-franc carmine-tinted rose. Substandard impression; cross-hatching is too large; $21^2/5$ mm instead of 22 mm; consequently, the two inscriptions are about $1/2$ mm too narrow.

The 1-franc orange. (1) Same manufacture; same characteristics. (2) Crude forgery. The double frame seems single, and the inner frame merges with the very fine line delimiting the upper tablet. (3) A forgery from a clandestine printing (?) on original paper; shade, dimensions, and design are not in conformity with original (lion shading); comparison is very necessary here.

1919. "T" overprint on 1915 postage stamps. Nos. 17–25 (Yvert) overprinted with a "T" about 16 mm high by 9 mm wide are the only official ones. All the other overprints are fantasies. There are a few forged overprints on Nos. 17–25. Make comparison.

IV. Telegraph Stamps

1866. Octagonals. Leopold I. Nos. 1 and 2. These stamps are rarely centered: 50M, 50U. No known blocks of four. Imperforate stamps (Rothschild): very rare. Stamps with SPECIMEN in black, blue, or red: rare.

Reprints (1895): perforated; 50-centime brownish gray; 1-franc pale yellow-green. Comparison is indicated.

1899. 25-franc red and green. No. 10.
Fake: cancellation punch holes were changed.

Forgery: a good photolithographed forgery exists, but the dimensions are inexact. The regular, delicately traced, red lines of the original are coarse and uneven in the counterfeit. The lettering of FRANCS is too bold, especially the "A"; the pearls are too large and too close to each other, and the first and last ones are about the same size. On the original, the first and sixty-fourth pearls are half as small.

V. Parcel Post

1882–94. Perf 15. 1- and 2-franc. Nos. 13 and 14.
Forgeries: perf 14 or imperforate. Some clandestine reprints are well executed and require design comparison; inexact shades; the forgeries are poorly executed.

1902. Perf 15. 1-franc. No. 39. *Forgeries:* crude; compare shade, perforation, design (little lions, inscriptions, etc.). A few postmarks on the 1-franc forgeries (Nos. 13 and 39) are so much like the originals that one wonders whether they are not used forgeries with postmarks obtained from the parcel post department.

1915. Overprinted stamps with winged wheel. Nos. 48 to 57. *Forged overprints:* very numerous. A few are really very deceptive. Minute comparison is indispensable.

VI. German Occupation

Forged overprints: very numerous on Nos. 8 and 9 (occasionally on canceled Nos. 1–7, overprint over cancellation!), on Nos. 21–25 (23a!), on Nos. 33–37, and all Eupen and Malmedy stamps.

The bad forgeries (dull inks, the "5" figures with upper stroke definitely raised) are easily spotted. Likewise, the No. 25 overprint when the stamp has only twenty-six perforations top and bottom instead of twenty-seven. However, a few clever fakes require comparison.

Benin

1892. Stamps overprinted BENIN. Nos. 1 to 13.
Originals: four types — Type I, letter "B" broken at bottom; Type II, first "N" broken, bottom right; Type III, normal; Type IV, normal, with an accent on the "E"; the top of the right downstroke of the second "N" curves inwardly slightly; cancellation using a wooden hand device. Very numerous forged overprints, most of them not resembling any of the original types. Comparison is indispensable, or at the very least, use of the template. The forged overprints were applied either on original stamps or on 1881 counterfeits, described in French Colonies. The forged Geneva set comprises Nos. 1–13 and the four values of postage due stamps (the latter printed in a single block of four); the letters of the two types of forged overprints are much too thick; the forged cancellation is GRAND POPO, 7 NOV. 92 BENIN (with date, double circle, inner circle broken, interchangeable figures).

1892. Same, with new value as overprint. Nos. 14 to 17. *Originals:* the new value designation does not coincide, or barely coincides, with the figures of the former value. Forged overprints are very numerous. Comparison is necessary.

1892. Peace and Commerce type. Nos. 20 to 26. *Forgeries:* see French Colonies for copies of this type (Geneva).

Postage due stamps. See the first issue.

Bermuda

1865–73. 1-, 2-, 3-, 6-pence, and 1-shilling. Nos. 1 to 8. *Originals:* where the center background shading stops is the only facial contour indication (see the illustrations of the 1-shilling "Bahamas"). There are six short, oblique shade lines under the lower lip; the ear lobe is covered with fine oblique shading.

Forgeries: all are lithographed without watermark. Four different sets, two of which do not include all values; their usual characteristic is a more or less thick line defining the face contour. Set No. 1: the center point of the "M" of BERMUDA descends to the bottom of the letter; two short lines under the lower lip. Set No. 2: no shading under the lower lip; the ear lobe is white. Set No. 3: no shading under the lower lip; five short lines shade the nose. Set No. 4: (Genoa) the nostril as in the forgery of the 1-shilling "Bahama Islands"; the lower lip is formed with a short, thick line.

1874–75. Overprinted stamps. Nos. 9 to 14. A great many forged overprints; the worst among those that look more or less presentable have blurred areas and even forged lines (Nos. 12 and 14), but there are good ones that must be compared; the original overprint measures 23 1/2 mm. The most widely circulated one is the THREE PENCE on 1-penny rose (No. 12). There is also the Genoa forgery of the 1-shilling with forged overprint, Type II (No. 14), on piece, to hide the absence of a watermark.

Bolivar

See Colombia.

Bolivia

1867. First issue. Nos. 1 to 8. *Originals:* recess print engraved.

Early forgeries: lithographed with very arbitrary design; the outer frame is thin. The 50- and 100-centavo stamps also are found engraved; in the former, the upper corners of the inner frame are rectilinear instead of rounded, and in the latter, the value tablets do not touch the inner frame and the lower ones are positioned like those above, and thus are wrong way up. All values also were photolithographed; the absence of embossing is enough to rule them out.

Clandestine reprintings made with the original plates. The shades are dull and must be compared with originals; 5-centavo dark violet; 10-centavo brown; 50-centavo dull yellow; 50-centavo dull blue; 100-centavo blue (instead of gray-blue or dark blue); 100-centavo green (instead of dark yellow-green or dull green).

1868–71. Nine or eleven stars. Nos. 9 to 18. The originals are engraved with finesse; the center circle background is made up of fine horizontal hatch lines.

Forgeries: the circle's background is full; the oval's horizontal hatch lines (center circle) are too far apart; letters "L" and "I" of BOLIVIA are not joined.

1894. Engraved stamps. Nos. 39 to 45. *Originals:* thin paper; perf 14½.

Forgeries or clandestine reprints: as many and whatever you like on original plates; thick paper (80–85 microns); perf 13, 13½, sometimes 11. A part of this Paris printing was sent to the Bolivian government (!) and was placed in circulation; thus stamps canceled on thick paper are valuable on complete cover; the rest, mint or barred (very thin or very thick bars), are valueless.

1897. 2-boliviano. No. 72. *Original:* lithographed, perf 11¾ x 12; 23 1/10 x 29¾ mm.

Forgery: very deceptive Geneva lithograph; perf 11½; 23 x 29 mm (see the various distinctive marks of original and forgery in the illustration).

The forged Geneva cancellation is a triple rectangle with two laterally adjacent rectangles and BOLIVIA in the middle.

1899. Overprinted with "E F 1899." Nos. 54 to 58. *Forged overprints:* comparison is necessary. Also (Geneva) on originals are forgeries of 1894.

1899–1901. Perf 11½. Nos. 59 to 66. *Geneva forgeries:* comparison with 1- or 2-centavo easy-to-find originals reveals a not very clear-cut hatched background; the coat of arms and the upper inscription are executed poorly; the stars above and below are touching.

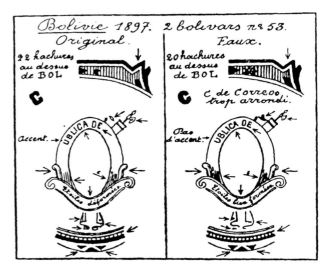

Top: Bolivia, 1897. 2-boliviano. No. 53. Original; 22 shade lines above BOL; accent over U; distorted stars. Forgery; 20 shade lines above BOL; the "C" of CORREOS is too rounded; no accent; well-formed stars.

Borneo [North]

1883–86. POSTAGE on top. Nos. 1 to 9. *Genoa forgery:* 2-cent. (This is the only value I have seen; there probably will be other values in "cents" from the same cliché): red-brown shade, red more pronounced (less chocolate color) than the original; perf 14; 22 mm high instead of 22⅓ mm; rose transparency instead of nontransparency; the boat's dotted line on the left under the background hatching and the stippling in the bottom of the escutcheon, between the groups of curved lines representing waves, are not very visible or are partly missing.

Geneva forgery: 50-cent. The shield's horizontal hatch lines and those of the loincloths of the two human figures are not parallel; half of the inscription lettering, PERCO ET PERACO, is touching the top of the banderole; the "T" is touching the bottom, and the "R" of PERACO, which is too large, is touching top and bottom. The forged Geneva cancellation is round, with date (27½ mm): SANDAKAN 23 JUN 1886.

1884–87. Stamps overprinted "3," "5," "8," and EIGHT CENTS. Nos. 12 to 15. *Original overprints:* they were applied only on the three values of 1883 and 1884, perf 12.

Forged overprints: very numerous; comparison is indispensable. A forged overprint of the "5-cents" with small "s" (as in Type I of the "3-cents") and with an almost horizontal lower bar, comes from Geneva. The EIGHT CENTS forged overprint (10 mm instead of 10½ mm long) with long and pointed serifs of the horizontal bar of the "T" letters was applied on the 2-cent Genoa forgery and on originals. The overprints applied on original stamps, perf 14 (aniline colors), are forged. The overprint "and Revenue" of Nos. 16 and 17 also was forged; comparison is necessary.

1888. 25-cent, 50-cent, $1, and $2. Nos. 30, 31, 33, and 63. Wishing to copy the rare 1883 values, Nos. 24–27, Fournier, lacking models perhaps, really counterfeited more common refashioned types. His model for the $1 stamp was No. 63, which was copied instead of No. 32. Except for a few details, its photolithographed forgeries are very well executed; the easiest way to recognize them is to compare shades: 25-cent is dark greenish blue instead of slate; the 50-cent, dark violet instead of violet-blue, and the $2 original is dark green and not green. In the 50-cent forgery, the height is 31⅓ mm instead of 30⅘ mm, and the design is coarsely drawn (see illustration). The faces of the two human figures are white; that's one way to save face! The forged cancellation is SANDAKAN 23 JUN (one circle), as in the first issue, but partly applied (without millesime); also barred oval.

1889–90. ½- to 10-cent. Nos. 34 to 42. POSTAGE inscription and REVENUE at bottom. *Originals:* 19 x about 22¾ mm; paper about 70 microns thick.

Forgeries: good general appearance; noncongruent shades; allowable perforation; slightly transparent paper, about 50 microns thick. The distinctive marks of each value follow (see the illustration also).

½-cent. Height, 23½ mm; cross designs on the left are off-center in their frames; rose red instead of carmine-tinted rose.

1-cent. Slight deviation of the cross designs; ochre-yellow instead of ochre.

2-cent. Triangular sail moved to the right; lower left corner design, left deviation; reddish brown; thin lettering.

3-cent. Irregular lower right corner design; the triangular sail has become trapezoidal; reddish violet instead of dark violet.

4-cent. Upper corner design defects; height, 23 mm; excessively dark rose.

5-cent. Upper right corner defective design; this square is not joined or is joined poorly to the tablet of the word BORNEO. Height, 23⅕ mm. Loop of the "5" extends only ⅒ mm beyond the figure's vertical line instead of ¼ mm; gray shade, not dark enough.

6-cent. Poorly executed mainmast; the two oblique ropes on the left do not touch it and are almost parallel. The sail contour lines are too straight. A hatch line is missing in the banderole above the "B" of BRITISH; flattened lower loop instead of round.

8-cent. Triangular sail as in 2-cent. The two cross designs on the left are left deviant and unsuccessful in execution. Under the boat, the wave lines form spots. Green shade contains a little too much yellow.

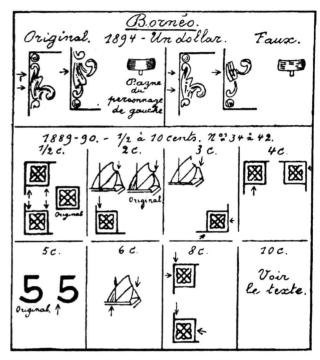

Top: Borneo. Original. 1894 — one dollar. Forgery. Loincloth of human figure on left. Middle: 1889–90. ½- to 10-cent. Nos. 34–42. Bottom: See the text.

10-cent. Height of figures is 1⅗ mm instead of about 1¾ mm. The right triangular sail line is too pronounced, the sail appearing as in the 2-cent stamp. The letter "S" of CENTS often is defective near its middle. Blue instead of dark blue.

1890–91 to 1899. Overprinted stamps. Nos. 43 to 48 and 86 to 97. *Forged overprints:* comparison is necessary.

Forged Geneva overprints: 4 CENTS, "Two cents," and 6 CENTS (the last two, on forgeries also).

1916. Red Cross. Nos. 150 to 162. *Forged overprints:* comparison is necessary. In the Geneva counterfeits applied on originals, the rose color is too carmine-tinted; the apexes of the four triangles are too thick.

Bosnia

First issue (June 1879–1898). Nos. 1 to 9. This is one of the most interesting issues for specialists because of the diversity of types, shades, perforation, plates, papers, etc. It shows that, in the beginning, manufacture was difficult — here as in all other countries — and that it took time to produce successful modern stamp sets with identical (and often uninteresting) examples.

There are three plates:

Plate I (1879–94): lithographed, Nos. 2 to 9; pointless shield at bottom. Watermarked BRIEFMARKEN until 1890 (once in each sheet) and ZEITUNGSMARKEN from 1890 to 1900. The 15-novcica stamp has two types, which can be identified by the figures on the right: Type I, thick figure "1," figure "5" with horizontal bar; Type II, thin figure "1," figure "5" with oblique bar.

Plate II includes No. 1, lithographed (end of 1894), and Nos. 1 to 9, typographed (1895). The shield point is visible. A second watermark, also once per sheet. The figures differ somewhat from those of Plate 1; for example, figure "2" on the right (No. 3) is in three pieces with a horizontal bar; figure "1" on the right (No. 6) is not so high, and the oblique bar is very visible.

In this plate, the 10-novcica stamp is found in two different types, figure "7" on the left of the second type being thicker. These two types are equally valuable, but the stamps of the second type, which have a small cross in the upper right triangle of the shield, are in demand (Type II appears ten times per sheet of 100 stamps).

Plate III has only the 5-novcica stamp in a red brick shade.

Reprints (1911): the whole set, perf 12¹/₂, duller shades. Compare with the original shades with the same perforation.

Forgeries: see the original stamps of the second issue in the illustration, and compare the stamp centers, outside the comers.

Second issue (1900–1901). Nos. 10 to 23. Production was modernized: fewer varieties. Watermarked ZEITUNGSMARKEN once per sheet in the first printings of the values in heller, then no watermark. No types, no plate varieties. A few perforation varieties: the 2-heller stamp, perf 12³/₄ x 13¹/₄, and the 10-heller, 12¹/₂ x 10¹/₂. Both are rare.

Reprints (1911): like those of the first issue.

Forgeries (V.): a set of modern forgeries, inexpertly

executed, with blurred impression; adequately described by the illustration. The lion is wearing a pastry apprentice's beret. The three large format values have similar differences. (Look especially at the stippling of the shields; also, there is little or no light on the right of the saber.)

Second issue (1901–7). Same type. Nos. 24 to 28. Perf 6¹/₂, 9¹/₄, 10¹/₂, and in combination, as well as imperforate stamps: 10 francs; on cover: 20 francs.

Forgeries: as in the preceding issue.

Subsequent issues. Nothing to point out.

Forgeries: the 1912 issue was counterfeited in large format typographed representations that do not resemble, even remotely, the engraving of the original stamps.

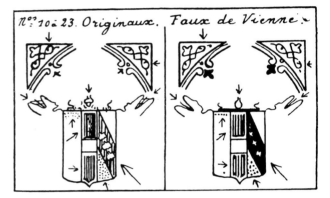

On the left, original stamps of the second issue, Nos. 10–23, compared with Vienna forgeries (right).

Brazil

There are a great many forgeries of imperforate Brazilian stamps. It would take too long to study them in detail; moreover, it is quite useless to concentrate on figure, frame detail, etc., when the background cross-hatching provides a quick, reliable diagnosis.

First issue. 1843. Nos. 1 to 3. *Originals:* the background is composed of a quincunx of lozenge-shaped dots. With the help of a magnifying glass, one can observe that each group of nine or sixteen angular shapes is separated from the others by a curved white line, which more or less encroaches on the sides. A study of the cross-hatching with regard to the two large white globes and the ornamental design of the bandeaux shows that the engraver of the firm of Perkins, Bacon, and Company engraved the figures of the 60-reis upside down on the reproducing matrix. Paul Kohl's *Briefmarken Handbuch* [Volume 1 of the eleventh edition of *Kohls Grosser Katalog und Briefmarken*

Handbuch (Chemnitz, 1907)] omits any mention of this peculiarity.

Forgeries: there are several sets whose quincunx is made up of groups of nine, twelve, sixteen, and even of as many as twenty-five round, rectangular, or lozenge-like dots. The spaces between the groups are too large or are almost missing. There are completely fantastic designs (see the illustration).

Second issue. 1844–46. Nos. 4 to 10. *Originals:* the cross-hatching is as finely executed as that of the first issue. This time, it was the engraver of the mint in Rio de Janeiro who made the error of engraving figures "90-," "180-," and "600-"reis upside down in relation to the cross-hatching of the 10-, 30-, and 60-reis.

Forgeries: the counterfeits sketched are grotesque. Three sets from three different workshops of photoliths that are blurred and lack relief. Usually, there is a single cliché per set, the cliché reproduced with figure changes. The Geneva set has three different clichés for the 180-, 300-, and 600-reis stamps, and they are just as fantastic (see the illustration). A comparison of the design with the original's upper left corner will be sufficient.

1850 and 1854. Nos. 11 to 20. *Originals:* this time, the background design, which is identical in all respects, allowed no engraving inversion of the figures.

Reprints: all values in black, on very thick paper. First-class printing on cleaned plates.

Forgeries: numerous sets, one of which is complete, made in Geneva (including Nos. 19 and 20), with arbitrary corner designs, which are sometimes different in each corner! Photolithographed with embossing.

Fakes: reprints that have been thinned uniformly. Compare paper texture.

Issue of 1861. 280- and 430-reis. Nos. 21 and 22. *Originals:* the recess print engraving, with its deep cuts, left a serious, perceptible color deposit, especially on the shaded figure lines.

Forgeries: poorly executed lithographed stamps. The two values were inexpertly counterfeited in Geneva, with thirteen horizontal shade lines, top left; eleven, bottom left; and only five curved lines in the three globes shown in the illustration. The forged Geneva cancellations on this set and on the preceding one are the early postmark with horizontal bars and parentheses of New Wales and Tasmania; barred oval; dots and partial round postmarks, double circle CORREIO, etc.

Clandestine reprinting of the 280-reis in claret on horizontally laid paper (original plate).

1866. Perforated. The originals are perf 13½.

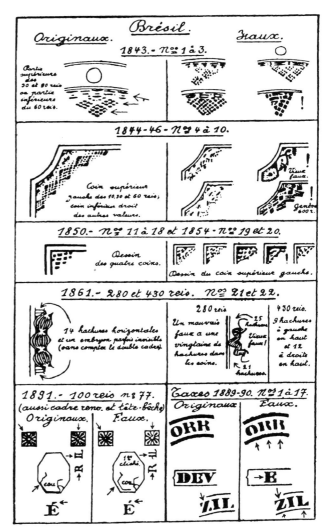

Top: Brazil. 1843, Nos. 1–3. Originals. Upper part of the 30- and 90-reis or lower part of the 60-reis. Forgeries. Second: 1844–46. Nos. 4–10. Upper left corner of the 10-, 30-, and 60-reis; lower right corner of the other values; early forgery; Geneva, 600-reis. Third: 1850, Nos. 11–18, and 1854, Nos. 19 and 20. Design of the four corners. Design of the upper left corner. Fourth section: 1861. 280- and 430-reis. Nos. 21 and 22. 14 horizontal shade lines and an embryonic line that is invisible at times (double frame, not counted). 280-reis: A bad forgery has about 20 shade lines in the corners. 25 shade lines; early forgery; 21 shade lines. 430-reis: 9 shade lines, top left, and 12, top right. Bottom, left: 1891. 100-reis. No. 77 (also inverted frame and tête-bêche). Originals. Forgeries. First cliché. Neck. Bottom, right: postage due 1889–90. Nos. 1–17. Originals. Forgeries.

1891–92. 100-reis. No. 77. *Originals:* dual-color typographical impression. One should note that the red shade lines covering the inscriptions are not limited by a red line at their extremities.

Geneva forgeries: deceptive-looking dual-color photoliths. The red shade lines are limited by lines that run along the sides of the ornamental corners near the stamp's interior. In a first cliché for the red impression, the portrait is separated from the octagonal frame by about ¹/₂ mm at the bottom and along the hair, but it is connected with this frame by the shoulder strap (forgery of a common single stamp and of a tête-bêche). In a second cliché, the portrait was lowered down to the octagonal frame's lower line; so, the forgeries from this rectified cliché are more deceptive. (See other details in the illustration.) The shades are fair: pale ultramarine and rose red — which focuses immediately on the forged tête-bêche, the original tête-bêche being blue and red; perf 12 x 12 or 14 x 14. The forged cancellation: (one circle, with date 23³/₄ mm) ITAJARY 23 ABR 1891 (S. CATHA) or (double circle, 20¹/₂ mm) ADM. DOSCNO PARANA (EXP.) 13 JUL 92.

1894–97. 100-, 300-, and 500-reis. Nos. 82, 84, and 85. *Used postal forgeries* (Rio de Janeiro) 100-reis: the letters of CORREIO evidently are too thin, and the bandeau that contains this inscription is too far away from the last "S" of ESTADOS. 300- and 500-reis: in the originals, the "S" of REIS, on the left of the value figure, is higher than the others; in the forgeries, in contrast, it is smaller, too narrow, and further away from the "I." Dimensions are arbitrary.

1900. 200-reis. No. 118. *Used postal forgery.* CORREIO is not positioned symmetrically in the bandeau. It is too low. This inscription is about 1 mm too wide because "RR" evidently is too wide.

Postage due stamps, 1889 and 1890. Nos. 1 to 9. *Originals:* fine, regularly sketched burelage.

Geneva forgeries: printed in sheets, each vertical strip of which has the nine values. Crude burelage with defects and ink clogging spots at line intersections; as a whole, nevertheless, the counterfeits look good. The illustration shows a few lettering defects. Allowable paper thickness; arbitrary, excessively dull shades in the 1890 set. Forged cancellation, ITAJARY, as in the 1891–92 issue (this one is the most frequent).

1898. Postage stamps, Nos. 91 to 100, and stamps for newspapers, Nos. 1 to 18. *Forgeries:* letters in CORREIO are not so thick, and the letters "RREI" are not joined at the bottom; in BRASIL, same defect for the letters "RASIL." Serious defects in the lower left corner design. Width, 27–27¹/₃ mm instead of 26¹/₂–26²/₃ mm.

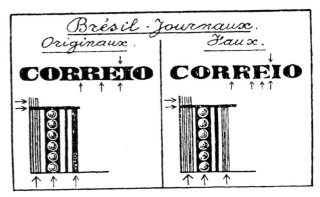

Brazil newspapers. Originals. Forgeries.

British Central Africa

1891. Nos. 1 to 16. The *original overprint* is more or less thick in Nos. 1–10. The South African 5-shilling to £10 stamps with fiscal cancellation often are *faked* by cleaning and subsequent impression of a forged overprint.

Forged overprints: comparison is necessary (Geneva and Fournier cancellation).

1895 and subsequent issues. Higher values: *faking* by scraping off the word SPECIMEN, followed by repainting or forged cancellation.

British Columbia

1861–65. Portrait. Nos. 1 to 5. A few early lithographed forgeries, in which the face contour is sketched by a more or less thick line. Lining or cross-hatching is defective; dividing frame lines; etc.

1865–67. "V" and crown. Nos. 6 and 7. *Originals:* typographed; watermark "CC" crown; perf 14 or 12¹/₂. On the crown's top sides, there are six pearls; in the middle, under the cross, three pearls; on the bandeau, seven pearls between two fine lines.

Early forgeries: no watermark; dividing frame lines. (a) On top, five pearls, three in the middle, seven lozenges on the bandeau, "UMBI" of COLUMBIA is touching the oval's fine lines; imperforate set. (b) Same number of pearls as in the set a; the seven lozenges are larger; almost all the inscription letters are touching the oval's fine lines; perf 13. (c) A better forgery, usually labeled FALSCH; middle lines in the "M" of COLUMBIA extend to the bottom of the letter; the "G" of POSTAGE is more like a "C"; perf 13¹/₂.

Engraved modern forgeries (Genoa): good photographically reproduced set; no watermark in benzine; perf 13 x 13¹/₂; color relief is sufficient to spot the forgery. Note: All forgeries, other than the 3-pence, are provided with forged overprints.

British East Africa

1890. Overprinted stamps, Nos. 1 to 3. *Forged overprints:* comparison is necessary. (Geneva, HALF, 1- and 4-anna.)

1890–91. Values in rupees. Nos. 15 to 20. *Originals:* not very transparent paper of variable thickness (about 55–75 microns); perf 14, 14½, and 14 x 14½.

Geneva forgeries: small sheets on very transparent thin paper, perf 14.

Genoa forgeries: same, on transparent, very white, thick paper (about 90 microns). (See the illustration.)

1891–95. *Forged overprints,* made by handstamp, and manuscript overprints: comparison is indispensable.

1895. Overprint on three lines, Nos. 29 to 43. *Forged overprints:* comparison will be useful. The values in rupees, counterfeits of 1890–91, received a forged overprint in Geneva, along with the Fournier forged cancellation (double circle, 23 mm).

1895. Overprint "2½," No. 44. *Forged overprints,* especially Geneva.

1896. Second overprint on three lines, Nos. 45 to 59. *Forged overprints* of Geneva, etc.

1896. Overprints "2½," Nos. 60a and b. Types II and III overprints are reprints in red-brown of 1897 overprints.

1897. Third overprint on three lines, Nos. 84 to 91. *Forged overprints* of Geneva, etc. Comparison is necessary. The overprints with a dot after AFRICA are reprints.

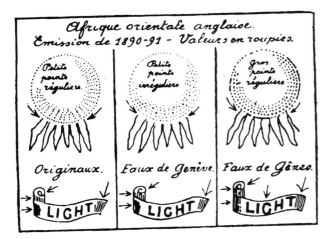

British East Africa. Issue of 1890–91. Values in rupees. Left: small regular dots, originals. Middle: small irregular dots, Geneva forgeries. Right: large regular dots, Genoa forgeries.

British Guiana

1850. Circular delivery stamps. Nos. 1 to 4. *Originals:* typographed on paper showing a kind of close wire-mark structure. The letters of British Guiana are 2 mm high, the value figures, 1½ mm. The "4" is closed. The "c" of "cents" measures about 1½ mm wide and high. The word is well aligned with the figure. The period is placed a bit too high, except in the 2-cent.

Forgeries: three kinds, all lithographed. (a) Letters are from 2½–2¾ mm high; figure, 2 mm high; "c" of "cents," 1¼ mm wide by 2¼ mm high. No dot after this word ("12 cents"). (b) Another early set which is very easy to check, because a signature, E. Lew (English manuscript), is lithographed like the rest; the value figure with "cents" is positioned very obliquely in relation to the figure; and because a kind of parenthesis emphasizes the signature. (c) Geneva set: letters are 2½–¾ mm high; figures, 2½ mm high (the "4" is 3 mm high and is open). The letters of "cents," except the final "s," are upright instead of slanted. Forgeries a and b are stippled paper; forgery c, on wove paper. The cancellation of the Geneva set is A 0 3, grayish ink, noncongruent handstamp impression.

1851. 1 and 4. Nos. 5 and 6. *Originals:* 19½ x about 28⅔ mm. Figure "1" has no terminal line and the "4" is closed. The "M" of VICISSIM is under the "U" of PARTIMUS.

Geneva forgeries: dimensions are somewhat too large; figure "1" has a terminal line; "4" is closed; the "M" is under the space between "U" and "S"; arbitrary shades; cancellation: A 0 3.

Reprints: perf 12½.

1853. Imperforate with millesime. Nos. 7 to 11. *Forgeries:* I have seen only a few forged copies; they are lithographed and, consequently, not close to the original engraving. One can recognize them right away by the almost illegible oval inscription; the lower bar of the "E" of POSTAGE is terminated by a short vertical line instead of a rather thick blank triangle.

Reprints: perf 12 and 12½; orange-red, pale blue; paper is thinner than in the originals.

1856. Rectangular stamps. Nos. 12 to 14. *Originals:* typographed (indention is quite evident); the frame lines do not touch each other, except occasionally in the lower left corner; the "Q" of "QUE" is a capital letter.

Geneva forgeries: lithographed; the frame lines meet; the "Q" of "QUE" is a lowercase "q"; the inscription letters frequently touch each other, particularly the "M" of DAMUS. Cancellation: A 0 3. There are also forgeries with similar defects, with the lithographed signature, E. Lew, and various cancellations.

1860–75. Millesime "1860." Nos. 15 to 26.
Originals: typographed with various perforations. The oval inscription is DAMUS PETIMUSQUE VICISSIM in well-shaped letters. The millesime figures are placed exactly in the middle of their frames. The "O" is flattened slightly on top. The terminal curl of the "R" of BRITISH turns up a bit higher than the lower serif of the "I."

Forgeries: a half-dozen lithographed sets which can be eliminated right away by comparing with the original designs. Check the ship, the horizontal background shade lines in the oval, and the inner corner burelage. The following serious inscription defects also may be noted: figure "1" is moved to the left; figure "O" is quite oval-like; RETIMUSQUE; PETIMUSQUE; the "A" in DAMUS has no median bar; full oval background; the curl of the "R" of BRITISH turns down or is horizontal in relation to the base of the "I." The imperforate stamps are essays.

1862. Provisional stamps. l-, 2-, and 4-cent. Nos. 27 to 29. *Originals:* the four inner frame lines do not touch, and the lines under BRITISH and POSTAGE are broken. The stamps have the red signature of the postmaster in their centers. (If there is no signature, they are unissued stamps.) The 1- and 2-cent stamps belong to Types a, b, and c in the catalogues (see the ornamental frame); the 4-cent belongs to Types d, e, f, and g only. Usual cancellation: one circle, with date, or A 0 3.

Forgeries: various sets whose inner frame lines touch each other and in which the vertical lines are unbroken. In general, imperforate instead of rouletted. The center inscriptions are frequently B M; C H; E Lew; C W; or "nor por" in black on two lines. Fournier (Geneva) reproduced seven types of each of the three values without signature, imperforate, and often with cancellations A 0 3.

1863–75. Millesime "1863." Nos. 30 to 32.
Originals: typographed, perf 10, 12, 13, or 15. The center background shading lines are finely drawn, parallel lines and have two small clouds on the left of the words and one on the right. There is a dot after GUIANA and CENTS. Between the B. GUIANA tablet and the circular bandeau, there is a blank dot above the "U" of PETIMUSQUE and another above the "Q." The imperforate stamps are essays.

Forgeries: a half-dozen sets, which have the following characteristics: (a) perf 13½; no cloud on the right of the mast; VICISSJM; blank dot above the "M." (b) Perf 13½, no dot over the "U." (c) Perf 13; no dot after GUIANA. (d) Perf 12; very faint dot after GUIANA. (e) Perf 12; no dot after GUIANA and CENTS. (f) Perf 11½; same defect, and "XXIV" is printed "24." Comparison with a used original of the rather common 24-cent stamp instantly will reveal the serious design defects (ship, horizontal background, corner lines) of all these sets. Some forgeries are perf 9½ or 11½; the value figure and CENTS are close together and are about 1 mm less in width and height.

1876–82. *Forgeries:* no watermark.

1882. SPECIMEN in oblique perforation. Nos. 61 to 64. *Geneva forgeries:* 27 mm instead of 25 mm; no dot after CENT; the foremast points toward the "T" of BRITISH (three-mast type).

Official stamps. Original overprint in black. The "O" of the overprint of one good counterfeit is too rounded.

Postage-revenue stamps. Nos. 1 to 15. *Genoa forgeries:* cleverly and deceptively counterfeited with overprint, particularly of values in dollars; however, they are lithographed, without watermark, and are dot perf 15.

British Honduras

1866. Perf 14. Nos. 1 to 3. *Originals:* very carefully typographed.

Forgeries: early lithographed forgeries from various sources, including Geneva; very mediocre execution which a second's comparison with common stamps (2- and 3-centavo on 1-penny rose and 3-pence brown, Nos. 26 and 27) will reveal; a full line defines, at least partly, the face and neck contour; letters are touching the oval. The 3-pence was counterfeited in the same way. Usually perf 13; deplorable perforation.

1871–87. With watermark. Nos. 4 to 17. Same forgeries as above, without watermark. Note: There exist fakes of the king and queen types in the major values which were obtained for more common values. The 5-dollar stamp, with the portrait of King Edward (other values also, probably), was counterfeited without watermark. Comparison of the facial features with those of a common stamp in the set will be sufficient.

British Somaliland

See Somaliland Protectorate.

British South Africa

1891. Perf 14. Nos. 6 to 11. *Fakes:* fiscal cancellations (stamp or pen), cleaned.

1891. Overprinted stamps. Nos. 12 to 15. *Forged overprints:* comparison is necessary. The 8-pence

(Geneva) with forged round cancellation (Geneva): FRANCESTOWN I MY 95 S. AFRICA.

1895. Overprinted Capetown stamps. Nos. 12 to 48. *Original overprint:* 9 mm high; SOUTH AFRICA: 14³/₄ mm wide.

Forged overprints on originals (often "used" in Capetown): comparison would be useful. Forged Geneva overprint, three types.

Brunei

1906. Labuan stamps overprinted BRUNEI. Nos. 1 to 12. Comparison with the authentic overprint is indispensable.

Buenos Aires

See Argentina.

Bulgaria

The first issues are interesting until about 1900; then we get into mass-produced new stamps.

1879. Values in centimes and francs. Nos. 1 to 5. Typographed. Perf 14¹/₂ x 15. Sheets of 100 in four panes of twenty-five stamps (5 x 5). Printed and issued May 1, 1879, at St. Petersburg, except the 50-centime stamp which was issued later, wherefore its rarity.

Select: stamps centered. Little variety in shades.

Varieties: 25-centime imperforate and 5-centime black and orange, inverted frame: very rare.

Forgeries: a set very crudely counterfeited in Genoa (I.) on thick paper without watermark or laid paper. Typographed. The figures and lettering of the oval are shapeless; the left forepaw of the lion is touching the oval; numerous white spots in the oval background of the inscription; noncongruent perforation. The second issue was counterfeited in similar circumstances.

Pairs: 3U; blocks of four: 12U.

1881. Value in stotinki. Nos. 6 to 11. Sheets and impression like the previous issue.

Varieties: a few minor shade varieties, especially the 5-stotinka in black and yellow and in black and orange. This stamp exists with a black and yellow double lion, the second one being inverted: very rare.

Pairs: 3U; blocks of four: 8U.

Forgeries: see the previous issue.

1882–85. Same. Colors changed. Nos. 12 to 20. Sheets, impression, etc., as above. The 1- and 2-stotinka were printed in 1885. All perf 14¹/₂ x 15.

Shades: two for each stamp, except the 10-stotinka carmine, scarlet, and rose, all three with a pale rose background.

Varieties: the 5-stotinka error, printed in the 10-stotinka shades, is rarer mint than used. The 5-stotinka has three types: Type I, no color dots above the tongue; Type II, with one dot; Type III, with two dots. Type III is less common. There is also a plate flaw in the 5-stotinka — a printer's error on the first "A" of BULGARIA.

Pairs: 2U; blocks of four: 6U.

Fake: the 10-stotinka was doctored so as to create an error of it. Not at all successful: a quick look through a magnifying glass will tell the story.

1884–85. Overprints. Nos. 24 to 27. The "3" overprints on the 10-stotinka, and the "5" on 30-stotinka are 7¹/₂ mm high; the "15" overprints on the 25- and 50-stotinka in one sheet are 12¹/₂ mm high. The first three are either lithographed or typographed; the last is lithographed only. The carmine overprints are typographed; the vermilion ones are lithographed. The "5" on 30 is printed in the carmine shades of the 10-stotinka stamp, whereas the lithographic overprint was applied only in the rose shade. Canceled stamps with date: 2U.

Varieties: there are inverted and double overprints: very rare. Expertizing is indicated. There are printer's waste sheets.

Forged overprints: as numerous as rabbits in Australia. Detailed comparison is absolutely indispensable; however, some of the overprints are so well counterfeited that expertizing seems impossible. (Clandestine printing?)

Subsequent issues. There is nothing very interesting to say about them.

1901. Commemorative stamps. Cannon type. Nos. 48 and 49. Sheets of 100 stamps (10 x 10), lithographed. Perf 13. Transfer block of five stamps in a horizontal strip.

Forgeries: the illustration gives adequate information on the Geneva forgeries (P.). The counterfeits have none of the transfer defects of the five original types, and the ground under the cannon is not stippled. Perf 11¹/₂.

1902. Commemorative stamps. Battle of Chipka Pass. Nos. 62 to 64. Sheets of 100 stamps (10 x 10), lithographed. Perf 11¹/₂. Transfer block of two stamps in a horizontal pair.

Forgeries: the Brussels forgeries are very widely circulated. Perf 11¹/₂, like the originals. Lithographed. The distinctive characteristics are shown in the illustration. Note that the distinctive transfer flaws of the two original types are missing.

1903. Overprints. Nos. 65 to 68. An inverted or double overprint is possible. There are pairs with only one stamp overprinted.

Forged overprints: most of the overprint varieties have been counterfeited; the same may be said regarding the 1892, 1895, and other issues. Comparative study is necessary.

Postage Due Stamps

The first three issues are lithographed. The very dark shade of the 50-stotinka is from the first plate; the pale blue shade, from the second. The 25-stotinka exists with zigzag rouletting and perf 11½ on the same stamp. The serpentine rouletting requires comparison.

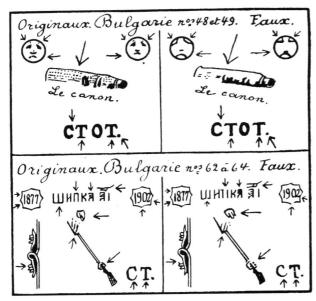

Top: Bulgaria Nos. 48 and 49. Cannon type commemoratives of 1901, originals, forgeries. Bottom: Battle of Chipka Pass set of 1902, originals and forgeries.

Burkina Faso — Upper Volta

Forged overprints on Nos. 18, 19, 20, 38, and 39. Comparison is necessary.

Bushire

Forged overprints. Comparison and even expertizing are indispensable.

Cameroun

First issue. 1896. Nos. 1 to 6. Numerous *forged overprints;* comparison is necessary. Also, one finds the forged overprint KAMERUN on German counterfeits of 1889 (Geneva). See German Colonies. The forged Geneva cancellation is round with date: KAMERUN 3 2 98 and star at the bottom; 24½ mm.

1900. Perf 14. Values in pfennig. Nos. 7 to 15. Steamer type *forgeries.* See German Colonies.

1915–16. Overprinted stamps. Nos. 25 to 66. Numerous *forged overprints*, the majority of which can be spotted immediately by making a good template measurement of the originals. As for the doubtful ones, detailed comparison is necessary.

Canada

1851. Specimen. No. 3 stamp on wove paper is known thus; it also is known without that red overprint (thin paper, gumless). A *reprint* is involved.

1855. 10-pence blue, No. 8. A *reprint* also bears the overprint SPECIMEN in red. Some essays of the 6- and 7½-pence have the same overprint, which occasionally was removed by fakers, but traces remain. Paper comparison will reveal them.

1857. Perf 12. Nos. 9 to 11. *Fakes* created by forged perforation of Nos. 4–6 of the preceding issue. There also are forgeries that are perf 13 and 14. The green is a *reprint.*

1899. Inverted overprints of the 2-cent. Nos. 76 and 77. *Forged overprints:* comparison is necessary (Geneva, two types).

Envelopes. The original envelopes, with queen's portrait (5- and 10-cent), were *reprinted* (measurements a little smaller than the 140 x 83 mm of the originals).

Forged envelope cutouts by Fournier on brownish yellow paper; same values. The portrait, which is 11 mm wide from nose to chignon instead of about 10 mm, is out of place in the oval.

Cape Juby

First issue. 1916. Forged overprints.

Cape of Good Hope

Triangular stamps. There are a great many forgeries of the Perkins and De La Rue sets, of woodcut engravings, and of rare errors of the latter. A detailed description would be tedious; in most cases, they are reproduced from a single matrix, a description of the typical defects of which is sufficient.

Sets from 1853 to 1858. *Originals:* all of them have the anchor watermark. (The 1-penny red also has the "C C" watermark; very rare.) The 1851 set (1-penny and 4-pence blue) is on blue-tinted paper whose shade is quite visible on the stamp's back.

Forgeries: no watermark. Almost all lithographed.

a. Early counterfeit of the 1853 set. Good general appearance, but the paper has a greenish tint. There often is a dividing frame line 1 mm from the stamp's edges. Examination of the "P" of POSTAGE, the "F" of OF, and of the burelage surrounding these letters will be decisive. Some counterfeits on white paper of the Perkins and De La Rue values (Nos. 3 to 6b) in several shades. The 1-shilling is found also on greenish paper.

b. Early poorly designed forgeries; 1-penny and 4-pence on very thick white paper. The background is formed by wavy, crisscrossed lines spaced about 1/3 mm apart. The inscription CAPE OF GOOD HOPE gradually increases in height to the right. See also the Figure *b* sketch of the ornamental square for each value in the illustration.

c. Geneva set, lithographed in blocks. All values in the several shades on yellowish or white paper; numerous design defects. See Figure *c*. The 1-penny has a color dot inside the "C" of CAPE. This set usually is canceled by a barred square with "21," or with a British foreign post office postmark with figure "1"; also with a barred lozenge with a white circle in the middle.

d. Geneva set, recess print engraved; very pronounced relief; De La Rue appearance; design defects. See Figure *d*. The anchor's diamond forms an acute angle. Forgeries are found usually on piece with forged British foreign cancellation "A 91."

e. Various incomplete sets of forgeries that are identified easily by comparisons with authentic designs and by the absence of a watermark.

f. Photolithographed stamps. Various values that would require comparison and measuring if they had a watermark. In the 1-penny (De La Rue), the stamp base is about 3/4 mm too short. The bottom of the goddess's skirt is broken into four pieces above her foot. The lines limiting the anchor are blurred. In the ornamental lower left corner design, the line near the corner is formed from three broken pieces of lines, and it is too short.

g. Finally, an engraved set with watermark is rather deceptive, but the background cross-hatching, which is so regular in the originals, is replaced by a multitude of infrequently long, straight lines, especially on the right of the goddess. Paper is too yellowish; margins are often too wide; arbitrary shades. The triangular base is not exactly long enough.

Set of 1861. Woodcut engraved stamps. Nos. 7 and 8. *Reprinting* of 1883 on wove white paper (no laid paper), with white gum instead of yellow; the errors were not reprinted.

So-called reprints of 1883 were typographed, not woodcut engraved. Glossy paper, arbitrary shades, differences in inscription lettering.

Forgeries: see preceding "g"; Geneva set. Lithographed on forged laid paper or on yellowish wove or white paper in blocks spaced 3 to 4 mm apart; 1-penny and 4-pence, including the errors. Grotesque design; lettering is poorly reproduced. The "S" of POSTAGE is a "B"; the "A" of the same word is a Russian "D" (Д), and the "A" of CAPE, a Greek delta (δ). The "H" and the "O" of HOPE are joined to the white line surmounting them. In the ONE PENNY (regular or error), the second "N" of PENNY is

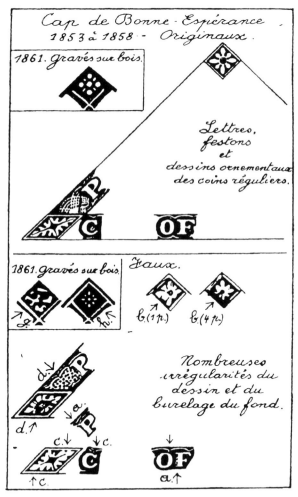

Top: Cape of Good Hope, 1853–58, originals. Rectangular insert: 1861; woodcut engraved. Trimmed triangular insert: regular corner lettering, scallops, and ornamental designs. Bottom: forgeries. Rectangular insert: 1861; woodcut engraved. 1-penny and 4-pence; numerous irregularities in the design and background burelage.

surmounted by a color dot in the margin. (See also Figure *g* in the illustration.)

h. Early forgery; heavy color frame. The word CAPE is evidently less high than HOPE.

i. Early forgery of a poorly executed 4-pence; the goddess's chignon is not prominent enough. See also the original design of the ornamental square.

j. Early set with very arbitrary design; the bottom inscription seems to form only one word; noncongruent lettering.

Overprinted stamps. Nos. 13 to 15 and 22. *Forged overprints:* ONE PENNY; FOUR PENCE; ONE HALF-PENNY, which are rather numerous on canceled originals. Some of them are ludicrous; others are better executed (No. 22 with "O" just above the hyphen); still others require comparison with an original.

Anglo-Boer War. Numerous forged overprints. Comparison is necessary. Nos. 1 to 20 overprints were counterfeited in Geneva.

Cape Verde

Crown type issue, 1877–81. Nos. 1 to 4. *Originals:* see details in the illustration for Portuguese Colonies.

Reprints: all values on pure chalky white paper, without gum, always perf 13½.

Geneva forgeries: the "C" and "R" of CORREIO almost are touching the bottom of the tablet. The cross, the crown bandeau, the ornamental design under the upper right corner square and (other) corner squares show differences. See the illustration under Portuguese Colonies.

Forged Geneva cancellations: (1) double circle, with date, CORREIO DE PORTO GRANDE 6/3 1881; PORTOPRAIA /12 1878. (2) Large double oval postmark: CORREIO 10 NOV 81 CIDADE DA PRAIA.

Caroline Islands

First issue, 1899. Nos. 1 to 6. *Forged overprints:* numerous forgeries of rare overprints (forty-eight-degree angle inclination); the inclination is variable and the overprint typographical characters are also variable. Make comparison. Forged overprints also are found on Geneva forgeries (see German Colonies), with rare inclination; lithographed. The forged cancellation of this set is YAP 7/1 99 KAROLINEN, one circle (27½ mm).

1910. 5-pfennig overprint. No. 20. *Forged overprints;* expertizing is necessary.

Castellorizo

French occupation. Nos. 1 to 14. Numerous forged overprints; make comparison. See also French Colonies for Nos. 12, 15, 25, 26, and 34, Merson type.

Caucasus

See Transcaucasian Federated States.

Cayman Islands

Forged overprints. Comparison is necessary for Nos. 17, 20, 31, and 49.

Ceylon

Issues of 1855–67. Rectangular design. *Originals:* recess print engraved; regular cross-hatching in which four ovals made of broken white lines are perceptible; a fifth oval is visible only above the head and in front of the neck. The white line (near the interior of the stamp) bordering the upper squares ends at the colored line which borders the background oval. Regular lettering. Face and neck covered with dotted lines, which are quite distinct in the good impressions. Watermark, except in the 1862 issue.

Early lithographed forgeries: no embossing; usually imperforate; 1-penny, 2-, 5-, 6-, and 10-pence. See design defects in the illustration.

Modern engraved forgeries: good appearance; thick paper (90 microns); margins, 3–4 mm wide, but trimmed by ½ or ¾ mm to preserve verisimilitude. Irregular design; the broken white line ovals are visible only in the 5-pence. (Only three of them are made of excessively thick lozenge dots.) Face and top of neck are in continuous shading. Defects in the white or colored line (2-pence) of the upper squares. The "O" of POSTAGE is too small; no watermark; arbitrary shades; 1-penny, 2-, and 5-pence, but I think there is a whole set.

Same. Octagonal design. 4-, 8-, 9-pence, 1-shilling 9-pence, and 2-shilling. *Originals:* eight horizontal shade lines above the POSTAGE tablet, the last one touching it; eight lines under the portrait's oval, the last one touching it.

Early forgeries: the 1-shilling 9-pence is known to exist lithographed; poorly executed. Other values do not merit description. The number of shading lines is the best identification mark.

Engraved forgeries: bad engraving with four thick shade lines above and five below. (See illustration.) That is the way the 4- and 8-pence stamps looked; the set possibly may have been completed. There were no *reprints.*

1868. 3-pence rose. No. 46. *Original:* typographed on glossy medium paper; watermarked "C C"; perf 12½ or 14.

Early forgery: lithographed on thin paper, without watermark, perf 12¼ (small holes). The fine center background and face hatching is confused — not entirely successful. Inscriptions are irregularly positioned in their tablets; the "Y" and "L" of CEYLON, in particular, are touching on top. Arbitrary purplish red shade.

1885–88. Various overprinted stamps. *Forged overprints* on used originals, especially Geneva. Comparison is necessary.

1903–4. 1.50-rupee, and 1910–11, 2-rupee. Nos. 153 and 176. *Forgeries:* bad lithographed stamps; no watermark or forged watermark. Portrait and background hatching examination will be adequate. The other major values probably will be forged also.

1918. War stamp on 2-, 3-, and 5-cattie. *Forged double and inverted overprint* on the 5-cattie. Comparison is necessary.

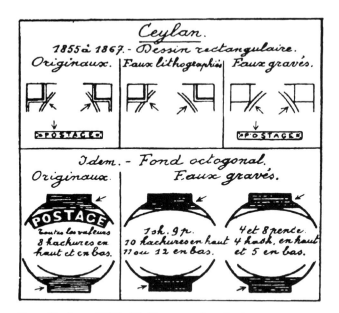

Top: Ceylon. 1855–67. Rectangular design. Originals, lithographed forgeries, engraved forgeries. Bottom: same. Octagonal background. Originals, engraved forgeries. All values — 8 shade lines top and bottom. 1-shilling 9-pence — 10 shade lines on top; 11 or 12 at bottom. 4- and 8-pence — 4 shade lines on top and 5 at bottom.

Official stamps. *Forged overprints* on canceled originals, especially Geneva, overprint ON SERVICE, etc. Comparison is indicated.

Chile

Imperforate issues. *Originals:* recess print engraved, except the lithographed transfers of 1854. Figure watermarks (see the catalogues); 19½ x about 22⁴⁄₅ mm. The center background cross-hatching displays only small symmetrically arranged white spaces, which form groups as in Figure *a* of the illustration. Each group contains two thin white lines (use magnifying glass), all of which form broken circles around the portrait. There are five of these groups between the hat and letters "LON" of COLÓN.

Early forgeries: lithographed without watermark. The design is arbitrary. See the upper left corner. The cross-hatched groups are shapeless; there are excessively visible white spots that are cut by a few lines of color.

Forged cancellation: quadruple circle with six inner bars, about 19 mm in diameter.

Forged photolithographs: 5- and 10-centavo, very successful with forged watermark, but figures are too large. The "errors" of watermark "1" are found on the 5-centavo; watermark "5" and "20" on the 10-centavo (figure "5," left line, is too long). No relief; minor design defects; arbitrary dimensions.

Set of 1867. 1- to 20-centavo. Nos. 11 to 15. *Originals:* admirable recess print engraved set; no contour line for the portrait, it being delimited by where the curving lines of the cross-hatching stop. The latter is visible between the letters of CHILE and under those of COLÓN. Perf 12.

Early forgeries: bad cross-hatched lithographs, composed of almost straight lines; nothing between the CHILE letters and a simple succession of white dots under COLÓN; thick color line (about ½ mm) around the portrait.

1900. Overprinted large figure "5." No. 41. *Inverted and double forged overprints* (Geneva). Comparison is necessary.

Postage due stamps (1895). 2- to 40-centavo. Nos. 1 to 9. *Geneva forgeries:* on common dull yellow or brownish yellow paper; perf 11½ (usually imperforate at top) instead of 13¼.

Forged cancellation, MULTADA, in a rectangle. A round cliché for the 10-centavo (letters PARAIS are touching the circle) and two clichés for the other values with interchangeable figure. In one, the "D" of MULTADA is inverted; in the other, the two strokes of the "L" of MULTADA are curved. There are other counterfeits; comparison is necessary.

Postage due stamps (1895 and 1896). Nos. 16 to 21 and 28 to 33. *Originals:* lithographed, 20 x 26¼–½ mm, depending on values and printing; regular background line structure.

Geneva forgeries: lithographed in two plates of seventy-two stamps (8 x 9). The first comprises rows (8 x 2) of the 20-, 40-, and 50-centavo stamps, and three rows of the 60-centavo. The second, three rows (8 x 3) of the 10- and 80-centavo and 1-peso stamps. About 20 x 26⅕ mm. The impression shade is an excessively dull red and the paper shades also are arbitrary: excessively pale yellow or buff yellow. The background lines are blotchy or are broken in places. The portrait is not congruent. There is a color protuberance on the upper left square. Three small color lines prolong the upper right square (see the illustration). Defects in lettering and stars. The 1895 set is perf 11½ instead of 11; that of 1896, an allowable 13½. Despite everything, these forgeries look good to the amateur: they are much in evidence.

Forged Geneva cancellations: postmark with date, two circles (22½–23 mm), TALCA 5 ABR 95; LINARES 30 NOV 95; VALDIVIA 1 FEB 97; CONCEPTION 30 DEC 97; PISAGUA 4 DIC 97, all with CHILE at the bottom. Large German-style postmark (26 mm), SANTIAGO 31 I 95 (with "1" figures sideways on sides and CHILE at bottom). They also are found with the preceding MULTADA framed (27 x 8 mm).

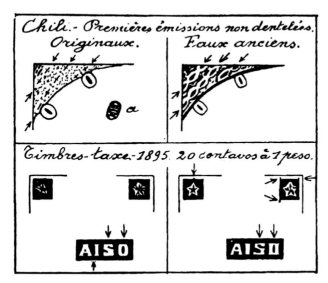

Top: Chile. First imperforate issue. Originals. Early forgeries. Bottom: postage due, 1895. 20-centavo to 1-peso.

China

First issue, 1878. Nos. 1 to 3. *Originals:* three plates for these values; they have different dimensions, and the stamps themselves vary in width and height; thin to thick paper. An essay of the 3-candareen stamp is recognized by the five well-formed pearls (instead of black dots) under the dragon (three on the left, one near the middle, and one on the right). No reprintings.

Second issue, 1885. Nos. 4 to 6. *Originals:* the shell watermark provides adequate identification. There are copies of the 3- and 5-candareen without watermark and with a red, four-character overprint; they are essays for Formosa.

Subsequent issues. *Overprinted stamps.* A few forged overprints, especially among the NEUTRALITY overprints (Nos. 109–20), postage due stamps (Nos. 26–31). Comparison is indispensable; likewise, with regard to the used values of Eastern Turkestan, issue of 1915.

1914. The 10-candareen, 50-candareen, and 1-dollar (perhaps also other values) were counterfeited to defraud the postal service. Noncongruent perforations and arbitrary design details (make comparison). In the 1-dollar, the two characters on the right in the Chinese inscription are about ⅓ mm apart instead of being very close, and the inscription tablets are touching the frame, top and bottom.

China (British Post Offices)

A few values with fraudulent overprint "C. E. F." on canceled stamps of British India from 1882 to 1911. Likewise, with respect to the overprint CHINA on canceled Hong Kong stamps (values in dollars). Cancellation provides useful information and clues; when it does not provide this information, comparison is necessary. The "C. E. F." overprint was counterfeited in Geneva.

China (French Post Offices)

Practically all overprints were counterfeited on postage stamps and postage due stamps; even millesime figures were reproduced. Many counterfeits require comparison and some of them, detailed expertizing. See French Colonies for Merson type forgeries, "Peace and Commerce," and postage due. The 16-cent overprint of 1901, large figure "5" (No. 34), overprint CHINA of 1902 and 1904, and overprint A PERCEVOIR, with a somewhat open "C," were counterfeited in Geneva.

China (German Post Offices)

1898. First issue. Nos. 1 to 6. The first overprint (forty-five-degree inclination) frequently was counterfeited. Comparison is indispensable.

A *forged overprint* also was applied on the Geneva forgeries (see German Colonies); Nos. 1–6, forty-five-degree inclination. This set has the forged cancellation: TSCHINWANGTAU 16/2 97 DEUTSCHE POST.

The second overprint (fifty-six degrees) is considered rather easily to be original, but there are counterfeits, particularly on stamps canceled by German cities. The original overprints themselves are found in thin, medium, or heavy impressions; specialization is advised.

Overprints of "5-pf" on 10-pfennig. Nos. 7 and 8. Numerous counterfeits (also Geneva). Comparison is necessary.

Subsequent issues. Nos. 9 to 48. Most of the values received forged overprints either on German stamps canceled in Germany for the horizontal CHINA overprint (Geneva), and the overprints of 1905–13 (usually 1-, 2-, and 3-mark, Nos. 35–37, 45–47), or on mint stamps for Nos. 23–28 (1900, CHINA is oblique). This last set also was overprinted fraudulently in Geneva with the following forged cancellations: round, with date, KAUMI 17/12 oo CHINA; TIENSIN 10 10 00 DEUTCHE POST; SHANGHAI 8/13 oo DEUTCHE POST, and TSINGTAU 16/12 oo KIAUTCHOU; 27 mm.

China (Italian Post Offices)

Numerous *forged overprints,* particularly of the first issue of 1918 (Pechino and Tientsin); comparison is indispensable. The Pechino set (Nos. 12–21) was overprinted fraudulently in Genoa on used Italian stamps. With a little concentration, one can identify the cancellations (ROMA FERROVIA; BAEZA; etc; or else the date, 1902 to 1917) as being invalid with regard to the overprints.

China (Russian Post Offices)

Forged overprints on all issues, including that of Kharbine (Harbin), most often on canceled stamps (especially on values overprinted in 1917; also on mints for rare overprints and varieties). The forged overprint in Russian was applied in Geneva (the accent on the last letter is not in its place) in black, red, and blue on canceled Russian stamps. A specialist in Russian stamps or a native Russian easily will recognize the cancellations of Moscow, Odessa, Kichineff, etc., and will sometimes run across the postal branch postmark which does not exist in China. The overprint also was applied inverted. A second Russian overprint from Geneva is somewhat better. The mints with forged rare overprints received the following forged cancellations: postmark with date, double circle (29 mm), with date in the middle, between two transversals and two stars and italic letter "A" at bottom: ΠΟΡΤ3-АРТУРЬ 27 5 04 and λ IAY-R (inverted) H L (with horizontal bar at top) b 30 8 04.

Cilicia

All overprints were *forged,* including Type II, air mail. Evidently, the higher priced values tempted the counterfeiters most. These values must be compared carefully with easily accessible common originals.

Cochin China

Numerous *forged overprints* of the issue's four types: detailed comparison is indispensable. Fournier counterfeited Type *a* (medium-size figure "5"), Type *b* ("5 C. CH"), and the "15/15" of 1888; I have not run across the large "5," Type *c*. These counterfeits were applied on mint or canceled originals and also on stamps of 1881 (see French Colonies).

The *Geneva forged cancellations:* double circle with a broken inner circle, with date, COCHINCHINE 6 OCT 76 SAIGON (inner circle pearled), SAIGON (at top, this time) 3ᵉ / 7 NOV 86 COCHINCHINE (inner circle with broken lines), both with ornaments between circle on the right and left of the postmark; SAIGON CENTRAL 2ᵉ / 24 OCT 92 COCHINCHINE; MYTHO 2ᵉ / 16 AOUT 92 COCHINCHINE; BACLIEU 1ᵉ / 27 JUIN 92 COCHINCHINE.

Colombia

Grenadine Confederation, 1859. Nos. 1 to 3. 16 x 31 mm. The red shade stamps with value figure on the left only are essays.

Forgeries: lithographed, easily identifiable by the inscriptions, whose lettering is not aligned, and by their arbitrary dimensions.

1860. Nos. 4 to 9. *Originals:* same dimensions; the wavy lines of the background burelage are printed delicately and quite visible (2 1/2-centavo, forty-two lines); the isthmus hatch lines (bottom of the escutcheon) are curved or oblique; there is a dividing frame line between the stamps.

Early forgeries: 2 1/2-centavo, fifty-six pearls instead of forty-three; background line structure is made of vertical lines; in the isthmus, horizontal hatch lines; letters "COR" of CORREOS are placed in the top horizontal strip; figure "2" under the escutcheon is too large and is touching the inner frame, as well as the "2" of the fraction. The other values have defects that are just as crude and as easily checked; in the 20-centavo, for example, there are forty-five pearls instead of forty-four; in the isthmus, dots instead of lines; regular background line structure; forty-four burelage lines above and thirty-eight below instead of forty. There was a *reprinting* for the peso; no dividing frame lines between the stamps; second "O" of CORREOS is joined to the outer frame; letters "ED" of CONFED are joined to the inner frame. The 1-peso on blue paper is an essay.

United States of New Granada, 1861. Nos. 10 to 14. Although this set has perplexed many collectors, there is nothing difficult about it.

Originals: lithographed on thin (about 40 microns) white or yellowish, slightly transparent paper; 20¼–20½ x 25 mm; nine eight-point stars. The extension of the inner frames upper line would not touch the "O" letters of the upper corners. The extension of the shield's axis just would touch the right of the "E" of DE. The first "O" of CORREOS and the "E" of NACIONALES do not touch the oval. In the first "A" of NACIONALES, the right downstroke is much thicker than the left. The top and bottom horizontal lines of the "T" of ESTADOS are equal in length. In the bottom of the shield, one finds a sort of circle or round figure, cut at the top seemingly by a color spot. There are fourteen color shading lines in the upper corners and fifteen below (without counting the frame). On the stamp's right side, the shortest lines often are connected. The "E" of NUEVA does not touch the top of the "V." See the arrangement of the first shade lines in the upper corners and the first shade line of the shield in the illustration. In the 2½-centavo, the value inscription is "21½," and in the peso, UN PESO. No *reprints*.

Early forgeries: a. An early set that is hardly worthy of description: no stars under the shield; the three parts of the shield are blank.

b. Thick paper: "DE" is printed "BE"; nine malformed stars (2½-centavo, value designation, same as in original).

c. An early set: "DE" is under letter "N"; the "E" of NACIONALES is touching the oval; the latter does not encroach upon the shield's inner frame; the bottom of the shield has no mark in it; in the shield's center strip, there is a funeral urn; eight approximately round stars; fifteen shade lines, top left, eleven, top right; yellowish, slightly transparent paper (55 microns); height, about 24⁴⁄₅ mm; the 2½-centavo value is designated "2 1 2."

d. Geneva forgeries: the extension of the top inner frame line touches the "O" letters in the corners; the upper bar of the "E" of NUEVA is almost touching the top of the "V"; the right part of the top bar of the "T" of ESTADOS is much longer than the left: in the bottom of the shield, a large comma; eight stars; the well-spaced corner hatching is too fine; fifteen shade lines, top left, and thirteen, top right; twelve or thirteen, bottom left, and ten or eleven, bottom right. Thin paper of allowable thickness, but a little more transparent than the original. The 2½-centavo is

designated "2 1 2," and the 1-peso, "I PESO"; height, 24¾ mm. Forged cancellations: BOGOTA, straight line, printing type is 3¾ mm high; "..OGA..," printing type, 7 mm high.

e. Photolithographed forgeries: they are among the most deceptive, but their shades, and especially the thick (about 70 microns, not including gum) yellowish paper identify them quickly and easily. The shield's bottom design is not congruent; the points of the nine stars are less blunt; the corner horizontal hatching is more regular than in the original; the "D" of DE is apparently not as tall as the "E" — it is ⅓ mm away from the "E" instead of ¼ mm. The right downstroke

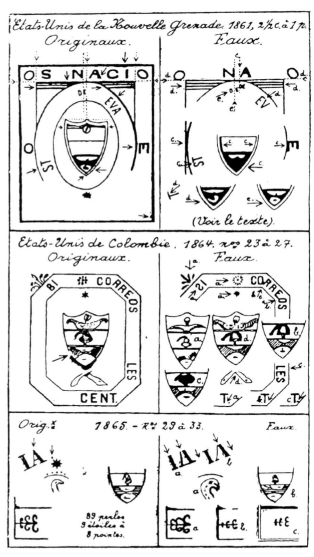

Top: United States of New Granada, 1861. 2½-centavo to 1-peso. Originals. Forgeries. Middle: United States of Colombia, 1864. Nos. 23–27. Originals. Forgeries. Bottom: 1865. Nos. 29–33. Originals; 89 pearls; 9 eight-point stars. Forgeries.

of the "N," if extended, would pass between those two letters; the measurements are nearly congruent; the 2½-centavo is designated "21½," but the fraction's bar is missing and the base of the fraction's "2" is horizontal. The 1-peso is designated correctly UN PESO.

f. In another early set, the "E" of NUEVA is too close to the "V," and there is a large star after NACIONALES.

g. In a rather deceptive forgery of the 2½-centavo of Colombian origin, there is no dot after GRANADA; the "N" and "T" letters of CENTAVOS are touching; 19¾ x 25½ mm.

United States of Colombia, 1862. Nos. 15 to 18. In the *originals,* which are lithographed, 16½ x 21–21¼ mm, one finds a small bulb-shaped design (two diagonal hatch lines, three tapering lines at the top) surmounting the horns of plenty, which does not touch the top of the shield. The background, which is full of herringbone hatching, has rather visible stars with a white dot in their centers. Forty-five pearls, the three highest of which, under the middle star, are not very visible.

Early forgeries: the design above the horns of plenty is made of a perfect circle with a center color dot. The circle is touching the top of the shield. The background hatching is vertical or slightly curved and the stars are almost invisible. In another rather deceptive set, there is a dot after NACIONALES; 17 x 21 mm.

Fantasies: 10-centavo on bluish paper and 20-centavo on green.

1863. Nos. 19 to 22. *Originals:* lithographed; at the top of the shield, a design that is similar to that of 1862, but the horn ends do not touch the sides of the shield; the lines dividing the latter are double (and very close together). At the top, the star between frames is formed by a dot and eight oblong rays. The nine six-point stars are arranged on two lines forming an elongated oval. The "E" of "E. U. DE.." and the "S" of NACIONALES are on the same horizontal. 16⅘ x 21¼ mm.

Early forgeries: eight-point stars; the horns with their embracing curve are 1 mm away from the sides of the shield. An oval surmounts the horns and almost is touching the shield's point. The shield is divided by single lines. The "S" of NACIONALES is evidently higher or lower than the "E" of "E.U.DE..," etc.

Geneva forgeries: all values are better executed, but the measurements are ¼ mm too large. A forgery of the 50-centavo red error often is paired with a 20-centavo. Height: 21 mm; only ½ mm, instead of 1 mm, between CORREOS and NACIONALES. In another deceptive but apparently jumbled set, the stamps measure only 16¾ x 20¾ mm.

Fantasies: 20-centavo green, or red on blue, and 50-centavo green on white paper.

1864. Nos. 23 to 27. *Originals:* lithographed; 17 x 21 mm; the star between frames and the nine six-point stars are arranged as in the preceding issue; likewise, the shield's double dividing lines; about 1 mm between the words CORREOS and NACIONALES. Thin paper (45 microns). No *reprints.*

Early forgeries: a half-dozen sets whose principal distinguishing characteristic is that the shield's frame is not broken on the left (see illustration of the original):

a. Completely arbitrary design forgery.

b. An early set whose "OR" and "EO" letters of CORREOS are not touching at bottom.

c. An early set with the same defects, but different designs in the shield (no better); the shield's dividing lines are single; "E" and "S" of NACIONALES are touching.

d. Much better forgeries, but the extremities of the horns of plenty are touching the shield frame; the interior designs of the latter and some streamers below it are different.

e. A design almost like that of the preceding forgeries, but the horn of plenty extremities do not touch the shield frame. The first "O" of CORREOS is definitely oval in shape; the one in the preceding forgery is too large and too wide.

f. Various dissimilar forgeries with defects similar to the previous ones, especially the b and c types. As for the 5-centavo and other values, either the first or the second type of original figure was copied.

g. The 20-centavo, 1-peso, and perhaps other values were counterfeited in Geneva with noncongruent star and shield designs. In all forgeries, check the distance between CORREOS and NACIONALES.

1865. Nos. 28 to 33. *Originals:* lithographed on white or slightly bluish paper; 17½ x 22½ mm. The top of the "A" of COLOMBIA is sharply pointed; there is a dot after E.U. COLOMBIA., CENT., or PESO. As for the escutcheon and the value tablet ornamental designs, see the illustration. No reprints.

Forgeries: a. a very well-known early set; seventy-three partly invisible pearls; no dot after the "O" of COLOMBIA; shapeless or misplaced stars under "E.U." instead of "E," under "C" instead of the "E" of DE, under the second "O" of COLOMBIA instead of under the "L"; the streamer above the escutcheon is touching the oval on both sides.

b. Rather deceptive forgery, especially of the 50-centavo, Type II: seventy-six pearls (see the illustration).

c. Thick, yellowish paper; no dot after "E.U." and COLOMBIA: bird of prey with a duck's head; full background escutcheon top; in the bottom of the latter, two horizontal lines and a curved one, no more; outer frame is ¼ mm away; pearls and stars are practically invisible; very bad.

d. Sixty-two pearls; in the escutcheon, ten or eleven horizontal hatch lines and a blank semicircle; the beak of the bird of prey is turned to the left.

e. Eighty pearls; dots after "E" and "U," but not after COLOMBIA and the value designation; six-point stars.

1867. 5- and 10-peso. Nos. 39 and 40. *5-peso original:* lithographed on thick (75 microns) glossy paper; 17¼ x about 22¼ mm, ten laurel leaves on the right and nine on the left; vertical lines, right and left, not including the inner frame lines; the arabesques of the oval bandeau — one might just as well say they are all separate.

Very bad *early forgery:* "5 PESOS" is printed on the lithographed counterfeit (see the illustration also).

Geneva forgeries: glossy paper, 85–90 microns; 22½ mm high; arbitrary arabesque design; laurel leaves do not appear in the bottom of the oval bandeau; this forgery is encountered most often with a small hole perforation, ½ mm in diameter; ten frame lines.

10-peso original: same paper as in the 5-peso; 17¼ x 22¼ mm; shaded condor head; square dots after "E," "U," COLOMBIA, N^les, and PESOS (the dot after this

word is more like a horizontal line); nine eight-point stars, the two highest ones not touching the edges.

Bad *early forgery:* 17³/₅ x 22²/₃ mm; (see the illustration for the condor design); eleven five- or six-point stars, no dot after "E," COLOMBIA, and N^les; in the middle section of the shield, a sort of lantern with five vertical hatch marks instead of a Phrygian bonnet, six hatch lines in the upper part of the shield instead of eight, etc. *Geneva forgeries:* same paper as the preceding one; 17½ x 22½ mm; very good appearance; no dot after "U"; the other dots are round (see the illustration for the bird of prey).

1868–77. Nos. 41 to 47a. *Reprints:* 10-centavo, mauve instead of violet. 50-centavo, the bar of the lower left "5" is touching the white line of the left frame in two places. 1-peso, on the right and left of the original stamp, mid-height, there is a figure-"1" shaped design which divides the inscriptions; this design has a white environment that is missing under "E" and "A" in the reprints. 5-peso, the "C" of CINCO is separated from the arabesque on its left by a black line. 10-peso, an oblique exterior line is seen at the top of the stamp on the left and is touching the oval arabesque in the stamp's corner.

Originals of the 5- and 10-peso: lithographed. 5-peso, five-point blank stars, the lowest ones almost touching the wings; on the left, the banderole is touching the "C" of CINCO; under the wings, dots and curved hatch lines. All around the stamp there is a fine black stippling between the frame lines (this in the 10-peso, too). The "S" of CORREOS is normal; the banderole inscriptions under the eagle are legible (10-peso, also). 10-peso, five-point stars, but malformed (stippled in part with supplementary lines or dots); the two dots before and after CORREOS are the same.

Typographed forgeries: indention is quite visible sometimes. 5-peso, copied from the reprint; so, the "C" of CINCO is separated from the arabesque by a black line; the second "O" of COLOMBIA is a "D"; the "L" of NACIONALES is an "I"; full-bodied stars with eight distinct points; the two lowest ones are ½ mm from the wings; the hatching is horizontal under the latter; the "S" of CORREOS is inverted. 10-peso, full-bodied stars; the dot after CORREOS is only partly visible. In the two values, the banderole inscriptions are illegible. Dimensions of originals: 5-centavo, 17½ x 24 mm; 10-centavo, 19 x 24 mm; 20-centavo, 18½ x 24½ mm; 50-centavo, 17½ x 23 mm; 1-peso, 19 x 23½ mm. The forgery dimensions are arbitrary.

1870–79. Nos. 48 to 53. Measurement of *originals:* 1-centavo, 18 x 23 mm; 2- and 10-centavo, 18½ x 23½ mm; 5-centavo, 19 x 23 mm; 25-centavo, 19 x 23½ mm. 1-centavo, *reprint;* green on laid paper, and other shades (rose, carmine); the "A" of COLOMBIA has no horizontal bar.

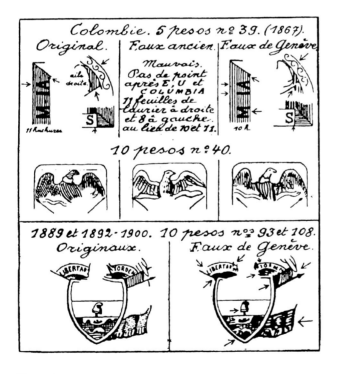

Top: Colombia. 5-peso. No. 39 (1867). Original, right, 11 shade lines. Early forgery; bad; no dot after "E," "U," and COLOMBIA; 11 laurel leaves on the right and 8 on the left instead of 10 and 11. Geneva forgery, 10 shade lines. Middle: 10-peso. No. 40. Bottom: 1889 and 1892–1900. 10-peso. Nos. 93 and 108. Originals. Geneva forgeries.

1-centavo forgery: letters "UU" do not touch at top; the Phrygian bonnet has no support; the line below it appears to be single and thick rather than double; the ship above the isthmus is shapeless.

2-centavo forgery: "EF" instead of "EE" (top left); in the banderole, above these letters, the word LIBERTAD is illegible.

25-centavo originals: loop of the "2" is closed; black on blue, rose and yellow.

25-centavo reprints: various shades, green on greenish, yellowish, or bluish paper; blue, carmine, and ultramarine on white paper; black on yellow, dark rose, rose, and pale blue. The loop of the "2" is open, and the dot before it is almost touching the white line.

25-centavo forgery: eleven unsuccessful stars instead of nine; the stars are too close together, and there is no dot after NALES.

1876–80. Nos. 54 to 58. The *originals* of the 10- and 20-centavo measure 19 x 23¹/₂ mm and the 5-centavo, 19¹/₂ x 23¹/₂ mm. With respect to these three values, there is good reason to beware of countless essays and printer's waste stamps; only the cancellation is conclusive here.

Forgeries: inscription, CORREOS NALES, almost on the white line; the "C" is ¹/₂ mm from the left inner frame; the "S" of NALES has a much wider lower thin loop than the upper loop; no dot after this word. The eyebrow arch is formed with a thick line which extends into the center background; the cheek hatch lines are slanted downwards too much; the stamp's background is strewn with large white dots; the "S" of CENTAVOS resembles an "8." In addition, some counterfeits have an outer dividing frame line. This set comprises the 5- and 10-peso reengraved stamps, which are similar to the 1870 types (Nos. 46 and 47a): 5-peso, original, reengraved with vertical hatch lines in the flag; 10-peso, original, reengraved with five-point stars; 5-peso, reprinted; the "C" of CINCO is separated from the ornament on its left; the ornament on the left of the "C" of CORREOS is barely touching the "C"; 10-peso, reprinted; the outer circle containing figure "10" is broken under "OS" of UNIDOS.

1879. Provisional Cali issue. Nos. 59 to 64. These stamps (typographed; 24 x 14 mm) are like typical overprints; they therefore must be compared with reliable originals. Besides, there are so many different varieties that specialization is recommended. Four successive printings were required to obtain a correct surface print: in the first one, the five plate types have the grammatical error "No hai" with an inverted "N" (the 1-peso is designated "1 PESO"). In the second printing, the second and fourth types were corrected (1-peso is designated UN PESO). In the third printing, the "N" of "No" was inverted again. Finally, the fourth

printing is correct. The "1-PESO" is known to exist only in the first two printings.

1881. Nos. 65 to 67. Originals: 19 x 24 mm.

Reprints: 2-centavo, on left of figure "2 " (lower right corner), there is a curl with a supplementary curved line on top; 5-centavo, the bottom of figure "5" (upper left corner) is traversed by a curved line. Errors in paper tinting are considered to be essays.

1883–89. Nos. 73 to 81. Numerous unofficial perforations, various essays; no *reprints.* The 10-peso has stars above the eagle.

Republic of Colombia, 1886. Nos. 84 to 88. Very numerous printer's waste stamps, perforation essays, and shades. Stamps on white and greenish paper are classified as reprints.

1890. 10-peso. No stars. No. 93. *Geneva forgery:* see the preceding illustration for the distinguishing characteristics of the forgery and original.

1892–1900. 10-peso. No. 108. *Geneva forgery:* the forged cliché used for No. 93 was reused here. The 50-centavo, Type II (No. 105a) also was counterfeited in sheets of fifty stamps; paper almost violet instead of lilac; imprint is too pale; comparison would be useful.

1902–3. Nos. 118 to 132. The 5-centavo blue on azure-tinted paper and the 20-centavo brown on buff officially were counterfeited; they are recognized by the inscription lettering, REPUBLICA DE COLOMBIA, where the letters are not high enough and are aligned poorly in the 5-centavo; the first of these words is designed inexpertly in the 20-centavo. Comparison is necessary.

5-peso forgery: the word VALIENTE is illegible.

10-peso forgery: letters "P" and "B" of REPUBLICA are too high, and so are "E" and "Z" of DIEZ.

1902–3. Barbacoa provisionals. Nos. 134 to 136. A set that lacks official status. Numerous forgeries.

1902–3. Perforated or rouletted stamps. Nos. 137 to 144. Numerous forged perforation fakes on imperforate stamps; comparison with easily obtainable original perforations: 10-centavo claret and 20-centavo violet.

1903. Nos. 165 to 169. *Forgeries:* 5-peso, poorly executed; see lettering design of REPUBLICA DE COLOMBIA. In the ornamental design below CINCO and PESOS, the five vertical hatch marks are executed poorly; the word VALIENTE, bottom of stamp, is illegible. 10-peso, "DE" above COLOMBIA is invisible.

1909. Overprinted stamps. Nos. 190 to 200. *Forged overprints:* comparison is necessary, especially for the

20-centavo, 1-peso, and 10-peso. Compare with the two types of the 1/2-centavo stamp.

Stamps for Registered Letters

1865. Nos. 1 and 2. *Originals:* thin, white paper (40 microns); Type R: the lower loop of the "S" letters of CORREOS, NACIONALES, and CENTAVOS is wider than the upper loop; the line after "E" is 1/2 mm long; thirty-two overlap lines (see the illustration). Type A: the left branch has eight, quite visible pieces of fruit; the right branch, five acorns, one of which is well formed.

No *reprints.*

Forgeries: white or yellowish paper; 50, 60 microns, and more. Type R: early forgery; thirty-one overlap lines after the right foot of the "R"; the cross-hatching does not touch figure "5"; the "C" of COLOMBIA resembles a "G"; this letter and the "S" of NACIONALES are touching the star's outer line.

Geneva forgeries: very widespread (see the illustration); Type R: the line after "E" is 4/5 mm long; the upper loop of the "S" of CORREOS is higher than the lower one and thus seems inverted; the two loops of the other "S" letters are of equal width; twenty-eight or twenty-nine overlap lines. Type A: the white lines of the "A" are evidently too thick; the left branch displays only four pieces of fruit; there are three acorns on the right.

1870. Nos. 3 and 5, 4 and 6, Types R and A. *Originals:* grayish white paper about 80 microns thick. Type R: the second "O" of COLOMBIA is lower than the other letters; the dots after "EE" and "UU" are not touching the other letters (use magnifying glass).

Forgeries: allowable dimensions; white or yellowish paper, 65–70 microns; Type R: the "C" of CORREOS often is joined to the "R" by a horizontal line; the dots after "EE" and "UU" are touching the letters that follow; the right foot of the "A" of COLOMBIA is touching the right frame; the bottom of "5" is touching the tablet; only traces of hatching can be seen in the center background; see the illustration for other defects. Type A: the right section of the bar of the "5" extends to the top of the tablet; the "A" of COLOMBIA is touching the right frame (see the illustration). In both forgeries, Types R and A, the background hatching is vertical, but only traces of it can be seen.

Reprints: the background is cross-hatched or there is no hatching; white or bluish paper.

1881. 10-centavo. No. 7. *Original:* thin or medium paper (40–60 microns); dividing frame lines or their traces; 32 1/2 x 37 mm, axis length, scalloping included; the outer oval line is thicker than the inner oval line; the top of the first "A" and of the second "D" of RECOMENDADA are joined by a thin guideline (use magnifying glass).

Geneva forgeries: paper about 80 microns; 32 1/4 x 36 1/2 mm; main defects are shown in the illustration. The outer oval is no thicker than the inner one on the left, near the middle of the stamp ("EE. 10 Cs"). One finds a stippled line above the right sections of the condor's wings; there is no hairline between the top of the first "A" and the second "D" of RECOMENDADA; the shade is lilac instead of violet or dark violet.

1889. The 10-centavo was counterfeited in Geneva. The "C" of COLOMBIA is touching the horizontal line under the tablet; irregular lettering, especially "M"; the white line is broken under the "O" of CENTAVOS; perf 14.

1902–4. The overprint "A R" in a circle has no official status on the 50-centavo and the 1-, 5-, and 10-peso.

Postage Due Stamps

1865. No. 1. Original: 22 mm, laterally. Figure "1" of the fraction has an oblique line; dot after "E"; short line after "U"; 116 apexes in the outer frame; the "C" of CENTAVOS is shaped like a "D."

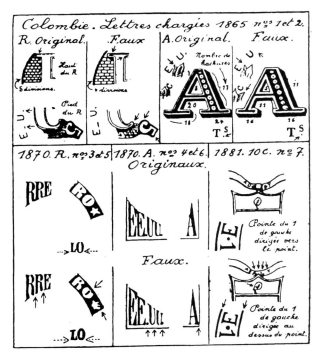

Top: Colombia. Registered letters, 1865. Nos. 1 and 2. "R" original, top of "R," five divisions; forgery, 4 divisions. "A" original, 17 shade lines; forgery, 11. Bottom: 1870, "R," Nos. 3 and 5. 1870, "A." Nos. 4 and 6. 1881, 10-centavo, No. 7. Originals, point of the "1" on the left is pointed toward the dot. Forgeries, point of the "1" on the left is pointed above the dot.

Early forgery: dots after "E" and "U"; eighty-six apexes in the frame; the letters of COLOMBIA are no larger than those in the other inscriptions; letter "I," between "2" and "$^1/_2$," is as high, dot included, as figure "2"; figure "1" in the fraction has no oblique line.

Geneva forgeries: 116 apexes; dots after "E" and "U"; figure "1" of the fraction has no oblique line; the "C" of CENTAVOS is rounded.

1870. No. 2. *Originals:* lithographed on wove or laid paper; 19 x 23$^1/_2$ x 30 mm; the loop of the "2" is closed, with dot in middle; hairline under CORREOS.

Very bad *early forgery:* the thin lines of the "U" letters are as thin as possible; no hairline under CORREOS; open loop, figure "2."

Reprint: magenta shade on wove or ribbed paper.

1873. 25- and 50-centavo. Nos. 3 and 4. *25-centavo original:* dot under the "S" following CENT; dot outside the frame under the above dot.

Early forgery: the two figures are equal height; regular background horizontal hatching, without breaks; no dot outside the frame. Geneva forgery: Phrygian bonnet is open on top; no dot under the "S"; no outer dot.

50-centavo early forgery: same type as the 25-centavo, with horseshoe-shaped inscription, SOBRE PORTE.

Geneva forgery: the top of the "5" is touching the inner octagon; the lines that join the two octagonal frames terminate at the inner frame instead of leaving about $^1/_2$ mm; the line to the right of the value designation cuts the "S" following the "C" and the dot is placed under the left side of the "S."

Antioquia

1868. Nos. 1 to 4. *Originals:* the shield design is first class and regular; inscriptions are traced regularly. 5-centavo: "M" and "B" of COLOMBIA touch at bottom. 10-centavo: dot after CORREOS and under the "S" after 10-centavo.

Early forgeries: poorly designed shield; irregular inscriptions; 5-centavo: "M" and "B" are not touching; blue dot above the "E" of DE (bottom of stamp); 10-centavo: no dots after CORREOS or under "S."

Other forgeries: 2$^1/_2$-centavo, letters "I" and "A" of COLOMBIA do not touch at bottom; 5-centavo, yellowish paper instead of white; there is a dot instead of a short line under the "S" after "U." In another forgery of the same value, which is also on yellowish paper, the star on the left is incomplete. Finally, there are photolithographed forgeries requiring comparison.

Reprints: there are lines over the whole design (plate withdrawal); slightly bluish paper.

1869. Nos. 5 to 10. *Originals:* thin paper; the "Q" of ANTIOQUIA has a terminal line. 5-centavo: dots after "E" and "S" (bottom of stamp). 2$^1/_2$-, 10-, and 20-centavo: dots after CORREOS, COLOMBIA, and ANTIOQUIA; the "C" of COLOMBIA is positioned between the two "R" letters of CORREOS.

Early forgeries: thick paper; the "Q" is an "O." 5-centavo: no dots after "ES" (below); 2$^1/_2$-, 10-, and 20-centavo: one or two dots missing after the words mentioned above.

Other forgeries: 20-centavo, the lowercase "s" letters are missing after "EU." 1-peso, arbitrary shield design, red shade instead of carmine or vermilion.

Reprints: same paper as for the 1868 reprints; the 10-centavo blue is a reprint.

1873. Nos. 12 to 19. A set of bad forgeries, undeserving of description.

Stamps for Late Arrival Letters

No. 1. *Geneva forgery:* inscription lettering is not well aligned; in the millesime, the "9" figures are higher than "18"; also arbitrary shade.

Bolivar

1863–66. Nos. 1 to 3. *Originals:* eight-point stars; two types of shades for the 10-centavo: Type I, nine stars; Type II, eight stars (five at bottom instead of six). Principal characteristics: inner frame only is quite visible between the two rows of inscriptions, but, with the aid of a magnifying glass, one sees guideline tracings of the inscriptions almost everywhere; the final "O" of CORREOS is separated from DEL by a greater distance (1-peso, more than 1 mm) than that separating the inscription lettering below (about $^1/_4$ mm). In the three values, the ninth star is touching the "V" of BOLIVAR; it is less successful than the others; 10 x 12 mm.

Forgeries from a variety of sources, whose main characteristics follow:

1. The inner frame and the two guidelines parallel to it seem to form a quite visible triple inner frame.

2. The final "OS" of CORREOS and the word DEL must have struck the counterfeiter as one and the same word, OSDEL, of "unknown" origin; he left exactly the same space between the letters everywhere. The same situation is found in the Geneva forgeries, a first, very unsuccessful cliché of which has an entirely blank median shield strip; after letters "EU," the lowercase "s" letters and the dots under them seem to form capital "I" letters; the shapeless stars have six points; in the 1-peso, the value is written "1 P^o"; 10 x 11$^3/_4$ mm. In the second cliché (Type I of the 10-centavo in green and red), which is much better executed, the inner triple frame defect is still there, along with that of

OSDEL, whose "O" often is printed as "U"; $10^2/_5$ x $12^1/_2$ mm; eight-point stars; the bonnet in the middle of the shield looks like a ham that has been planted in an upright position; the counterfeits have nine stars; a good counterfeit of the 10-centavo green has twenty-one blank spaces in the left frame instead of twenty and measures $10^1/_4$ x $12^1/_3$ mm.

1880. Nos. 23 and 24. *Geneva forgeries:* the side escutcheons are almost blank; only the right half of the face is shaded; forged cancellations in blue, MEDELLÍN, straight line, and BOGOTÁ, in an oval.

1903. Nos. 76 to 78. The three values were very poorly counterfeited lithographically, without any finesse in rendering details; imperforate or partly rouletted.

Stamps for Registered Letters

1903. Nos. 3 to 5. *Forgeries:* the "E" letters of DEPARTEMENTAL have practically no median bar; the horizontal line structure of the oval background is too pronounced, or else it is executed inexpertly. Forged overprint or cancellation "AR" in black in a circle of chain links or large round postmark (36 mm) in green: CORREOS-DEPARTEMENTAL-CARTAGENA.

Other Colombian States

In addition, there are counterfeits in the other Colombian states, notably Cúcuta (1900), Cundinamarca (1883), Honda (overprint), Garzon (1904), and Rio-Hacha (1901), which require comparison with reliable originals.

Cauca, 1890. No. 5. This stamp probably has no official origin.

Tolima, 1870. Nos. 1 to 3. *Forgeries* (so-called "reprints"): composite creations made in Tolima, even strips containing two types of each value or blocks forming tête-bêche stamps; ribbed or wove blue paper; wove white paper with blue lines, and laid white paper (5-centavo). The "A" of VALE is too large in the two types of the two values. In the second type of the 5-centavo, CORREOS is printed EORREOS; in the first type of the 10-centavo, ESTADO is printed EETADO (an error found in the originals, also) and in the second type, the zero ("0") is touching the "C" of CENTS.

1871. Nos. 4 to 7. *Reprints* of the 10-centavo, 50-centavo, and 1-peso, from the dies bearing the oblique lines of the tweezers used to void the dies; 10-centavo, line traversing the figure "1" on the right, extending into the escutcheon; 50-centavo, line cutting the "D" of DE, penetrating the escutcheon; 1-peso, lines cutting the "D" of DEL, the "U" of UN, etc.

Forgery of the 5-centavo, so-called "reprint," which comes from a rebuilt cliché in which there is a different

escutcheon design; this design (dot in a circle), on the right and left between the inscriptions, is shaped like a kind of star. They even made a 5-peso from this cliché. Note: There are other poorly executed Tolima forgeries (nonaligned inscriptions, etc.) which do not deserve description.

1886. *Reprints* (1888): perf $11^1/_2$ instead of $10^1/_2$; 50-centavo dull pale green and 1-peso bright red-orange.

Geneva forgery: 1-peso, shapeless stars; red dot in the "O" of ESTADO; perf $11^1/_2$.

Comoro Islands

See French Colonies, "Peace and Commerce" type. Fournier's forged cancellation is a double circle ($21^1/_2$ mm), with date, MORONI G^{DE} COMORE.

Cook Islands (Rarotonga)

First issue, 1892. Nos. 1 to 4. *Originals:* perf $12^1/_2$; typographed. The whole ornamental framework, including the outer frame, originally made from imperfectly aligned and spaced printer's type, has an indistinct imprint and breaks between the type. There are no color spots on the white background.

Forgeries: 1-penny, $2^1/_2$-, and 10-pence. Nos. 1, 3, and 4. Typographed in Geneva. Usually imperforate; allowable measurements; produced by photoengraving, but, as is almost always the case in this method, there are zinc defects (spots, color dots, and flawed lettering; see the illustration). Photography and the successive cliché building operations also have filled in the little ornamental framework breaks in many places.

1899. ONE HALF PENNY overprint. Forged normal, double, or inverted overprints. Comparison is necessary.

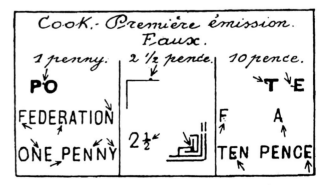

Top: Cook. First issue. Forgeries. 1-penny, $2^1/_2$-pence, 10-pence.

1921. RAROTONGA overprint, Nos. 20 to 24.
Forged overprints: principally on used fiscals of New Zealand, with postal cancellation of that colony or cleaned fiscal obliteration. Comparison is necessary.

Córdoba

See Argentina.

Corfu

Italian occupation: the difference in prices between Italian overprinted and nonoverprinted stamps suggests that counterfeits will not be long in appearing. As always, comparison is prudent.

Corrientes

See Argentina.

Costa Rica

First issue, 1862. Nos. 1 to 4. a. *Early forgeries:* lithographed; bad creations lacking the finesse of the original engraving. The four values were counterfeited (see the illustration for the defects of this set). The set is found imperforate and saw rouletted. On top of an essay? of this counterfeit, one finds PORTE I PESEDA, and on bottom, UNA PESEDA.

b. *Early forgery of the 1-peso:* very bad lithography; the first and fifth stars do not touch the ornamental motifs, but the second spear, top left, is single instead of double and is almost touching the left frame. No ornaments on the sides of UN PESO. Perf 12½.

c. *Other inexpertly executed early forgeries* have only three spears, top right; no hatch lines, or a single one, after RICA. An essay of the 1-real in light brown; perf 12, like the originals; three pearls on the bells of the horns of plenty (above "N" and "A" instead of "4" or "6").

1881–83. Overprinted stamps. Nos. 5 to 11.
Forged overprints: most often comparison with originals is sufficient. All overprints were counterfeited in Geneva. The 10- and 20-centavo without "U.P.U." were not issued. The 5-centavo red overprints with thin-printed "5" and right-hand bar are fantasies.

1907. Inverted centers. Fakes made from two cleverly repaired pieces.

1911. Stamps overprinted "73" to "93." Forged overprints of rare varieties; comparison is necessary.

Top: Costa Rica. First issue. Originals. Early forgeries.

Official stamps. Numerous *forged overprints,* especially (Geneva) on 1889 and 1892 stamps; comparison is necessary. OFICIAL overprints with an "O" that is almost round and a period are fantasies: third type overprint, 3 mm high, 19 mm long, including dot.

Guanacasta. These *overprints,* which are numerous and varied, require specialization. They were counterfeited extensively, especially in Geneva, in four types on 1883 stamps and in two types on 1889 stamps, Nos. 8–16 and 19–22.

Crete

I. British Post Offices

1898. Four-line inscription. No. 1. Thin, white paper; yellowish paper, less common. Hand-printed in violet, those stamps were used for two months only.
Printing order: 3,000.
Forgeries: there are a few forgeries, one of which is especially deceptive. Like the others, it can be identified by comparing inscriptions. The left side of the first downstroke of the Greek "pi" (π), first letter at top, is properly placed parallel to the stamp's edge as in the original, but here it is uniformly thick: it should gradually get thinner from bottom to top.

1898 (December). Square format. Nos. 2 and 4. 1899, Nos. 3 and 5. Lithographed. Sheets of 100 (10 x 10). Transfer block of ten stamps 2 x 5 (vertical) for the 1898 issue, and 5 x 2 (horizontal) for 1899. The overprint is a control mark. No. 2 exists either vertically or entirely imperforate. The French post office cancellations are in demand; for example, double circle with date, the outer circle composed of dashes, SAN NICOLO, date, year, and CRETE.
Forgeries: the set was well counterfeited in Geneva with congruent perf 11½. See the accompanying illustration. The copies are frequently provided with a forged control overprint.

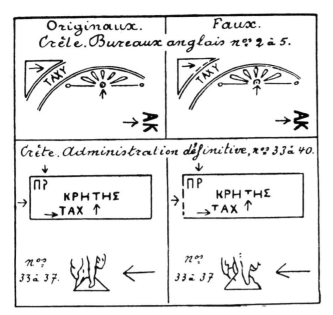

Top: Originals and forgeries of the British Offices in Crete, Nos. 2–5. Bottom: the Administration of Crete, Nos. 33–40.

II. Russian Post Office of Rethymno

1899. Handstamp impression, eagle type. Nos. 6 to 13. Authenticity can be claimed only for stamps bearing the Russian control postmark (double circle with Russian coat of arms and inscription in Russian: "Expeditionary army corps in the Island of Crete") applied to each block of four stamps, in violet on the 1-metallik blue and 2-metallik rose, and then in blue. Wove, laid, or cross-ruled paper. The 2-metallik rose is found on thin or thick paper. The 2-metallik blue is a color error.

Geneva forgeries (F.): the whole set was inexpertly counterfeited. In the type bearing French inscriptions, the "Y" of RETHYMNO forms a "V"; the "B" of TIMBRE, an "E"; the final "R" of PROVISOIRE a "P." The "A" of METALIK is too small, and the "E," "T," and "L" are slanted to the right.

In the Greek inscription type, the crossbar of the "H" goes beyond the letter on the right (upper inscription), and the lower inscriptions are very irregular: they touch the tablet edges, the top of the omega (ω), and the bottom of the left downstroke of the "A" of TAXYAP. The first lambda (λ) of METAλλIK extends to the edge, and the ornament above the figure on the left resembles the one on the right. The counterfeits are furnished with a forged control mark (without small escutcheons) and with the forged straight-line cancellation, PEOYMNON. Wove paper.

Paris forgeries (A.?): in this set, the "theta" (θ) of RETHYMNO is congruent and does not form an "O"

as in the previous sets; however, the ornament above the figure on the left forms an acute angle, the right side of which is not bent back. Also, forged control mark and forged cancellation. Comparison would be useful.

1899. Trident type. Nos. 14 to 16. Perf 11½. Thick paper. Sheets of twenty stamps (4 x 5), lithographed. Transfer block of four types in a horizontal strip. In the June issue, Nos. 14 to 34, there are no stars. Small control mark in violet, frequently omitted. Not very interesting. In Nos. 26, 36, and 46, the control mark is black.

Forged set: stamps are always well-centered on nonglossy grayish paper. Traces of the cross used as a reference guide for perforation are usually visible in the originals; in the forgeries, they were thought to be useless. Thin, transparent paper; no trace of hatching in the white (blank) circle surrounding the lower figures.

The lower part of the trident's shaft is cylindrical in form, whereas it should be shaped like the bottom part of a cone. On the 1-grosion, the line over the lower inscription is broken above the gamma (γ). Photolithographed; perf 11¾; forged violet-black control mark, visible on back; forged cancellations, RETHYMNO 10 JUIN 99 and 8 MAI 99.

III. Definitive Cretan Administration

No reprints.

1900. 1-lepton to 5-drachma. Nos. 1 to 9. Sheets of 100 stamps (10 x 10), perf 14¼.

Printings: 1-, 2-, and 5-drachma: 50,000; 50-lepton: 300,000; 10- and 25-lepton: 1 million; 1-, 5-, and 20-lepton: 500,000. Nos. 1 to 4, bistre-olive, are fiscals; are the imperforate stamps (Nos. 1, 2, 4, 10, and 13) essays?

Overprints: Nos. 10 to 20. The first one was created in vermilion.

Printings: 25-lepton: 100,000; 50-lepton: 25,000; 1-drachma: 7,500; 2-drachma: 5,000; 5-drachma: 2,500.

The second overprint (black) was executed in London in two printings: black and gray-black.

The 1-drachma exists with an inverted red overprint: very rare; the 50-lepton, with an inverted black overprint: very rare.

Forged overprints: not very numerous. Comparison is necessary.

1905. Revolution stamps. Nos. 33 to 40. Nos. 33 to 37: very striking double center circle, made with a handstamp; numerous errors (no control mark, control mark inverted, double prints, tête-bêche, etc.); stamps intended for the collector's purse.

Nos. 38 to 40 (November 1905).

Geneva forgeries (F.): issued in large quantities. The illustration provides sufficient information on their characteristics; in addition, on Nos. 38 to 40, one should note that the map of Crete is drawn arbitrarily. Forged postmarks made with wooden handstamps, OEPIZON I ZEN 1905. This cancellation was half-applied on each stamp: mass production job!

1905 (December). Crete in chains or portrait. Nos. 41 to 46. A set that was printed in Athens; perf 11½; less interesting, because all values were reprinted clandestinely by the printer in considerable quantities on the original stones after the first printing. Lithographed. These forgeries may be identified by examining the shades, the rays or shade lines of the inner circle (much less sharp, wear), and, finally, the forged cancellations. One of them (Geneva) is OEPIZON 5 OCT 1905.

1908–10. Various issues. Nos. 49 to 85. Numerous *forged overprints.* Very careful comparison is needed, especially for the inverted overprints, the double overprints (25-lepton, 2-drachma, 3-drachma, on Nos. 54, 57, and 58), the quadruple overprints (No. 59), and for errors in lettering.

IV. Austrian Post Offices

A few forged cancellations on Nos. 4 to 7, 10, 11, 13, and 14.

V. French Post Offices

Nos. 13–15 were reprinted clandestinely in Paris. Compare the printing shades. The overprints in piasters were forged in Paris (A.); the letter "R" is ⅕ mm too wide.

VI. Italian Post Offices

The original overprint is 15⅕ mm long and 1.9 mm high. A forged Geneva overprint, "La Canea," was applied to nonoverprinted Italian stamps Nos. 3 to 19; it measures 14½ x 2 mm. Italian cancellations often are seen under it. Another set of Italian origin measures 15½ x 2⅕ mm.

Cuba

1873. 12½-, 25-centavo and 1-peso. Nos. 1 to 4.
a. *Early forgeries:* the color line surrounding the oval is full instead of being formed by short horizontal lines (use magnifying glass); no tilde over the "N" of ANO; right below the portrait, "E. Julia" is missing.

b. *Genoa forgeries:* first, second, and third, as above; vertical corner shading instead of horizontal; the top shading is 1 mm away from the upper inscription.

1875. 12½-centavo and 1-peso. *Genoa forgeries:* fantastic design; no ornaments in the outer frame corners; background line structure is very crude (breaks); the tower and the necklace are practically invisible in the escutcheon.

1876. 12½-, 25-, 50-centavo and 1-peso. Nos. 13 to 16. *Typographed forgeries:* rather well counterfeited, but the CORREOS words, right and left sides of the stamp, are illegible; the hair contour is perfectly round.

1883. Overprinted stamps. Nos. 52 to 54. Type C (Yvert) was especially well counterfeited with the help of hand-applied original clichés; so the imprint is less sharp than in the typographical printing using the plate of 110 overprints including Type C; the indention is also less even. The other types also were forged so as to counterfeit overprint errors: comparison is indispensable. The five types were counterfeited in Geneva.

1883–88. Various values were reengraved. They are classified in the catalogues as Type II. The oval around the portrait is consistently thin except at top right, and Type II also has a rounded hairline above the temple instead of an acute angle.

Used postal forgeries: in imitation of the 5-centavo, Type II; grayish instead of white paper; perf 14½ instead of 14; the rounded hairline above the temple points toward the "U" of CUBA and not toward the "C"; the external ear is defined by an excessively thick white line; the oval is uniformly thick as in Type I.

1890. 5-centavo olive-gray. No. 76. *Used postal forgery:* perf 14½ like the preceding one instead of 14; arbitrary brownish shade; 19 mm wide instead of 18½ mm.

1898. 80-centavo, 1- and 2-peso. Nos. 114 to 116. a. *Genoa forgeries:* no shading line on the forecheek between nose, mouth, and right eye extremities. The short shading lines are missing above the upper inscription ("U," "B," and "9") and above "C" and "V" of the lower inscription. The back of the neck is quite concave; the face, neck, and ear shading is formless; no stippling at the base of the neck. The "Y" is touching figure "9" in the upper inscription.

b. *Forgeries of the 1-peso:* lithographed; cheek shading is hardly any better than in the preceding forgeries (a few almost invisible shade lines) and shading above the inscriptions as in the preceding forgeries; 2 mm margins; allowable perforation. Despite the inordinate margins, this forgery may belong to a copy of one of the Geneva blocks.

c. *Geneva forgeries:* perf 14; from a distance the cheek and the bottom of the neck appear to be blank, but using a magnifying glass one can see an area of small irregular specks with a few shade lines between the eye and the mouth and in the bottom of the neck. The "C" of CUBA is slanted to the left and the "A" is lower with respect to the other letters in the upper inscription. The inner circle is broken or is joined to the second blank circle, especially in the lower left quadrant. The forged Geneva cancellations are round

(27 mm) with date: HABANA 2 JULIO 1898 YSLA DE CUBA; SANTA-CLARA 3 ENERO 1899 YSLA DE CUBA; MATANZAS 7 DIC 1898 YSLA DE CUBA.

1899. Overprinted stamps. Nos. 117 to 135. Very numerous *forged overprints:* detailed comparison is indispensable. Geneva forged overprints (figures "1," "2," "3," and three types of the "5," none of which is congruent) were applied on originals and on forgeries of the same origin; the stamps were given the previously described forged cancellation.

Cundinamarca

See Colombia.

Curaçao

See Netherlands Antilles.

Czechoslovakia

This country's modern stamps generally are printed better than those of other newly created states. Many issues have large numbers of stamps, whose standardized mass production requires little study or research, and overprints, many of which have been counterfeited expertly and will be more so in the future. With regard to the latter, the best advice is to give the overprints a wide berth unless you are engaged in specialization.

1919. Set overprinted POSTA. Catalogued at about 310 francs in 1921, this set, Yvert Nos. 43–61, was purchased for about 150 francs (paper), which at 45 francs to the pound sterling made 80 francs (gold). In today's catalogues, it is worth about 350 francs, which is really 150 francs, or 26–27 francs (gold). Dead loss: 50 gold francs.

1919. Air mail. Set catalogued at 1,250 gold francs in 1921 and exactly the same today [1927] . Thus, one lost 200 gold francs if it was purchased for 300 gold francs in 1921.

1919. Overprint on Hungarian stamps. A similar calculation shows that rare stamp Nos. 65, 71, 80, and 94, which were quoted at 5,550 francs in 1921, are appraised today at no more than 5,325 francs. The calculation also points up a two-thirds loss in their gold value.

The money (or the gold) obviously went somewhere. The above examples have no other purpose than to

suggest to collectors that certain modern stamps (after World War I) are far from being a sound investment: "in all things, the end result must be considered."

1920–25. Nos. 118 and 126 were counterfeited to defraud the postal service. Perf 12½. Bad design, which is easily seen by comparison.

Dahomey

1899, 1900, 1901–5, 1912. Nos. 1 to 17 and 33 to 42. Peace and Commerce type and same overprinted type. See full treatment of these forgeries under French Colonies.

1906–7. Balay type. Nos. 30 to 32. *Forgeries:* see French Colonies.

1915. Red Cross. Triple overprints. *Forged overprints* requiring careful comparison. Note: A forged Geneva cancellation, double circle (21½ mm) with date, PORTO NOVO DAHOMEY (interchangeable date) is found rather frequently on forgeries from 1899 to 1912.

Danish West Indies

1855–71. 3-cent. Nos. 1 to 3. *Early counterfeits* on different papers, including yellowish; gum usually white. Impressions in various shades, including purplish brownish red, carmine-tinted red, etc. The same cliché was used from the outset, but it was retouched inexpertly to give more width to the upper branch of the "K" and to the right side of the "R."

The illustration shows the principal defects; in addition, the lower corner horn resembles a snail. The crown details, which are very fine in the originals, are executed very poorly. The fist has six perpendicular lines at the axis; the lines should be oblique.

1873–79. 7-cent. No. 9. *Early forgery,* 21 mm high instead of about 20²/₅ mm; imperforate, partly perforated, or perf 13; yellow or dark yellow.

Same issue, 14-cent. No. 12. *Genoa forgery,* perf 13. Height, 20³/₄ mm instead of 20½ mm. The corner ornaments are executed inexpertly; the "S" of CENTS resembles a "5."

Postage due stamps, 1902. Nos. 1 to 4. *Geneva forgeries:* letters of DANSK are too close at bottom; the "S" is too high; the second "O" of PORTO is executed poorly, top right; the circle radiuses are not symmetrical.

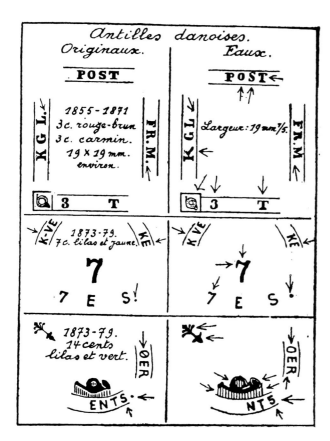

Top: Danish West Indies. Originals. Forgeries. 1855–71. 3-cent red-brown; 3-cent carmine. 19 x about 19 mm. Width: 19¹/₅ mm. Middle: 1873–79. 7-cent lilac and yellow. Bottom: 1873–79. 14-cent lilac and green.

Danzig

The most recently overprinted stamps have been causing quite a stir, because all of the overprints, especially the double ones, have been well counterfeited. In most of the more recent issues, inverted centers and color errors based on real errors on earlier stamps were usually created for avid collectors. This would be only half bad if we knew exactly what to expect; unfortunately, however, contemporary plates make possible a never-ending series of new printings, which sometimes are clandestine (see Russia).

We think we should advise collectors to avoid these stamps unless they are interested in professional specialization. A splendid Europe collection can be assembled even though one completely ignores the overprinted and doctored or speculative issues.

Reprints: none.

Forged overprints: everything that is catalogued as being more expensive with an overprint has been more or less well counterfeited. A crude set of 1920 with lithographed overprints can be identified by the lack of typographical indention ["bite"]; however, the rare values were also very well counterfeited. Comparison is necessary.

Dedeagh

See Levant, French Post Offices.

Denmark

I. Imperforate and Rouletted

Handmade paper: sheets of 100 stamps (10 x 10), with a marginal watermark, "KGL POST-FRMK" ("Kongellig Post Frimaerke," or "royal postal stamps"), as well as a crown in the upper corners and a horn in the lower corners. In addition, each stamp had a crown-shaped watermark. The cross above this crown is smaller in Nos. 1–6 than in Nos. 7–10. The 4-skilling stamps are found with inverted watermarks.

Security burelage: the imperforate stamps were first given a security impression made with a burelage beginning diagonally from the upper left corner in Nos. 1–3, and from the lower left corner in Nos. 5–10. (In No. 4 and in Nos. 3 and 5, it can be found both ways.) The shade of this burelage is yellow-brown, orange, sometimes reddish, or yellow. The other shades are discolorations resulting from age, gum, or successive printings.

In Nos. 1 and 2, the burelage is copper engraved or typographed. What was engraved is quite visible and is easily recognized, whereas one must look very closely sometimes to see what was typographed.

Control marks: the "S" above the lower right horn. In addition, the "2" (often like a "1") above the lower left horn in Nos. 3–6 and 7; the "4" in Nos. 2, 4 (second corrected plate), 8, and 10; and the "8" in No. 9 (this figure sometimes made into a "6" or a "5").

Secret marks: the initial of the engraver's name (Ferslew) in the horn of No. 1, and in the garland under the "M" of FRIMAERKE in No. 2; also, engraver Buntzen's initial in the garland under the first downstroke of the "M" in the inscription, "F.R.M."

Cancellations: Types A (Numerals 1–286) and B: common. Type A without numeral: rare. Pen cancellations: rare. Dated postmarks, one circle, which were used in 1850, had their inscriptions changed in various ways after that date; they were applied on envelopes, more rarely on stamps. The combined Type F postmark appeared about 1854 (rare on Nos. 1–10).

Later one finds Type D (in demand), and rare postmarks; for example, Type E, Holstein, and rural mail postmarks.

First issue. April 1851. Nos. 1 and 2. The Yvert numbering is irregular, the 4-rigsbank-skilling having been issued on April 1 and the 2-rigsbank as late as

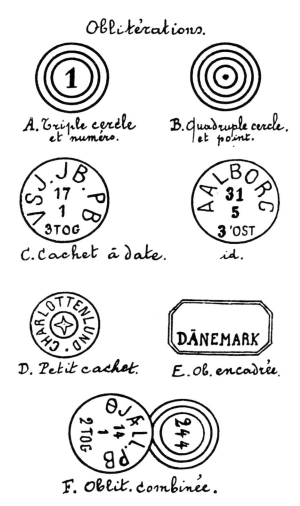

Obliterations.

A. Triple cercle et numéro. B. Quadruple cercle et point.

C. Cachet à date. id.

D. Petit cachet. E. Ob. encadrée.

F. Oblit. combinée.

Cancellations found on the imperforate and rouletted stamps of Denmark. A. Triple circle and numeral. B. Quadruple circle and dot. C. Dated postmark ("id.," or "same"). D. Small postmark. E. Framed cancel. F. Combined cancel.

April 28. The 2-rigsbank was the postage for Copenhagen; the 4-rigsbank, for the rest of the kingdom.

Select: the margins of No. 1 must be 1 mm wide; of No. 2, ³/₄ mm. The steel die of No. 1 was molded in plaster, then clichés were made from a metal alloy casting. Ten clichés formed a vertical transfer block (2

x 5) that was reproduced ten times by stereotyping. The blocks, welded together and mounted on a mahogany base, formed the plate. With careful observation, one can identify the ten types, even though the successive plating operations occasionally changed the distinctive marks or caused a few flaws, especially in the second and tenth block of the plate.

Type I: the "g" of "skilling" is malformed.

Type II: slight break in the base of the figure near the ascending loop; left extremity of the base is pointed.

Type III: the "G" of KGL is often open on top.

Type IV: the first "R" of FRIMAERKE is faulty; the white circle gets thinner under "KE."

Type V: the "O" of POST is open.

Type VI: the letters "AE" of FRIMAERKE are defective; the baseline of the "2" forms a smaller angle with the figure.

Type VII: the first "R" of FRIMAERKE resembles a "K"; the terminal line of the "2" is short.

Type VIII: the vertical downstroke of the "F" (secret mark) is thick.

Type IX: the final "E" of FRIMAERKE is open on top.

Type X: the same letter is open below, the secret mark usually being quite visible.

Varieties: No. 1, engraved background, Prussian blue instead of dark blue: 50M; 25U. No. 2, typographed background, maroon shade, is very rare — mint: 20U; the last printing (1853) of the gray-brown or pale brownish yellow shades is worth 3M, 50U; No. 2, with unofficial perf 12 or 13, on cover: 30U.

Pairs and blocks: No. 1: very rare; block of four: 20M; No. 2: 5U; strip of four: rare.

Cancellations: on No. 1, Type A, Copenhagen No. 1. The others are irregular and rare. On No. 2, Types A and B. All the others are rare, including a Copenhagen hour cancel.

Reprints: 1886: No. 1 with security burelage on yellowish paper and without burelage on white or yellowish paper. No watermark. Reimpression from the original plate.

No. 2 with security burelage on yellowish paper is from a rebuilt cliché, and shows design differences, notably no hyphen after POST.

1901: No. 1 on thin paper with burelage, no gum. Same remarks.

Forgeries: all of them early, without watermark. None noteworthy. Comparative study is needed.

Type I: blue frame, ³/₄ mm from the four sides; flattened crown, 5¹/₄ mm wide, without control mark.

Type II: same, on medium laid paper (the originals were on paper 100 microns thick); horn too wide.

Type III: a little better; corner designs not congruent; value figure broken on top. In the center inscription, the "G" has a long, oblique line, the "A" is too wide, the lower right downstrokes of the "K" letters are too long; no control mark. Occasionally cancellation Type A, No. 102.

Type IV: lithographed; the "R" of RIGSBANK is as high as the "I"; the letters "L L" are too far apart; no dot after SKILLING.

Type V: lithographed, with forged watermark that does not conform to the original; the first "I" of SKILLING lacks terminal lines.

Second issue. May 1854–60. Nos. 3 to 6. *Select:* four margins, ²/₃ mm wide. The paper is thin, medium, or thick. A thick, yellowish gum often gives a parchment effect. The thin paper is not common; No. 4: 2U; others: 50U. A single die, without numerals at the bottom, was used to constitute the four secondary matrices for the 2-, 4-, 8-, and 16-skilling stamp. Plate composition as above, but using the electrolytic method.

Varieties: No. 5, blue-green: 2M, 2U; good prints are not common. No. 4, very defective prints: 2U. Good prints of No. 7: rare. No. 3, no value figure: rare; unofficial perf 12 or 13. No. 4, 20U on cover. Perf 12 was used in Copenhagen (Ballin firm), and perf 13, in Altona (cancellation Type A, No. 113). The very rare perforations were frequently forged.

A few printing flaws are found; for example, No. 3, printer's error in the stippled background above the lower left horn, dot after the "G"; No. 4, no dot after "R," color dot in the "T" of POST, with an excessively long right terminal bar; No. 5, dot after "F"; etc. No. 6a is an unissued stamp. Its shade is always rose-lilac, like the first usual shade of No. 7 (1863), while No. 6 is purplish gray. No. 7 in dark lilac-rose is not very common, mint or used. No. 7 on cover is worth 2U.

Pairs: 4U. No. 4, blocks of four: rare. The combined franking of this issue with that of 1864 is rare.

Reprints: 1886: the 2- and 16-skilling stamps on yellowish paper without burelage, watermark, gum. Occasional unofficial perforation. In 1924, the 4- and 8-skilling stamps were reprinted the same way.

Fakes: in the days when the catalogues were quoting the unissued, canceled (!) No. 62 at higher prices than No. 7, the rouletted stamp was trimmed. The opposite operation sometimes has been performed since by changing the 6a mint, and even No. 6 mint or canceled, into a rouletted stamp. Comparison of margin width will tell the story.

Forgeries: Nos. 6 and 7 were ludicrously counterfeited in Geneva. No watermark, control marks, or secret marks. Forged cancellations: Type A, Nos. 31, 34, and 75. The early forgeries of Nos. 5, 6, and 7 are crude and have no watermark.

Repaired stamps: the paper of the first Danish stamps lent itself better than others to rebacking because it was thick, and the gum was thick, too. Remember that the watermark of the original stamps is always transparently visible. In the repaired stamps, it is much less visible. (If need be, use benzine to determine this.) In partially repaired stamps, the watermark is much less visible in the parts that have been restored.

Third issue (1857). Wavy background. Nos. 8 and 9. New stamp die with wavy background, without value figure. The dot after the "R" was forgotten, but the engraver, correcting errors in the previous issue, added exact control figures in the lower left corners.

Varieties: No. 8 is found with a small or large cross watermark. The 4-skilling brown-black: 2M, 5U. No. 8 with security background on reverse side: very rare. Thin paper becoming more frequent. Nos. 8 and 9, perf 12 or 13: very rare.

Cancellations: Type A: common; with date: 50U. Type A in blue (No. 122, etc.): rare.

Pairs: as above.

Reprints: 1886: as above, without watermark, from original plates.

Rouletted stamps: Nos. 4, 5, and 9 are found unofficially rouletted by the same machine used to roulette No. 10.

Fourth issue (1863). Rouletted stamps. Nos. 7 to 10. See the 1857 issue for the distinctive characteristics and fakings of No. 7, rouletted 11, which is worth 400 francs mint.

II. Perforated Stamps

Thinner, machine-made paper.

Issue of 1864. Large format. Nos. 11 to 15. The sole stamp die engraved by Batz lacks value figures. The frame was broken in the middle of the four sides and joined with the fine curved lines in the corners. The 4-skilling was printed first and was issued in that state, but the frame was retouched before the secondary dies were made for the other stamp values with engraved value figures, letter "S," and corner burelage. Medium or thin paper, so heavily stippled at times that it looks like laid paper. Sheets of 100 (10 x 10), with marginal watermarks as above.

Varieties: No. 13 carmine: 3M, 4U. Nos. 11, 12, 14, and 15, perf 12½ instead of 12¾ to 13¼: 2M, 2U. Fine impressions (50M, 2U) and very defective ones are in demand. Stamps with filigreed marginal letters: 2M, 2U. The 4-skilling frame may be either thin or thick; when it was thin, it was retouched by adding a second thin line. This stamp also is found with traces of wear either in the corners or the frame.

Plate varieties: the 8- and 16-skilling with a dot between the sword and the scepter; the 16-skilling with a printer's error before the "K"; the 4-skilling without a dot near the oval on the left of "4 S."

Imperforate stamps: unissued. However, the 4-skilling exists with cancellation: very rare. These

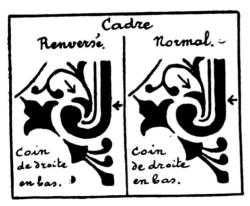

Inverted and normal frames, issue of 1870–71, Nos. 16–21, showing detail of the lower right corner of the design.

stamps are naturally identical with the others and have watermarks. They should be bought in pairs, because trimmed perforated stamps are being offered for sale, especially marginal copies, which often are larger. Value: No. 11, 35 francs; No. 12, 50 francs; No. 13, 25 francs; No. 14, 200 francs; No. 15, 150 francs. Only No. 15 is rare as a pair: 4M. Minimum format: 21½ x 25½ mm. Also, check single stamps for added margins.

Cancellations: Type A: common; Type C: less common; Type D: 2U; Type E: 3U; Type A, in red: 3U. Postmark Type D may have other place names: GJENTOFTE, etc. Pairs: 3U; blocks: rare.

Reprints: 1886: yellowish paper; no watermark; Nos. 11, 12, 14, and 15 in blocks of twelve (2 x 6); tête-bêche with 11¾ mm gutters.

Issue of 1870–71. Nos. 16 to 21. Watermarked as in the previous issue. Values in skillings. These stamps must be centered, with bright, clear shades, especially the 48-skilling. Sheets of 100 (10 x 10), printed twice. Two master dies were produced, one for the frame and one for the center, without value indication. The value figure was engraved afterward in the center and in the oval band of the secondary dies used to produce the center plates.

Inverted frames: detailed examination of the frames has revealed a few minor differences in the top left and bottom right corner designs; it also has revealed the existence of inverted frames (see the accompanying illustration).

It is not a question of sheets printed originally on an inverted frame plate, but of frame transfers that were erroneously placed upside down on the plate. Present-day research apparently has established that there were three inverts per plate. This minor error is not very easy to detect; in time, it will probably be judged much less rare than it seems now. In our view, it is less

interesting than the inverted backgrounds of Russia, which are more visible, but much less so than the inverted centers of the same country (1873–79 and 1883), in which the frame inscriptions show the error immediately.

Varieties: numerous secondary center and frame shades exist. The variety without a dot after POSTFRIM or after "SK" exists in all stamp values. This comes from plate fouling or color clogging. The 4-skilling can be found without horizontal perforation: very rare.

Imperforate stamps: all values: mint, 25 francs, except the 4-skilling carmine and the 48-skilling: 30 francs; used: rare.

Reprints: 1886: on white paper; imperforate reprints without watermark or gum.

Subsequent issues. All values are in Danish ore. From 1912, they are also in kronen.

1875–79. Very thick paper is rare in the 4- and 8-ore stamps; 3-ore: 5 francs; 12-ore: 3 francs. All values except the 5- and 20-ore exist imperforate: rare. Same remarks as above with regard to inverted frames. There are inverted watermarks, and marginal copies without watermark are found.

1882. Comparison is necessary to distinguish between Nos. 32–34 (small figures) and Nos. 35–37 (large figures). The inscription letters of DANMARK are clearly less thick in the latter. In addition, the extremities of the letters are widened, the vertical lines in the background are spaced farther apart, the circles around the figures are more generously spaced. Stamps with faked figures easily can be avoided by examining these details.

1915. Forged overprint on official stamp, No. 86: "80"-ore on "8." The authentic overprinted stamp has a 12½ perforation (official, No. 8); the stamps overprinted on No. 8a, perf 14 x 13½, therefore are forged. To this time, they have been easy to avoid, because the lateral ornaments are irregular and the "S" is upside down.

1918. The 27-ore overprint was counterfeited on Nos. 87 to 100 and on No. 102, used.

The space measurement between the figure and the four words varies. Comparison is indicated.

III. Newspaper Stamps

1915. There is no reason why we should deal with the figure repair job that transformed the 29-ore orange into a 38-ore orange, because the rarity of the latter will probably warrant scrutiny through a magnifying glass. Moreover, the shade of the 29-ore is orange-yellow and that of the 38-ore, orange, which proves once again that a little comparative study can be useful.

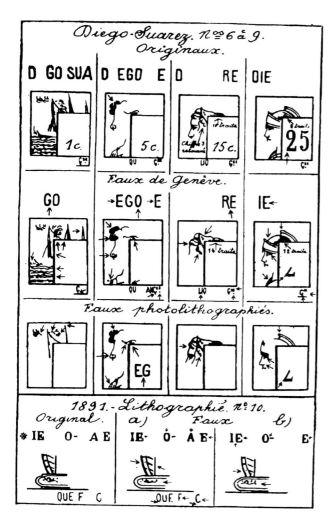

Top: Diégo-Suarez. Nos. 6–9. Originals. 1-centime. 5-centime. 15-centime, 10 lines, reversed figure "3." 25-centime, 8 lines. Second section: Geneva forgeries. 14 lines. 12 lines. Third section: Photolithographed forgeries. Bottom: 1891. Lithographed stamp. No. 10. Original. Forgeries.

IV. Official Stamps

1871. The first issue is interesting because of its perforations, or lack of them, and its inverted watermarks. Could the imperforate stamps be watermarked proofs that did not go through control?

Reprints: imperforate; no watermarks; no gum.

1875–1902. All values have an inverted watermark.

Diégo-Suarez

See French Colonies for wholly forged stamps (1881 and Peace and Commerce type).

1890. Stamps overprinted "15." Nos. 1 to 5.
Forged overprints: comparison is indispensable. The *original overprint* is 7 mm high. (Also, Geneva; figure "5" with excessively long horizontal bar.)

1890. Lithographed stamps. Nos. 6 to 9. *Originals:* lithographed on very slightly grayish white paper about 65 microns thick; the imprint is more gray than black, and, in the color lines, there are small white spots (use magnifying glass) that may be attributed to lack of indention, to the not very fluid ink used, and probably also to the texture of the paper. On average, 20 x 30 mm, the 25-centime stamp, a little less than that; inner frame, $11^1/_2$ x about 15; the frame on the left of the value is not over $^2/_5$ mm thick; the "D" of DIEGO is shaped like a rectangular "O." 1-centime, the wavy line of the highest wave is touching the ship's stern; check the small curved lines which form the clouds. 5-centime, check the hair on the negress's forehead; the right section of the latter's eye is rectangular. 15-centime, there is a reversed "3" on the helmeted portrait's temple and a second, rather well-shaped figure "3" in the dragon's head on top of the helmet. 25-centime, figure "2" forms a right angle, bottom left. (See the illustration for a few additional characteristic details.)

Geneva forgeries: in sheets of sixteen, comprising four strips of four, each having the four values; thick, yellowish paper (80 microns); the "D" of DIEGO is shaped like a "D"; allowable dimensions; the imprint is too black; left frame of the value is $^1/_2$ mm thick and more. The illustration brings out this set's serious defects.

The forged cancellations: double circle (24 mm) with date, Diégo-Suarez; same (23 mm) MADAGASCAR, with interchangeable dates in the center: 1 SEPT 92; 15 MARS 90; 28 SEPT 91; 27 SEPT 90; etc., in black or blue.

Various forgeries and photolithographed forgeries: paper is often too yellowish, also grayish, sometimes too gray; 55, 65, 70 microns thick; in general the impression is too black, but also gray or too gray; lines frequently are blurred with defects (very large white spots), caused by using coarse grain stones; frequently noncongruent dimensions (too high); the inscription lettering is rather successful, but, in a good set, one will notice the following: 1-centime, the "A" of FRANC is touching the bottom of the "N"; 5-centime, the "E" of FRANÇAISE is a little less high than the "S"; 15-centime, the letters of FRANC gradually increase in height as in the 25-centime original; 25-centime, the lower bar of the "E" of DIEGO is $^1/_4$ mm away from the "G" instead of $^1/_2$ mm. The frame on the left of the value is $^1/_2$ mm thick, but I have seen it with its normal thickness. The illustration will inform the reader on the commonest forgeries; they are so common that all albums have some of them. In case of doubt, they must be compared with reliable originals.

1891. Lithographed stamp. No. 10. *Original:* 17²/₃ x 21¹/₄ mm; the first figure of the millesime is a little less high than the last one; the "8" does not touch above, but the "9" touches rather often; the imprint is clear-cut; the various frames are regular (thin or thick); the sword hilt is not touching the arm (¹/₂ mm away); on the right of the millesime, the ornamental design forms, in its right section, a sort of figure "4," which is slanted to the left; the upper bar of the "5" is only 1¹/₂ mm wide. (See the illustration also.)

Forgeries: (a) mediocre creation in light gray; the design on the left of DIEGO is shapeless; the rosette above POSTES has an oblique line on top pointing toward the sun; the latter's second ray on the right is horizontal instead of concave and is no longer than the third; the serif at the bottom of the "E" of POSTE is touching the ornamental design on its right; the outer frame is consistently too thick; 18 x 21¹/₂ mm; various forged cancellations: round with date, in blue, Diégo-Suarez 28 SEP. 91 MADAGASCAR.

(b) Deceptive photolithographed forgery: 18 x 21¹/₂ mm; the design on the left of DIEGO is formless; the left downstroke of the "U" of SUAREZ is touching the top line; the rosetta above POSTE encroaches upon the inner left frame; the "8" and the "9" of the millesime are touching the line above them; the upper bar of the "5" is about 1³/₄ mm wide; the design on the right of the millesime is executed poorly; white or yellowish paper, instead of slightly grayish white; the imprint is black, sometimes slightly purplish, or a too vivid black; the outer right frame is drawn irregularly. Various forged cancellations, among which we find 1 SEPT 91 with very diluted gray-black ink.

1891. Overprinted stamps. Nos. 11 and 12. *Forged overprints:* comparison is necessary.
Original overprints: frame 17¹/₂ x 21¹/₂ mm; millesime, 4¹/₂ mm long.

1892. Stamps overprinted DIEGO SUAREZ. Nos. 13 to 24. The *original overprint* measures 2¹/₂ mm high by 19 mm long.

Very numerous *forged overprints:* normal, inverted, or double, in black or red; first, ascertain whether the stamp itself is a forgery (see French Colonies, 1881). The completely forged Geneva set with forged overprints in black or red has forged cancellations: Diégo-Suarez 28 SEPT 91 (or 1 SEPT 92) MADAGASCAR, in black or blue.

1892. Peace and Commerce type. Nos. 25 to 50. *Forgeries:* see French Colonies.

Postage due stamps, 1891. Nos. 1 and 2. *Originals:* 17¹/₂ x 21¹/₃₋¹/₂ mm, depending on impression; the "A"

of SUAREZ is higher than the other letters; the bottom inscription is like that of No. 10 (regular postage stamp), and the "S" of FRANÇAISE is also characteristic. There is a cedilla under the "C"; the inscriptions are regular as in the No. 10 stamp; the thickness of the thin or thick frames is quite distinctive; the paper is white.

Geneva forgeries: mere measurement of these counterfeits will justify their rejection; 5-centime, 17¹/₄ x 20¹/₂ mm; the bar under PERCEVOIR is straight instead of scalloped; 50-centime, 17¹/₄ x 20¹/₄ mm; the "A" of SUAREZ is no higher than the other letters; in FRANÇAISE, the last five letters are higher than the first four; no cedilla under the "C." Photolithographed forgeries also exist for which comparison and measurement are necessary.

1892. Overprinted stamps. Nos. 3 to 13. Numerous *forged overprints,* normal or inverted; comparison is indispensable. The forged postage due stamps (see French Colonies) also were overprinted fraudulently, especially in Geneva.

Dominica

1874–86. 1- and 6-pence and 1-shilling. *Originals:* perf 12¹/₂ or 14; watermarked "C C" or "C A" Crown.
Early forgeries: two sets easily identifiable by the single face contour line, the face shading which does not terminate at the line, and by the very indistinct bandeau jewels; the inscription circle is touching the value tablet or penetrates it slightly. Pin perf 13 or rouletted.

Dominican Republic

1862. Coat of arms. Nos. 1 and 2. *Originals:* typographed; the same twelve varieties in both values; nineteen horizontal shade lines, top left of the shield, and eighteen, which are horizontal or vertical, in the other three quarterings; the four frame lines do not touch each other.
Early forgeries: lithographed; seventeen shade lines, top left, with twelve on the right and thirteen at bottom, closed frame; the top of the Phrygian bonnet is slanted more to the right than to the left; the cross is shaded; "medio" is printed "medto"; etc. There is no correspondence between these counterfeits and any of the original types.

1865. Same. Nos. 3 and 4. *Originals:* typographed on laid paper; the first plate of the ¹/₂-real has twelve varieties; Plate II comprises five varieties for the two values. Eleven scallops on top; see the 1862 issue for the shield design.

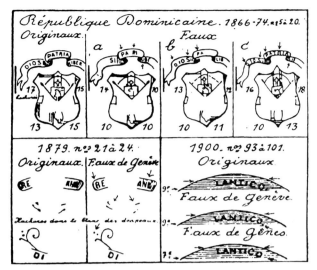

Top: Dominican Republic. 1866–74. Nos. 5–20.
Originals. Forgeries. (Numbers refer to shade lines.)
Bottom left: 1879. Nos. 21–24. Originals. Geneva
forgeries. Hatching in the white of the flags. Bottom
right: 1900. Nos. 93–101. Originals. Geneva
forgeries. Genoa forgeries.

Early forgeries: lithographed, with arbitrary wire-
thread pattern; (a) fifteen shade lines, top left, thirteen
on right, fifteen, bottom left, and fourteen on right; the
"C" and the two "O" letters of CORREOS are too
small. (b) Shade lines in the following order: sixteen,
thirteen, twelve, and fourteen; ten scallops on top.

1866–74. Nos. 5 to 20. *Originals:* 15$^1/_2$ x 25 mm;
because the CORREOS inscriptions (12$^1/_2$ mm wide)
and the value were printed after a first typographical
impression of the stamp, there is no good reason for
expertizing emphasis on the various shifts in inscription
placement; the shield axis passes between letters "T"
and "R" of PATRIA. The illustration will give
information on the principal features to be examined.
The figures indicate the number of escutcheon
quartering shade lines (bottom left: count the heavy line
on the right; bottom right: count the heavy top line and
the bottom thin line, which often is done poorly.)

Early forgeries: three sets, whose dissimilarities are
presented adequately in the illustration: (a) 15$^2/_5$ x
about 24$^3/_4$ mm; (b) *Geneva forgeries:* good
dimensions, large dot, printed, cancellation or irregular
eight-bar figure; the principal defects may be found in
the illustration; there are a few differences in
inscriptions, depending on values and imprint; the half-
circle above the cross sometimes resembles a full line;
(c) 15$^3/_5$ by about 25$^1/_5$ mm; the eighteen or nineteen
shade lines on the shield's top right include the dotted
lines and the broken or short lines; there often are
traces of hairlines in the base of CORREOS.

No *reprints.*

1879. Perf 12$^1/_2$ x 13. Nos. 21 to 24. *Originals:*
typographed.

Geneva forgeries: allowable dimensions; perf 13$^1/_2$
(see the illustration for the distinctive characteristics).
In the 1-real, the shading at the extremities of
REPUBLICA DOMINICA is a little more successful
than in the $^1/_2$-real. Arbitrary shades. Forged
cancellation with date, double circle: SAN DOMINGO.
A first Geneva set on tinted paper is perf 11$^1/_2$; the
flagstaffs are unbroken, except in the 1-real; the cross is
nearly $^3/_5$ mm thick and 2$^1/_2$ mm high; noncongruent
shading.

1880 and subsequent issues. 1-peso (gold).
Original: 19$^2/_5$ x 24$^1/_2$ mm, color rouletted.

Typographed forgery: 19$^3/_4$ x 25 mm; imperforate or
too pronounced rouletting — the stamp seems to be perf
10; a line instead of stippling above CORREOS; the
two "R" letters of this word are joined at bottom; the
inscription, DIOS PATRIA LIBERTAD, is especially
bad, formless lettering, illegible in part, many letters
touching the top and bottom edge of the tablet. The
lines on the sides of the shield are ill-formed. I have
seen only the 1-peso stamp. This forgery "supposedly"
was issued by Fournier; it comes from another
workshop, however.

1883. Overprinted stamps. Nos. 43 to 60. *Forged
overprints,* particularly on the 1-peso (gold).
Comparison is necessary. See the forgery of this value
in the preceding issue. The overprint errors also were
counterfeited.

Forged burelage (Nos. 51–60) on all values
sometimes is composed only of diagonal lines; compare
with burelage in the rather common Nos. 33–36
originals. The overprint, 5 FRANCOS, Type I, for
FRANCOS, and Type II for the figure (!), was made in
Geneva without a final period.

1900. Geographical letter-cards. Nos. 93 to 101.
Originals: Nos. 93–97, perf 14; Nos. 98–101, perf 12;
32$^3/_5$–$^3/_4$ x 20$^1/_2$ –$^3/_4$ mm. Dot after ATLANTICO;
letters "A" and "N" of this word are touching the third
shade line; "L" and "I" extend from the fourth to the
seventh line; the "O" extends beyond the ninth, and the
period is astride the tenth.

Geneva forgeries: 32$^1/_4$–$^1/_2$ mm in width; 1-, 10-,
20-, and 50-centavo, perf 13; "A" and "N" do not
touch the third shade line; the "O" does not go beyond
the ninth, and the period is between the ninth and tenth
lines. Forged cancellation with date, double circle,
SAN DOMINGO 20 ENO 02....

Genoa forgeries: 21 mm high; perf 11; "L," "A,"
"N," "T," and "I" are touching the second shading
line; no period.

Dutch Colonies

See Netherlands Indies, Curaçao, and Surinam.

Eastern Rumelia (South Bulgaria)

1880. Overprinted Turkish stamps. Nos. 1 to 6.
This is another issue that should be completely ignored unless you intend to make a specialty of it. Forged overprints are so numerous that one wonders how it is possible for any mint Turkish stamps of the issue of 1876–80 to be extant! It would be useless to give detailed information on the counterfeited overprints; there are too many of them! Minute, detailed comparison is absolutely indispensable.

Types: there are two types of the "R. O." overprint: Type I is the normal; Type II has wider spaced letters.

Varieties: inverted overprints: 50M, 50U. No. 2, with overprints "a" and "b" (Yvert) exists with the two overprints doubled: 25 francs. Stamps not catalogued in Yvert can only have forged overprints. The 10-para black on lilac, 1-piaster black and blue, 2-piaster orange, all three with overprint "R. O.", are unissued stamps. The 10-para black with overprint ROUMELIE ORIENTALE (without "R. O.") is an essay.

1881. Eastern Rumelia inscription. Nos. 7 to 11.
Stamps perf 11¹/₂ are unissued. The imperforate stamps must be bought with wide margins. There are tête-bêche stamps, one copy of which has a color background imprint that is inverted in relation to the impression.

Fakes: the colored background of the 10-para was chemically faked to create a rose shade (rare error). Comparison with a 20-para will reveal the fraud. As usual, tête-bêche stamps were manufactured with two single stamps; here, watermark fluid will do the trick.

Forgeries: remarkable photolithographed counterfeits of the whole set were made in Geneva (F.) by means of five clichés, plus a cliché for the background coloration. These clichés also were used to counterfeit the five values of 1885. Format 19 or 19¹/₄ x 22¹/₂ or 23 mm (originals 19–19¹/₅ x 22¹/₂–³/₄ mm); perf 11¹/₂ (the 1880 set is frequently canceled — the forger was too inexperienced to know better!); thin, transparent paper that is very similar to the original or to thick paper. The illustration will inform the reader about the set's general defects. It should be noted that in the forgeries of the 20-para the letters of "HA" are joined at the bottom and in the forgeries of the 10-para, the inscription ANATOAI is almost congruent; one also can note that the letters "AL" in ORIENTALE are jointed

at bottom in the originals and are well separated in the forgeries, except in the 20-para stamps. The forged cliché of the background coloration is too wide and too high and extends as far as the outer frame of the black impression. In the authentic stamps, the format is a little smaller. (See Turkey, also.)

These forgeries have had several worldwide circulations, which probably is the reason why the originals have invariably brought lower prices (in gold) in the last ten years or so.

188S. Same type. Perf 11¹/₂. The 20-para, 1- and 5-piaster stamps are unissued.

Varieties: 10-para, perf 11¹/₂ x 13¹/₂: rare, the unissued stamps are found imperforate.

Forgeries: see the preceding issue. Well-reproduced shades.

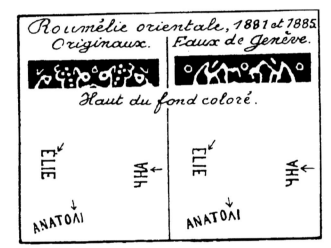

Eastern Rumelia, 1881 and 1885. Originals. Geneva forgeries. Top of colored background.

South Bulgaria

A country with many overprints where forgeries are plentiful. My advice is to forget it or to go in for thorough specialization.

1885. Unframed overprints. Nos. 1 to 5. Two different clichés were used in applying the overprints by hand. Thus, many overprints are poorly printed and are not very visible. It is a good idea to reject them whenever study is not possible.

The *two types* have a double-lined tail. In Type 1, the lion's left front leg has four claws; Type II shows only three. In Type I, the heel of the hind paws is quite prominent. The lion's tail is hairless in Type II. Type I, total height approximately 14¹/₂ mm. Type II: about 16 mm. Both in blue or black stamp pad ink.

Categories of overprinted stamps: Western Rumelia 1881, perf 13¹/₂; 1885, perf 11¹/₂ and 13¹/₂.

Type I. Blue ink, perf 13½ (1881), 5-, 10-, 20-para; 1-piaster.

Blue ink, perf 11½ (1885), 5-, 10-, 20-para.

Black ink, perf 13½ (1881), 1-piaster.

Black ink, perf 11½ (1885), 10- and 20-para.

Type II. Blue ink, perf 13½ (1881), 20-para; 1- and 5-piaster.

Blue ink, perf 11½ (1885), 5-, 10-, 20-para.

Blue ink, perf 13½ (1885), 5-para.

Black ink, perf 13½ (1881), 1- and 5-piaster.

Black ink. perf 11½ (1885), 20-para.

Black ink, perf 13½ (1885), 5-para.

The 10-para, Type I, exists with an inverted blue overprint: very rare. Authentic cancellations are rare.

Forged overprints: bad copies can be identified by comparing design and ink (single-lined tail, etc.). The best ones come from the Levant and even from Sofia. The whole set was counterfeited in Geneva in a glaring gray-black or blue. Make comparison.

1885. Framed overprints. Nos. 6 to 11. Black overprints on the same Rumelian stamps.

Type III: the end of the lion's tail is double-lined.

Type IV: the end of the tail is single-lined and not so wide; the cross on the crown is given prominence; the figures are higher.

Types III and IV have an appreciably similar format: 15 x 19 mm. No. 6 is known to have an inverted overprint.

Categories of overprinted stamps:

Types III and IV 1881, perf 13½. All five values.

Types III and IV 1885, perf 11½. The 5-, 10-, and 20-para.

Types III and IV 1885, perf 13½. The 5-para.

Forged overprints: design and ink comparison needed. The ink is duller than in the first issue. The forgeries have the same origins. In the Geneva set, Type III is 20 mm high and Type IV, 23 mm high.

Note: The Geneva overprints were applied not only on original Rumelian stamps, but also on forgeries of bogus issues.

Ecuador

First issues, 1865–72. Imperforate stamps. Nos. 1 to 4. *Reprints:* stereotyped in blocks of various categories; the work was executed poorly, either because the reproductions come from one or several oxidized reject clichés or because of unskilled workmanship. For the 4-real stamp, there must have been at least a partial photographic reproduction before plate construction; otherwise, it is difficult to explain the discovery of single stamp reprints in which the condor is facing right and which appear normal when placed side by side with others. The lateral outer frames of the ½- and 1-real stamps still are executed crudely, especially the left frame which usually is doubled or very thick (two lines very close to each other). The outer frame sometimes is doubled on three or four sides; shades and gutters between stamps are arbitrary; thin, transparent paper. The original stamps are typographed.

½-**real. No. 1.** *Original:* 18⅘ and 19¼ x 22⅗–⅔ mm; a sun with seventeen rays; thirteen very visible leaves on the left of the oval; seventy pearls not touching each other

Reprints: 19½ x 23½ mm; see information on the left frame above; no laid or cross-hatched paper; the first reprints (sheets of ninety, 1890) are more successful than those of 1893 (sheets of 100), in which most of the stamps have the defects shown in the illustration, especially the large blue dot on the blank circle.

Early forgeries: very crude; sun with twenty-eight or thirty rays; there are three elements in the Greek ornament instead of five; in the oval, the boat is suspended in space and is carrying a sort of palm tree on the right; there are about twenty shade lines in the inner corners instead of about thirty; the letters of MEDIO REAL are too high and too thick; between these words there is space of only 1⅕ mm.

Another forgery: like the one shown for Nos. 2 and 3.

1-real. Nos. 2 and 3. *Originals:* 19–19⅕ x 23–23⅕ mm. Seventeen sun rays. Seventy-eight pearls.

Reprints: 20 x 24 mm. Outer frame defect already mentioned; no laid or cross-hatched paper, except for No. 3, which sometimes is found on cross-hatched paper. I also have run across blue-tinted paper with foolscap lines in blue on the back of the stamp for this value. The reprints of the two values have forged shading lines between the sun and the ship (see the illustration); this can be seen in the good impressions; when the imprint is blurred, they cannot be seen. It is true that the forged lines in question also are found on originals; only the doubling of the left frame ensures decisive identification of the reprints. The two long sun rays on the left frequently are broken.

Early forgeries: (1) same features as for the forgery of the ½-real; three elements in the Greek ornament; fantastic sun; too few shade lines in the upper corners; more than 100 small pearls; no dot before and after UN REAL. (2) Another set originating in Geneva, whose crude oval design is shown in the illustration under that of the forgery; seventy-five pearls; at bottom, under the circle, fifty-five vertical shade lines (including two lateral inner frames) instead of seventy-four; three curved color lines in the flags on the left of the oval instead of four; there are nine or ten leaves above this design instead of thirteen. Note: A 2-real stamp also was counterfeited; forty vertical lines under the circle; the boat is nose-diving. There are reprints with forged cancellations (dots and FRANCA, etc.).

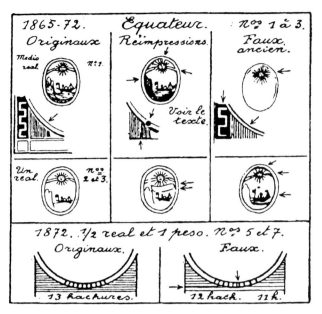

1865–72. Ecuador. Nos. 1–3. Originals. Reprints. Early forgery. ¹/₂-real. No. 1. See the text. Middle: 1-real. Nos. 2, 3. Bottom: 1872. ¹/₂-real and 1-peso. Nos. 5 and 7. Originals. 13 shade lines. Forgeries. 12 shade lines; 11 shade lines.

Real. No. 4. *Originals:* 23 mm high; various widths, from 18¹/₂ to 20¹/₂ mm; typographed stamps produced from a woodcut; white paper; greatly reduced gutters with almost no margins.

Reprints: on generally grayish paper of poor quality; in sheets of ninety (1890) or of ninety-six (1893); 23¹/₂ mm high; stereotype impression with color spot defects in various places; rather wide gutters with more or less normal margins; no frame line all around the sheets; in the original sheet, there is a color line 1–2 mm away from the marginal stamps. In a few copies of the large sheets, the condor is facing right! There is a 1 mm dividing frame line on the stamps' sides; the sun has six short horizontal strokes on four lines (2, 2, 1 [longer], 1); two types, one with a large blank "circle" (really an oval whose axes measure 14³/₄ x 16 mm); the tablet of CUATRO REALES has a small perfect blank circle about ²/₃ mm in diameter at each end instead of the curved line seen in the originals. In the second type, the large oval measures 14 x 15³/₄ mm; the circles at each end of the lower tablet have a color dot inside them. The first type has five vertical shade lines on the right and left of the upper legend; the second one, four on the

left and three on the right. In the two counterfeit types, the upper legend lettering is too thin and the shade is too dark. The forged cancellation frequently is a dot lozenge with large figure "3154."

1872. Perf 11. Nos. 5 to 7. *Originals:* lithographed; thirteen horizontal shade lines, top and bottom; eighty-seven blank dividing elements in the circle for the ¹/₂-real, and eighty-three for the 1-peso; 19¹/₂ by about 22¹/₂ mm; the sun is positioned a bit too far to the right in the oval; in the 1-peso, letter "U" of UN is square.

Geneva forgeries: twelve shade lines in the inner top corners; in the left corner, the twelfth line exists only in embryonic form (see the illustration for the lower corners); sixty-eight dividing elements, one of which is too wide in the bottom of the circle; three shade lines above the condor's neck (the third one is touching the neck); there are five of them in the ¹/₂-real. To execute the 1-peso, they used the ¹/₂-real cliché by simply changing the bottom of the stamp, which explains why neither the corner ornaments nor the value tablet touch the outer or inner frames or the Greek ornaments; the bottom of the "U" of UN is quite round; 20 x 22¹/₄ (¹/₂-real) or 22¹/₂ mm (1-peso); the sun is in the middle of the oval; perf 12¹/₂ or pinpoint perf 13. The forged Geneva cancellation most often is a square of large square dots. Among the other cancellations of the same provenance, we should mention the postmark with date, double circle (22 mm); QUITO 18 MARZO 81 FRANCA and two stars on the sides. A good counterfeit of the ¹/₂-real from another source exists, identifiable by its dimensions: 19¹/₂ x 22 mm. Perf 11 or 14; dull blue shade; thin paper.

Original, 1-real, No. 6, lithographed; seventy-eight horizontal lines, including the two inner frames; in addition, a much closer horizontal line structure between the lateral foliage.

Geneva forgeries: the outer frame is too far from the inner one; sixty-nine horizontal lines (count on the right); these shading lines are continued between the foliage with similar spacing: perf 12¹/₂.

1883. Stamp overprinted DIEZ CENTAVOS. No. 14. Compare the overprint; the inverted overprints are forged.

1894–96. Nos. 30 to 37, 38 to 40, and 69 to 75. The Seebeck reprints, whose shades and paper are different, are being sold as originals. Comparison is necessary and specialization is desirable. These reprints are found most often with the following forged postmarks: double circle (27 mm), CORREOS DEL ECUADOR 1904 SEPT 22 YBARRA; same, CORREOS DEL ECUADOR SEPT 1897; same (24 mm) DIRECCION GENERAL DE CORREOS Y TELEGRAFO QUITO U.P.U. FEB 2 1898, at bottom, ECUADOR; double circle with CORREOS DEL

ECUADOR, black star in the middle, and, in the circle, ENCOMIENDAS; double circle with black circle arc 2¹/₂ mm wide at the top of the inner circle: ADMINISTRACION DE CORREOS, in middle ENCOMIENDA ...; double postmark (32 x 22 mm), CORREOS DEL ECUADOR FEB 18..9....

Commemorative stamps, 1896. *Geneva forgeries:* very poor lithograph execution, identifiable by the background line structure whose horizontal lines are broken in numerous places and are not too equidistant; by the stippled shading of the portraits (dots too large, too few in number, and large blank spaces on the forehead and cheeks); by the unbroken lines which extend from the eye toward the nostril in the three-portrait type; finally, by the forged cancellations: double circle (25 mm) with date, ADN ... DE CORREOS DE GUAYAQUIL ECUADOR, and in the center, GUAYAQUIL U.P.U. MAR 12 189....

1897. Stamps overprinted "1897–98." Five original overprint varieties. One finds the forged overprints of the higher values, especially of the original overprint measuring 18 mm wide ("1" figures on left, "7" and final "8" are not high enough). Comparison is necessary.

1897. Perf 15, 16. Nos. 109 to 116. *Reprints:* compare with originals; lighter shades; thicker paper.

Official stamps. *Forged overprints:* comparison necessary; a forged overprint, OFICIAL, measuring 17 x 5 mm, is a fantasy.

The *original overprint* of Nos. 1–10 measures 22 x 3¹/₄ mm.

Postage due stamps, 1896. Nos. 1 to 7. *Reprints:* recumbent Phrygian bonnet watermark; thick porous paper. Sometimes the originals have the same watermark.

Egypt

1866. Nos. 1 to 7. *Originals:* lithographed with pyramid watermark (1-piaster, typographed, without watermark); 18 x 21 mm. Also 1-piaster, 18¹/₂ x 21¹/₂ mm; perf 12¹/₂, 12¹/₂ x 13, 12¹/₂ x 15. 5-piaster, center flower, fourteen petals. 10-piaster, twenty-eight circles around the oval. 20-piaster, the "A" letters of the upper left corners are pointed; figures are ¹/₂ mm away. 1-piaster, ninety-six pearls; square dot between "P" and "E" bottom right. 2-piaster, very visible dot after "E" in the upper left corner; 5-piaster, seventeen-petaled center flower, eleven pearls on top, twelve below; 10-piaster, dot after "E" in the upper left corner.

Early forgeries: no watermark, imperforate, or arbitrary perforation. 5-piaster, center flower with

nineteen petals; 10-piaster, twenty-seven circles; "1" figures with terminal lines; 20-piaster, upper left corner, the top of the second "A" is horizontal; ³/₄ mm between the upper right corner figures and ¹/₄ mm between those in the lower left corner; 1-piaster, eighty-four pearls, faint round dot between "P" and "E," bottom right; 2-piaster, very small dot after the "E" in the upper left corner, the median bar of the letter is shorter than the others; 5-piaster, various counterfeits and counterfeits of counterfeits; six boldly printed petals; ten pearls above and nine or ten below; 10-piaster, no dot after the "E" in the upper left corner; center oval is cross-hatched vertically and horizontally, nothing more.

1867. Sphinx in the middle. Nos. 8 to 13. *Originals:* perf 15 x 12¹/₂; star and crescent watermark, produced by embossing; lithographed; about 19 mm high. The inner corner cross-hatching around the center oval is executed finely and quite visible. Over the pyramid, above the sphinx, are four lines of marks or broken lines and a dot near the top of the pyramid. There are twenty or twenty-one horizontal shade lines on the left of the pyramid, depending on the type (5-piaster, nineteen), and nineteen or twenty on the right.

Early forgeries: lithographed, no watermark, height, 19¹/₂–20 mm; arbitrary perforations or dot rouletted; the cross-hatching of the inner corners is executed poorly; there are three lines of marks and a dot above the sphinx; one set has twenty-two shade lines on each side of the pyramid; another, twenty-one; a forgery of the 5-para stamp has twenty-two on the left and twenty-one on the right; in this forgery, the value tablets are no wider than the lateral tablets. 5-piaster, Geneva forgery: imperforate or arbitrary perforation; 19¹/₄ mm high; twenty-one shade lines on the left of the pyramid.

1872. Sphinx on the left. Nos. 14 to 22. *Originals:* 24 x 19 mm; perf 12¹/₂, 12¹/₂ x 13¹/₂, or 13¹/₂ x 12¹/₂; watermarked; the "T" of POSTES, lacking the right section of its top bar, looks like the figure "1"; the sphinx's head has three wide white lines and a fourth one on the right, divided by two horizontal color shade lines.

Early counterfeits: no watermark; shapeless perforation or rouletting; arbitrary measurements; five white lines on the sphinx's head, in the headdress, above the face; the "T" of POSTES has a normal bar; the "A" of EGIZIANE is an "R"; there is no fine white line above this inscription.

Modern forgeries: Geneva, the whole set; no watermark; 19¹/₅–¹/₂ mm high; at times, allowable perf 12¹/₂; bottom inscription lettering is too thin; between the bottom of the "S" of POSTES and the "T" ("1" in the originals), there is a ¹/₂ mm space instead of ¹/₅ mm; the blank oval is only ¹/₅ mm wide above the upper horizontal shade line instead of $^1/_3$ mm; on the left, below the mouth, there is a cross instead of dots; and there are traces of dividing frame lines about 1 mm from the stamp corners.

1879 and 1884. Stamps overprinted "5," "10," and "20-para." Nos. 21, 22, and 31. *Forged Geneva overprints* on forgeries and inverted overprints on forgeries and originals. Comparison is necessary.

1926. PORT FUAD overprints. Nos. 11 to 114. *Forged overprints:* comparison is indispensable. The original overprint is 23$^3/_4$ mm high; the lettering of the 50-piaster is clear-cut and is horizontal in the bottom of the stamp.

Postage due stamps. There are a great many forgeries of the first three postage due stamp issues. Specialization is desirable.

1884 and 1886. Nos. 1 to 9. *Originals:* first issue with star and crescent watermark; 22$^1/_2$ x 19 mm; perf 10$^1/_2$; the dots are square in the Egyptian inscriptions.

Geneva forgeries: the whole set with or without embossed watermark; width, 22$^1/_4$–$^2/_5$ mm (20-para, up to 22$^1/_2$ mm); perf 11; Egyptian inscription dots are more rounded; A PERCEVOIR is drawn somewhat obliquely in the tablet, and in the 10-, 20-para, and 1-piaster, especially, the bottom of the "P" is $^1/_6$ mm from the line underneath it, instead of $^1/_4$. Forged cancellations: one circle, EBNOUL, with star and crescent, and double circle with double bar in the middle, SEDF... 26 MAI or 301... (figures interchangeable). Another forged set: also with or without watermark; minor lettering differences, but the best distinguishing mark is measurement; 22$^1/_4$ x 19$^1/_2$–$^3/_4$ mm. Perf 11 and 11$^1/_2$.

1888. Perf 11$^1/_2$. Nos. 10 to 14. *Originals:* 22$^1/_2$ x 19 mm; paper thickness, 65–70 microns.

Geneva forgeries: perf 11$^1/_2$ but also 11 x 11; paper thickness, 55–60 microns. A few characteristics of the various values follow:

2-millieme. 18$^3/_4$ x 22 mm; the first bottom inscription character on the left, under the first "M" of MILLIEMES, instead of being uniformly curvilinear, forms a recumbent "E," whose top bar joins the first of the three dots above it.

5-millieme. 19 x 21$^4/_5$ mm; the second inscription character has no white dot in the middle of the circle.

1-piaster. 19 x 21$^9/_{10}$ mm; a white line cuts the lower left frame obliquely; it starts above the "T" of POSTES and ends in the lower frame, about 1 mm from the corner.

2-piaster. 19 x 21$^3/_4$ mm; the "P" of PIASTRES is too thick.

5-piaster. Two different clichés: One is 18$^3/_5$ x 21$^3/_4$ mm; between POSTES and PIASTRES, the fine frames are $^1/_4$ mm away from the thick frame; likewise, on the

right. The second cliché measures 18$^1/_4$ x 21$^3/_4$ mm; the thin frame surrounding the thick inner frame is only about $^1/_8$ mm away from it.

Another forgery: 5-piaster, 19$^1/_4$ x 22$^1/_4$ mm; gray paper of poor quality; the "O" of PERCEVOIR is really a "C" (use magnifying glass); the first character, lower left, ends on the right in a horizontal line with a small hook at its end, and the fine frame on the right of the thick inner frame, under the Egyptian inscription on the right, is further from the thick frame above it than below it.

Suez Canal. Nos. 1 to 4. *Originals:* 25 x 19$^1/_2$–$^3/_4$ mm; lithographed. See the illustration.

No *reprints.*

Forgeries: a dozen different sets are known to exist; a detailed study of them would be very tedious. We shall limit our treatment to the doubtful stamps with the distinguishing features shown in the illustration of the originals; none of the stamps has every mark. Examine especially the following features: the shading of the four circles; the small transfer plate flaws found inside the latter; the arrangement of the circles with respect to the hatching; the line shading of the inscription ovals; the letters described; the "S" letters of POSTES; the crisscrossed hatch lines above "PO" and under "EZ" of SUEZ; the ornamentation on the right of SUEZ; the arrangement of the masts, oriflammes, ropes, people, or tackle, and the smokestack, especially on the left where smoke conceals a part of the mizzenmast. The Geneva forgery, with outer framework 1$^1/_4$ mm away, has two types; one cliché with a person on the ship's bow; another, without anyone. There are numerous forged cancellations on these forgeries and on the originals.

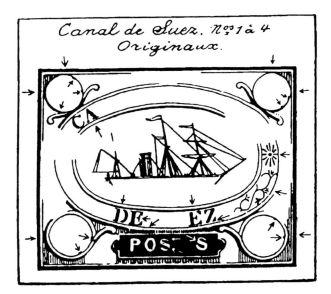

Suez Canal. Nos. 1–4. Originals.

Epirus

This is not a very interesting region. In addition to the stamp value in black, the 1914 provisional stamps must have a blue control postmark. Forgeries must be examined by comparing shades and design, especially the skull and the eagle. The 10-lepton exists tête-bêche.

1914. Perf 14¹/₂ Laid and wove paper. The values on wove paper are controversial. A set of them (Medallion types, Nos. 22–27) that brought fifty gold francs in 1916 is worth one gold franc now.

1915–16. Overprinted Greek stamps. Nos. 38 to 64. Most of the values were fraudulently overprinted in Greece. Thus, comparative study is necessary. The 1915 issue was officially overprinted in black only.

Eritrea

A country known for overprints, which were counterfeited on many values, especially rare inverted overprints. When the stamp is canceled, examine the cancellation first; it may be sufficient to spot the overprint forgery; then, compare with a reliable original overprint, available at low cost in almost all issues. The 5-lira, No. 11, was counterfeited completely; the portrait's right ear (on the left, looking at the stamp) is executed poorly: compare the lines with a low-value stamp.

The forged cancellations on this stamp: one circle, MASSAUA 12, 11, 99 (ERITREA).

Parcel post stamps: forged Genoa overprints; lettering 1¹/₄ mm instead of 1¹/₃ mm high and insufficient indention. The forged Geneva cancellations: one circle (26 mm) with date, MASSAUA 7-2-98 ERITREA or MASSAUA 7 6 98 (ERITREA), both with two stars on the sides.

Estonia

1919. Various frames. Nos. 10 to 16. *Forgeries:* more than ¹/₂ mm too wide. The spears of the five warriors under the sail of the drakkar (Viking ship) are too thick and are touching their heads (or their hair?); in the originals, the spears are slender and are separate from the heads, except in the case of the first warrior in the foreground.

The whole set of values in marks was counterfeited in Argentina. The inscriptions (lettering and figures) are not congruent. In the forged 15-mark, the "1" on the left is obviously too thick and the lower curl of the "5" curves inward on the same side.

1919. Overprints. Nos. 25 to 33. The whole set is rare, but it was expertly counterfeited. Detailed comparative study is all the more indispensable because we do not know whether the matrix was destroyed.

1923–24. Air mail. Nos. 62 to 73. These stamps should be acquired on authenticated cover, for there are a few forged postmarks.

Ethiopia

First issue types (portrait or lion). Nos. 1 to 7. *Originals:* perf 14 x 13¹/₂ 18 x 22 mm; very fine typographical execution; the illustration describes the portrait facial details. In the lion type, we note that all of the pieces of mosaic in the center background have two, sometimes three, short lines.

Geneva forgeries: in sheets of sixteen; perf 14; width, 17³/₄ mm (portrait), 17¹/₂ mm (lion) by about 21³/₄ mm high. Face examination may be adequate for forgery identification of the portrait type (see the illustration). As for the lion type, the easiest way is to examine the center background overlapping, each part of which has only one dot or one line; the parts under the oriflamme on the right have no dot at all.

Other forgeries, portrait type: very bad execution (see the illustration). Four postmarks forged in Geneva, 25–26¹/₂ mm in diameter, one of which is a broken line circle, DIBRE-DAOUA, star, 10-06 ABISSINIE; the others, double circle with two transversals, interchangeable dates, Ethiopian characters on top, ENTOTTO, HARRAR, ADIS ABEBA, at bottom.

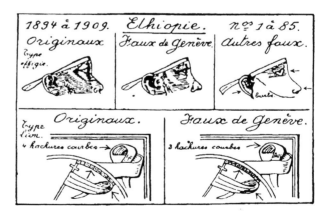

1894–1909. Ethiopia. Nos. 1–85. Originals. Geneva forgeries. Other forgeries. Portrait type. Bottom: Originals. Lion type; 4 curved lines. Geneva forgeries. 3 curved lines.

Issues of 1900–1908, Nos. 8 to 85, and postage due stamps, 1896–1909, Nos. 1 to 35a. There are forged overprints on originals; comparison is necessary;

also, one finds all these counterfeit overprints on Geneva forgeries; in this case, it is enough to ascertain the stamp's authenticity.

Forged Geneva cancellations, applied on forged postage stamps or postage due stamps; double circle, cut by two bars for the date (German type); 25 or 26 mm, with Ethiopian characters on top, and, at bottom, ENTOTTO, HARRAR; ADIS ABEBA, and various dates; also broken line circle, 26½ mm; DIRREDAOUA, star, 10-.. 06 ABYSSINIE.

Far Eastern Republic

An abundance of overprints, many of which have been copied: detailed comparison is indispensable.

Fernando Po

First issues. *Originals:* No. 1, 20-centavo brown (1868), 17³/₅ x 21⁴/₅ mm; Nos. 2–4 (1879), 17½ x 22½ mm.

Forgeries: crude lithographed copies that are executed so poorly they do not deserve description; the center background shade lines, which evidently are printed too boldly, frequently are broken and touch the circle.

Geneva forgeries: No. 1, good typographical execution (blocks); identified most easily by dimensions: 18¼ x 21½ mm. The inner white frame is broken in numerous places. Two forged Geneva cancellations with date, double circle, 25½ mm, SANTA ISABEL 21 APR 99 and CABO DE SAN JUAN 19 MAY 00, both with FERNANDO POO at bottom.

1885–1900. HABILITADO. Nos. 9 to 11 and 23 to 34. *Forged overprints* on originals and on forgeries; most of them executed poorly. Comparison is necessary.

The 5-CEN. overprint in an oval also was counterfeited, notably in Geneva, and requires comparison also.

1896–99. Fiscals. 10-centavo de peso. *Originals:* typographed; 26½ x 33 mm.

Forgeries: 26¼ x 32½ mm; lithographed; no accent on the first "O" of POO and MOVIL; broken background horizontal shade lines; the escutcheon's top vertical lines are touching the horizontal line delimiting their quartering; the escutcheon's lion has neglected to put his crown on his head; the two blank spheres on the right and left of the value tablet are separated from the latter instead of touching it.

1899. Perf 14, Nos. 40 to 57. Also 1900. Perf 14, Nos. 67 to 85. *Forgeries:* the large values 60- and 80-

centavo and 1- and 2- peso stamps, as well as the 3-milésimo, and probably other values, were counterfeited in blocks in Geneva. The inscription lettering is blurred; the right downstroke of the "N" letters of FERNANDO is longer than the left one; the "S" of CORREOS is touching the bottom of the tablet; the face is shaded insufficiently on the prominent parts of the forehead, cheek, and chin; the fine shade lines above and below the horizontal inscriptions are unsuccessful or missing. (See the Philippines.)

The 3-milésimo stamp comes from a different cliché; black-gray shade; perf 13¾. Forged cancellation: CABO DE SAN... 17 MAY.

Fiji

1870–71. Fiji Times Express. Nos. 1 to 5. *Originals:* 1870, typographed, 22½ x 18½ mm, grid paper (except the 9-pence); 1870, all values on laid, bâtonné paper. Dot rouletted (20); the horizontal frames are thicker than the vertical ones and do not touch them; the dividing frame lines between the stamps are composed of dots; the total length of the word TIMES is about 8½ mm and of FIJI, about 4¾ mm. The frame interruptions facilitate stamp location in the sheet. The value figure stands alone, except in the 1-shilling, where it is shaded by a fine line. 1-pence, the figure is 4 mm high; 3-pence, same; 6-pence, 7 mm; 9-pence, 4¼ mm; 1-shilling, about 6¼ mm.

No reprints. The so-called private reprints of the Fiji Times Express measure 22½ x 16 mm; typographed in black on tinted paper; TIMES is 7½ mm long instead of about 8½ mm; dot after FIJI; etc.

Essays on wove yellow paper.

Forgeries: sets easily identified by the fact that the horizontal frames are of the same thickness as the others. (a) On thick wove paper, purplish rose; 1-penny, value figure is 5¾ mm high; the frame lines are touching each other; 3-pence, value figure is surrounded by an ornamental line; 6-pence, value figure is 5 mm and has an ornamental line; 9-pence, value figure is 6 mm high. (b) Counterfeits called "San Francisco" on vertically laid paper; imperforate or pin perforated; the dividing frame line is made up of lines, not dots; TIMES is only 7 mm wide and FIJI, about 3½ mm; the inscriptions of these counterfeits often are manuscripted with ink.

End of 1871. 1-penny, 3-, and 6-pence. Nos. 6 to 8. *Originals:* typographed; the very finely executed design has horizontal shading lines in the center background which do not touch the circle (use magnifying glass); the base of the crown is horizontal and the bandeau has the same design in all three values;

in the 6-pence, the center background shade lines, which are broken on the right and doubly broken on the left, reveal a blank hexagon (use magnifying glass). The number of pearls and the circle design are shown in the illustration. Perf 12½, about 18⅓ x 21⅔, 22, 21½ mm; in the 1-penny, the "P" of POSTAGE and the "Y" of PENNY almost are touching the lateral tablet edge; the base of the "P" has corners cut off on the left; in the 6-pence, the blank triangle above POSTAGE and PENCE was embellished, as in the 3-pence circle, by color dividing lines.

Forgeries: the center background shading lines are touching the circle and the crown's base is rounded. Set (a) The three values have the same circle design! 1-penny, 18½–¾ x 22 mm; the "P" is touching the tablet edge; 2-pence, 22½ mm high; 6-pence, almost 23 mm high; imperforate or dot rouletted, 14½ to 15½ mm. (b) 1-penny, crown design that is just as bad and fifty-two pearls instead of sixty. (c) Bad copy of the 1-penny (see the illustration); bottom inscription letters are almost all touching the tablet; height, 22½ mm, perf 11. (d) 6-pence, the bottom of the crown is rounded; the center background hexagon is there, but only four sides of it can be seen, the horizontal shade lines of the other sides not having been reinforced. In Type "a," the forged cancellation is a quadruple circle with six bars inside or a barred circle; Type "c," large, heavy bars

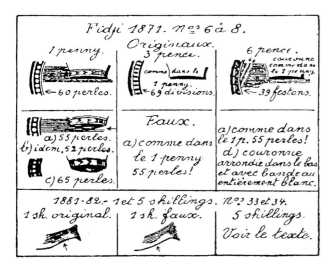

Fiji. 1871. Nos. 6–8. Originals. 1-penny, 60 pearls; 3-pence, as in the 1-penny, 69 division marks; 6-pence, crown as in the 1-penny, 39 scallops. Middle left: forgeries. (a) 55 pearls, (b) 52 pearls, (c) 65 pearls. Middle center: (a) as in the 1-penny, 55 pearls! Middle right: (a) as in the 1-penny, 55 pearls! (d) bottom of crown rounded and with entirely blank bandeau. Bottom: 1881–82. 1- and 5-shilling. Nos. 33 and 34. 1-shilling original; 1-shilling forgery; 5-shilling, see text.

spaced about 4 mm apart. Note: The three original values are found imperforate, but they are printer's proofs that were never issued; the same may be said for the following overprinted issues.

Types overprinted "C.R." (1872–77). Nos. 9 to 24. First of all, determine whether previous forgeries with forged overprints are involved. With respect to originals, overprint comparison becomes necessary. The "V.R." overprints were especially well counterfeited; expertizing is necessary if reliable originals are not available. The ornamental lettering type was counterfeited in Geneva without dots after the letters.

1878–80. "V.R." Nos. 25 to 32. These stamps were reproduced from stamp Nos. 1–3, with letter changes. Further discussion seems unnecessary.

1881–82. Large format. 1- and 2-shilling. Nos. 32 to 34. *1- shilling, original:* typographed; 27 mm high; perf 10; 11 x 10; 11 or 11 x 11¾.

Forgery: typographed in Geneva in blocks of sixteen (4 x 4), very deceptive; the shading lines at the base of the neck are not congruent and there is a very large blank space forming a spot; 26¾ mm high; on the right and left, outside the stamp, one often sees a very fine line created by excessive indention; perf 11 x 11; 11 x 11½; forged cancellation, one circle: NAOPOPIPOR 5 MAR 1902 FIJI.

5-shilling, original: lithographed on tinted paper; perf 10; there are eleven pearls above FIJI, the last one of which on the left is touching the value figure framework; the center shade is salmon pink.

Forgery: (a) typographed; bad copy; the eleventh pearl is not touching the frame of the "5"; the center is pink; perf 11½ x 11; moreover, the portrait is surrounded by a full, unbroken line; (b) another counterfeit was made in black-gray and orange; perf 10; 11¾; imperforate; very well executed (clandestine imprint?); its cancellation is open 15 DEC 00.

5-shilling, originals: (1) lithographed with COWAN watermark over the width of the five stamps; (2) typographed; the lower left star is touching the value inscription frame; watermarked NEW SOUTH WALES GOVERNMENT.

Finland

I. Imperforate Stamps

1856. Oval format. Wove paper. Nos. 1 and 2. These stamps were printed by the Finnish Treasury in sheets of ten in two rows arranged horizontally in tête-bêche fashion. Only about 120,000 copies of the 5-kopeck stamp were issued, in two printings. In the second, somewhat rarer printing (20M, 25U), the horn pearls are larger, especially the one on the left. Some

400,000 copies of the 10-kopeck were issued. The stamps are typographed (letterpress printed).

Select: for this issue, a select stamp is rectangular, with about 2 mm on each side.

Cancellations: rectangular or circular postmarks with city name and date are most frequently encountered. All others are rare.

Pen cancellations: 5-kopeck: fifty percent of the usual price; 10-kopeck: forty percent of the usual price. A stamp that is both pen canceled and regularly postmarked is worth the full price.

Pairs: rare.

Reprints: 1862, 1872: white paper, different shades, no gum. 1893: lithographed, same characteristics, thin, white gum. The 5-kopeck large-pearl type belongs to the second printing.

Fakes: these have been made by trimming envelopes. The 1856 envelope has pearls in the horns, but the paper is laid diagonally with wire marks 1²/₃ mm apart; other envelopes have no pearls in the horns; they are on wove paper like the original stamps, and there is good reason to avoid them when the cancellation is applied over the two pearls.

One finds fine tête-bêche pairs that have been made from separate stamps. These can be identified by examining the back of the stamps.

Early forgeries: on various kinds of paper (bluish white for the 5-kopeck, also), amateurishly executed and easily recognizable by comparing designs. The shield point does not fall in the middle of the angle formed by the openings of the mouths of the horns; sometimes there is no dot after the "1" on the right, no dots at all, or else round instead of lozenge-shaped dots; the third letter of KOP (on the right side of the stamp) is the Russian character for "P" not joined at top; pearl, horn, and crown designs differ from the originals. Forged lithographed stamps obviously don't show the "bite" that is typical of typographed (letterpress-printed) stamps. There are various forged cancellations, including pen cancellations.

Modern forgeries are known from various sources. These have many major design errors: the closed mouth of the lion formed by a single heavy line; an ape-like or bird-like head; a caudal appendage that differs from the original; etc. As an example, one can mention the Geneva (F.) forgeries, a few defects of which are shown in the illustration.

The 5-kopeck was honored by two different clichés. The first one (for the 5- and 10-kopeck) has small pearls, all of them with an inside dot or with a line passing through them; the second cliché (5-kopeck, second printing) has the large round pearls, but also certain defects that are shown in the illustration.

Forged cancellations: on Geneva forgeries: double circle (9 and 27 mm in diameter), HELSINGFORS,

with year date in the center; rectangular cancellation (36 x 11 mm), HELSINGFORS, without year date; same type (23 x 16), WIBORG 11-1 (date done rather inexpertly).

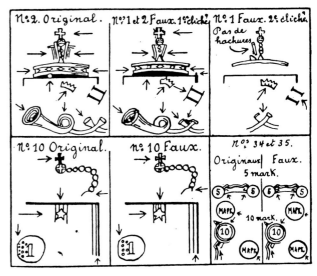

Finland. Top: No. 2. Original. Nos. 1 and 2 forgeries. 1st cliché. No. 1 forgeries. 2nd cliché; no shading. Bottom: No. 10. Original. Forgeries. Nos. 34 and 35. Originals. Forgeries. 5- and 10-mark.

II. Serpentine Rouletted Stamps

1860. Typographed stamps. Nos. 3 and 4. Paper: thin or average. Values in kopecks.

Select: well-centered stamps with all their "teeth."

Rouletting: two types: I, depth about 1¼ mm; II, about 1³/₄ mm (see illustration). 10-kopeck, Type II: 2M, 50U.

Varieties: 10-kopeck, thick paper: 3M, 3U; bâtonné paper, watermarked with parallel lines 8 mm apart: rare; 5-kopeck, milky, imperforate vertically: rare.

Pairs: rare in good condition because of the fragility of the rouletting.

Cancellations: small and large single circle postmarks with date; rectangle, narrow or wide, with city name and date; pen cancellations; all others: rare.

Reprints: 1893. Lithographed; thin paper. 5-kopeck pale blue; 10-kopeck bright rose. Thin gum. Type I rouletting. Slight differences in the inscriptions. Value: 3 francs.

Fakes: white, chemically bleached paper. The genuine 10-kopeck was printed on thick paper that was very slightly tinted.

Early forgeries: these are so bad that they do not deserve description.

1866–71. Typographed stamps. Nos. 5 to 12. Penni and markka values. *Select:* stamps that are centered.

Rouletting: Types I–IV (see illustration). Type III has a denticulation depth of 2 mm or more; Type IV, spatulate-shaped perforations, has a depth of 1.5 or 1.7 mm. The fine perf 10½ is extremely rare.

Values of the roulettes: 5-penni, Type III: common; Type I: 25M, 50U; Type III: 10M, 10U. Laid paper, Type III: common. Type II: 2M, 2U; Type I: 4M, 5U. Very thick laid papers are found: usual price, except Type III: 2M, 2U.

8-penni, Type III: common; Type II: 50M, used common; Type I: 3M, used common. The 10½ perforation is very rare. The three types are found on vertically ribbed paper; Type II: usual price; Type I: price doubled; Type III: mint, price doubled; used, tripled.

10-penni, Types I, II, III: same prices; Type I, however, is less common used; laid paper, Type II: common; Type I: 3M, 4U. All three types are found on very thick wove paper; Type II: same value; Type I: 6M, 3U; Type III: 3M, 2U.

20-penni, Type III: common; Type II: same; Type I: 3M, 2U; Type IV: very rare mint, and 12U.

40-penni, Types II and III: common; Type I: 8M, 4U; Type IV: very rare mint, and 50U. Ribbed papers (Types I–III) are common. Perf 10½ or 10½ x 8 is very rare.

1-markka, Type III: common; Type II: 25M, 25U.

Cancellations: with date, single- or double circle, in black or blue: common; large rectangular postmark: less common; narrow rectangle: 50U. FRANCO on one line: rare.

Pairs: 4M, 4U; strips and blocks: rare.

Reprints: 1893. Lithographed on wove, nonstriated paper. Different, paler shades: 5-penni, bistre-lilac; 8-penni, yellow-green paper; 10-penni, dark yellow, not ochre-yellow; 20-penni, blue; 40-penni, carmine-rose; 1-markka, light brown. Slightly different inscriptions. Value: 3 francs; the 1-markka: 8 francs.

Early forgeries: very crude. One 8-penni has twenty-seven vertical hatch lines instead of twenty-three, and sixty-four pearls instead of 106, etc. The 10-penni black on yellow was photoengraved; the design is too sharply etched, the dimensions too large.

Modern forgeries: the whole set, including the 10-penni error, is hardly more impressive than the preceding ones. Compare the crown design: there is a double-lined cross in the original penni values; the globe has unbroken horizontal and vertical lines at the top; the vertical line is missing in the 20-penni. Compare also the shield, fretwork, and inscription designs.

Special mention must be accorded the 1-markka Geneva (F.) forgery, which is a remarkable photolithographed achievement. The illustration gives information on its defects. Forged cancellations on this forgery include: rectangular, medium format WIBORG; single circle, with date, small postmark in black and blue NYSLOTT 21 10-5 71; single circle, with date, large postmark, HELSINGFORS 2 1876 I.

III. Perforated Stamps

1875. Figures in four corners. Nos. 13 to 20.
Shades: numerous: No. 14, dull pale red; No. 14a, bright red; No. 15, yellow-brown (dark brown: rare); No. 15a, always brown or dark brown; No. 17, rose; No. 17a, dark carmine; No. 18, always in a dark shade; No. 18a, pale shade; 8-penni, dark transparent green: rare.

Varieties: perf 11 on the left side and 13½ on the other three sides: rare; 1-markka tête-bêche with 1½ cm space between stamps: rare; "taller" stamps can be found (No. 13a); various values have a vertical line in the side margin; the 32-penni is found on medium, thick, thin, and transparent paper.

Cancellations: framed, with city name and date; same, with FR. KO: in demand; circle with six bars or large square dots (nine or twenty-five); circle with twelve small dots inside; other dotted circles. In addition, cancellations with date, blue cancellations, ordinary cancellations.

Reprints: 1893. Perf 12½ 8-penni, dark green; 10-penni, brown; 20-penni, blue; 25-penni, carmine; 52-penni, rose and carmine; shades and gums differ from originals.

Forgeries: 1-markka: crude design. Compare with original.

Fakes of perforations have been found on large-format originals, and on a 1-markka essay, with a wrong shade.

1884. Same as 1875. Color change. Nos. 21 to 27.
Perf 12½; the 5-penni emerald is not common used; the 25-penni on laid paper is rare; the 5- and 25-penni are found with shaded lion.

Reprints: none.

Genoa forgeries (I.): 1-, 5-, and 10-markka. Inscription MARKKA instead of MARKKAA immediately identifies the 5- and 10-markka forgeries. With respect to the 1-markka and the penni values (tête-bêche of the 5- and 20-penni), the photolithographic impression was not very successful. The upper right star of the shield is shapeless; the lion's tail, which ends in a plait, is unique; the saber, which looks like a stick, is truncated in some examples; the shapeless burelage is especially characteristic of these forgeries. Perf 11 or 13½ with small holes.

1889–95. Numerals at top only. Nos. 28 to 35. The fine 12½ perforation is common. The poorly executed perforation is rare. The 20-penni orange, imperforate vertically, is rare. Typographed.

Shades are numerous. The 5-penni olive, 20-penni yellow, and 25-penni blue are rare perf 12½: 2M, 3U.

Forgeries: look at a few expertizing points of the 5- and 10-markka originals in the illustration. The photolithographed forgeries don't resemble the originals; examination of the background burelage will provide sufficient evidence of forgery. The saber often rests on the crown instead of going through it; the stars are shapeless; the background is composed of uniform dots with a few vertical lines. Compare with an authentic 1-markka, and verify the inscriptions, too, especially those at the bottom.

Forged cancellations in German, Finnish, and Russian.

1891. Russian stamp types. Nos. 36 to 48. *Official forgeries:* a few current values and the 1-ruble. No watermark; infantile design; crude line drawing: rare.

Geneva forgeries (F.): 3½- and 7-ruble. 3½-ruble black and yellow; also, 3½-ruble black and gray on vertically laid paper. The latter, however, is not well known. Russian stamps, including the 3½- and 7-ruble without thunderbolts of the 1883 issue (Nos. 36, 36a, and 37), and those of 1889–1904 (Nos. 50, 50a, 51, and 51a) also were counterfeited.

In general, they look like very successful counterfeits, but the laid lines of the paper are spaced only 1.5 mm apart, compared to spacing of approximately 1.8 mm in the originals. No wavy line watermark. One laid line per stamp is perpendicular to the others, thus proving that a commercial paper was used. These laid lines were the principal argument in favor of the belief that these were authentic marginal copies, but the spacing of the laid lines surely destroys that legend, which was based on insufficient observation. A few of these forgeries were occasionally provided with a forged bold wavy line. This is all too visible when the stamp is dry, but it disappears almost completely when it is immersed in watermarking fluids.

The second frame of the double inner frame of the Finnish forgeries is thicker; the "W" shaped ornaments around the center oval are not as wide as in the originals; the pearls and the inscriptions are blurred; in the 3.50-ruble, the curl at the base of the "Y" is too far from the head of the letter. Perf 13¼.

Forged cancellations: I. On stamps of Finland, double circle, German model cancels:

1. KUOPIO I IV 83 I KYONIO (error — it should be KYONIO).

2. WIBORG WIIPURI (same error). 11. XI. 87. 9 1 BBIBOPFB.

3. HELSINGFORS HELSINKI 5. III. 00. FEABCNHIOOPCB (third error).

These three postmarks, engraved on wood, were applied to Brussels forgeries of Nos. 34 and 35. Thus do forgeries help one another!

II. On Russian stamps:

1. Single circle (26 mm) ATBHBI 7 HOA 18.

2. Double circle (25 mm) CMETE PBPFB 21 MAR 1888.

3. Single circle (25 mm) MOCKBA 11/12 AEB 1888 HMKOAHC.

1901–16. Values in pennia and markkaa. Nos. 49 to 60. *Official forgeries:* 10- and 20-penni, better executed than the preceding ones. Compare designs, particularly burelage, perforation, and format.

Forgeries: 10-markka. The Geneva (F.) counterfeit of typographed No. 60, with the letter "K" of MARKKAA open at the bottom, is best. Photolithographed on the same paper as the 3.50- and 7-ruble forgeries of the preceding issue. The absence of a watermark is quite natural here, because there is none in the originals (in a previous article, we had declared mistakenly that this forgery is identified by the absence of a watermark; let us hope that this misinformation does not make the rounds of the philatelic press); the oblique stroke of the numeral "1" is too short, and the serifs are more or less drowned in the background color. Perf 13¾.

1918. Mesa. Nos. 83 to 90. The imperforate stamps are reprints.

Helsingfors locals. The 10-penni in brown and blue; green and red shades are not well reproduced; stippled lozenge cancellation (see F. Serrane, "Faux de Finlande," *Philatéliste belge,* No. 54 [March 15, 1926]: 115–19).

Fiume

The Fiume collection includes many pretty stamps, but, unfortunately, it also has many, many overprints. Obviously, the average collector should abstain, because professional specialization is needed to cope with this situation.

1919. Overprinted Hungarian stamps. Nos. 1 to 28. The whole set (especially Nos. 1 to 23) was well counterfeited several times, including overprint varieties. So-called "original reprints" of Nos. 1–23 were sold all but openly (with offers in most of the philatelic journals): "Original reprints [of the overprint] with postal cancellation [are sold by everybody as perfectly authentic stamps] *[sic]* at 20 lire for the set, a minimum of five sets [for each customer]"!

This is the work of Genoa (Sestri Ponente); the overprinted set forged in Geneva is good, but the ink is too grayish, etc. Comparative study is necessary. (The overprint reproduced in the Yvert catalogue of 1926 is an example of bad overprinting: letters "M" and "E" joined at bottom; median bars of "F" and "E" halfway up the downstroke.)

No reprints, nor any subsequent issues.

1919. Overprinted postage due Hungarian stamps. Nos. 29 to 31. Forged overprints. Comparison is necessary.

1919. Fiume legend. Nos. 32 to 48. *Trieste forgeries:* Nos. 32–41 were photoengraved in sets of 50,000. This suggests that these common stamps find their way into collections under false pretenses. There are few differences in design, but the paper and gum are too white. In the originals, the paper is yellowish white and the gum is thick and yellowish.

The 10-corona also was well counterfeited, along with, probably, all of the flag-type values, Nos. 42–48. Photolithographed in small sheets of ten. Hairline above the "10" on the right, and the frame reinforced below this figure (flaws from the photographic cliché?); the white line that frames the escutcheon is visible only on the left, above; lack of hatch marks in the left border of the sailor's collar; the ear forms a white point instead of a half-oval; etc.

Subsequent issues. All rare overprints and overprint varieties were counterfeited more or less well. The following may be mentioned: the PRO FONDATIONE STUDIO inverted overprints (1919); likewise, FRANCO inverted overprints; Nos. 124–31 and the overprint varieties of that set (1920); the 1-lira GOVERNO PROVVISORIO (1921); Nos. 182–93 (1924); Nos. 3 and 4 special delivery stamps (the "S" should not have the horizontal bar of the postage stamp overprint); postage due stamps (first issue); and, finally, all Arbe and Veglia stamps. Detailed comparison with the originals is indispensable.

Formosa

1887. A large format stamp, 33 x 77 mm, is very rare. It is typographed in red and black.

1885. Perf 14. Nos. 1 to 3. *Originals:* 30½ x 32 mm, engraved; all details, especially the wavy background, the dragon and horse designs, are executed with the utmost finesse.

Forgeries: 29½ x 30½ mm; wavy background lines that are almost straight; irregular pearls with a single dot in the middle; crude design; etc.

France

I. Imperforate Stamps

Issue of 1849–50. Tinted paper. Nos. 1 to 7. *Sheets* of 300 stamps, typographed. Ceres portrait.

Select examples are those with four margins, minimum width ½ mm. Four margins, 1 mm wide: 2U.

Shades: the following are in demand: 15-centime yellow-green on yellowish green; 20-centime black on rosy white: 5U; black on dark buff: 50U; gray-black (more gray than black): 5–10U; 25-centime blue on white, dull blue, blue-black; 40-centime vermilion-orange: 25U; orange-red, almost brick red: 50U; 1-franc claret: 50U; cherry red: 2U.

Varieties: small printing defects in lettering, figures, dots, etc., along with printing blemishes. Priced according to the importance of the defect. Backgrounds lined horizontally or vertically. The 20-centime on pelure paper: 10U; the dark buff on thicker paper; grayish paper on the back side. The deep black stamp is in demand: 50U. The 25-centime, silky paper, very slightly striated, *solé,* thin: in demand; pelure paper and ordinary, distinctly transparant paper: 10U.

Retouching of the 40-centime stamp is recognized by the oblique bar of the "4," which is 1⅓ mm long instead of 1¼ mm, by the angle it forms with the horizontal bar (forty-five degrees instead of seventy degrees), and by the horizontal bar itself, which extends ¼ mm farther beyond the vertical downstroke than in the unretouched type.

Fine impressions exist, especially of the 20-centime deep black and the 25-centime blue on yellowish: 2U. They may be recognized by the facial shading and by the burelage dots, all of them executed with considerable expertise.

Pairs are worth two and one-third to three times a single stamp, according to the rarity of the stamp; blocks of four, mint, five to six times a single, except the 15-centime green: very rare, used; 10-centime: 5U; 15-centime: 12U; 20-centime: 30U; 25-centime: 80U; 40-centime: 10U; 1-franc: 12U.

On cover: not much increase in value for the 20- and 25-centime stamps; others: 25U.

Cancellations: Types A, B, C are common, except Type B on the 20-centime: 6U, and Type C on the 15-centime: 10U, and on the 20-centime: 6U. Type C, without numerals, is rare (see French Colonies).

Dated cancellations on all values are rare; on the 20-centime, small (thimble) cancel: 3–8U; average size: 5–8U; large: 8–30U. Cancellation Types E, F, and G are in demand; Type G on 20-centime: 5U.

All cancellations in blue and red are rare, and all cancellations of a different pattern are very rare. Consult the specialty catalogues.

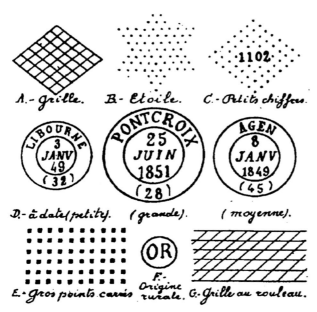

Cancellations found on the imperforate issues of France, Nos. 1 to 18. A. Grill. B. Star. C. Small numerals. D. Datestamp — small, large, medium. E. Large square dots. F. Rural origin. G. Roller grill.

Reprints (1862): the 10-centime: bistre (ochre) shade without visible yellow or brown always appears much paler than the originals; width 18¼ mm (originals are 18½ mm).

The 15-centime: bright light green on less tinted paper, which can be seen by comparing the burelaged areas of the corners and the white parts of the face; height 22 mm or a little less (originals are 22¼ mm).

The 20-centime: heavier, grayish paper (never yellowish or white); height 22⅖ to 22½ mm (originals are 22¼ to 22⅓ mm, according to which plate they are from).

The 25-centime: blue or rather bright blue; height 22⅖ to 22½ mm (originals are 22⅙ to 22¼ mm).

The 40-centime: orange shade that seems dull beside the original orange; paper less tinted; general appearance of a worn plate, details of the corner burelage and of the eye shading, not very visible; height 22⅓ rnm (originals are 22¼ mm).

The 1-franc: very close to the original shade, dark carmine; height 22⅖ to 22½ mm (originals are 22¼ mm).

The printing of the reprints is rather fine, and they have transparent gum. In the originals, the gum is brown and thicker. Color is well-distributed in the reprints, whereas it generally is thicker in the originals — see especially the center background. Printer's waste exists in the form of trial sheets of the 20-centime, thin paper, gray shade on the back.

Originals: the delicacy of design of these well-printed stamps is impressive; it facilitates the identification of all poorly executed forgeries; comparison of the burelaged areas in the corners, particularly the lower left corner, will provide sufficient evidence. In the originals, the wavy lines, which are finely drawn, form three arcs along the side of the fretwork; the dots between these lines, which are finely drawn, touch them only in printings that are less well done. See the accompanying illustration.

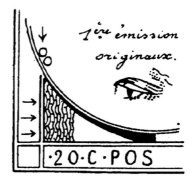

First issue. Original. The delicacy of the design facilitates identification of the originals.

The white line dividing the burelage from the lower left fretwork ornament points toward the middle of a pearl; the large pearls are so close together that they occasionally touch; in general, quite a few of them touch the white circle. The shadows of the eye are formed by fine dotted lines: four lines and one dot on the temple above the eyebrows, three lines under the right juncture of the eyelids.

If you look at the design very carefully, you will notice that the "C" of FRANC is connected with the bottom of the tablet by a small white line, which is visible especially in the 20-, 25-, and 40-centime, at times in the 1-franc, rarely in the 15-centime stamps, when the printing is not clogged or blurred; you will also see a small curvilinear line, beginning above the right foot of the "R" of FRANC, which rises as it goes around the bottom of the upper loop of the letter. This is visible in the 25-centime, sometimes in the 40-centime, more rarely in the other values. The inner frame of the 20-centime has a break above the right side of the "2" on the left. One should remember this when scrutinizing a good forgery of the 20-centime tête-bêche.

These three characteristic features may be considered as secret marks useful in expertizing. See the illustration "Originals of 1849."

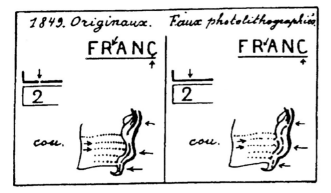

Originals of 1849 compared with photolithographic forgeries.

Finally, it will be observed that the fifth shadow line of the neck is the only one that goes as far as the Adam's apple and that it is curved; the two lines below it are made up of double dots near the hair, on the right.

There are eighteen grapes in the bunch (sixteen in the Bordeaux issue), and ninety-seven pearls around the center background.

Fakes: one finds forged cancellations — especially rare cancellations — on reprints as well as on 20-centime originals. The 15-centime reprint was worked over in various ways, and the paper was slightly tinted to make a new stamp. Likewise, the 1-franc carmine was darkened to make a No. 6b carmine-brown, or else bleached and repainted in vermilion.

Among the fabricated fakes, the tête-bêche stamps made from two units must be mentioned. Postmark traces on lightly canceled originals were scratched out; then the backs of the stamps were reinforced to conceal the places that had been thinned by the scraping process; finally, the new creations were regummed.

The figures of the 40-centime retouched stamp were doctored. A look through a magnifying glass will show this.

Forgeries: all values were lithographically forged several times, including tête-bêche copies of the 10-, 15-(!), 25-centime black, 25-centime blue, 40-centime (!), and 1-franc carmine and vermilion. The 40-centime was counterfeited with retouched figures. For identification, see the illustration in which "Originals of 1849" and "Photolithographed Forgeries" are compared. Neither the dimensions nor the shades of these forgeries are congruent with the originals.

Forged lithographed set: this is very deceptive; recognized experts have been fooled by it. Nevertheless, it is easily identified (good shades, good paper thickness) by the various distinctive features shown in the illustrations, particularly by the design

of the neck line (third and fourth shade lines), and by the design of the hair.

It may also be observed that in the laurel frond behind the head, the center vein of the leaf under the laurel berry is sectioned (small broken line near the point); this appears only rarely in the originals. Also, the "C" of FRANC is not curved enough at the top, and it is slanted too much. Finally, the design as seen through a magnifying glass appears to be less sharp. The cheek and neck dots are fuzzier, and many burelage dots touch the wavy lines. Measurements: width $18^{1}/_{2}$ mm; height $22^{3}/_{5}$ mm, with very few differences, depending on stamp values.

Forged cancellations on forgeries: one finds noncongruent grills, stars, small numerals, and, on the vermilion, a small dated postmark, PARIS 23 JANVIER 49 (60), etc.

Unissued stamps: the 1-franc pale vermilion, called "Vervelle," which probably came from a sheet that was rejected because of its shade or that was a color trial. The 20-centime blue or dark blue on lightly tinted paper, or blue on azure. width $18^{1}/_{2}$ mm, height $22^{1}/_{5}$ mm. The reprint of this stamp has the same blue shade of the 25-centime reprint ($18^{1}/_{3}$ mm x $22^{1}/_{4}$ mm).

Issue of 1852. minted paper. Nos. 9 and 10.
Inscription: REPUB-FRANC. The "B" is under the neck.

Sheets and margins: as above.

Shades: the 10-centime bistre-yellow, bistre-brown, dark bistre-brown.

Varieties: lined backgrounds: 3U; 10-centime, with dividing frame line in the margin: 2U; 25-centime: 6U; the 25-centime is found on grayish or slightly greenish paper rather than bluish paper; thin, transparent paper: 2U; 10-centime, very thick paper: rare.

Pairs: 3M, 3U; blocks of four, 10-centime: extremely rare; 25-centime, mint: 300 francs, used: 125 francs; 10-centime on cover: 25U.

Cancellations: Type C: common; Types B and E: in demand; Type A, 10-centime: 2U; 25-centime 10U; Type D, 10-centime: 2U; 25-centime: 20U; Type F. 10-centime: 2U; 25-centime: rare; Type G: 2U; Type H (large numerals) on 25-centime: very rare; Type A (occupation of Rome) on 10-centime: 2U. (See these types in the following issue.)

All cancellations are rare in color.

Reprints: the 10-centime is unadulterated bistre, without yellow or brown, and seems paler than all the original shades; width, $18^{1}/_{5}$ mm instead of $18^{1}/_{2}$ mm; the 25-centime is rather dark blue on yellowish gray; width, $18^{1}/_{4}$ mm instead of $18^{2}/_{5}$ to $18^{1}/_{2}$ mm.

Originals: comparison with a common 25-centime, especially the burelage, will adequately reveal the 10-centime forgery. The original has eighty-eight pearls.

Fakes: the 10-centime reprint with an Italian grill or other cancellation. When the top tablet, from a scrap of a 10-centime, was added to a repaired 10-centime of the following issue, the result was enough to open one's eyes; the collector will not be surprised to notice that the letter "B" under the neck is missing.

Forgeries: the 10-centime was very amateurishly counterfeited (fretwork ornaments, white lines under the top tablet, and, above the bottom one, doubly thick lines, etc.). Forged cancellation with a square (!) of large dots with average-sized numeral "23." A modern Paris photolithographed forgery can easily be analyzed by comparing it with a 25-centime (eye and cheek shading, dimensions).

Issue of 1853–60. Nos. 11 to 18. *Inscription:* EMPIRE FRANÇAIS.

Sheets and margins: as above.

Shades: the 1-centime bronze-green is the shade in which yellow is predominant; the paper is greenish gray, whereas with the other shades it is definitely bluish. The 5-centime light green (blue-green without a trace of yellow) is rare: 2U. The 10-centime yellow-brown shade on off-yellow is not very common. The 20-centime, the stamp on greenish paper, appears in two shades: blue on light greenish (first printing) and dark blue on more accentuated greenish (second printing, rarer). The 25-centime is not very common in dark blue.

The 40-centime, numerous shades; buff paper coloration comes from a brown gum. The 80-centime rose, from pale (50U) to dark; gooseberry red: 2U; pale to dark carmine, pale carmine (50U); garnet is a bright, warm-toned, dark carmine (2U); vermilion-tinted carmine is rare (10U); rose-carmine is a bright shade of rose containing some carmine; rose-tinted paper (rosy white instead of thicker yellowish white); the coloration of the buff paper (80-centime carmine) comes from the gum. The bleached 40-centime exists in brown and black-brown, and the 80-centime, in all purplish blue shades (less value).

Varieties: the 1- to 80-centime and the 5-franc stamps have horizontal lines in the background. Vertical lines are rare. A few values exist on thick paper (80–90 microns); 1-centime: 3U; 20-centime on azure: 10U 80-centime: 3U; thin paper: not very common; printing flaws. The 5-, 10-, and 20-centime are rare with dividing frame line in margin; 5-centime: 10M, 2U; 10-centime: 2M, 10U; 20-centime: 5M, 2 franc, used; major stamp values, twenty-five to fifty percent increment; 40-centime, striated paper: not very common.

On cover: the 1-centime: 2U; the 5-centime and 1-franc: 50U. Split stamps (20-centime, half of the 40-centime, and 10-centime, half of the 20-centime) and the 80-centime printed on both sides or with double

impression are exceedingly rare. The 80-centime is rare with control mark in the bottom corner of the sheet.

Unofficial perforations: see the specialty catalogues.

Pairs: mint: 3M; but 80-centime: 4M, used: 3U; 20-centime on azure or milky blue: 5-francs; 40-centime: 10U; 80-centime: 5U. Blocks of four: 6M, except the 25- and 80-centime: 8-10M, used: 8U, except the 10-centime: 10 francs; 20-centime: 5 francs; 40- and 80-centime: 100 francs.

Pairs on cover: the 1-centime: 2U; the 10- and 20-centime are common; the rest: 25U.

Retouched stamp (Delacourcelle). the 25-centime: deformed cross-like designs at top; the inscription EMPIRE FRANC is printed in lightface type; the ascending oblique stroke of the "M" is formed with two lines; the "M" and "T" are not as high as the other letters; the right downstroke of the "R" is touching the white line below it; the top bar of the "F" of FRANC is half as long as it should be; the "A" is touching the white line above; the "N" is not as wide as in the original. The top of the cliché is quite worn.

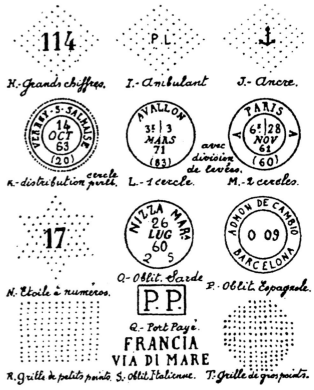

Additional cancellations found on Nos. 1–18.
**H. Large numerals. I. Traveling post office.
J. Anchor. K. Pearled circle. L./M. With mail collection numbers. N. Star with numerals.
O. Sardinian cancellation. P. Spanish cancellation.
Q. Post paid. R. Small-dot grill. S. Italian cancellation. T. Large-dot grill.**

Cancellations: Type C: common (on the 1-centime: 25U); Type D (small): common on the 1- and 5-centime; Type B: rare on the 1-centime; Types A, E, F, G: rare; Type H: common, except on the 1-centime: 50U, and on the 80-centime carmine: rare, 10U. Grill cancellations, Types R, T, and similar types; foreign cancellations, Types O, P, S, etc.; Sardinian cancellations, and those of military expeditionary forces, ships, and from the Levant are in demand or rare. Consult the Yvert catalogue, *France and Colonies.*

Reprints: the 25-centime in bright dark blue on well-tinted paper; width, $18^{1}/_{4}$ mm (originals measure $18^{1}/_{2}$ mm). The 1-franc is much closer to the original, and reprints are found that have been signed by the best experts. The easiest way to expertize is to measure the width, which, to repeat, is $18^{1}/_{2}$ mm in the originals and $18^{1}/_{4}$ mm in the reprints.

The paper of the reprints is grayer, the printing finer. The burelage dots and the burelage itself are more clearly defined, more visible; the almost vertical thin line that parallels the outer ear for about a millimeter is separated from it. This is not the case in the original.

Reprints of the 80-centime exist, but I have never seen any.

Originals: in the first issue, they can be identified by the delicacy of the burelage and by the shading on the face. Compare with a well-printed 80-centime stamp.

Used postal forgeries (Bayonne): the 20-centime: $22^{2}/_{3}$ mm high instead of 22 to $22^{1}/_{4}$ mm; greenish blue; noncongruent burelage; inscriptions likewise; dots in the bottom tablet missing: very rare. The 20-centime was photolithographically counterfeited in Toulouse (P.). The format differs from that of the original; comparative study is necessary.

Forgeries: the 1-franc:

1. Early, well-executed forgery, but it has a "1 FR" (reminiscent of a previous forgery of the first issue?) instead of a "1 F."

2. Geneva forgeries (F.), $18 \times 21^{4}/_{5}$ mm (original: $18^{1}/_{2} \times 22^{1}/_{4}$ mm); very unsuccessful burelage, especially in the upper left corner (breaks in the fourth and fifth wavy lines; inner frame line broken and too thick); value tablet protuberance above the vertical downstroke of the "F." A second cliché of the same stamp ($18^{1}/_{2} \times 22$ mm) corrects these gross defects, but leaves untouched all the other design blemishes (crude burelage, excessively heavy line under the eye, etc.). It was counterfeited as a tête-bêche.

3. Marseilles forgeries. Well-executed in carmine-red on yellowish paper, $18^{1}/_{4} \times 22^{1}/_{4}$ mm; photolithographically reproduced from a reprint. The excessively thick inner line of the outer ear joins the vertical line seen in the reprint. Figure "1" on the left is slanted to the left; the long goatee hair on the right

has only just begun to grow up above; the lower line of the eye itself is full and heavy as in the Geneva forgeries (dotted in the reprints and broken midway in the originals). Finally, the dots under the neck are small and round (almost like the reprint), but they are almost invisible in the left half (of the neck). These dots are always visible in the originals, and, especially on the right, they look like inverted incisors.

Fakes: the paper of the 20-centime has been chemically doctored to obtain greenish, lilac, or rose-colored paper shade varieties; comparison of shades is indicated. The reprints of the 15-centime and 1-franc stamps often have forged cancellations. Geneva forgeries are canceled with a dot lozenge small numeral "1032," a forged postmark also used for the first-issue forgeries of Greece.

Fakes have been created by fitting together portions of various issues to make a 25-centime, the 1-franc as a single stamp, or the 1-franc tête-bêche. Like all rebuilt stamps, they can be recognized.

To make the 1-franc tête-bêche, the faker joined together two 80-centime carmine stamps of the same issue, lower portions of defective originals of the 1-franc, or portions of forgeries. The faked tête-bêche of the 80-centime was formed from two stamps. However, it also has been made from a pair. The printed image was scraped off of one stamp, then a thinned original was affixed to the front of the stamp in an inverted position. Such fakes have no value whatsoever; their authors should be prosecuted for fraudulent misrepresentation of the merchandise offered for sale.

II. Perforated Stamps

To merit a highest-quality rating, all perforated stamps must be perfectly centered.

Cancellations are very numerous and it would take too long to give a detailed description of them here. The specialist will try to obtain all of those that are somewhat unusual. He will become aware of the rarity of a few of them only after long experience.

1862. Empire without laurel crown. Nos. 19 to 24. There are a few shade varieties. The 80-centime purplish blue resulted from bleaching. Well-centered stamps are not common.

Varieties: defective impressions are in demand. Stamps with horizontal lines in the background are worth about 5 francs; with vertical lines, 10 francs. The 1-centime on very thick paper is rare. The 80-centime is known to exist with burelage doubled at the bottom right. The 20-centime exists in pairs imperforate between.

Pairs: 3M, 3U, except the 40-centime: 6U.

Blocks of four: 5–6M, except the 10-centime: 12M, and the 80-centime: 8M; 1-, 5-, and 10-centime, used:

4 francs; 20-centime: 2 francs; 40- and 80-centime: 25 francs.

On cover: 1- and 80-centime: 50U. The rest are common.

Fakes: the tête-bêche stamps must be studied, for sometimes they are made from two single stamps and, consequently, they are considerably less rare and valuable!

Used postal forgeries: the 40-centime, used at Bayeux, is very rare. It can be identified by the design of the face and by the perforation.

1863–71. Empire with laurel crown. Nos. 25 to 33.
Shades are rather numerous. The 4-centime yellowish gray shade must resemble that of the 10-centime bistre-brown of 1849.

Varieties: defective impressions are in demand. The lined background, which is common in the 20-centime stamps, is rare in all other values. The 2- and 4-centime have been slightly retouched. The 2- and 80-centime are found on thick paper (rare); the 4-centime on thick, heavy paper (rare); and the 4- and 80-centime on thin, almost pelure, paper: 2U. Stamps with lined backgrounds are rare, except the 4- and 30-centime values.

There are some rather amusing plate defects:

1. The 20-centime with an animal's horn on the nose. (Before the cliché began to deteriorate, the horn did not touch the nose: very rare.) Value: 5 francs. This stamp is rare in pairs, blocks, and on cover.

2. The 20-centime with the laurel crown terminals forming a horseshoe.

3. The 20-centime with a horn on the forehead.

4. The 20-centime with white stars in the center background.

5. The 1-centime with a cigarette-shaped spot in front of the mouth, etc.

A few values are printed on the back (See and Son, etc.): rare.

The 5-franc stamp: there are four or five shades, from gray to mauve, with a like number for the "5 F." There are three varieties of the figure "5" and two of the "F" postmarks in color are rare on this stamp.

Imperforate stamps (Rothschild): these should be acquired with wide margins. Value of the set: 100 francs. A milky blue 20-centime, different from the 20-centime Rothschild, is rare (Lebaudy).

Unissued stamp: the 10-centime, with large numeral "10" in blue, No. 34.

Pairs: 3M, 3U; 30-centime: 8U; 40-centime: 16U; blocks of four, mint: 6M, except 30-, 40-, and 80-centime and 5-franc: 10M; used stamps, 1- and 2-centime: 20U; 4-centime: 10U; 10-centime: 3 francs; 20-centime: 1 franc; 30-centime: 25 francs; 40-centime: 40 francs; 80-centime: 25 francs; and 5-

franc: 10U. On cover, 10- and 20-centime: common; others: 50U.

Reprints: the 1-centime (Granet reprint), imperforate, dark bronze-green on green.

Forgeries: the 4-centime, single or tête-bêche, Toulouse forgery. Design comparison will reveal the forgery, which will be confirmed and reinforced by the arbitrariness of its perforations and format.

The 5-franc original: the leaves of the inner corner have five very distinct lobes; sixty-four pearls; the cedilla under the "C" is finely printed; in the inner frame, as in the shaded circle, the shade lines are much thicker than the white dividing lines. There are eight well-drawn, equidistant lines on the nose. The eyelid shading is almost horizontal.

The 5-franc forgery: forgeries, whether early or modern, are not congruent with the original. An early lithographed forgery on wove or laid paper has only sixty-three pearls and the leaves are shapeless. A Geneva forgery is not congruent. For example, the cedilla is as thick as the body of the letter "C" and the shade lines are incorrect throughout. In addition, the lowest of the horizontal lines at bottom left has no dots. Forged cancellation on this counterfeit: VERSAILLES 2e/28 AVRIL 71 (72).

1871. 5-centime without laurel crown. No. 35.
Printed on azure paper like that of the 1-centime of 1863–71, but with a slightly stippled appearance; green or dark green shade; the latter: 2U. Defective impression: 2U; blocks of four: 6M, 20U.

It is best to buy this stamp with a dated cancellation, checking at the same time whether it really may be a No. 25, canceled between 1862 and 1870.

1870–71. Siege of Paris. Nos. 36 to 38. These stamps were printed using the plates of the 1849 issue; the retouched 40-centime and the tête-bêche of the 10- and 20-centime are found among them.

Shades: the 40-centime yellow and dark yellow are not common. The brown shade was produced by bleaching.

Varieties: defective impressions are rare, especially the 20-centime. The 40-centime with its retouched figures often lacks a bottom dividing frame line. Pair with the two types retouched: 4U. The 10- and 20-centime with background lines are rare. Formats differ slightly depending on the plates from which they were printed.

Pairs: 3M, 3U; blocks of four: 6M; No. 36: 12U; No. 37: 3 francs; No. 38: 13 francs. On cover, 10-centime: 2U; others: 25U.

Reprints: imperforate; 10-centime, very yellow-bistre; 20-centime, very milky or dark blue. Value: 10 francs.

III. Imperforate Stamps (after 1870)

1870–71. Bordeaux. Nos. 39 to 48. The issue called "Bordeaux" truly one of the most interesting for specialization. The color and type varieties (20-centime); the lithographic, transfer, and impression varieties; and the defects are numerous. The obviously defective impressions, the eye shading, the bold white line defining the head contour, etc., invite one to engage in numerous research projects.

These lithographed stamps cannot be mistaken for those of the French issues of 1849 and colonies (1871–76), which are typographed. In case of doubt, examine the spikes at the end of the crown of grain, which protrude much less on the forehead than in those issues. Exception: the 20-centime, Type 1, the bad impression of which allows it to be classified easily.

Sheets: 300 stamps. The plate was made by laying down twenty transfer impressions from the matrix, the latter itself being obtained by the transfer of fifteen vignettes from the on-stone design (20-centime, Type I), or from the on-stone engraving (different values).

The transfer defects enable one to reconstitute the transfer block. All of the distinctive transfer features, with sufficient illustration, were published in *L'Écho de la Timbrologie* from December 15, 1922, to December 31, 1925. (See F. Serrane: I. *Stamps of the Bordeaux Issue. History, Description. Transfer Blocks. Distinctive Marks. All Shades in Color. Cancellations. Varieties. Forgeries, etc.* 190 pages. 176 sketches. 11 color plates. 40 francs [for sale by the author]. II. *The Reconstitution of the Bordeaux Plates.* 120 pages. 265 sketches. 15 francs.)

Plates: The 1-centime. Plate I. Stippled eye shading. Fine white hair contour line.

The 1-centime. Plate II. Broken line eye shading. Heavy white line.

The 1-centime. Plate III. Shading same. No white line.

The 2-centime. Unretouched plate. Transfer not stripped.

The 2-centime. Retouched plate. Transfer stripped.

The 4-centime. Unretouched plate. Color prominent inside the left vertical stroke of the figure on the right.

The 4-centime. Plate retouched. Figure on the right corrected.

The 5-centime. First state: eye very shaded.

The 5-centime. Second state: eye partly shaded.

The 10-centime. Unretouched plate. Normal inner frame.

The 10-centime. Retouched plate. Reinforced inner frame.

The 20-centime. Type I. Plate unretouched. Short oblique line connected externally to the top right frame. Gross transfer flaws uncorrected.

The 20-centime. Type I. Plate retouched. Right frame rectified. Gross transfer defects corrected.

The 20-centime. Type II. Plate I. No white contour hairline.

The 20-centime. Type II. Plate II. With white line.

The 20-centime. Type III. Plate I. Normal inner frame.

The 20-centime. Type III. Plate II. Reinforced inner frame.

The 30-centime. A single plate.

The 40-centime. A single plate.

The 80-centime. A single plate.

Value of copies from various plates: the 1-centime Plates I and II: about four times rarer than those of Plate III — double value.

The 2-centime. Stamps showing the stripped transfer are rare, but due consideration being given their rarity, only regular prices should be paid for shades; there is no reason why a supplement should be charged.

The 4-centime. Retouched-plate stamps are very rare and are worth three to four times their usual value.

The 5- and 10-centime. No supplement.

The 20-centime. Type I. Retouched plate, rare, used: 50U.

The 20-centime. Type II. No supplement.

The 20-centime. Type III. Plate I, about twenty times rarer than Plate II: 3M, 5U.

Rare shades: the 1-centime Plate I. Gray-green on gray-green paper: very rare; pale olive-gray: rare.

The 1-centime. Plate III. Very dark olive on blue paper.

The 1-centime. Plate III. Black-olive: rare. Pale off-olive-green: rare. Bronze-green, mint: very rare. Bronze-brown: rare.

The 2-centime. Transfer not stripped. Chocolate red-brown, intermediate shade: very rare. Bright brick red: very rare. Pale red-brown: rare.

The 2-centime. Transfer stripped. Dark chocolate: very rare.

The 4-centime. Plate unretouched. Dark lilac-gray: rare. Very dark gray: very rare. Gray-black: extremely rare. Yellowish gray on off-yellow: very rare.

The 4-centime. Plate retouched: still very rare.

The 5-centime. Dull gray-green (sage): rare. Emerald green (very dark blue-green): very rare. Dark green on blue: rare.

The 10-centime. Plate unretouched. Very pale bistre. Orange-brown: very rare. Light brown: very rare.

The 10-centime. Plate retouched. Lemon: extremely rare. Dark bistre-yellow: very rare. Bistre-orange: rare. Dark orange-yellow: very rare. Bistre-brown and yellow-brown: very rare.

The 20-centime. Type I. Dull blue (greenish) on off-yellow. Blue-black: extremely rare. Bright dark blue.

The shades are less varied in the retouched plate; dark blue is not common; very pale blue: very rare.

The 20-centime. Type II. Plate I. Bright dark blue. Steel blue: very rare. Sky blue: very rare. Royal blue: very rare. Dull greenish blue: very rare. Intermediate ultramarine: extremely rare.

The 20-centime. Plate II. Milky blue. Dark blue (gray or greenish). Steel blue: very rare. Intermediate ultramarine: extremely rare.

The 20-centime. Type III. Plate I. Pale blue. Dark greenish blue: very rare. Blue-gray: very rare. Intermediate ultramarine: 10 francs.

The 20-centime. Plate II. Steel blue: extremely rare. Blue-gray: very rare. Royal blue: very rare. Velvet blue: very rare. Very dark blue ("Chinese blue"): very rare. Intermediate ultramarine: very rare.

The 30-centime. Very pale brown or very dark black-brown are rare.

The 40-centime. Dark orange-yellow: rare. Dull orange-red. Bright vermilion: very rare. Intermediate blood red: very rare. Pale blood red: extremely rare. Bright red: extremely rare. Lemon(?): extremely rare.

The 80-centime. Very pale rose: very rare. Rosy red. Flesh red: very rare. Carmine shades (thin, transparent paper): very rare.

(The rare shades shown in general catalogues, which are familiar to specialists, are not mentioned here unless a particularly rare shade occurs in a plate).

The ideal comparison stamp for the ultramarine shade is the 25-centime blue and ultramarine of the 1913 Ivory Coast issue.

Varieties: transfer plate flaws, which appeared once every fifteen stamps in all printings of a plate, are in demand when they are visible and characteristic. Examples: 30-centime, the right base stroke of the "R" of REPUB is elongated; 20-centime, the Type I inner frame is broken above the "T"; 80-centime, the left branch of the "T" is missing; etc.

Transfer flaws, which occurred once in each printing of a plate of 300 stamps, are much rarer. Examples: 20-centime, Type II, Plate II, FRANE for FRANC; 30-centime, first-class impression, nose lowered right in front of the mouth; 80-centime BEPUB, or with "88" on the right; etc.

Printing flaws are interesting only when they are visible and extensive. Examples: color mishaps; printing failure; printing failure caused by paper fold-over (creating an accordion effect); partial or total double impression.

Retouched stamps: stamps that were retouched on the matrix before printing have no added value at all, because all stamps will have the retouching. Examples: scratching out of eye shading to make broken lines; reinforcement of the white contour hairline; reinforced inner frame. Retouching that was made only on a few positions (or on a single position) on the matrix are of average rarity. Examples: *very heavy* white line in the 4-, 5-, and 30-centime and in the 20-centime Type II, Plate II; retouching of the small bars in the fifth overlap line, top right; retouching of the inner left frame (5-centime).

Retouching made on the large litho stone, showing letters and frames visibly retouched, is rare. Finally, some extremely rare retouching performed on the same stone near the end of its use. Examples: 20-centime Type I, upper left overlapping entirely red one; 20-centime Type II, Plate I, same, or inner frame retouching, top right.

Fine printing: this must not be confused with first-class printing. The former shows all the finely traced lines of the design; it is in demand. The latter is usually made from a stripped transfer, with resultant thinning down of the burelage, and, consequently, greater prominence of the Ceres head. The quality of first-class printing is usually enhanced by expert workmanship.

Fine printing, which is always rare, is found in the following values: 1-centime, Plate III; 2-centime red-brown and 2-centime brown-red (transfer not stripped); 4-centime gray; 5-centime yellow-green or green (all broken lines under the eye are quite visible, first condition of plate); 10-centime bistre, plate unretouched; 20-centime, Type II, Plate I, blue; 80-centime pale rose. An average fine printing can be identified in the 20-centime, Type I, plate unretouched in blue or dark blue.

First-class printing: 1-centime pale off-olive-green, Plate III, second condition of plate, and Plate II, final condition; 2-centime (transfer stripped) red-brown and chocolate; 4-centime gray; 5-centime pale yellow-green, eye partly shaded; 10-centime bistre; 30-centime brown on more yellowish paper, but this is both fine and first-class printing; 40-centime orange-red.

Used plates: copies from well-used plates, with the burelage visibly worn, are always rare. For example: 1-centime, Plate I; 5-centime dark green; 10-centime bistre; 20-centime, Type I, plate retouched (not to be confused with stripped transfers); 40-centime orange; and 80-centime rose.

Pairs: not especially rare: 3M, 3U; 5-centime dark green: 4M, 4U; 20-centime, Type I, and 30-centime: 4U; 20-centime, Type III, Plate I: rare; Plate II: 5U; 20-centime, Type II: 10U.

Strips of three: not especially rare: 4M, 4U; 2- and 40-centime: 5U; 5- and 30-centime: 6U; 10-centime: 10U; 20-centime, Type I: 6M, 12U; 20-centime, Type II: 6M, 30U; 20-centime, Type III: 5M, 30U.

It should be noted that strips of three, four, and five have a value proportional to that of pairs and blocks of four.

Strips of four: not especially rare: 5M, 6U; 2-, 4-, 30-centime: 8U; 5- and 40-centime: 10U; 20-centime, Type I: 8M, 24U; 20-centime, Type II: 10M, 60U; 20-centime, Type III: 8M, 60–100U.

Strip office: not especially rare: 6M, 7–8U; 4-centime: 9U; 5-centime: 12U; 10-centime: 8M, 30U; 80-centime: 7U.

Blocks of four: not especially rare: 5–6M, 8U; 2-, 4-, and 30-centime: 10U; 5-centime: 10M, 15U; 40-centime: 15U; 10-centime: 12M, 40U; 20-centime, Type I: 10M, 40U; 20-centime, Type II: 15M, 150U; 20-centime, Type III: 10M, 150–200U.

On cover: the 1- and 2-centime: 2U; the 4-, 30-, and 80-centime: 50U; others: 20U. The 20-centime covers are common.

Cancellations: large numeral cancellations: common. With date, double circle: common in the minor values; 10- and 30-centime: 50U; 40- and 80-centime and 20-centime, Type I: 2U; Type II: 3U; Type III: 15U. Small numerals: 2U; 1-, 10-, and 20-centime, Type II: 3U; Type III: 10U. Mobile post office (small letters and numerals): 2U; 10- and 40-centime: 3U; 20-centime, Type II: 4U; Type III: 15U.

Anchor: rare on minor values; not very rare on the 40- and 80-centime. On the 20-centime, Type I: 2U; on the 10-centime: 3U; on the 20-centime, Type II: 4U; on the 20-centime, Type III: 6U.

Small (thimble) postmark with date: not very rare on minor values. On the 10-, 30-, and 80-centime: 2–3U; on the 20-centime, Type II, and 40-centime: 5U; on the 20-centime, Type III: 10U; on the 20-centime, Type I: very rare.

Triple circle with date, outer circle made of pearls: rare on all values: 3–5U. On the 20-centime, Type II: 10U; on the 20-centime, Type III: 30U. Star with or without numeral: always rare: 3–6U; Types II and III: 12U. Large numeral Levant cancels: 2–3U; less rare on the 40-centime stamp. All other cancellations — "O.R." (rural), mobile (railway) with date, station, Monaco, Levant with date, foreign, color, etc. — are rare.

Perforated stamps: all values are found rouletted and perf 13; the 20-centime, Type III, has a long-tooth rouletting pattern attributed to Avallon. These should be acquired on expertized covers. See the values in the specialty catalogues.

Split stamps: the following are found: 10-centime, split diagonally; 20-centime, Type III, split four ways (Limoges); 80-centime, split four ways (Clerval).

Reprints: none.

Official forgeries: the 20-centime, Types II and III, forgeries were used in the postal service. Type II, of Italian origin (?), was used in Marseilles. Lithographed. An indefinable type classified as Type II by the form of the "C" letters and the distance of the pearled circle from the top tablet. Letters not well aligned, not congruent (the "2" on the right resembles a "Z"), and a little higher than on the originals. Shapeless corner design; fretwork ornaments without shading are reproduced right up to the white lines. Intermediate ultramarine shade. Thin paper. On cover: 300U.

With respect to the 20-centime, Type III, the best-known forgery is the one that gave rise to the Aix-en-Provence lawsuit. Sketches A and B in the accompanying illustration will provide sufficient information. Thin paper (55–60 microns, including gum); bad copy of the 20-centime, Type III, Plate II (inner frame reinforced). On cover: 500U; mint: valueless. Large numeral "2240" (Marseilles) cancellation, March 10 to April 15, 1871; also, Lorgues (Var), La Seyne-sur-Mer, etc.

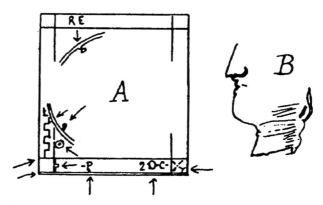

The best-known forgery of the 20-centime, Type III, gave rise to a lawsuit.

Forgeries: the secret marks (pearls connected in front of the nose; small bar missing in the fifth overlapping) can only be useful in spotting a few early forgeries of the 2-, 20-, and 40-centime stamps.

These marks are useless for modern photolithographed stamps (Toulouse), and a knowledge of the original transfer defects is indispensable, for these forgeries are much more difficult to identify than engraved copies. (It took five years of ardent discussion and a court action to decide between the Belgian amateurs with respect to the 1914 lithographed Red Cross stamps!)

Naturally, transfer characteristics are not always clear-cut on authentic stamps, but a little study will quickly authenticate them, with shade, measurement, and paper data used as confirmation of the authenticity.

The 20-centime Type I: there are two modern forgeries. The first one, with the neck dots, resembles Type I; however, its bottom inscription resembles that of Type III. The left "C" appears larger than the "20"; heavy color lines in the fretwork ornaments. Canceled

"2240E." Very poor quality gray paper. The second one is on a "woolly," stippled paper (85 microns) with threads visible on back, ½ mm shorter than the original, and a little less wide; ultramarine shade; bad copy of Type XII from the unretouched plate; the "P" of REPUB is too high, too thick; the "A" of FRANC is too small.

The 2-centime: there exists an early forgery with a color dot in front of REPUB, the forger having neglected to finish the job. The rest of the design is arbitrary in several places.

In February 1923, I discovered forgeries of the 2- and 10-centime in Nice. (See F. Serrane, "Faux de France," *L'Écho de la Timbrologie,* No. 652 [February 28, 1923]: 185–86.) These counterfeits were executed photolithographically in pairs, strips, and blocks in Toulouse (P.). The design was correctly reproduced; however, a lack of finesse in the shading of the eyebrow, the neck, and under the chin is noticeable. The measurements are good, but the forger left a 2 mm gutter on all sides: again, neglect of what is essential.

The paper did not receive the security impression, which gives the forgery a flat look, like that of original stamps that have been cleaned too much. Sometimes the paper is reddish on both sides; it is a modern paper, which in processing on wire gauze acquired a slight resemblance to stippled paper with numerous well-aligned transparent dots.

The shade is dull red-brown, which blends with the paper shade, and the Ceres is even less prominent than in the respectable, honest copies. Other arbitrary shades exist.

A few additional points may be useful in identifying the 2-centime Toulouse forgery:

1. Counterfeit of Type III of the transfer plate. The circle is clearly broken on top, but the almost invisible supplementary line attached to the inner frame above the figure on the left is poorly executed; the color dots after "2," "C," and POSTES are white inside. There is a thin, vertical line in the right margin, about 1 mm from the outer frame. Copper shade. Like the next two, this forgery is on thin paper (60–65 microns).

2. A copy of the same transfer type, which shows that exclusive use was made of a Type III authentic copy to create the forgery and that transfers of the latter were made to manufacture pairs, strips, and blocks. This time the circle is unbroken, but the line attached to the left frame is quite visible. The dot after the left figure has almost disappeared, and the dots after the "C" and POSTES are not very visible. No shading under the eye, pale reddish shade, dull tone.

3. A third Toulouse forgery has a color line attached to the top of the lower loop of the "B," an oblique line connected with the middle of the oblique downstroke of the "N," and above this downstroke there is another,

descending, unattached oblique line on the left under the lower eyelid line. The inner left frame is broken below the left figure and is formed by an oblique line above the base of the figure. Letters "O" and "S" are joined on top; the top of the first "S" of POSTES is thicker; the burelage lines, which are rather oval-like, are white in the middle. Light brownish copper-red shade, grayish paper on back. Various cancellations, one of which is dated: TOULOUSE 2e/20 SEPT 71 (30).

The "first-class printing on yellowish paper" of the 2-centime was counterfeited. Two types, presumably from different sources:

1. The median bar of the "E" of REPUB is oblique and is slanted downward; the vertical extends to the upper frame. The "F" and the "R" of FRANC are clearly separated on top. Other differences in design can be pointed out, especially a small vertical in the third burelage line of the upper right corner, a little to the left and below the dot after FRANC.

2. The loop of the "R" of REPUB is not connected with the middle of the vertical downstroke; the left downstroke of the "U" has a concavity, top left; the figure "2" on the left has a color concentration, top right, near the middle of the outer line of the loop of the "U"; the "C" after the figure ends below in a color dot.

This forgery does not have the lithographic security imprint, and its paper is tough; the burelage is made of dots; the grape leaf veins are made of well-defined dots. There is a trace of a white contour hairline. The inner right frame is almost as thick in its upper half as the outer frame. I have seen large numeral cancellations "709" and "822."

The 4-centime: a Toulouse forgery has a heavily inked impression, without security background. Same paper as for the similar forgery of the 2-centime. It is found in an extraordinarily bright purplish blue shade.

There are various forged postmarks, one of which is large numeral "3982."

The off-yellow 4-centime, with figure on the right retouched, was well counterfeited, but the measurements and design of the stamp differ.

The 20-centime, Type II: one forgery resembles the 20-centime, Type II, with respect to the bottom inscription; however, the top letters are too wide. The distance from the "R" of REPUB to the left side of the tablet is only 1 mm or less; no white line; a few vertical lines of dots from the eye to the nostril. All of the pearls look rectangular. The first overlapping lines on the left are made of straight lines, etc. Dubious "2240" cancellation. (Recent use of an authentic canceling device....)

I also have seen a dark blue 20-centime, Type II, with a white line, heavily printed, with a back imprint made of small, curving, irregular, blue lines. It is a single off-cover stamp with dubious cancellations. I imagine it came from printer's waste or from a rejected sheet on which trial inking was applied on the back.

In the bottom left corner, the first small overlapping has only two horizontal separations instead of four; the upper frame often is broken on the right of the left ornamental square, and the lower frame is not connected with the left lateral frame. This forgery is found pin rouletted and sometimes is provided with the lozenge-dotted cancellation often encountered on counterfeits.

The 40-centime: there is a rather curious forgery of unknown origin; it is probably an early one, for better work is done today.

Photolithographed on machine-made, glossy white paper (65 microns); no lithographed security imprint. Its shade resembles that of the Bordeaux 40-centime orange, but with a touch of ochre, enough to give it, at first sight, the appearance of certain 10-lepta Greek stamps.

The burelage is starred with dots; the eye and neck shading is made of dots. (Bordeaux: lines, broken lines, and more lines.)

Measurements: $18^1/_2$ x $22^1/_2$ mm. Dimensions exceed those of the Bordeaux stamps.

So, let's say we have before us a possible forgery of the 1849 stamp or of a colonial stamp, but the bottom tablet is reproduced from the 40-centime Bordeaux (Type V of the transfer counterfeited, as evidenced by the shape of the figures). From this I conclude that the forger, wishing to counterfeit the 40-centime 1849, and having available only a piece of this stamp in which a bottom tablet is missing, sticks a cut-out tablet from a 40-centime Bordeaux under the piece. This is confirmed not only by the tablet's transfer type identification, but also because the width of the tablet, which is shorter than in the 1849 issue, allows for no agreement of the lateral frames. The counterfeiter had no idea of all that when he photographed this curious ensemble and would be astonished to be told today exactly how he went about it!

Thus, this forgery is a hybrid that may be described as a forgery of the 1849 issues, of the colonies (1871), and of Bordeaux (1870). I do not think an all-purpose forgery was intended, for this would have been even more curious! It never went through the postal service, and has a forged cancellation of dots and small bars with large numerals (the numeral "3" is not congruent with the one used in that period).

I wanted to give some emphasis to this forgery, for although it does not withstand careful examination, collectors have occasionally been fooled by it.

Another, more deceptive forgery, which probably comes from Toulouse, has a reddish ochre shade. It is a crude counterfeit of Type XIV of the transfer plate.

The small white line attached to the base of the "R" is missing; the "C" after the "40" on the right is printed thin except at its base, where it is thick (the opposite is true in the original); the white line is heavy.

The inscription letters, which are equally thick in the originals, are poorly drawn and too thin, especially the "F," the upper bar of which is half as long as its normal length. The median bar and the two baselines of the "R" of FRANC are nonexistent. The "P" of REPUB is definitely open at the top, and the two "R" letters occasionally have the same defect.

The upper right corner rosette is very faint, as is the fretwork ornament on the same side. The feet of the two "4" figures are sometimes extended as far as the bottom of the tablet.

This counterfeit was stamped with various postmarks — for example, large numeral "532" and star without a numeral. It exists on piece.

Forged cancellations: in addition to the forged large numeral (Toulouse) postmark "3982" and other previously mentioned cancellations, about forty others are known to have been applied on the Toulouse forgeries alone. All of the Marseilles and Paris forged postmarks must have been used!

Fakes: it is fruitless to emphasize the faking of the perforated stamps of the Siege of Paris or of 1871–75, which had their teeth removed when they were transformed into imperforate Bordeaux stamps! Likewise with respect to the imperforate Granet reprints of 1887 (10- and 20-centime) and the imperforates of the French colonies (issues of 1871 and 1872–77), which are occasionally offered for sale as Bordeaux stamps. A look at the eye-shade stippling and the height of POSTES (1-, 2-, and 4-centime) is enough to dispel any doubt about these typographed forgeries.

IV. Perforated Stamps (after 1870)

1871–75. Ceres. Nos. 50 to 60. For the 4-centime yellowish gray, see my remark on No. 27, "Shades."

Stamps with lined background or defective impression are in demand. The 25-centime blue is found with various plate defects: worn upper tablet; heavy white line in the center background; fractured edge of the cliché above the left figure; worn frames; etc. There are retouchings of the upper tablet frame. A not-very-common retouching shows this frame entirely redone. There is general retouching of the frame, especially the upper one.

Pairs: 3M, 3U, except No. 51: 4M, 10U; Nos. 54–60: 5U; blocks of four, No. 53: 10M, used: 4 francs; Nos. 54–57: 10M, used: 10–15 francs; No. 59: 16M, used: 5 francs; No. 60: 6M, used: 1 franc; others: 8M, 8U. The 1- to 4-centime and the 80-centime are worth 2U on cover.

Imperforate stamps: with the exception of Nos. 54 and 55, the whole set is known imperforate (rare) in shades that are slightly different from those of the colonies.

Reprint: 25-centime blue, imperforate.

Official forgeries: Nos. 55 and 60: very rare. No. 60, canceled "5051." Comparison of face stippling is sufficient to reveal forgery.

Fakes: the 15-centime error, brown on rose, was faked using a No. 54 on which the zeros were changed to "5"; the tête-bêche 10-, 15-, and 25-centime were made with two single stamps, as explained previously in the discussion of the 1853–60 issue.

1876–1900. Peace and Commerce type. Nos. 61 to 107. No. 84, 1-centime black on Prussian blue, must have the light Prussian blue shade of the No. 4 stamp. There are chemical fakings of No. 83c. Compare shades and study the bogus paper, which is almost never entirely impregnated.

Pairs: 3M, 3U; except Nos. 64, 66, 68–72, 91, and 104, rarer used: 5U. Pairs of the adjacent 25-centime stamps, Types I and II, are exceedingly rare (gutter).

Strips: proportionate prices for pairs and blocks of four. For example, No. 62, strip of five: 10U. No. 68, strip of four: 60U. No. 71, strip of four: 30U. No. 91, strip of four: 80U.

Blocks of four: mint: 6–8M, except No. 92: 20M. Used: 8U, except lower values: 1–2 francs, and Nos. 76 and 95: 12U. No. 81: 16U. Nos. 64, 65, 93, and 104: 20U. No. 70: 30U. Nos. 66, 69, and 71: 40U. No. 72: 60U. Nos. 68 and 91: 120U.

Varieties: defective impressions exist, as do stamps with inverted impressions on the back. A few stamps are known on pelure paper: rare. No. 101 with double cross-ruling is rare. No. 103 with double impression is rare. Nos. 102 and 103, vertical pairs with Types I and II dividing strips: 5 francs, mint. The 20-centime blue, Types I and II, are unissued stamps.

Imperforate stamps: most values are known imperforate. Wide margins are necessary to ensure that the "imperfs" are not perforated stamps that have been trimmed. All are rare on cover.

Reprints (Granet, 1887, Type II): imperforate; shades differ from the originals.

Used postal forgeries: perfs are not congruent (originals are 14 x 13$^{1}/_{2}$), and neither are the dimensions (originals are 18 x 22 mm).

The 25-centime milky blue, noncongruent lettering and figures: very rare.

The 15-centime blue:

1. Crude design, perf 12.

2. Another forgery in very light blue with irregular design (compare) and the unsuccessful inscription J.A. SAGE INV.

3. The better-known Chalons forgery — the frontal bandeau of Mercury is made of two almost straight lines; full dots before and after the bottom inscription.

The word MOUCHON is inscribed between the two frames and not astride the inner frame. On cover: 40 francs.

Fakes: forged anchor cancellations; large numbers of forged year-date cancels, many of which are very well executed.

Issue of 1900. Nos. 107 to 123. The twice-printed stamp values, 10-, 20-, 25-, and 30-centime, with value figure too light or too dark, must have figures that are in sharp contrast with the rest of the printing. The 10-centime is found with printing in orange and figures in carmine.

The 10- to 30-centime stamps that have no figures are workshop rejects; they never went through control.

Fakes: the 40- and 50-centime, with background shade chemically or physically reduced. These fakes were then offered on piece with registry label, and provided with forged circular cancellations dated: VERDELAIS 1-3 19.. GIRONDE.

Forgeries: the 5-franc, which comes from a clandestine printing, like the Nos. 24, 25, and 26 forgeries from the French Levant bureau. Thus, it is not really a forgery, but, lacking any legitimacy, it cannot be assigned a place in collections. It is rather pointless to scrutinize the small hatching and shading differences resulting from different printing press pressures during the unauthorized printing. Paper verification is also not within the reach of everyone. However, there are shade differences, and the most distinctive characteristic is still the noncongruent perforation, the state's perforation machines having refused to cooperate.

1902. Retouched Mouchon type. Nos. 124 to 128. *Used postal forgeries:* the 15-centime, crude design. Comparison is indicated. Noncongruent perforation (originals are 14 x 13$^{1}/_{2}$), as well as perforation errors.

1903. Sower. Nos. 129 to 145. Imperforate examples of Nos. 137–43 come from sheets that did not go through control and that were sold to a few dealers by a stamp shop employee (Paris lawsuit, 1910). A great many shades are extant for most of the values. One example will show the range: No. 138: carmine-tinted red, light red, carmine, dark blood red, pale dull red, dark rose, vermilion, pale vermilion, poppy red (rare), scarlet, salmon red, orange-yellow (very rare without faking). The claret stamp is a chemical fake.

Official forgeries: the 10-centime rose, No. 129 (1907). Compare background lining at the places where the rays of the sun appear. Perf 14 x 13 instead of 14 x 13$^{1}/_{2}$.

The 10-centime, No. 138 (Torino): well counterfeited after a few corrections of a bad cliché (female sower with a death's-head; Toulon lawsuit). A few characteristic features, especially Nos. 1, 2, and 3 of the description that follows, recall the 25-centime forgeries, which are probably from the same source. Perf 13.

The 25-centime, No. 140: I discovered this counterfeit in Nice. (See F. Serrane, "Faux de France," *L'Écho de la Timbrologie*, No. 652 [February 28, 1923]: 185–86.) Principal identification marks:

1. The last "E" of REPUBLIQUE does not form an "F" as in the original, but an "E," the curved lower bar of which penetrates the hair.

2. The thumb on the right hand is formed by an oblique descending — rather than ascending — line.

3. The original female sower has five shading lines above the left elbow; in the forgery, there are only four, the two highest ones forming a spot.

4. The upper bar of Mouchon's "E" is too short and the "N" is too small; perf 12³/₄ x 13. Stamps on cover are rather rare, despite the fact that the postal authorities issued 8 million copies in about two years.

1914. Red Cross. No. 146. *Forged overprints:* comparison will identify those that are poorly executed. However, there are some that require the most precise measurement, along with comparisons of shade and color.

1917. Orphans. Nos. 148 to 155. The 5-franc + 5-franc has been faked by chemically reducing the overprinted 1-franc stamp (No. 169). Look for binding at the places bearing the overprint. Known with a forged large circle ROCHECHOUART cancellation.

War stamp. Valenciennes. 1914. *Forgery* (Paris, B.): compare shade, design, format. Perf 13¹/₄ instead of 11¹/₂.

V. Newspaper Stamps

Forgeries: the whole set was counterfeited in Geneva on yellowish paper. See the accompanying illustration for the identifying marks.

Forged cancellations on these forgeries: 1. 1870, figures 5 mm high, then a horizontal bar 4¹/₂ mm underneath, and, finally, 7¹/₂ mm further down, we see

the upper half of "E" and "I" (total height, 3 cm; the "E" is 3¹/₂ mm thick and the "I," 5¹/₂ mm).

2. Same kind: 1870, horizontal bar and upper half of "R O" or "B O" (3¹/₂ mm thick).

3. Same kind: 1869, horizontal bar and upper half of "S" (4–7 mm thick).

Note: The large cancellation letters frequently conceal the small horizontal line in the second "U" of JOURNAUX, this defect being quite obvious.

VI. Duty-Free Stamps

"F M" overprints were well counterfeited straight, inverted, or with varieties. Comparative study will isolate the bad ones.

VII. Postage Due Stamps

The 10-centime. No. 1. Lithographed. This stamp is from the issue of January 1, 1859. January cancellations are in demand (on cover: 2U). For differences between the lithographed and the typographed stamps, see the accompanying illustration. Dimensions: 2 x 2 cm.

Forgeries: this stamp was counterfeited several times. See the measurements in the sketch.

The 10-centime. No. 2. Typographed. Issue of March 5, 1859. White paper is in demand. Dimensions: 2 x 2 cm, typographed, or 1.95 x 1.95 cm, electrotyped. Varieties: errors in lettering are a result of type wear.

Rouletted or perforated (unofficial): on-cover purchase recommended, with expertizing.

Forgeries: same remark as for No. 1.

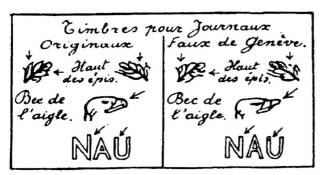

Distinguishing features of newspaper stamps. Originals. Geneva forgeries. Top of grain spikes. Eagle's beak.

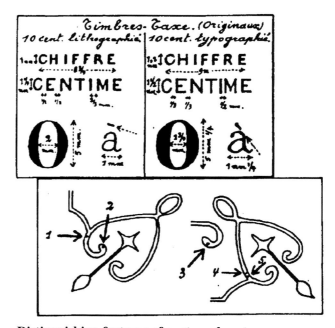

Distinguishing features of postage due stamps.

The l5-centime. No. 3. Typographed. *Original:* in the "5," the upper bow is ½ mm from the lower loop; the accent on the "a" forms an oblique angle of about forty-five degrees. There is a plate defect in which the trip bar of the "5" is broken. This is very rare.

Perforations: for this stamp and all those that follow, same remark as above.

The 15-centime. No. 4. Lithographed. Deep black shade. The upper bow of the "5" is only ¼ mm from the lower loop. The accent on the "a" has only about a thirty-degree angle of inclination, and, if it were extended, it would not touch the letter. In addition, there are secret marks (dots), which are shown in the illustration, that will be sufficient for identifying all the crudely executed forgeries. Those that are photolithographed require comparison of format, paper, and gum.

This stamp was executed in Bordeaux (1871) from a wood engraving and transferred ten times onto a mother-stone that was used to make up the sheet of 150 stamps in three panes of fifty (5 x 10), divided by a gutter.

Forgeries: Nos. 5–9. All values were counterfeited, especially Nos. 7, 8, and 9, and given forged cancellations. The shape of the letters — above all, the shape of the "a" and the accent positioning, which is similar in all values — facilitates recognition of most of the forgeries. For others that are better executed, it is necessary to compare and measure, and cancellation expertizing is indispensable for Nos. 7 and 8.

Perforated postage due stamps. Nos. 10 to 27. *Fakes:* the 2- and 5-franc red-brown from the colonies, furnished with a forged perforation. Check this perforation and also the cancellation, if need be. Do the same for the 1-franc rose on straw color. Also compare the shade.

Forgeries: see the distinctive features of similar stamps from the French colonies in the illustration. Same for Nos. 35 and 36.

Forged cancellations on Geneva forgeries: postmarks with date: PARIS 2 ? 82 60; NANTUA 3e/15 JUIL 72 AIN; FIGEAC 1/10 NOV 91 LOT; UZES 2e/1 Nov ? GARD; and hexagonal postmark with inner circle: MONS-EN-PUELLE MAI ? NORD.

VIII. Telegraph Stamps

Forgeries: the whole set was well counterfeited in Geneva (F.), despite the arbitrary paper, shades, and printing.

Distinctive features: 1. The "U" of OUDINE is not as tall as the other letters.

2. The base of the "T" of TELEGRAPHES is touching the white oval.

3. The crown has a single line on top, not a double line.

4. The first leg (not to be confused with the mandible) of the bee at top left is missing.

In the 2-franc stamp, the "2" on the right is touching the oval shading.

Forged cancellations on these forgeries: octagonal postmarks with inner circle: CAEN 12 JUIN 69 (one star); LE HAVRE 8 FEVR 68 (one star); MOLSHEIM 12 JUIN 69 (three stars). Same postmark, but smaller format: METZ 10 FEV 69 (three stars).

Alsace and Lorraine

The specialized collection of stamps of this territory is particularly engaging, because it was put into circulation concurrently with the advance of German troops.

1870. Postes, centimes, and large figures. Perf 13½ x 14½. *Sheets* printed twice, first burelage and then text. Numerous variations and defects in lettering and in the width of the words POSTES and CENTIMES originated in the typographical impression. Misplaced with respect to the letters, the figures allow us to situate the types to be discussed further on.

Various *plates* exist, at least for a few of the values; this question has not yet been adequately investigated. Type II of the 10- and 20-centime stamps comes from the first plates; Types III and IV of the 4-centime and Type IV of the 20-centime stamp appear likewise to belong to these plates, but the errors must have been corrected when the work was being done.

Burelage: all stamps have a burelage, which is occasionally inverted, but the 10-centime stamp has a partial burelage now and then, or it is not very visible because of wear: 10U.

Shades: a few shades of each value; vivid ultramarine is not common in the 20-centime: 3U. The bistre-yellow of the 10-centime appears only in the Plate II set.

Large format: 25 mm high instead of 24, imperforate; 5-, 10-, 20-, and 25-centime: 8U.

Stamps on cover: 2U. Franking rare: 1-, 4-, and 10-centime on cover; 2-centime and a pair of the 4-centime stamps. Combination French and German frankings are in demand; also, letters struck with a postage due stamp (for example, figure "20" in blue: 20 francs).

Pairs: 3U; the 1- and 4-centime stamps are less common; strips of three, 1- and 2-centime: 6U; 4-centime: 8U; 5- and 10-centime: 10U; 20- and 25-centime: rare. All blocks of used stamps are rare; blocks of mint stamps are in active demand.

Cancellations: the specialized catalogues, particularly Yvert, deal with this question in detail. (See Yvert catalogue, *France and Colonies.* Serrane consulted the 30th edition [1925–26] for Volume I of his study.) The following main subdivisions can be indicated:

1. French postmarks used in Alsace-Lorraine: circular or scalloped with date, bearing the departmental identification at the bottom. They are all rare, because they were replaced by German postmarks at the beginning of 1871. (Intrinsic value: 3–25 francs; they must be quite legible). Lozenge postmarks with dots, large or small figures, are rarer: 10–40 francs; straight line city or town names: 20–50 francs.

2. French postmarks used in French territory in communities occupied by the Germans. Same postmarks as above, same rarities, and provisional German postmarks with blank center or year date "1871" (Amiens, Epinal, and Rouen).

3. German postmarks used in Alsace-Lorraine, circular with date, with time indication at the bottom. Generally less rare than those of No. 1 (above). Rare: all postmarks with double circle, without time indication, especially Aumetz, Corny, Delme, Gertzheim, Rodemachern, and Scherweiler; and ordinary postmarks Roeschwoog, Merzweiler, and Westhofen im E: 10–30 francs.

4. Prussian, Bavarian, and Wurtemberger postmarks: circular, rectangular, or half-circle with "Feldpost" (military mail) indication. Rare: circular Type III postmarks, Nos. 63 and 64; rectangular, Nos. 4 and 75; Bavarian, Type VI, and Wurtemberger. Value: 20 francs.

5. Postmarks of German railway post offices, with or without frame, inscription on three lines: 3–10 francs.

6. Incidental postmarks on stamps, such as army corps, arrival, French railway, etc. Little value.

Types of stamps. The specialized catalogues say that the various types can be recognized by the position of the figures relative to the words POSTES and CENTIMES, and that this position can be ascertained by extending the axis or one of the sides of the figures.

This method makes for uncertain calculations and errors, because the printed text of POSTES or CENTIMES is more or less wide, depending upon the space assigned to it.

We have tried to make the solution of this little problem more exact by using the position of the figures relative to their distance from the left edge, rather than from the letters. The accompanying sketch illustrates both procedures, so that the specialist can evaluate them and, if need be, verify each by the other.

1-centime: Type I. Common. Boldface figure, $1\frac{1}{4}$ mm wide. The figure's body is $8\frac{1}{2}$ or $8\frac{1}{4}$ mm from the left edge; so its position relative to the word POSTES, which varies from $11\frac{4}{5}$ to $12\frac{1}{2}$ mm in width, can be slightly different.

Type II. Less common. Lightface figure, 1 mm wide. The figure is 9 mm from the left edge.

2-centime: no varieties worthy of mention. The word POSTES varies from $11\frac{4}{5}$ to $12\frac{1}{2}$ mm in width.

First row: 4-centime — Type I, common $\frac{4}{5}$. Type II, rare $\frac{1}{5}$. Types III and IV, exceedingly rare. Second row: 5-centime — Type I, common $\frac{14}{15}$. Type II, rare $\frac{1}{15}$. 10-centime — Type I, common $\frac{3}{5}$. Type II, less common $\frac{2}{5}$. Third row: 20-centime — Type I, common $\frac{2}{3}$. Type II, less common $\frac{1}{3}$. Type III, rare $\frac{1}{20}$. Type IV, exceedingly rare. Fourth row: 25-centime — Type I, common $\frac{2}{3}$. Type II, less common $\frac{1}{3}$. 1-centime — Type I, boldface figure, common $\frac{3}{4}$. Type II, thin lightface figure, less common $\frac{1}{4}$.

4-centime: Type I. Common. The axis of the vertical stem of the figure goes through the "I" of CENTIMES; or, the base of the figure is directly above TIM. The figure is $6\frac{1}{2}$ mm from the edge, and the "C" of CENTIMES is 2 mm away.

Type II. Rare. The axis of the vertical stem passes to the right of the "I" and is very close to it. Figure "4" is 7 mm from the edge; it has been shifted $\frac{1}{2}$ mm to the right because of the abundant space allowed to the left in typographical composition. When POSTES is abnormally wide, $12\frac{3}{4}$ mm instead of $11\frac{3}{4}$ to $12\frac{1}{2}$ mm, the "T" is to the right of the figure's top, instead of to the left. This might permit the listing of a subtype, but it is better, in order not to complicate things, to mention this case among the rare varieties of the word POSTES.

Type III. Exceedingly rare. The axis of the vertical stem of the figure passes to the left of "M" and is very close to it; or, the figure's base is directly above "IM."

We must point out right away that the figure is where it should be, $6^{1}/_{2}$ mm from the edge, as in Type I; it is CENTIMES that has been moved, $^{1}/_{2}$ mm to the left, the "C" being $1^{1}/_{2}$ mm from the edge instead of 2 mm.

This measuring procedure unquestionably establishes type identification. Judging by copies exhibited in Paris that supposedly belonged to this rare type, but that were really Types I and II, we can see that the old method was wrong. Type III is exceedingly rare.

Type IV. Extremely rare. The axis of the vertical stem of the figure cuts the "T" of CENTIMES; or, the figure's base is above the letters "TI." Here, the figure itself is definitely moved to the left, because its distance to the left edge is only 5 mm. This defect, like that of Type III and Type IV of the 20-centime stamp, must have been corrected on the second set of plates.

5-centime: Type I. Normal. Common. The extension of the left side of the oblique branch of the "5" goes through the "S" of POSTES. The top of the "5" is $7^{1}/_{2}$ to $7^{3}/_{4}$ mm from the left edge.

Type II. Rare. The same extension of the oblique branch finds the "S" on its right. The figure's left deviation is $7^{1}/_{2}$ mm from the edge.

Note: Both methods are equally good in examining this value.

Incentive: Type I. Common. The prolongation of the right side of the figure traverses the "O" of POSTES and the "N" of CENTIMES. Figure "1" is $5^{1}/_{2}$ mm from the left edge.

Type II. Less common. The same prolongation passes to the right of "O" and "N"; or, the figure is exactly above the "N." Moved to the right by the interposition of larger spaces, the figure is $6^{1}/_{4}$ mm from the edge.

Note: Slight differences in the position of the figure with respect to the letters is due to the greater or lesser width of POSTES.

20-centime: Type I. Common. The base of the "2" begins right above the "E." The base is $4^{1}/_{4}$ mm away from the left edge.

Type II. Less common. The base of the "2" begins above the "C." The figure is moved to the left; its base is $3^{1}/_{2}$ mm from the edge.

Type III. Rare. The base of the "2" begins above the middle of the space between the "C" and the "E." The figure's base is 4 mm from the edge.

This procedure in measuring is especially useful; the old way frequently induced the amateur to engage in wishful thinking.

Type IV. Extremely rare. The "20," which definitely is out of place in its elevated position, is separated from POSTES by only about 1 mm, whereas it is about $3^{1}/_{4}$ mm from CENTIMES. In other types, the space is $2^{1}/_{4}$ mm above and 2 mm below.

25-centime: Type I. Common. The prolongation of the left side of the oblique part of the "5" leaves the "T" of POSTES on its left; or, the prolongation of the left side of the vertical of the "T" does not touch the top of the "5." With values of this sort, types are most difficult to identify by the old formulas, because the figure is always located the same distance from the left edge, while POSTES varies in width. Measurement of this word will be decisive in determining the type under examination. One should measure from the middle of the lower curve of the "S" letters; measurement from the bottom may be faulty because of the serif of the "P." POSTES here measures 12 mm.

Type II. Less common. The extension of the left side of the oblique part of the "5" goes through the "T" of POSTES; or, the prolongation of the left side of the vertical of the "T" just touches the top of the "5." POSTES measures $12^{1}/_{2}$ mm.

Forgeries: the burelage imprint of the Alsace-Lorraine stamps was entrusted to various printers, which explains the difference in shades. It is made of almost concentric interlacings of double wavy lines, and is called "points-down" when the convex parts of the arcs are turned downward and "points-up" when they are turned in the opposite direction.

Originals: the distance from the "P" of POSTES to the left edge is 3 to $3^{1}/_{2}$ mm. The gum of the mint copies is colorless, of fine quality, and transparent.

Hamburg forgeries, called "reprints": the whole set has points-up burelage (the 1-centime with points-down burelage is rare); the gum is similar, but thicker. These forgeries were manufactured in 1885 from the original plate of the burelage. All others are definitely forgeries, the printing materials having been destroyed in 1872.

Everybody knows this set. The distance from the "P" to the left edge facilitates identification of these forgeries, it being only $2^{3}/_{4}$ mm. Using a well-known trick of the trade, one can draw a diagonal line from the upper left corner; it bisects the "P" at about the middle of the vertical. In the originals, it barely touches that letter's base. Being smoother in texture, the paper makes the burelage stand out. Perforation as in the originals.

Geneva forgeries (F.): produced in complete sets, with the addition of a 4-centime Type IV.

1. First cliché: a set with points-up burelage; gaps quite visible where the color margins meet.

2. Second cliché: same set with points-down burelage.

3. Third cliché: same set with points-up burelage, but the gaps have disappeared. The correction was made simply by filing the first plate.

4. Fourth cliché: same set with points-down burelage, without gaps.

There are also reasonably good forgeries deriving from the retouching of the first and second clichés, in which a few blanks have disappeared. Vertical or horizontal gaps are found in the same stamp value.

Note: Originals can be found that have some of these gaps in one corner or another.

The paper of these forgeries is the same as that used for the Swiss forgeries of 1862, made by the B.F.K. firm in R...(Isere). Sometimes the trademark "B.F.K." is watermarked in letters $2^1/_2$ cm high. The perforation having been made in four passes through the perforating machine, irregularities appear, especially at the corners.

The best way to identify these forgeries is to examine the burelage. In the accompanying sketch, Figure I, greatly enlarged, represents a pair of arcs with wavy line burelage. In the originals, the distance A–B is $9^3/_8$ mm; in the Geneva forgeries, it is $9^3/_4$ mm.

Moreover, in the originals, the cross-hatching of the scalloped pairs of lines forms a lozenge-like figure at the crest of the wave (Figure II, A, C, D, B). Each of these figures is divided into four lozenge-shaped parts (Figure III; the figure's lines were inked more heavily) and a curved crest, the distance E–F being very small, $1/_8$ mm or a mere gap. These four imitation inner lozenges are not found in the Geneva forgeries, where the distance E–F is $3/_8$ mm.

The distance from the "P" of POSTES to the edge is the same as in the originals; perf $13^1/_2$ x 14; $13^1/_2$; 14; brownish gum.

These are the most deceptive forgeries known. Specimens with points-down burelage have gotten into many albums. Experienced collectors have been fooled by the 4-centime stamp, Type IV.

Early forgeries: crudely executed, with points-up burelage.

1. Paris forgeries. "Apple pie" burelage; distance A–B (Figure 1), 9 mm; distance E–F (Figure III), none. The distance from the "P" of POSTES to the edge is $2^1/_2$ mm. The "E" of CENTIMES is not as high as the "C." Perf $13^1/_4$.

2. Brussels forgeries. Very bad workmanship; POSTES, too wide, 13 mm; perf $13^1/_2$.

Forged cancellations. On Geneva forgeries (engraved on wood):

Circular postmarks, single circle (24 mm):
Metz 30/6 71.
Geispoldsheim 11/1 71 4-5 N.
Bolchen 20 6 71 4-5 N.
Egisheim 13 2 71 2-3 N.
Urbeis 31 2 71 2-3 N. (Amusing error, February having only 28 or 29 days.)
Diedenhofen 9/6 71 4-5 N.
Kayserberg 18 12 70 2-3 N.
Forbach 30 12 70 2-3 N.
Strassburg im Elsass 10 12 70 4-5 N. (26 mm.)
Rectangular postmark, 15 mm high:
K. PR. FELD-POST RELAIS [Field Post Routes], No. 3. 10. 70.
Double circle postmark (black or blue):
K. PR. FELD-POST RELAIS, No. 19 3 11 (the last three figures, one under the other, in the inner circle).
Provisional German postmark:
EPINAL in blue (Type O in Yvert catalogue, *France and Colonies*); crude execution of lettering and ornaments; uneven ink shading.
Horseshoe postmark (Type U in France and Colonies):
COLMAR 30 Aug 71 10-11 U. The "30" figures in an oblique position with respect to "Aug"; stars poorly executed.

Note: All of these canceling devices have interchangeable dates; the ones listed above have canceled a very large number of forgeries, "reprints," and even 1-, 2-, and 25-centime originals.

Other forged postmarks. There are many other forged postmarks from many sources; they are found most often on "reprints" and on the authentic 1-, 2-, and 25-centime stamps. The following list is probably incomplete:
Single circle:
Erstein 6 4 71 10-12 V and 22 4 71 3-4N.
Bischweiler 20 1 71 10-12 V.
Lucy 17 10 71.
Hayingen 28/6 71 7-8 V.
Metz 5/7 71 7-8 V.
Metz 11/10... (blue).
Forbach 18 3 71 5-6 N.

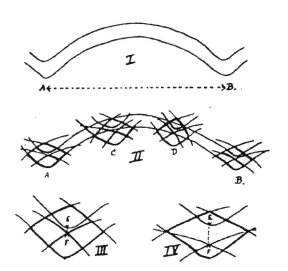

Winzenheim 29/12 20 3-4 N.

Mariakirch 5/5 71 6-7 N.

Ptsch 17 12... 11-12 V.

Metzerwisse 2 10 70 9 10 V. (Also, 7 3 71 and 28 7 71.)

Mulhausen im E. 29 11 70 and 2 5 71 2-5.

Oberberkheim 31/12 71 1-2 N.

Munster im Elsass 15 6 71.

Sentheim 27/2 71 4-5 V.

Steinburg 2 6 71 6-7 N.

...ler de Thann 31 12 71 7-8 V.

Ensisheim 21 4 71 2-3 N.

Finstingen 3.3 71 5-6 N.

Boofzheim 12....

Mutzig 15/4 71 2-4 N.

Wasselnheim 22 10 71 12-1 N. (Also, 1 2 71 and 13 5 71.)

Mulhausen. Elsass-Lothringen (nothing in middle).

Mulhausen. Elsass-Lothringen (date in middle).

Hochenfelden 14 10 71 3-4 N.

Farschweiler 29 11 71 5-6 N.

Rappolsweiler 21/11 70 11-12 V.

Thann 9. 2-7 (on a second line!).

Small French postmark:

Cirey-s-Vezouze 24 Nov. 70 (52) and 30 Nov. 70 (52).

Double circle (French or German postmarks):

Mulhausen 16-8-71.

Strassburg 71.

Reichshofen 1ᵉ20 Sept. 70 (67?).

Metz 16 Dec. 70 (53).

Amiens 1871 Poste.

Hagenau (nothing in center).

Commercy 29 March 71; 22 Sept. 71; 3ᵉ/24 Jan. (with or without division of collections, and so with interchangeable centers).

Thann 1ᵉ/23 NOV 70.

Soissons 21 DEC 70; 4ᵉ/16 Jan. (interchangeable center).

Ars-sur-Moselle 10/10 Nov. (without year date) (55) also 11/10 and 14/10.

Avricourt 5 Feb. 71.

Fontois (with nothing else).

Armée du Nord POSTES (general headquarters) (in blue).

K. PR. Feld-Post relais No. 11 21 1.

K. PR. Feld-Post relais No. 64 20 1.

Postmark type U (Yvert catalogue, *France and Colonies):*

Gebweiler 12 June 71 IV.

Large figure dotted lozenge:

2841, 1177.

Triple circle, beaded outer circle:

Chatenois 1ᵉʳ 23 Nov. (67).

Single line postmark, unframed:

Brune; Incwiller; Saint Nicolas (in blue); Thiaucourt (in black and blue).

Three-line postmark, unframed:

Strassburg 19 4 1 Avricourt.

Avricourt 16 4 11 Strasbourg.

Framed rectangular postmarks:

K. PR. Feld-Post relais No. 2 9 2.

Saarburg Lothringen 11 4 71 4.

Strassburg Bahn Post Bur (?).

K. PR. Feld-Post relais No. 23 10.

K. PR. Feld-Post Relais No. 27 11 3 (black and blue).

K. PR. Feld-Post Relais No. 43 2/12 (black and red).

Réunion

Statement on the classification of 1852 types. The originals of the 15- and 30-centime (Nos. 1 and 2) come from two typographical compositions, each comprising four types. The absence of whole sheets, of side-by-side pairs of the two values, and even of single horizontal pairs of the same value has induced all writers and philatelic works up until now to enumerate the types arbitrarily. For example, Marconnet: "The arrangement of the clichés is unknown. The sheet probably contained eight stamps in two rows of four. One of the rows probably contained the four clichés of the 15-centime, and the other row, the clichés of the 30-centime" (1897, p. 371). And Baron de Vinck de Winnezeele: "Each of the two values was printed in *sheets of four* on a single horizontal row (4 x 1)" (1928, p. 134). For the reasons given below, I believe that Marconnet is right.

In 1866, there appeared a first reprint, which was produced in blocks of six, three types of the 15-centime on top and three types of the 30-centime at bottom. Marconnet (p. 372) tells us that "the original plates had been stored in a cellar for some time," and that "the clichés were somewhat damaged by rust," and that "two of them (the fourth stamp varieties) were unserviceable." This may seem peremptory. When Marconnet used the word "plates," it surely was a slip, in view of his statement on page 371; it must be admitted that he meant "compositions." Likewise, when he spoke of "fourth stamp varieties," evidently two Type IV varieties are not involved but the types missing in the reprint sheet, which, as we have just said, contains only three. Note: Marconnet was only half mistaken: a look at the plate indicates that it was indeed the "fourth stamp varieties" (the first two of the sheet's inverted impression) which had disappeared.

Not being able to situate the original types exactly, our authors confined themselves to numbering the types of the reprinted sheet from I to III (from left to right); then they applied those designations to the originals of the same type and called the unreprinted variety of each value "Type IV."

15-centime. Lot 304 of the twelfth Ferrari sale had a superbly margined mint original which had, on its right, a marginal copy, 16 mm wide, with the trimming characteristic of sheet extremities. This stamp unquestionably is the Type IV of the original sheet, and, since it is the same type as the stamp on the right in the reprinted sheet, the reprint types evidently are II, III, and IV, in that order, and Type I must be reserved for the unreprinted original.

30-centime. Type designation for this value was made in the same way: I, II, and III for the reprinted types, and IV for the unreprinted original. The latter is easy to identify, for it has an "error": one of the characters of the center ornamentation is upright instead of prone as in the other types.

The erroneous numbering is more serious here; it is the result of insufficient observation, for a detailed study of the various types has shown me that the so-called "Type IV" is really in the reprint sheet: it is the last one on the left in that sheet.

The design error was corrected at frame replacement time, before reprinting, by an exacting printer who reestablished, in its normal prone position, the character that has assumed its unusual upright position in 1852.

To be convinced that this is so, it will be sufficient to make a detailed examination of the stamp on the left in the sheet reprinted in 1866: numerous distinctive marks of the erroneous original type will be found, in particular, the two large defects pointed out in the illustration. This stamp, therefore, is Type II; the adjacent stamps on the right in the reprint must be numbered III and IV, and the unreprinted stamp is Type I. In summary, the types should be numbered II, III, IV in each value from left to right in the reprint sheet; the same types, the same originals, must have the same numbers, and the unreprinted originals belong to Type I.

If it is objected that the original plate types could have been transposed during the frame change, I shall answer in the negative, because of three facts: (1) one type of each value was oxidized excessively; it is thus logical to admit that the original plate contained the four types of each value (block of eight) and that it was the two Type I clichés that oxidized, the right side of the plate having been stored for fourteen years against a cellar wall. They cannot be Type IV, proof to the contrary being furnished by the marginal copy of the 15-centime from the Ferrari sale. (2) Four reprints were issued in blocks of six from 1886 to 1889 without any transposition of types; moreover, for the fifth reprint, issued a little later, they eliminated the two types on the left, leaving only a block of four of Types III and IV of

each value; that amputation, which is identical with the one carried out in 1866, produced no change in the arrangement of the remaining types. (3) The finest mint copies of the Ferrari collection have lateral margins that are almost 4 mm wide — half of the space between the

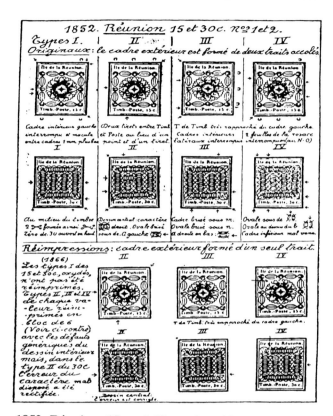

1852. Réunion. 15- and 30-centime. Nos. 1 and 2. Originals: the outer frame is formed with two closely set lines. I. Inner frame is broken and ink spot between frames 1 mm below break. II. Two hyphens between "Timb" and "Poste," instead of a dot or a hyphen. The "T" of Timb is very close to the left frame. Inner lateral frames are broken. III. Two leaves of the rosette are broken (northwest). Second row: I. In middle of stamp, two characters are formed this way. "0" of "30" is open on top. II. Center design character on right: broken oval under "de." On left. III. Broken frame under "m"; broken oval under "n." Bottom right. IV. Oval under "de." Oval above "b." Lower frame: poor execution. Bottom section: reprints: outer frame is formed with a single line. 1866. The oxidized Type I, 15- and 30-centime, was not reprinted. Types II, III, and IV of each value were reprinted in blocks of six (see text) with the typical defects of the inner design, but in Type II of the 30-centime, the error of the poorly positioned character was corrected. Center design: the error is corrected. "T" of Timb, very close to left frame.

stamps — and this dimension, when doubled, corresponds to the lateral gutters of the reprints, bearing in mind, of course, that the two lines of the early outer frames were replaced by a single line of lesser thickness, with the probable addition of an outer typographical interline to replace the second line and to help the locking up of the forms.

This irrefutable argument will guide my description of the following 1852 values.

1852. Imperforate, 15- and 30-centime. Nos. 1 and 2. *Originals:* typographed on slightly glossy bluish paper; a plate of eight clichés, four of which are 15-centime stamps, and four, 30-centime, the latter placed under the former. The thick lines of the outer frame of each stamp are formed by two bold-printed, side-by-side lines, together being ³/₅ mm average width; one of these lines is somewhat wider than the other, and you can see a gap between them in places. (Use magnifying glass for illustration.)

15-centime. 18¹/₅ x 23¹/₅ mm, on average. The types of the 15-centime stamp are identified by various typical defects shown under each of them in the illustration. They also can be identified by using the method developed in 1892 by the British writer, the Reverend R.B. Earee *(Album Weeds; or, How to detect forged stamps.* London, Stanley Gibbons, 1882. Serrane probably had access to the third revised and enlarged edition: London–New York, Stanley Gibbons, 1905, two volumes.) Examine the arrangement of the small crescents in the nine circles of the design.

Type I. The three bottom crescents are open on top; the one in the upper right corner is open at bottom; the top inner frame is touching the right frame.

Type II. The three top crescents are open at bottom; one of the small rosette leaves (on the right and above the median left crescent) is broken at its extremity (see the illustration; be sure to use magnifying glass).

Type III. The three crescents on the right are open on the left; there are breaks in the inner frame lines at the place indicated.

Type IV. The three bottom crescents are open on top; the upper right corner crescent is open on the left. Two leaves of the center rosette (north-northwest) are broken at their extremity.

30-centime. 17¹/₂ x 22¹/₂ mm, on average.

Type I. Inner right frame is broken above the lower ornamental circle. Lower right corner is broken. Smudge at the left extremity of the lower frame. See the illustration.

Type II. Corners on left are broken. Ornamental character error: upright instead of prone, and so forth.

Type III. Lower right corner is broken. Right branch of the "X" design is executed imperfectly above figure "3." Letter "c" is slanted a bit more to the right than in the other types.

Type IV. Inner lateral frames are broken (see illustration); various defects in the ornamental design; smudge at the extreme left of the lower frame.

These stamps sometimes were canceled with a sixty-four-dot lozenge in blue (Ferrari collection, two used copies), but more frequently they were canceled with pen and ink — bars or irregular cross-ruling — on arrival, and many mint stamps that had circulated received no cancellation whatever. Note: The lateral margins of the mint copies must be about 2 mm wide (minimum) in order to be judged "select." The used stamps often were trimmed by shippers: a fine copy at the Ferrari sale, lot 309, small dot cancellation, had four margins about 1¹/₂ cm wide.

Reprints: 1. 1866: 15-centime, 17⁴/₅ x about 22²/₅ mm. 30-centime, 17¹/₄ x about 22²/₅ mm. Outer frame, ²/₅ mm thick. Reprints ordered by Moens. Type I stamps were omitted in the original plate; correction of the Type II error of the 30-centime stamp; replacement of the double line outer frames by single line frames, and good impression in blocks of six (Types II, III, and IV of the 15-centime on top and the same types of 30-centime at bottom). Thin, gray-blue paper. Distinctive marks as in the originals, with the exception of the outer frames and a few deviant inner frames.

Subsequently, responding to other dealers' requests, they executed other "reprints" that are less interesting than the first one (the catalogue lists and quotations are valid only for the latter) because of the alterations and various defects that had affected the distinctive original characteristics of the stamps. Nevertheless, we shall enumerate them with their principal characteristics.

2. 1880: block of six; thin, bluish gray paper; good impression like those of 1866;

15-centime, Type II, the outer frame lines meet in the upper right corner; Types III and IV, no dot after Réunion and the disappearance of the dot after Timb in Type IV. 30-centime, Type II; the frames no longer meet in the upper left corner; Type III, they meet in the corner; Type IV, the dot after Timb has disappeared.

3. 1886: block of six; thin, grayish paper; bad impression. Type II of the 15-centime, altered; the circles and crescent of a few elements were replaced awkwardly (after a temporary loss of four of them); the two crescents, top right, are open on the right; the one on the left in the middle is open on the left.

4. 1885: block of six; bluish pelure paper; bad impression, pronounced print-through; same defects in Type II of the 15-centime as in the preceding reprint.

5. 1889–90: bluish pelure paper; good impression. Since complaints probably were made concerning the alteration of Type II of the 15-centime stamp, the printer of the reprints, who was not very anxious to get into such philatelic details, decided quite simply to amputate the Type II from each value and to print

blocks of four containing Types III and IV of the 15- and 30-centime stamps. To compensate and satisfy his customers, he produced a good impression and placed the two types of the 15-centime in a tête-bêche position.

Note: All the reprints being typographed, there is more or less evident indention; the distinguishing marks of the originals, which occasionally are executed poorly, still are present because of the impression. Nonglossed paper. In reality, there are no official reprints; however, the word "reprint" seemed preferable to the use I made of it in the five preceding printings, so that the reader could distinguish these creations from the counterfeits which never came from the printing presses of Réunion.

Forgeries: a. early fantasy of the 15-centime; lithographed on gray paper, with REUNION ISLE at the top and a floweret in the corners.

b. 15-centime, typographed on thin lilac paper, easily identifiable by the triple frame (thick outer one, and two thin inner ones regularly joined); crescents replaced by the open circles, all openings facing the middle of the stamp.

c. 15-centime, typographed on grayish paper; three frames as in b; a copy of Type IV, but with lower left crescent open on the right and numerous secondary defects.

d. 15-centime, typographed on thin bluish paper; "R" of Réunion is resting on the circle; rosette is touching this circle and the two lateral circles; triple frame as in b, and thin outer dividing frame line about $1\frac{1}{4}$ mm from the thick frame; no dot after Timb, but a hyphen which is too close to the two letters; the "i" of Timb is connected with the "T" at bottom; figure "1" has an oblique terminal line on top. The crescents are very faint; sixteen blank dots in rows of four in the star in the center of the stamp.

e. (Geneva) 15-centime, lithographed on bluish pelure paper; triple frame and dividing frame as in d; the "R" of Réunion is $\frac{1}{2}$ mm from the upper center circle; the "a" of "La" is connected with the bottom of the "R"; no dot after Réunion; the "i" of Timb has no dot and forms a four-branched "m"; no hyphen after Timb and the dot following this word is resting on the serif at the base of the "P" of POSTE; the center star has eight oblique lines with about ten pearls among them; the rosette is touching the circles, top and bottom. Counterfeit executed in small sheets containing four 15-centime stamps and four 30-centime, both values being side by side in each quarter of the sheet; FACSIMILE, 8 mm, above each stamp.

f. 30-centime, lithographed from a sheet described under e. Two frames (one thick, one thin) and a dividing frame line $1\frac{3}{4}$ mm away; letter "e" of "de" is a "c"; no dot after Réunion; the "i" of Timb has a dot and is connected with the base of the "T" and the "m"; no hyphen and dot placed as in e; the "e" of Poste is a "c."

g. 30-centime, fantasy with REUNION ISLE as in a.

h. 30-centime, typographed; same set as the 15-centime, Type d; closely resembles 30-centime, Type f (connected frames and dividing frame lines), but there is a dot after Réunion and no dot after the word in a secondary type. In the upper inscription, the words are $\frac{1}{2}$ mm from each other instead of about 1 mm, and the final "n" is $\frac{3}{4}$ mm from the right frame instead of about $1\frac{1}{2}$ mm. Timb and Poste are 1 mm apart instead of 2 mm, and for this reason the hyphen is above the dot following Timb; the "c" after the value figure is a small capital letter.

i. 30-centime, typographed on bluish paper; the two frames are joined; no hyphen after Timb; no accent over "e" of Réunion; inner design is not congruent.

j. 30-centime, lithographed; dark ultramarine shade impression on thick bluish paper; two frames; outer frame is about 1 mm thick; figure "3" with rectilinear top; no dot after Réunion; no hyphen after Timb.

k. There are other lithographed stamps from various sources; they are identified by the lack of indention and by many defects in lettering and design. Comparison with the originals in the illustration will be sufficient.

l. Likewise, there are collotypes that are more deceptive in their overall appearance, but they come from "reprints"; lettering and design defects, arbitrary measurements, and noncongruent paper will enable one to spot them.

m. Finally, there are photographic fantasies (same observation as above) and various photographic papers.

Subsequent overprinted issues. A great number of overprint types and varieties require specializing. Specializing is all the more appropriate since most of the stamps of these issue received *forged overprints,* some of which are executed very well; detailed comparison is indispensable, except for a few early fantastic counterfeits. All necessary information can be found in the works of Marconnet (1897, pp. 360–66) and de Vinck (1928, pp. 135–38).

1885. "52" overprint on the 40-centime stamp. Marconnet says (p. 370) that it was the postmaster general of the Réunion postal service who had the four sheets of 100 of these fantasies executed. There are some on piece, with complimentary original cancellation, which probably are from the same source. The 5-centime of Réunion was counterfeited inexpertly in Geneva, occasionally with the forged Geneva cancellation: double circle (22 mm), with date, REUNION 2 SEPT 84 ST BENOIT.

1891. REUNION overprints. Nos. 17 to 31. The *original* overprint is 15 mm wide (no variety); the letters are $2\frac{1}{2}$ mm high.

Forgeries: check whether the 1881 type of forged stamps is in question (see French Colonies).

Numerous *forged overprints, especially Geneva.* Comparison is indispensable. The forged Geneva cancellation is double circle (20 1/2 mm), with date, REUNION 23 SEPT 21 Sᵀ BENOIT.

1892–1900; 1900–1905; 1912. Peace and Commerce type. *Forgeries:* under French Colonies, see whether forged Geneva stamps of this type, which are sometimes provided with the forged cancellation in black described under "postage due stamps," are in question.

1915–16. RED CROSS as overprint. Nos. 80 and 81. *Forged overprints:* frequently inverted; detailed comparison is indispensable and even expertizing for the most deceptive counterfeits. The "Black Cross" (No. 80) was counterfeited right in Réunion and canceled with an original postmark (1917).

1917. "0.01" overprints. No. 83. *Forged overprints* (with varieties) executed in Réunion, occasionally canceled like the 1915 "Black Cross."

1889–92. Postage due stamps. Nos. 1 to 5. A single typographical composition was used for the printing of all values. The various typical defects of this composition are indicated in the illustration, except for certain letters ("p" and "c" of percevoir, "e," "i," and "s" of centimes), in order not to confuse the design exposition; there are others of lesser importance that the reader can find by using a magnifying glass.

Following the alterations that were executed for a change of figures after the printing of each value, certain defects disappeared, or else new ones were created; some of these are indicated below.

1889. A printing of four values; 5-, 10-, 20-, and 30-centime, in that order, on yellowish paper; $17 1/3 – 2/3$ (according to type) x $21 1/2$ mm. Good impression. The distinctive marks (defects) are the same in the four values, but beginning with the 10-centime (inclusive), the letters of "Centimes" are alignd better in Type I, and beginning with the 20-centime (inclusive), the space between "t" and "i" in Centimes is reduced in Type II ($2/5$ mm instead of about $2/3$ mm; the misplaced "a" on the right side is under the "i"),

1892. A printing of four values; 5-, 15-, 10-, and 30-centime, in that order, on rough white paper. The 5- and 15-centime were printed first and the alteration of the value figures caused the disappearance of "ti" of Centimes; it also caused the shifting of letters "mes" to the right, the absence of "a" and an evident enlargement of Type II. The oxidized or clogged plate and the inferior quality paper produced a rather defective impression, which we find again in the 10- and 30-centime stamps. In these two values, Type II was corrected, but the "a" is placed almost under the "n" of Centimes and the final "N" of REUNION is

moved about 1 mm to the right (about 1 1/2 mm between "O" and "N") and is touching the top right inner frame.

In the illustration of the ten types of the 1892 printing, arrows indicate a few changes in the defects of the first printing. The same holds for the other three values, with a few secondary changes, however, and bearing in mind what we just have explained regarding Type II.

Forgeries: (a) so-called "reprint"; they can be identified by a somewhat detailed study of the characteristics described for the originals; noncongruent paper. (b) Lithographical or photolithographical reproductions (no indention) with arbitrary dimensions, on noncongruent paper, with various small additional defects. (c) Set and single typographed stamps to be identified by dimensions and paper (see a). (d) Geneva

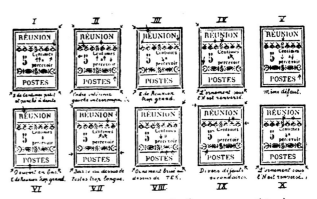

1889–92. Réunion. Postage due stamps. Nos. 1–5. Typical defects of typographical composition.
(1) 1889. First printing, 5-, 10-, 20-, and 30-centime. I. "s" of Centimes is too small and is slanted to the right. II. Inner left frame is broken. III. The "E" of REUNION is too large. IV. The ornament under the "N" is inverted. V. Same defect. VI. Bottom "O" is open. "E" of REUNION is too large. VII. Bar above POSTES is too long. VIII. Broken ornament above "TES." IX. Various secondary defects. X. The ornament under the "N" is inverted. (2) 1892. Second printing, 5-, 15-, 10-, and 30-centime (same comparison).

set; all values in a single block of five on very white paper; 17 x 21¼ mm; the "S"-shaped ornaments, under the first "N" of REUNION and above the "S" of POSTES, have no black balls at their extremities; 10- and 15-centime, the "s" of Centimes is ridiculously small; 20- and 30-centime, the first "e" of the same word, likewise; in all values, the first "r" of percevoir is too large and the excessively wide Centimes almost touching the inner right frame (except in the 5-centime). Forged cancellation on this set: double circle, with date, REUNION 2ᴱ/20 JANV 1892 ST BENOIT, in blue. (e) Very widespread typographed set; bad impression, similar to that of the 1892 printing, but the types do not correspond to any original type; 17½ x 22 mm; POSTES is 10¾ mm wide, instead of 9¾–10 mm; letter "O" of this word is ⅓ mm too low; frames are broken in the four corners; grayish paper.

1890–1903. Parcel post stamps. *Originals:* typographed frames; inner inscriptions are handstamp printed.

1890. Double frame, total width, 1 mm (heavy frame line, ⅗ mm thick, and a thin line); these frames do not meet in the corners; the whole stamp is surrounded by a thin dividing frame line, 1¼ mm from the double frame. Pelure paper (30 microns); orange-yellow; dimensions of the thick frame: 32⅓ by about 33½ mm. The outer circle of the handstamp printed impression measures 27½ mm; the inner circle, 19½ mm; TIMBRE is 11¾ mm wide at top; 11⅕ mm at bottom; 2½ mm high; figure "10" is 2¼ mm high; CENTIMES is 14 mm long, 1¾ mm high. There are two half-shade lines in the ornaments between circles.

Forgeries: on excessively thick paper; lithographed; inexact measurements. Fournier counterfeited this stamp on yellow-ochre; the outer frame is 1½ mm thick. The dividing frame line is 1 mm from the other frame; the letters of CENTIMES are 2⅓ mm high. No shading in the ornaments; forged cancellation like that of the postage due stamps.

1898. No. 2a. Blue frame similar to the preceding one, but different dimensions (30 by about 33½ mm); orange Bristol paper (153 microns); dividing frame line about 1¾ mm away.

1903. No. 2. Pale blue frame on thick yellow paper and on very thick paper (125 microns). The timer handstamp impression of Nos. 2 and 2a is the same as that of No. 1, but with occasional slight differences in measurement and differences due to indention which are found in all hand-applied impressions.

France — Offices Abroad

Alexandria

1899–1900. Nos. 1–18. The overprint was counterfeited on all values. Comparison often is indispensable. Also counterfeited in Geneva.

1921–23. Nos. 35–50 and 57–60. Forged overprints pullulate to such an extent that the 60-millieme on a 2-franc Paris overprint has become common. Comparative expertizing is indispensable.

1915. Red Cross. Counterfeited in Geneva and elsewhere. Upright, inverted, and double overprints are found.

See French Colonies for Nos. 31–33 and 47–50.

Canton

First three issues. An abundance *of forged overprints* (also Geneva first overprint), particularly for values above 25 centimes (also 5-centime dark green, No. 4). Many are unsuccessful, but there also are a great number of fantasy errors.

1919. For the values overprinted in piasters, see the same issue under Indochina.

Cavalle

See Levant, French post offices.

1893–1900. Nos. 1 to 9. *Numerous forged overprints.* Comparison is indispensable. Naturally, there are poorly executed forged overprints, some that are badly printed (smudging), but there are others that are quite successful. Canceled French stamps have been overprinted, which facilitates the recognition of the fraud.

1902–3. Nos. 15 and 16. See the complete repertory of forgeries of the Merson type, with forged overprints, under French Colonies.

Hoi Hao

1901, 1903–4. Nos. 1 to 31. Check first to see whether the stamp itself is forged (see French Colonies, Peace and Commerce type); next, make a detailed comparison of the overprint with originals. The forged Geneva overprint (1901) was applied on original and forged stamps.

1906–8. Nos. 32 to 47. Comparison of the overprint is indispensable. For the 75-centime and 5-franc, see French Colonies, Peace and Commerce type.

1919. Nos. 81 and 82. For the overprints of the values in piasters, see the same issue under Indochina.

Kwangchowan

1906. Overprinted stamps. Nos. 1 to 17. *Forged overprints:* comparison with the impressions of the two original printings (brilliant or dull ink) is necessary. As for the 75-centime and the 5-franc stamps, make sure first whether forgeries of the Peace and Commerce type are involved (see French Colonies). With regard to the 2- and 4-piaster overprint on 5- and 10-franc, Nos. 50 and 51, see also the 1919 issue of Indochina.

Mongtseu

1903–6. Stamps overprinted MONGTZE. Nos. 1 to 16. Numerous *forged overprints:* comparison is necessary. The overprint errors are clandestine fantasies.

Forgeries: see French Colonies, Peace and Commerce type.

1906–8. Stamps overprinted MONG-TSEU. Nos. 17 to 32. *Forged overprints:* see French Colonies, Peace and Commerce type.

Forgeries of the Peace and Commerce type (75-centime, 5-franc), likewise.

1908. Overprints in carmine or blue. Nos. 34a to 50. Comparison of the overprints is useful.

1919. Stamps overprinted in CENTS and PIASTERS. Nos. 51 to 67. *Forged overprints* of the 2- and 4-piaster: see the same issue under Indochina.

Pakhoi

1903–4. Overprinted stamps. Nos. 1 to 16. *Forgeries:* check first whether the values of the Peace and Commerce type are forgeries, as described under French Colonies.

Forged overprints: comparison is necessary; the errors and varieties are clandestine fantasies. The PAKHOI overprint and various overprints in Chinese coin money values were counterfeited in Geneva.

1906. Overprinted in two words. Nos. 17 to 33. *Originals:* typographical overprints — black or red, shiny or dull, depending on the printing.

Forgeries and forged overprints: same observation as above.

1908. Overprinted stamps. Nos. 34 to 50. Compare the overprints of the 5- and 10-franc stamps.

1919. Overprinted stamps. Nos. 51 to 67. *Forged overprints* of the 2- and 4-piaster on the 5- and 10-franc. See French Colonies.

Port Lagos

1893. Stamps of France overprinted PORT LAGOS. Forged overprints are numerous. Comparison is necessary. (See Cavalle and Dedeagh.)

Port Said

1899. PORT-SAID overprint. Nos. 1 to 18. *Originals:* typographical overprint with dieresis over the "I" or with a single dot on the left only.

Numerous forged overprints; comparison is indispensable for all canceled values (examine cancellation) and for a few mint values. The overprint was counterfeited in Geneva

1899. "25" and VINGT-CINQ overprints on 10-centime. The "25" overprint was made by handstamp in vermilion or black. The VINGT-CINQ overprint is typographed in red; the hyphen is made with a short, thick line or with a longer line that is less thick.

Very numerous *forged overprints,* especially lithographs (arbitrary dimensions and shades, lack of indention, and so forth); detailed comparison is indispensable and the use of the template is indicated for the large overprint. The latter was counterfeited in carmine-tinted red in Geneva, but the hyphen was considered superfluous.

1902–20. Values in francs. Nos. 32 to 34. *Forgeries:* see Merson type under French Colonies.

1915. Red Cross. No. 35. Typographical overprint in carmine.

Subsequent issues. Postage stamps and postage due stamps. A great number of overprints were counterfeited, occasionally with expertise; the most detailed comparison is absolutely indispensable.

Tchongking

1902. TCHONG KING overprint. Nos. 1 to 31. Unofficial overprints. Handstamp impression. Black or vermilion-tinted red overprint. Numerous forged *overprints:* comparison is necessary. The 1903 overprint was counterfeited in Geneva.

Subsequent issues. Nos. 32 to 98. *Original overprints:* typographed. In the 1903 issue, the distance between the name and the Indochinese characters varies.

Forged overprints: comparison is indispensable. As for the forged overprints, "2" and "4" piasters on 5- and 10-franc, Nos. 97 and 98, see Indochina.

Forgeries of the Peace and Commerce type: see French Colonies.

1903. Postage due stamp. Nos. 1 to 10. *Forgeries:* see forged postage due stamps under French Colonies.

Forged overprints: on originals and on forgeries; comparison is indispensable.

Yunnan Fou

1903–4 YUNNANSEN overprint. Nos. 1 to 15. *Originals:* black overprint; the Chinese characters are those of the China issue of 1902, with which they should be compared; there are *forged overprints* (especially Geneva), and forged overprints and overprint errors that were printed clandestinely. Forgeries of the Peace and Commerce type: see French Colonies.

1906. YUNNAN-FOU overprint. Nos. 16 to 32. The overprints are red or black; shiny ink in the first printing and dull in the second.

Forged overprints: comparison is necessary. Forgeries of the 75-centime and of the 5-franc, Peace and Commerce type: see French Colonies.

1908. YUNNANFOU overprints. Nos. 33 to 49. *Original* typographed *overprint* in carmine or blue.

Forged overprints: comparison is necessary.

1919. Same, overprinted in CENTS and PIASTERS. Nos. 50 to 66. *Forged overprints* of the 2- and 4-piaster stamps: see Indochina.

French Colonies

These stamps do not usually belong in a European collection, but the specialist should be acquainted with them to avoid confusion with imperforate stamps of the mother country or with reprints.

There are no overprints in the French colonies, whereas the colonies properly so called have an abundant supply of them, and, naturally, forged overprints are plentiful. The time has passed, unfortunately, when a simple notation — for example, "the original overprint measures x mm, and the forged one, x plus 1 mm" — could be used effectively in tracking them down.

Forgers have made tremendous progress, and overprints that have been cleverly copied with the same kind of ink, identical type, acquired in the country of the stamp's origin, or, sometimes, original type clandestinely forged, and with very exact gutter measurements, are no longer the exception. All of them must be compared carefully with reliable original overprints. It also is necessary to ascertain whether the stamp itself is forged completely. Thus, it is wise to recommend that only those who are interested in specializing collect these stamps.

1859–65. First issue. Eagle type. Nos. 1 to 6.
Originals: see the distinctive features in the illustration.
Sheets of 360 stamps in two panes of 180 (18 x 10).
Select: four margins $^1/_2$ mm wide. Mint stamps may be gumless.
Varieties: the stamps on white paper are from the first printing. The 20-centime is found on yellowish gray paper (rare) and the 40-centime on buff paper. This coloration, which apparently is not caused by the gum, may be attributable to the fact that there was printing on the fly leaves that were inserted to protect

Distinctive characteristics of the originals, Nos. 1–6. Outer circle: 112 pearls. Inner circle: 96 pearls. In the center: thirty-nine horizontal shading lines, one of them under the cask. Bottom left: the letter "S" is higher than the other letters.

the stamps during shipment. No. 2: Figure "5" on the right is almost always in parentheses; however, these were removed occasionally by a dirty plate; the same is true in regard to the cedilla under the "C" of FRANÇAIS on all stamp values. Stamps that have a background of lines are not common.

Nos. 1–6, which are pin rouletted (Cochin China), require expertizing.

The double impressions are printers' waste.

Reprints (Granet): 1887. The originals' shades are those of the France issue of 1862. Brighter shades, no gum, thicker paper; the 80-centime is bright carmine on well-tinted rose paper. All are rarer than the originals.

Cancellations: this matter belongs to specialization in each colony.

Pairs: three units; block of four mint: 6M; used: 8–12U.

Originals: see the distinctive characteristics in the accompanying illustration.

Forgeries:

I. Early forgeries: the whole set on thick yellowish paper, 114 and 92 pearls; thirty-two hatch lines; no dot before the "C" of COLONIES.

II. Same. The entire set on thick paper; the cross moved too far to the right; 115 and 92 pearls; no finesse in the hatching.

III. Geneva set (F.). On white or glossy colored paper, different shades; no dot between the value figure and the following "C"; the left downstroke of the "M" is slanted toward the pearl on the right of the cross instead of between the two pearls; the design of the feathered part of the wings is crudely executed. (Note: These counterfeits have the dot, the secret mark in the upper right corner of the ornamental design.)

IV. Brussels set. Crown slanted to the right; noncongruent background lines. Corner design comparison should be sufficient for making a determination.

Official forgeries: lithographed on rosy paper of which the laid lines are scarcely visible. No secret mark; 116 and 92 pearls; thirty-six poorly executed hatch lines; seemingly imitating a worn plate. Cross leaning to the right; the bird of prey's eye is a white dot. The upper curl of the first "S" of POSTES is too large; moreover, the letter is the same height as the other letters, whereas in the original it is higher. On cover, expertized: 100 francs. Also, this forgery was circulated in the postal system; it also is found single with a forged cancellation of generally large dots.

1871–72. Second issue. Napoleon portrait. Nos. 7 to 10. *Select:* four margins ³/₄ mm wide. The 1-, 30-, and 80-centime mint may be confused with the Rothschild issue (less rare, except the 1-centime stamp). Compare the shades.

The 5-centime original yellow-green on yellowish green does not bear comparison with No. 12 of France, with its consistently finer printing; few distinct dots between the center background hatch lines; the corner burelage, especially that at the bottom, seems to have been printed from a slightly worn plate; adequate margins and the cancellation (should the occasion arise) prevent this stamp from being confused with the perforated France No. 20...trimmed perforation. A rose-colored essay of the 30-centime exists; it follows that one should always check the "8" figures in No. 10.

With regard to the pin rouletted stamp (Cochin China), same remark as for the previous issue.

The 1-centime was reprinted (Granet), 1887, imperforate, green, dark bronze on green, no gum: rare.

There are a few printing varieties, especially in the background lines.

Pairs: 3U; blocks of four, Nos. 7 and 10: 8U; others: rare.

Fake: France perforated No. 20, with trimmed perforation; no margins or margins added after complete remounting of the stamp; check the cancellation also.

5-centime forgery: bad lithograph, green on greenish paper; four small pearls in the corners instead of St.

Andrew's crosses; the center background pearls are too far apart; the lettering is much too thin.

80-centime: fake of the 30-centime essay in rose; check the figures which sometimes are painted over in this essay.

1871. Ceres. Nos. 11 to 13. *Select:* four margins, minimum width ¹/₂ mm. Rather numerous shades; Nos. 11–13 were rouletted. Granet reprints (1887): same characteristics as for the Eagle type. No. 13 with retouched "4" figures adjacent to normal ones is worth double. Steamship cancellations are in demand.

Pairs: 4U; blocks of four: 8U.

Forgeries: No. 11 was counterfeited in Geneva (F.): yellowish paper, bistre-yellow impression — not very important, because paper and shades may be changed. The principal distinctive mark is the poorly executed burelage, particularly the bottom left corner, where the wavy lines are almost straight, too large, and have almost no dots between them. The tête-bêche was counterfeited by the same printer. For more information, see France, first issue.

Forged cancellations on these forgeries: black or blue anchor cancellation or postmark with date, double circle, COCHINCHINE SAIGON 6 OCT 76, in black or blue (the two tête-bêche stamps are found in this set); anchor is too thick in a dot lozenge that is too large. See also (France) photolithographed forgeries of the first issue.

Faking of No. 13: France No. 38, with perforation trimmed off, was affixed to a piece of cover with its original cancellation and provided with a forged cancellation, SAINT DENIS DE LA REUNION 7 OCT 79, on both stamp and piece. There are other fakings of this kind to create colonial Nos. 14–45.

Also stamps of France, with trimmed perforation, with forged wavy circle cancellation, SAINT DENIS 7 OCT 79 LA REUNION, applied on the French cancellation (on piece, usually; Geneva).

Granet *reprints* (1887): same characteristics as for the Eagle type; see first issue France reprints in France.

1872–77. Ceres. Large figure stamps. Nos. 14 to 17. *2-centime original:* The paper of No. 15 is rather similar to that of France's No. 51, while the 2-centime essay is on white instead of very slightly yellowish paper. The essay was colored, rebacked, and gummed to create a new No. 15 stamp.

2-centime forgery: lithographed on dark yellow paper; no dot before the "R" of REPUB.; bottom of chin is suggested by a single curved hatch line.

4-centime: No. 16 was faked by applying a forged cancellation on the 4-centime essay (dark gray, white paper). This cancellation obscures an almost imperceptible spot on Ceres's cheek. Formerly, the 4-centime France imperforate (pale gray) was used by fakers. The 4-centime always has the Cochin China cancellation, but the fakes do, too (ink too fresh, too grayish).

Also, *4-centime fake:* essay of dark gray 4-centime, on grayish instead of white paper, with forged cancellation; this essay is only about 55 microns thick instead of 70 microns; small color spot on the cheek. Of course, the 2- and 4-centime of France (4-centime pale gray) had their teeth (perforation) removed in order to qualify as colonial stamps.

4-centime forgery: the "E" of REPUB. is too close to the other letters; the lower bar is too long and its median bar is too low.

Note: The spot on the cheek of the 4-centime essay is nearly 1 mm long, oblique, and is found near the middle of a line beginning at the lip juncture and ending at the bottom of the ear; a little lower, under the spot, there also are two almost imperceptible small dots; the spot frequently was scraped off; the essay is wider than the colonial stamp, $18^1/_{10}$ mm instead of about $17^7/_8$ mm.

Pairs: 3U; blocks of four: 6M, 8U.

Select: four margins, minimum width $^3/_4$ mm, to avoid trimmed perforations. There are lined backgrounds.

Large, thick figures. Nos. 18 to 21. Pairs and blocks as above. Background lines. Four margins, $^1/_2$ mm wide. The bistre-yellow (No. 19) and pale brown (No. 20) shades are in demand, as are the stamps with lines in the background.

Reprints: one may consider the 15-centime imperforate, dark brown or bistro on white, a reprint of France No. 55, and the 80-centime imperforate, pale rose, a reprint of No. 57, both less rare than the colonial stamps.

Forgeries: 10- and 15-centime. (For corner burelage, see first issue, France.)

In the 10-centime: same remark as for No. 11 concerning the burelage; the large "1" figures extend right down to the white line. Same forged cancellations and black grill design of France! The 15-centime forgery, like the preceding one, can be recognized by the burelage and by the absence of the expertizer's secret marks that are described under the first issue of France.

Also, a bad 30-centime forgery has no dots before or after the tablet figures and words; it is $^4/_5$ mm too wide.

Small figure stamps. Nos. 22 and 23. *Original:* 15-centime, printing often less blotchy or defective; Granet *reprints* of the 25-centime in milky blue.

The 15-centime often bears evidence of a dirty plate or flawed printing. There are stamps with background lines.

Select: four margins, $^3/_4$ mm wide.

Pairs and blocks: as above.

Forgeries: see first issue, France, for the various sets of forgeries of the 25-centime, and even of the 15-centime, printed in bistre instead of green; one should include with these a good counterfeit of the 15-centime stamp in which the median bar of the "F" of FRANC is certainly not what it should be; the "C" letters have no serifs; the lettering is too thin; noncongruent corner burelage; frequent large dot lozenge cancellation with "2240" (Marseilles).

1877 and 1878–80. Sage type. Nos. 24 to 45. *Select:* four margins, 1 mm wide. No. 35 was used only in Guadeloupe and Senegal; No. 43, in Madagascar (Nossi-Be, Mayotte, Tahiti) and in Réunion.

Pairs: 3U; blocks of four: 8–20U. Blocks of four of No. 32 are rare mint.

Reprints: 1. The imperforate stamps of the French Peace and Commerce (Sage) type of the 1876–77 issues may be considered reprints. Comparison of shades is indicated, colors being sufficiently different. The 25-centime, for example, is black on rose, like the imperforate French stamp, but an imperforate black on dark red exists.

2. Granet reprints (1887), French Peace and Commerce type, may be confused with the mint colonials; make comparison. The 25-centime has a deeper red, more carmine-tinted background than the colonial stamp, which has a more brownish-red shade.

Fakes: sometimes stamps of France are offered for sale as colonials with perforations removed and an illegible cancellation. Comparison is necessary. Different shades; insufficient or rebuilt margins. This trap can easily be avoided by accepting only select stamps with adequate margins.

1881. Perforated stamps. Nos. 46 to 59. *Forgeries:* the whole set was counterfeited in Geneva (F.), but real colonial overprints being more expensive, the counterfeits generally are fraudulently overprinted and canceled. (In each colony, we show the forged cancellation [woodcut; interchangeable dates; in black or blue].)The accompanying illustration shows the best distinguishing characteristics of the forged stamps: (a) arrangement of hatching above the hair; (b) white bar under COLONIES; (c) lower left corner frame; (d) final "E" of REPUBLIQUE; (e) arrangement of hatching on the bottom of the right forearm; (f) hair design encroaching upon the flagpole; (g) right arm shoulder strap. In general, the perforation is 14 x $13^1/_2$, but one finds $13^1/_3$ x 14, too. Printed in blocks of twelve. There are Geneva forgeries in sheets which do not have all the distinguishing marks shown in the illustration, but the few that are shown provide adequate identification.

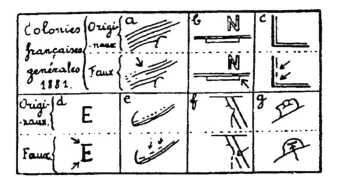

French colonies perforated issue of 1881. Originals. forgeries.

2. Another forged set; usually perf 12; in the originals, the color line of the flag (upper left corner) is indicated simply where the large horizontal hatch lines stop, but here there is a well-defined contour line; the hair completely covers the flagpole; the white line under COLONIES is shaded heavily below and on the right side; there is only a single hatch line on the right forearm; the goddess is unconvincing; most of the fine lines are missing; under the ship, likewise.

Forged cancellations: these do not fall within the scope of this work, being applied, in general, on individual colonial overprinted stamps. Nevertheless, familiarity with them is useful: wood engraved, black or blue, interchangeable dates.

Benin. Nos. 1–12 and postage due stamps 1–4.
GRAND POPO 7 NOV 92 BENIN.
Cochin China. Nos. 1, 2, 3, 5.
SAIGON 3ᶜ/7 NOV 86. COCHINCHINE.
HANOI 3ᶜ/27 FEVR 86 TONKIN.
MYTHO 2ᶜ/16 AOUT 92. COCHINCHINE.
Diégo-Suarez. Nos. 6–9, 10, 13–24, and postage due stamps, Nos. 1 and 2, and three similar postmarks bearing the inscription DIEGO-SUAREZ MADAGASCAR and the dates: 1 SEPT 92; 15 MARS 90; 28 SEPT 91.
Guadeloupe. Nos. 14–26.
ST LOUIS 2 JUIL 91 GUADELOUPE.
BASSE TERRE le/21 JUIL 92. GUADELOUPE.
POINTE A PITRE 2/21 JANV 91. GUADELOUPE
Guyane. Nos. 16–28.
CAYENNE 2 JUIN 92 GUYANE.
Indochina. Nos. 1, 1a, 1b, 2.
INDO-CHINE (the rest is illegible).
New Caledonia. Nos. 21–34.
NOUMEA 19 MAI 92 Nelle CALEDONIE.
NOUMEA 2e/3 SEPT 92 Nelle CALEDONIE.
Obock. Nos. 1–11, 12–20, and postage due stamps 16–18.
OBOCK 27 MARS 92 COLONIE FRANCse.
OBOCK 26 SEPT 92 COLONIE FRANCse.

Saint-Pierre and Miquelon. Nos. 18–30.
ST PIERRE ET MIQUELON 12 SEPT 92.
ILK AUX CHIENS 2 AOUT 92. St PIERRE ET MIQ.
Tahiti. Nos. 7–18.
PAPEETE 18 AOUT 9. TAHITI.

1892–1900–1912. Special issue for each colony. Peace and Commerce type with colony designation at bottom. Deceptive *forgeries* made in Geneva in sheets of thirty, each stamp having a different colony name in its lower tablet, from SULTANAT D'ANJOUAN to the twenty-ninth and thirtieth stamps which have SOUDAN FRANÇAIS. The forged overprints of 1912 were counterfeited and applied upright, inverted, and wide spaced on these forgeries and on originals. Perf 13³/₄ x 13³/₄ instead of 14 x 13¹/₂. The illustration gives information on the three most defective aspects of the design, reproduced photographically: (a) left hand of the goddess; (b) Mercury's right hand; (c) his navel; (d) one or both of the breast nipples of the goddess are missing.

The forged cancellations applied on these forgeries will be described in connection with various colonies.

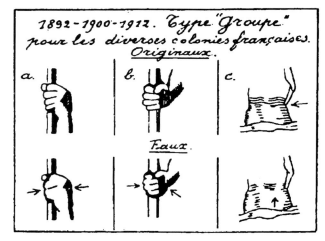

1892–1900–1912 Peace and Commerce type for the various French colonies. Originals. Forgeries.

Postage Due Stamps

1884–92. French type postage due stamps. Nos. 1 to 17. 1-, 2-, and 5-franc black, format about 17³/₄ x 21¹/₄ mm. Identification of the distinctive characteristics of original stamps Nos. 1–14 is facilitated by the accompanying illustration. The ornament under the "E" of CHIFFRE is separated from the double line by a gap.

Early forgeries: a few ludicrous counterfeits. One of them, a typographed creation, has only one frame; format 17¹/₂ x 21³/₄ mm; high-value stamps, and the 60-

centime stamp. In others, the inscriptions are arbitrary; comparison with an original easily will permit identification; check especially the "C" of CHIFFRE, whose lower extremity ends in a horizontal line, whereas in most and modern counterfeits it is cut obliquely, its prolongation touching the foot of the "R." In various modern sets, it also should be observed that the paper is too yellowish at times; the accent on the "A" is horizontal, or else it is oblique and is touching the letter; the fine framework above the tablets of CHIFFRE and TAXE is missing; some letters are too wide ("R" of CHIFFRE) or too high (second "E" of PERCEVOIR), etc.

Separate mention of the very common overseas forgeries follows:

I. *Geneva forgeries (F.).* 1-, 2-, and 5-franc black and red-brown, *first cliché*. Lithographed; 17 x 21¼ mm. The ornament under the "E" is ¼ mm from the double line. See sketches b, d, f, and h in the illustration. Common white, grayish, or yellowish paper. These perforated forgeries were used to fool collectors of French postage dues.

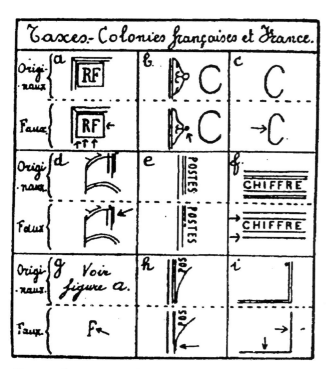

Postage due stamps of the French colonies and France, 1884–92.

II. *Geneva forgery (F.). Second cliché.* Photogravure. 17⅘ x 21⅕ mm. The ornament under the "E" touches the double line. See sketches a–e in the illustration. Same value, same paper, similarly perforated, to fool collectors of French dues.

Also, the first set comprises all values, beginning with the 1-centime stamp.

III. *Other series.* The most insidious is a photolithographed forgery. See sketches b, f, and g in the illustration. The very fine line above the tablet of CHIFFRE is too close to it and merges with it in places. There is a very fine line that tops the cartouche of the word TAXE, although some say it is invisible and blends with the cartouche. Well-proportioned.

Another set with excessively white paper (85–95 microns, gummed), most deceptive of all, copied from the 1882–92 reprints; 1-, 2-, and 5-franc black, Nos. 12–14 (France Nos. 22–24, under France); 55–60 microns instead of 50–55 microns for France postage due stamps; width, 17½ mm. (See the illustration for principal defects.)

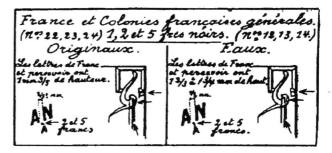

France (Nos. 22–24) and French colonies (Nos. 12–14). 1-, 2-, and 5-franc black. Originals. Letters of FRANC and PERCEVOIR are 1⅗ mm high. Forgeries. Letters of FRANC and PERCEVOIR are 1⅔–¾. mm high.

The most distinctive characteristic of all these forgeries is the fuzziness of the impression, especially above and below the streamer that bears the value, including the curl or spiral under the number. These forgeries don't compare to the original typographed impression, which resembles gravure.

See below for canceled forgeries.

Postage due stamps. Nos. 24 to 26. 60-centime brown, 1-franc rose, and 1-franc carmine. The forgeries have the characteristics of the preceding stamps.

Forged cancellations in black or in blue on Nos. 7–11 and 12–14, also on the lower values, Nos. 1–8 (original).

DAKAR 11 JUIL 92 SENEGAL.
CONCENTRA 2e/24 OCT 92 COCHINCHINE.
NOUVELLE CALEDONIE 2e/3 SEPT 92 NOUMEA.
MYTHO 2e/16 AOUT 92 COCHINCHINE.
(Based on a report in *L'Écho de la Timbrologie,* March 15, 1925.)

Forged millesimes: rather numerous. There is good reason to beware, especially of unframed pairs, which should be acquired with millesime only, after comparing the millesime's year shade. Specialization is indispensable.

Forgeries of France. Merson type: 1-, 2-, and 5-franc. This is not a general French colony type; it was used, however, in several colonies with various overprints; it is appropriate to mention it here since that often will dispense with tedious detailed overprint examination. The counterfeiter began by reproducing the three France stamp values; paper is too yellowish; good perforation; a few dissimilarities which probably come from defect retouching made on the photographic reproduction (see the illustration); then, secondary reproductions were made in which POSTES and REPUBLIQUE FRANÇAISE were replaced by the colony's name and POSTE FRANÇAISE; finally, forged overprints and cancellations were applied.

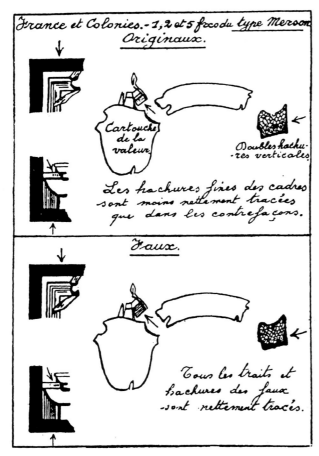

France and colonies. 1-, 2-, 5-franc Merson type. Originals. Value tablet. Double vertical hatching. The fine frame hatching is executed less sharply than in the counterfeits. Bottom: forgeries. All lines and hatching of the forgeries are executed sharply.

Balay type forgeries. 1-, 2-, and 5-franc. For French West Africa. The principal identification marks of these phototypographed forgeries, especially the 5-franc follow: (1) regular perf 14 x 14 instead of 14 x 13$\frac{1}{2}$; (2) overall dimensions, including perforations, 39$\frac{1}{2}$ x 24 mm instead of an average 40 x 24$\frac{1}{2}$ mm; (3) thin (50 microns) transparent paper, instead of 75 microns half-transparent paper; (4) 5-franc dull red, instead of carmine-tinted red or a warm shade of carmine; (5) the palm tree in the upper left corner is shapeless, and it is suspended in space with its broken trunk; the palm trees on the left above the negress look like feather dusters; in the large double-trunk tree, the foliage is shapeless, and the trunk on the right has only two or three oblique shade lines instead of five; (6) round dots on the portrait's forehead and cheek instead of square or rectangular ones; (7) the nose and shaded cheek lines (portrait) are doubly thick; (8) the horizontal shade lines are $\frac{1}{2}$ mm from the circle and the shaded cheek line instead of touching or leaving a gap; (9) the cabin shading is missing in places; (10) above the negress, the uncolored frame line is too thin on the left ($\frac{1}{10}$ mm instead of about $\frac{1}{6}$); (11) the negress: a single oblique shade line on her forehead; bust shading is broken or spot-forming; breasts running together to form a spot; in the loincloth, large shade lines form long spots and half of the fine lines are missing; (12) the colony's name also is reproduced photographically and the bright herringbone typography of the originals is replaced here by letters with rounded extremities (use magnifying glass); use the magnifying glass also for accents and hyphens.

Various forged cancellations.

French Congo

1891–92. Nos. 1 to 7. Numerous varieties which make specialization indispensable. The works of Marconnet (1897, pp. 263–68) and of de Vinck (1928, pp. 61–62) give amateurs enough information on the variety types and their measurements. *Numerous forged overprints,* varieties included; comparison is absolutely indispensable. (Geneva, three types of figure "5.")

1892. Nos. 8 to 11. Same comment as above. CONGO FRANÇAIS must be 18$\frac{1}{2}$ mm long.

1892. Peace and Commerce type. Nos. 12 to 24. For a full statement of these forgeries, see French Colonies.

1900. 15-centime overprint. Nos. 25 and 26. *Forged overprints;* detailed comparison is indispensable. The overprint was counterfeited in Geneva.

1900. Peace and Commerce type. Nos. 42 to 45. *Forgeries:* see French Colonies.

1903. 5 and 10 overprints. Nos. 46 and 47. *Forged overprints,* comparison is necessary. (Geneva, also.)

1916. Red Cross. No. 65 and varieties. Very numerous forged overprints, particularly the double and inverted ones. Very detailed comparison is necessary.

Parcel post stamps, 1891. No.1. *Original:* relatively dark blue-green paper strewn with bluish dots (use magnifying glass), some of which border on blue-black; paper, about 85 microns. The three types are identified by the arrangement of the upper ornaments.

Geneva forgeries: sheets of twenty (4 x 5); the seventh stamp is inverted (tête-bêche); all of them belong to Type I (upper ornaments, normal); paper is tinted yellowish green with blue silk threads inserted in the paper pulp; 75 microns. Bad forgery: they did not even take the trouble to obtain identical printing type. The illustration shows the grotesque defects; there are others in the frame and lettering.

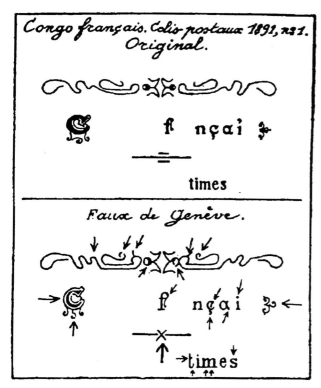

French Congo. Parcel post stamps. 1891. No. 1. Original. Bottom: Geneva forgeries.

Forged Geneva cancellations: (1) round (22¼ mm), with date, LIBREVILLE 13 NOV 92 GABON-CONGO; (2) round (21½ mm), with date, LIBREVILLE 10 MARS 00 CONGO FRANÇAISE ("00" is smaller than the date figures; no hyphen after CONGO). LIBREVILLE IE/15 DEC 86 CONGO FRANÇAISE. Dates interchangeable; postmarks applied so as to disguise FRANÇAISE and CENTIMES.

French Guiana

1886–88. Overprinted stamps. Nos. 1 to 9. Comparison of overprints is absolutely indispensable; the forged overprints are very numerous. (Geneva; overprint of Nos. 1 and 2.)

In the *original overprints,* the words GUY FRANC measure 14 mm in Nos. 1 and 2; 11 mm in Nos. 3 and 5; 10 mm in No. 4; 17 mm in Nos. 6 and 7; 15 mm in Nos. 8 and 9. The 1886 overprint is found in two different types: (1) accent on the "é" does not touch the letter and figure "1," with top oblique terminal line; (2) accent touching the letter and figure without terminal line.

1892. GUYANE overprint. Nos. 10 to 28. Overprint comparison is indispensable. For overprints of 1881 stamps (Nos. 15–28), first make sure whether the stamp itself is or is not forged (see French Colonies), the whole set having been counterfeited in Geneva and supplied with a forged overprint and forged cancellation: CAYENNE 2 JUIN 92 GUYANE; interchangeable dates or without date.

1892. Peace and Commerce type. Nos. 30 to 48. *Forgeries:* of this type, see French Colonies.

1912. Overprinted Peace and Commerce type. Nos. 66 to 72. *Forgeries:* see French Colonies.

1915. Red Cross. No. 73. Expertizing or detailed comparison is indispensable, for there are a great many forged overprints, even in the original vermilion shade. Do not rely on articles that give information on one or several forged overprints, for there are always others that are occasionally more dangerous; comparison alone is trustworthy.

French Guinea

1892 and 1912. Peace and Commerce type. Nos. 1 to 17 and 48 to 62. *Forgeries:* see French Colonies, forgeries of the Peace and Commerce type.

1906–7. Balay type. Nos. 45 to 47. *Forgeries:* see the counterfeits of this type under French Colonies.

The forged Geneva cancellation on forgeries and originals: double circle (23 mm), with date, broken inner circle, KONAKRI 29 NOV 10 GUINÉE FRANÇAISE; interchangeable date.

French India

1892–1907. Peace and Commerce type. Nos. 1 to 19. *Geneva forgeries:* see the forgeries of this type under French Colonies; forged cancellation: double circle (22 mm), with date, PONDICHERY. 1 FEVR 92 INDE.

1903. 0,15 overprints. Nos. 20 to 23. Great numbers of *forged overprints;* minute comparison with an original and application of the template are necessary.

1915–16. Red Cross. Nos. 43 to 47. Same remark as above. Typographed overprints: check the indention. In No. 47, the normal width is 10^1/$_2$ mm; one stamp in each sheet is only 9^1/$_2$ mm.

French Polynesia

1893–1906. Peace and Commerce type. Nos. 1 to 20. *Geneva forgeries:* see counterfeits of this type under French Colonies.

1915. EFO overprint. No. 38. Typographed overprint. *Forged* inverted *overprints:* comparison with original is necessary.

1915–16. Red Cross. Nos. 39 to 42. Typographed overprints of Nos. 39 and 40 in vermilion; No. 41, typographed in dark red, and No. 42, typographed in carmine.

Forged overprints, particularly inverted forged overprints which detailed comparison can identify.

1916–1921–1924. Overprinted stamps. Nos. 43 to 46 and 65. Same observation with respect to overprints. I have not seen the inverted forged overprint, No. 65a, but I am informed that it exists and is well done, and...I have no hesitancy in believing this is true.

French Somaliland

1894. Overprinted stamps. Nos. 1 to 3. *Forged overprints:* comparison is necessary; stamps with original overprint are canceled "554" (No. 1; also forged Geneva overprint).

1894–1900. 25- and 50-franc. Nos. 20 and 21. *Geneva forgeries:* bold print cross-ruled watermark, less visible in benzine; vertical bar of the "F" of "F^{cs}" is triangular instead of rectangular; there is a dot instead of a comma under the "S" the zero of "50" is as large as the "5," but it should be visibly smaller; both forged values are found with the figure omitted.

Forged Geneva cancellations: (1) wavy postmark with broken circle inside: DJIBOUTI 18 OCT 99 POSTES; (2) double circle postmark, inner circle broken: DJIBOUTI 10 AOUT 97 COLONIE-FRANC^{se}; (3) similar postmark: CÔTE FRANÇAISE DES SOMALIS 7 MARS 04 DJIBOUTI, the latter on the OBOCK 25- and 50-franc, and on piece (see

Obock). The three postmarks in blue or black with interchangeable figures; 25 SEPT. 99 also is found often.

1899–1902. Overprinted stamps. Forged overprints, mainly for the expensive varieties. Comparison is necessary. (Geneva forged overprints: Nos. 22 and 23.)

1902. Various subjects. Nos. 37 to 52. *Forgeries* that are counterfeited deceptively on very thick paper, with irregular perforation (examine the corners): blurred printing, easy identification when compared with the three original types.

1903. Same subjects. Nos. 53 to 66. So-called reprints: from a clandestine printing; shade comparison with reliable originals both in normal copies and in copies with inverted centers is indispensable.

French Sudan

1894. SOUDAN F^{AIS} overprint. Nos. 1 and 2. *Forged overprints:* detailed comparison is indispensable, for the original overprint is lithographed like a few counterfeits. Differences in the horizontal line should not cause concern, for it differs according to type. The two types were counterfeited in Geneva on originals or forgeries of 1881 with forged cancellation: double circle (24 mm) with date, on the left, KAYES, on the right, SOUDAN FRANÇAISE, and in the middle, 3^E 7 FEVR. 93.

1894–1900. Peace and Commerce type. Nos. 3 to 19. *Geneva forgeries:* see the forgeries of this type under French Colonies.

Gabon

1886–89. Overprinted stamps. Nos. 1 to 13. Ascertain first whether the postage stamps or postage due stamps are originals themselves (see French Colonies).

Originals: GAB is 9 mm wide; the figures are 5^1/$_2$ mm high; shiny ink. On originals from the French colonies, there are very numerous forged overprints (the ink is often lusterless); comparison with reliable originals (Nos. 3, 8, and 13 still are available) is indispensable. In the first issue overprint (thirteen or fifty-six dots), the "A" of GAB is a little less high than the other letters and is slanted to the left. Overprints GAB, GABON TIMBRE, and figures "15" and "25" were counterfeited in Geneva.

1889. Imperforate; typographed; overprinted GAB. Nos. 14 and 15. *Originals:* very thick or Bristol paper (120–60 microns); pink or slightly bluish green;

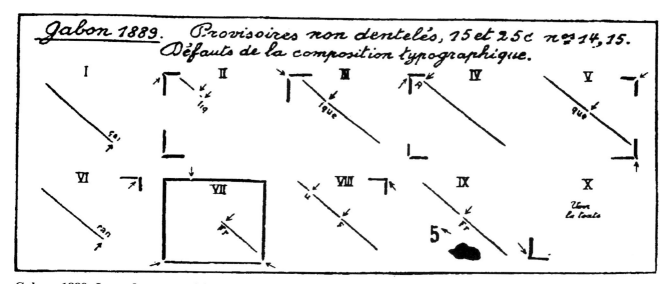

Gabon. 1889. Imperforate provisionals. 15- and 25-centime. Nos. 14, 15. Defects in typographical composition.

$25^{1}/_{2}$–$26^{1}/_{2}$ x about 22 mm. In the good impressions and in most of the ten types, the frame lines have beveled ends and are not connected; there is a space of about $^{1}/_{2}$ mm or less between them; (northwest corner of Type III stamps and northeast corner of Type V, a little more; see also the bottom of the Type VII stamps in the illustration); in the heavy-printed impressions, they often are connected. In RÉPUBLIQUE FRANÇAISE, the letters often are drawn crudely or printed faintly; likewise, in POSTES and the cedilla under the "C" POSTES is $1^{3}/_{4}$ mm high; the hyphen between GABON-CONGO is about 1 mm long and the lowercase letters of these words are about $1^{1}/_{4}$ mm high. The handstamped overprint, "GAB" surrounded by six dots, is identical on all types and exhibits, in this overprint's good impressions, the characteristics shown in the illustration.

Geneva forgeries: in blocks of six or twelve, medium paper, 25–85 microns, which indicates that there were several printings whose total must be at least ten times the number of copies in the original printings of 1,000 and 1,500. 15-centime, on approximate rose shade, but also on salmon-pink-tinted rose and salmon pink; 25-centime, on very light green or yellow-green. Each value was classified in types, which are reducible to two distinctively different types for each value, with vertical tête-bêche stamps with $1^{1}/_{2}$ and 1 cm gutters. First cliché of the 15-centime, $26^{1}/_{3}$ x $22^{1}/_{4}$ mm; second, about 26 x $22^{2}/_{5}$ mm. First cliché of the 25-centime, $26^{2}/_{5}$–$^{1}/_{2}$ x 22 mm, second $26^{1}/_{4}$ x 22 mm. Typographed; the illustration gives information on the frame defects of the two most typical clichés of each value; in the other stamps of the sheets, these defects are changed slightly or reproduced unsuccessfully. The 15-centime was copied from the Type IX original in

which the upper bar of the "5" ends in a more or less beveled shape; in the same value, the letters of POSTES are about 2 mm high instead of $1^{3}/_{4}$ mm.

The hyphen between GABON-CONGO is only about $^{1}/_{2}$ mm long; the "C" of CONGO is $1^{1}/_{4}$ mm wide instead of $1^{1}/_{3}$ mm; the imprint of RÉPUBLIQUE FRANÇAISE is always well done, as is the cedilla under the "C" in the 25-centime, figure "2" is too wide (see the illustration) and is separated from the "5" by more than 1 mm instead of $^{1}/_{2}$ mm; the "5" of the first type is counterfeited rather well; in the second type, this figure is like the "5" of the 15-centime stamp. The overprint GAB was applied with a handstamp, as in the originals, but it is not congruent (see illustration), and the two dots below GAB are *always* too faint. Note: The same thing happened on originals when the handstamp was held obliquely. Forged cancellations on these forgeries: double circle postmark with date (22 mm), LIBREVILLE 13 NOV 92 GABON-CONGO and (21 mm) LIBREVILLE 20 mai 89 GABON, with interchangeable dates: also 6 août 86 on fraudulently overprinted forgeries of the first issue.

1904–7. Peace and Commerce type (Nos. 16 to 32) and 1912 Peace and Commerce type overprint (Nos. 66 to 78). See French Colonies for forgeries of this type.

1910. Negress type. Nos. 46 to 48. *Originals:* typographed; 2-franc. $20^{7}/_{8}$ x $35^{1}/_{2}$ mm; 5-franc, $21^{1}/_{8}$ x $35^{3}/_{5}$ mm.

Forgeries: thus far, I have seen only the 2- and 5-franc forgeries; there probably will be others, since it is unlikely that the counterfeiter would want to stop there. In case one should decide to undertake a comparative study, the photolithographed forgeries have an overall

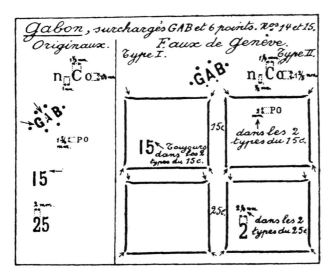

Gabon. Stamps overprinted GAB with six dots. Nos. 14 and 15. Originals. Geneva forgeries.

duller appearance and their shades are too pale. 2-franc, $20^2/_5$ x $35^2/_5$ mm; 5-franc, $20^7/_8$ x $35^3/_8$ mm. The fine white frame surrounding the whole colored background is too thick, especially on the left of GABON. In the L. COLMET inscription, under the stamp, the second "L" is down too far, and in the 5-franc, the lower branch of the two "L" letters is too short. In the earring on the right, the outer curved line evidently is quite remote from the cheek, whereas in the originals there is only a gap; the first necklace definitely is rounded on the right in the genuine stamps, but here it forms a sort of rectangle, the top of which clearly is broken near the neckline and is continued by an unbroken line instead of a dotted line (use magnifying glass); further on, on the left, the upper line of the same necklace is missing on the right and left of the place where the second oblique shade line ends (starting from the top of the neck on the right).

1916. Red Cross. Nos. 79 and 80. Comparison is indispensable because overprints are involved and there are different types in the sheet.

Gambia

1869–87. Embossed impression. Nos. 1 to 19.
Originals (1869): Nos. 4 and 6, imperforate, without watermark; the subsequent issues with watermark. Embossing is visible in all its details, especially in the first two issues and in the mint stamps (crown, hair, chignon, lettering, etc.). Note: The color dot on the chignon (see illustration) is not always visible.

Gambia. 1869. Embossed impression. Original. Forgeries.

Forgeries: electrotyped stamps which seem to be well executed; I say "seem," for if they are subjected to a two-minute inspection, they turn out to be quite the opposite. $18^3/_4$ x about $22^1/_5$ mm; the inscription lettering is somewhat too high ($1^2/_3$ mm instead of about $1^1/_2$ mm) and too thick, and the "A" letters in GAMBIA are not symmetrical (see the illustration); the colored line under GAMBIA and the one above the value figure are only $1/_5$–$1/_4$ mm thick, instead of $1/_3$ mm; the blank circle line is only $1/_4$ mm thick instead of about $2/_5$ mm: the color dot is missing in the chignon; the inner corner ornaments are too thick; embossing generally is not very accentuated. The height of the portrait, from the diadem point to the neck point, is 14 mm instead of about $13^1/_2$ mm. In imitation of the first issue, these counterfeits almost always are imperforate. No watermark. The forged cancellations are usually a barred circle or a square of large dots.

Georgia

1919. Russian stamps of 1918. Nos. 1 to 3. The perforation is not official. Buy only on cover. Rare.

Subsequent issues. Almost all the overprinted stamps were very well counterfeited (see Russia). Comparative study is necessary. Nos. 28, 29, and 30 in the Yvert catalogue are unissued stamps.

On the whole, a rather uninteresting region.

1920–21. Overprinted stamps. Nos. 19 to 30.
Forged overprints: comparison is necessary. For some of the forged overprints. general, overall comparison will suffice; for other more deceptive ones, which probably are clandestine creations, the indention and the ink are the best features for comparison. The same may be said with respect to subsequent issues and other Russian overprinted stamps, most of which are reoverprinted endlessly until the customers' thirst really is slaked.

German Colonies

The German set of 1886 (Nos. 44–50) was well counterfeited in Geneva and the following sets were overprinted fraudulently: East Africa (Nos. 1–10); Southwest Africa, Cameroon, Carolina Islands, China, Levant, Mariana Islands, Morocco, Marshall Islands, New Guinea, Togo (all of them, Nos. 1–6, except Levant, Nos. 6–10); and Samoa (Nos. 36–41). The illustration shows the main defects of these photolithographed forgeries.

Top: originals (18¼ x 21⅕ mm). Forgeries (18–18¼ x 21 mm). 3- and 5-pfennig. Bottom: 10-, 20-, 25-, and 50-pfennig.

In each one of the colonies, one also should examine the forged cancellation that was applied on the forgeries. There is no need to give an elaborate description of a second forged *set:* the inexpertly lithographed stamps are only 17¾ mm wide instead of about 18¼ mm, and they are perforated 13½ x 14 instead of 13½ x 14½; the hatch lines on the left of REICHSPOST are no higher than the top of the "R"; the crown is almost blank. This set generally is found unused. Note: Obviously, the forged Geneva overprints — and many other overprints — were applied on original German stamps. Comparison is indispensable.

Finally, to complicate things even more, *reprints* of the overprint essays were made in 1897. These essays, which previously were printed on originals in sets of five bearing, consecutively, overprints DEUTSCH-NEU-GUINEA, DEUTSCH-SUDWEST-AFRICA, MARSCHALL-INSELN (with "C"), TOGO, and CAMEROON, were reproduced, so to speak, in blocks of ten (5 x 2) bearing ten names of colonies: SAMOA, KAROLINEN, DEUTSCH-OSTAFRICA, CHINA, and MARIANEN also, in a different order and with names

spelled differently, like second-issue stamps, for DEUTSCH-SUDWESTAFRICA and MARSHAL-INSELN (without "C"). Despite the fact that the overprint printing type is generally not so thick, it is possible to make sense out of the eight others only by comparing shades with the overprinted originals of each colony. That requires specialization.

1900–1916. Steamer type. *Originals* typographed; 18⅗–⅔ x 22⅔ mm: perf 14; watermarked issues after 1906.

Genera forgeries: bicolor photoliths on wove paper of peso, cent. helter. and pfennig values. 18½–⅗ x 22⅓–⅔ mm; perf 13–13½ x 13½ fleecy paper: no watermark. The most visible defects are shown in the illustration; the poorly executed rosette, top right, has no white dot under it; the ensign is not defined by a curved line on the left, and the cross is touching the bottom; there is no horizontal white line to set off the top of the smokestack; there is a single vertical line on the smokestack and sometimes traces of a second line; no white hatching (or traces) on the lower part of the mainmast; there are other less important defects in design, value inscriptions, figures, and colony names. Comparison of all these things only will confirm the verdict.

1900–1916. German colonies. Steamer type. Originals. Geneva forgeries.

German East Africa

The first two issues (see Germany, 1889). having been counterfeited in Geneva (see German Colonies), can be found with forged overprints from other sources. Forged Geneva cancellation, one circle (30 mm), WILHELMSTHAL DEUTSCH-OST-AFRIKA 15/10 1. See German Colonies for steamer-type forgeries also.

Belgian occupation. The only official sets are those overprinted RWANDA and URUNDI; there are at least two sets *of forged overprints;* comparison is indispensable. A rare official reprint was run off. The so-called KIGOMA and KAREMA overprints are cancellations. A forged cachet, TAXES, was applied to Nos. 28–35; comparison would be useful.

German Southwest Africa

1897. First issue. The 3-, 5-, 10-, and 20-pfennig, as well as the unissued 25- and 30-pfennig, were *reprinted.* Thicker overprint; 3-pfennig yellow-brown; 5-pfennig dark yellow-green; the other values are very close to these shade.

Geneva forgeries: see German Colonies. Perf 13½ x 14. Forged cancellation: GIBEON 1/5 1898 (round).

Forged overprints: Geneva, two types, one of which is very bad.

1898. Second issue. Nos. 7–12. *Geneva forgeries:* as previously, with second forged overprint and cancellation BETHANIEN DEUTSCH-SUDWESTAFRICA 1/5 99 (round, 28 mm).

1900. Steamer type. *Forgeries:* see German Colonies.

British occupation. Many forged overprints.

German States

Baden

I. Imperforate Stamps

Sheets: No. 1, 45 stamps (5 x 9); Nos. 2, 3, 4, 90 stamps (10 x 9); No. 5, first printing, 50 stamps (5 x 10); Nos. 6, 7, 8, 100 stamps (10 x 10). Typographed.

Select: four visible margins, minimum width ½ mm: 2U; with four margins shoving part of the adjoining stamps: 3–5U.

Cancellations: quintuple circle, black, Type A: common, but certain numbers are rare: 40, 61, 97, 134, 147: No. 1: 2U; the others: 3–10U; Nos. 165 and 168 are very rare. In red, Nos. 28 and 115: 50U; Nos. 48, 121, 125, etc.: 2–5U. In blue, Nos. 4, 10, 17, 41, 60, 65, 66, 92?, 100, 104, 117, 123, 130, 162, etc.: 3–10U. In green, No. 92: rare. The dated cancellation, Type C, is very rare: 100 francs (minimum); on No. 1: 2U. Types F, G, H, etc., are rare: 3U (minimum). (See illustration.)

1851–52. Black on colored paper. Nos. 1 to 4. 1851: thin, transparent paper (50–60 microns); 1-kreuzer buff: 3-kreuzer orange: 2M, 50U; 6-kreuzer blue-green: 2M, 2U; 9-kreuzer old rose: 4M, 2U. 9-kreuzer green, color error, three copies known. 1852: nontransparent paper of average thickness (60–90, 95 microns); 1-kreuzer brownish buff; 3-kreuzer yellow; 6-kreuzer green; 9-kreuzer rose.

Stamps on cover: 50U.

A.- quintuple circle. B.- idem. exterieur dent.

Cachets à date (Ortsstempel).
C. Un cercle D. double cercle E. id rapproché

F. ob. Chemin de fer. G. Roue dentée. H. Obl. rare.
(Bahnpoststempel) (Uhrradstempel)

BRETTEN.
9. Sep.
I. oblitération barre.
(Balkenstempel)

PFORZHEIM
10. Apr.
J. idem. encadrée.
(Eingeradbmter Balkenstempel)

K. oblit ovale
(Postablage.)

A. Quintuple circle. B. Same, "sawtooth" exterior circle. C. Single circle. D. Double circle. E. Same, circles close together. F. Railway cancel. G. Cogwheel. H. Rare cancel. I. Bar cancel. J. Same, framed. K. Oval cancel.

Mint copies with gum: these usually are worth fifty percent more than the prices quoted in general catalogues. Yellowish gum; the 6-kreuzer green is very rare with gum.

Pairs: No. 1: 3U; Nos. 2 and 3: 4U; No. 4: 6U. Blocks of four: very rare; No. 2: 100U. A strip of three of the 6-kreuzer stamp for 18-kreuzer postage is rare: 10U.

Reprints (1866): white gum; No. 1 brown, and No. 2 yellow, thicker paper: No. 3 grayish blue-green, thin paper. Value: 10 francs.

Fakes: the 1-kreuzer made from the 1-kreuzer black on white soaked in tea, coffee, etc. The process left traces on the back of the stamp. If the paper is thick and the shade is light (pale buff), like that of the 1851 issue, the contrast is unmistakable. The 9-kreuzer stamp was bleached, then tinted green; same comment.

Forgeries: for a connoisseur, inspection of the burelage — so superbly executed in the originals — and of the engraver's secret marks is sufficient. The 1- and 6-kreuzer are good lithographed counterfeits. On the 1-kreuzer, a dot after the "1" is ¹/₂ mm away instead of 1 mm; the "F" and "K" of FREIMARKE and the dot over the "I" are touching the top of the tablet; the dot that should be on the right of the "6" (6 April) is touching this figure. When the stamp is not trimmed excessively, a second frame can be seen ¹/₂ mm from the outer frame. In the 6-kreuzer, the same defects in lettering are encountered; the dots after the Gothic "V" and the "6" of the tablet on the right have disappeared. (See F. Serrane, "Faux de Bade," *Philatéliste belge,* No. 51 [Dec. 15, 1925]: 51–55.)

Forged cancellations: on reprints of the No. 1 stamp.

1853–58. Black on colored paper. Nos. 5 to 8.
Paper of average thickness or thin paper; thin paper: 25U. Nos. 7 and 8 on very thin paper, almost pelure (40 microns): 2M, 2U.

Stamps on cover: 50U.

Mint copies with gum: 50M.

Shades: two shades per value, depending on the paper. The 1-kreuzer on ivory, very good grayish print; 2M, 4U. This value is known in tête-bêche with a margin between the stamps: extremely rare. No. 7 on pelure paper is grayish blue.

Pairs: 4U; strips of three, Nos. 5 and 6: 6U; Nos. 7 and 8: 12U; blocks of four, No. 5: 60U; No. 6: 100U. The others: very rare.

Reprints: finer printing than the originals; thick paper except the 6-kreuzer; white gum; the 3-kreuzer stamps have slightly different shades. Value: 10 francs.

Fakes: the poorly printed 1-kreuzer stamp was often faked to make a No. 1; the reprint was also faked; its paper is not uniformly thick.

Forgeries: see the first issue for the distinguishing characteristics. The shades are arbitrary.

Forged cancellations: on No. 5, faked to resemble No. 1, and on the reprint of this value.

II. Perforated Stamps

Sheets of 100 stamps (10 x 10). No reprints. Stamps generally badly centered; stamps in which perforation does not touch any frame line are rare.

1860–62. Background of lines. Nos. 9 to 15. Gum, yellowish or white. Nos. 9 and 10 (ultramarine) are found with rose-colored gum; mint: very rare; used No. 9: 8U; No. 10: 4U.

Shades: 1-kreuzer deep black (good impression): 50U; 3-kreuzer Prussian blue: 8M; 9-kreuzer dark rose: 50M, 50U. 1-kreuzer, perf 10, gray-black: 8M.

Varieties: No. 10 dark blue, very defective printing, greasy, and transparent. In demand: the fine impressions of the 1-kreuzer black, the 3-kreuzer dark ultramarine, the 6-kreuzer red-orange. and the 9-kreuzer carmine. The color of the 9-kreuzer is rarely fresh.

Cancellations: Type B, in demand: Nos. 24, 52, 37 (this last looks like a No. 87); Types F and H: 2U; Type G: 3U for Nos. 1–25; Nos. 26–45: rare; Type I: 3U; Type J common perf 10, but rare in blue. Type K is rare.

The stamps of Baden with Prussian cancellation are very rare. Stamps on cover: 50U.

Pairs: 3U; Nos. 11 and 12: 4U; strips of three: 5U; Nos. 11 and 12: 6U; blocks of four: rare.

Early forgeries: lithographed. Centered! The escutcheon's dots are irregular and faintly printed. The headband has only seventeen vertical lines instead of eighteen; the downstroke of the "A" of BADEN is too narrow; the lower line of the "E" of the same word is too long. Various shades.

1862–65. White background. Perf 10. Nos. 16 to 21. The 3-kreuzer, perf 13¹/₂ is from an 1862 issue.

Shades: 1-kreuzer gray: 3M; Prussian blue: rare, mint, 50U; the ultramarine and the bright blue are common; 18-kreuzer yellow-green, dark green: 50M, 25U. The dark green stamp, second printing, has whiter paper.

Varieties: the 3-kreuzer, No. 18, is known imperforate: 200 francs; the 9-kreuzer bistre, printed both sides, is very rare.

Stamps on cover: 18- and 30-kreuzer: 2U.

Cancellations: Types A, C, D: common; Types B, F, H, I, J: 2U; Type K: 3U; Type E: 4U.

Pairs: Nos. 17–19: 3U; Nos. 20–22: 4U. Blocks: rare.

Early forgeries: the attention of forgers was directed especially to the 18- and 30-kreuzer stamps, which were counterfeited by engraving and lithography.

The forged cancellations of four concentric circles spaced 2¹/₂ mm apart are to be rejected right away.

Usually there are not eighteen lines in the shield's bandeau; the left side of the diagonal of the "N" of BADEN ends right above its left base; the eagle on the right seems to be wearing a custard pie instead of a crown. Also, comparison of the shading of the shield would be useful.

In the engraved 18-kreuzer, the upper bars of the two "E" letters of VEREIN are longer than the lower bars; in the "K" of FREIMARKE, the oblique strokes cut the vertical instead of having their point of intersection connected with the vertical line by a short horizontal line. (Same remark with respect to the lithographed stamps.)

The other early forgeries do not deserve description. The original is 22$\frac{1}{5}$ mm square.

Fakes: in Geneva (F.), originals of the 3-kreuzer rose, No. 17, were chemically bleached, while the cancellations were kept intact; then the stamps were reprinted as 30-kreuzer stamps, with careful erasure of the orange imprint on the cancellation. Thus, perforation, cancellation, and paper are original, but the marks identified as "a" and "b" in the accompanying illustration and traces of the orange imprint on the cancellation reveal the fraud.

No. 17 went through the same process to make an 18-kreuzer stamp. Design comparison will be sufficient. (See also *early forgeries,* above.)

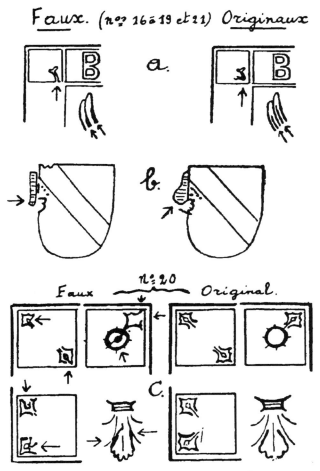

Distinguishing features of the forgeries, left, and originals of Nos. 16–19 and 21 (above) and No. 20 (below).

Modern forgeries: Nos. 16–21 (including No. 17a) were forged in 1899 by an engraver named V..., from Turin, then printed and fraudulently canceled by F..., in Geneva. The same cliché was used for all values except the 18-kreuzer, which was honored with a special cliché.

The paper is stringy, white or yellowish, and is 75–85 microns thick instead of the 55–65 microns of the originals. But this has only a relative importance, for paper may improve in other forgeries, and the same may be said with regard to perforations and shades. The perforation is most often 11$\frac{1}{4}$ to 12, but perf 10 also has been found. No. 17a was perf 14. The shades are not entirely exact: the 30-kreuzer is too reddish.

All values except the 18-kreuzer were printed in blocks of sixteen imperforate stamps (4 x 4), which were then perforated in ten successive operations. The sheets of sixteen were frequently canceled before perforation, which, with regard to mass production, makes one think of the basic principles of Taylorism.

Some of the defects of the impression are indicated as "a" and "b" in the illustration.

The counterfeiting of the 18-kreuzer stamp was done with particular care by the engraver and by the printer, who succeeded in printing it in the exact green and dark green shades. These forgeries were printed in blocks of four imperforate stamps, then perforated six times. In general, the perforation is a quarter of a dot too large; the paper, first yellowish and transparent, was printed in green and yellow-green; then the forgers used a relatively transparent, thin (55 microns) white paper with printing in dark green. See "c" in the illustration. (Also see F. Serrane, "Faux de Bade," *Philatéliste belge,* No. 51 [December 15, 1925]: 54.)

Forged cancellations: the forged Geneva postmarks, wood engraved, are:

1. Quintuple circle with numbers: 8, 12, 60, 79, and 109.

2. Dated postmark. single circle: RASTATT 14 OCT 5-10 V.

3. Dated postmark, double circle: KEHL 2 NOV 6-7N; HEIDELBERG 2 OCT; FREIBURG 4 APR 2-7 M; OPPENAU 10 Aug.

4. Cogwheel time postmark.

5. Double line postmark, framed: KARLSRUHE 2 MRZ.

These postmarks were spread not only over forged stamps Nos. 16–21 and counterfeit envelope cutouts (6-kreuzer blue and yellow; 18-kreuzer vermilion), but also over originals and noncounterfeit postage due stamps. A great number of additional forged cancellations are found on the 30-kreuzer stamp and on postage due stamps.

1868. "K R" inscription. White background. Perf 10. The 7-kreuzer pale blue (sky blue) is worth 2M, 3U. Good impression: rare. The 3-kreuzer with white line connected with the top of the "3" 10M, 10U (plate flaw).

Cancellations: with date: common.
Pairs: 3U.

III. Postage Due Stamps

Sheets of 100 stamps (10 x 10). Thin paper; the 1- and 3-kreuzer stamps on thick paper, too. Perf 10. The 12-kreuzer printing was limited to 1,500 copies; only about three percent are extant.

Stamps on cover: 12-kreuzer: 3U; others: 50U.

Varieties: No. 2 with the first "O" of PORTO broken above and below (plate flaw): 10M, 4U. No. 3 was bisected; on cover: 1,000 francs; on piece: 750 francs. No. 1, thick paper: 4M, 50U; No. 2: 6M, 3U.

Forgeries: often counterfeited on thick paper — watch out for this! The best thing is to get a moderately expensive authentic 1- or 3-kreuzer stamp on thin paper and use it as a reference. Notice that the leaves on the right and left near the middle of the stamp are not connected with their branches or twigs; notice also that the scrolls at the top and bottom of the stamp are connected by a wavy line that touches them only on heavily printed copies; two almost vertical small lines issue from the bottoms of the scrolls. The garland interruptions also should be noticed. These secret marks make a sound judgment of the stamp possible. Likewise, the ornamental ivy leaf design is enough to eliminate the counterfeits; in this design; there are unnatural, triangular-shaped leaves attached to the ornamental frame.

The three values must be examined by experts in this field.

Bavaria

I. Imperforate Stamps

Sheets of the large numeral values (1849–62) have 180 stamps divided into four panes of forty-five (9 x 5); in the 1867–68 issue, the sheets have 120 stamps, which are divided into four panes of thirty (6 x 5).

Select: Nos. 1–14, four margins extending right up to the dividing frame lines; Nos. 15–22, four margins, 1 mm wide, minimum.

Silk thread: Nos. 2–22 have a red silk thread, which is vertically incorporated into the pulp of the paper and spaced 21 mm apart; sometimes two threads are found on a single stamp and sometimes none at all. These varieties are valued in pairs or in strips, the single stamp occasionally being faked by removing the thread.

Paper: pelure paper: 30–40 microns; thin: 41–60; medium: 61–80; thick: 81 microns or more, up to 105–110 microns. All papers are handmade; the very thin paper is rare.

Cancellations: before 1849, a small dated postmark, Type D, was used: rare.

Type A postmarks (single circle) have numbers from "1" to "608"; triple circle postmark, from "1" to "922"; in general, they are common, but the ones from small localities are rarer, the single circle postmark possibly being worth 100 francs, the triple-circle (numbers above "800"), 20–100 francs and 50–200 francs (numbers above "900"). No. 922 is rarest of all. These postmarks, in red or blue, are very rare.

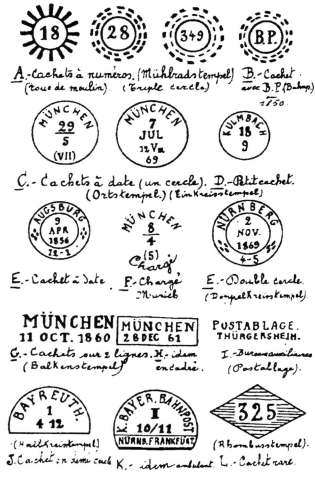

Cancellations: A. Numeral postmarks — cogwheel and triple circle. B. Postmark with "B.P." or "1850." C. Dated postmarks (one circle). D. Small postmark (thimble). E. Dated double circle postmarks. F. Registered (Munich). G. Postmarks on two lines. H. Same, framed. I. Branch offices. J. Half-circle postmark. K. Same, mobile. L. Rhomboid, rare.

Type B with "B.P." (railway cancel) is found on the 3- and 6-kreuzer stamp; it is rare on the 1-, 12-, and 18-kreuzer stamps. This postmark is found with 1850 year-date: 10 francs on No. 2.

The dated cancellations, Type C, are not common on the first three issues; Type A becomes very rare after 1870. Type J is common, but becomes rare with the "Bahnpost" indication (Type K). Types G and H are not common, except Munchen (Type H). "Bahnhof" (Type G): rare. Type I is always rare; in red or blue, very rare. Types F and L: very rare.

The pen cancellation on No. 1 is worth 75 francs.

1849. 1-kreuzer black. The deep black comes from the first printing: good impression. The gray-black shade must have been ordered to remedy the poor visibility of cancellations on deep black. Also, the plate was getting worn; this can be seen at the bottom of the figure on the left, in the cross-hatching of the ornamental squares and in their framework, as well as in the cross-hatching of the large bureled square. At the time of the last printings, the wear is visible also at the end of the large figure's oblique line. From 1850 on, this value was replaced by No. 4 in rose.

Varieties: first-class impressions are in demand. The stamp with silk thread is a rare essay. The tête-bêche is always a marginal copy on the left. There is a gray-black stamp with double print. A few plate flaws can be pointed out: the upper half of the "E" of EIN displays a white spot; FBANCO for FRANCO; etc. No. 1 was used bisected on printed matter wrappers.

Forgeries: there are a great many forgeries. Instead of cataloguing them here quite uselessly, we suggest that the reader ascertain whether the stamp has the characteristics and measurements described in the accompanying illustration of the original. In most of the forgeries, the upper line of the figure parallels the tablet, and the figure itself is too high, too narrow, too wide, misplaced, etc.

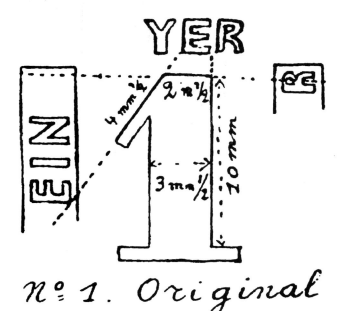

No 1. Original

A few early forgeries are so poorly executed that a child could recognize them; they usually have Type A and B cancellations. The chemical forgeries of Nos. 4 and 9 to make No. 1 are speculators' fantasies; check out the center burelage and the silk thread. A modern Geneva forgery does not bear up under comparison; it is a mint copy or is canceled with forged postmarks, Type A, Nos. "757," "249," "267," "269."

1849–50. Nos. 2 and 3 (3- and 6-kreuzer). Broken circle. *Shades:* No. 2 mint or used is rare in pale ultramarine. No. 3 is rare in yellow-brown and bright light brown, and rare used in red-brown and dark brown. The 3-kreuzer dark blue is worth 3M, 4U; the 6-kreuzer dark brown: 50U.

The gum of Nos. 1–3 is yellowish or brownish at times and was spread with a brush in the first issues; circumspection is obviously indispensable, for the gum is white and machine-applied in later issues. The two values are known to have red gum (Type A cancellation, one circle, No. 1).

Pairs: 4U; the 3-kreuzer is not known to exist in a used strip of three; a block of four is worth 75 francs.

6-kreuzer: it has been claimed that the matrix of No. 3 was lost; however, the plate change in No. 5 may be explained also by the engraver's desire to obtain a better product. In No. 5 (end of October 1850), the ornamental motifs in the arcs of the circle were expanded so that they would completely encircle the figure; the frames of the small corner squares are carefully traced.

Because a cogwheel cancellation may possibly conceal the broken circle of No. 3, and, moreover, because the used plate of No. 5 has broken-circle imprints, the accompanying illustration shows the distinguishing marks of both plates. Notice particularly in "b" the white hatching curving around the figure "6," bottom left, in the lower left square of No. 5.

Varieties: Nos. 2, 3, and 5 were used with red gum (unofficial) by the Allotting office (No. 7). No. 2 plate variety with a white line traversing the large "3" from the "E" of EIN to the "N" of BAYERN, or from the same "E" to the "O" of FRANCO. Nos. 2 and 3, printing defects: a figure that is almost blank; the ornaments surrounding the figure have entirely disappeared: 2U. Nos. 2 and 3 with visible silk thread on the reverse side and with double silk thread are in demand. The 6-kreuzer was bisected diagonally. Copies of this value with albino second impression have been found.

Cancellations: No. 2 with postmark Type B (year-date "1850"): 15U; No. 3, blue cancellation: 2U; pen cancellation: 50U.

Official forgeries: No. 2, without silk thread. The corner numbers are illegible; the design of the letters and ornaments is defective.

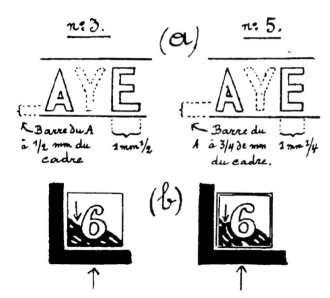

For No. 3, the bar of the "A" is ¹/₂ mm from the frame. For No. 5, the bar of the "A" is ³/₄ mm from the frame.

Regular circle. Nos. 4 to 8. The expression "regular circle" is perhaps improperly used for the 1-kreuzer stamp, because the circle is rarely closed as in the other values. The same may be said for a pale shade of the 6-kreuzer (No. 5, end of the plate), which is often offered for sale as No. 3. (See the preceding illustration.)

Shades: 1-kreuzer dark rose (1858): 2M, 2U; 6-kreuzer yellow-brown, red-brown, and chocolate brown: 3M; 9-kreuzer blue-green: very rare mint, 4U; bright green: very rare mint; 18-kreuzer dark yellow: 2M, 50U. The 12-kreuzer vivid dark yellow is rare.

Varieties: No. 5 with blank figure (arabesque wear): 15U; bisected, on cover: 600 francs. The 9-kreuzer, pelure paper: 2M, 5U. The 9-kreuzer with upper frame unbroken at the left end (Type I): rare; with broken frame (Type II): 2U; with frame thinned down (Type III): common.

Cancellations: Types C or E: 50U: Type B: 3U; Types G, H: 2U; Type G. Bahnhof: 3U; Type J: 2U; Type K, and all others: rare (except, of course, the A types).

Pairs: 4U; strips of three: 8U, but No. 5: 50U; blocks of four, No. 4: 80U; No. 6: 100U; others: very rare.

Forgeries: the 12- and 18-kreuzer stamps of this issue and the following one were counterfeited in Geneva (F.) either with silk thread stuck on the back, with thread drawn in red ink, or without thread. The accompanying sketch shows the identification marks.

Dull shades, not like originals.

The same values were counterfeited without silk thread in Nuremberg; the embossed imprint is quite

pronounced — look at the border of the ornamental squares with a magnifying glass; figure "1" is touching the circle at lower left.

The card cutouts (Munich exhibition, 1914) have no silk thread; the machine-made paper is too thick.

Forged cancellations: on Geneva forgeries. Type A (single circle). numbers "249," "257," "269," "757"; (three circles), No. "269" with larger figures and dated postmark: PASSAU VII 19; PASSAU 7 A-8.

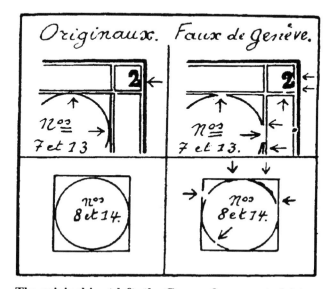

The original is at left, the Geneva forgery, at right.

1862–64. Color change. Nos. 9 to 14. The 3-kreuzer, No. 10, belongs to Type I, broken circle.

Rare shades: 1-kreuzer sulfur yellow: 10M, 3U; 6-kreuzer ultramarine: 800 francs. mint, 500 francs used; 12-kreuzer blue-green: very rare mint, 20U; the 18-kreuzer, No 14, has a vivid color even when it is pale; No. 14a has a dull orange-vermilion tint: 2M. This stamp is less rare than No. 18 in used condition.

Varieties: the 6- and 12-kreuzer stamps were bisected: 150 and 500 francs on cover. The whole set exists with silk thread on the obverse side: 2–4U; thin paper: 2U; 3-kreuzer: 2M, 8U.

Cancellations: Type A: common; with date: 50U: common on 1-kreuzer; Types D, F, I, L on Nos. 9–12: 3U; on Nos. 13 and 4: 50U.

The 12-kreuzer on cover is worth 2U; mixed frankings of Bavarian stamps with those of other states — for example, Austria — is rare.

Pairs: 4U; but 6- and 9-kreuzer: 8U; strips of three: 6U, but 6- and 9-kreuzer: 20U; blocks of four: rare: 1-kreuzer: 30U.

Forgeries: see Nos. 4–8.

1867–68. Coat of arms. Silk thread. Nos. 15 to 22. The background lines of most of the stamps of this issue are blurred; there are defective impressions. Try to obtain first-class prints.

Shades: 1-kreuzer blue-green: 2M, 2U; 6-kreuzer pale ultramarine: rare; 7-kreuzer Prussian blue: 3M, 4U; 12-kreuzer, two shades—pale violet, lilac-rose: 25M, 25U; 18-kreuzer bright red: rare mint, 2U.

Varieties: plate defects: lines or white spots touching or traversing the figures. On the l-kreuzer, an oblique line (top left figure); on the 3-kreuzer, white spots on the bottom globe; on the 7-kreuzer, same, on the terminal line of the figure; on the 12-kreuzer, same, spot at the same place. The last three (bottom left figure): 5–10U. There are other minor varieties. Marginal copies (minimum 3 mm): 2U.

Stamps with silk thread on the obverse side and the greasy prints of Nos. 15, 16, 19 (rare), and 21 are in demand.

The 6-kreuzer brown on very fine vertical laid paper: 2U. Nos. 17 and 18 were bisected diagonally: rare. No. 16, printed both sides: extremely rare. Nos. 15, 16, 18, 19, 21, and 22 were rouletted (not officially). Expertizing is recommended.

Cancellations: Types C, E, J: common; Type J on Nos. 20–22, less common; Type A (single circle) in black on Nos. 18–22: 2U; in red: 3U; Type I and framed postmarks: rare. Pen cancellations are worth fifty percent less.

Stamps on cover: 12-kreuzer: 2U; 18-kreuzer: 5U. The cancellation of the 12-kreuzer with the 3-kreuzer is rare on cover.

Pairs: 4U; but 6-kreuzer blue, 3-kreuzer brown, and 12-kreuzer: 5U; 1-kreuzer dark green and 3-kreuzer: 10U; 7-kreuzer blue: 20U. Strips of three of the 1- and 18-kreuzer stamps: 5U; others: 10U, except 3-kreuzer: 5 francs; 7-kreuzer blue: 40U. Blocks of four are rare; most common 3-kreuzer stamp is worth 50 francs.

Reprints: (1873): without silk thread; line traced with red ink, rare: 100 francs each. 1-, 3-, 6-kreuzer brown; 7- and 12-kreuzer (brown) also exist.

(1896): 1- and 7-kreuzer blue, with silk thread, still rarer; different shades; machine-made paper.

Fakes: mint copies of the next issue, with crossed line watermark, repaired on the reverse side by adding a silk thread between the two papers with forged gumming. Margins usually trimmed short; the watermark, which would remain invisible in a simple transparency examination, is brought out by benzine. Nos. 23–27 and No. 30 were faked this way.

The l-kreuzer without silk thread is a cutout money-order stamp.

II. Perforated Stamps

1870–72. Watermark lozenges. Perf 11½. Nos. 23 to 30. Two sets that can be distinguished on the basis of a 14 mm (1870) or 17 mm (1872) measurement of the main diagonal of the lozenge watermark. The 9- and 10-kreuzer (14 mm): very rare.

Varieties: vertical or horizontal laid paper; wove paper (less common). The 7-kreuzer with plate flaw, as in the preceding issue: 100 francs mint. The 12-kreuzer is found in two shades, red and violet-lilac, the second being less common. Other defects are evident: figures "3" and "10" are barred in the upper-right corner.

Stamps on cover: 25U; 7-, 9-, 10-, and 12-kreuzer (1870): 75U; 18-kreuzer (1872): 5U; 9- and 10-kreuzer (1873): 10U; 18-kreuzer: 20U.

Pairs: 4U.

Reprint. a few sets, which were expertly executed for the Vienna Exhibition of 1873. are not really reprints, but originals from a special printing. Different shades. Very rare. The 12-kreuzer with the 12 mm watermark — not present in the original — is thus the only true reprint. Mauve shade. Value: 100 francs.

Fakes: 1. cutout money-order stamps, with faked perforation and cancellation; shade too dark; faked watermark; found on piece with faked cancellation NURNBERG 15 DEC VORM II, etc.

2. The dishonest doctoring of No. 21 — forged watermark and perforation.

Forgery of the 12-kreuzer: crude. No watermark. Make comparison.

Forged cancellations: numerous on the 12-kreuzer stamp. No Type A cancellations in this value.

1874–75. 1-mark. Watermarked lozenges. Nos. 36 and 37. Imperforate No. 36 must have four margins with a minimum width of 1 mm if collection of a No. 37 with split perforation is not desired. The dark shade is very rare mint: 5U. Horizontal laid paper: 50U. Plate flaw: "M" and "A" joined at bottom: 2U.

Pair: 3U; a single on cover: 6U; blue cancellation: 2U. The dark shaded No. 37 is worth 50M, 50U; on cover: 10U.

1875. Watermarked wavy lines. Nos. 31 to 35. The 7- and 8-kreuzer on cover are worth 3U; 10-kreuzer: 8U. A cliché of the l-kreuzer stamp, misplaced in the plate of the 3-kreuzer stamp, shows traces of the corrected figure "1" in the "4" figures: rare.

1875–76. Value in pfennigs and marks. Nos. 38 to 47. Like the 2-mark stamp, the 50-pfennig red is quite rare on cover: the l-mark: 4U.

Reprints: Nuremberg Exhibition. 25-pfennig yellow-brown; the corresponding shade is dark yellow-brown; 50-pfennig dark brown, very similar to the original. Comparison with a canceled stamp is necessary.

Subsequent issues and new stamps. Much less interesting; from 1919, the stamps of these issues are valueless. The same may be said of official stamps.

Forged overprints: on Nos. 116–51. Crudely executed. Comparison will expose them. Overprints on

Nos. 1 and 5 of the official stamps: compare ink and indention on the reverse side of the stamp. There are numerous forged overprints.

III. Postage Due Stamps

1862. No. 1. Imperforate. Silk thread.
Typographed. *Select:* four margins, minimum width, $^{1}/_{2}$ mm.

Errors: "EmpfangE": 3M, 2U. Less visible errors: "Bom" instead of "Dom," etc.: 50M, 50U.

Forgeries: the early ones are easily identified by comparing the little inscriptions. The early forgeries and the modern ones (Geneva, Nuremberg) have no silk thread, or the silk thread is really ink-drawn or stuck on the reverse side. The original gum is brownish. The Geneva forgeries were executed on papers of various shades, from white to buff, in three plates:

1. Numeral "3," 8 mm high instead of $9^{1}/_{2}$.
2. The second "A" of ZAHLBAR has the shape of an inverted "U."
3. The inner frames are broken: bottom left, top left, bottom right.

The second cliché was made for typography; the others for lithography.

The forged cancellations described for the 1849–50 issue reappear.... [Translators note: Incomplete sentence and text. Instead of completing the sentence, the typesetter repeated the preceding paragraph, "The second cliché was made for typography; the others for lithography.]

1870. Watermarked lozenges. Perf 11$^{1}/_{2}$. Nos. 2 and 3. There are a great many forged cancellations. Expertizing is advised.

Geneva forgeries: like No. 1. No watermark; perforation and paper not like the original. Same characteristics as No. 1 for the 3-kreuzer stamp. In the l-kreuzer, the "H" of ZAHLBAR is touching the inner frame, which is broken 1$^{1}/_{2}$ mm to the right and left of the touching point. Same forged cancellations made in Geneva.

Bergedorf

The small Bergedorf set, which is composed of five values, is perhaps not very interesting to a collector who is satisfied with a single copy of each stamp, but its interest is very great for the plater. The study of these stamps will allow everyone to make a judgment by examining originals, official and unofficial reprints, and forgeries. (The unofficial reprints were made by Moens by means of transfers from the matrix stone, which he had acquired, along with some stock remainders. See J.B. Moens, *De la falsification des timbres-poste, ou nomenclature générale de toutes les imitations et falsifications, ainsi que des divers timbres d'essais de tous pays* [Bruxelles: Moens, 1862], 34 pages.)

The illustrations give information on cancellations, the principal characteristics of the originals, and the official reprints; as for forgeries — there are too many! One should bear in mind, however, that all values from the original stone have fifty-five intertwined circles (pearls) and that this number is frequently different in the forgeries.

The abundance of private reprints and forgeries is due to the small original print order; this was cleverly exploited by Moens, who brought out several sets of reprints. These pseudo-future rarities were very successful. It was one of the first philatelic speculation mysteries — and it was not the last: Cinderella collectors hare possibly become aware of that. Presently, the mint original set is worth 25 gold francs; in blocks of four: 125 francs.

By contrast with reprints and forgeries, authentically canceled stamps are rare.

Select: four visible margins; wide margins are exceptional. The 4-schilling must have 1 mm margins extending to the dividing frame lines.

Originals, reprints: one can set up a progression for each value, starting from the uniformly first-rate impression of the original (and of the essay) and proceeding to Moens' poorly transferred last reprint and its cross-hatched background, which has partly disappeared following matrix cleansing. The Moens reprints, which are not expensive. are good reference stamps, useful for comparative examination before official reprints, originals, and essays are acquired.

Essays: all are rare. The $^{1}/_{2}$-schilling lilac (No. 1, Yvert): 300 francs; 1-schilling white: 200 francs; 1$^{1}/_{2}$-schilling deep yellow: 150 francs; 3-schilling claret (No. 5, Yvert): 400 francs; 4-schilling light brown: 400 francs.

Cancellations: the Bergedorf territory comprised the city and the communities of Geesthacht, Kirchwserder, Kurslach, and Neuengramm. Before adhesive stamps were available, a Type B postmark (BERGEDORF, with two "F's") and a rectilinear postmark, BERGEDORF, spelled the same way and with date underneath, were used. A similar postmark with a single "F," which has V MITTG or N MITTG on a third line, is very rare. The Bergedorf straight-line cancellation, standing alone, is always fraudulent. The Type A postmark was almost always struck twice on domestic letters and once on letters addressed abroad; however, the latter also had Type B on cover.

Type B: 50U; Type C: very rare; Types D and E (Kirchwaerder or Geesthacht): 2U; in blue: very rare. Long postmarks, double-lined octagonal shape, with inscriptions BLPA (Bergedorf) and Kw. L. P. (Kirchwaerder) are very rare. All Bergedorf cancellations must be checked: forged postmarks are very numerous.

Bergedorf cancellations on foreign stamps are rare on cover: for example, North German Postal District, 1-groschen; Denmark, No. 3: 30U; Nos. 17, 19, and 20: 50U; Holstein, Nos. 1 and 2: 50U; No. 3: 3U; Schleswig, No. 2: 3U; No. 3: 8U; 3a: 2U; No. 4: 3U.

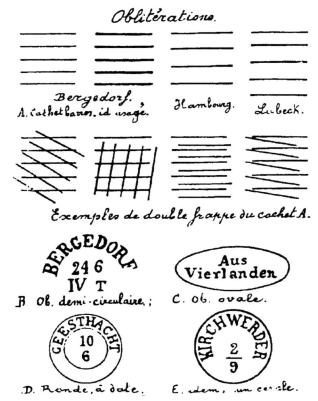

Cancellations. First row: A. Barred postmarks of Bergedorf, Hambourg, and Lubeck. The two Bergedorf cancellations saw the same use. Second row: Examples of double imprints of the postmarks shown above. Third row: B. Semicircular cancel. C. Oval cancel. Fourth row: D. Circular cancel with date. E. Same, single circle.

Stamps on cover: the ¹/₂- and 1-schilling: 3U; 1¹/₂-, 3-, and 4-schilling: 5U.

The ¹/₂-schilling black on pale lilac. This stamp is an essay: rare.

Fake: No. 2 mint, degummed, paper chemically tinted and regummed.

The ¹/₂-schilling black on blue or light blue. Nos. 2 and 2a. Sheets of 200 stamps from vertical transfer blocks of twelve (2 x 6); each half-sheet contains eight of these transfers plus four stamps at the bottom of the sheet on the right and left of a 1 mm center gutter.

Printing figures: No. 1, 180,000; No. 1a, 20,000 (1867).

The accompanying illustration shows the characteristics of the originals. The reader will also notice that the tower roof on the left has two shading marks, and that there are four black marks at the top of the shield and five white ones at the bottom. The shading of the eight circles touching the inner frame is quite visible.

On each stamp there are small transfer flaws that may help to place the stamp in the transfer block; sometimes there are transfer flaws that can situate it on the plate. The same is true for the other values. (Note: One should not stress the importance of a single mark. for the printing process may have eliminated, lengthened, or deformed it.)

Obviously, the essay in black on pale lilac has the same characteristics.

Official reprinting of the essay: executed in 1867 in black on pink lilac. After the transfer stones were cleaned, new vertical transfers (2 x 4) were made. Distinctive mark: a black dot over the "N" of EIN. Value: 5 gold francs.

The Moens reprint (1873): unofficial. The ¹/₂-schilling black on blue, gumless. Marks: the "H" and "A" of HALBER are barred by an almost vertical thin line; the base of the "R" is detached. Value: 10 gold centimes.

Second Moens reprint (1887): the ¹/₂-schilling black on purplish blue; in dimensions, ¹/₄ mm more; no finesse in impression; type too bold. Value: 2 gold centimes.

The 1-schilling black or gray-black on white. A sheet of 180 stamps made up of eighteen vertical transfers of ten stamps (2 x 5); there is a top transfer, then two panes of four transfers; same arrangement occurs at the bottom of the sheet, the six panes being separated by a 2 mm gutter. The bottom right pane is transferred in an inverted position, producing twelve tête-bêche stamps. Another anomaly: the figures were so poorly drawn on the matrix that they did not transfer to the mother-stone of ten stamps; they were drawn by pen on the latter — all of which helps plating.

Printing: 90,000.

Originals: the left tower roof structure has two short vertical shading lines at the bottom; the top white shield has five bottom vertical shade lines, the fifth one being paired. One can see the dots or lines that were used as reference in executing the figures.

Essay in black (thick paper). Value: 25 gold francs.

Moens reprint (1873): gumless, yellowish paper. New vertical transfer (2 x 4). Figures were redone with terminal lines at base: 50 gold centimes.

Second Moens reprint: bad printing. Dimensions excessive: 16³/₈ x 16¹/₄ mm. Figures are too large; worn center background burelage. Value: 5 gold centimes.

Third Moens reprint: very poorly executed. Figures are too thin; center background is definitely worn. Value: 2 gold centimes.

The 1¹/₂-schilling black on dark or pale yellow. The black on dark yellow is rare as a mint stamp. The shade of the 1¹/₂-schilling is sulfur yellow.

An essay on thick paper (dark yellow) is rare: 50 gold francs. It had the "SchillingE" error on it, which was corrected before the final printing.

Sheets of 200 stamps in two panes of eight vertical transfers of twelve stamps (2 x 6), plus four stamps joined laterally to the half-sheet; these four stamps, transferred in an inverted position, are tête-bêche copies.

Printing: 100,000.

Originals: the figures of the lower left corner were enlarged; this produced the marks shown in the illustration. On the right of the right tower, above the parapet passageway, there are three small dots; under the left claw of the beam clamp, two small dots are near the link. The horn opening suggests a serpent's head. First-rate burelage in the center background.

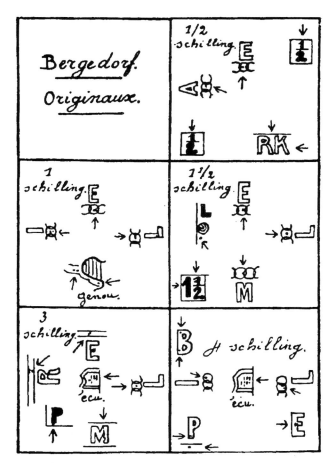

Identifying characteristics of Bergedorf originals: *genou* [knee]; *écu* [escutcheon].

The essay-error *"schillinge"* naturally has the same distinctive marks. The deep yellow paper is thick.

Moens reprint (1873): "SchillingE"; defective printing; center background is worn. Value: 5 centimes.

The 3-schilling blue on pink. Sheets of 160 stamps in two half-sheets of eight horizontal transfers of ten stamps (5 x 2), separated by a 4 mm horizontal gutter. A rare essay on claret exists; value: 175 francs.

Printing: 80,000.

Originals: five white vertical lines in the shield's base, the one on the left is often embryonic, the one on the right, broken in the middle. A fine horizontal line on the left of the base of the "H" in the inner corner. The paper is pink, but seems purplish because of the blue printing. Essay: same characteristics

Official reprinting of the essay (1867): black on lilac; two black dots near the middle of the "S" of POSTMARKE. Value: 8 francs.

Moens reprint (1873): blue on purplish transparent paper; eagle head without any shading; center background has traces of wear. Value: 10 centimes.

Second Moens reprint (1887): pale blue on lilac-pink. The burelage of the center background is even less complete. Value: 10 centimes.

Third Moens reprint (1888): shades of blue on paper that is almost purple with silk threads. Value: 2 centimes.

The 4-schilling black on buff or dark buff. There exists a very rare essay, black on rosy buff: 250 francs. Sheets of eighty stamps in two half-sheets separated by a 5 mm gutter. Each contains four horizontal transfers of eight stamps (4 x 2), and at bottom two half transfers.

Printing: 80,000.

Originals: a burelage line ends in a dot on the right of the right tower near the middle of the window; underneath, on a level with the parapet passageway, there is a dot between two lines of the burelage.

The Moens reprint (1873): black on brownish buff. Printing not so good: the distinctive characteristics have partly or totally disappeared. The center circle has a heavy ascending oblique line that begins at the link under the "I" of VIER. Value: 1 franc.

Second Moens reprint (1874): same paper. Printing a little better than the previous reprint, except for the burelage, which is beginning to show signs of wear, particularly in front of the upper part of the wing. No oblique line in the circle. Value: 60 centimes.

Third Moens reprint (1887): similar paper, but reddish; inscription lettering is very unsuccessful, especially top and bottom. A line in the circle. Value: 2 centimes.

Bremen

All canceled stamps are rare.

Stamps on cover: 3U, except Nos. 10 and 12: 2U. Covers with different issues: very rare.

Pairs: mint, 3U; canceled, 4U, minimum. Used strips of three are very rare.

I. Imperforate Stamps

Select: four margins, 1¹/₂ mm wide for Nos. 1 and 3, 1¹/₄ mm for No. 2, and 1 mm for No. 5. Marginal copies are very rare: No. 4: 2M or 2U.

Cancellations (for the first three issues): a few cancellation types are shown in the accompanying illustration; however, there are many others, which generally are rare. Type A: usually in black, very rare in blue; Type B: 10U; in blue: 30U, but VEGASACK BAHNHOF: very rare in blue and black; Type C: FRANCO unframed (often applied twice, sometimes crossed), rather common; Type D: same: Type E, quite visible: 30U; Type G: 50U (Hanoverian railway postal service). This last mentioned type is found with "G M = H V R" at the top and BREMEN on the third line. Type H: 20U; in blue: very rare.

There is a four-circle cancellation, No. 182, of the Prussian postal service. In the Hanoverian service, Type A, unframed and half-moon postmark with BREMEN and date; Type A, unframed; Type A with scalloped frame and various circular postmarks with date and BREMEN. In the Thurn & Taxis service, large semicircular postmark; quadruple circle, No. 301; Thurn & Taxis postmark with date in one circle and the dated postmarks with inscription BREMEN TH u TX. For the central post office, large circular postmarks with a key; Type A, framed and unframed postmark BREMERHAFEN with date; finally, postmarks with inscription AMERICA USER BREMEN.

Forged cancellations: very numerous. Expertizing is necessary. We can mention a few forged Geneva cancellations (engraved on wood): Type A, BREMEN 20 6-3 4; Type D, BREMEN 5 8 5-6; Type H, BREMEN, and BREMEN 25 5.

Types: the identification marks of the original stamps shown in the accompanying illustration indicate the differences between the three types of the 3-grote stamp and the two types of the 5-grote.

Early forgeries: in complete sets (London, Hamburg, Neuruppin). All of them amateurishly executed. Comparison with the distinctive characteristics of the originals will easily expose their fraudulence.

Modern forgeries: numerous, and many are no better than the preceding forgeries. We shall indicate a few differences of the most deceptive forgeries, without going into a time-consuming, lengthy discussion. The distinctive characteristics shown in the illustration are adequate for recognizing all counterfeits. With the

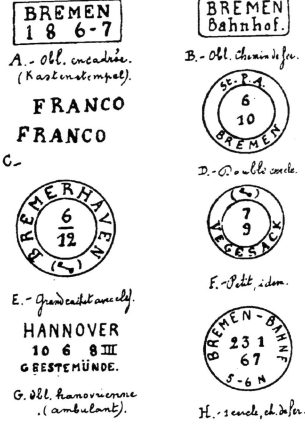

Bremen cancellations found on the first three issues: A. Framed cancel. B. Railway cancel. C. FRANCO (paid). D. Double circle. E. Large postmark with key. F. Small postmark with key. G. Hanoverian cancel (mobile). H. Single circle, railway.

exception of the so-called "reprint" of the 3-grote described below, these forgeries never have the finesse of the authentic original stamps.

Reprints: none exist, but sometimes facsimile stamps (forgeries) are called unofficial reprints made on rebuilt plates (!). These can be identified like other counterfeits.

No. 1. 3-grote black on blue (three types). 1855. *Sheets* of 120 stamps (12 x 10); the three types follow each other in each horizontal row. Horizontally laid paper; vertically laid paper: 50M, 50U. The dot at the top of the crown (secret mark) is not always visible. One stamp in each sheet has a black line under STADT POST AMT: 50M. 50U. The paper of the first printing had a manufacturer's mark, a large double-lined fleur-de-lys (very rare). A strip of three stamps containing the three types: 5M. (Postage for the Bremen region was three grote.) In the original Type III, the eighteenth line of hatching of the shield sometimes touches the edge; this type is only 19 mm wide instead of 19¹/₄.

Forgeries: generally on wove paper. The so-called "reprint," on grayish laid paper, is ¹/₂ mm higher than the original; the shading line is continuous under the "EM" (first downstroke) and "EN" of BREMEN, but in the original it is broken between the letters.

One early forgery has no white dots in the large figures; the "T" of AMT touches the "M." With regard to Geneva and early forgeries (Neuruppin, etc.), careful study of the illustration drawings will suffice. All nonlaid paper must be rejected.

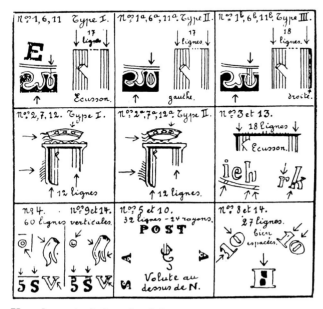

Key characteristics of originals, Nos. 1 to 14: *lignes* [lines], *éscusson* [escutcheon], *rayons* [rays], helix above "N," *bien espacées* [well-spaced].

No. 2. 5-grote black on rose (two types). 1855. Sheets as in No. 1. Four scarcely visible black dots outside the corners of each stamp, at the intersection of the extension of the frame lines, and a dividing frame line 1¹/₄ mm away from the extension. Five rote was the postage for Hamburg.

Pairs: both types joined: 3M. Double print: very rare. In the two original types, there are twelve shade lines in the shield, but in Type I, the line on the right is in slightly bolder print. Rather well-made *forgeries* of Nos. 2, 7, and 12 do not have the four external dots; the curved inner line is not broken at the bottom before it reaches the lower horizontal line under the "f" of "funf"; the upper horizontal lines of the second "f" and of the "t" of "rote" are not very visible on the left. Other forgeries do not have any dividing frame line, have a closed "G" at the bottom, etc. In a crude Geneva forgery, there is no burelage between the crown and the escutcheon, and the lines on the left of the shield are almost horizontal.

Fake: No. 7, with trimmed rouletting. The maximum width and height of this fake are 23 mm and 26¹/₂ mm, respectively. This shows why wide margins in imperforate stamps are necessary.

No. 2b, *error.* unissued precisely because of the error, is the best reference for Nos. 2, 7, and 12. However, the external dots are sometimes lacking. A block of four stamps: 6M.

No. 3. 7-grote black on yellow. 1860. Sheets of thirty-five stamps (7 x 5). Dividing frame lines. Seven grote was the postage for Mecklenburg and Lubeck.

Forgeries: no black dots in the "k" or "r" of "Marke" The left corner ornaments. especially the one on top, are too far from the frame. The "b" of "Sieben" is closed below. The left shading of the shield is too far from the edge. In the Geneva forgery, the poorly copied burelage overlaps a few of the inscription letters, and the dots above the corner ornaments are too far apart.

No. 4. 5-silbergroschen. Green on white, dark green. 1861. Sheets of thirty-six stamps (4 x 9), with colored frame lines about 1 mm from the stamp. The 5-silbergroschen was the postage for England. Medium glossy paper, brown gum, but regular blue-green gum is found on the thick (about 90 microns) chalky paper. The dot after "Sgr." is always definitely square; copies without a loop on the right of the key proper are sought after; there are copies with the blank inner oval broken about 2 mm above the left loop of the stem; sometimes the "V" on the left has a little curved line at its foot that is convex at the bottom.

Forgeries: thin, transparent paper. The bar of the "5" extends beyond the belly of the figure. The strokes of the "V" on the right are too close (¹/₆ mm instead of ¹/₄ mm), and the inner line of the right branch is slanted toward the latter's left branch. The drapery on the right is as in No. 9.

Geneva forgeries: the figure "5" and the letters "5" and "Q" touch the line above them.

Fake: No. 9, trimmed rouletting. The reader is referred to the illustration. The paper is thinner and is slightly transparent.

II. Arc Rouletted Stamps

These stamps should be centered, except, possibly, those with visible dividing frame lines (Nos. 7, 10. etc.), because these lines were used to guide the rouletting.

Same types as Nos. 1 to 4, except No. 9, which is somewhat different. Sheets as previously; Nos. 5 and 8, sheets of thirty-six stamps (4 x 9). The rouletting of Nos. 5, 6, and 9 is somewhat different from that of Nos. 7 and 8.

The 2-grote stamp is found in orange and orange-red shades. It was created to cover postage between Bremen and Vegesack. The 10-grote was the postage for Holland.

2-grote. 1863. Slightly glossy white paper, or grayish white paper.

Originals: fine parallel shading in the side tablets. Superb burelage. The tablet line ends are not very clearly printed; the right half of the one at the top of the lower tablet is almost invisible. The "G" resembles a "C."

Forgeries: 1. The dots are replaced by lines in the "A" of STADT and the "S" of POST; the others are missing; tablet lines are in bold print; the helix above the "N" of BREMEN is not broken; wavy shading in the lateral tablets.

2. Another forgery. The helix above the "N" is single instead of double; the opening of the helix under the "T" of POST faces right instead of downward; the well-formed, double-pointed white scallop that surrounds the loop of the key is replaced here by a single scallop.

3. Geneva forgeries. No dots in the "A" and "S"; no shading in the ornaments above the figures. The center burelage is $^1/_4$ mm from the inner frame; it should almost touch it.

3-grote. 1863. Horizontally laid paper: 2M, 2U. With a line under "Stadt Post Amt": 50M, 50U.

Fake: the arc rouletting of No. 1 was forged.

5-grote. 1862. This stamp, like the following one, sometimes has an outer dividing frame line; more rarely, two of them. Pairs unrouletted between stamps are found, but are rare.

10 grote. 1861. *Originals:* the double line cross-hatching that provides the background for the BREMEN and ZEHN POST inscription is very fine. There are six lozenges on the right and left, near the middle of the stamp, but the right side of the right lozenge on the right is not entirely complete.

Forgeries: 1. The "10" figures are not congruent. The cross-hatched background lines do not extend beyond the frame under the "10" on the left. The background is inexpertly drawn. The loop of the key touches the oval.

2. Geneva forgeries, two different models: (a) no trace of shading in the "10" on the right; four lozenges instead of six. (b) No shading in the figures; the two shade lines on the left of the left loop of the key are too close together.

5-silbergroschen. 1863. The vertical shading extends somewhat beyond the line under BREMEN (except in the worn plate).

Varieties: double rouletted: rare. Worn plate — disappearance of most of the vertical hatch lines: 25M, 25U.

III. Perforated Stamps (1866–67)

First-class stamps. Centered. There are two kinds of perforation, clean-cut and not so clean-cut; the former is in demand. The 2-grote is orange-red instead of orange-yellow: 75M, 50U. The 3-grote is always laid horizontally; there are copies of this one with no bottom perforation; with a line under "Stadt Post Amt": 50M, 50U. The 5-grote is found in pairs with no perforation between stamps: rare. The 7-grote stamp on cover is exceedingly rare. It has two slightly different shades.

Forgeries: see the previous issues. The envelope cutouts, 1-grote black on white. pale blue, or lilac-blue are worth 40 francs on cover for white paper, and 300 francs, for colored paper. They were counterfeited in Geneva with the forged postmarks already affixed. These counterfeits can be identified by the paper. the dimensions of the oval, the inscriptions, and the crown, which is broken diagonally.

Brunswick

Nos. 1 to 11 were printed in sheets of 120 stamps (12 x 10); the others, including the 4/4-gutegroschen, in sheets of 100 (10 x 10). Plating is difficult because of the scarcity of pairs and blocks; even marginal copies are rare. With respect to Nos. 4–11, the watermark may help in plating. Two plates of Nos. 1 and 3 are recognizable because of the width of the stamps: No. 1, $20^3/_4$ mm and $21^1/_4$ mm; No. 3, $21^2/_5$ mm and $21^4/_5$ mm.

First Issue. January 1, 1852. Nos. 1 to 3. The bright shades are worth 20M, 20U. Mint stamps are very rare, especially those with the original rose-colored gum: 2M. Watch out for pen cancellations that have been cleaned and regummed.

Paper: machine-made, without watermark, medium thickness, tough, very light yellowish white shade.

Select: four margins about 1 mm wide. Exceptional stamps with four wide margins are worth as much as 2U.

Varieties: No. 1, SIL3 instead of SILB: 50U. A dot above the value figure: 25U. No. 2, circle arc above the "2" on the right: 25U. No. 3, SIL3 or SIBB instead of SILB: 50U. There are less important varieties; for example, No. 2 with an "H" that is broken on top, and No. 3 with a dot over the "I" of SILB. These are either printing or plate fouling flaws. Good impressions with full vertical lines are in demand. Albino stamps are found in the three values. No. 2 is known bisected (Ferrary).

Cancellations: the principal postmark models are shown in the illustration. Type A and B cancellations in blue: common; Type E in blue: in demand; Type A in black: 25U; Types B, C, and J in black: 50U; Type D: very rare. There is also a small oval cancellation (major axis: 18 mm) with the hour inscription: 50U; also, early postmarks (Type A, but without bottom inscriptions or with middle manuscript inscriptions). They are rare, as are foreign cancellations. Pen cancellations: fifty percent.

Principal cancellations of Brunswick: A. Double circle, without year date. B. Half circle. C. With year date. D. FRANCO (paid). E. Rectangular framed cancellation. F. Unframed. G.-H.-I. Barred cancellations with numerals. J. Buckle-shaped cancel. K. Rare cancel.

Stamps on cover: 2U.
Pairs: No. 1: 4U; Nos. 2 and 3: 5U.
Originals: first, three wood-engraved matrices were made from them, three copper matrices were produced. These were used to cast the 120 typograph clichés of each plate.

There are a few minor differences between Nos. 1, 2, and 3: No. 1 is narrower and not so long as Nos. 2 and 3. There are also very slight differences between die clichés in the same plate.

It has been claimed that the plates for Nos. 7 and 11, 8, 9, and 10 were rebuilt. This argument was based on the fact that the varieties of Nos. 1, 2, and 3 are no longer found in the above numbered stamps. In my

opinion, the same plates were used. The marks caused by dirty plates disappeared after cleaning, but the distinctive stamp characteristics show no variation whatsoever.

In fact, if you examine the marks shown in the illustration, you will see that the marks of Nos. 1 to 3 all reappear in Nos. 7, 7a, 11, 8, 9, and 10, except the break in the oval on the right of No. 1, which is no longer found in Nos. 7, 7a, and 11. This may be attributed to slight cliché wear. The same may be said of No. 8 with respect to the banderole and the inner top right frame: likewise, with regard to the hatch lines of the oval on the right in Nos. 3 to 9.

So it was the heavier print impression that eliminated these flaws in the second issue; wear helped. Regular plate cleaning sufficed to remove the flaws caused by dirty plates.

Besides, if you examine the printings of Nos. 1, 2, 3, up to Nos. 10 (1862) and 11 (1864) one after another, you will notice that the plates produced more and more complete prints, which, however, diminished progressively in quality. The outer frames of Nos. 10 and 11 show this quite well.

It should be noted that the paper color change (1853) and the creation of a watermark were specifically intended to eliminate counterfeiting.

Forgeries: the early forgeries of German origin do not have the marks described for the originals. As for modern forgeries, one Geneva set is no better: the hatch lines in the center oval are oblique on the right of the crown; the hatch lines that overlap the end of the tail are too far apart; and the three clichés (Nos. 1–3, which were also used for Nos. 7, 7a, 11, 8, 9, and 10) are about 1 mm too narrow — $20^{1}/_{8}$ mm. The first quality of a forger should be to have good visual perception of measurement!

Forged Geneva cancellations (F): although there is little danger from forged stamps, we call attention to forged cancellations, because they were applied to original Nos. 12 to 16. Type A: WOLFENBUTTEL 7/ 1; $8^{1}/_{2}$-9 (the fraction bar touches the center circle); BRAUNSCHWEIG 1/ ... (bar 2 mm away from the center circle). Type C: BRAUNSCHWEIG 11 NOV 1865 8-10 A; same. 17 ... 1866-12 A. Type G: No. 32. Type H: No. 8. Hour cancellation, "1–$1^{1}/_{2}$," and French cancellation. "1104," with large figures in a stippled lozenge. Naturally, there are other forged postmarks.

Reprints: none.

Second issue (1853–63). Watermarked. Nos. 4 to 10. The $^{1}/_{2}$-groschen. short-tailed horse, is a new type.
Select: four margins, 1 mm wide.
Paper: handmade. various thicknesses, the extremes (thickest and thinnest) are in demand: No. 4, thin paper: 20U; No. 5, thick: 40U; No. 6, thick: 2U; No.

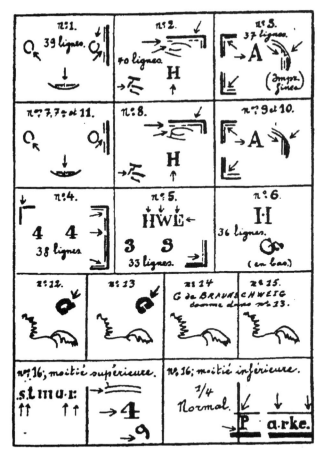

Identifying characteristics of Brunswick, Nos. 1 to 16 of the first issue: *lignes* [lines]; *impr. fines* [fine print]; *en bas* [at bottom]; **G** *de Braunschweig comme dans No. 13* ["G" of Braunschwieg as in No. 13]; *mottlé supérieure* [upper half]; *moitié inférieure* [flower half].

7, medium (60–70 microns): 50U; Nos. 7a and 8, very thick (more than 100 microns): 50U.

Watermark: framed post horn, various types, rather difficult to identify. No. 7 is found with the mouthpiece opening sometimes on the left, sometimes on the right; others, inverted watermark (mouthpiece opening on the right, when stamp is viewed from the back): 2–3U.

The framed post horn watermark can be found with the mouthpiece opening both to the left and to the right.

Gum: Nos. 4, 5, 7, 8, and 9: yellowish; Nos. 6, 10, and 11: white.

Varieties: the ⅓-silbergroschen with inscription SII.BR instead of SILBR and two broken banderole lines: rare. The 1-silbergroschen orange, 1-silbergroschen yellow, and 2-silbergroschen bisected: very rare (the 2-silbergroschen on cover: 250 francs). The 3-silbergroschen black on rose, clear, bright shade, is very much in demand. The 3-silbergroschen rose on white with a dot between the "S" and the "C" of BRAUNSCHWEIG: rare. No. 10 is known double-printed, but is very rare.

Cancellations: Type G cancellations in black are predominant: forty-eight post offices. Most common is No. 8 (BRUNSWICK-CITY). Having been damaged, No. 9 (BRUNSWICK-STATION) was replaced in 1863 by a large figured Type I: rare. Same cause, same effect, with respect to No. 36 (SALDER), replaced by Type H, with its finely drawn bars: rare. Type E in blue: 25U; in black: rare; Type G in blue: 50U; Types J, K, etc.: rare. Type C in black with millesime appears right at the end of the watermark issues.

Stamps on cover: 2U; No. 5: 3U, but a single on cover: 6U.

Pairs: 3U, but No. 7: 4U; strips of three: 5U, but No. 7: 8U. Blocks of four: rare (¼-silbergroschen and 3-silbergroschen rose on white: 12U; 3-silbergroschen black on rose: 24U).

Reprints: none. The so-called "unofficial reprint" of the ⅓-silbergroschen made in 1856 without watermark is sometimes classified in this category.

Forgeries: most of the forgeries are of German origin, but none, whether lithographed or typographed, deserves detailed description. General characteristics: no watermark. The horse's tail often touches the first or fourth shading line, whereas, in the originals, it touches the second one, except in the ½-silbergroschen and the 2-silbergroschen (first shade mark is a dot), where it touches the third. Irregularly shaped ovals and figures. Noncongruent format, generally too small. Compare with the distinctive characteristics of the originals shown in the illustration.

1864. Sawtooth rouletting. Nos. 4 to 11. Same details as in the previous issue. The rouletting of all sawtooth rouletted stamps should be expertized. This rouletting was discontinuous in the originals and continuous in the crude counterfeits. Some counterfeits, however, are very good.

Stamps on cover: the ½-groschen, No. 6: 4U; others: 2U.

Pairs: 3U; strips of three are very rare (No. 11: 10U).

Line-rouletted stamps: the 1-silbergroschen black on yellow, No. 7c, is worth about 400 francs, but 2,000 francs on cover. The 1-silbergroschen yellow, on cover, is worth 2U. The 3-silbergroschen, No. 10b, is worth 1,200 francs, but on cover: 8,000 francs (exceedingly rare).

Issue of 1857. Oval format. Nos. 12 to 15. Sheets of 100 stamps (10 x 10); machine-made paper; brown or white gum. Rouletted on all four sides.

Varieties: there is a demand for the carmine shades of the 1-groschen, and for the ultramarine variety of the 2-groschen. Nos. 13 and 14 were used bisected (very rare). No. 13 is found with the bottom of the letters "B R" broken; No. 15, with a white spot between the crown and the neck of the noble war horse (plate flaw, one per sheet).

Imperforate stamps: they must be at least 21³/₄ mm wide by 25¹/₃ mm high. The claret shade of No. 15 is rare.

Pairs: 3U; imperforate: 4U.

Stamps on cover: 2U; No. 12: 3U, on cover: 5U.

Cancellations: Type G in black: common; in blue: 50U; Type C in black: 2U. Expertizing usually is necessary.

Reprints: none.

Forgeries: fine counterfeits of Nos. 12 to 15 were made in Geneva (F.). See the distinctive marks of the originals: tail and mane, no relief, crude burelage, and rouletting. No. 12: 19¹/₂ instead of 20 mm wide (minor axis); No. 14: 20¹/₂ mm instead of 19¹/₂–19³/₄ mm. Rouletting is continuous.

Forged cancellations: see the first issue.

1857. No. 16 and unissued No. 17. The margins must be about ³/₄ mm wide. Sheets of 100 stamps (10 x 10). The paper of No. 16 is the same as that of No. 4. No. 17 was made to replace No. 16, which was too dark, but it turned out to be useless because of Brunswick's entrance into the North German Confederation. The printing of No. 17 is almost always defective.

Varieties: No. 16, thin paper: 50U; minor printing defects: "pfonnige" for "pfennige"; "8" instead of "3"; etc.: 20U.

Pairs: halves and quarters. One quarter (¹/₄): 2 francs; on cover: 5 francs, but on cover alone: 40 francs; two quarters (²/₄): 5 francs; on cover: 10 francs; three quarters (³/₄): 10 francs, on cover: 25 francs; a whole unit (⁴/₄) is worth 2U on cover; likewise, five quarters (⁵/₄); six quarters (⁶/₄) are worth 50U, on cover: 3U; a pair (⁸/₄) is worth 2U, on cover: 4U; ten quarters (¹⁰/₄): 4U, on cover: double.

Cancellation: with date: 50U.

Early forgeries: Nos. 16 and 17. No watermark, and they do not have the marks described in the illustration.

Modern forgeries: Geneva. Same characteristics. The fraction bars touch the ovals.

Forged cancellations: numerous on No. 16 (expertizing is indicated); also on No. 17, which should be discarded without further examination.

Fake: No. 17 transformed into No. 16 by chemical paper tinting and by impression oxidation. Result: black-brown (deep brown), or more or less mottled brown. On this fake, the cancellation is always forged.

Hamburg

I. Imperforate Stamps

1859. Wavy line watermark. Nos. 1 to 7. *Sheets* of 120 stamps (12 x 10), typographed. The watermark is always visible (use watermark fluid if necessary). Sometimes only traces or a fragment of a wavy line attached to the straight border line of the watermark is visible. This is due to the paper having been improperly aligned with the plate during printing.

Secret marks: there are small design flaws in each value. Some of them are so sharply etched (dots) that they make one think they are really engraver's secret marks. (See the illustration.) Use a magnifying glass to examine the stamp.

Select: four margins: ³/₄ mm, top and bottom, and 1³/₄ mm on the sides (up to the dividing frame lines). Mint stamps with the original brownish yellow gum are worth double. Compare the gum with that of a mint stamp of good quality.

Shades: very little variation. No. 5 green and blue-green. No. 7 orange and orange-yellow.

Varieties: the stamps with numbers in the margins (marginal copies) are in great demand: 3M, 3U. No. 5 is found with very clear-cut double print: 3M. One-half of a bisected No. 1 was used with No. 2 to make a 1¹/₄-schilling (1864): rare. 9-schilling, with thicker dividing frame line, plate flaw: 50M. The same value from worn plate can be found.

On cover: 1- and 2-schilling: 2U. ¹/₂-, 3-, and 7-schilling: 3U. Others: 4U

Cancellations: Type A (22–24 mm long): common. In blue: very rare. In black, about 40 mm long: very rare. Type B: 2U. Type C: 2U, but with other inscriptions ("St. P.A."): very rare. Type D (always in blue): 50U. A framed rectangular postmark with two wavy lines on the sides: very rare. Likewise for dated thimble cancellations in black and blue, foreign postmarks, mobile cancellations (on three lines, unframed) and all the postmarks not shown in the illustration, such as the Bergedorf bars (1861), etc.

Pairs: mint: 3M. used: 4U. Used strips and blocks: extremely rare.

Reprints: none.

Forgeries: very easily identifiable. 1. *No watermark:* no secret marks. Obviously, either of these may be missing or poorly executed in the originals because of printing flaws. The illustration shows enough distinctive characteristics to allow one to make a sound decision. Since they are lithographed, the forgeries do not have the typographical indention or "bite" on the reverse that is especially noticeable on mint stamps. Sometimes there is a boldface forged watermark.

Forged cancellations: Type B was counterfeited in Geneva: HAMBURG.. R 1866. Type A and D in black also are found, as well as various dated postmarks, which were applied not only on the forgeries but also on Nos. 1, 5, and 7, stamps that always require cancellation examination.

Fakes: your imperforate stamps will not turn out to have come from trimmed perforated stamps if you are careful to acquire them with adequate top and bottom margins (minimum format: $21^{1}/_{2}$ x $25^{1}/_{2}$ mm).

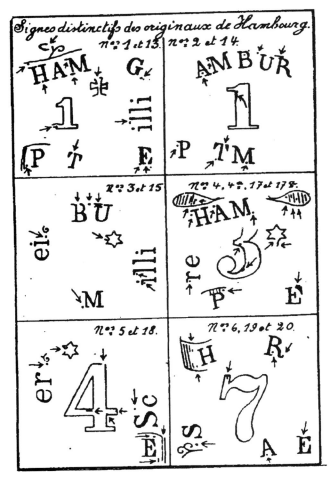

Distinctive marks of genuine Hamburg stamps.

1864. Same watermark. Nos. 8 to 10. *Sheets* of 192 lithographed stamps in two panes (12 x 8). The $1^{1}/_{4}$-schilling had two matrices and the $2^{1}/_{2}$-schilling only one (Plate II stamps are perforated), the matrices being composed of twelve transfers (4 x 3). Thus, it is possible to reconstitute the plate transfer blocks by means of distinctive transfer flaws. Transfer defects occur twice per sheet: rare.

Select: four margins, 1 mm wide, extending to the dividing frame lines. Mint examples of $1^{1}/_{4}$-schilling have yellowish gum; the $2^{1}/_{2}$-schilling, white gum.

Distinctive features of the originals: see the illustration.

Shades: numerous lilac and violet shades (No. 8); a mauve shade is less common. No. 8a is slightly blue-tinted gray. No. 8b, which is rare, is slightly greenish blue. No. 9 is dull greenish gray. No. 10 has a handsome dark green shade, but from the final printings, it has a duller, somewhat more yellowish color.

Varieties: small transfer flaws are found once every twelve stamps; transfer flaws (for example, a star-shaped white spot above "KE" of POSTMARKE), once every ninety-six stamps: 2M, 2U.

Pairs: 3M, 4U. On cover: 2U. Nos. 9 and 10: 3U.

Cancellations: usually Type E. Dated cancellations on the $2^{1}/_{2}$-schilling are very rare.

Reprints are found without (1872) and with watermark (1880). The watermarked reprints, which were made by means of new transfer plates, do not have the same defects that occur in the first transfers. This points out the importance and usefulness of plating. The two kinds of reprints, carelessly executed, are bad impressions. They do not show design details as sharply as in the originals (see illustration). Many are dotted with color specks. Shades differ.

Forgeries: no watermark. The imperforate and perforated stamps were photolithographically counterfeited in Geneva. The $1^{1}/_{4}$-schilling is identified by the fact that the thin, oblique upstroke of the "M" of HAMBURG is scarcely visible. In the $2^{1}/_{2}$-schilling, the cross under the "B" merges with the tablet's blank or is separated from it only by a very thin line. Counterfeited in yellow-green (erroneously), then in blue-green.

Forged Geneva cancellations on forgeries and reprints: Type D in black or blue; Type B in black, and Type F in blue and black.

Fakes: the perforated stamps with trimmed margins often are offered for sale as imperforate stamps. Thus, it is absolutely necessary to insist upon four wide margins when buying imperforate stamps. Moreover, verification of transfer plate characteristics enables one to identify exactly these fakes from the second plates.

II. Perforated Stamps

1864. Perf $13^{1}/_{2}$. Watermark. Nos. 11 and 12. Same characteristics as the preceding issue, but stamps are from Plate II. No. 12 is lighter green, yellower, than No. 10. It has no watermarked reprint.

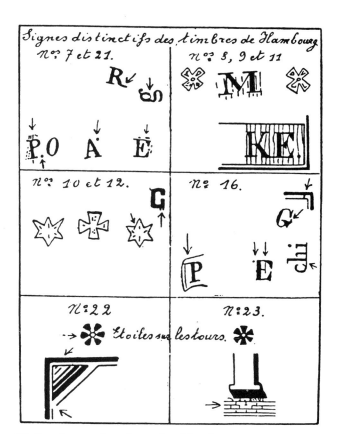

Distinctive marks of genuine Hamburg stamps.
Étoiles sur les tours [stars on the towers].

Cancellations of Hamburg: A. Bars. B. Parentheses.
C. Oval. D. Wavy line. E. Thurn & Taxis; three
circles. F. Single circle, with date. G. Two circles,
with date. H. Circle with stem. I. Official-stamp
cancel.

Cancellations: Types E, F, G: common. Type G.
with no year or hour designation, or with BAHNHOF:
very rare.

Pairs: 3U. On cover: 2U.

Forgeries: as above. Well executed in Geneva and
Charlottenburg, but without watermark; secret marks
are missing or defective.

Forged Geneva cancellations on forgeries and
reprints: single circle, with date: HAMBURG
BAHNHOF 21-11-66 8-10 1/2 N; HAMBURG 5-16-66
6-7 N, and Types B and D.

Another forged cancellation frequently found on
forgeries and reprints of Nos. 11 and 12, as well as on
the originals of the following issue, is Type H (irregular
cancellation on stamps, despite the fact that it is found
on late letters and sometimes on official stamps).
Moreover, it is not congruent with letters "H" and "M"
(too narrow, too tall) in the illustration.

1864–65. 1859 types. Watermark. Nos. 13 to 21.
Same characteristics as the first issue. Perf 13½.

Shades: 2-schilling pale red, red, dark red; 2½-
schilling olive-green, dark yellow-green; 3-schilling dull
pale green, yellow-green. The 3-schilling imperforate
ultramarine is worth the usual price.

Distinctive characteristics: see the illustration for
No. 16. In this issue, the characteristics are
occasionally less clear-cut than in the first one: No. 13,

curved line closed above "HA"; lower bar of "E"
likewise. No. 14, line at bottom of the "M" restored.
No. 17 likewise, and upper bar of the "E" also
restored.

Varieties: marginal copies with marginal numbers:
2M, 2U.

Cancellations: Type A in black or blue: common.
Types C and D: rare. Type G: common in blue. Foreign
cancellations, HELIGOLAND, SCHLESWIG, THURN
U. TAXIS, etc.: very rare. On cover: 50U. Nos. 17, 20,
and 21: 3U.

Pairs: 3U, No. 17: 4U. 7- and 9-schilling: very rare.
Blocks: rare.

Forgeries: ½-, 2½-, and 7-schilling. All without
watermark.

Fakes: the imperforate 7-schilling with forged
perforation.

Forged cancellations: numerous on the ½-, 2½-, and
9-schilling. A forged Geneva cancellation is Type B.
HAMBURG 1 MAI …

Reprints: none.

1866. Rouletted stamps. Nos. 22 and 23. *Sheets* of
100 stamps (10 x 10). No watermark.

Distinctive marks: see the illustration.

Cancellations: Type F in blue, etc.

Pairs: 4U. On cover, No. 22: 2U. No. 23: 2.5U.

Shades: 1¼-schilling violet, purple. Same value.

Variety: plate defect, 1¼-schilling, "3" instead of "B": 3M, 3U.

Reprints: 1¼-schilling, 19 x 22⁴/₅–23 mm instead of 19²/₅ x 22¹/₅ mm. The four stars in the inscription's bandeau are full and unbroken. More or less brownish red-lilac shade. 1½-schilling, 22¹/₅ mm high instead of 21⁴/₅ mm; red shade instead of carmine-tinted rose. The two reprints have a very pronounced printing indentation ("bite") and are on yellowish paper.

Forgeries: 1¼-schilling, photoengraved. Slate shade. 19½ x 22⁴/₅ mm. The distinctive marks of the originals are missing.

Envelopes (covers). Cut squares (1866, 1867) of stamp type No. 22 (½-, 1¼-, 1½-, 2-, 3-, 4-, and 7-schilling) were also counterfeited. Compare design and measurements.

1867. Official stamps. Nos. 1 and 2. A single type: roulette or perf 13½ x 14.

Cancellations: Types H or I in black.

Hanover

Select: four margins, minimum width 1 mm.

Sheets of 120 stamps (10 x 12).

Marginal numerals: Nos. 3–5, 1–13, and 13a have numerals 1–10 at the top and bottom of the sheets, while Nos. 2, 8, 10, 11, and 13–26 have numerals 1–12 in the side margins. Numeral in margin: double value. Nos. 9–13 with inscription fragments of "Koniglich Hannoversche Franco-Marken": triple value.

1850. 1-groschen black on blue. No. 1. *Watermark:* one rectangle per stamp, but only two sides usually are visible; margin copies: 2U.

Paper: blue or gray-blue. The latter is rarer. Rose-colored gum.

Cancellations: Type A: very rare. Types B, C, D, or F, common in black. In blue: 25U. Type I (HAMBURG or BREMEN), and Type A with FRANCO inscription: rare. Pen cancellations: 50 percent.

Pairs: 3U. Block of four: 50U. On cover: 50U.

Reprints (1864): in blue-gray, without watermark. In small sheets of four (2 x 2), without gum, or with slightly yellowish gum.

Forgeries: see the following issue. (Blue paper for No. 1.)

Fakes: No. 2, chemically tinted in blue. Different watermark!

1851. Oak Crown watermark. Nos. 2 to 5. *Shades:* No. 2, yellow-green; green: 50M, 50U. No. 3, more or less dark old rose: salmon pink. No. 5, yellow, dark yellow (No. 5a). The latter, which is almost imperceptible, should be judged comparatively.

Cancellations of Hanover: A. Semicircle. B. Name on one line. C. Name, date. D. Date, double circle. E. Large postmark. F. Date, single circle. G. Name and date, framed. H. Name, date, hour. I. Hamburg cancellation. J. Special postmark: Geestemunde. K. Railway postmark.

Varieties: No. 3 is found with inverted watermark.

Cancellations: Types D, E, F, G and H. rather common in blue. Rarer in black: 50U.

The rarity of these cancellations is affected by their color and place of origin. For example, CELLE, date and hour designation in black, etc. Types B and C: less common. Type I HAMBURG, in blue: 2U. Type G in red: very rare. (See illustration.)

Pairs: 3–4U. Strips of three: 8U. Blocks of four: very rare. No. 2: 200 francs.

Reprints: no official reprints. There is a "private printing" (i.e., *a forgery*) of the ¹/₁₀-thaler, no watermark, different shade and gum. The other values without watermark are essays.

Forgeries: the whole set was lithographically couterfeited several times without watermark. The illustration shows a few distinctive marks of the originals and of the two best forged sets. The latter, provided with a forged burelage background, were used for the unwatermarked Nos. 10–13. The set with inscription FINI instead of FINIRE is from Geneva (F.).

Forged Geneva cancellations (F.), engraved on wood.

1. Double circle, with date, in black or blue: FREIBURG 17 10 +; HANNOVER 8 11 4-5;

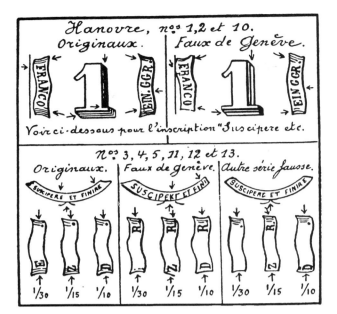

Hanover, Nos. 1, 2, and 10. Originals. Geneva forgeries. Top row: see below the inscription "Suscipere," etc. Bottom: Nos. 3–5 and 11–13. Originals. Geneva forgeries. Another forged set.

HANNOVER 3 11 4; HANNOVER 24 11 N 9-10 B; HAGE 6 2; LUNEBOURG (without center inscription); OSNABRUECK 21 9 8-9; CHUTTORF 16 5. The last two have a horizontal bar in the center circle, the first six lack a horizontal bar. The figures of the HANNOVER cancellations are interchangeable. With the same dated postmark: STPA (Stempel PostAmt = post office cancellation) 29 7 BREMEN.

2. Single circle, with date: HANNOVER 8 1 (with horizontal bar) 1-2.

3. Mobile (railway) on three lines: EMDEN 10 5 7 HANNOVER.

These postmarks also were applied to the forgeries of the following issues on genuine Nos. 14–16 and 21–23.

1853. With watermark. No. 8. Select: four margins, $^3/_4$ mm wide. Same for Nos. 9, 14–16. Two shades: rose and lilac-rose (rare).

Reprints (1864): no watermark, colorless gum, thin paper, dull rose instead of rather bright rose.

Forgeries (Geneva): with forged watermark printed on back in gray. Good measurements. Yellowish white paper. See the next issue for distinctive features.

1855–56. Burelage background. No watermark. Nos. 9 to 13. The mint stamps must have rose-colored gum.

Varieties: stamps with letter inscription in the top margin: 3U. The $^1/_{10}$-thaler was bisected to make a $^1/_2$-groschen: extremely rare. The $^1/_{15}$-thaler was bisected diagonally or vertically to make a 1-groschen: extremely rare.

Burelage: wide, made of elongated, side-by-side hexagons measuring about $2^1/_2$ mm wide by 1 mm high: a slight separation exists between each stamp's burelage, and all the sheet burelages are surrounded by two lines between which can be seen a burelage strip in the shade of each value which is $5^1/_2$ mm wide. The narrow-margined single stamps which bear the first of these lines, therefore, are margin copies.

Burelage: close-set, same characteristics, but the hexagons more elongated, looking like biconvex lenses, $1^1/_2$ mm long by $^5/_8$ mm at the minor axis.

The first printing (1855) of the $^1/_{10}$-thaler has a close-set burelage in very pale lemon shade: 50M, 3U. The second is ochre-orange.

Cancellations: most common are the rectangular postmarks with date in blue, Types D, F, G, H, Type K, mobile (railway): 2U. Bremen cancellations are in demand.

Pairs: 3U. No. 12: 8U. Strips of three: 8U. Blocks of four: very rare. Nos. 9 and 9a: 10U. No. 10: 250 francs; No. 13: 24U.

Reprints (1864): with colorless gum instead of rose. These reprints are almost as rare as the original stamps, except that of No. 9. Value: one-fifth that of the originals. The burelage shades are different. No. 9 light rose, blurred, confused burelage. No. 10 light green. No. 11 very pale rose. No. 12 dull blue. No. 13 light orange. All of them with wide burelage. The values with close-set burelage are essays. There is a "private printing" of No. 13, which is similar to that of No. 5. Same characteristics, same blemishes in the design.

Forgeries: the Geneva (F.) set was rather successful. Special consideration of its ultramodern paper or of its burelage shades, which may be changed, seems unjustified.

See the second issue for Nos. 10–13.

The measurements of the forgery of No. 9 are good, but the design and the burlage have a few defects (see illustration). The same cliché was used for Nos. 8, 9, and 14.

Forged cancellations on forgeries: see above.

1859–63. No watermark. Various types. Nos. 11 to 21. Select: Nos. 17–21 must have four margins no less than 1 mm wide.

Shades: 3-pfennig (1859) rose and dull rose, carmine-tinted rose, lilac-rose: 4M, 2U. Claret: 8M, 4U. 3-pfennig (1863) green; $^1/_2$-groschen (1860), rose-colored gum: 2M, 25U, or colorless gum. 1-groschen dull rose or dark purplish blue-carmine: carmine-tinted rose on thin, transparent paper: 2M, 2U. 2-groschen ultramarine and dark ultramarine on thin transparent paper. 3-groschen yellow; light yellow: 50M, 50U. 3-groschen (1861), shades between brown and dark brown; black-brown: 2M, 50U. 10-groschen (1861) green and yellow-green.

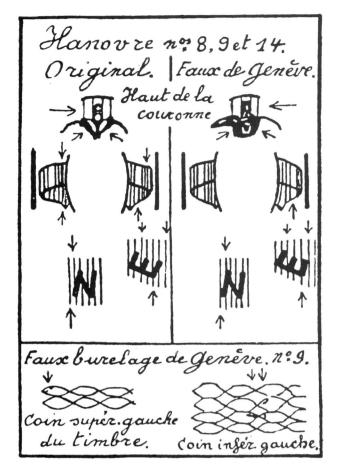

Hanover. Nos. 8, 9, and 14. Original. Geneva forgery. Top of the crown. Bottom: forged Geneva burelage, No. 9. Upper left corner of stamp; lower left corner.

Varieties: fine impressions are in demand. They are identifiable by the delicacy of the lines in the portrait and by the background lines, the corners of which seem whiter. In the 1- and 2-groschen, the background lines touch the value figure. The stamps at the bottom of the sheet which have year dates "1860," "1861," and "1862" are rare. 1-groschen, No. 17, is found with temple and neck shade lines broken in the middle, a plate defect which reappears in No. 24: rare. An olive-green shade, first printing of the 10-groschen: rare. The 3-groschen dark brown, very thick paper with thick rose-colored gum: rare, mint. Nos. 17 and 18 were used bisected: extremely rare.

Pairs: 3–4U (Nos. 15 and 18–20). Blocks of four: very rare (No. 14: 24U, No. 17: 300 francs, No. 19: 50U, etc.). On cover: 50U, except Nos. 15, 16, and 21: 2U. No. 21 alone on cover: 3U.

Cancellations: Types D, E, F, common in blue; in black: 50U. Types G, H: 50U. BREMEN and HAMBURG in blue, Type I: 50U; in black, rare. Types

J and K: rare. Type G. in green (HOHNSTORF): very rare. Types B and C: rare.

Reprints: no official reprints, just "private printings" (G.) of Nos. 14–16 (including a tête-bêche), 19, and 20. Colorless gum or no gum, different shades, no margin numerals, thick, not as rough surfaced paper, impression not so fine. The $^{1}/_{2}$-groschen original, whose shade cannot be compared and which was issued also with colorless gum, is on thick (80–85 microns), ungummed paper instead of the thick or thin (70 micron) paper on which this reprint was made in order to pass it off as the original. The illustration will facilitate recognition of this kind of fraudulent operation.

Used postal forgeries: No. 17, forged carmine-tinted rose, was used in the postal service: extremely rare. Compare the design; see illustration.

Fakes: No. 22 with rouletting trimmed to make No. 15. Moral: acquire the 3-pfennig green with sufficient margins, minimum format $21^{1}/_{2}$ x $24^{1}/_{2}$ mm. No. 15 (brown gum) is darker than No. 22.

No. 18 is known to have been subjected to color and numeral doctoring to make the 10-groschen green.

Forgeries: a few early forgeries do not withstand examination. In Nos. 17–21, these counterfeits have only fifty-one or sixty-seven vertical lines instead of eighty-two. A somewhat better executed set has only seventy-one. The No. 14 and 15 originals have thirty-two vertical shading lines. No. 16 has seventeen lines in the horn's bell.

A forgery of the $^{1}/_{2}$-groschen was made by direct photographic reproduction on exceedingly thick card paper (190 microns). It is $18^{1}/_{2}$ x $21^{1}/_{2}$ mm instead of 19 x 22 mm. A 10-groschen from Hanover (G.) was well counterfeited (in blocks of fifty), but the scratching off of FACSIMILE gives it away. Another forgery of the same value is poorly executed: it bears the word FALSCH (false).

The Geneva set (F.) was well counterfeited lithographically. The 3-pfennig rose is identical with the forgery of No. 9; however, it has no burelage. (See illustration of Nos. 8, 9, 14; see the following illustration for Nos. 15–21.) A first cliché had thirty-three vertical shading lines in Nos. 14 and 15. There are three clichés for No. 16. (The illustration gives information on the best one.) The 10-groschen was executed in two shades with colorless or rose-colored gum. (Take your choice; they're the same price.) There even are printer's waste copies of this forgery with double impressions.

Forged cancellations: Nos. 15 and 21 require cancellation expertizing; the forged Geneva cancellations were described above.

1864. Same types. Arc-rouletted stamps. Nos. 22 to 26. *Shades:* 3-pfennig green (June) and dark yellow-

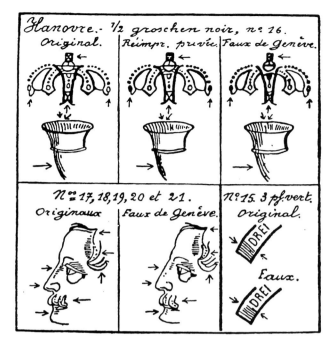

Hanover. ¹/₂-groschen black, No. 16. Original.
Private printing. Geneva forgery. Bottom: Nos. 17–
21; No. 15, 3-pfennig green.

green. 1-groschen rose and carmine-tinted rose. 3-
groschen, usual dark shades.

Varieties: the 1-groschen rose with rose-colored gum
is worth 2M, 2U. The 2-groschen with rose-colored
gum is exceedingly rare. 3-groschen: 2M, 2U. The 3-
pfennig on thin paper (colorless gum): 2M, 3U. The 2-
and 3-groschen are found imperforate on one side: 2M,
2U. Cleaned plate copies (very good printing) are in
demand; 2-groschen: rare.

Pairs: 3U. Strips of three: 6U. Blocks of four: very
rare (No. 22: 40U. No. 24: 150 francs. No. 25: 80U).
On cover: 50U.

Cancellations: as in the preceding issue, Types H
and K: 50U.

Reprints: "private printing" of the 3-groschen. See
preceding issue. Defective impression; corner lining
seems darker; 18⁴/₅ x 21⁴/₅ mm instead of 19 x 22¹/₅
mm. The rouletting is not congruent.

Fakes: canceled No. 16 was fraudulently rouletted to
make a No. 23. Likewise, the 1- and 2-groschen mint of
the preceding issue. There are a few rose-colored gum
fakes. Make comparison.

Koehler has drawn attention to a very amusing fake:
on a No. 24, very pale shade (sheet corner with margin
numeral "12"), the faker stuck a very thinned down No.
25. Then the design of No. 12 was painted on it in blue,
and the cancellation was lined up. Moral: check each
stamp with a magnifying glass and watermark fluid,
and measure thickness, if need be. All of these

operations take no more than two minutes, that is, ten
times less than the time spent at a bank teller's window
to obtain a 100-franc certificate.

Forgeries and forged cancellations: see previous
issue.

Envelopes: the four-leaf clover and horse-type
stamps were counterfeited in Geneva on yellowish
paper, offered for sale as 3 x 3 cm cut squares, with the
forged cancellations described above. Comparison of
lettering, horse, and horn under the four-leaf clover is
necessary.

Lubeck

Sheets of 100 stamps (10 x 10), with oval control
mark at bottom. The 4-schilling has the inscription
"Druckerei H.G. Raghtens in Lubeck" in the four
margins, and a control inscription, "Stadt-Post-Amt-
Lubeck," at top.

Cancellations: see the illustration.

Type B is common on the first issue and the Type A
postmark with date is common on the others. Postmark
with date on the first issue: 25U. (The Travemunde
postmark is Type A small format or Type E, large
format, both with an ornament instead of inscriptions at
bottom.) Type C or D (letter "L") on first issue: 50U,
but Type D (letter "T"): 2U. Type E on second issue:
25U. Same value on this issue for Type D (letter "T").
Type F on second issue: 2U. Type G is rather common.

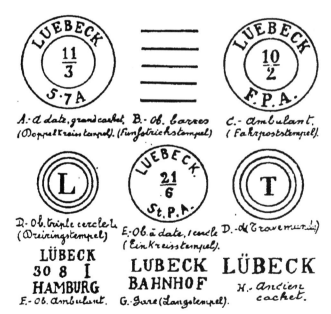

Lubeck cancellations: A. Large postmark with date.
B. Barred cancellation. C. Mobile post office
cancellation. D. Triple circle "L." E. Single circle
with date. D. "T" (Travemunde). F. Mobile post
office cancellation. G. Train station cancellation.
H. Early postmark.

Type H is rare. Foreign postmarks also are rare. (Thurn & Taxis, "F," "Th. u. Th.," or quadruple circle postmark; likewise, Denmark, letter "K," "D," "O," "P," "A," etc., and the Schleswig-Holstein postmarks.)

On cover: 3U.

I. Imperforate Stamps

Select: four margins, minimum width ¹/₂ mm.

1859. Little flower watermark. Nos. 1 to 5.
Lithographed on small-grained white paper.

Watermark composed of five-petal flowerets, about twelve flowerets per stamp.

Printing figures: No. 1, 40,000. No. 2, 20,000. No. 3, 138,600, of which there were 2,772 errors, No. 3a. No. 4, 50,000. No. 5, 150,000.

Errors: the ninety-sixth and ninety-seventh stamps (bottom right) of the 2-schilling sheet have inscription "Zwei ein halb" instead of "Zwei" (resulting from a transfer plate error), but figures "2¹/₂" were removed from the stone before any printing and replaced by noncongruent "2" figures.

Paper: thin (40–50 microns).

Shades: ¹/₂-schilling dark lilac, lilac, and pale lilac: very rare. 1-schilling orange and dark orange, 2-schilling and 2¹/₂-schilling (error) dark red-brown, 2¹/₂-schilling rose and bright rose; 4-schilling green, blue-green, yellow-green: 2M, 2U. This variety is worth 10U instead of 3U on cover.

Variety: No. 4 with transparent impression.

Gum: the stamps of the first two issues are worth fifty percent more than the catalogue prices when they have their original gum.

Reprints (1872): the five values were reprinted on thin, wove paper without gum and with no watermark, ten sheets of twenty-five (5 x 5) for each value. Rare: 20 francs each. Shades are too bright.

Fakes: Nos. 6 and 7 were given a forged watermark to make Nos. 1 and 2 stamps. Watermark and even shade comparison is indicated. There are countless forged cancellations and regummings. Make comparison.

Engraver's secret marks: look for color dots above and below the line in the middle of the lower portion of the stamp. Other distinctive design marks of each original value may be considered as expertizing "secret marks." (See illustration.)

Forgeries: very numerous counterfeits: six entire sets. All require detailed examination of design, paper, and watermark. It should be noted that only Nos. 2, 3, 5, and 7 have a dot after SCHILLING in the originals (No. 4 has none). Only Nos. 4 and 4a do not have any dot after POSTMARKE. Nos. 1, 2, 4, 6, and 7 have seven shading lines at the bottom of the shield. Nos. 3 and 5 have only five lines; the eagle's tail should not touch the banderole.

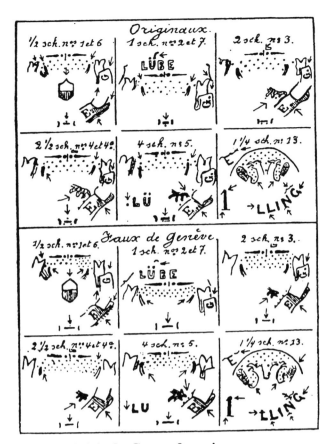

Lubeck. Originals. Geneva forgeries.

1. An early set. All values have three dots under the line at the bottom of the stamp and the right eagle's beak is touching the schilling bandeau. No watermark.

2. Hamburg set. Crudely done; make comparison. The ¹/₂- and 2¹/₂-schilling have a dot after SCHILLING. No watermark.

3. London set. No better than the Hamburg set. No watermark. Compare the eagles and the dots between their heads, etc.

4. Dresden set. Eagles are too large. Forged watermark. Background stippling and lettering are noncongruent. Occasionally marked FALSCH.

5. Vienna set. Photolithographed with engraver's secret marks, but very arbitrary shades, except the 4-schilling, which is comparable to the rare original shade. Design doesn't match; make comparison.

6. Geneva forgeries (F.): this set deserves special commentary, not only because it is better executed than its predecessors, but also because there is less clashing between shades. Consequently, superficial, less-observant collectors run the risk of adding these fantasies to their collections. The illustration gives easily accessible information on the principal defects. The same kind of study of other forgeries will identify

still more defects and, incidentally, provide a valuable exercise expertizing.

Forged cancellations: usually Type B, but width and spacing are not congruent. Also found are the triple circle numeral cancellations and a rectangle, 1.8 x 10 mm, containing three double stroke "I" imprints.

Geneva forgeries have Types A and C forged postmarks.

1861 (September). Same type. No watermark. Nos. 6 and 7. *Printing figures:* No. 6: 110,000. No. 7: 50,000,

Shades are lighter. No. 7 in yellow and dark yellow, but never in dark orange-yellow like No. 2.

Gum: with gum: 2M. The yellowish shade of the paper comes from the gum.

Reprints: rare. See first issue. The 2-schilling is orange.

Forgeries: see first issue and preceding illustration.

1863 (July). Oval type. Embossed. Nos. 8 to 12. *Printing figures:* 1/2-schilling, 120,000. 1-schilling, 80,000. 2-schilling, 120,000. 2 1/2-schilling, 50,000. 4-schilling, 80,000.

Sheets: 100 stamps (10 x 10), typographed.

Rouletting: 11 1/2 but 200 sheets of the 1-schilling were rouletted 10 (rare).

Shades: 1/2-schilling blue-green, yellow-green. 1-schilling orange-red, dark orange-red, orange. 2-schilling carmine-tinted rose. 2 1/2-schilling ultramarine; 4-schilling bistre.

Varieties: Nos. 1–10, marginal copies: 2M, 2U.

Cancellations: Type A: common. Others: rare.

Envelope cutouts: the 2-schilling rose and 2 1/2-schilling blue: extremely rare.

Fakes: envelope cutouts (for example, 1/2-schilling green, etc.), new or with forged cancellation and oblique scratching out of inscription "…schilling post convert…." Forged rouletting and noncongruent shades.

Reprints (1872): embossing is scarcely visible; imperforate. As rare as the preceding ones (250 copies of each reprint). Cruder printing than that of the originals. Gray instead of transparent gum. The 1-schilling is found on medium or thick paper.

Different shades: 1-schilling orange. 2-schilling purplish red. 2 1/2-schilling Prussian blue. 4-schilling dark bistre-brown.

Forgeries: imperfect early set. Compare paper and eagle (no embossing). Imperforate, perf 13, or with forged rouletting.

1864 (April 1). Same type. 1 1/4-schilling. No. 13. Lithographed, imperforate. 104,200 stamps in two equal printings. Very fine outer frame lines.

Shades: pale brown, red-brown (maroon), dark brown.

Paper: wove, medium.

Varieties: unofficial rouletting. Buy only on cover.

Reprints: none.

Forgeries: an early forgery on pelure paper has seven vertical lines of shading instead of six. A Geneva forgery is poorly executed, but its general appearance is good, and because of this, has caught many amateurs. Thin, stippled paper (see illustration). In the original, the eagle's tail is not touching the frame, even though it is very close to it. Use magnifying glass.

1865 (November 23). Same type. Octagonal 1 1/2-schilling. No. 14. Typographed. *Two equal printings,* the second one in May 1867, rouletted 11 1/2. First printing, purplish red-lilac; second printing, red-lilac.

The *envelope cutout* was used as an adhesive: extremely rare.

Reprint (1872): like the preceding ones. Violet shade. Imperforate. Not embossed. Rare.

Mecklenburg-Schwerin

Cancellations: postmark with date, Type A: common. Less common when post offices of lesser importance are involved: Sulze, Waren, Malchin, Wismar, Bruel, Stavenhagen, etc.

The same ones with inscription BAHNHOF at bottom are rarer: Schwerin and Rostock BAHNHOF. Friedrich FRANZBAHN, etc. Names of cities on one or two lines, Types C and D: 25U. Tessin is rare. Type E postmark with city name framed: 2U. The blue cancellation of Rostock, Type B: 2U.

1856. Buffalo head and inscription. Imperforate. Nos. 1 to 3. *Sheets* of 100, with marginal Nos. 1–10.

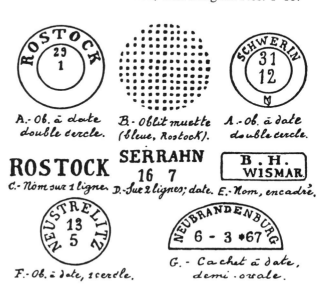

Mecklenburg-Schwerin cancellations: **A. Double circle dated cancel. B. Dumb cancel (Rostock, in blue). C. Place-name, on one line. D. Two lines, with date. E. Place-name in frame. F. Single circle, with date. G. Half-oval, with date.**

Select: four margins, ³/₄ mm minimum width.

Shades: No. 1, stippled background, red and dark red. No. 2, yellow and orange-tinted yellow. No. 3, blue; dark blue: rare.

Varieties: No. 1 in one-quarter, one-half, and three-quarters must be on expertized cover. One-quarter alone on cover is very rare. The ⁵/₄, ⁶/₄, ⁷/₄ stamps are in demand. Stamps with original gum: 50M. A brown tint on front of stamp comes from a brown gum. Stamps with marginal numbers: 2M, 3U.

Pairs: 4U.

Reprints: none.

Forgeries: see below. Forged cancellations, likewise.

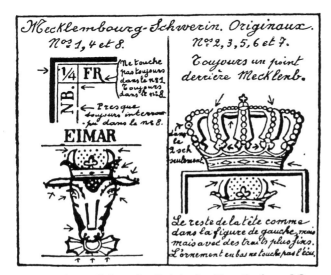

Mecklenburg-Schwerin Originals. Nos. 1, 4, and 8; Nos. 2, 3, 5, 6, and 7. Left: does not always touch in No. 1; always touches in No. 8. Almost always broken in No. 8. Right: always a dot after Mecklenburg. In the 2-schilling only. The rest of the head as in the sketch at left, but with finer lines. The bottom ornament does not touch the shield.

1864–67. Stamps rouletted 11¹/₂. Nos. 4 to 8.

Shades: ⁴/₄-schilling red, stippled background, paper slightly laid (1864). 2-schilling violet-red (October 1866); lilac-gray (September 1867), and lilac-blue (end of 1867): 30M for the lilac gray. 3-schilling yellow, margins about 2 mm (June 1867): common; yellow, margins about 1 mm (September 1865): 4M, but more common used than the stamp with wide margins. 5-schilling brown (1864), doe brown and gray-brown. This value is found on thin or thick paper; ⁴/₄-schilling red with white background (1864), red and old rose.

Varieties: the top right figure "2" of the 2-schilling (lilac-gray) has no terminal loop, and the inner frame under the second "R" of FREIMARKE is broken. The right frame of the 5-schilling is dotted with white

specks. Envelope cutouts of the 2-schilling blue and 3-schilling brown, on cover showing official use: extremely rare. Marginal numbers: 2M, 3U.

Pairs: 4U. Strip of four of No. 8 is rare. Mint pieces, Nos. 4 and 8: proportional value.

Reprints: none.

Forgeries: there are many early and modern forgeries, especially of No. 4. The Geneva (F.) set has two different clichés for each value. It would be a waste of time to describe these forgeries in detail. It will be sufficient to arm oneself with a good magnifying glass and to ascertain whether the stamps examined are completely congruent with the original designs in the illustrations. In particular, count the pearls, check the stippling — which is always regular and diagonally aligned — and, finally, check the dots indicated by an arrow in the illustration. Naturally, one can find one or two places in an original where these marks are not identical (as a result of printing flaws), but such differences in the forgeries tend to dispel any doubt about them.

One should note also that the impression of authentic imperforate stamps is always finer than that of rouletted stamps. The 5-schilling blue, the 2-schilling violet-red, and No. 1 are best for comparative study.

Forged cancellations on Geneva forgeries: Type A: ROSTOCK 24/1; WISMAR 13/11; GUSTIOW 22/10; SCHWERIN 24/11; SCHWERIN 1/8 BAHNHOF. These counterfeit postmarks were applied to Nos. 5a, 6, 7, and 8 originals and to the whole Strelitz set! When expertizing the cancellation, the above numbers should be compared, for there are other forged postmarks.

Fakes: the rouletting of Nos. 1 and 2 is forged. With this kind of faking, the margins are too narrow. The paper of the faked No. 4, which was made this way, is not laid, and the shade of the faked No. 6 is orange and is always darker than the orange-tinted yellow of No. 3.

Mecklenburg-Strelitz

1864. Embossed impression. Rouletted 11¹/₂. Nos. 1 to 6. *Shades:* vermilion-tinted red; pale vermilion-tinted red; orange: 2M, 2U. ¹/₂-silbergroschen green and dark green: 2M, 50U. 1-schilling violet; pale violet: very rare, used.

The 1-, 2-, and 3-silbergroschen carmine, ultramarine, and bistre have hardly any different shades.

Varieties: Nos. 3–6 with marginal Nos. 1–10: 2M, 3U. Gumless stamps: 50 percent. No reprints.

Cancellations: all types other than F and G are exceedingly rare. The whole set requires cancellation expertizing.

Forgeries: Nos. 4–6. Early, lithographed embossing not very marked, no embossed vertical lines between the crown and the shield. These lines are almost always quite visible in the mint originals. The cross, the crown, and the shield point should not touch the inner oval. Noncongruent inscription lettering. In the 1-silbergroschen, the "R" of STRELITZ resembles a "B." In the 2-silbergroschen, there is a dot between the "E" and the "I" of ZWEI.

Forged cancellations: there are some very deceptive ones. Expertizing is indispensable.

Memel

Except for the 1923 issue, Memel has only overprinted sets. Eighteen issues were spawned in four years with the desired varieties and errors of all kinds.

We sometimes have been criticized for advising against certain *new* stamps. The reproach is undeserved with regard to genuine, unhoarded, new stamps which, like their older counterpart, surely have a place in collections. But such an avalanche of uninteresting overprints — clearly without any interest for the collector — really is excessive. Let the reader judge on his own whether it is not in his true interest to say: "You have manufactured all those varieties, all those inverted overprints, etc., just to make money at my expense. Well, you can keep them!"

Right here in Memel, a dealer almost perfectly counterfeited several millions of gold marks worth of inverted overprints of the 1921 Flugpost issue (Nos. 45, 46, 49–51), and 1922 (Nos. 77, 78, and 82). Regular inverted overprints are themselves obligingly manufactured for speculation.

Besides, dealers have sold practically everywhere Nos. 29, 30, 31a (Type II), 33, 38 (inverted overprint), and 44 (inverted overprint), which were so well counterfeited that it was only when the forgers brought out Nos. 42 and 43 with inverted overprints (a simple error on their part, these overprints never having existed) that the experts were able to spot the other forgeries, which had been released and sold everywhere, particularly in Switzerland, France, and Germany.

Nos. 209–12 with wide numerals were likewise well counterfeited, and the less well-executed forgeries of many values are countless.

Well then? So? What can be done about it?

Oldenberg

I. Imperforate Stamps

Select: four margins at least 1 mm wide.

1852–55. Black on colored paper. Lithographed, Nos. 1 to 4. *Paper:* medium and thin, the latter: 25U.
Types: the $^1/_{30}$-thaler has three types. Type II: 2M, 2U. The $^1/_{15}$-thaler, three types, also. Types II and III: 50M, 50U. The $^1/_{10}$-thaler, two types, Type II, retouched: 2M, 2U. (See illustrations.)

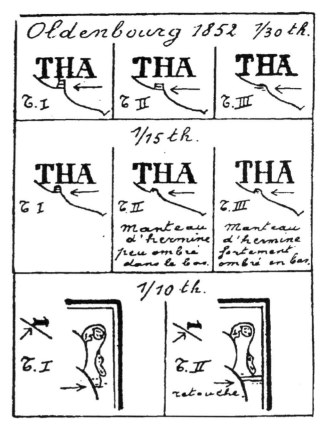

Oldenburg 1852. $^1/_{30}$-thaler. Second row: Type II, ermine cloak not shaded very much at bottom. Type III, ermine cloak heavily shaded at bottom. Bottom row: Retouching.

Shades: $^1/_3$-silbergroschen black on green. $^1/_{30}$-thaler, black on dark blue; light blue: 25U. $^1/_{15}$-thaler, black on rose; pale rose. $^1/_{10}$-thaler, black on yellow; on lemon color (thin paper): 50U.
Varieties: $^1/_{30}$-thaler, all three types in one strip: extremely rare. Fine impressions exist: rare. Defective impressions: 25U. Worn-plate copies: rare.
Cancellations: Types A and B in blue: common: in black: 25U. Type D: 50U. Branch post office cancellations. KLEINSIEL, SENGWARDEN, FEDDERWARDEN, etc., are rare. Type A in red (Dedesdorf): very rare. Dated circular cancellations: very rare.

Pen cancellations in red also are found: very rare. Oval cancellation of DELMENHORSTER HAUSCHEN: very rare.

Foreign cancellations, BREMEN, BRUNSWICK, etc., are very much in demand.

The $^1/_5$ and $^1/_{30}$-thaler somtimes have a "2$^2/_5$" postmark (ABBEHAUSEN): very rare (height of the numeral and of the fraction about 16 mm.)

 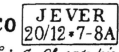

LŎNINGEN

Oldenburg cancellations: A. Frame cancel, town name, date. B. Unframed FRANCO. C. Framed, place, date, hour. D. Unframed, name of town. E. Double circle with date. F. Delmenhoster Hauschen cancel.

Pairs: 4U. No. 2, strip of three, all three types: 12U.
Reprints: none.

Originals: figure "1" of the center fraction does not touch the ermine evening cloak's stippling, except in the $^{1}/_{30}$-thaler stamps. This figure has a terminal line, top right, in the $^{1}/_{15}$-thaler. The shield point is touching the top of the Oldenburg tablet near the left downstroke or the middle of the "N." No dot after Oldenburg, except in the $^{1}/_{10}$-thaler. The lateral inscriptions do not touch the tablets. The "A" and the "L" of THALER are joined at the bottom only in the $^{1}/_{30}$-thaler, Type III, and in the $^{1}/_{15}$-thaler; the lettering of this word always has serifs.

In the $^{1}/_{3}$-thaler, the upper line of the cross in the small shield does not touch the left oblique line; the "L" and the "D" of Oldenburg are joined at the bottom; and the serif of the "G" touches the tablet edge.

Old and modern forgeries: a detailed study of all of the counterfeits would in itself furnish enough material for a small book: there are about fifteen different counterfeits, half of which exist in complete sets!

It will be sufficient to check all the characteristics of originals described previously, with type details given in the illustrations, to identify forgeries. Most of the forgeries, either lithographed or typographed, are poorly executed, with excessively thick shading. Comparison of paper shades and thickness also will prove useful.

1858. Larger format. Black on colored paper. Nos. 5 to 8. Lithographed, imperforate. Values in groschen.

Shades: 1-groschen blue and pale blue. 2-groschen rose and pale rose.

Varieties: No. 8, with transfer plate flaw: OLBENBURG: 2M, 2U. Some retouching of the 1-groschen can be found, for example, repairing of the

upper left corner of the frame, etc. The 1-groschen is found with single or double lines under the figure on the left.

Cancellations: Type A in blue: common. Types B, D, or E, on 1-groschen: 50U; on the other values: 25U. All other cancellations: very rare.

Pairs: 4U. No reprints.

Originals: the four values have dots randomly placed in the lateral ovals (see illustrations). The set was abundantly forged, most often lithographically. It would take too long to give a detailed description of the copies. The fine cross-hatched design of the upper tablet will be a reliable guide in tracking down all the forgeries. See the illustrations.

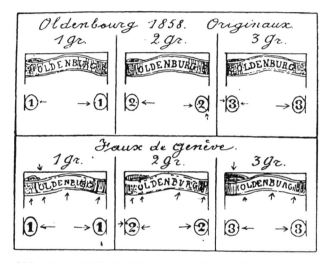

Oldenburg 1858. Originals and Geneva forgeries.

The number of shade lines on the left of the "O" of OLDENBURG and on the right of the "G" follows:

$^{1}/_{3}$-groschen. Thirteen lines on the left; the thirteenth is touching the "O"; twelve lines on the right; the last one is touching the serif of the "G."

1-groschen. Twelve on the left, the last one touching the "O"; ten on the right, the last one touching the serif of the "G."

2-groschen. Twelve on the left; the last one is not touching the "O": ten on the right, the last one very near or touching the serif.

3-groschen. Thirteen on the left (the first three, poorly executed); the last one is touching the "O"; eleven on the right, the last one touching the "G."

Forgeries: the set was forged almost as often as the first one. Design comparison will always show up crude execution; design shades are not congruent.

A listing of the number of shade lines on the left and right of OLDENBURG in the best known forgeries follows. We should point out that there are almost never any lines which go through the word's letters (see illustration of originals).

¹/₃-groschen. Ten lines on the left, the last one touching the "O"; seven on the right, the last one touching the "G." Eleven lines on the left which do not touch; nine on the right with no touching; six lines on the left with no touching; nine on the right with no touching; typographed.

1-groschen. Six lines on the left and eight on the right; the ones near the word are embryonic and the last ones are far from the letters. Innumerable lines, very bad sundry forgeries.

2-groschen. Ten and nine lines, the last ones touching; fifteen and eleven lines, the last ones touching; eleven and nine lines, the last ones touching; five and seven lines, the last ones not touching; fourteen and seven lines on the right, not touching.

3-groschen. Three and four incomplete lines, not touching; six and nine lines, the last ones not touching; fourteen and eight lines on the right, not touching.

One can single out for special mention the modern set of Geneva forgeries (F), Nos. 6–8, because the design is usually a little better and the black dots are reproduced in the ovals (see illustration). The paper's shade is far from exact, but this can be changed.

Forged cancellations: bars and Types A and B on the old forgeries.

On Geneva forgeries: Type A, VAREL, 16/6. Type B. Type E: OLDENBURG 16/10.

1860. Sarne type. Color on white paper. Nos. 9 to 14. *Shades:* ¹/₄-groschen orange-yellow, dark orange-yellow; ¹/₃-groschen pale blue-green, dull green, bright moss green: 2M, 50U. ¹/₂-groschen red-brown, dark brown. 1-groschen blue, dull blue, dark blue (steel colored): 2U, ultramarine-blue. 2-groschen red, dull red. 3-groschen yellow, lemon color: 50M, 50U.

The moss green is a relatively dark yellow-green and is always bright. Impression is generally much more distinct. The moss green stamp is 17³/₄ mm wide instead of 18 mm. Same differences in the ¹/₂-groschen dark brown.

Varieties: defective impressions are rather numerous, especially of No. 14. There are a few transfer plate varieties (one per sheet): No. 10 (blue-green or dull green): OLDEIBURG, DRITTD, DRITTO, DRITTE, OLDEFBURG, "8" instead of "3," all of them: 3M, 3U. Nos. 12 and 14, printed on both sides: extremely rare. No. 10 (blue-green or dull green) exists with a broken frame near the middle of the bottom (transfer flaw): very rare. There are a few more similiar flaws. Cancellation of two pieces of ¹/₄-groschen on cover is extremely rare. No. 10 with a dot between "L" and "G": 25U.

Fakes: some doctoring of Nos. 10 and 11 to obtain transfer plate defects 10b to 10d and 14a. Examine transparency with a magnifying glass.

Pairs: very rare.

No reprints

Cancellations: Type A: common. Type B: rare. Postmark with date. Type E, is becoming less rare. Others: very rare. The cancellations on Nos. 9, 10, 10a, and 11 must be expertized, for there are very cleverly counterfeited postmarks.

Originals: the ¹/₃-, 1-, 2-, and 3-groschen stamps have the same characteristics as the preceding issue: upper table shading and dots on ovals (see illustration).

The ¹/₄-groschen has eight shade lines on the right and left of OLDENBURG, which do not touch "O" or "G"; one line cuts through the middle of the "O" and "BURG."

The ¹/₂-groschen has six lines on the left and seven on the right: the seventh one on the right is touching the serif of "G."

Forgeries: most of the forgeries, which are lithographed, do not bear the secret marks in the figure ovals (see illustration). Nor does the ¹/₃-groschen have a dot on the right of the upper loop of figure "3" on the left, nor the dot in the oval on the left above figure "3" on the right.

Naturally, all the forgeries of the preceding issue were redone in color on white paper, including the modern Geneva forgeries (see illustration).

The characteristics of other forgeries which were specially executed for the 1860 issue follow.

¹/₄-groschen:
    9 shade lines on the left, 7 on the right (seventh touching "G")
    5 shade lines on the left, 7 on the right (GROSCHE*U*)
    10 shade lines on the left, 6 on the right
¹/₃-groschen:
    8 shade lines on the left, 6 on the right
¹/₂-groschen:
    4 shade lines on the left, 7 on the right
1-groschen:
    10 shade lines on the left, 9 on the right (last ones touching)
2-groschen:
    20 shade lines on the left, 6 on the right
    14 shade lines on the left, 8 on the right (typographed)
    13 shade lines on the left, 11 on the right
3-groschen:
    No shade lines on the left, 6 on the right (typographed)
    10 shade lines on the left, 3 or 4 on the right (dot after the "G")

In addition, there are forgeries which have no shading on either side and some which have none at all; it is sometimes impossible to count the lines, which are often incomplete. The inscription lettering is not congruent with the original.

Forged cancellations on Geneva forgeries. They also are found on forgeries of the preceding issue and on originals of the following issue: Type A, RASTEDE 18/11, VAREL 16/6, ABBEHAUSEN 11/VI; Type E, OLDENBURG 16/10 1-2N.

II. Rouletted Stamps

1862. Typographed oval. Embossed. Nos. 15 to 19. *Sheets:* 100 Stamps (10 x 10).

Rouletted 11½: mint stamps are rare: 4M. Rouletted 10: mint stamps are common (prices quoted in general catalogues); used stamps are worth double the catalogue prices. The 1-groschen: 4U. Make comparative check of rouletting, for the rouletting of some stamps are doctored.

Shades: ⅓-groschen green, yellow-green. ½-groschen orange and bright orange. 1-groschen rose (pale to dark shades). 2-groschen blue and ultramarine (the latter, rouletted 10); 3-groschen bistre.

Varieties: the marginal copies are numbered 1 to 10 on all four sides of the sheet: 2M, 3U. The 1-groschen was split to be used as a bisected stamp. Imperforate stamps are essays; 1-groschen orange-red, green, blue, bistre, and brown.

Pairs: rare because of the fragility of the rouletting: 4U; a strip of three of the 1-groschen is worth 8U. Mint blocks are becoming rare.

Cancellations: Types A and E in blue or black, common; Type C in black, common; all others: rare. Foreign cancellations. BREMEN, Type A, etc., are in demand. All cancellations must be expertized.

Envelope cutouts: cut round or rectangular: rare on cover; the 3-groschen, extremely rare. These cutouts are found stuck on letters of the period with forged cancellations.

Prussia

1850–56. Cross-hatched background. Laurel tree watermark. Nos. 1 to 5. *Sheets* of 150 stamps (10 x 15). Nos. 2–5 with marginal numbers 1–10 at top and 1–15 on the left.

Select: four margins at least ½ mm wide.

Shades: 4-pfennig (1856) yellow-green; dark green: 50M, 25U. 6-pfennig vermilion-tinted red; pale orange-red; less common. 1-silbergroschen black on pale rose; on bright rose: 2M, 50U. 2-silbergroschen black on blue; 3-silbergroschen black on yellow; on bright yellow; on ochre: 2M, 2U.

Varieties: marginal copies with number: 3M, 5U. Without number: 2M, 3U. 1-silbergroschen on fire red: rare. 3-silbergroschen on thick paper: less common. This value is found with marginal inscription PLAT: very rare. The 1-silbergroschen is known with inverted watermark: very rare. The 2- and 3-silbergroschen, same variety: extremely rare. The 6-pfennig is known with inscription "Platte No. 7" in the right margin: extremely rare. The 2-silbergroschen is found bisected: extremely rare. A few retouched stamps: rare. The

Prussia cancellations: A. Framed name of town and date on too lines. B. Four circles and number. C. Mobile (railway) cancel on three lines. D. Double circle with date. E. Station postmark. F. Single circle with date.

reprint of the 6-pfennig is known canceled on cover.

Cancellations: Types A and B: common. Type A with inscription on three lines (BAHNHOF) is in demand. Type B, red: rare. On Nos. 3–5: 10U (Nos. 107, "1748," etc.); in blue: same value. Type D: 2–4U, except No. 1. All other cancellations, for example, name of city on one line and foreign cancellations, are rare.

Pairs: 4U. No. 3: 3U. No. 4: 8U. Strips are rare and blocks of four, including the 1-groschen, very rare.

Reprints: 1864: no watermark. The 6-pfennig (rare) does not have the security burelage. This can be checked by immersing it in a sulfur solution. Examples of the 1,500 reprints are not very common.

1873: with watermark. Shades less bright for Nos. 1 and 2, altered paper tints for Nos. 3–5. Thin, white gum (Goldner issue); shabby appearance. The paper shade of Nos. 3–5 is dull pale rose, dull pale blue, and dirty yellow. The reprint of No. 1 is 18 x 21⅓ mm (give or take ⅒ mm) instead of 18⅓–½ x 21½–⅔ mm. The paper is less tinted. The reprint of No. 6 is 18 mm wide instead of 18⅓–½ mm, and 21⅓ mm high instead of 21½–⅔ mm.

The 3-silbergroschen black on gray is an essay.

Fakes: the reprints were occasionally given a new chemical coloration to make new stamps out of them. The same operation was performed on essays and watermarked printer's waste. One must remember that reprint dimensions are smaller: No. 4 is 18¼ mm wide, whereas the original is 18½ mm.

Some watermarked reprints were fraudulently canceled, Type B, "1190," etc.

Early forgeries: no watermark; arbitrary format, design, and inscriptions. Silbergroschen values also were typographed in color on white paper!

1857. Same type. No watermark. Plain background. Nos. 6 to 8. *Sheets* as above: 150 stamps (10 x 15), but with marginal numbers on all four sides.

Select: four margins, ³/₄ mm wide.

Shades: 1-silbergroschen rose; bright rose: 50M. 2-silbergroschen ultramarine blue; dark ultramarine blue: 25M, 25U. 3-silbergroschen orange-yellow; yellow: 25M; lemon yellow: rare.

Varieties: Nos. 6–13 were provided with a colorless vertical burelage over their entire surface. Occasionally you can see its pale gray tone through a magnifying glass. This control device was intended to prevent fraud. The black or brown burelage becomes quite visible only in copies that have undergone a sulfur-based chemical test. Obviously this is a way of guaranteeing the stamp's authenticity: no value increment.

There are faintly visible retouchings in the corner vertical shade lines; small vertical lines around the inscription; curvilinear shading in the middle of the neck. In the 2-silbergroschen, there are some plate flaws: right frame broken in two places at top: SILBE*P*.GR. There also are impression defects.

Stamps with marginal numbers: 2M, 4U. The 3-silbergroschen is known to exist with unofficial perforation: very rare.

Pairs: No. 6: 4U. Nos. 7 and 8: 5U. Blocks of four: very rare.

Fakes: the stamps of the following issue (cross-hatched background) were faked by applying color on the cross-hatching. A trained eye, aided by a good magnifying glass, is not fooled by it. Check the mint stamps also, particularly the 1- and 2-silbergroschen, for lightly applied cancellations, or for pen cancellations that may have been cleaned.

Reprints: none.

Forgeries: 1. A set of so-called "reprints" appeared in 1864. (The plates and dies were destroyed.) Strips of three containing the three values exist. The shades are carmine, ultramarine, dark yellow; the crude inscription design and the absence of a dot over "2" after SILBERGR will identify them satisfactorily. No gum.

2. A second set of this fantastic issue appeared in 1876; same arrangement, but the value indication is missing. Shades: carmine-tinted red; dark blue; yellow-brown; black. No gum.

3. Set of so-called "essays" — after the fact! — from Berlin (F.). 3- and 4-pfennig; 2- and 3-silbergroschen, and 6-kreuzer black on white, imperforate. No gum.

Various forged cancellations on the forgeries and reprints.

1858–60. Same type. No threads. Cross-hatched background. Nos. 9 to 13. *Sheets* as in the 1856 issue, with marginal numbers.

Select: four margins at least ³/₄ mm wide.

Paper: medium, thin (less common). 4-pfennig, very thin: 50U.

Shades: 4-pfennig green; pale yellowish green. 6-pfennig bright vermilion and vermilion-red. 1-silbergroschen, from pale rose to bright carmine-tinted rose. 2-silbergroschen blue and indigo blue. 3-silbergroschen light orange-yellow and orange-yellow.

Varieties: the color of No. 10 occasionally was changed to brown: less valuable.

Various minor plate flaws.

Cancellations: Type A on two or three lines, common in black; in red: 3U. Type B: 2U. Type C: 2U; in red: 5U. Type D: common, Types E and F: rare.

In demand: Hamburg, Saxony (grill) cancellations, and all foreign cancellations (SWINEMUNDE PER DAMPFSCH), Lubeck, etc.

Pairs: 1-silbergroschen: 3U; others: 4U. 2-silbergroschen: 5U. Blocks of four: rare. 4-silbergroschen, mint with gum: 12M.

Reprints: none.

The first reprint of No. 2 must not be confused with the No. 10, mint. The original No. 10 is 18³/₄ mm wide by 21³/₄–22 mm high. This fraudulently canceled reprint also must not be confused with the used No. 10.

1861–65. Rouletted stamps. Embossed. Nos. 14 to 20. *Sheets* as above, with marginal numbers.

Shades: rather numerous. Rare: 3-pfennig carmine-tinted lilac: 2M, 2U. 1-silbergroschen bright carmine-tinted rose: 2M, 2U. 1-silbergroschen Prussian blue.

Varieties: stamps with marginal numbers: 3M, 3–5U. The imperforate stamps are essays. Some of them were used in the postal service. Stamps with inscriptions on the back also are essays.

Cancellations: Type A: common; in blue: 2U. BREMEN BAHNHOF in blue: 3U. Type A with inner dividing line (inscription on three lines) occurs rather often. Type B: 3U. Type D: common in black and blue. Type F: common in black and blue.

HAMBURG cancellation with date: 2U. BERGEDORF in half-circle (1861–64): very rare. LUBECK: rare.

Pairs: 3U. Blocks of four, mint: 6M, used: 8U, except No. 18: very rare, and 1-silbergroschen rare. This last value is not common in strips of three. Strips of five of No. 18 are rare.

Reprints: none.

Used postal forgeries: Nos. 19 and 20. Comparison is indicated. Eagle, burelage, and inscription design: very rare.

1866. Large figures. Nos. 21 and 22. Do not put these stamps in water.

Select: four margins at least ¹/₂ mm wide and all inscriptions visible.

Canceled, well-preserved stamps are rare, and are worth more than the catalogue prices, especially on cover.

Early forgeries: the originals were expertly printed. Using a magnifying glass, one can see the very regular frame structure, ornaments, inscriptions, and the inscriptions in the body of the figures. There are twenty inscription lines in the background (20- or 30-silbergroschen).

The forgeries of these two values were poorly executed: especially the PREUSSEN inscription. The background inscriptions are illegible (only nineteen lines). The inscriptions in the figures are irregular.

For forged cancellations on originals, expertizing is necessary.

Fakes: for cleaned pen cancellations and forged cancellations, expertizing is necessary.

1867. Octagonal type. Rouletted. Nos. 23 to 27. *Sheets* of 150 (10 x 15). Nos. 1–10 and 1–15 in the margins.

Shades: two shades for each value: ordinary shade, or dark or bright shade. 2-kreuzer dark orange: 50U.

Cancellations: as in the 1861 issue. Name of city framed on one line: 2U. Type C: 2U (thinner type impression), etc.

Essays with inscription on back.

Envelope cutouts: when used as adhesives, valuable only on a large piece or on entire cover.

1851–52. Head in an oval or octagon with silk thread, 1- to 7-silbergroschen. All rare, especially the 6- and 7-silbergroschen.

1853–54. 1- to 4-silbergroschen without silk thread. Only the 4-silbergroschen is rare.

1861. Type of inscription slants to top right. 1-, 2-, 3-silbergroschen: rather common.

1863–65. Same type with double inscription across the vignette. 1-, 2-, 3-silbergroschen: common; 3- and 6-pfennig: rather rare.

1867. Same type; value in kreuzer. 1-, 2-, 3-, 6-, and 9-kreuzer: rather common.

Telegraph Stamps

The set exists in two shades: gray-black and dark bistro. The whole set is rare. No reprints.

Punch stamp cancellation in "T" shape removes a good part of the stamp; purchase of mint stamps is recommended.

Saxony

I. Imperforate Stamps

1850 (July 1). Stamp for printed matter. No. 1. *Sheets* of twenty stamps (5 x 4). Typographed. Dividing frame lines in the gutters. Margins, minimum width ³/₄ mm.

Printing figure: 500,000 were printed, of which 36,922 (stock remainders) were burned. Thus, this stamp is ten times rarer than Nos. 1 and 2 of Belgium. However, this proportion definitely is increased by the fact that printed matter is destroyed much more often than letters. Mint stamps with gum: 50M.

Shades: red, brick red, brownish red.

Pairs: 3U. Blocks of four (?). (Two vertical pairs coupled — stamp Nos. 13 and 18; and 9 of the sheet — forming a block of four on piece were purchased for 15U at the Ferrari auction.)

Cancellations: usually Type D (with year-date in center also) and Type B (also unframed, on one or two lines in black or blue). Type A is very rare.

Saxony cancellations: **A. Solid grill. B. Framed cancel. C. Grill with number. D. Dated double circle with time indication. E. Dated single circle. F. Double circle.**

Originals: the paper is white, medium-thick wove. Typographical strike-through of inscriptions is quite visible. See illustration for the most important distinctive marks.

Forgeries: this stamp was especially tempting to forgers; more than twenty counterfeits of it are known. This does not mean that it is more difficult to expertize than others. What frequently is lacking is a genuine stamp on which a comparison can be based.

All of these forgeries are lithographed, with the exception of a single recess-printed forgery. This suggests that mere examination of the impression (does it lack indention?) often is enough to decide an item's status. Paper examination also will reveal differences; most of the early forgeries are on yellowish paper. Finally, design comparison is so conclusive that eighteen specimens out of twenty can be rejected at first sight. Among the best of the lot, let us list the following, with certain distinctive characteristics:

1. "R" and "A" of FRANCO joined at the bottom: "NNI" joined on top. No curving lines in the ornaments. Horizontally laid paper.

2. "C" and "O" of FRANCO are as large as the other letters. Forged cancellation, grill, Type A.

3. SACHSEN moved to left in the tablet. "A" of FRANCO pointed at top. Tiny "3" figures in the large figure "3."

4. "N" and "I" of PFENNIGE joined at top. Four curved lines in the four ornaments.

5. Recess print type (relief instead of indentions). "O" of FRANCO slightly slanted to the left, like the seventeenth stamp of the original sheet. No curved lines in the ornaments.

6–12. Various types, all of which have four curved lines in the corner ornaments.

13–17. Various types without any curved line in the ornaments.

18. Hugo Griebert drew attention to a more deceptive early forgery that had its day of success. The upper left serif of the "N" of SACHSEN and the lower left serif of the "N" of FRANCO are so short that the "N" seems further away from the adjacent letters than in the originals. This countefeit, which was copied from the third stamp of the sheet, was printed in sheets of eighteen, in which there were three tête-bêche stamps (Dresden, F.).

Among the modern forgeries, we must mention the Geneva forgeries (F.).

Cliché 1: broken frame under the "I"; "G" and "E" of PFENNIGE are joined at bottom. The tablet frame is broken twice above the "E." The inner frame line is 1 mm from the outer frame.

Cliché 2: same positioning of the frame line. This time it is much too thick. The inner frame no longer is broken under the "I." The background cross-hatching does not touch the large figure "3" shading above the "F" of PFENNIGE.

Finally, a rather recent photolithographed counterfeit (Chemnitz) is identifiable by the lack of indention and by the upper tablet line of FRANCO, which has a gap above the "O," as in the sheet's stamp number 9. Comparison would be useful here.

Forged cancellations: Types A and B (Bautzen, Anneberg, "Freiburg" for Freiberg, Herrnhuth, Lobau, Leipzig, Dresden, Marienberg, Meissen, Reichenbach, Riesa, Zwichau, etc.). Type E on Geneva forgeries (SEBNITZ 1/8 15–3. 52. 5–3 V.).

Fakes have been made by regumming uncanceled mint stamps from printed matter wrappers or removing pen cancellations. As on all rare stamps, one finds extensive repair work. This is how the worst kind of rubbish has usurped a special place in many an album.

1851. 3-pfennig. Coat of arms. No. 7. *Select:* four margins, minimum width ¹/₂ mm. Typographed.

Shades: blue-tinted green, dark green; yellow-green: 50M, 25U. The paper is thin (50–70 microns), transparent or nontransparent. However, the blue-green is found on very thin (40 microns) and very transparent paper: 5U. The first printings with first-class

impression and sharply etched frames are in demand.

Pairs: 3U. Strips of three: 4U. Blocks of four: rare.

Cancellations: usually Types A, C, D, and F.

Forgeries: 1. Geneva (F.). Machine-made, white paper (55 microns). Dull, very pale yellow-green impression, which can, of course, be altered. A bad copy from a defective impression. Forged cancellation Type F, LEIPZIG II MAI 53.

2 and 3. These forgeries are of German origin. See illustration.

Saxony. 3-pfennig. No. 1. Original. Top, left: curved line; inscription DREI too high; not always; no curved line. Center: SACH inscription a little too low; "S" and "A" almost always joined at bottom; right downstroke of the "N" is concave (except seventeenth stamp). Right: no curved line; broken curved line; inscription PFENNIGE is too high; no curved line. Bottom: "A" and "N" joined at bottom, except sixth, thirteenth, and sixteenth stamp of the sheet; letters "C" and "O" not as high as "AN." Bottom box: 3-pfennig green. No. 6. Original: dot after SACHSEN; seven pearls in the crown's outer branches. Geneva forgery. Early forgeries: I. Ten pearls in the crown's outer branches. II. No dot after SACHSEN.

1851 (end of July). Head facing right. Nos. 2 to 5.
Select: four margins, minimum width $^3/_4$ mm.
Engraved.

Varieties: the error of the $^1/_2$-neugroschen on pale blue paper must be expertized by paper comparison. The bright shades of the 1- and 3-neugroschen stamps are in demand. Slightly worn impressions (lower left corner) are found. The dark blue 2-neugroschen is from the 1852 issue.

Pairs: rare: 5U. Strips of three: 8U, except $^1/_2$- and 3-neugroschen: 10U. Blocks: very rare. On cover: 2U.

Cancellations: Type C: common. 133 numbers in all. Nos. 1 and 2, very common. The others are in demand or are rare. Type A: in demand. Type D: common on the 2-neugroschen pale blue. Type E: 25U, but 3U, on 2-neugroschen dark blue: in blue: 50U. Color grills, Type B, and Chemnitz triple circle cancellations are rare.

Fakes: $^1/_2$-neugroschen with an erroneous blue shade. The 2-neugroschen pale blue with the three "2" figures scratched out and replaced by "$^1/_2$" fractions — also erroneous.

Forgeries: there is a bad German set, which even one of today's children would not want.

1855 (June 1). Head facing left. Nos. 7 to 10.
Same margins. Engraved like the preceding issue.

Shades: $^1/_2$-neugroschen gray, blue-gray. 1-neugroschen rose, old rose, and dark rose. 2-neugroschen blue, green-blue, dark blue: 2M. 3-neugroschen yellow, bright yellow, dull yellow; yellow-ochre: 2U.

Varieties: $^1/_2$-neugroschen, the "1" figures of the left fraction are either above the middle of the "2" or moved to the left. 1-neugroschen, the oblique line of the "1" is long, concave, or very short (two plates?). The $^1/_2$- and 2-neugroschen stamps are found with single or double inner left frame, and the frame occasionally was reinforced by appropriate retouching.

A double impression of the $^1/_2$-neugroschen is known.

Pairs: 3U, but 2- and 3-neugroschen: 4U. Strips of three: 10U. Blocks of four of the $^1/_2$-neugroschen: 150 francs; of 1-neugroschen: 50 francs; others: rare. On cover: 50U.

Cancellations: Type C: common (Nos. 1–212; a few numbers are rare: 205, 212, etc.). Type F: less common; in blue: 50U. Mobile (railway), other types, and color cancellations: rare.

Forgeries: bad set, as above.

1856 (April). Same type on white paper. Nos. 11 and 12. Margins, engraving, cancellations, as above.

Shades and paper: 5-neugroschen pale red, medium paper, last printing, engraving often slightly worn: 2M, 50U. Rather bright red on thin paper; same, on very transparent paper: 2U; carmine-tinted red; brown-red:

3M, 3U. There are intermediate shades. 10-neugroschen blue and dark blue on medium paper; blue on thin paper, common, mint: 25U.

Varieties: the two values with double impression: rare.

Pairs: 3U. On cover: 2U, but No. 12: 2.5U.

Forgeries: the originals are so expertly designed that a second's comparison with common No. 7 or 8 stamps is enough to track down the counterfeits. In one early forgery, the mouth is made of a full line and the foliage is really bad. The modern Geneva forgeries are hardly any better: in the 5-neugroschen, there are five heavy shade lines in the top right banderole, instead of six: in the 10-neugroschen, the first cliché displays a background that is almost full on the left of the head, and a second cliché is no better. Both have shapeless shading in the aforesaid banderole. Lithographed. Type A cancellations. Finally, some forgeries of German origin have defects that are just as serious. For example, 5-neugroschen, noncongruent inscription lettering; the three shade lines after GROSCH have become four: the dot between the second and third line is missing. 10-neugroschen, same defects; "10" figures are too large. An early lithographed forgery has an ultramarine shade; the shading inside the ear forms a question mark; the bottom "10" is slanted; the upper eyelid line is straight! In case of doubt, compare the shades, and then, before any decision is made, see whether you are looking at a common lithographed stamp without any color relief, as is almost always the case.

Fakes: a few acid baths of No. 11 to make No. 11a.

II. Perforated Stamps

1862–63. Embossed coat of arms. Nos. 13 to 19.
Typographed. Perf 13.

Rare shades: 3-pfennig yellow-green, mint: 8 francs, 50U; $^1/_2$-neugroschen red, mint: 8 francs; 3-neugroschen yellow-brown, mint: 8 francs. The $^1/_2$-neugroschen lemon color and the 1-neugroschen carmine are essays.

Varieties: pairs of No. 15 imperforate between: rare.

Pairs: 3U. On cover: 50U.

Cancellations: as above. Type B (rectangular) is becoming common. Mobile (railway): rather common. There is an active market for military postmarks: rare. Numerous forged cancellations.

Envelopes: envelope cutouts (head), used as adhesives, are rare. The 10-neugroschen green was counterfeited crudely.

Schleswig-Holstein

Cancellations: Type A is usual on Nos. 1 and 2. (There are forty-two cancellation numbers. more or less rare, depending on locality.) The Danish Copenhagen cancellation (triple circle, No. 1) is very rare on these stamps. On subsequent issues, we find Type B on various values: different numbers, from 6–206. There are rare ones; No. 2 (Hamburg) and No. 3 (Lubeck) are in demand. Type C is rare. Like Type B, it is found without a dot in the middle. Type C also is found with a dot that is twice as large and with five circles and a dot. Type D is usual on these issues. Types E and F are less common. Foreign country cancellations are rare; for example, the encircled "L" of LUBECK. Straight-line inscriptions are always rare. Franking with stamps of Holstein and of Schleswig is rare. Color cancellations are in demand.

Watch out for forged Schleswig-Holstein cancellations on Nos. 1–3, 5–7, and forged Schleswig cancellations on Nos. 6 and 7.

Schleswig-Holstein cancellations: A. Number and barred circle. B. Three circles and number. C. Four circles and dot. D. Two circles, with date. E. On two or three lines, framed or unframed. F. One circle, with date.

I. Schleswig-Holstein

1850. Embossed coat of arms. Nos. 1 and 2. Imperforate. Typographed. Four margins, ½ mm wide. Blue silk thread in the paper pulp.

Printing figures: No. 1: 1,300,000. No. 2: 700,000.

Shades: dark blue, blue, and Prussian blue; rose and pale rose. Gumless stamps: less valuable. Copies with pronounced embossing are in demand.

Pairs: 3–4U. On entire cover: 3–4U.

Originals: the horizontal lining is finely printed and regular. The eagles' feathers are designed expertly and are no more than 1 mm from the lateral frames. The "S" shading of SCHILLING is touching the "C," and "H" and "I" are joined at top.

Forgeries: these rare stamps often were counterfeited, but never successfully; none of the counterfeits is really deceptive. First, examine the silk thread; then, the embossing; finally, the design.

1. Early forgeries: The "S" of SCHILLING is about 1 mm from the "C"; "H" and "I" are not joined at top. There are only three horizontal shade lines above the eagles' heads.

2. Same. Thick, grayish paper of poor quality. No embossing. Traces of marginal lines.

3. Hamburg forgeries: The "silk thread," which is drawn with red ink, and the noncongruent inscriptions obviate the necessity of a more thorough examination.

4. Paris forgeries: same remark. No silk thread.

5. Geneva forgeries: on wove or laid paper (½ mm). Blue silk thread stuck on the back or between paper layers. The coat of arms crown is flat on the shield. Seven or eight horizontal lines above the eagles' heads. The "S" of SCHILLING is not touching the feather above it. Ovals are bordered by a line. (See illustration.) Four forged cancellations: rectangles of sixteen, nineteen, twenty, or twenty-four excessively thin bars with a circle or a blank oval in the middle.

6. Forgeries of German origin (2-schilling): instantly identifiable by the ovals of "S" and "H," which are positioned much too low. The left eagle's feathers are touching the outer frame. The "H" and the "I" of SCHILLING do not touch each other.

7. Private reprints (1894): noncongruent embossed impression. No silk thread.

1865. Oval. Embossed impression. Nos. 3 to 7. Rouletted 11½. Marginal numbers from 1 to 10 (also "Holstein" and "Schleswig"): 2M, 3U. The 1½-schilling is known to exist imperforate and in pairs unrouletted between. The 1¼-schilling split diagonally for the ½-schilling: very rare.

Pairs: 3U. On cover: 2U, but 4-schilling: 4U.

Forged cancellations on originals, on singles or pairs, especially on the 4-schilling, where we find Type B (No. 191), as well as the Danish thimble cancellation, with one circle, D.P.S.K. 10, also forged, and all the forged postmarks mentioned below.

II. Holstein

Note: Holstein stamps were current in Bergedorf from 1864. They are rare with Bergedorf cancellation.

1864. Square stamps. Nos. 1 to 3. Nos. 1 and 1a. Lightface type. Lateral inscriptions a little far from the ornaments. Dots on the "I" letters of SCHILLING. Gray burelage with "P" in white, in the middle. Type I (No. 1), corner wavy lines set close together. Type II, same, but lines far apart. Imperforate.

Select: four margins, 1 mm wide.

No. 1, bisected: 20U. On cover, No. 1: 2U; No. 1a: 4U.

No. 2. Boldface type. No dots on the "I" letters. Same burelage. No dot after "F.R." On cover: 2U.

Bisected, on cover: 15U. The rouletting (9½) is not official.

An early forgery of No. 2 is crude. No burelage. Letters of CHILLIN are joined at bottom. Dots on the "I" letters of SCHILLING. "R" and "T" touch.

A modern forgery of the same stamp is not much better. Compare ornaments, garland, horns, and wavy lines.

No. 3. Rouletted 8. Rose burelage. Bisected, on cover: 12U.

Pair: 3U. On cover: 2U.

Note: The usual cancellation on Nos. 1–3 is Type B.

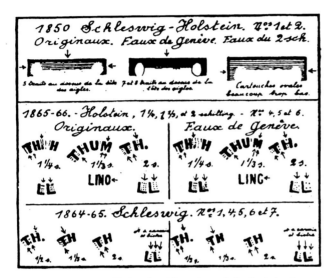

1850. Schleswig-Holstein. Nos. 1 and 2. Originals: five lines above the eagles' heads. Geneva forgeries: seven or eight lines above the heads. 2-schilling forgery: oval tablets, much too low. Second row: 1865–66. Holstein. 1¼-, 1⅓-, and 2-schilling. Nos. 4–6. Originals. Geneva forgeries. Third row: 1864–65. Schleswig. Nos. 1, 4–7. 4–schilling carmine and bistre.

1865–66. Oval. Embossed impression. Nos. 4 to to 10. Nos. 4–7 (plain frame) are from 1865–66. Nos. 8–10 (pearled frame) are from 1865 (November 1). Inscription: HERZOGTH-HOLSTEIN. Rouletted 8. There exist essays of 1-, 2-, and 3-schilling stamps in various colors. The 1¼-schilling, No. 4, bisected, on cover: 200 francs. On cover: 2U.

Pairs: 3U, except No. 8: 4U.

Geneva forgeries (F.): Nos. 4–6. Lithographed (no indention). Paper is too thick (75 microns, instead of 40–55 microns), and it lacks the transparency of the original. The 1¼-schilling is bright violet; the 1⅓-schilling, brownish dull red; the 2-schilling, somewhat too dark. The preceding illustration will give enough information on design defects.

Forged Geneva cancellations: Type B, three circles, No. 191. Type F, BRANST 27 6 1865 and WESSELBUREN 24 11 …

III. Schleswig

1864–67. Same type. Nos. 1 to 7. The 1¼-schilling green and 4-schilling carmine are from 1864, the others from 1865, except the 1¼-schilling gray (1867).

Shades: 1¼-schilling, from yellow-green to dark green. 1¼-schilling lilac, from pale lilac to blue-lilac. 1¼-schilling lilac-gray is worth 150 francs, mint; gray, mint, half of that. On the other hand, canceled gray: 2U. These two stamps are rouletted 10; the others, 11½.

Pairs: 3U, except , 2-schilling: 4U. On cover: 2U, except ½-schilling: 3U.

Geneva forgeries (F.): ½-, 1⅓-, 2-, and 4-schilling carmine and bistre were executed like the preceding ones. Same paper. Shades are arbitrary: ½-schilling pale green; 1⅓- and 4-schilling, same shade as that of the 1⅓-schilling Holstein forgery; 2-schilling dark blue and 4-schilling light brown instead of bistre.

Forged Geneva cancellations: Type B, three circles, No. 23. Same type with "L" (Lubeck). Type D, HUSUM 19 6 12-1N. Type E, FLENSBERG 10/1 U … and ELMSHORN 26–5–67.

1920. Plebiscite. Recent stamps in sets.

1920. Same. Nos. 33–35 were overprinted fraudulently. Comparison is necessary.

1920. Official stamps. Forged overprints. Detailed comparison is indispensable.

Wurttemberg

Cancellations: Type A, dumb cancels: (1) four circles without a number (the ones with numbers are from Baden, and other places: rare). (2) Barred lozenge, as in the illustration, or seven bars (TUTTLINGEN). (3) Circular cancellation which is rather similar to Type A of Bavaria, but without inner circle or number. Two types: small and large sun (Keulen). All of these cancellations are found on the first issue, usually on the 3-kreuzer stamp and are worth 20–50 francs.

Type B, in black or blue, rather common on the first issue, rarer on the following ones: 2U on common values. Straight line with date (CAIW, etc.): rare. The POSTABLAGE cancellations are rare.

Type C, common in black or blue on the first issue and in black on the following ones up to the rouletted issues, on which it is less common.

Type D, less common on the first three issues (in blue on the first: 25U). Then it is found more rarely on the following issues until 1875, when it is rare. This type is not to be confused with a Bavarian postmark, UNTERTURKK, found sometimes on the 1-kreuzer, No. 1 (see Bavaria, Type J), or with other Bavarian postmarks of the same model in the following issues, which are always rare.

Type E is common up to and including the rouletted stamps of 1866, after which it becomes rare.

Type F (several modules) is common in black on the two rouletted issues, less common in red.

Type G (black) is not common on the rouletted issues of 1866, but became common in black, blue, green, and violet on the rouletted stamps of 1869 and the following issues. It is found with or without a bar under the place name. STUTTGART is common; the others, GMUND, HEUDENHEIM, etc., are in demand.

Type H is not common on the 1866 rouletted stamps, but became so subsequently. Essay, registered letter, and foreign cancellations are rare.

A.-*Oblit. muette.* B.-*Nom de ville et date.* A.-*Ob. muette.*

C.-*a date triple cercle.* D.-*Double cercle coupé.* E.-*Date, 2 cercles.*

F.-*a date, 1 cercle.* G.-*Trapézoïdale.* H.-*Avec bande horiz.*

Wurttemberg cancellations: **A. Mute cancel.**
B. Place-name and date. C. Triple circle, with date.
D. Double circle, cut. E. Double circle, with date.
F. Single circle, with date. G. Trapezoid.
H. With horizontal band.

I. Imperforate Stamps

1851. Black on color. Nos. 1 to 5. Figure on cross-hatched background (1-kreuzer, cross-hatched; 18-kreuzer, with lines).

Select: four margins, minimum width: 1 mm.

Shades: 1-kreuzer buff and light buff. 3-kreuzer yellow, dark yellow-orange: 12M, 6U. 6-kreuzer green; blue-green: 50M, 50U. 9-kreuzer rose and old rose; 18-kreuzer violet. The mint stamps with original gum, which brought amateur prices until the 1862 issue, are very rare. The 9-kreuzer dark rose is rather common mint.

Paper: Nos. 1–5 have medium or thin paper. Among the stamps on thin paper there are clear-cut transparent impressions, especially Nos. 2 and 3. The medium paper is not very strong; one must always unstick the gummed hinges with great care, using water, and only when this is absolutely necessary.

Varieties: there are numerous typographed inscription varieties.

I. WURTTEMBERG, 18–20 mm, final period included. In the 1- to 9-kreuzer stamps. it is usually 18 mm; in the 3- and 6-kreuzer, 18½ mm, and 19 mm in the 1-, 3-, and 9-kreuzer stamps. Top dimensions are abnormal.

II. A single dot over the "U" (1-kreuzer).

III. The dot after POSTVEREIN is in four different places with respect to the serpentine ornament under it.

IV. 6-kreuzer green, various inner frame cracks; thin or thick frame above FREIMARKE. Bad retouching, or rather bad type replacements. Good retouching.

V. Impression defects. Inscriptions on right, no dot after "6" (3- and 18-kreuzer), no dot after "V" and "U" (3-kreuzer).

VI. Dots also are lacking in the inscription on the right.

Pairs: 1-kreuzer: 3U. 3-kreuzer: 12U (No. 2a: 5U). 6-kreuzer: 6U. 9-kreuzer: 8U.

Strips of three: 5U, 50U, 20U, 16U, and 5U for the five values respectively, and 12U for No. 2a. On cover: 50U; 18-kreuzer: 2U.

Reprints (1864): in reality, they are official forgeries made on retouched plates (lettering). The "W" of WURTTEMBERG is ½ mm from the left frame instead of 1 mm, comparison shows differences in the printing type. The flower-shaped ornaments in the lower tablets also were changed. Shades, in the order of the five values: brownish yellow, flat yellow, yellow-green, rose, and reddish violet. (See illustration on page 142.)

Originals: 22–22¼ x 22⁴/₅–23²/₅ mm high. In the heavily inked impressions these measurements are somewhat increased. Inscriptions are regular and are symmetrically arranged in the tablets. In the first-class impressions of the 1-kreuzer, the right curl (or loop) of the lower left ornament is broken. In the 18-kreuzer, the figures are touching the twelfth horizontal shade line, counting from the top. Counting from the bottom, they touch the fourteenth line.

Forgeries: 1. Very bad early set, Decalcomania process (useless to describe it).

2. 1-kreuzer Geneva forgery (F.) which makes a good impression ... at first sight. That is why its characteristics are shown in the illustration. Lithographed, 22½ x 23 mm, often on transparent pelure paper (about 35 microns), whereas the thin paper of the originals is 45–50 microns, and the medium paper, about 75 microns. The word WURTTEMBERG is 1 mm too wide and is positioned too low; no dot after "1850." Two clichés. Framework ½ mm from the stamp.

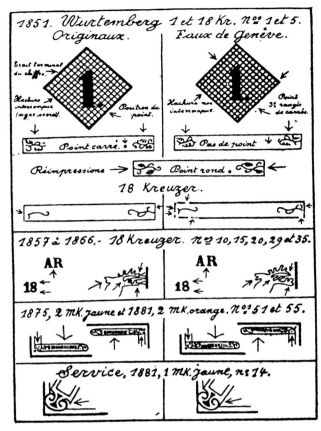

1851. Wurttemberg. 1- and 18-kreuzer. Nos. 1 and 5. Top: originals (at left). Counterclockwise from left: 1. Figure's terminal line. 2. Broken hatching (secret mark). 3. Square dot. 4. Reprints: round dot. 5. Position of dot. Geneva forgeries (at right): 1. Hatching not broken. 2. No dot. 3. Dot in third row of squares. Bottom: 1857–66. 18-kreuzer. Nos. 10, 15, 20, 29, 35. 1875. 2-mark yellow. 1881. 2-mark orange. Nos. 51 and 55. Official, 1881. 1-mark yellow. No. 14.

3. 6-kreuzer. A single dot over the "U"; the "F" is touching the frame.

4. 18-kreuzer. A value that was frequently tackled...but so inexpertly that these lithographs are really not dangerous. The best characteristic for expertizing purposes is figure placement: their tops are touching the tenth, eleventh, and fourteenth horizontal lines of the background, or they fall between the eleventh and twelfth lines. The bottoms of the figures are touching the tenth, eleventh, twelfth, or thirteenth shade lines, counting from below. Naturally, there are differences in the rest of the design (lettering; arbitrary number of lateral tablet scallops; dots instead of ornaments in the lower tablet; etc.). Dimensions and shades are arbitrary, etc.

A photolithographed Geneva forgery (F.) is more successful: 22 x 22$^2/_3$ mm high; most often on pelure paper as in the 1-kreuzer. In the original, the background lining does not touch the figure inscription squares, but here most of the shade lines are touching. There are a few differences in lettering design. Two clichés possibly. Also, see a few quite obvious distinctive features in the illustration.

Forged cancellations on forgeries and reprints: these easily can be checked by examining the stamp. A Type D cancellation, BLAUB 17 AUG. 1858, is found on the Geneva forgeries. This also was used for the 18-kreuzer forgeries of the 1858 issues.

Fakes: there have been various attempts to doctor other values to make the 18-kreuzer stamp. Warm water, watermark fluid, and even a magnifying glass will expose the fraud.

1857. Embossed coat of arms. Nos. 6 to 10.
Orange-colored silk thread in the paper pulp.

Paper as thick as 120 microns; medium (70 microns): rare.

Margins: the margins of these stamps, which occasionally are only $^1/_2$ mm wide, resemble those of Tuscany or Thurn and Taxis. The stamps, therefore, are select copies when the frame is not touched. Four margins, $^1/_2$ mm wide: 3U.

Shades: 1-kreuzer brown (reddish); dark brown: 25M, 50U. 3-kreuzer orange: 50M; orange-tinted yellow. 6-kreuzer yellow-green; blue-green: 25M. 9-kreuzer rose: carmine-tinted rose. 18-kreuzer blue, pale blue.

Varieties: impressions with colored medallion are in demand.

Pairs: 3U, except the 9-kreuzer: 4U. Strips of three: 5U, but 9-kreuzer: 8U. Blocks: very rare. On cover: 50U, but 18-kreuzer: 2U. 18-kreuzer single on cover: 2.50U.

Reprints (1864): red silk thread. The 6-kreuzer also with yellow thread. The gutters are 1$^3/_4$ mm wide.

Shades: Gray-brown, orange-yellow, gray yellow-green; carmine-tinted rose and carmine; blue — all are rare.

Originals: both dimensions, about 22$^1/_2$ mm.

Geneva forgeries (F.): 18-kreuzer, both dimensions, 23 mm. Paper (70–80 microns) with silk thread stuck on back or else two thicknesses of thin paper with the silk thread in between. The shade is indigo blue or dull dark blue. A line almost separates the left lion's tail from its rump. The white lines in the cross-hatched background are less wavy than in the original. The white, rectilinear, outer frame is not "heart-shaped." The end of the banderole extends to a point just above the "E" of KREUZER. (See illustration.)

Other forgeries: poorly executed. The banderole extends to a point just above the middle of the "R."

Forged Geneva cancellations: (1) see the first issue. (2) Type C, WANGEN 20 10 59 (the bottom design is not congruent); TOTTLINGEN 2 APR. 1867 3 N 6 (a cancellation reserved for the forgeries of Nos. 29 and 35, including the following cancellation); SCHELINGE 21 1....

Fake: No. 20, with trimmed perforation. Noncongruent shade; paper 50 microns, and silk thread is removable.

1858. Same. No silk thread. Nos. 11 to 15. *Select:* four margins, $^2/_3$ mm wide.

Shades: as above, but each number having nearly the same value.

Varieties: 3-kreuzer, second "R" of KREUZER with a long tail. Various impression defects: the "E" of KREUZER joined to the "U," etc.

Pairs: No. 11: 3U. Nos. 12–14: 5U. No. 15: 4U. Strips of three of Nos. 12–14: 10U: of No. 11: 5U; of No. 15: very rare. Blocks all are rare. On cover: 50U; 18-kreuzer: 2U.

Reprints (1864): 1-kreuzer yellow-brown. 3-kreuzer orange-yellow and pale yellow. 6-kreuzer dark green, blue-green, and grayish yellow-green: rare. 9-kreuzer bright rose and carmine. 18-kreuzer dull blue, bright blue. All are rare.

Forgeries: see preceding issue.

Fakes: No. 20, trimmed perforation. Nos. 27, 32, and even 33, same, with figures doctored. Paper too thin (50 microns). Shades arbitrary (except for the 6-kreuzer, No. 32): a bit of watermark fluid will reveal the fraud.

II. Perforated Stamps

Select: the stamps must be centered: rare. No reprints.

1859–61. Same. Perf 13$^1/_2$. Nos. 16 to 20. The remaining stock of thick paper (about 80 microns) was used first for the 1859 printing comprising Nos. 16b, 17a, 18a, and 19b. Then the 1861 issue was printed on thin paper (about 50 microns).

Shades: the mint stamps on thick paper all are rare, particularly the 1-kreuzer gray-brown: 2M, 50U; and the 9-kreuzer claret: 2M, 2U. There are two shades of each value (same price) on thin paper, except for the 1-kreuzer, where the dark sepia is rarer, and for the 9-kreuzer claret, more common mint. The 18-kreuzer is dark blue. The shades of the 9-kreuzer are brighter on thick paper than on thin.

Pairs: 3U. Strips of three: 5U. Blocks of four: very rare. On cover: 50U; but 18-kreuzer: 2.50U.

Forgeries: see the 1857 issue. Allowable perforation.

Fakes: Nos. 27, 32, and 33 were faked to make the 18-kruezer stamp. See the preceding issue.

1862. Same. Perf 10. Nos. 21 to 24. The 9-kreuzer claret is rare, but a carmine-tinted red shade is worth double.

Pairs: 3U, but 9-kreuzer: 4U.

1862–64. Altered shades. Nos. 25 to 29. *Shades:* 1-kreuzer yellow-green, dark green, moss green (rare). 3-kreuzer rose, carmine-tinted rose; claret: 4M, 10U. 6-kreuzer blue, pale blue. 9-kreuzer bistre, bistre-brown, and black-brown: 2M. 2U. 18-kreuzer yellow and orange-yellow. All perf 10.

Pairs: 3U. On cover: 5U, but No. 28a: 2U.

Forgeries: see the 1857 issue. Perf 11$^1/_2$; 13. Geneva forgeries: allowable perforation.

1866–68. Rouletted stamps. Nos. 30 to 35. Rouletting must leave four margins about $^3/_4$ mm wide when the stamp is not off-center.

Shades: 1-kreuzer pale yellow-green, yellow-green, dark yellow-green. 3-kreuzer pale rose, carmine-tinted rose. 6-kreuzer blue; pale blue (almost milky): 2U. 7-kreuzer (1868) blue, dark blue, indigo blue (blue-black): 50M, 50U. 9-kreuzer bistre, bistre-brown; fawn (reddish): 25M, 2U. 18-kreuzer (1867) yellow; orange-yellow (rare).

Varieties: there are defective impressions and the shield may or may not be colored, as in the preceding issues.

Pairs: 3U. The 7-kreuzer is rare in strips of three: 8U. On cover: 50U, but 9-kreuzer: 2U, and 18-kreuzer: 2.50U.

Forgeries: 18-kreuzer. See 1857 issue. See also an early forgery of the 9-kreuzer stamp.

Fakes: a few childish attempts have been made to fake No. 29, in bad condition, with rouletting made to order. Use watermark fluid.

1869. Modified Ape. Nos. 36 to 42. Rouletted 10. No. 42, perf 11. Nos. 36–41, perforated, are essays.

Shades: 1-kreuzer yellow-green, dark yellow-green; dark blue-green: 2M, 50U. 2-kreuzer (1872) dull orange; bright orange, less common. 3-kreuzer various rose shades. 7-kreuzer light blue and dark blue. 9-kreuzer (1873) bistre and bistre-brown. 14-kreuzer (1869) yellow and orange-tinted yellow; pale yellow: 2M, 2U. The 1-, 3-, and 7-kreuzer are from the end of 1868. The perforated 1-kreuzer is from 1874. No. 37, dull shade, has the No. 25 Luxemburg shade. The 14-kreuzer stamp possibly exists in orange, the shade of the 2-kreuzer?

Pairs: 3U. On cover: 50U, except 14-kreuzer: 4U, and 7-kreuzer, which is rare.

1873. 7-kreuzer. No. 43. Printed in small sheets of six stamps with single- or double-stippled dividing lines. Select stamps must have margins that extend to the stippling.

Shades: red-lilac (double stipple); violet (single).

Pairs: 3U. Very rare on cover: 4–10U, depending on whether a card, piece, or a letter is involved.

Forgeries: crude early German counterfeits and publicity stamps, which are no better. One of the latter has the dealer's name on the left and STUTTGART on the right! In another crude counterfeit, all the white parts are too large, including the corner stars (1¹/₂ mm maximum width); the stag's mouth is closed; and the embossing is not prominent enough. The word FALSCH is found in lowercase type at top, etc.

Subsequent issues. Sufficiently detailed information may be found in the general catalogues.

1875. 2-mark. No. 51. *Original:* 18¹/₂ x 21¹/₄ mm; perf 11¹/₂ x 11.

Geneva forgeries (F:): very deceptive photolithographed cliché, but 18 x 21 mm, and it has the differences described in the illustration. Perf 12; thin paper. I do not know whether it was used to counterfeit No. 52, with forged overprint on back.

Forged Geneva cancellation: Type C, SCHELINGE 21-1-1875.

1881. 2-mark. No. 55. A forgery. The same cliché, or a transfer from the latter, was used to counterfeit No. 55, which is lithographed, in the same format, but the value figure is typographed. It is found perf 11¹/₂, instead of 11¹/₂ x 11, or imperforate, in yellow or in orange.

1881, 5-mark. No. 56. *Original:* 18¹/₃ x 21 mm. Perf 11¹/₂ x 11.

Geneva forgery (F.): 18 x 20⁷/₈ mm. Perf 11¹/₂. Also photolithographed. The shade hatching of the inner frames is not as symmetrical as the originals; it is rather like pleating, giving an accordion effect. There is a mint "color essay" of this counterfeit, or it may be found canceled on grayish paper, with dull greenish blue impression, but the "definitive printing" is in the right shade on white paper.

Nos. 51 and 52 are worth 2U on cover. No. 56: 3U. With telegraphic cancellation, No. 56 is worth only fifty percent.

Nos. 57 and 61 were counterfeited to defraud the postal service. They are so poorly executed that appraisal with the naked eye is possible.

III. Official Stamps

Except for the first four issues, these stamps are not very interesting. Nos. 38–125 are available in great quantities. It is better to look for a fine copy of the 1-kreuzer brown (postal service, Nos. 6, 11, 16, or 21), for it easily can be exchanged in twenty years for a whole collection of official stamps dating from 1907 to the present.

1881. 1-mark orange-yellow. No. 14. *Original:* 18¹/₂ x 21¹/₃ mm; perf 11¹/₂ x 11. On cover: 2U.

Geneva forgery (F.): 18²/₃ x 21¹/₂ mm; perf 11¹/₂. Fair, somewhat ochre shade. Paper is too thick. but this can be changed. Serious design defect at bottom left (see illustration); same defect, upper right corner.

Forged Genera cancellation: large circular postmark with date, URACH.... OCT 1 (letter "b," on left, in the middle).

1906. Commemorative stamps. A few forged overprints. Make comparison. There also are forged overprints of No. 61 (1919), the only modern creation that is not extra common.

Germany

I. Office of Thurn and Taxis (Northern and Southern States)

In fine condition, mint stamps of the first two issues (1852–59) are rare, especially with original gum, except the 5- and 10-silbergroschen, 15- and 20-kreuzer. Those from other issues often are more common mint than canceled because of the sale of remainders; Nos. 12–15, 20–31, 40, 41, and 45–52 often have forged cancellations.

Select imperforate stamps must have four visible margins (¹/₄ to ¹/₂ mm). Those with full margins are doubly valuable and those whose margins encroach upon the stamps beside them are worth at least triple. Marginal copies are rare. Shades sometimes have been changed by exposure to light. Compare front and back of stamps.

Cancellations: cancellation numbers from 1 to 424 have four circles, except Nos. 104, 220, 270, 360, 363, 370, 381, 382, 384–86, 388, and 390–93, which have only three. Rare number in black, 390 and 406; very rare, 372 (500 francs). In blue, 2 to 5U, but No. 80 is rare and No. 424, very rare. In red, rare, to 10U; Nos. 69 and 238, very rare. In addition, one finds green cancellations, which are rare.

Postmarks with a date are double in value. There are rare ones, notably those in blue; in red, very rare. One- or two-line postmarks, framed or unframed, always are rare, as are those used in railroad mail service, the round "T u T," and foreign cancellations (Hanover, etc.).

On cover stamps are worth about 50U, except Nos. 2, 12, 13, 26–30, 40, and 41: 2U; Nos. 1, 17, 14, and 26 (¹/₄-silbergroschen), used alone: 4U.

Envelope cutouts that have been used as adhesives are known but rare.

North (1852–58). Nos. 1 to 6. The 2-silbergroschen, No. 5, generally has no dot after TAXIS. This has no

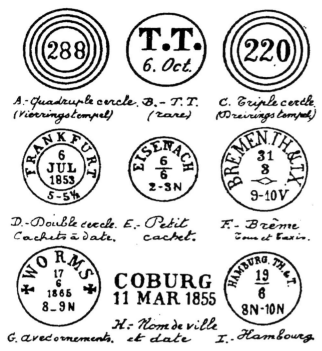

Germany cancellations: A. Quadruple circle. B. T.T. (rare). C. Triple circle. D. Double circle with date. E. Small postmark. F. Bremen, Thurn and Taxis. G. With ornaments. H. Name of city with date. I. Hamburg.

value in the other issues either, except No. 24. No. 3 was bisected.

Pairs: 4U; strips of three: 6U; blocks of four, No. 1: 20U; No. 3: 30U; the others: very rare. The 1-silbergroschen stamp has three different shades: blue, gray-blue, and dark blue, and the 3-silbergroschen, two shades: yellow and ochre-yellow.

1859–61. Nos. 7 to 13. *Pairs:* 4U; strips of three: 6U; blocks: very rare.

1862–64. Nos. 14 to 19. Buy these stamps with sufficient marginal space so that you can be sure they are not copies of subsequent issues with trimmed rouletting. The 1-silbergroschen rose-colored stamp was bisected diagonally. Pairs: 3U; strips of three: 6U, but Nos. 14 and 18: 8U; blocks of four, No. 19: 16U; No. 14: 32U; the others, very rare.

1865. Nos. 20 to 25. The canceled stamps require rouletting authentication, for No. 20 can be a No. 14 that was fraudulently rouletted in white, and the whole set may have been faked from the new issue of 1867 with a forged cancellation added.

Pairs: 3U; strips of three: 5U; blocks: rare (No. 23: 20U).

1867. Nos. 26 to 31. No. 29 exists in pairs, imperforate between: rare. A few stamps of the two

preceding issues are known with margins added and painted-on rouletting. Block of four, No. 29: 30U.

South (1852–58). Nos. 32 to 35. Same shades of paper as in Nos. 1–6. The 6-kreuzer stamps have no dot after POSTVEREIN. The 3-kreuzer was bisected.

Pairs: 4U, except 33a: 8U; strips of three: 6U; block of four: rare (No. 32: 40U).

1859–60. Nos. 36 to 41. No. 36 in blue-green is worth 2M. No. 39, printed both sides: very rare. Nos. 40 and 41 are found with unofficial rouletting.

Pairs: 4U; strips of three: 6 to 10U; blocks of four: rare (No. 36: 50U).

1862–64. Nos. 42 to 44. Same remark as for Nos. 14–19. No. 43 is known printed on both sides: very rare.

Pairs: 4U; strips of three: 6U; blocks of four: rare.

1865. Nos. 45 to 48. Same remark as for Nos. 20–25. Pairs: 3U; strips of three: 5U; blocks of four: rare.

1867. Nos. 49 to 52. *Pairs:* 3U; strips of three: 5U; blocks of four: rare.

Reprints: Nos. 1–11, 14–19, 22 and 23, 32–39, and 42–45 were reprinted in 1910 (Nos. 4 and 33 in two shades). Colors slightly different from the originals, no gum, letters "N D" in violet on reverse side. The set is worth 25 francs.

Early forgeries: in addition to the crude forgeries (Nuremberg, etc.), the following should be noted:

$^1/_4$-silbergroschen, four lithographed types. (a) FREIMARKE is spelled FREINRARKE; (b) the "$^1/_4$" fractions in the comers are scarcely visible and the "4" of the fraction in the lower tablets is smaller than the inscription's lowercase letters; (c) the "S" of DEUTSCH does not have a top serif; (d) a very successful forgery, but the lower right horn is inverted, the bell pan being directed toward the bottom of the stamp.

10-silbergroschen, two lithographed types. (a) THURN and UND form a single word; (b) the tall consonants of "Silb Grosh" are not as high as the capitals; the "K" of FRIMARKE is $^1/_2$ mm from the upper edge of the tablet instead of coming close to it; the bottoms of the horns and of the small "10" figures in the center background are very poorly executed (hatching); the "10" figures in the four corners are too large.

30-kreuzer. The "T" of TAXIS has a single vertical serif instead of two at the top.

Modern forgeries: all of the values except the 5- and 10-silbergroschen and the 15- and 30-kreuzer were counterfeited with ten clichés made in Turin. The paper tinting (semigloss modern) was done in Geneva, as were the printing and the quadruple circle cancellations, Nos. 6, 9 (sometimes 6 and 9 are upside down), 34, 95, 142, 195, etc. These cancellations also were applied on the originals. One can find all sorts of shades, but they are rarely consonant with the shades of the originals, the paper being tinted as orders were received. The characteristics of these forgeries and of the originals are shown in the accompanying illustration.

Thurn & Taxis, north and south: left columns, originals; right columns, Turin forgeries.

Forged cancellations: in addition to the forged number cancels already mentioned (Geneva), some come from other places (Saxony, Berlin, Alsace, Paris); the quadruple circled "18" and "39" are especially well executed. There are also about thirty dated cancellations, the best of which are Bremen Th u Tx; Blomberg; Frankenberg; Hamburg Th u Tx; Ilmenau; and Marburg. A few were struck on whole covers made with paper of the period. The less attractive ones can be identified easily by an occasional bad arrangement of the conventional markings (letters or figures, slanted: time figures, too small; letters not concentric with the circle; letters whose axis does not pass through the cancellation center; etc.), and the cancellation ink, being too new, draws attention to all of these things.

These forgeries are found on all mint stamps, the last of the remainders, and therefore on those that were not reprinted, and also on No. 2, which is much less rare mint than used.

II. North German Postal District

1868. Rouletted, typographed stamps. Stamps on cover are worth 2U. Pairs: 3U; strips of four: rare; blocks of four used are rare — for example, Nos. 3 and 9: 25 francs. Some rouletted stamps are wider and occasionally higher than others (21 x 25 mm); imperforate stamps are made from these. It is best to buy the imperforate stamps in pairs (rare) or as singles on cover: 3U. Imperf No. 4: 50 francs: No. 7: 100 francs; No. 8: 75 francs; No. 9: 50 francs; No. 10: rare; a used pair: 500 francs. Essays are available: No. 4, in black. No reprints known. Stamps with marginal numbers are rare: minimum, 50 francs.

Cancellations: all unusual ones are rare — for example, a dumb cancellation struck in Hamburg (machine cancel) on No. 4: 25 francs; Saxony cancellations: 3 to 10U, according to value; railway post mail; Konigl. Preuss Post Amt Cassel.

Forged cancellations: a few on No. 11, which is rarer used than mint.

Forgeries: Nos. 4 and 5 were crudely counterfeited in Geneva (F.). Very different shades. Lithographed.

1869. Perf 13½ x 14, Typographed. Stamps on cover: 50U; No. 22: 2U; pairs: 3U, but No. 22: 4U: blocks: rare, No. 12: 25 francs. No reprints known.

Cancellations: see the preceding issue.

Fakes: Nos. 1, 8, and 11 were fraudulently perforated to make Nos. 12, 19, and 22.

Forged cancellations: rather numerous on Nos. 19 and 22.

Forgeries: Nos. 15 and 16, usually mint. See the preceding issue.

Official forgeries: lithographed; nonconcentric center inscription; irregular value inscription; difficult to read. Rare.

1869. North German Bezirk postal inscription; perf 14 x 13½. On cover: 2U; pen canceled and dated postmark: 30U; pairs and blocks: rare.

Fakes: Nos. 23 and 24, pen canceled, frequently were cleaned to make mint copies. Make a comparative check of the gum and look for traces of ink on the reverse side. (Photography is sometimes necessary to see the traces.) Spongy paper is a good indication of cleaning.

Forged cancellations: not rare on No. 24.

1870. Official stamps, perf 14 x 13½. *On cover:* 50U, but Nos. 8 and 9: 3U. Pairs are not very common: 4U.

Cancellations other than the circular one with date, ordinary black, are rare — for example: K.P.R. Kriegsgerich-Commission zu Glatt.

Forged cancellations: numerous on values in kreuzer (Southern States).

1869. Telegraph stamps, Perf 13¹/₂ x 14¹/₂. Usually pen canceled. Worth about double with postal cancellation.

Fakes: the pen cancellations of Nos. 3, 5, 7, and 8 were cleaned.

III. German Empire

No known reprints.

1871–72. Small shield, perf 13¹/₂ x 14. Nos. 1 to 11. No. 5, imperforate: extremely rare. A few stamps are known to have crude perforations: 2M; 5U. On cover: 50U, No. 11: 2U; pairs: 3U; blocks of four mint: 6M; 10U. 5-groschen stamp: 20U. Common values: 5 francs.

Cancellations: circular with date: common. All the others are rare: color; railway post; straight line, for example, Emden; foreign: Bavaria, Saxony, Holland, etc. No. 8 has a forged cancellation.

Fakes: see the *large shield* issue [which follows].

1872 (July). 10- and 30-groschen. Nos. 26 and 27. With pen and postal (machine) cancellation: 30U. On cover: 2U.

Forged cancellations: very numerous (Murrow, etc.).

1872. Large shield. Nos. 13 to 25. On cover: 50U; 18-kreuzer: 2U. Pairs: 3U; No. 21: 4U; blocks of four: 10U; No. 19: 30U; common values: 5 francs. The 2-groschen brown is an unissued stamp.

Cancellations: see the preceding issue. Levant cancellations are in keen demand.

Forged cancellations: on Nos. 21, 24 (red-brown), and especially No. 25.

Fakes: most of the "large shield" stamps were reembossed to make small shields, and the contrary operation was performed on No. 8 (orange); this fraudulent operation is revealed by the crumpled paper and the noncongruent defects in the design. With regard to canceled stamps Nos. 21 and 25, the issue date is conclusive evidence of fraud. Stamps with inverted centers are fantasies.

Forgeries: the whole set, imperforate, was forged in Berlin. Crude workmanship. Offered for sale sometimes as reprints.

1875. Overprints, 2¹/₂- and 9-groschen. Nos. 28 and 29. No. 28 with figure "1" of the fraction out of place 1 mm to the left: 20 francs. No. 28, block of four: 30U; No. 29: rare.

1875. Pfennig. Perf 13¹/₂ x 14¹/₂. Nos. 30 to 35. Blocks mint are rare; Nos. 30–33: 15M; Nos. 34 and 35: 10M. No. 35a, dark bronze-green, and No. 35, pale gray, are rare mint: 100 francs; the other shades, gray-black, gray, olive-gray: 50 francs.

1880. Pfennig. Nos. 36 to 41. The mints from the first printing (dull shades, thicker paper) are much

sought after: 5M; 25-pfennig mint: 20 francs; the rare shade of No. 41a (first printing): 20 francs; the olive-gray is worth only 5 francs; the common stamp last printing) is dark bronze-green.

10-pfennig, imperforate: 50 francs; 50-pfennig: very rare. It should be noted that these are perforated stamps of larger format than the others, 22¹/₂ x 23¹/₄ mm, perforation included, and that the imperforate stamp must therefore be 21¹/₂ x 22¹/₂ mm, minimum. 50-pfennig with circular blank ornaments at the top: 10 francs M, 5 francs U.

Blocks of four canceled stamps: Nos. 36–39: 5 francs: Nos. 40 and 41: 7 francs 50 centimes.

Forged used postage stamps: No. 38, 10-pfennig, Strasbourg forgery: very rare canceled. Poor workmanship; center comparison is enough to reveal the forgery. No. 41, 50-pfennig, Bremen forgery: 75 francs canceled (October 1882 to March 25, 1883); height measured from the middle of the stamp: 21¹/₂ mm instead of 21³/₄ mm; the blank divisional design between the two scrolls to the left of DEU is touching the oval; the secret marks are missing.

1875–82. 2-mark. Figure. Perf 13¹/₂ x 14¹/₂ No. 43. No. 43a, dark purple shade, dates from 1875.

1889–1900. Figure or eagle in the center. Perf 13¹/₂ x 14¹/₂. Mint, imperf, 3-pfennig: 40 francs; 10-pfennig: 75 francs; 25-pfennig: 50 francs; 50-pfennig (brown): 50 francs. Plate defects, 2-pfennig, with error REIGHSPOST (for REICHSPOST): 10 francs; 10-pfennig, with elongated line on the "T" of the same word: 5 francs. No. 41 is rare on cover: 5 francs.

Forged official stamps: 10-pfennig Hochst forgery: 30 francs canceled; on cover: 40 francs. Dull rose and red, the latter shade being less common. Shades and perforations not consistent with originals. 10-pfennig. Mayence forgery: 75 francs. Brick red, same defects.

When the arbitrary shades have been recognized, comparative design study will reinforce doubt concerning the authenticity of the stamps. This will be corroborated by studying format and perforation.

Forgeries: the whole set was counterfeited. See below.

1900. Germania. Reichspost. Perf 14. Nos. 51 to 64. 5-pfennig blue, color error: very rare, 200 francs mint. 10-pfennig, imperforate: 10 francs mint. 5-mark, Type III, plate retouched: 50M; 50U.

1901. 5-pfennig. Bisected vertically for 3-pfennig. No. 65. Not very official overprint. The mint stamp is not recommended. The on-cover canceled stamp is worth 500 francs; single: 300 francs.

Forged overprints: numerous. Geneva overprints appear on the entire stamp, unbisected. The expertizing of this stamp's overprint and cancellations is absolutely necessary.

1902–4. Deutsches Reich. Nos. 66 to 80. The 3-mark stamp in Gothic is rare on cover: 3U.

Fake: error 67a, DFUTSCHES made by scraping; magnifying glass and transparency examination indicated.

Official forgeries: 60-pfennig olive, Berlin forgery (2), perf 13; the lines of the face, neck, and background do not have the finesse of the original. Make comparison.

New stamps. Forged overprints. 1921: No. 136, 5-mark on 75-pfennig: green shade and figures, not congruent; stars too small; make comparison. No. 137, 10-mark on 75-pfennig: irregular type letter "M" higher than the figures); make comparison.

1923: overprinted set, Nos. 252–90. A few single overprints, notably Nos. 269 and 270, were counterfeited. Great quantities of overprint errors were copied in Munich. Make comparative study.

The 800-thaler on 100, on 300 (dark green), and on 500 (red) are unissued stamps.

1923: overprinted set, Nos. 310–19. A few values were copied, especially No. 310, which may have been used. Comparison is indicated.

Official stamps. 1923: Nos. 37–47; a few forged overprints. 1923: Nos. 48–61; there are no inverted original overprints.

Telegraph stamps. Same comment for pen canceled stamps that have been cleaned as for the telegraph stamps of the North German Federation.

Polish occupation (1919). Nos. 1 to 7. The three higher values were counterfeited extensively, as were the inverted overprints of Nos. 6a and 7a. Comparison is indispensable, for very good forgeries are known.

German colonies. The German set of 1889 (Nos. 44–50) was well counterfeited in Geneva (F.). It has been indicated erroneously, particularly by Zumstein, that this set was reprinted. (Note: *Zumstein Europa,* a standard work in Europe for a long time, probably was Serrane's source. Zumstein and Co., *Europa. Briefrnarken-Katalog,* 8th edition, 1925.) It rarely is found without the forged colonial overprints. The illustration shows the design's principal distinguishing marks. Thus, it is not necessary to take up the arbitrary shades, the paper, or the perforations, all at variance and all of which may be changed tomorrow.

For whatever use they may be, and despite the fact that they do not logically belong to this study, let us mention the fraudulently overprinted sets and the forged handstamps that were used to print them. (A circular handstamp, with date, engraved on wood).

Eastern Africa: 1893, a set in pesas, Nos. 1–5; 1896, German West Africa set in pesas, Nos. 6–10.

Southwest Africa: 1897, German Southwest Africa set, Nos. 1–6, cancellation Gibeon 1/5 9. 1898,

Originals measure 18¹/₄ x 21¹/₅ mm; forgeries, 18 to 18¹/₄ x 21 mm.

German Southwest Africa set, Nos. 7–12, canceled Rethanien Deutsch-Sudwestafrica 1/5 99.

Cameroons: 1896, Cameroon set, Nos. 1–6, canceled Kamerun 3 2 98.

Caroline Islands: 1899–1900, Caroline Island set. Nos. 1–6, canceled Yap 7/1 99 Karolinen.

China: 1897–1900, China set, Nos. 1–6 with the two corners of the overprint, canceled Tschimvangta 16/2 97 Deutsche-Post.

Levant: 1889, a set in para and piaster, Nos. 6–10. Various cancellations.

Mariana Islands: 1899, Mariana Islands set, Nos. 1–6, the two corners canceled Saipan 18/11 99 Marianen.

Morocco: 1899, Morocco set (centime values also), Nos. 1–6.

Marshall Islands: 1897, Marshall Island set, Nos. 1–6, canceled Jaluit 8/18 97 Marschall-lnseln.

New Guinea: 1896, German New Guinea set, Nos. 1–6, canceled Stephansokt [sic] 18-5-99.

Samoa: 1900, Samoa set, Nos. 36–41, canceled Apia 1-2-00 10-11 V (Samoa).

Togo: 1897, Togo set, Nos. 1–6, canceled Klein-Popo 5-11-98.

Naturally, the forged overprints and cancellations also were applied on originals.

Gibraltar

The early English stamps canceled "G," "A 26" and sometimes GIBRALTAR with date belong to this British colony's collection.

1886. Overprints. "C.A." watermark. Nos. 1 to 7. Forged overprints being numerous, all overprinted stamps must be given a careful comparative examination. Examine the watermark also: the 6-pence stamp was used in Gibraltar with the "C.A." watermark only. Thus the 6-pence variety dark violet of Bermuda (1865–73) with "C.C." watermark has a forged overprint). The 1-shilling Bermuda is bistre-olive; the one used in Gibraltar is bistre-brown. The same holds true for the 4-pence orange Bermuda (1880), "C.C." watermark, and for the 1-pence rose (1865–73), "C.C." watermark. Cancellation is often a good indication because many forged overprints are applied to canceled stamps of Bermuda.

Forgeries: 4-pence (Genoa, I.). The inner ear, the nostril and its shading, the shading under the lower lip, etc., form color spots instead of the original's fine design. The overprint is executed poorly and the watermark is printed on the back of the stamp in a reddish tone. The 6-pence was counterfeited without watermark, with little improvement in design and noncongruent perforation. Finally, the 1-shilling was forged on a chemically bleached 1-penny stamp. Thus, paper, perforation, and watermark are original, and the overprint, too, but all this finagling left traces. Comparison of shading design will leave no doubt about this.

1886. Second issue. Nos. 8 to 14. *Fake:* 1-peseta of 1898 with value cleaned and forged impression of one shilling, in bistre shade. Compare the original stamp's shade with the latter and with the reprint.

The 1-penny was bleached completely to receive a forged imprint of the 4-pence and 6-pence, and the 1-shilling stamps. Compare design.

1889 (September). Overprints. Nos. 15 to 21. The overprints of Nos. 15, 16, and 18 were expertly forged. Compare.

Forged cancellation: GIBRALTAR A P 28 89.

Subsequent issues. The high-value stamps are less common used than new. Most of them are rare on cover. Revenue cancellations have been removed to make stamps appear to be unused, but traces remain. Then, a forged postal cancellation would be applied.

Gold Coast

First three issues. Nos. 1 to 20. GOLD COAST, on sides.

Early forgeries: bad lithographed forgeries; no watermark; a few dots on forecheek and nose instead of the fine original shading; a thick line defines the face and neck contour (see the illustration of the first Bermuda Islands issue); dot perf 13.

No. 21. ONE PENNY overprint and bar. Forged overprints. Comparison is necessary (Geneva also).

Great Britain

With its varieties, types, plates, colors, cancellations, etc., Great Britain offers more opportunities for specialization than most other countries of Europe.

The cancellations on early British stamps all must be examined carefully; some of them are extremely rare. Such examination is so important that we will begin by listing the cancellations from the British colonies and foreign post offices which are found from time to time on British stamps. Interesting British cancellations will be described at the end of the treatment of each issue.

Cancellations (colonies and foreign) that may be found on British Stamps

A01 Jamaica	C36 Peru
A02 Antigua	C37 Chile
A03 British Guiana	C38 Peru
A04 British Guiana	C40 Chile
A05 Bahamas	C41 Ecuador
A06 British Honduras	C42 Peru
A07 Dominica	C43 Peru
A08 Montserrat	C51 St. Thomas
A09 Nevis	C56 Colombia
A10 Saint Vincent	C57 Nicaragua
A11 Saint Lucia	C58 Cuba
A12 St. Christopher	C59 Haiti
A13 Tortola, Virgin Islands	C60 Venezuela
A14 Tobago	C61 Puerto Rico
A15 Grenada	C62 British Colombia
A18 Antigua	C63 Mexico
A25 Malta	C64 Mexico
A26 Gibraltar	C65 Colombia
A27–A78 Jamaica	C79 Hong Kong
A80–A98 Mailboats	C81 Brazil
A99 Virgin Islands	C82 Brazil
B Mailboat	C83 Brazil
B01 Alexandria, Egypt	C86 Dominican Republic
B02 Suez, Egypt	C87 Dominican Republic
B03 Mailboat (Africa)	C88 Cuba
B12 Mailboat	D14 Singapore
B13 Mauritius	D17 Penang, Straits Settlements
B27 Gold Coast	D22 Venezuela
B31 Sierra Leone	D26 St. Thomas
B32 Argentina	D27–D30 China
B53 Mauritius	D47 Cyprus
B54 Gold Coast	D48 Cyprus
B56 Gold Coast	D74 Peru
B57 Mailboat (Africa)	D87 Peru
B62 Hong Kong	E06 Jamaica
B64 Seychelles	E30 Jamaica
B65 Mauritius	E53 Haiti
C Constantinople	E58 Jamaica
C28 Uruguay	
C30 Valparaiso, Chile	
C35 Colombia	

E88 Colombia	196 Jamaica
F69 Colomia	199 Jamaica
F80 Jamaica	201 Jamaica
F81 Jamaica	247 Fernando Po
F83–F85 Pueno Rico	554 Gold Coast
F87 Smyrna, Turkey	556 Gold Coast
F88 Puerto Rico	582 Puerto Rico
F95–F97 Jamaica	598 Jamaica
G Gibraltar	615 Jamaica
G06 Beirut, Syria	617 Jamaica
G13–G16 Jamaica	622 Jamaica
H Mailboat	631 Jamaica
L Lagos, Nigeria	640 Jamaica
M Malta	645 Jamaica
O*O Crimean War	647 Jamaica
S Stamboul	942 Cyprus
T[I] Turks Islands	969 Cyprus
172 Malacca	974–75 Cyprus
193 Jamaica	981–82 Cyprus

Cancellation rarity of the several values can be determined by consulting the specialty catalogues.

[Editor's note: Serrane's listing of British Empire numeral cancellations is incomplete and occasionally inaccurate. Readers are referred to the Rev. H.H. Heins's *Numeral Cancellations of the British Empire,* Third Edition, London: Robson Lowe, 1967, available in the American Philatelic Research Library.]

I. Imperforate Stamps

1840. 1-penny black and 2-pence blue. Nos. 1 and 2. *Plates:* 240 stamps in four panes (6 x 10) with letters in the lower corners arranged in horizontal strips of twelve: AA, AB, AC, etc., up to AL, reaching the bottom of the sheet with TA, TB, etc., up to TL. The same arrangement for Nos. 3, 4, 8–15, 26, and 27.

Select: Nos. 1 and 2 must have four margins at least $\frac{1}{2}$ mm wide. Copies with wider margins bring higher prices.

Shades: the 1-penny is found in black, deep black, gray-black. The 2-pence comes in blue, dark blue, pale blue.

Varieties:1-penny. Eleven different plates, with very fine impressions from the first printings. Specialist prices. Copies from Plate 11 with transfer flaws, retouching, etc., are in demand. On blued paper: 4U. Double letter in one corner: 5U. Guideline in the corners: 50U. Guideline across the value: 2U. Inverted watermark: 4U. Thin paper: 50U.

2-pence. Double letter in the corners: 10U. Guideline in the corners: 2U. Across the value: 4U. Inverted watermark: 4U.

The reader is referred to the many specialty works in which the stamps of Great Britain have been described.

Cancellations: Type A in blue on No. 1: 10U. No. 2: 3U. Orange on No. 1: 3U. Violet: 6U. Yellow: 10U.

Great Britain cancellations: **A. Maltese cross.**
B. Dated cancel. C Maltese cross, with numeral.
D. Various numeral cancels. E. Circular datestamp.
F. Cancels of British offices abroad.
G. PD = postage paid. H. Military postmark.
I. Small dated postmark.

Type C on No. 1: 20U. No. 2: 4U. Dated cancellation in black on No. 1: 8U. No. 2: 2U.

Type A is not very common in black on No. 1. Name of city and "Penny Post" in italics on two lines: rare.

Pairs: 4U. Blocks of four, No. 1: 16U. No. 2: extremely rare.

Reprints: there is no reprint of No. 1, but there was one, called "Royal," of No. 26, done in black (large crown inverted watermark, 1864).

Faking of No. 2: in the original, the background burelage is separated from the words POSTAGE and TWO PENCE only by the blue line of the tablets of these two words ($\frac{1}{8}$ mm). In the fake, the blue line is about $\frac{1}{2}$ mm thick. It includes the white line which has been changed to blue. Nos. 1 and 2, mint, are rare; check for traces of cleaning.

Forgery No. 1: lithographed, no watermark. No dot after PENNY. No. 1, engraved with forged boldface watermark. Easy to detect!

1840. Official 1-penny black. No. 1. This stamp has "V R" (Victoria Regina) in the upper corners and the letters that ordinarily should be placed at the top are in the lower corners. This is an unissued stamp.

Forgeries: same forgery as above *(Forgery No. 1),* but with letters "V R." Traces can be seen of rosettes that have not been entirely scratched out.

Fake: the original No. 1 with upper rosettes, scratched out and "V R" substituted.

1841. 1-penny and 2-pence. Nos. 3 and 4. Rather numerous shades exist of No. 3. Copies on very blue-tinted paper and worn-plate copies (3U) are in demand. The 2-pence has two white lines.

Varieties: 1-penny — inverted watermark: 20U. Guideline on the value: 20 francs. Double letter in one corner: 30 francs. 2-pence — guideline in the corner: 2U. On the value: 3U. Inverted watermark: 10U.

The 1-penny rouletted 12 (Archer) is extremely rare (500 francs) and perf 16 (Archer): 75 francs mint, 150 francs used. Should be acquired only on cover.

The 1-penny is found with vertical silk threads. This is an unissued stamp and is rare.

Pairs: 4U. Strips of three: 6U. Blocks of four: 16U.

Cancellations: Type A in red is very rare (100 francs). In black: 2U. In blue: 12U. In green or violet on 1-penny: 50 francs; on 2-pence: very rare. Type C: 6U. Cancellation with date in black: 5 francs.

1847–54. Octagonals. Nos. 5 to 7. *Plates:* 6-pence, forty stamps (4 x 10). 10-pence, twenty-four stamps (4 x 6). 1-shilling, twenty stamps (4 x 5). Two Dickinson silk threads 5 to 5½ mm apart in each of the 1-shilling and 10-pence stamps (handmade paper). The 6-pence is on handmade paper and has the "V R" watermark in all positions. The plate numbers, preceded by "W W," appear at the base of the neck.

Shades: the 6-pence dark violet and the 1-shilling dark violet: 50U.

Varieties: the three values are found with embossed double print (R.). Difficulty in accurately spacing the embossing caused many stamps to touch one another. Copies with four clear margins are in demand. Octagonal cutouts in good condition are worth one-twentieth of the value of a full-margin copy.

Pairs: 3U. The pairs and strips of three of the 1-shilling are rather common.

Fakes: an envelope stamp, with inscription on the color background and figures in three small white circles, sometimes is offered for sale after front and back inscription repair to produce an apparently transparent stamp. No watermark. Laid paper "W W 5" at base of neck.

Repair: corner rebuilding currently is being practiced. Check using watermark fluid, and remember that the paper of the original 6-pence is handmade.

II. Perforated Stamps

To merit a "select" rating, perforated stamps must be perfectly centered. A pronounced off-centering, where the perforations cut into the design, reduces value by sixty to eighty percent.

1854–55. 1-penny and 2-pence perforated stamps. Nos. 8 to 11. Small crown watermark, as above.

Perforation: beginning with this issue, the reader will notice that British stamps are about 2 cm wide. Thus, to ascertain perforation, one can count the holes — there's no need to use a gauge [since the perforation standard is the number of denticulations per 2 cm].

1-penny, Type II. A retouched type from a die created from the original die. The shading of the eye is better and the nostril and mouth lines, as well as the forehead bandeau, are more visible. In case of doubt, refer to Nos. 12 and 14, which come from this die.

2-pence, plates: No. 9 comes from Plate 4 (small letters in the bottom corners) and from Plate 5 (larger letters). Plate 5: 3M, 3U. Same remark for No. 11. Plate 5: 50U.

Varieties: Nos. 8 and 10 are found with an inverted "S" (R.). No. 8a is known to exist imperforate. Nos. 8 and 10 on heavily tinted blue paper are in demand.

Pairs: 3U. Blocks of four: rare when they are well centered.

1855–58. 1-penny and 2-pence perforated stamps. Nos. 12 to 15. Large crown watermark.

Nos. 12 and 14 belong to Type II, described above.

Nos. 13 and 15 are from Plate 5 (larger letters) or from Plate 6 (same letters, but the white lines are thinner). Same value, mint: used, 25U.

No. 14 imperforate is very rare (250 francs M or U). On white paper: 150 francs used.

Same for pairs and blocks.

1855–57. No letters in corners. Nos. 16 to 20. *Plates* of twenty stamps. Thus, margin copies are numerous and are worth one-third less because they are felt to make an awkward appearance in albums.

Watermark: heraldic *fleurs* except for the 4-pence, which has small, medium, or large garter watermarks.

The medium and large garter watermarks are rather easily confused. Remember that the medium garter has only one dot instead of a vertical bar at the top, that it has a bar that is concentric with the two lines of the oval in the second part of the garter on the right (beginning with the lower part) and, finally, that the bottom has a horizontal line that is not found in the large garter. Watermark fluid always will expose these distinctive marks.

With this issue, one begins to find trimmed marginal stamps and stamps that have been reperforated to obtain well-centered stamps. The corner letters in these stamps attract one's attention.

Varieties: No. 18, thick glossy paper: 10U. No. 19, on blue-tinted paper: 20M, 30U. No. 20, on blue-tinted paper: 5U.

1862. Small letters in corners. Nos. 21 to 25. Same watermark. The 4-pence with large garter.

Shades: numerous in the 3- and 4-pence.

Imperforate: 4-pence and 1-shilling: very rare.

Varieties: 3-pence rose with white dots before and after POSTAGE, in the upper part of this word's tablet. 9-pence, Plate 3, with oblique white lines in the corner squares. These two varieties: mint, exceedingly rare; used, 1,500 gold francs. 1-shilling, imperforate, Plate 2, or perforated with letter "K" in a white circle (lower left corner): 200 gold francs. The 3-pence with lined background is an unissued stamp.

1858–64. Large letters in the four corners. Nos. 26 and 27. *Plates:* as in the 1-pence and 2-pence of the preceding issues, but the letters AA, BA, CA, up to LT, are in the top corners.

Remarks: unissued Plate 70 is extremely rare. Plate 77, likewise, with only a few copies known. Plates 75, 126, and 128 do not exist.

Varieties: large crown watermark with an oval below it. The oval's upper line is not doubled (watermark error) on stamps with letters MA or ML (HA or HL if the watermark is inverted) in Plates 72–74, 78, 83–85, 87–93, 96. Plate 81 is known to exist with an inverted "S."

Imperforates: purchase in pairs. Nos. 79, 81, 90, 92, 97, 100, 102–4, 107–9, 114, 116, 122, 136, 146, 158, 164, 171, 174, 191: extremely rare. Used pairs: 500 francs.

Fake: Plate 225 of the 1-penny must be examined closely; the figures have been tampered with.

1865. Large white letters in the four corners. Nos. 28 to 32. Same watermarks as in the issue of 1862.

Varieties: the 9-pence, Plate 5, and the 10-pence of the following issue, erroneously printed on the 1865 issue's paper (silk thread, heraldic *fleurs*) are exceedingly rare.

1867–69. Large white letters in the four corners. Rose stem watermark. Nos. 33 to 39. *Shades:* rather numerous for the 6-pence. The 10-pence dark brown: 50M, 50U.

Varieties: 6-pence, Plate 10; 10-pence, Plate 2, and 2-shilling blue, Plate 3: exceedingly rare. The 1-shilling, Plate 7, pairs imperforate between: extremely rare.

Used postal forgeries: 1-shilling, Plate 5. No watermark. Copied from a stamp with letters "S," "K"

on top; "K," "S" on bottom. Found with circular Stock Exchange cancellation.

Fake: 2-shilling brown fraudulently printed on a bleached 3-pence. Compare design with a 2-shilling blue.

1872–73. Same. 6-pence. Nos. 47 and 48. An early forgery, without watermark. Very poorly done.

1867–82. Large format stamps. Nos. 40–46. The 5-shilling, Maltese cross watermark, Plate 2, is worth 2U.

Fakes: the paper of No. 46 was treated chemically to give it an azure shade. Comparison is needed.

The 10-shilling, anchor watermark, (No. 44) and the £5 were forged on chemically bleached postal revenue stamps of 1862. The arbitrary perf 15 and design comparison (diadem, hair, lining, ornaments) will facilitate identification of these bogus creations.

Forgeries: a lithographed counterfeit of the £5 is known, with no watermark. The space between "£" and "5," bottom left, is too large and is almost nonexistent on the right.

1870. ¹/₂-penny. Half-size. No. 49. *Plates:* 480 stamps in twenty rows of twenty-four. Letters AA, AB, etc., at the bottom of the stamp, then BA, etc., CA, etc., to TX.

Varieties: "Half penny" watermark inverted: 4U. Stamps without watermark are marginal copies. There are imperforate copies from Plates 1, 4–6, 8, and 14: rare (50 francs).

Fakes: plate numbers. have been doctored to obtain Plate 9. Check paper transparency — the giveaway to a possible alteration — using a magnifying glass and watermark fluid.

1870. 1¹/₂-penny. No. 50. The 3-shilling 2-pence mauve on blue-tinted paper is an unissued stamp. The 183rd stamp of the sheet containing 240 stamps has the "OP" error (instead of "CP") at top.

Subsequent issues. 1875. Plate numbers 3 and 17, on the 2¹/₂-pence rose, globe watermark, were obtained by doctoring other numbers.

1876–80. No. 58, 4-pence vermilion, Plate 16, and No. 59, 4-pence green, Plate 17, are very rare, mint; used: 600 and 500 francs. An 8-pence purplish blue-brown, large garter watermark, is an unissued stamp: 200 francs.

1881. No. 73, 1-penny lilac, sixteen pearls, printed on both sides: 400 francs.

1883–84. Fake. No. 84, 9-pence green obtained by forged impression on a bleached 2¹/₂-pence stamp. Compare portrait design.

Forgeries: photolithographed, no watermark, shade and perforation don't match the original.

Note: Nos. 76–85, perf 12, and No. 82 with a line under the "D" letters. instead of a dot, are unissued stamps.

1884. Large format. The 2-shilling 6-pence, 5-shilling, and 10-shilling stamps were doctored chemically to produce the blue-tinted paper variety. Front and back comparison is indicated, as well as comparison with the original blue-tinted shade.

1887–1900. The 3-pence dark brown on orange is worth 100 francs mint and 40 francs used.

1902–4. Forged £1. Crude execution; check the portrait design (beard, hair, lines) and the crown. Perforations and watermark don't match the original. Forged circular thimble cancellation with date: GUERNSEY.

III. Official Stamps

All overprints were more or less well counterfeited on single stamps or in sets as in Geneva (F.) and elsewhere; likewise, with respect to the Board of Trade perforations.

It follows that prudence is mandatory, and detailed comparison with the original overprints is indispensable.

Greece

I. Imperforate Stamps. Large Hermes Head. Nos. 1–54.

A few years ago, I had evolved a practical way of classifying stamps by progressive elimination procedures (*Catalogue du Spécialiste d'Europe,* 1922). I still value that method, perhaps wrongly, because it helps the average level-headed amateur to extricate himself rapidly from collecting problems.

Here is a summary of the steps to be taken in establishing a tentative classification. Place all the Large Hermes Head stamps (Yvert, Nos. 1–54) in rows in the following order:

1. Stamps on cream-colored paper (Nos. 43–54).

2. Stamps on stippled paper. Very numerous "light dots" forming well-aligned broken lines are seen when this paper is held to a light (Nos. 33–38).

3. 30- and 60-lepton stamps (Nos. 39–42). Stamp Nos. 1–32 remain to be classified.

4. Remove the stamps whose impression is as fine as that of No. 39, with emphasis on cheek and neck shading. This will help you find Nos. 1–6a (Paris impression), among which the 5-, 20-, 40-, and 80-lepton stamps have no numerals printed on back; conversely, the 10-lepton has large numerals.

5. Next, take out those that generally look alike, but whose cheek and neck shading is not so fine and which have control numbers printed on back. The unshaded lines of these numbers are very slender, sometimes partly invisible, whereas the shaded lines are more

boldly printed. That is the first-class Athens impression (Nos. 10–16).

6. Take the 5-. 10-, 20- and 40-lepton stamps whose shades and paper resemble the stamps of the two previous issues, but whose printing is duller, slightly oily, with cheek shading done in full lines and control numbers exactly like those of the preceding issue. Provisional Athens printing (Nos. 7–9). Nos. 17–32 now remain to be classified.

7. The 20-lepton sky blue of the new makeready has a very characteristic appearance, with its broad white areas in the bureled corners and cheek and neck shading that seems less wide. The cheek and neck shading of this stamp can be used to identify No. 31.

8. Take out next the stamps whose cheek shading is made of fine, unbroken. unblurred lines and whose general appearance is evidence of well-cleaned plates (Nos. 24–30).

9. What remains must belong to the less carefully executed Athens impressions of 1863–71 (Nos. 17–23). The cheek shading is made of unbroken, frequently blurred lines, and all the lines of the control numbers are bolder than in the provisional, first-class Athens impression. The "5" control number has a single-line vertical bar.

This tentative sorting is followed by a definitive classification based on the study of each stamp's paper, tint, shade, fineness of the impression, control numbers, and value inscription printed on back, dated cancellations, etc.

Proceeding slowly — Is five minutes per stamp on the average too much? — the varieties, exceptions, etc., gradually will be isolated.

For each issue, there are always stamps that are very easy to classify and thus are the best reference stamps:

1861. Paris. No. 6a, 10-lepton orange, large control numbers.

1861–62. Provisional Athens stamps. 5-lepton green with special control numbers.

1862. First-class Athens printing. 80-lepton, with control numbers in vermilion.

1863–68 and 1871. Second-rate Athens printings. No. 22b, claret on gray, distinctive shade.

1869–70. Cleaned plates. No. 25, 2-lepton light bistre, distinctive shade.

1870. New makeready. No. 32, white areas in the angles.

1872–76. Thin, stippled paper. Nos. 37b or 38b, distinctive shades.

1875–76. 30- and 60-lepton stamps.

1876–82. Cream-colored paper. Nos. 51–53. Special shades for these values.

All that seemed clear enough to me, but readers have pointed out that the classification of the 1- and 2-lepton remains difficult because they have no control number.

That is quite true. I will deal with this in the definitive classification when I go into the printing question more deeply.

As is known, all stamps of 1861–82 were printed from the same plates. The greater or lesser care taken in printing the successive issues caused the change in the stamps' general appearance. This is especially evident in the cheek and neck shading, whose characteristics can be summarized under four different types, *a, b, c,* and *d* in the illustration.

Having completed our tentative sorting, let us take up the issues in their chronological order.

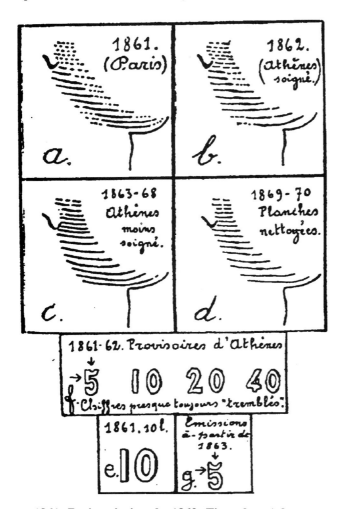

a. 1861. Paris printing. b. 1862. First-class Athens printing. c. 1863–68. Less careful Athens printing. d. 1869–70. Cleaned plates. f. 1861–62. Athens provisionals. Figures almost wavy. e. 1861. 10-lepton. g. Issues from 1863.

Definitive Classification

1861. Paris printing. Fine impression. Look at the sketch of Type *a.* All the shadow lines under the ear end in dots, either on the right only, or on both sides. The unbroken lines gradually become thicker over a rather extensive width and very artistically emphasize the cheek shading.

The 1-lepton is maroon brown, more or less dark, or chocolate brown. One stamp per sheet (in the bottom left corner) is less finely printed. The shade, its general appearance, and the shadow lines eliminate it from the first-class Athens printing.

The 2-lepton of the first printing is bistre, very finely printed, with fine, well-etched dots in the burelage. It closely resembles No. 1a of France. The second printing bistre-olive copies are rarer. Examples from the third and last printing are slightly fawn bistre-orange and are sometimes found on very thick, Bristol paper.

The 5-, 20-, 40-, and 80-lepton have no control numbers. This, along with the quality of the impression, is an unquestionable criterion for definitive classification.

The 10-lepton has a special control number and is 8 mm high (Figure *e*). This is fortunate, for it is the least finely printed stamp in the set. The cheek shading of many copies resembles the first-class Athens printing and some of them (rarities) have only unbroken lines on the cheek. The 5-lepton is found with a broken circle on the right at eye level.

Finally, I wish to point out that the 5-lepton also is found with four color dots on the circle around the pearls in the same place and that in other copies the circle is thinned down, always in the same place, by a quarter of its usual width. (Does this indicate the beginning of wear in a cliché?) Oddly enough, I have found 20- and 40-lepton stamps with the identical flaw. The 1-lepton exists with a circle break of about ½ mm in front of the mouth.

As far as I know, these last defects have not been reported in any specialty catalogue.

1861–62. Provisional Athens printing. The cheek shading is made of unbroken lines, with a few gaps. The control numbers are "wavy" (Figure *f*). The stamps' general appearance is not very far from that of the stamps of the next issue, but the color tones are duller, flatter.

1862. First-class Athens printing. Look at Figure *b*. The cheek shading is no longer made of dots, so to speak, but of small broken lines. This applies to the good and very good printings, for in most of them mark lines seem unbroken from one end to the other. Careful scrutiny of the design requires the use of the magnifying glass.

154

If these stamps are compared with those of the Paris printing, you will notice that the latter, *viewed from a distance,* seem to have only the reinforced lines of the cheek shading, the dots that terminate the shading being so fine (except in dhe 10-lepton) that one can hardly see them. On the other hand, in the first-class Athens printing, these dots, which have become little lines, enable one to see, even at a distance, the whole extent of the shading. Moreover, you will note that the thick part (cheek shading) of the unbroken lines is not as long as in the Paris printing, and, immediately to the right of this reinforced part, the unbroken lines break or become so thin that a kind of line of light models the cheek contour.

These observations concern primarily the 1- and 2-lepton stamps; control numbers are an even more reliable criterion for the other values.

These numbers are like those of the provisional Athens issue: their unshaded lines are so slender that they seem to be missing at times (particularly the left line of the "0" of 80); the shade lines are proportionately thicker.

The shades of the 1-lepton are different from those of No. 1 except a dark chocolate brown (which is very rare). The 2-lepton has an intermediate shade between Nos. 2 and 2a. It is a very slightly orange-tinted or fawn-colored bistre-brown. It also is found in a very pale bistre, like the 10-centime Bordeaux of that shade. The 80-lepton exists on buff paper (discoloration due to the gum?).

1863–68 and 1871. Less carefully executed Athens printings. These printings are characterized by the unbroken shading lines of the cheek and neck (Figure *c*), which have no finesse whatsoever, even in the first printing. And, if the lines do not touch each other in the first printings, the plate clogging and the lack of careful workmanship in the later printings caused them to become thicker and thicker and to touch at the bottom of the cheek, and sometimes give the stamp a very heavily shaded look. In this case, a color spot forms an angle whose second branch terminates under the Adam's apple.

It should be noted that beginning with this issue, the more or less different control numbers are no longer as finely drawn in the unshaded lines; the shaded lines are thick enough. Later, numbers become thicker so that finally the nonshaded and shaded lines are almost equally thick.

The 1-lepton shades go all the way from rather light red-brown to dark red-brown (light chocolate). The 2-lepton is rather comparable to the pale bistre of the preceding issue, but it is a little more orange-tinted. It also is found in bistre-brown. These two 1-lepton shades are found in the last printing of 1871. Here, however,

the paper is more yellowish and the cheek lines are spotted with color dots.

Starting with this issue, the 5-lepton assumes a new control number (Figure *g*).

The 10-lepton is found in dull orange-tinted red on blue and in bright orange on greenish paper. The 20-lepton ultramarine also is found in blue on greenish paper. These four shades with the 40-lepton claret on rose-gray are good references for the not very carefully executed Athens printings.

The 80-lepton is carmine, while No. 30 is more or less bright carmine-tinted rose.

Quite deliberately I have avoided establishing a separate classification for the Athens issue of 1871: it would cause confusion within the framework of this study. Aspiring specialists can study it separately, and from now on separate out the 1- and 2-lepton on yellow, the 5-lepton emerald and yellow-green of the same printing, the 10-lepton red on greenish paper mentioned above, the 20-lepton indigo, the 40-lepton lilac on azure, and Nos. 22c and 22d in the Yvert catalogue.

1869–70. Cleaned plates. Figure *d* shows that the cheek shading is composed of unbroken lines, which are finer and more slender than in the usual Athens printings. There are no smudges in these lines and they rarely touch each other. One encounters a slight thickening in the cheek contour, as in the first-class Athens printing. The control numbers eliminate confusion with the latter.

The 1-lepton is dark maroon-brown and often is found vertically lined. The 2-lepton is pale bistre-yellow on yellowish paper, but the bright bistre shade is best for reference.

1870. New makeready. It is easy to obtain a sky-blue, bright blue, or a dark vivid blue 20-lepton whose corner burelage was damaged (it is more or less blank) by poorly done makeready. You will notice immediately that the neck and cheek lines taken together resemble the Paris printing. They appear narrower, however, the dots being less numerous at the ends of the lines.

The 1-lepton, which is very light maroon, gives the same impression of narrowness in the neck lines. It has almost no dots on the right of the shading, but there are some that are very irregularly placed near the middle of the neck.

1872–76. Printing on thin, stippled, transparent paper. Most of the stamps in this issue are very easily identified by their thin, transparent paper. However, all stamps tentatively classified as from this issue must be subjected to a careful transparency examination, since thicker, stippled, nontransparent paper is found.

The cheek shading is like that of Figure *c*, but since the clichés were a little worn, the lines are more uniformly thick. As a whole, the stamp impresses one as rather amateurish work. There are practically no dots left in the corner burelage (except in No. 37 blue), and those that are left form dashes in the clogged printing.

The 1-lepton is brown, gray-brown, or red-brown on yellowish paper. The 2-lepton is pale bistre. These two values have irregular stippling.

Copies of all values exist with oily printing.

The shades of the 5-, 10-, 20-, and 40-lepton are numerous and sometimes odd. The 10-lepton exists in brick red on blue-tinted gray, the 20-lepton in indigo on greenish paper. The 40-lepton olive on blue (No. 38b) has numerous shades, some of which come from bleaching. The ink used for this stamp issue also was used for the control numbers on a few sheets of Nos. 38 and 38a.

1875–76. Paris and Athens impressions. 30- and 60-lepton. The 30-lepton olive-brown from the Paris printing is a first-class impression which closely resembles that of stamps Nos. 1 and 6. The 60-lepton blue-green on greenish paper is not so fine (neck shading and dots in the burelage).

The 30-lepton from the Athens printing resembles the less careful Athens printings (neck shading), except No. 41c, more carefully printed, which is always olive-brown and is always on the light buff paper of No. 39. The others are on more intensely tinted yellowish or grayish paper.

The 60-lepton of Athens is dark green or Russian green on cream-colored paper.

1876–82. Local printing on cream-colored paper. Classification is made easy by the paper shade. The cheek shading is sometimes rather clear-cut, without approaching the fineness of that of the cleaned plates of 1869, however. On other occasions, as in Nos. 46 and 46b, the dirty plate produced substandard impressions in which a compact ink blob separates the neck from the mask-like face.

The control numbers on a few stamp values are so blurred that one can hardly tell whether their lines are shaded or not; they frequently are malformed.

Classification is facilitated by shades and cancellations.

The 1-lepton (various shades) and the 2-lepton (dull pale bistre) often have lines instead of dots in the corner burelage. This recalls the overlapping of the Bordeaux stamps.

With their shades, paper, printing and control numbers, as well as with their innumerable varieties, not to speak of cancellations, the first Greek stamps are "splendidly" interesting. (See F. Serrane, *"Méthode de classement des timbres grecs à tête de Mercure,"* *L'Écho de la Timbrologie,* No. 709 [July 15, 1925]: 1024–26.)

1861. Paris issue. Nos. 1 to 6. *Sheets* of 150 stamps.

Shades: 1-lepton: brown. maroon-brown, chocolate brown. 2-lepton: bistre-yellow (shade of France No. 1), first printing; bistre-olive R., second printing; bistre-fawn (reddish), third printing. 5-lepton: bright green, first printing; yellow-green, second printing. 20-lepton: dull blue or dark blue, first-class printing, first printing; blue and dark blue, dark blue on thin, transparent paper R., second printing. 40-lepton: mauve, first printing: violet, second printing. 80-lepton: bright rose, first printing: carmine-tinted rose, yellowish gum, second printing. The 10-lepton red on blue is an unissued stamp.

Select: the stamps of this issue and of all the Large Hermes Heads (Nos. 1–54) must have four margins. a minimum of ³/₄ mm wide.

Varieties: thin paper, Nos. 3, 4, 6: 2U. No. 4, dark blue (steel), thin or thick paper: 3U. Plate flaws: broken circle with white curl penetrating the Greek ornament framework. 5-lepton: 3M, 3U; thin circle, 5-, 10-, 20- and 80-lepton: 3M, 3U; white spot in the Greek ornament framework (see sketch), 20-lepton: 3M, 3U.

From left: broken circle; thin circle; white spot on Greek ornament.

The 10-lepton also is found with two white dots instead of a single one after the word ΓΡΑΜΜ, the 40-lepton, with entirely white cross, top right, no dot between the cross bars, and the 20-lepton with the outer right frame line too far removed from the inner one: 2U.

The large control numbers of the 10-lepton normally are shaded on the right side (looking toward the numbers). Number "1" inverted (shaded on the left): 3U. Number "0" inverted: 3U. The two numbers inverted: exceedingly rare. No control number (133rd stamp of the sheet): 3M, 10U.

The 5-lepton is found with thick numbers; the vertical bar is too wide.

Pairs: 3U. Blocks of four: 5M, 6U. This is the same for all the Large Hermes Heads issues. We will return to them only when important exceptions require it.

Cancellations: the first two issues are usually canceled with postmark Type B; the others are rare.

Beginning with the third issue, there are about as many Type A cancellations as Type B. Later (1873–74), the number of Type A postmarks is greater, and, beginning with the issue on cream-colored paper, hardly any but Type A or C cancellations are found.

Foreign postmarks are in demand: Turkey, Nos. 95–99, 103, 105, 135; Romania, Nos. 52, 100, 102, 133; Crete, Nos. 9–11. Value: 2–10U.

Dated cancellations in color are rare.

On the issues subsequent to the Large Hermes Heads, one finds Types D, F, G, H, and I, or similar postmarks, as well as elliptical or circular ones used by steamship companies, or with the name of national Greek ships inscribed on one line, without framing.

Greece cancellations: A. Double circle with date. B. Lozenge of dots with numeral. C. Single circle with date. D. Divided double circle. E. Greek foreign post offices (Smyrna, Turkey). F. Mobile post office markings (Piraeus-Athens). G. Name of city (customs markings). H. Municipal mail marking. I. Registry marking.

Essays: a great number of essays, whose shades are only slightly different from the original shades, are offered for sale as new stamps. They are on white paper. Comparative study is indicated. The 10-lepton stamp has no numbers on its back.

Early forgeries: lithographed, without numbers on the back (not even the 10-lepton), or with numbers in imitation of the first-class Athens issue. Seventy-five pearls, sometimes fewer, instead of eighty-eight. Pearls poorly drawn. Few, if any dots between the corner burelage lines. Lettering and figures not very congruent.

Other forgeries are so badly done that a moment's comparative study is sufficient to identify them. The 20-lepton was counterfeited in dark blue on thin paper, without dots in the burelage, no nostril, etc.; the 80-lepton, likewise. Check dimensions also.

It should be noted that in all well-printed originals the first three wavy lines on the left are separated from the inner frame by a gap (top and bottom), while in the forgeries these lines, being thicker, touch the frame.

Geneva forgeries: the whole set was counterfeited without control numbers. However, this may come to be considered an advantage in the future, since this set may be used to forge *all* Large Hermes Heads. The neck shading is not similar to any of those issues. (Examine with magnifying glass.) However, from a distance it will seem to be related to the cleaned plate shading. (See illustration.)

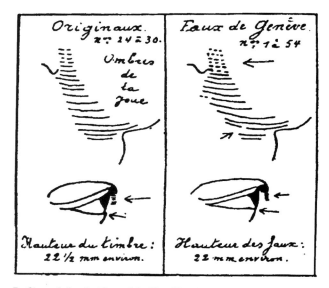

Left: originals Nos. 24–30. Cheek shading. Stamp height about 22¹/₂ mm. Right: Geneva forgeries. Nos. 1–54. Height of forgeries about 22 mm.

Again, one should note that these forgeries do not have the fineness of the originals, that the burelage lines are almost straight, and that the dots between these lines are very poorly executed. In the bottom left corner, the burelage lines do not touch the thick shading of the white circle. The 80-lepton had two clichés, the very bad first one of which was retouched. However, in the second cliché, there is still a vertical line between the value tablet and the lower right square.

Forged cancellations on Geneva forgeries: Type B. Nos. 140, 1032: Type A, AΘHNAI 6 AΠP6 10 Π 1896; ΠΓOΣTOΛION 3 IOYΛ 77 (110); ΩAEOI I NOEM 75, and cross-shaped design; Type C, KOPINEOΣ.

Fakes have been made from essays fraudulently gummed or canceled; originals of subsequent issues with control number scratched out, and sometimes also the cheek shading to make dots; forged large control numbers printed on the 10-lepton. A good magnifying glass will prove useful.

1861–62. Provisional Athens printing. Nos. 7 to 9.

The first stamp printed in Athens was the 20-lepton. It had no control number (Yvert No. 8b), very dark blue bordering on indigo on slightly blue-tinted or grayish paper. Ordinary, or thin, transparent paper, the latter being rarer. This stamp still has traces of the small white spot in the background cross-hatching, which eliminates the possibility of confusion with No. 14 which has no control numbers (an error).

The other values may be identified (1) by their frequently greasy appearance; (2) by the Hermes Head which seems larger than in the other issues (resulting from wavy printing and spots along the hair, accentuating the optical illusion); (3) by the frequent occurrence of other white spots or color blobs in the center background; with oxidation, this sometimes produces different or metallic-looking shades; (4) by the control numbers which almost always exhibit similar blobs; these numbers are very fine on one side and heavily shaded on the other.

Shades: 5-lepton, blue-green; yellow-green: 50M, 50U. 10-lepton, yellow-orange on azure paper or vermilion-tinted orange on azure paper, but yellowish green paper on the front: 50U (the control number is often visible in front). 20-lepton, dark blue (several printings), gray-blue (intermediate ultramarine): 2U; very rare, mint. 40-lepton, violet; mauve: 25U.

Varieties: 5-lepton, control numbers slightly doubled: 3U. 10-lepton, control number "1" or "0" inverted: 5U; same, numbers spaced further apart: 2U. 20-lepton with "0" inverted: 5U.

Pairs: 3U, strips: extremely rare.

Forgeries: see Paris issue. Count pearls, compare design, shade and paper.

Fake: 5-lepton of subsequent issues with forged control number "5," first type. Shade and control number faking must be compared.

1862. First-class Athens printing. Nos. 10 to 16.

See the illustration for cheek and chin shading, especially in the 1- and 2-lepton stamps. As for the other values, when the shades and the general appearance seem to indicate Paris printings, these stamps must be assigned to the first-class Athens printing when numbers are found on the reverse.

No greasy appearance. No white or color spots as in the provisional printing. Control numbers are well drawn and well shaded, but without uniform distribution of color.

The cheek shading. frequently composed of small broken lines, especially at the top, is the chief characteristic of this issue. These lines are reinforced at the cheek contour, which, consequently, is finely (and visibly) drawn.

Stamps with a fineness of design similar to that of the Paris issue: double value.

Shades: 1-lepton dark chocolate, similar to the Paris stamp, plain background: 3M, 3U. The basic dark brown shade, lined background, is most common. An amber bistre-brown, plain background, is rather like the 2-lepton, and could very well have come from mixing the inks used for the two values: 50M, 2U. Finally, there are two intermediate shades, a light brownish shade, lined background, with play of iridescent purple or crimson, and a very light chocolate. Both have the same value as the amber bistre-brown.

2-lepton. Bistre-fawn like that of the Paris issue and pale bistre, which is a little less common. An amber bistre-gray (due to the ink mixing mentioned above?) is very rare: 20M, 20U. Some believe this stamp came from the provisional printing.

5-lepton. More or less dark green, often with the shade of the yellow-green paper on front.

10-lepton. Orange; dark orange: 25M, 25U; with yellow-green paper on front instead of blue-tinted paper: 2M, 2U.

20-lepton. Dark blue (intermediate steel blue or bright dark blue, the latter having very dark control numbers). The first closely resembles the Paris stamp. Yellow-tinted paper on front: 25M, 25U.

40-lepton. Violet like the Paris violet shade, control numbers darker than the stamp.

80-lepton. Rose or carmine-tinted rose with orange control numbers (first printing). The carmine-tinted rose is less common. I have run across a rose-colored stamp on yellow-tinted paper (paper from the provisional printing) with spots in the center background. Finally, rose-carmine and carmine shades belonging to the definitive Athens printings are found.

Varieties: 1-lepton, striated: 2U. This paper variety is also found in subsequent issues. 2-lepton, pale bistre on thin paper; rather common. 5-lepton, broken circle: 3U, double control number: 6U. 10-lepton. "1" or "0" of the control number, inverted: 2U; with "01" 3U; with numbers 8 mm apart: 2U. 20-lepton, no numbers on back: 8U; with "0" of control inverted: 2U. 80-lepton, control number "8," inverted: 3U; no control number: 10U. The 10- and 40-lepton stamps are found with double impressions caused by movement of the paper during printing.

The figures are not always in the same place in the lower tablet. It is anomalous that one of the figures should be well placed and the other much too low, as in the 80-lepton where the "80" figure on the right is touching the bottom of the tablet.

Pairs: 10-, 20-, 40-, and 80-lepton: 4U. Mint: rare.
Forgeries: see first issue (1861).

1862–68. Definitive Athens printings. Nos. 17 to 23. The succession of printings reveals, first of all, rather finely printed copies which come close to the quality of the least successful first-class Athens stamps, and occasionally to that of the cleaned plate stamps (1870). However, the cheek shading (see Figures *b*, *c*, and *d*), made of full, unbroken lines (or almost so), lines that are uniformly thick, removes any possibility of confusion. Afterwards, the plates got dirty and the shading became thicker until it finally turned into spots.

The control numbers no longer show any pronounced contrast between the finely printed parts and the number shading. The 5-lepton has a new control number with a single vertical downstroke.

In case of doubt, comparison with the 5-lepton on greenish paper, with the 10-lepton on blue (paper of the 40-lepton), and with the 40-lepton claret on gray paper, or salmon pink on greenish paper will provide a very n liable reference procedure.

Yvert included this issue with that of 1871. This has caused a very regrettable confusion. The latter came *after* the cleaned plate and new makeready issues. The sequence of issue date will be basic for those who wish to make a collection of these stamps.

Shades: 1-lepton brown (1862), reddish gray-brown (1863) — these two shades exhibit a more or less visible whitish lining in the center background — red-brown (end of 1864) with center background white spots instead of lines; chocolate brown or purple-brown (June 1865), jumbled design; dark red-brown, very good impression (1866), finely printed and shorter cheek shading, rare: 8M, 4U. Chocolate brown on thin, transparent stippled paper (1871).

2-lepton. Bistre (June 1863); dull bistre-brown, paper more highly tinted, heavy impression (1865); yellow-brown (September 1865), very dark shade for a 2-lepton — it is probably a printer's waste stamp, released erroneously for distribution — rare: 20M, 50U. Pale bistre on unstippled ordinary paper (1871), heavy or blurred printing.

5-lepton. Green on blue-green (1863), yellow-green (1864), with well-shaded control number. The impression in these two printings is blurred, but there is one that is very good: 2U. Emerald green (1871) on nontransparent, unstippled, really green paper. A rather yellowish gray light green on unstippled, transparent paper is from a second printing of 1871.

10-lepton. Orange on azure paper (beginning of 1863), control numbers almost without shading. This stamp was used very belatedly until about 1880. Orange on blue (end of 1864); brick red on blue (end of 1865), red on blue-tinted paper (end of 1866), red on greenish paper (1871), stippled and thin, inferior impression.

20-lepton. Ultramarine (shades) (1862), blue control number; blue on greenish paper (middle of 1866), blue or dark blue control number, the former being from a paler impression. Subsequent printings: pale blue, blue control number; dark slate blue bordering on indigo (1867), with blue-black control number. All these shades are found in the 1871 printings either on thin or on thick, stippled, nontransparent paper.

40-lepton. Lilac on azure paper (May 1862), shades, control numbers, darker than the front impression and not shaded very much: dull gray-lilac on azure paper (end of 1865), control number, same as the preceding stamp. Another printing is rosy gray-lilac; claret on rosy gray paper (1866), control number same as that of the stamp. Red lilac (end of 1868), shade much darker than the preceding ones, bad impression. Next, one finds more or less dark violet on stippled, nontransparent blue paper (1871).

40-lepton. Flesh color or salmon pink on greenish paper, three printings: (1) salmon-tinted red on blue-tinted paper, rare: 2M, 6U (end of 1868); (2) dull flesh color on greenish paper (1871), often bleached; (3) dull pale bistre on light greenish paper (end of 1871). All three have carmine control numbers.

80-lepton. Rose, vermilion-tinted orange control number (1862); dark rose (rare); carmine (1865); dark carmine, fine impression (1866): 3M, 3U. Rose and rather dull carmine on common paper, bad impression (1866).

Varieties: 1-lepton, striated paper: 2M, 2U. White spot on the pearls, under the neck point, forty-fourth stamp: 3U. White spot in the hair, behind the lower ear, fifty-fifth stamp: 3U. These two varieties were in circulation only from 1865. The gray-brown stamp with very defective impression: 50M, 50U.

5-lepton. Broken circle: 4U. Thin circle: 2U. No control number: 50U. Doubled control number: 20U. 19b with control number visible on front: 5U.

10-lepton. Thin circle: 2U. No control number: 100U. "1" or "0" inverted: 2U. "10" inverted: 10U. Space between figures: 3U. "01" on back: 20U. "01" on front only, very rare: 200U. Figures faintly doubled: 5U. Double print on front: rare.

20-lepton. No figures on back: 100U. "0" omitted: rare. "80" instead of "20": 300U; "02": 50U; "0" inverted: 2U. Figure doubled: 100U. Figures 9$\frac{1}{2}$ mm apart: 3U. A few control plate defects are found: broken figures (also in the 10- and 40-lepton): 2U. White spot in the Greek ornament: 10U.

40-lepton. No control number: rare. Double print, front of stamp: rare. Doubled figures: 20U. Space between figures: 5U. "2" overprinted with a "4" to make "40" instead of "20" on back: 50U. "0" inverted: 5U. With right dividing frame line too far away, or upper right cross without center dot: 2U.

80-lepton. No control number: 30U. Figures with spaces: 5U. "8" or "0" omitted: 12U. "8" or "0" inverted: 3U. Double print on front: rare.

There is often a color spot on the cheek.

The 10-lepton, split diagonally, was used in place of a 5-lepton: extremely rare.

Pairs: 3U. 40-lepton, 4U.

Forgeries: see first issue (1861).

1869–70. Cleaned plates. Nos. 24 to 30. The cleaning of the plates removed the flaws of previous printings. The imprint from these cleaned plates is sharp and clean, but wear is perceptible. If you compare with the first-class Athens printing, you will notice that the neck lines, which are made of unbroken, regularly spaced lines, are thicker and that consequently the shade thickening of the cheek contour is less pronounced (Figure *d*).

In addition, the corner burelage, cleansed of impurities, seems whiter than in the printings from 1863 to 1868. The control numbers are only slightly shaded. The 2-lepton flesh color, which is so similar to the 40-lepton of the same shade (1871), is an excellent inference stamp.

Note: This issue is catalogued "1869–70," but the plates of the 1-lepton and a few shades of other values were cleaned before or after that period.

Shades: 1-lepton, red-brown or yellowish gray paper (1867?); grayish brown. 2-lepton, pale bistre (1870); bistre flesh color (1872). 5-lepton, emerald green (1868), blue-green control number; light green, yellow-green, or sage green control number (1870); dark red on blue paper and flesh-colored red on greenish paper, both fine impressions (1869): 2M, 4U. Orange on azure paper (1870) and vermilion on azure, both with unshaded figures. 20-lepton, blue, unshaded figures. 40-lepton, mauve, figures same shade. 80-lepton, carmine-tinted rose, bright carmine-tinted rose: 2M, 50U.

Varieties: 1-lepton with background lines; white spots (cliché wear), Nos. 44 and 45: 3M, 3U. 5-lepton. broken circle: 5U. Control number faintly double: 10U. "15" instead "5": 10U. 10-lepton, "1" or "0" inverted: 3U. "01"; 20U. Figures with spaces: 5U. 20-lepton, "02": 30U. Faintly double control number: 30U. No control number: 100U. Figures with spaces: 10U. "0" inverted: 3U. 40-lepton, "4" on "2": very rare, 80U. Double print in front: very rare; fine impression: 2U. Doubled control number: 20U. 80-lepton: "8" or "0" inverted: 3U. "8" instead of "80"?: very rare.

Forgeries: see first issue (1861).

1870. New makeready. Nos. 31 and 32. Because of unsuccessful makeready in the printing process, the cheek shading in the 1-lepton is too restricted, and the shading on the left of the cheek contour is almost always reduced to a few dots. In the 20-lepton, the inner corners display extensive, definitely white spots in the burelage.

Shades: maroon-brown on slightly yellowish paper, paler maroon-brown, sky blue, bright sky blue. These last two shades, same value. Dark sky blue: 50M, 2U.

Varieties: the cheek shading in a few clichés of the 1-lepton is complete: 50M, 50U. 1-lepton, with cliché wear: 2M, 2U. 20-lepton, with cutout encroaching on the outer framework: 2U. "0" inverted: 3U. "20" inverted: 25U. "02": 25U. Doubled control number: 30U. Thin paper: 3U.

In stamps of this issue, as well as in the preceding one, one finds control numbers straddling two stamps, either laterally or above and below. Always rare.

Pairs: 20-lepton: 4U.

1872–76. Transparent stippled paper. Nos. 35 to 38. This issue is identified by the paper, which is thin, transparent, and stippled.

Shades: 1-lepton brown on straw-colored paper (1875); bistre-gray; pale red-brown on opaque paper. The 2-lepton is on ordinary unstippled paper. The 5-lepton is found in gray-green or very transparent sage green (1872): yellow-green (1872), of which there is a printing in dark yellow-green, with heavy, occasionally greasy impression, and, finally, a late printing (1875) in emerald green: rare, 2M, 4U. 10-lepton brick red on blue-tinted paper (1872); brick red on purplish blue-gray (1873); indigo on blue (1874), rare; dark Prussian blue on greenish blue paper (1876); figures on back, same shade as stamps. 40-lepton lilac on azure paper and dull pale violet on azure (1872); control numbers, same as stamp shade. The bistre shades on blue date from the beginning of 1872. Shades from a very pale, scarcely visible bistre to bronze brown through various olive-green shades have been created by bleaching. The excessively pale shades come from inks that have been thinned down too much with oil. There is a reddish, relatively rare, dark violet stamp.

Varieties: stamps on nontransparent stippled paper are rarer, and are worth double. 1-lepton, cliché defect: 3U. 5-lepton, broken circle: 3U. Bottom of "5" broken: 6U. Transparent figure in front: 3U. "15" instead of "5": 15U. Doubled control number: 10U. 10-lepton, no control number, very rare: 80U. "1" or "0" inverted: 3U. "10" inverted: 10U. "1" only or "0" only: 10U. Doubled figures: 20U. Figures spaced 8½ mm apart: 3U. "01": 15U. "110": very rare. 20-lepton, doubled figures: 50U. No figures: 80U. "0" inverted: 5U. Figures with spaces: 10U. 40-lepta, very pale olive-green control number on a dark lilac or lilac stamp: 4U. No control number: 10U. Doubled control number: 8U.

In this issue, as in the preceding ones, there are control numbers, one of which is more or less high in relation to the other one, or whose figures ("5"; "0" of 10; "2" and "0" of 20; "4" and "0" of 40) are broken: 3U.

1875. Paris printing. Nos. 39 and 40. Executed in Paris. Sheets of 150 stamps.

Shades: 30-lepton, first printing, olive-brown; second printing, dark olive-brown on ordinary paper and dark olive-brown on thick paper, the latter rare. 60-lepton, first printing, blue-green on green paper; greasy paper: second printing, green on green paper. The first printings with finer impression are in demand.

The 30-lepton yellow-brown is a rather rare essay. The 30-lepton with double print is from printer's waste.

Pairs: 30-lepton: 4U.

Fake: the cheek shading of the 30-lepton of the Athens printing has been doctored to create a stamp from the Paris printing! Compare shades and use a magnifying glass to look for traces of scraping.

Geneva forgeries (F.): the paper and impression shades prove that the target was the Paris printings, but these counterfeits are poorly executed. The illustration will give adequate information on the printing characteristics of the 30- and 60-lepton clichés. Dimensions: about $18\frac{1}{2}$ x 22 mm (as in the originals of the preceding issues), whereas the format of the new value originals is $18\frac{4}{5}$–19 by about $22\frac{1}{2}$ mm.

The forged cancellations are the same as for the forgeries of the preceding issues (see first issue, 1861), with an additional cancellation, a double circle postmark with date:

(A) ΡΓΟΣΤΟΛΙΟΝ.

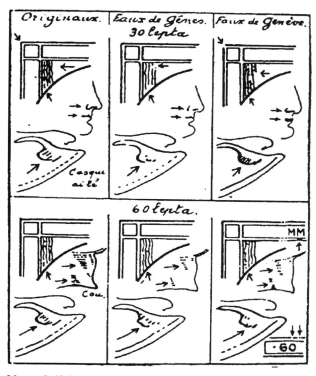

30- and 60-lepta. Originals. Genoa forgeries. Geneva forgeries.

3 ΙΟΥΛ 77 (110).

Genoa forgeries (I.): these are two very deceptive creations, especially the 30-lepton. Ninety-nine out of one hundred collectors would be fooled by it. The dimensions are good, except that the 30-lepton is a bit too high ($19\frac{1}{5}$ mm). The forgery's shade and the shade of its paper are good. The shade of the 60-lepton is too dark or too gray, and the paper's shade is far too blue-green, but this can be changed. The paper of the 30-lepton is too thin, 50 microns including the gum, whereas the original is 50–60 and 70 microns with gum. As for the 60-lepton, thick paper. 75–90 microns with gum, whereas the original is 45–55 microns without gum, but that too can be changed.

The illustration shows the distinctive features of the two categories, it being understood that the originals, in which the impression is less fine (especially the 60-lepton), may not exhibit the neck shading as fully as in the sketch, which shows the complete shading of the very good impressions. The 60-lepton forgeries also may or may not have thick shading. Evidently counterfeits of the two values may be offered as Nos. 41 and 42 after a color or paper change.

1876. Athens printing. Nos. 41 and 42. *Shades:* 30-lepton, first printing, fine impression, olive-brown on the paper of the Paris printing. More or less fine impressions are found, but the off-olive-green shade and the thin, transparent paper leave no doubt about the Paris printing. Second printing, brown on cream-colored, transparent paper (the paper of No. 42): 25M, 50U. Then there are printings that range all the way from dark brown to black-brown, with defective impressions in which the back of the head has disappeared. These have thin, transparent, slightly greasy paper resulting from excessive inking. Finally, we get to the red-brown stamps on nontransparent white paper (a light bistre-red is rare: 2M, 12U), and on thin, transparent paper: 50M, 50U.

60-lepton, more or less dark green (Russian green) on cream-colored paper, which is greasy at times. Again, excessive inking has occasionally blotted out the back of the head or the inscription lettering.

Varieties: dark brown, double print: 30U. Red-brown, printed both sides: 2M, 20U.

Forgeries: see the preceding issue.

1876–80. Issue on cream-colored paper. Nos. 43 to 45. *Figures on back of stamps.*

Shades: 5-lepton yellow-green; dark green; yellow-green, greasy impression. 10-lepton orange, vermilion, brick red (rare); orange and vermilion on greasy paper. 20-lepton dark ultramarine; dark blue (light indigo); Prussian blue (first-class impression); royal blue: 4M, 6U. Dark blue, greasy impression. 40-lepton salmon pink, greasy impression: 2M, 2U.

Varieties: there are rather fine, first-class impressions of the 5-, 10-, and 40-lepton stamps: 50M, 2U. 5-lepton, double print: 3M, 4U. Double print: 3U. Doubled control number: 5U. 10-lepton, double print: 3M, 8U. "110": 20U. Figures spaced 4 mm apart: 6U. Figures astride: 8U. 20-lepton, "2," "0," "20" inverted: 60U. Doubled figures: 80U. 3 mm spaces between figures: 15U. Figures astride: 20U. Small control numbers: 25U.

Forgeries: see the preceding issues.

Fakes: forged control numbers have been added to the 5- and 10-lepton of the printing with no control number. Compare the shades: No. 44 is redder than the faked No. 49 orange. No. 4 dark green measures $18^{1}/_2$ by about $22^{1}/_3$ mm instead of $18^{2}/_3$–19 by about $22^{1}/_2$ mm.

1878–82. Issue on cream-colored paper. Nos. 43 to 54. *No control number.* As in the preceding issue, these stamps are easily identified by the paper.

Rare shades: 1-lepton, very pale russet brown: 3M, 4U. Dark maroon on yellow paper: 4M, 5U. 5-lepton, very dark green: 2M. 20-lepton, slate blue-gray: 2M, 2U. 30-lepton, milky pale blue-gray 2M, 2U.

Varieties: 1-lepton, worn clichés: 10U. Cross-ruled background (sieve pattern): 20U. 20-lepton, aniline blue, transparent impression with ivory head: 2M, 4U. 30-lepton, cross-ruling background (sieve): 10U.

Ribbed paper, double prints, and fine impressions are found.

Pairs: 3U. No. 54: 4U.

Official forgeries: a few copies are known of a 20-lepton with only sixty pearls.

Forgeries: see the preceding issues.

II. Imperforate Stamps. Small Hermes Heads

Electrotyped plates of 300 stamps in six panes of fifty (10 x 5). Plate flaws: 10-lepton. white spot on the middle of the top tablet; left double-lined zero on left side, with no color between the two lines; 25-lepton, white spot in the inner, top right, angle; 50-lepton, no dividing frame line on top. Value: 4M, 10U.

1886–88. Belgian impression. Nos. 55 to 63. The Belgian issue (Marines) is characterized by fine lines in a very clear-cut design, without blobs in cheek shading and with finely traced ornaments in the upper corners (Figure *a)*. The initials of the engraver, A. DOMS, almost always appear, at bottom right.

Shades: there are no shade varieties except a 25-lepton pale milky blue: 5M, 8U. The other shades evidence only a slight gradation from the dark shades of the 1-lepton and 10-, 20- (bright), and 40-lepton stamps to the pale shade of the 50-lepton. This is true to such an extent that the forgeries described below may be

recognized immediately by their noncongruent shades, despite good design execution.

Varieties: 25- and 50-lepton and 1-drachma with background lines.

Pairs: 3M, 3U. Blocks of four: 6M, 10U.

Geneva forgeries (F:): well executed. There is no good reason why we should deal with their shades. which are slightly different from those of the Malines printings, or the yellowish paper, both of which may be changed from day to day. These counterfeits resemble both the Malines impression with its fine neck shading and the Athens impression with its upper corner ornaments (Figures *a* and *b*). The illustration also shows the forgeries' distinctive features. Notice, in particular. that the horizontal line underneath the shading below the "A" is hardly visible except in the originals of the 25-lepton of Malines and Athens.

1889–99. Athens impressions. Nos. 77 to 100. Shades are very numerous due to the staggered printings and the various kinds of paper.

Four important printings: 1. 1889–90. All values, except the 25-lepton blue and the 1-drachma, on thin,

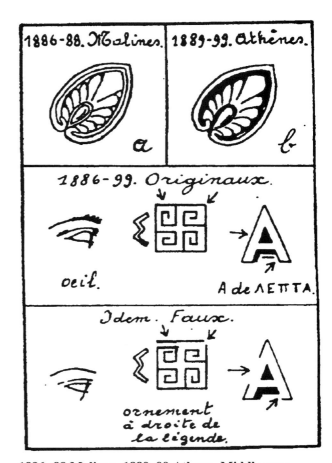

1886–88 Malines. 1889–99 Athens. Middle row: 1886–99 Originals. Eye. Bottom row: Forgeries. Ornament on the right of the legend.

yellowish gray paper. Bad impression, but clear-cut. The l-lepton black-brown, the 20-lepton aniline rose, the 25-lepton ultramarine, and the 40-lepton violet appear only in this printing. Examples on glossy paper are in demand. Pelure paper: 2U.

2. 1892–93. Thick, rough, yellowish white paper; bad impression. All values, except the 40-lepton violet.

3. 1894–95. Cleaned plates. Thin or thick paper, but very white and slightly glossed, which distinguishes it from the preceding slightly yellowish paper. All values except the 25-lepton blue or ultramarine and the 40-lepton violet. Very good impression, approximating the quality of that of Malines.

4. 1898–99. Same paper, but bad impression, which is occasionally quite defective; same exceptions.

Perforated stamps: all values were perf 13$^{1}/_{2}$ and 11$^{1}/_{2}$. The whole set, except the 40-lepton violet, is known perf 9. The 1-drachma was perf 13. Unfortunately, there are a great many forged (and clandestine) perforations.

Pairs and blocks: as above.

Varieties: the 1- and 5-lepton are found with double impression: rare.

Used postal forgeries: 20-lepton aniline (about twelve varieties); 25-lepton blue and violet; 40-lepton blue and l-drachma gray; imperforate or perf 11$^{1}/_{2}$. Value, 20-lepton: 10 francs. 1-drachma: 30 francs. Others: 20 francs. Dimensions easily identify these forgeries: 19 x 22$^{2}/_{3}$ mm instead of 18$^{1}/_{2}$ x 22 mm. They also are easily identifiable by the lithographic impression and by the very thinly printed inscriptions.

Forgeries: see the preceding issue.

Fantasy: the 25-lepton rosy red is a chemically produced color alteration.

III. Perforated Stamps

1896. Olympic Games. Nos. 101 to 112. *Varieties:* 60-lepton gray (first printing), gray instead of black: 2M, 2U. 2-lepton without engraver's signature, twice per sheet, on a vertical pair: 5M, 5U. 2-drachma, no perforations between stamps of a pair: rare. The 1-drachma with white spot (plate flaw) under the triangle on the right of the value tablet: 5M, 5U.

Forgeries: the 40- and 60-lepton, and the 2-, 5-, and 10-drachma were counterfeited in Genoa (I.), and given forged cancellations in Geneva (F.)...not to speak of other places!

These photolithographed counterfeits have little of the finesse of the originals. They are on grayish white paper, perf 14$^{1}/_{2}$ x 14 instead of 13$^{1}/_{2}$ x 14.

The background of the originals of the 40-lepton and 2- and 5-drachma is composed of small, well-designed squares, each of which has two small parallel lines. The background of the counterfeits is made of rings or blank ovals rather than squares, and a dot or a line rarely

appears in them. In the 5-drachma, the blurred "H" of MOUCHON resembles a "W."

The sky above the Roman chariot or the Parthenon in the originals of the 60-lepton and 10-drachma stamps is made of a very regularly arranged field of dots. In the counterfeits, these dots are missing in places. Perforations are arbitrary.

Forged Geneva cancellations: circles with date, one circle:

ΟΡΙΝΟΟΣ (Corinth) 2 ΝΟΕΜ Ⅎ 1896 M

ΑΘΗΝΑΙ (Athens) 22 ΑΠΡ 10 Π 6 1896 6

ΑΡΓΟΣ (Argos) 7 ΦΕΒΤ 1900.

With date, double circle: ΑΡΤΑ (Arta) 13 ΜΑΡΤ 99.

Fakes: the 5- and 10-drachma overprints (issue of 1901) were doctored in Athens to remove the overprint. A magnifying glass and watermark fluid will easily reveal the traces of this operation and of the subsequent repairing.

1900. Overprints. Nos. 113 to 145. *Interesting varieties:* No. 113, pale violet instead of violet: 50M, 50U. Nos. 114 and 199, 40-lepton, on No. 25 (cleaned plate): 8M, 8U. Nos. 117 and 122, 5-drachma, on No. 38 (stippled paper): 2M, 2U. No. 141 with error "Δ" instead of "A": 3M, 3U.

There are double overprints and letter errors. The 50-lepton on the 2 drachma is known to exist with double black and red overprint.

Forged overprints: very numerous. The lithographed forgeries easily recognized by the absence of "bite" typical of typographed stamps. Nos. 115 and 115a were given forged overprints by the Athens firm, Z....

Forgeries with forged overprints: Nos. 144 and 145. See preceding issue.

1901. Giovanni Bologna Hermes. Nos. 146 to 159. *Varieties:* the whole set, except the 2-, 3-, and 5-drachma, exists imperforate; the l-drachma is imperforate horizontally. There are clandestine reprints on average white paper, with 1- to 5-drachma stamps in brilliant shades.

Essays in black. The whole set is imperforate, with *no watermark.* Value: 5 francs each.

1906. Olympic Games. Nos. 165 to 178. The whole set, up to and including the 1-drachma, except 40-lepton, exists imperforate. The set: 100 francs.

Subsequent issues. These are adequately described in general catalogues.

1912. Well-executed forged overprints. The whole set in black or red lithographed overprint (no "bite"); make comparison, especially overprint varieties.

IV. Postage Due Stamps

The first two issues have many different perforations. Some of them are rare.

Shades: first issue, two sets 10½; green and black, and black and gray-green: 2M, 2U. Second issue, green and black, yellow-green and black.

Varieties: 1-drachma, with wide "M" (first issue), 1-, 2-, 40-, and 60-lepton, 1- and 2-drachma, with center inverted (second issue).

Numerous inscription varieties, misplaced centers, double perforations, etc.

Geneva forgeries (F.): first two issues. Rather grayish paper; perf 12½, first issue, and 12½ x 12½, second issue; yellow-green shade. Respective heights 23½ and 22½ mm, like the originals, but width 20 mm, whereas the originals are only 19¾ mm in the two issues. The Greek "Pi" of the center inscription is about 1 mm wide in original Nos. 1–12. In the forgeries, it narrows at the bottom where it is less than 1 mm wide. In Nos. 13–24, it is about 1⅕ mm (originals) and 1⅓ mm (forgeries). Other design defects are described in the illustration.

Note: Occasionally, there is a dot in the lower left corner square (forgery Nos. 1–12), but it is very faint.

Forged Geneva cancellations: (1) with date. single circle. Like those described for the 1896 issue with interchangeable dates. (2) With date, double circle:

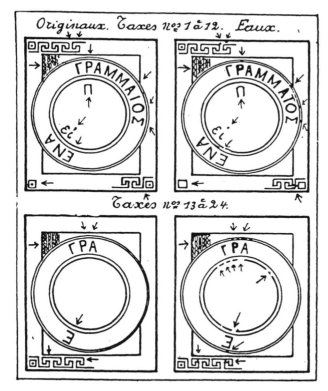

Postage Due Stamps. Nos. 1–12. Originals. Forgeries.

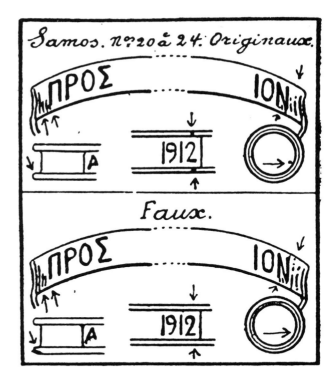

Samos. Nos. 2–24. Originals. Forgeries.

ΑΡΓΟΣΤΟΑΙΟΝ (Argostoli); 3 NOEM 77(110); the initial "A" is missing. (3) Lozenge of dots cancellation without numeral.

Fakes: a few underhanded operations transformed the 1- and 2-lepton into 1- and 2-drachma, and manufactured expensive stamp values of the next issue.

1902. Postage due stamps. Nos. 25 to 38, etc. Nos. 26–28, 31, and 35 are found imperforate. The whole set was reprinted on common white paper. The major values of 1912 were given forged overprints.

V. Occupied Countries

Most of the sets were overprinted and forged overprints abound. Comparative study is indispensable, for some sets are almost perfect.

Mytilene. The overprint was counterfeited on the entire set in Geneva. Its falseness is revealed by the second downstroke of the "N" letters, which is vertical and uniformly thick throughout its length.

Samos (1912). Bristol paper. Several sets were counterfeited. The best one is identified by the "O" of SAMOS, which is round instead of being rather square, and by the "E" of MEION, whose center bar placement is normal, whereas in the originals it is too low.

Hermes (1912). Nos. 4–8 were well counterfeited (likewise, Nos. 9–14 and 15–19 with forged overprints).

The shading lines in front of the eye are short and poorly executed; in the originals there are six wider, well-spaced lines. Moreover, sufficient proof is provided by measuring the stamp's width: it must be 21$^1/_2$ mm; the forgeries are 21 mm.

Monument (1913). Nos. 20–24 (also 25–36, with forged overprints). See the distinctive characteristics of these forgeries in the illustration.

Grenada

1860–65. 1-penny and 6-pence. Nos. 1 to 6.
Originals: engraved, 19$^1/_2$ x 22$^1/_2$ mm, first issue (1860). imperforate without watermark, thick paper; the other issues, perf 14–16 with watermark, thin paper.

Forgeries: medium paper, no watermark, perf 12 or 13 or imperforate; the ornamental squares in the corners are square or rectangular instead of forming a Maltese cross; the bottom of the diadem is composed of three rows of pearls instead of the inner row being composed of odd-shaped jewels; the foot of the "P" is as long as it loop, instead of being only one-third or one-fourth of it height.

Fakes: in the following issues, fiscal cancellations on the major values were cleaned, and the values then were ornamented with a forged cancellation. Comparison of cancellations is necessary. No. 1 is known to exist as an imperforate essay.

Griqualand

Overprints are plentiful, and as the overprint is composed of only one or two letters, people have taken their fill of them. Only one way to deal with that: compare, or have someone else compare, with a specialist's originals. Neither the best references in print nor a public sale are worth as much as that kind of guarantee. With respect to fiscal cancellations, see the preceding remark in Grenada in this connection (Geneva: Types I–V were copied by Fournier).

Guadeloupe

1884–94. Postage stamps. Nos. 1 to 54. *Original overprints:* impossible to enumerate here the different types of overprints and the multiplicity of varieties of the stamps of Guadeloupe. Specialization is necessary; amateurs will find the necessary details and illustrations in the work of Marconnet (1897, pp. 283–96) and in the fine work of de Vinck (1928, pp. 72–107). In the issue of 1891, the word GUADELOUPE is 16 mm long.

Forged overprints: very numerous. particularly in the 1891 issue, Nos. 14–26 were manufactured in Geneva (see French Colonies, 1881, "forgeries") with forged

overprints and *forged cancellations as* follows: round, with date, St LOUIS 2 JUIL 91 (and 92) GUADELOUPE; BASSE-TERRE 21 JUIN 92 GUADELOUPE; POINTE A PITRE 2^E 21 JANV 91 (and 92) GUADELOUPE; interchangeable figures. Fournier also counterfeited the overprints of 1888, with CENTIMES measuring 12$^2/_5$ mm, and of 1889, with CENTIMES measuring 10$^3/_4$ and 12 mm; interchangeable figures.

1892. Peace and Commerce type. Nos. 27 to 44. *Geneva forgeries:* see the counterfeits of this type under French Colonies.

Postage due stamps (1876). Nos. 1 and 2 with CENTIMES. *Originals:* plates of twenty typographical clichés (4 x 5), 13$^1/_2$ x 15$^2/_3$–$^3/_4$ mm. The same composition first was used for the 25-centime, then for the 40-centime, after figure changes. Afterwards. the word CENTIMES and the figures were removed and replaced by larger figures with "C" (40-centime, on white; 12- and 30-centime, Nos. 3–5).

The illustration gives information on the principal typical plate defects, which are restricted, however, to those found in the continuation of the various values.

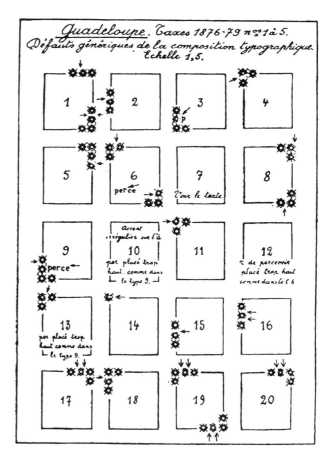

Guadeloupe. Postage due stamps. 1876–79. Nos. 1–5. Typical defects of typographical composition. Scale: $^1/_5$.

25-centime on yellowish paper, 40-centime on blue; good, clear-cut typography; printing type characters are well aligned; value figures are $2^{1}/_{2}$ mm high x 2 mm wide with a $^{1}/_{2}$ mm space between. Lettering is 1 mm high. "Centimes" is about $8^{1}/_{4}$ mm wide. The grave accent on the "a" is oblique and forms a triangle whose base is above the letter; the "a" is $^{1}/_{4}$ mm from "centimes" and "percevoir."

Forgeries: 1. Geneva. They do not look like any original type. 25-centime, allowable measurements; figures, 3 mm high by $21^{1}/_{4}$ mm wide; blurred impression on white paper; rounded scallops in the frame; 40-centime, $13^{3}/_{4}$ x about 16 mm; sharper impression; frame without any of the defects shown in the original types; figure "4," same height as those of the 25-centime forgery; the "0" is $3^{1}/_{4}$ mm high by $2^{1}/_{4}$ mm wide. The "m" of "centimes" frequently is closed at the bottom; the "a" is closed. White or yellowish paper for the 25-centime, which was printed in blocks with that value indication, as well as the 40-centime on white and the 30-centime without "C." The 40- and 15-centime were printed together on blue paper in blocks of two values. The types in these blocks from a single forged cliché per value thus are always alike in each value (see illustration).

2. *So-called reprints:* see the following issue.

3. Other counterfeits are so fantastic that they do not merit description.

4. A few photoengraved counterfeits which are recognizable by the blurred, defective printing, the excessively dark imprint, and by the arbitrary paper and measurements. Note: The 25-centime with large figures is a fantasy.

1877?–79. With "C." Nos. 3 to 5. *Originals:* same composition as Nos. 1 and 2, but the value figures are larger and are followed by "C," replacing "centimes." 40-centime, on yellowish white paper; 15-centime, on bright and light blue; 30-centime, on thick, yellowish white and on thin white. Same measurements as previously for the stamp and lettering. Value figures are $4^{5}/_{6}$ mm high by $2^{1}/_{3}$ mm wide, with a space of $^{1}/_{2}$ mm, except in the 15-centime ($1^{1}/_{2}$ mm). The "C" is larger than the other letters (see the illustration).

Forgeries: 1. Geneva. Allowable dimensions; white paper; figures $4^{3}/_{4}$ mm high; no type like the twenty original types; various frame defects; letter "C" is $2^{1}/_{2}$ mm high. The other letters are only about $^{3}/_{4}$ mm high; the "a" usually is closed and the accent is more or less round and is touching the letter. The 30-centime is found without "C" or a period with 1 mm space between the figures. The forged cancellations are the same as on the overprinted stamps of 1881, but they conceal the millesime.

2. Other forgeries. Poorly executed; they easily may be identified by the information we have just given on the originals. A 40-centime closely resembles the Geneva forgeries (value figures, the same height, and the following "C," too), but the "4" is separated from the "0" by $1^{2}/_{5}$ mm and from the "C" by about 1 mm; the "a" is executed better and the accent is oblique without touching the letter; lettering is the same height as in the Geneva forgeries, but "percevoir" is only 7 mm wide instead of about 9 mm. Faultless frame. It is quite possible that Fournier simply copied this forgery to fulfill his production quota.

3. *So-called reprints:* two compositions of eight clichés (4 x 2) made for the 25-centime, No. 1, and the 40-centime, No. 3, executed probably with the original typographical characters for the frame, figures, and the lettering, but none of the types corresponds to the previously described original types, and the "a" letters, although their measurements are good, frequently are provided with an almost vertical accent that is round or oval in form. The following defects will enable one to identify these counterfeits:

a. 25-centime composition. The "4" and "8" types are too low in relation to the others; Type I, figure "2" is too wide ($2^{1}/_{2}$ mm instead of about 2 mm); Type II, the frame rosettes on the right and left of the top figure "25" are broken at bottom; in Type III, the same rosettes are blunted on top and the rosette on the left of the "p" of "percevoir" is pruned on the left of that letter; Type IV, the rosette in the upper left corner is half clipped at bottom; figure "2" is slanted to the right; Type V, figure "5" is slanted to the left; Type VI, the "c" of "centimes" is touching the rosette; the rosette on the right of the "R" is blunted on that side; Type VII, "5" is slanted slightly to the left; Type VIII, figure "5" is evidently too thin; the rosette on the left of "percevoir" was moved $^{1}/_{4}$ mm to the right, and the rosette on the right of "percevoir" was clipped in its southeastern part.

Top: Guadeloupe. 1876. Postage due stamps, with "centimes." Nos. 1 and 2. Originals. Forgeries. Bottom: 1878?–79. Postage due stamps, with "C." Nos. 3–5.

b. 40-centime composition. The "3" and "7" types are clearly higher than the others. Type I, the upper right corner rosette is blunted on the left, and the one underneath it is blunted top and bottom; Type II, figure "40" definitely was moved to the left; the "a" is under the blank part of the "0"; the lower right corner rosette is broken on top; Type III, upper left corner rosette was ruined (poor execution), and its neighbor on the right is blunted on the left; Type IV, no letter "a"; rosettes are placed on the right above the "C," and on the left of the horizontal bar of the "4," and their tops are damaged; Type VI, the syllable "voir" (of "percevoir") is slanted upward to the right as in Type II; the upper left corner rosette is spread out to the right, and the one underneath it is narrowed at the top; Type VII, the value figures are moved to the left, but less than in Type II; the lower right corner rosette is $^{1}/_{4}$ mm too low; Type VIII, the "0" is somewhat wider than in the other types, its blank interior evidently being too wide, thus emphasizing the defect; the rosette on the right of "percevoir" does not have any frame divider in its southwestern part. The paper is thinner and whiter than in the originals.

1884. Nos. 6 to 12. There are seven different types for each value, except for the 35-centime. The 50-centime blue-green exists only in Type I. For details, see the works of Marconnet and de Vinck.

1903. Overprinted stamps, Nos. 13 and 14. The works of Marconnet and of de Vinck are put to good use by specialists here. The forged *overprints* are identified easily.

Guam

1899. Nos. 1 to 11, and postage due stamp No. 1. *Forged overprints* from various sources, well executed at times; among them one finds a set which was manufactured in Geneva by applying a forged overprint on canceled U.S. stamps. Comparison is necessary.

Guanacasta

See Costa Rica.

Guatemala

1871. Nos. 1 to 4. *Originals:* engraved, $18^{1}/_{2}$ x $22^{1}/_{2}$ mm, perf 14 x $13^{1}/_{2}$; a sun with thirty-six noncolored rays; at the top of the escutcheon, six vertical blank bars and an embryonic bar, top left.

Forgeries: three poorly lithographed sets, perf 13: (a) thirty-one rays and seven complete bars; (b) thirty-four rays and five bars plus two parts of bars on the right and left; (c) about thirty-three rays and five complete bars plus an almost complete bar on the left.

1872. 4-real and 1-peso. Nos. 5 and 6. The *originals* are lithographed, $18^{1}/_{2}$ x $22^{1}/_{2}$ mm, perf 12

Forgeries: good-looking lithographed forgeries, but no shading on the page in the middle of the shield, a bird with a duck's head, perf $11^{1}/_{2}$, poor quality yellowish paper. Most amusing is the fact that this forgery has "facsimile" in lowercase white characters in the shaded background under the shield (use of magnifying glass is necessary).

1875. $^{1}/_{2}$- to 2-real. Nos. 7 to 10. *Originals:* engraved, 16 x 26 mm, perf 12 or imperforate, the "A" letters of the inscriptions have an almost imperceptible median bar (use magnifying glass).

Geneva forgeries: lithographed, perf 13, the "A" letters have no horizontal bar, and the white of the eye is not shaded.

1878–81. Indian woman's portrait. Nos. 11 to 14. *Originals:* typographed, perf $13^{1}/_{2}$, occasionally there are watermark fragments of the trademark of LACROIX FRERES; twelve quite visible pearls in the necklace; the bird's eyes are quite visible.

No *reprints.*

There are imperforate *printer's waste stamps,* stamps printed front and back, etc.

Forgeries: lithographed, perf $12^{1}/_{2}$ or 13, birds without eyes, fourteen completely visible pearls in the necklace; the two feathers or leaves on the head, which are pointing toward "O" and "A," are touching the inner oval instead of the outer one.

1881. Overprints in centavos. Comparison is indispensable, since these overprints were counterfeited recklessly.

1881. Dual color stamps. 1- to 20-centavo. Nos. 22–26. *Originals:* expertly engraved by the American Banknote Company of New York; perf 12.

Forgeries: very poorly lithographed; arbitrary shades; usually imperforate; the bird has an owl's head; etc.

1887–94. Engraved. Perf 12. Nos. 44–51. The stamps are easily distinguishable from the lithographed stamps of 1886; the four upper horizontal shading lines above the locomotive evidently are printed more heavily than the following ones; all details of the bird's plumage, especially on its head, are quite visible (use magnifying glass).

Official stamps (1902). Nos. 1 to 5. The whole typographed set was forged childishly: letters irregularly spaced; in FRANQUEO the "R" frequently is touching the "A"; the dot after GUATEMALA often is too close to the final "A," etc. Perf 11½ instead of 12.

Other official stamps. Overprinted stamps of 1924, etc. The overprints were forged out of all proportion. Scott does not classify them.

Haiti

1881. Liberty type. Nos. 1 to 6. *Originals:* 18 by about 21¾ mm; very regular inscriptions; the cut of the neck frequently is indicated by a white line above the escutcheon bearing the value which is 1½–2 mm long.

Forgeries: first set (Geneva), 22 mm high; rather crude lithographed impression; thick outer frame; ¼ mm instead of about ⅛ mm; the color circle is broken on top and between letters "I" and "Q" of REPUBLIQUE; the inner circle is broken under "D," under the apostrophe, and under the right downstroke of the "A" in D'HAITI; there are numerous incorrect lines in the design; see especially the cheek shading in the illustration. This set is canceled frequently with a double circle (21 mm) postmark with date: CAP HAITIEN 13 SEPT 82 HAITI. Second set, 18¼ x 22 mm, much better appearance than the first set; the terminal curl of the "R" of REPUBLIQUE evidently is too oblique; the "Q" of the same word is touching the color circle above it; the curved ornament, on the left of the escutcheon, is broken near its middle; one finds *toujours* in the bottom of the value escutcheon, and, as shown in the illustration, two rather thick lines, whereas

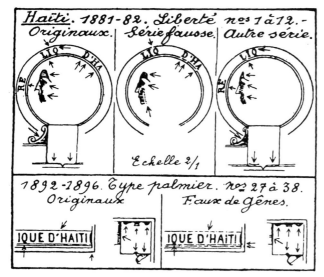

Top: Haiti. 1881-82. Liberty. Nos. 1–12. Originals. Forged set. Another set. Scale: 2/1. Bottom: 1892–96. Palm tree type. Nos. 27–38. Originals. Genoa forgeries.

in the originals, depending on type, there is only a fine hairline, or else nothing at all, in that place; defects in the facial shadows (see especially the forehead shape). These two sets almost always are found imperforate, the second one with wide margins.

1882. Same type. Perforated. *Forgeries:* see first issue.

Used postal forgeries: in circulation in Cap-Haitien in 1882; perf 14 and 15¾–16 (original perf 13 and 13 x 13½); comparison of facial features will identify them. Buy only on cover. Value: 25–100 francs or a value proportional to rarity.

1892–96. Palm tree with drooping branches. Nos. 27 to 38. *Originals:* width, 19½–¾ mm; thick paper, about 90 microns; slightly yellowish; perf 13, well engraved.

Forgeries of recent manufacture (Genoa): two issues, inexpertly photolithographed; too wide; imperforate or perf 11; thin paper, about 50 microns; arbitrary shades; numerous defects in the design (see illustration); the serif of the "Q" is touching the line above the letter. A quick comparison with an original will eliminate these ludicrous creations.

1898. "R.H." watermark. Nos. 39 to 44. The 1-, 3-, 7-, and 20-centime are speculative stamps. Buy on cover only.

1902. Overprinted stamps. Nos. 62 to 76. Parisian, Genevan, and other forged *overprints.* Comparison is necessary. Forged Geneva postmark as in the first issue, sometimes with date changed, 1 …JUIN 02.

1904. Holy Year stamps. Nos. 77 to 83. *Forgeries:* the whole set was counterfeited by P. in Lausanne; allowable perforation; bad photolithography; comparison of the two women is necessary; see also the following issue.

1904. Same. External postal service. Nos. 84 to 89. *Originals:* perf 13½, 14; slightly grayish paper; design details are drawn quite sharply, especially the cannon and their gun carriages The 1-centime has PARIS as an inscription under the right value figure; the other values have the "1903" millesime.

Forgeries (or clandestine reprints): very white paper, perf 13, the place name under the left figure is incomplete, and under the right figure, the "0" of 1903 is too small.

Same set with blue overprint. Nos. 84 to 89a. *Forged overprints,* especially Geneva, the whole set forged in blue or red on originals or on reprints. Comparison is necessary. Forged Geneva cancellation as in the preceding issue.

Subsequent issues with overprints. A few forged overprints. Comparison would be useful.

Hawaii

1851–52. Nos. 1 to 4. *Originals:* typographed, 19½ x 28 mm, on bluish wove pelure paper. Two types for each value: Type I, the vertical downstroke of the "P" of POSTAGE, if extended, would pass between the two verticals of the "H" of HAWAIIAN; Type II, the vertical line of the "P" is just under the left vertical of the "H." The outer frame has one or two corners in which the lines do not meet.

Forgeries: lithographed on medium white paper; always? Type II; the four frame lines meet; the ornamental designs in the corners do not resemble those of the originals (see the illustration for one of the best counterfeits); the dots over the "I" letters of HAWAIIAN are touching the inner frame (in the genuine stamps, they are ½ mm away from the frame).

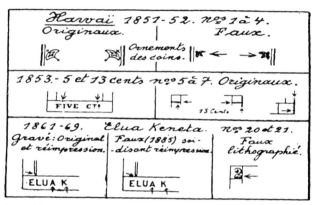

Top: Hawaii. 1851–52. Nos. 1–4. Originals. Forgeries. Corner ornaments. Middle: 1853. 5- and 13-cent. Nos. 5–7. Originals. Bottom: 1861–69. Elua Keneta. Nos. 20 and 21. Engraved: original and reprint. Forgery (1885): so-called "reprint." Lithographed forgery.

1853. Portrait. Nos. 5 to 7. *Originals:* recess print engraved on thick (80 microns), yellowish, wove paper, or very thick paper (110 microns). No. 7, on azure-tinted paper of the least possible thickness; 5-cent, 19 mm wide; 13-cent, 18¾ mm; both 24½ mm high. The person's dolman or tunic has six buttons on each side; there are five lines in the collar. In the 5-cent, one notices two color dots attached to the portrait's lower frame, one of them between "F" and "I," the other above the small "s" (see illustration). There also are two small color dots on the left of figure "5" on the right which are attached to the line, and near the top and bottom of the figure. In the 13-cent, the right frame is made up of two adjacent lines, and the lines under the top "13" figures are also double (use magnifying glass, see illustration). The base of figure "3," top left, is

flattened slightly; the dot after "Cts," in the left tablet, is touching the figure framework; the one after "Cts" in the lower right corner is thin and is touching the right frame.

The so-called *reprints* are really forgeries which were printed from newly engraved plates in 1889; width of the two values, 19¼ mm; thick paper; shades are too pale; sometimes they bear the word REPRINT. In the 5-cent, the protuberances of the portrait's lower frame are missing; moreover, they are not found in any of the other forgeries; the two dots on the left of the right-hand "5" frequently are missing, or else they are almost imperceptible. In the 13-cent, the right frame has a single line; the lines under the top "13" figure are indeed double but are so close together that they appear to form a single line. The base of the top left figure "3" is rounded; under this figure, the dot after "Cts" is not touching the line; no dot after the "Cts," bottom right.

Forgeries: all of them are lithographed, making for easy identification. There are about a half-dozen counterfeits of each value. The following are good indications for spotting them: 5-cent, on thin bluish paper, seven indistinct buttons on the right; on thick white paper, ten buttons on the left; pale blue, stippled, seven buttons on the left and three on the right; pale blue on thin paper, only three lines on the left side of the collar; blue on white paper, the two "I" letters of HAWAIIAN form an "N," and there is only one dot over the letters; on thick white paper, no buttons at all on the right; blue on white and black (!) on blue, full portrait background. 13-cent, defects of the same kind, with the following: five buttons on the left and no dot after the "Cts" in the left tablet; no dot after the lower right corner "Cts"; in the left tablet, one finds HAWAИIAN(!) and a fantastic color error creation in blue. These forgeries' paper often is laid or stippled.

1859–67. Figures. Nos. 8 to 15. *Originals:* each value has ten typographed types; 20 by about 26 mm; medium blue-gray paper; with a few rare exceptions, the outer or inner frames do not touch in one or two of the corners; there is a dot after POSTAGE and LETA and a larger dot after CENT or CENTS. The paper is thin. This, with the shade, color, impression, and paper indications given in the general catalogues, is adequate for tracking down all the *forgeries*. Among the latter, the following defects may be noted: frame lines always joined; one, two, or three dots missing; letter "H" of HAWAIIAN has no median bar or else the word is printed HAWANAN; outer frame lines are spaced 1½–2 mm apart; the base of figure "2" is made of a straight line; paper is too thick. In a good set in which the frame lines do not meet, the bar of the "t" of "Cents" sticks out on both sides of the vertical downstroke, instead of slightly to the right, and the curve at the foot of the letter is quite pronounced instead of curving slightly. All these forgeries are lithographed except one recess print engraved set of the values, in which the frame lines consistently meet.

1864–68. INTER-ISLAND on the left. Nos. 16 to 18; and 1864–67, 5-cent blue, No. 19. *Originals:* same comment as previously regarding the frames; the 5-cent is found in two compositions of ten types: (1) with INTER-ISLAND on the left; (2) with HAWAIIAN POSTAGE on both sides. The four values do not have dots after the inscriptions or after the value figure.

Forgeries: lithographed; same comments as above; the 5-cent is found typographed, in ultramarine, with the southeast corner only being closed. The 5-cent was counterfeited in Geneva with the two left corners open; 20 x 25½ mm.

1861–69. ELUA KENEIA. Nos. 20 and 21. *Originals:* 1861: lithographed, horizontally or vertically laid white paper; jumbled imprint; no reprints; 1869: recess print engraved; unissued; thin, wove, yellowish paper; 19⅛ x about 24¾ mm; see the distinguishing features in the illustration.

Reprints of the engraved stamp (1889): same distinctive characteristics as the original, but the external line on the right of the "2" figures is visible, whereas it is scarcely perceptible in the lithographed or engraved originals; the floral ornamentation is retouched (it is now more complete); thick paper; 19¼ mm wide; inscription CANCELLED, SPECIMEN, or REPRINT under the beard.

Forgeries of 1885 (so-called *reprints*): engraved; the bar of the "A" of KENETA is longer (see the illustration also for the vertical line on the right of the left tablet); the curved line on the right of the "2" figures is more complete and so goes up higher than in the reprint; 19¼ x 24½ mm.

Another *forgery* of the engraved stamp was lithographed; the left figure "2," instead of being in the middle of the rectangle, is moved markedly to the right (see illustration); no dot after KENETA; the dot after LETA is ¼ mm away from the vertical line limiting the upper tablet on the right instead of ⅗ mm.

1864–71. Perf 12. Nos. 22 to 29. *Originals:* recess print engraved; the value figure inscription tablet background is composed of quite visible lines.

Forgeries: crude, early lithographed creations; dividing frame line traces; bad perforation or perf 13; figures set on unbroken or almost unbroken background.

Heligoland

Sheets of fifty stamps (10 x 5).
Shades: the originals shades are open so little different from certain reprints that the gradual

establishment of a reference file of these stamps is indispensable. In most cases, such a file will help one make a quick decision.

Chignon curl and neck point: three different types, with Type III only in the 1-schilling perforated stamp. In Type I, the portrait is ½ mm higher than in Type II. See the illustration.

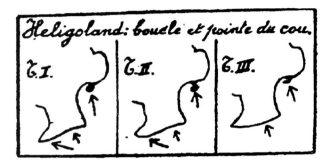

Heligoland: curl and neck point.

Cancellations: the usual cancellation is circular, with date, HELGOLAND top and bottom, and two concentric circle arcs (in two slightly different types).

In addition, one finds postmarks that were mistakenly applied on arrival: (1) in segments with the inscription AUS HELGOLAND. (2) Rectangular postmark with inscription on two lines, AUS HELGOLAND USER CUXHAVEN.

A straight-line HELGOLAND postmark is rare, as are all foreign cancellations.

Pairs: 3U. On cover: 2U. First three issues, 5-mark: 3U.

1867 (April 11). Rouletted stamps. Nos. 1 to 4.
Printing figures: ½-schilling (Type I): 20,000. Type II: 10,000. 1-schilling: 40,000. 2-schilling: 200,000. 6-schilling: 100,000. A single printing was made of each value. Shades are palpably similar in each printing.

Paper: thin and transparent, especially in No. 3.
Originals: Type I: ½-, 1-, 2-, and 6-schilling. The first two were printed three times, which caused deviation in the oval and inner frame placement. The last two and the ½-schilling, Type II (1868), were printed twice (inner frame and oval intact), and so there was no oval center deviation. The ½-schilling, Type II, which is very difficult to distinguish from the reprint, requires comparison.

Shades: the five printings, including the ½-schilling, Type II, have a characteristic slightly carmine-tinted (lilac) rose shade; the green shades are dark green for the ½- and 1-schilling, less dark blue-green for the ½-schilling, Type II; yellow-green for the 2-schilling and slightly blue-tinted green for the 6-schilling.

Reprints: Berlin, 1875: ½-schilling dark green and rose. 1-schilling rather bright red and yellow-green, both Type II. Berlin, 1879: four stamp values, imperforate (rare), rouletted, and 2- and 6-schilling perf 13½ x 14¼.

Shades: ½-schilling dark yellow-green and rose; 1-schilling bright red and yellow-green; 2-schilling slightly vermilion-tinted rose and off-olive-green; 6-schilling, a grayer green than the original and rose without the purplish carmine point of the originals.

Forgeries: there are a few poorly executed early forgeries, which usually are imperforate. An examination of the inner corner ornaments (and of the fraction bars of the ½-schilling) will expose the forgery. The same is true for a few imperforate, perforated, or rouletted modern forgeries. Shade comparison will always corroborate one's judgment.

1869–74. Perforated stamps. Nos. 5 to 9. *Papers:* until 1873, the ½- and 1-schilling were printed on wove paper, but beginning in June 1873, all values were printed on a thick paper, cross-ruled with fine wire threads, which is found only in the original stamps. Stamps on this paper are therefore reliable references.

Printing figures: ½-schilling (1873): 65,000 on cross-ruled paper, and, end of 1874, 100,000 on ordinary paper (unissued). ¼-schilling, error, No. 5a (1873), 25,000. ½-schilling, 100,000 (1869–72) in six printings on ordinary paper, and 40,000 (1873) on cross-ruled paper. ¾-schilling (1873), 50,000. 1-schilling (1871–72), 30,000 on ordinary paper in two printings, and 30,000 on cross-ruled paper (1873). 1½-schilling (1873), 50,000 on cross-ruled paper.

Originals: ¼-schilling, Type I, first printing (rare), bright carmine, with lily of the valley green center; second printing, dull rose and blue-green, rose and olive-green (1874 printing). ¼-schilling, error (Type I) yellow-green, with deep carmine center. ½-schilling (Type II), stamp shades on ordinary paper are rather different. Light blue-green, with corners in dark carmine in the first two printings, then, dull dark green and rose; light yellow-green and dark rose, finally, off-olive-green and carmine. The light yellow green (rare) has little white specks in the inner corners, like the preceding printing. The last printings are on cross-ruled paper; lily of the valley green, with dark carmine corners; pale blue green, with dark carmine corners. ¾-schilling (Type I), light yellow green and dark rose. 1-schilling (Type II), dark rose, green corners with little white specks; rose, with bright pale green corners (rare), and dark rose, with pale green corners on cross-ruled paper (1873). 1½-schilling (Type I) dull yellow-green or bright green with carmine center.

Reprints: ordinary paper. ¼-schilling (1875), Type II, bright rose, olive-green; (1884), lilac rose, olive-green. ¼-schilling, error (1875), Type II, dark off-olive-green and red-rose; (1884), dark green and dark lilac-rose. ½-schilling (1875), Type II, dark green with

rose corners; (1879), see first issue. ¾-schilling (1879), Type II, green and red; (1884), dark green and dark rose. 1-schilling (1875), red and yellow-green; (1879), see first issue; (1884), carmine, yellow-green corners. 1½-schilling (1875), Type II, green and dark rose; (1879), Types II and III, dark green and carmine-rose; (1884), dark green, with dark lilac-rose oval.

There is ample justification for adding to the above the set of Leipzig reprints (1888) that easily is identified by the pin perforation and the noncongruent shades, as well as a bright red, green-gray, or dark green-gray. Nos. 1–4 were also reprinted in those shades and rouletted. The 6-schilling, however, has a rose-colored center.

The Hamburg reprints, perf 14 x 14, as well as Nos. 1–4 rouletted and the ½- and 1-schilling imperforates were printed between 1891 and 1895 in decidedly arbitrary shades which are obvious at first sight. The impression is often defective, and the embossing of the head is insufficient. Ordinary wove or thick paper. It should be noted that the ¼-schilling stamps of 1891 have a Type I head and those of 1895, Type II.

All varieties that have not been mentioned are stamps from printer's waste.

Forgeries: there are a few not-so-formidable early forgeries and some Geneva forgeries of the 1-schilling, Type I.

Forged cancellations: very numerous. Expertizing is necessary.

1875. Values in pfennig. Nos. 10 to 15. *Printing figures:* 1-pfennig: 300,000. 2-pfennig: 200,000. 5-pfennig: 120,000 in three printings. 10-pfennig: 490,000 in six printings. 25-pfennig: 100,000. 50-pfennig: 100,000 in two printings.

Plate flaw: the 50-pfennig is known with a dot after "6."

Originals: perf 13½ x 14½. 1-pfennig dark red and dark green; 2-pfennig green or dark green and dark carmine-tinted red. The reprints of the other values are much rarer than the originals.

Reprints: perf 14 x 14. 1-pfennig (1882), light red, with vermilion point, dark green center; (1883), a little brighter red than the original and dark green; (1888), Leipzig, bright red and dark green; (1891), Hamburg, imperforate.

2-pfennig (1883), pale yellow-green and red; (1888), Leipzig, more or less dark green-gray and bright red.

The 5-, 10-, 25-, and 50-pfennig, as well as the 20-pfennig of the following issue, were reprinted in 1890. Rare, four sheets of fifty stamps of each value. Perforations like the originals. Shades differ slightly. The 5-pfennig is very difficult to identify. The 25-pfennig, with its excessively dark carmine-tinted rose, is easy.

Forged cancellations: very numerous. They are especially frequent in the reprints. Expertizing is necessary.

1876. Coat of arms. Nos. 16 and 17. *Printing figures:* 3-pfennig: 80,000. 20-pfennig: 420,000.

Originals: perf 13 $\frac{1}{2}$ x 14 $\frac{1}{2}$.

3-pfennig dark green and red, and yellow, first printing; yellow-green, bright red and apricot, second printing. Both common.

20-pfennig, first printing, dark carmine-tinted (purplish) rose, dark green, and yellow, No. 16a, rare; second printing, bright red, dark green, orange-brown, also rare. The following printings are more common: rose, green-black, and yellow; bright aniline red, gray-green, and straw yellow; flesh red or brick red, gray-green and straw yellow (fifth, sixth, and seventh printings), finally, a brownish red tint, light green, and canary yellow.

Reprints: perf 14 x 14. 3-pfennig (1880), Berlin, green, bright red, and apricot; (1885), gray-green, brick red, and straw yellow.

20-pfennig (1890): rare. See the preceding issue.

1879: 5-mark. Nos. 18 and 19. *Printing figures:* 1-mark: 15,000 in two printings. 5-mark: 10,000.

Originals: 1-mark green and pale vermilion-tinted red; dark green and carmine; dark green and bright carmine (unissued). 10-mark green and pale vermilion-tinted red.

The stamps perf 11 $\frac{1}{2}$ are nothing more than proofs — which is proved by the fact that the "H" of HELGOLAND was corrected before definitive printing of the 1-mark. In the 5-mark original, the letter is closed on top.

Reprint: very rare; twenty-five copies in all (1890). Good perforation: 13 $\frac{1}{2}$ x 14 $\frac{1}{2}$. The green shades are too light.

Honduras

1865. Black on color. Nos. 1 and 2. *Originals:* lithographed on thin paper, gray-blue and rose; 17 $\frac{3}{5}$ x 18 $\frac{1}{4}$–$\frac{1}{2}$, mm; the oval is touching the end shade lines, top and bottom; the lowest line is split in two under the left figure "2" (use magnifying glass); there is no dot after REALES or after LIBERTAD; the left side of the pyramid is twice as thick as the right side; in the oval, there are two well-formed five-pointed stars; the pyramid's apex barely is touching the bottom of the timer inscription between letters "N" and "Y.

Forgeries: a half-dozen lithographed sets with arbitrary shades in which the lowest horizontal hatch line is not split in two on the left. They have one or several of the following defects: the oval does not touch

the end shade lines; the pyramid's apex is too near the "N" or the "Y" or is touching it; UNION is printed ONION; there is a dot after REALES; no stars; the Phrygian bonnet is replaced by a triangle; the outer oval is too wide, less than $\frac{1}{2}$ mm on the left and less than $\frac{2}{3}$ mm on the right; the waves under the triangle are made of horizontal lines; the inscription lettering is not comparable. These counterfeits usually are canceled or overprinted. There are many forged cancellations on originals.

1877. Overprinted stamps. Nos. 3 to 13. Ascertain first whether previously described forgeries are involved. Next, make a comparative check of the overprint or have it expertized. MEDIO REAL, UN REAL, and DOS REALES overprints were counterfeited in Geneva and applied on original stamps of 1865.

1896. Portrait. Perf 11 $\frac{1}{2}$. Nos. 76 to 83. *Originals:* lithographed on slightly transparent, thin paper.

Reprints on thick, nontransparent paper; usually obligingly handstamped in sheets with a HONDURAS postmark between two bars.

Forgeries: Paris or Genoa? Perf 11; in the upper left rosette, the "U" is larger than the other two letters; the ear is completely blank, and the forehead is frequently like that, too. Chalky paper.

1898. Locomotive. Nos. 84 to 91. Originals: perf 11 $\frac{1}{2}$; lithographed.

Geneva forgeries: the tablet frame and the right outer frame are touching on the right of the lower loop of the "S" of HONDURAS; on the right of CORREOS, the upper frame is touching the first shade line under it; the landscape background and the locomotive's smoke are made of dots and are confused; visible clouds (originals apparently have no clouds).

Paris or Genoa forgeries: perf 11; chalky paper; photolithographed.

1913, 1913–14, 1919, and 1925. Various overprints. Comparison of the overprints is indispensable.

Official stamps (1898). Nos. 23 to 27. The Geneva forgeries (see "1898" previously) received the forged overprint, OFICIAL. and a forged postmark: AD$^\pi$ DE CORREOS TEGUCICALPA 25 May, in blue.

Same. 1911 and 1916. Overprinted stamps. Nos. 28 to 42. Comparison of overprints is indispensable.

Hong Kong

1862. Perf 14. Nos. 1 to 8. *Originals:* typographed; background of ninety horizontal shade lines which do not touch the lateral inner frames; since there is no contour line, where these lines stop forms a "contour" for the forehead, nose, and front of the neck; the neck's point rests on the fourth shade line.

Forgeries: (a) Geneva set; bad lithography; seventy-three shade lines touching the lateral frames; the neck point rests on the third shade line; perf 12½; no shading on the cheek below the eye; the chignon has two large color spots inside it, surrounded with white, and the whole thing, seen from a distance, seems to form a quite visible "8" (the 18- and 48-cent stamps are somewhat more successful here); no watermark; forged cancellation, B 62. (b) Similar set with the same characteristics (even the same number of shading lines; the neck point rests on the third line; no shading under the eye), but the shading, although too close to the frame, does not touch them; the forehead, nose, chin, and neck are defined by a full, unbroken line; the chignon is better drawn than in the preceding set; no watermark; perf 12. (c) Genoa set; engraved; seventy-seven fine shade lines which do not touch the inner frames; the neck point rests on the second line; there is practically no cheek shading under the eye; in certain values, the whole front part of the face and neck is defined by a thin line; in others, it is defined as in the originals by horizontal shading. From a distance, the portrait seems to have an ear, but if a magnifying glass is used at close range, it disappears. No watermark or with forged embossed watermark; perf 13½ x 12½.

1863–74. Same type. Watermarked "CC" Nos. 8 to 21. *Forgeries:* a few values were forged as above (sets a and b); no watermark.

1876–80. Overprinted stamps. Nos. 22 to 28. *Forged overprints* on canceled originals; comparison is necessary. Forged overprints also on forgeries. especially the four overprints of the 5-, 10-, 16-, and 28-cent stamps in Geneva.

1885–90. Overprinted stamps. Nos. 46–56. *Forged overprints:* same as above; the 7-, 20-cent, and $1 stamps were counterfeited in Geneva, and overprints were applied on canceled originals and on forgeries.

1891. Jubilee. No. 57. Overprint comparison is necessary; it was counterfeited in Geneva and applied upright or inverted on canceled originals. Check the cancellation millesime.

1903, 1904–9. Portrait of King Edward. Nos. 71 to 76 and 88 to 94. *Forgeries:* the best way to identify the counterfeits is to compare the facial features with a common original (1- to 10-cent).

There *was faking* of the major values of these issues and of the following ones by replacing fiscal obliterations with forged ones.

Hungary

Select: the stamps must be well centered. This is a rare quality in the first two Hungarian issues, and the stamps in which there is no encroachment of the perforations into the design are worth double the prices quoted in catalogues.

Cancellations: the usual postmark on the first issues is a single circle with date, with the day and month separated by a short horizontal bar. The year often is indicated ("71," "72," "73," etc.).

Some of the postmarks have the name of the town in Hungarian, followed by the name in German. There are Austrian cancellations with or without ornaments at the bottom.

The oval, rectangular, or square postmarks with corners trimmed, with the same data, are less common.

The circular German-type postmark, with two horizontal bars and vertical shading lines, is not common on the second issue. It is common, however, on the third.

All other postmarks are rare, especially those of the Levant, steamers, military posts, etc., as well as postmarks in color. (See Austria.)

1871 (May). Lithographed stamps. Nos. 1 to 6. This set is recognized by the impression, the absence of indention on the back of the stamp, and by the shades, which are perceptibly different from the recess-printed engravings. The reader will notice that the beard seems more bushy, so much so that the chin looks like a small white spot that usually is devoid of the oblique shade lines seen in the engraved stamps. The distinctive marks (transfer plate flaws) are useful; we do not yet have enough information on them.

Shades: 2-krone, more or less dull ochre-orange; yellow: 4M, 3U. 3-krone, yellow-green or dark yellow-green. 5-krone rose; red: 50M, 50U; brick red: 2M, 2U. 10-krone, from pale blue to dark blue in a number of varieties — milky blue, ultramarine blue, etc.: same prices. 15-krone brown; light brown, rare, mint: 50U. 25-krone rose-lilac, lilac, bright violet, rare, mint: 25U.

Paper: white. semithick (70–80 microns). Colorless, thin gum.

Varieties: Nos. 2 and 5, printed on both sides: extremely rare. There are defective impressions. The imperforates (good impression) are essays.

Pairs: 5-krone: 4U; blocks of four: extremely rare: 12–16U.

Essays: slightly different shades. These stamps, which might be offered for sale as originals, may be identified by their forged perforations and an occasional forged cancellation.

Fakes: Strip cutouts, post cards, or envelopes, fraudulently perforated, sometimes are offered as originals. In the case of the design and cancellation being original, exclusive attention should be given to the paper and the shade of the impression; perforation frequently is arbitrary. It may, however, be congruent.

2-krone (strip) is on thinner, visibly grayish paper; made of yellowish, thick post card paper, even though a layer was removed to adjust thickness. The shades are quite arbitrary: orange-red and pale ochre-orange.

The 3-, 5-, 10-, and 15-krone come from cutout envelopes; the paper is a little thinner (65–70 microns), but not having been gummed, it seems more pliable. The shade is grayer, especially in the 3-krone, and, with the stippled effect on the face, this paper gives all these fakes a spoiled look. The 3-krone seems gray-green, the 5-krone is too pale, the 10-krone (deceptive) looks good, blue or milky blue, the 15-krone is pale brown.

One should note that the perforations are always clean-cut, whereas in the originals there usually are circular punch-outs that still are attached. Moreover, the background cross-ruling ends in an indistinct shaded part (on the crown's sides), whereas in the authentic, original stamps it touches the crown.

Turin forgeries: lithographed. The inner line of the coat of arms is consistently parallel with the latter instead of forming a recessive curl, aimed toward the inner shield's point. Very arbitrary shades. Perf 11½.

Paris forgeries: lithographed in somewhat better shades, but with serious design defects, especially the "R" of "KR," with very horizontal top, without concavity on the right of the vertical foot of the letter. Perf 10–12.

Pest forgeries: a lithographed forgery of the 3-krone. Format, design, perforation are noncongruent with the original.

Vienna forgeries: lithographed. Very deceptive. Different format. Minute design comparison is necessary.

Geneva forgeries (F.): these are well-executed photolithographed stamps, originating in an envelope copy. They can be identified by the white horizontal line, beginning at the "O" top right; by the pointed vertical line which terminates the oblique bar of figure "1," and by the cheek that is covered with blue dots right up to the eye.

After what we said above, these distinctive marks will suffice. However, there also are serious transfer plate defects: top of skull open near the middle, a consequence of the failure to complete a laurel leaf; ornamental white circle with a 2 mm break (upper top left corner). Clean-cut perf 9½. Card paper (160 microns) of appropriate thickness.

1871 (July) 1872. Engraved stamps. Nos. 7 to 12.
Shades: visibly brighter and sharper than in the lithographed stamps, except in a few printings made with excessively fluid inks. 2-krone pale yellow: 8M,

2U; dark orange, ochre-orange, ochre. 3-krone green, dark green, dark blue-green, dark yellow-green. 5-krone carmine-tinted rose, vermilion-tinted rose: 25M, 25U. 10-krone blue, dark blue. 15-krone yellow-brown, transparent paper: 2M, 2U; red-brown, chocolate brown, black-brown: 25M, 2U; copper red-brown: 5M, 10U. 25-krone gray-violet, violet.

Paper: medium thickness (70–80 microns) to very thick (120 microns): 50M, 2U. The yellowish paper, which is in demand, comes from a gum of the same shade.

Varieties: 3-krone, printed on both sides: extremely rare. All values are known with double print. Defective impressions are in demand.

Reprints: 1885: on watermarked paper of the fourth issue, perf 11½, shades duller and paler; the set: 25 francs. 1890: Same watermark and perforations, bright aniline shades; the set: 10 francs.

Pairs: 3U. No. 12: 4U. Blocks: rare.

Fakes: the 2-, 3-, and 25-krone have been chemically altered to create shades.

1874 (October). Figures on cover. No watermark. Nos. 13 to 17. An interesting set with its perforations, retouching of engraving, and numerous shades.

Perforations: 12½, 13, and 13½ are common. 11½, 12, and composite 11½ x 13 or 13 x 11½ are rare. The 3-krone, perf 9½ and the 5-krone, perf 9 x 13, are very rare.

Varieties: all values are found with double print: very rare.

The values with arbitrary shades are essays.

The 5-krone had two plates. In the first, the top left triangle is accurate. In the second one, there is a curved line under the circle arc side.

Plate defects: 5-krone, one or two dots over the second "A" of MAGYAR; second dot after the "R" of KIR. Bottom double-lined inscription lettering (printing flaw). Various errors in printing, especially in the 3- and 5-krone stamps.

Retouched stamps: these retouchings are very numerous, especially in the background hatching of the 3- and 20-krone and the 10-krone, Nos. 16 and 21. This retouching, which is more or less extensive, is worth from 5 to 20 francs on Nos. 14 and 16, and from 10 to 20 francs on No. 17, depending on the degree and kind of retouching. Retouching is classified as that done with a straightedge or that done freehand. The latter is rarer.

A very nice collection of relatively common stamps from this issue can be formed with defective copies (those showing white spots) placed opposite copies in which the defect has been corrected by retouching.

The illustration will give information on some examples of retouching, thus familiarizing the reader with it somewhat.

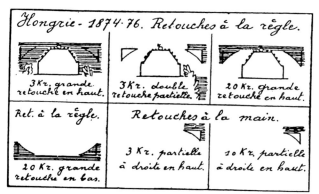

Hungary, 1874–76. The top three boxes show retouching accomplished with a straightedge. From left, the 3-krone with extensive retouching on top; 3-krone double partial retouching; 20-krone extensive retouching on top. At bottom left is a straightedge retouch of the 20-krone, showing extensive retouching at bottom. The remaining two boxes show freehand retouching of upper right portions of the 3-krone and 10-krone.

One also finds retouching of border pearls, especially in the 10-krone with pearls entirely redesigned top and bottom, and partly on the sides.

When the retouching becomes relatively worn, attentive examination is sometimes necessary to detect it.

Used postal forgeries: 5-krone carmine. Very unsuccessful, confused design. The center casing measures about 11 mm instead of 10½.

Fakes: there are narrow, very wide, and very tall copies. The latter are sometimes offered as imperforates after removal of the perforations.

1888–91. Saline watermarks Nos. 23 to 36. Nos. 23–26 and 32 are imperforate: rare. Buy in pairs.

Numerous *shades.* Nos. 24–26, 28, and 31 with this watermark (1888) are rare. Variable thickness in figures is found. Same remark as above with regard to wide and tall stamps.

1898. Crown watermark in a circle. Nos. 23 to 34. The thin, almost pelure, transparent paper is rare. Numerous shades.

Subsequent issues. These usually are well classified in general catalogues. The minor values, and stamps from issues after 1915 ("new" category), are available in great quantities.

No. 99a, error, must be compared. Its color tone should be exactly that of No. 100. There are chemical fakes of No. 99, with bleached impression and paper tinting.

Forged overprints: these are poorly executed in general, but nevertheless are found in many collections, amateurs not being sufficiently wary of less expensive stamps. To be watched particularly are: 1-krone red-brown (1914); 5-krone red-lilac (1915); 1.50-krone and

4.50-krone air mail (1918); 5-krone black-brown and brown (1919, overprint on a 1916–17 stamp); the sets overprinted MAGYAR (1919); and grain-head spikes. Comparison with an original is necessary.

The same applies to a few postage due stamps, especially the 1922–23 set.

As for occupation overprints ARAD, BACSKA, BARANYA, DEBRECZEN, and SZEGEDIN, only professional specialization can provide some security, for everything was so perfectly counterfeited from Paris to Budapest that one wonders whether the original overprint clichés were not completely ignored.

Newspaper Stamps

1871 (May). No. 1. Mouthpiece on the right. *Shades:* red, bright red, brick red.

Varieties: transparent, greasy impression: 2U.

Cancellations: straight-line and Lombardy cancellations are in demand.

Forgeries: two out of three of the vertical lines (on the left, under the crown) touch the mouthpiece. There are seventy-six pearls instead of seventy-seven (in the lithographed originals).

1872. No. 2. Mouthpiece on the left. *Shades:* dull to bright red; rose and carmine-tinted rose.

Cancellations: see above.

Varieties: this stamp is found with double print: very rare. Very transparent impression: 4U. Printed both sides: extremely rare.

Reprint: on official paper of the third issue with watermark "KR."

1874. No. 3. No watermark. *Shades:* from very pale dull red to bright red; orange-yellow; dark yellow: 2U; lemon: very rare.

Iceland

For details not given here, the reader is referred to Denmark.

Sheets of 100 (10 x 10).

1873–74. Crown watermark. Nos. 1 to 4. *Printing figures:* values in skillings. 2-skilling: 40,000; 4-skilling: 100,000; 8- and 16-skilling: 40,000; 3-skilling: 25,000.

The first printing (1873) includes the 3-, 4-, and 16-skilling, perf 12½. The printing of 1874 includes the 2-, 4-, 8-, and 16-skilling, perf 14 x 13½.

Shades: in each issue, there is not much difference in shades. Differences are perceptible especially between the same values perf 12½ and 14 x 13½.

Varieties: imperforates are relatively common, except the 3-skilling, which is rare.

Cancellations: dated cancellations are common. Those with the name of the town on one line are less common. Color or foreign cancellations earn different degrees of rarity.

Reprints: none.

Forgeries: all lithographed, no watermark. Compare lettering, dots, vertical corner hatching. In the originals, the vertical lines in the oval background touch neither the inscription oval nor the ornaments.

Forged cancellations: various, among which one finds REYKJAVIK JAN 73, which frequently was applied to originals. Cancellations on Nos. 1–4 must be compared or expertized.

1876. Values in aurar (eyrir singular). Nos. 12 to 17. Nos. 12–15 are dated July 1, 1882; Nos. 16 and 17, October 1892.

Rare shades: 20-aurar ultramarine: 2M, 2U; slate: 50M, 25U.

1897. "3" and PRIR overprints. Nos. 18 and 19. Four different overprints, none of which resembles another. The "3" numerals also are different. Comparative expertizing is absolutely necessary, for there are some very well-executed forged typographed overprints.

Originals: the values perf 14 x 13½ are worth twice as much as those perf 12½.

Forged overprints: the lithographed overprints have no indention on back. The "I" of PRIR has a dot instead of an accent, etc.

1897–1902. Crown watermark. Perf 12½. This issue comprises the 3-, 5-, 6-, 10-, 16-, 20-, and 50-aurar, Nos. 12a, 13a, 7a–9a, 14a, and 16a, perf 12½.

Reprints: the whole set, as well as Nos. 15 and 17, Nos. 21 and 22 of the following issue. The whole 1902 set was GILDI overprinted. Official stamp Nos. 3–9 and the entire official set overprinted GILDI were reprinted in 1904 with the great crown watermark of the portrait values (1902–4).

1900–1902. Same, perf 12½. Nos. 20 to 22. No. 20 comes from a new plate with larger figures than in Nos. 12 and 12a.

Reprints: see issue of 1897–1902. These are described as varieties in the Yvert catalogue.

Subsequent issues. These are adequately described in the general catalogues.

The official error, 20-aurar blue (Yvert No. 22a), really comes from the sheets of the 20-aurar blue, No. 40 (two plates per sheet, 2,000 stamps in all).

Official Stamps

1873. Values in skillings. Nos. 1 and 2. *Printing figures:* No. 1: 50,000; No. 2: 30,000.

Varieties: Nos. 1 and 2 with white spot after ISLAND. Imperforate stamps — No. 1: common (10 francs). No. 2: 20 francs.

The copies on thick paper without watermark are essays.

Issue of 1876–1901. Nos. 3 to 9. *Varieties:* 3-aurar yellow, thin paper, perf 14 x 13½: 3M, 3U; 5-aurar, imperforate: 20 francs. Nos. 4–7 on thick paper without watermark are essays.

Reprints: see postal issue of 1897–1902.

1902. Issue overprinted GILDI. Nos. 10 to 14. Same remarks as for the corresponding postal issue.

Reprints: see postal issue of 1897–1902.

India

1852. Embossed imprint. Nos. 1 and 1b. *Originals:* No. 1, wove white paper; No. 2, wove white paper of variable thickness; No. 3, red glossy paper on back only. The word ANNA does not touch the inner circle.

Forgeries: (a) the loop does not touch the thin circle in the bottom. (b) Another set: the thin circle is missing; the outer circle, therefore, is single, not double. (c) From a German source; rough paper; figure "1" of the fraction is touching the bottom of the center shield. In case of doubt, comparison would be useful.

1854. Nos. 2 to 5. *Originals:* thick yellowish paper with watermark fragments. Nos. 2 and 3, lithographed; Nos. 4 and 5, typographed.

Reprints of the five values on glossy white paper; without watermark and gum (1887). These reprints usually have SPECIMEN on back. There is also a reprint of the 4-anna, made in 1867–68 with marginal dividing lines in red or blue, and another one of the 2-anna, perf 12½, on bluish laid paper, without watermark.

Various *forgeries:* ½-anna red, lithographed on thin or medium paper without watermark; 8¼ color cones on the left side; 7¾ on the left; 7 on the right and 7¾ on the left; 8 on the right; and a recess print engraving with 8 cones on each side, whereas in the original there are 9½ cones on each side.

Geneva forgeries: thin, dark yellow paper; cancellation "112." ½-anna blue, on pelure or medium paper; 7¾ cones on the left; black imprint; the original has 8 cones on each side. 1-anna red, very thin, thin, or medium paper; three rows of dots in the neck cut, with two rows of insufficiently aligned dots or no dots at all; in the original, there are two lines of well-aligned dots. 4-anna, Geneva forgery, executed in blocks; portrait upright or inverted; medium paper; extremely pointed nose; the first "A" of ANNAS is touching the blank circle above it, and the second "A" is touching it below it. The eighth oblique white line on the left of the circle (count from bottom) is thick and penetrates the blank circle, which does not occur in the twelve original types. Another early Geneva forgery, which is framed and canceled "21," does not deserve to be described.

Faking of the 4-anna to make a rare stamp with inverted portrait by removing the portrait imprint and then printing an inverted portrait in its place; detailed design comparison will prove adequate in checking this creation.

1856–60. Azure-tinted paper. Nos. 6 to 8. *Fakes* made by tinting chemically the paper of the stamps of the following issue, especially the 8-pence.

1866. POSTAGE overprint on fiscal stamp. No. 26. *Forged overprints* (Geneva, Type I).

1888. 12-anna brown on red. No. 42. *Used postal forgeries:* lithographed, not typographed; no watermark; gray shade, not brown.

1891. "¹/₄" overprint. No. 44. Inverted *forged overprint* (Geneva). Comparison is indicated.

Official stamps. 1866. SERVICE overprint. Nos. 1 to 11. *Forged overprints:* detailed comparison is indispensable, for there are clever, deceptive counterfeits and fantastic creations (Geneva).

1867. Overprinted stamps. Nos. 12 to 17. Same statement as previously. The question is complicated by more or less official reprints of the overprint: characters and measurements are different. Note: overprints GOS, GPS, GWS, etc., which may be found on these stamps, have no official status.

Telegraph stamps. The Type II TELEGRAPH overprint was counterfeited in Geneva.

Indian States

Important note: the stamps of these states have not been counterfeited extensively, and the counterfeits, with rare exception, are crude lithographed productions. In case of doubt, measurements may prove decisive. The numerous varieties of types, shades, perforations, and reprints make specialization desirable. Excellent pointers can be found in the British catalogue, Stanley Gibbons' *Native States of India,* and the Calman study [*A Catalogue for Advanced Collectors of Postage Stamps, Stamped Envelopes and Wrappers* by Henry Collins and Henry L. Calman, 1890–91] will give useful information on the numerous types of the various plates reproduced there.

Alwar

1877. Lithographed; 24 x 21 mm. Stamps with watermark are in demand.

Bamra

1899. First issue. Wove paper; 1-anna blue, plate of seventy-two varieties; 2-anna green, plate of eight varieties; ¹/₂-anna red, 4-anna yellow, and 8-anna rose:

plates of ninety-six varieties. ¹/₂-anna yellow and ¹/₂-anna rose (1890). Nos. 1 and 2 (Yvert), plates of sixteen varieties (8 x 2).

So-called *reprints* of Nos. 1–6 (Yvert) executed on new plates with twenty types (5 x 4), with the shortest banderole line pointing horizontally to the right. Wove paper.

Early *forgeries* in rose, green, yellow, and blue, 2-anna type (the third letter of the inscription resembles a reversed "R" in this type), but the bottom banderole rather resembles the 4-anna type. Thin, stippled paper (Geneva).

Bhopal

Nos. 1 to 5. Lithographed. One plate, twenty types per value; two plates for No. 5. Wove white paper.

1878–79. Lithographed. One plate, thirty-two types per value.

1881–82. Nos. 13–17. A single plate of twenty-four types for all values (value change only). Lithographed.

1886–90. Nos. 18 to 23. Lithographed. (1) A plate of thirty-two types (8 x 4); various kinds of paper, imperforate or perf 7. (2) A plate for the ¹/₂-anna pale red; thirty-two types with larger characters and BECAN instead of BEGAM. (3) A plate of twenty-four types for the 4-anna; thicker characters; one plate of thirty-two types for the ¹/₂-anna black with error BECAN. (4) A plate of twenty-four types for the 1-anna brown and the 4-anna yellow. (5) A plate of twenty-four types for the ¹/₂-anna black; perf 8 or imperforate. (6) A retouched plate of ten types (5 x 2) for the 8-anna blue. (7) A plate of twenty-four types for the 2-anna blue-green; smaller letters. (8) A plate of thirty-two varieties for the ¹/₂-anna red. (9) A plate of ten varieties for the 8-anna blue-green (1891, laid paper). Evidently specialization is rather desirable. Amateurs will find all the information desired in Calman's (Collins and Calman, 1890–91) fine work.

Bhor

1879. Nos. 1 and 2. Handstamped impression on thin, grayish, laid paper. No. 1: axes, 32 x 25 mm; No. 2, 31 x 25 mm.

Bundi

Specialty catalogues must be consulted.

Bussahir

Same remark.

Chamba

Very numerous forged overprints, especially on used stamps. Nos. 1–13, 17–23, and official Nos. 1–10, 12, and 13 were overprinted fraudulently in Geneva;

CHAMBA is 10$\frac{1}{2}$ mm wide, as high as the bar of the "A"; the blank part above this bar is half as large as the "A" of STATE and the right side of the "A" is double the thickness of the left side. STATE is only 7$\frac{3}{4}$ mm wide in this set and the lower bar of the "E" is much thicker than the upper bar. A second Geneva type is no more successful (lettering is too thick). Specialists in British East Indies stamps still think that the cancellations provide a reliable criterion for judging these stamps. The forged Geneva cancellation is round (26 mm), with date; CHAMBA 13 MA. 00; a top banderole has CHAMBA-STATE.

Charkhari

1896–97. Nos. 1 to 5. The stamps on tinted paper are essays.

Geneva forgeries: recognizable by the dot after the "0" in the upper right corner. Double circle cancellation, 28 mm, CHARKHARI (on top), 2 JV 97 P M (between two bars in the center), and B-C INDIA (bottom).

Cochin

1892. Nos. 1 to 3. Lithographed on grayish wove paper; 19 x 20$\frac{3}{4}$ mm.

Duttia

Comparison is indispensable for Nos. 1–4 and 10–14.

Geneva forgeries: Nos. 5–8; the first "T" of STATE is joined with the "A" at its base; same, for the "I" and the "A" of DUTIA; the "P" and "O" of POSTAGE almost are touching; the frame is broken in the four corners.

Faridkot

1879–80. Nos. 1 to 3. Typographed; bad handstamped impression; 1-folus, 17$\frac{1}{2}$ x 14 mm; 1-paisa, 19$\frac{1}{2}$ x 25 mm; No. 3, thick, double, white, outer frame, 20$\frac{1}{2}$ x 26$\frac{1}{2}$ mm. Wove white paper; Nos. 1 and 2 also on laid white paper. Note: The square stamps are postal fantasies. Also postal and official forged overprints FARIDKOT STATE on British India stamps. Comparison is necessary.

Gwalior

1885. Overprinted stamps. Nos. 1 to 8. *Originals:* the two overprints are about 13$\frac{1}{2}$ mm long; the Indian characters are 13$\frac{1}{2}$ mm wide.

Reprints of the $\frac{1}{2}$- and 1-anna with overprint lengths of 13 mm; sometimes they have SPECIMEN on them.

Forged overprints: numerous; comparison is indispensable; in dealing with the used stamps, verify the cancellation — that is always good expertizing procedure. The whole set was overprinted fraudulently in Geneva, but the second line of the overprint, instead of GWALIOR, is a five-letter Hindu word.

1886–1900. Overprinted stamps. Nos. 9 to 28. Overprint comparison is indispensable. In the original overprints, the Indian word is 14 mm wide.

Reprints of the $\frac{1}{2}$-, 2-, 4-anna, and 1-rupee with red overprint; the reprints frequently bear the word REPRINT.

Forged overprints: numerous. In the red or black forged Geneva overprint, all the letters of the Hindu word are joined on top, and the vertical line of the "G" is missing (bottom right).

The SERVICE overprint also was copied in Geneva. The forged Geneva cancellation: one circle (25 mm) with date, GWALIOR-STATE 7 oc 01 AGAR, and ornaments.

Hyderabad

1866. No. 1. *Original:* recess print engraving on wove white paper; 29$\frac{1}{2}$ x 20$\frac{1}{2}$ mm; perf 11$\frac{1}{2}$; forty-eight rows of horizontal white lines.

Reprint: perf 12$\frac{1}{2}$; shade is too light; reprints with perforation trimmed off are offered as imperforate stamps. The stamps in other shades (red and ultramarine), perf 12$\frac{1}{2}$, are sometimes used postal(?) fiscals.

Forgery: lithographed; dot perf 13$\frac{1}{2}$; thirty-five rows of horizontal white lines.

1871. Nos. 2 and 3. *Originals:* engraved; perf 11$\frac{1}{2}$; laid white paper, 240 types, 17 x 20$\frac{1}{2}$ mm.

Reprints: perf 12$\frac{1}{2}$. $\frac{1}{2}$-anna, 135 types, in orange-tinted brown only instead of brown; 2-anna, 240 types in bright green or blue-green instead of sage green.

1871–1904. Nos. 4 to 10. Perf 12$\frac{1}{2}$; 19 x 21$\frac{1}{2}$ mm.

Official stamps. Numerous forged overprints; many are very deceptive, especially for the 1869–71 issues, and require detailed comparison. Investigate quartz-lamp expertizing.

Jaipur

1904. Nos. 1 to 5. Comparison is indispensable.

Jhalawar

1887–90. Nos. 1 and 2. Lithographed on laid white paper; No. 1, 18$\frac{1}{2}$ x 22 mm, and No. 2, on various kinds of paper (1890), 21$\frac{1}{2}$ x 25$\frac{1}{2}$ mm.

Jind

1875. Nos. 1 to 5. Lithographed on thin white paper; 18 x 20 mm. For each value, a plate of fifty slightly different types (10 x 5).

1876. Nos. 6 to 11. Same; on thick, bluish, laid paper; fifty types per value; the $\frac{1}{2}$-anna, imperforate or perf 12.

1882–84. Nos. 12 to 25. Lithographed on various papers, depending on printing. $^1/_4$-anna orange, 15 x 16$^1/_2$ mm; the others, 18 x 21$^1/_2$ mm. $^1/_4$-anna orange, three plates: (1) fifty varieties; (2) reengraved plate of fifty varieties; (3) plate of twenty-five varieties or types; the other values, a plate of fifty types. See also Jind.

1885. First issue. Nos. 26 to 31. *Originals:* JHIND overprint is 9 mm wide, STATE, 9$^1/_2$ mm.

Reprints: JHIND, 8 mm wide, and STATE, 9 mm.

Forged overprints: very numerous, especially (Geneva) all the overprints on postage stamps. Comparison is necessary. In the Geneva forged overprints, the total width of STATE is 10$^1/_2$ mm in one type and 10 mm in a second one.

Subsequent issues. Numerous *forged overprints.* Comparison is necessary. (Geneva, Nos. 32–37.)

Official stamps (1885). Nos. 1 to 3. *Reprints* of the three values. Same remarks as for the 1885 postage stamps. The SERVICE overprint of 1887–1903 (Nos. 7–13) was counterfeited in Geneva and applied on canceled originals. Note: The forged Geneva cancellations: one circle (26 mm), with date, SANGRUR MA 14 03, and, above the circle, a circular strip with the words JHIND-STATE.

Kashmir

Jumbo (1866). Nos. 1 to 11. Handstamped impression on grayish or brownish thick, laid paper. Two types for the $^1/_2$- and 1-anna; Type I, 23 mm in diameter; Type II, 24 mm. The printing type characters in these types differ slightly. The $^1/_4$-rupee (a bar and a crescent in center) is found in black, blue, and ultramarine.

1867. Nos. 16 to 25. Handstamped impression with three clichés (three types) of the $^1/_2$-anna and one cliché of the 1-anna. Same paper; 21 x 24 mm.

Kashmir. Nos. 26–34. Handstamped impressions; one for the $^1/_2$- and 2-anna; one for the 4- and one for the 8-anna. Numerous varieties and papers. Consult the specialty catalogues.

Jumbo and Kashmir (1878). Nos. 35 to 43a. Typographed, 19 x 22 mm. Various plates; $^1/_2$-anna, fifteen types; 1-anna, twenty types.

1879. Nos. 44 to 49. Typographed; 22 x 24 mm; $^1/_2$-anna, fifteen types; 1- and 20-anna, twenty types; 4- and 8-anna, eight types.

1883–94. Nos. 50 to 66. Same.

Official stamps. As in the issue of 1878. *Reprints* of the stamps for Jumbo (Jammu) and Kashmir (Srinagar) on various wove or laid machine-made papers instead of handmade laid paper; greasy imprint; Nos. 1–34.

Forgeries: recognizable by the paper and dimensions; in case of doubt, compare with the originals' design, which is executed very crudely here.

Kishangarh

Comparison is useful for all the rare stamps. Forged Geneva cancellation: one circle (26 mm) with date, KISHENGARH 23 AP 04 RAJ · PO.

Nabha

A country with abundant overprints: specialization definitely is recommended, Numerous *forged overprints,* for which comparison is indispensable. The overprints of the postage stamps and the first overprint of the official stamps were counterfeited in Geneva.

1885. Oval overprint. Nos. 1 to 6. (and) **1885. "Official" oval overprint. Nos. 1 to 3.** So-called "official" *reprints:* NABHA and STATE are about 9$^1/_2$ mm long (originals: 11 and 10 mm).

1887. Overprint on two lines (regular postage and official stamps): $^1/_2$-, 1-, 2-, 4-, 8-anna, and 1-rupee; official stamps: the first three values only; the so-called "official" *reprints* bear the word SPECIMEN.

Nepal

Lithographed on various papers; 17 x 20 mm.

Nowanuggur

1877. Nos. 1 and 2. Typographed on wove white paper; 17 x 16$^1/_2$ mm.

1880. Nos. 3 to 5. Specialization is indispensable. Eleven plates for the 1-dokra, thirteen for the 2-dokra, and nine for the 3-dokra, each plate having ten to fifteen types.

Patiala

Numerous *forged overprints;* comparison is indispensable.

Reprints of overprints: 1885, the five values with STATE being 7$^3/_4$ mm wide instead of 8$^1/_2$ mm and usually having the supplementary REPRINT overprint; 1886–87, official reprinted overprints having the same characteristics, but the $^1/_2$-anna green, No. 4, is overprinted in red. All overprints, except the OFFICIAL overprints of 1913–27, were counterfeited in Geneva.

Poonch

Handstamp impressions on various papers: Type a (Yvert), 20$^1/_2$ mm square; a similar type (1-anna with circle and dots in the upper right corner and broken circle in the inner square), 21$^1/_2$ x 21 mm; Type b, 21$^1/_2$ x 21 mm; Type c, 21 x 19$^1/_2$ mm; similar type, but well-formed character in the upper left corner (2-anna),

$22^{1}/_{2}$ x $21^{1}/_{2}$ mm; Type d, 20 x 19 mm; Type e, 4-anna, $27^{1}/_{2}$ x 23 mm.

Rajpeepla

1880. Nos. 1 to 3. Lithographed on wove white paper. 1-penny, perf 11; 18 x $18^{1}/_{2}$ mm; sixty-four types; 2- and 4-anna, perf $12^{1}/_{2}$; 18 x $22^{1}/_{2}$ mm.

Scinde

See India, Nos. 1 and 1b.

Sirmoor

1879–80. Nos. 1 and 2. Lithographed; perf $11^{1}/_{2}$; the $^{1}/_{2}$-anna on wove white paper (1879) and the $^{1}/_{2}$-anna blue on laid white paper.

Originals: $21^{1}/_{2}$ x 24 mm; green, pale green, blue, dark blue; the first line has nine Indian characters, and there is no accent or protruding line above the third character of the bottom line.

So-called *reprints* (or second printing); 23 x 26 mm; printed perf $11^{1}/_{2}$; yellow-green, blue-green, and ultramarine; thick paper; very thick outer frame.

Forgeries: eight Hindu characters in the first line and an accent extending over the bottom line, above the third character.

Soruth

No. 1. Handstamp impression on azure-tinted, laid paper.

1870–78. Nos. 2 to 6. Specialization is necessary. Typographed. Two plates of twenty varieties for the 1-anna and three plates of twenty types for the 4-anna, plus three plates of each of the values in sixteen, sixteen, and four types, respectively.

1878. Nos. 9 to 14. Lithographed. 1-anna, 21 x $17^{1}/_{2}$ mm; two plates of fifteen and twenty varieties; 4-anna, $19^{1}/_{2}$ square; two plates of five types.

Travancore

1888–1900. Nos. 1 to 9. Typographed; 20 x 25 mm.

Wadhwan

No. 1. Lithographed; 30 x 27 mm.

Indochina

1889. Overprinted stamps. Nos. 1 and 2. *Forged overprints:* comparison is indispensable. First determine whether the 35-centime stamp is the 1881 forgery described under French Colonies. This forgery was overprinted fraudulently in Geneva (Nos. 1 and 2, with varieties) in black or in red and provided with the following forged cancellations: double circle (24 mm)

with date, NAM-DINH 1 OCT 92 TONKIN, which also was used on the following issue and on the fraudulently overprinted stamps of Annam and Tonkin; (24 mm): HANOI 3^{e} 27 FEVR 93 TONKIN, which also was used on the forgeries of the following issue, on the Annam and Tonkin forgeries (same date, but millesime "88"), and on this issue (1889), the millesime and the figures being interchangeable.

1892–98. Peace and Commerce type. Nos. 3 to 21. *Geneva forgeries* of the Peace and Commerce type; see French Colonies. Forged Geneva cancellation: double circle (22 mm) with date, HA-NOI 2^{E} 21 JUIL. 92 TONKIN and (23 mm) HA-NOI 2^{E} 20 AOUT 92 TONKIN.

1912. Stamps overprinted "05" or "10." Nos. 59–64. *Geneva forgeries,* Peace and Commerce type, fraudulently overprinted: see French Colonies.

1914–17. RED CROSS. Nos. 65 to 68. *Forged overprints:* meticulous comparison is indispensable, particularly of the double, triple, and quadruple overprints which were manufactured specially for amateurs.

1919. Stamps overprinted PIASTRES. Nos. 88 and 89. *Forged overprints:* note particularly the defective final "s" of PIASTRES (blurring). The same values were overprinted fraudulently on stamps from Indochinese post offices in China (Canton, Hoi-Hao, Kwangchowan, Mongtseu, Pakhoi, Tchongking, and Yunnan Fou).

Ingermanland [North]

New stamps in sets.

Fake: center cut out and stuck upside down on the 10-mark brown and lilac, No. 14. Use magnifying glass for front examination, benzine for the back.

Inhambane

1895. Overprinted stamps. Nos. 1 to 14. *Forged overprints:* especially in Geneva. Easily identifiable by comparison or by template measurement.

Ionian Islands

No. 1, wove paper. No. 2, with watermark "2." No. 3, with watermark "1."

Originals are expertly engraved. Although very close, the chignon does not touch the oval. The ornament in the front of the diadem is a Maltese cross, of which only two prongs can be seen; the cross does not touch the oval. The third ornament is a cross, the other two are fleurs-de-lys. The face and neck shading is made of curved and parallel lines of dots. The center background, which is made of lozenge designs, is a very fine burelage.

Cancellations: FRANCO in an oval or double circle cancellation with name at top. All others are rare.

The cancellations on these stamps always require expertizing. Examples on cover are very rare. Pen cancellations exist. On single stamps, off cover, they are worth nothing.

Forgeries: all stamps lithographed, with or without the ludicrous watermark; imperforate or perf 11–12. Various sets have the following principal defects: the chignon is touching the oval; it is almost 1 mm away from it; the three ornaments on the right...diadem [Translator's note: Incomplete text. Obviously, the typographer dropped some text, probably a parenthetical element ending in "diademe."] are crosses; the last one on the right is a pearl; the left cross is touching the oval; a curved line connects the tops of letters NIKON KPAT; shading lines instead of dots down to the bottom of the neck (back part); various unstippled places in the face and neck; full center background on the right.

Forged cancellations: dot lozenges, cancellation with date, British style; four-circle cancellations with horizontal lines or numeral in center; "B 62" British cancellation (Geneva, F.); framed cancellations; etc. These forged cancellations are found on authentic single stamps as well as on stamps on cover.

Ireland

There is nothing to point out. The difficulty experienced in locating the distinctive Irish type explains why there are no forged overprints — which, however, will probably not be long in coming. Right now, comparative examination is strongly advised, at least for the overprints of the first issue. Good collection management implies foresight!

Italian States

Modena

This is an extremely interesting country for the stamp specialist because of the number of varieties, errors, and cancellations.

Select: Modena stamps must have four margins, a minimum of about 1 mm in width, measuring right up to the dividing frame line.

1852 (June 1). Eagle and crown. Black on colored paper. Black on white for the 1-lira (watermark Type A). Imperforate stamps. Nos. 1 to 6. *Sheets* of 240 stamps in four panes of sixty. Typographed.

Paper: handmade, thin, or medium, with slightly stippled appearance; 25-centesimo on thick paper, first printing: 3U.

The 5-, 10-, and 40-centesimo stamps have a dot after the value figure.

Shades: 5-centesimo, first printing, no dot, blue-green; with dot, blue-green, green: common. Olive-green: 8M, 4U. 10-centesimo rose, bright rose. Last printing, with dot, dull rose. 15-centesimo light yellow (canary); dark yellow; lemon: rare. 25-centesimo more or less light buff. 40-centesimo sky blue: very rare (first printing); dark blue; last printing, with dot: dark blue.

Varieties: broken cliché: unprinted line traversing the middle of the stamp horizontally, No. 1: 3U (stamp No. 174 of sheet). Various printing flaws: foliage partly missing; space between the "T" and the value figure is more or less large, particularly in the 5-centesimo ($2^{1}/_{2}$–$3^{1}/_{2}$ mm); letters or figures not aligned. Frequently in the last printings of the 10- and 40-centesimo, and the 5-centesimo olive, figures do not touch the lower frame line. All of these defects are minor errors, which become valuable only when the defect is quite visible, especially in a pair, next to a normal stamp.

One can classify in the same category the dots of various sizes before or after the figures. Some of them are microscopic ($^{1}/_{8}$ mm in diameter), usual ($^{1}/_{4}$ mm), medium ($^{1}/_{3}$ mm); large ($^{1}/_{2}$ mm), and very large ($^{2}/_{3}$ mm). The large dots are rare: two units. "Commas" which may be printing flaws are also found.

The dots occasionally are misplaced. The one after CENT. is very close to the "5" or to the "4" of "40." The same dot is out of place on the left between "N" and "T," the "T" being moved to the right near figure "4." The dot after the figures is near the top of the "5" and "10" of the 5- and 10-centesimo stamps, or misplaced on the left between LIRA and "1": very rare. These quite visible errors are worth four or five times the stamp's value. The same is true for juxtaposed letters or figures: "T5," or those with extra spaces: "N. T 4," mentioned above: 10M, 10U; or elevated (10-centesimo). The dot after the figure is sometimes missing in the 5-centesimo olive-green, the 10- and 40-centesimo stamps, and after the "T" in the 10-, 15-, 25-, and 40-centesimo, including the sky blue stamp. The 1-lira stamp exists with a foreshortened figure "1" (no baseline).

All of these distinctive marks, with other design features and the errors treated below, are quite useful in plating.

Errors: real errors in value lettering or in transposed figures are called "errors" here: No. 1: ENT; CENT ("E," prone); CNET; CEN1. No. 2: EENT; CE6t; CENE; CNET; CENT 10 ("1," inverted). No. 3: CETN. No. 4: CENT 49; CENE; CNET; CE6T; CENT 4C; C... (three letters omitted), and the whole value figure omitted in the 5-centesimo (very rare). These errors are assigned values in the general catalogues.

Printing flaws? CCNT 5; CENL 5, and when figure "5" is not there, they are classified in the same category. Also, CEBT 10; CENT 8; CEZT 10; CCNT 15; CINT 15; CLNT 15; CNET 15. In the 25-centesimo: CENT 1; CENT 2; CE T 25; C... 25; CENT .... In the 40-centesimo: CEBT; CENT....

Modena cancellations: A. Barred cancel.
B. Registered mail cancel. C. Large postmark, with date. D. Circles close together, with date. E. Large oval postmark of Reggio. F. Dumb cancel of Modena. G. Single circle, with date. H. Postage due at destination. I. Town name, on one line. J. Place-name in frame.

Cancellations: Type A, common in black; less common in blue: 25U; rare in red: 3U. Type B: rare (various varieties, word abbreviated or not). Cancellation ASSICURATO and time indication DOPO LA PARTENZA on two lines are rare.

Type C: 2–5U; in blue (GUASTALLA, etc.): rare. Type D in blue is common when applied to cover, rare on stamp. All post offices have the normal double circle postmark (26–28 mm), with date. Type E: 3U. Types F, G, I (several varieties), and J (several models): rare.

Type H in black: 2U; unframed: 3U; in blue: rare. Sometimes the date stands alone on one line: rare. The 1-lira always requires cancellation expertizing.

Pairs: 4U. Blocks of four, mint: 6M; used: very rare.
Reprints: none.
Fakes: the 40-centesimo sky blue must be expertized, especially when it is new; a dark blue 40-centesimo was used to make chemical fakes. One must be alert to minor errors such as misplaced dots, etc., that were sometimes added afterwards. One should also be attentive to large and very large dots.

The 25-centesimo green and the 5-centesimo yellow, which are found canceled at times, are essays on laid paper. The 1-lira, white laid paper, is a printer's proof. The 10- and 15-centesimo white and the 15-centesimo brown are chemical fakes.

Forgeries: numerous. Usually lithographed, occasionally typographed, the latter using a single cliché, with different lettering and figures applied afterwards.

Some early forgeries with a characteristic large format, 19–20½ mm wide by 22–24 mm high, deserve nothing more than mere mention. The margins are congruent, and dividing frame lines are 1½, and as much as 2½ mm (!) away from the stamp; the value tablet is occasionally 3 mm high(!). For other, better executed, early forgeries, one should examine the eagle's head (see illustration, "originals"), the upper tablet lettering, the crown, the eagle's head and feet (four, five, and six claws!). The large dot at the end of the foliage on the right, under the "N," often is missing. If the stamp's back monopolizes your attention, examine the paper (sometimes laid and stippled, most often thin and machine-made) in making a decision. Shade comparison also gives reliable information, as does the lack of a watermark in the 1-lira.

The illustration shows a few details of a set made in Genoa (I.). These stamps often are provided with a forged circular Modena postmark with date. A forged Florentine set has the word SAGGIO (specimen) in the lower tablet.

1859 (October 15). Savoy coat of arms. Imperforate. Nos. 7 to 11.

It should be pointed out that before this set appeared, Sardinian stamps Nos. 10a, 11b, 12a, 13, and 14a were used in the Duchy of Modena and are in demand with Modena cancellations. 80-centesimo: very rare.

Sheets of 120 typographed stamps in four panes of thirty. Dividing frame lines between the stamps.
Paper: white, thin, machine-made.
Shades: 5-centesimo green, blue-green, dark green. 15-centesimo brown, gray-brown, and gray. 20-

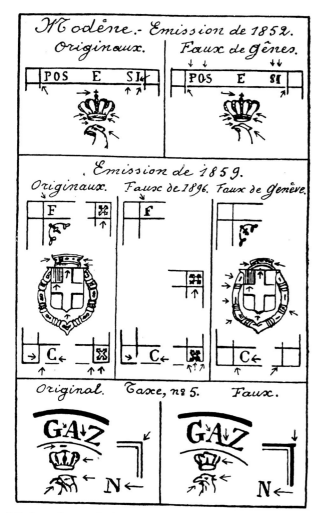

Modena issue of 1852. Originals. Forgeries. Middle: Issue of 1859. Bottom: Postage due.

centesimo reddish lilac and violet blue in various shades. 40-centesimo red-rose; bright Venetian red and brownish red. 80-centesimo orange-tinted bistre.

Varieties: the first printing of each value is of good quality and displays no defects, except, naturally, the errors. In the second printing, one notices a rather large number of defects, which may double the price of the stamp when they are quite visible. For example, 15-centesimo: CENT 5, CEST, CENI, CENT 14, CENI 16, etc. 20-centesimo: CENI, CENT 2, etc. 80-centesimo: CENT 8, CENT 0, CONT, CENI, CREY, etc.

Plate defect: no dot after the value figure in all stamp values: 2M. The 5- and 40- centesimo are found with a dot before the "C": 3M.

There are defective impressions.

Errors: 20-centesimo, ECNT: 8M, 5U; 40-centesimo: 5 CENT 40: exceedingly rare. The "N" of

the 20- and 80-centesimo is found inverted and is about $^1/_2$ mm lower than the other letters of CENT: 5M.

Pairs: 4U.

Cancellations: most of the preceding postmarks recur: Types A and B, entire word in kidney-shaped frame; sometimes "R" standing alone. Type C: very rare. Type F: very rare. Types H and J. A few types are modified: Type E (Reggio) becomes a double circle postmark with date, and Type J (Reggiolo, etc.) has a double frame. Type G was being used. All cancellations must be compared or expertized.

Special mention must be made of two rare postmarks. One bears the Savoy shield with a crown in the center of a 32 mm nine-barred rectangle. The other has the same characteristics, and, in addition, inscription POSTA LETTERE REGGIO, double circle in black or blue.

Reprints: none. See modern forgeries, below.

Early forgeries: there is no good reason why we should pause to study various crudely executed forgeries with full quartering shields, or with six vertical lines in the top quarterings instead of five, and five lines in the lower ones instead of six. The line under the value usually connects with the corner squares and the "I" of MODONESI does not form a sort of "T" as in the originals. One early forgery has a second outer frame that measures $21^1/_2$ x 24 mm.

Modern forgeries: I. so-called "reprint" of 1896 (Genoa, I.?); manufactured in sheets of twenty-four. No dot after the value figure; the letters of CENT. are not so thick; the figures are smaller ($1^1/_4$ mm instead of $1^1/_2$). The shades are relatively well imitated. The zero figures are closed (in the authentic stamps they are usually open). The paper is thin, the gum, not so thick. (See the preceding illustration for other details.)

II. Geneva forgeries (F.). Very thick yellowish paper. No dot after CENT. Arbitrary shades. See illustration. Closely set bar cancellation or dot lozenge.

Forged cancellations: very numerous on originals. Make comparison.

1852–59. Postage due stamps for newspapers. Nos. 1 to 5. Sheets of 240 stamps. Medium or thin paper which is so heavily stippled that it seems laid (Nos. 1, 2, and 5), or thin paper with blue silk threads and a few rose-colored threads incorporated in the pulp. Examine transparency.

Shades: Nos. 1 and 2, black on lilac-rose. No. 3, brownish lilac and dark lilac. No. 4, blue-tinted violet, and slightly rose-tinted violet; No. 5, black on yellowish white paper.

Characteristics and varieties: No. 1 (April 1853), large-letter "B.G." ($1^1/_2$ mm); letters of CENT. (1 mm); no dot after the figure. No. 2, small-letter "B.G." ($1^1/_4$ mm); letters of CENT. ($^3/_4$ mm); dot after the "9"; same cracked cliché as for No. 1 (see first issue). No. 3

(September 1855), no "B.G." letters; a dot after the value figure. Unissued No. 4 (November 1, 1857), no dot after "10." No. 5 (February 1859), new model. No. 2, no dot after the figure: 3U; very large dot (^{2}/$_3$ mm) after "9": 2U; "B" about 1 mm lower than the "G": 4U. No. 3, no dot after the figure: 3M; no dot above the foliage on the right: 2U. No. 4, error CEN1 10.: 15M, 10U (twice per sheet).

Reprints: No. 5 in gray-black only; circle broken under the "C" of CENT. There are proofs of Nos. 1–3 on laid white paper.

Cancellations: for stamps of foreign origin, before the issuing of Nos. 1–5, a double circle postmark (24^1/$_2$ mm) was used, bearing the inscription SPATI ESTENSI between circles; GAZZETTE ESTERE on two lines in the center, and CENT 9 at the bottom, between circles.

On No. 1, Type A: double circle with date MODENA: extremely rare; also pen cancellation. No. 2, cancellations common at that time; in blue: 2U. No. 4, Types A and F in black; Type D in blue and black. No. 5, Type D in black: extremely rare.

Forged cancellations: on No. 3, an unissued stamp! Also found on Nos. 4 and 5, whose cancellations must always be compared to known genuine ones.

Forgeries: there is a deceptive photolithographed forgery of No. 1. It was printed on the original paper of No. 3 (a margin copy) whose shade is browner than that of No. 1 and which contains silk threads. It is also found on gray-brown paper. Compare lettering and eagle design.

A modern forgery (Geneva, F.) of No. 1 can be identified by design differences (see illustration of the 1852 issue, "originals"). There is no line under the bottom inscription.

There are a few forgeries of No. 2, which are easily identifiable by paper shade and differences in design.

No. 5 on thin stippled paper (see illustration); lettering too high; bar of the "A" of GAZETTE, likewise; the right foot has four claws; the "N" of CENT is narrow. In another forgery, which is noncongruent in format, the fine horizontal line above the crown in the original is too long and too high.

Parma

1852 (June 1). Black on colored paper. Imperforate. Nos. 1 to 5. Fleur-de-lys in a circle surmounted by the crown of Parma.

Sheets: eighty stamps in four panes of twenty (4 x 5). Typographed.

Paper: machine-made, medium (60–70 microns) or thick (90 microns; last printings).

Select: four margins ^{1}/$_2$ mm wide.

Shades: 5-centesimo more or less dark yellow, bright yellow: 50M, 50U, and a greenish yellow (1855): 2M, 2U. 10-centesimo white; 15-centesimo white; 15-

centesimo more or less dull early rose. 25-centesimo more or less dark violet. 40-centesimo light blue: 4M, 50U, and blue. The impression shade is black or gray-black, which is visible especially in the 5- and 10-centesimo stamps.

Varieties: thick paper, 5- and 10-centesimo (1855): 50U. 15-centesimo, tête-bêche: extremely rare. 15-centesimo double print: very rare. 15-centesimo, thin, transparent paper (55 microns): 2M, 2U.

The Greek ornaments are usually ^{1}/$_4$ mm thick, but there are copies that have a wider ornament on either side or even on both sides (^{1}/$_3$ mm): 2–3M and U.

All values have defective impressions: inscriptions out of set, for example, CENTES 16, 18 (15-centesimo), or P RM instead of PARM (40-centesimo: 2M, 2U).

A quite visible dot between the "R" and the "M" of PARM: 25U.

The essays of the 10- and 15-centesimo in black on white were used in the postal service: extremely rare. Thick, handmade paper. The essays must be expertized.

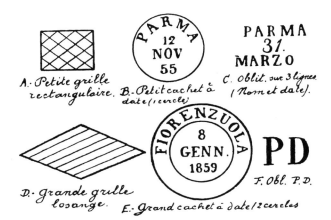

Parma cancellations: A. Small rectangular grill. B. Small dated postmark (single circle). C. Three-line cancel, with place name and date. D. Large lozenge grill. E. Large dated postmark (two circles). F. Postage due cancel.

Cancellations: Type B, small postmark: common, likewise, Type C. Type A: 50U; in red: 3U. Type E: 2U. Type F: rare (see illustration). Straight-line cancel with date, without name of city, is rare.

Pairs: mint, rather common. Used: 4U. Nos. 4 and 5: rare. Blocks of four, used: very rare. No reprints.

Fakes: 40-centesimo blue, chemically tinted to obtain light blue. Also, the 15- and 25-centesimo stamps were bleached white to obtain used postal essays! Examine the paper of the latter and the shade on the back of the 40-centesimo.

Originals: the illustration gives information on the most important details. The fleur-de-lys is touching the third hatch line in the lower part of the stamps.

Forgeries: like the forgeries of all the former Italian states and kingdoms, the Parma forgeries are especially numerous. A detailed description of each item would be time-consuming and tedious, and would interest only collectors of forgeries. The illustration gives data on a bad early forgery which is found in many collections, on a few well-executed Geneva forgery details, and on some other forgeries — a token description intended to demonstrate graphically that magic is not needed to identify counterfeits; all one has to do is *look*.

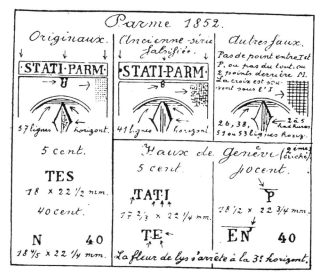

Parma 1852. Left: originals, 57 horizontal lines. Top center: early forged set, 41 horizontal lines. Top right: other forgeries. No dot between "I" and "P," or none at all, or two dots after "M." Cross often is under the "I." 2–5 shading lines, 26, 38, 51, or 53 horizontal lines. Bottom right: Geneva forgeries (second cliché). The fleur-de-lys stops at the third horizontal line.

In addition, there are a few particulars that deserve attention: they will help to spot all the counterfeits. There are about twenty different ones, almost all of them lithographed, and most of them in complete sets. Look for: Seven complete parts of the Greek ornament instead of eight; two ornaments of different thickness, especially in a forgery of Italian origin printed in sheets of twenty-five (5 x 5) with a tête-bêche; inscription letters not aligned, too wide, not high enough; dots missing before and after the words in the upper tablet (also, in the poorly executed originals, but very often there are traces of them that are exactly positioned because authentic dots are involved); the two Greek ornaments are anemic; behind the coat of arms, the

background is composed of color lines or of some kind of balding stippling effect; at times it also is composed of a field of dots with a few vertical lines; the top and bottom of the fleur-de-lys do not touch the horizontal shade lines at the places indicated; the number of these lines is not exact, nor is the number in the top sheet (from two to five), or in the median sheet below (from one to three); the crown is closed by a white line, bottom left; the circle is not normal — its bottom is flat; the cross is inexpertly formed and positioned, particularly in a Hamburg forgery, which was printed in sheets of twenty-five (5 x 5); the paper is too thin; the figures are not congruent (figure "4," often poorly drawn); dividing frame lines.

The Geneva forgeries were executed with two clichés. The first one is bad: no dot before STATI, but two of them after PARM. The second cliché comes from a rather successful photographic reproduction. However, there are defects in the inscriptions (see illustration, especially the 5- and 40-centesimo stamps).

Finally, there are reproductions in black which come from an original oxidized cliché. The tête-bêche stamps, except those of the 15-centesimo, and the stamps printed on both sides, are forgeries.

Forged cancellations: Types A, B, C (sometimes on two lines), Type D, all of them noncongruent. Also barred oval and widely spaced bars.

Type A is found on Geneva forgeries: postmark too large, the lozenges are square. Type D, lines too close. Type B, PARMA 15 MAG 1854, and 9 MARS 1858; COLORNO 4 MARZ 1852; BORGO 6 FEBR. 59. Modena barred postmark, etc.

1854 (January). Same type. Color on white paper. Nos. 6 to 8. As above. The impression is often slightly greasy. Paper is glossed on both sides.

Shades: 5-centesimo orange; yellow: 50M, 50U. 15-centesimo bright vermilion-red, vermilion-red, pale red: 2M, 2U. 25-centesimo red-brown, dark red-brown: 25M.

Select: four margins, 1/2 mm wide. No reprints.

Varieties: defective impressions are common; good ones are in demand. There are double prints of the 5- and 25-centesimo. Greek ornaments are wider (a single one or two of them) in the 15- and 25-centesimo.

Cancellations: Types B, C, and E: common. Type E in red: 2U.

Pairs: 4U. Strips of three of the 5-centesimo are very rare.

Forgeries: most of the forgeries of the first issue were printed in color on white paper, especially the early set with a poorly executed background (see illustration) and the forgeries with a cross-hatched background.

The 5-centesimo was well counterfeited in Geneva (F.) on paper not much thinner than the original, but not of the same consistency (see the illustration for a few distinguishing characteristics; however, examination of the printed image is difficult, for both originals and forgeries are crudely executed in orange-yellow). These forgeries usually are provided with previously described postmarks, among them those of the 1852 issue.

One modern forgery merits a more detailed description. Its impression is definitely chocolate, which contrasts with the color tones of the originals. The Greek ornaments, the white frame lines, and the white circle are too thin; they may appear to be not so wide in the originals as a result of plate clogging, but their real width still can be seen in a few places. Somewhat greater width: 18½ mm instead of 18–18¼ for the original after impression.

In this forgery, it also may be noted that the first two white lines under "T" and "PA," at the top of the crown, are not connected with the almost vertical white lines under the "I" and a little to the left of the "P." The forged cancellation occasionally is a red grill.

1857–59. "Duchy of Parma" inscription. Nos. 9 to 11. *Sheets:* sixty-four stamps. Typographed. Imperforate.

Select: four margins, minimum width: 1 mm.

Paper: medium (65–70 microns). 15-centesimo (1859), a little thicker. Slightly stippled, white, or slightly yellowish paper. Nos. 9 and 11 sometimes have striated paper.

Shades: 15-centesimo red, pale red. 25-centesimo pale lilac-tinted brown, lilac-tinted brown, and dark brown. 40-centesimo more or less dark blue. The 15-centesimo dark blue and the 25-centesimo green are essays.

Varieties: 15-centesimo, greasy impression: 2M, 2U. The minor impression varieties are numerous. The 40-centesimo is found with a narrow "O" (1¼ mm wide instead of 1½) twenty times per sheet: 50M, 75U.

Cancellations: Types D and E: common. All others: rare. There are some very rare ones, for example, POSTA MIL. SARDA, etc. Expertizing of all cancellations is indispensable.

Pairs: 4U. No reprints.

Originals: see details in the illustration. Notice that the crown's cross is placed in the middle, between "DI" and "PARMA," above the crown's median branch. The three leaves under the "CC" letters end approximately on the same horizontal.

Forgeries: very numerous. Most are in sets, all lithographed, with twenty-five, twenty-seven, thirty-one, and thirty-two shading lines in the oval. Figures and lettering are noncongruent, as are acorns and leaves. In a German forgery, sheets of twenty-five (5 x 5), the lower left acorn is almost horizontal; the lily leaf is touching the second, fourth, or fifth hatch line on top, the second or fourth one at bottom. Two

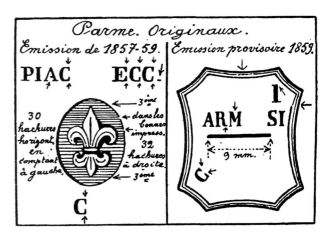

Parma originals. Left: issue of 1857–59, 30 horizontal shading lines counting on left; third line; in the good prints, 32 shading lines counting on right; third line. Right: Provisional issue, 1859.

forgeries have dividing frame lines between the stamps. The 25-centesimo exists tête-bêche, in which the line structure cannot be discerned and the upper right fleur-de-lys petal is not as high as the one on the left and has no vein.

Forged cancellations: numerous on originals; comparison is necessary. On the forgeries, one finds the same cancellations as in the first issue, except Types A and C. The barred circle is also found on these forgeries.

1859. Provisional government. Nos. 12 to 16. Note: The Sardinian stamps, 1855–61 issue, which were in circulation in 1859, are in keen demand with Parmesan cancellations.

Inscribed STATI PARMENSI and value in a triple octagonal frame with concave lines.

Sheets: sixty stamps (6 x 10). Typographed. Imperforate. Two plates for each value, except the 80-centesimo stamp.

Paper: about 65 or 70 microns, depending upon the printing.

Select: four margins, about 1½ mm wide.

Shades: 5-centesimo yellow-green, blue-green (first printing). 10-centesimo more or less dark brown. 20-centesimo blue to dark blue. 40-centesimo vermilion-tinted red; red-brown (first printing): 10M. 80-centesimo off-olive tinted bistre, orange-bistre: 50M.

Varieties: wide zeros in Nos. 13–16 (almost 2 mm instead of 1½), seven times in Plate I and six times in Plate II: 2M, 2U. A zero that is not so high (2 mm instead of 2½) is found only once in Nos. 13 and 14, Plate I: 3M, 3U. No. 13 with figure "1" inverted, once in Plate II: 3M, 4U.

There also are plate-wear defects that command an additional twenty-five percent when they are clearly visible: CFNTESIMI; CENTFSIMI; CFNTFSIMI; CENTESINI; CENIESIMI. Various letters (for example, the "A") and the zeros in the 10- and 20-centesimo, are broken at top and wearing thin at bottom. Minor flaws of this sort, along with flaws in the frames, facilitate plating.

Cancellations: Types B or E. Others are rare. All cancellations on this set must be expertized. Only three genuinely canceled examples are known of the 80-centesimo stamp. Covers franked with Sardinian stamps are very rare.

Pairs: 3M, 4U. Blocks of four, mint: 6–8M. Used: exceedingly rare. No reprints.

Originals: see preceding illustration.

Forgeries: about twenty early and modern ones, most of them in complete sets, and all of them lithographed, save for one typographed set. A few characteristic features will suffice for identifying all of them. Look for: Noncongruent inscription letters with no evidence of indention: letters too high, too far away from each other, "P" touching the frame, top of "A" sharp-pointed, "R" too thick, or with a tail on the right, "M" and "I" joined top and bottom, letters of PARM connected below; "I" of STATI with top left serif; bottom of "S" of PARMENSI flattened; "C" of CENTESIMI, no bottom serif (frequent, especially in the typographed set); arbitrary shades; figures noncongruent — wide, tall, narrow, too small; "4" of "40" closed on top or with oblique rectilinear line; dividing frame lines between the stamps; bars under PARMENSI too long, too short, too narrow (in one forgery that overcame the obstacle there is no bar at all); noncongruent frames with frequently equidistant median line or with rectilinear cut-off corners; different formats; paper also, especially thin paper, pelure paper, laid paper (typographed); PARMENSI must measure 12½–12⅗ mm (measure from the middle of the letter). In the Geneva set, the bar under PARMENSI is only 8½ mm long.

One finds forgeries printed in sheets of six (2 x 3), the two rows as tête-bêche; in sheets of twenty-five (5 x 5), and 100 (10 x 10), which is larger than in the Nicolet establishment or the official printing presses. One even finds values printed in black on white (printer's trial proofs, or counterfeiter's proofs?), and a 60-centesimo stamp that would be very rare if it were authentic.

Forged cancellations: most often a square or a dotted circle, a grill, various circular cancellations with date: PARMA 13 AGO 58; BORGO 6 FEVR. 59, both previously mentioned, and PARMA 18 AGO 59, etc.

Fakes: 40-centesimo red, mint, daubed with red-brown shades.

Postage Due Stamps for Newspapers

Like Modena, there is a handstamped postmark similar to double circle cancellations (24½ mm, PARMA, and 23½ mm, PIACENTA) with names of these towns at bottom and GAZZETTE ESTERI on top; in the middle, a single or double circle surmounted by a crown enclosing a fleur-de-lys; above the circle, inscription CENT. 9. This postmark is probably an arrival marking, with charge indicated.

1853–57. Preceding type. Postage due stamp for newspapers. Nos. 1 and 2. *Sheets* and design as above.

Paper: 6-centesimo, No. 2, thin paper (50 microns) for the dull rose.

Shades: 6-centesimo (1857), rose, dull rose; 9-centesimo (1853), blue, pale blue, grayish blue.

Varieties: same flaws in lettering as in the preceding issue: "F" for "E"; "A" split on top; etc. No reprints.

Cancellations: they must always be checked. Most frequent is postmark Type E (quite often, PARMA with two loop-shaped designs before and after the word). The 9-centesimo is exceedingly rare.

Forgeries: go back to the text dealing with forgeries in the preceding issue and compare with the illustration of the originals of that issue. Figures, paper, shades are not congruent.

Romagna

1859 (September 1). Values in bajocchi. Nos. 1 to 9. *Sheets* of 120 stamps in two panes of sixty (12 x 5). Imperforate. Typographed. Machine-made paper (60–70 microns), except 8-bajocco (85 microns). The brownish gum has sometimes altered the paper shade.

Select: four margins, to dividing frame lines: 1 mm.

Split stamps: 1-, 2-, 4- to 6-, and 8-bajocco, for half of their value, and ½-bajocco, for 1-centesimo. No. 3, bisected: 3U. No. 5: 10U. Compare cancellations, and purchase all only on cover.

Cancellations: eight-barred lozenge is common. Circular with date: 25U. All others: rare.

Pairs: 2.50M, 3U. 4-bajocco: 4U. Uncommon values: very rare. Blocks of four, mint, the set: 500 francs. Used are very rare. Romagna and Sardinia cancellations are very rare.

Essays on paper of different thicknesses are in different shades than the original.

Reprints (Brussels, Moens, 1892): unofficial, made with original clichés in a poor state of preservation, which caused plate clogging, letter splitting, corrections. The "R" and the "A" of FRANCO are joined at the bottom; also, often, the "T" and the "A" of POSTALE. The corner ornaments are blurred and the center circle of the upper right corner is closed. No gum, noncongruent format. Different shades, in the following order: bistre-yellow, dark gray, bistre-brown, dark green (less bluish than the original), reddish brown, bright lilac, pale green, rose, dull blue.

Originals: width: $18^3/_5-^3/_4$ mm, according to values. The 8- and 20-bajocco are a little narrower (about $18^1/_2$ mm). Height: $21^3/_5-^3/_4$ mm, the 6- and 20-bajocco about $21^1/_2$ mm. See the illustration for the distinctive characteristics. Inscription letters do not touch each other. However, because of the slight distance between the serifs of the "R" and "A" of FRANCO, these letters occasionally do touch at bottom in heavily inked impressions.

The marks indicated by arrows are not always visible, of course, particularly the small breaks or cracks in the serifs when the impression is not so good. In addition to these, there are one or two uniform marks in each value that also may serve as expertizing indicators: $^1/_2$-bajocco, the dot in the upper right corner is rarely visible. 1-, 2-, and 3-bajocco; special figure shape. 4-bajocco, serif of the second "L" of BOLLO is often broken at bottom, as in the first "L," and the inner frame frequently is broken on the right above the last "O" of BOLLO. 5-bajocco, the left downstroke of the "N" of FRANCO is almost invisible or is broken; the small circle in the upper left corner is broken where it touches the center circle. 6-bajocco, an unprinted dot in black in the upper frame above the right stroke of the first "O" of BOLLO. 8-bajocco, a break in the inner frame above the "E" of POSTALE. 20-bajocco, a color line joining the two frames under the right foot of the "R" of ROMAGNE, and a black dot above the horizontal bar of the "A" of FRANCO.

Forgeries: five sets of early forgeries, lithographed. Comparison with illustration will make clear that the center circle of the upper right ornament is usually complete, and that there are defects so minor that they cannot be considered serious. The "R," "A," and "N" of FRANCO are touching. The dots after BAI are round or else are too high or too low. The tops of the "A" letters are pointed. ROMAGNE is printed in ordinary capital letters. The inscriptions are not aligned and do not show the marks indicated in the illustration. The figures and the format are not congruent, the shades are arbitrary, etc. The same may be said for a few isolated forgeries that usually are of Italian origin. One of these sets comes from Hamburg.

Genoa forgeries (I.): this modern set is certainly the best and the most widely circulated. One cliché was manufactured for the nine values. It lacks the upper right ornament break in the center circle (engraver's secret mark, since a mere design flaw due to caliper slippage would not explain the break in *two* circles). The forged cliché then was retouched crudely to make a mark resembling the original. The illustration shows this and gives information on other defects in these counterfeits.

Romagna originals. Forged Genoa set; open or closed.

Forged cancellations: they are extremely numerous on originals as well as on so-called "reprints" and forgeries. The ones found on originals must be given comparative expertizing, and, when buying single stamps, only those covered by a large part of the cancellation should be accepted.

Forged Geneva cancellations are very widespread on originals and Genoa forgeries. The forgers are creating several new ones to attract collectors looking for something new. Let us hope that the results will convince them that their efforts have been futile.

Circular cancellations with date: FAENZA 20 DIC; RAVENNA 5 APR 59; TORINO 6 JUIL 59; RIMINI 7 NOV 59; PISANI.... Lozenge cancellation with six bars inside. Barred cancellation (four heavy bars, 15 mm long, spaced 3 mm apart!). Straight-line cancel in capital letters: MEDICINA, CESANA, ASSICURATO; interchangeable dates. Note: Some of these forged postmarks also were used for Roman States stamps.

Powell's Bookstores Chicago

AbeBooks.com

SHIPMENT TRACKING ID: PWL641822

|||||||||||||||||||||||||||||||||||||||||

SHIPPING **INTERNATIONAL**

DATE

Pierre Bellemare
192 Main
PO Box 12014
Ottawa, ON K1S 1C2
CANADA

SKU	TITLE
BR12007	The Serrane Guide: Stamp Forgeries of the World to 1926

Thank you for your order from Powell's Bookstores, Chicago through AbeBooks.com!

If you have any questions about this order, please contact us at **catorders@powellschicago.com**.

Thank you for shopping with AbeBooks.com, the world's largest online marketplace for books. Whether it's new, used, rare, or out-of-print, you can find it here! **AbeBooks - Because you read.**

Roman States

I. Imperforate Stamps

First issue. 1852. Nos. 1 to 11. *Plates:* the different types were letterpress-printed from stereotypes in sheets of 100 in four panes of twenty-five (5 x 5), except Nos. 10 and 11, which were done in sheets of fifty.

Gutters, margins: Nos. 1, 2, 4, 5, and 9 have a single frame, separated from the adjacent stamps by a $^1/_2$ mm gutter. That suggests that the stamps with four margins are as rare as the Thurn and Taxis stamps with the same gutter measurement. The stamps with a frame very close to the adjacent stamps are exceedingly valuable: 2–3 units. Nos. 3, 6, 7, and 8 have a double frame and gutters about $^3/_4$ mm wide. Marginal copies are not rare: 25U; corner copies: 2U.

Paper great diversity in thickness: wove, laid, stippled. The 7-bajocco is found laid and striated (slightly ribbed), both having been produced at the same time.

Printing: Nos. 2–10 were printed in 1854 with a gray ink that is occasionally so oily that it shows through the back of the stamp.

$^1/_2$-bajocco: the rose-violet shade is rare: 4M, 4U. The tête-bêche is from the first printing. Bisected to make a $^1/_4$-bajocco: very rare.

1-bajocco: shades: gray-green, dark yellow-green, blue-green. Printed both sides: rare. Bisected ($^1/_2$-bajocco): 20 francs. This stamp has two varieties, depending upon whether the horizontal framework is continuous or not.

2-bajocco: this stamp exists on thick paper; pale green shade. Bisected (1-bajocco): 10 francs.

3-bajocco: brownish buff, yellowish ochre, light yellow. No dot after BAJ (fourteenth stamp on the sheet): 15 francs M, 5 francs U. Trisected (1-bajocco): 75 francs. Bisected ($1^1/_2$-bajocco): very rare. Thick paper is not very common. Printed both sides: 60 francs.

4-bajocco: the new lemon shade is worth double the straw-yellow. Quartered (1-bajocco): very rare. Bisected (2-bajocco): 50 francs. Printed both sides: very rare.

5-bajocco: rosy white: 3M. This should be checked, for the rose shade occasionally was bleached. Bisected ($2^1/_2$-bajocco): 200 francs. Printed both sides: very rare.

6-bajocco: trisected (2-bajocco): 100 francs. Bisected (3-bajocco): 75 francs. Printed both sides: very rare.

7-bajocco: bisected ($3^1/_2$-bajocco): very rare.

8-bajocco: white or yellowish-white paper. Bisected (4-bajocco): 200 francs.

Split stamps: on cover, these are found used singly or in combination with complete stamps; the latter have greater value. Horizontally split stamps: twenty-five percent more. Numerous fakes: buy only on whole cover, expertized.

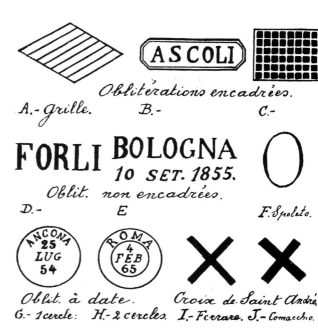

Roman States — cancellations of the first issue. A. Grill. B/C. Framed. D/E. Unframed. G/H. Dated. I/J. St. Andrew's cross. K. Comacchio L. Lozenge. M. Oval.

Varieties: there are many secondary varieties such as tiaras, tufts, broken letters, and frames, etc.

Cancellations: there are a great many different cancellations. The limited number illustrated shows the amateur that the field for research is far from being restricted to common cancellations A or D and the somewhat less common Type G. Many rare cancellations are valued from 10–100U, depending on the rarity of the canceling postmark. Examples: Type E, ACQUAPENDENTE, APPIGNANO, etc., are worth 10 francs on No. 2 or No. 3 on cover; Type A in blue: 2U; in red: 3U; fine Bologna grid: 5U; Types D or E in red: 3U; in blue: 5U; Type I: 50U; Type J: less common. Type K dumb cancellations are not very common. Type L was used on the second issue: common. Type F: rare; on No. 4: 20 francs. Type M oval cancels: value depends on where they come from. ASSICURATA (insured), straight line, in red; "P L" in a circle; "P P," etc.: rare.

Note: The 1-scudo was used only in Rome.

Pairs: 3–4U; blocks of four mint: 6M; used blocks: rare (for example, No. 3: 20 francs). A strip of four of the 6-bajocco is rare.

On cover: 25U; Nos. 10, 10a, and 11: 2U.

Reprints: none.

Used postal forgeries: Nos. 2, 6, and 9 were lithographically counterfeited in Bologna. The method of printing facilitates their identification. The paper is too thick. Comparison of design, lettering, and general characteristics will supply a third proof of forgery. Genuine cancellations on these stamps are rare; No. 2: 10U; No. 6, 12U; No. 9: 25U. It is desirable to acquire these stamps on cover. In case of doubt, cancellations should be expertized.

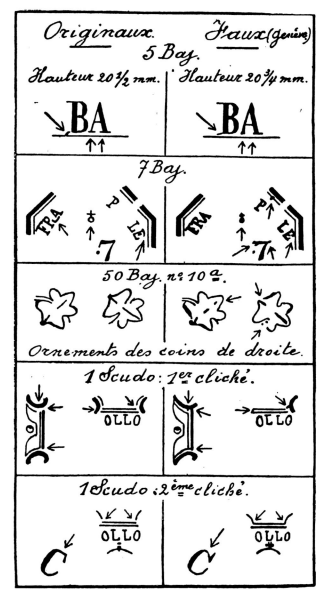

Characteristics of the first issue and Geneva counterfeits. 5-bajocco, height 20½ mm, original; 20¾ mm, forgery. 7-bajocco. 50-bajocco, No. 10a, right corner ornaments. 1-scudo.

Varieties of the forged 5-bajocco with the "A" touching the "J," and of the 8-bajocco with thin-printed "J," are worth twice the usual value.

Early and new forgeries: comparative study facilitates the identification of all stamp forgeries. The accompanying illustration gives information on the Geneva (F.). counterfeits, which are especially widespread and relatively well counterfeited, and on the 5-bajocco printed both sides. The characteristics of values shown in the illustration may be useful in spotting other forgeries.

Noteworthy among the deceptive forgeries are the following:

½-bajocco, dark brown, the left frame almost touching the oval and the acorn trimmings touching the pearl above the "B." This defect is found on the right in another copy.

1-bajocco, without dots in the lateral ornaments of the tiara (these dots cannot be seen in the heavily printed originals, either); the paper lacks the stippled effect of the original (examine for transparency).

5-bajocco. See the illustration.

7-bajocco. See "Geneva forgeries" in the illustration. The second and third wavy lines of the tiara meet; this flaw persists, like the others, in a second cliché in which the globe of the crown, the spacing of the "E" of POSTALE with the inner frame, and the horizontal bar of the figure were inexpertly corrected. Paper insufficiently stippled.

8-bajocco, with a single inner left frame unthinned above the terminal loop of the key, etc.; in another one, the key stems are broken.

50-bajocco, No. 10. The originals are about 26¾ to 27 mm wide by 20 mm high (measure from point to point, middle of stamp); one forgery is 26½ mm wide; the terminal line of the right downstroke of the "A" of BAJ. is double that of the left stroke; another on laid paper measures 26½ mm; the letters of FRANCO are too high, 1¾ mm instead of 1½ mm; the design of an Austrian forgery is not congruent with that of the original (see illustration); the serifs of "P" and "T" of POSTALE of an engraved Breslau forgery are too short; finally, Geneva forgeries of Nos. 10a and 10 exhibit the characteristics shown in the illustration.

1-scudo. Numerous forgeries — it would take too long to describe them. Compare with the distinctive marks of the originals (see illustration). Also, note that the originals have gaps or breaks, which can be considered to be secret expertizing marks, in the following places: the "N" of FRANCO (dot at top on left of letter, right downstroke of letter broken at top); the "T" of POSTALE (top bar broken on both sides of the vertical, or on one side only); the "U" of SCUDO (break at bottom; figure "1" also broken on right of stem); first ornamental frame, above the "A" of

POSTALE; same frame, printing failure under the figure and a break 3 mm from this spot, where the frame reascends.

For Geneva forgeries of No. 11, see the characteristics of the two clichés in the illustration; the second of the clichés, although mended, is perhaps even worse than the first.

Forged cancellations: various kinds are found on the forgeries and on both forgeries and originals of the 1-scudo. The Geneva-fabricated forged postmarks, engraved on wood, were affixed on No. 11 originals: Type A: grill crudely executed, with rounded corners; Type D: CALDARO; Type H: ROMA 17 AUG 56, "56" changed subsequently to "66"; RIMINI 17 NOV 59.

Fakes: all stamps split for one-half, one-third, or one-quarter of their value must be closely examined, on cover or on piece of cover, because posthumous cancellations (those made at a later date) are numerous.

Second issue. 1867, September 21. Nos. 12 to 18. This set was made necessary by a monetary change from bajocchi/scudo to centesimi/lira.

Plates: formed as previously, but in four panes of sixteen (4 x 4).

2-centesimi: no dot after CENT: 3M, 2U.

5-centesimi: blue or green. Blue-green: 50M, 25U. No dot after "5": 4M, 2U.

20-centesimi: no dot after "20" or CENT, mint: 20 francs; used: 10 francs.

40-centesimi: yellow or yellow-ochre, with or without dot after "40": no increase in value.

80-centesimi: this value may have a small or large dot after "80": 6M, 20U. Two dots: printing flaw.

There are numerous secondary varieties.

To be considered select examples, stamps must have the fine double line of the framework intact.

Reprints and forgeries: see below, in connection with the following issue.

II. Perforated Stamps

1868. Same type. Nos. 19 to 25. Sheets of 120 stamps (8 x 15), except the first printings of the 3-, 10-, and 20-centesimi, which were printed as in the previous issue, in sheets of sixty-four stamps. Perf 13¼.

2-centesimi: no dot after CENT: no value increment.

5-centesimi: same: 8M, 6U.

10-centesimi: nontransparent paper: 8M, 50U.

20-centesimi: no dot after "20" or CENT, mint: 60 francs; used: 15 francs.

80-centesimi: the purplish rose stamp is unissued. No dot after "80": 20 francs.

The 5- and 40-centesimi without a dot after the figure are common. The 80-centesimi exists without vertical dividing frame line; with a large dot: same value as without dot; with small dot: double value.

The 10-, 40-, and 80-centesimi also are found imperforate horizontally; the 2-, 5-, 10-, and 20-centesimi, imperforate vertically; the 2-, 3-, 10-, 20-, and 80-centesimi, with double horizontal perforation. The 5-, 10-, and 20-centesimi exist entirely imperforate.

Reprints (second and third issues): printed from plates amateurishly reproduced from the original plates; the imprint is flattened by excessive pressure and has many flaws. Shades, paper, and, occasionally, perforations differ. Not being official, these reprints must be considered forgeries. The forgers repeated the operation four times to meet the demand.

1878–79 (Usigli). Imperforate, thick paper, perf 11½ to 12.

1889 (Moens). Imperforate, with and without gum, also perf 11½ and 13. The 10-, 20-, 40-, and 80-centesimi are found on glossy paper, as well as on nonglossy, matte paper.

1890 (Cohn). Imperforate, paper slightly glossy, perf 11½.

1890 (Gelli). Imperforate, and perf 13.

Only specialization will enable one to make a sound decision by comparing perforations, shades, paper, and, above all, printing, which is always better in the imperforate originals, only a little better in the 1868 perforated stamps. Bright shades.

Forgeries: also, several additional sets of forgeries are known (Pisa, Genoa, etc.) that must be judged by comparing the design, which is never congruent with the originals. The Genoa set looks good in general, but the shades are too bright and the printing is more blurred, even more defective than in the so-called "reprints." Details and lettering are poorly done; the frames or the inner ovals are too thick; etc. The Pisa forgeries were given forged cancellations in Geneva.

Pisa forgeries: glossy, wove, or stippled paper (10- and 40-centesimi); measurements rarely agree with originals.

2-centesimi. Outer frame malformed in the upper right corner; base of the "2" is oblique with respect to the lower frame; the acorn above "G" forms a crow's foot (this flaw was corrected in a second cliché, but the acorn then became too narrow).

3-centesimi. Frame broken above "N" and malformed to the right of "M I" (two clichés).

5-centesimi. First cliché: very bad, numerous broken letters, breaks in the outer frame. Second cliché: the horizontal bar of figure "5" does not curl up as in the original; the "O" of FRANCO is broken, upper right; and the "B" of BOLLO is much larger than the "O." Third cliché: same flaws, but the "B" has been reduced to normal size.

10-centesimi. The inner left frame is joined with the curved frame on top. (This defect was corrected in a second cliché.) The curved frame is broken on the right of "T," as in the original, but here the curve is joined to the scallop. "T" appears almost as in the "reprints"; in the originals, it is less complete.

20-centesimi. The design, although acceptable, is not as fine as in the original.

40-centesimi. In the original, the "4" is slightly elevated with respect to the "O," and its base is extended by a line. The dot after the "T" is too low.

80-centesimi. Inner frame broken above the "C" of FRANCO. The bottom left acorn forms a crow's foot, as in the reprints. There are four fringes in the original.

Forged cancellations on Pisa forgeries: Type A: grill. Type B: MASSA; MEDICINA AROL. Type C: (with date) ROMA 1 AUG 67 and 1 DEC 68; TERRACINA 4 APR 67; VITERBO 6 DEC 67; CIVITAVECCHIA 10 NOV 67. "P.D." (postage due), framed.

Forged cancellations: numerous other forged postmarks were applied to original stamps. Expertizing is useful.

Sardinia

The Sardinian collection is one of the most attractive with its cancellations and the wealth of color shades in the 1855 issue.

I. Cavallini

The former postmarks called "Cavallini" have been assigned a separate category by Sardinian specialists. Three values: 15-centesimo (circular), 25-centesimo (oval), 50-centesimo (octagonal), applied by handstamp (1819), or machine-stamped (1820). Value of mints: 30, 60, and 80 francs; used stamps of the period: 15, 50, and 60 francs; used after 1836: 10, 25, and 15 francs. The mints of 1820 are worth a little less. Sheets folded in two with various watermarks; the half-sheets or pieces are worth much less.

Forgeries: identifiable usually by the sexless war horse that adorns them. Design and paper comparison are necessary. The paper is not the same, or else the forgeries are printed on pieces of the original paper.

II. Imperforate Stamps

1851 (January). Lithographed. Nos. 1 to 3. *Select:* four margins, $1/2$ mm wide.

The very difficult task of reconstructing the plates is not finished. Thick (80 microns+), machine-made, white paper. No reprints.

Shades: 5-centesimo black, gray-black. 20-centesimo dark blue; pale blue: 50M. 40-centesimo rose; carmine-tinted rose. The purplish rose is worth: 50M, 50U.

Varieties: good impressions of the first printing are in demand. The 20-centesimo is found with the transfer flaw "8 OLLO." The 5-centesimo has some center oval

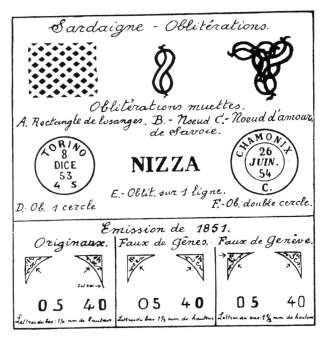

Top: Sardinian cancellations. A. Rectangle of lozenges. B. Knot. C. Love knot of Savoy. D. Single-circle. E. Straightline. F. Double circle. Bottom: Issue of 1851. Originals. Genoa forgeries. Geneva forgeries.

retouching. The retouched spots are rare, having been made at the end of the plate's use.

Pairs: 4U. Blocks are rare.

Cancellations: Type A (several styles): common. Types B and C, essay cancellations, rare: 2U on No. 2. Cancellation with date is rare. Color cancellations are rare. Pen cancellation: 50 percent.

Reprints: none.

Originals: format, 5-centesimo, $19 1/4$ x 22 mm. 20-centesimo, $19-19 1/2$ x $21 3/4-22$ mm. 40-centesimo, $19-19 1/4$ x $21 3/4$ mm.

Fakes: pen cancellations cleaned.

Official forgeries: the lettering form in the three values is arbitrary; compare letters, hair, beard with a 20-centesimo stamp. Noncongruent format. Stamps with an authentic cancellation are rare.

Forgeries: 1. Early lithographed set without dot after POSTE. Different lettering, especially the "C" and the "O," which are round. The beard is too straight and too short.

2. Rather successful forgeries of the 5- and 40-centesimo, which are identifiable as official forgeries. Noncongruent shades.

3. Genoa set (I.). See the illustration for distinctive characteristics. Format 19 x $21 1/2$. White paper (70 microns). The 5-centesimo is deep black; the 20-centesimo, indigo blue; 40-centesimo rose and bright

rose. The neck stippling is quite visible. The eye line comes down as far as the nostril. Forged cancellation, Type A.

4. Geneva set (F.). Format 19¼ x 21½ mm. Tough, yellowish, thick (75 microns) paper. Shades are too pale and dull. The excessively short beard ends above the "O" of BOLLO. No Adam's apple. Forged cancellations: TORINO 13. GEN (on two lines); a large Neapolitan cancellation, NAPOLI 17 NOV 185..; Type F, AIX-LES-BAINS 24 NOV. 51.

1853 (November 1). Dry offset impression. Nos. 4 to 6. *Select:* four margins, minimum width: 1 mm.
Sheets of fifty stamps (10 x 5).
Shades: 5-centesimo blue-tinted green. 20-centesimo light blue. 40-centesimo dull rose. Dry, embossed offset impression on colored paper.
Pairs: 4U. Blocks: rare.
Cancellations: almost always Types D and F. Cancellations of Savoy and of the County of Nice are in keen demand; their rarity varies according to whether the delivery localities were more or less populated (NIZZA MARITTA is common). Some of them are very rare. All other types of cancellation are rare.
Originals: format 19 x 21¼-½ mm (measure between depressions, outside the pearls). Thick paper (about 50 microns).
Genoa forgeries (I.): 19¼ mm wide. Chalky presses produced a horizontal stippling in the paper. Also, wove paper (80 microns). The line after POSTES does not appear in any of the values. The 5-centesimo has no dot after the value figure. (A first cliché of the 5-centesimo had an embossed vertical line before "05" and after the first bottom "C.") Noncongruent shades: green, blue, purplish rose, etc. The error (!) "05" is found on blue paper!

The difficulty of studying and achieving this kind of impression tempted counterfeiters. However, the forgeries are unsuccessful. The pearls of the outer frame, the inscriptions, and the corner ornaments are most often not very visible; likewise, the head contour line. Everything is quite visible in the originals.

Forged cancellations: a list of the forged cancellations on Genoa forgeries follows: PINEROLO; GENOVA; forged postmark, Type A, large lozenge; TORINO 28 OCT 53 10 M; BIELLA 13 MAR 53 10 M; BIELLA 15 FEBR 53 ..S; NOVARA 26 DIC 53 ..S; PALLANZA 13 AGO 53; VERCELLI 14 GIU 53 1 M. The dates are interchangeable. For example, one finds TORINO 2 AGO 53, etc. The forged postmarks described under the following issue also were used here.

Private reprints made by the printer are on stippled paper or excessively thick paper. For these forgeries and for others from various sources, the arbitrary shades provide the best criterion. These so-called "reprints" were canceled fraudulently with different postmarks.

The Florence (U.) and Berlin (C.) forgeries also can be identified by the arbitrary shades and by the absence of embossing.

1854 (mid-April). Blank center. Nos. 7 to 9. Dry offset impression embossed on white paper. Lithographed framework. Margins, minimum width: ¾ mm.

Shades: the 5-centesimo olive-green is rare, mint. 20-centesimo light blue: 3M, 3U. The indigo and greenish blue are less common than the ordinary blue stamps. The 40-centesimo dull pale rose is most common, mint or used; carmine-tinted rose and brownish rose: 50M.
Cancellations: see the preceding issue.
Pairs: 4U.
Originals: the embossing is almost always quite visible everywhere, including the head, to such an extent that hair, ear, and beard details stand out clearly. In the best dry offset impressions, one can see the horizontal line after POSTES. We particularly recommend the copies possessing that primary guarantee of authenticity. The second guarantee is the cancellation, when it is good. The paper is white, medium (55–75 microns). Format, 5-centesimo, 19 x 21½ mm; 20-centesimo, 19½ x 21½–22 mm; 40-centesimo, 19¼ x 21½ mm.
Stock remainders: paper is grayer. Format is smaller: 5-centesimo, 18¾ x 21¼ mm; 20-centesimo, 18¾ x 21 mm; 40-centesimo, 18⅗ x 21⅛ mm. The prices quoted in the catalogues are for mint stock remainders (dull shades) with less pronounced embossing. The others are much rarer.
Private reprints were done by the printer himself. Shade comparison is necessary. The reprints are almost congruent, but brighter, and the paper is grayer. Other "reprints" were made later in Florence and Berlin. Different papers and paper often stippled as in the preceding issue. Format 5-centesimo, 19 x 21¼ mm; 20-centesimo, 19 x 21½ mm; 40-centesimo, 19½ x 21½ mm. The embossing is not very visible.
Genoa forgeries (I.): this set is so widespread that except for the forgeries executed in Genoa on excessively soft, congruently thick paper, there must be a large number of so-called "second reprints" that took the Genoa road to acquire a forged cancellation. All these undesirables are often stuck on pieces of contemporary paper exactly the size of the stamp. There are very amusing value "errors": 5- and 40-centesimo blue; 20- and 40-centesimo green; 5- and 20-centesimo rose. The dry offset impression is absolutely inadequate; comparison will show it. Numerous shades, many of which are arbitrary. Various formats: 5-centesimo, 19 x 21–21½ mm; 20-centesimo, 19⅕ x 21½ mm; 40-centesimo, 19–19½ x 21¼–¾ mm.

Forged cancellations are numerous on stock remainders, the so-called "reprints," and on forgeries. Beware of on-cover stamps. A list of counterfeit Genoa postmarks with interchangeable dates — the inner inscriptions are much too close — follows: ALESSANDRIA 3 OTT 54 10 M; CASALE 17 GIU 54 4 S; CHIAVARI 24 LUG 54 10 M; GENOVA 23 LUG 54 7 S; MONTE ROTONDO 14 DIC; NIZZA MAR 54 7 S and 15 AGO 54 10 M; NOVARA 14 FEB 54 10 S; PINEROLO 18 FEB...; SALUZZO 25 AGO 54 4 M; SAVONA 3 OTT 54 3 M; SUSA (with "61" inverted); SUSA 13 SET 54 7 S; TORINO 12 SET 54 7 S; TORTONA 14 AGO....; VERCELLI 29 LUG 54 7 M. Also, one finds "P D" unframed in red, blue, and black.

Note: These forged postmarks have been applied to genuine stamps.

1855–58 (June). Head-only embossed. Nos. 10 to 14. This set has a great many shades for each value, many of which are rare. One can find a gamut of ten different shades just for the 80-centesimo value. This and the 10-centesimo value are from the 1858 issue, the others from 1855.

Sheets as above. Paper of various thicknesses. Typographed.

Select: four margins, minimum width ³/₄ mm.

Rare shades: 5-centesimo yellow-green, first printing: 60 francs, mint; 4 francs, used; green-black (myrtle): 100 francs, mint, 10 francs, used; emerald green: 80 francs, mint; 10 francs, used. 10-centesimo purplish brown and black-brown: 12 francs, mint; 6 francs, used; umber (first printing): 25 francs, mint; 3 francs, used; olive-brown: 3 francs, mint; 1 franc, used. 20-centesimo cobalt and sky blue (first printings) are worth 80 francs, mint; 5 francs, used; milky blue: 100 francs, mint. 40-centesimo, the vermilion shades are worth from 25–50 francs, mint; 4–5 francs, used; dull rose: 15 francs, mint; 3 francs, used; rose: 2 francs, mint; 1.50 francs, used; purplish rose is worth 25 francs, used; mint: very rare. 80-centesimo, the orange shades are worth 10 francs, mint, 20 francs, used; yellow-ochre: 8 francs, mint, 10 francs, used; orange-yellow and bright yellow are common mint, 8 francs, used.

Varieties: 20- and 40-centesimo, with outer frame line: 2–3U. Various plate defects are found in the lettering and figures. Heads out of place, and with double and triple impressions. The canceled stamps with inverted head all are rare; naturally, there are many forged cancellations. The 20-centesimo exists without head, the 5-, 10-, and 40-centesimo, with double head, one of which is inverted. The 10-, 20-, 40-, and 80-centesimo stamps were bisected for half their value: rare. The 80-centesimo was split for a quarter: very rare.

Pairs: in demand, because it is easier to read cancellations. Blocks: rare.

Cancellations: the cancellation varieties are as numerous as those of the shades. Types D and F are common; rare in red or blue. Type A, circular dumb cancellation: rare. Type E (SICILIA; NIZZA in red, etc.): rare. There is an active market for the following cancellations: Parma, Modena (bars), Lombardy, the small Italian grill (1861); the Neapolitan cancellations (ANNULATA in parentheses and in a circle; ANNULATA framed; cancellation with date of Sicily-Messina, etc.); those of San Marino: 5U; those of Savoy, County of Nice, Monaco, mobile (railway) cancels, Italy, Marseilles, Type E postmark with date; steamship cancellations (PIROSCAFI POSTALE FRANCESI in blue; COL VAPORE, etc.), and the stamps of previous issues which continued to be used long after issuance. Foreign cancellations (Italian postal service in Tunis, Egypt, etc.) are rare, as is Tunis in blue. French arrival cancels are found, usually large figure "2.240" (Marseilles). Many are very rare. Consult specialists before selling.

Reprints: unofficial, lithographed. Details of hair, ear, and beard embossing are not well done. Some 5-, 20-, and 40-centesimo stamps are imperforate or perf 11¹/₂.

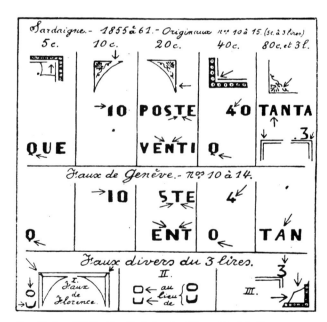

Sardinia, 1855–61. Originals. Nos. 10–15 (5-centesimo to 3-lira). Middle: Geneva forgeries. Nos. 10–14. Bottom: various forgeries of the 3-lira. I. Florence forgeries. II. instead of.

Originals: a few matrix plate reproduction defects may be considered as secret expertizing points. (See illustration.) The "S" of POSTES is slanted to left; the "O" letters have an octagonal shape.

Forgeries: there are many forged cancellations on stock remainders. Mint stamps from the latter are so inexpensive that it is astonishing to find this issue completely counterfeited.

1. Geneva forgeries (F.): they do not have the expertizing points of the originals. The illustration shows the other principal defects. Forged cancellations on these forgeries: Type D, PIAC... 6 OTT 57; Type E, on two lines, ANNE... MAR; TORINO 13 GEN; Type F, BOLOGNA 21 GEN 59.

2. Genoa forgeries (I.): they do not have the expertizing points either. The "S" of POSTES is erect and straight. The embossing is more visible than in the preceding forgeries, but the nose is more rounded because the hollow above it is too low and the nose's end extends beyond the moustache. The set exists with head inverted. Forged cancellation: Type D, NAPOLI 19 MAGG 61 12 M.

Fakes: a few stamps have been doctored chemically to create rare shades. General appearance and comparison will expose the faking.

1861 (January 1). Same type. 3-lira. No. 15. See the preceding issue for margins, sheets, cancellations, etc. There are two slightly different shades. Mint stamps on not very transparent thick paper: 2M. The 3-lira with inverted head is a printer's proof. The perforated copies are stock remainders.

Forgeries: three different kinds, the distinctive characteristics of which will be found in the illustration. The Florence forgery, with straight "S" of POSTES, is most widely known and circulated.

Forged cancellations: extremely numerous. Compare to original cancellations or have them expertized.

1861 (January 1). Stamps for printed matter. Nos. 16 and 17. Embossed figures. Lateral inscriptions: GIORNALI, STAMPA (newspapers, printed matter).

Sheets of 100 (10 x 10).

Shades: numerous. Margins must be 1 mm wide. The embossing error, figure "2," with frame of No. 16 (UNO) is very rare canceled.

Fakes: numerous because of the flattening of the embossed figure with the consecutive reembossing of this inverted figure or of the figure error. When this happens, the center is crumpled and traces of the first operation are found.

Forged cancellations are abundant. Make comparison. (See F. Serrane, "Faux de Sardaigne," *Echangiste universel,* May 1, 1925, 71. Serrane discussed Sardinian forgeries also in *Philatéliste belge,* No. 52 [January 15, 1926]: 71-73.)

Tuscany

This is a very interesting area for shades, paper varieties, and cancellations.

Select: margins are always very narrow ($^{1}/_{2}$–$^{2}/_{3}$ mm for the lateral margins and $^{3}/_{4}$–1 mm for the horizontals), so we must be satisfied with four visible margins, no dividing frame line being touched. Copies with four margins of more than $^{1}/_{2}$ mm are considered extraordinary and command very high prices.

Cancellations: Types B and D are common on the three issues. There are other styles of Type B: close-set bars, large bars, three bars spaced far apart; the latter is rare. Type A is common on the first issue, but rare in red. It has other styles, for example, small square dots: rare (2U for the common stamps). Type C: 2U on common stamps, rare in red. Type E, LIVORNO, FIRENZE, same value. Type F is common on the first two issues; less common in red: 50U on common stamps. Type G is common; in frame, a little less common, and in red: 50U. Type H is the natural accompaniment of the third issue. Type I, likewise; the latter is in active demand: 50U.

There are other cancellations — mute, rare, an ovoid "SA FA" (*strada ferrata* [railway]): 3U on common stamps. Large postmark with date with "PD" at top: rare. The cancellations of other Italian States are always rare. Roman States grill: 10U on common stamps; dot and number lozenge (France), etc. Franking with foreign stamps in Tuscany is rare.

Tuscany: Mute cancellations. **A. Lozenge grill. B. Bars. C. Large grill. D. Large postmark with date. E. Heart shape. F. With date and oriflammes. H. Thimble with date.**

1851–52. Sitting lion. Nos. 1 to 9. *Watermark:* crown fragments; horizontal lines.

Sheets of 240 stamps in three panes of eighty (16 x 5). Typographed.

Paper: the paper frequently is blue-gray or gray, but the first printings were made on a definitely blue paper, which is rare and in demand. The paper shades intensify the stamps' color tones, which although bright seem quite dark. No. 4 becomes a bright dark carmine; No. 5, bright dark blue; No. 7, blue-black; No. 8, dark violet. Paper is medium or thick (60–85 microns). The 6-crazie stamp is found on 75-micron transparent paper: rare.

Shades: 1-quattrino (September 1, 1852) on azure-tinted paper: 25M, 25U. 1-soldo bistre or orange-tinted ochre; bistre or dark yellow on azure-tinted paper: rare, mint, 25U. The 2-soldo is always on azure-tinted paper. 1-crazie (July 1, 1851), various carmine shades: purplish carmine on azure-tinted paper (Yvert No. 4a): rare, mint, 50U; bright dark carmine on blue (first printing): rare. 2-crazie, various blue shades, gray-blue, green-blue, etc., true blue on azure-tinted paper: rare, mint, 2U. 6-crazie, various shades of blue, indigo, slate; blue-black: rare, mint, 50U. 9-crazie (July 1, 1851) lilac-brown; dark violet: 3M, 50U; dark violet on bluish paper: rare, mint, 2U. 60-crazie on bluish gray (November 1, 1852). The 1- and 2-soldo and 2-, 4-, and 6-crazie are from the issue of April 1, 1851.

Varieties: the true blue paper (first printing): very rare, mint, 2–3U. Sometimes there are marginal copies, practically without watermark. Plate defects are found in all values. For example, 1-quattrino, top of "1" is thick; 1-crazie, upper right corner is rounded; 4-crazie, color spot between the lion's head and the left paw. Slight cross-hatching of the background (trace of press blanket) is not rare.

Pairs: 1-, 2-, and 9-crazie: 3U; others: 4U. Strips of three in good condition are rare. Blocks of four are very rare.

Reprints (1866): 2-soldo and 60-crazie on original paper of the last printings (grayish) with watermark, but the repaired value inscription is not congruent, nor are the shades. Make comparison. Thus, these reprints are part counterfeit and should go into reference albums. Essay stamps of all values (except the 60-crazie) exist on white paper, which time often has turned yellowish; no watermark, thick paper (85–90 microns). The set: 30 francs. Some of them have gone through the post.

Originals: width, about 19 mm, height, 22½–¾ mm (sometimes, almost 23, 1-soldo), in conformity with printings and paper. See the principal expertizing points, which are indicated by arrows in the illustration.

It also will be noted that the lower frame is broken on the right and left of the value tablet, except in the rare cases of blotchy printing. Also, the frame line is

1851–59 Tuscany Issues. Originals, Nos. 1–16. Counterclockwise, from top: 1. Cross under the left terminal line of the "T." 2. Three jewels. 3. Four toes. 4. Four toes. Four toes. 5. Pearls are visible only in the good impressions.

rarely of the same thickness as the sections of the lower frame under the corner ornaments. The inscription letters are aligned; they do not touch each other. They are 1¼ mm high and the value letters are 1½ mm high. Finally, the watermarked crown lines are ½–¾ mm thick. The horizontal lines (or the vertical line) are half as thick and are spaced about 7 mm apart. The pearls in the top of the crown are 7 mm in diameter.

Forgeries: a small book would be needed to describe in detail the characteristics of 100 or so counterfeits of the first two Tuscany issues. Such a description would be both tedious and useless: all of them can be judged quite rapidly by using the eliminative method. With respect to this, as well as to many other things and people, one can say, "From a distance, it looks good; up close, it's hardly worth a second look." A suggested eliminative method procedure follows:

1. Examine the watermark first; more than half the counterfeit sets do not have any. There are many originals that have a few traces of watermarks or none at all, but they are rare — a fact that should be emphasized. Essays do not have watermarks either, but their white paper is enough to identify them.

2. Next, check the center design with the illustration and check the inscriptions against a common original.

3. Check whether the paper is really handmade, furrowed on the back, suitably tinted, and of proper thickness.

4. Compare, if possible, the impression and paper shades with originals.

5. Examine for indention — the "bite" characteristic of typographed stamps; lithographed stamps do not have any.

If carefully followed, this five-step procedure will isolate the intruding counterfeits. The characteristic features of the forgeries, which often are found incomplete and sometimes are printed in small sheets, are listed below. All forgeries are lithographed, except for a single engraved stamp.

1. Arbitrary format, often more or less than 19 mm in width.

2. No watermark.

3. Noncongruent watermark. Same thickness of crown and rectilinear lines, the latter spaced 5, 6, 8 mm apart. Pearls on top of crown are 5 or 6 mm in diameter.

4. Paper too thin.

5. Paper untinted (often yellowish), sometimes vertically or horizontally laid.

6. The lion's face resembles a squirrel-monkey's snout, or the face of a closely related animal: man.

7. The eye, nostril, and cheek lines are arbitrarily drawn or are missing.

8. Two or three toes of the three paws are visible.

9. The shield's outer line is not rectilinear, or its lines are too long or too short.

10. The dots are totally or partly missing between the shield frames.

11. The interior ornamentation of the latter is not regular and sometimes touches or almost touches the inner frame.

12. The dots and lines on a level with the lion's "knee" are too long, too short, parallel, or are missing.

13. The line above the value is much too thick.

14. The lower frame is not broken.

15. The stippling on the body and the lion's hindquarters does not resemble what one sees in the originals.

16. The crown is tipped (higher on one side than on the other). The cross on top of it is more or less than $1/2$ mm from the frame, or else it is placed under the body of the "I," or under the right terminal line. The crown branches are poorly drawn. The bandeau lines are rectilinear and not curved. The jewels are missing, or else there are four or five of them.

17. The beams of the corner crosses are too long and they are not thickened at ends. At times, there are no circles in the ornamental squares.

18. The lettering is too high, too low, too wide, too thin. Letters "O" or "Q" are round, not oval. Some letters touch each other.

19. Noncongruent figures, notably "1" (quattrino), too narrow, or placed variable distances from the tablet edge. (For the 1-quattrino it should be $1/2$ mm, for the 1-crazie and 1-soldo, 1 mm.)

20. There is a dividing frame line in the upper margin ($1/2$ mm), or dividing frame lines all around the stamp (about 1 mm).

Finally, there are perforated counterfeits, or flagrant "errors" such as "9 CRAZIA" or no figure before the word "CRAZIE."

Photolithographed forgeries: these counterfeits, which are among the most recent, are better than their predecessors in design, but the lithographed impression, the format, the paper, and the forged watermark will quickly identify them.

The so-called Florence (?) set, which was supplied with forged postmarks in Geneva, is on parchment-like paper: rather thick (80–90 microns), occasionally thin (60 microns), and similar to tracing paper (6-crazie). Height, about 23 mm, width $18^3/4$–$19^1/5$, depending on value. Dull shades. Forged watermark with heavy rectilinear lines.

Fakes: doctoring of the figure of No. 4a and of the final "A" of CRAZIA to make the 60-CRAZIE. Magnifying glass examination of transparency and shade comparison are indicated. Essays were given a forged watermark by applying pressure or by thinning on the back or by printing with a greasy substance. It should be noted that in the doctored stamps the watermark is much less visible in the parts that have been doctored.

Forged cancellations are very numerous on the counterfeits. All kinds are found, and often, when it is a question of early forgeries, it is quite useless to pursue the matter further.

The forged cancellations on Florence counterfeits: Type A, circular; Type B, nine bars spaced 2 mm apart, or six, $2^1/2$ mm apart; Type D, large postmark with date: LUCCA 23 GIU 54; S. MINIATO 25 NOV 185.; ROSSIGNANO 10 AGO 1856; PISA 16 FEB 1854; PONTEDERA .. SETT 18..; Type F, 8 MAG 1856 LIVORNO; Type G has an octagonal frame.

1857. Same. Wavy line watermark. Nos. 10 to 16. Same characteristics, same design as for the preceding issue. Imperforate.

Watermark: wavy lines forming "lemmas" about 28 mm long by 6 mm, maximum width. These "lemmas" are 9 mm apart at their extremities (including the line thickness), and 3 mm in the middle. There is a demand for copies containing pieces of the inscription I I E R R POSTE TOSCANE on a double-lined postmark.

Paper: grayish white, same thicknesses as previously. The thin paper (55–60 microns) sometimes is transparent.

Format: $18^1/2$–$3/4$ x $22^1/2$–about $4/5$ mm.

Shades: much less numerous than in the first issues. Usually the shades in the catalogues, or a lighter version thereof. The 2-crazie, also in blue-gray and greenish blue; 6-crazie in blue, true blue, and dark blue.

Varieties: a few plate defects in lettering and figures. Also, a large color spot between the thigh and the mane, covering the entire width of the lion's body: 2U; but 1-soldo: 50U, and 9-crazie: 25U.

Pairs: 3U. Blocks: rare.

Forgeries: what we said about the first issue is applicable to this one in which the stamps were counterfeited much less. However, one should be on his guard against good photolithographed forgeries of the 1-quattrino and 9-crazie stamps with a noncongruent forged watermark. In the very successful 1-quattrino, the "R" of QUATTRINO is open in the middle and the "lemmas" of the watermark are only 8 mm apart at their extremities and about 2 mm in the middle. Dark gray paper. Three or four dots on the left knee. Good dimensions.

It should be noted that the impression of the originals is definitely not as good as in the first issue. Well-executed copies, especially those with pearls above the crown, are in great demand.

Fakes: essays with counterfeit watermark.

1860 (January 1). Coat of arms. Nos. 17 to 23. Issued by the provisional government. Coat of arms of Savoy. Decimal values.

Sheets, paper, and *watermark,* as in the preceding issue.

Shades: 1-centesimo, from pale lilac (common) to dark brown-lilac. 5-centesimo green; olive-green: 3M, 25U. 10-centesimo, from purplish brown to dark brown and chocolate. 20-centesimo, from dull blue-gray: 2M, 25U, to dark blue. 40-centesimo more or less bright carmine-tinted rose. 80-centesimo dull rose (flesh). 3-lira ochre.

Varieties: a few minor plate defects, for example, No. 18, with figure "6" or "8." The 40-centesimo exists bisected (used at Terni and at Orvieto in 1861): very rare.

Cancellations: the Roman States grill is very rare on this issue. It should be purchased only on cover.

Pairs: 3U. 80-centesimo: rare. Blocks: very rare.

Originals: 18½ mm wide by about 23 mm high. With respect to inscription lettering, corner ornaments, and lower frame breaks, see the two preceding issues. The watermark is like that of the second issue.

There is a dot after letters "S" and "T" of the value. The shield has five quite separate vertical shade lines in each quartering. They are well aligned horizontally at the top and in the middle of the shield. At the bottom, they follow the curve; none is joined to its neighbor. In each quartering the right and left lines are thicker than the others. At the top, the shield line extends beyond the lateral edges. The vertical beam of the cross is under the "T," a little to the left of that letter's axis. There are five jewels in the crown bandeau.

One also should note that in the 1–20-centesimo stamps the value inscription is too low in the tablet; it almost touches the lower frame.

This set's impression is hardly any better than that of the preceding issue. In the good copies or in the 3-lira, whose shade does not help, paper and watermark study are important aids in stamp analysis.

Forgeries: all are lithographed. Most have no watermark or the watermark is noncongruent, made by embossing or heavy, greasy impression. Poorly executed lozenge design. Shapely parallel wavy lines whose measurements differ (sometimes 1½ mm wide!). Without wavy lines, but with portion of double-lined letter. As above, compare with a common original.

Shade lines are too short, too long, or are joined. Paper is yellowish, not grayish white. Paper occasionally is laid. There are dividing frame lines in the margins. The cross is under the axis of the "T" or is too far to the right, sometimes much too far to the left. Three jewels in the crown bandeau, or none at all; the bandeau is sometimes formed by a single line. FRANCO BOLLO is printed as two words. The "A" letters are pointed at top. Noncongruent lettering. A dot is found after the value, too close to the final letter, or two dots, or none at all. Corner crosses are not congruent and are without circles.

There is a set (including the 3-lira) with embossed blank parts. Another set (without the 3-lira?) has the same curiosity. In one set, the line under the value is much too thin. In a German set in sheets of twenty-five (5 x 5), the figure "5" has become "6."

Most of the sets extend only to 40- or 80-centesimo stamps, the counterfeiters often not having the access to the 3-lira original.

Reprints (1866): private reprints exist of the 3-lira, 2-soldo, and 60-crazie (original paper, but noncongruent value inscription and bright yellow shade).

Fake: after looking for 10-centesimo stamps whose secondary shades (purplish brown) could harmonize more or less with those of the 1-centesimo, the swindlers scraped out the "0" of "10": they thought they had played their trump card. Yes...but the distance from figure "1" to letter "C" is 2 mm in the 1-centesimo original and 3 mm in the faked 1-centesimo, as in the 10-centesimo stamp. Let us not forget Columbus' little egg (F. Serrane, *Catalogue du Spécialiste d'Europe,* 1922).

1854 (November 1). Postage due for newspapers. 2-soldo on thin, yellowish tracing paper (50 microns). Sheets of eighty stamps (10 x 8). The format is rather different, from 40 to about 45 mm laterally. The stamps are divided by a red ink line. The tête-bêche is worth 25M.

There are essays on white paper.

Forgeries are numerous. Comparison is necessary.

Noncongruent format. No red framing. Diameters are arbitrary, for example, large circle, 22¹/₂ instead of 23 mm; small circle, 14¹/₂ instead of 15 mm. Yellow or pink slightly transparent paper. Inscription letters touch each other, or are more than 2¹/₄ mm high.

Two Sicilies

The kingdom of the Two Sicilies was divided into two parts, with different postal administrations:

1. All the territory in the southern part of the Italian peninsula as far north as the Roman States.

2. Sicily proper, which formerly was called "Trinacria" because of the island's triangular shape, with its three jutting capes.

I. Naples

1858. Trinacria stamps. Nos. 1 to 7. Plates: 200 stamps engraved in two panes of 100 (10 x 10). Handmade paper, white, porous, thick, often more than 100 microns. Watermark: forty fleur-de-lys designs in the sheet, framed by two fine lines joined by a wavy line; between these lines, on the sheet's four sides, one finds this inscription: BOLLI POSTALI. The inverted watermark is common.

Secret marks: on all stamp values, there is a microscopic letter from the engraver's name, G. MASINI. It is often difficult to see this on stamps of a pale shade or with light impression.

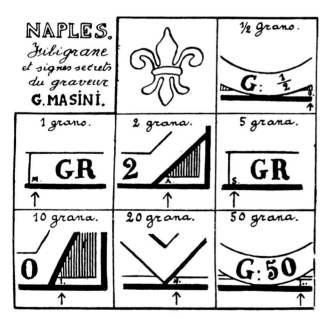

Naples. Watermark and secret marks of the engraver, G. Masini.

Select: four margins about 1¹/₄ mm wide. Numerous shades, from pale rose to dark carmine. The lilac-rose and the rose-red are in demand. One must not mistake the red-brown or the dark carmine shades for discoloration caused by oxidation (very deep brown, or black-brown). Nos. 3 and 5, rose-brown: 50M, 50U; however, this shade is common in Nos. 6 and 7. It should not be confused with the brownish coloration of the paper, which is sometimes caused by the gum.

Double prints: these exist on the 1-, 2-, 5-, 10-, and 50-grano stamps; they must be very clear-cut (see the accompanying illustration); those that are caused by sheet slippage have only a halo and are not very interesting. No. 3: 5U; No. 4: 2U; others: rare. No. 4 is found with triple and even quadruple impressions; in this case, one or two of the impressions are jumbled and were caused by paper play. There are stamps that are only partly printed.

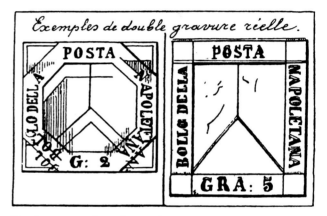

Naples: examples of true double prints.

Cancellations: Types A and B as shown in the accompanying illustration are common, but specialty catalogues reproduce a few rare serpentine cancellations. Red and blue cancels: 3U; green: 5U. Type C cancels, with date, are in demand; blue cancels: rare; double-lined oval postmark with date (UFFICIO, etc.): rare. Type D, rare: 4U. Sicilian cancellations are very rare: No. 2: 4U; No. 3: 8U.

Pairs: mint: 3U; used: 3U to 4U. Strip of four of No. 3: 8U. Mint or used blocks are rare. No. 7 on cover: exceedingly rare.

Reprints (1898): unofficial, made in Turin with the original dies. Fine printing on handmade white paper, without watermark. These cannot be confused with the originals because of shades. Do not pay more than about 20 francs for the set, and if you buy them, use them only as reference stamps. One should not encourage work of this sort: it is often followed by reprints bearing forged rare cancellations, etc.

Postal forgeries: the 2-, 10-, and 20-grano were forged by intaglio engraving and canceled in Naples, usually with Type A postmark, to defraud the postal service. The handmade paper is of various thicknesses.

No watermark, but traces of a manufacturer's trademark can be found. The three values may be on vertically or horizontally laid paper, and the 10- and 20-grano stamps may also be on stippled paper.

Oblitérations.

A.- *Encadrée*   B.- *Serpentine.*

B. - N-B. *On trouve, de ces oblitéra-tions, un grand nombre de variétés.*

B. -

C.- *à date.*

ASSICURATA
D. *ob. chargé.*

Cancellations found on the issue of 1858, Nos. 1 to 7. A. Framed. B. Examples of serpentine cancellations. C. With date. D. Registered

Mint copies evidently are rarer than canceled ones; in our opinion, however, they are valuable only as reference stamps, as it is the original postal cancellation applied to a forged stamp that alone gives it value.

2-grano: two types, two retouched types. The right band (APOLET) of none of them is as wide as the left band (LO DELL). No control mark.

Type I (see the accompanying illustration): very rare in rose-carmine; the others in purplish blue shades are worth 50 francs.

Type II: lettering, lines, and frames are reinforced, and the eight sections of the inner octagon are shaded.

Type III: very bad — nothing more than a rough sketch; the top left oblique strip is too narrow.

Type IV: same band flaw; lettering and frames have been traced over. The horse's mane and tail, which were too bushy and which formed white spots that were separated from the body in Type III, have an equine look again.

Used postal forgeries, showing retouches. There are six types and two retouched types of the 20-grano. Letters, frames, and inscriptions "GRA 20" are too bold. Corner ornaments are different.

10-grano: five types, printed in a special reddish shade. There are double impressions.

Type I: too high, horse's head is flattened — this is the rarest type of all; the others, on horizontally laid paper: 60 francs; on vertically laid paper, very rare: 150 francs.

Type II: horse's head almost touching the frame.

Type III: the Medusa's lower "leg" has a reinforced "heel" resembling that of the upper leg. The horse's mane is separated from its head by a heavy line.

Type IV: not as high as the original; the "knee" of the Medusa's right "leg" is too large; defective lettering.

Type V: not so high; the horse's back is shaded by a heavy line.

20-grano: good counterfeits; eight types, two of which are retouched; excessively vivid rose shade. The defective lettering and inscriptions are printed too boldly. Make a comparative study of the design, especially in the stamp's corner. One of the types, in which the "B" of BOLLO is too large and is placed too low beside the "O," is rare on laid paper. Value on wove paper: 50 francs; on vertically laid paper: 125 francs; on horizontally laid or stippled paper: rare.

Early forgeries: almost all are lithographed. Arbitrary shades. Poor design (and drawing), easily discerned by comparison.

$^1/_2$-grano: the fraction bar is oblique; no watermark or secret mark; the horse is a male, and this is made abundantly clear; the vertical hatch lines are not broken by a horizontal line in the lower right corner; the Medusa has three flat "feet"; vermilion shade.

1-grano: no secret mark or watermark; the letters of POSTA are too large and too wide.

50-grano: I. no watermark or control mark; same manufacture as the forgery of the $^1/_2$-grano — three flat "feet," unbroken hatch lines, vermilion shade. II. Yellowish, handmade paper; manufacturer's trademark as watermark; counterfeited control mark; the horse seems bisected by the shading lines on its thigh; four groups of shading lines on the horse's shoulder; a Medusa head that is not in conformity with the supplementary lines on the two upper "legs."

Modern forgeries: like the previous ones, they have no watermark; this is enough, despite their improved manufacture, to invite comparative research in noteworthy differences of design and inscription. All values were counterfeited several times.

Faking and forgery: $^1/_2$-grano: original paper from a minor value (2-grano) original, bleached with forged reprint of the $^1/_2$-grano; it has the forged secret mark; seventeen vertical shade lines between the knee bend and the circle under the "L" of NAPOLETANA; originals, sixteen. The use of chemical reagents in paper inspection is effective. Very deceptive forgeries.

II. Provisional Government

1860 (November 6). $^1/_2$-tornese blue. No. 8. Issued following the reduction in printed matter postal rates, this stamp comes from the plate of the $^1/_2$-grano, No. 1, on which a scratched out "G" has been replaced by a "T." Traces of the "G," which came up in printing, are visible on all of the plate's stamps. So there are 200 varieties.

This was a temporary stamp, used for one month, created during Garibaldi's dictatorship, known as "Trinacria." It is more valuable when it is on a piece of cover or on a newspaper.

Fakes: very cleverly executed by forged printing on the original paper of Nos. 1, 2, or 3 (very pale shades), bleached without touching the cancellation. The study of design differences (hatching, inscriptions, center, retouching of the "G") and differences in format is indispensable in circumventing swindling.

Early or new forgeries: compare with No. 1 and check the following:

1. The secret mark ("G") of the engraver, which is sometimes not visible in the very pale shades of Nos. 1–7, but is always visible in No. 8.

2. The watermark.

3. The retouching of the "G." (In most copies, there is no longer any trace of it, except in a good Geneva forgery with no watermark.)

4. The fraction "$^1/_2$" (position of the figures, width of the bar).

5. The corner shade lines, which should be equidistant and twenty-six in number; the horizontal frame should show a printing fade-out between the first and second line in the upper left corner.

6. The lettering design.

7. The center design.

8. The cancellations on Geneva forgeries, Types A or D, are so poorly executed that, in general, they are quite obvious.

1860 (December 6). Cross of Savoy. No. 9. The provisional government lost no time in having the coat of arms of Naples scratched out so that the Cross of Savoy could be substituted. Vestiges of the former engraving, which was not completely effaced, reappeared in the printing. Thus, there are 200 different types. However, same paper, watermark, secret mark.

Fakes: as in the procedure for the previous stamp, check the design of the new impression. This stamp was also remade on a No. 1 by giving the design an entirely new shade; the "Trinacria" stamp (No. 8) was redone in the same way. These fantasy stamps are not seen very often. Design differences facilitate inspection and checking.

Early and new forgeries: same remarks as for "Trinacria." It should be pointed out, moreover, that crosses without any trace of the former design are forged; the shading lines of the four segmented triangles must be more or less wavy, and there must be eleven of them, or twelve, if the cross line, accurately traced, is counted. This stamp (Cross of Savoy) was counterfeited in Geneva (F.) with three different clichés.

First cliché: no watermark or secret mark; thirteen rectilinear shade lines in the circle, top left, instead of eleven; the "G" is as visible as the "T."

Second cliché (first cliché, retouched): same; blue dot in the center; blue dots in the "O" of POSTA, between the "O" and the "S," and between the "T" and the "A"; the important printer's error in the shading above the "A" of POSTA was corrected here.

Third cliché: still no watermark; control letter counterfeited; the bottom line of the "2" is shorter than the figure's curl at the top; this time, there are only ten shade lines in the two parts of the circle containing them. The engraving correction has shown up: The "G" is still quite visible.

Forged cancellations: numerous. One of them, a red one with date, single circle, is well-executed: NAPOLI 6 LUG 61.

1861. Embossed impression. Nos. 10 to 17.
Because these stamps belong to the United Italy collection, they are described under Italy.

III. Sicily

1859 (January 1). Head of King Ferdinand. Nos. 18 to 21. The pretty Sicily stamps called "Ferdinands" are in demand by specialists because of their rich shades and varieties, and because of plating. Same values as in the Naples issue.

Printing figures: 1/2-grano, 2,350 sheets from two plates; 1-grano, 5,400 sheets from three plates; 2-grano, 16,500 sheets from three plates; 5-grano, 2,000 sheets from two plates; 10-grano, 1,000 sheets from one plate; 20-grano, 1,000 sheets from one plate; 50-grano, 250 sheets from one plate.

The stock remainders were, respectively, 975, 970, 1,729, 1,046, 211, 580, and 178 sheets of 100 stamps. This explains why the 50-grano canceled stamp is so rare.

Arrangement of a specialized collection of "Ferdinand" stamps: if the specialist has a stamp from each plate, a select stamp, or one that is not rare because of retouching, variety, or printing flaw, he may affix it on a white sheet of paper divided into twenty-five quarter sections corresponding to stamp measurements, or a little higher so that an annotation can be placed under the stamp, and with wider or higher marginal sections so that marginal copies can be placed in them.

He will have a sheet for each plate value, thirteen sheets in all. Because the sheets are large and difficult to handle and annotate, interchangeable album sheets that can hold twenty-five stamps are frequently used. These are then labeled at the top with descriptive notes like "1/2-GR. Plate I. Top-left section."

The specialized collection can be arranged this way in an album having fifty-two pages, reserving a large blank space at the bottom of each page, or one or two blank pages after every four pages from one plate. Thus, the stamps from a whole plate can be made available for inspection by spreading out four pages.

Having numbered each stamp slot, the specialist lays aside the stamps acquired, those preferred with retouching or in a shade different from the stamp types already in his collection. As soon as he is certain of the plate, the number retouching, etc., he puts the stamp in its place with annotation. Of course, it is not necessary to get all the stamps from each plate; this would be onerous. The specialized collection can be considered complete with a stamp type in each plate section, each being of a different shade. All of the interesting retouched stamps and stamp varieties are then assigned their places little by little.

Plates: some soft metal clichés were taken from the original die engraved by T.A. Juvara. The best of them were assembled either in four panes of twenty-five (5 x 5), or in panes of 100. The whole thing was electrolytically coated with a thin layer of copper, and

To identify the plates: 1/2-grano, Plate I — gutters 2 mm; two left groups, two right groups. 1/2-grano, Plate II — gutters 1 1/2 mm. No white dots in background. 1-grano, Plate I — vertical lines 2 1/2 mm, horizontal lines 2 mm. White dots on stamps. Middle: 1-grano, Plate II — horizontal lines 1 mm, vertical lines 2 1/2 mm, except Nos. 1, 2, and 98. 1-grano, Plate III — gutters 1.5 mm. No white dots. No white line under beard. Sharp impression. Olive-green. 2-grano, Plate I — vertical lines 1.5 mm, horizontal lines 2 mm. *En haut* [top]; *en bas* [bottom]; *groupe de gauche/droite* [group at left/right].
Bottom: 2-grano, Plate II — vertical lines 1.5 mm, horizontal lines 2 mm. Difficult to distinguish from Plate I without plating. Sometimes a dot on the nose in stamps of lower-left group. 2-grano, Plate III — vertical lines 1.5 mm, horizontal lines 2 mm. Sharp impression. No white dots or lines. No retouching. A white dot behind the ear. 5-grano, Plate I — vertical lines 1 1/2 mm, horizontal lines 1 3/4 mm. 5-grano, Plate II — vertical lines 1 1/2 mm, horizontal lines 2 mm. First-class impression. No white dots. Vermilion is the only shade.

this layer, removed with great care and reinforced with hard metal, formed the plate. During cliché manufacture, bad press operations caused the cliché reproduced on the die to be struck twice in succession. That made double prints, which thus are really reentries. (See this word under Belgium.)

Retouching: to reinforce the design, much retouching was done before each printing. There was additional retouching after plate wear. (Note: The accompanying illustration identifies the places one should look for retouching. The retouched design is not always faithfully reproduced, especially in plates where retouching has been frequent.)

Varieties: there are a great many varieties — white spots, color spots, etc. I have shown the most striking ones. Their value is the same as for marginal copies: 25M, 25U, except for the 2-grano: 50M, 50U. White, machine-made paper; medium paper thickness, rarely thin; no watermark. The first printings were on yellowish-white paper and often have a transparency that is attributed to oily gum.

Pairs: very much in demand for plating: 3M, 3–4U. Blocks: rare. Nos. 24 and 24a on cover: extremely rare.

Cancellations: beware of forged cancellations, especially on the ¹/₂-grano, the 5-grano vermilion, and the 50-grano. Expertizing is essential. Blue cancellations: very rare; red: extremely rare. Expertizing is necessary.

¹/₂-grano: Olive-yellow, Plate I	2,500	1,100
Yellow, light yellow, Plate I	150	180
Orange-yellow, Plate I	135	160
Yellow-orange, bright orange, Plate II	125	180

Sheets of 100 stamps in four panes of twenty-five (5 x 5). The mark that identifies Plate II (inner frame under the "A") is often missing in Nos. 81–100.

Essays: the ¹/₂-grano was used as the color essay for all values (bright colors, thin or very thick paper). An essay in blue of Plate II is known to be canceled.

Varieties: Plate I: No. 76 is incomplete in upper left inner corner; there are copies with a small horn behind the head, and others in which the second "I" of SICILIA is elongated upward as if it were given a dot, etc. Plate II: printed on both sides: 1,000 francs. Stamps with Roman numerals in the right margin, plate identification: extremely rare.

Retouched stamps: No. 69: 2.5M, 2.5U; Nos. 19–99: 75M, 75U; others: 50M, 50U. Plate II has no retouched stamps.

1-grano:	Red-brown, Plate I	1,250	275
	Olive-brown, Plate I	1,000	200
	Olive-green, Plate I	1,200	750
	Olive-brown, Plate II	125	50
	Brown, Plate II	125	100
	Olive-green, Plate II	75	35
	Olive-green, Plate III	35	30

Plate I: the "S" and the "T" of POSTA are not always connected on top as in the illustration; the background of No. 8, above the tuft, is recast.

Retouched stamps: Nos. 7, 24, 31, 51, 53, 57, and 59: 10M, 25U; Nos. 32, 34, and 78: 25M, 75U; Nos. 5, 18, 24, and 27: 2M, 3U. No. 16: very rare. Stamps retouched after the plate was placed in service are worth 2M, 4U. No. 18, head has been done over almost entirely; No. 34, heavy grid lines above the tuft; No. 55, eye is done over, as are lines in the background facing it; No. 78, head entirely done over; No. 87, eye done over, and previous retouching reinforced.

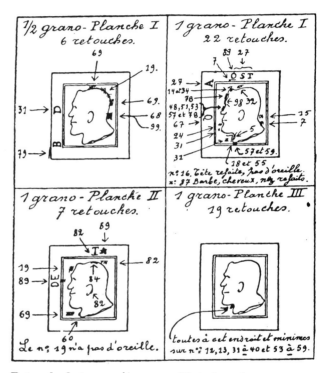

Retouched stamps. ¹/₂-grano, Plate I — six retouches. 1-grano, Plate I — twenty-two retouches. No. 16: head redone, no ear. No. 86, beard, hair, and nose redone.

Bottom: 1-grano, Plate II — seven retouches. No. 19: no ear. 1-grano, Plate III — nineteen retouches. All are minimal retouches at the spot indicated, on Nos. 12, 23, 31–40, and 53–59.

Plate II: reentries. POSTA, lightly double-printed and wider, olive-green, Nos. 30 and 32: mint, 125 francs; letters "P T A," the "A" of SICILIA, and figure "1," definitely double-printed, olive-green: mint, 200 francs. The 1-grano, double print, olive-brown: extremely rare; the lower frame of the second impression blocks out letters and value figure; the white frame above the head blocks out POSTA; etc.

Retouched stamps: No. 60: 50M, 50U; Nos. 69, 82, and 89: 75M, 75U; Nos. 19, 59, and 84: 2M, 2U.

Plate III: still olive-green. No. 85 has a variety: a color spot on the inner frame below the "E" of DELLA. Stamps with Roman numerals in the margin: very rare.

2-grano:	Cobalt-blue, Plate I	200	27.50
	Ultramarine-blue, Plate I	200	20.00
	Blue (shades), Plate I	15	6.50
	Cobalt-blue, Plate II	125	30.00
	Ultramarine-blue, Plate II	125	20.00
	Blue (shades), Plate II	17.50	8.00
	Pale blue, Plate II	17.50	8.00
	Dark blue, Plate III	400.00	40.00
	Blue (shades), Plate III	12.50	5.00

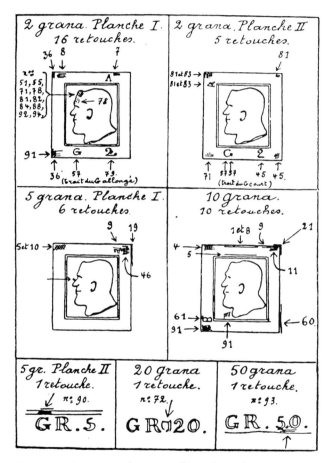

Retouched stamps. 2-grano, Plate I — sixteen retouches. Horizontal line of "G" elongated. 2-grano, Plate II — five retouches. Short horizontal line of "G."
Middle: 5-grano, Plate I — six retouches.
10-grano — ten retouches.
Bottom: 5-grano, Plate II — one retouch, No. 90. 20-grano — one retouch, No. 72. 50-grano — one retouch, No. 93.

The blue-green shade is a result of a chemical reaction with the gum. The 2-grano is found printed on both sides (very rare) but, the two impressions not being from the same plate, a sheet reject is involved, which was used for a different plate or for starting another press run. The explanation for this, and for the used $^1/_2$-grano essay, may be found in some printer's scheme to sell these waste sheets or to frank letters with them.

Retouched stamps: hair corrections: 50M, 50U; other corrections and retouching of Plate II: 3M, 3U.

Varieties: Plate I: No. 42, large white spot under the neck above the figure. Plate II: No. 79, white spot on the figure. Plates I and II: No. 25, large white spot above the head, under the "A" of POSTA; No. 100, white spot on the "G" of "GR." These major blemishes: 25M, 25U. There are other minor, insignificant flaws. Roman numerals in margin: very rare.

5-grano:	Dark carmine, Plate I	180	160
	Carmine, Plate I	160	120
	Light carmine, Plate I	135	110
	Blood red, Plate I	450	275
	Red-brown, Plate I	1,500	350
	Vermilion, Plate I	100	135
	Vermilion, Plate II	80	175

Plate I, No. 62, reentry: extremely rare. Double print: extremely rare.

Retouched stamps: Plate I: Nos. 5, 9, 10, and 46: 50M, 50U; others: 20M, 20U. Plate II: 60M, 50U.

Varieties: Plate I: No. 99, color spot above the eye and on the head under the "S." Plate II: large color spot on "C I" of SICILIA: 25M, 25U. Roman numerals in margin: very rare.

10-grano:	Indigo	120	90
	Very dark blue	100	75

Only one plate; gutters $1^1/_2$ mm in both directions. Double print: extremely rare.

Retouched stamps: 50M, 50U; No. 91: 2M, 2U. The canceled pairs are rare:

20-grano:	Black	300	200
	Slate gray	100	120
	Dark purplish gray	150	135

One plate only; gutter $1^1/_2$ mm.

Retouched stamp: 2.5M, 3U. The color of the greenish 10-grano was altered by exposure to light: lower value.

50-grano:	Dark red-brown	200	800
	Chocolate	275	1,000

One plate; gutters $1^1/_2$ mm.
Reentries: Nos. 43, 62, and 70: 2.5M.
Retouched stamp: 4M, exceedingly rare used.
Variety: greasy paper. On cover: 2U.
The cancellation always requires expertizing.
Early and new forgeries: there are entire sets of early

or modern lithographed forgeries. This printing method is so inferior to the fine engraving of the "Ferdinands" that a cursory examination is enough to eliminate all of them. In case of doubt, comparison with an authentic 2-grano (inscriptions, cross-ruled background, eye, cheek shading, hair, etc.) will settle it.

The same comparative procedure will always be effective for the best of the forgeries, even those that are engraved. Among the latter, we must mention the following: a $^1/_2$-grano photoengraving, copied from Plate II, orange shade too bright, paper too thick, noncongruent design.

A 5-grano bright vermilion, Plate II, has the same flaws; this stamp exists also in a light brown shade, engraved with ideal cross-ruling, but the ear lobe is made with spaced dots (inner edge of the lobe); the temple and cheek shading is made with regularly spaced dots and the lower curl of the "B" of BOLLO is higher than the upper curl; the dot is missing after SICILIA; etc.

A recent lithographic production from Genoa (I.) was modeled on this forgery; a 2-grano original mint would not have overburdened the enterprise's budget, however. A more successful 10-grano stamp was made in the shade of the original; the paper is too tough; the background did not come out well; it is a copy of the retouched No. 61 from Plate III — and that is enough to give it a good going over.

Among sets of forgeries that look good when engraved, two Italian productions (Genoa, V.?) must be mentioned. The second of these is only an improved version of the first one and can be recognized by the neck shading (in front, under the beard) made of equidistant lines without any burelage counter line.

It should be noted that the originals always show traces of the joining of the value band with the rest of the design either in the stamp or in the margins. These traces are found only in photographically produced forgeries.

Italy

We place the Neapolitan issue of 1861 here for the following reasons: Naples and Sicily, annexed by Italy following Garibaldi's expedition in 1860, have been a part of the kingdom since that time, and the Neapolitan province has been ruled by Prince Eugene of Savoy, lieutenant of King Victor Emmanuel II, from January 1862. Their stamps no longer bear the Trinacrian design or the fleurs-de-lys watermark of the House of Bourbon, nor do they have King Ferdinand's portrait, which has been replaced by the portrait of the King of Italy, and the cross of Savoy is now found in the four corners. They must therefore be assigned a special classification entitled:

I. Nonunited Italy

1861 (February). Head of Victor Emmanuel II. Nos. 1 to 8. Lithographed. Nos. 10–17 of the Two Sicilies are imperforate.

Sheets of fifty stamps (5 x 10) composed of:
$^1/_2$-tornese, five transfer plates of ten types (5 x 2).
$^1/_2$-grano, ten transfers of five types (5 x 1), two plates.
1-grano, five transfers of ten types (5 x 2).
2-grano, Plate I, five transfers of ten types (5 x 2).
2-grano, Plate II, three transfers of fifteen types (5 x 3), and at the bottom of the sheet, the top transfer strip (Types I–V).
5-grano, five transfers of ten types (5 x 2).
10-grano, ten transfers of five types (5 x 1), two plates.
20-grano, five transfers of ten types (5 x 2).
50-grano, ten transfers of five types (5 x 1), two plates.

Select: four margins, 1 mm wide.

Shades: this set is extremely rich in shades. It is not possible to catalogue all of them, for there are indefinable intermediate shades. Sometimes, when they come from small printings, these are quite rare. As an example of the gamut of shades, one can take the 50-grano, which generally is catalogued in two shades, gray and blue, whereas in reality there are shades of gray from pale pearl gray to an intermediate slate tone and shades of blue-gray from a pale bluish gray to dark steel blue.

The important, well-defined shades are: $^1/_2$-tornese yellow-green, olive-green, green, emerald green; $^1/_2$-grano gray-brown, brown, bistre-brown; 1-grano black-gray, black; 2-grano blue, indigo blue: 2M, 2U, ultramarine blue: 3M, 3U; 5-grano vermilion, lilac-rose: 10M, 5U, lilac: 20M, 8U, dark lilac: 30M, 15U, carmine-tinted red: common; 10-grano dark yellow, bistre-yellow, lemon: 5M, 5U, orange-yellow; 20-grano orange-yellow, pale yellow; 50-grano gray, blue-gray: 50M.

Varieties: machine-made paper, medium thickness (first printing) and thin. The $^1/_2$-tornese and $^1/_2$-grano are found on thick paper.

As in all lithographed stamps, there are numerous transfer, plate, and printing flaws. For example, $^1/_2$-grano: G*P*ANO. 1-grano: the "O" of BOLLO or of FRANCO, cut by an oblique line, forms an "8"; etc. Very defective impressions, showing worn spots in corners, are found on the 1-, 2- and 5-grano: 2U. Transfer plate flaw, 10-grano: BOLIO instead of BOLLO, etc.

Portrait: the whole set exists with inverted head, except the 10- and 50-grano mint or used, which come from the original sheets in which one or two (?) stamps with inverted head may be found. The used stamps are very rare because the authorities must have done something about these errors as soon as they saw them. On the other hand, entire sheets (or blocks) with the inverted head come from press rejects or those culled by inspection. The heads that are shifted out of place are not rare. Double or triple impressions of the head are rare, used. The 5-grano lilac in this form was used in Bari, the doubling not being as visible as in certain proof rejects. Values with no head, occasionally with gum on the front, are printer's waste. The 1- and 2-grano are known to have been issued that way (by a fraudulent printer-lithographer operation?). One should be on the lookout for forged cancellations, especially on similar varieties.

Printed both sides: 5-grano: extremely rare.

Bisected stamps: ¹/₂-grano, to serve as a ¹/₂-tornese; 2-grano for 1-grano; and 5-grano for 2-grano: very rare.

Color errors (?): ¹/₂-tornese black, and 2-grano black. Value, mint: 50 francs; used, extremely rare (the ¹/₂-tornese brought 1,000 francs at the Ferrari sale). Not having been put into regular circulation, these errors must be considered as printer's waste. The impressions in black on pelure paper (40–45 microns) are printing proofs. There also are essays.

Cancellations: the Naples postmark with date in a single circle is common (see Type I, illustration). The dated double circle postmark (Type III), and Type C of the Two Sicilies cancellations (see Two Sicilies) are less common. Type B of the Two Sicilies is worth 2U. The small grill, Type II, is rare. Type IV is in active demand.

I. Oblit. à date, un cercle. II. Petite grille.

III. a date, double cercle. IV. Ob. ovoïdale.

Italy cancellations: I. Circular, dated cancellation. II. Small grill. III. Double circle, with date. IV. Oval cancellation.

The composite Italian and Two Sicilies cancellations are in demand.

Pairs: 3U. Blocks: rare.

Originals: see Figures a and b in the illustration for the distinctive features. Each value has a few defects originating in the transfer plate of the sole matrix. Obviously these defects, which are attributable to defective impression or wear, are not always visible in all copies. The secondary matrices were themselves transferred five or six times to form the transfer block (which, by the way, facilitates reconstruction of the transfer), and the block was itself transferred five or ten times to form the sheet. Measurements: 18¹/₂–19 x 20³/₄ –21¹/₄ mm, depending on printings and values.

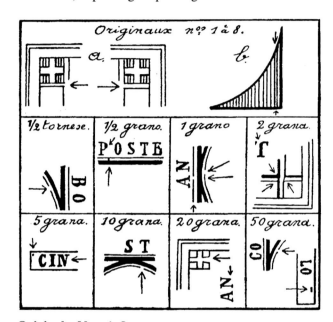

Originals. Nos. 1–8.

Early forgeries: crude. No distinctive features as in Figures a and b. Letters too high, especially in the 50-grano, or too wide. Design defects, etc.

Used postal forgeries: 2-, 5-, 10-, and 20-grano (2-grano, too dull: extremely rare. 5-grano: rare. 10-grano bistre-yellow: 3U. 20-grano yellow: 40U). These have neither the features designated by Figures a and b, nor those that are peculiar to each value. The letters are too wide, especially the "A" letters. The "G" of GRANA is defective; the "E" of VENTI is too high in the 20-grano; there are three or four vertical lines of hatching along the crosses instead of two; etc. Mint stamps are rarer than used ones, the counterfeiter having tried to liquidate his stock. The former are interesting only as reference stamps for expertizing, since it is the original cancellation that gives value to forgeries.

Modern forgeries: two well-counterfeited photolithographic sets.

I. Genoa forgeries (I.): all values, normal or inverted head. The width is within possible limits, but a few values are over 19 mm. Average height 21 mm (50-grano, 19½ x 21½ mm). White paper (50 microns). The Figure a and b features are well reproduced, but the expertizing marks for the different values (see illustration) are missing. (The "N" letters of the 5- and 20-grano are fair) and the defects resulting from any block transfer obviously do not occur either.

II. Geneva forgeries (F.): all values, normal head. Here, too, the width is fair, but a few values are over 19 mm. Some are too high: 21⅓–½ mm. The expertizing marks also are missing; paper (45–50 microns). Relief of the head is not curved enough on top and hair not visible enough.

Forged cancellations are numerous on all values; comparison is needed. The wood-engraved Geneva cancellations are found on both forgeries and originals: (1) ANNULATO, framed (the fine inner frame line is missing). (2) ASSICURATA, straight line with capitals. (3) Six bars spaced 1.8 mm apart. (4) Type C cancellation with date (see Two Sicilies), NAPOLI 17 NOV 1861. (5) Same, NAPOLI 3 GIU 1861. (6) Neapolitan cancellations, with date, Type I, NAPOLI 12 AGO 61 3 S. (7) Cancellation with date, double circle, Type III (22 mm), FAENZA 20 DIC (without year date). (8) Same cancellation, FAENZA 5 SETT 61. Interchangeable dates; ink too gray.

Fakes: printer's waste, with no head in center, occasionally gummed on front, were given forged cancellations, Type I, NAPOLI 29 OTT 61 1 S (Geneva), and other forged postmarks.

II. United Italy

1862 (May 1). Newspaper stamps. No. 1.
Imperforate 2-centesimo with embossed figure.

Shades: bistre-brown and light yellow: 50M, 50U. This stamp, with its inverted figure, was not used in the postal service. There are numerous forged cancellations. Expertizing is necessary.

For the 1- and 2-centesimo black, see Sardinia.

1862 (March 1). Perforated stamps. Nos. 4 to 7.
Sheets of fifty stamps (10 x 5), imperforate at bottom.

Shades: very numerous. 10-centesimo: from bistre-yellow to dark bistre off-olive; intermediate shades from ochre and brown to dark off-olive-brown. 20-centesimo, various shades of blue; intermediate ultramarine blue, indigo blue. 40-centesimo, red shades. 80-centesimo, yellow, dull yellow, bright yellow, and orange-yellow.

Varieties: copies imperforate at bottom: 50M, 50U. 40-centesimo, with outer frame line: 50M, 50U. The 5-, 10-, and 20-centesimo were used bisected: rare. The stamps perf 7½ are perforation essays.

Cancellations: dated Italian cancellations, single or double circle, are most common. Those from other countries are rarer. There exists a rather large number of rare cancellations: grill, large numeral (France), VIA DI MARE, etc. Consult the specialty catalogues.

Cancellation expertizing is necessary because there are a great many forged cancellations on Nos. 5, 6, and 7.

Pairs: 3U. Blocks of four: 8–12U.

Fakes: a number of Sardinian stamps of corresponding values were fraudulently perforated. Thus, shade comparison would be useful, not to mention perforation examination. Consequently, Sardinian postmarks must receive some attention also.

Unissued stamps: 5-centesimo green and 3-lira, perf 9½, 10, 12½, 13, 13½, and 14 instead of 11½ x 12.

Forgeries: there are a few forgeries of Italian origin. Compare inner corners, inscription, and embossed portrait design. Perforations are not congruent.

1862. Unissued stamps. Preceding type altered.
This is a much better executed set than that of Sardinia (1855). Five values, imperforate: 5-centesimo yellow-green; 20-centesimo gray-brown; 20-centesimo blue; 40-centesimo red; 80-centesimo orange.

The stamps can be identified by the much more distinct design that was altered in all its parts (see illustration). "C" and "O" are much wider and higher than in the Sardinian set; this facilitates identification. The set was not issued because of a major robbery, which was kept concealed until very recently. In our opinion these stamps are not very interesting, with the exception of a few (very rare) postally used copies to which cancellation gives value, like that of all "official forgeries." The administration's stock remainders were incinerated because of the robbery.

1863 (January 1), 15-centesimo imperforate. No. 8. Lithographed. Various ultramarine shades. *Select:* four margins ½ mm wide.

Varieties: transfer flaw in the lower left ornament: 4M, 5U. A few retouched stamps exist; quite distinct ones are rare. Frame double print: rare. Inverted head or no head: extremely rare, used.

1863 (February 9). New type. Imperforate. No. 11. *Select:* four margins, 1 mm wide.

Lithographed. The transfer plate of five stamps was transferred to make a stone of 100 stamps in two panes of fifty, Plate I (the "C" in front of QUINDICI is closed), and to make a stone of 200 stamps in four panes, Plate II (the "C" is open and the inner frame is broken under the "Q").

There are a few rather evident transfer flaws: the closed "C" ("O") and the unbroken frame under the "Q" in Plate II; the last "I" of QUINDICI is occasionally formed by two or three dots; etc.

The type was corrected in the corners (white circle, inscriptions, "C" and "15") of the matrix of Plate II.

Stamps printed on both sides are essays.

Cancellations: see the first issue.

Official forgeries: these can be recognized by shade and design, of which there are numerous varieties. One of the first categories (Rieti and Aquila, used) is slate blue; the other (Naples) is blue. Make comparison.

1863 (December 1) to 1877. Crown watermark. Nos. 12 to 21. *Sheets* of 400 stamps in four panes of 10 x 10.

The 2-centesimo brown, No. 13, belongs to 1865, the 10-centesimo blue to 1877. The stamps overprinted SAGGIO are essays.

Shades are not very numerous. They vary from pale to dark.

Varieties: Nos. 12–14, 17, and 18 imperforate are rare.

1865. 20-centesimo. Surcharged on 15-centesimo. No. 22. Three types: Type I, normal 15-centesimo stamp. Type II, reworked with a dot above and below the ornaments between the inscriptions. Type III, same as Type II, with the addition of two white dots at design extremities in the stamp's corners.

Varieties: Type I imperforate: rare. Type III with inverted overprint: rare. As a pair with a nonoverprinted stamp: rare.

1867 (May) and 1877 (August). 20-centesimo. Nos. 23 and 24. 20-centesimo blue and 20-centesimo orange. Types are almost alike. Nothing special to point out.

1878 (January). Overprinted Official stamps. Nos. 23 to 30. The inverted overprints frequently were counterfeited, sometimes in black instead of indigo. Check whether cancellation is on top of or beneath the overprint. Comparison is sufficient. A few overprint impression varieties exist.

The 2-centesimo with wavy line brown impression and blue value impression on brown is an essay.

1879 (August). Head of Umberto I. Nos. 33 to 39. Various shades.

Varieties: No. 35, perf 10½: very rare.

Cancellations: Nos. 37 and 39 always must be expertized and should be collected only on entire cover.

Subsequent issues. *Varieties, cancellations, etc.:* the 40-centesimo, No. 41, in pairs with no perforations between: rare. The 5-lira, No. 45, canceled, must be expertized. The 5-centesimo, No. 40, has a plain background and a white inscription; No. 57, a lined background and inscription in black. The 5-lira of 1889, No. 45, was crudely counterfeited. Compare the head. There is no watermark and the perforations don't match the original. A fake printed on a bleached 5-centesimo of 1879 is hardly any better. Nos. 46, 48, and 50, overprinted VALEVOLE PER LE STAMPE, exist with inverted overprint. The first one: 5 francs. The others: rare. No. 52, 2-centesimo on 5-centesimo green, with thin-tailed numeral: 15 francs, mint; 5 francs, used. There are a few forged overprints of Nos. 51 and 54.

Double head stamps with inscription NOZZE D'ARGENTO are fantasies (5-centesimo green and 20-centesimo red). The same, with inscription ROMA 24-8-96, are unissued stamps.

No. 56, imperforate: rare. No. 63, canceled, needs to be expertized. Nos. 64 and 65, imperforate: unusual.

No. 65, with double print, 2 francs.

There are essays of No. 66 with watermark, in different colors (imperforate without gum); an essay in green, forged perforations; comparison of shades.

No. 71, 45-centesimo imperforate, rare. No. 73, error, value inscription 1 LIRA UNA in green: rare.

Nos. 76 and 77 are known imperforate, with double print, and with double print in which one of the impressions is inverted. The latter, like a great many varieties of this sort which originate in other countries, is a fantasy intended for collectors, who have proliferated since about 1900, when speculation began to enjoy exuberant growth. No. 73, with its obviously misplaced frame, can also be mentioned.

No. 78, imperforate: 10 francs; or in pairs, imperforate in middle.

Nos. 79–81, imperforate: 1 franc. Pair of 25-centesimo, imperforate vertically: 2 francs; 25-centesimo, printed both sides: rare.

Subsequent values exhibit numerous varieties of this sort. They are so numerous because they were intended to be so, and many were not subjected to official scrutiny.

No. 87, 10-lira, has been counterfeited. It has no watermark and perforations don't match the original. Forged overprints have been made of the issues of 1916, 1922 (Congress of Trieste), and of 1924 (overprint, 1-lira.)

Used postal forgeries: Nos. 66 (Naples) and 67 (Milan), lithographed. No. 70 (Catania), typographed. All three lack watermarks and have noncongruent perforations. Same defects as the following:

No. 76, zincographed, with very poorly executed head (make comparison). No. 76, same, more successful, both in carmine instead of rose. In spite of the places where these counterfeits were found, they (and the following ones) may well come from the counterfeiting workshops of Genoa, which did such an admirable job on the 30- and 60-lepta of Greece (see that country).

Nos. 77 and 104, said to be from Milan, on 50–70 microns paper, also have no watermark. The horizontal lines in the background, behind the neck, do not touch the neck or the oval. There is a single space between two lines in the top white inner frame. The nostril is not bent forward. The letters are unevenly spaced and the space varies between them and the edge of the tablet. Carmine and dark gray shades. Perf 11½.

Red Cross, 15-centesimo, 1915. No watermark, arbitrary perforation, crude design.

Special Delivery Stamps

No. 1 exists imperforate: mint, 2 francs; used, 15 francs. No. 8 with double overprint, one of which is inverted: a fantasy intended for collectors. No. 8, imperforate.

Used postal forgeries: No. 1, ascribed to Milan, vermilion-tinted red, no watermark, noncongruent perforation. The background lines touch neither the head nor the oval. There are five lines of hatching in the shield quartering instead of seven.

Official Stamps

These is nothing special to be noted about these stamps.

1921. Advertisement cover stamps. The official Italian catalogue rightly says that these stamps belong to collections of entires rather than to those of postage stamps. The overprints were counterfeited in London.

Parcel post stamps. Cancellations on Nos. 5 and 6 must be expertized.

III. Postage Due Stamps

1863. Imperforate stamp. No. 1. Three principal shades: yellow, light brown, and ochre-red, with a few intermediate shades. Sheets of 200 stamps.

The cancellation of this stamp always requires expertizing.

Worn-plate copies exist.

Forgeries: numerous sets in all shades. The stamp shown in the illustration, an early forgery, is very well known. It has fifty-one U-shaped ornaments in the

frame. The lines under TASSA are not congruent with the original. The shield's right belt buckle on the right of SEGNA is on the same level as the one on the left. Another early forgery has only forty-nine ornaments instead of fifty and figure "1" is placed too low.

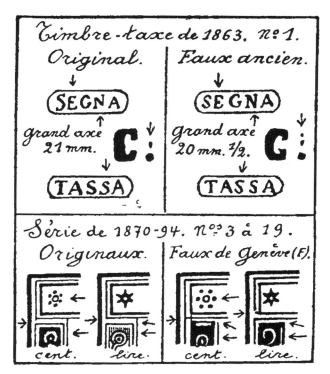

Postage due stamp, 1863. No. 1. Original. Early forgery. *Grand axe* [major axis]. **Bottom: Set of 1870–94. Nos. 3–19. Original. Geneva forgeries (F.).**

A more successful forgery with congruent dimensions comes from Genoa (I.). It does have the fifty ornaments, but the "N" of SEGNA is normal; it must have been copied not from an original but from an early forgery, because the defect (an extra white dot) above the dot after "C" is there. The paper is too thin, but this can be changed. I shall not discuss the generally arbitrary shades for the same reason.

Forged cancellations: very numerous. A forged circular postmark with date, RIETI 21 LUG 63, often is encountered.

1869. No. 2. There is nothing to say about this one. Crown watermark, vertical.

1870–94. Same watermark. Nos. 3 to 19. *Varieties:* Nos. 6 and 18 with inverted watermark. Nos. 6, 7, and 13, imperforate. No. 16 with double figure. Stamps with misplaced figures are not rare, although those with figures outside the oval are less common.

Forgeries: the whole set was poorly counterfeited in Geneva. The illustration gives information on the stamp's upper left corner. I think it is useful to mention these forgeries. Because they are stamps of little value, the collector tends to pay little attention to them and sometimes fails to notice that the watermark is missing.

Fakes: inverted impressions have been made on bleached-center originals.

1890. Overprints. Nos. 22 to 24. Nos. 23 and 24 are known to exist with inverted overprint: very rare.

IV. Foreign Occupation Stamps

The general catalogues contain sufficient basic information on these stamps.

Forged overprints are found of the whole Trentino set (1919), Nos. 1-18, with the errors. Quite well counterfeited in Genoa (I.) The whole set of Venezia Giulia (1919), Nos. 1-18, with the errors, was poorly counterfeited in Geneva (F.), and better in Genoa (I.).

The whole set of Venezia Giulia (1919), Nos. 19-29, was well counterfeited in Paris (H.) and in Genoa (I.), along with the postage due set, Nos. 1-7. On the forged Paris set, overprints applied on canceled stamps, one finds Italian cancellations dating from 1904 (!) to 1918, and on a few the year date itself received a forged overprint. The regular mail and postage due set of Genoa was provided with forged postmarks. Comparison with originals is necessary. This should emphasize paper differences, with or without silk thread, and differences in shades between the nonoverprinted and the overprinted stamps — all of which proves once more that specialization is useful.

Italy — Offices Abroad

Tripoli

The TRIPOLI DI BARBERIA overprint was counterfeited well. Comparison is necessary, especially for the 1- and 5-lira stamps and for the Special Delivery stamps. This overprint was counterfeited in Geneva and affixed on mint and used originals.

Ivory Coast

1892 and 1900. Peace and Commerce type. Nos. 1 to 17. Completely forged (Geneva); see French Colonies.

1904. ".05" overprinted on 30-centime. No. 18. *Forged overprints:* comparison is necessary.

1906-7. Balay type. Nos. 36-40. All sorts of *forgeries* were overprinted fraudulently in Geneva (see French Colonies) with normal or spaced overprint; forged Geneva cancellation: double circle with date (inner circle is broken), with collection branch indication, GRAND-BASSAM (a small star) 25 MARS 15 COTE D'IVOIRE.

1915. Red Cross. No. 58. *Forged double overprint,* which is found sometimes on cover. Comparison is indispensable.

Parcel post stamps. Numerous *forged overprints:* comparison is very necessary, and specialization is recommended if one wishes to establish some kind of rationale for good judgment. The forged overprints were applied on originals but mainly on forged stamps, especially in Geneva, Nos. 5 and 6; No. 7, Type I; Nos. 9 and 10.

Jamaica

1863-83. Nos. 1 to 24. *Originals:* typographed; perf 14.

Early forgeries: crude lithographed execution; the set comprises the six types of the first issue; no watermark; no shading on the cheek; the forehead, chin, and the front of the neck frequently are defined by a full, unbroken line.

Postage-revenues. *Fakes* obtained by removing fiscal obliterations and then replacing them with *forged cancellations.*

Japan

General observation. Specialization is recommended. The following information will facilitate the checking of all forgeries, but, with respect to the first issues, if there still is any doubt, since the cancellation question is based on facsimile indications or on distinctive marks, the reader may wish to consult the types described in the Calman study (Collins and Calman, 1890-91), the best of the forgeries having no well-defined type.

1871. First issue. Nos. 1 to 4. *Originals:* engraved on indigenous thin, laid paper, or on wove paper; the illustration (use magnifying glass) shows the details of the frame ornamentation: ten Greek ornament elements, or rather five double elements on each side, not counting the corner ornaments; in the 48- and 500-mon stamps, there is a dot in the center of each of the top and bottom lozenge-like forms under the Greek ornament; four dots in the 100-mon and five dots

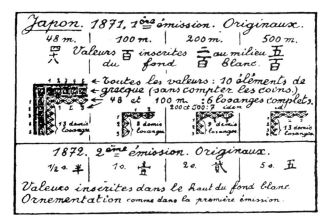

Japan. 1871. First issue. Originals. Values inscribed in the middle of the white background. All values: ten Greek ornament elements (corners not counted). Bottom: 1872. Second issue. Originals. Values inscribed in the top of the white background. Ornamentation as in the first issue.

(frequently only two dots and a line can be seen) in the 200-mon. No *reprints*.

Forgeries: (1) so-called "official counterfeits," identifiable by two microscopic Japanese marks (reproduced in the catalogues), which are found either in the blank background or in the design. These sometimes are hidden by a cancellation. (Obviously, the whole stamp should be examined through a magnifying glass.) The design is more clear-cut than in the originals; the paper is white instead of grayish and is less transparent; finally, there are design errors, especially in the Greek ornaments in which the elements are too wide in relation to others. These counterfeits are engraved. (2) Typographed counterfeits: same paper defects; the corner ornaments (one or several corners) are not properly aligned; the Greek ornaments are defective (height, spacing, or width) in a few places; the design is etched too sharply; finally, there occasionally are more serious defects, which are mentioned among the distinctive features of the lithographed forgeries. (3) Lithographed forgeries: the paper usually is too white; transparency generally is better; jumbled, confused design (dragon details often have disappeared). 48-mon: (a) eleven Greek elements, top and bottom; (Geneva) Japanese characters, which are grayish and blurred. (b) Eight elements, top and bottom, and twelve half-lozenges on the right. (c) The dots inside the lozenges are replaced by small circles. 100-mon: nine Greek elements, top right; one forgery, steel blue shade, is well done, but the lozenge dots almost always touch the four sides of the lozenges. 200-mon: 7½ lozenges on top (the superfluous half is on the left). 500-mon: (a) eleven Greek elements bottom right and left; six whole lozenges on top and two halves at

each end. (b) Thirteen half-lozenges on the sides, but the lowest one is much too small (sharper angle). (c) Nine lozenges, top and bottom, and the half-lozenges on the sides end in large, unbroken spheres. (d) Geneva: eleven Greek elements on top, etc. Note: In the forgeries of the No. 3 stamp, the white background inscriptions almost always are lithographed in a grayish shade (originals and forgery of No. 1, in deep black) with numerous white dots, due to a print failure and smudging.

1872. Perforated stamps. Nos. 5 to 8. *Originals:* perf 11½; 1- and 2-sen, 19 x 22½ mm; 10-sen, 21 x 24 mm; 20-sen, 22½ x 25½ mm; 30-sen, 24 x 27 mm; thin laid or wove paper; the 5-sen, also on wove paper. Ornamentation and lozenges as in the first issue; see also details given there.

Reprints (1896): 1- and 2-sen, imperforate; white paper instead of yellowish and better imprint; they are the only Japanese reprints and are very rare.

Forgeries: inexpertly perforated (pin perforated or rouletted) or noncongruent perforation. See the first issue for general details. ½-sen: eleven Greek elements, top and bottom right.

1-sen: nine elements, top and bottom; the thin frame surrounding the Greek ornaments externally was forgotten.

2-sen: (a) eleven elements, top and bottom left, and 10 half-lozenges on the left; (b) 7½ lozenges on top (the half, on the left) and 9 half-lozenges on the right; (c) 6 lozenges and two halves, top and bottom; six halves on the right and five on the left.

5-sen: (a) eleven Greek elements top and bottom, and six lozenges plus two halves, top and bottom; (b) nine half-lozenges on the right and left. The Geneva forgeries on white pelure paper or very transparent yellowish-white paper have eleven or nine Greek ornamentation elements at the top (still not counting the corner elements), and there are four forged Geneva cancellations: (1) large circle, 1½ mm thick (22 mm) with Japanese characters?; (2) a cork, 18 mm in diameter, intersected by a white cross about 2 mm wide; (3) a cork, 23 mm in diameter, forming a large circle, which is broken in eight pieces, and a small inner circle made of four triangular pieces; (4) triple rectangle, 21 x 18 mm, the smallest one 13½ x 10 mm, with Japanese characters.

1872–73. With chrysanthemum. No plate number. Nos. 9 to 19. *Originals:* engraved; perf 9½–12½; 6-sen, 20 x 22½ mm. Thin wove or laid paper, except No. 15, 2-sen, on thick laid paper, and Nos. 16 and 17, 4- and 30-sen, on wove paper.

Forgeries: the best executed ones are the so-called "official forgeries" that have microscopic characters indicating "facsimile," which identifies them sufficiently; if the characters are hidden by a forged cancellation, the stamp and its design must be studied as follows.

First, examine the paper and the perforation (most of them will be rejected on this basis); then, examine the impression, which usually is lithographed (no embossing or indention); finally, examine the design, which was executed for the originals by excellent designers and engravers; thus, it should have clear-cut, symmetrical features without smudges or undesigned lines. The center chrysanthemum always must have sixteen petals.

The best-known forgeries have the following characteristics: 2-sen orange, No. 11, northwest corner flowers, ten radiating lines; southwest, six lines and seven lines on the right. 10-sen green, chrysanthemum with fifteen petals. 20-sen, No. 13: (a) the chrysanthemum is too close to the top frame; in the leaf on the right above the "E" of SEN, there are only two well-drawn veins instead of three; (b) bottom figure "2" is touching the tablet and the "0" is touching its lower line. 30-sen, Nos. 14 and 17: the lower inner frame under the value is touching the Greek ornament, especially on the right, and the two "3" figures are touching the tablet's lower edge. In this forgery and in another that is better executed, the Greek ornamentation elements are very uneven. 4-sen rose, Nos. 16 and 19: (a) the two extremities of the branches are unbroken; (b) the center of the left corner designs is shifted to the right; (c) the chrysanthemum is not round and two opposite petals are half as wide as the others.

1874. Same. With plate numbers. Nos. 20 to 31.
Originals: the numbers are found at the bottom of the stamp at the branch intersections, between the dragons' tails (10-sen), under the curl on the right of SEN in the 6-sen and above the "0" of "20" on the left of the left leaf in the 20-sen. Perf 11½. Thin laid paper for Nos. 20–23 and thick wove paper for the others.

Forgeries: same remarks as in the preceding issue. Perforation is better at times. I have not seen any forgeries on this laid paper (remove the paper that sometimes is laid on the back of the forgeries).

½-sen, No. 24: chrysanthemum with seventeen petals; dot perf 14; plate designated with poorly drawn figure "2."

1-sen, No. 25: three counterfeits which have the required sixteen petals, but (a) on thin wove paper, perf 14, the left branch is touching the left tablet (by a five-veined leaf) and the left inner corner ornament; two Japanese characters instead of four in the center, plate number is indecipherable; (b) same defect in the left branch; four characters in center; thin wove paper, Plate 2, random traces of SPECIMEN outside the top of the branches; (c) medium yellowish paper, Plate 14, the right branch nowhere touches the right tablet.

2-sen, No. 26: (a) the characters in the left tablet are different from those on the right, Plate 15; (b) same; on thin wove paper, Plate 17.

4-sen, No. 27: (a) counterfeit "c," already described under "stamps without plate numbers" (previously), Nos. 16 and 19 (Yvert), but this time we have Plate 1; there are six lines of characters in the white background; allowable perforation; (b) imperforate; chrysanthemum with 14? imperfect petals; (c) fake using a stamp from a strip with plate number in a hexagonal frame.

6-sen, No. 28: (a) chrysanthemum with fifteen petals; medium wove paper; Plate 14, but this figure forms a closed Gothic "P"; (b) chrysanthemum with same number of petals; thin wove paper; in the flowers of the left corners, radiating lines on the left are missing; (c) three pearls instead of four in the bandeau on the right of the "6." All three have allowable perforation.

20-sen, No. 30: lilac and violet with fifteen-petal chrysanthemum.

30-sen, No. 31: (a) medium paper; formless perforation; the upper flower of the right branch is moved away from the chrysanthemum; the inner right frame is touching the Greek ornament; (b) thin, nonlaid paper; the flower almost is touching the chrysanthemum; almost similar defect in the inner right frame; allowable perforation. All stamps are lithographed, except the so-called "official forgeries."

1876. Birds. Nos. 32 to 34. *Originals:* delicately engraved; perf 9–13.

Forgeries: (a) a so-called "official" set with the two facsimile marks in very small characters (use magnifying glass). In the 12-sen stamp, the marks are 1 mm from the middle of the bird's neck, right and left; in the 15-sen, in the center background, they are about 1 mm below "15 SEN"; in the 45-sen, about 1 mm above the ground on which the bird is standing and 1 mm from the circle defining the center background. These forgeries seem clever and deceptive; they are found in many general collections. Procedures for identifying them, even when the facsimile marks intentionally are hidden by a cancellation:
(a) 12-sen, the chrysanthemum on top has fifteen petals; 15-sen, thirteen petals; 45-sen, fourteen or fifteen petals; (b) a lithographed set, inexpertly dot perf 13, Plate 1, but the two lines are touching in this figure; 12-sen, thirteen petals, no dot in the lower left corner; 15-sen, eighteen petals; 45-sen, seventeen petals; upper left corner flower is too small.

1875. With plate numbers. Nos. 35 to 44.
Originals: same perforation as previously; the 6-sen is orange; the 20- and 30-sen, small format; 5-, 10-, 20-, and 30-sen, 19½ x 22 mm. The 1-, 4-, and 5-sen are found without plate numbers (Nos. 42–44, Yvert).

Forgeries: ¹/₂-sen, No. 35: Plate 2; see forgery of No. 24.

6-sen orange: (a) Plate 9; this plate exists only in the violet-brown of No. 21; the ornament of the inner left corner is shifted to the right; (b) Plate 17; three pearls in the banderole under the value, bottom of the stamp (there should be four).

10-sen, No. 39: chrysanthemum with fourteen petals.

20-sen, No. 40: (a) the double center circle is too thick on the right and is touching the right tablet; under the plate number there are three pieces of leaves; only the leaf in the middle has the necessary veins; (b) fourteen-petal chrysanthemum; good impression; allowable perf 11¹/₂; six lines of characters in the center background; (c) fourteen petals; poorly executed dot perforation.

30-sen, No. 41: (a) generally inferior imprint; the bottom branch extremities are full and unbroken, instead of line shaded; (b) plate number-like figure "11"?! Bottom figure "3" evidently is wider at its top than at its bottom; (c) fifteen petals; no plate number.

5-sen, No. 44: (a) with Plate 17! The loop under the "N" of SEN is shaded with single, uncrossed lines; (b) no plate number; same defect; and the shade lines under SEN are not crossed either; (c) fourteen-petal chrysanthemum; this forgery has two different types: (1) the left corner flowers are touching the inner frame; (2) they are not touching, and in the oval's sides, there is a third Japanese mark that is smaller than the two customary marks and different on each side. In this type, the line shading is partly crossed.

1876–77. Various types. Nos. 47 to 59. *Originals:* perf 8¹/₂–10¹/₂ (common) and other rare perforations; see the catalogues.

Forgeries: the whole set was lithographed inexpertly with rare perforations in Japan. The double circle cancellation also was lithographed on the 1-sen black; in other values, notably the 5-sen, the cancellation then was applied more or less successfully. Since most of the stamps of this set are common, comparison with an inexpensive original (10-sen for the 12-sen, and 15- or 20-sen for the 30- and 45-sen) easily will expose these counterfeit creations (shade lines and Japanese characters, crossed lines for the numbers of the 30- and 45-sen).

Karelia

Nothing interesting. The set was counterfeited lithographically; irregular stippling in the center background, very regular in the originals. The corner stippling should be compared, too.

Kiauchau

1900. Nos. 1 to 13. *Forged cancellations!*
Geneva forgeries: steamer type, values in pfennigs (and in cents for the other two issues), no watermark; perf 13¹/₂ (see German Colonies). Forged Geneva cancellations: one circle (27 mm), TSCHINWAN 16/2…DEUTSCHE POST.

1905. Value in cents and dollars. Nos. 14 to 23.
Values in cents — *Geneva forgeries:* see first issue.

Values in cents — *Genoa forgeries:* lithographed, perf 13¹/₂ instead of 14; frame hatching is confused, especially the banderole shade lines connecting the upper inscription with the figures; there are no visible shading lines in the top of the banderole curls bearing the CENTS words. The black impression also is lithographed (uncolored dots in the characters and the figures); letters "ENTS" of CENTS are joined.

Values in dollars — expertly *reprinted;* these values should be collected on dated cover before November 1905 after cancellation expertizing.

1905–11. Lozenge watermark. Nos. 24 to 33.
Geneva forgeries: values in cents; see first issue.

Korea

1884. Nos. 1 to 5. *Originals:* typographed, perf 9, 10; 8¹/₂ x 9; 9 x 9¹/₂; 9¹/₂ x 10; the 10-mon stamp, also 8¹/₂.

Reprints: 5- and 10-mon in enormous quantities (probably the other three values also) with perf 8¹/₂, 9, and 11–12. Comparison with the original shades is indispensable.

Forgeries: 5-mon, lithographed in dull red on thick paper, perf 11¹/₂. The small corner lozenge is replaced by a sort of comma.

Kuwait

1923–24. Overprinted stamps. Nos. 15 to 26. This set, as well as the corresponding official stamp set, is unissued. Inverted *forged overprints:* comparison is necessary.

Labuan

1892–93. No watermark. Nos. 32 to 45. *Originals:* 1892 set: engraved (Nos. 32–38). 1893 set: lithographed (Nos. 39–45); the forehead, nose, and the front of the neck are defined by a thin line (about ¹/₁₂ mm thick); the bottom of the chignon is formed by two spindle-like curls whose lines almost always are touching and which are joined to the chignon; the inner corner ornaments do not touch the inner frame or the oval; these ornaments end in the corners with a small arrow made of two lines separated by a gap (use magnifying glass).

Lithographed *forgeries* — confusion with the original engraved set is obviated by the lithographed impression: (1) a set of Italian origin, photolithographed in blocks of ten (5 x 2); lines in front of nose and neck are too thick ($\frac{1}{6}$ mm); the chignon curl has lines that are separated; the curl only rarely is connected with the chignon, and the lower oblique line is only $\frac{1}{4}$ mm long instead of about $\frac{1}{2}$ mm; the small arrows in the bottom inner corners are not broken; there are numerous gaps in the thin frames of the four tablets; the line defining the mouth on the right frequently is too bold. (2) *Geneva forgeries:* also photolithographed and much more successful; however, the frame and oval lines are smudged; the arrows in the bottom inner corners are not broken. In dealing with this last set, it is useful to compare the arbitrary shades; this also should be done when working with the preceding set. Note: The two forged sets have allowable paper thickness, dimensions, and perf 14.

1895–99. Overprints on Borneo. Nos. 57 to 61 and 86 to 94. *Forged overprints:* comparison is necessary. (See Geneva also on originals and on the forged $1 stamp.)

Lagos

1885–86. Values in shillings. Nos. 24 to 26. Clever *forgeries* on original watermarked paper. Comparison of the center background hatching and of the portrait lines with a common stamp is sufficient.

Latvia

This is a country with a plentiful supply of new stamps. Mint sets can be had at will and this delights collectors who go in for numbers. Unfortunately, the albums are worth more than their contents.

Forgeries: 1918: 5-kapeika carmine. Crude center design and format, and, as for No. 2, the perforation doesn't match the original. 1920: Nos. 51 and 52 (50-kapeika and 1-rublis), imperforate. Compare hatching and ornament design on the sides. 1920–21: overprints, 2-ruble on 10- and 35-kapeika were counterfeited. Make comparison.

Lebanon

Regarding the Merson type values, 1-, 2-, and 5-franc (France), Nos. 12–14; 17, 18; 40–42; 45 and 46; check whether the forged stamps described under French Colonies are involved.

Leeward Islands

1897. SEXAGENARY overprints. Nos. 9 to 16. *Forged overprints:* comparison is necessary. Geneva, two types: (1) 16 mm, lower curl traversed by a diagonal line; (2) same dimension instead of $15\frac{1}{2}$; a horizontal line traverses the whole curl on top, and the "R" of SEXAGENARY almost is touching the inner circle.

Levant

Most Levant issues have overprints and thus require a thorough comparative examination, for there are a great many counterfeit overprints and forged cancellations on both originals and reprints, as well as forgeries with forged overprints.

I. German Post Offices

The issues of the North German Postal District (Nos. 12–17, 23, 24), those of the German Empire (Nos. 1–6, small shield; 13–19 and 28, large shield; 26 and 27), and the issues of 1875, 1880, and 1875–82 (Nos. 30–43) were used without overprinting in Constantinople.

The 1-, 2-, and 5-groschen and the 20-pfennig are most common: 5–20U. The $\frac{1}{4}$- and $\frac{1}{2}$-groschen are rare: 20–50U. The rectangular stamps are very rare.

1884. Overprinted German stamps of 1880. Nos. 1 to 5. The principal characteristics of this set are tabulated below. With this information it is possible to relegate reprints and most forged overprints to a reference function. Comparison and the study of cancellations are still necessary. As an example of the latter, a stamp canceled COELN (Cologne) would be classified with forgeries.

Measure the overprints starting on the left of figure "1" or on the left of figure "2" and ending at the right of the last figure or fraction bar. When the overprint impression is heavily inked, it may vary slightly in width.

The set of reprints is worth 5 francs. Its fraudulent cancellation is a large postmark with CONSTANTINOPLE preceded and followed by a star.

Subsequent issues. Check overprints by comparing them.

OVERPRINTED GERMAN STAMPS of 1880		ORIGINALS Plain center background. Dull ink. Type I	Type II	REPRINTS Background not plain. Shiny ink, Pearls defective at times.
10-para	Shades	Violet		Violet red
	Figure height	3½ mm		3⅗ to 3⅔ mm
	Overprint width	15¾ mm		16 mm
20-para	Shades	Rose: rare: 2M, 3U	Dark rose	Rose
	Between O,P	¾ mm	1 mm	1 mm
	Overprint width	16½ mm	16⅞ mm	17 mm Pearls defective
1-piaster	Overprint width	13½ mm		13½ mm Pearls defective
		PIASTER 1⅖ mm from base of figure		PIASTER 1⅖ mm from base of figure
1¼-piaster	Shades	Brown Red-brown (1884-85) "4" figures touch fraction bar	Red-brown "4" figures do not touch	Brown "4" figures do not touch (Type II)
	Between P and fraction bar	½ mm	½ mm	1 mm
	Overprint width	15¼ mm	15 mm	16¾ mm
2½-piaster	Shades	Olive-gray (1884-86)	Olive-gray Bronze-green (1888)	Dark green (black)
	Between P and fraction bar	½ mm	½ mm	1 mm
	Overprint width	17 mm	17 mm	18 mm Pearls defective
	Extension of fraction bars	Goes through P loop	Goes over loop line of P	Goes over loop line of P

Varieties: No. 6, with figure "10" positioned too low. No. 19 has two types: PIASTER, too low (Type II). No. 25, same. Nos. 22 and 28 are found with overprint doubled: extremely rare. No. 33 with figure "1" not high enough (plate flaw): 6M, 10U.

Cancellations: Nos. 34, 35, 38, 40, 50, and 54–56 must be expertized.

II. British Post Offices

The overprints that require special attention belong to the first issue, No. 4 (40-para on ½-penny), No. 25 (1-piastre on 2-pence, Beirut), and the two types of Levant overprints. Make comparison.

Cancellations: common: "C" (Constantinople); "S" (Stamboul [Istanbul]); postmark with date, double circle, BEYROUT (Beirut); postmark with date, single circle, BRITISH POST OFFICE CONSTANTINOPLE, etc. Less common: "B 01" (Alexandria); "B 02" (Suez); "F 87" (Smyrna); "G 06" (Beirut); and all other postmarks. The Egyptian ship cancellation PORT SAID is rare. Stamps of Great Britain with Levant cancellation are in particularly active demand. Consult the specialty catalogues.

Remarks on the various issues: All the rare values have been fraudulently overprinted.

1885. No. 1 (40-para on 2½-pence lilac) was well counterfeited in Geneva, but the overprint is somewhat too wide: 17 mm instead of 16½–¾ mm after printing. The 12-piastre on 2-shilling 6-pence lilac, blue-tinted paper, is very rare.

1887–96. No. 4 (40-para on ½-penny red) requires comparative expertizing, especially the ink. The original handstamp was used to make forgeries, so having an original cancellation on cover or piece is very helpful in this case. The canceling device was used for five days at the end of February 1893.

No. 5 (40-para on 2½-pence) exists with double overprint: very rare.

1902–5. The 24-piastre (No. 24) belongs to this set. The 4- and 12-piastre overprints are found on chalky paper: same value.

1905. Levant overprinted stamps, Nos. 12–21. The overprint was well counterfeited. Compare overprint, impression, and even paper shades. Nos. 14, 15, and 21 are found on chalky paper.

1906. The 2-piastre, No. 23, is also found on chalky paper.

1906. Beirut overprint, No. 25. Compare and expertize. A few bad copies, one of which comes from Beirut, can be identified by comparison alone.

1909–10. No. 32, a second type with a more finely printed figure "4," is worth 5M, 5U.

1911–14. No. 36, two types, overprint $2^1/_2$ mm high: common. Overprint 3 mm high: 2M, 4U. No. 45, a second type of figure "4" (as in No. 32) is worth 20 francs, mint and used.

1916. Special issue for Salonika. Nos. 49–56. This issue is rare, having been in use for only fifteen days, with military postmarks. One finds double overprints and pairs in which one stamp is overprinted. These are speculative fantasies of the military office in charge of printing. Dangerous forgeries. Expertizing is necessary. As a rule, buy on cover only.

1921. Nos. 57–74. There is nothing to say about them.

III. Austrian Post Offices

The Lombardy-Venetia stamps, eagle type of 1863–64, Nos. 18–27, are very much in demand with Levant cancellations. There are many of these, proceeding alphabetically from Alexandria to Volo. (See Lombardy-Venetia, "cancellations.")

1867. Head of Franz Joseph. Value in soldi. Nos. 1 to 7. A very pretty collection can be built with just the shades, perforations, types, and the cancellations of this issue.

Cancellations: all Turkish post offices can be found. A few postmarks are very rare, depending on the office of their origin and the color used. The postmarks of the Lloyd agencies and of steamship companies are always rare: 10–100U.

Types: all values are classified in two types according to whether the beard is fine or coarse. Prices are the same for the two types, except for the 50-soldo, perf $10^1/_2$, which is worth 1.50 francs with coarse beard, but which is extremely rare, used; with expertly executed beard, same perforation, it is worth 10 francs, mint, and 5 francs, used.

Perforations: $9^1/_2$: common. 5- and 10-soldo, perf 9: rare, mint, 25 francs, used (fine beard). 50-soldo: 30 francs, mint, and 15 francs, used (coarse beard). 10-soldo, perf $10^1/_2$ x 9: very rare, mint; 40 francs, used. 50-soldo: very rare; 10- and 15-soldo, perf $10^1/_2$: rare, mint. 10-soldo: common, used. 15-soldo: 15 francs; perf 12: 5M, 50U.

Varieties: the whole set, except the 3- and 50-soldo, is found with very transparent impression: 30M, 20U, except 25-soldo: 3U.

50-soldo in pairs, imperforate between: rare.

The 25-soldo, slate gray-black shade is rare.

Reprints: 10-soldo dark blue, perf $10^1/_2$ on grayish paper.

Fake: fraudulently perforated envelope cutout of a 25-soldo. The paper is too white and indention is quite evident.

Forgery: the 25-soldo was well counterfeited in Geneva (F.). Comparison of hair on temple and bottom of neck, and of beard, will reveal the counterfeit. Paper slightly transparent. Perf $11^1/_2$. Almost always canceled with date, single circle.... OTIN 5/7.

Forged cancellations: very numerous. Check and compare (especially the rare cancellations) with the cancellations of an extensive specialized collection of this issue.

1883–86. Black numeral. Value in soldi. Nos. 8 to 14. *Sheets* watermarked BRIEFMARKEN. (See Austria.) Copies with pieces of this watermark are in demand.

Perforations: all values: $9^1/_2$. Perf 10: 3-soldo green [with 10-para] overprint (Vienna); 5-soldo: 20 francs, mint; 5 francs, used. Perf $10^1/_2$: 10-soldo: very rare, mint; 30-francs, used.

Varieties: two types can be specified depending on the width of the "D" of SLD; also, there are several other types related to differences in the numeral "5."

No. 14, overprinted: Type I (Vienna), $15^1/_4$–$^1/_2$ mm. The "P" is $1^1/_2$ mm from the zero. Numbers and letters aligned at bottom. Type II (Constantinople), $15^3/_4$–16 mm. The "P" is 2 mm from the zero. PARA positioned too high.

Overprints are found out of place (for example, at the top of the stamp), which explains why one can find vertical pairs in which one stamp is not overprinted.

Forged overprints: numerous in Type II. Comparison is necessary.

1888. Overprinted Austrian stamps (kreuzer). Nos. 15 to 19. *Varieties:* the 1-piaster is found perf $13^1/_2$: rare. 10-para with misplaced overprint. There are no inverted or double overprints.

1890–92. Overprinted Austrian stamps. Nos. 20 to 27. Numerous perforations. Rare: Nos. 20, 26, and 27, perf $9^1/_4$; Nos. 21–23, perf $10^1/_2$ x $12^1/_2$; Nos. 21, 23, 24, 26, and 27, perf 11; No. 20, perf $12^1/_2$.

Varieties: No. 23, PIAS; No. 23 without figures on the right; overprints misplaced.

Fakes: the imperforate fakes were perforated stamps before they had a trip to the dentist's.

Forged overprints. Nos. 24–27. Comparison is necessary.

1891–96. Same. Nos. 28 to 31. *Perforations:* numerous. Not very common: Nos. 28 and 29, perf $12^1/_2$ x $13^1/_2$; No. 31, perf $12^1/_2$, and No. 30, perf $11^1/_2$. Rare: No. 28, perf $9^1/_4$; Nos. 28 and 31, perf 11; No. 29, perf $12^1/_2$ x $10^1/_2$, and No. 30, perf $12^1/_2$.

Varieties: Nos. 28 and 29 with misplaced overprint: rare.

Forged overprints: on No. 31, used, Austrian cancellation underneath the "overprint," and on No. 31. Make comparison.

1899–1900. Same. Nos. 32 to 38. Many different perforations. Nos. 36–38 are rare, perf $9^1/_4$ or $10^1/_2$.

Nos. 33 and 36–38 with composite (10½ x 12½) or reverse cancellations. No. 36 is found in pairs, imperforate in middle: rare.

1903. Same. Nos. 39 to 42. The stamps without shiny lines are rare with perf 9¼; 9¼ x 12½, or reverse; 10½ and 12½ x 10½.

1906–7. Same. Nos. 43 and 44. Same remarks as on perforations for the 1903 issue.

1908. Same. Nos. 45 to 53. Stamps perf 9¼ are unissued.

Postage due stamps. In 1879, stamps perf 8½ with notation "Delivery Tax 20-para: S O" on five lines were affixed on letters; 20-para black on violet or black on white. These are very rare on cover.

1902. Overprinted Austrian postage due stamps. Nos. 1 to 5. Perforations 10½ x 12½, or reverse, and 12½ x 9½ are rare.

IV. French Post Offices

French stamps with Levant postmarks, small numerals 3704–9, 3766–73, 4008–19; large numerals 5079–5107, and 5119, 5121, 5129, 5139, 5153, 5154–56, and postmarks with date from 1876 are very much in demand. Some of them are very rare. Beirut is the oldest Levant French post office (1840).

1885. Overprinted French stamps. Nos. 1 to 3. Nos. 2 and 3 belong to Type II.

1886–1900. Same. Nos. 4 to 8. Two overprinted types for No. 8: width 15.7 mm and 16.2 mm. They are a little wider when the impression is heavy. Overprints are found straddling two stamps (1- and 2-piastre).

No. 6, with PIASTR*FS*, printing variety: rare.

No. 6, bisected: very rare.

No. 7, 3 PIASTRES 8, printing variety: rare.

Forged overprints: numerous on Nos. 8 and 9. Make comparison.

1902–6. Levant. Nos. 9 to 22. There are a few varieties of letter positioning in relation to figures. Forged overprints on Nos. 21–23 originals and on the 5-franc stamps printed clandestinely. (See France.)

1906. No overprint. Nos. 24 to 26. Clandestine impressions of these stamps exist; a few minor differences in printing and shade. This set should be acquired on entire cover.

1905. BEIRUT overprint. No. 27. The issue lasted only eleven days (January 17–28, 1905). Overprint in very dark green. Good counterfeits. Make comparison.

1921–23. Overprinted French stamps. Nos. 28 to 40. Postmarks printed by hand. Quantities printed were 2,500 of No. 38 and 7,500 of Nos. 39 and 40.

Cavalle, Dedeagh, Port Lagos. 1893–1900. Clandestine overprint impressions were made in Paris

with the original matrices. Likewise for Vathy. Make comparison; the ink shade is slightly different. These should be bought on cover only.

Clandestine impressions of Nos. 14–16 of Cavalle and Dedeagh. There are a few slight differences in design and shade. These counterfeit creations slip into collections with the greatest of ease, since they meet all the general buyers' requirements. On-cover acquisition is advised.

V. Italian Post Offices

The nonoverprinted Italian stamps with Levant cancellations (Tunisia, Egypt [Alexandria], Tripoli, and Red Sea) are in active demand.

Cancellations: numerals in an octagon of small lozenges or in a barred circle: "234" (Alexandria), "235" (Tunis), "3336" (La Goulette), "3365" (Sousse), "3051" (Tripoli), "3840" and "3862" (Assab and Massaua, Red Sea). Most common are Nos. "234" and "235."

Cancellation PIROSCAFI POSTALI ITALIANI in a rectangle: 50U.

Rarer are the cancellations with point of origin indication on one or two lines: TRIPOLI, DA TUNISI, DA MONTEVIDEO (or BUENOS-AIRES), COI POSTALI ITALIANI, BAJA DI ASSAB, etc., or special postmarks, for example: rectangular postmark MASSAUA SERVIZIO ITALIANO DEL MAR ROSSO, with date and year on the left of that inscription, etc.

1874. Figures or head. ESTERO overprint. Nos. 1 to 11. *Sheets:* 200 stamps in two panes (10 x 10). 2-lira: sheets of 100 stamps.

Types of similar Italian stamps with corner ornaments altered. (White in the four corners; the 2-lira with white-petaled flowers.)

Overprint: usually deep black. Outside, 6 mm curve radius; inside, 4¼ mm.

Varieties: oversight or defects in corner alteration: 1-centesimo (two or three dots, top right); 5-centesimo, untouched bottom right. 10-centesimo (examine the four corners). One finds copies without any alteration, like the 30-centesimo stamp. This last variety exists also untouched top left and bottom, right. All are rare.

No overprint: 1- and 2-centesimo, unissued.

Double overprint: 30-centesimo.

Forgery: 2-lira on original watermarked paper. Compare line structure and the corner florets.

Forged overprints: on Italian stamps with doctored (scraped) corners and on Italian stamps with corners that have not been altered. They are obviously ridiculous, except for the rare varieties of the 10- and 30-centesimo with unaltered corners, which must be thoroughly examined and compared.

Fakes: unaltered corner repair varieties have been obtained by adding one or several Italian stamp corners of the same shade to a Levant stamp.

Forged cancellations are very numerous on 1-, 2-, 30-, 40-, 60-centesimo and 2-lira stamps. The ink is too new, design and spacing are noncongruent, arbitrary numerals, etc. Comparison is necessary.

1881–83. Head of Umberto I. Nos. 12 to 17. Same overprint; corners altered.

Varieties: 5-centesimo, poor retouching of bottom right angle. 20-centesimo, double overprint. The 2-lira is really an unissued stamp.

Forged cancellations: numerous. Nos. 15 and 16 require expertizing. No. 17, Tunis complimentary cancellation.

Subsequent issues. All Constantinople overprints were made with the sole purpose of raiding the unsuspecting collector's pocketbook. Keep away from them. There is an abundance of forged overprints.

All subsequent issues were fraudulently overprinted every time the forgery made it worthwhile (for example, in the 1909–11 issue, all the 20-piastre stamps were overprinted on the 5-lira). One can say that half of the overprints, from No. 18 to the end of the series, require comparative expertizing, especially Nos. 24–38, with varieties.

VI. Polish Post Offices

1919. The values in penni were fraudulently overprinted.

1921. The whole set was poorly overprinted. Comparative examination would be enough.

VII. Romanian Post Offices

Black overprints on 5-ban blue, perf 13½ and 13½ x 11½. Same perforations on the 10-ban green and the 25-ban violet (the latter, also perf 11½). Note: Black or violet overprints on stamps perf 11½ and composite are rare.

Violet overprints on 5-ban blue, perf 13½, 11½, and 13½ x 11½; 10-ban, perf 13½; and 25-ban, perforated like the 5-ban.

Numerous double, inverted, and error overprints. No. 1, double black overprint, and No. 2, with 10-para black overprint, exist in vertical pairs, imperforate between.

Forged overprints are very numerous. Make comparison.

VIII. Russian Post Offices

Imperforate Stamps. Among the stamps of the Levant, the Russian post offices occupy a special place because the first issues are composed of imperforate stamps, created especially for use as imperforate stamps, and almost all of them rare. Research on the various types has increased interest in these handsome stamps.

1864. Large format stamp. No. 1. *Select:* four margins about 2 mm wide.

Typographed in sheets of four stamps.

First printing (1863, St. Petersburg) in vertical strip of four, normal type, on thin paper. Used for the first time by the Russian Navigation and Commerce Company, January 6, 1864. Second printing (1864) in dark blue, in blocks of four, whose transfer plate flaws (see illustration) make it possible to locate the type (Types I and II, top pair; Types III and IV, bottom pair). Thicker paper than that used for the first printing.

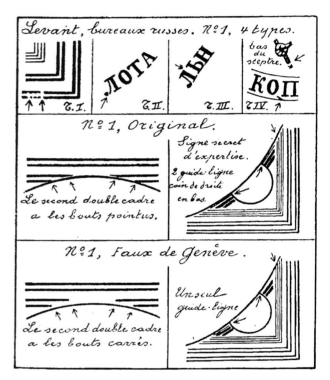

Russian offices in the Levant, No. 1, four types. Lower part of scepter. Middle: No. 1, original. Second double frame lines are pointed; expertizing secret mark; two guidelines, bottom right corner. Bottom: No. 1, Geneva forgeries. Second double frame lines are squared at end; a singled guideline.

Shades: dull pale blue, dark blue, and indigo (1865?). The last two shades are found in unissued stamps.

Cancellations: single circle with date, Constantinople (in Russian), first six months of 1864. This cancellation is very rare on Russian stamps. Double framed Franco, 20 x 12 mm, small blue postmark of 1865, which is also very rare on Russian stamps.

On subsequent issues, one encounters either a black dotted lozenge (14 mm on one side); very rare in blue; a double circle (30 mm) consular cancellation, which is very rare; or a cancellation with date.

These cancellations are exceedingly rare on Russian stamps, as is the framed FRANCO (rectangle 35 x 12¹/₂ mm), with corners cut off, in black.

Forgeries: there are inexpertly done early lithographed forgeries, one of which ("S") is not on chalky paper, and has unbureled half-moons around the center circle. The other one bears the word FACSIMILE, which sometimes has been erased.

It should be noted that neither these forgeries nor the following one have dots in the blank spaces above the half-moons surrounding the center circle.

Modern forgery (Geneva, F.): more deceptive. See the illustration for the identification marks.

In a first cliché, there were two shading lines in the right horn's bell and three in the one on the left. In a retouched cliché, the lines were arranged in normal order: three on the right, two on the left. However, above "O T," the two median lines of the four horizontals are touching the blue circle. Finally, in a cliché that was corrected a second time, these shade lines no longer touch. The two shades were counterfeited.

1865. Steamer type. Nos. 2 and 3. *Select:* four margins 1¹/₂ mm wide.

Sheets: twenty-eight different types (7 x 4). Russian Navigation and Commerce Company. Lithographed in Odessa. The types are identified by transfer plate flaws (especially frames and scepter).

Cancellations: see first issue.

Pairs: the 2-piastre pair is exceedingly rare. There is one pair in the Tapling Collection; one pair, Ferrari; and one strip of four, Mavrogordato.

Forgeries: the two values were relatively well counterfeited. However, the following defects should be noted: 10-para: the dots following the inscription letters are not square; the curl-shaped design on the right under the ship has two white protuberances inside the curl; the burelage is far from being as fine as in the original. 2-piastre: the boat frame under letters "P" and "O" is much smaller than in the originals and most of the small oblique frame shading lines are missing or are poorly executed. In the two values, the ship itself, its masts, flags, ropes, and funnel are not congruent with the original type. There are other very inexpertly executed forgeries. Comparative procedures will be adequate.

Reprints: there was an unofficial reprint in sheets of ten (5 x 2) with a 9 mm gutter between the two rows of five and a lateral gutter of 22 mm between the stamps. Each stamp has a frame line which is 1¹/₂ mm from the vignette. The paper is yellowish. The shades vary. No gum.

1866. Similar types. Lozenge burelage. Nos. 4 and 5. *Sheets* of twenty-eight types (7 x 4) as in the preceding issue. The burelage is made up of lozenges with a horizontal major axis; lozenge axis length is approximately 1.2 mm and 0.5 mm. The same is true for the next issue.

For some unknown reason, the lozenge burelage ends at the plate's third horizontal row, but reappears ¹/₄ mm further on. This occurred, possibly, only in the second printing. Is the explanation to be found in a partially rebuilt plate?

Copies with double marginal lines on one or two sides are found. This resulted from improper juxtaposition of transfer plates.

The first printings have shading in the upper inscription tablets (Yvert Nos. 4 and 5). Shading differs according to type.

These shade lines (Nos. 4a and 5a) disappeared in the last printing (end of 1866?). It may be noted that the blue and rose of Nos. 4a and 5a are duller than those of Nos. 4 and 5. If a plate which was corrected by retouching the shading of Nos. 4a and 5a is involved, it can be called a retouched plate, but if the matrix was retouched and a new plate was made for each value, we would have to classify Nos. 4a and 5a as a new issue, a modified type, done at the end of 1866 or beginning of 1867.

Cancellations: see first issue. Consular cancellations are very rare.

Reprints (1867): unofficial reprints exist of both values, without gum.

Forgeries: there exist a few crudely executed forgeries which can be exposed immediately by comparative examination of steamship or wave details. Also, the more expensive stamps of the next issue with vertical burelage were counterfeited most frequently. See next issue.

Originals: width: 16 mm; height: 21²/₅–³/₅ mm.

1868. Same type, vertical burelage. Nos. 6 and 7. The burelage is identical with that of Nos. 4 and 5, except that it is positioned vertically, that is, the lozenge's major axis is vertical. Lozenge measurements are the same as in the preceding issue.

Cancellations: canceled examples of No. 6, which are very rare, are worth fifteen to twenty times the value of the mint stamp.

Forgeries: the burelage measurements are not congruent with the original. They usually exceed those of the originals, which are about 16 mm by about 21¹/₂ mm. Moreover, comparison with ship and wave details in stamps of the preceding issue (Nos. 4 and 5), which are not so expensive, will identify the counterfeits. A rather common forgery of No. 6 has a horizontal red line under the "P." Another forgery of No. 7 has a line under the "O," making it resemble a "Q." Both of these forgeries are on thin, yellowish paper.

1868 (May). Large center numerals. Nos. 8 to 11.
This issue and the following ones were made on official Russian state paper with wavy line watermark and were issued by the Russian government.

Shades: the four values have the shades indicated in the catalogues, with darker shades. The 5-kopeck burelage is blue or pale blue. In the 10-kopeck, it is green or dark green.

Perforation: 11½. This eliminates confusion with the next issue, which is perf 14½ x 15. Nos. 9 and 11 are known to exist imperforate: very rare.

Cancellations: black or blue, with date or numerals and stippled lozenge. The green ones are rarer: 50U.

Pairs: 4U. Blocks: rare.

1872. Same type. Perf 15. Nos. 12 to 15. *Paper:* laid horizontally or vertically.

Shades: common or dark color tones.

Varieties: pairs of No. 13, imperforate between, exist: rare.

1876–79. Overprints. Nos. 16 to 18. Stamps overprinted in blue or black. Two numeral "7" types (thick or thin). Numeral "8," a single type, on stamps of the preceding issue only.

The stamps overprinted on vertically laid paper, in black on No. 17, in blue on No. 16, and in black or blue on Nos. 18 or 18a, being rare, are worth double.

Forged overprints: numerous. Comparison is indicated.

Even the 10-kopeck of the 1868 issue, perf 11½, was overprinted.

1879 (June) to 1884. Same type. Nos. 19 to 25. A few shade varieties. Imperforate Nos. 22–25 are unissued stamps.

Subsequent issues. There is nothing special to be pointed out, except a few forged overprints on Nos. 34 and 35 (these being originals or fraudulently overprinted stamps, see Russia), the inverted Beirut overprint, and the 50-piastre Romanoff, identifiable by the word PIASTRES, whose end letters do not encroach upon the left and right frames as they do in the original overprints. Postwar values no longer have known printing figures, inflation being the rule in the prices specified. The same is true with respect to the inflated prices of various errors and of all Russian stamps of recent years.

If you are a person who does not believe the moon is made of green cheese, refrain from buying these stamps. All values of the Wranger Army stamps were fraudulently overprinted.

Liberia

1860–64. Nos. 1 to 6. Typographed; perf 12, 11, 11½, x 12. The 1860 stamps are on thick wove paper; imperforate stamps are found; Nos. 4–6 are on medium wove paper.

1867. Nos. 7 to 9. Lithographed; same perforations; thin wove paper; there are imperforates; the perforated 6-cent green and the imperforate 24-cent red are essays. The stamps of this issue have an outer frame that is 1 mm away from the usual triple frame.

Nos. 1 to 9. *Originals:* 6-cent, 22⁴/₅–23 x 27³/₄–28 mm. One can see the five toes of the right foot; the latter is 1 mm horizontally from the circle; looking at them from a distance of 50 cm, the clouds are barely visible. 12-cent, 22½–¾ x 27¹/₃–½ mm. The left foot is ½ mm from the circle and it has crisscrossed hatching in its rear part. Two toes with a trace of a third appear on the right foot. The large cloud above the ship is sufficiently visible. 24-cent, 23¹/₅ x 28 mm. The right foot has five toes that usually are visible. At the

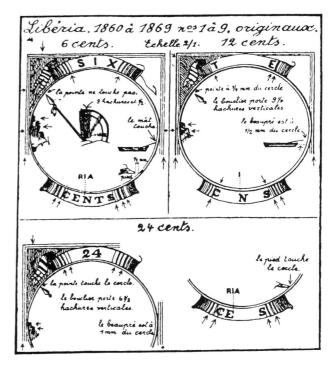

Liberia. 1860–69. Nos. 1–9, originals. 6-cent: The spear point is not touching. 9½ shade lines. The mast is touching. Foot. 12-cent: Spear point ¼ mm from the circle. The shield has 9¼ vertical shade lines. The bowsprit is ½ mm from the circle. Bottom: 24-cent: The spear point is touching the circle. The shield has 6½ vertical shade lines. The foot is touching the circle.

ship's prow, the waves cannot be distinguished easily from the land; clouds as in 6-cent.

Forgeries: very numerous; five sets of the three values and various singles; since it would take too long to give a detailed description of them, we prefer to emphasize the originals' characteristics. When one compares with the illustrations of the three values, the differences become quite evident. One also should pay attention to the following: 6-cent, thick outer frame; the distances from the spear, the left foot, and the bowsprit mast to the circle are not consonant with what one finds in the originals; five, six, or seven vertical shade lines in the shield; outer frame is $1^1/_2$–$^3/_4$ mm away from the shield; the circle does not touch the inner right circle; 12-cent, thin outer frame; no shading lines are touching the inscription lettering; shapeless feet; the spear is touching the circle; six, seven, or eight vertical lines in the shield; inscriptions are placed too high in their tablets; shield curves are noncongruent; 24-cent, the left foot does not touch the circle; outer frame line fragments in the corners; five or nine vertical lines on the shield; very thick outer frame.

We want to point out also that the three values of the two early sets (with or without clouds above the ship, perforated or imperforate, with or without supplementary frame) have oblique rectilinear lines on the corners; the second "I" of LIBERIA is above the middle of the "N" of CENTS; these sets frequently are canceled with a round postmark: MONROVIA and LIBERIA.

The *Geneva set,* executed in imperforate blocks and perf $12^1/_2$, has a corner burelage resembling that of the 24-cent stamp (see illustration) for the three values from 1860 to 1867, all of which immediately focuses attention on the 12-cent. In the 6-cent, the mast is $^3/_4$ mm from the circle and in the 24-cent, the foot is the same distance from the circle, and the second "I" of LIBERIA, if extended, would touch the left side of the "N" as in the 6-cent.

Forged cancellation: one circle (23 mm), with date, MONROVIA 7 JAN 64 LIBERIA; it was applied on forgeries and originals.

Probably as a result of his customers' demands, Fournier made more deceptive copies of the three values, with or without the 1 mm outer frame. This *second Geneva set* is identified by the following characteristics: 6-cent, $23^1/_5$ x about $27^1/_2$ mm in the bureled corners, diagonal cross-hatching forms quite visible, rather large lozenges, especially in the upper corners; the spear's point and the foot are touching the circle; 12-cent, $22^1/_4$–$^2/_5$ by about 27 mm; this time the corner burelage is correct and the overall appearance of the stamp is very deceptive; the top of the tablet does not encroach upon the inner frame; the shield has only $6^1/_2$ or $7^1/_2$ vertical shade lines; the outer right frame is broken at the bottom, about 4 mm from the corner; the outer left frame always is executed unsuccessfully or is broken on the left of the rock; 24-cent, $22^3/_4$ x $27^1/_2$ mm; same lozenges in the corner burelage as in the 6-cent; on the left of "24," one finds 1, 1; 2, 2; and 3 shade lines (instead of 1, 1; 2; 3; 2; see illustration). Same forged cancellation as in the preceding set.

1880. Same type. Perf $10^1/_2$. Nos. 10 to 14.
Originals: lithographed on ordinary paper; the 6-, 12-, and 24-cent, same type as those of the preceding issues.

Geneva forgeries: 1-cent, milky blue; corner burelage as in the first forged set described previously; the spear is touching, the foot is not touching, the circle; 2-cent, dull carmine; corner burelage as in the second forged set; the spear and the foot are touching the circle. The other three values also were counterfeited imperforate or perforated; the 6-cent, as in the first set, and the 12- and 24-cent, as in the second forged set. Arbitrary shades.

1902. ORDINARY overprints. Nos. 54 to 72.

1916. Various overprints. Nos. 116 to 139.

1918. Red Cross. Nos. 153 to 165 and official stamps. Regular or inverted *forged overprints* (a few other varieties also) on most values. Comparison is indispensable.

Libya

Forged overprints on first-issue stamps (Nos. 1–13), mainly canceled stamps (the cancellation millesime often antedates 1912); on No. 19; on canceled postage due stamps, Nos. 8–10 (values in lira), and on parcel post stamps. Comparison is necessary. The forged Geneva overprints on values of lira of the first issue and on postage due stamps evidently are too thick. The Red Cross overprint of the 15-cent + 5-cent was reprinted and requires comparison.

Liechtenstein

Beginning with the second issue, these very uninteresting stamps have been available in great quantities.

Forgeries: the first three issues (1912–18) were counterfeited imperforate or with noncongruent perforations. Compare the center hatching and the format.

Forged overprints are known of the 1920 set, which can be identified by comparison.

Lithuania

This country's stamps are hardly more interesting than the preceding one's. The same is true for Central Lithuania, whose nonoverprinted stamps of 1920 would have difficulty in competing with bottle labels.

Lourenco Marques

1895. Overprinted Mozambique stamps. Nos. 14 to 30. *Forged overprints:* S. ANTONIO, etc., especially in Geneva; comparison is useful, but template use is sufficient.

1898. 50-REIS overprint. No. 31. *Forged overprint:* make comparison.

1902. Overprints of new values. Nos. 52 to 64. *Forged overprints:* comparison is necessary.

Luxembourg

This is an extremely interesting country in which to specialize.

I. Imperforate Stamps

1852 (September 10). Watermark "W." Nos. 1 and 2. Recess engraving. Yellowish gum.

The sharpness of the engraving can be observed especially in the 10-centime stamp.

The deep black first printing, called "velvet black," is of superb quality. The color relief gives the stamps a special look. The subsequent printings (1853, 1854, 1855) also are black, but only the first two can be considered fine impressions (1853–54, greenish black, deep black). The first printing is recognized by the uniformly quite visible letter contours (use a magnifying glass), and by ornament and head details, all of which are very well executed.

The last printing in black (1855?) is not so good. Although the thinnest lines are always visible, they are now less clear-cut.

One can say that all the printings in black display stippling at the point of the neck.

Next, we come to a succession of printings in gray (end of 1855 to September 1858) with secondary varieties in gray-black, black-gray, and dark gray. From the very beginning of the printings in gray, the thinnest lines are blurred and fade out. No more than a few vestiges of neck-point stippling can be found, and the contour of the first "S" of POSTES is now hardly visible. Later, these defects spread to all stamp details, notably to the contours of letters "O S T" and to the

shade lines between these letters. At this stage of plate wear, the neck-point shading has disappeared.

Again, it can be pointed out that in the fine and good impressions the two curvilinear shade lines appear continuously, without any interruption, under the neck. (See below a few distinctive features of the No. 1 and 2 originals.)

Printing figures: 10-centime: 2,122,200 (eleven printings). 1-silbergroschen: 716,800 (nine printings).

Paper: usually thick, or very thick, in the first printing, and medium and thin, slightly transparent, in the last printings. However, the 10-centime gray-black is found on very thick paper (125 microns).

Shades: 10-centime. (See above, "recess engraving.")

1-silbergroschen, first printing (1852), brownish red; fine impression. Nostril curve and the seven shading dots forming a circle arc on the right of the curve are quite visible. Second printing (1853), vermilion. Third, fourth, and fifth printings (1854–55), red-brown. The nostril and the seven dots are blurred or are incomplete. Sixth printing (1856?) dull pale rose (flesh color). Finally, the last three (?) printings (1857–58) are basically carmine, ranging from pale carmine-tinted rose to dark carmine. In these last printings, the wear is much less visible than in the 10-centime stamps of the same period, appearing only in the shadow stippling, especially on the temple and nape of the neck.

There are numerous secondary shades, which enable one to build some extremely pretty color arrangements. Some of the secondary shades are very rare, for example, the cherry red shade, which is rather like the similar shade of the 1-franc stamp of France (1849).

The gum is responsible for the paper's yellowish tint.

Watermark: double-stroke letter "W." Regular watermark, with double stroke on the left, looking at the back of the stamp. Reversed, single stroke on the left: rare; inverted (head down), only on the 10-centime: very rare.

Varieties: the 10-centime is found with a horizontal line 2 mm long, which begins above the left zero and ends above the "P." (Plate defect or reentry?)

Essays: 10-centime black on yellowish card paper, blue-tinted black on white. To these must be added a greenish black on horizontally laid paper, without watermark, a canceled copy of which has been found. However, this stamp may come from a sheet of printer's waste accidentally slipped in among the sheets intended for control inspection. 1-silbergroschen black on yellowish card paper.

Cancellations: 1. Dumb: Type A (1852) in black: common. Green: 2U. This type is also found on the 10-centime in blue and red: 3U. Type B (Remich): 2U. Type C (Ettelbruck): 3U. Type F (Frisange), 10-centime: 4U. Type D (1853): common with nine bars.

Less common with seven (Kap) and six (Mersch, Type E). Type G. Various styles: common (Vianden, ten bars). Blue bars: 4U. Type J. 10-centime: 4U. Type I. Postmarks "PP" and "PD," applied to stamps, were done in error.

2. Cancellations with date: Type H (end of 1854), then a smaller style in 1860. On 10-centime: 2U. On 1-silbergroschen: 25U. Red or blue: very rare.

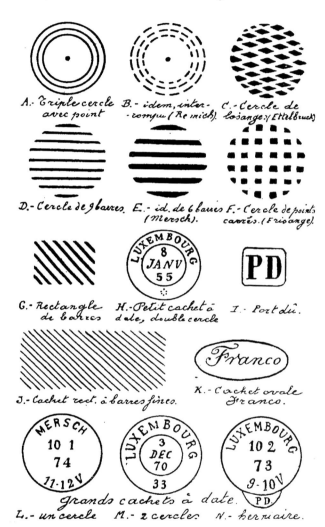

Luxembourg cancellations: A. Triple circle with dot. B. With broken line (Remich). C. Circle of lozenges (Ettelbruck). D. Circle with nine bars. E. With six bars (Mersch). F. Circle of square dots (Frisange). G. Rectangle with oblique bars. H. Small double circle postmark with dots. I. Postage due. J. Rectangular postmark with fine, oblique bars. K. Oval "Franco" postmark. L. Single circle. M. Two circles. N. Hernial (with sack).

Pairs: 3U. Strips of three: 5U. Blocks of four: 12U.
Fakes: fraudulently canceled reprints.

Reprints: there is nothing official here. Fouré executed a printing of the original plates on unwatermarked paper, the 10-centime greenish black stamp.

Another printing (1906) was made in Stuttgart with a few original clichés on watermarked paper. Poor execution: misplaced, inverted watermarks; white gum instead of yellowish; etc.

Examine the background cross-ruling through a magnifying glass. Half of the squares are ink-clogged, whereas in the original the cross-ruling is everywhere quite visible. The outer frame has smudges on it. Vertical lines appear in the side margins. The 1-silbergroschen is always of a very slightly brownish dull pale red shade. The two stamp values are studded with small dots of color.

Forgeries: the two values were created by F. of Geneva. Lithographed without watermark, bad impression on yellowish paper. See the illustration for design defects.

The 10-centime is black; the 1-silbergroschen is pale vermilion-tinted red. Both were made from a 10-centime gray-black, which is verified by the interruption of the curved lines under the neck, which are uninterrupted in the No. 2 original, and by the crude lettering of UN SILBERGROS.

In the two values, one finds three inexpertly executed lines in the upper left corner instead of the four quite visible vertical shading lines in the originals. In addition, two early forgeries are known to be so poorly executed that a beginner could not possibly be fooled by them.

Forged cancellations: on these forgeries, Lubeck bars! and Spanish oval grill!!

There are a great many forged cancellations on the so-called "reprints."

1859–64. Coat of arms. Frankfurt printing press. Nos. 3 to 11. *Paper:* white, no watermark. Typographed.

Select: the stamps have very narrow gutters, 1–1½ mm. They may be considered "select" when their four margins are ½ mm wide.

Shades: No. 3 (1863) is bistre. When placed next to No. 16 red-brown and No. 12, it seems to be a yellow-brown. No. 4 (1860) is black, but its shade is always lighter than No. 40. No. 5 is light yellow (canary) (1860) and yellow-ochre (1864): 2U. (No. 14 is of a more vivid yellow shade which seems off-orange next to the 4-centime of 1860.) No. 6 (1859), blue, pale blue, dark blue (1861): 50U. No. 7 (1859), more or less carmine-tinted rose. No. 8 (1859), maroon. No. 9 (1859), purplish red, less bright than No. 21. No. 10

(1859), green. No. 11 (1859), dull pale orange, orange-red, vermilion-tinted orange-red (No. 23) is vermilion-tinted red. No. 25, dull orange, more or less pale with fuzzy impression.

Varieties: 30-centime, double print: very rare. 12½-centime with letters "NTIM" broken at bottom (seven scallops), the word CENTIMES being printed CENIIMES or CEMITES: 2U. In the 10-centime, the value inscription always has CENIIMES. 37½-centime, with CENTINES, plate flaw: 2.50U. The 12½-centime is also found with CENIIMES: printing flaw. Also, the "C" is incomplete. The values printed on both sides are printer's waste. 1-CENTIME, final letter too high, plate flaw: rare. It is also rare in the following issues.

Cancellations: Type H, common on all values. Types A, D, and G, less common: 25U to 2U. Type K: 2U. All others: rare.

Pairs: 3U. Nos. 9, 10, and 11: 4U. Strips of three: 5U. Blocks: rare.

Fakes: there hardly exists any issue that has been more faked than this one, by removing the rouletting or the perforation of the following issues and by bleaching of the color rouletting. With a little close attention, all the undesirables can be tracked down, however. Prior consideration should be given to the following matters:

1. Shade (see above, "Shades," and compare).

2. Cancellation. From 1859 to 1864, the stamp is not faked when the cancellation bears one of those year dates…and when it is original! Forged cancellations are found on mint stamps with trimmed perforation from the following issues. It obviously is possible to find Nos. 3–11 with 1865 cancellations, etc. But they must attract your attention.

3. The paper is medium thick (65–70 microns), relatively tough, and nontransparent. The colored line-rouletted stamp paper is less tough, a little less thick (60 microns, with exceptions, however), and, in general, slightly transparent compared to the imperforates.

4. Impression. Very good on the imperforate stamps. The background cross-ruling and all the shield details are clear-cut and quite visible. All the lion hatching can be seen well. This may serve as a means for differentiating the issues, particularly the 12½- and 40-centime stamps. From a distance, as in the color line-rouletted stamps, the outer frame dashes do not seem to form a continuous line.

In the common values, one should consider the shading under the inscription tablets and under the center background. In the imperforates, the shading is very fine. In the following issues, it is less fine. Finally, in the end, it seems to merge into a thick, continuous line in the so-called "first-class" Haarlem impression! This is especially visible in the 2-centime black, less

visible in the 1- and 4-centime yellow and green because of the color used. (See illustration.)

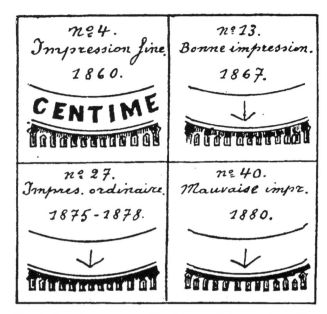

No. 4, fine impression. No. 13, good impression. No. 27, ordinary impression. No. 40, bad impression.

Essays: 10-centime lilac on white paper with watermark, and 10-centime lilac on yellowish paper without watermark. Imperforate.

Reprints: none.

Early forgeries: two well-executed sets, the better ones, photolithographed (see illustration). The paper is too thin, which is why these counterfeits are often found stuck on pieces of old writing paper. There is a rectilinear framework around the stamp proper, about ¾ mm away from it. In the least acceptable set, the word LUXEMBOURG is placed too high in the tablet. The letters "X E M," "U X E," "M B" (bottom right), and "U R" along the top are too large. The line at the opening of the "G" (bottom right) curves down to the right. In both sets, the word CENTIMES is normal. This immediately identifies the 10-centime stamp. Early cancellations include forged quadruple circle, "PD" unframed, bars, and various postmarks.

Modern forgeries (Geneva, F.): this photolithographed set is much more successful in design than the previous ones. The slightly transparent paper is often too thin, and the shades are arbitrary. See the illustration for the distinctive characteristics. See also the sketch of the oval lines surrounding the word "G.D." DE LUXEMBOURG. It is not congruent in the Geneva forgeries; the cross on the crown is unconvincing: it looks like a young girl *(vierge)*…or a chess pawn. The lion does not have all the visible vertical shading lines of the original, and his rear left leg is deformed.

Forged cancellations on Geneva forgeries: 1. Triple circle postmark with "L" in black or blue. (See Lubeck!)

2. Type D of eight or nine bars, medium thickness, between Types D and E, in black or blue.

3. Type A with a center dot that is too large.

4. Thimble cancellation with date, double circle (20½ mm), black or blue. LUXEMBOURG 10 DEC 62 (the year-date numbers, which are too large, are touching the inner circle), LUXEMBOURG 7 DECEMBRE 63; REMICH 8 MAI 61; WILTZ 8 MAI 61. Interchangeable dates.

See the other forged postmarks in the following issues.

These postmarks and other forged cancellations are found on Nos. 3 and 4 originals.

Note: It is a good idea to check the issue dates of these and the following issues.

1852 Originals. Geneva forgeries. Figures at right. Middle: 1859–64 Originals. Early forgeries. Letters separated; letters U, X, E attached. Bottom: 1859–64 Originals. Geneva forgeries. Upper left corner; upper ornaments.

II. Line Rouletted Stamps

1865–74. White line rouletted stamps. Nos. 12 to 15. *Shades:* 1-centime (1865) red-brown, a shade that is not very different from that of No. 16. 2-centime (1867) black. 4-centime orange-yellow, brighter than No. 5, and lemon yellow (1867). 4-centime dark green and slightly yellowish green (1871).

Varieties: 1-centime, imperforate (identical shade). Buy in pairs only: rare. 2-centime double print: 4M, 4U.

Cancellations: Types H, L, and M are common. Type H in blue: 50U. Type N is in demand. All other cancellations are rare.

Pairs: strips and blocks are rare because of the fragility of the rouletting.

Fakes: the perforation of No. 28 was trimmed and replaced by a formless kind of line rouletting to create a dark green No. 15 stamp. In this, the design is crude: shading at the bottom of the inscription tablets, and the left line of the ornaments on the left, often are ink-clogged.

Forgeries: the 1- to 4-centime stamps, yellow or green, were well counterfeited in Geneva, but the margins of the 2- and 4-centime, which are always narrow in the white line rouletted stamps, are about 1½ mm wide on all four sides! As for the distinguishing marks, see the illustration of the same values in the preceding issue.

Forged Geneva cancellations: same postmarks as the preceding ones, with changed date and millesime: LUXEMBOURG 6 DEC 66, 8 DEC 72, 6 DEC. Also, ECHTERNACH 12 AVRIL 66. Since the figures are interchangeable, other dates may be found.

1864–74. Colored line rouletted stamps. Nos. 16 to 24. The margins of the color line rouletted stamps are ½–1 mm wide. To merit "select" classification, the rouletting must be entirely visible.

Shades: first printing (1867) orange-brown. Second printing (1868) pale red (rare, worth about double the orange-brown). Third printing (1869) orange-yellow. Next printings, red-brown (1871), dark to pale shades.

10-centime. Numerous printings, three principal shades: mauve (1865) (pale and dull reddish lilac): 2U. Red lilac (1868). Slate (blue lilac) (1871); dark slate: 2U.

12½-centime. Bright carmine (1873): 2U. Carmine-tinted rose (1865); pale carmine-rose (1868): 50U.

20-centime. brown (1869). Light yellow-brown (1867). Gray-brown (1872).

25-centime. Bright dark ultramarine (1865). Pale ultramarine (1866). Dull blue (1872).

30-centime. Bright lilac red (1864).

37½-centime. Bistre (1866) and dark bistre (1871). Total number of copies of this stamp printed: 24,100.

40-centime. Vermilion-tinted red, No. 23 (1866). Dull orange-red, No. 25 (1874). Very pale dull orange-red (flesh color), No. 25 (1874).

37½-centime. Overprinted UN FRANC. Printing: 75,800 (1873).

Varieties: defective impressions due to ink clogging. These are interesting when the shade is changed: 20-centime grayish dark brown; 10-centime dark mauve; 40-centime, No. 23, bright vermilion red. Value: 2–3U.

Note: The No. 25 impression is always mediocre, with its blurred cross-ruling. There are copies with horizontal lines in the upper and lower margins, between the vignette and the rouletting: 50U.

The overprint of No. 24 is frequently out of place. The final dot is round or square.

The 37½-centime exists with a plate flaw, CENTINES: very rare.

The 10-centime still has the original flaw, CENIIMES. The 12½-centime is rare with this flaw.

Cancellations: with black date, Types H, L, M: common. Type N: in demand. With blue date: less common: REMICH, GREVENMACHER, HOSINGEN, MAMER, KAP, ECHTERNACH, etc. The early postmarks are all rare, for example, Types G, I, K are worth 3U on common stamps, and 2U on rare ones; 50U on No. 22.

Pairs: 3U. Nos. 20a, 21–25: 4U. Blocks of four: rare. Nos. 16–19: 16U. On cover: 2U.

Reprints: none.

Forgeries: the whole set was counterfeited in Geneva with clichés used for the 1859–65 set. See preceding illustration. There is also a forgery of the 37½-centime bistre, whose "X" and "E" letters are a little further apart at bottom than in the originals, their serifs being too short. The small burelage lozenge under the "I" of CENTIMES does not touch the inscription bandeau. This forgery was fraudulently overprinted UN FRANC, no dot after FRANC.

Forged Geneva cancellations: the reader is referred to the ones already mentioned. In addition, there is a circular cancellation, Type I: LUXEMBOURG 8/11 77 7-8 N, and LUXEMBOURG 16/12 76 5-6 N.

Fakes: the rouletting of Nos. 18, 21, 23, and even 25, was trimmed or bleached to create imperforate stamps. Also, the overprint of No. 24 was quite obviously cleaned to make a virgin No. 22. Compare shades and impression.

III. Perforated Stamps

1874–79. Local printing press. Perf 13. Nos. 26 to 39. *Select:* perfectly centered stamps: rare. They are worth fifty percent more than the prices quoted in the catalogues.

Shades: 1-centime (1878) brown, dark brown, dark brown greasy impression: 3U. 2-centime gray-black

(1875), black (1878); 4-centime blue-green, imperforate (1874, Yvert No. 36b); same shade perforated (1875); dark green (1876): 50U. 5-centime lemon, imperforate (1876, No. 37), lemon, perforated (1876), bright yellow (1877–78), ochre (1878): 4M, 4U. 10-centime gray, imperforate (1875, No. 38); gray, perforated (1875–76); blue-gray and slate-tinted dark blue-gray (No. 30a): 2M, 5U (1876); rose-tinted pale gray (1878): 2M, 3U. 12½-centime pale lilac rose (1877), reddish lilac rose (1876), bright carmine-tinted rose and light carmine-tinted rose (1879); 25-centime dark blue (1877), Prussian blue: 2M, 2U (1879). 30-centime dull purplish red (1878); 40-centime orange-ochre (1879); 37½-centime bistre, imperforate (1879), unissued (No. 39), bistre, perforated (1879), unissued (No. 34). Overprinted UN FRANC, bistre (end of 1879). This overprinted stamp is always well centered with FRANC as well as with PRANC.

Varieties: thin paper, thick paper, especially the 5-centime stamp. Defective impression, especially the 10-centime (No. 31a) with white spots in the cross-ruling, shapeless lion, etc. Error UN PRANC on 37½-centime: extremely rare, twice per sheet at the beginning of the printing. 25-centime blue, perf 11½ on top: very rare. The 4-centime imperforate exists with a dividing frame line between the stamps. This stamp is found printed on both sides, as is the 12½-centime perforated.

Pairs: 3U. Used blocks: rare.

Cancellations: Type L (single circle): common. Types H and M, less common. Blue cancellations: 50U. A rectangular LUXEMBOURG postmark is not very common. All others: rare.

Essays: 1873: 10-centime black, occasionally imperforate. 1874: 4-centime black, light or dark green on card or thick paper. 1875: 2-centime black, perforated at times; 4-centime black; 10-centime lilac-violet or deep lilac on white paper, medium or thick, on buff or yellowish paper. No reprints.

Fakes: imperforate Nos. 36b, 37–39 from this issue are sometimes perforated, or, from the following issue, the 5- and 10-centime stamps. Shade comparison for the 5- and 10-centime of 1880 and the absence of margins in the locally printed fakes are adequate criteria for identification. Check also for possible forgeries. Overprint UN FRANC was scratched out on No. 36 to make a No. 34, or the "F" is scratched out to make a rare error, UN *P*RANC. Finally, a forged overprint was applied on an unissued No. 34 original, then a forged cancellation was added to conceal the faking.

Geneva forgeries (F.): the whole set, perf 13½, same identification marks as in the forgeries of the preceding sets. The 37½-centime bistre, also with a forged overprint ("N" separated from "F" by 2⅙ mm instead of 2¼ mm). The shades are not always well executed, but the 1-, 2-, 25-, and 37½-centime stamps are very deceptively counterfeited.

Forged Geneva cancellations: Type H: HOSINGER 21 JUIN 75. Type L (single circle): LUXEMBOURG 30/1 82 7-8 N; DIEKIRCH 25/2 82; DIEKIRCH 7/9 76; LUXEMBOURG 2/6 80 2-3 S; GREVENMACHER 25/8 80 4-5 S; ECHTERNACH 2/6 80 7 (!!)-3 S; WILTZ 3/6 83 2-3 S (the "S" is really an inverted "2"). All in black.

1880–81. Haarlem printing press. Nos. 39a to 46. These stamps are identified by the greater care taken in printing and by their wider margins, 1 mm and more, especially at top and bottom, sometimes less on the sides.

Shades: not very distinctive.

Perforations: 13½, all values, except the 30-centime: common. 12½ x 12, all values, except 5-centime: common. 12½-centime: 2M, 2U. The left stamp of each row of the sheet that is perf 12½ x 12 is perf 11½ x 12: 2M, 2U. 12½ x 12½, all values, except 1- and 2-centime: 50M, 2U.

Cancellations: as previously. There also are large format postmarks with date, Type M, 28 mm in diameter.

Varieties: the 10-centime stamps will have CENIIMES as previously. There are printing or plate flaws. For example, 12½-centime, no dot over the "i," "t" not crossed; 30-centime, "C" and "S" letters broken, etc.

Reprints: none.

Forgeries: the whole set (Geneva, F.), perf 13¼. See preceding issue and illustration.

Forged Geneva cancellations: see preceding issue.

1882. Allegorical group. Nos. 47 to 58. *Perforations:* as in the preceding issue. Typographed. But the 12½ x 12½ stamps are found with common or pin perforations.

Same remark with respect to the first stamp on the left of the rows perf 12½ x 12: 2M, 2U.

Some uncommon perforations: 1-, 2-, and 10-centime, perf 13½. All stamps perf 11½ x 12: 2M, 2U.

Shades: various.

Reprints: none.

Forgery of the 5-franc: yellowish or fleecy white paper, possible shades. Geneva forgery, perf 12½ or 14; the other forgery, 12½ x 12¾. These counterfeits look extremely deceptive, but comparative study using a magnifying glass will very quickly strip the grackle of his borrowed feathers! (See illustration.)

Forged cancellations: beginning with this issue, we find, especially on official stamps that have been fraudulently overprinted, circular dated cancellations,

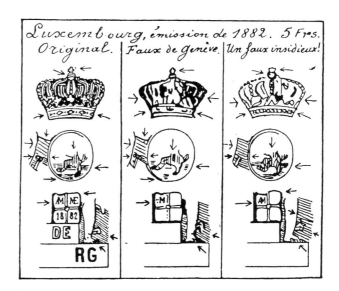

Luxembourg issue of 1882. 5-franc. Original. Geneva forgery. A deceptive forgery.

Type L: LUXEMBOURG, ECHTERNACH, RUMELANGE, ETTELBRUCK MERSCH, etc., and double circle: LUXEMBOURG-VILLE, RODANGE, and D'ESCH SUR ALZETTE. Date, year, and time indication, all are interchangeable. Grayish ink.

1891–92. Prince Adolph portrait. Nos. 59 to 68. Engraved. Perf 11, 11½, 12½, and 11½ x 11. No. 61a (color error) must be perf 11½ x 11½.

Fakes: chemical faking of the color error. Make comparison; the shade is never that of the original.

Forgeries: 2½-franc purplish black. Lithographed, perf 12 x 11. Comparison with an original would be sufficient.

Subsequent issues. Complete sets of these can easily be obtained.

1895. Thin or medium paper.

1921. The 10-franc green should be catalogued among color errors.

Forged 10-franc green (Paris, C.): the total height of the original, including the dividing frame lines, is 24 mm; width 37½–⅗ mm. Very fine impression, including the corner burelage. The "0" of figure "10," seen from a distance, seems broken on top and bottom. The house windows are drawn with two lines.

The forgeries have none of this finesse and the dimensions are not congruent with the original. They have not yet appeared on the market, but future penetration is possible, like the appearance of the Bordeaux forgeries (France, 1870), in spite of the arrest of counterfeiter P. and the seizure of his equipment and working stock.

IV. Official Stamps

1875–81. Rouletted official overprints. Nos. 1 to 9. (1) In normal overprints, the tops of the letters are turned toward the upper left corner, in all values; (2) irregular overprints, tops of letters turned toward upper right corner, No. 9: 3M, 3U. (3) Normal inverted overprints, top turned toward the inner right corner, 1-centime red-brown and orange: 50M, 50U. 2-, 12½-, and 20-centime, 25-centime dull blue, 30-, 40-centime (No. 25), and 1-franc on 37½-centime. (4) Irregular inverted overprint, top turned toward the inner left corner, 2-centime black: 3M, 3U. The different angles of the overprint are a job for the specialist. Double and triple overprints are printer's waste.

Forged overprints exist of all values. It would be useless to study all the known forged overprints in detail, for in addition to the crude creations which are usually spotted immediately by the connoisseur, there are very successful ones. It is best to measure and compare with a common original stamp. Moreover, it is useless to collect Luxembourg official stamps unless serious specialization is envisaged. Otherwise, one would risk making costly mistakes today and especially tomorrow, since the art of forging overprints has been making real progress.

Two rather well-counterfeited sets are known: Nürnberg, lettering noncongruent, and Geneva, letter "L" broken ¼ mm near the final up stroke of that letter. Upright or inverted forged overprints were applied on originals, and the Geneva forgery is found applied on forgeries with all the other previously described forged cancellations.

Official rouletted overprints on 1874 stamps (local printing press). Nos. 10–17. (1) Regular overprint: all 1874 values, except Nos. 33–35. Nos. 33 and 35 may have been overprinted as essays. 5-centime yellow and ochre: 2M, 2U. 10-centime gray and pale rose-tinted gray: 2M, 2U. 12½-centime, both shades. (2) Regularly inverted overprint: same values, except the 5-centime. 10-centime gray and pale rose-tinted gray: 2M, 2U. 12½-centime, both shades.

Varieties: same remark as above regarding double and triple overprints; likewise, incomplete overprints.

Forged overprints: numerous. Some are found even on values in the Haarlem impression, except the 25-centime. Make comparison and verify perf 13.

Same, on 25-centime (Haarlem printing press, 1880). No. 18. 25-centime blue, perf 13½, 12½ x 12, 11½ x 12.

1878–80. OFFICIAL overprint in narrow capitals. Nos. 19 to 30. 1. On color rouletted stamps. Regular overprint: 1-, 20- (gray-brown), 30-, 40-centime (No. 25), and 1-franc on 37½ centime. Inverted overprint: same.

2. On stamps of 1874 (local printing press, perf 13). Regular overprint: 1-, 2-, and 4-centime blue-green and green; 5- and 10-centime gray and rose-tinted gray; 12½- and 25-centime. Overprint inverted: same values, except 5-centime and 10-centime gray (rose-tinted gray only).

Forged overprints: what we have said concerning the first overprint is appropriate for all the rest: it is always measurement, comparison of ink, perforation, shades, sometimes also of the transparency of the original overprints, and the presence or absence of indention which enables one to arrive at a good judgment in this complicated business.

1881–82. "S.P." [Specimen] overprint (lightface, lowercase type). Nos. 31 to 43. 1. On 40-centime, No. 23. Upright and inverted overprint.

2. On stamps of 1874 (local printing press, perf 13). 1-, 4-, 5-centime, and 1-franc on 37½-centime.

3. On stamps of 1880 (Haarlem). 1-, 2-, 5-centime, 10-, 12½-, 20-, 25-, and 30-centime. The 5-centime also has an inverted overprint like the 10–30-centime stamps.

Forged overprints are numerous. Make comparison, as above.

1882. "S.P." [Specimen] overprint (boldface type). Nos. 44 to 66. 1. On 40-centime, No. 25.

2. On 2-, 4-, 5-, 12½-centime, and 1-franc on 37½-centime of the local issue, perf 13; the last one with inverted overprint also.

3. On Haarlem issue: 1-, 2-, 5-, 10-, 12½-, 20-, and 30-centime.

4. On allegorical group, all values.

Regarding the fourth, "allegorical group," category, same comment as above in connection with inverted or double overprints, etc. There are plate defects — dots are missing, etc. Some overprints have a larger "S" (Nos. 54 to 60). There is one instance of this per sheet: 4M, 4U, depending on which printing it is. Overprint values are more or less bright.

5. On 5-franc, allegorical group, slanted boldface overprint: No. 66.

Forged overprints are numerous. Make comparison. A boldface forged overprint is also found on the 5-franc. Geneva forgery.

1892–95. 1891 and 1892 issues. "S.P." [Specimen] overprint (tall letters). Nos. 67 to 81. All values. Numerous forged overprints.

Subsequent issues. These can be obtained in sets. Almost all overprints and perforations have been counterfeited.

Macao

1876–85. Crown type. Nos. 1 to 9 and 16 to 21.
Geneva forgeries: the whole set. See the distinctive characteristics of the originals and of these forgeries in the illustration for Portuguese Colonies. One also should notice that in the counterfeits the inner corner ornamentation, top right, is touching the upper tablet line under the "I" of CORREIO and under the corner's ornamental square.

Forged cancellations: double circle (26½ mm), with inner rectangle, with date, CORREIO 13 NOV. 84 BOLAMA.

Reprints, 1885: the whole set; glossy, chalky, pure white paper (originals: yellowish or grayish paper); no gum. 1906: reprints for the King of Spain, with gum, perf 13½, and very rare.

1884–85 and 1887. Overprinted stamps. Nos. 10, 11 to 15, 22 to 28. *Forged overprints:* comparison is necessary. First, make sure the Macao stamps are not forged themselves (see previous issue), for the stamps of the set counterfeited in Geneva received forged overprints (the whole set), along with the following forged cancellation: double circle (26½ mm) with inner rectangle, with date, CORREIO 10 JAN 87 MACAU in blue and black.

Madagascar

1889–91. Overprinted stamps. Nos. 1 to 7.
Originals: overprinted by handstamp.

Forged overprints are very numerous; comparison is indispensable. Check first whether the stamps themselves are forgeries of the 1881 issue (see French Colonies). Overprint "05" of No. 4 and overprint "5" of Nos. 6 and 7 were counterfeited in Geneva and applied on forgeries and originals, along with the forged cancellation: double circle (23 mm), with date, TAMATAVE 25 JANV 91 MADAGASCAR, which also was used to cancel forgeries of the following issue.

1891. Large format. Nos. 8 to 13. *Originals:* typographed on tinted paper. The 1- and 5-franc stamps have an original background impression in the paper shade. All values were executed with the same typographical composition. The accompanying illustration shows the composition's principal defects, some of which are visible only in the last values printed and even only in the 5-franc stamps. This may be attributed to figure alteration after the printing of each value and to general printing press operations. In the 5-franc value, the value inscription was executed by triple application of a handstamp.

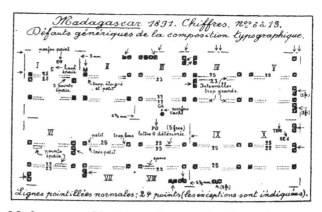

Madagascar. 1891. Value figures. Nos. 8–13. Typical defects of the typographical composition. Normal dotted lines: 24 dots (exceptions are indicated).

The illustration gives information on the arrangements of the dotted lines with respect to the circles' ornamental frames and on the number of dots in each type, on lettering defects, and on the breaks in the dividing frame lines, it being understood that in the heavily inked impressions small breaks sometimes are diminished or eliminated. The dimensions (ornamental circle lines included) average 22–22¼ x 28¾ mm, with some variation in each type due to typographical composition. No *reprints.*

Forgeries: first set, 22½ mm wide, but 1- and 5-franc, 22⅓ mm; 29 mm high, except the 5-centime, which is only 28¾ mm. All of them are lithographed, including the background of the 1- and 5-franc. The 5-, 10-centime, and 1-franc appear to be copied from Type VIII, if one relies upon the *arrangement* of the dotted lines, but these dots are, respectively, twenty-one, twenty-two (the third and twenty-first are split into two parts), twenty-three, and twenty-three dots, counting from the top; the 15- and 25-centime are copied from Type IV, judging by the dotted line spacing, despite the fact that the third line is further to the right with respect to the fourth; twenty-two or twenty-three, twenty, twenty-two and twenty-two dots; the 5-franc might correspond to Type X because of the arrangement of the third and fourth dotted lines; in the first line, twenty-two or twenty-three, but dots often are missing on the left; twenty-four, twenty-three, twenty-one. Naturally, no value shows lettering or frame defects; the dots are shaped inexpertly (dashes, small oblique lines, "double" dots, small dots); in the left frame the first circle encroaches upon those of the upper frame and the bottom one encroaches on those of the lower frame. Paper: 40–50 microns. Forged cancellations: TAMATAVE 15 OCT 91 MADAGASCAR; TAMATAVE 25 MARS 92 MADAGASCAR, double circle, outer diameter, 23 mm.

2. Second set (just as bad), also lithographed; lettering of POSTES is thicker than that of FRANÇAISE; twenty-two or twenty-three dots; twenty (last one on the right is faint); twenty or twenty-one; twenty-one or twenty-two; really, they can be counted only with great difficulty because, in general, they are lines rather than dots and two or three lines often are joined. No correspondence with any type; the two end circles of the upper frame evidently are lowered. Forged cancellation of TAMATAVE MARS 96, but also …91 — I have seen those two millesimes on two different postmarks applied on the same forgery!

3. 1-franc, photolithographed from Type IV with typographed background burelage. Figure "1" is 4 mm from the left frame (instead of being a little more); the third dotted line starts 2 mm from the frame, and the fourth, 1½ mm, instead of 1¾ mm, in the original of this type; these lines are just as near the right frame. Height: 29 mm; wove paper, 65 microns. 5-franc, clever, deceptive forgery of Type VIII; photolithographed with faintly printed background that seems to be lithographed; the original type's defects are present. Height: 29 mm; soft, slightly stippled paper, 65 microns; "5-FR" is handstamp printed; the loop of the "5" forms one 4½ mm circle instead of about 5 mm. 5-franc, with dotted lines that evidently are too thick; vertical diameter of the loop of the "5," about 4½ mm, the loop being quite thin near the vertical line of the figure; horizontal bar of "F" is scalloped instead of being straight.

1895. Overprinted stamps. Nos. 14 to 22.
Originals: typographed overprinting (indention) in vermilion. Make comparison. First, find out whether forgeries of the Peace and Commerce type (described under French Colonies) are involved.

1896. Ellipses as overprints. Nos. 23 to 27.
Originals: handstamp imprint; the handstamp used for the overprint of the 25-centime is wider than the stamp. Comparison is absolutely indispensable.

Forged overprints: numerous; there are very good ones with a forged cancellation in which the "T" of ET and the "P" of P^ES are close together, whereas the authentic cancellation has a space of 1½ mm between its top and bottom. Check also whether forgeries of the Peace and Commerce type are implicated. Comparison or, at the very least, template measurement is necessary. The ellipses were counterfeited in Geneva with the double circle (23 mm) forged cancellations: TAMATAVE 7 SEPT 96 MADAGASCAR.

1896–1906. Peace and Commerce type. Nos. 28 to 47.
Geneva forgeries: see description under French Colonies; same forged cancellation as on the preceding issue.

1902. Overprinted stamps. Nos. 48 to 60.
Various *forged overprints.* Comparison is necessary. First step: ascertain whether you are dealing with forgeries of the Peace and Commerce type (see Diego Suarez for [Madagascar] Nos. 59 and 60).

1904–6. Split and officially canceled. Nos. 78 to 93.
Originals: handstamped impression. Comparison is necessary.

1912. Stamps overprinted "05" and "10." Nos. 111 to 120.
Check the possibility of the involvement of forgeries of the Peace and Commerce type (see French Colonies), which were overprinted fraudulently.

Forged overprints on originals of the Peace and Commerce type (errors and figures spaced): comparison is necessary; forged overprints on Geneva forgeries.

1915. Red Cross. No. 121.
Originals: the overprint is carmine.

1921. Overprinted Zebu type. No. 124.
Forged overprint: comparison is indispensable; same: No. 126a, "25-C" on 35-centime.

Postage due stamps (1896). Nos. 1 to 7.
Typographed *original overprints* (indention). First, determine whether the stamps are forgeries (see postage due stamps, French Colonies). The overprint was counterfeited in Geneva and applied on forgeries and originals; the forged cancellation, described in the ellipses issue, likewise.

Majunga. *Forged overprints:* comparison is absolutely indispensable. Nos. 1–5 must have the "25 February" cancellation, according to de Vinck. The forged Geneva cancellation, which was applied at times also on postage stamps and postage due stamps of 1896: double circle (23 mm), MAJUNGA 28 DEC 96 MADAGASCAR.

Madeira

It may be said that, practically speaking, having been overprinted for Madeira, all stamps of Portugal received a great number of *forged overprints.*

Comparison is indispensable, particularly for the first three issues. The reader may find guidance in the following relevant details. There are three kinds of overprints: (1) about 15 mm wide by 3 mm high; (2) 14½ x 2¾ mm; (3) 14¼ x 2½ mm.

Originals: Type I overprints on the first two issues; on the 1871–79 issue, Types I, II, and III are found, depending on values and perforations (consult the specialty catalogue of Portugal); on the 1880 issue, Type III.

Reprints: 1885 and 1906 (very rare), always Type II. In the imperforate reprints (first issue), one finds the 5-reis black, 10-reis yellow, and the 25-reis rose, which subsequently was perforated for the second issue. The forged MADEIRA overprint was created in Geneva in two types: one in lightface type, 14¼ mm wide at the letter's base; the other in boldface, a rather deceptive one which, however, being 15 mm wide, exceeds somewhat the allowable measurement.

Malaya

Johore

1876–91. Overprinted stamp. Nos. 1 and 2. *Forged overprints:* comparison is necessary and specialization is useful if you want to get somewhere with these.

Malacca [see Yvert, Straits Settlements]

1867. Overprinted stamps. Nos. 1 to 9. The value of the 3/2-cent stamp is printed in letters [THREE-HALF-CENTS]; the crown is different from that of the other values. It is found in black with figure "2" on top (very rare).

Numerous *forged overprints;* comparison is indispensable.

1868–91. Queen's portrait. Nos. 10 to 21 or 31 to 43. *Originals:* watermarked "CC" or "CA" Crown, perf 14; typographed; the horizontal shading lines of the background are clear-cut and do not touch the portrait's frame; the ear details are quite visible through a magnifying glass; the line in front of the eye is concave.

Early counterfeits, inexpertly lithographed, notably those made in Geneva, with background shading touching the frame; formless perforation; no watermark; traces of dividing frame lines outside the margins.

Modern *engraved forgeries,* called *"sans oreilles"* [earless]; various perforations; 14 x 12½; 14 x 13; 11; forged embossed watermark. Very good general appearance, but these counterfeits are easy to spot because the ear, apparently visible at a distance, practically disappears in the 5-, 10-, and 30-cent stamps when it is observed through a magnifying glass, and it is executed inadequately in the other values; one also may notice that the line in front of the eye is vertical, not curved.

1879–82. Overprinted stamps. Nos. 22 to 30 (and)
1883–94. Overprinted stamps. Nos. 44 to 64. Numerous *forged overprints.* Comparison is indispensable. No. 29 has seven overprint varieties; No. 30 has twelve. Obviously, specialization would be useful.

Pahang

Very numerous *forged overprints,* several of which are executed rather well; comparison is indispensable and specializing is recommended because of the varieties of types. The Type II PAHANG overprint was counterfeited in Geneva.

Perak

There is an abundance of overprints in this country; some of them, especially that of 1878, No. 1, were counterfeited expertly. Comparison is indispensable, especially for the rare varieties; specializing is recommended. The less common values of the issue of 1895 had their fiscal obliteration cleaned off and replaced by a *forged cancellation,* or they were offered as mints.

Official stamps: the "P.G.S." overprint was counterfeited in Geneva...and elsewhere. Careful comparison is indispensable.

Selangor

1878–82–90. Nos. 1 to 6. *Forged overprints:* rather numerous, some of them deceptive; detailed comparison is indispensable and specializing would be quite useful. The overprint of Nos. 1 and 2 was counterfeited poorly in Geneva.

1895. Values in dollars. Nos. 21 to 25. *Forged cancellations* on stamps which had a cleaned fiscal obliteration.

Geneva forgery: $1 with right frame usually broken in several places and various small defects in the background design; easily detected by comparison.

1900–1901. ONE CENT overprints. No. 26. *Forged overprints:* I am familiar with only one forged overprint type — no dot after CENT. There may be others; comparison is useful.

Sungei Ujong

An abundance of overprints, most of which were well forged. Specializing is not only recommended, it is necessary. All overprint types can be found illustrated with measurements in the Calman catalogue (Volume 3, Straits Settlements; Sungei Ujong, pages 969–73). The overprint of No. 1 was counterfeited in Geneva.

Trengganu

1917. Red Cross. RED CSOSS error. *Forged overprints:* comparison is necessary.

Fakes produced by removing fiscal cancels on values in dollars, especially on the $25 to $100 stamps of 1921–26, and by replacing them with forged cancellations.

Maldive Islands

1906. Stamps overprinted MALDIVES. Nos. 1 to 6. *Forged overprints* on new or used originals of Ceylon. Comparison is necessary.

Malta

Cancellations: well-known postmarks are usually found on the first issues: Type "A 25" in a barred circle; capital "M" in a barred oval, and sometimes a thimble cancellation with date, MALTA A (20 mm), erroneously applied. Next, the dated postmarks: MALTA F, VICTORIA, VALETTI, etc., as well as the horizontally barred postmark with MALTA in the middle. Finally, later, there is the round Maltese cross postmark and the large double circle with date (30 mm).

1860–63. No watermark. Perf 14. No. 1. 1/2-penny, blue-tinted paper (1860), bistre-buff, No. 1a.

1/2-penny, white paper (1861 to the end of 1863), pale rose-tinted bistre: common; gray-bistre: 2M, 2U; rose-tinted bistre: 2M, 2U.

Forgeries: crude. Perforations don't match genuine. Comparison will be sufficient.

Fakes: the white paper of No. 1 was chemically doctored to make No. 1a. Make comparative examination of the paper on the stamp's back and examine edgewise.

1868–71. Watermark "C.C." (Crown colonies). Perf 12-1/2. No. 2. 1/2-penny orange-tinted bistre (1868). One finds pairs that are imperforate in the middle. These are very rare; yellow-bistre (1871).

Forgeries: crude. No watermark. See No. 1, above.

Fakes: No. 3 with doctored perforations to make a No. 2a.

1863–81. Watermark "C.C." Perf 14. No. 3. About ten printings of the 1/2-penny, 1863–81.

Common (No. 3, Yvert): yellow (1881); orange-tinted yellow (1879). Less common: orange-yellow (1864): 2M, 50U; then, bistre-yellow and bistre (1875–76): 2M, 2U. Rare: red-brown (No. 3b, Yvert) (1867): 4M, 3U; then, orange (1870); bistre-orange (1873), and buff-rose (1863), all of which have about the same value: 3M, 3U. The rarest one is the golden yellow, sometimes called "saffron yellow," whose aniline color frequently tinted the stamp's back (No. 3a, Yvert): 5M, 4U.

1/2-penny bistre-yellow, perf 14 x 12 1/2 is from 1878: 3M, 3U. Watch perforation faking: check the stamp's width.

1882. Watermark "C.A." (Crown agents). Perf 14. No. 4. 1/2-penny bistre-buff: common; red-orange: 5M, 5U.

1885. Various types. Watermark "C.A." Perf 14. Nos. 5 to 11. 2 1/2-pence blue: 2M, and ultramarine: common.

Imperf-between pairs of the 4-pence brown are very rare. The 5-shilling rose has watermark "C.C."

A few sheets of the 6-pence lilac of Great Britain (1865), without watermark (?), were used in Valetta. They may be classified in the Maltese collection like the other British stamps used in that colony.

One must remember also that SPECIMEN stamps are found in the first printing of each value, with some exceptions, thus providing a degree of certainty in a truly chronological classification.

Forgeries: there is a forgery of the 5-shilling, which is very poorly executed. Design comparison would be sufficient for identification. No watermark. Noncongruent perforations.

1899–1900. Watermark "C.A." Perf 14. Nos. 12 to 16. These stamps have no history.

1902. 2 1/2-pence, 1885, overprinted ONE PENNY. No. 17. The overprint is interesting only because of the error, ONE PENNY, once per sheet of sixty stamps. Printing: 12,000. In demand in pairs or blocks with normal overprint.

The overprint error appears in the three printings of this value. It is rarer, however, in the bright ultramarine printing with white gum.

Forged overprint: the original overprint is deep black. The forged overprint, at least the one that was counterfeited so abundantly, is gray-black and shows no evidence of "bite" from the type. (Sometimes the overprint is found applied over the cancellation.) These are the only indications of fraud, for the measurement of printing type impression is quite close to the genuine.

1921. The 10-shilling was faked by cleaning the revenue cancellation and adding a forged cancellation. The cleaning operation left visible traces.

1922. SELF GOVERNMENT. A few forged overprints on the 2-shilling and the 10-shilling, No. 16.

1925. Counterfeit POSTAGE overprints, especially on the 4-pence, 2-shilling, and the 2-shilling 6-pence. The measurements match the genuine. However, the copies that were printed with a handstamp can be identified by the very pronounced "bite" of the last letters of the overprint, whereas in the originals the indention is everywhere the same. The "G" is slightly different. Also, in blocks, all the overprints are quite symmetrical, which is not the case in the fraudulent overprints.

Postage Due Stamps

1925. Typographed. The whole set has been counterfeited singly and tête-bêche. Comparison and measuring will be adequate to identify the counterfeits. In the originals, there is a gap in the four corners. Medium paper. The dot after the value is irregular in form. In the forgeries, there is no gap in the corners; thick paper; very regular dot.

Mariana Islands

Spanish occupation. *Forged overprints:* comparison is useful; Philippine cancellations will reveal the overprint forgery; this test is all the more effective if the cancellations were applied after November 1899.

German occupation.

1899. Overprinted stamps. Nos. 1 to 6. *Forged overprints,* some of which are very deceptive, especially a hand-painted set in which the dot over the "i" is square instead of round. Comparison, and even occasional expertizing, is indispensable. Expertizing of the cancellation is also necessary for the overprints with a 56-degree inclination.

Forgeries: the whole set was counterfeited (48-degree overprint inclination) in Geneva (see Germany, issue of 1889) with forged cancellation: SAIPAN 18/11 99 MARIANEN (one circle, 26½ mm).

1900. Ship type. Nos. 7 to 19. Numerous *forged cancellations.* Expertizing is necessary.

Geneva forgeries: values in pfennig; see German Colonies.

Marienwerder

This is another mine of forged overprints, made worse by the fact that clandestine counterfeits were made with the original equipment. Evidently identification of these counterfeits is possible, but only by experienced specialists. The average collector should avoid them. Sets of forged overprints from various sources exist. The color overprints are essays.

Marshall Islands

1897. MARSCHALL-INSELN overprint. Nos 1 to 6. Wide variation in prices according to whether the stamps are canceled with the first postmark, MARSCHALL (with "C") INSELN (very rare) or with the second MARSHALL (without "C"). As for the mints, the Bern post office set (difference in pressure applied in impression) is most in demand.

Forged cancellations of the first type and of the second (especially on the 25- and 50-pfennig stamps).

Geneva forgeries: completely manufactured (see German Colonies, forgeries of 1889) with forged overprint and forged cancellation, JALUIT 8/6 97 MARSHALL INSELN (one circle, 27 mm).

1900. MARSHALL-INSELN (without "C"). Nos. 7 to 12. These stamps are rare and are in demand with the first cancellation.

Forged overprints: comparison is necessary.

Forged Geneva cancellation: one circle (27 mm), JALUIT MARSCHALL-INSELN (these words on two lines) 12-2-98.

1900. Ship type. Nos. 13 to 25. Numerous *forged cancellations.* Expertizing is necessary.

Geneva forgeries: see German Colonies, steamer type.

1914–15. Stamps overprinted "G.R.I." Numerous *forged overprints:* comparison is indispensable and so is specialization, for there are different types and a great many varieties on which the Stanley Gibbons Catalogue gives the necessary information.

Martinique

1886–92. Overprinted stamps. Nos. 1 to 30. *Originals:* specialization is recommended; for type and varieties, consult Marconnet's book (1897, pp. 312–24) and de Vinck's book (1929, pp. 116–20).

Forgeries: as a first step, determine whether the stamp itself is a forgery of 1881 stamps (see French Colonies).

Forged overprints are numerous: comparison and template measurement are indispensable.

Originals: typographical overprints (indentions). No. 1, value figure, 5¾ mm high; variety with "c," 4 mm. No. 2, lettering, 5½ mm high; variety, 4½ mm; there are copies with the dot after "c" placed on a level with the top of that letter. No. 26 also has this variety. All overprints were counterfeited in Geneva on forgeries and on fraudulently overprinted originals.

Forged Geneva cancellation: double circle (24½ mm), outer circle with breaks, with date, ST-PIERRE 1ᵉ / 11 JUIN 92 MARTINIQUE.

1892–1906. Peace and Commerce type. Nos. 31 to 51. *Forgeries* of this type (Geneva); see French Colonies.

Forged Geneva cancellation of the preceding type (23½ mm), FORT DE FRANCE 6 MAI 94 MARTINIQUE.

1903–4. Nos. 52 to 60. Typographed overprints.

Forged overprints: comparison is indispensable. Check first whether the stamps belonging to the Peace and Commerce type or the No. 60 postage due stamp type are counterfeits.

1912. Overprinted stamps, Peace and Commerce type. Nos. 78 to 81. *Geneva forgeries:* see counterfeits of the Peace and Commerce type under French Colonies.

1915. RED CROSS. No. 82. Typographed overprint. There are counterfeits on the used 10-centime of 1908; check the cancellation millesime.

Overprinted stamps of subsequent issues. Comparison is useful, especially in dealing with rare varieties.

Mauritania

1906. Balay type. Nos. 14 to 16. *Forgeries:* see the forgeries of this type under French Colonies.

1915. RED CROSS. No. 34. Double *forged overprints.* Detailed comparison is indispensable.

1906. Postage due stamps. Nos. 1 to 8. *Forged overprints:* "T" in a triangle; comparison is indispensable.

Mauritius

1847. Post office. Nos. 1 and 2. *Originals:* recess print engraved, with traces of color on the blank parts due to inadequate plate cleaning; twelve types, 3 x 4. Crisscrossed background (vertical and oblique lines); diadem with crosses alternating with fleurs-de-lys.

Forgeries: various typographed or lithographed reproductions made by dealers, easily identifiable by their kind of impression. A few early forgeries: (a) typographed with such fine background lines that the background seems solid, unlined; (b) lithographed on brownish paper with a single bandeau instead of a diadem; (c) Geneva lithograph (2-pence) with background composed of oblique, crossed, white lines whose intervening spaces form squares of color.

1848–58. Post paid. 1- and 2-pence. *Originals:* recess print engraved; paper usually stippled, showing clusters of four dots transparently. Background of boldly printed oblique lines crossed with less boldly printed vertical lines. Diadem of alternating crosses and fleurs-de-lys. Plates of twelve types (3 x 4); in the 2-pence, the PENOE error (instead of PENCE) is in the seventh stamp. Four principal successive plate conditions: (1) very fine engraving with clear-cut reproduction of background lines with excellent recess cut (May 1848 to the end of 1851), thick, yellowish paper and thin, yellowish, bluish, or white paper; (2) intermediate

engraving with all the oblique background lines entirely visible, but few of the vertical lines are visible (1852 to the end of 1855); (3) worn engraving; diagonal lines visible but without relief and disappearance of these lines at the shallowest recess cut places (1857 and 1858); (4) end of plate, very worn engraving; only traces of oblique lines near the portrait remain. The types are identified mainly by the inscription lettering (see the catalogue of the second Ferrari sale with its reconstituted plates).

Forgeries: (a) lithographed, with thick vertical lines and thin oblique ones; (b) photolithographed with FACSIMILE for the 1-penny in a twelve-type plate, worn plate, on very thick paper.

One finds *essays?* in black from the retouched plate, or rather from the plate that was rebuilt for reengraving (with different diadem), and *reprints* in orange-red from the same plate, both on white paper instead of yellowish or tinted paper.

1859. Portrait with bandeau. No. 7. Recess print engraving, reconstructed on the 2-pence plate of the POST PAID stamps; the portrait has only one bandeau; irregular crisscross background.

Forgeries: (a) lithographed copy of Type X (no dot after PAID); (b) lithographed in dark ultramarine on bluish paper. These forgeries are easily identifiable by their lithography. There also are essays? in black or white paper (instead of bluish paper) of the entire plate, and *reprints* on white paper from the same plate.

1859. Dog head. No. 8. *Originals:* recess print engraving. Three plate conditions: (1) very fine engraving; (2) background lines, partly worn; (3) worn plate; background lines, now vestigial. In the stamp's background, one finds vertical, horizontal, and oblique shading lines.

Forgeries: lithographed; no horizontal lines in the background around the portrait, and no oblique lines in the inscription background.

Note: There is an illustrated reconstruction of the POST PAID and Nos. 7 and 8 plates in the Calman Catalogue (1901).

1859. Portrait with Greek ornaments. Nos. 9 and 10. *Originals:* lithographed on yellowish white, horizontally laid paper. Note: Regrettably, the transfer plate has not yet been reconstructed. Admittedly, this is far more difficult than the reconstruction of engraved plates. The publication of the distinctive characteristics of the transfer plate would be extremely useful, for that is the only way to identify good forgeries made on similar paper. The plate must have been constituted by direct transfers from the matrix of the two values without multiple reproduction from transferral on a large matrix-transfer stone. In my opinion, the number of types is rather small (twelve?) if we go by the wide-neck variety of the 2-pence (important retouching of the shading on the right of the neck), a variety that is found rather frequently since the Stanley Gibbons Catalogue lists it only at about three times the price of the common, normal stamp. In the same value, there is other minor retouching.

Early forgeries: on wove white paper.

1854. Overprinted Britannia type. No. 11. The original overprint, FOUR PENCE, is engraved.

Forgery: see the following issue. The overprint was counterfeited in Geneva with lower horizontal bars of the "E" letters that are too long.

1858. Same type. No value indicated. Nos. 12 to 16. The reader is asked to look at the illustration given for stamp Nos. 1–5 of Barbados.

Originals: the bonnet has a five-pointed star and the top button is shaded; the corner design and the side and background burelage are similar to those of the Barbados stamps. Recess print engraved.

Forgeries: (a) early lithographed set; shapeless bonnet, the whole top of which is blank; no star or button; the spear point almost is touching the top interlacing; crude creations; (b) lithographed set, better executed, but the bonnet button has no shading; the spear point has a single thick shading line; the hand that holds the weapon has only three fingers instead of four; the burled background does not resemble the original design; (c) recess print engraved; no button or star on the bonnet; spear point with shading, except the two extremities of the background burelage which encroach upon it; this fantastic engraving looks good; it easily is recognized by a double scalloped line (outer parts concave); the space between the scallop and the outer frame being totally blank; (d) Geneva set lithographed in blocks; see details in the following issue which comes from the same forged cliché.

Fakes obtained by chemical alteration of the shades of Nos. 15 and 16 mints, unissued, in green and red-violet, to make Nos. 12 and 14 stamps. Usually comparison is sufficient; if not, use of a quartz lamp is indicated.

1858–62. Same type. Value indicated. Nos. 17 to 22. *Originals:* see preceding issue.

Forgeries: 6-pence, lithographed in various shades; imperforate or irregular perforation; the bonnet star forms an inverted-edge oval; colored dot instead of shading in the bonnet button, or else the latter is entirely blank; two shade lines in the spear point; formless background.

Geneva forgeries: lithographed in blocks, like the forgeries of the preceding issue; imperforate or perf about 13^1/$_2$; the bonnet button is small and round and has a color dot in the middle; the spear point has a large, curved shading line near the middle, except in the

two shades of the 6-pence where there are two; single small white spot on the front of the bonnet; four visible fingers on each hand, but they are so thin that one might say they are claws; the background is made of a field of white dots.

Forged cancellation: quadruple circle (24 mm in diameter) instead of original cancellations, B53 PAID, in one circle, or quintuple circle (16^1/$_2$ mm).

1860. No watermark. Perf 14. *Originals:* typographed; the face contour is realized simply by the cessation of the fine hatching of the center background; the ear shade lines are horizontal.

Forgeries: 6-pence, Nos. 26 and 27; lithographed; dot perf 13; face shading is missing; the bottom of the diadem is divided in three parts by vertical lines; comparison with a 4-pence rose of the following issue would be adequate. 9-pence, No. 28, lithographed; perf 11; full, unbroken line as face contour; oblique shade lines on the ear; some inscription letters are touching the tablet's edges.

1863. Watermarked "CC." Nos. 33 to 40. *Originals:* see the preceding set.

Forgeries: the center background is made up of small dots; the face shading is missing; perf 13; no watermark.

Overprinted stamps of subsequent issues. A few *forged overprints,* especially of Nos. 42b, 42c, and inverted or double varieties: comparison is necessary. The TWO CENTS overprint of 1891 (No. 79) was counterfeited in Geneva (single or double).

Mayotte

1892–1912. Peace and Commerce type. Nos. 1 to 31. *Geneva forgeries:* see the forgeries of this type under French Colonies.

Forged Geneva cancellation: double circle (21^1/$_2$ mm), broken inner circle, DZAOUDZI 2 AOUT 98. MAYOTTE.

Mexico

It is strongly recommended that collectors interested in this country specialize. Recommended also is the utilization of the Calman Catalogue which gives a ninety-page, in-quarto description of all overprints (with illustration, measurements, shades, split stamps, etc.), information we cannot possibly reproduce here, even in abridged form.

1856–61. Imperforate stamps. Nos. 1 to 12. *Originals:* recess print engraved; paper about 50 microns; the oval's background has close-set horizontal lines with oblique shade lines (northwest to southeast) on the left side of the portrait; however, these lines are hardly visible, except in the reprints; the shirt has two buttons; the ornamental background is formed with fine oblique shading lines (northeast to southwest); a thin line runs along the bottom of the letters of CORREOS MEJICO; the value background is made of frequently not very visible crossed lines, except in the reprints; the whole face (forehead, nose, cheeks, and chin) is well shaded.

Reprints (1888): the five values of the 1856 issue, color on white, plus a 2-real rose, a 4-real on ribbed paper, and an 8-real gray. Thicker paper (65 microns); the blank parts of the stamp's front (use magnifying glass) are slightly bluish; they were printed on cleaned, worn plates, and, because of this, the face shading is reduced (forehead, nose) and the lines of the center, ornamented, and inscription backgrounds, being reduced in width, are more visible. The five values of the 1861 issues also were reprinted: 1/2-real, black on pale brown; 1-real, black on green and black on rose; 2-real, black on yellow and black on rose; 4-real, black on yellow and red on yellow; 8-real, black on brown and green on brown. Here, with respect to imprint, it is more difficult to distinguish between originals and reprints, but it can be done by comparing the slightly different, more vivid shades and the thicker paper which has fewer transparency specks. Note: The reprints sometimes bear district names.

Fakes: reprints with forged names — compare the overprint; forged or unforged cancellation.

Forgeries: several lithographed sets, the first three of which have the following serious defects: Sets (a) CORREOS MEDICO [MEJICO]; the large oval is unbroken; (b) CORREOS MEJIOS [MEJICO]; with dividing frame lines around the stamp; (c) upper inscription is spelled accurately, but the lettering is colored on a white background! Three other sets are better: (d) upper inscription is very defective (see the illustration); lines or segments of dividing lines; the nose is formed with a large thick line; the upper lip, with a thick line doubled with a thin line; frequently there are three buttons on the shirt instead of two; (e) photolithographed Geneva set, successful in its details, were it not for the arbitrary shades; the center background shade lines are limited by a curved line beginning under the "S" of CORREOS and ending on a level with the bottom of the ear; see the illustration for a few defects in the ornamentation under the oval; the background of horizontal lines in the oval, on a level with the mouth, measures only 11 1/2 mm wide instead of 12; the ear forms an inverted "8"; the right eye terminates at the face's contour line; (f) defects in the ornamentation under the oval (see illustration); the nose and the eyebrow of the right eye (on the left looking at

the stamp) is formed with a heavy unbroken line; twelve curved shade lines in the coat's right lapel instead of about sixteen and ten in the coat's left lapel instead of sixteen; (g) a few values including the 2-real; crude

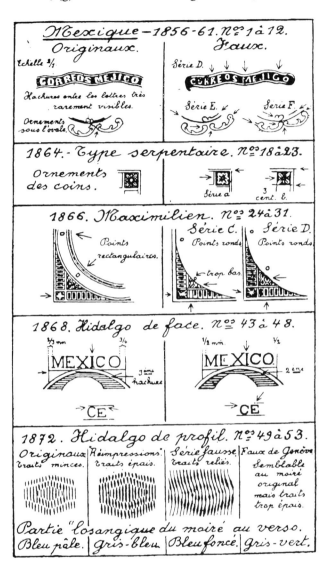

Mexico. 1856–61. Nos. 1–12. Originals. Shade lines between letters are rarely visible. Ornaments under the oval. Forgeries. Second section: 1864. "Serpentaire" [Eagle] type. Nos. 18–23. Corner ornaments. Set a. Set b (3-centavo). Third section: 1866. Maximilian. Nos. 24–31. Rectangular dots. Sets c and d, round dots. Fourth section: 1868. Hidalgo, full-face. Nos. 43–48. 3rd shade line; 2nd shade line. Bottom: 1872. Profile of Hidalgo. Nos. 49–53. Originals, thin lines, pale blue. Reprints, thick lines, gray-blue. Forged set, lines joined, dark blue. Geneva forgeries, like the original moiré, but the lines are too thick, gray-green. "Lozenge" of the moiré on back.

photolithographed set in which the value lettering is not much larger than that of the top inscription; (h) again, I am informed of the existence of a few values which have only eight or nine shade lines in the top tablet instead of eleven, with the portrait's nose unshaded; this set probably was engraved, but not having seen it, I assume that reprints (?) with a poorly executed upper inscription background are involved. See the 1867 issue also.

Forged overprints with rare district names: comparison is necessary. Fournier counterfeited the SALTILLO overprint.

1863. Perf 12. Nos. 13 to 17. Very numerous *forged cancellations*. Only the Saltillo, Paso del Norte, and Monterrey postmarks are valid; they must be expertized. Fournier obliterated these values with the following forged postmarks — single circle (24 mm): (1) FRANCO 29 OCT 18..? MEXICO; (2) FRANCO 7 DEC 1863 MONIERREY; (3) FRANCO 2 OCT 1863 SALTILLO; (4) double oval in red (28 x 17 mm): FRANCO EN TUXILA CHICO; (5, 6) on two lines, lettering about 5¼ mm high: FRANCO ADALAJA; FRANCO ANTEPEC; (7) a design resembling a Savoy knot (see Sardinia, for illustration).

Forgeries: very deceptive engraved set provided with various cancellations mentioned above; the 1-real was given a forged "¹/₂" overprint. Perf 11½; no dot in the small circles which terminate the value tablet; six black shading lines in the collar under the chin instead of five.

Forged overprints: "¹/₂" on 1-real (No. 17, unissued); comparison is necessary; the oblique line of the "1" and its terminal line, in the forged Geneva overprint, are too short; the fraction bar is bent back too much at its ends; gray ink. Also, forged overprint, SALTILLO, with three "L" letters of different widths.

1864. Eagle type. Nos. 18 to 23. *Originals:* recess print engraved; color traces frequently are found over the whole surface of the stamp due to careless printing; with regard to the corner rosettes, see the illustration; the serpent's head is visible and is pointed toward the "E" of Mexico; in the "X," the left downstroke is twice as wide as the right one.

Forgeries: (a) crude lithographed set with dividing frame lines; headless serpent; what is supposed to be its head is pointed toward the "M"; the two downstrokes of the "X" are of like thickness; the ornamental square illustration is adequate for identifying these creations. (b) I have seen only the 3-centavo stamp, but the whole set may be extant; more successful lithography; the ornamental squares are executed scarcely better than in the preceding set; the oval bandeau background apparently is solid under the inscriptions; the serpent's head is pointing toward the right foot of the "M"; the top of the "X" is touching the "E"; etc. (c) So-called

"reprint" of the 3-centavo, obtained from printing with an original cliché whose value lettering was retouched; yellowish-brown shade, nonoverprinted.

1866. Maximilian. Nos. 24 to 31. *Originals:* the center background is made of vertical and horizontal crossed shading lines; the inscriptions' background is made of fine concentric lines, which easily can be seen through a magnifying glass in the *engraved* stamps, less easily in those that are *lithographed*. The bottom of the beard is divided into two points, one of which is separated from the neck point by about 1 mm. The whole portrait is well shaded, and the neck cut displays crossed lines. See the illustration for corner ornamentation details.

No *reprints.*

Forgeries: all sets are lithographed with a solid oval background. There are two sets in which the beard ends in a single point, where the distance to the neck point is minimal: Set a, well executed on thick paper; MEXICANO is printed MEXIOANO; there are two square and two round dots between the value indications and the inscriptions; Set b, crudely executed set on yellowish paper; thin lettering; the four dots are missing. In two other sets, the beard is presentable. Set c, most widely circulated set, in which the dots are round, the ones after the "c" letters being placed at this letter's base; dividing frame lines; very poorly copied corner design (see illustration). Set d, Geneva, much better photolithographical execution; 21²/₃ mm high; the four dots are round; the letters are too thin; see a few of the corner ornamentation defects in the illustration. This set frequently was overprinted with MEXICO (at bottom), "78" (top left), and "1866" (top right), and given the previously described forged cancellations, without visible millesime. The 25-centavo blue is an essay.

1867. Stamps overprinted MEXICO. Nos. 32 to 42. There are *reprints* without watermark: ¹/₂-real black, 2-real dark green, and 4-real rose, on excessively thick paper and in more vivid colors than the originals (¹/₂ real).

Forgeries: see the first issue; the 8-real stamp also was executed very cleverly on paper resembling quite closely that of the first issue (less chalky, however); Nos. 37 and 38 with overprint also were counterfeited well, and, likewise, the 1- and 4-real stamps of the 1867 printing on thin, azure-tinted paper with forged watermark, "R.S.P." Design comparison, measurements, and the slightly dissimilar shades will help to identify these counterfeits.

Numerous *forged overprints:* comparison is necessary. (Geneva, also.)

Fake: reprint of the ¹/₂-real, fraudulently overprinted with MEXICO.

1868. Hidalgo, full-face. Nos. 43 to 48. *Originals:* the center background shading lines are small and thin; the "I" of MEXICO is evidently thicker than the other letters; the top of the skull is touching the third line (the first one frequently touches the circle); the "C" of CENT, which is higher than the other letters, comes closer to the top of the value tablet.

No *reprints.*

Forgeries: lithographed; the center background shading lines are too thick; the skull is touching the second line; the "I" of MEXICO is no thicker than the other letters; the feet of the "X" are touching the circle (at times only in one place); the "C" of CENT is no higher than the other letters. Other counterfeits, which are similar, easily are identified by comparing them with the characteristics of the originals described in the illustration; none has the small line which begins on the left of the upper part of the oval, forming a tangent with it.

Forged overprint, ANOTADO, often with forged rouletting. Comparison is necessary. Remember that the ANOTADO overprinted stamps belong to Type II (thick figures), like the color errors, and also that their cancellation usually has millesime "1872."

1872. Profile of Hidalgo. Nos. 49 to 53. *Originals:* 19^1/$_2$ x 24 mm; paper, 55 microns thick; watermarked copies are rare; the outer frame is formed with a single thick line on the outer surfaces of the corner ornamental squares and above the inscriptions; everywhere else it is double. The background lines generally are quite visible, but there are thick places and gaps. The thin line, which limits the horizontals above CENTAVOS on the left, often is unsuccessful or almost is invisible; the shade lines on the right and left of CORREOS and MEXICO are vertical in the 6- and 25-centavo and horizontal in the other values.

Reprints (1888): 19^2/$_3$ x 24^1/$_2$ mm; paper, 65 microns. First-rate impression with finer, more successful shading than in the original. The network of fine wavy lines (moiré) on the back of the stamp is forged (see illustration). No watermark. The essays have no moiré effect on back.

Forgeries: lithographed; (a) widely circulated early set; 19^1/$_4$ x 23^1/$_2$ mm; paper, 70–75 microns; no overprints. These forgeries do not look bad despite their serious defects: uniformly thick outer frame; the 6- and 25-centavo stamps have horizontal shade lines on the right and left of CORREOS and MEXICO; same, in the ornamented inner corners; the word SEIS (6-centavo) is inverted in its tablet (bottom of letters up toward stamp's interior); the oval's line pattern is made of excessively thick lines, etc. (b) Geneva photolithographed forgeries; 19^1/$_2$ x 24^1/$_3$ mm; paper, 70–75 microns; well executed, but shades are arbitrary;

the background lines and the inner line of the dual-lined frame are etched too sharply. With respect to the moiré effect, see below.

Forged Geneva cancellations: (1) one circle, with date, FRANCO 29 OCT 18.. MEXICO; (2) red oval, FRANCO EN TUXILA CHICO; (3) on two lines, FRANCO DAL.. ANTEPE.

Forged overprints on reprints and forgeries; comparison is necessary. One usually finds the following forged overprints on Geneva forgeries: VERACRUX 50 73; URES 50 73; SALTILLO 49 73. Moiré effect on back of stamps: the illustration gives information on the principal defects; the original moiré shading provides the means for quick expertizing; by way of supplement, we should add that when the original's back is examined with the naked eye at some distance, the lozenge-like forms of the design cannot be seen; their rudimentary shape can be perceived in the reprint; they are quite visible in the Geneva forgeries — and, in the early counterfeited set, they can be seen at a distance of more than one meter.

1877–82. President Juarez. Nos. 61 to 73. The nonoverprinted stamps are stock remainders that were sold as mints and provided with various cancellations or *forged overprints.*

1884–85. Hidalgo. Corner figures. Nos. 77 to 100. Same remark for Nos. 87–89 (50-centavo to 2-peso), whose stock remainders were sold in large quantities.

1886–93. Figure in an oval. Nos. 101 to 130. *Reprints* (1891): 20-centavo (No. 109) in lilac-brown, watermarked "1891"; 12-centavo red on ribbed instead of wove paper and white instead of brownish gum. The overprint, "IIIII Vale. I Cvo," is a fantasy made by a postmaster for dealers.

Subsequent issues. *Forged overprints* on 1914 stamps: VICTORIA DE TORREON ABRIL 2-1914, Nos. 223a–229a; and on 1915 stamps: "Vale 4" or "20 centavos 1914," Nos. 286–88. Detailed comparison is needed. Stamps of the latter set are from a semiofficial issue.

Official stamps. Most of the overprints must be compared with reliable original overprints.

Chiapas. *Originals:* 25 x 17 mm.
Forgeries: 30 x 20^1/$_2$ mm with oval postmark FRANCO CHIAPAS.

Cuernavaca. *Original:* 25 mm in diameter. A disputed stamp, due to the lack of official documentation.

Guadalajara. *Originals:* 21 mm in diameter, handstamp impression; yellowish wove paper; crisscrossed paper; laid paper; paper with spaced watermark lines (*bâtonné*); various shades; imperforate or perf 42 in circle.

No *reprints.*

Forgeries: (1) so-called "reprints," made with the original stamp for the circle and the inscription FRANCO EN GUADALAJARA but with forged value and millesime; arbitrary shades and paper; (2) Geneva set: 22 mm, 1-real (1867) in four paper shades with forged cancellations; oval or large double-lined "8," or else cancellation on two lines, FRANCO.. ADALAJA.... From the same source, the 2-real (1867), with most of the letters touching the circle; (3) various sets from several sources. All of these forgeries, including the so-called "reprints," easily are identified by drawing a straight line under the millesime; in the originals (1867), it will cut the left side of the "O" and about the middle of the "A" of FRANCO; in the 1868 originals, it will cut the two letters near the middle — which is never the case in the forgeries. All of this, without prejudice to the arbitrary paper, shades, and perforations.

Patzcuaro. *Original:* handstamp imprint; 22 mm, similar to that of Guadalajara but without value or millesime designation. An unclassified stamp, due to the lack of official documentation, like those of Chalco, Chihuahua, Morelia, Oaxaca, Queretaro, and Vera Cruz, which already have been classified, however, as fantasies by Calman.

1875. "Porte de Mar" (sea shipment) stamps. Nos. 1 to 8. *Originals:* lithographed black on yellow; plates of forty-nine stamps including all values (fourteen of 10-centavo, seven of 25-, 35-, and 50-centavo, four of 75- and 85-centavo, and three of 60- and 100-centavo).

1875. Black on white. Nos. 9 to 19. *Originals:* lithographed on various kinds of paper; with or without district overprint; value figures, 7 mm high; CENTAVOS, 7 1/2 mm wide; 25 1/2 x 31 1/2 mm.

Forgeries: various counterfeits, one set of which with allowable measurements seems good, but no value figure has the white frame or traces of it as seen in the originals (except in the 10-centavo and in the "1" figures of the 12-centavo and the "0" of the 20-centavo) around the figures, due to the fact that the figures were changed on the plate for a second impression; one also should notice that the shade lines do not always agree. In the forged set with acceptable dimensions, the "S" of CENTAVOS evidently is too high; there is only one dot, instead of two, under the "P" of PORTE above the lower left corner ornament. Other forgeries have the two dots. These stamps were counterfeited in Geneva, with or without forged overprints, URÈS, SALTILLO, etc.; forged cancellations in blue or black.

1875. Same, with larger figures. *Originals:* figures are 8 mm high; CENTAVOS, 9 1/2 mm; 25 1/2 x 32 mm; no longer any white framing around the value figures, each of the values having a different plate.

1879. Color on white. Nos. 26 to 31. *Originals:* lithographed on wove white paper; 19 x 25 mm; watermarked ADMINSTRATION GENERAL DE CORREOS MEXICO in the sheet.

Forgeries: a good set, but with arbitrary shades; about 19 1/5 mm wide; still only three dots in the small white circle between MEXICO and MAR, and the dots above the second "R" of CORREOS are arranged poorly in the corner ornaments; two lines almost are touching the volute instead of two dots on a horizontal plane; above the "E" of CORREOS, a large dot and a small one instead of two dots of the same size; above the "X" of MEXICO, the right dot is touching the volute on its right; a single dot under the "A" of MAR instead of two; no dot after the inverted comma on the right of the large volute in the lower left corner.

Moheli

1906 and 1912. Peace and Commerce type. Nos. 1 to 22. *Forgeries:* Geneva; see forgeries of this type under French Colonies.

Forged Geneva cancellation: with date, double circle (22 mm), FOMBONI 4 NOV 09 MOHELI.

Monaco

The Monaco collection began rather late, in 1885. The specialist is confronted with two groups of foreign stamps bearing the cancellations of that principality.

I. Sardinian postmarks. Double circle with date, MONACO and MENTONE: very rare.

II. French postmarks. Lozenge with small numerals, "4222" (1860): very rare. Lozenge with large numerals, "2387" (1862): rare. Lozenge with small numerals "2.387": very rare. French postmarks with date, various models (MONACO), 1860–85, very much in demand. In addition, one finds a dated postmark, MONTE-CARLO (1884); mobile (railway), MONTE-CARLO VINTIMILLE; MONTE-CARLO MONACO MENTON, and the MONACO telegraphic postmark. In view of the value increment, forged cancellations have been added to French stamps that are common in mint conditions.

Issue of 1885. Perf 14 x 13 1/2. Nos. 1 to 10. *Sheets* of 150 stamps in six panes of twenty-five. (The 75-centime was printed in four panes of twenty-five.) Portrait of Prince Charles III. First printing, July 1, 1885, of the 5-, 15-, and 25-centime stamps; other values: September 1885.

Shades: 1-centime bronze-green, olive-brown; 2-centime various violet shades; slate: 50M, 50U.

5-centime blue. 10-centime brown on yellow; on light yellow: 25M, 25U. 15-centime rose, carmine-rose: 6M, 50U. 25-centime green. 40- and 75-centime blue or black on rose; blue or black on lilac: 25M. 1-franc black on bright yellow; black on yellow: 25M, 25U. 5-franc bright carmine on blue-green: 25M, 25U; carmine on green.

Varieties: mint stamps with brown gum (first printing) are in demand. There are a few varieties, such as the printing failure in the cheek of the 2-centime. The 15- and 25-centime mint are much rarer than the used stamps, especially the 15-centime carmine, but the used 75-centime, 1- and 5-franc stamps are rarer than the mint. The 5-franc on piece or cover is extremely rare.

Cancellations: the usual postmarks of Monaco and Monte Carlo.

Real value of first issue stamps and blocks. The market for the principality's stamps having been subjected to extensive and intensive cornering from 1919 ("orphans"), the market for earlier issues reflected this phenomenon, and so the prices quoted in catalogues do not mean very much. We reproduce below the real current prices at a public sale in Nice, the most important market for these stamps, in 1926, with values in gold:

	Singles		Blocks of Four	
No.	Mint	Used	Mint	Used
1	0.20	0.25	1.25	1.50
2	1	1	5	3
3	2	1.50	10	7
4	4	3.50	25	20
5	6	1.50	35	20
6	15	5	150	
7	5	4	25	
8	8	8	40	
9	60	50	(600)	
10	500	425	(6,000)	

Reprints: none. Imperforate essays on cardboard paper (230–40 microns) exist for the entire set.

Forgeries: the major values, 40-centime to 5-franc, often were counterfeited lithographically and photolithographically. These more or less successful counterfeits become quite deceptive when the shade, paper, and perforation closely approximate the authentic original. No counterfeit can really be said to be comparable to an original; careful scrutiny of the stamp's design or of the illustration will convince one that this is true; moreover, shade, format, and perforation will justify immediate rejection of most of the forgeries made in Italy, Belgium, Paris, Switzerland, Marseilles, etc.

A comprehensive description of all the forgeries would take too long and would be tedious. However, the matter concerns so many collectors that a detailed study of a few counterfeited sets may help them in their comparative research. Paper furnishes good data, especially if one has access to a good microscope capable of magnifying fifty times.

The forged Monaco stamps are so numerous that it may justifiably be said that there are two forgeries of the 1- and 5-franc stamps for every authentic one in albums.

I. Geneva forgeries (M.). In general, these appear least impressive: 40-centime blue-gray on dull rose; 75-centime, good shade. 1-franc, good shade. 5-franc carmine-tinted red on slightly greenish white paper. Crude design (see illustration). On comparing, one finds other marks, especially in the hair and the goatee, that are as distinctive as those shown in the illustration. A few cliché corrections were subsequently made in Turin without any improvement to speak of.

Measurements: $18^{1}/_4$ x $22^{1}/_5$ mm; paper (65 microns); perf 14 x $13^{1}/_2$; 14 x 14; 13 x 13. Nontransparent, fleecy paper.

Forged cancellations on these forgeries: double circle with date: MONACO 27 DEC 89 PRINCIPAUTÉ; MONACO 3e/17 MARS 91 PRINCIPAUTÉ; MONTE CARLO 12 OCT … MONACO; MONACO 16 MAI 89 PRINCIPAUTÉ. The dates are interchangeable.

II. Florence forgeries. The paper shade of the 75-centime is good. In the 5-franc, it is yellowish white with very little green, but this may be altered, of course. On the other hand, the shades are not congruent: the 5-franc is too red; in the 75-centime and 1-franc stamps the black impression seems darker than in the originals because it is cruder. The design can be compared to that of the Geneva forgeries (see illustration), especially with respect to the opaque eye shading. One of the two clichés was made for the 5-franc stamp. The top line of the "E" of PRINCIPAUTÉ is thinner than the top bar of the "T." Measurements: 18 x $22^{1}/_8$ or $21^{3}/_4$ mm (5-franc). Paper (60–70 microns). Perf $13^{1}/_4$ x 14; 14; or imperforate. Nontransparent paper. The names, D. DUPUIS and E. MOUCHON are $^{1}/_3$ mm from the lower frame (about $^{1}/_4$ mm in the originals and other forgeries).

III. Marseilles forgeries. 1- and 5-franc. See the illustration for the most important features. Executed in blocks of four imperforate stamps, then perforated six times, the perforation being noncongruent. Slightly transparent paper like that of the originals, but somewhat thinner, about 50 microns; the paper of the 1-franc is too yellow; that of the 5-franc is yellowish green. Measurements: $17^{2}/_3$ x $21^{2}/_3$ mm. Sometimes these forgeries are sold as "reprints" at exorbitant prices. Real value: 10 centimes each. (See F. Serrane, "Faux de Monaco," *L'Écho de la Timbrologie,* no. 717 [November 15, 1925]: 1588–89.)

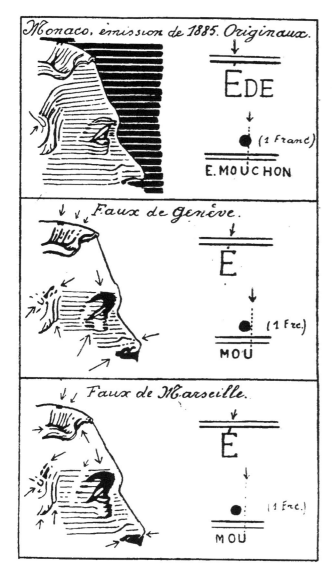

Monaco. Issue of 1885. Originals. Middle: Geneva forgeries. Bottom: Marseilles forgeries.

Originals: 17⁴/₅–18 x 21³/₄–21⁴/₅ mm, depending on the printing. However, the 15-centime carmine and the 40-centime stamps are found with a height of about 22 mm. Slightly transparent paper; perf 13¹/₂ x 14. Very thin-stroked impression (see illustration). The upper frame is about ¹/₃ mm from the top line of the tablet, whose thickness is double that of the outer frame. In the forgeries, except those of Florence and Brussels, the distance is only ¹/₅ mm and there is little difference in line thickness.

Forged cancellations: in addition to the Geneva forged cancellations, there are two or three other completely forged postmarks, for example, MONACO 16 MAI 89 (PRINCIPAUTÉ), etc.

Fakes: with occasional use of the microtome, the cardboard paper essays were thinned and then perforated. Thickness is usually not congruent. Less transparency in watermark fluid than in the originals.

The shade of the 1-franc on card is an excessively bright yellow. That of the 5-franc is usually pale carmine on yellowish green paper. This essay, however, exists also in bright carmine. The latter, especially, was faked most often. The 1-franc measures 18 x 22 mm; the 5-franc, 18¹/₆ x 22¹/₄ mm in the pale carmine and 18¹/₁₀ by about 22¹/₁₀ mm in the bright shade.

The 5-franc was faked also by chemical erasure of the figures of the 15-centime carmine, followed by impression of "5 F" value indications and chemical tinting of paper. Blocks of four of the 5-franc must be carefully examined with this in view. One must not forget that the formats of the 5-franc and the 15-centime rose are similar, but faking with the latter gives a noncongruent color tone; with regard to color tone, the 15-centime carmine is perfect, but its format is a little too large, about 18¹/₆ x 22 mm.

1891–98. Prince Albert portrait. Same perforation. Nos. 11 to 21. *Sheets* of 150 stamps in six panes of twenty-five; beginning with the second printing, millesime numbers appear between the panes in the middle of the sheet. First printings (1891), except the 40- and 75-centime values (1894).

Shades: three or four shades for each value.

Real value in gold of single stamps and blocks of four in 1926:

No.	Singles Mint	Singles Used	Blocks of Four Mint	Blocks of Four Used
11			0.10	0.10
12			0.10	0.10
13	1.25	0.50	6	
14	2.50	1.50	8	6.25
15	1.75	0.25	12	
16	7.50	1.75	(120)	
17	0.25	0.20	1.50	1
18	0.50	0.30	3	1.50
18a	1.50	1	9	3
19	1	1	6	
19a	2	2	10	
20	0.75	0.60	5	
20a	2.50	2.50	15	
21	6	4	35	30
21a	20	12	100	

Varieties: there are defective impressions; 40-centime with transparent printing: 2M, 2U. The 15-centime with double print is an essay. The 1- and 5-franc imperforates, thick paper, paper color of stamp, are essays.

Cancellations: various postmarks of Monaco and Monte Carlo.

Issue of 1901–3. Same type. Nos. 22 to 25. A few shades; the 5-centime dark yellow-green is from a 1903 printing.

	Singles		Blocks of Four	
No.	Mint	Used	Mint	Used
22			0.25	0.15
23	0.25	0.10	1.25	0.50
24	0.20	0.15	1.25	1
25	0.60	0.15	3	2.50

1914. Red Cross. No. 26. Unit value: 60 centimes. Block of four: 3 francs.

Millesimes: consult the specialty catalogues for millesimes after the first issue.

Subsequent issues. The market for almost all stamps was cornered to keep prices high in spite of the large number of stamps printed. Abstention is advised.

1919. Nonoverprinted "orphans." A printing of from 25,000 to 48,000 stamps. 50-centime: 12,000; 1-franc: 9,000; 5-franc: 3,500. Compare the prices of Nos. 47 and 48 of Gabon from a 3,000 stamp printing.

1920. ORPHANS overprinted. A printing of about 15,000 for all values, except the 15-centime + 10-centime (25,000), the 25-centime + 15-centime (34,000), and the 5-franc + 5-franc (1,050). Obviously, the latter is really rare, and the counterfeiting of its overprint was excellent. Make comparison: upper loops of the "2" figures, etc. To compare values, see the price of the No. 1 of Madagascar, printed in 1,000 copies.

1921. Albert type. Nos. 44 to 47. Modified shades; the 5-franc mauve is not very common.

1921. Early overprint types. Nos. 48 to 50. No. 48 (300,000); No. 49 (100,000); No. 50 (42,000).

1922. Overprints on stamps of 1891–1901. Nos. 51 to 53. Nothing interesting here.

1922–23. Monuments series. Nos. 54 to 61. Recess print engraving. Printings: No. 54 (72,000, for comparison, see the prices of Réunion No. 76, same number of copies printed); No. 55 (95,000, see Dahomey No. 2, also, for prices); No. 57 (200,000, see New Caledonia No. 110, same); No. 58 (76,000, see Réunion No. 76, same); No. 59 (550,000); No. 60 (1 million); No. 62 (240,000, see Comoro Islands No. 22, same); Nos. 62 and 64 (48,000, see St. Pierre and Miquelon No. 37); No. 63 (67,000, see Gabon No. 39).

There are a few shades, as in worldwide issues, no more, no less. A few values have as watermark the firm trademark "B.F.K.R." (Blanchet Brothers and Kleber, in Rives-Isère). These are no more interesting than issues from other countries where similar trademarks are found in the paper.

The whole set exists imperforate — "errors" intended as a rip-off of the collector.

The information given on these issues and on the frequently speculative postage due stamps in general catalogues is adequate.

The Prince Louis set has the following printing figures: No. 65 (850,000). No. 66 (650,000). No. 66 (650,000). No. 67 (500,000). No. 68 (1.6 million). No. 69 (750,000).

Montenegro

Sheets of 100 stamps watermarked ZEITUNGS MARKEN in the middle of the sheet, lettering 23 mm high.

1874 (May). Perf 10$^{1}/_{4}$, 10$^{3}/_{4}$. Nos. 1 to 7. *Paper:* thick, nontransparent. Stamps typographed.

Perforation: large holes, about 1$^{1}/_{2}$–1$^{3}/_{4}$ mm in diameter. The explanation of this may be seen in the fact that the perforations end in points. In the following issues, the holes are medium-sized, about 1$^{1}/_{4}$ mm in diameter, and the perforations are either rounded or straight.

Printing figures: 10,000 copies, except Nos. 1 and 3 (20,000) and No. 25 (5,000). No reprints.

Shades: 2-novcic yellow, usually poor impression resembling lithography. 3-novcic yellow-green, often poorly printed also, and blue-green, much better impression, rarer mint: 2M. 5-novcic dull rose-red and rose-red. 7-novcic pale lilac. 10-novcic blue and light blue. 15-novcic more or less bright bistre-brown. 25-novcic lilac-tinted gray (stone color). The first printing had brownish gum.

Cancellations: the customary, common postmark is round with date (thimble cancellation, about 20$^{1}/_{2}$ mm). All other cancellations are rare.

Pairs: 4U. Blocks of four: very rare.

Secret marks: the secret marks and a few expertizing marks, 1874 type, are shown in the illustration.

Research in these marks is interesting since it is related to issue classification. In the 3-novcic, the break in the frame line above the Russian "tche" is no longer visible after the first issue, each time there is a large impression. 5-novcic, first issue, there is a dot on the left of the small slanted line under the lily-leaf shaped ornament in the upper left corner. In the following issues, the dot, which now coincides with the line, is rarely visible. 7-novcic, first issue, a dot is sometimes visible near the middle of the same left ornament, lower left corner. 10-novcic, beginning with the second issue, the two dots in the upper left corner are rarely visible. 15-novcic, the two vertical hatch lines that connect the upper and inscription frames can be seen only in the first issue. This defect was rectified by retouching (erasure), which can be seen in No. 13 where the space between frame and tablet is larger at this place.

Similar marks recur in the issue of 1894 (different values). The 1-florin has the two dots of the 25-novcic in the upper right corner ornament. The 30-novcic has just a single dot at the same place, etc. Curiously enough, other writers have said nothing about this.

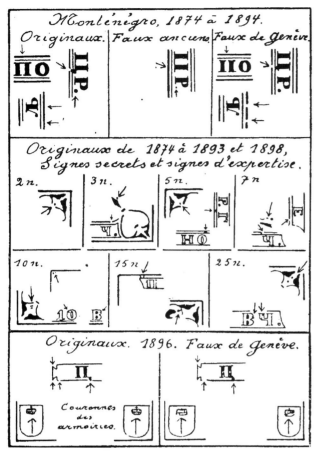

Montenegro. 1874–94. Originals. Early forgeries. Geneva forgeries. Middle: Originals, 1874–93 and 1898. Secret and expertizing marks. Bottom: Originals, 1896. Geneva forgeries. Crowns of coat of arms.

Forgeries: I. Very poorly counterfeited early forgeries. A quick comparison with an original will easily expose the fraudulence: fantastic portrait; first letter of the inscription on the right forms an "H"; inscription on the left is inverted, the top of final letter "A" being on the right, near the portrait.

II. Early lithographed set. Passable design; medium transparent paper. The set exists imperforate, irregularly rouletted, or perf 12½. See the illustration for a characteristic distinguishing mark. It should be noted that in the original 3-novcic the upper bar of the first letter of the right inscription connects the vertical lines, the only exception to the rule in all the other values, whereas in this set the letter appears in the 3-novcic stamp as shown in the illustration.

Forged cancellations on this set include a closely barred circle, large dot lozenge, and double circle with date.

III. Geneva forgeries (see illustration). There was wholesale counterfeiting of the 1894 issue in particular, but the clichés also were used to counterfeit the preceding issues (forged circular date cancellation).

Issues of 1875–80 and 1893. Same type. Nos. 8 to 14. 1875–80 (Nos. 8a–14): perf 12, 12½, 13, on various thick papers, perforations with medium size holes. Composite perforations are rare. The irregular perf 12 is very rare, mint. All of those with teeth have a wider cut than in the first issues.

1893 (Nos. 8a–14): perf 10½ and 11½ on thick paper. On thin paper: Nos. 8–14.

Shades: rather numerous. It is a good idea to use them as references in classifying the various printings and issues.

Cancellations: see first issue. There also are dated cancellations, single circle (25 mm).

Varieties: defective impressions are in demand. No. 8a exists with double print.

Pairs: since they enable one to ascertain marginal width with the naked eye, they are in demand.

Forgeries: see first issue.

1893. Overprinted stamps. Nos. 15 to 23. *Perforations:* 10½ and 11½.

A nice collection can be made here of perforations (narrow and wide margins), papers (thin or medium, and transparent), overprint varieties (normal, inverted, double), and errors ("1495," " 893," "18 3," "1493," "14 3," "149 ," " 493," etc.), and varieties in which one or the other year date is lacking.

Reprints (1898): Perf 10½ except the 15-novcic which is perf 11½. Overprint in carmine.

1897. Same type. New values. Nos. 24 to 29. *Perforations:* 10½, 11½, and 11 (rare). Imperforates exist (rare).

Forgeries: the whole set was photolithographically counterfeited in Geneva (F.), perf 11¼. See the preceding illustration for the distinctive marks.

Forged Geneva cancellation: circular postmark with date: CETTIGNE 10/7 (26 mm). The fifth and sixth Russian letters are connected at the top (flaw).

1896. Panoramic view. Nos. 30 to 41. *Perforations:* 10½ x 10½ and 11½ x 11½. The normally canceled stamps are worth three times the price of mint. 1- and 2-florin: 5U. Forged cancellations are plentiful.

The 3-, 5-, 10-, 20-, 30-, 50-novcic and the 1-florin are sometimes imperforate: rare. The 3-, 5-, 10-, and 20-novcic are found partly perforated: rare.

Varieties: inverted centers, double print of the center or of the frame, and printing on both sides are printer's trial proofs.

Geneva forgeries: the whole set, perforated or imperforate. 33 x 21$^1/_5$ mm, instead of 33$^1/_5$–$^2/_5$ x 21$^1/_2$ mm in the originals. Perf 11$^1/_2$ x 11$^1/_2$ as in the originals. Lithographed in occasionally similar shades. See the illustration for the distinctive marks; the trees in the foreground, bottom left, are shapeless. In the originals, they have clear-cut tree-like shapes. Same forged cancellation as above.

1898. Early type. Nos. 42 to 48. *Perforation:* 10$^1/_2$, 11$^1/_2$.

Varieties: the 14-novcic imperforate, the 15-novcic with double print, and the 3- and 7-novcic printed on back are printer's proofs. The 3-novcic is found with very transparent impression: 10M, 20U. But this variety has fakes.

The following issues are adequately described in the general catalogues.

1902. The whole set exists imperforate (printer's proof), with single or double impression, except Nos. 55 and 56.

1905. An enormous quantify of varieties, wantonly created for the use of collectors.

Montserrat

1876. Overprinted Antigua stamps. Nos. 1 and 2. *Originals:* see Antigua. The 6-pence emerald (blue-green) is not known to exist as a used stamp.

Forgeries: crude lithographed copies, with forged overprint; no watermark. The bisected 1-piaster must be on entire cover; when one-half of the stamp, on cover or not, is overprinted with the fraction "$^1/_2$" in black, that forged overprint shows that it is a fake.

Morocco

1. German Post Offices

1899. Single MAROCCO overprint. Unissued set.

1899. Oblique overprint on two lines. Nos. 1 to 6. *Original overprints:* classified in boldface and lightface categories.

Forged overprints: comparison is necessary. Examine first whether forged stamps of Germany (1889) are involved.

1900. Overprinted REICHSPOST. Nos. 7 to 19. *Forged overprints.* Make comparison.

Forged cancellations on overprinted originals: expertizing is indicated. The forged Geneva cancellation: one circle (26$^1/_2$ mm), with date, TANGER (MAROCCO) 6/3. 01. DEUTSCHE POST.

1905–11. Overprinted stamps. Nos. 20 to 27. Same observation.

Note: In Nos. 16, 17, and 19 originals, the value is positioned higher than the bottom of the lateral inscriptions or is level with it. In No. 8, the "T" is pointed or not; in the stamp values in marks of the last three issues, the value is placed either level with the lateral inscriptions or higher; finally, from 1903, the "M" letters in the values in marks of 1900 are thicker.

2. British Post Offices

There are *forged overprints,* especially of the first three issues and of their rare varieties. Comparison occasionally is necessary; overprint study is easy, however, British overprints being well executed in general.

3. Spanish Post Offices

Same observation for the first three issues. Comparison is indispensable. The overprint of 1903–9 (Nos. 1–13) was counterfeited in Geneva and applied generally on used stamps whose *Spanish* cancellation is original. Two types were created: the first one with letter "M" under the first "R" of CORREO; the second one is better. The forged Geneva cancellations: double circle (30$^1/_2$ mm), with date, TANGER (between two stars) 2.. ..NE 04 MARRUECOS.

4. French Post Offices

There are a great many forged overprints (current types and varieties); comparison frequently is obligatory and specializing is indicated. A few details in the various issues are offered here for the attentive collector: typographed overprints have an even, regular indention; in hand-applied overprints, it may be more pronounced on one of the four sides, with occasional light slippage. When the mint French stamp is expensive, examine the French cancellation closely to see whether the date is prior to the overprint issue or whether it is found under the overprint.

1891–1900. CENTIMOS and PESETA. Nos. 1 to 11. Typographed overprint. The 25- and 50-centimo, Type II, and 1-peseta are from the issue of January 1, 1891. The 5-centimo green, Type I; 10-centimo, Type II; and 20-centimo are from January 1, 1893. The 5-centimo yellow-green, Types I and II, and 10-centimo, Type I, are from 1899. The 50-centimo, Type I, and the 2-peseta are from 1900. The vermilion overprints, 5-centimo green, Type II, and 25-centimo are from April 1895. The overprint of the 2-peseta was counterfeited cleverly, but figure "2," which is too thick, has in its loop an oval, the major axis of which is vertical instead of slanted to the left; this does not mean that when the axis is slanted to the left the overprint is always original.

1893. TIMBRE POSTE. Nos. 12 and 13.
Handstamped impression with carmine ink.

February 3, 1893. Check first whether the postage due stamp of France is a forgery (see France and French Colonies).

1902–3. MAROC type. Nos. 14 to 20. Typographed overprints. In the double overprint, No. 14b, the indention of the two overprints must be the same.

Forgeries of the 1- and 2-franc, Merson type (see French Colonies).

1903. "P.P." overprint. Nos. 21 and 22.
Handstamp impression, still carmine. The overprint is really a cancellation (indication of *postage paid*) and should be accepted only on cover of October 10, 1903, the stamp having been used on that day only (TANGER). The 5- and 10-centime postage due stamps of France were overprinted in Geneva (and not the postage due stamps of Morocco with carmine overprint) by using the framed "P.P." which was used to cancel Swiss forgeries.

The *forged Geneva cancellations:* double circle (25 mm), broken line inner circle, with date, TANGER 5 FEV 93 MAROC.

1907–10. Nos. 23 to 27. Typographed overprint.

1911–17. MAROC type with arabic overprint. Nos. 28 to 39. Typographed overprint. In the widely spaced figures, the distance between the figures is $1/2$ mm greater in the 10-centimo and about $3/5$ mm greater in the 20-centimo than in the normally spaced figures. For No. 39, see *forgeries,* Merson type, under French Colonies.

1914–21. PROTECTORATE FRANÇAIS. Nos. 40 to 54. Typographed overprinting. The 15-centimo is from 1919 and the 1-centimo, gray-black, and the 25-centimo are from 1921. See the preceding issue for the widely spaced figures. For Nos. 53 and 54, see *forgeries,* Merson type, under French Colonies.

1914–15. Red Cross. Nos. 54a to 59. Note: These overprints have been the object of unremitting solicitude from counterfeiters. Detailed comparison of the cross, value figure, and lettering, as well as ink, is indispensable. No. 56 ("Oudja") comes from a handstamp, carmine ink; the others, from local typographical overprinting. In No. 55 (on No. 43), the horizontal bar is composed of two typographical characters; in the others, of a single one. In No. 57 (on No. 43), the overprint is vermilion.

1915–27. Red Cross. Nos. 60 to 62. Typographed overprints.

1918–24. TANGER overprints. Nos. 80 to 97.
Typographed overprint.

Fake: the rare variety of the 25-centimo without TANGER was obtained by scraping off the overprint of the 25-centimo, No. 35, of 1911.

1922–27. Airplane. Nos. 98 to 108. *Faking* of the 75-centimo green, No. 102, in blue to make No. 101, 75-centimo blue. Most often the shade obtained is the blue-green of the 50-centimo, but to be absolutely sure, compare with the shade of a 75-centimo blue original.

1923–27. 1917 types. Nos. 109 to 133. Heliogravure impression. Comparison with the impression of the 1917 set is necessary, for the reference, "Helio Vaugirard" (under the stamp, bottom right), was scraped off on major value heliogravure stamps.

Postage due stamps. All overprints are typographed.

Mozambique

1877–85. Crown type. Nos. 1 to 14. *Originals:* 21 x 24 mm.

Reprints, 1885: on thick wove paper, perf 13$1/2$, usually gumless; 20-reis in yellow-brown; 20-reis, dull rose; 50-reis, pale green; 100-reis, pale lilac. For 1881–85: 10-reis, green; 20-reis, pale rose; 40-reis, pale yellow; 50-reis, blue; shades differing somewhat from the original colors. The same may be said for the other values; comparison is useful. 1895: very rare; compare the shades with the originals and the reprints of 1885.

Geneva forgeries: Nos. 1–14. See details concerning the forgeries, with illustration, under Portuguese Colonies. The inner top ornaments are touching the line under the upper inscription: (a) under the "O" of COR; (b) under the right ornament; no cedilla under the "C" of MOCAMBIQUE. The forged Geneva cancellations: one circle (26 mm), with date, CORREIO DE BEIRA 6/10 1878 (MOCAMBIQUE) and double circle (26 and 15 mm), with date, CORREIO DE MOCAMBIQUE 1/9 1885.

1886. Embossed impression. Nos. 15 to 23.
Reprints (very rare) of the 5-, 25-, 40-, 50-, 100-, and 300-reis (1905).

Originals: 21 x 24 mm.

1893. Stamps overprinted JORNAES. Nos. 24 to 26. *Forged overprints:* comparison is necessary.

1894. Nos. 30 to 42. *Reprints* (very rare) of the 2$1/2$-, 25-, and 80-reis stamps.

1895–98. Overprinted stamps. Nos. 43–54. *Forged overprints:* comparison is useful. The overprint of the 2$1/2$-reis (No. 53) was counterfeited in Geneva.

1902. Overprinted stamps. Nos. 70 to 91. *Reprints* (very rare) of "65" on 40-reis; "65" on 200-reis; "115" on 5-reis; "115" on 50-reis; "130" on 25-reis; "400" on 100-reis.

1915–16. Stamps overprinted REPUBLICA.
Forged overprints, especially on No. 173 ("115" on 5-reis black) and No. 193 (75-reis purplish brown). Comparison is necessary.

Postage due stamps, overprinted REPUBLICA.
Forged overprints: comparison is indispensable.

Mozambique Company

Among the forged overprints, we should single out for special mention those of 1917 (Red Cross).

Reprints (very rare) of the set of 1892–94, except the 100-reis; the 20-reis is in carmine; 40-reis, in chocolate; 200-reis, in lilac. Comparison of the other shades is necessary.

Natal

1857–58. Embossed impression. Nos. 1 to 7.
Reprints in 1866, 1873, and 1893. Some of these reprints are recognized easily by shade (compare similar shades); for example, 1-penny rose-lilac or pale rose (instead of rose, No. 1); 1-penny yellow and white on back (instead of buff, No. 3); 6-pence yellow-green (instead of blue-green, No. 5); 9-pence pale blue and 1-shilling yellow (instead of buff); there are others that are so similar, in spite of their somewhat accentuated embossing, that the Stanley Gibbons Catalogue took the wise precaution of listing them only as canceled stamps. The other stamps that are tinted on only one side and the ones that are perf 12½ are fiscals. The imperforate 3-pence, No. 3a, must be bought with very wide margins, for there are perforated stamps with fine margins; the imperforate 1- and 3-pence, with star watermark, are essays.

1859–64. Portrait in an oval. Nos. 8 to 13.
Originals: 18½ x 22 mm, recess print engraved with oval background made of extremely fine shade lines; the diadem has three rows of more than twenty pearls. Star watermark for the 1862 issue and "C C" Crown for that of 1864.

Forgeries: lithographed, crude counterfeits with shapeless center background and lateral ornaments; the diadem has three rows of nineteen or twenty pearls in one row, seventeen and nineteen in the others. Imperforate or arbitrary perforation. No watermark. The 1-penny was counterfeited in Geneva, also without watermark; 18¾ mm wide; the center oval shade lines are touching each other; the pearl above the letter "E" is misshapen.

Fiscals: different shades.

1867. 1-shilling green. No. 14. *Fiscals:* shades other than green.
Fake: shade of the fiscals changed to green.

1869–70. Overprinted stamps. Nos. 15 to 26.
Forged overprints: comparison is indispensable.

Official stamps (1904). Nos. 1 to 6. Same observation.

Netherlands

I. Imperforate Stamps

1852. Portrait of William III. Nos. 1 to 3. *Sheets* of 100 stamps in four panes of twenty-five, divided by a 1 cm gutter.

Select: four margins, about 1 mm wide. The margins are indispensable for plating.

Watermark: post horn, one per stamp.

Paper: handmade, wove, very thick (135–55 microns), but the paper used for the 5- and 10-cent, which seems thick by comparison, is not so thick (85–120 microns).

Essays: black, no watermark, on white card paper, very fine impression (5-cent). There also are watermarked essays on blue-tinted paper, without gum: four shades for the 5-cent, six shades for the 10-cent. One watermarked essay of the 5-cent is black.

Plates: distinctive plate features include many exceptions. Since a detailed description of them would take too long, the reader is referred to specialized works. See the illustration for characteristics that differentiate copies from the various plates.

Plates and shades: 5-cent, Plate I (1852), dark blue and steel blue; first printing, dark blue on cream-colored paper: very rare. Plate II (1853–54), less contrasting steel blue (slate tint), and intermediate steel blue. Plate III (1856–57), very dark blue (blue-black or indigo); rather bright dark blue; cobalt; blue and pale blue (in all the dark blue shades, the paper is heavily tinted on the back of the stamp by the impression). Plate IV (1859–61), greenish pale blue, milky blue, and various blues. Plate V (1861?), greenish blue and cobalt. Plate VI (1862), dark green-blue on the usual paper, and the last printing, blue and pale blue, on thinner paper. Plates I, V, and VI (thin paper) are less common.

10-cent, Plate I (1852), good impression; bright shades in the first printings, followed by duller tones. Plate II (September 1853), bright shades. Plate III (October 1854), bright and dark carmine-tinted shades; also brownish ones from oxidizing or gum. Plate IV (April 1865), same shades, also rose red and bright carmine-tinted rose. Plate V (August 1857), carmine-

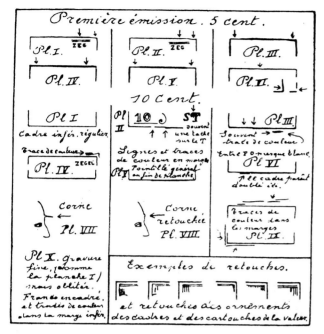

Netherlands first issue. 5-cent. Left column: lower frame normal. Color spot. Horn. Plate X, fine engraving, like Plate I, but FRANCO framed, and traces of color in lower margin. Center column: often a spot on the "T." Lines and traces of color in margins. Plate V: general stippling, end of plate. Horn retouched. Right column: often color trace. Almost blank between "P" and "O." Frames seem double here. Traces of color in margins. Examples of retouching and retouching of ornaments, frames, and value tablets.

tinted red on yellowish paper; carmine-tinted shades and reds, also light carmine-tinted rose on cream-colored or white paper, dull rose, pale rose. Plate VI (October 1860), light carmine-tinted rose, bright and dark carmine-tinted rose. Plate VII (May 1861), horns on forehead; bright carmine shades, carmine, and carmine-tinted rose; field of dots over entire stamp surface in the last printing. Plate VIII (August 1861), retouched horn; dark carmine and carmine-tinted rose; frequent dot fields, but less pronounced than in Plate VII. Plate IX (January 1862), rose red and relatively dull pale rose red. Plate X (June 1862), light rose and dull rose. The bright carmine-tinted rose and the bright reddish rose are rare.

The stamps of Plates I, II, VI–X (thin paper only) are least common. Those from Plates V and X (usual paper) are most common. Plate IX stamps are very rare mint, and are not very common used.

15-cent, a single plate: dark orange, orange, orange-yellow, and pale orange-yellow. There are various retouchings done to repair the top and bottom frame.

Value of shades: a few shades are very rare, depending on the plate they belong to. Only specialization can help one to recognize them.

5-cent milky blue: 2M, 3U. Steel blue: 4M, 4U. Blue-black: 50M, 50U. Intermediate steel shade (Plate II): 3M, 2U.

10-cent dull red (Plate V): 50M, 2U. Bright carmine-tinted red: 50M.

15-cent. The saffron-tinted shades are in demand.

Varieties: quite visible retouching: 50M, 2U. Rare retouching, on the 10-cent: 50M, 3U.

Thin paper: 50U. Worn plate: 50M, 2U. No. 1, double print: very rare.

Pairs: 4U. Blocks of four (5-cent): 8M, 60U; 10-cent: 8M, 80U; 15-cent: 6M, 25U.

Cancellations: first of all, there is the early Dutch Type A postmark without a year date: 50U, followed by Type B, with year date, from the beginning of 1852. This type was changed in 1854 (Egyptian typeface and larger FRANCO). In 1860, Type E, FRANCO is framed (rare on Plate III of the 5-cent). A smaller format cancel was used experimentally from 1856 (?). There are also Type C cancels of various kinds, rare: 3U. Type D, small, unframed FRANCO: 3U; in blue, 5U. Cancellations with date, Type B, in red or blue: 5U. Mobile (railway) cancellations, N. R. SPOORWEG, or H. SPOORWEG, rare: 6-8U.

Fakes: lightly canceled stamps are cleaned with solutions and regummed. It seems quite useless to present a detailed description of the process here. Sometimes gold-filled traces of the operation can be seen. Use a magnifying glass or a microscope.

Reprints: Moesman (1895). Plate IV of the 10-cent, not very clear-cut impression, thick, unwatermarked, white paper. Various shades. Other reprints, which were made from a lithographic reproduction of a block of twenty-five stamps of Plate IV, have the word NADRUCK on their back.

Perforated Stamps

1864. POSTZEGEL inscription. Perf 12½ x 12. Nos. 4 to 6. Sheets of 200 stamps in two panes (10 x 10).

Select: stamps centered. Copies in which the perforations do not encroach upon the frame are exceptional.

Paper: (1) handmade, hard, thick, wove: Utrecht printing (July 1864, 5-cent; May 1864, 10-cent; January 1865, 15-cent). (2) Machine-made, thin, wove: Haarlem printing (December 1866).

Shades: 5-cent, Utrecht: blue, bright blue, dark blue, greenish blue; Haarlem: indigo blue and very dark blue. 10-cent, Utrecht: more or less carmine-tinted rose; Haarlem: all carmine shades to dark carmine. 15-cent, Utrecht: orange, bright orange, dark orange; Haarlem: orange-yellow; saffron-tinted yellow.

A.- Ob. a date, sans millésime. B.- id. avec millésime

APELDOORN

HOOG · SOEREN

c.- Nom de ville sur une ligne

FRANCO
FRANCO
FRANCO

D.- Franco, non encadré. E.- Franco encadré. F. id. non encadré, grandes lettres.

:·: 44 ·:·
AMSTERDAM
ROTTERDAM 3 APR 70 8-5N

G.- Chiffres et points. H.- Nom de ville encadré. I.- Petit cachet à date, 2 cercles.

AMSTERDAM 18 NOV 98 5-6N
ZWOLLE 11 NOV 72 FRANCO
APELDOORN 21.1.14. 7-8N 2

J.- Grand cachet à date. K.- à date, avec Franco. L.- Cachet moderne.

Netherlands cancels: A. Date cancel, no year.
B. Date cancel, with year. C. Name of town on one
line. D. Unframed FRANCO. E. Framed FRANCO.
F. Unframed, large capitals. G. Numerals and dots.
H. City name framed. I. Small postmark with date,
two circles. J. Large postmark with date. K. Dated,
with FRANCO. L. Modern postmark.

Varieties: the principal varieties are engraving defects and their retouching, which occur especially in the left frame of the 5-cent: 3–5U. Sometimes they are found in the right frame: rare. The whole outer frame, redrawn: very rare. 10-cent, left frame redone: 2–5U; others: rare. 15-cent, a few frame repair defects. Nos. 4 and 6, double print: very rare.

The occasional brownish paper coloration comes from the gum.

Cancellations: Type E: common. Type I: very rare, 20U; 15-cent: 10U. Type C in red: 8U. All others: very rare.

Pairs: 4U. Strips of four are very rare. Blocks of four, 5-cent: 12M, 80U; 10-cent: 10M, 120U; 15-cent: 12M, 30U.

Reprints: none. There are essays on card in the Utrecht set: rare.

1867 (October 1). Portrait facing left. Nos. 7 to
12. *Sheets* of 200 stamps in two panes (10 x 10).

Emission de 1867. T. I. Planche de Voorschoten.
(les parties blanches seules reproduites ici.)
→5 (5c) 1 (10c) 15 (15c) →2 (20c) 2 (25c) (50c)
T. II. Planche de Haarlem.
→5 1 15 →2 2

Netherlands issue of 1867. Type I. Voorschoten plate
(only white parts reproduced here).
Type II. Haarlem plate.

Plates: recognizable by the value figures. Voorschoten printing (J.W. Van Kempen firm), Type I or Plate I. Haarlem printing (Enschede firm), Type II or Plate II. (See illustration.)

The 20-, 25-, and 50-cent stamps were issued October 1, 1867, the other values after depletion of the values of the preceding issue.

You will observe that in Plate I the top lines of the "1" or "5" are not well joined. (See illustration; use magnifying glass.)

Perforations: $12^1/_2$ x 12; $10^1/_2$ x $10^1/_4$; $13^1/_2$; 14; $13^1/_{12}$ x 14. These perforations are more or less rare, varying not only with the values, but also with the plate. The following scale can be used as a base for rare types; the price range for other values is as in the general catalogues:

Perf $12^1/_2$ x 12, Plate I, 5-cent, mint: 7 florins, used: 7 florins; 10-cent: used: 0.50 florins; Plate II, 10-cent, mint: 12 florins.

Perf $10^1/_2$ x $10^1/_4$, Plate I, 10-cent, mint: 250 florins, used: 75 florins.

Perf $13^1/_2$, Plate I, 5-cent, used: 3 florins; 25-cent: very rare.

Perf 14, Plate I, 5-cent, mint: very rare, used: 35 florins; 25-cent: very rare, mint or used.

Perf $13^1/_2$ x 14, Plate I, 5-cent, mint: rare, used: 2 florins.

Varieties: one finds white, yellowish, or blue-tinted paper in the second plates of the 5- to 20-cent stamps, perf 14 and $13^1/_2$ x 14. Same prices.

All values exist imperforate (Type II). Buy in pairs: there are larger format stamps. Each set of pairs: 200 florins. A few plate flaws, chiefly color dots in the lettering or in the rest of the design: 25U.

Cancellations: Types G and E: common; with date: in demand. Type D: rare. Type H: 3U. Others: rare.

Reprints: none.

The 5-cent perforated black is an essay of Type I; the 25-cent red, an essay of Type II.

Pairs: 3U. Blocks of four, 5-cent, mint: 15 florins, used: 6 florins. 10-cent, mint: 20 florins, used: 12

florins. 15-cent: extremely rare, mint and used. 20-cent, mint: 200 florins, used: 150 florins. 25-cent, very rare, mint and used. 50-cent, mint: 100 florins, used: 75 florins.

Forgeries: the 50-cent stamp was well counterfeited in Brussels (G. de S.). The inner corner and center background cross-hatching is too visible (vertical lines, which are not very visible in the original). The dotted lines between the temple and the ear are neither parallel nor regular. The same is true for the bottom of the neck, where an unshaded area (not in the original) can be seen. The left edge of the lettering is not as fine as in the originals. Perf 12½ x 12. Often canceled, Type C, No. "91." The whole set was typographically counterfeited very deceptively by means of clichés that were quite similar to the one used for the Brussels forgery. The vertical lines of the cross-hatching are too visible in the corners and around the circle (compare with an original). Noncongruent format; good shades, reasonable perforations. Forgeries manufactured in blocks; offered for sale both perforated and imperforate.

1869–71. Coat of arms. Nos. 13 to 18. *Sheets:* as above. Stamps for printed matter were typographed.

Shades: ½-cent brown; dark brown: 2M, 2U. 1-cent black; 1-cent green; pale green. 1½-cent rose; bright rose; 2½-cent lilac; dark lilac: 50U.

Varieties: numerous plate flaws, most of them not very interesting; special: 1-cent black with a dot after CENT.: 2M, 2U. No dot in the lower left corner: same value. 1-cent green, same flaws: 5M, 5U.

Blue-tinted paper, perf 13¼: double value.

The ½-, 1-, and 2-cent stamps are found on striated paper. The 2½ cent, on thin paper. The ½-cent black and the 1-cent on very thick paper are essays. All values exist imperforate. Buy them in pairs. Value: 4 florins M and U.

Perforations: 13¼ and 13½ x 13¼; usual value. Perf 14: ½-cent brown: rare, mint, 20 florins, used; 1-cent green: 10M, 10U. 1½-cent: 2M, 2U; 2-cent: 2M, 2U; 2½-cent: very rare: 50M, 30U.

Cancellations: Type K, common. Type C: rather common. Types B, I, H: 2U. Type D: 3U. Others and color cancellations: rare.

Pairs: 3U; blocks of four, mint: 10M, used: 10U for Nos. 14, 16, and 18; 20U for the others.

1872–88. Portrait facing left. Nos. 19 to 29. *Sheets* of 200 stamps (10 x 20); the 2½-gulden, sheets of fifty (10 x 5). Typographed.

Shades: numerous.

Perforations: 14, 13¼; 13¼ x 14; 12½ x 12; 11½ x 12, all with small holes. The 5- and 20-cent, perf 14 are very rare. Large-hole perforation: 14; 13½ x 13¼; 12½ x 12; 11½ x 12; 12½; 20- and 50-cent, perf 14: very rare.

Varieties: a few plate flaws — white spots in the hair, frames, etc.

The 5-, 20-, 25-, and 50-cent stamps are found on thin paper. The imperforates are essays.

Blocks of four: 6M, 8U.

Cancellations: Types I, G: common.

1876. Large numerals in circle. Nos. 30 to 33. Sheets of 200 stamps (10 x 20), typographed, from a woodcut. Stamps for printed matter.

Perforations: various. The ½-cent, perf 14: very rare.

Varieties: the ½-cent has two types: Type I, thick fraction bar (8¼ mm long); Type II, thin bar (9 mm long). The latter is rare in all perforations. A few plate flaws, spots, lines, or black or white dots are known.

1891–97. Portrait without diadem. Nos. 35 to 38. *Sheets:* like 1872 issue. Values in gulden. Sheets of fifty (10 x 5). Numerous shades.

Perforations: 12½; 50-cent and 1-gulden, perf 11 and 11 x 11½; 2.50-gulden, perf 11, 11½, and 11 x 11½; 5-gulden, perf 11.

Varieties: a few plate flaws. The 5-cent orange essay is known canceled: rare. The 5-cent blue and the 20-cent green on coarse, yellowish paper are essays.

Cancellations: Type J: common.

Official forgeries: 5-cent blue, lithographed. This one seems crude if it is compared with the original's design and line finesse; the word CENT and the format are not congruent.

Forgeries (Geneva, F.): 5-gulden olive and red, imperforate or with noncongruent perforation. Olive-green pearl circle; first "D" of NEDERLAND is too high; nostril lines are too short; etc.

1898–1907. Portrait with diadem. Nos. 49 to 64. *Sheets* of 200 stamps (10 x 20), but dual color stamp sheets: 100 stamps (10 x 10).

Varieties: numerous plate flaws.

Subsequent issues. These are adequately described in the general catalogues.

1913. Paris forgeries (C.). 10-gulden orange on yellow, recess printed. The cross-hatched background of the original is very well defined and has well-formed squares, whereas the forgery has dots of varying dimensions that are more often round than square. The eye is made of a full, heavy line, and all the face and neck shading lines are almost as thick as the thick lines inside the ear (half as thick in the authentic stamps). Large dots are touching the edge of the pearls in the pearl necklace, whereas in the originals these dots are quite small (use magnifying glass) and do not touch the pearls, except, occasionally, the fourth pearl, counting from the left. The nostrils of the lion on the right are made of a slanted line (right nostril) which is too far from the dot that forms the left nostril (in the originals, there are two close-set slanted lines). The stamp's lace border is made of quite rectilinear sections in the authentic stamps; this is very inexpertly executed in the counterfeit. Finally, one can note that if the widths are practically the same, the forgery is about $^1/_3$ mm higher.

1919. Fake. 5-gulden, No. 97, with cleaned overprint. That acid-treated bastard still has traces of the cleaning on it.

III. Postage Due Stamps

1871. 5-cent and 10-cent. Nos. 1 and 2. 5-cent brown on orange and 10-cent violet on blue. No. 1 brown on yellow is worth 30M and 20U; the shade is light yellow. No. 2, perf 12$^1/_2$ x 12, is worth 4M, 4U. The imperforate stamps are essays.

Forgeries: lithographed on thick paper. Noncongruent design, especially the rings and the inscriptions.

1881. Same type. Blue on white. Nos. 3 to 11. There are four types:

Type I. 34 rings. The "T" of BETALEN in the middle of a ring.

Type II. 33 rings. The "T" of BETALEN between two rings.

Type III. 32 rings. The "T" of BETALEN on the left of a ring.

Type IV. 37 rings. The rings not so wide; word PORT is thicker.

Forgeries: 1-gulden, No. 12. Lithographed, perf 11 x 11. Inscription lettering differences: center stroke of "E" of "TE" as long as the bottom stroke, upper stroke of the first "E" of "TE" as long as the lower stroke, letters of GULDEN much too thick; frame white lines too thin; etc.

The whole set was specially counterfeited in Geneva (F.) for the Indies, Curaçao, Surinam, and also for the Netherlands, Type III. Neither the rings nor the white frame lines nor the white circles have the uniform thickness of the originals. Perforations don't match the originals. Comparison of lettering, especially the "E," will quickly expose the fraud. Width 18–18$^1/_4$ mm instead of 17$^3/_4$–18 mm, and height 22–22$^1/_4$ mm instead of 21$^4/_5$–22 mm. Slightly yellowish gray-tinted paper.

Fakes: center cut out and replaced by the center of a higher value stamp!

Subsequent issues. Forgery of the 6$^1/_2$-cent ultramarine, No. 18. Comparison indicated.

Forged overprints of Nos. 26 and 40. A few counterfeits of overprinted Nos. 27–39. Comparison is necessary.

Telegraph stamps, stamps for steamship safes, and for money orders are not in demand.

Netherlands Antilles (Curaçao)

1873–89. King's portrait. Nos. 1 to 12. *Originals:* typographed; bluish (first printing) or stippled white paper, about 70 microns thick; 18$^3/_4$ x 22$^3/_4$ mm; various perfs, from 11$^1/_2$ to 14. The whole portrait (forehead, nose, ears, cheek, and neck) is covered with fine shading; in the center background, the thick or fine horizontal shading is regular; in the background, the burelage not only has large lozenge-like dots, but all the lines are less accentuated also.

Early forgeries: wove, yellowish paper of allowable thickness; wide margins (1 mm); 19–19$^1/_4$ x 23 mm; perf 11$^3/_4$ x 13$^1/_4$. No finesse in execution; face and neck, totally or partly lacking in shading; the top of the head, under letters "AC," has a white spot. The shade lines of the center background often are jumbled on the left and broken on the right. The large background dots are oblong rather than lozenge-like. The rest of this background is insufficient (a few small round dots scattered around, except under CENT, where the design is more successful). Dull shades. Forged cancellations (with outer circle arcs; see the following "Postage due stamps") are unevenly or partly applied.

1896. 2$^1/_2$-CENT overprint. No. 25. *Forged Geneva overprint* applied on forgeries.

Postage due stamps, 1899. Nos. 1 to 10. *Originals:* stippled white paper. Width, 17$^3/_4$ mm: yellowish green shade or stippled yellowish paper; width, 17$^7/_8$ mm, yellow-green shade. Height, 22 mm. Perf 12$^1/_2$. The printing of the design has left traces of indention (look at the back of stamps, especially the new ones). The figure terminal lines are finely executed (figures "1" to "4"). The corner design under "TE" is regular; the inscription letters are sharply incised. There is a rather regular color rectangle (see the illustration) in the loop of the "P" and in the "O" of PORT.

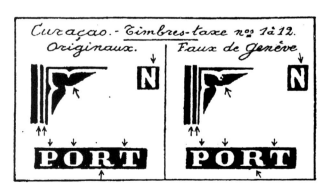

Curaçao. Postage due stamps. Nos. 1–12. Originals. Geneva forgeries.

Geneva forgeries: the whole set was photolithographed from the cliché used for the Netherlands Indies counterfeits, but, either because of a bad transfer or bad retouching of the cliché's defect under the letters "TE" (see Netherlands Indies), there is, under these letters, a no less serious defect in the triangular-shaped blank design. Wove paper, allowable shade and thickness; Type III; 18 x 22 mm. Perf 12¹/₂. Somewhat too pale yellow-green. Irregularly drawn letters: see the "N" of BETALEN and PORT.

Forged cancellation of the model described for the Netherlands Indies (woodcut, excessively gray ink): CURAÇAO 5 3 1890 and PARAMARIBO 2 7 1890.

Another photolithographed set: well executed and really deceptive, but perf 12¹/₂ x 12. The paper is too yellow, too common; figures are lithographed.

Finally, a *third photolithographed set* on real yellow paper, with vertical stippling, perf 11¹/₂ x 11¹/₂; 18 x 22 mm. Figures also are lithographed. On the left, near the middle of the stamp, the second and third green frames are touching and the blank circle between the center background and the chain links, on the same side, is broken.

Netherlands Indies

1864–65. Portrait. Nos. 1 and 2. Originals: recess print engraved; the relief, therefore, is proportionate to the depth of the cut (examine with magnifying glass, holding the stamp obliquely); traces of inking in the margins. The background shade lines around the portrait are crisscrossed, except top left where only horizontal lines are found; on the right of the "T" of CENT, there are four shade lines of unequal length; the shade is a relatively dark carmine; the paper is thick and yellowish, but the gum, which is thick and brownish, often modified the original shade. The perforation of No. 2 is 12¹/₂ x 12.

Early forgeries: two lithographed types, consequently no colored embossing. Type I: yellow paper and design that is so crudely drawn that even beginners could not go wrong in this sort of graphic transfer; the background shading is formless. Type II: thin, white paper; shade is too reddish; the whole background is formed with crisscross lines, and the four shade lines on the right of CENT are of equal length. Comparison of the portrait's nose and of the epaulette will reveal perceptible differences. Imperforate or noncongruent perforation.

1870–86. Portrait of William III. Nos. 3 to 16. *Originals:* typographed; very thick (first printings), or stippled white paper (about 60 microns); various perforations; 18 by about 22 mm; eighty-seven round pearls. In the lateral tablets, the caduceus wings have

four notches in them; the serpents' mouths and eyes also are quite visible (use a magnifying glass). Also, see the illustration.

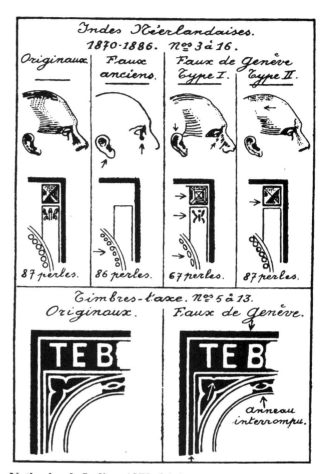

Netherlands Indies. 1870–86. Nos. 3–16. Originals, 87 pearls. Early forgeries, 86 pearls. Geneva forgeries: Type I, 67 pearls; Type II, 87 pearls. Bottom: postage due stamps. Nos. 5–13. Originals. Geneva forgeries, broken link.

Early forgeries: the whole set was lithographed. Poorly executed copies whose defects are made accessible in the illustration; round dot under the eye; the outer ear and the earlobe are unshaded; the inscription lettering is too thin; the caduceus wings have only two notches; the serpents are blind; and other parts of the design are formless. Eighty-six excessively small, irregularly formed pearls. Thick paper; imperforate or pin perf 13. Often canceled with a large circle postmark with date, a semicircle FRANCO.

Geneva forgeries: Type I. Lithographed set. Soft, downy, yellowish paper (about 70 microns). Perf 13, 14; irregular perforations. Flat, noncongruent shades. Sixty-seven oblong or rectangular pearls; this is enough to identify the set. 18 x 21³/₄ mm on average; the "2 G

50" is 22 mm high. (See the illustration, also.) The forged cancellations are semicircles (24 mm), with FRANCO at bottom, like the second type of Dutch cancellations, with millesime and date. The dates are interchangeable. One finds:

SOERABAJA	...	...	1870	FRANCO
SEMARANG	23	12	1870	FRANCO
MAOASSAR	...	...	1870	FRANCO

Type II. A photolithographed set that is much more deceptive than the preceding one. Whiter, sparsely stippled paper about 80 microns thick. Same dimensions; eighty-seven well-executed pearls. Pin perf 14. This set has the usual defects associated with the lithographic process: finesse in rendering the design is crude or is lacking completely. (See the illustration.) The cheek and neck shading frequently is composed of a succession of dots rather than continuous lines; that is caused by the lithographic stone's texture.

Forged cancellations: as in the preceding; in addition, a small square dotted polygon with interchangeable center figure (often "9" or "6").

Fake: having undergone a chemical color change, the 1-cent is found in red-brown.

1902. "¹/₂" on 2-cent, and "2¹/₂" on 3-cent. Nos. 38 and 39. Single, double, inverted *forged overprints.* A fashionable sport. Comparison is necessary.

1908. JAVA and BUITEN BEZIT. overprints. Make comparative check, as above.

1912–13. 1- and 2¹/₂-gulden. Nos. 106 and 107. *Fakes:* the corresponding values of the Netherlands 1903–8 issue (Nos. 58 and 59) were changed chemically to blue. There also are secondary fakes made with ink. Compare shade and ink spread.

Official stamps (1911). Nos. 2 to 8. "D" (Dienst) *forged overprints:* the whole set of 1891 (Nos. 23–30) was given an upright or inverted forged overprint, and, being exceedingly well counterfeited, it is found in a great many collections. The circle conforms to an allowable dimension, but the letter "D" is a bit less wide than it should be; the ink, which is somewhat too greasy, is too transparent; the irregular indention suggests that a handstamp was used; no doubt wishing to give good measure, the counterfeiter also overprinted No. 28 (30-cent). Compare as for the provisionals of 1902.

Postage due stamps. No. 1. *Fake:* the Netherlands postage due No. 1 was bleached chemically to make a rare Netherlands Indies postage due stamp, but the former is perf 13 and the latter, 13 x 14; this information, along with the arbitrary shade, easily will expose the fraud.

Postage due stamps of 1882. Nos. 5 to 13. *Originals:* stippled paper, various perforations; four

types, rose or vermilion-tinted rose shades. The inscription lettering is regular and clear-cut; the links are regular; the inner lateral frames are thin; and the corner ornaments have quite regular white reentrants (directed inwardly); average width, 18 mm.

Geneva forgeries: lithographed dual color stamps, reddish rose shade. As a consequence of the printing method used, neither the frame nor the black figures show any trace of indention. These counterfeits belong to Type III; they are rather deceptive, and, the originals being common usually, they easily find their way into collections. Width, 18¹/₈ mm; insufficiently stippled paper, allowable thickness, perf 11¹/₂ x 13¹/₂. Principal design defects: the "B" of BETALEN is slanted to the right; colored inner frames are too thick; corner ornament white reentrants are less pronounced than in the originals; the one under "TE" clearly is defective (see the illustration). The links are irregular; the one under the "B" of BETALEN frequently is broken (transfer plate flaw); a similar break is found in the original copies, but this minor plate defect is located more to the right. The figures also are noticeably different, but what we have just indicated concerning the rest of the design allows us to omit consideration of these.

Forged cancellations: double circle (24 and 13 mm), inner circle broken at bottom, and externally, at the four cardinal points, three small concentric circle arcs, with interchangeable dates:

BATENGLENTJIR	29	6	1886
WELTEVREDEN	6	7	1890
MAOASSAR	29	2	1888
PALENBANG	30	7	1886

Photolithographed forgeries: these forgeries are more successful than those of Geneva in that their defects are not as characteristic, but their yellowish paper, shade, perforation, and arbitrary dimensions enable one to identify them easily; compare the characteristics of the "E" letters of BETALEN (Types I and III).

Nevis

1861–79. Nos. 1 to 16. Four values, engraved or lithographed. Engraved stamps: embossing from engraving, which is visible through a magnifying glass by holding the stamp obliquely; 1861: Nos. 1–8 on grayish or bluish paper, perf 13; 1886: Nos. 9–11 (no 6-pence), on white paper, perf 15; the 4-pence is orange instead of rose.

Lithographed stamps: no embossing; perf 15 in the four values, and, in addition, vermilion-tinted 1-penny (1876), perf 11¹/₂. So, it is possible to confuse only the 1-, 6-pence, and 1-shilling of 1866 and 1876 if you cannot distinguish between an engraved and a lithographed stamp, but the 1-penny of 1866 is pale or dark red, whereas that of 1876 is pale or dark red-rose, or else vermilion-tinted; the 4-pence of 1866 is pale or dark orange and that of 1876 is orange-yellow; the 1-shilling of 1866 is blue-green or yellow-green and that of 1876 is pale or dark green.

Originals: all values have twelve slightly different types. To give an example, the lateral burelages in the 1-penny have a curve that terminates at the inner corners of the ornamental squares: the curve may terminate a little more to the left or to the right on occasion. Medium paper thickness, 75 microns. Average height, $22^1/2$ mm; average width, 19 mm, except the 1-shilling, $18^1/4$–$^3/4$ mm. (Do not measure the height of the 1-shilling stamp from the middle of the stamp, but on its sides). See the illustration for the characteristic features of the original stamps.

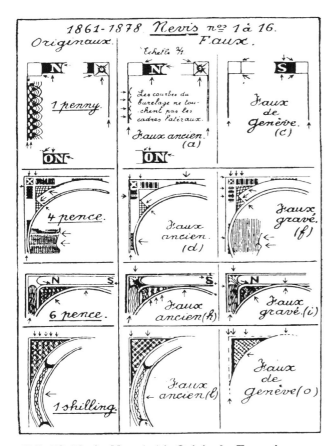

1861–78. Nevis. Nos. 1–16. Originals. Forgeries. (Scale 2:1) 1-penny. Early forgery (a). The curved lines of the burelage do not touch the later frames. Geneva forgery (c). Second row: 4-pence. Early forgery (d). Engraved forgery (f). Third row: 6-pence. Early forgery (h). Engraved forgery (i). Bottom: 1-shilling. Early forgery (l). Early Geneva forgery (o).

1-penny: the lateral frames are doubled along the burelages; the water falling from the spring is quite visible; the right hand of the sick woman is touching the ground.

4-pence: the crossed horizontal and vertical shade lines on the left of the kneeling person are characteristic; likewise, the fine and the thick lines that surround the stamp.

6-pence: the illustration shows some of the design finesse; the sick woman's right hand has no visible fingers, and its extremity is $^1/2$ mm from the inner circle; you scarcely can see anything but vertical shade lines on the left of the kneeling person; however, in the lithographed stamp and in a few engraved types, horizontal lines are visible on the left of the skirt.

1-shilling: the sick woman's right hand is touching the inner circle; the corner burelage, which is slightly different, depending on type, is a good control check point, each vertical chain of double-lined lozenges having been engraved in succession, one after the other; the outer angles of the lozenges do not always coincide with the tops of the adjacent chains.

Forgeries: 1-penny: (a) very widely circulated early forgery; lithographed; width, $19^1/5$ mm; paper, 60 microns; dark red or red-rose; perf 12, 13, or $13^1/2$; dividing frame line, $1^1/2$ mm from the outer frame; the sick woman's right hand evidently is resting on the bottom of her skirt; the vertical shade lines in the bottom of the rock on the left are rectilinear or nearly so, instead of being wavy (see illustration). (b) Another early forgery with quite visible round clouds; the rock is as dark as the persons; the nurse has an egg in her left hand, not a cup; perf 13; vermilion-tinted; the formless burelage does not show the blank lozenges seen in the originals. (c) Geneva forgery; lithographed; $18^1/2$ x $21^3/4$ mm; common, grayish paper, allowable thickness; perf $13^1/2$ x 14; dull red-rose; the spring water is not very visible; lateral frames are formed with a single line (see illustration).

4-pence: (d) early lithographed forgery; light rose, orange-yellow, or bright orange-yellow; 23 mm high; thin, transparent paper, 50 microns, or medium, 70–80 microns; dividing frame line, $1^1/2$ mm away; imperforate or perf 12–13; see the illustration for a few defects; the vertical shade lines, on the left of the kneeling person, evidently are heavier than the horizontal lines; the sitting person's right hand has a very visible thumb. (e) Forged lithographed stamp from the same source; medium paper; carmine-tinted red; same dimensions; the right hand of the sitting person has no thumb. (f) Engraved forgery; vermilion-tinted red on azure! (possibly printed also in lilac-gray); height, $22^3/4$ mm; thin, transparent paper, 50 microns; perf $11^1/2$; no horizontal shade lines on the left of the kneeling person (see illustration); the sick woman's right hand seems about to touch the inner circle! (g) Geneva forgery; dull ochre; very bad imprint; $18\frac{1}{4}$ x $21\frac{3}{4}$ mm; for paper and perforations, see forgery "c" (1-penny, above); inner circle broken in various places; absolutely formless border of thin and thick lines.

6-pence: (h) Early forgery; $19\frac{1}{4}$ x $22\frac{4}{5}$ mm; in dark gray on thin, transparent white paper (50 microns), or in pale purplish blue on medium white paper; imperforate, or perf $12\frac{1}{2}$–13; but the perforation rather resembles a line perforation; dividing frame line, 2 mm away; the right hand of the sick woman has three fingers; it is about 1 mm from the inner frame; the "S" of NEVIS was retouched (see illustration). (i) and (j) Engraved forgery, counterfeited from Type V of the sheet; $18\frac{1}{2}$ x $22\frac{1}{2}$ mm in black-gray on bluish paper (or 19 x 22 mm in gray on white paper, a lithographed reproduction of the same stamp); perf $11\frac{1}{2}$; medium, nontransparent paper (60 microns), or thin, slightly transparent paper for the lithographed forgery. In the two forgeries, the sick woman's right hand has the thumb exposed and the hand is $\frac{1}{4}$ mm from the inner circle. The "E" and "C" of PENCE are only 1 mm high, while "N" and "E" (second "E") are $1\frac{1}{4}$ mm high. See the illustration, but only for the burelages and the "N" of NEVIS. (k) Geneva forgery, lithographed in dull violet; allowable dimensions; paper and perforation as above; right hand of the sick woman is 1 mm from the inner circle; very crude, spot-forming impression.

1-shilling: (l) early lithographed forgery, $18\frac{1}{2}$ x $22\frac{1}{3}$ mm; dark emerald green (blue-green); paper, 60 microns; dividing frame lines, $1\frac{1}{2}$ mm away; imperforate or arbitrary perforations; the two chains sketched in the oval bandeau are shifted slightly to bottom left (see illustration). (m) Crude lithograph on thick yellowish paper; dot perforated; the value tablets are pointed at their extremities instead of being round. (n) Lithographed forgery in excessively pale yellow-green; allowable perf 15; noncongruent, irregular corner burelage; dots (or specks) on the persons' arms, without any line. (o) Geneva forgery, lithographed in yellow-green; the corner burelage and the outer frame are executed very crudely (see the illustration); the inscriptions are too thinly printed, especially the "I" of NEVIS, the "O" of ONE, and "SH" of SHILLING; $18\frac{3}{4}$ x $22\frac{1}{2}$ mm; paper and perforation like the preceding forgeries from the same source.

Note: The forged Geneva set frequently is canceled with the British postmark A 09 in a barred oval. I am informed by a correspondent that there also are engraved forgeries of the 1-penny. If such a stamp appears, comparison with the illustration of the originals will identify it. An engraved forgery of the 1-shilling (Geneva) measures $18\frac{1}{2}$ x $22\frac{2}{3}$ mm; the corner crisscrossing is made of double lines which go from one frame to the other; perf $11\frac{1}{2}$.

Fakes: chemical tinting of the gray paper of 1861 to make bluish paper. The fiscals, overprinted REVENUE (1876, 1-penny red or rose, 4-pence orange, and 6-pence gray; 1882-83 1-penny lilac-mauve, 4-pence blue, and 6-pence green) had their fiscal obliteration cleaned off and then were canceled fraudulently again. Comparison of the cancellations is necessary, for these six stamps possibly were circulated through the regular postal service (see Stanley Gibbons Catalogue). The REVENUE overprint sometimes was scratched off, especially on the gray 6-pence stamps of 1876 and the green 6-pence of 1883.

New Brunswick

1851. Crown type. Nos. 1 to 3. *Originals:* expertly recess print engraved, with quite visible embossing (hold the stamp obliquely); bluish paper, 85–90 microns; with the word BRUNSWICK at the top, the width is $22\frac{1}{2}$–$\frac{2}{3}$ x 22–$22\frac{1}{2}$ mm high. In three places, the crown almost is touching the single octagonal frame around it; the flower stems are pointed toward the points of the stars surrounding them; the inner point of the value squares is confused with the point of the white curved lines defining the four floral designs; this point frequently is closed. (See the illustration for certain details.)

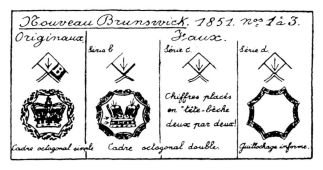

New Brunswick. 1851. Nos. 1–3. Originals, single octagonal frame. Forgeries: set b, double octagonal frame; set c, tête-bêche arrangement of figures; set d, formless cross-hatching.

Reprints (1890): rare; on slightly yellowish paper, 70 microns; gumless. The 3-pence is pale orange instead of red; the 6-pence is black-blue and the 12-pence or 1-shilling is a dark slate color.

Forgeries: set (a) successfully engraved on paper about 90 microns thick, yellowish white for the 3- and 6-pence, and bluish for the 12-pence. There are a few minor differences from the original engraving, but the shades are arbitrary, and, what is much more important, these counterfeits are much too large; width,

23¹/₂–³/₄ x about 23¹/₂ mm; the diagonal measures 33 mm, which exceeds by about 1¹/₂ mm the diagonal length of the originals. Then there are three lithographed sets and one that is engraved. (b) Crude set, easily identified by the design around the crown (see illustration); the rays of the four stars are straight instead of concave. (c) A set that was counterfeited even more crudely, with, in addition, a double octagonal frame around the crown; figures positioned in a tête-bêche arrangement, the ones on the sides being recumbent in relation to those on the top and bottom. (d) A rather successful set, on bluish paper, about 80 microns; 22 by about 22 mm; see the principal defects in the illustration; the fine machine-made crisscrossing of the originals is replaced here by dots (visible especially in the secondary stars between the flowered white stars). (e) Engraved; 23 x 23 mm; the word POSTAGE measures 14¹/₂–³/₄ mm instead of 14 mm.

1860–63. Nos. 4 to 10. *Originals:* recess print engraved; perf 12; yellowish white paper.

Early forgeries: inexpertly lithographed; perf 13; white paper that usually is too thin; fragments of dividing frame lines in the gutters near the corner of the stamps. 1-cent, the background around the oval contains horizontal and oblique shade lines; the latter are oriented northwest to southeast, instead of northeast to southwest; 2- and 5-cent, the diadem's center ornament is almost completely blank (no trace of the original cross); the crudely executed shade lines of the center

background frequently touch each other; in the 2-cent, one finds crossed shade lines in the figure ovals instead of horizontal lines only, or else the background appears to be solid. With or without hyphen after NEW; 10-cent, the Roman numerals are surrounded by a single blank circle: it should be double; 12¹/₂-cent, the smoke is behind the masts: it should be in front of them; 17-cent, the "N" of CENTS is cut, top left; the two almost vertical white lines beginning near the collar point should not touch it; they are pointed toward the middle of the "T," instead of the "N," and thus are not sufficiently oblique.

No reprints: could the imperforate stamps be essays?

New Caledonia

1859. Lithographed stamp No. 1. *Originals:* printed in sheets of fifty (10 x 5), each type being different; grayish, thick, wove, white paper; impression in black or black-gray; imperforate; gumless. The upper legend is N^LE CALEDONIE, with or without dot under "LE"; lower legend is "10 C. POSTES," 10 C. appearing everywhere with dots, but one of the dots may be missing, depending on type. The outer lateral frames are formed with a heavy thick line which divides the stamps (consequently, no lateral gutters), and with two lines with circles between them; the stamps are divided top and bottom by a line that is somewhat less

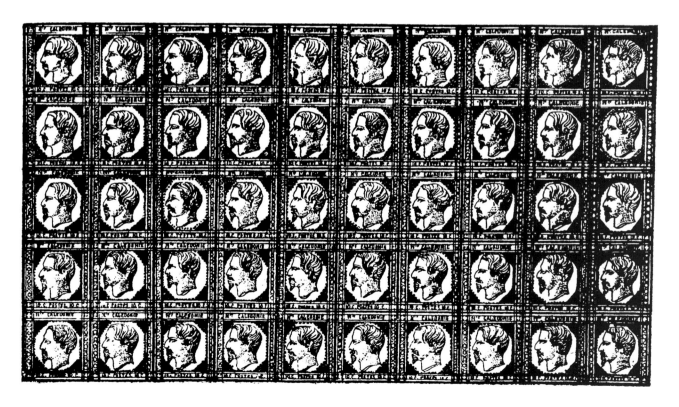

thick than the lateral frame lines. The portrait's eye most often is formed by a double line representing the eyelid, with an oblique line at each extremity; a curved line, which represents the eyebrow, touches the reentrant angle (inward directed) between the forehead and the nose line. The arrangement of the portrait in its inner octagonal frame and the eye design (see the illustration for the various types) will facilitate the identification of a great number of these crude counterfeits. Three cancellations are used regularly: (1) round, solid, but with a white cross in the middle, crossroad or ribbed cork type, like certain U.S. cancellations. (2) Postmark of blurred dots, made with the split cork model. (3) PP, this being an arrival cancellation. Franking for Europe frequently was made on passing through Sydney, Australia, with the addition of a 1-penny red stamp of New South Wales in current use. The lithographed stamp of 1859 was eliminated in 1861.

Forgeries: the many counterfeits may be divided into five main groups.

1. Direct photographic reproductions whose types evidently are similar to the original types; they easily are identified on their front by the more or less glossy layer of silver bromide, or by their shade, and, with respect to modern paper, by the grayish or brownish shade of the parts that should be white. The measurements are arbitrary ninety-nine times out of one hundred.

2. Imitation modern petit-point reproductions. Ludicrous forgeries, which are found, nevertheless, in certain collections; a magnifying glass examination of the blank parts reveals a great many symmetrical dots, which will justify the immediate rejection of these fantasies. The illustration was executed this way.

3. Lithographical or photolithographical reproductions on excessively white paper, or on yellowish paper, impression in gray, pearl gray, deep black with various defects identifiable by type examination (see especially the eye, neck stippling, lower inscription dot, dots sometimes placed near the middle of the inscription instead of at the bottom); certain designs do not correspond to any of the fifty types; noncongruent measurements; paper usually is thin or medium.

4. Photoengraved reproduction. The types are consequently congruent and the counterfeits are rather deceptive, but the paper is yellowish and thin with deep black impression. Noncongruent measurements; a few design details were affected by the impression and the inking; light indention.

5. So-called "reprints," made for the author of the original plate about 1862 with definitely different types. The printing was limited to a few sheets, one of which was in the Ferrari collection. Lacking any official status, these stamps are really forgeries.

1881–86. Overprinted stamps. Nos. 2 to 10. *Originals:* typographical overprints; in Nos. 2–5, "NCE" measures 14 x 4 mm, and in Nos. 6 and 7, 17¹/₂ x 4 mm.

Forged overprints: rather easily identifiable; comparison of lettering, ink, and print-through is useful. With regard to Nos. 9 and 10 of 1876, determine first whether the 1-franc is forged (see French Colonies, 1881). The overprints of Nos. 2–10 were counterfeited in Geneva.

1891–92. Framed overprints. Nos. 11 to 13. Large figure "10" (No. 12) measures 11¹/₂ x 7 mm, with slight differences, when the impression was applied obliquely. The two types of overprints also were counterfeited in Geneva. Nos. 12 and 13 must be checked to see whether 1881 forgeries are involved.

1892. N^LLE CALEDONIE overprint. Nos. 14 to 34. *Originals:* two types of overprints made by handstamp impression: (1) final "E" of CALEDONIE is broken (the terminal line of the top is oblique and the bottom line is too short [rare]). (2) The "E" is normal; overprint, 22 x 3 mm. As for the Peace and Commerce type (1881), make sure first whether the stamps themselves are forged. The whole forged set of this type (Geneva) was overprinted typographically by Fournier, with a single line under "LLE" and "D" with a lozenge-shaped white dot near the middle of the letter's curved line. Note: Some original stamps also received this forged overprint.

Forged Geneva cancellations: double circle, with date — (1) 24¹/₂ mm, with collection branch indication, NOUVELLE CALEDONIE 2^E/26 FEVR 92 NOUMEA. (2) Same, 22¹/₂ mm, with broken line inner circle, NOUVELLE CALEDONIE 2^E/3 SEPT 92 NOUMEA. (3) Same form, 21¹/₂ mm, without collection branch indication, N^LLE CALEDONIE 19 MAI 92 NOUMEA, in blue or black.

1892–93. Ornamented overprint "NCE." Nos. 35 to 40. *Originals:* handstamp imprint.

Unofficial *reprints* of the inverted overprints with the original impressions. That is why these overprints bring high prices on entire original covers which are dated 1892 or the beginning of 1893. The "5" and "10" overprints (no value indication) were counterfeited in Geneva. Nos. 36–40 should be checked for the possible involvement of 1881 forgeries.

1892–1900. Peace and Commerce type. Nos. 41 to 53 and 59 to 64. *Geneva forgeries:* look for these under French Colonies.

1903. Fiftieth anniversary. Nos. 67–87. *Originals:* typographical overprints.

Forged overprints (usually jumbled) on Nos. 72–80, and particularly on rare varieties. Comparison is indispensable.

1912. Stamps overprinted "05" and "10." Nos. 105 to 109. *Forgeries:* see Peace and Commerce type under French Colonies.

1915. RED CROSS. Double overprint. No. 111a. Forged double overprints on No. 111 and on No. 92 (with two forged crosses). Comparison is absolutely indispensable.

Postage due stamps, overprinted "T." Nos. 1 to 7. Numerous *forged overprints*; comparison is absolutely indispensable. First see whether the stamp is a forgery of the Peace and Commerce type.

1903. Fiftieth anniversary. Nos. 8 to 15. *Forged overprints:* see the postage stamp issue with that overprint. With regard to the 60-centime, 1-, and 2-franc, determine whether the stamp itself is forged.

Newfoundland

1857–60–62. Square, triangular, and rectangular types.

1. Square types. 1-penny and 5-pence. Nos. 1 to 5. *Originals:* recess print engraved on hard, medium, or thick yellowish paper; 1-penny, 22¹/₅ x 22²/₃ mm; 5-pence, 22²/₃ x 22¹/₅ mm; measure with the value at bottom. There are measurement differences, depending on printing and paper. As a consequence, the types are not square; it seems that after establishing an identical frame for the two values, the engraver began his work for the 5-pence on the wrong side. The illustration will give information on the principal distinguishing characteristics.

Forgeries: three lithographed sets, easily recognizable by the lack of embossing, the very unsuccessful design sketching, the dull shades, which occasionally are too dark, and by the paper, which is too finished or not hard enough. (a) Thick, yellowish paper; the point of the white curved lines does not reach the angle of the ornamental squares; the main body of the apostrophe accent is much too large; shapeless crown and flowerets. (b) White, or medium bluish white paper (65 microns instead of 85); the cross above the crown is touching the curved line above it; six pearls on the left of the crown; the upper right floweret design is arbitrary. (c) Thin, white paper; the bottom of the crown is open on the sides and contains nothing but five heavy lines; impossible to count the pearls. In addition, there is one set engraved on yellow paper of allowable thickness; 1-penny, 22¹/₄ x 22¹/₂ mm; 5-pence, 22¹/₄ x 22³/₅ mm; dark chocolate brown shade; about ten pearls on the crown's left side; very poorly executed cross; the "S" after JOHN is wider on top than on the bottom; the two curved lines above POSTAGE do not terminate in a point; figure "5"

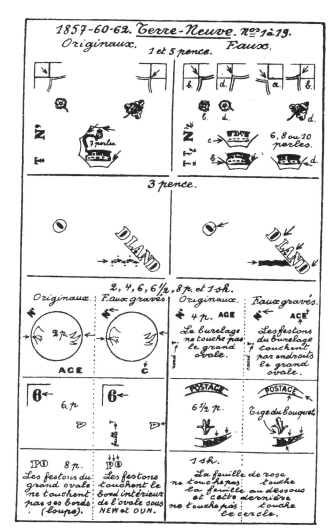

1857–60–62. Newfoundland. Nos. 1–19. 1-penny and 5-pence. Originals. 7 pearls. Forgeries. 6, 8, or 10 pearls. Second section: 3-pence. Third section: 2-, 4-, 6-, 6-¹/₂-, 8-pence, and 1-shilling. Originals. Engraved forgeries. 2-pence. 4-pence. The burelage does not touch the large oval. The burelage scallops touch the large oval in places. Fourth section: 6-pence. 6¹/₂-pence. Bouquet stem. Bottom section: 8-pence. The scallops of the large oval do not touch its edges (use magnifying glass). The scallops touch the inner edge of the oval under NEW and OUN. 1-shilling. The rose leaf does not touch/touches the leaf under it and the latter does not touch/touches the circle.

(5-pence), in the lower left corner, is upright instead of slanted to the right and is only 1³/₅ mm high instead of 1³/₄ mm.

2. Triangular type. 3-pence. No. 3. *Original:* base, 43¹/₂ mm; the other two sides, 31 mm; recess print engraved; normal spacing between NEWFOUND and

LAND; the oblique line of the "3" figures almost closes the figure's loop; the "H" of THREE is open at the bottom; the comma in front of this word resembles the apostrophe of Nos. 1 and 5.

Forgeries: well lithographed; the dot under the "T" of ST is almost invisible; the curl of the apostrophe-dot in front of the "S" is not wide enough; the "H" of THREE is closed at the bottom and the preceding comma is square; the space between the "D" and the "L" of NEW FOUNDLAND is obviously too large; base, 44 mm; left side, $31^1/3$ mm; right side of the triangle, 31 mm (see the illustration).

3. Rectangular types. 2-, 4-, 6-, $6^1/2$-, 8-pence, and 1-shilling. Nos. 2, 4, 6 to 9, and 10 to 19.
Originals: recess print engraved. Measurements vary according to printing and paper; the bouquet does not touch the center circle (use magnifying glass) or the oval of the 6-pence; in the top flower, all the lines that separate the petals, which form the five rays of a sort of center star, usually touch the petal extremities; the oval's burelage scallops, bearing the name of the colony, do not touch the inner or outer edges of this oval bandeau (a few exceptions are indicated below); finally, finesse in the printing of details is so striking that comparison with a copy of the 4-pence or 1-shilling carmine, very common mint stamps, immediately will expose all the lithographed forgeries.

Forgeries: the lithographed forgeries will be designated by "L" and the engraved forgeries by "E."

2-pence (L): bright red, red-brown, or purplish red; the lateral petals of the rose (sometimes the other petals, too) are too short; the bottom of the bouquet is touching the circle in two places; the large oval burelage is touching the edges everywhere; the letters of TWO PENCE are 2 mm high instead of $1^3/4$ mm. (E): the ovals in the burelage of the original, above and below the center circle, are lozenge-shaped; seven rather visible lozenges above and eight below.

4-pence (L): on yellowish paper; a few bouquet leaves are entirely blank; the rose is touching the circle; the dot under the "T" is square. (E): in addition to the characteristics shown in the illustration, there are numerous forged strokes crossing the letters.

6-pence (L): The white circle that surrounds the figures is very poorly executed and very weak; the rose petals do not touch the edges of the former; the burelage scallops touch points on the oval. (E): the burelage scallops are very far away from the edge of the oval under NEW and above SIX.

$6^1/2$-pence: (E): very insidious forgery; 19 x 25 mm; in addition to the characteristics referenced in the illustration, it will be observed that in the upper left corner the figure "1" is printed in lightface, and its base is not touching the oblique bar; the "2," bottom left, has no terminal loop and is touching the bar on

top; in the lower right corner, the base of the "1" is not touching the "6"; the figure "2" has a terminal loop, whereas in the original it terminates in an oblique line; in the rose, the top (north) petal is slanted to the right of the vertical downstroke of the "T" of POSTAGE instead of prolonging it; the petals of the first flower, bottom left, hardly can be counted (in the original, fourteen petals).

8-pence (E): the word POSTAGE is executed poorly (see the illustration for letters "P" and "O"); the top of the "S" is narrower than the lower loop, this word's tablet is rounded on the right, and because of this, the bottom of the tablet measures no more than 10 mm from point to point, instead of $10^1/2$ mm. The forgery measures $18^2/3$ x $24^1/5$ mm; the center circle is only $11^1/4$ mm high instead of $11^1/2$ mm; the curved shade lines in the figures are too pronounced and too visible from a distance; the apostrophe is too far from the "N" because it is not thick enough; the bottom of the "J" of JOHN is half-concave instead of flat. In the original, the burelage scallops are very near the edges but do not touch them; here they usually are too far away.

1-shilling, typographed in vermilion; numerous press failures in the delicate design structure; FALSCH at the top; no shade lines in the letters of POSTAGE. (L): no trace of shade lines in the letters of POSTAGE; the base of the "L" of NEW FOUNDLAND is oblique and is somewhat too low; the foliage on the right, under the rose foliage, is almost entirely blank; the two main bars of the "E" of POSTAGE are of equal length, whereas in the original the upper bar is shorter (Paris forgery). (E): the apostrophe is oval-like and is too narrow; no shading in POSTAGE; the rose leaf, top right, is touching the leaf underneath it; this leaf extends almost to the circle.

The average measurements of the originals: 2-pence, 20 x 26 mm; 4-pence, $19^3/4$ x $25^1/2$ mm; 6-pence, $19^3/5$ x $25^1/3$ mm; $6^1/2$-pence, $19^1/2$ x $25^1/2$ mm; 8-pence, $18^1/2$ x $25^1/4$ mm; 1-shilling, $19^1/2$ x 25 mm. As has been pointed out already, they vary with paper thickness; thus, for the 1-shilling vermilion, we have $19^1/2$ x $25^1/2$ mm; same measurements for the stamp on horizontally laid paper; $19^1/4$ x 25 mm for the good orange impression; 20 x 25 mm for the stamp on vertically laid paper.

1866–71. Various subjects, perf 12. Nos. 20 to 26.
Forgeries: various early lithographed counterfeits having nothing in common with the fine engraving of the originals; they easily are identifiable at sight (except the forged "c" of the 5-cent, which is deceptive); the paper usually is thin; perf 13 (exceptions noted below).

1-cent, perf $12^1/2$; 1 mm space between NEW and FOUNDLAND; ten white shade lines in the plaid instead of fourteen; the oval does not terminate in a point above the upper tablet.

2-cent. (a) Perf 12½; figures and inscriptions on a solid background. (b) Perf 11½, or imperforate; dividing frame line 1 mm from stamp; TWO on a reasonably solid background; three single shade lines between the fish's tail and body instead of three double lines.

5-cent. (a) 26¼ mm wide instead of 26½ mm; perf 14; the mouth is defined by a white line instead of a black one; the figure's background is executed poorly, the four fine white shade lines on each side of the figure cannot be seen; the vertical downstroke of the figures does not touch the blank loop. (b) Perf 13½, with a seal with undivided tail; top right, the seagulls or albatrosses are placed exactly one above the other. (c) Deceptive photolithographed forgery; 25⁴⁄₅ mm wide; perf 14; the fine color shading in the white line under the two FIVEs is invisible; the left fin (of the seal) has two visible "claws" instead of three; the icebergs under "L" and "A" are almost indistinguishable.

10-cent, yellowish paper; rather good counterfeit, but there is one line of pearls instead of two in the bottom of the collar under the crown.

12-cent. (a) Crude early forgery on yellowish paper with dividing frame line; no dot lines on the nose; the cheek lines do not terminate at the hair; the dot after "D" is ½ mm from that letter's shading (it should touch it); in the bottom, the curl penetrates the oval background and touches its first two shade lines. (b) More successful, but the dot after "D" does not touch the letter shading and we see only three pearls in the diadem instead of five; other defects are almost the same as those of "a" (12-cent, above).

13-cent. (a) Yellow, with dividing frame line; the three pearls above "UN" are missing; the mainmast is touching the curved line above it; rectangular and blank colors; letters "H," "I," and "R" of the value do not touch each other. (b) Orange, with the same defects but with traces of a dividing frame line in the corners and with name designation on a practically solid background.

24-cent, imperforate, or perf 13, with dividing frame line; heavy color line on the right of the nose instead of fine shading; letters "L," "A," and "N" are well separated; background horizontal shade lines are executed poorly and spaced too far apart, with oblique shade lines northwest to southeast instead of northeast to southwest; no vertical shade lines between the letters of CENTS; in the bottom of the necklace, no jewel is touching the octagon.

Fake: 5-cent blue, No. 28, chemically changed to black.

1868–79. 3-, 5-, and 6-cent. Perf 12 or rouletted. Nos. 27–34. *Forgeries:* 3- and 6-cent; lithographed on thin paper; perf 13; in the center background, no vertical shade lines on the right of the portrait, in front

of the face and neck; figures and stars are on a practically solid background; in the lower arm, there are two shade lines, then a heavy line formed by three lines in the originals; 5-cent (see preceding issue).

1880–87. Various subjects. Nos. 35 to 42. *Reprints (1896):* perf 12, like the originals; yellow gum; 1-cent, No. 35, in dark brown instead of gray, brown, or purplish brown; 2-cent, No. 36, in dark green instead of green or yellow-green; 3-cent, No. 37, dark blue (originals, same shade, but slightly different or pale blue); ½-cent, No. 39, vermilion instead of reddish rose; 3-cent, No. 42, very dark brown instead of brown.

1897. ONE CENT overprint. No. 62. *Forged overprints.* Comparison is necessary.

New Guinea

1896. Overprinted German stamps. Nos. 1 to 6. Determine first whether the stamps belong to one of the two categories of forged German stamps described under German Colonies. The forged cancellation of the Geneva set is one circle, with date, STEPHANSOKT 16-5-99, and a star.

1915. Overprinted G.R.I. Nos. 1 to 15. Numerous forged overprints. Comparison is indispensable.

New Hebrides

1920. Overprinted stamps. Nos. 58 to 69. *Forged overprints:* comparison is indispensable.

1924. Overprinted stamps: "50-c." on 25-centime. No. 75. The "50-c." was applied on 25-centime stamps of the 1911–12 issues with multiple watermark "C A" and with watermark "R F." These stamps fraudulently were provided with a multiple forged "C A" watermark in boldface and with a forged overprint to pass them off as No. 75 stamps. Overprint comparison usually will eliminate these unorthodox products; watermark comparison will speed up the diagnosis.

New Republic of South Africa

The stamps of this state were printed with a rubber handstamp. Depending on whether the hand pressure was heavier on one or the other side, there are thicker or thinner frames, letters, ornaments, like hand-applied overprints. Evidently, this impression must be considered as an oversize overprint and must be compared with reliable originals, since it was counterfeited. Specialization definitely is indicated. The 1-penny was printed in black on yellow, January 9, 1886 (very rare), and in violet on the same date.

1886. Nos. 1 to 18. *Originals:* violet on yellow; average dimensions, 24 x 32$\frac{1}{4}$ mm; perf 11$\frac{1}{2}$. Violet on gray with short line threads in the paper pulp, Nos. 19–37; same, 1886-87, Nos. 38–65. In the embossed coat of arms, the escutcheon is about 1 mm wide; other characteristics, same as Nos. 19–37.

In the stamps with embossed coats of arms, the original Dutch inscription is EENDRAGHT, REGTVAARDIGHEID en LIEFDE; the stamps are found with inverted coats of arms.

Forgeries: no correspondence with the facts given above in most cases; otherwise, make comparison. Nos. 1 (1-penny, November 3, 1886), 19 (1-penny, November 3, 1886, and June 30, 1886), and 22 (4-pence, no date) were counterfeited in Geneva with lateral frames shifted on the outer left, middle, and inner bottom right.

New South Wales

1850. 1-penny, 2-, and 3-pence. Views of Sydney.
Originals: engraved; 1-penny, Plate I, no clouds; yellowish or bluish paper; retouched plate with clouds, very yellowish, gray, bluish, laid paper, plate of twenty-five types (5 x 5).

2-pence, Plate I, vertical burelage. The worn engravings (observe the almost complete disappearance of the fine lines, clouds, and so forth) are worth about half as much as the first-class engravings. This plate was retouched (Types 10, 12, and 13–24); same value. Plate II, horizontal burelage; small dot in the center of the corner stars; bale with millesime. Plate III, no dots in the stars; bale without millesime and surrounded by a single line (Types 7, 10, and 12, double bale rope lines). Plate IV, bale surrounded by a double line; small circle in the middle of the stars; wove blue or yellowish paper and paper laid vertically. Plate V, vertical line in the fourth leaf of the fan (bottom of the circle) and a dot in the small circle that connects the fan's leaves. Same paper as for Plate IV. Twenty-four types in each plate (12 x 2).

3-pence, plate of twenty-five types (5 x 5), yellowish, bluish, grayish, wove paper, but also paper of the same shade laid vertically. No emerald shade in the last paper variety.

The three values are recess print engraved; specialization is recommended; consult special works, such as the Calman Catalogue (Volume 1, 559–62, and Vol. 3, "New South Wales") on types in the various plates; useful information concerning paper, shades, and varieties also can be found in the Stanley Gibbons

Catalogue (pp. 298–310). Imperforate stamps. No reprints.

Forgeries: 1-penny. Plate I. No clouds: (a) early lithographed forgery, thick white paper; fantastic counterfeit of the 3-pence with color cross on white cross in the corners and a single frame strip on the sides with interlacing circles; legends, POSTAGE and ONE PENNY, in red on a white background; in the circle, SIECILLUM instead of SIGILLUM. (b) Recess print engraved; no people and no legend in the bottom of the center circle, under the landscape. Retouched plate, with clouds. (c) Early lithographed forgery on thin, transparent, or nontransparent paper; SICILLUM for SIGILLUM; POSTAGE and value in lettering, 2 mm high, instead of about 1$\frac{1}{2}$ mm. (d) Early lithographed forgery, without people or legend in the bottom of the circle under the landscape.

2-pence. Plate I. Vertical burelage: (e) early lithographed forgery with SICILLUM and illegible millesime on the bale; full star in the corner. Plate II. Horizontal burelage, small dot in the center of the stars. (f) The bale has double-lined crossed ropes; millesime is illegible; burelage with single concentric curves; the inscription on the right under the right landscape is ET RURI or ET RURA instead of ETRURIA; in the blank circle, the word CAMB is barred with a blue line on top; thin, transparent, white paper. Plate III. No dot in the stars. (g) Fantasy of the 3-pence, as in Type a (above) of the 1-penny stamp. (h) Engraved, as in Type b (above) of the 1-penny. (i) Engraved; inscription SIGILLUM NOV CAMB. AUST. is placed entirely in the lower half of the blank bandeau surrounding the center background. (j) Lithographed in dark gray on thin, transparent, white paper; crude counterfeit of Type 18; the total width of the "P" of PENCE is only 1$\frac{1}{4}$ mm instead of about 1$\frac{3}{4}$ mm; the dividing line between the fifth and sixth leaf of the fan is double; no blank or colored line above POSTAGE and under the value.

3-pence. (k) Fantastic counterfeit of the 3-pence, which is similar to Type a of the 1-penny and Type g of the 2-pence; horizontal shading lines above and below the center circle instead of curved burelage; no bale, no people, and no inscriptions under the landscape. (l) Engraved, like Type b of the 1-penny stamp. (m) Lithographed; seven horizontal lines between the circle and the value; the bale has a large spot near its middle. Note: if other forgeries or more refined modern ones were found, consultation of the reconstituted plates would be indicated if paper and shade examination reveal nothing troublesome-which is more than improbable.

1851–54. No watermark; imperforate. Nos. 8 to 15. *Originals:* engraved; plates of fifty types (10 x 5). Various kinds of paper: see Stanley Gibbons Catalogue (1928).

Forgeries: 1-penny. Lithographed, no watermark; crude counterfeit printed from the 3-pence since it has a colored line above and all along the POSTAGE tablet; the white line above the value tablet is $1/2$ mm wide instead of about $1/10 - 1/8$ mm. This forgery, which was printed in blocks, has several varieties.

2-pence. Bad lithographed counterfeit which does not have, under NEW and WALES, the half-dozen circle arcs that are seen joined to the frame of the tablets bearing these words. No watermark.

3-pence. Lithographed; no watermark, like the preceding ones; twelve leaves in the laurel diadem instead of fifteen; the small star rays are insufficient in number, and the chignon does not have the characteristic double-headed book form or the form of an inverted "S" shown in the originals.

6-pence. Lithographed; background of crossed lines without curved lines. Recess print engraved; very visible vertical background lines crossed by oblique lines that are not so visible; usually bluish paper; the line above SIX PENCE is heavier than that of the inner frame above it.

8-pence. Engraved on bluish paper; margins almost 3 mm wide; corner stars not very visible; value tablet is oval, as in the 1-penny, 2-, and 3-pence stamps, not rectangular; vertical line background instead of wavy lines. On the engraved stamps, triple oval cancellations; axes of outer oval: 29 x $18\frac{1}{2}$ mm, with letters "N.S.W" without a period after the "W."

There is a set of so-called "reprints," which are really private reprints on stolen plates, having no official status. However, they may serve as references for the types; plates of fifty types (10 x 5), except for the 6-pence, twenty-five types (5 x 5) with various minor differences produced by retouching or reengraving; paper is too thick; gumless; the 2-pence, in dull blue instead of dark blue; the 6-pence, in very dark brown, or in pale brown on azure instead of brown or yellow-brown; the 8-pence, dull yellow instead of yellow or orange, the latter also on azure. The 8-pence blue is an essay...of those forgeries, printed in 1885.

Same issue with watermark. 1-penny, 2-, and 3-pence. Nos. 16 to 18. See the forgeries previously described; they lack a watermark, which is enough to check them out.

1856. Portrait with diadem. Imperforate. Nos. 19 to 25. (and)

1860. Portrait with diadem. Perforated. Nos. 26 to 35. *Forgeries:* 5-pence, early lithographed forgery; the center background is solid instead of being stippled; the "T" of POSTAGE is exactly in the axis of the "T" of SOUTH instead of being a bit to the right; no stippling on the front part of the neck.

5-pence, engraved, very deceptive; 25 x $25\frac{1}{2}$ mm instead of 25 mm square; forged embossed watermark;

on the left of NEW, there are five small lines in the blank circle instead of three; four shade lines on the white of the eye; the curl above the "F" of FIVE and the burelage on all four sides are not in conformity with the originals; in case of doubt, compare with a very common No. 29. Same cancellation as on the preceding engraved stamps.

5-shilling, No. 32, crude lithographed counterfeit; no watermark; the very poorly constructed background of horizontal lines has blank spaces and colored spots; no shade lines on the front of the face and neck; the ear forms an "O" and the hair around the ear is enclosed on a sort of blank half-oval.

Fakes: the 1860 perforated stamps often were transformed into imperforates of 1856 by adding margins.

Reprints (1872): 1-penny, with crown watermark and "N S W" on paper of 1871, and 2-pence, with single line watermark on paper of 1862–64; these reprints often are found with the SPECIMEN overprint.

1882–85. Nos. 45 to 58. *Reprints* of all values, except the 5- and 9-pence, Nos. 49 and 52, and 10-shilling, No. 56. All of them with REPRINT overprint. The stamps overprinted with official "O S" also were reprinted.

Geneva forgeries: 5-shilling, No. 55; the "W" of NEW, on the left, is shaped very poorly; the "U" of SOUTH is too small; defects in the corner burelage; center horizontal shade lines are not parallel; no watermark.

Stamps for registered letters. Nos. 1 to 3. *Originals:* plates of fifty types.

Reprints: (1) 1870: in the two shades of the value with white gum, imperforate, often with the SPECIMEN overprint. (2) 1887: in the two shades, without gum, dark shades; imperforate; on yellowish paper. (3) 1891: in red and blue; perf 10; REPRINT overprint. Numerous forged cancellations on the reprints that have no overprinting.

Official stamps (1880–92). Nos. 1 to 24. Numerous forged overprints, especially the red overprints of 1880–86. Detailed comparison is necessary.

New Zealand

First issues. Portrait, diadem, and necklace (1855–72). Nos. 1 to 36. *Originals:* recess print engraved on various kinds of paper, with various perforations and watermarks as described in the catalogues; average dimensions 19 x 25 mm. Not exactly facing the observer, the head is turned slightly to the right (to the left, looking at the stamp).

Early lithographed forgeries of 1-penny, 2-, 4-pence, and 1-shilling. The 1-penny and 4-pence stamps on yellowish paper, imperforate, or inexpertly perf 12$\frac{1}{2}$– 13; the 2-pence, on thin, bluish paper, imperforate, or dot perf about 17; the 1-shilling, on greenish paper, imperforate. All four without watermark. Lithography is far from rendering the finesse of the original engraving, in particular, the burelage of the center background, of the corner design, or of the outer background; a moment's comparison with an easily accessible original like the 2-pence blue of 1864 will be sufficient for making the decision to reject these creations. The portrait is presented full-face; there are only four or five color dots on the ermine of the left shoulder instead of seven, and nine on the right shoulder instead of ten; in the 1-penny, the "P" of POSTAGE is touching the top tablet; in the 2-pence, the same word's tablet is shifted to the left; it starts from the first downstroke of the "W" of TWO instead of starting in the middle of that letter; in the 1-shilling, on the other hand, it is shifted to the right and starts from the right downstroke of the "N" of ONE instead of starting from its middle. The same may be said for the 4-pence, where the "E" of POSTAGE is above the space between "N" and "C" instead of being above the "N."

Revenue postage stamps. Numerous forged cancellations on stamps whose pen-and-ink fiscal obliteration has been removed; microscopic examination often will reveal traces of this; if not, comparison of the postal cancellation is necessary.

Nicaragua

1862–77. Perf 12 or rouletted. Nos. 1 to 12.
Originals: Nos. 1 and 2 (1862); 22$\frac{1}{2}$ x 18$\frac{1}{2}$ mm; medium yellowish paper, the others on thinned, slightly yellowish white paper. Recess print engraved; the finesse of the very parallel shading lines which form the sky and the regularity of the lettering, without smudges, easily identify the lithographed forgeries.

Reprints (1897): perf 12 and rouletted on pure white paper. Although the shades are slightly different, comparison with reliable originals and measurement are necessary.

Early lithographed forgeries: crude counterfeits, easy to detect by the irregular sky hatching, the mountain stippling, and by the irregular, smudged lettering. One set has the word PORTE on the left instead of CORREOS. A few details of the forgeries in which the inscription is correct follows: 1-centavo, no trees in the lower left corner; 2-centavo, sky shades are not parallel; 5-centavo, (a) the two "C" letters of CINCO are too high; in one of the varieties of this forgery, the "O" of the same word is too large and the trees in the lower left corner are missing; (b) some of the value letters are

touching the top of the tablet; 10- and 25-centavo, traces of dividing frame lines; the sun rays can be seen a meter's distance away; the two bottom trees are imperceptible or are missing.

1892–93. Nos. 40 to 59. The stamps having a shade that is different from the one shown in the catalogues are not errors; they are telegraph stamps that were mistakenly nonoverprinted or intentionally nonoverprinted with a speculative purpose in view.

1896 and 1897. Geographical map. Nos. 81 to 98. *The reprints* (1899) are on thick porous paper and rarely have a watermark. The originals are on medium ordinary paper.

1898. Perf 12. Nos. 99 to 109. *Reprints* (1899): same observation.

Subsequent issues. Overprinted stamps. *The forged overprints* are rather numerous (likewise, official and telegraph stamps), and there is good reason to compare them with reliable original overprints each time; the overprinted stamp is more expensive than the stamp without overprint. 1901: the 2 CENT on 1-centavo without lateral ornaments as overprint is a reprint (No. 134). 1901: stamps overprinted CORREOS 1901, with millesime on top (overprint of Nos. 155–61) are forgeries. 1901: Overprints with CENTAVOS instead of CENT (Nos. 142–54) are forgeries. 1902: Nos. 176–78, imperforate, are essays.

1903–4. Black center, Nos. 179 to 186. The so-called "color errors" of Nos. 179–82 are illegally sold, unissued stamps.

1908. CORREOS–1908 overprint. To be compared especially on the 1-centavo, for this stamp was overprinted fraudulently in blue with a handstamp, 35 mm.

Note: The original stamps of the first issues, especially on the higher value stamps of 1869–99, frequently were given the forged Geneva cancellation: double circle with a supplementary, thick, outer circle (30$\frac{1}{2}$ mm), with date, ADMINISTRATION DE CORREOS 18 JUL. 18.. NICARAGUA, and two stars.

Official stamps (1896–98). Nos. 62 to 90. *Reprints* on thick porous paper with or without watermark.

Postage due stamps (1896–97). *Reprints* on thick porous paper in orange-red for the 1896 issue and on reddish violet for that of 1897. The 1-, 2-, and 20-centavo of 1896 are rare with watermark (mints), like the 10-centavo of 1897; the 20-centavo of the same issue is rare without watermark.

Cabo and Zelaya. Numerous *forged overprints;* comparison is indispensable.

Niger Coast Protectorate

Forged overprints on the first three issues, Nos. 1–19, and on Nos. 26, 33, and 34. Make comparison.

Nigeria

The cancellations of the higher value stamps must be examined carefully, for there are fiscal obliterations.

Niue

1902. Handstamped overprint. No. 1. The overprint must be compared meticulously in dimensions and ink shade.

1902–16. Overprinted stamps. Nos. 2 to 11. Nos. 1a–6 require specialization in view of the great variety of overprint types.

North West Pacific Islands

Original overprints. Three types on Nos. 1–10. Type I: the two "S"s of ISLANDS are normal (the letter's two loops are alike). Type II: the top loop of the first "S" is not as high as the bottom one; the second "S" is normal. Type III: the two "S"s are like the first "S" of Type II. Great variation in price depending on variety. Overprints on Nos. 11–20: Type I only.

Forged overprints: comparison is necessary. In a rather widely circulated set, the distance between "N" and "W" is more than 3 mm instead of 2³/₄ mm; the three lines of the overprint are divided by a 2 mm space instead of 1³/₄ mm, and the word ISLAND is 15¹/₂ mm long instead of 14¹/₂ mm. So the Type I counterfeit can be found on all values.

Norway

1855 (January 1). Lion type. Imperforate. No. 1. *Sheets* of 200 stamps in two panes of 100 (10 x 10). Typographed, lion watermark. There are seven transfer plate types, which are identifiable by the vertical shading lines.

Paper: medium, coarse, or thin paper, 2U.

Select: four margins, minimum width, 1¹/₂ mm.

Shades: blue, dark blue: 2M, 50U; gray-blue, greenish blue: 50U, and ultramarine-blue: rare.

Varieties: the abundance of plate varieties facilitates plating. The lion with a right rear double paw is the principal one: 12U. This variety was corrected after the first printing. The other varieties usually are found in the corner ornaments: white spots or design defects (lettering, blue background, etc.). A few examples are shown in the illustration.

The gummed mint stamp is exceedingly rare.

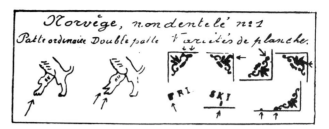

Norway, Imperforate No. 1. From left: Usual paw, double paw, plate varieties.

Cancellations: Type A, barred circle (eleven to thirteen bars): common; in blue: 2U; Type B, with date, less common; in blue: 2.50U; Type C, three concentric circles and numeral, a little rarer: 25U (Nos. 1–354; Nos. 1–382, after June 30, 1859); in blue (No. 333, etc.): 2U.

All others are rare. A black circle with fraction "L/S" in white in the middle and black dots spread around the black circle is very rare. Pen cancellations: rare.

Pairs: 5U; strips of three: 10U; strips of four: 20U. Blocks of four: extremely rare.

Reprint: an imperforate reprint (1924) in dark blue without watermark for the work of Anderssen and Dethloff on Norwegian stamps.

Forgeries: I. Bad design, crown too wide; thirty-seven horizontal lines instead of thirty-nine, and twenty-

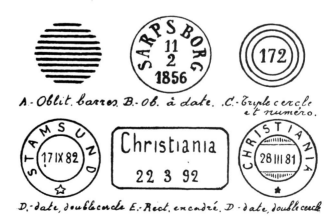

A. Barred cancel. B. With date. C. Triple circle with number. D. Double circle with date. E. Framed rectangle.

one vertical shade lines in the shield instead of twenty-four. All lines are too thick; as a result, the blank spaces are less wide than they are. Lithographed.

II. Modern forgery, lithographed; similar design; yellowish paper; lion's mouth open; figure "4" closed; thirty-five horizontal shade lines, twenty-two vertical ones.

1856–57. Portrait of Oscar I. Perf 13½. Nos. 2 to 5. *Sheets* of 100 stamps in four panes of twenty-five (5 x 5).

Paper: medium, coarse, sometimes transparent.

Shades: 2-skilling light orange-tinted yellow; orange-yellow; dark orange-yellow: 50U; 3-skilling gray-lilac: 50U; lilac; 4-skilling pale to dark blue; 8-skilling pale to dark carmine-tinted rose; bright carmine-tinted rose: M (rare), 2U.

Varieties: the 4-skilling exists imperforate: rare; also with a more or less wide ray of light in the neck; 4-skilling, bisected: very rare; 8-skilling, bisected: very rare; the last two should be bought only on cover or large piece. No. 5 with very transparent impression: 2U. The 3-skilling yellow and blue on laid paper is an essay: rare. The 3-skilling lilac-gray is a pale slate shade; when discolored by light exposure it is true gray; same shade when it is chemically faked; chemical bath too intense: dirty gray-green. 8-skilling imperforate: rare.

Reprints: the whole set (1924) on wove white paper, perf 10¼; 3-skilling pearl gray; 4-skilling dark blue; 8-skilling carmine-tinted red.

Cancellations: Type B, with date: common; in blue: 2U. The usual postmark has a horizontal bar between the day and month numerals which are all smaller. Type A, bars: 2U; Type C: 25U. Others, and foreign cancellations: rare.

Pairs: 3U; block of four: 16U. Strips are not common.

1862–66. Figure on the left only. Nos. 6 to 10. *Sheets* of 100 stamps in four panels of twenty-five. Lithographed.

Paper: less coarse than the preceding paper.

Perforation: 14½ x 13½.

Shades: 2-skilling yellow; 3-skilling dark lilac; 4-skilling blue, pale blue; 8-skilling very pale rose; rose red: 2U; 24-skilling brown, yellowish brown, reddish brown.

Varieties: the initial die had four types, which are identifiable by the figures. The 4-skilling had two plates. There are retouched 4-skilling stamps. Defective impressions: 50U. Nos. 6–9 are found with SPECIMEN in blue.

Cancellations: with date: common; in blue: 2U; Type C: 2U. All others: rare, especially ship cancellations (ALTO SCHIFFS, etc., oval). On cover: 50U.

Pairs: 3U; strips and blocks are rare.

Forgery: a crude 3-skilling counterfeit, which is not worthy of description.

Genoa forgery (I.): a typographed modern forgery, measuring 16¾ x 20⅕ mm instead of 16½–¾ x 20¼–⅖ mm.

Very white stippled paper, with wide margins (minimum width: 1½ mm); visible print-through; perf 14 x 14.

The lines which form the crown's bandeau jewels are too thin and the curvilinear lines above them cut the second and third ornament (counting from the right). It should be noted that the shading does not encroach upon the inner frame. Slightly lilac-tinted gray shades. Fine impression.

1867–68. Figure repeated. Nos. 11 to 15. *Sheets* of 100 stamps (10 x 10), perf 14½ x 13½. Typographed. Background of vertical hatch lines, not crisscrossed as previously.

Paper of various thicknesses.

Shades: 1-skilling gray-black; deep black: 50M, 50U; 2-skilling orange; 3-skilling dark lilac; lilac-gray; 50U; 4-skilling blue (various shades); 8-skilling carmine-tinted rose; pale rose (the shade of No. 9): 50U.

Varieties: 1-skilling, perf 13 x 13½: rare. 2-skilling, split, having served as a bisected stamp: very rare. Generally dark, defective impressions: 50U. A few minor retouchings of white spots, crown shading (3-skilling), and of the crown (8-skilling), etc.

Pairs: 3U; used blocks: 12U.

Cancellations: with date, common; Type C: 3U. All others, rare, including the HAMMERFEST-HAMBURG ship cancellation.

Reprints: (1924): 8-skilling bright carmine, perf 15, on very white paper. (See the Anderssen-Dethloff work for this reprint and for those of the preceding issue.)

1872–76. Figure in a horn. Horn watermark. Nos. 16 to 21. *Sheets* of 100 stamps. Values in skilling. Perf 14½ x 13½.

Shades: 1-skilling yellow-green; dark green; emerald green: 20M, 3U. 2-skilling dull blue-gray; dark ultramarine; pale ultramarine. 3-skilling, from carmine-tinted rose to bright shades. 4-skilling mauve; dark violet: 10M, 50U. 6-skilling red-brown. 7-skilling brown. A few secondary shades.

Varieties: the 1- to 4-skilling stamps have twelve different types; the 6-skilling, fifteen types; the 7-skilling, ten types for Plate I and twenty-two types for Plate II. Types are identifiable by the value lettering. 1-skilling, transparent: 50U. The dark green stamp is always transparent. 1-skilling, "E.EN": 20M, 10U.

Pairs: 3U; blocks of four: 10U.

Cancellations: round, with date: common.

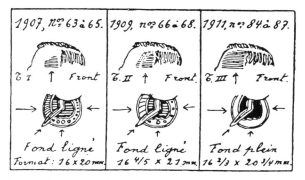

Norway issues of 1907, 1909, 1911. *Front* = forehead; *fond ligne* = lined background; *fond plein* = solid background.

1877–78. Same. Values in ore. Shaded horn. Nos. 22 to 31. This set is identified by the shaded horn and the letters of NORGE which lack terminal strokes.

Shades: very numerous.

Varieties: all values have six different types, except the 3-, 5-, 10-, and 20-ore which have twelve, and are identifiable by the value figures. The 5-, 10-, 20-, 35-, and 60-ore stamps exist without a dot after POSTFRIM: 2M, 2U; the 60-ore with a double dot after the word: rare.

Cancellations: with date, Types B and D: common, color cancellation: 2U. Others: rare.

Pairs: 3U; blocks of four: 8U.

1878. Same. Portrait of King Oscar II. Nos. 32 to 34. These three values belong to the preceding issue. No different types. They are often found with the Type E cancellation, which frequently is encountered on the subsequent issues.

1882–93. Type of 1877–78. Unshaded horn. Nos. 37 to 45. Identified by the unshaded horn. The NORGE lettering, as above. This set really comprises two different issues:

1. 1882–84. Nos. 37b, 37c, 38–42, and 44a (Yvert). Clichés 21 mm high. The 20-ore always lacks a dot after POSTFRIM.

2. 1886–93. Nos. 35a (Plate I); No. 35 (Plate II); No. 36 (eight types); No. 37a orange-red (Plate I); No. 37 orange-yellow (Plate II); No. 37 orange (Plate III), four types in each plate; No. 38 (four plates: four types, four, eight, and one types); No. 39 (six plates: the first three, four types; the last ones, one type); No. 43 (five plates: the first three, four types; the last two, a single type); No. 44 (four types of each of two varieties of small and large bottom figures). The types can be identified by the bottom inscription figures.

The 5-, 10-, 20-, and 25-ore are found without a dot after POSTFRIM.

1893–1905. Same type. NORGE lettering with serifs. Nos. 46 to 59. *Shades:* numerous. Two sets are

possible on the basis of the bottom figures (I. Central Printing Press; II. Knudsen Printing Press). A slanted line goes across the horn under the crown. This is not found in the 1910–20 issue.

Cancellations: Type D: common; Type E: less common; a triangular type PAKKEPOST with town and date: 2U.

For subsequent issues, see the general catalogues.

With regard to the three portrait issues of 1907, 1909, and 1911, the illustration will help identify them. The 2-krone, No. 86, has a little larger format than the others.

1905–8. Forged overprints of the 1-, 1.50-, and 2-krone stamps. Make comparison.

Nossi-Bé

One finds a multitude of overprints here. It would serve no useful purpose to describe the abundant forged overprints, for if there are forged overprints on single stamps, there are many that are mass-produced; some could be omitted; others will continue to be manufactured. Most of them are crude and can be judged easily by comparison; the best ones should be measured with the template and subjected to a detailed comparison. Practically all the overprints more or less were counterfeited felicitously in Geneva.

Forged Geneva cancellations: double circle (22½ mm), with date, NOSSI-BE 10 OCT 91 (and 95) MADAGASCAR; HELVILLE 22 AVRIL 09 NOSSI-BE.

1889. Nos. 1 to 9. *Originals:* Nos. 1 to 6, figures are 6²/₅ mm high; Nos. 7–9, about 4³/₄ mm.

Reprints: the overprints in ultramarine and indigo do not really belong to the regular printing in pale blue, despite the cancellations with which they obligingly were supplied. They are found on cover, but that does not disprove our contention, the overprints having been made locally right in the post office; it was the post office which, for a price, used this means to satisfy collectors whose requirements went far beyond the normal needs of the postal service.

Forgeries: for Nos. 2–6 and 8–9, ascertain first whether forged stamps of 1881 are involved. (See French Colonies.)

1890. Overprinted stamps. Nos. 10 to 18. *Originals:* the "N S B" overprint of Nos. 10 and 11 measures 8½ x 3½ mm; that of Nos. 13–15, 9 x 2¼ mm. Typographical overprints.

Forgeries of 1881: same remark as above.

1893. Stamps overprinted NOSSI-BÉ. Nos. 19 to 22. *Originals:* typographical overprint; NOSSI-BÉ measures 13½ mm; the figures are 7 mm high.

Forgeries of 1881: same remark as above; likewise, for Nos. 23–26.

1894. Peace and Commerce type. Nos. 27 to 39. *Geneva forgeries:* see the forgeries of this type under French Colonies.

Postage due stamps. Nos. 1 to 17. 1881 type *forgeries:* see French Colonies. Regarding the forged *overprints,* same observation as for the postage stamps.

Nova Scotia

1852–53. Nos. 1 to 4. *Originals:* recess print engraved; bluish paper; paper thickness and dimensions, as in the first issue of New Brunswick, but the 1-shilling stamp is somewhat smaller (22 1/3 x 22 mm); the crown type value design is like that of the Brunswick stamps, except that the rose under the crown is replaced by a flowering branch bearing four olive-shaped fruits. The apex of the corner squares, turned inwardly, frequently is broken, which means that the apex of the large uncolored curves also is broken. In the 1-penny, the center and legend backgrounds are formed with a delicate, machine-made crisscrossing.

Reprints (1890): thin, white paper; gumless. The 1-penny is brown instead of red-brown; the 3-pence is overly dark blue; the 6-pence is dark green (this shade exists in the originals, but it is different); the 12-pence is intensely dark violet.

Lithographed forgeries: crude early counterfeits which are recognizable by their lack of embossing: 1-penny, formless crisscrossing; 3-pence, nice ultramarine fantasy, in which the pearls of the crown, which is only a bit wider on top than on bottom, are more than 1/2 mm from the octagonal frame; 1-shilling, same defect; legends on a background which is not divided by a line from the rest of the stamp; this forgery is found in rose, lilac, and deep violet; 6-pence, no lines inside the letters of POSTAGE; unconvincing crisscrossing. In a good forgery of the 6-pence, the corner squares are rectangular instead of square.

Engraved forgeries: (a) same kind of expertly engraved counterfeits as those described under New Brunswick; printed in blocks of four on white paper of allowable thickness; steel blue shade; dimensions evidently excessive, 23 1/2 x 23 mm high (measure by placing SCOTIA on top). (b) Another engraved forgery; although I have seen only the 6-pence, a set probably exists; expertly engraved, but execution is less satisfactory than the preceding ones with respect to certain details; bluish paper of allowable thickness; 22 1/2 x 22 mm; the inner apexes of the figure squares are not pointed toward the apexes of the large white curves; the ornamentation surrounding the octagonal frame is not comparable to that of the originals (see the illustration under New Brunswick); there is a field of small dots which is noncongruent with the original background, under the "I" of SCOTIA and the "A" of NOVA.

1860–63. Perf 12. Nos. 5 to 10. *Originals:* recess print engraving; thick, yellowish or white paper. 1-, 2-, 5-cent, the neck point resting on the third horizontal line in the background is 1/2 mm from the blank circle surrounding the shade lines on the left. 8 1/2-, 10-, and 12 1/2-cent, background of fine horizontal shade lines, surrounded by a blank circle containing two exceedingly delicate, unbroken colored circles (use magnifying glass); the two rows of pearls have, respectively, twenty-three and twenty-eight pearls in them.

No reprints.

Early lithographed forgeries: perf 12 1/2–13. (1- to 5-cent), set (a) center background shade lines are surrounded by a circle; nose and forehead contour is indicated by a thick line; set (b) neck point is resting on the second shade line and is touching the blank circle on the left; the lower part of the eye is formed with two parallel lines (only one is needed); the colored line under the value tablet is only 1/6 mm from it, instead of 1/2 mm. 8 1/2- to 12 1/2-cent, cross-ruled center background (use magnifying glass); dot figure shading; less than twenty pearls in each necklace strand.

Geneva forgeries: rather well executed on grayish white or yellowish paper; perf 10; the word SPECIMEN often is typographed in red in the bottom of the center background (this overprint sometimes is scratched off). 1- to 5-cent, the neck point is resting on the fifth shade line; the "O" of NOVA is elevated; the "V" is closed on top; the bottom of the eye frequently is formed with two short lines (instead of a single one joined with a curved line for the front of the eye) which are separated by a thick, oblique line forming the front of the eye. 8 1/2–12 1/2-cent, necklace, first strand, fifteen or sixteen pearls, second strand, twenty or twenty-one; the two delicate circles in the blank circle surrounding the center background hatching are nothing more than vague sketches. Another engraved set is on thin grayish paper, perf 14; similar defects.

Nyasaland Protectorate

1916. Stamps overprinted "N.F." Nos. 25 to 29. In use in the Tanganyika region (German East Africa) during the British occupation. There are only six copies of the double overprint of the 3-pence in existence.

Forged overprints: comparison is indispensable.

Nyassa

1898. Stamps overprinted NYASSA. Nos. 1 to 26. Forged overprints on the 2½- and 5-reis and inverted forged overprint on the 50-reis, No. 7. Comparison is necessary. The 2½- , 5-, 25-, 80-, 150-, and 300-reis were reprinted in 1906 (very rare) for the King of Spain.

1919 and 1921. Overprinted stamps. Nos. 64 to 94. *Forged overprints:* comparison is indispensable.

Obock

1892. Stamps overprinted OBOCK. Nos. 1 to 20 (and)

1892. Postage due stamps with same overprint. Nos. 1 to 18. *Originals:* handstamp overprinted, with defective lettering imprint. The curved overprint measures about 12½ mm wide (middle to the left of letter "O" as far as the reentrant angle formed by the two downstrokes of the "K"); the height of the first "O" is nearly 4 mm.

So-called *reprints:* the curved overprint on the 4-centime postage stamp, No. 3, and on the 5-centime postage due stamp, No. 1. They are fantasies, the result of a dealer's agreement to have these impressions of the two rarest values made, as if by chance, into upright and inverted overprints. Fortunately, the rubber, burdened with years of use, had shrunk, and the first "O" was scarcely more than 3 mm high and the width was no more than about 12 mm. Although the original stamp impression is involved, it was an error to catalogue these fantasies and especially to quote prices on them, first, because their printing figure is unknown, and then because tomorrow or the day after tomorrow someone else had "reprints" that were just as special or just as unofficial made with a stamping device hardened by age, that would augur a fine future for philately...or for speculation.

Forgeries: first of all, check whether the postage or postage due stamps are forgeries. (See French Colonies.) The two forged Geneva sets (postage and postage due) were provided with forged overprints: in the carved overprint, the lower loop of the "B" evidently is higher than the upper one; in the straight overprint, which measures almost 18 mm instead of 17½ mm, measuring up to the right foot of the "K," the upper oblique line of the letter is too short. Forged cancellations on these sets: double circle, inner circle broken, with date: OBOCK 27 MARS 92 COLONIE FRANÇAISE, and the same words with 26 SEPT 92 in blue or black.

Forged overprints: numerous; some of them are executed very well. Detailed comparison is indispensable.

1892. Overprints with large figures. Nos. 21 to 31. *Original overprints:* handstamp impression applied twice on Nos. 27–31, in black, vermilion, and violet.

Forged overprints on originals with upright overprint (Nos. 12–20), especially on Nos. 22 and 27–31, as well as forged inverted and double overprints. These forged overprints also are found on the previously described forgeries. Comparison of figures (measurement, spacing) and of ink is necessary.

1892. Peace and Commerce type. Nos. 32 to 44. *Forgeries:* see the counterfeits of this type under French Colonies.

1893–94. 2- and 5-franc. Nos. 45 and 46. 5-franc original: format, 45 x 37 mm.

Forgeries: there are good counterfeits of this value; measurement identification is best.

1894. Cross-ruled paper. Nos. 47 to 64. *Geneva forgeries:* of the 25- and 50-franc stamps with forged boldface lithographical cross-ruling, shiny in light, but disappearing in benzine. Arbitrary shades. The curved line imitation perforation is broken in many places on the right side. In the tablet of "R F," there is a small white ornament with three small oblique shade lines in the lower corners (in the originals, the ornament on the right, a mask-like form, has only two lines). These counterfeits were manufactured with normal arrangement or with a 1–2 cm displacement of the center. I also have in my possession a bisected 25-franc stamp, on piece with forged cancellation OBOCK, illegible center, and at bottom, REPUB FRANC^{SE}.

Orange Free State

1868–1900. Orange tree type. Nos. 1 to 31. *Originals:* typographed; perf 14; 19 x 22¾ mm; paper, 60 microns (1868–78), 70 microns from 1883.

Forgeries: always examine the stamps, overprinted or not, to determine authenticity, and then, if they are genuine, subject the overprints to detailed comparison: forged overprints are very numerous.

Early forgeries: Nos. 1–3, perf 12½, sometimes on one side only; lithographed; 18⁴/₅ x 22²/₃ mm; paper, 55–60 microns; often canceled with an oval grill; the bottom of the "J" of ORANJE is joined with the "N" and the dot is touching the inner frame. Also, see the illustration for varied details of shading and of the horn under the foot of the orange tree. These forgeries appear to come from Geneva; they subsequently were retouched slightly and issued in arbitrary shades; always seventy-four shade lines; the "J" of ORANJE almost is

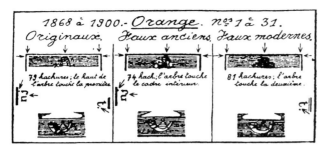

1868–1900. Orange. Nos. 1–31. Originals. 79 shade lines; the top of the tree is touching the first line. Early forgeries. 74 lines; the tree is touching the inner frame. Modern forgeries. 81 lines; the tree is touching the second line.

touching the "N"; the dot almost is touching the left frame; the "J" of VRIJ has a flat bottom instead of a rounded one; the 4-pence blue of 1878 similarly was counterfeited.

Modern forgeries: relatively recent, lithographed on very white paper; 6-pence and 1-shilling of 1868, 5-shilling of 1878, 1-shilling of 1898; all values probably will be forged in the future, and as the stamps are well counterfeited, all the known forged overprints will be applied quickly on them; allowable perf 14; $19^1/_5-^1/_4$ x $22^7/_8-23$ mm; paper, about 80 microns; the dot after STAAT is about $^1/_2$ mm from the "T" (instead of $^1/_4$ mm); see the illustration for various details; the horizontal shading lines are well executed and well spaced, but the counterfeiter, to give good measure, added a line on top and bottom (eighty-one instead of seventy-nine).

Subsequent issues: most of the overprints were counterfeited on originals or on forgeries, and thus require rigorous comparison. Types I and III of the 3-pence, No. 9, and the 1900 ORANGE RIVER COLONY overprint were counterfeited in Geneva.

Telegraph stamps. Same observations as above. *Geneva forgeries:* 1-shilling, No. 6, with the two "A"s of STAAT clogged at the top, noncongruent burelage, and forged overprint TELEGRAAF.

Panama

I. Colombia

1878. Nos. 1 to 4. *Originals:* lithographed on white paper; $18^1/_4-^1/_2$ x $23^1/_5-^1/_4$ mm; 50-centavo, $22^1/_2-^3/_4$ x 27 mm; paper of various thicknesses, 50–65 microns; the 5-, 10-, and 50-centavo, about 80 microns. The stamps have a dividing frame line that is not very visible; shades: 5-centavo green or blue-green; 10-centavo blue; 20-centavo rose; 50-centavo dark

orange. The inscription letters do not touch each other, except the value letters in which a few are joined by their serifs. In the corner escutcheons, the shade lines of the upper strip are equidistant; all lines are thin-printed and the imprint is good.

Reprints: 5-centavo yellow-green; 10-centavo blue-gray; 20-centavo red; 50-centavo yellow. Blurred impression, especially in the bird's plumage, the isthmus, and in the bottom of the circle under the ship.

Geneva forgeries: lithographed on white or yellowish paper (5-centavo), the 10-centavo with quite visible dividing frame line $^4/_5$ mm from the frame; the other values do not have this. The shade lines of the four shields are not equidistant; the lines between frames are much too pronounced; those in the peninsula are irregularly crossed. 5-centavo dark olive-green; $18^1/_2$ x 23 mm, paper 70 microns; the bird's right foot, on the left in the stamp, has only two claws; the "E" of ESTADOS is touching the bottom of the "S"; no shade lines in the upper half of the left frame, except a few dots scattered about under the shield. 10-centavo ultramarine blue; the bandeau in the eagle's beak has two heavy color lines instead of one; the value letters have practically no serifs. 20-centavo pale or dull brownish red with or without very transparent impression; the "S" and the "T" of ESTADOS are touching at top; in the sea below, the ship's masts are slanted too much to the right.

1887. Perf $13^1/_2$. Nos. 5 to 10. *Originals:* always perforated on all four sides. 1-centavo dark green or green-blue; 2-centavo rose; 5-centavo blue; 10-centavo dark yellow or lemon; 20-centavo lilac; 50-centavo brown on yellowish white paper. Average dimensions, $24^1/_2$ x $21^1/_4-^1/_2$ mm.

Reprints: gumless; perf $13^1/_2$, but frequently partial perforation; 1-centavo yellow-green; 2-centavo dark rose; 5-centavo dark blue; 10-centavo straw color; 20-centavo violet; 50-centavo light brown.

Subsequent issues. *Forged overprints:* especially of No. 20c and of Nos. 2–8 and 11–18, registered letter stamps. Comparison is necessary.

II. Independent Republic

1893–1904. Overprinted with RÉPUBLICA DE PANAMA. Nos. 1 to 7. *Originals:* handstamp impression; first line, 18 mm, second, $12^1/_2$ mm wide; total height, about 5 mm.

Forged overprints: very numerous; comparison is necessary. Also, under this heading may be included the private Panama reprints of the original model (but with RÉPUBIICA) and those of COLON ($16^1/_2$ mm, 11 mm, and 4 mm high) that were issued in arbitrary shades and were put in regular postal circulation. They have no official status, and they may be catalogued as used postal forgeries.

Subsequent issues; registered letters; Canal Zone.
Very numerous *forged overprints* that require detailed
comparison. Specializing is recommended. The
CANAL ZONE overprints on one and two lines (Nos.
1–4, 10–15, and postage due stamp Nos. 1–3) were
counterfeited in Geneva.

Papua
(Papua New Guinea)

1907–8. Stamps overprinted PAPUA. Nos. 9 to 24.
The *original overprints* measure 11 mm and 10³/₅ mm,
including the period. The first one was counterfeited on
the 4-pence and the second one in various double
overprints; comparison is indispensable.
    1901. 2-shilling 6-pence. No. 8. *Fake:* 2-shilling
6-pence of 1908 with small overprint scratched off and
replaced by a cancellation, a heavy bar of which covers
the scraped area; the use of benzine, or, for
transparency, the use of magnifying glass, will show up
the fraudulent operation.

Paraguay

1870. Lithographed. Nos. 1 to 3. *Originals:*
imperforate; paper, medium thickness (70 microns); 19
x 24¹/₂ mm (the 2-real is ¹/₄ mm higher; the 3-real,
¹/₅ mm wider; measure from the middle of the stamp).
1-real, each figure contains three dots, the middle one
of which is larger; the terminal point of the figure is
curved and slightly rounded at the end; eight shade lines
in the bonnet, which does not touch the circle; a few
background shade lines penetrate the inner circle (use
magnifying glass). 2-real, the bonnet extends a bit
beyond the sixth horizontal shade line; it has twelve
curved lines; in the corners, the letters in DOS do not
touch their frame (top right, the "D" very nearly does
touch), or the large white dot. 3-real, the background
horizontal lines encroach upon the inner lozenge in
places; the bonnet is touching the fourth line; the
northwest and southeast circles are not touching the
outer lozenge. There is no shade line between the
bonnet and the top of the lion's head in the 1-real; there
are three in the 2-real, and four in the 3-real, not
counting the one that is touching the bonnet. The pole
on which the bonnet is placed is shaded everywhere in
the 1- and 3-real stamps, but, in the 2-real, one sees
only short lines which leave a line of light on the left.
Forgeries: various counterfeits, a detailed description
of which would take too long; all lithographed; none of
them showing the distinctive marks identified with the
originals. The most widespread forgery is the 1-real,
with bonnet touching the inner circle; the "1" figures

with oblique line finishing in a point; thin paper, 50
microns. Forgery (or "private reprint," 1898) of the
2-real stamp without any official sanction, produced
from the original lithograph plate; porous paper, 80
microns; bright instead of dull blue.
    1878. "5" overprint. Nos. 4 to 6. *Original
overprints:* Types I and II overprints in dull black and
dull blue.
    Forged overprints: so-called "reprints," with no
official status, of Type I, large "5," in deep black or in
bright blue, with the vertical line of the "5" broken.
There are other forged overprints from various sources;
detailed comparison is indispensable. The overprint of
Nos. 1–6 was counterfeited in Geneva.
    1879. Lithographed. Nos. 10 and 11. *Originals:*
perf 12¹/₂; smooth, white paper.
    Forgeries: so-called "private reprints," printed on the
original plates; forged yellowish, stippled, excessively
thin paper, with gum; arbitrary shades: excessively pale
brown and dark yellow-green instead of emerald green;
forged perf 11¹/₂; 13¹/₂ (too regular) and imperforate.
    1881. "1" and "2" overprint. Nos. 12 and 13.
Forged overprints: comparison is indispensable. The
"1" overprint was counterfeited in Geneva with a
baseline that is printed too boldly and the "2" overprint
with a wavy baseline.

    Subsequent issues and official stamps. *Forged
overprints,* especially for the varieties of No. 48 and for
the official stamps, all of which must be compared
minutely.

Persia

A. No figure between the lion's paws

    1868. Essays. Four types of values were engraved in
Paris (Barre) and sent to Persia with essays: 1-shahi
violet, 2-shahi green, 4-shahi blue, and 8-shahi
vermilion or carmine; first-class impression — the fine
white line underlining the white bar on which the lion is
resting is quite visible; 18¹/₂ x 22 mm, perf 12¹/₂. The
2-shahi green (No. 1, Yvert) is known to exist canceled,
which can make it somewhat valuable, but that is no
proof of its official circulation as a mint; it is an essay
like the other three; in fact, other catalogues, notably
the Scott Catalogue, do not list it either as mint or
used. Besides, there are essays of this sort, with good
impression, often imperforate horizontally, the other
sides perf 13 (for example, 1-shahi red, 2-shahi violet,
8-shahi green, and so forth) which are rather
widespread and are valuable only as reference stamps.
    1870. Nos. 2 to 5. From these four clichés (the
values engraved in Paris), the following four *original*

values were printed in Teheran in 1869–70: 1-shahi violet, 2-shahi green, 4-shahi blue, and 8-shahi vermilion or carmine; imperforate; same dimensions as the essays of 1868; crude impression, thin paper. The 1- and 8-shahi carmine are known to be printed on both sides; and there is a 2-shahi tête-bêche.

Fakes: the above essays with trimmed perforation, first-class impression, not crude, fine white line under the entire white bar, not broken or poorly executed.

Forgeries: lithographed and easily recognized by comparing with an essay; lion's nose is open on top; no color spot in the end of the lion's tail; left forepaw, $\frac{1}{2}$ mm wide on top, instead of 1 mm; arbitrary shades; dimensions, likewise; 4-shahi with a sort of figure "2" in the circles (top loop is closed on right), positioned obliquely, instead of the visible Arabic figure in the illustration.

B. With figure between the lion's paws.

The various issues and printings (1875–76–78) come from the clichés described previously; it is therefore useful to study them concurrently.

Originals. 1875. Nos. 6, 7, 9, and 10 (Yvert). 1-shahi black; 2-shahi blue; 4-shahi vermilion; 8-shahi green; typographed in strips of four (4 x 1) on thick paper; imperforate; about 18 x 22 mm; bad impression in which half of the fan lines formed by the sun rays are invisible or poorly executed. For each value, there are four types identifiable by the shape and the positioning of the figures between the lion's paws (see illustration). Note: The bottom line, on the right of the figure, represents the lion's right rear paw; its shape is irrelevant; what is relevant is the distance that separates it from the value figure or from the large white bar. The four values are found rouletted; the 1- and 8-shahi, arc or dot rouletted.

1876. Nos. 6–11 and 12 (Yvert). 1-shahi black; 2-shahi blue; 4-shahi vermilion-tinted red and carmine-tinted red; 1-kran carmine; 4-kran yellow and orange-yellow. These values have four types like the preceding ones, but they were typographed in blocks of four (2 x 2); the 1- and 4-kran, printed like the 1- and 4-shahi, comprising thus four types of figures between the lion's paws; the vertical pairs are Types I and III, or else II and IV. Same paper as for the issue of 1876, or slightly bluish paper; same impression; imperforate, or the same perforations; same average dimensions. The 1-kran carmine and the 4-kran yellow and orange-yellow are known to exist on laid white paper (still four types); the 1- and 4-kran, printed on both sides; the 1-kran was printed in yellow (color error); finally, the 4-kran is known to exist in tête-bêche.

End of 1876. Nos. 7 and 8 (Yvert). The 1- and 2-shahi are printed this time in vertical strips of four (still four types in each one) on grayish white paper;

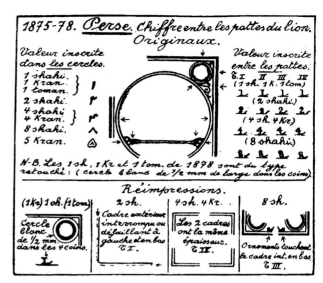

1875–78. Persia. Value figure between the lion's paws. Originals. Top, left: value inscribed in the circles. Top, right: value inscribed between the paws. Note: The 1-shahi, 1-kran, and 1-toman of 1878 belong to the retouched type (blank circle $\frac{1}{2}$ mm wide in corners). Bottom section: reprints. (1-kran), 1-shahi, (1-toman): blank circle $\frac{1}{2}$ mm wide in four corners. 2-shahi: outer frame broken or missing on left and at bottom. 4-shahi, 4-kran: the two frames have same thickness. Type IV. 8-shahi: ornaments are touching inner frame at the bottom. Type III.

horizontally rouletted; the 2-shahi is known to have the tête-bêche arrangement. This last value is considered as a color error by certain authors.

1878. February. No. 18 (Yvert). 4-kran blue or blue-gray in strips of three, Types I–III, like Types I–III of the 4-shahi of 1875.

1878. Nos. 17, 19–22 (Yvert). 1-kran carmine; 5-kran violet; 5-kran gold on white paper; 1-kran carmine on yellow; 1-toman bronze on blue, four types, the 1-kran and the 1-toman were printed from the 1-shahi of 1875 but retouched in the four corner circles (colored circle surrounded by a blank circle $\frac{1}{2}$ mm wide instead of $\frac{1}{8}$ mm); the 5-kran stamps are printed from the four types of the 8-shahi, the "8" between the lion's paws having been changed rather inexpertly into "5." In this value, the types are recognized by the more or less oblique position of the figures, by their distance from the lion's paw and the white bar; in the block of four of the 5-kran, the top pair is Types I and IV, the bottom pair, Types II and III. As in the 1876 set, the values are printed in blocks of four of the four types.

1879. January. No. 20 (Yvert). 5-kran reddish or purplish bronze, printed like the 5-kran of the preceding printing (18 by about $21\frac{1}{2}$ mm).

Note: See the illustration for various distinctive features of the original design; the end of the lion's tail always has a large colored dot; the ornamentation does not touch the lower frame, except when there is blurred impression; the pearls are regular; the white bar under the lion does not touch the pearls. In view of the number of types, paper varieties, perforations, and crude impression, the study of these stamps is rather difficult and is complicated still more by new reprints or reprints that were ordered canceled and by rather well-executed forgeries: specialization definitely is recommended.

Reprints (1885). The 1-shahi, 1-kran, and 1-toman were printed from Type IV of the 1-shahi of 1878, with corner circles retouched; figure "1" is a Roman numeral (I), and the upper horizontal line is encroaching upon the vertical line of the value figure on the right and left; see the illustration. The 2-shahi come from Type I; the exterior frame is broken or totally missing on the left and on the bottom; 17–17$\frac{1}{2}$ x 21$\frac{1}{2}$ mm. The 4-shahi stamps belong to Type IV with the large plate defect, thick white line on the bottom ornament; the two frames are uniformly thick; 17$\frac{3}{4}$ x 21$\frac{1}{2}$ mm. The 8-shahi stamps are printed from Type III; the two terminal loops of the bottom ornamentation are touching the inner frame; 17$\frac{3}{4}$ x 22 mm. The 5-kran stamps also come from Type IV; 17$\frac{3}{4}$ x 21$\frac{3}{4}$ mm. There also are reprints of the 1-kran and of the 1-toman of Type III. All values gumless or with white gum. A list of papers and shades follows.

1. Imperforate; thick, wove, yellowish white paper; 1-shahi deep black; 2-shahi ultramarine; 2-shahi black; 4-shahi orange-red; 8-shahi yellow-green; 1-kran rose bordering on carmine.

2. Imperforate; thin, white paper; 1-shahi deep black; 2-shahi blue-gray bordering on ultramarine; 2-shahi black; 4-shahi bright red; 1-kran black; 1-kran rose bordering on carmine; 4-kran yellow, 4-kran gray-blue; 5-kran gold, bronze, lilac, or bright violet; 1-toman gold. In this set, the 2-shahi blue; 4-shahi, 1-kran black or yellow; 5-kran black or yellow; 5-kran gold or lilac; and the 1-toman also are found perf 13$\frac{1}{2}$; the 1-kran is found in brownish red, imperforate, with yellowish background tint on the front of the stamp.

3. Imperforate; on colored papers; 1-kran carmine-tinted red on yellow, orange-yellow, blue, and lilac paper (the latter, cross-ruled); 1-toman gold on blue-gray, lilac, and yellow. All reprints were canceled to order for sale to collectors; however, they also are found in the mint, uncanceled state.

Forgeries: (a) we will mention first a counterfeit of the 8-shahi green-blue and ultramarine from an original cliché of the 5-kran, in which the bottom of the figures in the corners was scratched off; thin paper. (b) Early forgeries; lithographed on thick white paper;

imperforate or perf 13; the lion's chin is beardless; the white line is touching the pearls; the end of the lion's tail is entirely blank; shades and measurements are arbitrary. (c) Geneva forgeries; 1-shahi black; 2-shahi blue; 4-shahi red and 8-shahi green on white paper, about 60 microns. The impression is better than that of the originals; the fan of sun rays recalls that of the 1870 stamps; the ornament under the top right circle is touching the inner frame; 18$\frac{1}{2}$ x 21$\frac{3}{4}$ mm; lithographed; the 1-shahi is copied from Type IV; the 2-shahi, from Type II; the figure of the 4-shahi is open on top; the 8-shahi is Type II, but sharply printed value figure everywhere; forged cancellation: large dotted square. Forged Geneva cancellations: (1) 6 x 7 rectangle with large square dots. (2) One circle (27 mm), with date, TEHERAN 21 10, and Persian inscription. (d) Other forgeries from a variety of sources; it would be tedious and take too long to give a detailed, perhaps incomplete, description of them; they easily can be checked with the preceding information. Pay particular attention to the figures between the lion's paws which practically are never congruent, the dimensions and shades which frequently are arbitrary or whimsical, the gum in the mint stamps, cancellation in the used ones, ornament, frame, lion design, and so forth. All these counterfeits are lithographed.

1876. Portrait. Value figures at bottom. Nos. 13 to 16. *Originals:* typographed in black on a bureled color background; 17$\frac{1}{2}$–$\frac{3}{4}$ x 22$\frac{1}{2}$ mm; various perforations (see the catalogues); the lion has two short horizontal lines in the middle of its forehead; its tail has an inside black line; the shah's mouth is formed by an almost horizontal line; the tuft clasp is formed by a cabochon at the bottom (one large pearl surrounded by nine or ten small ones, the latter not always visible); then there are eleven pearls and in the top of the clasp, a twelfth pearl shaped like a comma (use magnifying glass).

No *reprints.*

Forgeries: lithographed on a crudely counterfeited bureled background; allowable dimensions and paper thickness; dot perf 12$\frac{1}{2}$; no horizontal lines on the lion's forehead; the curved shade lines in the center background frequently are broken; the shah's mouth is formed by an inverted circumflex accent; the tuft clasp is made of about ten large pearls forming a circle with one pearl in the middle; 2-shahi, the loop of the "2" figures is 1$\frac{1}{4}$ mm wide, instead of 1$\frac{1}{2}$ mm, and its end points downward instead of curving to the right; 10-shahi, the left figure "0" is rectangular and is 1$\frac{1}{10}$ mm in width, instead of 1$\frac{1}{4}$ mm.

Forged overprints: 5- or 10-shahi or overprint on horizontal half of this value; Teheran postmaster general's fantasies.

1879–80. Same type with color border. Nos. 23 to 28. No *reprints.*

Forgeries that are more or less official, considering the fact that they occasionally have complimentary cancellations; they prove to be outright forgeries when one examines their design. The top of the tuft is touching the inner circle; the tuft is much less shaded (compare with a common value); the finer center background shade lines seem to be spaced too far apart; perf 12 and 12½ x 13 mm; the 2- and 5-shahi and the 1- and 5-kran are known to have nearly congruent shades; also the 2-shahi, with background burelage in blue instead of yellow; the 5-shahi, same in red instead of green; and the 10-shahi in red-lilac instead of violet.

1881 (June). Lithographed; sun type. Nos. 32 to 34. *Originals:* recognizable by their overall finesse, which, in the engraved stamps of the following issue, is entirely successful: especially the four fine shade lines coupled with the lateral frames near the middle of the stamps; the top ornamentation, between the circles — visibly doubled lines; the ornamentation under the circles; the value tablet's cross-ruled background, forming here single thick lines or a solid background; 22½–23 x 26½–¾ mm; perf 12, 13, or 12 x 13.

Forgeries: see the following issue.

1882 (January). Engraved. Same type. Nos. 29 to 31. *Originals:* 22½ x 26 mm; the 25-shahi, 22¼ x 26½ mm; perforated as preceding; easily identifiable by the engraving's embossing (see the following detailed description of the visible aspects of finesse in execution).

No *reprints.*

Deceptive *forgeries* of the 5- and 25-shahi; arbitrary shades; the sun's rays are alternately thick and thin in the southeast corner of the sun ray framework; in the 5-shahi, the extension of a line drawn on the left of the oblique line in the upper left circle would go over the middle of the figure "5," whereas in the originals it goes near the middle of the value letter. Dimensions, 22¼ x 26 mm for the 5-shahi; 22 x 26⅕ mm for the 25-shahi.

1882. Portrait. Persian postal service. Nos. 35 to 40. 5- and 10-franc *originals,* expertly engraved: 5-franc, 22 x 27½ mm; fine curved shade lines in the plume's tuft; the bonnet is not limited by a line on the left; ten shade lines in the banderole above "PO" of POSTES; thirty-seven horizontal lines in the value circle. 10-franc, 29 x 36 mm, nine shade lines in the banderole above "PO" of POSTES; thirty-three horizontal shade lines in the value circle; the three fine lines surrounding the whole stamp are well executed and are quite parallel.

No *reprints.*

Forgeries: 5-franc, lithographed; rather deceptive; allowable measurements; single traces of shade lines in the plume; vertical line on the left of the bonnet; perf

11½; nine shade lines in the banderole above "PO"; twenty-eight horizontal lines in the value circle; 10-franc, lithographed: (a) twenty-three shade lines in the value circle; seven shade lines in the banderole above "PO" of POSTE; in PERSANE, the median bar of the first "E" and the bar of the "A" do not touch the body of the letters; the word FALSH is inscribed in white in the lower red border, but it is sometimes shaded with red. (b) 29 x 35¾ mm; the stamp, perforations included, is too wide, the red borders being 1¾ mm wide instead of 1¼ mm; perf 11½; eight shade lines above "PO"; twenty-two horizontal shade lines in the value circle; the blank part of the zero of the value is 1¾ mm wide instead of 2¼ mm; the triple outer frame lines frequently touch each other; the bonnet does not have the curved lines seen in the original; the whole background of the stamp, near the frames, seems solid and is far from resembling the remarkable finesse in the cross-ruling and line structure of the original background. (c) Geneva forgery of the 10-franc; 28½ x 35 mm; two almost similar types, one with stippling on the garment above SANE of PERSANE, the other, not stippled; twenty-nine crudely executed shade lines in the value circle; lithographed.

Fantasies: 10-shahi 50-centime and 2-franc overprinted with Persian characters. Likewise, the 50-centime and 1-franc, overprinted with a large "5."

1882 (end). Sun type of 1881. No. 41. *Originals:* engraved; value on white background; two types according to the Persian inscription on the right of POSTE PERSANE; Type I, about 9 mm wide; Type II, about 9⅓ mm wide; the latter is rare.

1901–2. Overprinted stamps. Nos. 123 and 124 to 145. The two overprints were counterfeited in Geneva. Comparison is indispensable.

1902. Meched provisional stamps. Nos. 192 to 198. *Forgeries* of No. 195a; inverted center of the 5-centime black; these forgeries probably are deceptive — I have not had a chance to see any of them and only can recommend detailed comparison.

Peru

1858–61. Lithographed stamps. Nos. 1 to 7. No *reprints.*

Forgeries: 1-dinero blue, copied from the 1-dinero of 1858, No. 1; eight shade lines on the four sides (the original has nine on the bottom); thirteen horizontal lines in the shield quartering containing the llama, instead of sixteen; inscription lettering is same height, whereas in the original, the "U" of UN is set lower and the "D" and "N" of DINERO are not as low as the other letters.

1-peseta rose, copied from No. 7 (1860), without dot after CORREOS, but very easy to recognize, the bottom inscription being UN PESETO instead of UNA PESETA; there are pearls around the center background instead of a broken line forming blank triangles.

1/2-peso yellow, copied from the 1/2-peso of 1858, No. 3. The original is dull orange-tinted yellow on white paper, about 65 microns; 21 1/4 x 20 7/8 mm; the first setting for the center background is formed with about forty lines, half of which are short, and at times seem to form pearls; the other half are about 1 mm long. These lines alternate; the inner corner burelage is formed with vertical wavy lines.

Forgeries: (a) greenish yellow on thick white paper, about 90 microns; fourteen shade lines instead of thirteen in the quartering of the llama; FALSH printed in green at the top. (b) Like the forged UN PESETO described in the preceding; yellowish paper; CORREOS on the right and left instead of MEDIO PESO on the left and 50 CENTIMOS on the right; (c) brownish yellow or purplish rose (error) on thin paper, about 50 microns; large zigzag inner corner shade lines; twelve lines in the llama quartering.

1862. Typographed stamps. Nos. 8 and 9.
Originals: 21 mm square; quite visible coats of arms, the 1-peseta coat of arms with flags. No. 13 (1868), same. No. 15 (1871), same.

1866–67. Nos. 10 to 12. *Originals:* first-class engravings; perf 12.

Forgeries: two crudely lithographed sets, perf 12. 5-centavo, the "U" of PERU is closed at top; the two banderoles of CORREOS PERU and PORTE FRANCO are touching at their extremities. In the 10- and 15-centavo stamps, the mountains are far too visible. 10-centavo, the black llama is one-eyed. 20-centavo, (a) two heavy lines on the right side of the highest mountain; "2" figures are broken in the northwest and southeast corners. (b) The black llama is blind, or, rather, it has no eyes.

1871–73. Locomotive or llama. Nos. 14 and 16.
Originals: No. 14, carmine and vermilion-tinted red; 20 1/2 x 21 mm; No. 16, slate (gray-blue), dark ultramarine; 17 3/4–18 x 19 1/2 mm. The left frame is narrower than the others; thick, yellowish, white paper; average impression: small color protuberances like "smudges" in the frames, in llama's contour lines, and in the lettering.

Reprints of No. 16; paper is a little thinner (80 microns) and whiter; less pronounced embossing impression, but better; the left frame is as thick as the others; 18 1/8 x 19 3/5 mm; dull pale blue or pearl gray.

Forgeries: dark gray (copied from the reprint) on paper of allowable thickness, but grayish and of poor quality; the four frames are too thick; 18 1/4 x 19 4/5 mm;

embossing is less accentuated, especially the embossing of the llama; lateral inscription lettering is executed poorly, because of bad impression; the "D" of DOS resembles an "O," the "E" of CENTAVOS is too narrow, and the "N" is too small; the llama's tail is touching the inner frame, and this often is the case in the reprint.

1874–79. Nos. 17 to 25. *Originals:* engraved, perf 12; embossed grill on the back of the stamp.

Forgeries: values in CENTAVOS; inexpertly perf 13, imperforate, or dot perforated; lithographed; no embossed grill. 2-centavo, the sun rays form nine white bands, undivided at top, which extend to within 1/2 mm of the oval, instead of about 1 mm; three cannonballs under the left cannon's muzzle, instead of five; bright violet instead of violet or mauve. 20-centavo, nine white sun ray bands that terminate at the oval instead of remaining separate from it; the llama's head is touching the top of the shield; in the bottom of the latter are six oblique shade lines around the cornucopia instead of twenty-one vertical lines.

1880–84. Overprinted stamps. Nos. 26 to 74. Very numerous *forged overprints;* comparison is necessary.

Original overprint, UNION POSTAL, and so forth, PLATA LIMA, in an oval: the letters of PLATA measure 2 1/2 mm high; the horizontal bar of the "T," likewise; *reprints?* of the overprint: PLATA 3 mm high; the horizontal bar of the "T" likewise; (Nos. 26–37 and 67–71, as well as postage due stamps, Nos. 6–10).

Original overprint of the Chilean coat of arms (Nos. 42–47); the star is 3 1/2 mm, outer diameter; the shade lines are touching the shield; numerous clandestine counterfeits. The *original triangular overprint* on Nos. 59–74 is found in five different types. Comparison is necessary. The overprints of all these issues were counterfeited in Geneva.

1884–86. 1-sol brown. No. 82. *Forged cancellation:* with date, double circle (26 mm), CORREOS DEL PERU...SET 05 LIMA.

Official stamps. *Forged overprints,* especially Geneva (GOBIERNO, framed or unframed).

Postage due stamps. LIMA CORREOS overprint. Nos. 12 to 16. This overprint was *reprinted* copiously. Redder, greasier ink, and the overprint is thicker than the original. Compare with the overprint in blue, which is a reprint variety. This also is applicable to other issues or values on which this overprint reprint might be found, especially Nos. 27–31.

Arequipa

1882. AREQUIPA overprint in a circle. No. 3. In the original overprint, the "P" resembles an "F."

1883. No. 6. *Reprints* on thin paper in orange-red or brick red.

Original: 19 1/4 x 24 mm.

1883–84. Nos. 8 to 10. *Reprints* of the 10-centavo and 1-sol: slightly bluish paper; the 1-sol is dark brown instead of brown.

Forgery: 10-centavo, typographed in pale blue instead of slate on thick nontransparent paper, instead of thin, transparent paper; frequently with FALSH in red in the middle of the shield. The 25-centavo was counterfeited crudely; compare the stippling in the upper corners and the details of the shield's design.

1885. Nos. 11 and 12. *Originals:* 5-centavo olive-gray, 20 1/2 x 26 1/2 mm; 10-centavo, slate, 20 1/2 x 27 1/2 mm.

Reprints: no overprint; pale olive and pale slate; white gum.

1885. Nos. 13 and 14. *Originals:* 5-centavo, 20 x 25 1/2 mm, blue; 10-centavo, 20 1/4 x 26 1/4 mm, brown or olive brown.

Reprints: no overprint; 5-centavo, pale blue; 10-centavo, pale olive; white gum.

Cuzco

1881–85. Nos. 1 to 3. *Original overprint:* the word CUZCO measures 16 x 3 1/2 mm and the oval, 25 1/4 x 17 mm.

Forged overprints: make comparison. In a good early forged overprint, CUZCO is 17 mm and the oval is too large.

Puno

1881–85. Nos. 1 to 14. *Original overprints:* in three types. Outer circle: Type I, 19 mm; Type II, 23 mm; Type III, 20 mm. Letter M: Type I, 2 1/2 mm wide; Type II, 3 1/2 mm; Type III, 3 mm.

Pacific Steam Navigation Company

1857. Imperforate. Nos. 1 and 2. *Originals:* the Pacific Steam Navigation Company circulated only the 1- and 2-real stamps on azure paper. These stamps were used before the first Peruvian issue (1858); they were accepted by the Peruvian government and, therefore, should be placed in a primary position among this country's issues. The only regular cancellations are those of Lima with date, in one circle; LIMA, CALLAO (Lima's port), and CHORILLOS, in an oval with dots above it; finally, figure "4" in a barred oval (19 x 25 1/2 mm), like the British postmarks, A 0 1, B 0 1, and so forth; figure "4" was the Pacific Steam Navigation Company's postmark. Recess print engraved; average dimensions, 25 2/3 x 20 3/4 mm; the two lines of the large oval are very close; the center oval line is hardly more than 1/5 mm from the scalloped part; the steamer's flag is almost rectangular and has three horizontal shade lines; its hull scarcely rises above the horizontal line defining the sea.

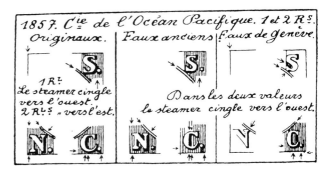

1857. Pacific Steam Navigation Company 1- and 2-real. Originals. 1-real: the steamer is headed west; **2-real:** it is headed east. Early forgeries; Geneva forgeries: In the two values, the steamer is headed west.

Essays: the same stamps are found on wove or laid white paper, about 60 microns, in blue (2-real, laid), in carmine (1-real, laid), in yellow and green (both values), and in brown (2-real). These stamps are not listed in the Scott Catalogue, and rightly so, it would seem, since they were ordered for a private company, and in contrast to stamps on azure paper, they received no official recognition.

Forgeries: a great many counterfeits in all the arbitrary shades imaginable, on white or yellowish paper (1-real blue, also on bluish paper — Geneva); they may be divided into two sets, one for early forgeries and the other for Fournier, both of them lithographed — which enables connoisseurs to identify them at first sight. The illustration will inform the reader on the various defects of these creations.
(a) Early forgeries, 26 x 21 mm; the center oval is more than 1/4 mm away from the scallop; the smoke is shaped like a cigar; the flag, shaped like a circumflex accent, has a solid background; dividing frame line, 1 1/2 mm from the outer frame. (b) Geneva set, 25 3/4 x 21–21 1/5 mm; flag too curved with its solid background; dividing frame line, about 1 mm away (see the illustration for further defects). In the 2-real stamps of the two sets, the ship is sailing westward! (c) 2-real typographed early forgery, the ship is sailing eastward, as in the original; the shading of the dot after the "C" does not touch the first shade line; the oval's two lines are spaced widely; this oval does not touch the lateral frames; the flag has no hatching; the vertical lines are too far apart and are irregular.

Philippines

1854. Large portrait. Engraved. Nos. 1 and 4.
Originals: crude recess printed engraving; one plate of forty stamps (5 x 8) for each value; forty stamps

engraved differently in each plate; 18–18¹/₂ x 21¹/₂–22 mm; imperforate; white or yellowish white paper. The CORROS error of the 1-real is the twenty-sixth type of the sheet. Note: In the 1-and 2-real, the

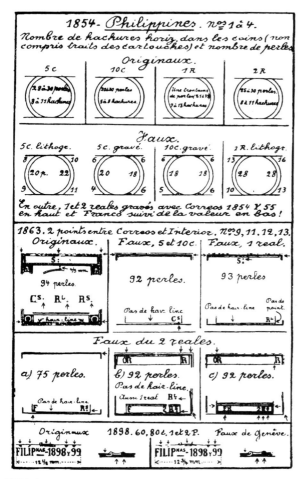

1854. Philippines. Nos. 1–4. Number of horizontal lines in the corners (not counting tablet lines) and number of pearls. Originals. 5-centavo, 28–30 pearls, 8–11 shade lines. 10-centavo, 20–30 pearls, 5–8 shade lines. 1-real, about 30 pearls (25–33), 7–13 shade lines. 2-real, 25–30 pearls, 8–11 shade lines. Forgeries. 5-centavo (lithographed), 5-centavo (engraved), 10-centavo (engraved), 1-real (lithographed). In addition, engraved 1- and 2-real with CORREOS 1854–55 on top and FRANCO followed by the value at bottom. Second section: 1863. Two dots between CORREOS and INTERIOR. Nos. 9, 11–13. Originals. 94 pearls, hairline. Forgeries. 5- and 10-centavo, 92 pearls, no hairline. 1-real, 93 pearls, no hairline, no dot. 2-real, (a) 75 pearls, no hairline; (b) 92 pearls, no hairline, also 1-real; (c) 92 pearls. Bottom: originals. 1898. 60-, 80-centavo, 1- and 2-peseta. Geneva forgeries.

value is found at the top of the stamp and CORREOS, etc., and the rest at the bottom.

Forgeries: from various sources; the illustration will show the number of pearls and horizontal shade lines in the inner corners. In case of doubt, or if you have before you counterfeits that have not been described, consult the illustrations given for the originals (the number of pearls indicated may include half-pearls at the extremities of the half-circles), or compare with the forty types that are reproduced in the Calman Catalogue (Volume 2, page 630). The lithographed forgeries easily are identified by the absence of embossed impression.

1855. Same. Lithographed stamps. Nos. 5 and 5a. *Originals:* two types: Type I, the tablet of CORREOS, and the rest, is 2²/₅ mm high; in Type II, the tablet is only 2 mm high, and the letters are, therefore, not so big. Type I comprises four different types in blocks of four (2 x 2); the two stamps on the left measure 19 x 22 mm; those on the right, 19¹/₄ x 22 mm; in the first and fourth stamp of the block, the second "5" of "55" is touching the top tablet and there is no dot after the figure; in the second and third stamp, the figure is not touching and there is no dot. Type II, reengraved (the oblique eye line is touching the bandeau; a cross is missing on the diadem on the right of the chignon); 18-¹/₄ x 21 mm. Being of an entirely different type, this stamp should have a special number.

1856. Spanish West Indies stamps of 1855. The 1- and 2-real stamps of the West Indies were used officially in the Philippines; they only can be identified by the cancellations used in that country. There are *forged cancellations.*

Forgeries: see Spanish West Indies.

Small portrait. Lithographed. A. Single frame; two small bells and a fraction in the lateral bandeaux; tablet of CORREOS and the rest is 2 mm high; that of FRANCO, 2¹/₂ mm.

1859 (April) and 1860. Nos. 7 and 8. *Originals:* a single outer frame line, but the first printing (1859) has an additional dividing frame line which is ¹/₂–³/₄ mm from the former; in the 1860 printing, this frame line is not always present; the stamps of each block of four have four different types identifiable by the figures, by the hair, and so forth. The letters of CORREOS are 1¹/₄ mm high; those of FRANCO, 1¹/₂ mm. Width of stamps: 18²/₅–³/₄ mm, according to type; height: 22³/₄–23 mm. The sixty-five pearls are made of thick, short lines. Thick or thin white paper in the two values; the 5-centavo on yellowish thick or thin paper, or thick ribbed paper. Numerous shades in the 5-cuarto stamps.

Forgeries: a crude lithographed counterfeit of the 5-centavo can be related to that issue because of the height of the letters of CORREOS and certain frame details, but it also can be considered a forgery of the 5-centavo (August 1862), for it has three small bells and a fraction in the lateral bandeaux; seventy-five pearls as dots, and FRANCO is only 1¼ mm high, like CORREOS.

1861. No. 7a. *Original:* this stamp has nothing in common with the preceding one and should be assigned a special number. The legends are larger; letters of CORREOS, 1½ mm high; tablet of FRANCO, 2½ mm high, and its letters, 2 mm high. Seventy-nine pearls shaped like small dots, or thin, very short lines; the frame and the inner corner design (oyster shells) are thicker than in the 1859–60 issue; the same may be said concerning an outer dividing frame line which is ½ mm from the stamp itself. The latter measures 19¼ x 23¼ mm and has only one type.

B. Double frame, the usual frame line and a very thin line on the outside (use a magnifying glass); the top and bottom legends have special tablets; the tablet for the top legend, CORREOS INTERIOR, is 1⅗ mm high; the bottom one for FRANCO and the value, 1½ mm high.

1862 (August). No. 10. *Original:* this 5-centavo stamp is different from the preceding one and the following set; it should be catalogued under No. 9 and in 1862 (the four values of 1863 are under Nos. 10–13); a single dot after CORREOS; thick paper; 19¼ x 23½ mm; the clearly visible corner burelage is less dense than in the following issue; there are two unbroken shade lines in the neck under the ribbon whose end is on this side of the shaded part of the neck; three small bells and a fraction in the lateral bandeaux; thick white or yellowish paper; with or without a dot after FRANCO.

Forgery: lithographed in red-brown on thin paper; two lines of dots in the neck under the ribbon which terminates right at the neck shading.

1863 (January). 5-, 10-centavo; 1- and 2-real. Nos. 9, 11 to 13. *Originals:* four small bells in the lateral strips; two dots between CORREOS and INTERIOR; ninety-four pearls set very close together; the word FRANCO is resting on a hairline which diminishes the tablet's height and continues on to the right, passing through the blank circle of the lower right corner (use magnifying glass); 19 x 23¼ mm; the inner corner design is made of small, densely set oyster shells. There is a dot after the "S" of C^S or R^L or R^S on a level with the base of the letter. The hairline, which underlines the value, goes through the right circle in the 5- and 10-centavo stamps; in the 1- and 2-real, it often goes through the left circle. The distance between CORREOS and INTERIOR is about 1½ mm in the 5- and 10-centavo stamps and less than 1 mm in the values in reals; the "F" of FRANCO is 1 mm from the line on the left in the 1- and 2-real stamps and a little

less (⅔ mm) in the 5- and 10-centavo. (See the illustration for frame details.)

No *reprints.*

Forgeries: two principal characteristics for all values. (1) No hairline under the value inscription and the dot is placed *under* the "S" of C^S, R^S, or under the "L" of R^L. (See the illustration for the other distinctive marks.) In the first forgery of the 1-real, the letters of CORREOS gradually increase in height on the right; this forgery is typographed, all the others are lithographed; letters "NT" of INTERIOR evidently are too large. At times, one finds the word FALSCH printed in blue above the value tablet. In the forgeries of reals, there is no dot after INTERIOR; the forgeries illustrated under "b" in the illustration constitute a set, with the forgeries of the 5- and 10-centavo. The "c" counterfeit seems to be a retouched type of the preceding forgery; it is even worse.

1863–64. 1-real silver. No. 14. *Originals:* lithographed; green-gray and dark green-gray on white paper and green-gray on yellowish paper. Dot before and after CORREOS. In 1864, this reengraved stamp was issued in green, yellow-green, and emerald green, without dots before and after CORREOS.

1864. Spanish issue type (1864). Nos. 15 to 18. Typographed; 18¾–19 x 22–22¼ mm. The outer frame is thick on the right and at bottom; the inner frame is just the opposite; no pearl is touching the bandeau borders. See the details of this impression in Spain.

Forgeries: (a) crude lithographs; paper tinted on front only; frames are uniformly thick; pearls are touching the bandeau; no dot after CENT or before CORREOS. (b) Lithographed on thin paper; most of the pearls are touching the bandeau borders.

1869–74. HABILITADO overprint. Various numbers. A few forged overprints, especially on No. 9. Comparison is necessary.

1877. Overprinted stamps. Nos. 49 and 50. *Forged overprints,* especially Geneva.

Subsequent issues. The reader is referred to the details of these issues given in Spain and Cuba.

1881–88. HABILITADO overprints. Nos. 68 to 108. Comparison is indispensable. The overprint of Nos. 85 and 86, DE DOS RLES, was counterfeited in Geneva.

Same observation for *fiscals* and the *telegraph stamps.*

1898. Postage stamps, perf 14. Nos. 172 to 175. *Originals:* 18 x 21½ mm. Typographed. The fine shade lines in the lettering of CORREOS and TELEGRAFOS (on the stamp's sides) and in the second "E" of TELEGRAFOS are quite visible (use magnifying glass). (See the previous illustration.)

Forgeries: the four higher value stamps were counterfeited in Geneva in blocks of four with wide margins; imperforate, or allowable perforation; grayish, rather soft paper. $18^{1}/_{5}-^{1}/_{2}$ x $21^{1}/_{2}-22$ mm, according to values. The shading lines of CORREOS and TELEGRAFOS usually are executed poorly and the accent is too faint. The four values are found with or without shade lines in the bottom of the ornament supporting the value tablet.

Forged Geneva cancellations: double circle ($26^{1}/_{2}$ mm), with two cross bars in the inner circle, with date MANILLA 12 DIC 98 FILIPINAS and CAVITE 21 DIC 98 FILIPINAS.

1899–1904. PHILIPPINES overprint on U.S. stamps. Nos. 176 to 203. Numerous *forged overprints* on all less expensive nonoverprinted stamps. Detailed comparison is indispensable. Examine the cancellation. The overprint was counterfeited in Geneva and applied on U.S. canceled stamps.

Republic of the Philippines

1899. 8-centavo de PESO. No. 4. *Original:* thirty-three equidistant shade lines in the center circle, not counting those above and below which often merge with the circle line; figure "1" on the left has a very visible oblique line extending over six shade line spaces; the extremity of the figure is above letter "O" of GOB^{NO}.

Forgery: thirty-seven shade lines (plus two) in the center circle; the oblique line of the "1" on the left is not very visible and is not long enough (four shade line spaces); the bottom of the figure ends above the letter "N." The three "k" letters evidently are too large; the letters of GOB are too wide. Nos. 1 and 3 were counterfeited in Geneva; they hardly deserve description since their defects easily can be judged by comparison.

Poland

1860 (March 16). Wavy line watermark. No. 1. Russian stamp type of the 1859 issue.

Shades: pale blue and pale rose; blue or blue-green and rose; dark blue and dark rose: 50M, 25U. This stamp is less expertly executed than the Russian stamps; centered copies are rare.

Cancellations: triple circle with numeral: common; dot lozenge and figure: in demand. All others: rare, especially Russian cancellations.

Fakes: one finds stamps that have been cleaned to remove pen cancellations.

Forgeries: various sorts, all without watermark. Comparative study will suffice.

Recent stamps. What can one say about recent Polish stamps? Most of the nonoverprinted sets are cheap; the overprinted sets have been extensively counterfeited, and it is difficult to recommend sets that are made for stamp speculation — twenty-one issues from 1918 to 1925, twelve of which appeared in 1918 and 1919!

Forgeries (Warsaw, 1919): Nos. 206–12. Crude workmanship. Compare portrait design and inscriptions.

Official forgeries (Warsaw, 1920): 20-marka, dark green instead of olive-green; too high (almost 23 mm instead of 22); "0" (zero) is $^{1}/_{2}$ mm too small. It will be enough to compare design, horses, and lines.

Forged overprints are practically innumerable. Avoid the overprinted stamps unless you are interested in professional specialization. A detailed description of forged overprints would be time-consuming and tedious, for the best counterfeits must be compared with originals. A few fraudulent creations are obvious and ludicrous.

1919. Austria Nos. 74–107, all of which were more or less well counterfeited. The 2- and 10-korona, Nos. 90–93, on silk thread paper, are always forgeries.

1919. Same. Lublin overprint. This is a good Geneva counterfeit, but, as a result of a cliché flaw, there is always a small black accent mark about 2 mm above the "P" of POCZTA, and a small "airplane" under the outer left ornament.

Local postal service (Warsaw): No. 1 has been doctored to create 1a. Overprints and varieties of Nos. 8–11 have been forged.

Ponta Delgada

All values of the 1892 issues were *reprinted* (1906); reprints for the King of Spain (very rare). Perf $13^{1}/_{2}$; slightly different shades; comparison is necessary.

Portugal

There is a demand for Portuguese stamps issued between 1853 and 1869 that are bar canceled with numbers of the Azores: 48 (Angra), 49 (Horta), 50 (Ponta Delgada), 51 (Funchal). After 1869, the same postmarks are oval, thick bars, with Nos. 42 (Angra), 43 (Horta), 44 (Ponta Delgada), and 45 (Funchal). The former are rare; the latter, very rare.

I. Imperforate Stamps

1853. Embossed impression. Nos. 1 to 4. *Shades:* 5-reis orange-brown; yellow-brown. 25-reis pale blue to dark blue; blue is most common. 50-reis yellow-green; blue-green: 25M, 25U. 50-reis light lilac; mauve-lilac: rare, mint; 25U.

A.-Oblit. barres B.-Oblit. cercle C.-Cd a date
et numéro. de points et numéro. double cercle.

Portugal cancellations: A. Barred cancel with number. B. Dotted circle with number. C. Double circle with date.

Varieties: the 5-, 25-, and 50-reis are found on thin paper; same prices, except 5-reis: 50M, 25U.
5-centimo, retouched type, curl less prominent, Adam's apple protruding, etc.

Select: four margins, with minimum width of 2 mm.

Cancellations: Type A (fifteen and twenty bars); name of town on one line: rare. Type A in blue: 25U.

Pairs: 4U. Blocks of four: very rare.

Fakes: in this and the following issues, there are fraudulently canceled reprints. Also, watch out for stamps on which the portrait portion of the design has been replaced with another.

Reprints: 1864. The whole set. White gum; no brown gum. White paper; no slightly yellowish-gray paper. Thin paper. No. 1 is always a retouched type, vermilion-tinted red-brown. No. 2, a single shade: blue; more uniform inking in the frame; engraver's initials are often quite visible. No. 3, yellow-green; frame broken above the second "O" of CORREIO; engraver's initials not very visible. No. 4, very pale lilac; initials not very visible.

1885. Very white paper, too thick, no gum. No curl under the chignon. The four values are found pen barred. 25-reis sky blue. 100-reis purplish red.

1903. Smooth, glossy, thin paper; no curl under the chignon, light colored gum. Reprints overprinted with the word PROVA in black.

Forgeries: Portugal's stamps were not extensively counterfeited because of the difficulty of matching the look of the originals, but the reprints often are offered for sale as mint originals, or are fraudulently canceled in an effort to create rare used stamps.

1855. Portrait of Dom Pedro V facing right. Straight hair. Nos. 5 to 8. *Select:* four margins, with minimum width of 2 mm.

Shades: 5-reis reddish maroon. Others as in the first issue.

Types: 5-centimo, Type I, seventy-five pearls. Type II, seventy-six pearls and the "RR" letters of CORREIO not close to the circle. Type III, seventy-six pearls, "RR" touching the circle. Type IV, eighty-one pearls, letters and lower ornaments at some distance

from the circle. Type V, eighty-one pearls, but letters and ornaments are close together. Type VI, eighty-nine pearls. This last one is worth 25M, 25U.

25-centimo, Type I, pearls not close to the oval. Type II, pearls touching the oval: 5M.

There are defective impressions.

Pairs: 4U. Blocks: rare.

Cancellations: Type A (eleven, fifteen, twenty bars, etc.) and Type B. Others are rare.

Reprints: white paper (1885). 5-reis brown-black. The angle designs are replaced by lines; letters are thinner. 25-reis light blue has color dot in the ear. The 50- and 100-reis can be identified by the paper and the slightly different shades. Make comparison.

Fake: No. 6 head cut out and fitted on a No. 13. Found sometimes on cover, after cancellation alteration.

1856–57. Same type. Curly hair. Nos. 10 to 12.
Select: four margins, with minimum width of 2 mm.
25-reis blue, two types: I. Close, single line burelage; II. Wide, double line burelage. 25-reis rose, Type II.

Shades: 5-reis dark brown; maroon: 2M; yellow-brown: 2M; red-brown: 50M; shade similar to that of No. 5: 2M, 50U. 25-reis, Type I: blue, black-blue: 50U; Type II, pale blue to dark blue; 25-reis carmine-tinted rose to carmine.

Varieties: thick paper, 5-reis dark red-brown: 50M, 50U; 25-reis, Types I and II: same prices as for ordinary paper.

Cancellations: Types A (various models) and B. Others are rare.

Pairs: 4U. Blocks: rare.

Reprints: 1885: 5-reis dark brown, white paper. 25-reis more or less ultramarine blue, white paper. 25-reis rose with Type I burelage.

1906: on cream-colored paper, shiny gum; overprint PROVA in black.

1862–64. Portrait of Dom Luis I. Nos. 13 to 17.
Select: four margins more than 2 mm wide.

Paper: thin or thick. The latter is a little less common.

Shades: as in the previous issues. The 10-reis orange and orange-yellow; 5-reis brown and dark brown.

Varieties: 5-reis, two types: I. the "5" is almost touching the ornament on its left; II. the "5" is 1 mm away from the ornament. There are eight varieties of minor importance for the 25-centimo stamp.

Cancellations: as above. Type B is found with medium-size or large figures, especially No. 52 (Porto).

Pairs: 4U. Used blocks: 12U.

Reprints: 1885: the white paper, gum, and shades are different. 10-reis orange, 50-reis yellow-green; a white dot is touching the bottom of the "5" on the right.

1906: the whole set, except the 25-reis; with overprint PROVA. Essays of No. 17 exist in various colors.

1866. Rectangular format. Nos. 18 to 25. Letters "C W" under the neck.

Select: four margins at least $1^1/_2$ mm wide.

Shades: not very numerous. 10-reis yellow and orange-yellow; 25-reis rose and carmine-tinted rose; 120-reis blue and dark blue.

Varieties: 5-reis two types, and 25-reis, three types identifiable by the "5" figures in the upper and lower inscriptions. Nos. 18, 19, 21, and 25 exist rouletted (on-cover purchase recommended): rare.

All values, except the 20- and 50-reis, received a cross-in-lozenge perforation.

Cancellations: as above.

Pairs: 3–4U. Blocks of four: 10U.

Reprints: 1885: the whole set on excessively white paper. 5-reis deep black; 10-reis, good shade. The other values may be recognized by the shades and the impression. Make comparison. 50-reis, lower right corner is lightly trimmed.

1906: the whole set with overprint PROVA.

Fakes: the portraits were removed and replaced, sometimes with a part of the background near the oval, by heads from the following issue. This happened especially when a lightly applied cancellation struck only the head, which was then replaced by another to make a new stamp. If you want to avoid perforated stamps whose perforations have been trimmed, accept only imperforates with wide margins.

Forgeries: there are a few good ones in this issue, but identifiable by the figures (for example, on the 20-reis the "2" on the right and the zeros are too narrow), by the lettering, and by the positioning of the stippled background too far from the banderoles. (Because of this, there is a single line of dots instead of two on the banderole sides and three or four at the bottom of the stamp instead of four or five).

II. Perforated Stamps

1867–70. Same type. Perf $12^1/_2$. Nos. 26 to 34. Letters "C W" in the neck.

Select: stamps perfectly centered.

Shades: same shades as for the preceding issue. 100-reis light lilac and grayish lilac; 240-reis violet and mauve.

Varieties: 5-reis, two types: I. Upper right figure, thin, and some distance away from the edge and bottom of the banderole; Type II. The figure is thicker at bottom and closer to the bottom and edge of the banderole.

25-reis, two types: I. Top figure not so thick, the "2" on the left at some distance from the banderole edge; Type II. Thick figures, the "5" with a pronounced upper curl, and figure on the left close to the banderole.

100-reis, two types: I. Grayish lilac, zero at bottom right is some distance from the banderole; Type II.

Light lilac, zero at bottom right is very close to the end of the banderole.

The 5 and 25-reis, Type II, are less common.

Cancellations: as previously, but other barred types with numerals (Type A) with eight bars appear. Types A and B: common.

Pairs: 3U. Blocks of four: 8–10U.

Reprints: 1885: the whole set on white paper, perf $13^1/_2$ instead of $12^1/_2$. Perforations more sharply cut and holes are larger.

1906: the whole set overprinted PROVA.

1870–79. Same type. No letters under the neck. Nos. 35 to 49. *Select:* stamps well centered.

Shades: numerous.

Perforation: $12^1/_2$: common, except for the 25-reis mint; 80-reis vermilion: 5M, and 150-reis on ordinary paper: 3M. Perf $13^1/_2$: mint stamps are worth 2M on ordinary paper, except 5-, 10-, 50-reis green, which are worth triple; 150-reis blue: 8M, and 120-reis: rare. The 50-reis blue, 100-, 120-, and 150-reis blue, used, are worth 2U. Stamps perf 11 and 14, and horizontally ruled, thick paper are rare.

A kind of paper called "porcelain" (chalk-coated paper) is found among the stamps perf $12^1/_2$ and $13^1/_2$. Various prices.

Varieties: the two types of the 15-, 20-, 25-, and 80-reis are identified by the upper right figures, which are close to, or at some distance from, each other. One finds fine, thick, smooth, and very white paper known as "porcelain."

The 5-reis, 10-reis yellow; 15-reis, Type II (figures far apart, light maroon), and the 25-reis are known to exist imperforate.

Pairs: 3U. Blocks of four: 8U.

Cancellations: the eight-barred Type A often are seen. This type is found with nine bars and oval shape. Type C postmarks with date, circular or oval, also are seen. There is also a postmark with modern date, double circle, with date in a rectangle in the middle of the postmark.

Reprints: 1885: the whole set has been reprinted and is recognizable by the very white paper, the perforation ($13^1/_2$), and the noncongruent shades. Make comparison.

1906: as above.

Forgeries: the whole set. Distinguishing characteristic: fifty-seven pearls, some of which are touching the ovals, instead of sixty-one clearly detached ones. There are twenty-four shade lines in the top left corners and twenty-five at top right, whereas in the originals there are twenty-eight vertical lines in the four corners. (The last ones are made up of dots and are occasionally "blind." Use magnifying glass.) The bottom of the lower banderole is not as close to the frame as in the original, and the shading seems to be continuous in the middle. The white paper is too thin; perf 11½.

Subsequent issues. See the general catalogues.

1876. No. 50. The reprints of 1885 are perf 12½ or 13½.

1880. Nos. 51 to 54. 5-reis black, two types identifiable by the nostril. Type II, nostril drawn with a thick line; temple stippling not interrupted: 2M, 4U.

Reprinted in 1885, perf 13½, and in 1906 (royal reprint, like the previous ones).

1882–97 and 1884. Nos. 55 to 65. Nos. 55–57, 59, 61, and 62 were reprinted in 1885 and 1906, the others in 1906 only.

Nos. 59 and 62 were forged. Make comparison. Noncongruent perforations. Black and off-gray-black. Thick paper.

1892. Nos. 66 to 77. Reprinted in 1906. The 5-, 20-, 25-, 50-, and 80-reis on ordinary white paper, perf 13½. The others closely resemble the originals.

1892–93. Overprinted. All were reprinted in 1906. There are many forged overprints. Make comparison.

1894. Nos. 96 to 108. Not reprinted. Special postmark 1894 CENTENARIO 1894.

1895. St. Anthony. Nos. 110 to 123. Not reprinted.

Forgeries: the uncommon stamp values were counterfeited several times; design comparison will reveal them.

1. 50–100 reis: bad design.

2. 100–1000 reis (Geneva, F.): see the hands and the hatching (column pedestal on the left). In the prayer on the back of the stamp, "nunc" is spelled "nune." This set was fraudulently overprinted with AÇORES (and other colonies).

3. 150–1000 reis, a few differences in design, format more than 1 mm too large.

1898. Vasco da Gama. Ludicrous forgeries. Design comparison will be sufficient. With forged overprints for the colonies.

Postage due stamp (1898). Two forged sets. Stamps lithographed in London. Design comparison will be enough; arbitrary shades. Paris: noncongruent background design, inscriptions, and format.

Portuguese Colonies

Crown type. I think it is useless to deal with the early forgeries; they are executed so crudely that the least competent philatelist will have no difficulty in appraising them at first sight; very arbitrary shades; ludicrous inscription lettering; formless perforation.

Complete sets, which are infinitely more deceptive, come from Geneva. The occasionally arbitrary shades

of the Fournier *forgeries* are very close; the paper is a bit too yellowish; it is thin (50–55 microns), very transparent, or medium (50–55 microns), less transparent.

The paper of the *originals* is white (grayish because of age, at times), 55–60 microns, or thick, with thick yellowish gum. The imprint measurement difference in the forgeries is so slight that it hardly deserves to be mentioned; in contrast, the overall dimensions up to perforation extremities are 24–25 mm wide by 28+ mm (originals, about 24 x 27–27½ mm); the forgeries, which are perf 12½, also are found imperforate. The forged cliché designs, one for each colony, with interchangeable values, show dissimilarities which various illustrations will clarify. (We reproduce here the sketches of the distinctive marks of the various colonies because our clichés were used this way to illustrate articles.)

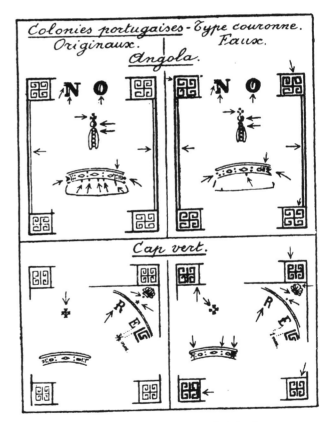

Portuguese colonies. Crown type. Originals. Forgeries. Angola. Bottom: Cape Verde.

Examination of the cross on top of the crown and of the five pearls under the globe supporting the cross will be decisive most of the time; the other marks can be used when a cancellation conceals the cross and the pearls. Note: The corner ornamental design for Angola is different. There is little point in taking up the

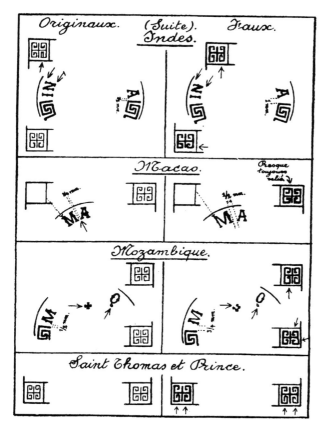

Portuguese East Indies. Originals. Forgeries. Second section: Macao. ¼ mm. ½ mm. Almost always connected. Third section: Mozambique. ½ mm. ¾ mm. Bottom section: Saint Thomas and Prince.

secondary figure and value inscription defects.

Reprints (1886): chalky, very white paper, perf 13½, gumless; (1906): reprints for the King of Spain, 168 sets (very rare); same perforation, white gum. See Angola, Cape Verde, Portuguese Guinea, Portuguese East Indies, Macao, Mozambique, Saint Thomas, Prince Edward Island, and Timor for special details and for forged Geneva cancellations.

The St. Anthony set of 1895 was counterfeited (see Portugal); stamps, therefore, must be expertized before colonial overprint examination.

The same is true for the Vasco da Gama issue of 1898, which is not worth describing, and for the 1898 postage due stamps.

Portuguese Congo

1902. Overprinted stamps. Nos. 29 to 36. A few forged overprints. Comparison is useful.

1914–18. RÉPUBLICA overprint on 75-reis stamp. No. 18. Same comment.

Portuguese East Indies

1871–77. Figure in an oval. Nos. 1 to 40.
Originals: typographed. See the catalogues for the various types, paper, and perforations. There is a dot under the "C"; the background line structure is irregular (thirty-three, forty-one, forty-three, or forty-four shade lines); cross-like design before and after INDIA PORT formed with four lines in the first issue and with five dots in the following ones.

No *reprints*.

Forgeries: all values lithographed; set (a) thick paper; perf 11½; no cross-like design or dots under the "C"; twenty-eight hatch lines; inscription lettering is too high; set (b) the background shading lines are composed of about forty very fine, excessively regular lines; medium paper; the oval does not touch the frame either at bottom or on the right; no dot under the "C."

1879–81. Crown type. Nos. 41 to 54. *Reprints:* see Portuguese Colonies.

Geneva forgeries: all values in blocks, but reproduced from a first defective cliché whose distinctive characteristics will be found in the illustration (see Portuguese Colonies); the ornamentation of a top inner right corner is touching the lower line of the square ornament. 21 x 24 mm.

1881–83. Figure overprints. Nos. 55 to 113. Extremely numerous forged overprints on original or forged stamps: detailed comparison and, occasionally, even expertizing are indispensable. "Two heads are better than one." The forged overprints are usually too black, and the "T" of stamp Nos. 87–113 is positioned exactly under the value figure. All overprints were counterfeited in Geneva and applied on originals and on blocks of forgeries; thus the authenticity of the stamp should be verified before examining the overprint.

Forged Geneva cancellations: (1) one circle (25 mm), with date, DAMAO 2 NOV. 82. (2) Same, but with date in an inner rectangle: DIRECCAO DO CORREO 14 JUIN 84 DE MACAU; double circle (same diameter), CORREIO DE DAMAO 6/3 1885.

1882. Crown type. Nos. 114 to 120. *Originals:* two types. Type I: the cross on the crown is entirely blank. Type II: its four branches are cut by a color circle with a white center.

1913–14. Overprinted stamps. Nos. 252 to 305. A few *forged overprints:* comparison is necessary.

Portuguese Guinea

1880–83. Stamps overprinted GUINÉ. Nos. 1 to 24. *Forged Geneva stamps:* see Cape Verde.

Forged overprints: very numerous, especially in the first issue: detailed comparison is necessary. In the two types of forged Geneva overprints (GUINÉ on originals and forgeries) the overprint is too wide and the accent is too large.

Prince Edward Island

1861. Perf 9. No. 2. *Original:* typographed; 19–19¹⁄₄ x 22¹⁄₂ mm; the face is shaded with dotted lines; the oval's background is made of nineteen horizontal rows of vertical lines and of as many rows of dots.

Forgery: crude lithograph; perf 12¹⁄₂, which corresponds to no original perforation of this issue or of the following one; face is shaded with solid lines; seventeen rows of vertical lines.

1864. Perf 11, 11¹⁄₂, 12, and composite. Nos. 4 to 9. *Forgery:* 3-pence blue; see preceding issue. A counterfeiter with a diseased imagination created a 10-pence of the same type.

Forged cancellations: very numerous; these stamps should be acquired on cover only, and this applies also to the following issue. There are numerous fantastic cancellations, with cork shapes cut out to form various designs and executed by the postmaster general from 1865 to 1870; and, naturally, fantasies of fakers trying to arbitrate between mint and used values.

1872. 4-cent green (1872). No. 14. *Original:* 19²⁄₅ x 22¹⁄₂ mm. The upper inscription lettering is quite regular and aligned; the figures do not touch their frame; the white of the eye is free from shade lines; the lower figure frames encroach upon the value tablet by about ¹⁄₄ mm.

Forgery: lithographed; perf 13; irregular inscriptions; the top figures are touching their frames on the right; the white of the eye is shaded; the bottom figure frames and the tablet are on the same level.

Reprints (1893): in black; imperforate. (1) Printed with engraved corners, 1-, 2-, 3-, and 9-pence of 1861–64 (Nos. 2, 5; 3, 6; 4 and 9); 1-, 3-, 4-, and 6-cent of 1872 (Nos. 11, 13–15). (2) Printed from typographed plates: 2- and 4-pence; 3- and 12-cent.

Puerto Rico

1873–76. With paraph as overprint. Nos. 1 to 12. With respect to the mints, make sure that not having been used for anything they do not have a hand-punch cancellation; if they do, benzine will reveal traces of the cancellation; make sure also that the stamp actually having been canceled was not given a special face-lifting; finally, with respect to Nos. 8–12, make sure that you are not dealing with a stamp with cleaned fiscal obliteration, which was provided with a forged cancellation that was intended to conceal the dirty trick. The four types of paraphs were counterfeited well in Geneva applied upright or inverted. Comparison is necessary with rather common canceled Nos. 1, 4, 8, and 11, which usually are available with authentic overprint.

Subsequent issues. If doubtful stamps were encountered, they should be compared with those of the similar issues of Cuba or Spain. The 10-centavo brown of 1879 was faked by changing the figure "9" to "8." The error 8-cent brown of 1882–84 should be collected paired with the 3-centavo. The 3-centavo, No. 101, of 1893 (interior postal service) was counterfeited in Geneva; there are few corner squares or they are invisible; the lower curl of the "3" on the right is forked; large white spot on the right of the person seated on the boat's right side.

1898. Perf 14. Nos. 131 to 150. *Originals:* typographed; small shade lines above the upper legend, as in the Philippines stamps (see the illustration for this country); face and neck are hatched entirely; the color circle surrounding the center background is drawn delicately and is unbroken.

Forgeries: values in milesimas. Yellow paper, allowable measurements and perforation; lithographed in a brown that contains an insufficient amount of red; no Adam's apple (quite visible in the originals); not any or too few shade lines on the forehead, cheek, and front of the neck; the bottom of the eye has two bold oblique lines on the forehead, cheek, and front of the neck; the bottom of the eye has two bold oblique lines directed toward the nostril; the color circle around the center background is broken in numerous places; no fine hatching in the upper tablet above the legends (same defect in the lower tablet); in the two "M" letters of MILESIMAS, the center point does not extend down to the letter's foot. The 80-centavo, 1-, and 2-peso stamps were counterfeited in blocks in Geneva with the same defects as the values in milesimas, but they are attenuated now; the Adam's apple is not very visible; short lines in the top and bottom tablets are missing (see also Philippines).

Forged Geneva cancellations: double circle (27 mm), with date, PLAYA DE MAYAGUEZ 10 NOV 98 Pᵀᴼ-RICO and SAN GERMAN 10 OCT 98 (Pᵀᴼ-RICO).

1899. The PORTO-RICO overprint was counterfeited in Geneva and applied on canceled U.S. stamps.

Queensland

The stamps of New South Wales were used in this colony until 1860; in that year the stamps of the issue of 1854–56 were in use: 1-penny, 2-, 3-, 6-, 8-, and 12-pence, with double line watermark.

1860–80. Full-face portrait. Nos. 1 to 40. (and)

1861–65. Same. Stamps for registered letters. No. 1. *Originals:* expertly engraved, except the 1866 and 1880 issues, which were lithographed from the original engraving, with a few changes in the legends and in the design in the oval bandeau of 1880 stamps; three "diadem" stamps are square with a pearl in the center and four oblique lines directed toward the corners; three rows of jewels, the first of which has twenty-six rather square stones; the second row, twenty-three, two of which are coupled under the left stone of the center square; and the last (bottom) row, twenty-seven stones, the last one of which on the left is just above the eyebrow, the last one on the right, shaped like a "V," finishing on the ear. The eyes are made of curved lines, turned downwards; an oblique line, shaped like a *diabolo,* is fastened below the lower line and surrounded by a perfect semicircle, whose left side is touching the line and whose right extremity is not touching it. There are two small curved lines in the middle of the necklace's center stone. The oval background cross-ruling is quite visible; one can count twenty-two vertical lines from the oval's left side to the earring. The legends are regular and equidistant from the two lines of the oval; the same is true for the arabesques separating them. The outer oval is touching the lower frame on all four sides; this frame is drawn more delicately in the tangential parts than everywhere else. The corner ornamentation is formed with vertical, wide, and narrow bandeaux containing a great many small and large lozenges, lozenges that are not very wide, viewed edgewise; the whole thing forms an inimitable characteristic design. The catalogues give information on the watermarks, perforations, and shades.

Reprints (1895): (1) 1-penny, 2-, 3-, 6-pence, and 1-shilling violet of the 1868–75 issue (Nos. 24–27 and 29); perf 13; with this issue's watermark; white gum; different shades. 1-penny orange-brown and orange instead of vermilion-tinted orange; 2-pence bright blue and dark blue; 3-pence dark brown; 6-pence dull yellow-green instead of yellow-green or green; 1-shilling bright lilac and dull violet. Less successful impression than in the originals (observe especially the center background). (2) 1-penny, 2-, 3-, 6-pence, and 1-shilling of 1876 (Nos. 30–34), perf 12, watermarked "Q" crown as in that issue: 1-penny vermilion-tinted red; 2-pence ultramarine or dull blue; 3-pence bistre-brown; 6-pence dull green; and 1-shilling gray-violet. White gum. (3) A stamp for registered letters, perf 12, white gum; star watermark (1868–75); dark yellow.

Various *fakes:* perforated stamps with perforation trimmed and remargined or entirely remounted with or without subsequent repainting to make rare imperforate stamp Nos. 1–3; higher value stamps with fiscal obliteration cleaned (especially values of 1-shilling and above) to make mints or else used stamps after adding a forged cancellation.

Forgeries: (a) engraved; $19^1/_3$ x $22^1/_2$ mm; no watermark; imperforate. The top of the diadem's center square forms a Maltese cross, the two very wide top oblique lines terminating in the cross-ruled background. Three rows of jewels: the first one has twenty-three stones; second one, about twenty, but those on the left are not edged; third one, twenty-three. The eye circle is shaded; there is a single line for the mouth; very poorly drawn necklace, especially on the left; the center stone has a pearl in the middle; one might say that the large oval is not touching the frame on the left (minor axis, $18^1/_4$ mm instead of about $18^2/_3$ mm) and the tangential points; the inner frame is uniformly thick. Letter "Q" is made with an "O" and a curved line coupled to the center background oval (instead of an oblique line touching the body of the letter, but not the oval); the middle of the arabesque on the left is touching (interruption of) the large oval. No stippling near the middle of the neck and chest. The corner design is not comparable to that of the original; on the right and left, especially, the three rows of small lozenge-like dots are missing and are replaced by dots, lines, or vertical lines. (b) Early set, inexpertly lithographed in all values, even the 5-shilling rose, including the stamp for registered letters (REGISTERED); no watermark; various perforations. The lithographical process easily is distinguished from the engraving of the originals. For doubtful cases, we shall indicate a few distinguishing characteristics: irregular inscriptions with letters occasionally touching the oval lines; the three rows of stones in the diadem are executed very crudely — impossible to count them; no fine white lines between the hairlines; the interior corner design is not comparable, particularly at the bottom; the cross-ruling of the center background is too wide and forms blotches of color in places. The 5-shilling of 1882 was counterfeited lithographically in Geneva, without watermark; the design of the diadem's square jewels and of the necklace pearls is formless.

Réunion

See France.

Rhodesia

1909. RHODESIA overprint. *Forged overprints* on the £1 dark violet and the £2 brown (Nos. 70 and 71) of British South Africa to counterfeit No. 15 (£2 brown, London overprint) and No. 20 (£1 black, local overprint). Comparison is indispensable.

1913. HALF-PENY overprint. No. 58. Forged overprints, especially of the inverted overprint; same observation as above.

Romania

A specialized Romanian collection is one of the most interesting because of its great wealth of rare stamps, color combinations, and varieties.

I. Moldavia

1858 (July 15). Inscription in a circle. Nos. 1 to 4. Wild ox head surmounted by a five-pointed star.

Sheets of sixteen stamps (8 x 2), printed with four different handstamp dies, one for each value.

Paper: medium, tinted. Laid almost perceptibly, except for the 81-parale.

Quantities printed: 27- and 108-parale: 6,000. 54-parale: 10,000. 81-parale: 2,000. One sheet of each value was delivered to the postal authorities. According to *Die Postmarke,* 3,691 copies of the 27-parale, 4,772 of the 54-parale, 709 of the 81-parale, and 2,584 of the 108-parale probably were sold. This explains the rarity of the 81-parale stamp. In all probability, there no longer exists a single canceled 81-parale that is in perfect condition. The remaining stock was lost.

Varieties: the 27-parale is known to exist tête-bêche. Stamps sometimes were cut round instead of square by postal officials. Consequently, such copies are not considered damaged if the design is not touched. Value: 30 percent.

Essays, on white paper: extremely rare. Three sets known.

Reprints: none.

Cancellations: the usual postmark is Type A in blue. See illustration.

Originals: the best way to identify them is to make a detailed comparison with the copies of the two clichés in the illustration: star, wild ox head (check shape, shading and direction of horns, ears, eyes, nose, and mouth), figures, and post horn. A few additional details for each value can be noted:

27-parale: unprinted small circle arc in the horn's mouthpiece. The second "O" on top is very finely printed. The last letter is too far away and is wider than the fourth letter of the second word. There are two shading lines on the left and three on the right, touching

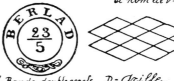

Romania–Moldavia cancellations: A. Moldavian. B. FRANCO, in various types with town name. C. Double circle, date, ornaments. D. Grill. E. Double circle, date, inscription. F. Thimble, single circle. G. Framed FRANCO. H. Rare Galatz registry cancel.

the cheek line. The bottom of the ox's muzzle does not touch the horn. Circle: 19½ mm.

54-parale: partial left ear, much higher than the one on the right. Nose lines are parallel. The ox's right horn (on the left in the stamp) is more concave than the other. Circle: 19½ mm.

81-parale: color dot between the star point and the ox's left horn (on the right in the stamp). The outer line of this horn is thinner than the one turned toward the star. There is an unprinted dot in the post horn's opening. Circle: 19⅔ mm.

108-parale: the circle is thinned down or broken on the right of the last letter of the inscription. The shading of the post horn is much worse than in the other values. Circle: about 20 mm.

Forgeries: there are many counterfeits, some of which are rather deceptive. Almost all of the early forgeries are crudely executed and easily identifiable by means of the following data:

27-parale: typographed. Thick, nonlaid paper. Defective lettering. Curve in the base of the "2." No dot after the "7." The ox's mouth is touching the post horn.

54-parale: (1) lithographed on laid paper. Upper star point directed toward the middle of the "K." Right ox horn directed toward the "C." (2) Lithographed, vertically laid paper. Star point directed toward the right foot of the "K." (3) Thin, nonlaid paper. Inscription too far from the circle. Left ox horn directed between "P" and "N." (4) Typographed on laid paper. Left ox horn directed toward the "N." (5) Typographed on thick, nonlaid paper. Dark green. Right ox horn directed toward the second "O." Right ear directed toward the "P."

81-parale: (1) typographed. Right ox horn directed toward the body of the "C." Star point directed toward the middle of the "K." Left ox horn, between "P" and "N." (2) Another forgery has the same characteristics, as well as many others. (3) Lithographed. The "81" figures are placed in the left half of the oval formed by the post horn.

108-parale: All stamps on nonlaid paper. (1) Lithographed. Left ox horn directed toward the "P." Inscriptions are much too fine. (2) Typographed. Ears form black triangles. (3) Typographed. The star point is directed between the "C" and the "K."

These forgeries are pen canceled: large circle; large, freakish, square dots. Sometimes not canceled. Forgeries also were fraudulently handstamped with an authentic JASSY postmark.

Modern forgeries: if the early forgeries are rather ludicrous, three modern sets are, by contrast, rather cleverly executed. Two of these are photolithographed (in one of them, the "81-parale" is missing). There are differences in format, paper, design, and shades. Comparison with originals is indispensable. We have not had the opportunity to see the third set, which has been offered for sale as "rare reprints": 27-parale on thick paper (also 54-parale); dark green (also 81-parale); and the 108-parale on lilac-tinted rose-colored paper with letter "O" circle broken as far as the post horn's opening. These probably are forgeries from a clandestine printing made with worn original handstamp dies, rather than forgeries made with completely new materials.

1858 (November 1). Same type. Rectangular format. Nos. 5 to 7. *Quantities printed:* on azure-tinted paper, 960; 7,040 and 2,816 copies respectively of Nos. 5–7; 7,136, 21,472, and 11,264 copies on white paper (1859).

Select: four margins, minimum width: 2½ mm.

Paper: pelure (20–30 microns); white or slightly brownish gum, also yellowish gum, which sometimes has given a pronounced yellowish shade to the paper. The 40- and 80-parale are found on slightly yellowish paper with white gum.

Sheets of thirty-two stamps (8 x 4). Eight tête-bêche stamps in the middle. The stamps, handstamp-printed like the preceding issue, usually have defective impressions.

Shades: a few shades of the 40- and 80-parale stamps.

Varieties: 5-parale, two types: Type I. lower frame unbroken. Type II. Lower frame broken below the "A" of HAP (Romanian abbreviation for PARA). Color spots often found on both sides of the head. The 5-parale on bluish paper is always Type I. Canceled, this stamp is probably of greater rarity than the 81-parale of the first issue. The 5-parale, Type I, on white paper (first printing) is rare used, and exceedingly rare mint. The 5-parale, Type II, is a stock remainder that has not been found canceled. The first printing on white paper of the 40-parale is blue-green, yellowish gum. Its printing is defective.

Cancellations: usually Type B. There are two FRANCO postmarks for Galatz, the second one being like the Jassy postmark, but with double oval, with one of the ovals pearled and inscription "No. 2" in the middle: rare. A dated postmark, Type A, is found on cover. Type B cancellations exist in blue, red, violet, and black.

Pairs: 4U. On cover: 2U.

Originals: the ox's muzzle does not touch the post horn in any of the values.

5-parale: this measures 15¼–½ x 18¼–½ mm; however, we have found a Type I, 15 x 18 mm. The bottom of the star is open and its upper branch is less tapered than in the others.

40-parale: top of star is open. The zero of the top "40" is somewhat wider than the bottom one. The tops of these figures are open, except in heavily inked impressions. The bottom "4" is a bit too low in relation to the zero and is slightly less high; format, 16½–17 x 19–19½ mm, depending on the printing.

80-parale: the "P" of the top inscription is further away than at bottom. On the other hand, "80 HA" is slanted to the right in the lower inscription. The two figures are of uniform height, except on top where the "8" is somewhat larger. The upper point of the star is half open; format 17 x 19¼–½ mm. The three values (5-, 40-, 80-parale) sometimes have color spots on both sides of the wild ox's head (in the 80-parale, they also are found on both sides of the lower inscription).

The three values display characteristics that are typical of handstamp-printed stamps (typical also of hand-applied overprints): double impressions or impressions deviating from one or the other frame each time the printing device was not held quite vertically, and often a halo shadow of the entire frame when the device was not applied firmly and sharply. For these reasons, defective impressions are frequent.

Forgeries: minute comparison with the cliché reproduced in the illustration and use of the preceding information will ensure quick identification of the forgeries. There are about twelve of these for each value. To give a detailed description of them would be tedious and useless. Suffice it to say: The star often has only five branches, or else six, but all of them well closed. The wild ox has ears that perceive with great difficulty the sounds coming from the Moldavian plains; its eyes have an excessively menacing look; its degenerate muzzle looks like a pig's snout. The top point of the star and the ox's horns and ears are deviant. The muzzle frequently touches the post horn. The figures are not congruent (the top "4" figure is closed at times). Lettering is not congruent either. Finally, a glance at the excessively small dimensions (5-parale, $15^{1}/_{2}$–16 mm wide!), or the excessively large ones (80-parale, $20^{1}/_{2}+$ mm high!), and at the medium or thick paper also will help to fish out a few more counterfeits.

A good-looking Paris set, but with noncongruent formats and inscription lettering is found in pairs, strips, and blocks (!) on white or azure-tinted paper, and sometimes on cover with relatively well-counterfeited forged postmarks. Compare. There is also a so-called "reprint" of the 5-parale (see preceding issue). Careful comparison is necessary. There are rare essays of the 40- and 80-parale stamps (regular octagon, five-pointed star, muzzle touching the post horn, etc.).

Used postal forgeries: hardly any better than the foregoing; noncongruent dimensions. 5-parale, the first letter of the upper inscription is formed by two "I" letters. 40-parale, the word SCRISOREI, which is too convex, does not follow exactly the slight curvature of the right frame. 80-parale, the "80" figures are only $1^{1}/_{2}$ mm high instead of $1^{3}/_{4}$–2 mm.

Forged cancellations are numerous on forgeries and originals. The latter's cancellation always must be compared. The crude forged Geneva set is provided with a circular postmark, 30 mm in diameter, with circular inscription, KASSA CLOWNA POCEYOWA on two lines.

Fakes: white paper rarely is found faked into bluish paper: make comparison. Remember that the 40-parale ultramarine and the 80-parale bright scarlet red and brown (a very rare shade) do not exist on bluish paper. Faking of the 5-parale, Type II, into Type I is more frequent, so compare paper, format, and gum to upset the applecart of fraud.

II. Moldavia-Walachia

1862 (June). Eagle and wild ox. Nos. 8 to 10.
Select: four margins, minimum width: $1^{1}/_{2}$ mm.

Sheets: first printing: thirty-two stamps (8 x 4), handstamp-printed as above; irregular gutters; eight tête-bêche stamps in the middle of the sheet. This printing is identified by the impression, especially the frames (see preceding issue). Examples sometimes are found without any gutter on one side. Sometimes, in the same sheet, there are very good impressions, and next to them, really defective impressions in which the eagle, the wild ox, and the post horn are nothing but a spot, and in which the two frames merge into a single one, especially in the 6-parale vermilion-tinted red, No. 9b.

Second printing (March 1863): typographed in sheets of forty (8 x 5). The stamps in the third horizontal row are wrong way up in relation to the others. There is a single tête-bêche in the middle of the sheet.

The stamps of the first printing are much rarer than those of the second. 3-parale: 3M. 6-parale (see prices of shade varieties, Nos. 9a and 9b). 30-parale white: 5M, 2U.

Paper: first printing: pelure, 25 microns to thick (3-parale and 30-parale, 40–55 microns), wove or laid horizontally. Second printing: wove pelure (6-parale, thick), horizontally laid, and blue-tinted wove (30-parale).

Shades: the 3-parale bright yellow belongs to the first printing, as well as the lemon and olive-yellow shades (rare). Likewise, the 6-parale vermilion-tinted red or bright and dark carmine. The second printing of the 6-parale has light shades of lilac-rose, rose, and carmine-tinted rose. Both printings have the 3-parale orange and the 30-parale light blue, blue, and dark blue.

Varieties: Nos. 9a and 9b are known bisected (to frank printed matter): very rare. The 3- and 6-parale, second printing, are known to exist with thick yellowish gum that has yellowed the paper. The tête-bêche stamps on laid paper are worth three times the value of tête-bêche on wove. The 30-parale on blue-tinted paper is found in two printings; it is very rare in the second. Minor lettering flaws: 50M, 50U. "E" of SCRISOREI broken at bottom, 30-parale "E" and "I" of the same word touching each other at bottom. Letter "R" of PAR with broken upper loop. (This is frequent in the 6-parale, less so in the 30-parale.) Large color dot under the "O" of FRANCO and on the "R" of PAR (6-parale). The 6-parale is known to exist with double impression: rare.

Pairs: 3U. See catalogue for pairs with one stamp wrong way up.

Cancellations: usually Types B or C, in red, blue, and black. All others are rare.

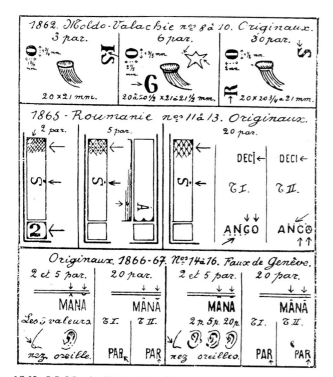

1862. Moldavia-Walachia. Nos. 8 to 10. Originals. Middle: Romania Nos. 11 to 13. Originals. Bottom: 1866–67. Nos. 14 to 16. Originals. Geneva forgeries.

Originals: see the distinctive features in the illustration.

Forgeries are rather numerous. Typographed or lithographed. The 3-parale was counterfeited on lemon-tinted wove paper, golden yellow, and orange, the two frames merging into a single one, or else with the "O" of FRANCO being $2^{1}/_{2}$ x $1^{1}/_{4}$ mm. With respect to the 6- and 30-parale stamps, the early forgeries frequently do not have dots after the figures. The word PAR touches the post horn, or the stars have six points. In a vermilion forgery of the 6-parale, the horn has vertical shade lines! Modern forgeries, especially the Geneva set, were more successful. The details of the authentic stamps shown in the illustration are adequate for spotting the forgeries.

Forged cancellations are very numerous. Comparison is necessary for all values. The 3-parale, laid paper, and the 3-parale of the second printing are not known to exist used. The 6-parale second printing (lilac-rose on thick, white paper, carmine-tinted lilac on thin paper, and carmine-tinted rose on pelure) is in reality an unissued stamp. The Geneva forgeries have a noncongruent Type B cancellation (JASSY).

III. Romania

1865 (January 1). Portrait of Prince Couza. Nos. 11 to 13. *Sheets* of 192 stamps. Lithographed. 20-parale, 200 stamps.

Select: four margins, minimum width: $1^{1}/_{2}$ mm.

Paper: medium, thick (2- and 20-parale). Vertically laid (2- and 5-parale); on azure-tinted and bluish paper (20-parale). The latter is very rare.

Varieties: the 20-parale has two types (see illustration). In Type I, the bottom of the oval is $^{2}/_{5}$ mm away from the framework. In Type II, the oval is touching the frame, or else there is a slight gap. The figures differ, depending on transfer plate flaws. 2-parale and 5-parale, on thin paper: 3M. 20-parale, on azure-tinted paper: 20M, 5U. 5-parale, on yellowish paper: 3M. 20-parale, on the same paper: 50M, 30U. The 5-parale and 20-parale are known with double impression: rare. The 20-parale was bisected: very rare.

Pairs and mint blocks: common. Pairs: 3U. Blocks: rare.

Cancellations: Types C, D, and F: common. Type C in blue is less common. Type B is not very common. Type G: rare.

Essays (Duloz): same portrait in a circle; Greek ornaments on sides.

Originals: see the illustration for the distinctive characteristics.

Forgeries: numerous, absurd, early forgeries. 2-parale, with figures more than 2 mm high. Moreover, to lend excitement to his adventure, the counterfeiter inflicted the erroneous "doua deci parale" (20-parale) upon the 2-parale, and, on the 20-parale, "doua parale" (2-parale). (This appeared in my *Catalogue du Spécialiste d'Europe,* 1922.) The other early forgeries are not much better. To spot them, examine the hair-net burelage and the distinctive marks shown in the illustration.

The set was lithographically counterfeited in Geneva (F.) with greater success, using two different clichés for each stamp value (20-parale, first cliché is Type I; second is Type II). None has the color dot under the "S" of POSTA. The set from the first clichés is crude. Respective dimensions: $18^{1}/_{2}$ x 21 mm; $18^{1}/_{2}$ x $21^{1}/_{2}$ mm; $18^{1}/_{2}$ x $21^{1}/_{4}$ mm. The set from the second clichés is much better, but comparison will show design defects and noncongruent shades. Respective dimensions of the forgeries: $18^{3}/_{4}$ x 21mm; 19 x 21 mm; $18^{1}/_{2}$ x $20^{3}/_{4}$ mm. Originals: 2-parale, $18^{1}/_{2}$ x 21 mm; 5-parale, $18^{3}/_{5}$ x 21 mm; 20-parale, Type I, $18^{1}/_{3}$ mm, Type II, $18^{1}/_{2}$–$^{2}/_{3}$ mm, both by about $21^{1}/_{4}$ mm.

Forged cancellations are frequent on the originals of the 2- and 5-parale stamps. Comparison or expertizing is indicated. Forged Geneva postmarks: Type C, GALATI 4/9 and BUCARESTI; Type F, JASSY FRANCA.

1866–67. Head of Prince Charles I. Nos. 14 to 16.

Select: four margins, minimum width: 1 mm. Beginning with this issue, the imperforate Romanian stamps have a very adhesive gum that is difficult to remove, even in hot water. Insistence on removing the gum will probably damage the stamp.

Quantities printed: 2-parale, 130,000; 5-parale, 160,000; 20-parale, 250,000. The stamps were lithographed.

Sheets: 204 stamps, also 200 (12 x 17; block of four in unprinted upper right corner) of the 20-parale from the second and third (?) plates.

Transfer blocks: the transfer matrix had six stamps (3 x 2). It easily can be reconstructed by means of transfer defects. Moreover, the sheets contain a rather large number of transfer flaws. (These are rarer, since they are found only once in sheets from the same plate.) These transfer defects are also called plate defects.

Two types of the 20-parale: Type I, the right Greek ornament begins under the "2." Type II, the right Greek ornament begins under the zero, etc. In the plates of 200 stamps, there are sixty-seven Type I stamps and 133 Type II stamps.

Shades: thin paper, 2-parale, yellow; very pale yellow and lemon yellow: 3M. 5-parale, light blue, dark blue, indigo: 50M, 50U. 20-parale, pale rose and rose. Thick paper, orange-tinted yellow: 3M. Bright yellow; dark blue. 20-parale, claret and purplish claret. The 2-parale is also found on medium paper.

Dot in the Greek ornament: the catalogues have exaggerated the value of the 20-parale (thick and thin paper) that has a dot inside and at the top of the right Greek ornament (Type II). This is a transfer flaw in that value's first plate (it is not found in the second and third plate sheets) and is no more interesting or important than the "broken" circle above the "D" (2-parale), the "broken" frame, bottom left (5-parale), or the center background traversed at neck level by a white line (20-parale). The double print of the 20-parale is much rarer.

Pairs: pairs and mint blocks are not rare, but blocks of six (the complete transfer block) are very much in demand. Pairs: 4U. Used blocks: very rare.

Cancellations: Type C: common in black, less common in blue, rare in violet. Type E: in demand. Type D: 2U.

Originals: see the distinctive characteristics in the illustration.

Early forgeries: crude. The accents on the "A" letters of ROMANA are missing, or else these letters, with tops trimmed, are smaller than the others. Two heavy lines form the lip. The Greek ornaments are much too thick, or, on the contrary, too thin. The poorly executed inscription lettering is not $1^4/_5$ mm high as in the originals, and the whole design is arbitrary.

Geneva forgeries (F.): better executed. The illustration will show a few defects. Measurements: 2-parale, $19^1/_4$ x $24^1/_2$ mm; 5-parale, $18^3/_4$ x $23^3/_4$ mm; 20-parale, Type I, 19 x 24 mm; Type II, $19^1/_4$ x 24 mm. There are two different clichés for the 20-

parale (two types) with eye, mouth, and ear differences. (The originals are 19 mm high and about $24^1/_4$ mm wide. However, we have found $18^2/_3$ x 24 mm for the 5-parale indigo.)

Forged cancellations: numerous on the 2-parale, and especially on the 5-parale. This canceled value is very rare: make comparison. For forged Geneva cancellations, see the preceding issue, as well as Type B, JASSY.

1868–70. Same type. Nos. 17 to 20. *Select:* Four margins about $1^1/_4$ mm wide.

Quantities printed: 2-ban, 120,000 (Plate I), 48,000 (Plate II), and 48,000? (Plate II, retouched, 1870). 3-ban, 100,000 (1870). 4-ban, 30,000 (Plate I), and an unknown number from Plate II. 18-ban, 170,000 (Plate I), and 120,000 (Plate II).

Sheets of ninety-six stamps (twelve transfers of eight).

Block transfer plate: eight stamps (4 x 2). Transfer flaws make it possible to reconstitute the *bloc report* for each plate. Plate reconstruction using single stamps is almost impossible, despite the fact that the transfer flaws (found once per sheet in a plate) allow one to locate a certain number of copies. Plating is feasible using blocks only, the sheets having only ninety-six stamps. The transfer matrix of the 4-ban (figures scratched off) was used to form the 3-ban transfer plate. Since the figures for the 3-ban were engraved one by one on the matrix stone, they are all different, and thus can be used, along with the transfer flaws of the 4-ban, to reconstitute the block transfer plate.

Plates: 2-ban, two plates: Plate I, yellow shades; Plate II, bright orange shades. 18-ban, Plate I, rose and carmine-tinted rose shades; Plate II, red and vermilion-tinted shades. 3-ban, several (five?) plates. This question has not yet been sufficiently studied. Single printings made from rebuilt plates with the same transfer matrix are involved, of course.

Paper: thin, medium, thick, white or yellowish: rare.

Shades: 2-ban, dull ochre-yellow to bright orange. The dark ochre and the dark orange-red are rare. 3-ban, various mauve and violet shades; the pale lilac-gray and the dark reddish dull violet are rare. 4-ban, dark blue and pale blue; sky blue is rare mint: 2.50M. A very dark blue, close to indigo, is in demand: 50M, 50U. 18-ban, many shades, from pale old rose to bright carmine (rare) and from pale dull red to vermilion and bright red (rare).

Varieties: 2-ban, laid paper: very rare. Some value is being assigned to certain very visible transfer flaws, for example, FOSTA instead of POSTA on the 2-ban. This is no more rare than design defects of the same importance. The 3- and 4-ban were bisected and are very rare. The 18-ban was unofficially rouletted. The 4-ban was retouched under the "4" on the right. The

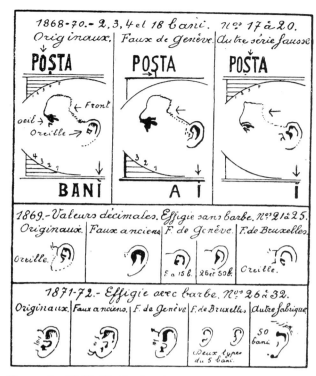

Romania. 1868–70. 2-, 3-, 4-, and 18-bani. Nos. 17–20. Originals: forehead, eye, ear. Geneva forgeries; another forged set. Middle: 1869 decimal values. Beardless portrait. Nos. 21–25. Originals, early forgeries, Geneva forgeries, Brussels forgery. Bottom: 1871–72 Portrit with beard, Nos. 26–32 originals, early forgeries, Geneva forgeries, Brussels forgery, another forgery.

hair and beard of the 2-ban were retouched. The worn plate 2-ban is rare. No. 19 on card paper is, perhaps, an essay?

Cancellations: Type C in blue, Type E in black: common. Type C in black: less common. There is also the small double circle postmark with date, usually applied on cover (22 mm in diameter, Graïova, etc.): less common. The small Type F postmark is in demand. Grill, Type D, in black or blue: 2U. Type G, FRANCO or RECOMMANDÉ, framed: 3U. All others are rare.

Pairs and blocks are very much in demand for plating. Pairs of the 2-ban: 4U. 3-ban and 4-ban: 5U. 18-ban: 6U. Pairs and mint blocks of the 3-ban are not rare. Mint pair of 4-ban: 4M. Blocks of four, used: rare; 2-ban: 16U; 18-ban: very rare.

Originals: the illustration gives information on the principal characteristics. You will notice that the forehead looks like a well-shaped mushroom.

Early forgeries: in one set the hairline is indicated by a heavy white line. The set has no dots or accents under the "S" of POSTA nor on the "A" letters of

ROMANA. The letters are only 1½ mm high instead of 2 mm. No dot on the "I" of BANI. Noncongruent ear.

Modern forgeries: I. Geneva set. (See the illustration for the principal characteristics.) Each value had two clichés. In the second, there are four lines of shading above the figure and two fine lines under POSTA; the "P" of POSTA is closer to the left edge than in the first cliché. In stamps from both clichés, the "mushroom" forehead is too elongated on the left and the ear is abnormal (see illustration). There are previously described cancellations, with the following additions: square or lozenge of large square dots, thin, barred circle, Type D, grill with irregular lozenges.

II. A set called "pointed mushroom" (see illustration). White line as hairline; all values on thin paper; the 4-ban also on yellowish paper. General appearance and shades are good; consequently, the set is found in many collections. Forged cancellation: Type F, BUCURESTI 18 JUN 71.

III. A very deceptive photolithographed set in which the head contour is too rounded and the shades are arbitrary (2-ban brownish yellow, etc.), yellowish paper (55 microns), and noncongruent format: 17¾ x 23 mm instead of 18 x 23¾–24 mm. Forged cancellation, Type C, JASSY, and date in hieroglyphs.

1869. Decimal values. Nos. 21 to 25. *Select:* four margins, 1 mm wide.

Sheets of 100 (10 x 10), or twenty-five times the transfer block of four (2 x 2). Beardless portrait, with sideburns only.

Rare shades: 5-ban dark orange (1870): 2M, 2U; dark red-orange: 3M, 3U; dull orange on yellowish paper: 3M. 10-ban sky blue: 50M, 25U; indigo: 2M, 50U; indigo on yellowish paper: 3M, 3U. 15-ban dull rose: 2M, 50U; blood red: 2M, 2U; vermilion-tinted red or blood red on yellowish paper: 3M, 3U. 25-ban orange-red and indigo: 50M, 50U. 50-ban dark carmine center: 50U.

Paper: white or yellowish (see above).

Varieties: attractive range of color shades, especially in the graduated color tones of the center and frame of the 25- and 50-ban stamps. The 15-ban was trisected for 5-ban (very rare). 50-ban, double impression of center: very rare (bad cleanup from a previous printing); 10- and 25-ban, retouched: 3–5M and U (white line corrections, hair contour, occipital area, and nape of neck). As in the other lithographed issues, one finds quite visible transfer plate or transfer flaws, for example, 15-ban, with a large dot before the "R" of ROMANA, Type 4 of the transfer plate; 15-ban, with a damaged "N": CIHCI; 25-ban, with a long "I" in DOUEDECI, etc. The 15-ban is known to exist with unofficial perforation. On laid paper this value is a stock remainder.

The 50-ban is known bisected: very rare. 10-ban, double impression: very rare.

Cancellations: Types C, E, and F: common in black or blue. Type C (or A), 22 mm. Thimble cancellation: less common. Type D: 2U. Type G in black or blue: 3U. Type H: 3U.

Pairs: 4U. 5-ban: 5U. 15-ban, on yellowish paper: 5U. Blocks are rather rare: 12U. 50-ban: 16U.

Originals: all values, except 5-ban, have a faint dot over the "I" of BANI (touching the tablet frame). The inscriptions are clear-cut, remembering, however, that we are dealing with lithographed stamps. POSTA and ROMANA are equidistant from the edges of their tablets. See the preceding illustration also for ear details.

Early forgeries: there is a bad set in which the letters of POSTA are much too close to the left side of the tablet; wide margins; noncongruent ear. No dot over the "I" of BANI. Forged cancellation with date or bars.

Modern forgeries: I. Geneva (F.). Relatively crude lithographed stamps; no dot over the "I" of BANI, all on yellowish paper; hair insufficiently evident on temple and behind the ear (see the illustration). Forged cancellations as above.

II. Brussels: very deceptive, photolithographed set. All stamps on yellowish paper; noncongruent ear; color dots in the inscriptions; noncongruent formats. The 15-ban (congruent format) is a copy of Type 3 of the transfer plate, but the ornament on the left of the "C" of CINCIS in the counterfeit is heavily damaged, in fact almost blank. In the 50-ban, the first "C" of CINCI has a cedilla. Height 24 mm instead of 23¾ mm, etc. Forged cancellation, Type F: ROMAN 20 SEP. Type C: BRAILA, circles 6 mm apart, etc.

1871. Bearded portrait of Prince Charles. Nos. 26 to 30. *Sheets* of 100 stamps. Transfer block of ten stamps (2 x 5). The transfer matrix of the 10-ban yellow was used for the 10-ban blue (December 1871). 15-ban, transfer block of eight (4 x 2).

Select: four margins, minimum width: 1 mm.

Rare shades: 5-ban pale rose: 2M, 2U; geranium: 4M, 50U; on rose-tinted paper: rare. 10-ban dark orange: 50U; yellow on yellowish paper: 2M, 2U. 10-ban ultramarine: 2M. 15-ban pale red: 50U. 25-ban light brown: 2M, 50U.

Varieties: the 15-ban with CIN6I is transfer plate flaw found on one stamp in eight. The 10-ban dark yellow is found with defective impression. Fine impressions of the 10-ban ultramarine and 25-ban very dark sepia are in demand. 10-ban yellow, bisected: very rare. Canceled marginal copies are very rare. 10-ban yellow on laid paper: very rare.

Cancellations: Type F, in black or blue: very common. Type E, in black or blue: less common.

Pairs: 4U. 10-ban blue: 5U. Blocks are rare.

Originals: the matrix plates of the preceding issue (frames and inscriptions) were used for this set of reproductions; consequently, the 5-ban has no dot over

the "I" of BANI; the portrait was entirely remade, curly hair, nose, eye, ear, beard, and neck nape shading in parallel lines (the 15-ban sometimes has a retouched nape — vertical lines: rare). As for the ear, see the illustration.

Fakes: a few beards painted on the 10- and 15-ban of the preceding issue. This is childish work. Comparison with the rest of the portrait will suffice. The latter is not shaped the same way and does not occupy the same place in the center oval.

Early forgeries: wide margins. POSTA is much too close to the left side of the tablet. In the 30-ban, the Greek ornament on the left is touching the inner frame, eye... "Persian." See the illustration for the ear. Barred cancellation.

Modern forgeries: I. Geneva (F.). The whole set on yellowish or rose-tinted paper (!) including the two 10-ban stamps on vertically laid paper. Rather crude; compare hair, beard, ear, neck nape shading — that will be enough. The 50-ban is like the other stamps of the set, which have three lines between the figures and the BANI inscription. Noncongruent shades. Cancellations as above with the addition of a thimble cancel, Type F, JASSY 10/8, 17 mm in diameter.

II. Brussels. Two different types of the 5-ban. (The rest of the set must have been or will be forged following these two types.) The top banderoles have no cross-hatching. The bottom of the "S" of POSTA is an unbroken line, whereas in the originals it is broken, except in Type 9 of the transfer plate or in blotchy impressions. Hair not well executed. Noncongruent upper inscription lettering.

III. Another (unidentified) forger. In the 50-ban the "C" of CINCI is touching the lower tablet and the "N" of this word is much too wide. The outer frames extend into the margins. The chin is straight; see the illustration for the ear. Figure "5" on the right is at some distance from the line on its left. The left Greek ornament has only five elements instead of six, etc.

IV. The 10- and 50-ban were photolithographically counterfeited, with noncongruent dimensions (originals: 19½ x 23¾ mm). Comparative study is necessary, especially of the ear.

1872 (end of August). 10- and 50-ban. Nos. 31 and 32. The 10- and 50-ban stamps of 1872 should be catalogued separately because a very different issue is involved. As a matter of fact, the frame of the 10-ban blue of 1871 and that of the 50-ban of 1869 were reproduced to form the matrix plates of these two stamps, but a vertical line to the right of the figure on the right and to the left of the figure on the left was added in both values. Moreover, the 10-ban has a blue line extending from the Greek ornament on the right, between letters "A" and "N," which connects the tops of the "N" and of the second "A" of ROMANA. In the 50-ban, one finds a short blue line above the left downstroke of the "N" of the same word. The portrait is the same as the one in the 1871 issue, but the latter was reproduced, unfortunately, from a bad impression with blotchy neck nape shading; this reduced the width of the lower part of the neck. Also, the head was tipped toward the right in the oval, and the back of the head is 1 mm from the tablet under "R O," instead of $1^{1}/_{2}$ mm, as in the preceding issue.

Paper: 10-ban, white, yellowish, and vertically laid. 50-ban, white.

Shades: pale to dark ultramarine. The latter, which is from a good impression (Paris), is rare. There are intermediate shades of ultramarine approaching milky blue. Light blue on yellowish paper: 3M, 2U. Shades of dark blue (more greenish than No. 28, blue): not very common. The 50-ban is very common mint (everything is relative!), with red center, but very rare, on the other hand, with original cancellation (95 percent of the cancellations are forged). As contrast, this value with dark carmine center almost never is found as a mint stamp: 3M. The 10-ban on laid paper is rare with authentic cancellation. Used pairs: 5U.

Varieties: 10-ban with a color line in the left margin (1 mm): 2M, 2U. 50-ban, with double frame impression: very rare. The 50-ban without the portrait is printer's waste.

Forgeries: see preceding issue.

IV. Perforated Stamps

1872 (January). Same type. Perf $12^{1}/_{2}$. Nos. 33 to 35. *Sheets* and transfer plate blocks are as in the issue of 1871 (100 stamps: 12 x 8, plus four, top right, for the 25-ban).

Shades: 5-ban carmine or carmine-rose: common; geranium: 5M, 3U; brick red: very rare; a pale rose is rarer still. 25-ban chocolate: 50M, 25U.

Varieties: 10-ban, pairs imperforate in the middle exist. The 10-ban was bisected: rare.

Fakes: wide-margin copies of the 10- and 25-ban were trimmed to make imperforate stamps of the preceding issue. Moral: buy the aforesaid imperforates with the fine imprint of the first impressions (ultramarine and dark sepia). Rare shades of the 5-ban must be examined carefully to ensure that they have not been fraudulently perforated.

Cancellations: as above.

1872 (October). ROMANIA inscription. Nos. 36 to 42. Paris printing. Perf 14 x $13^{1}/_{2}$.

Sheets of 150 stamps (15 x 10). Typographed. French control number.

Shades: rather numerous for each value. 5-ban olive-yellow is rare. No. 45a is really blue-black. Two tones of ordinary blue are found, not including the ultramarine shades. 3-ban, on blue-tinted paper: 8M, 4U. 25-ban, sulfur color, is rare.

Varieties: the 15-ban stamp is known printed on both sides. The whole set is known to exist imperforate; these are stock remainders. There are two 50-ban types: I. Left figure "5" with long top bar. II. Same, with short bar. 3- and 10-ban have been found bisected: rare. The imperforates without gum are printer's waste.

Essays: without gum in all values. In the originals' shade, one should mention: $1^{1}/_{2}$-ban on greenish paper; 5-ban imperf 13 [*sic*] top and bottom (overprint ANULLATA); 5-ban green; 10-, 15-, and 50-ban.

Cancellations: as on the preceding issue. However, there are rare cancellations on this issue and the following ones, for example: Type D in black or blue; Type F, thimble cancellation ISMAÏL in blue; CAHUL in blue; PITESTI in dark blue; BOTOSANI in red, etc. Also TYPE E (thimble) in black or blue; RECOMMANDÉ, etc.

1876–78. Same. Defective impression. Nos. 43 to 47. Bucharest printing. Perf $13^{1}/_{2}$, $11^{1}/_{2}$, and composite. There are quite a few composite perforations, as well as diverse varieties attributable to the bad printing. The 15-ban with the so-called "mask" portrait is in demand.

Shades: the $1^{1}/_{2}$-ban mint in olive-gray is not common.

Varieties: 5-ban error in blue. There is one error per sheet of the 10-ban. Many errors were removed from the sheets and overprinted ANULLATA. The 5-ban is known to exist imperforate with cancellation, and a few values are imperforate on one side. 5-ban and 30-ban, printed on both sides; 5- and 15-ban, printed on both sides and double impression: rare. The 30-ban was issued in 1878.

Reprint of the error in whole sheets, perf $11^{1}/_{2}$.

Fakes: (1) reprint offered as original error. (The impression of the reprint is better. Dark blue. Check the perforation.) (2) Chemical alteration of the 5-ban green of the following issue. (It is useless to describe here the chemical product in question.) (3) Faking by scraping off the ANULLATA overprint. Moral: buy the error in a pair in which there is an ordinary stamp.

Used postal forgeries: irregular inscriptions; perf 10.

1879. Change of shades. Nos. 48 to 54. Perf 11, $11^{1}/_{2}$, $13^{1}/_{2}$, and $11^{1}/_{2}$ x $13^{1}/_{2}$, and $13^{1}/_{2}$ x $11^{1}/_{2}$. Composite perforations are rare. Numerous shades.

Varieties: 15-ban, Plate I (Type I), figure "1" without oblique terminal line. Plate II (Type II), "1" is normal. Type III, "1" is shorter: 2U. Type I, mint: 2M; very rare in brick red, mint, or used. The $1^{1}/_{2}$-, 5-, and 10-ban are known imperforate. The 10-ban having been printed from the plate of the preceding issue, the 5-ban error is present in rose and carmine. A few used copies are known: extremely rare. Likewise, there are two types of the 50-ban. The 3-ban was bisected: rare. There are imperforate varieties, especially the 5-ban in a pair imperforate between.

Reprint of the error stamp in sheets are dark carmine and rose, on glossy paper like that of the preceding issue. The impression of the reprints is better than that of the originals. Buy the error only in a pair with a normal stamp. Copies overprinted ANULLATA come from the original sheets. The imperforate 50-ban yellow is an essay.

Fakes: as in the preceding issue.

Subsequent issues (1885 and 1887. Nos. 57 to 69.) *Geneva forgeries (F.):* the two sets, perf 11½ or 13½. These are of very good appearance even if the impression and paper shades are not always consistent. They belong to those reliable stamps of lesser importance that have an easy entrée into collections (via export across the Atlantic). The eagle's tail is shaped like a goblet. The format is 18½ mm high by 22 mm wide instead of 18½ x 22¼–½ mm. The illustration shows a few differences in design. All of these forgeries have no watermark; consequently, the 1889 set is not involved.

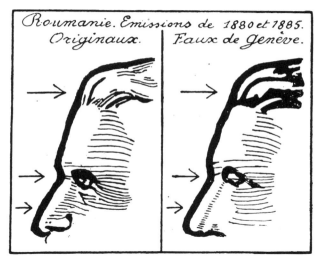

Romania issues of 1880 and 1885. Originals and Geneva forgeries.

Issue of 1891. Nos. 80 to 94. *Geneva forgeries (F.):* also well reproduced. However, comparison with an original will show differences in design, chiefly in the ornaments on white background on the right and left of ROMANIA, in the figures, and in figure "25" of the inscription. Perf 10½. Yellowish paper.

Forged cancellations: circle with date, double circle, 20 mm, BUCURESCI 23 MAI 91; also, 22 MAI 91. (The outer circle is broken between the "I" and the ornament between the circles.)

Issue of 1903. Nos. 137 to 151. The whole set was photolithographically counterfeited. The format and perforations don't match the originals and the paper is too thick. A Bucharest set is not nearly so good:

compare the design of the horses (Nos. 137–44) and of the portrait (Nos. 145–51); the latter is blotchy, with crackled gum.

1906. Charity. Nos. 156 to 167. *Geneva forgeries (P.):* good photolithographed stamps, perf 11½. Comparison will reveal design defects: female figure sketched with an excessively thin line (Nos. 156–59); foliage surrounding the value and the left boot (Nos. 160–63); woven fabric (Nos. 164–67).

1919–25. *Used postal forgeries:* 1-lei rose and 2-lei blue. Noncongruent shades: carmine-tinted rose and dark blue. Format too large; thick paper.

V. German Occupation

Forged overprints: No. 3 (40-ban on 30-parale) and the three sets overprinted by the Ninth German Army were counterfeited. Comparison with genuine stamps is necessary.

Rouad Island

1906. Stamps overprinted vertically. Nos. 1 to 3. *Original overprints:* (1) about 19½ mm wide (two words); ROUAD, 11¾ mm; height of letters, the highest ones, nearly 3 mm; "R" is broken, top left; bottom of the "U" is round; vertical downstroke of the "D" is broken; handstamp impression. (2) ROUAD, 11½ mm wide; normal letters, a little less high than in the first impression; no breaks or cracks in the letters. This last impression was used especially for collectors.

Forged overprints: rather easy to check by comparative procedures.

1916–20. Stamps overprinted horizontally. *Forged overprints:* on the 5-franc, and double overprint on the 3-centime.

Fake obtained by removing chemically the background color of the 50-centime to produce a rare variety, but there remain incriminating traces of the operation.

Russia

1857. Numeral watermark. No. 1. Imperforate. Typographed.

Select: four margins, 1 mm wide.

Pairs: 4U.

Cancellations: usually Types A, B, or circular cancellation with date; several styles of Type A (circular, rectangular, oval, lozenge, etc.); of Type B (framed straight-line inscriptions, unframed on one or two lines; small, medium, large printing type; etc.). The circular postmark with date also has several styles,

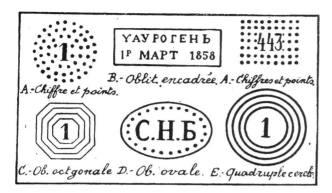

Russia cancellations: A. Number and dots.
B. Framed. C. Octagonal, with number. D. Oval.
E. Quadruple circle, with number.

beginning with the ordinary type of the following issues
and extending to very large postmarks: 35 mm in
diameter. Pen cancellations: fifty percent.

Fakes: pen cancellations often are removed to make
"mint" stamps; noncongruent gum; mint originals with
gum are rare.

Early forgeries: crude lithography. The background
is formed exclusively of inexpertly drawn vertical lines,
without the fine alternating lines made up of short
strokes or dots in the originals. No watermark.

1858. Same type. Perf 14¹/₂ x 15. Nos. 2 to 4.
Watermark: units of ten figures (large numerals, 14–15
mm high, read upside down by looking at the back of
the stamp). This watermark was produced not by paper
thinning, but by thickening.

Varieties: 30-kopeck on very thick paper: 2M, 2U.
Mint without gum: fifty percent.

Pairs: 4U. Blocks: rare.

Cancellations: Type A: common. Type B: less
common. Type B, unframed, and Type E: in demand.
With date: not very common on the 10-kopeck.

Forgeries: see the preceding issue. No watermark.
An early forgery of the 30-kopeck is bright carmine;
the corner ornaments are not separated clearly from the
background; the post horns are neither curved nor do
they have mouthpieces. Sometimes the forgery is
imperforate.

**1859. Same. No watermark. Perf 12¹/₂. Nos. 5 to
7.** *Shades:* 10-kopeck pale: 50U. 20-kopeck dark blue:
2M.

Varieties: 10-kopeck on thick paper: rare.

Cancellations: Type A and circular cancellations
with date: common. Types C and E: in demand. (Type
E is found also with letters "D P.") Color cancellation
and Type B: rare.

Forgeries: see first issue. Noncongruent perforation.

1864. Same type. 1-, 3-, and 5-kopeck. Perf 12¹/₂.
The 1-kopeck orange-yellow instead of yellow: 50M,

25U. A greasy impression is found in this value. Red
cancellations are in demand.

1865. Same type. No watermark. Nos. 11 to 16.
Perf 14¹/₂ x 15. Wove paper.

Varieties: 1-kopeck black on orange instead of
yellow: 50M. The 10-kopeck red-brown and also this
value on very thick paper: in demand. 20-kopeck on
same paper is rare. Stamps with inverted centers are
essays. The red cancellations with date and Type D are
in demand.

1866. Same. Wavy line watermark. Nos. 17 to 23.
Laid paper. The 1-kopeck black and orange: 5M, 50U;
rare on thick paper. 5-kopeck black and blue-gray: 5M,
3U. 10-kopeck, thick paper: rare. The 1- to 10-kopeck
stamps are found imperforate: rare. The 1-, 2-, and 10-
kopeck with background inverted are very rare.

**1875–79. Same. Horizontal bottom inscription.
Nos. 24 to 27.** Perf 14¹/₂ x 15. The 2-kopeck black and
red (Yvert No. 18) belongs to this issue (1875). The 10-
and 20-kopeck with inverted center are exceedingly
rare. The 2-, 7-, and 8-kopeck exist imperforate. The 7-
kopeck belongs to the 1879 issue. It is worth 2M in
gray and rose instead of gray and carmine. There was a
printing of this value at Perm on paper watermarked
with small hexagons.

Used postal forgeries: the 7-kopeck Moscow forgery
has no watermark; perforation is arbitrary. These
distinctive characteristics are sufficient for decision
making. However, design comparison will reveal
numerous defects and differences in format. The same
can be said for the other used postal forgeries.

1883. Change of shades. Nos. 28 to 35. Wavy line
watermark. Horizontally laid paper.

14-kopeck with inverted center: very rare. The
2-kopeck is known to exist without figures on the left.
The 1-, 2-, 3-, 7-, and 14-kopeck stamps are known
imperforate.

1884. 3¹/₂- and 7-ruble. Nos. 36 and 37. Post horns
without thunderbolts. Vertically laid paper. The
3¹/₂-ruble is found on horizontally laid paper.

Fakes: disappearance of the thunderbolts, followed by
embossing and repainting. Measure the horns' width,
which should be about 6 mm (3¹/₂ mm in the 1889–
1904 issue).

Geneva forgeries (F.): for a detailed description of
these forgeries, see Finland. The forged clichés have an
interchangeable milieu, which permits the production of
Finnish or Russian products at will. In the first clichés
of 3¹/₂- and 7-ruble, the outer frame was as thick as the
inner one. Some of the second clichés of these values
have a correct outer frame. Format: 25–25¹/₂ mm wide
and 28¹/₂–29¹/₂ mm high, depending on frames.
(Originals: 24³/₄ mm wide for the 3¹/₂-ruble, a little less

than 25 mm for the 7-ruble, and 29 mm high.) The paper is counterfeit. The 7-ruble stamp was printed in three shades: lemon yellow, yellow, and orange-yellow. There are copies with forged wavy line watermarks, which disappear in watermark fluid.

Forged Geneva cancellations: Postmarks made with woodcuts:

Single circle, 26 mm, ATBHBI 7 HOA 18..

Single circle, 25 mm, MOCKBA 11/12 DEB 1888 HMKOAHC.

Double circle, 25 mm, CMETEPBPFB 21 MAR 1888.

(See F. Serrane, "Faux de Finlande," *Philatéliste belge,* No. 54 [March 15, 1926]: 115–19.)

1889–1904. Thunderbolts in the post horns. Nos. 38 to 51. The 1-ruble exists perf 11^1/$_2$: rare. Also, 11^1/$_2$ x 13^1/$_2$ and 13^1/$_2$ x 11^1/$_2$: very rare. The 2-, 3-, 5-, 7-, and 10-kopeck without background coloration: rare. The 1-ruble is known on wove paper. The 2-, 5-, and 7-kopeck, imperforate: rare. The 3-kopeck is known with double impression. The 14-kopeck and the values in rubles are found with inverted centers, as are the 15- and 25-kopeck of 1904: very rare.

Used postal forgeries: 70-kopeck, 1- and 3^1/$_2$-ruble. No watermark. Design defects. Compare as in the 1875 issue. Same for No. 67 (10-kopeck, 1909).

Subsequent issues. The greatest caution is necessary when considering all the errors and varieties of stamp issues between 1909 and 1917, for the Russian government in power at that time did everything possible to help philatelic swindlers. The matrices, plates, etc., were available to everybody for printing the largest possible number of stamps. Most of the printing figures are unknown; it reasonably may be said that they were frequently astronomical.

The forgers went even further. They thought it was a good idea to copy philatelic *trivia*. We can mention 1921 (Nos. 139, 140, 144–49, and 150–52), 1922 (Nos. 153–56 and 176–79), 1924 (Lenin, Nos. 266–69). All of them can be identified sufficiently by comparing design and paper (too white). The 1917 set (crossed swords, etc.) came from the imagination of a man named T..., who came from Odessa, after the Russian Revolution, to serve the grand dukes residing on the French Riviera. This gave a kind of "official" scent to these lucubrations.

The air mail set of 1922 was overprinted fraudulently. Minute comparison is necessary.

With regard to armed forces issues including the Finnish occupation issue (AUNUS), almost all of the overprints were counterfeited well (and poorly). Keep away from all of these unless you are specializing.

Wenden

1862. Inscriptions in a circle. No. 1. Unissued, imperforate 2-kopeck blue on white or yellowish paper. Copies with yellowish gum: 5M. Tête-bêche (in the fifth row of the sheet): 10M. Some copies have dividing frame lines, others don't. Still others have double lines. The original lithographed stamp has an apostrophe to the right and above the "N" of WENDEN.

1863–64. Briefmarke or Packenmarke. Nos. 2 and 3. *Select:* four margins, minimum width: 1 mm. Black impression on cross-hatched color background; thick white paper (80–90 microns). In the 2-kopeck (Briefmarke), the burelage is a delicate rose; in the 4-kopeck (Packenmarke), it is green. In the second printing (1871), it is yellow-green: 2M, 2U. These stamps are almost always pen canceled. The 4-kopeck was bisected and is very rare thus. The stamps with inverted burelage, about fifteen small blank lozenges in the lower left corner instead of top right, are rare: 2M, 2U.

Originals: the background and frame burelage are extremely fine, all lines are equidistant from each other, and the excellent impression has no blanks in it. 28^1/$_2$ x 18^1/$_2$ mm, including the corner "squares." These "squares" are 1 mm wide by ^{4}/$_5$ mm high, except the one in the lower right corner that measures 1 mm sideways (upright burelage). The impression is a somewhat shiny deep black. The letters are all aligned and regular. The loop of the "d" of "des" is closed and there is a small oblique terminal line on its left (use magnifying glass). There is a dot after KREISES.

Reprints were made by the Wenden postmaster. 2-kopeck dark rose, a somewhat too bright rose, and pale rose. (The original shade is the rose of France.) 4-kopeck blue-green, pale yellow-green, and dark yellow-green. The hyphen after WENDEN is not double, and there are differences in the overprint inscription. The 2-kopeck is found with double overprint. These reprints are rare.

Forgeries: the authentic burelage is absolutely inimitable, so comparison with an original will immediately spot all the forgeries, with their white and color spots scattered around in the background. There are important differences in lettering in the overprint: "d" of "des," open or without oblique line on the left; "B" and "P" with loops that are too rounded; shape of the "K" letters, especially the "K" of KREISES; all the letters of SCHEN KREISES have long and extra fine serifs; the shading of the letters of WENDEN is not congruent.

Some additional characteristics of the three rather widely circulated sets follow:

1. 28 x 17^1/$_2$ mm. The background is lithographed in dull pale red. Corner squares are a bit too small,

including the lower right square. The inscribed crosses are too large. Tough, yellowish paper (70 microns). The overprint is lithographed in black or gray-black.

2. 28½ x 18–18¼ mm. Photolithographed. Paper about 85 microns. White gum. Shapeless cross-hatched frame. The three letters of "des" are truncated.

3. This set is so poorly executed that one cannot make out whether there is or is not a framework.

1863–71. Green oval. Nos. 4 to 6. No. 4 (1863). Small stars in the corners. Carmine-tinted rose and green. No thin red line frame around the oval. The oval's background is green.

No. 5 (1871). Larger stars. Carmine-tinted rose and dark green. Double thin red frame line around the oval.

No. 6 (1864). Small stars. Carmine and green. Thin green frame line around the oval, which contains a griffin.

The burelage of Nos. 4 and 6 is vertical and resembles the Hanover stamps' burelage (1856), but it is much more closely set. The burelage of No. 5 is made of intertwining lines, which are almost as delicate as in the ⅓-silbergroschen of Thurn and Taxis. (The one shown in the Yvert catalogue does not resemble it at all.)

No. 6 is rarest of all, and neither pairs nor blocks are known.

No. 4 has a thin green frame line around the green oval in the 1863 printing (rare). It disappeared in the 1866 and 1870 printings, in which the shades are rather more red than carmine-tinted. Value: 30 francs (gold). There is a tête-bêche without green framing.

These stamps are pen canceled. However, they sometimes are found with a partial postmark, on cover next to Russian stamps: rare.

Originals: Nos. 4 and 5 are identified by the burelage and the curved lines that surround the red oval ban. In No. 4, the curved lines are trimmed down below, the thickest line being on the right under BRIEFMARKE. In No. 5, these curved lines, which are more regular here, are formed from a succession of symmetrically trimmed thin and thick semiovals. In No. 6, the curved lines are like No. 4. The griffin's eye and ears are visible with its ears pointing upward, and the ground is represented by curved white shade lines.

Reprints: like the preceding ones, they are unofficial, having been made by the postmaster. No. 4, rose and dark rose; a thin, pink line surrounds the oval. No. 5, pale red and dark red; the oval is only 5 mm wide instead of 6. No. 6, pale rose and dark rose; a pink line surrounds the green oval. A different reprint of No. 5 was executed in 1893 by Postmaster Hirschheyt in pale rose and rose; worn plate. There also are essays.

Forgeries: the rarest stamp, No. 6, received the most attention. However, there is an early forgery of No. 4, with white gum instead of brown, curved lines around

the red oval band, the thickest part being on the left under BRIEFMARKE, and the oval line that interrupts the curved lines uniformly thick. A No. 6 stamp has the same defect, and the griffin looks like a small rat…without a saber. In another, the top burelage is imperfect; the eye is invisible; the ears are recumbent. Still another has over large inscriptions. All are easily identifiable by comparing burelage with a No. 4 stamp.

1872. Arm bearing a weapon in the oval. No. 7. Red burelage and frame. Red center. Oval and weapon-bearing arm are green. Perf 12½. One finds yellow-green and dark green: 50M, 50U. Paper is thicker than in the preceding stamps. The impression in black and red is an essay. The blue-green shade of the oval results from exposure to light.

1875–93. Same type. Nos. 8 to 10. Nos. 8 and 9, yellow-green or blue-green (less common) burelage and red oval. No. 10, black, green, and red. Sheets of twenty-eight stamps (7 x 4) for No. 8 (1875, without figures in the corners) in this value. Figure "3," top right, plate defect: very rare. No. 9 (1878, with corner figures) in sheets of 132 (11 x 12). This stamp is known to exist imperforate. No. 10 in sheets of 112 (8 x 14); also known imperforate; various printings from 1884 to 1893, with first ones with a small "w."

Reprints (1893): No. 9, various printings, all in gray-green and red. Perf 12½ and 11½.

1901. Panoramic view. No. 11. Oval in red-brown: 50M, 50U; in purplish red: rare. This stamp is known tête-bêche (brown oval), as well as imperforate. Sheets of 150 (6 x 25).

Saar

This is another less interesting philatelic region. The nonoverprinted issue of 1921 and the overprinted issue of 1920 can be found easily in complete sets.

With regard to the overprinted stamps of the first two issues, one can say that there are nine counterfeit overprints for each authentic one. These issues should be banned from one's album unless a very thorough specialized study is undertaken. The forged overprints are extremely well done; even comparative study leading to a decision is difficult. Quite probably there were clandestine impressions, for many of these counterfeits were sold even in post offices.

Nos. 51 and 52 are forged in the same way; however, they can be comparatively analyzed.

The inverted overprint of No. 76 has just been counterfeited. The distance between the value figure and the bars is ¼ mm too short. Make comparison.

St. Helena Values	Issue	Watermark	Perforation	Value Overprint Height	Width	Bar under the value
1-penny (I)	1863	C C	None	2½	16½–17½	16–17
1-penny (II)	1863	C C	None	2½	18½	18½–19-½
1-penny	1864	C C	12½	2½	17½	16–17
1-penny	1868	C C	12½	2½	17½	14–14½
1-penny	1871–73	C C	12½	3	17	16½–17
1-penny	1882–84	C A	14 x12½	2½	17	13½–14
1-penny	1882–84	C A	14	2½	17	14–14½
1-penny	1884–90	C A	14	3	17–17½	13½–15
2-pence	1868	C C	12½	3	15½	14–14½
2-pence	1871–73	C C	12½	3	18	18
2-pence	1882–84	C A	14 x14½	3	15½	14
2-pence	1882–84	C A	14	3	15–15½	14–14½
2-pence	1894	C A	14	3	15½	13½–14½
3-pence	1868	C C	12½	3	17–18	14–14½
3-pence	1871–73	C C	12½	3	18	16½–17½
3-pence	1871–73	C C	12½	3	18	16
3-pence	1882–84	C A	14½	3	17–17½	14–15
3-pence	1884–90	C A	14	3	17½–18	13½–14½
4-pence	1863	C C	None	3	16½–17	16–17
4-pence	1864	C C	12½	3	16½–17½	16–17
4-pence	1868	C C	12½	3	18–19	13–14½
4-pence	1882–84	C A	12½	3	17–17½	14–14½
4-pence	1884–90	C A	14	3	17–17½	13½–14½
1-shilling	1864	C C	12½	3	17½–18	16–17
1-shilling	1868	C C	12½	2½	16½–17½	14–14½
1-shilling	1882–84	C A	14 x 12½	3	17½–18	17½–18
1-shilling	1882–84	C A	14	2½	17	13½–14½
1-shilling	1893	C A	14	3	17½	17½
5-shilling	1868	C C	12½	2½	18	14–14½
½-penny	1884–90	C A	14	3	17–17½	13½–14
½-penny	1894	C A	14	3	15½	14

St. Christopher

1870–82. 1-penny and 6-pence. Nos. 1 to 3; 4, 7, 9, 10, and 15. *Originals:* typographed; expertly executed; perf 12½ or 14; watermarked "C C" or "C A" with crown.

Early forgeries: two bad sets of the two values; lithographed without watermark; thick paper; the value is inscribed right in the middle of the tablet instead of being moved to the left. (a) Full, unbroken line around the face contour; the first pearl of the diadem is on the right of the vertical downstroke of the first "H" of CHRISTOPHE; shade lines in center background and face frequently are broken. (b) Even worse; poorly perf 13; same defects; the pearl is under the middle of the letter "H."

St. Helena

1856–94. Recess print engraved stamps. Nos. 1 to 19. *Originals:* expertly engraved; 19¼–½ x 25½ mm. Check the catalogues for watermarks and perforations. POSTAGE is 1¹/₁₀ mm from the tablet's left edge and 1¹/₅ mm from the right edge; center background burelage is executed expertly: around the blank circle, there are thirty-nine small blank triangles whose bases form the circle's inner line. Overprints vary a great deal, at times even on the same value; specializing is recommended. The accompanying table will clarify the problem somewhat by measuring the height and width of the value overprint and the width of the bar under it.

Forgeries: several lithographed sets, usually on thick

paper; arbitrary dimensions, perforation, and overprints, or without overprint. POSTAGE is too near or too far from the tablet's lateral edges; irregular inscriptions; corner designs with large white spots in the most widely circulated set; in another set, a sort of overlapping in the same places; noncongruent center background burelage; thirty-six or forty blank triangles around the inner circle; at times there is a dot after POSTAGE. All in all, they are not very deceptive; they are easy to judge. There is a collotyped forgery of the 6-pence made in Genoa in carmine or other shades; a few of the ends of the leaves in the lower corner rosettes are broken; the second square jewel of the diadem is shapeless.

Engraved forgeries: rather deceptive; no watermark; thick paper; perf 12 or imperforate. "P" and "E" of POSTAGE are $1/2$ mm from the tablet's lateral edges; thirty-six triangles around the circle.

Fakes obtained from the removal of a violet cancellation on the stamps of the 1884–94 issue, Nos. 12 to 19.

St. Lucia

1859–84. Engraved stamps. Nos. 1 to 24.
Originals: $18^1/2$–$3/4$ x $22^1/2$ mm; look at "watermarks" and "perforations" in the catalogues. These stamps are engraved superbly; the corner and center background burelage, viewed through a magnifying glass, is an intricate, inimitable lacework. The inscription letters are regular and equidistant from the oval lines (about $1/4$ mm); the whole face is covered with curved lines composed of spaced dots; the ear is quite visible; a curl, which is part of a long curl (3 mm long, $3/4$ mm wide, pointed toward the end of the neck) is hanging under the chignon, side-by-side with a short curl ($1^1/2$ mm), which is a part of the longer one.

Forgeries: 1. lithographed stamps: a half-dozen clichés were used to counterfeit a like number of sets or single copies of Nos. 1–24 (Nos. 17–24 occasionally having forged overprints). They even were "dished up" in all the original shades, but usually with arbitrary color tones. A careful examination of the corner and center oval burelage will lead to their immediate rejection: numerous white spots in the corners and no well-defined design; in the oval around the portrait, on its left, a succession of thick, curved, vertical lines, and a shapeless design with a full vertical wavy line passing behind the chignon and terminating above the final "E" of POSTAGE. No watermark; bad perf 13 or imperforate. Irregular, excessively wide inscriptions; insufficient, noncongruent stippling on the face. We offer a few pointers on the various sets one may encounter. (a) Most widely circulated set; only the large

curl hanging from the chignon can be seen and it is triangular in shape; no earlobe; the front part of the eye socket is formed with a heavy line. (b) The "S" of S^T is touching the bottom of the oval. (c) Two curls are hanging from the chignon; the longer one almost is touching the oval below. (d) Practically no ear. (e) Letters of S^T LUCIA are $1/3$ mm from the inner oval line, instead of $1/4$ mm. (f) No vertical shade lines in the crown's bandeau; the top of the head is marked by a heavy line.

2. *Engraved forgeries:* 19 x $23^1/3$ mm; the corner and oval background burelage is formed similarly with a multiplicity of fine curved vertical lines, with a few oblique lines; the oval's lines extend slightly beyond it into the blank oval; the shade lines at the base of the neck are limited on top by a heavy line; only the large curl is hanging from the chignon, and, because there is no short curl, it is separated from the neck on a level with the ear by about 1 mm. Note: These forgeries received forged overprints.

Forged overprints: comparison is necessary.

Postage-revenues. *Forged postal cancellations:* sometimes after the removal of the fiscal obliteration.

Steamship stamps. Collections often have the 1-penny, 3-, and 6-pence stamps, respectively, in sky blue, lilac-rose, and violet; $21^2/3$ x $18^2/3$ mm; glossy white paper, usually mint with yellowish gum, with an oval containing this legend: "S^T Lucia Steam Conveyance C^Y Limited" and a three-masted ship sailing in a westerly direction; they are stamps issued in 1873 by a company serving Castries, Port Louis, and the coasts of St. Lucia. Not very valuable because of the large number of stamps remaining in stock.

Ste. Marie de Madagascar

1894. Peace and Commerce type. Nos. 1 to 13.
Geneva forgeries: check under French Colonies whether counterfeits of this type are involved.

Forged Geneva cancellation: double circle ($21^1/2$ mm), inner circle with broken lines, with date, S^{TE} MARIE 12 SEPT 95 MADAGASCAR.

St. Pierre and Miquelon

Very numerous overprints. About these, Marconnet, who gives a detailed description (1897, pages 375–87), says: "Some of them are quite genuine, especially the first ones, but how many others are there that conceal the shameless speculation practiced by postal employees and especially by dealers."

1885. Figure and "S P M" overprints. Nos. 1 to 3. *Original overprints* made by five handstamps: (1) the one used for No. 1 (height, 8¹/₂ mm; horizontal bar, 5 mm; curl, 6 mm wide) and for the "5" overprint of No. 2. (2) A figure "2," same height as the preceding impression. (3) and (4) Two for the figures of No. 3. (5) A small one for letters "S P M" (height, 2¹/₂ mm; length, 13¹/₂ mm).

Forgeries: No. 1; see forgeries of this type under French Colonies, 1881.

Numerous *forged overprints* on forgeries and on originals; detailed comparison is indispensable; there are some so-called "reprints" of Nos. 1 and 3, which perhaps were made with the original handstamp printing device, but with no official status; they must be included in these overprints; black ink instead of gray; No. 1 overprint is upright or inverted (Geneva types a and b, Nos. 2 and 3 and varieties).

1885. "5" overprint on 4-centime. No. 4. This overprint was published for the first time only quite recently in the 1927 edition of the Yvert catalogue; the Scott catalogue does not list it; de Vinck's work makes no mention of it, and Marconnet (1897, page 387) says: "Most of the catalogues draw attention to a '5' on 4-centimes with letters 'S P M' spaced further apart. We are skeptical about the authenticity of the stamp; it seems wholly improbable that the administration may have had a second stamp printing device made for a printing of 900 copies." That is also our opinion, for news of that would have gotten out, and if the letters ("S P M") were set closer together since then, the mingling of stamping devices furnishing the "reprints" of Nos. 1 and 3 had something to do with it. The overprints were counterfeited in Geneva.

1885. Figure, bar, and "S P M" overprints. Nos. 5 to 15. *Forgeries:* see forged stamps of 1881 under French Colonies ("05" on 20-centime; "15" on 30-, 35-, and 40-centime, Nos. 8 and 12–15).

Forged overprints: upright and inverted, rather easy to check by comparison. The four overprint types were counterfeited in Geneva.

1886. "P D," bar, and figure. Nos. 16, 16a, and 17. Concerning these stamps, the Yvert catalogue (1928, page 791) quotes Marconnet (1897, page 385): "The abundance of overprints had completely exhausted the colony's stocks. On January 22, 1886, the Count of Saint-Phalle had to decree that 'until stamps were received from France, letters intended for communication in the colony would be franked at the post office with P D.' On February 17, the postal service, implementing this decree, issued a set of paper squares with P D and 5-, 10-, and 15-centime value figures in a black overprint."

The quotation stops there, but Marconnet continues: "We cannot agree that these stamps were adequately authenticated by the January 22 decree, which, quite simply, authorized, *as was done many times before,* the affixing of the postmark P D right on the letter; until proof to the contrary is given, we shall consider these stamps as purely speculative products."

The reader will make his own decision. Not surprisingly, there exist counterfeits of these not very official products. The overprint was counterfeited in Geneva.

1891. "ST-PIERRE-M^on" overprint. Nos. 18 to 34. *Original overprints:* 23³/₄ mm wide; typographical overprint; numerous varieties because of press misses, the absence of letters, hyphen, and so forth. De Vinck says (1928, page 143) that these varieties have little interest for the collector; he makes an exception only for the absence of the "S" of "ST" in the forty-second overprint of the second composition. The Yvert catalogue, in contrast, thinks that all these varieties are worth two or three times the prices listed in the catalogues.

Forgeries: see 1881 forgeries under French Colonies.

Forged overprints: numerous on original stamps; comparison is necessary.

Forged Geneva overprints: 23–23¹/₄ mm long, on originals and forgeries of 1881, in black and red with the following forged cancellations: double circle (22¹/₂ mm), inner circle broken, with date, S^T PIERRE ET MIQUELON 12 SEPT 92, star at bottom; same (22 mm), ILE AUX CHIENS 2 AOUT 92 S^TE PIERRE ET MIQ^ON, in black or blue.

1891–92. New value overprint. Nos. 35 to 50. *Originals:* typographical overprints.

Forged overprints: rather easy to verify by comparison.

Forgeries: see French Colonies, counterfeits of the 1881 type on which forged overprints were applied.

1892. Postage due stamps with "T P" overprint. Nos. 51 to 58. *Original overprints:* typographed.

Forgeries: see the various types of forged stamps under French Colonies.

Forged overprints: this is where the forgers' imagination went wild — there are a great many forged lithographed and typographed overprints, not only on counterfeit stamps, which are easy to check, but also on originals of the 10-, 20-, 30-, 40-, even 60-centime black stamps. Comparison is necessary for the latter. The whole set was counterfeited on forged postage due stamps in Geneva, with typographed overprints.

1892–1912. Peace and Commerce type. Nos. 59 to 77 and 94 to 104. *Geneva forgeries:* see forgeries of

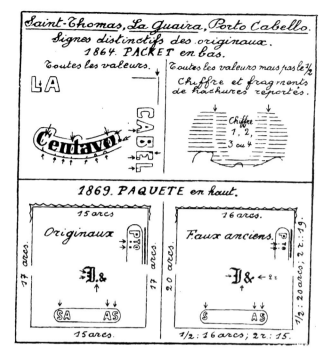

St. Thomas, La Guaira, Puerto Cabello. Distinctive markings of the originals. 1864. PACKET at bottom. All values. All values, but not the ¹/₂-reis; figure and shade line pieces are carried over. Bottom: 1869. PAQUETTE on top. Originals. Early forgeries.

this type under French Colonies. See the 1891 issue for the forged cancellations.

Postage due stamps (1893). Overprints. Nos. 1 to 9. *Originals:* typographical overprint.

Forgeries: see forged postage due stamps under French Colonies.

Forged overprints: comparison is necessary.

Parcel post stamps (1901). Nos. 1 and 2. Same remarks as preceding.

St. Thomas, La Guaira, Puerto Cabello

1864–70. PACKET at bottom. *Originals:* lithographed; 16³/₄–17 x 22 mm; transfer matrices of four stamps (4 x 1), thus four minor varieties per value; outer dividing frame line, ³/₄ mm from the frame; CENTAVO in all values; all legends have a period (final dot); the legend letters are about ¹/₂ mm thick; black impression on color; three printings: (1) 1864: ¹/₂-centavo black on yellowish white paper with shade lines crossing the figures; in the following values, the

lines do not cross them; 1-centavo rose; 2-centavo green; 3-centavo dark yellow; 4-centavo blue; (2) 1866: 1-centavo rose with retouched figure shading; (3) 1868–70: the shade lines cross the figures in all values; ¹/₂-centavo on grayish white; 1-centavo rose-violet; 2-centavo blue; 3-centavo orange-yellow; 4-centavo green. All these stamps were used in La Guaira and Puerto Cabello. See the illustration for the distinctive markings of the originals.

No *reprints.*

Forgeries: three bad sets of early lithographs, none of which has the distinctive characteristics of the originals (see illustration); (a) no dot after PACKET or after CABELLO; CENTAVOS with "S"; (b) no dots after PACKET and CABELLO; the horizontal shade lines are cut off sharply before the lateral arabesques; (c) doubled lateral frames; legend letters are 1¹/₂ mm high instead of about 1³/₄ mm.

Fake: 2-centavo green with letters "VO" of CENTAVO scratched out.

1864–69. PAQUETE under the steamer. *Originals:* ¹/₂-real rose and 2-real green (Nos. 7 and 9), three printings; transfer matrices of five stamps (5 x 1): (1) 1864: 18¹/₂ by about 23 mm; white or yellowish paper; rose and dark rose; yellow-green and blue-green; perf 12¹/₂. (2) End of 1864: types retouched with smaller corner figures; 19 x 23 mm; bluish white paper; rose, green, and yellow-green; zigzag dot rouletting, 9–10¹/₂, or sawtooth 11¹/₂, 12. (3) 1869: types still retouched, especially the word PAQUETE, which became PAOUETE; ¹/₂-real, about 18 mm wide; 2-real, about 18¹/₂ mm; white or bluish paper; rose, red, green, or yellow-green; zigzag dot rouletted 9–10¹/₂. All of them were used in La Guaira or Puerto Cabello.

The same values, but ¹/₂-real slate and 2-real orange (Nos. 8 and 10) had two printings: (1) 1864: 18²/₃ x 23 mm; white or yellowish paper; perf 12¹/₂; (2) 1869: dimensions as in the same issue of the two preceding values; types with PAOUETE retouched; rouletted 9–10¹/₂. These stamps were used in St. Thomas.

Reprints (1881): ¹/₂-real bright rose and 2-real bright yellow-green; PAOUETE retouched, naturally; rouletted 9–10¹/₂, on white paper; traces of plate wear in the clouds (white spots or faintly printed lines) and in the background burelage of the value.

Forgeries: lithographed on thin white paper; shapeless rouletting or rouletted 10¹/₂; final "E" of PAQUETE is wider than the first "E"; PAQUETE is printed with a "Q" with an oblique tail that does not extend beyond the letter on the right, but it touches, over ¹/₂ mm, the white line below it; it also is printed with an "O" (2-real); 19 x 23 mm; figure "1" in the upper left corner with more or less horizontal top line;

the upper curl of the "6" of the lower left corner is not as wide as the lower loop; no trace of colors on the mizzenmast; noncongruent background burelage.

1869. PAQUETE on top. *Originals:* lithographed; $18^2/_5$–$^1/_2$ x 23 mm, outer arcs not included; the latter only rarely touch the frame; the letters of CURAÇAO are $1^1/_4$ mm high; perf $12^1/_2$ or 10; green, dark green; red-rose or red; white or yellowish, sometimes brownish (because of gum) paper; (the illustration will give adequate information on the distinctive features to be examined); these stamps were used in Curaçao.

Reprints (1876): perf 15; $^1/_2$-real blue-green; 2-real dull red.

Forgeries: lithographed; $18^3/_4$ by about 23 mm; dot perf 13; the letters of CURAÇAO are only $1^1/_5$ mm high (see the illustration for the various marks).

1875. Hamburg-American Company. *Original:* center embossed; typographed; perf $12^1/_2$.

1875. Royal Mail Stamp Packet Company. *Original:* typographed; perf 13; the flagstaff is not touching the top inner circle; the "N" of TEN normally is spaced from "E"; the letters of the circular legend and the corner designs are regular.

Forgery: lithographed; center shade lines are too far apart; the flagstaff is touching the top blank circle; the "N" of TEN is much too far to the right of the "E"; the letters of the circular legend and the corner ornaments are irregular; perf $11^1/_2$.

St. Thomas and Prince Islands

1869–81. Crown type. Nos. 1 to 14. *Originals:* typographed; 21 by about 24 mm; accent on the "E" of THOMÉ; the following "E" evidently is wider at base than on the top; see the illustration under Portuguese Colonies. [Translator's note: The illustration of St. Thomas and Prince stamps under Portuguese Colonies does not show this.]

Reprints (1886): chalky white paper; gumless. All values perf $13^1/_2$; slightly different shades; the 5- and 50-reis green were reprinted only in Type II.

Early forgeries: three lithographed sets are executed so poorly that they hardly deserve description. (a) About $^1/_2$ mm between the lateral frames; the noncongruent "E" standing alone is under the first "R" of CORREIO instead of between the "R"s; "P" of PRINCIPE is under the second "R"; corner squares are not closed, the lines under CORREIO and above the value ending at the inner frame; crude rouletting rather than perforation. (b) Forgeries of the same kind, with similar defects, but with an accent on the "E" standing

alone; squares are open as above; crude $12^1/_2$ rouletting, or imperforate. (c) Perf $12^1/_2$; the letters of CORREIO are touching the top tablet; the ornaments of the ornamental squares do not form the usual design of two tête-bêche "E"s with a vertical line between them.

Geneva forgeries: much more deceptive; yellowish paper; perf $12^1/_2$; $20^3/_4$ x $23^2/_3$ mm; found in many modern collections; for the ornamental squares, see the illustration under Portuguese Colonies. The distance between the bottom of the "E" of PRINCIPE and the following ornament is $^1/_2$ mm; it is less in the originals; the inner top corner ornaments are touching the line under CORREIO in several places.

Forged cancellations on this set: (1) triple circle, inner circle with broken lines, usually illegible inscription, with date. (2) Double circle (22 mm), with date, SAO THOME 20/7 1875. (3) Double oval (43 x 25 mm, length of axes), CORREIO 16 OUT 84 SAO. ANTONIO; one circle (25 mm), ST. THOMAS 2/12 18.6.

Subsequent issues. There are a great many *forged overprints,* for which comparison is necessary, especially for the following: a set of 1889–90 (Nos. 24–34); 1899, "$2^1/_2$" brown; 1902, forged overprints on a few of the more expensive values with overprint; 1913–14, with REPUBLICA overprints, same remark.

St. Vincent

1861–97. Engraved stamps. The large format 5-shilling and the small format $^1/_2$-penny were not engraved.

Originals: recess print engraved; $19^1/_5$ x about $22^1/_3$ mm; yellowish white paper, about 70 microns. See the catalogues and specialty works for watermarks, perforations, and shades. Fourteen visible round pearls are found in the top of the crown's bandeau; the vertical downstroke of the "T" of S^T is as thick as the other letters; the dot under it also is just as large and is square-shaped (no counterfeit comes close to that); the shading behind the neck is thick, made of fine oblique shade lines, but this is not visible in all copies.

Forgeries: (a) early lithographed set; $19^1/_3$ x 23 mm; paper, 80 microns; perf 13; dividing frame line traces outside the corners; no watermark; vertical downstroke of the "T" of S^T is half as thick as the other letters and there is a small round dot underneath it; the face and neck stippling is too pronounced on the right, forming a spot that is visible from a distance, the rest appearing blank; eleven or twelve visible pearls; the ear is practically invisible. (b) Lithographed forgery of the 6-pence; 19 x $22^1/_4$ mm; perf 12; paper, 80 microns; eleven pearls in the top of the bandeau, the first ones being open at bottom; the oval, which is made of curved lines, has thicker white lines on the right than on the left and the background between the curved lines is solid; practically no stippling on the face; no watermark. (c) *Engraved forgeries:* much more deceptive; no watermark; dimensions excessive, 19½ x 23½ mm; yellowish paper; allowable thickness; heavy color embossing; imperforate with 3 mm margins, or perf 12 x 13. I have seen only the 1-penny carmine and black and the 6-pence yellow-green and dark blue-green, but I think that there will be engraved forgeries of the other values in the future. The tablet containing Sᵀ VINCENT is too high, being almost as high as the ornamental squares; these really are not squares, but Maltese crosses, the oblique lines being much too boldly printed. The dot under the "T" of Sᵀ is nearly ½ mm from the letter; it really is a horizontal hyphen placed a little higher than the base of the letters; about fourteen pearls in the top of the bandeau, the first seven ones on the left, except the fourth, are open on their left side and thus form "C"s.

5-shilling, large format. Nos. 18, 30a, and 38. *Originals:* 25¼ x 29½ mm; various watermarks; perf 11–12½; 12; 14. Expertly recess print engraved; blank frame; white ovals (outside the oval band of the legends) and quite visible corner burelage; small curved shade lines in the crown's pearls and in the cross-like ornaments in the large blank oval — all quite visible.

Forgeries: photolithographed; 24¾ x 29½ mm; perf 11; flat carmine shade; most of the details (blank frame, white ovals, and burelage) are merged together in color. FACSIMILE in black often is found on the ground.

1880–81. Overprinted stamps. Nos. 20 to 23. *Original overprints:* "½ d." on half of 6-pence. "1," "2," and "d." are 4 mm high; between "2" and "1": 2 mm; between "1" and "2": 2½ mm; between "1" and "d.": same; figures are 8¾ mm high, 1½ mm wide; "d." is 3 mm high; between "d." and "1," ½ mm. "4-d." on 1-shilling, "4-d." is 8½ mm high; loop of the "5" is 5½ mm high.

Forged overprints: some of them are deceptively counterfeited: comparison is indispensable.

1890–92. "2½ d." and "5 pence" overprints. Nos. 39 and 40. Same remark.

1902–11. Higher value stamps. *Fakes* obtained by cleaning fiscal cancels.

Salvador, El

1867. Perf 12. Nos. 1 to 4. *Originals:* expertly recess print engraved with traces of color over the whole stamp (plates not well cleaned); the background, on the left and right of the oval, is formed by repeating the value figures ("½" and "4") for Nos. 1 and 4, or in letters (UN and DOS) for Nos. 2 and 3.

Early forgeries: crude lithographed set, recognizable at a glance; in the four values, the background outside the oval is formed by a crossed burelage of three fine curved lines.

1874. CONTRA SELLO overprint. Nos. 5 to 8. *Forged overprints:* rather easy to identify by comparison.

1889. "1889" overprint. Nos. 22 to 26. *Forged overprints:* comparison is indispensable.

Subsequent issues. Overprinted stamps.

Overprinted official and telegraph stamps. Nos. 4 to 8. Detailed comparison is indispensable.

Note the overprints counterfeited in Geneva: QUINCE centavos, No. 144; TRECE centavos, Nos. 157–60; rosetta, Nos. 176–83; overprints of 1900 (Nos. 206–27); overprints of 1896–97 on official stamps; FRANQUEO OFICIAL in an oval, Nos. 40–92; same, 1900, Nos. 113–20 and overprints CONTRASELLO on telegraph stamp. Nos. 4–8. Forged Geneva cancellations: (1) one circle (18½ mm), S. SALVADOR; (2) triple circle, thick outer circle (29 mm), ADMINISTRATION DE CORREOS REPUBLICA 28 AG. SN SALVADOR (SAN SALVADOR).

Samoa

1877–81. First issue. *Originals:* lithographed; paper of various thicknesses but usually thick (thin paper also is found in Type III); yellowish white gum; gum applied after perforation (occasional traces of gum on front of stamp); 20 x 23½ mm. The sheets were not perforated marginally, which explains why the corner copies are perforated on only two sides and the marginal copies, only on three. In the sheets of ten (5 x 2), there is thus not a single stamp that is perforated on all four sides. The watermark of some stamps is the manufacturer's trademark (J. Whatman), with the millesime. The matrix design had the 6-pence value; other values come from transfers taken from that value with transfer of the new value.

Type I: first printing, 1877; 1-penny in sheets of twenty stamps (4 x 5), thus having six perforated stamps on the four sides. 3-, 6-pence, and 1-shilling in sheets of ten (5 x 2); perf 12½. The little line on the right above the "M" of SAMOA is normal and the white line above EXPRESS is normal, without any defect above the "X" (see illustration). Stamp Nos. 3, 8, 14, 16, and 17 of the plate have a dot after PENNY; in Nos. 2 and 4 of the 3-pence, there is no space between POSTAGE and THREE.

Type II: second printing, 1878. 1-penny, 3-, 6-pence, 1-, 2-, and 5-shilling. Same plates as previously; the 2- and 5-shilling, in plates of ten (5 x 2); for some unknown reason, probably as a result of a press shock or jolt, the matrix has a break in the white line above the "X" of EXPRESS, and a dot has been added on the right of the upper right terminal line of the "M" of SAMOA. On the right of the same letter, one of the dots over the upper inscription seems to have been reinforced. Perf 12½.

Type III: third printing, 1880. 1-penny, 3-, 6-pence, 1-, 2-, and 5-shilling. Perf 12½. The defect above the "X" was retouched poorly and the white line is positioned abnormally at that place; the dot on the right above "M" (Type II) has been connected with the letter's serif; however, since the dot was placed a little too low, it follows that the serif is bent obliquely; see the illustration where the defect has been made a bit too visible in order to show what is involved. Henceforth, all printings of originals and of reprints will have these two defects. 1880–81 (some authors say "May, 1881").

Fourth printing, Type III. 1-penny, 2-, 3-, 6-, 9-pence, 1- and 2-shilling. Perf 12. The 2-pence, which is not listed in some catalogues, is an unissued stamp. Note: With the exception of this printing, perf 12, the original stamps are perf 12½ with poorly executed perforation, the small paper rounds often remaining attached. The "12" perforation is itself an irregularity since the perforations of the reprints are regular.

Reprints: (1) 1882 or 1883; the eight values, including the unissued stamp, in sheets of twenty-one stamps (7 x 3); printing of Whitfield, King, and Company. (2) Perf 12. The question of this printing has been much debated by a few authors; some say that the fourth printing of the originals is involved; others talk of reprints; still others speculate on the basis of plates of twenty (5 x 4). We want to point out that "timbrological problems" always arise each time the original plates fall into the hands of dealers. The reprints have a dot which is quite faint at times (use magnifying glass), under the center branch of the "M"; depending on the color used and the impression, this dot often is connected with the curved line below it, forming a short vertical line. The dot also is found in the original, unissued 2-pence, but the latter is lilac-rose, whereas the reprint is bright rose or lilac-rose of a different shade; the dot also is found in the originals of the 9-pence, these being identified by the blind perf 12, as is explained in the preceding, whereas the reprints are cleanly perf 12 or 12½ and their shade is orange or brown-orange instead of brown-yellow.

1885; all values in sheets of forty (8 x 5) with sheets occasionally imperforate on edges; thus, imperforate stamps can be found on one or two sides, but, in general, the reprints are perforated on all four sides.

There was a printing of 25,000 copies of each value, except for 1-penny, 2-, and 3-pence (50,000, 35,000, and 30,000). White gum. Those who had the plates in their possession executed subsequently one or two printings, on which we have no information, and finally, they brought out the large printing of 1892, 100,000 copies of each of the eight values. The question is complicated even more by *essays,* which, however, are entirely imperforate.

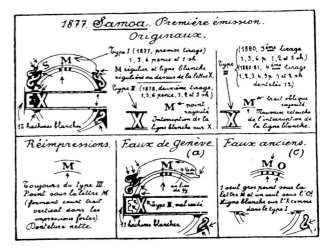

1877. Samoa. First issue. Originals. Type I. (1877, first printing) "M," regular, and white line above "X" is regular. Type II. (1878, second printing) "M"— dot added. White line over "X" is broken. Type III. (1880, third printing; 1880–81, fourth printing) Perf 12. "M"— oblique line added. Bad retouching of the broken white line. 12 white shade lines. Bottom: Reprints. Always Type III. Dot under the "M," forming a short vertical line in the heavily inked impressions. Clean-cut perforation. Geneva forgeries. (a) ⅕ mm instead of ⅓ mm. Type III, poorly executed. 11 white shade lines. Early forgeries. (c) A single large dot under the "M" and a single one under the "O." White line over the "X" as in Type I.

Forgeries: the question of reliable originals of Type III and of reprints already was quite complicated. Fournier came and complicated it still more by counterfeiting rather craftily the eight values in small sheets. (a) His set, called "de Geneve," is easily identifiable (see details in the illustration); this set is quite common, there are copies in almost all general collections, often with one side of the perforation trimmed off. The stamps are somewhat too narrow, about 19¾ mm. White, grayish, or yellowish paper of medium thickness; perf 11. (b) Early forgeries, very crude lithographs; allowable measurements; in the semicircular white bands, there are eighteen instead of sixteen color pearls, three of which are under the first "A" of SAMOA, and fifteen at bottom instead of fourteen; the two "S" letters of EXPRESS are square in form (top and bottom formed by horizontal lines); the white line above the "X" is thick and unbroken; in the upper left corner, there are only two curved ornaments instead of three (the smallest one is missing); no dots above SAMOA, only short lines, the first one of which begins above the "S"; the value inscription tablet, on the right and left, displays a wide blank triangle, with a 2½ mm base resting on the tablet and terminating at the usual blank volute. (c) Early set, easily identifiable since it has only a single large color pearl under the "M," and a single one under the middle of the "O" instead of two; the upper curls of the two "S" letters are larger than their lower curls (see other defects in the illustration); perf 11.

Fakes: scratching out of dot under the "M," repairing of white line above the "X" and one side of the perforation trimmed to help a reprint bridge the gap of authenticity. Magnifying glass examination is adequate for most cases.

Forged cancellations: rather numerous on originals, reprints, and forgeries. Comparison is necessary.

Forged Geneva cancellation: double circle (23½ mm), with date, APIA 1 21 85 SAMOA.

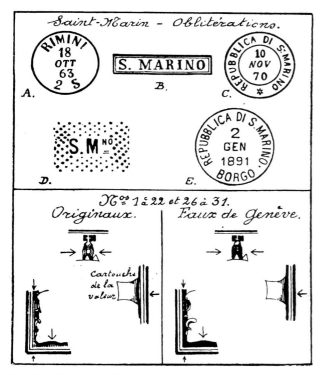

San Marino cancellations. Bottom: Nos. 1 to 22 and 26 to 31. Originals; value tablet. Geneva forgeries.

1894. "5 d" or FIVE PENCE overprints. Nos. 19 and 20. *Forged overprints:* comparison is necessary.

1894. Samoa Post. No. 21. *Geneva forgery:* lithographed instead of typographed; the letters of FIVE PENCE are only ⅙ mm wide instead of ⅓ mm. The letters of SAMOA POST are too thick and the crown displays practically no detailed structure. No watermark. The "5-d," Type II, and FIVE PENCE, Type I, overprints were counterfeited in Geneva.

1900. German stamps with SAMOA overprint. Nos. 36 to 41. *Forgeries:* see German stamp forgeries of 1889 under German Colonies; the latter, made in Geneva, received the forged SAMOA overprint and forged cancellation: double circle (26 mm), with inner strip, modern German postmark type, APIA 1-2 00-10 IIV SAMOA.

1900. Perf 14. 50-pfennig. No. 49. *Forgery:* lithographed; no watermark; cutout of a propaganda label bearing the stamp with perforation on a dark background; on the four sides of the stamp, the following words in white: *Vergiss nicht unsere Kolonien* [Don't forget our colonies]. Glossy paper. The cutout perf 14 and the lack of a watermark will identify adequately this fantasy. Other better counterfeited forgeries come from Geneva (see German Colonies, steamer type).

1914. "G.R.I." overprint. Nos. 59 to 71. *Forged overprints,* some of which are deceptive: comparison and, if need be, detailed expertizing are indispensable.

1914–25. Overprinted postage-revenue stamps. Nos. 78 to 82a. *Forged overprints:* on canceled stamps or on fiscals with fiscal cancels cleaned. Comparison is indispensable.

San Marino

Sardinian stamps, Nos. 10, 11, 13, 14, and 16 and Italian stamps of the first issues, Nos. 5, 8, 11, 12, 14, 15, and 17, canceled with Type A postmark (Type B, on cover) are in demand: about 15 francs. Type C on Italian stamps of 1863–77 is almost as rare, and Type D on these stamps is worth 5 francs. A few values are very rare. (See illustration.)

1877–91. Crown watermark. Nos. 1 to 7. Perf 14. The 5- and 25-centesimo stamps belong to 1891.

Sheets of 400 stamps lithographed in four panes of 100 (10 x 10). Watermarked upside down.

Varieties: the 2- and 10-centesimo were used bisected. A few shades can be found, for example, 5-centesimo dark yellow (first printing), orange-yellow (second printing), etc.

Cancellations: Type C: rare. Types D and E: common. Type E also is found with SERRAVALLE at the bottom or with a single star in that place. San Marino stamps with Italian postmarks are rare.

Forgeries: 1. A few values were printed fraudulently on common Italian stamps of the 1879 issue after the chemical alteration and removal of the original impression. Noncongruent inscriptions. See also the distinctive features of the originals in the illustration.

2. Poorly executed Genoa set (I.). Perf 11½. No watermark, or a forged watermark made by impressing a greasy yellowish gray blotch on the paper. Gaudy shades. A few inscription letters are touching the fine lines ("EP" of REP, bottom; "E" of POSTALE, top; "R" of LIBERTAS, bottom). Letters "TAL" are joined at bottom. The forged watermark disappears if immersed in watermark fluid. Thick paper (70–75 microns). Forged cancellation: large dotted square.

3. Geneva forgeries (F.): the whole set was photolithographed very successfully. The shades are slightly arbitrary: this matter concerns the specialist. Perforation matches the original and the paper is of appropriate thickness (45–50 microns like the originals), but it is too transparent. The dimensions are good: 22½–⅔ x 18½–¾ mm. No watermark, or else a forged watermark that disappears in watermark fluid. In the originals, the watermark is not always plainly visible. That is why we think it is a good idea to indicate a few design differences. (See illustration.)

Forged Geneva cancellations: Type D, a single thick line under NO. Type E: REPUBBLICA DI S. MARINO BORGO 7 JUN 1890.

1892. Overprints. Nos. 8 to 11. This set was one of the first products of a scheme set up by the state to defraud collectors. San Marino did not make much from it. The dealer who launched it made a great deal, and collectors lost as much as he made. All overprints were counterfeited and require comparison; the forgeries were overprinted no less fraudulently. Keep away from them, unless San Marino is a definite collection specialty.

Forged cancellations: see the following issue.

1892–94. 1877 type. Nos. 12 to 22. *Sheets* as above. The 5-, 30-, 40-, 45-centesimo, and 1-lira stamps are from the 1892 issue; the others, from 1894.

Medium paper, yellow gum, or thin paper, colorless gum, depending on the printing. Copies of the first printing are in demand (2-lira dark brown: 50M, 50U, and 5-lira purplish brown and green: 2M, 2U, instead of carmine-tinted brown on greenish paper).

Forgeries: the whole set was expertly counterfeited in Geneva, the 5-lira in the shade of the second printing. The lira values usually have a forged watermark. Forged postmarks, Type E: 5 APR 1892 BORGO; 7 MAR 1892 BORGO; 4 FEB 1892 BORGO; and 7 DEC 1892, with star at bottom. See first issue. Like the first issue, the set also was counterfeited in Genoa. Finally, there are forged impressions on original paper from bleached stamps, with watermark. Noncongruent design and arbitrary shades. Comparative study is necessary.

1894. Commemorative stamps. Nos. 23 to 25. *Watermark:* Cross of Savoy coat of arms.

1894 (December) and 1899. 1877 type. Nos. 26 to 31. *Sheets,* etc., as above. The 2-, 20-centesimo, and 1-lira are from 1894, the others, from 1899. The darkest shades of the first printings are in demand; others are common.

Forgeries: Geneva and Genoa. See first and third issues. There are very good forgeries of the 1-lira on original paper. See previous issues.

1903. Large format. Nos. 34 to 45. *Sheets* of 200 stamps in four panes of twenty-five (5 x 5). Crown watermark.

Forgeries: the whole set was photolithographically counterfeited expertly on original paper, but the impression lacks finesse, particularly in the horizontal lines. Also, one can observe that the three shade lines in the ribbon knot under the "S" are not of the same length in the lira values.

Subsequent issues. 1905. The error of figure "5" in the 1905 issue is encountered once per sheet.

1907. The imperforate 15-centesimo is an essay.

1911. The two values of 1907 were withdrawn (wider format, 19 mm). Impression not so good.

1917–25. Eleven issues in eight years! *L'appetit vient en mangeant.* [Eating stimulates the appetite.] Pay up, philatelists, pay up, if this kind of profitable philately continues to interest you.

Postage due stamps. The set of 1897–1919 was counterfeited well. Design comparison (corner ornaments, inscriptions, center figure) will be sufficient. The 1924 and 1925 sets — for which there was no perceptible need — probably will go through the counterfeiter's mill also.

Fakes: figure "1" chemically erased and replaced by a "5." Printing type not congruent in tone and design. One must assume that the 10-lira, No. 18, will experience the same fate.

Sarawak

1869. No. 1 and 1871–77. Nos. 2 to 7. *Originals:* 19 x 26½ mm, large format, No. 1; 20 x 22½ mm for the others, which have five types per value; lithographed.

Forgeries: I have seen only two lithographed fantasies, Nos. 1 and 7; an examination of the center background burelage will prove decisive. Arbitrary dimensions.

Overprinted stamp Nos. 28a and 70a. *Forged overprints:* inverted "2 C" on 12-cent, red on rose, and distinct error ONE C on 10-cent blue. Rigorous comparison is necessary.

Saudi Arabia — Hejaz (Arabia)

Numerous forged overprints. Make comparison.

Senegal

There are French colonial stamps overprinted with the word SENEGAL only, about 21$\frac{1}{2}$ x 4 mm, in black, blue, or red, upright or inverted overprint; according to Marconnet (1897, page 390), they are military cancellation postmarks. They were affixed to mints in connection with speculative operations.

1887–92. Overprinted stamps. Nos. 1 to 7. The numerous types of *original overprints* require specializing; Nos. 1–5 have a typographical overprint; Nos. 6 and 7, a handstamped overprint.

Numerous *forged overprints:* comparison is indispensable. Types II, V, and VI of the "5" (Nos. 1 and 2); III and V of the "10" (Nos. 3 and 4), and III and VIII (?) of the "15" (No. 5), and the overprints of Nos. 6 and 7 were counterfeited in Geneva and applied on originals and forgeries of 1881 (see French Colonies). The forged Geneva cancellations on this issue and the following ones are double circle, broken inner circle, two stars on the sides, with date: (1) 21$\frac{1}{2}$ mm, SENEGAL 2 SEPT 92 S^T LOUIS; (2) 22 mm, SAINT LOUIS 12 SEPT 92 SENEGAL; (3) 22 mm, DACAR 11 JUIL 92 SENEGAL; (4) wavy postmark without stars, maximum width, 25$\frac{1}{2}$ mm, S^T LOUIS A DAKAR 4 JUIN 92, and SENEGAL, inverted.

1892–1901 and 1912. Peace and Commerce type. Nos. 8 to 25 and 47 to 52. See the *forgeries* of this type under French Colonies (Geneva).

1903. Nos. 26 to 29. The two overprints were copied in Geneva.

1906. Balay type. 1-, 2-, and 5-franc. Nos. 44 to 46. See the forgeries of this type under French Colonies.

1915–18. Red Cross. No. 70b. Inverted *forged overprints.* The original overprint is typographed. Detailed comparison is indispensable, for there are good counterfeits both on cover and not.

Postage due stamps. Overprinted stamp Nos. 1 to 3. *Forgeries:* see forged postage due stamps under French Colonies.

Senegambia and Niger

1903. Peace and Commerce type. Nos. 1 to 13. *Forgeries:* see the forgeries of this type under French Colonies.

Serbia

1866 (May 13). Serbian coat of arms. Nos. 1 to 3. Provisional stamps for printed matter. Sheets of twelve stamps (4 x 3) with dividing frame lines. Typographed. Imperforate. Minimum width of margins must be 1$\frac{1}{2}$ mm. An unsuccessful reproduction allows one to establish that there are twelve types of each value and to reconstruct the sheets.

Printing figures: 1-para: 170 sheets; 2-para: 162 sheets for the first printing: very rare. For the second printing, 1,530 sheets of each value.

Varieties: 1-para dark green on purplish rose-tinted paper: 2M. 2-para red-brown on gray-lilac, thick paper: 2M. Copies with good embossing (showing indention on back) are in demand. The 2-para exists on thin paper: more common. The 2-para dark green on purplish rose (error) is very rare. The 2-para green on rose, paper tinted on back, is an unissued stamp. It is found on thick or medium paper; on medium paper: 25M.

Cancellations: three post offices used the Nos. 1 and 2: Belgrade, Alexinatz, and Kladowa. All canceled stamps are exceedingly rare. The postmark usually is rectangular: NAPLATCHEVO (FRANCO).

Originals: eleven horizontal lines in the upper corners and thirteen below. Seventy-seven pearls. Slight embossed effect on back.

Forgeries: Nos. 1 and 2 on paper shades that are too pale. Lithographed without either embossing or indention. Seventy-two pearls. Twelve horizontal lines above and below. Arbitrary shades. Another set, which we have not had a chance to see, comprises the three values. It also is lithographed, which facilitates its identification.

1866 (July). Portrait of Michael III. Nos. 8 to 10. 10-, 20-, and 40-para, perf 12. Typographed, Vienna printing. 10-para orange. 20-para pale rose and rose. 40-para dark blue. In the 20- and 40-para, two dots sometimes are seen under the "10" figures. 40-para bisected: very rare.

Cancellations: same postmark as above or city name on one line, unframed (3 ¹/₂ mm high).

Early forgeries: the whole set, including the 1- and 2-para. The part in the hair cannot be seen; the beard looks like a Japanese fan. 10-para bright orange, 20-para carmine or bright carmine, 40-para ultramarine blue. Irregular perforation or imperforate. (See illustration.) Barred circle cancellations, Lubeck bars, or circle postmark with date.

1866 (November). Same type. Nos. 6, 7, and 11 to 13. I. Nos. 6 and 7. 20-para rose, carmine-tinted rose, and rose on yellowish paper (yellowish gum); the latter: 3M, 4U; 40-para ultramarine. Perf 9¹/₂, medium or thick paper, Belgrade printing. The 20-para is found with "broken" CK letters (plate defect) and in pairs that are imperforate between. The 40-para is known bisected: very rare.

II. Nos. 11–13. Same values, plus a 10-para orange, same perforation, but pelure paper. The 10-para exists in orange and orange-red. The 20- and 40-para are known to exist in pairs that are imperforate between. Nos. 11–13 are from a second Belgrade printing.

Cancellations: as above, and with date cancellation.

Forgeries: same forgeries as for Nos. 8–10.

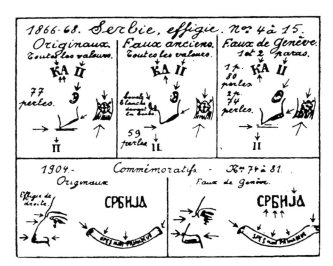

1866–68. Serbia. Portrait of Michael III. Nos. 4–15. Originals: all values; 77 pearls. Old forgeries: all values; white curl in front of beard; 59 pearls. Geneva forgeries: 1-para, 80 pearls, and 2-para, 74 pearls. Bottom: 1904. Commemoratives. Nos. 74–81. Originals. Geneva forgeries.

1867 (March). Same type. Nos. 4 and 5. 1- and 2-para, perf 9¹/₂. Stamps for printed matter. 1-para light yellow-green and a yellow-green olive shade. 2-para brown and dark brown. Rarely canceled. A few plate flaws: 2-para, NAPF instead of NAPE: 3M; as a pair with ordinary stamp: 5M.

Early forgeries: see Nos. 8–10 and illustration. The 1-para is meadow green or dark yellow-green; the 2-para is dark brown.

Geneva forgeries (F.): two somewhat different clichés for the two values. 1-para, four white shade lines cut the horizontal lines near the pearls in front of the nose. 2-para, three horizontal lines under the neck. The ear looks like a black velvet carnival mask. The bottom Cyrillic letter "П" often has become an "H." Perf 11¹/₂ and imperforate. Thin paper or transparent pelure. 1-para green, blue-green. 2-para bistre, red-brown.

1868. Same. Imperforate. Nos. 14 and 15. A continuation of the preceding printing of stamps for printed matter. 1-para dark green and pale green; olive-green: rare. 2-para red-brown; brown on yellowish paper: 2M. Same Cyrillic letter "П" defect as in the preceding issue; same value. Cancellations are very rare. There are many forged cancellations: comparison is necessary.

Forgeries: see the preceding issue.

1869. Same. Usual format. Nos. 16 to 24. *First printings:* most of the head details (hair, neck, and cheek shading) are rather delicately executed. The cheek and neck shading usually is visible enough. Stamps are spaced 2 mm apart, including perforation, resulting in narrow margins. Typographed.

Second printings: blotchy, often defective impression in which the back of the head quite often merges with the background. However, an exception must be made of the second printing of the 25-para blue, thick paper, which is much less blotchy. Stamps of the second printing are spaced 3–4 mm apart, perforation included, and thus have wide margins. The 20-para had several printings, but, except for the one mentioned above, the value of the various impressions is about the same.

Perforations: very numerous, ranging from 9¹/₂ to 13. They can be reduced to the three types indicated, which are quite sufficient even for a specialized classification.

Shades: very numerous. In order not to complicate things, we will mention only the principal ones. The amateur stamp collector can build a fine color display arrangement with them.

Paper: frequently medium or thin, sometimes thick. The yellowish paper shade comes from the gum. There are glossy papers and transparent, greasy or nongreasy, impressions.

The perforation, shade, and value variations of Nos. 16–24 of the first and second printings are summarized in the tabulation.

All values, except 1-para, also are found perf 12 x 9¹/₂: rare; and with composite perforations 11¹/₂ and

No.		Printing	Perf.	x Mint	x Used
16	1-p. yellow	1st	12	10	10
a			9½ x 12	4	10
b		2nd	12	5	(rare)
17	brown, bistre-brown	1st	9½	12	4
a			12	6	4
b			9½ x 12	6	4
c	red-brown, brown	2nd	9½	6	4
d			12	4	3
18	10-p. dark orange	2nd	12	0.5	0.6
19	15-p. orange	1st	9½	20	15
a			9½ x 12	20	15
20	20-p. blue shades	1st	9½	5	2
a			12	2	1
b			9½ x 12	2	0.5
c		2nd	9½	1	0.5
d			12	0.3	0.5
e			9½ x 12	(rare)	1
21	25-p. rose, carmine-rose	1st	9½	15	8
a			12	8	4
b			9½ x 12	2	1
c		2nd	9½	0.5	1
d			12	1	3
e			9½ x 12	0.5	1
22	35-p. green, blue-green	1st	12	15	10
a			9½ x 12	0.5	1
23	40-p. violet, dull violet	1st	9½	8	0.5
a			12	0.5	0.6
b			9½ x 12	0.8	0.6
24	50-p. green, dark green	1st	9½	3	1
a			12	1	1.5
b			9½ x 12	5	1.5

13, which are worth much more than the prices quoted in gold. Nos. 17 and 20 exist imperforate. There are pairs of Nos. 16–18, 20, and 21 that are imperforate between. Impression defect varieties are numerous: No. 23 with doubled figure, No. 24 with "56" instead of "50," etc.

Cancellations: rectangular (already mentioned) in black or blue: 50U; in blue: 2U. Straight line cancellation, unframed: 2–3U. Circular dated cancellation, double circle, is common in black and blue; in violet or in red: 50U.

Pairs: 3U. No. 19: 4U. Blocks: rare.

Early forgeries: the whole set. Good lithographed counterfeits. Perf 12½. The back of the neck always is delineated by a white line. There are thirteen ornamental lines in the bottom part of the stamp instead of fourteen.

Subsequent issues. 1872. 1-para yellow: imperforate. There are horizontally perforated pairs.

1873. 2-para black: with uncut "T," mint: 1 franc; used: 3 francs.

1880. King Milan IV: uncommon shades, mint; 5-para gray-green; 10-para lilac-rose; 20-pence yellow; 25-para dark blue; 50-para purplish brown; gray-brown; 1-dinar lilac.

1890. King Alexander: 15-para lilac-red: 3M. The whole set is found imperforate: rare.

1894. Same. Composite perforation 13, 13½, 11½ is rare (5-, 10-, 15-, and 25-para).

1900–1902. Horizontal inscription at top. Nos. 51 to 59. *Forgeries:* Geneva set (F.). The 3- and 5-dinar stamps were singled out for special attention. Lithographed. Good perforation and width, but 24 mm high instead of 23½ mm. An analytical comparison is based on center background stippling, forehead shading, and shading under the eye and in the collar. The ear is shapeless. Yellowish paper of approximately similar thickness, but with no transparency. Arbitrary shades. For cancellations, see "1904," below.

1903. Provisionals with overprint. Nos. 60 to 69. Lithographed overprints, 12 mm wide, on the 1-, 5-, 10-, 15-, 20-, 25-, and 50-para. Typographed, 10 mm wide, on the 1-, 5-, 10-, 25-, and 50-para and the 1-, 3-, and 5-dinar.

1904. Commemorative centenary stamps. Nos. 74 to 81. *Geneva forgeries (F.):* lithographed. Nontransparent, 55-micron paper, instead of transparent, 45–55 microns. Nos. 74–78 were counterfeited in two shades. Noncongruent cheek and neck hatching. For other features, see the illustration. Circular cancellation with date, rectangle in the middle: BEOF PAA 34 04 34 B BELGRADE.

1911. Military uniform. Nos. 93 to 104. *Genoa forgeries (I.):* photolithographed. Good perforation, but 19⅘ x 24¼ mm instead of 19½ x 24⅕ mm. Paper, 70 microns instead of 60. Small, white tunic lines, long lines from the top of the sleeve, irregular or faintly printed decorative lines. The goatee looks like a heron waiting for its prey. 1- to 5-dinar, including the error (!) of the 3-dinar, in yellow.

1912. With escutcheon. The stamps which have no escutcheon overprint are unofficial. They were never circulated.

1915. The whole set was probably counterfeited?

Postage due stamps. The catalogues give enough information.

Austrian occupation. Forged overprints are more numerous than stars in the sky. Specialize, or leave them alone. No middle ground.

1865–66. Shanghai. Nos. 1–19. Originals. (1) The outer frame lines do not meet. (2) The inner frame lines do not touch each other and do not touch the outer frame. (3) The center design is identical in all original stamps, and its frame, when it is visible, is rounded in the corners. (4) Outer right frame is broken in two places (not always visible). (5) Always seven lines under the mouth. (6) Always three curved lines (one long and two short), unattached or joined, depending on impression, which form the mustache. (7) First section of dragon has 19 scales; second, 24; third, 27. In the wove paper stamps: scattered white dots. Values in candareens: 2-candareen, Type I, Type II. 4- and 8-candareen, Type I, Type II. Early figures: 1, 2, 3, 4, 6, 8, 12, 16. Roman numeral: I (1-, 12-, 16-candareen). Modern figures: 1, 2, 3, 4, 6, 8, 12, 16. Second row: Reprints. Frame and center design as in the originals. Modern paper with broken, transparent, lines. (See text.) Third row: 1874. Official forgeries. 1-, 2-, 3-candareen. Type I: 1-candareen ultramarine, large modern figure. Two mustache lines. Very different tail shape. First section of the dragon: 25 scales; second, 22; third, 25, placed irregularly. Type II: 1-candareen ultramarine, small "1" modern figure. 2- and 3-candareen, with small or large modern figure. Nine lines under the mouth. Three long mustache lines and various defects. Bottom: Other forgeries.

Seychelles

Overprinted stamps. Double or inverted *forged overprints* of the 1893, 1896 (18 CENTS on 45-cent, double overprint), and 1901–2 issues. Comparison is indispensable.

Shanghai

1865–66. Large format. Nos. 1 to 19. *Originals:* typographed on local wove white paper whose transparency reveals only irregularly positioned tiny white dots; very transparent pelure paper (22 microns); thin (50 microns) transparent paper; medium (65 microns) yellowish paper; and laid paper (1- to 4-candareen). The center design is identical in all values (see the illustration). In the third section of the dragon's body, on the left, there is a triangular fish scale inserted between the two rows of scales, and, on the left of this peculiarity, two scales, which are unattached to the others on the left side, form a "3"; the center design is surrounded by a frame with rounded corners; in the early printings, or else later, when there is a more heavily inked impression, it can be seen quite well, but afterwards it is scarcely visible except on top and bottom, there being only traces on the sides.

The 1-candareen stamp has two types which are identified by the first top left Chinese character under the corner square; two types also for the 4- and 8-candareen stamps following the second Chinese character in the same tablet. The width of the center design varies from $17\frac{1}{4}$ to 18 mm, depending on impression; height, from $19\frac{1}{4}-\frac{1}{2}$ mm. The indention usually is evident; sometimes it is so pronounced that the thin inner frame lines cut the paper. There are numerous varieties (frames, lettering, Chinese characters, figures), classified in twenty-four categories in the Calman catalogue (volume 2, pages 870–74); obviously specializing is to be recommended.

Reprints: easily identified by the thin (40 microns) modern paper which was stippled by its passage through chalky presses; transparently, one can see white lines forming broken lines (seven per 3 mm of width; short lines in quincunx, staggered arrangement). The frame and center designs are identical with those of the originals; however, the impression is not as good, and there are blurred parts of the design, blurred figures, or blurred Chinese characters. Shades: (1) with early figures, 6-candareen brown; 8-candareen dark olive-green. (2) With modern figures, 1-candareen blue (various shades); 2-candareen dark gray; 3-candareen brown (various shades); 4-candareen yellow; 6-candareen olive-green; 8-candareen emerald green; 12-candareen vermilion; 16-candareen brownish red.

Except for the 1-candareen, all values have CANDAREENS (with an "S"). No perceptible differences in dimensions.

Official forgeries: some were used; the mints have little value; pelure paper (about 40 microns), with gum. The outer and inner frames, the Chinese characters, and the inscription lettering are rather similar to the original types. As for the inner design (dragon, and so forth), the original cliché, either because it was too worn or was lost, could not be used, and so a very different cliché was made (see illustration, Type I), with a six-point tail. But since this was not very impressive, particularly as an official copy, they made a second one that is much closer to the original design (see illustration, Type II), but, besides other defects, the first section of the tail has twenty scales, and second and third sections, twenty-five. The two types were printed in pairs: Type I, with modern figure "1," $1^2/_3$ mm high, and Type II, modern figure, $1^1/_4$ mm high; this type is 28 mm wide instead of $26^1/_2$–27 mm, the two thin vertical lines being about 1 mm from the dragon's frame. Both types have a very visible frame. In the 2-candareen stamps, one can distinguish two types — small or large modern figure "2" (see illustration); the small figure 2-candareen also is 28 mm wide; the impression of all these forgeries is rather good.

Other forgeries: (1) early lithographed forgeries from various sources on various kinds of paper; the dragon frame is 20 mm high in the 4-, 6-, 8-, 12-, and 16-candareen stamps.

1-candareen: with dot $1/_2$ mm away from "L"; very thin, yellowish paper; four close curved lines in the bottom of the center design; the left mustache forms a spot and is touching the ornament on the left; the right mustache is missing; in the first section of the dragon, twenty-four scales; in the second, twenty-three; and in the third, about the same number; the tail points are touching the ornaments, but none is touching the inner right frame; four dots instead of five; dull blue or dark green-blue.

2-candareen (reproduced in the illustration, easily identifiable with its numerous defects): eight lines under the mouth; the last two on the right are touching; large white circles under the eyes; mustaches (see illustration): sixteen, eighteen, and twenty scales. Another forgery of this value was printed in rose; the dot after the "L" is touching the terminal line of the "F"; two points of the dragon's tail are touching the inner frame; letters are too large.

3-candareen: the two triangles over the eyes extend beyond the dragon's frame, touching the inner left frame; the same is true for the left horn; there is a single "3"-shaped ornament in the upper right corner (dragon's frame); seven lines under the mouth, plus an

eighth line, forming a part of the mustache.

4-candareen: dark brown-red; inscriptions only 1 mm high, total width, 28 mm; dragon frame, 18 mm wide; the small sentry box in the middle of the stamp, under the dragon, is 7 mm from the dragon's left instead of about 8 mm; eight lines under the concave mouth; two-braid mustache; the "O" of the upper inscription is $1/_2$ mm from the line on the right; the center point of the dragon's tail is not touching the frame; twenty, twenty-three, and twenty-seven scales; yellow-ochre shade.

6-candareen: olive-green on grayish paper, copied from the 1-candareen official forgery (!) (Type I, tail with six points, and so forth); shade, that of the reprint with the modern figure. 8-, 12-, and 16-candareen stamps with defects similar to the preceding ones; eight or nine lines under the mouth; two mustache braids on one of the two sides; in the bottom of the design, under the sentry box, four well-spaced semicircles as in Type II of the official forgeries; number of scales: first section, twenty-one to twenty-three; second section, twenty to twenty-two; third section, twenty-nine. These forgeries are most common; there are others that the reader will recognize by the lithograph impression and by the various defects, which are as important as those just described for the various values. Comparison with the illustration of the originals is sufficient.

2. *Modern forgeries:* typographed; well-executed set of the 1-candareen in dark ultramarine, dark brown, dark olive-green, dark bistre, yellow, bright green, red, dull violet, and bright carmine; the value figure possibly was changed since to imitate the other values. Modern yellowish paper with lines of small, transparent broken lines (eight per 3 mm), similar to the reprint paper; yellowish gum; on the right, mustache formed by a short line and a long one with a circumflex accent shape at its end; the letters of "REEN" gradually increase in height to the right; all lines of the center design are too thick; scales: in the third section, all scales are connected (see illustration); the entire edge of the body has transversal hatch lines. There also are photolithographical forgeries (especially the 2-candareen, Type II), identifiable by the less sharply printed frames, the dimensions, the paper, and by a few minor defects which become evident from comparison. A forged Geneva cancellation, sometimes applied on forgeries of the following issue: one circle (24 mm), with date, SHANGHAI 4 APR 65.

1866. Dragon standing. Value in cents. Nos. 20 to 23. *Originals:* typographed; perf 12; the 2-candareen, also perf 15. 2-candareen rose, 19 x $23^3/_4$ mm; 8-candareen, 20 x 23 mm, blue-gray.

Forgeries: 2-candareen: a. early forgery, letters "L.P.O.," $1^1/_4$ mm high instead of 1 mm; the sides of the "O" are straight; crude center background burelage, made up of lozenges with a $1/4$–$1/2$ mm axis; height, $22 1/2$ mm; the upper left foot, on the right of the stamp, is shapeless and the square ornament on its right, in the tablet, does not have any inner horizontal line; curved base of the "2"; a dot after CENTS; dividing frame line, $1 1/4$ mm from stamp; perf $13 1/2$ x $12 1/2$.

b. Early lithographed stamps, $22 1/2$ mm high; dragon with a calf's head; the "S" and the "O" of the upper inscription are too high; the ovals of the center burelage are too large; the dragon's navel(?), or at least the design between the sections of its body, is formed by a single circle $1/2$ mm in diameter; the two top and bottom bars of the "E" of CENTS are the same length; perf $11 1/2$.

c. Geneva forgery, lithographed; dragon with a monkey's head with very prominent eyes; perf $12 1/2$; the "O" of the upper inscription is $3/4$ mm from the right side instead of $1/2$ mm, and the period is in the middle of the gutter instead of being very close to the vertical line. The burelage does not touch the reptile's rear "feet." Figure "2" is not as high as the letters of CENTS; stamp width, $19 1/2$ mm. 4-, 8-, and 16-cents: the center burelage finesse permits one to spot counterfeits with the naked eye — each detail is a defect.

A better executed forgery of the 8-cent stamp is identified by the following characteristics: gray shade; $23 1/4$–$1/2$ mm high; in the lower left corner, the B-shaped mark is touching the oblique line; the four small circles that should be found in the recesses of the center frame (use magnifying glass) were forgotten; the upper left "foot's" middle "toe" (right side of the stamp) is a rather long, oblique, descending line instead of being short and horizontal. Dot perf $12 1/2$ or $13 1/2$. This set and the following one were counterfeited in Geneva with a forged cancellation, a square of large round dots.

1867. Same. Values in candareens. Nos. 24 to 27.
Originals: typographed; 20 x $22 1/2$ mm; perf 15; in all values, the small crab-like design found in the center background in the middle of the dragon's body is the same.

Forgeries: 1-candareen (a) early forgery; lithographed; crudely perf 13; $19 1/2$ x $23 1/4$ mm; the "S" of SHANGHAI is touching the tablet on the left and the "G" is a "C." The right lateral tablet frame is triple instead of double; the corner and tablet circles do not touch the frame; in the upper right circle, the character is shifted to the right and its base is touching the circle on the right; thick, nonequidistant, vertical shade lines of the background; the crab-like ornament is shapeless and is on a blank background; the "C" of CAND is a "G." (b) Lithographed forgery; perf 12 x $12 1/2$; allowable dimensions; the background shade lines

do not usually terminate at the dragon; the horns come very close to the frame ($1/2$ mm required); the upper right "foot" (left side of the stamp) extends beyond the second vertical shade line instead of touching the fifth; no dot after CAND.

3-candareen, 22 mm high; the "O" is slanted to the right; in the inner corners, the three blank parts of the design are not connected with each other; the left horn ends quite near the oval instead of being about 1 mm from it; right "fist" with five quite unconnected "fingers" that cast no shadow; perf $12 1/2$ or dot perf 13.

6-candareen, lithographed; dot perf 13; no circles in the center of the flowerets bordering the inner frame (use magnifying glass); irregular, not very visible background line structure; figure "6" with upper curl shifted to the right of the lower loop.

12-candareen, shapeless "crab"; the small blank circles of the border (use magnifying glass) are practically invisible; crude hatching; lithographed stamps, dot perf 13.

1873. Overprinted stamps of 1866–67. Nos. 28 to 35. In the original overprint, the "D" of CAND is broken on top.

Forged overprints: very numerous; some of them are deceptive; detailed comparison is indispensable. The red overprints with unbroken "D" are forged.

1875–76. Dragon types of 1867. Nos. 36 to 42. *Forgeries:* the details given for the 1867 issue will identify sufficiently the forgeries of this issue.

1877. Preceding issue overprints. Nos. 43 to 46. *Forged overprints:* same remark as in the 1873 issue.

1877. Dragon types of 1866. Nos. 47 to 62. *Forgeries:* see details for the 1866 issue; they will identify the 20- to 100-candareen forgeries with values changed to CASH. In the 20-candareen lithographed stamp, no circle touches the frame; the design around the center medallion is shapeless; the center background shade lines are equidistant; however, they are broken. The other values experienced a similar fate. Dot perf 12, $12 1/2$, 13.

1884–86–88. Types of 1866. Nos. 56 to 60 and 69 to 73. *Forgeries:* same remark.

1879–86–88. CASH overprint. Nos. 53 to 55 and 61 to 67. *Original overprints:* total height of the overprint is $7 3/4$ mm (measure near the middle of the overprint) and the letters of CASH are $3 1/4$ mm high.

Forged overprints: comparison is necessary, for some of the overprints are executed well.

1893. Overprinted stamps. Nos. 108 to 114. *Forged Geneva overprint:* comparison is necessary.

Postage due stamps. Overprinted. Nos. 1 to 11. *Forged Geneva overprint:* same remark.

Siberia

KOLTCHAK overprints. Nos. 1 to 10. Numerous *forged overprints.* Comparison is indispensable.

Sierra Leone

1861–72. 6-pence. Nos. 1 to 4; 1876, No. 16.
Originals: typographed on azure or white paper; perf 12½ or 14; no watermark, except on No. 16, which is watermarked "C C" with crown; 18¾–19 x 22½ mm.

Early forgeries: poorly lithographed; no watermark; imperforate or perf 11½; dividing frame lines; ⅓ mm between SIERRA and LEONE instead of ¾ mm; irregular bureled background under SIX and above PENCE, formed as in the corners, instead of having only the three usual lines of lozenges in these places.

Modern forgery: typographed; perf 13½ x 13; no watermark; thick greenish azure paper; 18½ x 22⅕ mm; the background shade lines usually touch the octagon's sides; they are too thick and give the background an appearance that is hardly less dark than the inscription tablets; above the first crown jewel, the two shade lines are parallel instead of meeting; the corners around the octagon have lines of lozenges, as under SIX in the original, instead of a burelage of lozenges and dots; the "I" and the "E" of SIERRA are joined at top and bottom, and the two "R" letters are joined at the bottom; the eye, the earlobe, and the front of the cheek do not have any shading.

1872–95. ½-penny to 1-shilling. Nos. 5 to 15 and 17 to 28. *Originals:* watermarked "C C" of "C A"; perf 12½ or 14; 18¾ x 22½ mm; in the center background, the first three top shade lines and the last bottom two are not parallel; the one at bottom is ⅕ mm from the tablet; the nose point is 1¼ mm from the shade lines; the neck point is touching the sixth shade line. The final "E" of POSTAGE is normal; its median bar is placed at the midpoint of the letter's height.

Forgeries: lithographed; no watermark; value printed in the same shade as the stamp; (a) early set of the 1-penny, 2-, 3-, 4-pence, and 1-shilling stamps; formless perforation, background shade lines: four instead of six per millimeter of height; neck point on the third line; ½ mm between the corner squares and the inscription tablets; the "A" of SIERRA has a serif on top; no shading under the eye or on the front of the neck. (b) Early set of the same values, but a little better; the two "R" letters of SIERRA are open on top; poorly executed background shade lines with breaks and blank spots; same, with respect to the hair, and so forth; perf 11½. (c) Early set that is better, easily identifiable by the inner rectangle instead of a square in the right corner ornamental squares; see Type d for the other marks — Type c is related to it — but the lower line of the center background is ¼ mm above the lower tablet; fragments of dividing frame lines; perf 12 and 13. (d) Geneva; retouched type of Type c, with the addition of the ½-penny, 1½- and 2½-pence; a few of the face shade lines are lengthened; a line was added in the bottom of the center background, very near the lower tablet; allowable dimensions; perf 12½; these forgeries would be deceptive if they had a watermark; there are some with an embossed (stamped on) watermark or a watermark made with a greasy instrument — not visible in benzine; the top and bottom shade lines are equidistant; there is a single lip junction line instead of a forked line; the nose point is ¾ mm from the end of the shading; the neck point is touching the eighth shade line, but, a little to the right, the point descends to the seventh one; the final "E" of POSTAGE is irregular, with median bar placed too high, and the bottom oblique line is too near the vertical and is too long; the eye is looking fixedly at the end of the nose; blank space on the left of the neck shading.

1893–97. "½" and "2½" overprints. *Forged overprints:* very numerous. Comparison and, if need be, expertizing are indispensable.

Higher value stamps of issues from 1897 to 1928. *Fakes* obtained by removing fiscal cancels and replacing them with forged cancellations.

1-shilling green, overprinted SIERRA 5 S LEONE. This stamp is a fiscal (not issued by the postal service).

Solomon Islands

1907. Pirogue. No watermark. Nos. 1 to 7.
Originals: lithographed; perf 11; sheets of sixty (6 x 10); ½ and 2½ transfer matrices of three stamps (3 x 1) and transfer plates of six stamps (6 x 1) for the other values; 29 x 25¾–26 mm. On the right and left of the upper inscription, there is a volute containing four heavy white shade lines, which are thick and curved, and a fifth one, also curved, which is thin, except in Type I of the 2½-pence, where the fourth and fifth lines, because of transfer plate flawing, merge into one line; on the right and left of these volutes, right up against the inner frame, there are six or seven white horizontal shade lines; the "R" of BRITISH normally terminates at bottom right; the four palm trees on the right have a vertical white line, about ¾ mm long, in the middle of each of their trunks; two long color lines connect the top of the foliage of the first and fourth palm trees on the left, which is very close to the inner oval, under the "B" of BRITISH.

Forgeries: lithographed; allowable dimensions; perf 11$\frac{1}{2}$; three heavy curved lines and one thin one in the volutes on the right and the left of the upper inscription; outside these volutes, near the outer right frame, there are only four heavy horizontal shade lines, which are short and often are almost invisible; no vertical white lines in the middle of the trunks of the palm trees on the right, except in the 6-pence, where they are also too short; the "R" of BRITISH ends in a point, bottom right; the oblique color shade lines connecting the foliage of the first and fourth palm trees on the left are missing. The shades are dull and lifeless; the $\frac{1}{2}$-penny was printed in gray. The paddlers' heads are too large and cannot be distinguished as well as in the originals. No counterfeit has the defects of the various types of the transfers of each value: real philatelists will understand that this is proof positive of the inauthenticity of those stamps.

No *reprints.*

Somalia (Italian Somaliland)

1903. Crown watermark. Nos. 1 to 7. *Originals:* value in besas, 22$\frac{1}{4}$ x 28$\frac{1}{2}$ mm; values in annas, 22$\frac{1}{2}$ x 28$\frac{1}{2}$ mm.

Geneva forgeries: 1- and 2-besa, 22 x 27$\frac{3}{4}$ mm; 1- and 2-anna, 22 x 28$\frac{1}{5}$ mm; I have not seen the other values in annas — they may exist. In the elephant type, the letters "ALIA" of SOMALIA and "AD" of BENADIR are joined at bottom; the vertical shade lines under BENADIR are too short. In the lion type, the center background and stippling is incomplete; the shield's shade lines are too short and the ornamental design surrounding the shield is formless.

1906. Overprinted 5- and 10-anna of 1903. Nos. 8 and 9. (and)

1916. SOMALIA overprint, inverted on a red cross. (and)

1907. Postage due stamps. Nos. 1 to 11. *Forged overprints:* comparison is necessary. With respect to the postage due stamps, measure the distance from "Meridionale" to "Somalia Italiana": it is too small in the forgeries, and the characters are printed less boldly.

Somaliland Protectorate

1903. BRITISH SOMALILAND overprints. Nos. 1 to 19. *Forged overprints:* comparison is indispensable. The whole set was overprinted fraudulently in Geneva on canceled original stamps of the West Indies.

1904–5. Official stamps overprinted O.H.M.S. Nos. 1 to 15. *Forged overprints:* comparison is useful. The "On H.M.S." (Nos. 1–5) and SERVICE (Nos. 6–10) overprints also were counterfeited in Geneva.

South Australia

1855–77. Portrait in a circle. 1-penny, 2-pence, and 1-shilling. *Originals:* recess print engraved; star watermark; imperforate, or various perforations. In addition to stars, there are concentric circles in the ornamental squares; the circle does not touch the lower tablet and is about $\frac{2}{3}$ mm away from the tablet containing the words SOUTH AUSTRALIA; the face and neck are shaded finely with dots.

Early forgeries: no watermark. The center circle is almost touching the top tablet and is touching the value tablet; the corner design is arbitrary; white spots on the cheek and the bottom of the neck.

1859–67. 9-pence. No. 9. *Originals:* recess print engraved; star watermark. The oval is touching the frame at all possible points. There are sixteen double hatch lines in the oval, on the right and left of the frame.

Early forgeries: thirteen double hatch lines on the left and right. No watermark.

Spain

Spain is one of the most interesting countries in Europe for specialization. It has numerous early issues of different types, and an infinite number of shades, varieties, and cancellations.

I. Imperforate Stamps

Issue of 1850. Nos. 1 to 5. *Select:* four margins, $\frac{1}{2}$ mm wide.

Plates: the 6- and 12-cuarto: 255 stamps; the 5-real: 180 stamps; the 6-real: 150 stamps; the 10-real: 180 stamps. The two plates of the 6-cuarto can be distinguished by whether the "T" is attached to the "O" (Plate II), or unattached (Plate I).

Transfers: transfers from the original die were formed in panes of twenty-four, thirty-five, forty, thirty, twenty-five, and thirty stamps, respectively, for the 6-cuarto, Plates I and II, and for subsequent values. Each stamp provides enough variety for possible plate reconstruction. The distinctive marks of the transfer do not constitute varieties properly so-called, but flaws from plate transferral, which appear only once in each sheet, are rare.

Varieties: the 6-cuarto, Plate I: 2M, 2U; the 12-cuarto dark lilac: 50M, 25U. The 5-real pale red (rosy) and brownish dark red: 2M, 50U. The 6-cuarto, thin paper, Plate II: 50M, 3U. Other values: 2M, 50U. The 6-cuarto, Plate II, exists also on paper of medium thickness. There are numerous printing defects on the 6-cuarto: 3U.

Transferral flaws (one per sheet): one especially finds deformed letters or figures that are either attached or misplaced. The 6-cuarto: 5U. The 6-real: 3U. The 10-real, with year date: extremely rare.

6-cuarto retouched stamps: 10–25U.

Pairs: 3–4 units; blocks of four: 6–8 units.

Cancellations: Type A: usual and common in black; rare in blue. Type B, with date in red, was applied to stamps in January and February 1850 (also later, occasionally); on the 6-cuarto: 2U. The following types and those not shown in the illustration are rare.

Type C: letters "A" (railway post); "A S" (railway post); "0" (Zaragoza) (the zero is sometimes doubled); "C A," monogram (railway post). Type D: figures "6," "8" (Cuenca), "11" (Zaragoza), in blue and black, figure sometimes doubled; "14," "15," etc., different figure types, "I I" (Palma de Mallorca: rare). Types E, F, G (Parilla, Madrid).

Type J: various kinds of grills, three bars (Logrono), black or blue dots (Sevilla). Type H: "Post Paid" or "P.D.," postage due at destination. Type I: straight line; on two lines — for example, GALICIA PUEBLA and LUMBIER NAVARRA: very rare, etc. Framed town designation — for example, CAZERES, in a Type E

oval — and letter "C" surmounted by a crown are very rare.

Forgeries: the whole set was well counterfeited in Barcelona (1905). There are also early as well as modern forgeries that are done well enough to fool one at first sight. All forgeries, however, whatever they are, are easily identified either by comparing shades and design, if they are poorly executed, or by the absence of transfer plate marks, if they are good copies. (The reader is referred to the magnificent work of Hugo Griebert, *The Stamps of Spain (1850–54),* with a special study of the stamps of the first issue, 1850, including a full description of varieties, transfer errors, obliteration, etc. Illustrated by photographic plates. London, 1919. See the reconstruction of first-issue plates.)

Measurement of lithographed originals is not really conclusive, for the dimensions vary according to the type of transfer, the printing, the paper, and the plate. The 6-cuarto: $17^{1}/_{2}$–18 mm x $22^{1}/_{4}$–$^{1}/_{2}$ mm. A description of a few of the best forgeries follows.

6-cuarto: early engraved forgery. Ornaments on the side of the year date are symmetrically placed; figure "1," too tall, too thin; upper loop of the "8," too narrow, etc. Another early forgery: the squares of the cross-ruling are too large. A modern forgery (Plate II): bad cross-ruling behind the chignon; no line behind the neck; heavy line coming down to the lip junction line; the "0" of 1850, open at the top; poorly sketched eye.

12-cuarto: forgeries have inscriptions that differ from the originals. Comparison is indicated. Transfer defects,

Spain: cancellations found on the issue of 1850, Nos. 1 to 5. A. Rosette. B. Early dated cancel. C. Letters. D. Figures. E. Large grill. F. Small oval grill. G. Medium grill. H. "P.P." framed. I. Name of town on one or several lines. J. Open grill. K. Circle with numbers. L. Small dated postmark. M. Bars and number.

especially in this value, furnish the best references, for the shade does not always enable one to discern the design of the head; moreover, in the Barcelona forgery, the background cross-ruling appears to be larger, but in the pale lilac original on thin paper, it seems to be the same in relation to the usual lilac shade, because of the lighter impression of the former. Original dimensions: $17^{1}/_{2}$ x 21 mm; on thin paper: $17^{1}/_{2}$ x $20^{3}/_{4}$ mm.

5-real: 1. early lithographed forgery on thin, glossy paper; the neck extremity, which is too pointed, extends beyond the "0" of 1850 on the right; the ornament on the left of the year date is too narrow and is 1 mm from figure "1"; the corner ornaments form poorly executed St. Andrew's crosses, with the same colored cross inside.

2. A modern lithographed forgery; the extremity of the diadem is pointing toward the left of the "S" of REALES, whereas in the originals it is somewhat slanted toward the right of the letter; the crude eye is surrounded with big dots; the nostril is made with a straight line followed by a color triangle and a vertical line. Height, $21^{1}/_{2}$ mm. Originals: 18 x $21^{2}/_{3}$–$^{7}/_{8}$ mm.

6-real (Barcelona): dark ultramarine; thick, brown gum. The two serifs of the second "I" of CERTIFICADO are concave; a sharply etched, thick line is visible in front of and behind the neck and under the chin. The bandeau lines and hatching are thicker than in the original, as is also the case with respect to the eye, nostril, and mouth lines, and the face and neck stippling. In contrast with the original, the overall effect is harsh. Measurement: $17^{1}/_{2}$ x 21 mm instead of $17^{1}/_{4}$ x $21^{3}/_{4}$ mm. Inscription comparison is sufficient in studying the early forgeries of this stamp.

10-real: Poorly executed lithographed forgery; the cheek and hair lines are crude; the eye does not resemble the original; the outer line of the bandeau extends over the forehead. Dimensions of the original: $17^{7}/_{8}$ mm by about $21^{2}/_{3}$ mm.

Issue of 1851. Nos. 6 to 11. *Plates:* 170 stamps.
Paper: thin and transparent.
Select: four margins, $^{3}/_{4}$ mm wide.
Varieties: the 6-cuarto, gray, brown, or deep black: 2M, 50U. The 12-cuarto, gray: 2M, 2U. The 5-real, dark or bright rose: 50M, 25U. The 6-real, dark blue: 50M. The 10-real, dark green: 50M. The 2-real is orange-red. The 6-cuarto on very transparent pelure paper (30 microns) is rare; on average paper (first printing, 60 microns): 5U. The 5-real red-brown (color error?): 10M, 10U. The 6-cuarto, with bottom of "S" of SEIS deformed and touching the center background: 10U. Stamps with lined backgrounds exist.
Cancellations: Type A, black rosette, is common; in blue or red: rare. Type B with red date is rare. Type F, small blue grill, letter "C".... or others, and the other cancellations are rare. [Translator's note: Incomplete

text: the printer dropped part of a line or a whole line.]
Pairs: 3M, 3U; blocks of four: 6–8M, 8–10U.
Forgeries: there are a great many forgeries, and they usually are lithographed. It would take too long to describe them. Compare with a common 6-cuarto original; the other values are identical. Nos. 7–11 must be on thin paper.

Check especially the parts of the original design described in the illustration. Naturally, in this or that forgery, one of the distinguishing marks may be more or less like the original — that is why we are careful to show several.

Barcelona set (S.). The 2-real blue error in a block of four is found in this set. The lower right downstroke of the second "R" of CORREOS is more oblique (appearing longer) and bulges more in the middle than the downstroke of the first "R"; the "A" and "R" of CUARTOS and the "A" and "L" of REALES are not joined at bottom. The measurements are good: originals on average, 18 x 22 mm.

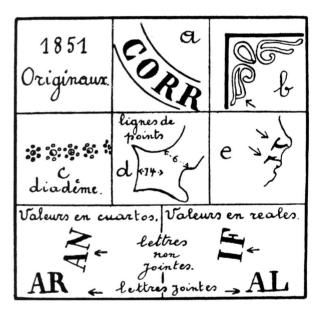

Forgeries of the 1851 issue, Nos. 6 to 11. Originals. Middle: Diadem; lines of dots. Bottom: Values in cuarto; values in real; letters not joined; letters joined.

Geneva set (F.). $17^{2}/_{3}$ x $22^{1}/_{3}$ mm. Not nearly as well executed as the Barcelona set. The vertical downstrokes of the "R" letters have no terminal lines; the "L" of REALES has no top serif; the "O" of CORREOS bulges too much on the right; the design of the hair is not comparable. (See the illustration.)
Fake: a 2-real, made with a "rebuilt" 5-real red. Shade not correct. The new stamp, faked this way, is so cleverly repaired that removal of the forged gum is necessary to ascertain that the stamp was altered.

Issue of 1852. Nos. 12 to 16. *Plates:* 170 stamps (10 x 17), typographed.

Select: four margins, ³/₄ mm wide.

Paper: medium thickness; the 6-cuarto is on thin paper that in some cases is oily.

Varieties: the 6-cuarto dark rose: 50M, 50U; bright carmine: 2M, 2U. The 12-cuarto purplish lilac: 75M, 2U. The 5-real dark green: 50M, 50U. The 6-real pale blue or dark blue instead of blue-green: 25M, 25U. The 2-real is pale, dull brownish red; the bright shade is extremely rare.

No dot after CORREOS, 6-cuarto: 3M, 10U; 5-real: 3M, 4U; other values: 2M, 2U.

Plate flaws: the 6-cuarto, the "A" of FRANCO has no top or the "2" of "1852" has a foreshortened horizontal bar: 2M, 8U. The 12-cuarto, upper tablet shading is incomplete on the left: 2M, 2U. The 5-real, figure slanted. The 6-real, the "s" of "Rs" forms an "8"; the upper or center bar of "E" (CERT^{DO}) is almost invisible.

Pairs: the 6-cuarto: 3M, 4U; other values: 2.50U. Blocks of four, 6-cuarto: 8M, 12U; other values: 8M, 6U.

Cancellations: Type F in black is common; in blue, it is in demand; in green or red, it is rare. This cancellation is found in black writing ink: 2U. All other cancellations are rare.

Forgeries: except for the 6-cuarto value, all stamps on thin paper are forgeries. The lettering of the poor counterfeits is neither aligned nor congruent with the original; in the early ones, the letters sometimes touch the top or bottom of the inscription tablet. Compare with a 6-cuarto and with the original design shown in the illustration.

Two sets are especially well done: 1. Barcelona (S.) forgeries. Format 17¹/₂ mm by about 22, but it should be 18 x 22¹/₄–²/₅. The value figures and the "5" of 1852 don't match the original.

2. Geneva (C.) forgeries. Executed in blocks of nine. Very deceptive, but 22¹/₂ mm high. Defects are reproduced in the illustration: the "N" of FRANCO slants too much to the right; corner ornaments are finer than in the originals; inscription tablets are placed too far to the left; a few white lines are missing near the middle of the right side of the chignon; the right nostril line is missing.

Official forgeries: these are not nearly so well done as the Barcelona and Geneva forgeries. Comparison of inscriptions will quickly identify them. They are rare with authentic cancellation. Forgeries of the 6- and 12-cuarto are known to exist.

Issue of 1853. Nos. 17 to 21. *Plates:* 170 stamps, typographed.

Select: lateral margins, ³/₄ mm wide; others, ¹/₂ mm wide.

Originals of the 1852 issue, Nos. 12 to 16, compared with forgeries of Barcelona and Geneva. Originals. Forgeries. *Largeur* [width].

Paper: thin. The 6- and 12-cuarto also are found on medium paper.

Varieties: the 6-cuarto carmine-rose, bright rose: 2M, 2U; medium paper: 4M, 8U. The 12-cuarto purplish gray: 2M, 2U; medium paper: 2M, 2U. The 5-real green or dark green instead of yellow-green: 50M, 2U. The 6-real dark blue: 50M, 25U. The 2-, 5-, and 6-real stamps are found without a dot under the "s" of "Rs": 50M, 50U. In addition, there are a few minor plate flaws.

Pairs: 3M, 3U; blocks of four, 12-cuarto: 8M, 8U; others: 6–8 M and U. Blocks of four of the 5-real are rare.

Cancellations: Type F, black, is common. The same type with writing ink: 50U. All others, including the colored ones, are rare.

Fake: the 6-cuarto azure is slightly tinged with blue. It often has been faked, sometimes chemically, and, if the requisite for comparison is not available, it always must be expertized.

Early forgeries: a few values in reals do not have the exact number of pearls on one or the other side of the portrait; the same applies to the number of heavy white lines, it being understood that the number of white lines shown in the illustration includes the white dot that forms the tenth or the eleventh line in the originals, but does not include the fine inner frame. Inscriptions and figures are defective. For example, in a good forgery of the blue-black 6-cuarto, the "3" has a vertical terminal line, not an oblique one. Dimensions are not congruent: originals are about 18²/₅ x 22–22¹/₂ mm.

Modern forgeries: Geneva set (F.). About 18 x 22 mm. Compare with the sketch or with originals. The hatching of the head and bandeau and the diadem ornaments are not congruent; all the shading lines are almost as thick as the nose and mouth lines, whereas in the originals they are half as fine.

In another set, of Spanish origin, the stamps are not quite wide enough (18 mm); the two long median shade

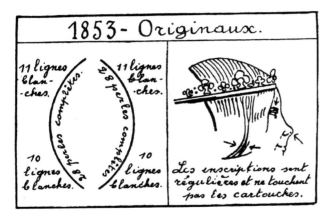

Characteristics of the 1853 issue, Nos. 17 to 21. Originals. Left: *Lignes blanches* [white lines]; *perles completes* [whole pearls]. Right: the inscriptions are regular and do not touch the tablets.

lines of the bandeau are not congruent. The eye design also lacks congruence.

Forged cancellations: as above, grill or rosette.

Issue of 1853. Local postal service (Madrid coat of arms). Nos. 22 and 23. *Sheets* of 170 stamps.

Paper: thin, transparent or nontransparent.

Shade: burnished bronze (copper-red), perceptible only in the oxidized copies. A second printing of the 1-cuarto was made in July 1854.

Varieties: there are a few plate flaws: broken white line under CORREO, or the "N" of FRANCO joined to the "C" by a line that makes an "E" of the "C." The 1-cuarto: 3.50M, 2.50U. The 3-cuarto: 2M, 50U.

Mint pairs: very rare; blocks of four: extremely rare.

Reprints (1870): rather dull, dark bronze-gray shade; paper more gray than yellowish; figure "3" (3 CUARTOS) has no curl below. A 2-cuarto was reprinted from a die made in 1853, but soon was rejected because of the appearance of the 2-cuarto of 1854 (November 1854). Like that of the reprints, the shade indicates that it is not an unissued stamp. Value, 1-cuarto: 35 francs; 2-cuarto: 35 francs; 3-cuarto: 100 francs.

Forgeries: the paper is usually thicker and the shade is different. The rather numerous forgeries do not have the exact number of color lines in the corners or of dots in the crown. In one of them, the "C" of CORREO is almost touching the frame on the left. Check whether your copies have the following characteristic features of the originals:

1. Ten color lines in the corners, counting the lines above and below the tablets.

2. The bear seems to be wearing a three-pointed crown; the lowest point usually touches the tree; the shading of the back is visible through a magnifying glass.

3. Regular and well-spaced inscription lettering.

4. Six points in the stars of the oval.

5. Except for the one below the top right star, the horizontal shade lines in the oval are straight and well spaced.

6. The laurel drapes are well formed, well shaded.

Fake: a look through a magnifying glass is enough to reveal the transformation of the 1-cuarto into a 3-cuarto. The addition of the lower bandeau of the 3-cuarto reprint was accomplished by repairing a 1-cuarto. Ridiculous.

Issue of 1854. Coat of arms. Background in color. Nos. 24 to 27. *Select:* four margins, $^{1}/_{2}$–$^{3}/_{4}$ mm wide.

Varieties: the 6-cuarto pale carmine: 2M, 2U; thick paper: 4M, 4U; thick azure paper, mint: 100 francs, used: 80 francs. The 2-real dark vermilion instead of common vermilion: 50M, 50U; red: 3M, 2.50U; pale dull red, mint: very rare; 4U. The 5-real pale green and dark green, and the 6-real dark blue: 50M, 25U. The 6-cuarto and the 2-real azure stamps must be expertized. The 2-real dark red brick and extra bright dark vermilion are rare; no dot after CORREOS: 2M, 2U.

Stock remainders: these were canceled with three black bars, with or without finer interlining. They have little value; No. 25a: 10 francs.

Cancellations: the black oval with bars is common; in blue: 50U. Others: rare.

Pairs: 3M, 3U; the 1-real dark blue: rare; blocks of four of the 6-cuarto: 12U; other values: 6M, 6U.

Forgeries: rather numerous. The following distinctive marks of the *originals* will help to identify all of them.

1. Crown pearls: five on the right and left, the highest of which is malformed, then seven on the right and left, finally three in the middle.

2. The inscription letters do not touch each other and the corner ornaments do not touch the frames.

3. The middle of the dot after 1854 is a little lower than the horizontal line of the "4." There is a dot after CORREOS (except in the 2-real exception).

4. Very fine shield hatching. The shade lines of the top right quarter of the shield do not end at the top, while those of the left quarter at the point of the shield all end at the horizontal line dividing the quarters.

5. The curves of the coat of arms, both on the right and on the left, have three and four oblique lines.

6. The small center oval is shaded with horizontal lines.

7. The ornaments of the necklace are all terminated by three rather clearly defined points; the ornament above and to the right of the value figure usually is touching the white line below.

8. The top bar of the "5" of 1854 clearly is concave.

9. The terminal line of the horizontal bar of the "4" occupies only about $^{1}/_{4}$ mm of the vertical body of the

figure. (The best set of forgeries of this issue is identified by this characteristic mark.)

Issue of 1854 (November 1). White background. Nos. 28 to 33. The 2-cuarto stamps do not have a year date.

Varieties: the 2-cuarto blue-green: 50M, 50U; fine impression: 2M, 75U. The stamp on azure paper has the fine impression. The 4-cuarto dark carmine: 2M, 3U; thick paper: 4M, 5U; the stamp on azure is on thick paper. The 1-real blue-black: 2M, 50U; the 1-real pale blue is on thick paper; the fine impression of No. 28 is recognized by the star points and the shadings.

Plate flaws: the 4-cuarto, no dot after CORREOS; the 2- and 4-cuarto, no dot after the value figure; defective lettering and figures; for example, 4-cuarto with "1354" (instead of "1854"), "1 54," figure "4" followed by a comma, the "8" of 1854 open at top, etc. Collector's price. [This term is used to indicate that such items may bring higher prices that bear little relation to their catalogue value.]

The 2-cuarto green with curl watermark is an unissued stamp; it is rare.

Cancellations: the small oval black grill is common; in blue: 50U; canceled with date in blue: 2U.

Pairs: 3M, 3U; blocks of four: 6M, 6U. Bar cancellations have minimal value; No. 29: 1 franc.

Originals: in the preceding issue, look at the characteristics of these numbers:

Nos. 1, 2, 3, 4, and 5. In the heavily inked impressions of this stamp, only three oblique shade lines are seen in the left curve of the coat of arms.

Nos. 6 and 7. In a deceptive forgery, the last chain link on the right is not connected with the following one; the middle of this last one is not as wide as it should be.

Nos. 8, 9, and 10. The cross on the crown does not touch the color line under CORREOS — use a magnifying glass — except in heavily inked impressions.

No. 11. Under the "C" of the same word, the corner ornamentation ends in a small, clearly visible four-branched design.

Regarding the 2-cuarto (Nos. 28 and 32), we should point out, moreover, that the inner right frame does not touch the line under CORREOS and that the small "s" on the right of the "C" is clearly slanted to the right.

Forgeries: the above characteristics will enable one to identify the best of the forgeries and the official forgery of the 4-cuarto stamp.

Fakes: the bar cancellation of the two shades of the 1-real frequently was changed to a grill; at times it even was dipped in acid to produce an entirely new stamp. Finally, the piecing together of two fragments of the bar canceled stamps produced a stamp without bars, the joining of the two fragments being masked by part of an oval cancellation. Like all other similarly doctored

stamps, this fake is quite susceptible to identification.

As for the 2-cuarto, sometimes it was given an azure chemical bath, which was unsuccessful, however, in transforming its thin paper (50 microns) into medium-thick paper (70 microns) and its generally crude impression into first-class printing.

1855. Curl watermark. Nos. 34 to 37. *Select:* for this issue and the next two, a select example is one with four margins, minimum width 1/2 mm.

Shades: 2-cuarto yellow-green: 50M, 50U; 1-real blue-green: 50M, 50U.

Varieties: No. 35, grayish shade, is found on medium paper. No. 37, on thick paper: 2M, 2U. Numerous flaws resulted from bad printing or from cliché wear: CORRIOS, PEALES, CORRFOS, CORRECS, C..ARTOS, CORRLOS, RFAL, CORKEOS, COKREOS, COKKEOS, KEAL, CORREO.., etc.: collector's price. The four values are found without a dot after the value figure, and the 1-real, without the figure "1" or with the figure reduced to its lower section; totally defective impressions.

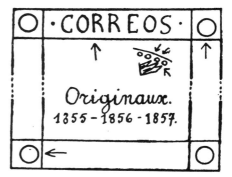

Characteristics of the 1855 Curl watermark issue, Nos. 34 to 37.

Cancellations: Types F and K are common; Type F in blue: 50U; with date, single or double circle: 50U.

Pairs: Nos. 35 and 36: 5M, 6U. Nos. 37 and 38: 3M, 2.50U. Nos. 37 and 37a (error): the pair is worth three times the error price; blocks of four, Nos. 35 and 36: 12M, 20U; Nos. 37 and 38: 8M, 8U.

Barred stamps: No. 36: 0.25 franc; No. 37: 0.40 franc.

Fake: the 2-real violet was worked over chemically to make a No. 37a, which never has the blue shade of the original. The same operation was performed on the 2-real of the following issue by fakers who did not know much about watermarks.

Used postal forgeries: several varieties exist of the 4-cuarto on thick paper:

1. No overlapping between the circle and the tablet lines of CORREOS and CUARTOS (with or without watermark).

2. The top left rosette is almost touching the lower line of the square; the one at top right is touching the line on the right; the "C" of CUARTOS is slanted to the right; the serif on the right foot of the second "R" of CORREOS is too long.

Forgeries: there are a few. Compare with an original 4-cuarto, and do not linger over the multiple printing flaws that may appear.

Originals: 1. the dot preceding the value figure is always higher than the one that follows (the 12-cuarto has only one dot).

2. The corner rosettes are not symmetrically placed in the squares.

3. The laurel leaves (foreground) are pointed toward the pearls, except the lower one of the three (see illustration).

4. The two letters "R" of CORREOS seem to be a little higher than the other letters, and the first one is slanted to the left.

5. Compare the inscriptions and the dots before and after them.

1856. Crossed line watermark. Nos. 38 to 41.
Paper: white or yellowish.

Varieties: 2-cuarto pale green: 50M, 50U; 4-cuarto azure, mint: 60 francs, used: 20 francs; 1-real blue or dark blue instead of dull blue-green (common): 50M, 50U; 2-real purplish maroon: 50M, 50U. A few printing flaws are in evidence.

Cancellations: as above. The red cancellation with date and the cancellation that is lozenge-lined are rare.

Pairs: 2-cuarto: 4M, 8U; others: 3M, 3U; blocks of four, 2-cuarto: 12M, 20U; others: 8M, 8U.

Barred stamps: No. 40: 2 francs; No. 41: 0.75 franc.

Used postal forgeries: 2- and 4-cuarto: various types, easily identifiable by the descriptive marks given for the preceding issue. One 4-cuarto stamp is on thick paper with a reinforced forged watermark; the second laurel leaf is touching a pearl; the "U" of CUARTOS is too close to the "C"; the other 4-cuarto stamps have no watermark.

1856 (April). No watermark. Nos. 42 to 46. *Paper:* wove, thick or thin. Nos. 43, 45, and 46, on thin paper: 50M, 75U.

Shades: 2-cuarto yellow-green or dark green instead of pale green, 1-real dark blue, 2-real dark violet: 50M, 50U. 4-cuarto, bluish paper, mint: 40 francs, used: 10 francs.

Varieties: the 2-cuarto was printed on back. The 4-cuarto was dot perforated in Valencia (unofficial): rare on cover. All values exist without a dot after the value figure, and there are defects like those of the preceding issue. There also are lined backgrounds.

Cancellations: as above. The dated cancellation is becoming common, but it is rare on the 2-cuarto.

Pairs: 3M, 3U; blocks of four, 2-cuarto: 6M, 12U; others: 6M, 6U.

Barred cancellations: No. 42: 0.25 franc; Nos. 45 and 46: 0.50 franc.

Official forgeries: the whole set, except the 12-cuarto orange. The characteristics given for the 1855 originals can be used in researching these forgeries.

Issue of 1860–61. Nos. 47 to 52. *Select:* four margins, $^3/_4$ mm wide.

Paper: tinted; thick, medium, or thin.

Shades: the 2-cuarto pale yellow-green or dark green: 2M, 50U; the 4-cuarto dark orange: 2M, 2U; azure: 30 francs, mint; 4 francs, used; the 12-cuarto bright carmine: 2M, 50U; thin paper, same; transparent pelure paper: 3M, 3U; the 19-cuarto dark brown: 50M, 25U. The 1-real pale blue: 2M, 50U; the 2-real violet: 2M, 2U; violet on azure: 8M, 5U.

Varieties: the 4-cuarto, perf 15$^1/_2$, mint: 100 francs; used: 5 francs. Some impressions are very defective. The 12-cuarto sometimes is bleached into violet. No. 51 on very transparent thin paper, and No. 52 on transparent pelure paper or on very thick paper are rare.

Plate flaws: the 4- and 12-cuarto with the "O" of CUARTOS worn down, top right: 4M, 6U.

Cancellations: Type K in black is common; in blue: 2U. The cancellation with date in blue is in demand: 2.50U. French cancellations are known to exist.

Barred cancellations: Nos. 51 and 52: 0.50 franc.

Pairs: 3M, 3U, except the 2-cuarto: 6U; blocks of four: 8M; used, 2-cuarto: 75U; 12-cuarto: 30U; 19-cuarto: 10U; others: 6U.

Used postal forgeries: Nos. 48, 49, 51, and 52 can be identified by comparing with the marks of the originals described below: check inscriptions, figures, and dots. In this issue, forgeries designed to defraud the postal service are numerous (a half-dozen different types for the 4-cuarto and 3-real stamps!). The characteristics of the originals will help to expose all the counterfeits and avoid confusing them with the very defective impressions that are not uncommon in the 4-cuarto.

Forgeries: there are a few forgeries of the 19-cuarto. The Barcelona version is deceptive enough to merit a brief study:

1. The first three shade lines on the right of CORREOS gradually diminish in size, the two marks following the word being higher and the sixth being too short.

2. The shading above the head is made up entirely of full, unbroken lines.

3. There are forty pearls on the left and forty-one on the right. Many of them form a "U," the shading being made with a full, unbroken line.

4. The chignon is divided into three pieces by the center background.

The other forgeries offer no problems when comparative study techniques are used.

Originals: 1. in the banderole of CORREOS, there are four groups of six shade lines; on the right of the "S" of CORREOS, six lines, four of the same length, the fifth one occasionally touching the top of the banderole, the sixth one touching one of its folds.

2. The shading above the head is made alternately of an unbroken or a dotted line.

3. There are forty-four pearls on the left, forty-three on the right. The convex part of their half-moon shading is turned to the right in the lateral frames and downward in the others. All of the pearls are quite distinct.

4. The letters, even "R" and "A" of the 4-cuarto, do not touch each other. (Use a high-powered magnifying glass.) Compare inscriptions and design with a 4-cuarto original.

5. In the 12- and 19-cuarto stamps, the dot after the "S" of CUARTOS is square.

1862 (August 1). Tower or lion in corners. Nos. 53 to 58. *Select:* four margins, 3/4 mm wide.

Shades: 2-cuarto dark blue: 2M, 50U; blue-black: 4M, 75U; 4-cuarto light brown or black-brown: 8M, 3U; on white paper, mint: 20 francs; used: 5 francs; 12-cuarto light and dark blue: 3M, 2U; thick paper: 6M, 3U; white paper: 20M, 6U; 19-cuarto, white paper: 3M, 2U. 1-real red-brown on buff: 4M, 50U; 2-real pale yellow-green and black-green: 3M, 2U.

Varieties: no dot before or after the value figure or after CUARTOS or REAL; sometimes only an embryonic dot; figure "4" malformed; another plate flaw similar to a printing failure under the tower or the lion at the top of the stamp. Collector's price.

Defective impressions, especially the 19-cuarto; the 4-cuarto with CUARTOS in thin, slender letters; same value perf 9½, 12, and 15. These should be acquired only on cover.

Cancellations: Types K, L, and M are common. Type F: 2U; Type K and L in blue: 2U. Type D cancellations (large numbers) and Madrid FRANCO with date in a double oval are very rare.

Pairs: 3M, 3U; 19-cuarto: 5U; blocks of four: 8M, 8U; 19-cuarto: very rare.

Barred cancellations: No. 57: 0.50 franc; No. 58: 0.25 franc.

Fakes: white paper must be expertized, for it was obtained by chemical treatment.

Used postal forgeries: the 2-, 4-, and 12-cuarto. These can be recognized immediately by the distinctive marks of the originals given below. In a 4-cuarto stamp, the letters of CUARTOS touch each other. In another type, the pearls are very poorly executed, and the tilde [˜] touches the tablet.

Forgeries: compare with the following distinctive marks of the originals:

1. Each of the ninety-one pearls has a half-moon shadow, the concave part of which is turned to the right.

2. The corner ornaments between frames and oval do not form a bisection of the angle, but curve concavely toward the oval.

3. The inscription letters do not touch each other.

4. There are thirteen pearls in the diadem. The two largest protrude from the hair on the left; the three on the right appear to be dots that are not connected with the ornament.

1864. Stars in the corners. Nos. 59 to 64. *Select:* four margins, 1 mm wide.

Shades: 2-cuarto dark blue: 50M; 4-cuarto carmine on flesh color: 8M, 3U; white paper: 30 francs, mint; 8 francs, used; 12-cuarto pale yellow-green: 2M, 2U; dark green: 5M, 2U; 19-cuarto, thin paper; 2M, 50U. 1-real brown on dark green: 50M, 50U; 2-real dark blue: 2M, 2U; white paper: 10M, 3U. Don't confuse with Nos. 59 and 64 of the same shade.

Varieties: the 12- and 19-cuarto, and the 2-real, no dot after the value figure. Defective impressions. Thin paper is rare. The 4-cuarto was perf 12½, 13, and 14.

Cancellations: as above. Dated cancellation in blue: 2U; in red: rare.

Pairs: 2-cuarto: 4U; others: 3M, 3U. Blocks of four: 6M; 2-cuarto: 8U; 12-cuarto: 20U; 19-cuarto: 10U; others: 6U.

Barred stamps: No. 63: 1.50 francs; No. 64: 1 franc.

Used postal forgeries: the 4- and 12-cuarto stamps. In the 4-cuarto, the two top circles do not go past the inner frame. The stop mark, after "Ctos," forms a cross. The eye is very poorly executed. The "1864" is not congruent with the original. The "S" of CUARTOS is too narrow. For the rest, look at the distinctive marks of the originals. The 2-cuarto and the 2-real stamps were probably used also.

Forgeries: the 19-cuarto was well-counterfeited in Geneva. The pearls around the center background are not regular, several of them being incompletely formed; the terminal line of the "4" forms a loop instead of rising vertically; the frames, and especially the thick, left inner frame, are inexpertly traced; yellowish or reddish paper. Forged cancellations from the same source have a circular postmark with date: SALAS DE LOS INFANTES 7 FEV 65 BURGOS. The other forgeries easily can be recognized by comparing them with the 4-cuarto stamp.

Originals: 1. the two top circles do not touch the upper frame, except in the heavily inked impressions.

2. The diadem has ten pearls; the first two stand out from the hair, the last one forms a dot.

3. Eighteen shade lines on the neck.

4. In the corner ornaments, the circle arcs are concentric and quite equidistant.

1865. Tower and lion at top only. Nos. 65 to 71. *Select:* four margins, 1 mm minimum width.

Shades: the 2-cuarto carmine and bright carmine: 2M, 2U; the 12-cuarto blue-black and carmine-rose: 2M, 2U; the 19-cuarto dark brown and carmine-rose: 25M, 25U. The 2-real rose is rarer than the salmon-pink; the 2-real rose-lilac, rarer than the lilac: 50M, 25U.

Varieties: No. 67a is the seventy-second stamp in the 100-stamp sheet. No. 66 is still Type I and is identified by the fact that the "S" of CUARTOS is not as high as in Type II. The latter, with a higher "S," along with Type I, is found in the following issue. Consult the illustration. In No. 72 (2-real salmon-pink), the "S" of "RS" was retouched at the top, where it looks like a Gothic "S": 10M, 5U; in pairs, with a normal "S": 15M, 10U.

Nos. 65 and 69 have defective impressions. The center is frequently out of place in the 12- and 19-cuarto stamps. The 12-cuarto shows evidence of a worn cliché, with the oval framing of the "C S" deformed on the left: rare.

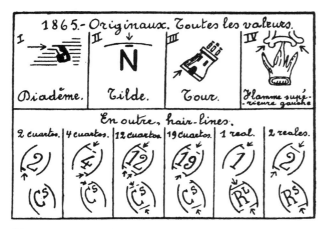

Characteristics of originals of all values of the 1865 issue. Note especially the hairlines in the lower tablets.

Cancellations: Types L and M are common. Type K is less common; with red date and "P.D." in red, in an oval: rare. Large oval with small lozenges (Philippine Islands): rare. The 12-cuarto with stippled lozenge cancellation "2.240" (Marseilles): 3U.

Pairs: 3M, 3U; blocks of four: 6M; 19-cuarto: 10M, 8U; but 12- and 19-cuarto: 10U.

Barred stamps: No. 68: 25 francs. No. 69: 2 francs. Nos. 70 and 71: 1 franc.

Fakes: the perforated 4-cuarto has had its teeth extracted to create a No. 66. If the "S" after the "C"

belongs to Type II, there is no further doubt; if it belongs to Type I, the width of the margins has to be checked. The 12-cuarto: inverted center applied to the front of an upright center; upright center completely removed and replaced by an inverted center, after which the entire back of the stamp is laminated. (This is a fake that is most often perforated, because the original is worth more in that form.) These two fakes are identified by the usual repaired-stamp research techniques. The same value is found with the original upright center chemically removed, and with an inverted center subsequently printed on it. Careful checking of the design is enough to spot the fake.

Used postal forgeries: the 12-cuarto, 2-real, and probably other values: the "S" after the "C" resembles the "S" of the 4-cuarto, Type II; the center shading lines are too far apart, etc. — see illustration.

Forgeries: this is probably the issue that has been counterfeited most successfully. Numerous early and modern forgeries: Barcelona, Geneva, Florence sets, etc. Compare with the salient features of the originals. None of these forgeries is congruent with the originals. In all of them, the forgers, who were anxious to execute perfect designs, eliminated the hairlines in the lower tablets.

The 19-cuarto was made with an inverted center in Geneva. The 4-cuarto (Florence) has superb margins and generally looks good, but, after what we have said, a quick look will suffice for forgery detection.

Forged cancellations: these are numerous on forged stamps. The same Geneva cancellations as for the preceding issue: circular, with date: CAMPILLOS 8 OCT 66 MALAGA; Type M, numeral 2; Type K, numeral 1.

II. Perforated Stamps

1865. Same type. Perf 14. Nos. 72 to 78. *Shades:* the 2-cuarto carmine instead of rose: 50M, 25U; light or dark carmine: 2.50M, 50U; the 12-cuarto dark blue and carmine: 50M, 50U.

Varieties: the 4-cuarto, Types I and II — see the accompanying illustration. Type II: 2M, 50U. In Type I, the "S" is like the "S" in the 2-, 12-, and 19-cuarto stamps.

Varieties, cancellations, pairs, blocks, and forgeries are as in the preceding issue.

Fakes: No. 74A: look out for optical illusions. All of the imperforate stamps except the 4-cuarto have received forged perforations.

Forgeries (official, early, and modern): consult the preceding issue and check perforation.

Issue of 1866. Nos. 79 to 84. The 19-cuarto dark brown: 2M, 2U; the 10-centimo-escudo dark brown: 2M, 50U.

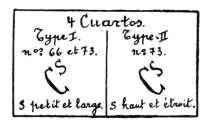

Comparison of the "C S" of Type I and Type II. Left: Small, wide "S." Right: High, narrow "S."

Pairs: 3M, 3U; blocks of four, mint: 6M, 6U, except the 2- and 12-cuarto: 8U, and the 19-cuarto: 10U.

Cancellations: double circle oval; "P.D." in one circle; red cancellations: rare. Canary Islands cancellations: very much in demand.

Originals: all forgeries may be identified by comparing the following typical features.

Type I. Cuarto value stamps:

1. The CORREOS inscription is printed inconsistently; the first "O" seems low with respect to the adjacent letters; the second "O" is too far removed from the "E" and the "S."

2. Under the word CORREOS, there are ten white lines of equal length, regularly spaced.

3. Cheek shade lines are regularly reinforced from the ear to the very end of the double chin. The horizontal and well-spaced shade lines of the center background are not very fine.

4. The top of the diadem is touching the fourth of the shade lines.

5. Perf 14.

6. The bottom serifs of the "A," "R," and "T" of CUARTOS are finer than the center background shade lines. The word CUARTOS is also farther from the top of the tablet than from the bottom.

7. The crown of the top left escutcheon is well formed; the second and fourth sections have two pearls; the center section, a single, larger one.

Type II. Stamp values in centimo-escudo: same characteristics as in Nos. 1 through 5 and 7 above.

Forgeries: see the distinctive features of the originals. On a good 19-cuarto Geneva forgery, the fourth section of the crown in the upper left corner is formed with a white line and incomplete pearls; in the second section, there is only one pearl; at the left of the crown, the small curl in the corner of the stamp is broken, so all that remains is a small circle arc; the cheek shading is not reinforced by the contour of the cheek; the dot after CUARTOS is more square than round (forged cancellation, CAMPILLOS, etc.).

Used postal forgeries: the whole set was forged; check the authenticating marks; with respect to the 12-cuarto, look especially at Nos. 4, 6, and 7 above (originals, Type I).

1866 (August 1). 20-centimo. No. 85. This stamp must be exactly similar to stamps from the 1864 issue. Dark shade, violet instead of lilac: 2M, 50U.

Issues of 1867, 1868, 1869. Nos. 86 to 101. *Rare shades:* the 19-cuarto, No. 90, carmine instead of rose: 2M, 2U; No. 92, the 20-cuarto gray instead of lilac: 3M, 2U; No. 95, the 25-milesimo blue and carmine or blue-black and rose instead of blue and rose: 4M, 3U.

Varieties: Nos. 87, 88, 91–94, and 98 exist without perforation: all are very rare. The 4-cuarto, No. 87, has two types: I, a blue line completely surrounds the center oval; II, the line is missing on the right: 10M, 10U.

Retouching: the 19-cuarto, Nos. 90 and 101. Letters "U" and "A" of CUARTOS, which were redrawn in one cliché, appear in color on a white background. No. 90: 20M, 10U; No. 101: 6M, 3U.

Used postal forgeries: the entire 1867 set (Nos. 86 to 92), except perhaps the 2- and 19-cuarto; the 50-maravedi of 1867 (July), No. 97; finally, the whole 1868 set (Nos. 98 to 101), except the 19-cuarto.

A few characteristic features of these forgeries follow: No. 87, dimensions too small, perf about 14³/₄. No. 88, too wide, "R" and "S" of CUARTOS not nearly high enough, other inscription letters noncongruent. No. 91, noncongruent inscriptions, three shade lines on the temple instead of five, perf 15¹/₄.

No. 97, the tilde is almost touching the oval; the line under the "s" of MILˢ is too close to that letter, which is flattened underneath; the line that forms the nostril is too short; the "E" of CORREOS is too narrow; the "D" letters of two "D.E." inscriptions are too wide, etc. Two other varieties have incorrect inscriptions also, and the perforation is noncongruent.

No. 98 is very poorly executed: noncongruent inscriptions; the two "M" printer's errors on the right, draw attention by their contortions; perf 14³/₄. Other varieties are recognizable also by noncongruent perforation. Likewise, No. 99 is recognizable by its noncongruent inscriptions. Finally, No. 100 is completely spoiled, the design of the portrait, including the diadem, being bad.

Forgeries: Nos. 86–101 were scarcely counterfeited at all; however, compare the rare values with originals, examining particularly the inscriptions, the cheek modeling, and the perforation; the perforation must be 14 and clean-cut. In each authentic stamp, you will find striking features: For example, in the 4-cuarto of 1867 (No. 87), there is always a gap in the ornament above the "S" of CORREOS and the color oval is reinforced at that spot; in the 10-centimo green (No. 91), there are four shading lines and the embryo of a fifth under the temple.

HABILITADO POR LA NACION *overprints*: very numerous, many of them well done. It would be prudent to "outlaw" all these provisional overprints if you are not going in for real specialization; if you are, each item must be subjected to serious comparative study: dimensions, inks, printing type, etc.

1870. Ceres. Perf 14. Nos. 102 to 104. *Rare shades:* the 1-milesimo maroon on white: mint, very rare, 10U; 10-milesimo carmine: 3M, 3U; 100-milesimo red: 3M, 2U; 200-milesimo sepia: 3M, 3U. The 50-milesimo imperforate is rare.

Pairs: 3U; blocks of four: 6M, 8U, but 1.600-escudo, 2-escudo, and 19-cuarto: 8M, 12U.

Early forgeries: a few crude early forgeries are easily identified by the perforation, which is often 13 instead of 14, by the center background lines, by the noncongruent inscriptions, and by the initials "E.J." of the engraver. See also the distinctive characteristics of the originals shown in the accompanying illustration.

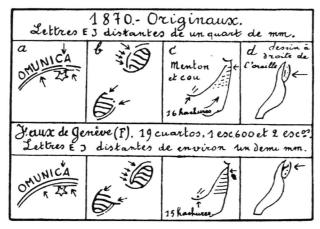

1870 Ceres issue. Originals: letters "E.J." $^1/_4$ mm apart; (c) chin and neck and 16 shade lines; (d) design on right of ear. Geneva forgeries: letters "E.J." about $^1/_2$ mm apart; 15 shade lines.

Official forgeries: a few values, among them the 50-milesimo blue, the 400-milesimo green, and the 1.600-escudo. They can be detected in the same way as early and modern forgeries. However, the cancellation is original.

Modern forgeries: the Geneva (F.) forgeries are best (1.600-escudo, 2-escudo, 19-cuarto). Initials are spaced $^4/_5$ mm apart, and there are fifteen shade lines in the neck, their right half unbroken, and, counting from the top, the third and sixth are single, solid lines. These forgeries were executed in imperforate units with color framing 1$^1/_2$ or 2 mm from the design, perf 14$^1/_2$ x 14. A retouched cliché of the 19-cuarto is slightly different.

1872. 2- and 5-cuarto large figures. Nos. 115 and 116. The 2-cuarto pale gray: 3M, 2U; dark gray: 6M, 2U. Imperforate: 75 francs. The 5-cuarto green-black: 2M, 2U.

1872. Portraits. Nos. 117 to 128. *Shades:* the 5-centimo carmine: 5M; the 10-centimo dark violet, the 50-centimo dark green, and the 1-peseta violet: 2M, 2U. The 6-, 10-, 40-, and 50-centimo and the 1- and 4-peseta imperforates are rare. On the 10-peseta, the left frame is broken under the first "C" of COMMUNICACIONES: 2M, 2U.

Pairs: 2.50U; blocks of four, mint and used: 5 units. With a few exceptions, the same holds for the following issues.

Early forgeries: no engraver's name, bad impression; compare especially the shading with a well-printed 10-cuarto ultramarine; noncongruent perforations. Also, examine the features described in the illustration.

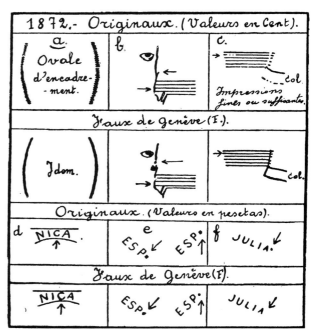

1872 Portraits issue. Originals. Values in centimos. (a) oval framework; (c) col. [collateral]; fine, or adequate, impressions. Second row: Geneva forgeries. Third row: Originals. Values in pesetas. Bottom: Geneva forgeries.

Official forgeries: the 10-, 12-, 20-, 25-, 40- (?), and 50-cuarto (?). To be identified like the preceding ones; the cancellation, however, is original.

Modern forgeries: Geneva (F.). See the main characteristics in the illustration. We can also point out that the name of the engraver, JULIA, is not visible at the very bottom of the oval in the centimo values; in the peseta values, the bottom left frame of the value tablet does not have the reinforcement evident in the originals; perf 13$^1/_2$ x 14.

Forged cancellations: round, engraved on wood, on Geneva forgeries, double circle: FIGUERAS 1 JUL 72

CATALUNA. PUYCERDA 21 OCT 72 CATALUNA. Interchangeable dates.

Fakes: telegraph cancellations (punch hole) in the major stamp values of this issue and of the following ones are not rare, and these values frequently were repaired and regummed to make "new" stamps. This shady business often is masked by a lozenge cancellation inside a stippled lozenge, the whole lozenge being applied so as to obscure the plugged hole.

For the following issues: *barring exceptions,* pairs are worth 2.50M, 2.50U; blocks of four: 5M, 5U. Forgeries become much less numerous.

1873. Liberty facing left. Nos. 130 to 139. The imperforate 10-centimo is worth 2 francs mint, 10 francs used. This stamp is known to exist as a used tête-bêche (one copy). The 20-centimo black, pair: 3M, 3U; block of four: 6M, 6U.

Originals: the lower right quartering of the shield has four groups of two well-spaced, very fine shading lines.

1874. Liberty facing right. Nos. 141 to 150. The 10-centimo purplish blue: 20M, 10U; the 50-centimo lemon-yellow: 5M, 3U; the 1-peseta blue-green: 4M, 4U; the 10-peseta deep black: 50M; the 10-centimo imperforate: 2 francs mint, 10 francs used; the 25- and 50-centimo, 1- and 10-peseta, imperforate: rare. The 1-peseta color error in black is known only with telegraph cancellation. The 20-centimo, pair: 3M, 3U; block of four: 6M, 6U. French cancellations 2240 (Marseilles) are not rare.

Originals: 1. The sword point goes through a double horizontal line, but the lower line does not touch the weapon on the left.

2. The dot after "D" (centimo values) is rectangular.

3. The center inscription letters do not touch each other and are regularly drawn; the "C," "D," "O," "P," and even the "S" are square in form.

4. There is a dot behind the head, separated from the lower part of the hair.

5. The toes of the right foot are well defined in the good impressions.

6. The value tablet on the left, which is hexagonal in form, is broken on the left on the level of the terminal lines of the figures.

Official forgeries: the 10-centimo blue: crude design; compare with the distinctive features described above. There are other values, but because it is the cancellation that determines their worth, it should be closely examined, and, if need be, expertized, so as to avoid acquiring modern forgeries with a more or less successful forged cancellation.

Forgeries: almost all of them are modern. Peseta values especially have been the center of attention. Compare with the characteristic features of the originals, as well as with a common original. The best

forgery is a good-looking 10-peseta stamp, in which the two "S"s of PESETAS are quite rounded (also, the "S" of COMUNICACIONES and the other letters mentioned above); the break in the value tablet frame on the left is missing (the forger's secret mark?); the sword hilt is too large. By looking carefully, you could find about fifty additional differences in the design.

Fakes: see the preceding issue.

1874. Coat of arms. No. 151. The price differential between the perforated and imperforate stamps is enough to forewarn the specialist that imperforate stamps must have adequate margins.

1875. Portrait facing right. Nos. 153 to 162. The 2-, 5-, and 10-centimo imperforates are rare. Stamps perfectly centered, no perforation hole touching the impression: rare, 2M, 2U; 4- and 10-peseta: 3M, 3U.

Originals: 1. very fine shading in the neck front and center background.

2. The inner corner stars have fine, quite visible points.

3. The inscriptions are congruent.

Official forgeries(?): the 20-centimo rose and all peseta values. See my remark in the preceding issue.

1876. Full-face portrait. Tower watermark. Perf 14. Nos. 163 to 171. A second printing of the 5-, 10-, 25-, and 50-centimo and the 1- and 10-peseta stamps was made in London. Slightly different type, a few retouched values, value figures a little higher; in the 1-peseta, slender figures. All values of the first printing are known imperforate: 10 francs mint, 20 francs used; the 4- and 10-peseta: 40 francs mint, used, very rare. Blocks of four, 20-centimo, 1-, 2-, and 4-peseta: 6U.

Used postal forgeries: the 25-centimo: very unsuccessful impression. The originals of this issue, of the preceding one, and of the following ones up to 1900 are practically inimitable marvels of design.

1878, 1879, 1882. Perf 14. Nos. 173 to 195. *Official forgeries:* the 25-centimo blue-gray, No. 187, perf 11. Comparison of ornament design, background lining, and facial features will reveal the forgery.

Forgeries: same remark as for the 20-centimo, 4- and 10-peseta stamps of 1878 [*sic;* probably should be 1875].

Fakes: as above, with regard to telegraph cancellations. A doctored essay of No. 175 (10-centimo, 1878) to make a 40-centimo will fool only novices.

1889–99. Alfonso XIII as a child. Perf 14. Nos. 196 to 211. *Forgeries:* the 4-peseta, Geneva (F.). The second "N" of COMUNICACIONES is slanted to the right; the "4" and the letters of PESETAS touch the tablet line and the lower frame; the ear shading doesn't match the original. Presumably the whole set was forged. The other forgeries require only a moment's comparative study.

Forged cancellations: on Geneva forgeries: rectangular postmark CERTIFICADO 14 MAY 9 COROGNA — which matches nothing genuine.

Official forgeries: the 15- and 25-centimo: ordinary forgery comparison is indicated, as is expertizing of the cancellation.

1905. Commemorative stamps. Nos. 226 to 235. *Forgeries:* the 10-peseta, Genoa (I.). Very bad lithographed design; the "U" of the engraver's name, MAURA, is almost closed at the top and the other letters are not congruent. Perf 11$\frac{1}{2}$. Rather gray cancellation, rectangular postmark: MADRID 5 MAY 1905. Forged control No. A.008.866. The whole set probably was forged in the same way.

1909–17. Portrait. Perf 12$\frac{1}{2}$ x 14. *Fakes:* the 15-centimo bistre-yellow, No. 246, in which the top of the "5" and the bottom of the "C" are scratched out. Subsequent repair to make an "O" and a "P" so as to obtain a 10-peseta, No. 254, in an arbitrary shade. The fraud can be detected by using a magnifying glass. Such use always should be kept foremost in one's mind.

1907. Madrid Exhibition stamps. These fantasies should not be collected.

III. Official Stamps

1854. Rectangular format. Nos. 1 to 4. *Forgeries:* the best set is old. It is 22$\frac{1}{2}$ mm high instead of 22 mm. The cross of the crown touches the horizontal line; the towers of the shield are too large (1$\frac{1}{4}$ mm and 1 mm instead of 1 mm and $\frac{3}{4}$ mm); the inner right frame, if extended, would pass to the right of the dot after "1854" rather than to the left, as on the original. Also, compare the shield with the features described for the postal issue of 1854; no forgery can stand up under that examination.

1855. Oval format. Nos. 5 to 8. *Forgeries:* in this case, the lithographed Geneva (F.) set was most successful. A few letters of CORREO are joined at the bottom hairline; the same with respect to the "O" and "F" of OFICIAL. The tail of the lion at top right touches the oval of the shield. This lion has a shapeless head (a juvenile creation?), and an oblique black line can be seen under the left hind leg. The value lettering was unsuccessful (compare).

The inner oval frame was exactly traced by the forger, with the result that the curves in his sketch extend beyond their intersection points; this is visible, above, to the right of the crown; below, to the left, under the first letter of the value inscription. Comparative study obviously would be useful in the quick identification of these forgeries.

Forged cancellations: one usually finds a barred oval for the two issues.

IV. War Tax Stamps

Official forgeries: the 5-centimo of the first issues and the 15-centimo of 1877. Acquire these only on cover.

Error: the 5-centimo blue (1876). This should be purchased as a pair with a 10-centimo because of chemical faking of the common single stamp.

V. Telegraph Stamps

Usually only mint copies are collected.

Fakes: the punch-hole cancellations were plugged by lamination, then the stamps were regummed to make "new" stamps. With this in mind, check the perforated and imperforate 20-real of 1865 and the 2-escudo carmine of 1866.

VI. Carlist Insurrection

1873. 1-real. Nos. 1 and 1a. *Originals:* No. 1: no tilde; brownish gum; lithographed. The horizontal lines of the entire background are unequal in length (bad lithographic stone texture). The shading line ends in a dot above the "E" of FRANQUEO. The shade lines on the left almost reach the "F," and one of them touches that letter on a level with the center bar. The eyes are composed of a whole field of dots in which it is very difficult to discern the engraver's initials, "M.C." (on the right of the right eye).

No. 1a: with tilde; white gum; cliché of No. 1 was retouched by insertion of the tilde, an indication of good Spanish pronunciation, and by correction of the corner hatching above "r. l. 1," [Translator's note: lowercase "L" in the middle] which is irregular in No. 1 and regular in No. 1a. In the two types, the terminal lines of the number "1" figures on the left are clearly marked, and the dimensions of the stamp are 18 x 24$\frac{1}{2}$ mm.

Forgeries: (Paris). 1. Crude so-called reprints. The eyes form a spot on both sides of the nose; the median bar of the "E" of FRANQUEO is horizontal instead of oblique; the letters of ESPANA are malformed, especially the "N," which is not as high as it should be. Good dimensions.

2. There are a few early forgeries. On these, the dimensions, shades, and designs are not at all congruent. Comparative study would be sufficient.

3. Photolithographed Geneva (F.) forgeries. In a first cliché (No. 1), the nose base is too high; the number "1" on the left has no terminal lines; the first shade line at the top does not touch the left frame; the shading of the center oval is too regular; the shade lines to the left of the "F" are all $\frac{1}{4}$ mm from it. Height, 23$\frac{1}{2}$ mm.

The second cliché (No. 1a) is less deceptive, for the shading above "r. l. 1" is like that of No. 1, and the tilde is made of a single straight line. The usual forged cancellations found on this forgery are PUYCERDA and VALENCIA, which have been described.

1874–75. Portrait. Nos. 2 to 4. *No. 2 originals:* 18 x 23³/₄ mm.

Brussels forgeries: these are 23¹/₂ mm high; photolithographed. Common, somewhat yellowish paper. The most delicate shading of the design (banderole of Spain; between eye and nostril; beard on cheek; ear lobe; neck) did not come out well (photograph taken on a day of national *"drache"*?). The nose ends in a very pronounced angle; dull shade, too dark. The figures seem smaller, but their actual height is the same. Forged cancellation is a double oval in red: ASTAOSA CORREOS GUIPUSCOA. We do not know whether its origin is the same.

Nos. 2 and 3. The 50-centimo and the 1-real. The figures and the letter that follows them (corrected errors) of the two values have been retouched: rare. They are found on thin or medium paper.

Early forgeries: poorly executed. In a forgery of the 1-real, the "N" has no tilde; the shade lines in the lower right corner are almost straight and do not come together with the circle's shading.

Cancellations: all cancellations on Carlist insurrection stamps must be properly expertized.

Cataluna and Valencia. Nos. 5 and 6. No. 5, the 16-maravedi rose (Cataluna), was typographed. The indention is quite visible and there are numerous transfer flaws. There also are forged cancellations.

No. 6, the ¹/₂-real (Valencia), must have four margins, 1 mm minimum width. There are two lithographed types. In Type II, the banderole of ESPANA VALENCIA is well executed on the right and left. In Type I, it is incomplete, especially on the right, where it is a single curved line pointing toward the corner of the stamp. Dimensions: 17⁴/₅ x 21 mm.

Forgeries: 1. an early forgery, 17 x 20¹/₂ mm, has thirty-three instead of thirty-one shading lines in the center background.

2. A better one, with thirty lines, has the "S" of CORREOS clearly larger than the other letters.

3. Geneva (F.) essays (!) exist in various colors (brown, green, rose, black, ultramarine, blue, etc.), thirty-one lines, good dimensions like the preceding one, but the impression is heavily inked. The top inscription letters are 1¹/₄ mm high instead of 1 mm; the tilde extends to the top of the right downstroke of the "N"; the "A" following this letter touches the bottom of the tablet; the beard is in a vertical relationship with the ear; etc.

Note: No. 7, the ¹/₂-real red, and No. 7a, the error 42-real, are forged fantasies. (See F. Serrane, *"Faux d'Espagne," L'Écho de la Timbrologie,* No. 702 (March 31, 1925): 455–56; No. 706 (May 31, 1925): 809–11.)

Spanish Guinea

The overprints on fiscal stamps of the Spanish possessions in Africa (Nos. 27–33c and 101–102c, Yvert, 1928) must be judged by comparing them with a reliable original overprint.

Spanish West Indies

1855–57. Nos. 1 to 10. *Early forgeries:* the three values have no watermark; seventy-eight pearls instead of seventy-three.

Geneva forgeries: 2-real, no watermark; figure "2" is 1 mm from the left side of the tablet instead of 1¹/₂ mm; no dot after the figure nor after the "F"; this forgery was overprinted "Y ¹/₄," with oblique fraction bar, Type I and II.

Used postal forgeries of the ¹/₂- and 1-real of 1857, Nos. 8 and 9; lithographed instead of typographed; the white dots in the corners are placed irregularly (compare with a Spain original); there are two varieties for each of the values: Type I, seventy-three pearls as in the originals, and Type II, seventy-nine pearls.

No. 4, overprinted. *Original overprints:* four varieties on the 2-real carmine: Type I, the "Y" is 4¹/₂ mm high; Type II, 5 mm; Type III, 5¹/₄ mm; and Type IV, 5¹/₂ mm. Type III also was applied on the red-brown shade. When found on Nos. 5, 6, and 7, these overprints always are forged.

No. 11, overprinted. The "Y" of the original overprint is 5¹/₄ mm high, the "1" being 1³/₄ or 2 mm, according to type. There is a forged Geneva overprint.

1862. ¹/₄-real black. No. 12. *Forgeries:* twenty-seven pearls above, twenty-nine on the right, thirty-one below, and twenty-seven on the left instead of thirty-six, forty-three, thirty-six, and forty-four, respectively.

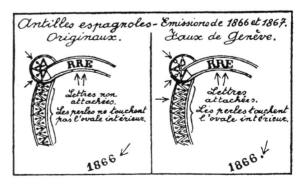

Spanish West Indies. Issues of 1866 and 1867. Originals. Letters not connected; pearls do not touch the inner oval. Geneva forgeries. Letters are connected; pearls are touching the inner oval.

1864, 1866, 1867. Nos. 13 to 25. Very unsuccessful *early forgeries.* The lateral bandeau pearls are touching the bandeau; the second "6" almost is touching the tablet edge (1866), or else the dot after the millesime is too near the edge. The diadem and center oval pearls are not very visible or are done very poorly. Letters "RRE" of CORREOS are shapeless, but they do not touch each other.

Geneva forgeries (1866, 1867): 18¾–19 x 22½ mm instead of 19 x 22¼ mm. Thickness, 70–75 microns instead of 60 (1866) and 50 (1867), and the latter perf 13 instead of 14 (see the illustration).

Forged Geneva cancellation: Spanish grill oval.

1868. Nos. 26 to 29. *Early forgeries:* no dot after "1868." Bottom right, letter "K" instead of "R"; on left, "R" is done poorly, resembling an "H." There are five hatch lines under the neck point instead of three. The forged HABILITADO overprints are rather numerous. Comparison is necessary (Geneva).

1869. Nos. 30 to 33. Same forged set as above. Also forged HABILITADO overprints, especially Geneva.

1870. Nos. 34 to 37. *Early forgeries:* design is executed inexpertly; figure "7" (1870) is uniformly thick; the neck is not shaded on the left; the engraver's initials are missing under the neck. Imperforate, or perf 12½.

1871. Nos. 38 to 41. *Early forgeries:* the dot after "D" is placed at bottom, like its placing after the "C" following the value; a dot is found after PESETA in No. 41. Thin paper, imperforate, or perf 13. The bar of the "A" is placed near the letter's middle instead of in its upper third.

Stellaland

1884. Escutcheon and star. Nos. 1 to 5. *Originals:* perf 11½; 12; 11½ x 12 on one side; all values, except the 1-shilling which is imperforate horizontally and vertically. Eight transfer plate types for each value; the 6-pence has nine. STELLALAND is about 18½ mm long and POSTZEGEL is 16¾ mm; the letters of POSTZEGEL are 1¾ mm high. The paper is transparent.

Essays are imperforate.

Forgeries: perf 12½; 13½; wide margins; paper is not very transparent; various defects are rendered perceptible by the illustration; STELLALAND is only 18⅓ mm; POSTZEGEL is 17 mm, and its letters are nearly 2 mm high. Shades allowable for the most part; the transfer plate marks of the originals cannot be found.

1884. TWEE overprint on 4-pence. No. 6. The original overprint is purplish red. *Forged overprints* on originals and forgeries: comparison is indispensable.

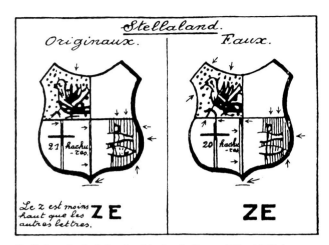

Stellaland. Originals. 21 shade lines. The "Z" is not as high as the other letters. Forgeries. 20 shade lines.

Sudan

1897. SOUDAN overprint. Nos. 1 to 8. *Forged overprints:* comparison is necessary. The whole set was overprinted fraudulently in Geneva on original canceled Egyptian stamps.

Official stamps. A few *forged overprints* in the 1905 issues (ARMY OFFICIAL, inverted overprint, and ARMY SERVICE); comparison is necessary. The "O.S.G.S." overprint was counterfeited in Geneva.

Postage due stamps overprinted SOUDAN. Nos. 1 to 4. Same observation.

Telegraph stamps overprinted TEL. Nos. 1 to 5. The five values, which were overprinted fraudulently in Geneva (the SOUDAN overprint) received the additional forged TEL overprint in a blue oval, axis lengths, 18 x 13 mm, with a 1½ mm break on the left of the "T"; the letters of TEL are 6 mm high.

Suez

See Egypt.

Surinam

1873–92. King's portrait. Nos. 1 to 15. *Originals:* typographed, various perforations (see the specialty catalogues). Fine shade lines cover the entire face, including the nose and the neck; the 2½-gulden has eighteen lines on the forehead; the whole ear is shaded; there are five vertical lines on the right of the center circle and four on the left, not including the inner frame.

Early forgery of the 2½-gulden; typographed; perf 13; allowable shades. This counterfeit's design is executed poorly: three vertical shade lines on the right of the circle, two, on the left; eleven or twelve lines on the forehead; none on the ear.

Geneva forgeries: the whole set was photolithographed on thin (40–45 microns) transparent paper; perf 14; 2½-gulden, perf 11½ x 13½ with dull, flat shades, dull ochre and green-gray (sage); the other values have arbitrary shades; the large blank spots devoid of any shading on the forehead, the nose, around the eye, in front of the ear, under the nostril, and on the front of the neck, characterize these somewhat attractive creations. What we have said regarding the Curaçao counterfeits applies to this set, but the general appearance of the latter is better, however; the center background shade lines are executed more successfully, although insufficiently clear-cut. The vertical lines are broken in places, especially in the 2½-gulden (the lines that are closest to the green circle). The forged cancellation is round (23½ mm), with date, with three curved outer lines in each angle of a square; the inner circle is broken at bottom, thus forming a horseshoe: PARAMARIBO 2/7 1890. Interchangeable figures. The forged "2½ CENT" overprint was applied to originals and forgeries of the 50-cent stamp. Of course, there are other forged overprints on the 50-cent mint original. Comparison is necessary.

Chemical *faking* of stamps perf 14 to counterfeit the bluish paper: the paper shade must be compared.

1893. Child queen. Nos. 23 to 28. *Originals:* 19¹⁄₁₀ x 23 mm; perf 12½; regular pearls.

Lausanne *forgeries* (Pasche): the whole set printed in blocks; 18¾–⅞ x 22¾–⅘ mm; perf 11; the center background and the portrait shade lines are not equidistant; the first center background shade line is practically touching the pearled circle; the pearls are irregular and are too small (½ mm instead of about ¼ mm); unshaded white spots in front of the middle of the ear, above and under the eye, in the top part of the temple, and an exceedingly wide white area all along the nose line; two white shade lines cut the ear; a center background line is touching the circle in its middle, on the left. Thick, very white paper; incongruous shades.

1898. 10 CENT overprints. *Forged overprints:* especially in Geneva on originals of the 15-cent and of the 25-cent ultramarine, and on forgeries of the six overprinted values.

1899. 1.00 1.00 SURINAME overprint. No. 35. *Forged Geneva overprint* applied on originals. Comparison is necessary.

1900. 50 CENT overprint on 2½-gulden. No. 40. *Forged overprint* on the forgery of No. 15. Poorly lithographed, which makes quick elimination possible. Beginners also can find confirmation by studying measurements, figures, lettering (see the bottom of the "n," the terminal loop of the "t," and so forth). The forged cancellation is the type described for the Curaçao postage due stamps: SURINAME 2/7 1900 (boxwood engraving, noncongruent ink; interchangeable figures).

1886. Postage due stamps. Nos. 1 to 8. *Geneva forgeries:* photolithographed frame. This time, they took the trouble to manufacture a new, better executed cliché (see Netherlands Antilles and Netherlands Indies). However, one should note that the color dots in the "B" of BETALEN are too round (use magnifying glass). Dimensions, 18 x 21¾–22 mm. Lightly, irregularly stippled yellowish white paper; transparency comparison is useful, for the counterfeit is deceptive. The specialist also will compare the arbitrary shade — a dull, flat color tone, a lilac that is too brownish. Perf 12½ x 12. The figures are typographed (look for indention) and reproduced more successfully: comparison is necessary. This suggests that the forger envisaged an extension of his operation into postage due stamp issues with CENT or GULDEN in the center, but his equipment since has been destroyed by the "Union Philatélique de Geneve." Forged cancellations, same model as above; I have found: PARAMARIBO..10 1894, and SURINAME 29 4 1892.

Swaziland

1889–92. "Swazieland" overprint. Nos. 1 to 9. *Original overprint:* 13½ mm; 1½ mm high, except "S," "1," and "d," which are 2 mm high.

Reprints (1894): ½-, 1-penny, 2-pence, and 10-shilling, black overprint with a dot after the word.

Forged overprints: rather numerous; comparison is necessary; the whole set was overprinted fraudulently in Geneva on used originals of the Transvaal state; 13¼ mm long; letters 1⅖ mm high, "d" 1¾ mm high.

Sweden

The first issues of Sweden are among the most interesting because of their rarity and the variety of their shades.

Cancellations: the illustration gives information on the postmarks commonly used on these issues; all others are rare. The later, more modern cancels are sufficiently well known. The thimble cancellation, Type A, is in demand. It exists in various styles, 18–21 mm. Type B is less common: 25U, and rare, second issue: 2U. Types A and C are most common on this issue. Types D and E are worth 2U on common stamps of the third issue. Type D is not very common on Stockholm locals. Type F is common on stamps used in the Stockholm local postal service (Type B postmark with inscription LOCAL-BREF, etc.).

Foreign cancellations are rare, as are many other postmarks whose description would take too long; for example, postmark Type B with double frame (corners cut off) with inscription AUS SCHWEDEN, etc.; triple circle postmarks with numbers, etc.

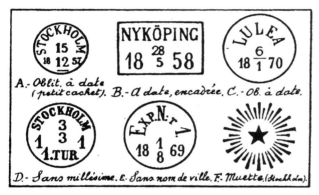

Sweden cancellations: **A. Thimble, with date. B. Framed, with date. C. Dated cancel. D. No year date. E. No town name. F. Dumb (Stockholm).**

1855 (June). Values in skilling. Nos. 1 to 5.
Perforations: 13³/₄ x 13¹/₂; 13³/₄; 14.
Sheets of 100 stamps, watermarked in corners or margins.
Shades: 3-skilling pale green, green, blue-green: 25U; 4-skilling blue (shades), blue-gray (pale ultramarine): 20U; 6-skilling gray, dark gray with intermediate shades of brown; 8-skilling pale yellow, yellow, orange; 24-skilling red and pale red. Rough, thin paper (about 50–60 microns) and thick paper (about 80 microns), the latter being rare mint.
Select: stamps centered (not very common in that state).
Varieties: 3-skilling yellow (error), a well-known stamp. One finds 8-skilling stamps with defective impression in which the figures seem to be fives or threes. The 3-skilling is known to exist with a short "V" in SVERIGE; the 4-skilling, with defects FYBA, PYRA, etc.; 8-skilling, with ATEE, etc. This value is found on very transparent paper.

Pairs: 3U. 24-skilling: very rare. Blocks of four: rare.
Reprints: 1865: perf 13¹/₂ x 14; 13¹/₂; rough paper. 3-skilling yellow-green; 4-skilling dark blue; 6-skilling purplish gray-brown; 8-skilling orange-yellow. 24-skilling bright red (1871), thin, glossy paper. Perf 14, shades nearly alike. These two sets have about the same value.
1885: perf 13, glossy paper. Shades different from the original ones, except the 4- and 8-skilling. This set is much rarer.
Note: Original cancellations are found on the three sets.
Forgeries: crude; compare the word SVERIGE with an original 4-skilling. Noncongruent perforations.

1858. Same type. Values in ore. Nos. 6 to 11.
Perforation: 14.
Shades: 5-ore yellow-green, green (a blue-green shade): 2M, 50U; dark green: 4M, 2U. 9-ore lilac, dark lilac. 12-ore blue, Prussian blue: rare; ultramarine: 10M, 4U. 24-ore, from yellow to orange-yellow: 50M, 50U. 30-ore, from pale brown to dark brown, red-brown: 50U. 50-ore early rose, carmine-tinted rose, bright carmine: 2M, 2U.
Varieties: 50-ore with transparent impression: 2U. 30-ore, imperforate: rare. There are defective impressions, especially at the top (SVERIGE; right figure "O" in "30 ORE") and at bottom, "24" and "50 ORF" (rare).
Pairs: 4U. Blocks of four: rare.
Reprints (1885): perf 13; the 12-, 24-, and 30-ore on thin and thick paper. Value of the set: 200 francs.

1862–66. Different type. Nos. 12 to 15.
Perforation: 14.
Shades: 30-ore brown, pale brown, yellow-brown. 17-ore gray (slightly slate), dark gray, true shade of gray: 25M, 25U. 17-ore red-lilac (No. 14), pale to dark shades; lilac-gray: 50M, 50U. 20-ore red and pale red, bright brick red: 50M, 50U; red-brown: 2M, 3U.
Varieties: the 20-ore is known to be imperforate. The 3-ore, printed on both sides and double impression.
Pairs and blocks: rare.
Reprints (1885): 3-ore brown, 17-ore gray, and 20-ore light red. All three perf 13. The set: 100 francs.
Fakes: some doctoring of the color of No. 14 to change it to gray. Very mediocre results and dead loss on No. 14.
Forgeries: 17-ore, in two shades. Childish counterfeits — a quick glance and the use of the perforation gauge will expose them right away.

1872–78. Figure in center. Nos. 16 to 27.
Perforations: 13; 14; also, 3-, 12-, and 20-ore, perf 13¹/₂: rare.

Shades: numerous. Rare mint: 5-ore emerald: 2U; 6-ore gray or slate gray shades: 3U; 24-ore lemon color: 2M, 2U; 30-ore red-brown: 2U. All perf 14.

Varieties: 3-, 12-, and 30-ore, imperforate. The 20-ore red is found printed a second time on the pale orange 20-ore: very rare, mint.

Pairs: 3U. Blocks: rare. 3- and 6-ore: 12U.

Reprints (1885): 1-riksdaler yellow-brown, perf 13.

Fakes: doctoring of the 20-ore to obtain the TRETIO error. Compare lettering with a 30-ore. Watermark fluid will expose the paper thinning. The nonerror inscription also was removed chemically, with the word TRETIO reprinted in its place. The cleaning process left traces: noncongruent counterfeit lettering; noncongruent distances to the "F" of FRIMARKE, to the "O" of "ORE," and to the two delicate circles.

Forgeries of error 20 TRETIO (Genoa, I.): $17^{1}/_{4}$ x $19^{2}/_{5}$ mm instead of $17^{1}/_{2}$ x 20 mm. The diaeresis over the "A" of FRIMARKE is touching the thin circle. Letters "RI" and "MAR" are touching each other at bottom. No dot after FRIMARKE. Very crudely executed burelage. Framing of SVERIGE letters too far away and sometimes midway between the letters. Paper too white. Dull red shade (ochre-like). Perf $13^{1}/_{2}$ (apparent intention to pass both for perf 13 and perf 14!). No one will be fooled by such a gaudy creation.

Stockholm Locals

These stamps were used more widely for domestic service and the 3-ore bistre was used occasionally on cover for foreign mail: very rare on cover.

1856. LOKALBREF. Perf 14. Nos. 1 and 2.

1-skilling black or gray-black. There is a correction on the lower frame, extreme right: very rare. The imperforate stamp is an essay.

3-ore bistre, olive bistre.

Reprints: 1868: 1-skilling gray-black, perf 14, wove white paper.

1871: 1-skilling gray-black, and 3-ore, perf 14. These reprints are worth 20 francs apiece.

1885: 1-skilling and 3-ore, perf 13, thick or thin paper: 35 francs each. The perforated reprints are comparatively identified by the slightly different shades and the paper. Forged cancellations often are found on the latter.

Subsequent Issues

The general catalogues give adequate information.

1889. Forged overprint, which was well counterfeited in Geneva (F.), upright and inverted on the two values, Nos. 39 and 40. Comparison is necessary.

1891. The 50-ore stamp exists in brown. Color error?

1918–19. Faking of Nos. 109 and 111 (overprinted 55- and 80-ore) to make nonoverprinted Nos. 101 and 103. Traces of the chemical cleaning can be seen at the overprint places. Microscopic examination will furnish undeniable proof.

1889. Official stamps. The 12- and 24-ore, overprinted "10 ÖRE" (Nos. 13, 14) are very rare with perf 14.

Switzerland

This is one of the best countries for serious specialization. The plating of lithographed stamps is possible and its cancellations are now countless.

Cancellations: there are about 1,000 different postmarks. If the differences in their value, which varies with the stamps on which they were applied, and their shades are taken into consideration, a collection of several thousand cancellations ultimately can be built.

The accompanying illustration simply shows the main categories, a detailed study not being within the projected scope of this work. Nevertheless, the following details for reader guidance are given:

Type A, five different styles on Geneva stamps. Common in red, rare in the other shades.

Type B, common in red on the Zurich stamp, less common in black, and rare in blue. This type is rather common in black, but rare in red on values arranged serially.

Type C is found in several styles. It also is found unframed.

Type D comprises various dot types that are more or less large, square, rectangular, or diamond-shaped in form, the ensemble forming an octagon, a square, a lozenge, or a framed circle. There are various ornamental designs (including a magpie or a duck?).

Type E has about thirty styles, with various square, rectangular, circular, or diamond-shaped formats.

Among the latter, Type F occupies a special position, for it comprises in itself about fifteen types with seven to fifteen more or less large bars.

Types G and H are found with letters of various sizes, with or without dots after the letters, unframed, or in a rectangle, a circle, or an oval, sometimes double letters (Type G, also with a single "P").

The same is true for Types I, J (also RECOMMANDÉ), and K (also with the city name on two lines with date, postmark framed or unframed).

Types L and M have various styles. There is a strong market for large early postmarks, 25–30 mm in diameter, with ornaments at bottom.

Finally, there are the familiar modern postmarks.

Forged cancellations: rare on early stamps that are rarer used than mint. However, there are some on

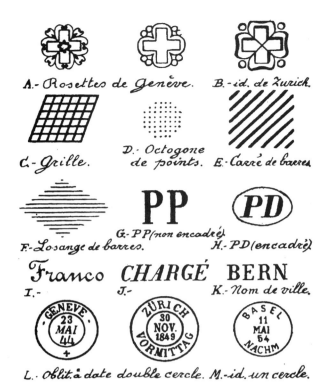

Switzerland cancellations. **A.** Geneva rosettes.
B. Zurich rosettes. **C.** Grill. **D.** Octagon of dots.
E. Barred square. **F.** Barred lozenge. **G.** Unframed
"PP." H. Framed **"PD." I.** Paid. **J.** Charge. **K.** City
name. **L.** Double circle with date. **M.** Single circle
with date.

stamps whose pen cancellations have been cleaned and
on forgeries, of course.

On cover: 10–25U (Basel). The "Winterthur": 2U.

Originals and forgeries: Swiss rarities were forged
so frequently that a sizable book would be needed to
deal with this question in detail. The question of forged
rare stamps is complicated further by minor differences
in the originals resulting from transfer flaws.

Naturally, no more here than in other countries are
there counterfeits which successfully withstand detailed
comparison, but difficulties often arise when terms of
comparison are lacking. So we thought it would be
useful to display enlargements of the various values,
thus facilitating, right from the beginning, the
elimination of counterfeits. However, the wise amateur
will make an additional comparison with some
colleague's original stamp. Works of art costing from
1,000 to 10,000 francs are not purchased without some
kind of serious guarantee. The maxim, "There is more
wisdom in several hands than in one," is universal in its
application.

Moreover, we shall indicate the places requiring
attentive scrutiny and a few characteristic features of the
best counterfeits. Among the latter, the

photolithographed stamps require that special attention
be given to design, format, shades, and especially to
paper, since it is sufficiently characteristic for possible
identification of all past and future counterfeits.

Special consideration also should be given to items
originating in plate cutouts, as studied in the admirable
work on Swiss stamps by Reuterskiold and Mirabaud,
Les Timbres-poste suisses 1843–1862 (Paris: Libr. impr.
reunies, 1898) and in the remarkable Zumstein
catalogue, *Spezial Katalog und Handbuch uber die
Briefmarken der Schweiz* (Bern: first edition, 1890).
Holland or Bristol paper, both too white, on which
these stamps were lithographically reproduced and other
details eliminate the possibility of confusion with
authentic stamps.

I. Local and Cantonal Post Offices

Select: four margins extending to the dividing frame
lines between the stamps. However, it is not necessary
to see the four dividing lines, for stamps of this quality
are very rare. The small eagle stamp must have four
visible margins, and the large eagle stamp must have
vertical margins that are about $1/2$ mm. Horizontal
margins must be visible.

Geneva

1843. Double Geneva. Nos. 1 and 1a. *Sheets* of
fifty stamps (5 x 10). Transfer of five in a horizontal
row.

Printing figure: 1,200,000 copies.

Shades: yellow-green, pale and dark yellow-green.
When in good condition, this stamp is worth 5,000
francs used; but, when the halves are reversed: 50M,
50U, and the vertical pair, formed by the two right and
left halves (really a pair of No. 1a), is worth 2M, 2U.
The half-double (postage for the city of Geneva) is
worth 1,000 francs used; two joined side-by-side halves
on cover, forming a double, are worth much more:
3–4U, depending on stamp condition.

Originals: left half, $14^{1}/_{2}$ (lateral) x $15^{2}/_{3}$ mm
(horizontal); right half, $15^{1}/_{2}$ x $15^{3}/_{4}$ mm, with slight
differences, depending on type; strip with words PORT
CANTONAL not counted. See the illustration for the
characteristic features.

Forgeries: noncongruent formats, paper, and shades
(sometimes blue-green, sage green, or true green). The
inner frames are not connected with the outer frame at
the places indicated. Five, six, seven, or eight lines
after TENEBRAS, or else four, and lines are not
congruent. No dots after GENEVE (or dots are not well
positioned after this word), after the figures, or after
the "C" letters. There are from twelve to sixteen
vertical shade lines in the shields' right section instead
of eleven.

The word FACSIMILE is printed on the back of two
counterfeits and on the front of another; obviously, this

inscription is often scraped off. The facsimile stamp manufactured for the Geneva Philatelic Exhibition also has that notation printed on the back in large upright capitals. With the green shade, a quite useless precaution: the six and five shade lines after TENEBRAS, and the parallelism of the first shade line of the half-shield in the stamp on the left.

The Reuterskiold reprints measure $14^1/_3$–$^1/_2$ x $15^2/_5$–$^1/_2$ mm for the left half, and $15^1/_4$–$^1/_3$ x $15^1/_2$ mm for the one on the right. The Zumstein reprint measures $14^1/_5$ x 15 and 15 x 15 mm.

Forged cancellations: the rosettas are not congruent.

Fakes: two defective halves touched up and joined to make a double. This fake is frequent on letters or printed matter of the period.

1845. Small eagle. No. 2. *Sheets* of 100 stamps (10 x 10). Block transfer plate of five stamps in horizontal row. The shade is yellow-green. The eagle feathers are not touching the inner frame of the coat of arms.

Stamps with four margins $^1/_2$ mm wide are worth double.

Pairs: 3M, 4U. A few plate transfer flaws (one per plate), TNNEBRAS, etc.: 25U.

Originals: 17 mm wide by about $19^1/_2$ mm high. (See illustration.)

Forgeries: shades of sage green, green, dark green, olive-green, blue-green, but also arbitrary yellow-green. Noncongruent formats (as much as 20 and 21 mm high!). The serif of the "P" of POSTE is touching the inner frame, but it does not go through it, or it does not even touch it. Inscription "JHS" (really "IHS") has become "INS" and "POST" has become "FIST." The last vertical shade line on the right touches the line limiting the right section of the shield. No dot after the "5," after GENEVE, or after CANTONAL. Inscription FACSIMILE in violet under the shield (scraped off). Thirteen quite straight lines in the shield's right section. An early counterfeit has eighteen of them; the eagle is crowned; and the dimensions are $14^1/_2$ x 15 mm! (Reduced in size for infants....) Another early counterfeit has the same number of shade lines. These lines and the ones around TENEBRAS are characteristic of photolithographed copies of Geneva stamps.

Reuterskiold reprint: $16^1/_2$ x 19 mm. Zumstein: $16^1/_2$ x $18^1/_2$ mm.

Forged cancellations: Types A, B(!), E (!), etc., noncongruent, in red or black. Also on piece with forged postmark, Type L, GENEVE 13 AOUT 45.

1846 (End). Large eagle. Nos. 3 and 3a. No. 3a (same plate) is from the August 1848 issue.

Sheets of 100 stamps (10 x 10). Block transfer of five stamps in horizontal strip. The eagle feathers touch the inner frame of the shield.

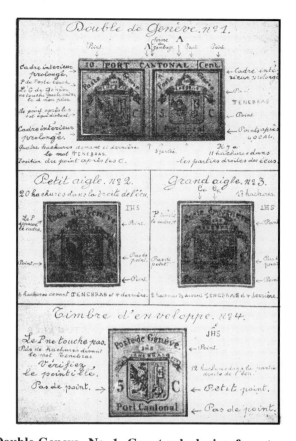

Double Geneva. No. 1. Counterclockwise, from top left: 1. Dot. 2. Inner frame extension. 3. "P" of POSTE touches frame. 4. The "G" of GENEVE does not touch frame, nor does "de." 5. Equidistant dot after the "5." 6. Inner frame extension. 7. Four shade lines before and after TENEBRAS. 8. Dot position after the "C" letters. 9. The "5" is slanted. 10. There are 11 shade lines in the shield's right section. 11. Dots after LOCAL. 12. Dot. 13. TENEBRAS. 14. Dot. 15. Inner frame extension. 16. Dot. 17. Dot. 18. Downstroke of "N."
Middle, left: Small Eagle. No. 2 (at left). Counterclockwise, from top left: 1. Twenty shade lines in shield's right section. 2. The "P" goes through the inner frame. 3. Dot. 4. Six shade lines before TENEBRAS and four after. 5. Dot. 6. No dot. 7. Dot. 8. IHS.
Middle, right: Large Eagle. No. 3 (at right). Counterclockwise, from top left: 1. "P" touches the frame. 2. No dot. 3. Two and a half shade lines before TENEBRAS and four after. 4. Dot. 5. No dot. 6. Dot. 7. JHS. 8. 17 shade lines. 9. The "e" shape.
Bottom: Envelope Stamp. No. 4. Counterclockwise, from top left: 1. The "P" touches the inner frame. 2. No shade lines before TENEBRAS. 3. Verify stippling. 4. No dot. 5. No dot. 6. Small dot. 7. Twelve shade lines in the shield's right section. 8. Dot. 9. Circumflex mark over the "H" of JHS.

Pairs: 3M, 3U.

There are transfer flaws in lettering and plate defects (accidental traces of printing tools) that are common on all lithographed stamps (long oblique black lines).

Originals: 16$\frac{1}{2}$–$\frac{3}{5}$ mm wide by about 19$\frac{1}{2}$ mm high. (See illustration.)

Forgeries: noncongruent formats and shades (grayish yellow-green, dull green, excessively dark blue-green). Some forgeries are 20 mm high with FACSIMILE printed on back, others with FACSIMILE in violet on front. In green on white paper for envelope, but large eagle type. No dot after GENEVE. Twenty vertical shade lines in the right section of the shield. No accent over the "E" of GENEVE. Noncongruent lettering, etc. (See illustration.)

Reuterskiold reprints: 16–16$\frac{1}{4}$ x 19 mm. Zumstein: 16$\frac{1}{4}$ x 19 mm.

1849 (June). Similar type. No. 4. Trimmed envelope stamp, used as an adhesive. The mint envelope is rather common: 25 francs; cutout on piece: 500 francs; same, on cover: 1,500 francs (3U). The black cancellation is rare. Forged cancellations (rosettes, etc.) are very numerous. Some very good ones exist on piece or cover. This stamp always must be given a very careful examination in the envelope area. There were three different envelope formats.

Originals: yellow-green on yellowish white paper; 17$\frac{1}{2}$ x 20$\frac{1}{2}$ mm. (See illustration.)

Forgeries: very numerous. Impression in various shades of yellow-green, green, dark green, blue-green. Eleven to sixteen vertical shade lines in the shield's right section. No dot after GENEVE, or the dot is too small, or is touching the "E." No circumflex accent over the "H" of JHS. The eagle definitely is not touching the shield's inner frame. There is a dot after CANTONAL, or after the "5." No shade lines after TENEBRAS. Terminal line above the "J" of JHS. The word "de" appears above this inscription. Noncongruent formats. PEST instead of POST. Violet-colored inscription of FACSIMILE above the shield, although frequently this word is scraped off. Finally, three to nine dots between the eagle's beak and wing instead of twelve. These dots are not always entirely visible in the originals, but their position must be examined.

A few forgeries were executed on the original envelope paper and then stuck on piece or on cover with expertly counterfeited cancellations. Detailed examination and, occasionally, photographic enlargement are necessary.

Reuterskiold reprint: 17$\frac{2}{5}$ x 20$\frac{1}{2}$ mm. Zumstein: 17 x 20 mm.

1849 (end). White cross in a circle. Nos. 5 and 6. Issued during the transition period between cantonal and federal issues, these stamps were circulated in the Geneva canton and the Nyon (Vaud) district. They are called "Vaud stamps" because the cross in a circle is part of the Nyon coat of arms.

Sheets of 100 stamps (10 x 10). Single stamp transfers. To make the 5-centime stamp, all "4" figures on the plate were scraped off and "5" figures, which are somewhat different from each other, were drawn (100 types). This value dates from the end-of-January 1850 issue.

Shades: black and gray-black. Circle in carmine-tinted red and red, the latter less common.

Varieties: circle out of place. White spot on the right, near the middle of the plate's stamp No. 26 (plate defect): 10U. There also are smaller defects. The 5-centime with red dot in the cross: 25U. Same defects as in the 4-centime, and some retouching of the horizontal shading on the stamp's sides. The 5-centime is known to exist with double impression: very rare.

Pairs: 3M, 3U. Blocks of four: 8M; 5-centime: 16U.

Cancellations: usually Types A and F: rare. Franking with other stamps is very rare.

Fakes: the reverse operation of that performed by the lithographer was executed by swindlers for their own profit: the "5," having been scraped off, became a "4." Examine transparency; evidence of thinning in that place is an indication of the probability of faking — a probability that often becomes certainty when one examines the "4," its exact position and its impression.

Originals: 21$\frac{1}{4}$ x 15$\frac{3}{4}$ mm. (See illustration.)

Forgeries: very numerous for the two values. Several of them have no dot after LOCALE (POSTE LOCALE), or else the dot is replaced by a recumbent comma. Twelve, thirteen, fourteen (on several stamps), fifteen, and sixteen lines coil around the post horn. Three large dots, instead of four, either on the left or on the right of the value inscription. (In one counterfeit, there is none at all on the right.) Horizontal bar of the "4" is as thick as the vertical downstroke. FACSIMILE inscription on back of stamp was scraped off. No outer frame line either on top or at bottom. Circle arc in upper right corner. Distorted lettering which is too large or too small. White cross framed by a black line (!). Red circle framed the same way, etc.

All of these forgeries are lithographed, but there is a very fine recess printed counterfeit (letter embossing very pronounced; no dot after LOCALE) in which the number of horizontal and vertical shade lines and of horn shade lines is double the number of lines in the original: a lot of work for nothing.

Reuterskiold reprints: 4-centime, 20$\frac{3}{4}$ x 15$\frac{1}{2}$ mm; 5-centime, 21 x 15$\frac{1}{2}$ mm. Zumstein: 4-centime, 20$\frac{2}{3}$ x 15$\frac{1}{2}$ mm; 5-centime, 20$\frac{7}{8}$ x 15$\frac{2}{5}$ mm.

1851. Cross in an escutcheon. No. 7. White cross on red escutcheon background. Stamp said to be from Neuchâtel. Black and gray-black. Lithographed in *sheets* of 100 stamps (10 x 10).

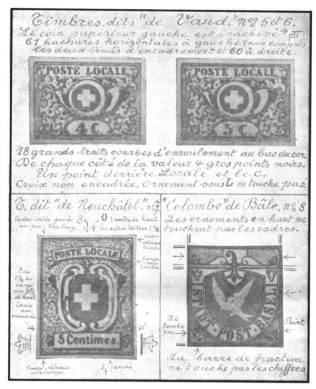

The "Vaud" stamps. Nos. 5 and 6. 1. The upper left corner is unfinished. 2. Sixty-one horizontal shade lines on the left (not including the frame lines) and sixty on the right. 3. Eighteen coiling lines in the bottom of the horn. 4. On each side of the value, four large black dots. 5. One dot after LOCALE and "C."

Bottom, left: The "Neuchâtel" stamp. No. 7 (at left). Counterclockwise, from top left: 1. Left frame, which is a little too long, is broken. 2. Shield 7½ mm wide, 9½ mm high. 3. Cross not framed. 4. Inner frame broken. 5. "S" slanted. 6. Banderole is touching. 7. "O," 1¼ mm high; the other letters, 1⅛ mm.

Bottom, right: Basel "Dove." No. 8 (at right). 1. The top ornaments do not touch the frames. 2. Does not touch. 3. The fraction bar does not touch the figures. 4. Dot.

Pairs: 5M, 4U. Franking with federal post office stamps: 50U.

Cancellations: often Type F. Others: rare.

Originals: 18⅕ mm wide by about 23⅖ high. (See illustration.)

Forgeries: numerous, from all sources. POSTE LOCALE is moved to the right, or the letter dimensions are arbitrary: 1, 1¼, 1½, 1¾ mm. The "O" of LOCALE is as high as the other letters. The escutcheon measures 6¼ x 9; 6¾ x 9½; 7 x 9; 7 x 10; 7⅖ x 10; 7½ x 9¼; 7½ x 9½; 7⅔ x 9½; 7¾ x 9½, 7¾ x 10;

etc. No dot after CENTIMES, or a dot that is too faint and which sometimes touches the tablet edge. The ivy-leaf ornaments on the right and left of the tablet of CENTIMES touch the inner frame or else have shapeless ornamentation. The inner frame occasionally is as thick as the outer frame or else the two frames merge into a single thick line. The left inner frame abuts on top against the outer frame or else does not touch it, bottom right. The ornament shaped like an "8," above the "L" of LOCALE, did not appear or did not come out well. The dot on the "I" is touching the tablet. One of the forgeries mentioned above has or had FACSIMILE in microscopic violet print at the top.

Reuterskiold reprint: 17⁹⁄₁₀ x 23 mm. Zumstein: 17⁴⁄₅ x 22¾ mm.

Basel

1845 (July 1). Basel dove. No. 8. The dove is embossed. Shades are black on greenish blue and dark carmine, or pale blue and carmine (first printing): 25M, 25U. The stamp in green and brick red is a rather common essay. There are a few plate flaws, white spots in the red background, cliché "cracking," and a black dot in the lower part of the "S" of BASEL.

Sheets of forty stamps (5 x 8). These stamps are so close together in the sheet (⅔ mm) that stamps rated as *select* simply have four visible margins.

Pairs: 3M, 4U.

Cancellations: usually circular with date in red or doubly framed FRANCO. Type C: rare.

Originals: 18⅔ mm wide by about 20 mm high. Thick paper. Dove embossing is quite visible. In the corners, there is a white curved line burelage on a blue background. The prolongation on the left of the "L" would fall between the "S" and the "T" of STADT. No letter touches the inner tablet line. The red frame is somewhat thicker than the heavy black frame lines and often deviates from its exact position. (See the illustration.)

Fake: the essay was doctored by painting the green corner parts blue and the background around the bird carmine.

Forgeries: numerous. All of them may be identified by the following defects: corners are not cross-hatched, or the layout is made of oblique white lines on a white background. At times there is nothing but white dots; at other times there is a field of blue dots on a white background. When the burelage is fair, the shade is arbitrary: blue-green instead of slightly greenish blue; one even finds true yellow-green, for the counterfeiter, not possessing authentic stamps, copied the essay. The frames are uniformly thick or they are misplaced (thick in place of thin and vice versa; see illustration). The red frame, which is either too thick or too thin, and rare displaced, is missing. The short lines between the words have become round dots. Sometimes they are too long or are missing. The value figures and the lettering touch the inner frame. Large figure "2" and small figure "1" occasionally touch the inscription's curved line. The bottom of the bishop's crosier is too far away from the small shield's point. The "O" of POST is slanted too much to the right. The "L" is too straight. One or both of the ornaments on top touch the inner frame. The dove is not sufficiently embossed, is not embossed at all, or is framed with a blue line!

One forgery had the violet-colored FACSIMILE inscription at the top. The format is not congruent; most of the stamps have margins that are too wide, even 3 mm! The counterfeiting done in Geneva (F.) used two clichés. In the first, the corner burelage is rather well executed, but the four lateral frames are uniformly thick. (This cliché also was used to counterfeit the essay.) In the second, the frames are congruent, but the corners are specked with blue dots on a white background. Various forged cancellations. On Geneva forgeries (F.), double circle in red with date, BASEL .. SEPT 1848.

Reuterskiold reprints: $18^{1}/_2$ x $19^{4}/_5$ mm. Zumstein: $18^{1}/_4$ x $19^{3}/_4$ mm.

Zurich

1843 (March). Large figures. Nos. 9 and 10.
Sheets of 100 (10 x 10). Block transfer of five stamps in horizontal row. Medium paper (50–60 microns).

Varieties: 6-rappen, large white spot in the cross-hatching under "ZUR" (Type IV): 5U. Retouched group of four shade lines under the "Z" (Type I): 2M, 5U. Bad retouching of two groups of lines under "ZU" (Type III), rare, end of plate: 8M, 8U. The 4-rappen was bisected to make a 6-rappen with another 4-rappen stamp: extremely rare. First-class impressions of the first printing with clearly visible red lines are in demand. Mint stamps without gum bring lower prices.

Cancellations: usually Type B in red or black; rare in blue. The two values were used in 1850 and 1851 after their official discontinuance. Franking with 1850 stamps is rare.

Pairs: 3M, 3U, but 4-rappen: 5U.

Originals: 4-rappen, $17^{3}/_4$–18 x $22^{1}/_4$–$^{1}/_2$ mm. 6-rappen, $18^{1}/_8$–$^{1}/_4$ x $22^{1}/_2$ mm, depending on type. Also, there are a few figure differences. Each type has a background cross-hatching arranged in groups of four oblique lines; the illustration shows the number of lines in the four inner corners. The cross-hatched corners have five large black dots. There is a leaf-like figure made of three lines in the lateral half-moons and a similar design juts out from the half-moon intersections. Observe the shading pattern inside the figure spaces. That is one of the best ways to ascertain the stamp's authenticity. There are seven horizontal black lines in

the tablet of ZURICH (4-rappen). Reuterskiold erroneously shows only six in Types II and III. This error recurs in all the publications that were slavishly copied from his work. In the lower tablet, there are eight lines, except in Type IV, where there are nine, and in Type V, where there are ten. In the 6-rappen stamp, there are eight lines on top and at bottom, except in Type V, where there are nine. In impressions that are not so good, one or two of these lines merge sometimes with the frame lines.

Red lining: this is composed of single lines spaced exactly $^{2}/_3$ mm apart (four lines in 2 mm, including the baseline). Between these lines, right in the middle, one invariably finds two lines drawn with the same finesse, spaced $^{1}/_8$ mm apart. This is one more mark that enables one to spot many forgeries. However, there are originals in which a part of the lining is irregular, due to plate, background, or retouching flaws.

Forgeries: very numerous. Their principal characteristics follow.

The early forgeries had figures "1," "8," "4," and "3" of the year date in the corners. Sometimes these are scraped off and replaced by black dots.

Noncongruent diagonal, horizontal shading or lining; the red lining sometimes flows over the black impression! No diaeresis over the "U." No dash before TAXE. Two dots after ZURICH, or one dot in an unknown type. Same, after TAXE in the 4-rappen. The number of half-moons is arbitrary. They are too flat or too tall; their ornaments are not congruent. A 4-rappen stamp has CANTONAL-TAXE at the bottom! All these forgeries are lithographed, except two engravings, one of which is on thick paper and the other of which has no red lining.

The Turin (U.) photolithographed stamps are all well done. However, they may be identified by the fuzziness of this kind of counterfeiting, the format, paper, and the noncongruent lining. Forged cancellations, Type B, in red or black, and Type G in black or blue, etc.

Reuterskiold reprints: 4-rappen, $17^{2}/_3$–18 x 22–$22^{1}/_4$ mm; 6-rappen, $17^{1}/_2$–18 x $22^{1}/_2$–$^{3}/_4$ mm; Zumstein: $17^{1}/_2$–18 x 22 and $17^{1}/_2$–18 x 22–$22^{1}/_2$ mm.

Reprints: thin paper; no red lining.

1850 (March). Cross in a horn. No. 11. *Sheets* of fifty (5 x 10). Transfer strip of five in horizontal sequence.

Varieties: broken letters or frames. Some frame retouching (lower right corner): 25U.

Cancellations: Type B, red or black; in blue: 25U. Type G; Types E and F are less common.

Pairs: 2.5U. Blocks of four: 10U.

Originals: $19^{3}/_4$ mm wide by about $15^{4}/_5$ mm high. A double black frame encircles the cross. The thicker outer frame is reinforced in certain places (see cancellation, Type B). The red lining has thirty-two

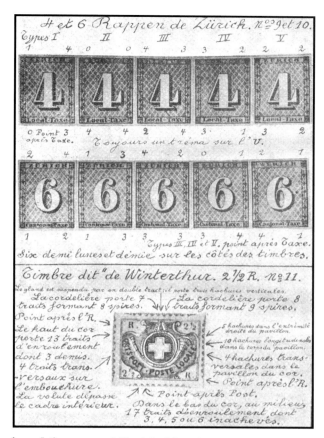

4- and 6-rappen of Zurich. Nos. 9 and 10. [The numbers above and below the 4- and 6-rappen stamps indicate the number of dots found where the numbers are placed.]

There is always a diaeresis over the "U" [of Zurich].[Under the 6-rappen types:] Types III, IV, and V, a dot after TAXE. 6½ half-moons on the stamps' sides.

Bottom: The "Winterthur" Stamp. 2½-rappen. No. 11. The acorn is hanging on a double line that has three vertical shade lines. Counterclockwise, from top left: 1. The suspension cord has 7 lines that form 8 twirls. 2. Dot after the "R." 3. The top of the horn has 13 coiling lines, 3 of which are half-lines. 4. Four transverse lines on the mouthpiece (end of horn tube and mouthpiece). 5. The volute goes through the inner frame. 6. Dot after POST. 7. Midway in the bottom of the horn, 17 coiling lines, of which 3, 4, 5, or 6 are incomplete. 8. Dot after the "R." 9. Four transverse shade lines on the horn's bell. 10. Ten longitudinal shade lines on the bell. 11. Five shade lines on the bell's right extremity. 12. The suspension cord has 8 lines that form 9 twirls.

horizontal lines between the top of the stamp and a point between the mouthpiece and tubular structure of the horn; thirty-nine lines from the bottom of the stamp

up to the bottom of the top inscriptions. This lining, which is too narrow and too high by about ⅓ mm, exposes blank spaces on the sides. The center circle is slightly brownish red. Nine spirals encircle the arrows which form dividing lines.

Forgeries: dividing lines with five to twelve spirals, black arrow or no arrow at all. Nine circles instead of spirals. Suspension cords with five, six, or seven lines on the right or left. A black dot in the upper branch of the cross. No dot after ORTSPOST. Dot out of place or too small. A dot after LOCALE. Two or three transverse lines on the mouthpiece tube. Mouthpiece itself too large and too flat. On the horn's tube, top middle, eight, twelve, seventeen coiling black lines, or none at all. At the bottom, six, eleven, fifteen, seventeen, eighteen, twenty, or thirty-one coiling lines. At the extremity of the horn's bell opening, six, eight, or ten shade lines instead of five. On the body of the horn's bell opening, nine or eleven longitudinal and five or six transverse lines. Lettering is too high or is noncongruent. Format is arbitrary. Inscription FACSIMILE in violet on back of stamp. Twenty-nine, thirty-one, thirty-two (etc.) horizontal red lines at bottom of stamp up to bottom of the "R"; the red lining sometimes encroaches upon the black impression! Forged cancellations are Type B in black, red, or blue; Type G in black or blue; Type C.

Reuterskiold reprints: 19⅗ x 15¼ mm. Zumstein: 19⅖ x 15⅕ mm.

II. Federal Postal Service

1850 (April). Local mail service (Poste Locale and Ortspost).

1850 (October). Rayon I and II. Nos. 12 to 19. Beginning with these issues, with the wealth of materials available, we are obliged to refer the reader to specialty catalogues for everything concerning varieties, types, and all details of minor importance. We shall give information only on things that one must know in order to make a sound judgment on appraisals.

Sheets of 160 stamps (16 x 10) in four transfers of forty (8 x 5).

Varieties: Poste Locale, No. 16, fine impression: 50M, 50U. Ortspost, No. 13: minor retouching in the right frame and cross: 25U. Rayon I, No. 14, numerous shades; thin paper; marbled background (also No. 18): 25U. Double impression, No. 14: 5U; No. 18: 4U. Rayon II, No. 15, orange-tinted brown: 2M, 2U; brown (tobacco): 3M, 3U; thin or card paper: 3M, 3U; marbled background: 2M, 3U; double impression: 30U. No. 19 with incomplete cross framing is worth 20–100 francs, used.

In the Ortspost stamp blocks, one finds types that are out of place in the transfer plate (very rare) due possibly to transfer paper tearing or to poor transfer impression.

There is nothing surprising about this, for the first Swiss stamps were printed with exemplary care. There are also transfer flaws: broken letters, frames, spots, etc., not to mention impression defects. Worn plate copies: 2–3U.

Cancellations: numerous and interesting. Types B–M in color or black and in various styles lending a greater or lesser degree of rarity to the stamps. See the specialty catalogues.

Pairs: 2.5M, 2.5U. Blocks of four: 8U, except No. 18: 12U; No. 14: 20U, No. 15: 30U. On cover: 25U, except Nos. 13, 16, and 17, 50U. Completely reconstructed transfers (forty types), select copies: 60U.

Originals: Poste Locale, 18 1/4–1/2 x 22 3/5 mm. Ortspost, 18 x 23 mm; Rayon I, 18 2/5 x 22 3/4–23 mm. Rayon II, 18 1/4–1/2 x 22 3/5–23 mm. Some difference in dimensions, depending on type. The forty types being different, one must rely on complete transfer reproductions to situate them exactly. Nevertheless, each value has a few generic marks, which are shown in the illustration. Except for questions of paper, format, shades, and impression, these marks will enable one to pick out and discard the forgeries.

Forgeries: Poste Locale: early forgeries which are wretchedly lithographed on yellowish paper. On the horn, one line on the left, then six lines. The shading at the bottom of the shield is shapeless. In another forgery, there is a mouthpiece shaped like a nozzle. The horn's circle is double on the left, but the lines are too far apart and there are four vertical lines in the bottom of the circle, which makes it look like a life buoy. Three heavy shade lines on the right under the shield. No line in the horn's bell. No dot after "Rp." Among the most recent forgeries, there is an engraved forgery in blue-black; otherwise, it is a good copy of Type 33, 18 x 22 3/5 mm. A lithographed forgery has a noncongruent horn with a narrow bell opening. The framework of heavy shading around the shield and the long frame suspension cord are shaped from a single, heavy, unbroken line. The Geneva (F.) photolithographed forgeries, which are printed on yellowish paper, are good copies of Type 7, but there are only two heavy shade lines under the shield on the left, and a single line inside the horn's bell opening; 18 2/5 mm wide by about 22 1/2 mm high.

Ortspost: same forgery as for Poste Locale with heavy shade lines and suspension cord frame formed from a single heavy black line. The bell opening is too narrow. The ORTS lettering is too high. "R" and "T" of ORTS are joined at top. Another forgery has no dot after POST, and the mouthpiece of the horn is black until it reaches the shading below. The heavily shaded framework is made from a single black line. The Geneva photolithographed forgeries are quite deceptive. First cliché, 18 3/5 x 22 3/4 mm, reproduction of Type 18.

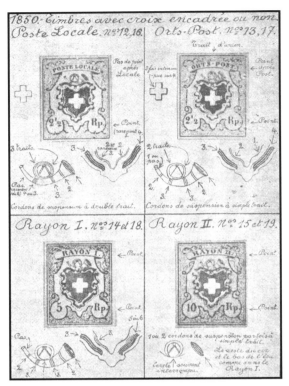

1850. Stamps with Cross Framed or Unframed. Counterclockwise, from left: Poste Locale. Nos. 12, 16 (at top left). 1. Three lines. 2. No lines; rarely one or two. 3. Four or three. 4. Double line suspension cords. 5. Two and two; rarely three. 6. Four; rarely five. 7. Dot. 8. No dot after LOCALE.
Ortspost. Nos. 13, 17 (at top right). 1. Broken three times out of four. 2. Two lines. 3. One line, or none. 4. Single-line suspension cords. 5. Dot. 6. Dot after POST.
Rayon I. Nos. 14 and 18 (at bottom left). 1. No lines. 2. Dot. 3. Dot.
Rayon II. Nos. 15 and 19 (at bottom right). 1. One or two suspension cords, sometimes single-lined. 2. Circle often broken. 3. The rest of the horn and the bottom of the shield are as in Rayon I. 4. Dot. 5. Dot.

(The two curved shade lines in the bell opening foreground are too short at bottom.) Under the shield, on the left, there are two finely etched shade lines (see illustration), but the higher one is broken near the middle and its left stub almost touches the line below it. The thin left suspension cord line does not terminate at the banderole coil under the "T." The second cliché, 18 2/5 x 22 4/5 mm, is a copy of Type 14. The line that limits the bottom of the horn is broken between the two curved shade lines in the foreground of the bell's opening. The middle line of the trio under the left suspension cord is broken. The bottom inner frame ends in two lines which are slanted toward the outer frame corners. When the cross is framed, the lower line of its left branch is thin.

Rayon I: bad modern forgery whose horn has one, two, two, and two transverse shade lines. No dot after the "I," light blue and bright carmine. A Geneva forgery (F.) (framed cross) does not correspond to any transfer type. The heavy shield shading forms a single line. The coil lines are broken below, as is the horn's line at that spot. The "R" of "Rp" is broken on top, in the middle. This forgery was occasionally retouched by those motivated by a false hope of making a better deal.

Rayon II: an early forgery, which is often canceled with Bergedorf bars. A single fine shade line on the left under the shield. The horn's transverse shade lines are two, two, two, and two. A modern photolithographed forgery, $18^2/5$ x $22^3/4$ mm, glossy paper, while apparently convincing with its seemingly deceptive appearance, the Roman numerals are joined neither at top nor at bottom; the loop of the "p" of "Rp" is broken at bottom; and this pale copy of the Type 30 stamp exhibits an almost perfect trefoil in the lower left corner! The Geneva photolithographed forgery (F.), $18^1/6$ mm wide by about $22^1/2$ mm high, is a good copy of Type 38; acceptable paper, good shades. However, the transfer is unsuccessful, and each group of the horn's transverse shade lines merges into a single line. The same is true with regard to the heavy shading around the shield and the suspension cord which is broken under the first loop on the right.

Reuterskiold reprints: Poste Locale: $18–18^1/4$ x $22^3/5-^3/4$ mm. Ortspost: $18–18^1/4$ x $22^3/4–23$ mm. Rayon I: $17^3/5–18$ x $22^1/2–23$ mm. Rayon II: $18–18^1/4$ mm by about 23 mm.

Zumstein reprints: in the same order, Poste Locale and Ortspost: $17^1/2–^3/4$ x $22^1/4–^1/2$ mm. Rayon I: $17^1/2$ x $22^1/4–^1/2$ mm. Rayon II: 18 x $22^1/2$.

Forged cancellations: on Geneva forgeries: Type B, black or red; Type F; Type G, large "PP," unframed; medium-size "PP," framed and in blue; small "PP" in slanting capitals; Type I in upright capitals; Type L, WINTERTHUR 2 MARS 1850 NACH M, in blue. Finally, the "hoax" type in black.

Fakes: faking of the framework and even of frame traces of the cross. Compare dimensions, ink shade, cross format according to stamp type. Check also whether the cross passes over the cancellation and whether it shows any strike-through.

1851 (February). Same type. Nos. 20 and 21.
5-rappen blue and red on white paper. Rayon I.

Sheets, etc. As above.

Varieties: ultramarine: 50U. Thin paper (40 microns): 2U. Both rare mint. Double impression: 20U; partial impression: 5U. There are various plate defects. Most of the stamps show traces of the cross framework. Bisected stamp, on cover: 150 francs.

Cancellations: usually Type F, in black; in blue: 50U; in red: 3U. Type E: 2U. The other types and postmarks with date vary in their rarity.

Pairs: 3M, 3U. Blocks of four: 8M, 16U. Transfer plate reconstructed from forty types: 50U.

Originals: $18–18^1/4$ x $22^1/2–23$ mm. Types similar to those of Rayon I, Nos. 14–18.

Geneva photolithographed forgeries (F.): $17^3/4$ x $22^1/2$ mm. Yellowish paper. Copies Type 25. The tablet's upper edge has a wide break above the "I." The loop of the "5" is too small. Well-framed cross.

Reuterskiold reprints: $17^3/5–18$ x $22^1/2–^3/4$ mm. Zumstein: about $17^1/2$ x $22^1/4–^1/2$ mm.

Fakes: inevitable doctoring of the cross framework. See preceding issue.

1852. Rayon III. Nos. 22 to 24. Small figure No. 22 and the type with "Cts." (No. 24) are from the January 1 issue; the large figure type is from the May issue. Thus, No. 24 regularly should be classified with the latter. The three values were printed from a transfer of ten (2 x 5) of the Ortspost plate (Types 2, 3, 10, 11, 18, 19, 26, 27, 34, 35), which is evident from the burelage, but the inscriptions have been changed and the shield has been covered with lines, shade upon shade.

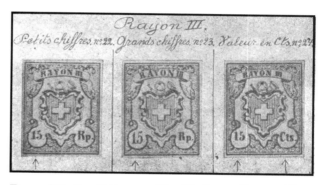

Rayon III. Small figures, No. 22. Large figures, No. 23. Value in "Cts.," No. 24.

Sheets as above. Red or dark red shades. A few plate defects: 25U.

Varieties: in this category are classified the large plate transfer flaws (one per sheet, in a single printing): thick figure "1" in No. 22 (Type 3); figure "1" with large hooks on left, top, and bottom. (The figure resembles a "7" that is slanted to the left.) Also in No. 22 (Type 6), etc. No. 23, thin paper: 50U. Upper right frame retouching in the three values and retouching of the vertical shading in No. 23: 2–3U. Bisected No. 23 is rare.

Cancellations: usually Type F in black or blue. All others are less common or rare.

Pairs: 2.50U. Blocks of four: 24U. Transfer of ten, reconstructed: 12U. On cover: 25U. Franking with stamps of the following issue or rappen values with centimes is rare.

Originals: 18 x 22$\frac{1}{2}$ mm. Large figure type, sometimes 17$\frac{4}{5}$ mm wide or as much as 23 mm high. The small and large figure types always have a dot after "Rp." In the "Cts." type, the dot is missing in Type 4, and there are two of them in Type 9: 25U. There are eighteen vertical shade lines in the small figure and "Cts." types, except in their transfer Type 6. In the large figure type, there are eighteen lines, except Types 5, 7, 9, and 10. The lines are correctly sketched with straight edge.

Geneva forgeries (F.): small figure type: twenty-three vertical shade lines. The extremities of the suspension cord, which are pointed toward the lower corners, are missing and are traced in red ink. Value in centimes; twenty-one shade lines; two dots spaced after "Cts." Large figure type: this forgery lays some claim to Type 5; eighteen lines, the sixth and seventh of which are too long at bottom; the shield border is missing there; two transverse shade lines instead of three on the horn, in the direction of the left suspension cord; letter "R" of RAYON is touching the top of the tablet.

Forged cancellations: Type L in red, BERN 7 APRIL 52 (cross at bottom). Type I, framed. Type F, in black or blue. Type M, MORGINS 27 MARS 51.

Reuterskiold reprints: 18 x 22$\frac{1}{2}$-$\frac{3}{4}$ mm. Zumstein: 18 x 22$\frac{1}{4}$-$\frac{1}{2}$ mm. Large figure type, a little narrower: 17$\frac{1}{2}$-$\frac{3}{4}$ mm.

1854 Helvetia seated. Imperforate. Nos. 25 to 32.
Imperforate. Typographed, embossed impression, silk thread in various shades. Printed in Munich and Bern. The Munich printing: good paper, good embossing, good impression, emerald green silk thread. The Bern printing: not so good, identifiable by the color spots in the background lining; thin, medium, or thick paper; silk thread of various shades.

Sheets of 100 (10 x 10). 100,000 copies of the 5-rappen red-brown, 150,000 of the 40-rappen yellow-green on thin paper (Munich), and 400,000 of the 2-rappen (Bern) were printed.

Select: four margins up to dividing frame lines.

Varieties: the 1854–62 issue alone makes it possible, even for collectors of modest means, to assemble a fine collection specializing in shades, silk thread, cancellations, paper, plate defects, retouching, pairs, and blocks.

The specialist will notice right away that the stamp's color varies with the color of the silk thread in the stamp's paper. Because silk thread colors might be faked easily, he must learn to recognize the original colors.

For further information on these varieties and on cancellations, consult the specialty catalogues. The 2-,

5-, 10-, 20-, and 40-rappen were bisected: 8U, except the 10-rappen: 20U, and the 40-rappen: rare.

Pairs: 3M, 3U. Blocks of four: 10M. 2-rappen and 1-franc: 12U. 40-rappen: 16U. (The Munich yellow-green is very rare.) 5-rappen: 50U. Others: 30U. On cover: 25U.

Cancellations: most common are Types L and M, and Type F in black. Type F in blue: less common, etc.

Forgeries: an early forgery of Swiss origin, 2-centime, 40-centime, and 1-franc. Poorly executed design (compare especially the background lining), bad embossing (in the 1-franc, there is embossing on the back of the stamp), bad paper, and "silk threads" traced on the back.

Geneva forgeries (F.): 2-rappen and 1-franc. Inner frame no thicker than the background shading, the latter being irregular in spots; in the shield's oval, twenty-one shade lines instead of seventeen. In a second, better-executed cliché, the inner frame is normal and there are seventeen shade lines, which, however, are too close. The one on the left is standing apart from the others, and the last one is touching the cross on the right, leaving a space of more than $\frac{1}{2}$ mm between it and the oval. "Silk thread" traced with ink, or real silk thread placed between thin layers of paper. Forged cancellations, Type F or M: BERN 14 DEC 9 VOR M. with "1862," halfway near the circle, on a level with the mouth.

Fakes: chemical fakes daubed in all the colors of the rainbow have been made to obtain No. 27 and error No. 26d. Verify the shade, which is never exact, the silk thread, and the impression.

III. Perforated Stamps

The general catalogues give adequate information on the perforated issues.

1862. *Geneva forgeries (F.):* first cliché: 2-, 3-, 30-, 40-, 60-centime, and 1-franc. With shield 2$\frac{3}{4}$ mm wide instead of 3$\frac{1}{4}$ mm. Various design defects in the background shading and in the lines above the seated female Swiss. These counterfeits usually can be identified easily by their bad impression. Lithographed. No watermark, or dry offset embossed forged watermark. The 30-centime measures 22$\frac{1}{3}$ mm high instead of 22 mm. Perf 11$\frac{1}{2}$, 11$\frac{3}{4}$. Second cliché: 2-, 3-, 40-, 60-centime, and 1-franc (gold or bronze); much better and really deceptive. Typographed. This time, the oval has the right width, but it is only partly printed, the bottom and top left parts are missing. Moreover, in the imperforate essays of these counterfeits, the cross has no horizontal lines, or, in the forgeries put up for sale, it has excessively large ones. The shades are sometimes slightly arbitrary. The forged watermark is still dry offset embossed, as above. Forged cancellations: see the 1881 issue.

Fake: daubing of the 2-centime olive in red-brown. This work of art belongs in the "Museum of Painting."

1867–78. Forged tête-bêche of the 15-centime yellow. This shade was chosen because design defects are more difficult to recognize when the stamp is yellow. Design defects are numerous and the watermark is missing.

1881. The mint stamps of this issue are so cheap that counterfeiters exclusively applied cancellations, which are always rare. A list of the postmarks counterfeited in Geneva follows. Because of dates, parts of these are found on the forgeries of the 1862 issue. Double circle with two horizontal bars in the middle, with date (German type): BERN 30 III 2 8 .. and Geneva cross encircled at bottom; BASEL 18 IX .... and BASEL .. VII 21 2, both with cross at bottom, and BRF EXP; CHUR 15 III 81 II, cross; GENEVE 13 .. 81 VIII, cross and EXP LET, at bottom; LUZERN... III 82 V, cross and EXP LET; MORGES 4 XI 81 8, cross and EXP LET; MORGES 9 IX 82 XII, with cross encircled only; ZURICH 18 IX 81 II, cross and BRF EXP; finally, AMBULANT XI III 81, and at bottom, No. 5 and small cross.

1904. 40-centime gray with double impression; the second impression (Paris) is counterfeited. It may be identified by the shade and by excessive deviation from the normal format, 1–2 mm, the forger having generously wished to give good measure. The 25-centime, No. 107, experienced the same fate.

1917–20. Forged air mail overprints. Make comparison.

Official stamps. Forged overprints. Beware! Consider with the greatest of caution!

Duty-free stamps. Counterfeited several times, occasionally in sheets of sixteen with the Gretis error. Dull lilac-rose; dark rose, yellow, etc. Make comparison.

Postage due stamps (1883). Chemical alterations of the following issue in an arbitrary shade of blue-green.

Telegraph stamps. 3-franc, No. 6a (without silk thread), brightly daubed to make a gold and carmine No. 8. Ludicrous.

Syria

1920. FAIÇAL overprints. Nos. 1 to 63. *Forged overprints:* comparison of the main characteristics and of the ink shades is indispensable.

French occupation. Very numerous *forged overprints* of all rare values, in particular, of the first issue (1919, Nos. 1–10), of air mail stamps (1920, Nos. 48–50), of the 1920 issue (Nos. 51–59, with varieties) and top-to-bottom overprint varieties, and of rare varieties of subsequent issues. Specializing is recommended and comparison is absolutely necessary.

Tahiti

1882. "25c." or "TAHITI 25 c." overprints. Nos. 1 to 3. *Original overprints:* handstamp impressions. Nos. 1 and 2: the bars measure 16 mm, and there is a space of 15 mm between them; figure "25" is 5³/4 mm from the upper bar.

Forged overprints: detailed comparison is indispensable.

1884. Stamps overprinted TAHITI "5c," "10c," and "25 c." on 20-centime and 1-franc. Nos. 4 to 6. *Original overprints:* handstamp impression. "5" and "10 c": TAHITI, 18 mm; bars, 16 mm; "25 c," impression of No. 3 with value changed: TAHITI, 17 mm long, 4 mm high. The strips, letters, and newspapers bearing these impressions — "5 c"; "10 c"; "10 + 5"; "25 c"; "25 + 5 c"; "25 + 10 c" — are rare and are in demand, according to Marconnet (1897, p. 397).

Forged overprints: very numerous; same observation as for the first issue. First, determine whether Nos. 4 and 5 are forgeries of the 1881 issue (see French Colonies). The three overprints were counterfeited in Geneva.

1893. TAHITI overprints. Nos. 7 to 18. *Original overprint:* handstamp impression.

Forgeries: make sure that forged 1881 stamps are not implicated (see French Colonies).

Forged overprints: extremely numerous — upright, inverted, and address varieties — some of them are very deceptive; comparison and template measurement will identify them; in case of doubt, expertize, two opinions being better than a single one that often is self-centered. The whole set of forged stamps was overprinted fraudulently in Geneva with an easy-to-check, inexpertly executed overprint with forged double circle cancellation (20 ¹/2 mm), PAPEETE 18 AOUT 93 TAITI; also, oval postmark with bars of the British naval stations with a "T" in the middle.

1893. 1893 TAHITI overprint. Nos. 19 to 30. Specializing is necessary because of a half-dozen different types.

Forgeries and forged overprints: same remarks as above. The forged overprint was counterfeited in Geneva on originals with forged cancellation, PAPEETE 7 MAI 93 TAITI. (20 and 21 mm, with same names and interchangeable dates.)

1903. Nos. 31 to 33. *Forged overprints:* inverted and double, counterfeited in Geneva.

1915. Red Cross. Nos. 34 and 35. *Original* typographical *overprint* (cross with three characters), vermilion shade.

Forged overprints: numerous, poorly executed. Template measurement will suffice, the distance between the cross and TAHITI being too small or too large.

Postage dues stamps overprinted TAHITI or 1913 TAHITI. Nos. 1 to 28. *Forgeries:* first, ascertain whether the stamps are not forged completely (see French Colonies).

Forged overprints: on originals or on forged stamps: detailed comparison and template measurement are indispensable.

Tasmania

1853. 1-penny and 4-pence. Nos. 1 and 2.
Originals: recess print engraving on paper of various thicknesses, wove, and also laid for the 4-pence orange of Plate I; twenty-four varieties (6 x 4); 1-penny, one plate; stamps with dividing frame line about $2/3$ mm from stamp; engraver's initials on the edge of the neck; 19 x 21 mm; 2-pence, no outer dividing frame line; engraver's initials; two plates of twenty-four varieties; in Plate II, the southwest line of the outer frame is thicker than in Plate I; $22^{1}/_{2}$ mm.

Reprints: printed on the three preceding plates in which the portraits were barred with two heavy graver strokes. Plate I (1879): perf $11^{1}/_{2}$; 1-penny, blue; 4-pence, Plate I, bistre-yellow. Thin paper; white gum. Plate II (1887): 4-pence, Plate II in red-brown and black; thick, gumless paper; imperforate. Plate III (1887): 1-penny, pale blue. 4-pence, Plate I, in yellow-bistre and black; Plate II, in yellow-bistre; white Bristol paper; imperforate; gumless.

Forgeries: 1-penny, early forgery, lithographed; very crude, and immediately recognizable by the center oval background which is formed with crossed oblique shade lines instead of heavy vertical lines; dividing frame line about $1^{2}/_{5}$ mm from stamp. No engraver's initials. My attention has been drawn to a good photolithographed forgery of this value; unfortunately, I have not had a chance to see it. 4-pence, (a) early forgery, lithographed on medium paper; the center background is solid; no engraver's initials; no accent between "N" and "S." (b) Early forgery, lithographed; the center background is formed with horizontal lines crossed by oblique lines instead of horizontal lines and dots; the circle under the inscriptions is $4/5$–1 mm from the center circle instead of $2/5$ mm; the engraver's initials form a spot; about 23 mm. (c) Forgery engraved on modern stippled paper;

the circle under the inscriptions is about $1/4$ mm from the center circle; the burelage is irregular on the left (compare with the right side). Poorly executed copy of a stamp from Plate II. The forged Geneva cancellation is a six-barred oval with TASMANIA in the middle.

1855–70. Portraits with necklace. Nos. 3 to 21.
Originals: recess print engraved; various watermarks; imperforate or various perforations (see the catalogues). The 6-pence and the 1-shilling have an octagon-shaped frame. $19^{1}/_{4}$ x $25^{1}/_{2}$–$^{2}/_{3}$ mm for the 1-penny, 2-, and 4-pence. A good reliable characteristic of all originals, reprints, and various essays: the first row of pearls under the crown is not very visible and merges with the jewels to such an extent that at first sight there seem to be only two rows of pearls.

Reprints I (1879): 1-penny, 2- and 4-pence on thin, white paper, without watermark, white gum; perf $11^{1}/_{2}$; 1-penny brick red; 2-pence bright green; 4-pence blue. With or without the word REPRINT. II (1871): 6-pence and 1-shilling on glossy white paper without watermark; white gum; perf $11^{1}/_{2}$. 6-pence lilac and 1-shilling vermilion. With or without REPRINT. III (1889): 6-pence lilac and 1-shilling dark red on Bristol paper; imperforate without watermark, gumless.

Various *essays*, some of which have the stamp's color, but with very different shades, dull color tones, on thin or pelure paper, tinted by the impression; comparison with the original shades will identify them.

Forgeries: the chief characteristics of all these forgeries are the absence of watermarks and the visibility of the three rows of pearls under the crown, the upper row being just as visible as the others. (a) Set of the 1-penny, 2-, 4-pence, and 1-shilling; early lithographs; imperforate or perf $12^{1}/_{2}$; $19^{3}/_{4}$ by about 26 mm for the 1-penny, 2-, and 4-pence. In these values, the blank oval, instead of being broken above MEN, extends somewhat beyond the upper frame; no break on the sides, either, where the oval almost is touching the left frame and remains $1/2$ mm inside the right frame. 1-shilling, on bluish thin paper; imperforate; twelve pearls instead of sixteen in the necklace; the ones in the middle are very small. (b) Engraved forgery. I have seen only the 1-penny red-brown that was made to counterfeit the stamp without watermark of 1856–57. However, since the other values probably will be counterfeited also, I think it is necessary to dwell somewhat on this particular forgery. $19^{2}/_{3}$ x $25^{4}/_{5}$ mm, with margins often attaining a width of 3 mm, thick paper, imperforate, or forgers' choice of perforation; chocolate red-brown; the "S" of DIEMENS is nearly 2 mm high instead of $1^{2}/_{3}$ mm; the "A" and the "N" of LAND are joined at bottom; the "D" is more than $1/2$ mm from the "N" instead of $2/5$ mm; the "T" of POSTAGE, which is larger than the other letters, is touching the tablet's upper edge; the neck base is $^3/_4$ mm from the edge instead of $^1/_2$ mm; the whole center background is saturated with color; the pearl in the upper part of the heavy ear pendant is missing; the pendant is cut on the left by a heavy graver's stroke; a few short, oblique lines are placed in the wrong direction under the right eye (left side of the stamp); the necklace's center stone forms a six-petal floweret instead of a round jewel and the stones on the right are not limited by lines on their sides.

Fakes: reprints or essays with trimmed perforation.

1870–78. Watermark figure or TAS. Nos. 22 to 34. *Reprints:* I (1871): Nos. 22–26, 31, and 33–34, on glossy white paper, without watermark; perf 11$^1/_2$; with or without REPRINT overprint. Different shades: the 3-pence is reddish brown; the 4-pence dark blue; the 5-shilling purple. II (1879): 4-pence dull yellow and 8-pence dull lilac with the characteristics of reprints I (1871). Finally, III (1889): 4-pence in blue with the same characteristics, but on very thick paper.

Official stamps. *Fakes:* some doctoring of higher value stamps by fraudulent perforation; they are identified easily by placing them perforation hole by perforation hole on an original, looking at them through a magnifying glass: the holes do not match. In case of doubt, have them expertized.

Thailand (Siam)

1883. 1-lotte, 1-att, 1-pynung. Nos. 1 to 3. *Originals:* recess print engraved with surface-tinted paper (edges) resulting from poor plate cleaning; good embossing; upper inscription on a background of horizontal shade lines, which are visible through a magnifying glass; two small curved shade lines under the pearl in the upper right corner; 2 mm below the pearl, the innermost lozenge contains two oblique shade lines; under the lozenge, there are seven vertical shade lines that form a frame (six of them, rather thick, and one very thin one on the left); on the forehead, above the eye, there are dots in the space between the lines of broken dashes; under the eye, on the right of the iris, there is a curved line and two not very curved broken lines; 20$^4/_5$ x 25 mm; as for the stamp printed in blue, slight variation in dimensions; perf 15.

Forgeries: perf 12$^1/_2$; 25$^1/_2$ mm high; very white paper; phototyping with color reinforcement and pronounced indention of the four circles; upper inscription on a solid background; horizontal white line in the bottom of the second character on the right; no lines under the pearl in the upper right corner; no hatching in the innermost lozenge; only six lines under the lozenge; in the center background, on the right of the portrait, the northwest–southeast oblique shade lines

cannot be seen; no dots above the eye in the space between the lines of dashes; under the eye, on the right of the iris, no line and the two lines of small dashes are spaced too far apart and are too convex; the seven oblique shade lines that form the mustache are almost invisible. This imperforate forgery was used to make No. 1a.

1885. 1-lotte overprinted 1 TICAL. No. 6. Numerous *forged overprints* on originals and on forgeries; some of them are deceptive. Comparison or expertizing is indispensable. Types I and II overprints were counterfeited in Geneva.

1890–99. Overprinted stamps of 1887–91. Nos. 16 to 25. *Forged overprints* of rare varieties; comparison is necessary.

1908. Equestrian statue. Nos. 77 to 83. *Forgeries* of the 10-, 20-, and 40-tical. Comparison with a common 1-tical stamp is sufficient, the counterfeits being poorly lithographed; only a child could mistake them.

1909–10. 2 SATANG overprint on 2a, No. 52. No. 87a. *Forged overprints:* comparison is necessary.

Thessaly

This is a set of distinctly minor interest that nevertheless was forged twice. Shades, perforation, and design of the forgeries don't match the originals. Comparison with an original stamp will suffice.

Thrace

This is a region where overprints are abundant. The majority of the overprints are unorthodox on the 1913 issues, which have nothing official about them. Complete abstention is best.

Timor

1885. TIMOR overprint. Nos. 1 to 12. *Forgeries:* see Macao for the completely forged stamps of Timor. *Original overprints:* 11$^1/_2$ mm long. *Reprints* of overprints on Macao stamps with thick, chalky, white paper, usually gumless (Nos.1–10); in black for Nos. 2–10, in red for No. 1. Perf 13$^1/_2$. The Macao originals are perf 12$^1/_2$ and 13. The reprinted overprint measures 12 mm. *Forged overprints* on originals: make comparison (Nos. 2, 4, 11, and 12). On forged stamps, the whole set was overprinted fraudulently in Geneva, TIMOR,

11³/₄ mm long, Nos. 1–10, as well as on originals and forged 10-reis green of Mozambique and Netherlands Indies to create Nos. 11 and 12. The forged cancellation on these forgeries is like that of Macao, CORREIO 12 NOV 85 DILLY in black or blue.

Tobago

1886. "¹/₂ PENNY" and "2¹/₂ PENCE" **overprints. Nos. 25 to 30.** *Forged overprints:* on Nos. 25–30, except No. 27 (¹/₂ PENNY on 6-pence bistre). Comparison is necessary; compare with No. 27.

First issue. Nos. 5 and 6 and postage-revenue stamps. *Fakes* obtained by removing the fiscal cancel, which occasionally was replaced by a forged cancellation.

Togo

1897. German stamps overprinted TOGO. Nos. 1 to 6. *Forged overprints:* checking with the template usually is effective; comparison is indispensable for the most deceptive ones. As for the used stamps, an overprint "on" any German cancellation often amounts to the disclosure of an agreeable joke.

Forgeries: ascertain first whether German forged stamps of 1889 are in question (see Germany); the latter were overprinted fraudulently in Geneva and provided with a forged cancellation: one circle, black: KLEIN-POPO 5-11-98, and a star in the bottom.

1914–15. Various overprints. Nos. 23 to 71. *Forged overprints* from various sources; detailed comparison is particularly indispensable since there are good counterfeits of the rare varieties.

Transcaucasian Federated States

First issue, 1923. Nos. 1 to 6. *Forged overprints:* comparison is necessary. The overprint of the first issue was counterfeited particularly well on the 3.50-ruble stamp. Comparison or expertizing is indicated. Presumably, forged overprints on the 10-kopeck and other values, including the 1-ruble, will not be long in appearing.

Transvaal

1870–75. Large format. Nos. 1 to 24.

1883. Same types. Perf 12. Nos. 70 to 73. Specializing is indispensable, because of the printings, shades, paper, and impressions and because all values were withdrawn by the engraver himself to be sold to collectors: so-called "reprints"; also, there are reprints of the 3-pence that are very difficult to identify and well-executed modern forgeries of all values. Measurement is not very useful in view of the number of printings and kinds of paper; on the other hand, shades will give the specialist effective aid in comparative appraisal, whereas a written or printed description may lead to an error. The illustrations following will prove useful only if well-printed copies are used (German or local impression), for in the heavily inked blurred impressions, reliable identification of originals is limited to shade and paper.

Originals: typographed; 1-penny, 6-pence, and 1-shilling, eagle with wings spread out. 1-penny, 21³/₄ x 25 mm; 6-pence, 21 x 24²/₃ mm; 1-shilling, 21 x 24¹/₂ mm, with differences in measurements due to printings (paper) and impressions (good or blurred); the eagle does not touch the flags; the flagstaff of the first flag on the right only rarely shows white line tracings; the anchor bills have only one hook inside; the anchor's ring is closed; fourteen shade lines in the oval, top left; twenty-five lines in the bottom of the oval, including the short line above the "R" of EENDRAGT, which touches the oval at times, and a faintly printed dot, top right.

Early and modern forgeries: a. crude early lithographed set, including a 3-pence with outspread wings; fifteen oval shade lines, top left, and twenty-seven lines and one dot in the bottom half-oval; legend under the oval: EENDRACT MAAKT MACT. The letters of EENDRACT are quite far from the top and bottom of the banderole, even in the 1-penny original value, where the legend frequently touches. Yellowish paper; bad rouletting or perf 13; occasionally, dividing frame lines. The warrior seems to be holding a glass of beer in his hand; the vehicle's pole is about 1 mm from the oval instead of about ¹/₅ mm.

b. 6-pence in blue-gray on thick paper, imperforate; no dot after the "Z"; the upper tablet is about 3 mm high instead of 2¹/₂ mm; the "P" of POSTZEGEL is ¹/₄ mm high instead of ¹/₂ mm, since this counterfeit was copied from the 1-penny; the horizontal line that divides the oval is not broken under the anchor.

c. A set copied from the so-called "reprints," including the 1-penny black; see the illustration for the anchor, the first flag on the left and the first two flags on the right, and the so-called "reprint" for the shading of the upper right corner and on the right of the warrior's foot.

d. 6-pence, in dark ultramarine on thick imperforate or rouletted paper; crude impression; no dot after "Z" or "AFR"; the letters of EENDRAGT are touching the top and bottom of the banderole; the pole is touching the oval; above the "I" of REPUBLIEK, the loop is half as small as it should be and the ornament underneath it is formed by two thin points.

e. 1-shilling, the first "E" and the "D" of EENDRAGT are touching the banderole; the lion's tail practically is separated from its body and the lion's head is shapeless; the front wheel of the truck is broken.

f. 1-penny, easy to recognize, the "1" figures being surrounded by a thin, blank rectangle; all the letters are too slender; almost all the shade lines are touching the oval and are too thick and heavy; the banderole legend is illegible.

g. 1-shilling, on very thick (100 microns) imperforate or perforated paper with EENDRACT; yellowish paper; the well-closed "S" of POSTZEGEL forms an almost perfect "8."

So-called reprints: identical framework, but inner design was reengraved by the engraver of the originals, which suggests that the differences are less perceptible (see some of the distinguishing marks in the illustration). The specialist will note that the paper of the various printings of these forgeries is either less thick and more transparent or thicker and less transparent than that of the originals; the shades are arbitrary, but sometimes they are close to the original color values and require comparison. Whereas the early forgeries are provided with a barred cancellation and the more recent ones with a quadruple circle without figures in black or blue, the so-called "reprints," which have been circulated quite widely, frequently have a triple circle, 19½ mm in diameter (exterior measurement); very thin concentric circles, 2 mm apart, with center figure (2, 6, 11, 12, 16, 19, 31, and so forth), 5 mm high.

3- and 6-pence, eagle with drooping wings. *Originals:* 3-pence, 21⅓ x about 24½ mm; dull violet, between a blue-violet and dark violet; thin and glossy paper for the rouletted stamp; a little thicker for the imperforate. No tête-bêche.

Reprints of the 3-pence; about 21⅙ mm wide; imperforate or rouletted 15, 15½. Tête-bêche. The shades are dull lilac-rose and a brighter lilac-rose. Most of the sheet's stamps have color spots in the lettering of the massive legends; one of the most curious ones has DRQE on the left and DROE on the right. There also are reprints in blue, dull rose, and so forth.

6-pence, original: in blue with Type II eagle, like the 3-pence. The eagle's eye is formed with an oblique line, as in that value; another oblique line goes along the neckline, back of the beak.

Reprints: 6-pence ultramarine, rouletted 15, 15½; in brown, too. Slight difference in the eagle's head lines: comparison with an original is necessary.

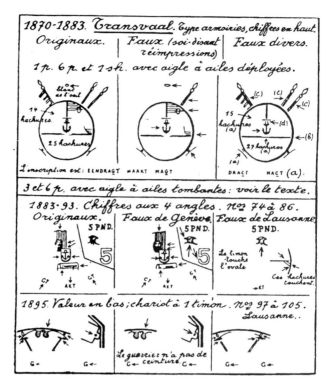

1870–83. Transvaal. Coat of arms type, figures on top. 1-penny, 6-pence, and 1-shilling eagle with outspread wings. Originals: White of eye. 14 and 25 shade lines. The inscription is EENDRAGT MAAKT MAGT. Forgeries (so-called "reprints"). Various forgeries: 15 and 27 shade lines. DRACT MACT. Second section: 3- and 6-pence, eagle with drooping wings: see the text. Third section: 1883–93. Figures in the four corners. Nos. 74–86. Originals. Geneva forgeries. Lausanne forgeries: The pole is touching the oval. The shade lines are touching. Bottom: 1895. Value at bottom; one-pole vehicle. Nos. 97–105. The warrior has no belt.

3-pence red and 3-pence black on rose, perf 12 (1883). *Originals:* 3-pence dull red-orange on thick, white paper, white gum; 3-pence black on lilac-rose, both perf 12.

Reprints: dark red-orange and dark black-brown on bright rose; thinner paper; yellowish white gum; perf 12, but really a bit too small (11⅘).

Forgeries: 3-pence, early forgery, poorly executed, like the preceding one; the left wing (on the right, looking at the stamp) is touching the flag; the point of the lowest placed of the two flags is touching the lateral tablet.

1877. V.R. TRANSVAAL overprint. Nos. 25 to 42. *Forged overprints:* a few counterfeits on originals, especially red, inverted overprints; numerous on so-called "reprints" or reprints of the 3-pence and on forgeries. Comparison of the stamp and of the overprint is indispensable. Type I, Nos. 25–29, was counterfeited in Geneva.

1882. 6-pence, "1 penny" overprint. No. 69. *Forged overprints* of the various types that are more or less successful. Comparison is necessary.

1885–93. Figures in the four corners. Nos. 74 to 86. *Originals:* 18½ x 22½ mm; perf 12, 13½. The oval shading is delicate and fine; most of the lines touch neither the oval nor the inner lines; the anchor is not touching its tablet; the anchor tablet's shadow is not touching the truck; the second shade line of the upper left quarter of the oval bends inwardly after a break and goes along the bottom of the lion's head; the anchor's bills are forked; the pole is not touching the oval.

Geneva forgeries: 18⅓–½ x 22½–⅔ mm, according to value; perf 12½ x 13½, and so forth, thin, slightly transparent paper; values up to the 10-shilling come from a first cliché; magnifying glass examination of the distinctive characteristics shown in the illustration (originals and forgeries) will enable one to identify these forgeries easily; all the shade lines are too heavy and most of them are touching the oval or the inner lines; the anchor ring frequently touches the line above it; the anchor bills are not forked, and the one on the left usually touches the vertical line; the pole is touching the oval; the truck shade lines are too short and their right extremities are joined; these shade lines are somewhat better in the 2½ pence stamps and in the 10-shilling; the "G" letters of the banderole legend look like the letter "C." In addition to these typical defects, which are inherent in all stamps from small sheets, there are secondary defects in the figures and legends; for example: 2½-pence with figure "2" of the fraction touching the oblique bar; 3-pence, with a lower bar of the final "E" of PENCE that is too long; 4-pence, with figure "4" lacking bottom terminal lines; 6-pence, with final "E" of PENCE with horizontal bars that evidently are too thin; 2-shilling 6-pence with figure "2," bottom right, that is not thick enough; 5-shilling, with noncongruent figures and nonparallel median bar of the second "E" of REPUBLIEK; 10-shilling, with shade lines too far to the right of the gun and figure "0" with an almost horizontal base. The £10 stamp comes from a more successful cliché; allowable dimensions, 18½ x 22½ mm; executed in blocks of sixteen; "G" and "T" of EENDRAGHT frequently are connected on top; the frame has numerous blurred edges (use magnifying glass) instead of sharp, clear-cut lines; the pole is touching the oval; all the oblique shade lines are touching the right side of the oval; the truck lines are more alike than those of the preceding forgeries; the anchor bills, likewise, but their tops sometimes are touching (see the illustration for the "5" figures and the

bird's head); dark olive shade on yellowish gray paper instead of dark green on white paper; thin, fleecy, very transparent paper; 12½ x 13½ mm. Forged cancellations of partially applied postmarks are described below (1895).

Lausanne forgeries (Pasche firm): £5; the other values probably will be forged, too; execution, also in blocks, is much better than that of the Geneva forgeries; the counterfeiting of this stamp, which is less common than generally is believed, is deceptive. Allowable measurements; very dark green shade, a rather blue-green color tone, whereas the original appears to be more of a dark yellow-green when the stamps are compared (see the illustration for the eagle's head); the warrior's right leg is separated from the body; the anchor bills are about the same as in the Geneva set; between the oval and the ground under the wagon, there are eight shade lines, some of which touch the ground or the oval, but the short shade line (or dot) on the right of the eight others is missing. Not very clear-cut perf 12.

1885–93. Various overprinted stamps. Nos. 87 to 96. Various *forged overprints* on originals, reprints, or forgeries; comparison is indispensable. The HALVE PENNY, TWEE PENCE Z.A.R., and 2½ PENCE (Type I) overprints were counterfeited in Geneva.

1895. Value at bottom. Nos. 97 to 105. *Originals:* 18⅖–⅗ x 22½–¾ mm, according to value and impression; perf 12½; there is a shade line on the right of the eagle's beak; the "G" letters of EENDRAGT and of MAGT are formed well.

Geneva forgeries: impression in small sheets; 18 x 22–22⅓ mm; allowable perforations; no shade line on the right of the eagle's beak; the "G" letters are shaped poorly (no horizontal bar; see illustration); the warrior has no belt; between the wagon wheels, the four vertical shade lines found in the originals are not visible, but, on the other hand, there is a small rectangle with a dot or a cross, like the Red Cross insignia — of Geneva. The shade lines do not touch the flagstaff tip of the first flag, under the "F" or under the wing.

Forged Geneva cancellations: double circle (23½ mm), with date: PRETORIA 6-AUG A 97 Z.A.R.; same (24 mm), PRETORIA 22 SEP. A02, and one star on each side; one circle (22 mm), with date, MAFEKING FE 11 00.

Lausanne forgeries (Pasche): I have seen only the 5- and 10-shilling forgeries; the rest probably will be forged in the future; 18¼–⅓ x 22½–⅔ mm; perf about 12¾; impression in blocks; the oval shading is too far removed from the oval line (about ⅛ mm), which explains why, at a distance, you see a blank space that is not found in the originals; the flagstaff tips and the flagstaffs of the first flags, under "F" and "L," are too short; under the "M" of MAGT there are four shade lines, only one of which is touching on top; the horizontal shade lines are too far from the flagstaffs and the wings above the oval.

1900. "V.R.I." overprints. Nos. 124 to 135. Upright and inverted *forged overprints* on various original values and on forgeries: comparison is necessary. This overprint was counterfeited in Geneva in two types.

1901. Black on color. Nos. 142 to 147. Stamps without signature are unissued stock remainders without much value.

1902. Portrait of Edward VII. No. 163. The £5 orange and violet was forged by chemical removal of a pale shade, lower value impression, followed by reprint from a forged cliché. Thus, only the impression is forged; orange-red instead of orange and excessively bright violet; the crown jewels practically are invisible; the portrait's forehead lacks adequate dot shading; the lateral rosettes are not congruent; compare with a lower original value.

Official stamps. "C.S.A.R." overprints. *Forged overprints* especially in Geneva; comparison is mandatory.

Telegraph stamps. *Forged overprints:* comparison is useful; the two types (a and b in the Yvert catalogue) were applied in Geneva on originals and on forgeries.

Trinidad

1847. No. 1. *Original:* unofficial; issued by the owner of the *Lady McLeod,* a steamer plying between San Fernando and Puerto de Espana (Trinidad); $18^1/_2$ x 23 mm.

1851–72. No value indicated. Nos. 1 to 5. Also, 1-penny of the following issues. Engraved; $18^1/_2-^1/_3$ x $21^1/_2$ mm; the shield (buckler) has about fifteen vertical shade lines, and in its left section, near the middle, there are two double horizontal lines and two oblique lines (also found on the right in the very good impressions), which represent the Union Jack. The ball on top of the bonnet is shaded; the spearhead has three vertical shade lines on the right; four fingers are visible in Britannia's two hands; her foot and toes are visible; the latter are touching the second shade line above the lower tablet; the ship, which has nine sails and a jib, is three-quarters visible; the burelage is fine and regular. A moment's comparison with a very common, canceled 1-penny of 1872 will facilitate identification of all the counterfeits.

Early forgeries: early lithographed sets. (a) A crude set which does have about fifteen shade lines, but they are too far to the right, which gives us a buckler that is blank in about one-third of its width on the left, and there is no trace of a Union Jack; the not-very-visible sails have only a few shade marks; a front view of the ship's hull is seen; Britannia's foot is practically invisible; blank ball on the bonnet. (b) Six visible sails; blank ball on the bonnet; crude general appearance. (c) Much better appearing set, but the bonnet ball has two or three horizontal half-lines on the right; spearhead without shading; eight sails, no jib; no star on the bonnet; oblique traces of the Union Jack (but no horizontal lines) on the buckler; $14^1/_4$ x 22 mm. A Genoa counterfeit, without value indication, is only 18 mm wide. The forged Geneva cancellation, applied on this forgery, is one circle (24 mm), with date: TRINIDAD MY 27 1851, with half-circle under the millesime.

1852. Lithographed stamps. Nos. 6 and 7. Blue. The characteristics described for stamps with no value indication can apply here, but due consideration must be given to the lithographed impression.

1852. Lithographed stamps with defective impression. Nos. 7b to 9. *Originals:* very bad lithograph transfers; their description would take too long and, moreover, would tend to be confusing; the three values must be compared with reliable originals or must be expertized, depending on the situation.

1859–72. Stamps with value indicated. Nos. 10 to 33. Except the 1-penny. *Originals:* engraved; same characteristics as the stamps with no value indication (1851); $18^1/_2-^2/_3$ x 22 mm.

Forgeries: lithographed sets. (a) $11^1/_2$ instead of $12^1/_2$ scallops are visible in the top of the stamp; the ones in the middle are more visible than in the originals, the word TRINIDAD being placed too low; six sails and other characteristics as in set b of stamps with no value indicated. (b) Same characteristics as set c of the stamps without value indicated; the 1-shilling is found in dark ultramarine and in dull dark blue; other counterfeits do not deserve description.

1879. Manuscript overprint "1d" in black. Expertizing of this overprint is indispensable.

1896–1914. Values in shillings and pounds. There are fiscal cancels, and, consequently, there is faking in their removal.

1914. Red Cross. No. 87a. *Forgery:* comparison is mandatory.

1917–18. War Tax stamp. Inverted overprints. *Forged overprints:* comparison is indispensable.

Official stamps. "OS" and OFFICIAL (1910) overprints were counterfeited and require comparison.

Tunisia

1888. Plain background. Nos. 1 to 8. A British writer, E.D. Bacon (*Reprints of Postal Adhesive Stamps and Their Characteristics,* London, Stanley Gibbons, 1899, p. 144) mentions reprints of this set which were made in 1893; the set had the same perforation and gray gum as the originals of the same original printing, and in it the 5-, 15-, 25-, and 75-centime stamps hardly can be distinguished, even in shades, from the originals. The 1-centime is black on bright blue instead of blue-gray; the 2-centime, dark brown-lilac on yellow instead of brown-red on American gray; the 40-centime, bright red on very pale yellow instead of pale red on American gray; and the 5-franc mauve on lilac instead of lilac on pale grayish lilac. The French catalogues have nothing to say about this.

The paper of a second impression may have been thicker with white gum. The 1-, 2-, and 5-centime only have colored paper with horizontal lines; the 1-centime is black on gray; the 2-centime, brown-red on yellow; the 5-centime, green on pale green instead of green on green; the 15-centime, blue on bluish white instead of white on grayish; the 25-centime, black on pale rose instead of rose; the 40-centime, red on pale red; the 75-centime, rose-carmine on pale rose, very close to the original; and the 5-franc, mauve on very pale lilac.

Postage due stamps. 1888–1901. "T"-perforated (Nos. 1 to 25). *Originals:* common perforation; Type I, 16 mm wide by 19½ mm high; Type II, rare perforation; five holes instead of six in height; Type III (Gafsa), small "T" (9¼ x 11¾ mm).

Forged perforations: very numerous (Type I); measurement and comparison are mandatory. The upright or inverted *forged Geneva perforation* measures 16¹⁄₁₀ mm wide x 19½ mm high. These forgeries have a date cancellation, whereas the originals mostly are hand-canceled with pen and ink.

The *forged Geneva cancellations* are double circle (24 mm), inner circle with broken lines, with date: at top, TUNIS; at bottom, REGENCE DE TUNIS, and in the middle, 7ᴱ / 9 AOUT, or 1ᴱ / 20 JUIN 94.

Turkey

Varieties of all sorts make the specialized collection of early Turkish stamps extremely interesting.

I. Imperforate Stamps

Black on color. Crescent or toughra. The stamps are printed as vertical tête-bêche with official control number in red or blue at the bottom of the stamp.

Pelure paper (25–30 microns) for the 20-para and 1-piaster; also thick paper (70–80 microns).

Select: four margins about 2 mm wide, or extending to the dividing frame lines between the stamps in the first printings (in the third printing, dividing frame line at top and bottom, only).

Cancellations: the most common type is a dotted rectangle with Turkish inscription resembling English capital "M" in black or blue. Less common: rectangular cancellations divided in four rectangular parts whose northeast and southwest quadrants are composed of twelve parallel lines; the northwest and southeast quadrants are composed of lozenge grills. All others are rare.

A. Postage Stamps

1862–63. Various frames. Nos. 1 to 4. *Shades:* 20-para yellow; dark yellow: 50M, 50U. 1-piaster gray; violet: 50U. 2-piaster blue-green or blue; dark blue: 2M, 2U. 5-piaster rose, carmine-tinted rose.

Varieties: 20-piaster and 1-piaster on thick paper: same price used; 25M. 1-piaster, on medium paper (50–60 microns): 2M, 2U. Errors of 1-, 2-, and 5-piaster are found printed in yellow and the 20-para in blue; this last one is very rare. The others: 20–30M and U. The tête-bêche stamps are worth 4M, 4U. There are copies with poorly executed background coloring (blank spots): 50M, 50U. 1-piaster, with background color on back: rare.

Border control varieties: normally the control is red, except for the 5-piaster, in which it is blue. No border control: 2M, 2U. With control on top and bottom: 50 francs (gold) each. Stamps with control on the value or on the top of the vignette are worth 25 francs (gold) each (no tête-bêche in these). Color errors of control in blue instead of red and vice-versa: 50 francs (gold). The ones in green, violet, and yellow are essays. Those with regular border on back: 150 francs. Finally, the ones with border in bronze (Sultan's stamps, unissued) are rare.

Pairs: 3–4U. Used blocks: very rare.

Originals: 20-para, 21¹⁄₅–½ x 25¼–½ mm, including corner squares. The shading at the bottom of the crescent is visible only in the very best impressions, which are rather well executed on thick paper. Figure "2" is thinner at bottom than at top; its lower part usually touches the ornament, except in light impressions. The corner ornaments are 1 mm away from the top inner frame and ½ mm from the inner laterals. See the illustration for other expertizing marks.

1-piaster. 19–19¼ x 25½–¾ mm. Same comment as above concerning the crescent shading. The extremities of the latter are about ½ mm from the corner ornaments. (See the illustration.)

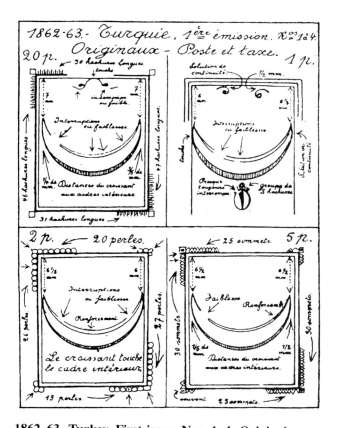

1862–63. Turkey. First issue, Nos. 1–4. Originals — postage and postage due stamps. All counterclockwise from top. Top left: 1. Thirty long shade lines. 2. 7 mm. 3. Breaks or faint print. 4. Forty-six long shade lines. 5. ¹/₄ mm distance from crescent to inner frames. 6. Thirty-one long shade lines. 7. ³/₅ mm distance from crescent to inner frames. 8. Forty-seven long shade lines. 9. 7 mm. 10. Broken or faint print. 11. Touching. Top right: 1. Gap. 2. 6 mm. 3. Breaks or faint print. 4. Touching. 5. Almost always broken. 6. Group of five shade lines. 7. Gap. 8. 5¹/₄ mm. 9. ¹/₂ mm. Bottom left: 1. Twenty pearls. 2. 6¹/₂ mm. 3. Twenty-six pearls. 4. Breaks or faint print; reinforcement. 5. Nineteen pearls. 6. The crescent touches the inner frame. 7. Twenty-seven pearls. 8. 6 mm. 9. Twenty pearls. Bottom right: 1. Twenty-five apexes. 2. 6¹/₂ mm. 3. Thirty apexes. 4. Faint print. 5. ¹/₅ mm distance from crescent to inner frames. 6. Often. 7. Twenty-three apexes. 8. Thirty apexes. 9. ¹/₂ mm distance from crescent to inner frames. 10. Reinforcements. 11. 6¹/₂ mm.

2-piaster. 19 x 24¹/₄–¹/₂ mm, including pearls. The number of pearls shown in the illustration does not include the corner pearls. Moreover, the latter are apparently design connectors, and their shape is different in each corner. The lines at the bottom of the crescent rarely are discernible. The leaves of the lower corner ornaments are about ¹/₂ mm away from the inner frames and the crescent; however, the one on the right comes very close to it.

5-piaster. 20 x 25¹/₄ mm, including ornaments. The crescent points are about ¹/₂ mm from the upper ornaments.

Forgeries: what we have said above, along with the information given in the illustration, is adequate for the identification of all extant forgeries. Nevertheless, we offer some additional information for the use of nonspecialists, who are always more like "doubting Thomases" than connoisseurs.

The forgeries' paper is often too thick (40 microns) and the impression is usually too black and too shiny. The stamp or control number shades generally are arbitrary; some seem possible. Color and control errors are not at all rare if one considers the number of counterfeits.

Practically speaking, one can say that there were only four fraudulent clichés, one of which was rebuilt. They were used for postage and postage due stamps. The counterfeits coming from these clichés are extremely widespread and are quickly identified by the lack of faintly printed spots in the crescent. The other forgeries, which usually are cruder, do not merit description.

20-para. 19³/₄–20 x 25 mm. Thirty-three long lines, top and bottom. Forty-two lines on the left, forty-five on the right. The top ornament in the middle of the stamp does not touch the frame and the corner ornaments are only ¹/₂ mm from it. Figure "2" is too large and the zero forms a four-pointed star, one point of which points downward.

1-piaster. The dimensions of this forgery are possible. The extremity of the left corner ornamentation is further from the left frame than that of the right ornament. The small circle above the value forms a "U." In another one, the ornaments' extremities are well placed, but the small circle above the value is an unclosed oval that is joined to the value's oval. Square dot to the left of figure "1"; the second right frame ends on a level with the third lower frame.

2-piaster. 18 x 24¹/₂, or, with rebuilt cliché, 19 x 25 mm only. The crescent does not touch the left frame. Its points end 5¹/₂ mm from the upper frame, on the left, and 6¹/₂ mm on the right. Down below, the left leaf is touching the frame, and the right leaf is touching the crescent. Twenty-two pearls on the short sides, twenty-nine on the long sides, the corner pearls not counted. The figure's bar is straight and does not even touch the circle on the right. The dot in the outer ornament is missing on the right of the figure's short branch.

5-piaster. 20 x 24¹/₂ mm. The crescent points are almost touching the upper ornaments. Twenty-nine apexes above and below; thirty-two on the left, thirty-four on the right. The crescent is ¹/₂ mm away from the left frame. In another lithographed forgery, the dimensions are fair, but there are twenty-five apexes above and below and thirty-one on the sides.

B. Postage Due Stamps

1863. Same. Nos. 1 to 4. Same characteristics and variety values as in the postage stamps of the first issue. The shades are brown and red-brown (in the 5-piaster, brown and rosy brown), but there is an almost brick red shade for the four values that is worth double the others. The rosy brown of the 5-piaster cannot be confused with the rose or carmine-tinted rose of the postage stamp: there is no brown in the latter.

Originals and forgeries: exactly like the postage stamps.

II. Perforated Stamps

The abundance of material available makes it necessary for us to pass lightly over the perforated values, which usually are studied in sufficient detail in the general catalogues. The shades and cancellations (especially local mail and contraband postmarks, "Catchak") of issues up to about 1876 are interesting. The triangular overprints of Mount Athos also are in demand. Most of the values were used bisected. Stamps should be purchased on entire cover only, for there was a great deal of doctoring. Pairs are worth 3U. Blocks of four are rare and are in demand.

Issues of 1865–75, Nos. 7 to 33, and postage due stamps, 1856–71, Nos. 5 to 24. *Originals:* typographed. 10- and 20-para, and 1- and 2-piaster measure 18¹/₄–¹/₂ x 21³/₄–22 mm. 5- and 25-piaster measure 18³/₄–19 x 22¹/₂ mm maximum, the matrices for these two value categories being different. The crescent is thicker and wider in the last two. The error of the 1-piaster yellow is in demand. Copies without black inscriptions or with inverted inscriptions and imperforate stamps are also in demand. The 1865 issue is perf 12¹/₂; 1867, 12¹/₂; 1869, 13¹/₂; 1871, 9 or 10; 1873, 12 (10-para); 1875, 13¹/₂ (10- and 20-para, 1-piaster). Paper (50–70 microns), usually somewhat transparent; the impression is frequently greasy in the issue of 1871.

Forgeries: the illustration will give detailed information on the originals and on the counterfeit set encountered most frequently; 19 mm wide, except for the 25-piaster, 19¹/₄ mm. All values about 22³/₄ mm high. The pearls often are irregular. Lithographed. The forty-two pearl set, which also is lithographed, does not deserve description. The outer frame of both is much

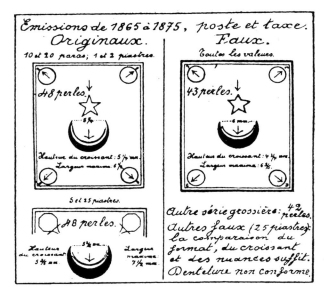

Issues of 1865–75. Postage and postage due stamps. Originals (at left). 10- and 20-para; 1- and 2-piaster. Left box, from top: Forty-eight pearls; 5¹/₄ mm; crescent height 5¹/₄ mm; maximum width 6¹/₂ mm. At bottom left: 5- and 25-piaster. Forty-eight pearls; height of crescent 5³/₅ mm; 5¹/₅ mm; maximum width 7¹/₂ mm. Forgeries (at right). All values. Forty-three pearls; 6 mm; crescent height 4³/₄ mm; maximum width 6³/₅ mm. At bottom right: Another crude set has forty-two pearls. Other forgeries (25-piaster): comparison of format, crescent, and shades is enough. Perforation is noncongruent.

too thick. There also are a few forgeries of the 25-piaster that have similar defects or that do not have the double inner shading in the crescent. The dimensions of the latter are always arbitrary.

Simple comparison of the inscriptions in black with a common stamp from each issue is almost always enough to classify these creations, none of which is really deceptive for a person who is willing to take the trouble to look at them.

Sometimes, rather successful shades are found. However, the specialist, aided by his reference stamps, frequently makes the "right" decision when he is at least a meter away from the stamp and thus cannot see its design, black inscriptions, perforations, or paper.

1876. Overprints, Roman numerals. Nos. 39 to 43.

1876–82. Same, without numerals. Nos. 34 to 38b. All errors (imperforate, tête-bêche stamps, and inverted overprints) are unissued stamps that have been rejected at control.

Originals: paper and impression as in the 1865 issue. Perf 13¹/₂. Stamps perf 11¹/₂ are unissued.

Forgeries: the whole set of 1876 (Nos. 39–43). Thus it will suffice to examine design, format, and perforation in order to locate the counterfeit forty-three-pearl set. Likewise, it also will suffice to compare overprints, Turkish inscriptions, and other crudely counterfeited inscriptions to arrive at a decision. The customary blue grill cancellation also is executed poorly. There are forged overprints of the value in black. Make comparison.

1876–77 to 1888–90. "Ottoman Empire" inscription and great crescent. Nos. 44 to 79. 1876–80. Nos. 44–53, perf 13½. The stamps perf 11½, the imperforate and tête-bêche stamps are unissued. The 1-piastre black and yellow error is rare.

1884. Nos. 34–60, perf 11½ or 13½; the 2- and 5-para, 13½ only; imperforate and unissued stamps exist. The 10-, 20-para, and the 1-piastre are found on thick paper: 50U.

1886. Perf 13½. Stamps perf 11½ and imperforate stamps are unissued. 5-para, 2- and 5-piaster on thick paper: 50U.

1888–90. Nos. 72–74, and 76 are perf 13½ or 11½. The others, 13½. The imperforate stamps are unissued. Nos. 80 and 82 were trimmed and overprinted in Baghdad.

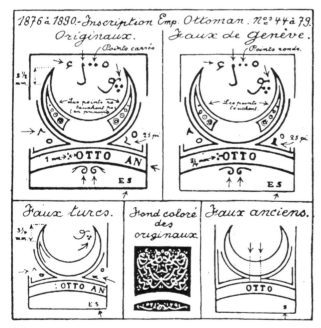

1876–90. Ottoman Empire inscriptions. Originals (top left): squared points; the dots do not touch. Geneva forgeries (top right): rounded points; the dots touch. At bottom (from left): Turkish forgeries; colored background of the original; early forgeries.

Originals: Typographed. 19 x 22¾ mm, with slight differences in printing stemming from light or relatively heavy, blotchy impression. Thin paper (50–55 microns), with the exceptions previously described. The value letters do not touch each other. The Turkish inscription dots are always square. For other details, see the illustration.

Forgeries: 1. Early counterfeits, especially of the 5- and 25-piaster stamps. Perf 12½. Lithographed in two colors. Paper is too thick. Bad design, the principal characteristic of which is shown in the illustration. The value letters frequently touch each other.

2. 25-piaster forgery of Turkish origin. Height, ¼ mm too short; a bit too narrow. The dots are round. The "S" of PIASTRES is slanted to the left. Letter "N" is too near the frame. The illustration shows the main characteristics of these apparently deceptive forgeries. Perf 11¼, sometimes 10¼. Thin paper.

3. Geneva forgeries (F.): all values, but rare copies of the 5-para, 5- and 25-piaster are known to be widely circulated. Paper of various thicknesses (40–75 microns), white or yellowish. Perf 13½. Very well executed and as deceptive as the preceding ones when they are on thin, white paper. Superb corner copy imperforates also have trespassed upon collections. The outer frame usually is too thin. See the illustration for expertizing points.

Note: The shades of these three categories of counterfeits only rarely are congruent, especially in the first one, and the colored background design is never congruent. (See the illustration and Eastern Rumelia.) Forged cancellations on Geneva forgeries: (1) Triple rectangle, 21 x 18 mm (exterior). (2) Double triangle. Both with Turkish inscriptions, and both in black or blue.

Subsequent issues. From 1900, sets resembling each other came off the press in rapid succession. From 1914, there is a veritable inflationary deluge: 400 new issues in five years. Many collectors rightly refuse to follow destitute states along this path.

Forged overprints pullulate; all the more reason why one should avoid involvement. As is the case for all overprints, the specialist relies especially on comparison in this area.

1914. 200-piaster. This stamp usually is found trimmed by customs employee shears. Soon afterwards it is offered for sale after repair work. However, the invisible repair work becomes quite visible in water and benzine.

Stamps for Printed Matter

Here again one must go in for thorough specialization to avoid collecting philatelic trivialities. A small book could be written just on forged overprints. It would be quite useless to study and classify all the bad overprints that seem attractive, for there are others that are really quite well executed. Only painstaking comparison can identify these. There also are clandestine printings in which the same kind of research is necessary.

1865. Private local mail service. Nos. 1 to 3. *Originals:* perf 14. Thirty-nine oblique lines above and below. There are many forged cancellations.

Early forgeries: the whole set with 5-para Turkish numeral in the top corners. Thirty-two oblique lines.

Nos. 4–7: there are forgeries of these stamps which must be studied comparatively, for there are different types in the sheets.

No. 8: Colors other than black on green are essays.

Turks Islands

1867–80. Portrait in an oval. Nos. 1 to 16. *Originals:* recess print engraved; very fine burelage, a vertical strip (2 mm wide) which runs right in front of the nose; this band contains horizontal lines of small lozenges, alternately five and six of them; on the right of the band are two vertical bands about 1 mm wide made of staggered lozenges; these bands are divided by a vertical white band $1/2$ mm in width which goes through the middle of the nose. The oblique shade lines of the neck cut are not limited at the top. All around the oval, the burelage is formed with small-dimension lozenges which make a regular design.

Forgeries: early lithographed counterfeits, all of them without watermark; burelage examination will be decisive. (a) A set whose band in front of the nose has five rows of vertical lines; the rest of the burelage is made with scattered dots forming a shapeless design. The first ornament of the crown is touching the oval line under the upper tablet; the second ornament has only three leaves instead of five. (b) Burelage hardly any better than the preceding one; the last two crosses of the crown are almost invisible; no ear; oblique shade lines of the neck cut are limited by a heavy line at the top, as in set a. (c) Same defect, but with a thinner line; the burelage is made of a dotted field, top and bottom, and with crossed lines along the lateral frames; the band in front of the nose has irregular lines made of comma-like shapes; no white line cutting the nose; mouth open; this set includes the 1-shilling stamp. Perf $11^1/2$.

1881. "$2^1/2$" and "4" overprints. Nos. 6 to 16. Very numerous *forged overprints,* especially of Nos. 10–16; detailed comparison is indispensable, for there are very deceptive counterfeits (Geneva: Types I and VII in the Yvert catalogue).

1917. WAR TAX stamps. Nos. 69 to 72. *Forged overprints:* WAR TAX, double and inverted overprints. Comparison is indispensable.

Ubangi-Shari (Oubangui)

1915–18. Overprinted stamps. Nos. 1 to 17. *Originals:* typographical overprint.

1916. Red Cross. Nos. 18 and 19. *Originals:* surface-coated paper; No. 18, handstamp printed in black; No. 19, carmine typographical overprint.

Forged overprints: numerous on originals, especially on rare varieties, Nos. 18a and 18e. Exacting comparison is indispensable.

Uganda

Comparison and even expertizing are indispensable for Nos. 1–35 and for the telegraph stamps.

Ukraine

We cannot advise too strongly that you refrain from collecting Ukraine if you have neither the skill nor the means to specialize.

All overprints were copiously counterfeited, first by German, Armenian, and Jewish counterfeiters, who added forged cancellations, then by countless fakers from all over the world; about thirty different overprints were manufactured in Geneva (F.) alone. The matrix plates are still extant and there probably will be clandestine printings in the future, which will complicate the Ukraine question even more.

Forged canceling devices were manufactured by the Germans during their stay in the Ukraine. There are about sixty of these woodcuts with interchangeable dates, from BIELIKI POLT to MIRGOROD (double circle postmarks with date), not counting the registry and supplementary fee postmarks.

On their withdrawal from the Ukraine, the Germans saw to it that these laboriously produced nonentities were admitted to the postal service.

United States of America

I. Postmaster Generals' Issues

What we have said concerning the similar issues of the Confederate States is valid here. Even if the following information seems adequate for stamps that one would like to acquire or identify with certainty, it is necessary to have them examined by a specialist in these issues, for most of the stamps are exceedingly rare, and better counterfeits than those present known may be made in the future.

Alexandria. *Originals:* 27 mm in diameter; thirty-nine or forty asterisks in the circle.

Baltimore. *Originals:* engraved; 16–17 x 53–54 mm; eleven varieties for the 5-cent, three for the 10-cent, on white or bluish wove paper.

Brattleboro. *Originals:* recess print engraved in sheets of ten (5 x 2) forming ten types; 21 x 14 mm.

Forgeries: lithographed.

New Haven. *Original:* handstamped, 26 x 31 mm.

Forgery: lithographed, 25^1/$_2$ x 30 mm.

New York. *Originals:* steel plate engraved; sheet of 100 (10 x 10), and signed "ACM" or "RHM," red ink flourish slanted to the right, 20^3/$_4$ x 27^3/$_4$ mm. Some copies have no signature.

Reprints: in black, but also in brown, green, blue, and red; 20^1/$_2$ x 28^1/$_4$ mm.

Forgeries: good counterfeits with FALSCH visible or scratched out in the bottom of the stamp. In case of doubt, comparison would be useful.

Providence. *Originals:* recess print engraved, sheet of twelve (3 x 4); eleven varieties of the 5-cent and one of the 10-cent (No. 3) in the same sheet; 28^1/$_4$ mm by about 20 mm; with or without blank dot after CENTS (10-cent, without dot); in the four corners, triangular ornaments with three curved lines of shading, the first two of which, almost forming a single thick line, join the frame lines; the third finer shading line is parallel to them; in the "O" letters of the inscriptions, the design is triangular.

Reprints: thin, yellowish or bluish paper or thick white paper; each of the twelve stamps of the sheet has one of the letters on its back (in the order of the types) of the person who executed these reprints: BOGERT DURBIN.

Forgeries: 27^1/$_2$ x 19^3/$_4$ mm; counterfeits of the 10- and 5-cent were made by reproducing Types 3 and 6 of the sheet (5-cent, without dot after CENTS); lithographed; 27^1/$_2$ x 19^3/$_4$ mm; paper similar to usual original paper, but thinner, more transparent; the large blank sphere in the middle of the right part of the stamp is equidistant from the frame and the oval instead of

closer to the frame; the inside of the "O" letters is oval-like.

St. Louis. *Originals:* recess print engraved; 1845: sheets of six (2 x 3); three types of the 5-cent on the left and three of the 10-cent on the right; 1846: same plate, but figure "5" of the two top stamps was scratched out and replaced by "20." Both of these printings on greenish gray wove paper; 1847: same plate, but they scratched out the "20" figures and replaced them by a "5," which is placed too low, almost touching the circle in Type I; it is too low and has been moved to the right in Type II; printing on pelure paper.

No *reprints.*

Forgeries: 2-cent, fantasy; 5-cent, deceptive counterfeit on grayish green paper; Type III copies: (a) the curved line above "OUIS" of LOUIS in the originals is missing here. (b) In the top right of the lower loop of the "5," there are only three dots instead of four; the curved line above "OFFI" of OFFICE ends above the space between "I" and "C" instead of above "I." Other forgeries of the 5-cent do not belong to any type, particularly a counterfeit on white paper where the bear's thigh penetrates the inner left frame whereas the bear's thigh on the right is about ^{1}/$_2$ mm from the inner frame; the two curved lines under SAINT and LOUIS are touching the "A" and the "I" at their extremities; the three lines under these curved lines are too long; those on the right almost are touching the horizontal line shading of the "5," which also is too large.

II. General Issues

1847. Nos. 1 and 2. *Originals:* 5-cent, the two figures practically are equidistant from the lower frame; the left side of the white necktie touches the oval almost between "F" and "I" on the right side, above the middle of the "V"; the mouth is somewhat too elongated toward the stamp's right. 10-cent, the two eyes are regular; the collar is shaded heavily and scarcely can be distinguished from the coat; on the left of the portrait (stamp's right), the hair normally is curly.

Reprints or, rather, official counterfeits made on reengraved plates; 5-cent: the "5" on the left is higher than the one on the right; the former is on the third horizontal shading line; the one on the right is under the second; the left side of the white necktie is touching the oval above the heavy vertical downstroke of the letter "F" and the right side of the necktie is above the left branch of the "V"; the mouth ends on the left (near stamp's right) with a color dot, and there are two short lines (use magnifying glass) which seem to form a second obliquely positioned color line; 10-cent, the right eye is not as high as the left eye; the less-heavily shaded collar becomes visible; on the left side of the face (right side of the stamp), you can see a small black circle with a vertical shading line (use magnifying glass) in the bottom of the hair curl. In the two values, letters "R," "W," "H," and "E" under the lower frame are less visible and legible than in the originals; no gum. The paper is wove in the 10-cent and the 5-cent reddish brown; it is laid in the 5-cent brown.

Early forgeries: so poorly executed that they need not be described.

Fakes of the 10-cent original, bisected, should be acquired only on cover, and the cancellations should be submitted to a specialist for expertizing.

1851–56. Imperforate stamps. Nos. 3 to 8. *Fakes* like that of the preceding issue made by bisecting the 10- and 12-cent stamps, Nos. 7 and 8, frequently with a forged cancellation of San Francisco, 1858.

1857–60. Perf 15. Nos. 11 to 17. *Reprints* (1875): easily identifiable by perf 12; the 3-cent is Type I, the 5-cent, Types II and III, the 1-, 3-, 10-, and 12-cent are printed from new plates; shades differ; gumless, very white paper. The 24-, 30-, and 90-cent imperforates are *essays:* very rare.

Forgeries of a few poorly lithographed values easily are exposed by imprint inspection; the 90-cent was counterfeited on several occasions (a) with horizontally shaded background only, dividing frame line, a single thick curved line above U.S. POSTAGE; (b) with very closely shaded background in which the vertical shading lines are quite visible through a magnifying glass; in the bottom of the stamp, a thin horizontal line and another thicker one, which is dot rouletted; the right eye seems to be made of glass; (c) in a better copied photolithographed forgery, the three horizontal lines in the bottom of the stamp are touching the outer curved lines instead of stopping at the faintly printed, almost invisible inner curved lines. The forgeries described in a and c (preceding) usually are imperforate stamps. In these three kinds of forgeries, the forehead, nose, the hair on the left temple, the left side of the chin, and the white necktie have blank spaces without any dot or line shading.

1861–66. U.S., in bottom of stamp. Perf 12. Nos. 18 to 28. Grilled stamps of various dimensions; 9 x 13–13$\frac{1}{2}$ mm; 11$\frac{1}{2}$ x 13 or 13$\frac{1}{2}$ mm; 12 x 14 mm; 13 x 16 mm; 18 x 15 mm; grill over the whole surface of the stamp (3-cent).

Reprints (1875): also perf 12; 1-cent ultramarine; 3-cent red-brown; 5-cent pale brown; 10-cent blue-green; 24-cent dark violet-brown; 30-cent orange-brown; 90-cent dark blue; the 2-, 12-, and 15-cent stamps in deep black instead of gray-black or black; very white paper, white gum. These reprints are not grilled and are rare.

Fakes: forged grills of various dimensions (also Geneva); some of them are deceptive and require additional specialized information. There are *essays* on card paper in the original shades of this issue and of subsequent issues — which laid the groundwork for *fakes* created by uniform thinning of the card paper followed by application of a forged grill.

1869. Embossed grill. Nos. 29 to 38. *Originals:* 9 mm square grill, or without grill.

Reprints (1875): no grill; tough, porous white paper. Same perforation as the originals; white gum instead of brown; slightly different shades.

Fakes: flattening of the grill to make it disappear; inverted centers obtained by remounting an inverted center or by applying an upright frame with forged embossed grill.

1870–73. U.S. POSTAGE. Nos. 39 to 57. *Originals:* grill, 12 x 13 mm, or without grill; perf 12.

Reprints: (1) 1875: gumless, perf 12, difficult to identify, but a specialist will manage by identifying a few shade differences and the plate wear in a few values; the whiter paper also will be indicative. (2) 1880: same indications, but a part of the printing is on porous paper. The reprints have no grill.

1882–83. Perf 12. Nos. 60 to 62. *Reprints* of the three values (end of 1883) on soft porous gumless paper; 2-cent pale brown; 3-cent pale green; 5-cent yellow-brown.

1916–17. 5-cent rose error. No. 203a. *Forgery:* the serif of the left downstroke of the "U" is triangular; no watermark; perf 11; the ear is indistinguishable; there is a long white line above the head.

Stamps for newspapers. Nos. 1 to 4. *Originals:* typographed, 51 mm by about 95 mm.

Reprints (1875): Nos. 2, 3, and 4; 10-cent in dark green and dark blue-green; 25-cent in bright vermilion-tinted red; 5-cent (white border) in dark blue. Same perf 12. These reprints still are recognized by the inscription, NATIONAL BANKNOTE COMPANY, NEW YORK, which is found at the bottom of the stamp, but here it is printed less boldly than in the originals. Tough, gumless, white paper; perf 12. The 5-cent was reprinted later in dark blue, dull dark blue, and purplish blue with the same characteristics, but on soft porous paper.

Geneva forgeries: 5-cent (with color border), perf 12$\frac{1}{2}$. The center background around the portrait is made of formless shading lines (see the 25-cent forgery); in the two large "V" letters, there are only six lines of shading and a dot instead of seven lines with an imperceptible dot.

10-cent, thirty-six horizontal colored shading lines instead of forty-one in the NEWSPAPERS inscription tablet; oval background around the portrait is made of horizontal lines $^1/_3$ mm thick instead of about $^1/_5$ mm; the curved hairline under the ear is invisible; the eyebrow and the eye form a black spot; the whole cross-hatching around the center oval is made of crisscrossing curved white lines, all of them executed delicately; no NATIONAL BANKNOTE COMPANY inscription at bottom of the stamp; perf $12^1/_2$ instead of 12.

25-cent, the frames on the left (white or colored) are not straight; the horizontal lines around the portrait are shapeless, made of occasionally curved, unequally thick shading lines which touch each other often and in which the blank spaces between them are as wide as the lines themselves; in the originals, these lines are regular, quite parallel, and the spaces are realized by very thin white lines; in the bottom inscription, there are two square dots after the "3" following MARCH instead of "3^D" (third). These forgeries have a round postmark, 33 mm in diameter, in red or black, with NEW YORK, and an ornamental design composed of a star and two arabesques at the bottom.

Other forgeries of the same values, perf $11^1/_2$; in the 10-cent, all the background lines around the portrait are touching each other and the thick color line surrounding them hardly can be made out; even on the portrait, they frequently are touching; the eye is indistinguishable; in the tablet of NEWSPAPERS, and so forth, the color shading marks are much thicker than the white lines that divide them; the inscription, NATIONAL BANKNOTE COMPANY, NEW YORK, is invisible; very pronounced fulling. 25-cent, same fulling which resembles hand-stamping. The background around the portrait appears solid. The inscription, NATIONAL BANKNOTE COMPANY, NEW YORK, is barely visible. One also can find counterfeits that are perf 11, $11^1/_2$, and $12^1/_2$; from 49–51 x $92^1/_2$–$94^1/_2$ mm; arbitrary shades; lithographed, but the blank parts subsequently were embossed to resemble a typographed printing.

1875–1885–1895. Perf 12. Nos. 5 to 53. *Reprints* (March 1875, two months after the original printing); very tough, gumless, white paper; perf 12. The shades are slightly different; 2- to 10-cent in gray-black instead of black; 12- to 96-cent in pale rose instead of rose; $3, scarlet; $6, dark ultramarine; $9, orange-yellow; $12, dark green; $36, brownish rose; $48, red-brown; $60, purple. The shades of the $1.92 and of the $12 must be compared. The $5 to $100 stamps of 1895 were reprinted in 1899 with the watermark of the 1897 issue (double line "U.S.P.S."), perf 12; with white instead of yellowish gum, and in different shades; $5, Prussian blue; $10, gray-green; $20, lilac-gray; $50, brownish rose; $100, purple-violet.

Forgeries: there are a great many counterfeits bearing the overprint FACSIMILE or FALSCH at the bottom of the inner frame, engraved with the stamp;

these inscriptions sometimes are scratched out and this was followed by remounting; the Indian type, 1- to 10-cent black, is recognized easily by the heavy oblique shading beginning below CALS and ending above CENTS, straight instead of curved lines; in the Goddess of Justice type, Nos. 13–20 rose, there are no dotted lines between the horizontal shading lines of the escutcheon. There are equally serious differences in the various types of Nos. 21–53; make comparison.

Special delivery stamps. Nos. 1 and 2. *Originals:* $34^3/_4$ mm by about 20 mm.

Geneva forgeries: $35^3/_4$ mm by about $20^2/_5$ mm; in No. 1, the vertical lines of the left frame (except two of them) are far from the horizontal line below them; one of the white shading marks of the upper frame extends on the right beyond the oblique line which limits the shading lines; the "S" of CENTS is slanted to the right. In No. 2, the "S" of CENTS is too large, crudely drawn, and visibly is slanted to the right.

III. Carriers

A. Official Issues

1851. Portrait. No. 1. *Reprint* (1875): (1) on original paper in dark blue on rose instead of dull or dark blue on yellowish rose; (2) on pale rose in the same shades (reprint more common). The two are gumless; the originals have brown gum and are printed more finely.

1851. Eagle. No. 2. *Reprints* (1875): (1) gumless, perf 12; (2) imperforate, gumless. The original with brown gum, blue or greenish blue shade; reprints are dark blue. Note: Nos. 1 and 2 orange are essays.

Forgeries: lithographed instead of engraved; dot instead of hyphen between PRE and PAID.

B. Semiofficial Issues

All of these issues should be expertized, for there are a great many counterfeits, most of the early collections containing many of them. It would take too long to describe them; the best advice is to assemble a small collection of reliable common stamps that can be used as references. In doubtful cases, consult a specialist.

Official stamps. *Reprints:* all government department sets were reprinted in 1875 on thick white paper with the word SPECIMEN (or, erroneously, SEPCIMEN) in carmine for Agriculture, State, Navy, and Post Office; in blue for the other departments. The dimensions usually are smaller, particularly in the STATE stamps.

The *originals* of the Department of State (STATE), values in dollars, measure $25^1/_2$ mm by about $39^1/_2$ mm.

Some very well executed *forgeries* measure $25^1/_4$ x 39 mm and have FACSIMILE at the top, usually just below letters "RTMEN" of DEPARTMENT. These forgeries are lithographed and perf $11^{1}/_{2}$.

Postage due stamps, 1879. Nos. 1 to 7. *Reprints* (September 1879) on soft, gumless, porous paper; perf 12. Brown-red shade instead of red-brown.

Return mail stamp. 1877. No. 2. *Original:* 43 mm by about $26^{1}/_{2}$ mm; regular cross-hatching.

Geneva forgeries: $44^{3}/_{4}$ mm by about $27^{2}/_{5}$ mm, with formless cross-hatching and arbitrary shades.

USA — Confederate States

I. Provisional Issues

Postmaster General, 1861

Numerous early forgeries, which usually are not very dangerous, but since an original most often is not available for comparison, specialization is useful, and even with the following furnished information, it is a good idea to have these little-known stamps checked by an experienced specialist.

Almost all the early collections contain poorly executed facsimile copies of these adhesives. We will describe a few of the better counterfeits further on. The Scott catalogue (1890?), in addition to the stamps listed by Yvert, gives information on a lot of envelopes which are in very keen demand in the United States; the prices for these vary from $25 to $500 for a few exceedingly rare varieties.

Athens. *Originals:* typographed; 21 x 25 mm; ATHENS measures 14 mm.

Forgeries: the dimensions are inconsistent; lettering is thick; ATHENS measures $15^{2}/_{5}$ mm.

Baton Rouge. 5-cent carmine with star background imprint in green.

Forgeries: stars are too close together; $3^{2}/_{3}$ mm from center to center instead of $4^{1}/_{4}$ mm.

Goliad. *Originals:* Type a, 21 x $23^{1}/_{2}$ mm; Type b, 24 x 22 mm; typographed or handstamped in black.

Forgeries of Type a are handstamped in dark violet on rose-tinted paper.

Greenville. *Originals:* Nos. 1 and 3, $21^{1}/_{2}$ x 27 mm; No. 2, $20^{1}/_{2}$ x $24^{4}/_{5}$ mm.

Forgeries of No. 2 with GREENVILLE in capital letters, as in Type a (Yvert).

Knoxville. *Originals:* typographed on laid paper; 20 x $24^{1}/_{3}$ mm.

Forgeries: lithographed on wove paper.

Livingston. *Original:* typographed, 24 x $26^{1}/_{2}$ mm; the inscription lettering is thick and irregular.

Forgeries: lithographed with thin, nonaligned lettering.

Lynchburg. *Original:* typographed, $20^{2}/_{5}$ x $24^{3}/_{5}$ mm.

Forgeries: (a) the dot is missing in the lower right corner; (b) another forgery with the inside of the loop of "5" entirely blank. Noncongruent measurements and shades.

Macon. A deceptive *counterfeit* of the 2-cent, No. 1, comes from a handstamp applied on sage-colored paper.

Original: typographed, black on green.

Memphis. *Original:* 2-cent, 22 mm by about $24^{1}/_{2}$ mm, typographed on thin paper; on the left above the "D" of PAID there is a full rectangle, which is a little narrower than the full squares in the background design.

Forgeries: 2-cent, on thin paper; a single line above and on the left of the "D"; in another forgery on thick paper, a complete square is found $1/_{2}$ mm on the left and above letter "D," from which it is separated by two lines; milky blue or dark blue, $21^{1}/_{2}$ x 24 mm; 5-cent, forgery with terminal curl of the figure about half as large as in the genuine stamp; in another forgery, the external scallops are regular (in the original, they are irregular); 5-cent, *reprint,* shade is too light; comparison is necessary.

Mobile. *Originals:* typographed, 18 x 20 mm.

Forgeries: noncongruent dimensions, and the star points do not touch the inner frame.

Nashville. *3-cent carmine original:* $21^{2}/_{5}$ x $21^{2}/_{3}$ mm; *forgeries:* noncongruent dimensions; outer frames are connected. In other forgeries, the dimensions are not in agreement and the shade is dull carmine-tinted red.

5- and 10-cent originals: blue-gray ribbed paper; *forgeries* on wove or laid paper.

New Orleans. *Originals:* lithographed; 2-cent, $19^{1}/_{3}$ x $24^{1}/_{2}$ mm; 5-cent, 19 x $23^{3}/_{5}$–$^{4}/_{5}$ mm, depending on type.

Forgeries: 2-cent blue, 19 x $23^{1}/_{2}$ mm; the "R" of ORLEANS is under the first "D" of RIDDELL instead of under the "I." In a more successful 2-cent red, with letters of POST OFFICE aligned, the same defects can be seen; the height, however, is allowable. 5-cent: (1) the lower left ornament displays a forearm with a four-finger open hand; (2) the "N" of NEW and the "S" of ORLEANS are touching the bottom of the tablet.

Petersburg. *Originals:* thick paper, 21 by about 25 mm; red.

Forgeries: shades of rose; fantasies in blue; noncongruent measurements; lettering of PETERSBURG is $1^{1}/_{8}$ mm instead of about $1^{2}/_{5}$ mm.

II. Regular General Issues

1861–62. Nos. 1 to 5. *Originals:* lithographed; 2-cent, 20½ x 26 mm; 5-cent, 21½ x 27 mm; 10-cent, 20 x 25¼ mm. The center background has crisscrossed horizontal and vertical shading; the vertical lines are spaced more widely in the 2-cent than in the other values; this especially is evident on the left of the head; in the 5-cent, you see the two points of the detachable collar and the "O" and "N" of CONFEDERATE are very close together.

Forgeries: 2-, 5-, and 10-cent, with horizontal shading lines only in the center background. In another forgery of the 5-cent, the inscription, CONFEDERATE, and so forth, is illegible; only the left point of the collar can be seen. In still another forgery of the 5-cent, the "O" and "N" are spaced like the other letters and only the right point of the collar is visible. There are other poorly executed counterfeits with arbitrary dimensions; they do not deserve description.

1862–64. Nos. 6 to 12. *Originals:* 5-cent, typographed, the shading of the center background is more serried than that of the face; the first "E" of CONFEDERATE has a very short median bar; in the second "E," the bar is as long as the other; the four stars are normal, same size, and they contain a perfect blank circle. 10-cent, engraved; the collar point ends exactly at the oval formed by the crisscrossed lines of the center background; on the left end and below figure "1," and on the right of the "S" of CENTS, there are four very thick shade lines. 20-cent, recess print engraved; dotted lines on the forehead; the vertical shade lines in the center background are well drawn and are quite visible; the almost imperceptible oblique lines crossing them can be seen with the help of a magnifying glass.

Forgeries: 5-cent, center background shading is spaced as in the face; the blank circle of the stars up above is larger than the one in the stars down below; in the first "E," the median bar is long, but it is short in the second. 10-cent, the collar point does not end at the edge of the oval of crisscrossed lines; the "C" of CENTS is narrower than the other letters; the "S" and "T" of POSTAGE are touching at the top; on the left of figure "1" and on the right of the "S" of CENTS, there are five shading lines. 20-cent, unbroken horizontal shading lines on the forehead; the center background is practically full. Bad lithographed stamp. No *reprints*. A 10-cent stamp with the portrait of Jefferson Davis, like the 5-cent blue, No. 9, was printed from the latter value's plate; it is a fantasy. Other rather deceptive forgeries of the 5-cent are typographed in dull blue-green; the median bar of the "F" of FINE is too short.

Upper Senegal and Niger

1906. Balay type. Nos. 15 to 17. *Forgeries:* values in francs; see the counterfeits of this type under French Colonies.

Forged Geneva cancellation: double circle (24 mm) with date, BAMAKO-KOULO 6 JAN 11 HAUT-SÊNÉGAL-NIGER.

Upper Silesia

Overprint country. One renders a service to collectors and particularly to amateur collectors by saying exactly what the situation is.

Upper Silesia: sets of 1920 and of the Plebiscite of 1920 — sixty percent are bad forged overprints, thirty percent are fair, and eight to nine percent are very good forged overprints. Remaining: one to two percent are original overprints. Two reasonable options: thorough specialization or total abstention.

In Eastern Silesia, the "S.O.S." distress signal also is obligatory, for the "SO" overprints are counterfeited well.

Uruguay

I. Private Issues of Sr. Lapido (With Approval of the Government)

1856–57. Diligencia. Nos. 1 to 3. *Originals:* 19 x 22¼ mm; 104 rays; the head is tilted slightly; lithographed plates of thirty-five types (transfer plate differences, 5 x 7); the inner white frame is broken in the upper right corner; the seventh vertical white line of the Greek ornament on the left is broken; see also various details in the illustration. A 60-centavo stamp is a very different type; no Greek ornaments; they are replaced by thirteen double vertical lines on the left and fifteen on the right; DILIGENCIA is as long as the top inner frame; fewer rays and in general they are further away from the circle; different head. For a long time this stamp was considered as a new type essay, and it is, perhaps, since the lucky find of on-cover canceled copies proves nothing.

Forgeries: a characteristic of all the counterfeits is the fact that the inner frame is whole and is unbroken in the upper right corner.

60-centavo. (a) The Greek ornament on the left has eighteen vertical lines; eighty rays; the "E" of DILIGENCIA is as wide as the other letters. (b) Greek ornament on the left has twenty-two vertical lines;

ninety-nine rays; wide "E." (c) Greek ornament on left has twenty-one vertical lines; ninety-eight or ninety-nine rays; a single one of these touches the circle on the right.

80-centavo. (d) $18^3/4$ x $21^1/2$ mm; upright head; the Greek ornaments have only seventeen vertical lines; 110 well-spaced rays; letters of DILIGENCIA are too thick; the "E" of this word is as wide as the other letters. (e) Geneva forgery; 19 x $21^4/5$ mm; rather well-executed in blocks; the principal characteristic is an oblique line in the middle of the forehead; see the illustration for the other chief characteristics; these forgeries do no have the transfer plate flaws of any type from the plate but appear to be copied from Type VII.

1-real. (f) Greek ornament on the left has eighteen vertical lines; the two branches of the "A" letters are equally thick. (g) Geneva forgery; $18^1/2$ x 22 mm; executed in blocks that seem to be reproduced from Type XVII; see various defects in the illustration; all stamps of the block have the RFAL error. The forged cancellation on the 80-centavo stamps and the 1-real Geneva forgery is formed of two interesting ovals (31 x 15 mm), with ADM. DE CORREOS at the top, DOLORES (underlined) in the middle, and REP. OR DELURUG at the bottom.

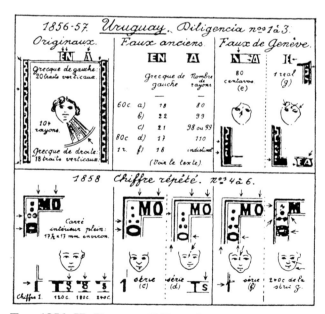

Top: 1856–57, Uruguay. Diligencia. Nos. 1–3. Originals: Greek ornament on left: 20 vertical lines. 10 rays. Greek ornament on right: 18 vertical lines. Early forgeries. Geneva forgeries: 80 centavos (e); 1-real (g). Bottom: 1858. Figure repeated. Nos. 4–6. Solid inner square: about $17^1/2$ mm by 17 mm.

Note: There are *essays* with DILIGENCIA extending over the length of the top inner frame with

seven shaded ovals in place of the Greek ornaments (1857; 180-centesimo green and 240-centesimo red).

1858. Value figure repeated. Nos. 4 to 6. Pending the arrival of the second issue, postage was paid in cash and two postmarks were stamped on the envelopes. The first one, double oval-shaped, took the place of the stamp; on top, it had ADM^{ON} DE CORREOS; in the middle, the date, the month, and "1857" or "1858"; and at the bottom, MONTEVIDEO between two stars; red or green. The second one included the framed word FRANCO and served as a sort of cancellation and indicated that the postage had been paid.

Originals: sheets of seventy-eight stamps (6 x 13) for the 120- and 180-centesimo stamps, tête-bêche at the No. 8 spot; a sheet of 204 stamps (12 x 17) for the 240-centesimo, with lithographed errors of the 180-centesimo red in the first printing: Nos. 41, 47, 101, 107, 161, 167, and 203; with these numbers blank in the second printing, the erroneous figurines having been pumiced out on the stone. A third printing did not comprise any value errors. Thin or thick paper; $23^3/4$–24 x $22^1/5$–$1/4$ mm, according to values and impression. MONTEVIDEO measures about $18^1/4$ mm in the 120-centesimo, $17^4/5$ mm in the 180-centesimo, and $17^1/2$ mm in the 240-centesimo. (Measure from the middle of the letters.) The "M" of MONTEVIDEO is set as in the illustration in the 180- and 240-centesimo stamps and a bit more to the left (just above the line that underlines CORREO) in the 120-centesimo. The "S" of CENT^S is touching the line above it in the 120- and 180-centesimo stamps. The balls all are shaded horizontally; in the 240-centesimo, those above the "C" of CORREO on the right almost are touching it.

Forgeries: there are good forgeries in these three values, but as the stamps are rare, certain counterfeits (notably the first Geneva set) are very widespread.

a. Lithographed set with the "M" of MONTEVIDEO beginning $1/4$ mm on the right of the line underlining CORREO and without any white tracing in the hair; with its thin-printed lettering and rather fine printing, this may be a set of essays of the counterfeits of set d (1856–57).

b. 240-centesimo, typographed in red-brown on grayish pelure paper; the shade lines of the balls are vertical.

c. Lithographed set, of which the 180-centesimo is best known; the balls are solid; the chin is pointed; allowable dimensions; the "M" of MONTEVIDEO has been shifted slightly to the left; the balls are too small or poorly arranged; the blank of the "O" letters and of the zero figures is too large; the "1" figures with an oblique terminal line; the "S" of CENTS is narrow and does not touch the line above it (180-centesimo). See the illustration.

d. A set whose impression is finer than that of the original; thin letters; spot between the eyes; balls with three shade lines; dividing frame line; no dot under the "S" of CENT^S.

Forged cancellations: double oval — ADM^{ON} DE CORREOS....60 REP-O-DEL URUG; round cancellation with "77" at bottom and cancellation on one line, *annul....*

e. Counterfeits that are rather similar to the forgeries of set f, with similar legend lettering but with "M" placed nearly as in the original; "S" of CENT^S, similar to that of set d, and dividing frame line $^3/_4$ mm from the stamp.

f. First forged Geneva set which seems to have been copied from the preceding set. To begin with, they made the 120-centesimo, and then its transfer plates were used to execute the other two values, with a simple change of value figures; the latter, which are positioned inexpertly, usually do not touch the line above them and they overlap the inner frame below them. The inner frame is double under CORREOS on the left; spot between the eyes; letters, not thick enough; dividing frame line. In spite of its defects, this set has been circulated very widely. The forged cancellation is a double oval with ADM^{ON} DE CORREOS on top, ARREGONDO (underlined) in the middle, and REP-O-DEL BRUG at bottom.

g. Second Geneva set. This set comes from two clichés, the first one of which was used for the 120- and 180-centesimo stamps — an excessively small cliché whose block reproduction gave stamps measuring $22^1/_2$ x $20^3/_4$–21 mm — which makes naked-eye identification possible. It also should be noted that the long rays are still 1 mm and more from the poorly executed inner circle, which is broken in many places on the left side; large color dot above the left eye; the nose has a line that is aimed toward that eye, and so forth. The second cliché gave the best forgery in this issue; $23^3/_4$ mm by about 22 mm; the long rays still are too short; the salient defects can be found in the illustration. The forged cancellation of this set, which also is affixed on the Geneva forgeries of the following two issues, is a double oval (29 x $18^1/_2$ mm, axes length), with ADMIN^{ON} DE CORREOS on top, NOV^{BRE} 15 1862 in the middle, and MONTEVIDEO between two stars at bottom.

II. Government Issues

1859. Lightface figures. Nos. 7 to 12. (and)

1860. Boldface figures. Nos. 13 to 17. *Originals:* lithographed in sheets of 204 stamps; $22^3/_4$–23 x 21–$21^1/_2$ mm, according to value and printing; the solid inner rectangle measures 17 mm by about 15 mm; MONTEVIDEO is about $12^1/_4$ mm long; all letters are $1^1/_2$ mm high; ninety-seven rays; the final "S" of

CENTESIMOS is slanted to the left and does not touch the extension of the solid inner rectangle; the second "E" of CENTESIMOS has an accent that does not touch the letter in the lightface set; in certain values, CORREO on the left often is spelled COBREO and even CORHEO at times (transfer plate flaws); the center circle is not in the middle of the rectangle; it is moved to the left and is slightly lower; the rays are alternately straight and wavy, and, in the good impressions, the wavy lines frequently are broken.

Forgeries: very numerous sets, most of which easily are identified by the following important defects: (1) no accent on the second "E" of CENTESIMOS (sets b, c, d, e, f, g); (2) the extension of the right side of the solid rectangle is touching or cuts the final "S" of that word (sets a, b, c, d, e); (3) the word CORREO on the right is as wide as the one on the left (sets a, c, e, f); (4) the center circle is right in the middle of the rectangle (sets a, b, c, d, e), or shifted slightly to the right (set f); (5) measurements and shades are arbitrary. See the illustration of the originals for a few typical defects.

The following defects will give further aid in identifying the forged sets:

a. Very thin paper; no ray is broken.

b. All rays are of equal length and the head is not in the middle of the circle.

c. A rather good-looking set, most widely circulated; $20^1/_2$ mm high; solid rectangle; $16^1/_4$ mm by 14 to about $14^1/_2$ mm; this set received the forged postmark ARREGONDO (described before) in Geneva.

d. No wavy rays (all rays are straight); the head is tilted to the right; it is too narrow (2 mm wide instead of about 3 mm) and is set too low; the two CORREO words are printed in capitals and are $10^3/_4$ mm wide on the left and 11 mm on the right; only one shade of the 180-centesimo lightface figure.

e. No wavy rays; most of the long rays are touching the circle; the letters of CENTESIMOS are $1^3/_4$ mm high; the forged postmark applied on this set is a double oval (38 x 24 mm), having at the top of the oval REPUBLICA DEL, in the middle, on three lines, CORREOS DE MONTEVIDEO, and at the bottom of the oval, URUGUAY.

f. $22^1/_4$ x 21 mm; the solid inner rectangle is 16 mm high; the inscription letters are only $1^1/_4$ mm high.

The *modern forgeries* comprise three sets:

g. Geneva, lightface figures, 60- and 100-centesimo carmine, but with large figures; 120-centesimo, in blocks of sixteen; the 60-centesimo, without accent on the second "E" of CENTESIMOS; the other values with accent touching the letter; for other defects, see the following set.

h. Geneva; the five values with boldface figures; this set, like the preceding one, is on thick yellowish paper;

all shades except the 120-centesimo blue are dull and flat; in the 60-centesimo (boldface figures), one can see a color line under the first ornament following MONTEVIDEO; letters "ORR" of CORREO on the left are touching each other on top; the left eye (on the right looking at the stamp) forms a spot; 80-centesimo, letters "IM" of CENTESIMOS are joined, top and bottom, and the "R" letters and the "E" of CORREO on the left are joined on top; same defect, left eye; 100-centesimo (carmine or rose), letters "NTE" of MONTEVIDEO are joined on top and CORREO on the right is spelled CORBEO; 120-centesimo, the first ornament on the left of MONTEVIDEO is open on top; a line connects the left eye to the hair; in the lightface figure value, the accent is not touching the "E"; in the transfers made with reinforced figures "1" and "2," which are larger than the zero, it touches it; 180-centesimo comes from a transfer taken from the 180-centesimo original, for the defect of the line connecting the eye to the hair reappears in this value; the "R" and the "E" of CORREO on the right are

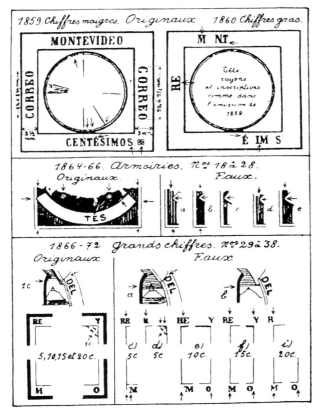

Top: 1859. Lightface figures. Originals. 1860. Boldface figures. Heads, rays, and inscriptions as in the 1859 issue. Second section: 1864–66. Coat of arms. Nos. 18–28. Originals. Forgeries. Bottom: 1866–72. Large figures. Nos. 29–38. Originals. Forgeries.

joined at the bottom. The forged cancellations on this set are the intertwining double oval DOLORES and the double oval of the 15 NOV 1862, previously described.

i. Well photolithographed, deceptive set with excessively lightface lettering and crude impression of the rays; the upper line of the "E" of CORREO (on the right) is concave instead of straight; measurements and shades are arbitrary.

1864–66. Coat of arms. Nos. 18 to 28. *Originals:* plates of 224 stamps in four pages of 56 (7 x 8); $18^3/_5$ mm by about 21 mm; two dots containing four vertical hatch marks before and after REPUBLICA ORIENTAL; accent on the second "E" of CENTESIMOS touching the top of the tablet; thin, blank circle under the first inscription; in the escutcheon, half of the right scale of the balance is missing; see the illustration also for a few details.

Early forgeries: easily spotted lithographed sets; they have no accent on the second "E" of CENTESIMOS.

a. The tablet of CENTESIMOS begins at the third shade line on the left and finishes at the second one on the right; no dots before and after the inscription; the blank circle under it is too pronounced; above the tablet of the CENTESIMOS, the background is shaded instead of solid, etc..

b. The background is solid especially in the top and has only a few traces of fine shade lines in the bottom; dividing frame line is about $1^1/_2$ mm from the outer frame; the dots before and after the inscription are formed poorly, too small, and lack shading; no blank circle under the inscription; embryonic accent on the second "E" of CENTESIMOS is touching the tablet.

c. A set that is almost as bad, with solid background in the top; the tablet of CENTESIMOS just is touching the inner frame on the left; no dot after ORIENTAL; the other one is not congruent; no blank circle.

d. The tablet of CENTESIMOS begins at the second vertical line on the left and ends at the third one on the right, no dots before and after the inscription; blank circle under "REP" and "NTAL" only; dividing frame line 1 mm from outer frame.

e. A set that is rather similar to set a, with shading above the tablet of CENTESIMOS; no dots before and after the inscription; too boldly printed blank circle. Comparison with an original will furnish additional significant information on the shield's bad design; the entire balance is placed on an unlined background; horse or mule resembling a sheep, its head touching the shield on the left; animals in the right quarterings are shapeless in general, the one in the bottom quartering being on an unlined background.

Forged overprints: not very numerous on originals of the 6-centesimo rose and 12-centesimo blue; forged inverted overprints and fantasies; comparison is necessary; also a few forged overprints on forged stamps.

1866–72. Large figures. Nos. 29 to 38. *Originals:* lithographed in sheets of 200, with two panes (10 x 10). 1-centesimo, 20 x 23½ mm. The other values, 19 mm by about 23½ mm, except 15-centesimo, 23–23¼ mm high, and 10-centesimo, 19¼ mm wide. Thin or medium paper; the perforated stamps of the 5- to 20-centesimo are also on pelure paper. The illustration will give information on a few characteristics of authentic stamps. 1-centesimo, the second "E" of CENTESIMO has an accent; this word's tablet has nine horizontally wavy lines and there is a small rectangular ornament before and after the word. 5-, 10-, 15-, and 20-centesimo: an extension of the inner left frame bisects the "R" of REPUBLICA and brushes against the left side of the "M" of MONTEVIDEO; an extension of the inner right frame bisects the "Y" and the "O" goes a little beyond the latter frame (see illustration). 5-centesimo, sixteen inscription lines, lower left, extending as far as the inverted inscriptions. The 10-, 15-, and 20-centesimo have twenty-five CENTESIMO inscription lines (count to the left). In the 15-centesimo, the bottom of figure "5" is not touching the "1." The 10-centesimo has a double inner frame line on top. Comparison with the designs in the center escutcheon will reveal numerous additional defects in the counterfeits.

Lithographed forgeries: see the characteristics shown in the illustration.

1-centesimo (a). Allowable dimensions; rather deceptive in appearance, but numerous defects; in particular, horizontal lines in the tablet of CENTESIMOS, no accent on the "E," no ornaments before and after CENTESIMOS; the horse's tail is ¼ mm from the vertical line instead of almost touching it.

b. See illustration; the horizontal shade lines go down under the "D" of DEL; the ox (lower right in the shield) looks like a sheep; no accent on the "E."

c. 5-centesimo, crude early forgery; twelve inscription lines, bottom left.

d. 5-centesimo, Geneva forgery in dark blue and ultramarine; allowable dimensions; the "R" of REPUBLICA is a "K"; previously described *forged cancellations:* DOLORES or NOV 15 with jumbled millesime; see recurring characteristic in the illustration.

e. 10-centesimo, bad early forgeries; only twenty inscription lines.

f. 15-centesimo, equally bad forgeries; seventeen inscription lines; the bottom of the "5" is touching the shading of the base of figure "1"; the "I" of MONTEVIDEO is separated from the top of the "V" by about 1 mm instead of ⅗ mm.

g. Geneva forgeries with the same cancellations as above; rather deceptive because of the shade, the details

not being easily distinguishable; 19 x 23½ mm; a few defects in the inscriptions; for example, the "S" letters all along the inner right frame merge with it, whereas in the original they simply touch it; on the right of the base of figure "1," the "T" letters are well separated from the base's shading instead of touching it; in the bottom of figure "5," the lower inner curved line never is broken; dark yellow and dark orange-yellow, noncongruent shades.

h. *Genoa forgery:* deceptive, but 19⅖ mm by about 24 mm; imperforate; the sun rays above the head are almost invisible; the two rays above the vertical lines of figure "5" do not touch the figure and the vertical lines of the same figure do not touch the allegorical head.

i. Bad early forgery; no "c" letters are seen on the left of the top of figure "2."

An additional deceptive photoengraved counterfeit of the 1-centesimo is known to exist; however, the horizontal shade lines largely are broken and the dimensions are not in conformity.

1877–80. 1-centesimo lithographed. The original is distinguished from the engraved stamp by figure "1," which is a little smaller and is on a background of horizontal shade lines instead of on a solid background.

1881–82. 1- and 2-centesimo. Nos. 46 and 47. *Originals:* 1-centesimo, 18¾ x 22½ mm; 2-centesimo, 19 x 22½ mm.

Forgeries: deceptive photoengraved stamps; 1-centesimo, 18½ x 22 mm; and 2-centesimo, 18½ x 22 mm; figures too thin; shades too bright.

Subsequent issues. A few *forged overprints,* especially 1889; 5-centesimo, violet PROVISORIO inverted; same, 1891 and 1892; Nos. 84–87, rare varieties; 1897, PAZ (forged in two types in Geneva). Comparison is necessary.

1908. Large format. Ship type. Nos. 174 to 176. *Originals:* one of the rare sets done in half-tone engraving; 40½ by about 27¼ mm (27 mm for the 5-centesimo). The lower loop of the "G" of AGOSTO is open; the "T" and "E" of TELEGRAFOS do not touch each other; the ship's main funnel is broken by five lines and there is a like number on the left of the second funnel; the prow of the hull is well shaded, and, somewhat in front of the mainmast, it has three black dots, and there is a dot under the mainmast, dots that are a little above the surface of the sea; shades: carmine, blue-green, and orange.

Geneva forgeries: half-tone engraving; 40 x 27 mm (39⅔ mm for the 5-centesimo); shades: rose, green, and ochre; the lower loop of the "G" of AGOSTO is closed; the "T" and "E" are touching; three and one-half lines traverse the main funnel; the dots on the hull are missing; no accent, or none that is very visible on the "U" of REPUBLICA.

1921. Air mail. Nos. 246 to 248. *Forged overprints:* comparison is necessary.

Official stamps. *Forged overprints:* OFICIAL, from various sources (Geneva 1881 and 1901). Comparison is indispensable.

Venezuela

1859–60. Small format. Nos. 1 to 3. *Originals:* lithographed; 13³/₄–14¹/₅ x 19³/₄–20 mm, depending on value and printing. In the printing of 1859, there is no dividing frame line in the vertical gutters of the stamps and the impression is first rate; in the second printing (1860), the impression is relatively crude; there is a vertical line between the stamps and the margins are narrower. The tablet of LIBERTAD is not closed by a top line.

Forgeries: two poorly executed lithographed sets, which are easily identifiable by inscriptions CORREO DE and LIBERTAD (see illustration). (a) Early set, 19¹/₂ mm high; arbitrary shades; the 2-real is occasionally chocolate colored; VENEZUELA is spelled VENEZULLA; in the escutcheon, the sheaf is only 2 mm high instead of about 2¹/₄ mm; the horse's head extends beyond the curved line, and the right side of the shield, if extended, would bisect the "A" instead of the "D" of LIBERTAD. (b) Geneva set; 14–14¹/₄ x 20 mm; canary yellow, dull red, dull dark blue, and dull red-brown, flat color tones; the stamp's background is made of crossed lines; in the right quartering of the shield, there is only one flag, mostly unfurled, with excessively short flagstaff, full flagstaff tip, but no trace of the second spearhead, which, in the original, is under the first one and almost is touching the line dividing the quarterings; the two banderoles under the tablet of LIBERTAD are blank or else have only a few vertical shade lines.

The *forged Geneva cancellations* are squares of round dots spaced 1¹/₂, 2, or 3 mm apart.

1861. Coat of arms. Nos. 5 to 7. *Originals:* lithographed; ¹/₄-centavo, 18¹/₂ x 21 mm; ¹/₂-centavo, 18¹/₄ x 21 mm; 1-centavo, 18 x 21¹/₄ mm. Dividing frame line, 1 mm from the outer frame; there always is a dot after VENEZUELA between frames in the ¹/₄- and ¹/₂-centavo; the dot is on the inner frame in the 1-centavo stamps; there always is a dot after CENTAVO; in the left quartering at the top of the shield, eighteen vertical shade lines in the ¹/₄-centavo, sixteen in the ¹/₂-centavo, and seventeen in the 1-centavo (count under the sheaf of grain, the dividing shade line included). In the illustration, see also the set of the "C" of CORREO and of the "A" of VENEZUELA in relation to the frame and the first pearl; see also the number of pearls for each value.

Forgeries: lithographed; in general, they do not have any dot after VENEZUELA, and some of them, no dot after CENTAVO. ¹/₄-centavo: (a) only fifteen shade lines in the upper left quartering of the shield. (b) The horse is shapeless and there are only eight or nine horizontal lines in the lower half of the shield. (c) Twenty-two pearls at bottom, which is enough to classify this counterfeit.

¹/₂-centavo: (d) fifteen shade lines in the upper left quartering of the shield; the dividing shade line is thicker than the others. (e) The "C" of CORREO is too near the frame (like the 1-centavo) and is touching the pearl; fifteen shade lines in the upper left quartering. (f) No dot after centavo and the shield is divided into four quarterings instead of three; consequently, the horse is cut by a vertical line.

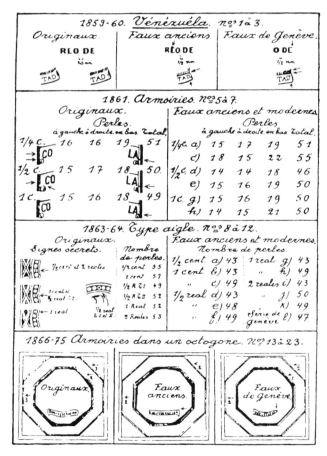

First section, top: 1859–60. Venezuela. Nos. 1–3. Originals. Early forgeries. Geneva forgeries. Second section: 1861. Coat of arms. Nos. 5–7. Originals. Early and modern forgeries. Third section: 1863–64. Eagle type. Nos. 8–12. Originals. Early and modern forgeries. Bottom section: 1866–75. Coat of arms in octagon. Nos. 13–23. Originals. Early forgeries. Geneva forgeries.

1-centavo: (g) forgery of the same set as b, same characteristics. (h) Under the shield, LIBERTAO for LIBERTAD. Cancellations with millesime "1860" or "1861" are forged.

1863–64. Eagle type. Nos. 8 to 12. *Originals:* lithographed; average measurements: 1/2-centavo, 18 x 21³/₄ mm; 1-centavo, 18 x 22¹/₄ mm; 1/2-real (Type I), 17¹/₂ x 21³/₄ mm; Type II, 18 x 22¹/₅ mm; 1-real, 18 x 22¹/₅ mm; 2-real, 18 x 22 mm. The inscription under the circle is VENEZOLANA; however, VENEZULANA, a printing flaw, is found, especially in the 1/2-centavo; the letters of FEDERACION and of the value are regular and are equidistant or reasonably equidistant from the tablets' lateral edges; they are very close to the top and bottom of the tablets; the vertical shade lines of the background are delicate and wavy and often are not very visible in the 1/2-centavo and the 1-real. In the 1/2-centavo, a pearl under the second poorly designed star seems double; likewise a third one under the third star; in the 1-centavo, the fifth pearl below the top of the eagle's left wing (on the right of the stamp) is too small. The stars do not touch each other; there is a dot after CENTAVO, REAL, and REALES. (See the illustration for the secret marks and the number of pearls.)

Forgeries: lithographed; they have no secret marks; irregular background shade lines and inscriptions; VENEZULANA often is found; stars are too large or too close together; allowable measurements; see the illustration for the number of pearls. Certain details of single stamps or of sets follow.

1/2-centavo (a) The fifth star is touching the sixth; letters of FEDERACION are 1 mm high instead of 1¹/₄ mm; no dot after CENTAVO.

1-centavo (b) VENEZULANA; early forgery with large blank spots on the eagle's body; the wings have a white border ¹/₄ mm wide, down to the bottom, and the top of the wings is too far from the circle. This forgery was produced in sets (see especially forgeries d, g, and i). (c) FEDERACION is not wide enough.

1/2-real (d) VENEZULANA; the background shade lines are thick and straight. (e) Bad forgery; counting pearls is enough; no secret mark. (f) The "F" of FEDERACION is more than 1 mm from the left side of the tablet instead of ¹/₃ or ¹/₂ mm, depending on type.

1-real (g) VENEZULANA; early forgery; see d. (h) UN REAL is too wide; there is only 1 mm on the left of "R" and 1 mm after the dot instead of 2¹/₂ and 1¹/₂ mm. This forgery forms a set with the c forgery.

2-real (i) early forgery; see b, d, and g. (j) Fifty pearls; bottom inscriptions are not high enough; no dot after REALES; letter "S" of this word is slanted markedly to the left; quite regular background line structure; good impression; sometimes pen-and-ink

canceled. (k) Same defects as j; this time, the "S" of REALES is slanted to the right. (l) The whole set was counterfeited in Geneva with or without the forged cancellations described under the first issue; the background shade lines are heavy, quite visible, and straight; no dot after the value inscription.

1866–75. Coat of arms in an octagon. Nos. 13 to 23. *Originals:* width, 20¹/₂ mm; height, 1/2-centavo and 1/2-real, 20¹/₄ mm; 1-centavo and 1-real, 20¹/₂ mm; 2-real, 20¹/₂–³/₄ mm. These are measurements of the outer frame about ²/₃ mm from the frame enclosing the design; the outer octagonal frame is entirely triple, but two of the lines, sometimes three of them, occasionally are merged on one or several sides into a thick line by printing press operation (use magnifying glass); the inner octagonal frame around the solid octagon is double. The first "U" of E. E. U. U. is just above the apex of the octagon, except in the 2-real stamp, where the apex is under the middle of the letter; the inscription, DIOS Y FEDERACION, is quite legible and its letters are about ³/₅ mm high in DIOS and ²/₃ mm in FEDERACION, with a space of about ¹/₅ mm above and under the letters.

Used postal forgeries. 1/2-real, two types: Type I, the horse has only one ear; its tail is ¹/₂ mm from the shield's edge; only the point of the horn of plenty on the left is visible and it is ¹/₂ mm from the circle. Type II, the horse has two ears; however, they are cut by the horizontal dividing line of the shield; the "L" of REAL has no serif on top. On the two types, there are double shade lines in the bottom of the shield. Cancellations are CARACAS or LA GUAIRA.

Forgeries: (a) early set with double (not triple) outer octagonal frame; the inner octagonal frame is double but very poorly executed (see illustration); the banderole bearing the inscription, DIOS Y FEDERACION, is almost rectangular instead of well curved; the "S" of LOS is touching the bottom of the "O"; the first "O" of CORREO evidently is too small; nine vertical shade lines in the upper left quartering of the shield instead of twelve, and nine horizontal shade lines below, which are thick and unparallel, instead of fourteen. (b) Geneva set, easily identifiable by the double (not triple) outer octagonal frame, by the single octagonal frame surrounding the solid octagon, and by the excessively short banderole carrying the inscription, DIOS I FFDERAOI (see illustration).

Original overprints: the overprint words are CONTRASENA with a tilde over the "N" and ESTAMPILLAS DE CORREO. They are repeated many times on the sheet and are found on two or three lines and in various positions.

Forged overprints: not very numerous; at times, inscription errors; comparison would be useful.

1880. Lithographed stamps. Perf 11¼. Nos. 24 to 28. *Originals:* thin, transparent paper and porous paper of various thicknesses; all around the stamp, about 1¼ mm from the outer frame, a dividing frame line is visible in a few places near the middle of the four sides (use magnifying glass).

Forgeries (so-called "reprints"): printed in sheets with tête-bêche stamps; hard, smooth paper; shades are too bright; color is spread evenly; the dividing frame line is present only in the corners, over a few millimeters; the frame and background shade lines were retouched or remade; they are too clear-cut.

1892. RESOLUCION overprints. Nos. 39 to 42.
Original overprints: the circle is 21½ mm in diameter; CENTIMOS measures 12 mm and UN BOLIVAR, 12½ mm. In the 25-centavo, the "C" of RESOLUCION almost is closed: there is an accent on the second "O"; only a comma between DE and I°; in the 1-bolivar, the "C" is as in the 25-centavo; no accent on the second "O."

Forged overprints: especially on the 5-centavo blue. There are serious errors, where comparison is indeed necessary.

1896. Miranda geographical map. Nos. 54 to 58.
Originals: perf 12; 5-centavo, 34½ x 24¾ mm; 10-centavo, 34¾ x 24½ mm; the other values, 35 x 24³⁄₅-⁴⁄₅ mm; the river which starts at the "N" of MIRANDA, flowing toward the Atlantic, is made of a heavy line on the right and on the left of several lines that almost always are visible; in the lateral frames, on the right and left of the three balls, there is cross-ruling whose vertical and horizontal lines can be seen; under "LA" of VENEZUELA, above ATLANTICO, there is a background of shade lines, the first of which is touching the color line under "A" in the corner; the second one is touching on top and on the right; the third one, in contrast, is touching neither top nor right. On the left, above the three balls, there is an ornament which has a small ball in its bottom section, then a branch ending in a concave ornament that is smaller than the ball.

Geneva forgeries: perf 11½; 34¹⁄₅-¼ x 24½ mm (width for the 50-centavo, 34³⁄₅ mm); the river is formed with two thick lines; in the inner right corner under "LA," the third shade line is touching the top right color line, except in the more successful 50-centavo; on the stamp's sides, on the right and left of the balls, there is a solid line without any trace of shading; on the left, above the three balls, the second branch ends in a ball that is larger than the one below it. All values were executed as tête-bêche stamps.

Forged Geneva cancellation: double circle (29 mm), CORREOS DE VENEZUELA 12 ENE 97 CARACAS.

1902. 1-bolivar gray without "1900" overprint. No. 76a. *Fakes* obtained by scraping off the "1900" overprint from the overprinted 1-bolivar gray of 1900.

Forgery created by using the 1-bolivar green of 1899–1902 (No. 63), whose green impression was bleached; the stamp then received a forged, excessively dark gray impression; comparison with a common stamp of the 1899 set will suffice; measurements are arbitrary; defects in inscription lettering, in the design, and in the shading. This fake frequently has a forged cancellation.

Postage-revenue stamps.

1879–80. 5-centavo, yellow. Nos. 15 and 23. *Used postal forgeries:* sixty-three pearls instead of sixty-eight; the vertical downstroke of the "L" of ESCUELAS is slanted to the left.

1903. INSTRUCCION vignettes. Nos. 93 to 98.
Originals: as overprint, they have a violet postmark with the coat of arms of Venezuela and inscription.

St. Thomas–Puerto Cabello–La Guaira. See St. Thomas, La Guaira, and Puerto Cabello.

Victoria

Reprints. A rather large number of stamps were reprinted in 1891 on paper watermarked with a crown surmounted by a "V," the watermark in use in that period; white gum or yellowish white gum; perf 12 or 12½; the word REPRINT, in red or black, is found most often printed as an overprint. See the reprinted values and the exceptions to the above procedure in each issue.

1850. Lithographed stamps. Nos. 1 to 3. *Originals:* 1-penny, background of fine curved shade lines producing a moiré effect; the moiré reappears in the two sides (frames); letter "E" is placed bottom left and "W" is on the right. 2-pence, background of crossed shade lines in strips of three; letters "T" and "H" in the lower corners. 3-pence, background like 2-pence, but the strips of shade lines are formed more often with four lines than with three; letter "E" in the lower left corner; an ornament in the right corner.

Reprints: perf 12½. 1-penny vermilion, Plate II, with dividing frame lines between the stamps; 2-pence brown, Plate IV, with lines between the stamps and cliché cancellation lines in the center of the stamp; 3-pence dark blue, Plate III, with lines between the stamps.

Early forgeries: lithographed. 1-penny, background copied from the 2-pence (groups of three shade lines); in the lower squares, there is a blank cross on a solid background; 2-pence, two types easily identifiable by the blank crosses in the lower corners; the second type is copied from the forged 3-pence; one still can see the top of the letters of the inscription, THREEPENCE, above the lower tablet; 3-pence, background copied from the 2-pence original; in the lower corners, a blank cross with center dot.

1852–54. 2-pence, engraved or lithographed. Nos. 4 and 5. *Originals:* the background is formed by groups of twelve or sixteen dots separated by dotted lines. The lithographed stamps were taken from transferrals of the engraved stamps, with various errors in lettering. See the specialty catalogues.

Reprints: engraved; 2-pence brown; fifty types as in the original sheets; perf 12, 11½.

Forgeries: lithographed; no trace of the throne appears under the skirt on the left. Type (a) a copy of the sixteenth stamp of the sheet (letters "Q" and "V"); no scepter. Type (b) a copy of the eighteenth stamp (letters "S" and "W"); background made of heavy-line lozenges with a color spot in the middle.

1854–60. Rectangular or octagonal stamps. Nos. 6 to 8. *Fakes* of the imperforate stamp, especially 6-pence, in various roulettings. Comparison is mandatory.

Reprint: 1-shilling pale blue, perf 12–12½.

1856–58. Star watermark. Nos. 13 and 14. *Reprints:* 1-penny pale yellow-green, and 6-pence dark blue, perf 12, 12½, and imperforate.

1861. Same watermark. Nos. 15, 18, 21, 23, and 26. *Reprints* of the 1-penny in bright yellow-green.

1861–66. No watermark or watermark in letters. Nos. 29 to 30, 32, 33, and 34. *Reprints* of the 3-pence in dull blue; 4-pence rose and 6-pence black.

Forgery of the 6-pence, No. 33; very bad; imperforate and without watermark; pale yellow shade.

Geneva forgeries: 3-pence, Nos. 29, 30, and 31; perf 11½, no watermark; the "T" of VICTORIA, the "G" of POSTAGE, and most of the letters of the value are touching the tablet; the two "E" letters of THREE are executed very unsuccessfully.

1864–73. Various types. Nos. 51 to 67. *Reprints:* all values (no overprints); the 5-shilling in carmine and ultramarine.

Originals of the 5-shilling blue on yellow and blue and carmine on yellowish white paper, Nos. 63 and 64. Typographed. Regular lettering, a little less high than the blank circle; details of the design and especially of the crown are quite visible, except, of course, when there was plate clogging; the top of the crown has a rectangular-shaped jewel with two crossed diagonal lines.

Forgeries: lithographed; no watermark; executed in the shades of Nos. 63 and 64. (a) Dot rouletted or perf

12; amateurish execution, details of the crown are not very visible (bandeau); a single globe on top; the laurel crown and the hair almost are indistinguishable.
(b) Imperforate or finely chiseled perf 12; the two curls shaped like kidneys on the left of the crown are connected by two short lines which form an acute angle, as on the right; and the curl down below, under the "H" of SHILLINGS, is inverted and has only a small vertical white line inside.

1873–81. Tinted paper. Chemical *fakes* of the ½-, 1-penny, and 2-pence, Nos. 70, 71, and 72 on papers of various color shades. The tinting usually is spread unevenly, with lighter spots in places, or else it is uniform but arbitrary; in the latter case, only comparison can reveal it.

1874–79. Various types. Nos. 70 to 75. *Reprints:* 1-penny in yellow-green; 2-pence in mauve; the others in approximate shades — which should be compared.

Geneva forgeries: 2-shilling, 20¾ x 24¼ mm (nearly 1 mm too large); the figures are upright and vertical terminal line at bottom; the bottom right figure is the only one that is slanted; the first pearl in the crown is touching the oval.

1881–84. Various types. Nos. 76 to 82. *Reprints* of the 2-pence brown; 4-pence dull rose and 2-shilling blue on yellow-green (No. 75).

1884–86. Various types. Nos. 83 to 93. *Reprints:* ½-penny bright rose; 1-penny yellow-green; 2-pence bluish lilac; 4-pence bright lilac; 6-pence ultramarine; 1-shilling dull blue on yellow.

Geneva forgeries: 2-pence, No. 85. The background horizontal shade lines do not end in a perfect curve; the forehead, the nose, and the front of the neck display an excessively extensive blank spot.

Forged cancellation: six-lined oval with the word VICTORIA in the middle (the "I" is too small and the following "C" is slanted to the right).

Postage-revenue stamps. Very numerous *fakes* obtained by removal of fiscal cancels and their replacement by forged ones.

Virgin Islands

1866. Lithographed stamps. Nos. 1 to 4. *Originals:* 1-penny, 18⅔ x 21¾ mm; the background shade lines are regular and are spaced ⅙ mm apart; the final "S" of ISLANDS is 1 mm from the end of the tablet; the value tablet is 1¾ mm high; thick (90–130 microns); white paper. 2-pence, 18½ x 21¾ mm; the curved shade lines of the background are regular and are spaced ⅙ mm apart; thirteen horizontal lines in the upper tablet and fourteen in the bottom one, counting those that almost touch the edges; the "S" of SIX is only 1 mm wide; the circle on the head is thin and does not touch the frame.

Geneva forgeries: lithographed, poorly executed; 1-penny, 18²/₃ x 21³/₄ mm and 19 x 21¹/₂ mm; the center background shade lines are spaced ¹/₄ mm apart; the final "S" of ISLANDS is ³/₅ mm from the end of the tablet and the value tablet is 1¹/₂ mm high. Thin or thick paper; imperforate or perforated irregularly; dividing frame line. 2-pence, the curved shade lines of the background are spaced ¹/₅ mm apart and are too finely drawn — which makes this background as deficient in coloring as the tablet; the top tablet had eleven horizontal lines; the lower one, thirteen; the "S" of SIX is 1¹/₂ mm wide; the circle on the head is about ¹/₂ mm thick and is touching the frame. About 18³/₄ mm by 22 mm; thin paper; imperforate, perforated, or rouletted; dividing frame line.

1867. Lithographed stamps. Perf 15. Nos. 5 to 7.
Originals: paper of various thicknesses; 4-pence, 20¹/₂ x 27 mm. 127 pearls. The front of the neck is blank and the right sleeve (stamp's left), starting with the hand, has no contact with the garment. At 50 cm distance, the small *blank circles* surrounding the inscriptions scarcely can be seen; the background of the inner corners is made of rosettes with a white dot in the middle; the lower right corner square is about 3 mm wide. 1-shilling (white border), 21 x 27¹/₂ mm, frame included, and 1-shilling (red border), 21 x 27 mm, measuring up to the red border. The "V" of VIRGIN is ³/₄ mm from the tablet's edge; the "I" of ISLANDS is slanted to the left, and the bottom of the "S" is 1 mm from the tablet's edge; the two "G" letters of the inscription are alike; the bar of the "A" is set low; in the background, under the upper inscription, there are thirty-six lines made of blank rectangles (³/₄ mm long) with a line and white dots inside. All around the Virgin, except when she is no longer centered, you see oblique white rays.

Geneva forgeries: lithographed. 4-pence, allowable measurements; eighty-two pearls; dividing frame line; imperforate or perforated irregularly; the front of the neck has a color spot that extends up to the mouth; the right sleeve is touching the garment under the right forearm; the large white dots surrounding the inscriptions are quite visible; the background of the inner corners consists of squares with a blank *circle* in the middle; the lower right corner square is 3¹/₂ mm wide. 1-shilling, with white border, 21 x 27³/₄ mm, or red, 21 x 26¹/₂ mm. The "I" of ISLANDS you might as well say vertical; the "S" is ¹/₂ mm from the end of the tablet; the horizontal bar of "A" is set near the middle of the letter; thirty lines of blank rectangles — they often look like ovals — which are ¹/₂–³/₄ mm long with a line inside; no rays around the Virgin; the "G" letters

are different; that of SHILLING is wider, thicker; imperforate, rouletted, or perf 12¹/₂; thin paper.

Forged cancellation: usually a square with more or less large, square or round dots.

1879. Watermarked "C C" crown. No. 8. *Forgery:* no watermark; see forgeries of the 1-penny, first issue.

Western Australia

1854–89. Rectangular type. POSTAGE at top.
Originals: the various values are reproduced with the 1-penny black, 1854, as model. Watermarked with swan, "C C," or "C A" crown; various perforations; see the catalogues. The originals are recess print engraved; the background cross-hatching is made of white crisscrossing curved lines; the base elements of the "W" of WESTERN are not pointed. See the illustration for the corner ornamental design, the cross-hatching (bottom left inner corner), and the swan's base. In the ONE PENNY, the "O" is noticeably closer to the ornamental square than to the right branch of the "Y," and in the 2- and 6-pence, the lower bar of the second "E" of PENCE is longer than the upper bar.

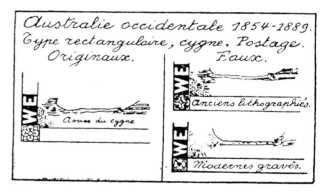

Western Australia, 1854–89. Rectangular type, swan, POSTAGE. Originals. Swan's base on water. Forgeries. Early lithographed. Modern engraved.

Forgeries: several lithographed sets. In the most widely circulated of these (Geneva), the two bottom elements of the "W" of WESTERN are pointed (see the illustration); the whole design is arbitrary; the ornamental squares are hardly larger than the height of the inscription tablets; the lettering design is blurred; no watermark. In the 1-penny, the "O" of ONE is as far from the square as the right branch of the "Y" of PENNY; in the 2- and 6-pence, the upper and lower bars of the second "E" of PENCE are equal in length. The 2-pence forgery received the forged green overprint ONE PENNY in Geneva and elsewhere. Triple circle forged cancellation with center dot, 24 mm, outer diameter.

In another set, the lower branch of the "G" of POSTAGE does not go beyond the upper branch on the right; no swan foot is visible; the forged design easily can be judged by a novice; no watermark.

In a second lithographed Geneva model (especially the 1-penny and 4-pence), the burelage surrounding the swan is a little better, but the ornamental square design is shapeless; the "S" of POSTAGE is slanted to the left; the "E" of PENNY is too high. No watermark.

An *engraved set,* with forged handstamp-applied watermark, is hardly more deceptive despite the forger's effort and good intentions; the swan is more elegant than the one in the original engraving. The cross-hatching can create an optical illusion at a distance of 50 cm, but, seen through a magnifying glass, there is nothing good about it; the ornamental squares are no larger than the height of the tablets and their design is fantastic (see the illustration). The *forged cancellation* is a copy of the usual cancellation with figure "1."

1854–57. Octagonal type. 4-pence. No. 3. This value was counterfeited fairly well lithographically either without watermark or with forged watermark in yellow on the back of the stamp and as invisible in benzine as if there were not any. The 2-pence was counterfeited in the same type, in brown on buff; the background stippling is formed by short uniform lines.

1857. Octagonal type with white background. 2- and 6-pence. Nos. 2 and 4. In the *original* of the 6-pence, which is lithographed, there are traces of a white line under the upper inscription. There is a watermark.

Forgeries: (1) no trace of the white line; no watermark; the swan is placed too far to the left. (2) No watermark; outer frame almost is touching the stamp's edges; there are curved hatch lines representing water. (3) Rather well-executed photolithographed set in silver gray and golden bronze; forged watermark printed on back in yellow; swan with duck beak; the top and bottom of the "S" of SIX are horizontal; the upper and lower bars of the second "E" of PENCE are $1\frac{1}{2}$ mm long instead of about 1 mm; the swan's tail is pointed toward the top of the water lily instead of above it.

1854. Oval type. 1-shilling. No. 5. Lithographed *forgeries* in brown and reddish chocolate; no watermark or with forged watermark. Inscription lettering is too heavy, especially the "W"; the "G" of POSTAGE and of SHILLING is too bold (in the originals it rather resembles a "C").

There are no *reprints* of the values previously described. Only the "Half-penny" on 3-pence brown of 1893–95 with double red and green overprint was reprinted on paper watermarked "C A."

1884–85. "$\frac{1}{2}$" overprint. Nos. 37 and 38. *Forged overprint* on canceled original stamps or on Geneva forgeries. Comparison is necessary.

Yugoslavia

There is an abundance of forged overprints of this modern stamp-issuing entity. Total abstention is advised or thorough specialization with minute comparison of everything that is overprinted, especially Nos. 1–26, 85–108, 145–49, as well as newspaper (Nos. 3 and 4) and postage due stamps.

Forgeries (1918) Nos. 31 to 34. Comparison of the hatching of the kneeling person's light ray lines will suffice. These stamps are found rouletted more often than perforated. In the 45-heller, the "5" figures are too large and too "square."

1920. Nos. 85 and 86. Clandestine printing forgeries, with noncongruent shades, format, and paper.

Carinthia

Despite the fact that the two overprinted issues are not very interesting, all overprints must be compared, especially those of Nos. 20–25, which are different for each stamp value: there were many printings of counterfeits.

Zambezia

1902. REIS overprints. Nos. 29 to 41. A few *forged overprints* on the $2\frac{1}{2}$- to 25-reis of 1894. Comparison would be useful.

Zanzibar

1896–97. ZANZIBAR or value overprint, Nos. 1 to 26 and 42. Numerous forged *overprints*; specializing is recommended and detailed comparison is indispensable (Geneva, for the ZANZIBAR overprint). The forged Geneva cancellation is one circle (19 mm) with three outside lines forming corners of a square, with date: ZANZIBAR M A. 17 96.

Zanzibar (French post office). For stamps emanating from this bureau, specializing is not only recommended, it is really indispensable, because of the numerous types in the 1894 and 1897 issues and the very numerous *forged overprints* in circulation; a good many of the latter are deceptive enough to fool people. The works of de Vinck (*Colonies françaises et bureaux* *à l'étranger,* 1928, pp. 32–44) and of de Reuterskiold (*Les Timbres du bureau français de Zanzibar* [Lausanne, Imp. Marchino, 1925, 28 pages]) should be consulted.

1894–95. Stamps overprinted in ANNAS. Nos. 1 to 11. *Forged overprints* from various sources. Most of these are spotted easily by template measurement. The 50-anna was counterfeited on a forged stamp in which the inscribed names of Sage and Mouchon are too small (comparison would be useful); allowable height; width, $17^3/_4$ mm instead of about 18 mm; the ANNAS overprint is 10 mm wide instead of about $10^1/_2$ mm.

1894. ZANZIBAR and value overprints. Nos. 12 to 16. *Forged overprints:* very numerous; detailed comparison is indispensable.

1896–1900. Value and ZANZIBAR overprints. Nos. 17 to 31. Same observation; there are forged Geneva overprints.

1897. Typographical overprints of the value. Nos. 12 to 36. Same observation.

1902–3. Overprinted Blanc, Mouchon, and Merson types. Nos. 47 to 57. *Forged overprints:* same observation. Forgeries of the Merson type, Nos. 55–57, see French Colonies.

1904. Various overprinted stamps. (and)

Postage due stamps. Various *forged overprints* on original stamps (comparison is indispensable) and on forged postage due stamps: see French Colonies.

Zululand

1888. Stamps of Great Britain with ZULULAND overprint, and Natal stamps with the same overprint (Type II). The *original overprint* on the stamps of Great Britain measures $15^3/_4$ x $2^3/_4$ mm.

Numerous *forged overprints,* especially the two Geneva types. Comparison is indispensable.

1894–96. Watermarked "C A" crown. Nos. 14 to 23. *Fakes* obtained by removing the impression of the

1-penny lilac and carmine and of the 1-shilling green, followed by impression of the 4-shilling green and carmine, No. 21. Comparison of facial features will expose the fake. *Forged cancellation.*

Postage-revenues. *Forged overprints:* comparison is necessary.

Fakes made by removal of fiscal cancel and its replacement by a forged one.

Useful References to the Detection of Forged Stamps

by Varro E. Tyler

The listing that follows is as complete as the author, a longtime collector of forgeries and literature pertaining to them, could make it; without question, there are many omissions. In addition to the inadvertent ones, articles that failed to convey significant, useful information were purposely omitted. Some of the titles are referred to with considerable frequency. In these cases, the reference has been designated as a comprehensive one (comp. ref.) and referred to simply by number. The complete citation is listed following these brief comments prior to the individual country references. The same is true for certain references of British North America (BNA refs.), Espionage and Propaganda (E. & P. refs.), Germany (Germany refs.), Russia (Russia refs.), and Spain (Spain refs.). Aside from these, the designations of books and periodicals are given in full each time they appear to avoid possible confusion. Following the periodical title, the volume number appears in boldface, then, if necessary, the issue number in

parentheses, followed by the inclusive pagination, and then the year in parentheses. Two general sections, "Forgers and Their Works" and "Forgery and Fakery (General Considerations)," are listed alphabetically among the countries.

In general, the work is not annotated, but a few comments are included in those cases where clarification was deemed desirable. All citations given are of value, but especially useful ones are designated with an asterisk. References covering a significant number of issues are designated "Broad Coverage." The listings under a single country heading are chronological beginning with the oldest issue and continuing to the most recent. Regular issues, commemoratives, semipostals, airmails, etc., are grouped together. Stamps of the various Offices and States, comprehensive listings of cancellations, unofficial items, and the like generally follow the basic listing.

COMPREHENSIVE REFERENCES (comp. refs.)

1. Aretz, F., *Know Your Stamps*, Marks Stamp Company Limited, Toronto, Canada, 1941, 102 pp.
2. *The Work of Jean de Sperati*, 2nd ed., Part 1, *The Text*, and Part 2, *Plates*, British Philatelic Association, London, 1956, 214 pp. and 143 plates plus plates A–J.
3. Bynof-Smith, H., *Forged Postage Stamps of:*
3A. *Africa and Asia (Excluding Colonies of European Countries)*, 1992, 145 pp.;
3B. *the Americas (Excluding British Empire)*, 1991, 206 pp.;
3C. *the British Empire*, 1990, 193 pp.;
3D1. *Europe and Colonies — Albania to Greece*, 1993, 230 pp.;
3D2. *Europe and Colonies — Hungary to Ukraine*, 1993, 213 pp.;
All volumes published by the author, Sydney, Australia.
4. Chemi, J.M., J.H. Beal, and J.T. De Voss, eds., *The Yucatan Affair: The Work of Raoul Ch. de Thuin, Philatelic Counterfeiter*, American Philatelic Society, State College, Pennsylvania, 1974, 523 pp.
5. Fletcher, H.G.L., *Postal Forgeries of the World*, Harry Hayes, Batley, West Yorkshire, England, 1977, 140 pp.
6. Johnson, A.C., *Forgeries Old and New:*
6 I. Part I, 1941, 47 pp;
6 II. Part II, 1945, 47 pp;
Both volumes published by Marks Stamp Company Limited, Toronto, Canada.
7. *Schach den Fälschungen:*
vol. 1. 1935, pp. 1–48;
vol. 2. 1935, pp. 49–96;
vol. 3. 1935, pp. 97–144;
vol. 4. 1935–36, pp. 145–92;
vol. 5. 1938, 31 pp.
All volumes published in German by Kurt Kayssner-Verlag, Bad Buckow, Germany.

Although authorship is not claimed, some or all of the volumes were apparently written by Dr. Arthur Schroeder.
8. Newall, A.S., *Airmail Stamps: Fakes & Forgeries*, Newall Consultants Ltd., no address given, 1990, 309 pp.
9. Ragatz, L., *The Fournier Album of Philatelic Forgeries: A Photographic Composite for Reference Purposes*, Janet van den Berg, Worthington, Ohio, 1970, 175 pp.
10. Schloss, H., *Distinguishing Characteristics of Classic Stamps: Europe 19th Century (Except Old German States)*, H.L. Lindquist Publications, New York, 1951, 200 pp.
11. Spying Eye [Reeves, B.], *Handbook of Philatelic Forgeries*, Maplewood Press, Chicago, 1948, 48 pp.
12. Stiedl, O.E., and F. Billig, *Grosses Handbuch der Fälschungen*, 44 parts, in German, Fritz Billig, Vienna, 1933–38, unpaged.
13. Tyler, V.E., *Focus on Forgeries: A Guide to Forgeries of Common Stamps*, Linn's Stamp News, Sidney, Ohio, 1993, 158 pp.

BRITISH NORTH AMERICA REFERENCES (BNA refs.)

1. Pugh, K.W., *Reference Manual of BNA Fakes, Forgeries & Counterfeits*, 3 vols. (11 releases), looseleaf, published by the author, Brandon, Manitoba, Canada, 1977–81, unpaged.
2. Smythies, E.A., *B.N.A. Fakes and Forgeries*, British North America Philatelic Society, Raleigh, North Carolina, no date, 104 pp.

ESPIONAGE AND PROPAGANDA REFERENCES (E. & P. refs.)

1. Williams, L.N., and M. Williams, *Forged Stamps of Two World Wars: The Postal*

Forgeries and Propaganda Issues of the Belligerents 1914–1918, 1939–1945, published by the authors, London, 1954, 52 pp.
2. Friedman, H., Propaganda Forgeries of World War II, *Linn's Weekly Stamp News:*
A. "Anti-Ley" Postcard, May 24, 1965, p. 32;
B. English "Hitler Heads," Sept. 20, 1965, p. 25;
C. American "Hitler Heads," Jan. 10, 1966, pp. 21, 39;
D. "Himmler" Parody, Jan. 17, 1966, p. 31;
E. "Witzleben" Parody, March 7, 1966, p. 49;
F. British-made Italian Parodies, April 4, 1966, p. 35;
G. Parodies of WWII French Stamps, April 11, 1966, pp. 16, 17;
H. German "D-Day" Sheet, June 6, 1966;
I. American "Death Head" Parody, July 11, 1966;
J. "Free French" Parody, Aug. 22, 1966, pp. 28–29, 34;
K. Nazi War Criminal Hans Frank, Oct. 10, 1966, pp. 42–43, 47;
L. British Government Forgeries of French Stamps, Nov. 14, 1966, pp. 104–5, 109.

GERMANY REFERENCES (Germany ref.)

1. Bohne, W.M., *Reference Manual of Forgeries*, 14 vols. in progress (42 releases to date), looseleaf, German Philatelic Society, Arnold, Maryland, 1975–98, unpaged.
2. Schloss, H., *Distinguishing Characteristics of Classic Stamps: Old German States*, H.L. Lindquist Publications, New York, 1948, 108 pp.
3. Gilgis, J.R., ed., *Old German States' Notes*, vols. 1–4(2) quarterly periodical, Fayville, Massachusetts, 1992–95.

RUSSIA REFERENCES (Russia refs.)

1. Ceresa, R.J., *The Postage Stamps of Russia, 1917-1923:*
1A.-vol.1, *Armenia,* 13 parts, 1978-1984;
1B.-vol.2, *Ukraine,* 26 parts, 1979-1988;
1C.-vol.3, *The Armies,* 24 parts, 1981-1991;
1D.-vol.4, *Transcaucasia,* 16 parts, 1992-1994.
1E.-vol. 5, *R.S.F.S.R.*, 12 parts, 1996-97.
All volumes published by the author, Ross-on-Wye, England; varying numbers of parts are bound together and paginated as a unit.

SPAIN REFERENCES (Spain refs.)

1. Graus, F., *Manual de Consulta de Falsos de España,* 7 vols. (14 releases), in Spanish, looseleaf, Graus, Barcelona, 1981-85, unpaged.
2. Graus, F., *Guia-Catálogo de Falsos Postales: España-Cuba Filipinas,* in Spanish, Graus, Barcelona, 1986, 233 pp.

AFGHANISTAN

Modern Issues: Patterson, Frank E., III, *Afghanistan: Its Twentieth Century Postal Issues,* The Collector's Club, New York, 1964, 208 pp.
1931-38 2p. Newspaper Stamps: Tyler, V.E., *Linn's Stamp News,* June 13, 1994, p. 6.
1932 National Council Commemoratives (Reprints): Tyler, V.E., *Linn's Stamp News,* December 26, 1994, p. 6.
1939 First Airmails: Newall, comp. ref. 7, pp. 2-3; Tyler, V.E., *Linn's Stamp News,* November 14, 1994, p. 6.

ALBANIA

1913 Eagle Overprints: Eckhardt, W.J., *The American Philatelist* 62:613-20 (1949).
1917-18 Double Eagles: Tyler, comp. ref. 13, p. 1; *Kremzar, M., *The American Philatelist* 111:1104-8 (1997).
1929 Airmail Overprints: Newall, comp. ref. 8, pp. 4-5.
1946 Women's Congress: Tyler, comp. ref. 13, p. 2.

ALSACE AND LORRAINE

1870 Numerals: *Stiedl-Billig, comp. ref. 12, Elsass-Lothringen; Schloss, Germany ref. 2.

ANDORRA — FRENCH ADMINISTRATION

1931 Overprints: Bennett, W.H. *S.P.A. Journal* 40:17-20 (1978); Jacques, W.A., *Andorra-Andorre,* Robson Lowe, London, 1974, 68 pp. plus 32 pp. suppl.

ANDORRA — SPANISH ADMINISTRATION

1928-42 Broad Coverage: Jacques, W.A., *Andorra-Andorre,* Robson Lowe, London, 1974, 68 pp. plus 32 pp. suppl.
1928-35 Overprints and First Designs: Fink, E. *The American Philatelist* 106:35 (1992).

1932 "Semi-Official" Airmails: Romo, C., *The American Philatelist* 97:1079-84 (1983).

ARGENTINA

1858 First Issue: Kimble, R.A., *The American Philatelist* 55:287-91 (1942).
1858 5c. First Issue: Tyler, V.E., *Linn's Stamp News,* November 29, 1993, p. 6.
1862-77 Various: Bynof-Smith, comp. ref. 2B, pp. 12-17.
1892 Discovery of America: Tyler, comp. ref. 13, p. 3.
1888-1910 Forged Proofs: Brazer, C.W., *Essay Proof Journal* No. 37:13 (1953).
1917-46 Selected Postal Forgeries: Batousek, A., *The American Philatelist* 94:526-27 (1980).
1917-22 5c. San Martin: Fletcher, comp. ref. 5, p. 11.

ARGENTINA — CORRIENTES

Broad Coverage: *Stich, L., *Corrientes: The Issues from 1856-80,* The Collectors Club, New York, 1957, 88 pp.

ARMENIA

Broad Coverage: *Ceresa, Russia ref. 1A.
1920 Eagle Pictorials (unissued): Tyler, comp. ref. 13, p. 4.
1922 and 1923 Pictorials: Barefoot, J., and A. Hall, *Forgery & Reprint Guide,* nos. 3 and 4, J. Barefoot (Investments), York, England, 1983, 20 and 12 pp.
1922 50r. Unissued Erevan Pictorial: Tyler, V.E., *Linn's Stamp News,* December 13, 1993, p. 8.
1922 300r. Unissued Erevan Pictorial: Tyler, V.E., *Linn's Stamp News,* March 6, 1995, p. 6.

AUSTRALIA

1932 2p. King George V: Fletcher, comp. ref. 5, pp. 14-15; Belknap, T.L., *S.P.A. Journal* 30:257-59 (1967).
1932 2p. Sydney Harbor Bridge: Fletcher, comp. ref. 5, pp. 12-13; *Walters, D.K., *Philately from Australia* 1:69-76; 109-15 (1949); *London Philatelist* 66:201-6 (1947); Anon., *West End Philatelist* 37:50, 142 (1947); Belknap, T.L., *S.P.A. Journal* 30:257-59 (1967).
1987 January 28 36c. America's Cup Color Error: Boyd, A., *Linn's Stamp News,* May 18, 1987, p. 10.
(Military Stamps)
1946-47 Military Overprints: Silvester, A.P., *The American Philatelist* 64:33-37 (1950).
(Unofficial Airmails)
1919 Ross Smith Stamp: Eustis, N., *The Ross Smith Air Stamp,* The Hawthorn Press, Melbourne, 1979, pp. 26-27.
(Australian States — Various)
Classic Issues, Selected Coverage of Forgeries and Fakes: Wynn, H., *The American Philatelist* 106:1008-20 (1992).

AUSTRIA

1850-1916 Various: Bynof-Smith, comp. ref. 3D, vol. 1, pp. 16-23.

1850 First Issue Types: Theimer, E., *The American Philatelist* 97:135-44 (1983).
1867-80 10k. Franz Joseph Stamp: Brownell, K.W., *The American Philatelist* 94:511 (1980); Theimer, E.T., *The American Philatelist* 95:432-33 (1981).
1916-19 Espionage & Propaganda Issues: Williams, E. & P. ref. 1, pp. 9-11.
1945 Overprints for Styria: Weihs, K., and E. Lewey, *Philatelic Magazine* 62:515 (1954).

AUSTRIA — DANUBE STEAM NAVIGATION CO.

Broad Coverage: *Hurt, E.F., and D.N. Kelly, *The Danube Steam Navigation Company,* American Philatelic Society, State College, Pennsylvania, 1950, 64 pp.; Barefoot, J., *Forgery & Reprint Guide,* nos. 7-8, J. Barefoot (Investments), York, England, 1983, 32 pp.

AZERBAIJAN

Broad Coverage: Hall, A., *Forgery & Reprint Guide,* no. 11, J. Barefoot (Investments), York, England, 1983, 24 pp.; *Ceresa, Russia ref. 1D, parts 1-5.
1917 Occupation Overprints on Russia Arms Types: Ashford, P.T., *British Journal of Russian Philately,* No. 11:341-48 (1953).
1919 First Issue: Tyler, V.E., *The American Philatelist* 97:60-61 (1983).
1921 Semipostals: Tyler, V.E., *The American Philatelist* 98:695 (1984).
1922 Second Issue: Ayer, M.A., *The American Philatelist* 91:541-42 (1977).
1922 150r. Blacksmiths: Tyler, V.E., *Linn's Stamp News,* December 27, 1993, p. 6.
1923 500r. Phantom Issue: Tyler, V.E., *Linn's Stamp News,* April 18, 1994, p. 6.

AZORES

1912-31 Ceres Overprints: Tyler, comp. ref. 13, p. 9.

BADEN

1851-68 Broad Coverage: *Bohne, Germany ref. 1; Schloss, Germany ref. 2, pp. 6-11; *Stiedl-Billig, comp. ref. 12, Baden.
1862-65 Regular Issue: Vervisch, R., *Balasse Magazine* No. 265: 284-85 (1982), in French.
1862-65 Fournier Forgeries: Gilgis, Germany ref. 3, vol. 1-1, pp. 3-4; Ragatz, comp. ref. 9, p. 11.
1862 Land-Post: *Gilgis, Germany ref. 3, vol. 3-3, pp. 25-36; Tyler, V.E., *Linn's Stamp News,* May 29, 1995, p. 6.

BANGLADESH

1971 Pre- and Post-Liberation Issues: Alam, K.S., and C.W. Drake, *The American Philatelist* 88:861-66 (1974).

BATUM

Broad Coverage: Ceresa, Russia ref. 1D; *Hughes, W.E., *The Postage Stamps of Batum,* published by the author, Edgware, England, 1835, 44 pp.

1919 First Issue: Spying Eye, comp. ref. 11, pp. 2–3; Tyler, V.E., *Linn's Stamp News,* September 6, 1993, p. 6; September 20, 1993, p. 6.

BAVARIA

Broad Coverage: *Bohne, Germany ref. 1; Schloss, Germany ref. 2, pp. 12–16; *Stiedl-Billig, comp. ref. 12, Bayern.

1865 Dead Letter Seals: Gilgis, Germany ref. 3, vol. 2-2, pp. 1–5.

BELGIAN CONGO

1886–1908 Broad Coverage: *Stiedl-Billig, comp. ref. 12, Belgisch-Kongo.

1886 5c. First Issue: Deneumostier, E., *E.I.C. — Les 5 Centimes de 1886,* Group d'Étude des Falsifications, Belgium, no date (ca. 1990) 16 pp., in French.

1886 10c., 25c., and 50c.: Deneumostier, E., *E.I.C. — Les 10–25 & 50Cs de 1886,* 1990, 23 pp., in French.

1886 5f.: Vervisch, R.: *Éléments d'Expertise des 5F Belge de 1878 et Congolais de 1886,* Editions de la Revue Postale, J. Henin, Farciennes, Belgium, 1978, 26 pp., in French; Vervisch, R., *Balasse Magazine* No. 258: 231–34 (1981), in French.

1887–94 10f. Regular Issue: Vervisch, R., *Balasse Magazine* No. 263: 182 (1982), in French.

BELGIUM

1849–1946 Broad Coverage: *Slagmeulder, M.G., *Les Timbres Faux de Belgique,* Editions Héraly, Charleroi, Belgium, no date, 157 pp., in French.

1849–1928 Broad Coverage: *Stiedl-Billig, comp. ref. 12, Belgien.

1865–66 1f. Regular Issue: Vervisch, R., *Balasse Magazine* No. 283: 276–77 (1985), in French.

1866–67 1c. Regular Issue: Vervisch, R., *Balasse Magazine* No. 284: 46–47; No. 285:104–5 (1986), in French.

1866–67 5c. Regular Issue: Vervisch, R., *Balasse Magazine* No. 264: 231–34 (1982), in French.

1875–78 5f. Leopold: Vervisch, R., *Balasse Magazine* No. 273: 92–93 (1984), in French.

1882–94 Parcel Post Issue: Tyler, comp. ref. 13, p. 11.

1893–1900 and 1905–7 2f. Stamps: Vervisch, R., *Balasse Magazine* No. 256: 144–45 (1981), in French.

1912 5f. King Albert I: Rompay, R. van, and R. Vervisch, *Belgique Émission de 1912 le 5 F. Lie de Vin,* Groupe d'Étude des Falsifications, Brussels, no date, 8 pp., in French.

1914 Red Cross Small Albert Heads: Dobes, H., *The Forgeries of the Red Cross Small Albert Heads of 1914,* published by the author, Carmel, California, 1989, not paged (12 pp.).

1914 Semi-Postals: *Vervisch, R., ed., *Belgique L'émission Croix-Rouge de 1914,* Groupe d'Étude des Falsifications, Brussels, 1990, 55 pp., in French.

1926–27 5 & 10f. Regular Issue: Deneumostier, E., *Les 5 & 10 F "Houyoux",* Phila Club Flemalle, Belgium, no date, 34 pp., in French.

1928–31 Newspaper Overprints: Vervisch, R., *Balasse Magazine* No. 255:89–90 (1981), in French.

1939 Precancels: Vervisch, R., *Balasse Magazine* No. 274: 142–43; (1984), in French.

BERGEDORF

1861–67 Broad Coverage: *Willing, R.S., *German Postal Specialist* 27:167–76, 251–59, 332–41, 368–77, 451–59 (1976); 28:13–17, 51–55 (1977); Gilgis, J.R., *Old German States Notes* 3:13–24 (1994); Stiedl-Billig, comp. ref. 12, Bergedorf; Gilgis, Germany ref. 3, vol. 3-2, pp. 13–24.

BERMUDA

1940 December 20 Halfpenny Provisional: Halward, P., *West-End Philatelist* 49:53–54 (1959).

BOLIVIA

1863–1937 Broad Coverage: Porter, H.S., *West-End Philatelist* 38:35–36 (1948).

1868–69 Regular Issue: Bynof-Smith, comp. ref. 2B, pp. 18–19; Tyler, V.E., *Linn's Stamp News,* May 2, 1994, p. 6.

1894 Regular Issue: *Dromberg, D.A., *London Philatelist* 72:202–7 (1963) and 73:9–12 (1964); *Gordon, D.L., *London Philatelist* 73:187–88 (1964).

1897 2b. Coat of Arms: Tyler, V.E., *The American Philatelist* 100:351–52 (1986).

1899 E.F. Overprints: Salinas de Lozada, J., *Pan American Philatelist* 3:99–102 (1957).

1930s Unissued Series: Bynof-Smith, comp. ref. 2B, pp. 20–21.

1939 Eucharistic Cong. Airmails: Bonilla Lara, A. *Chile Filatelico* 15:13–16 (1972), in Spanish; Newall, comp. ref. 8, pp. 9–10.

BOSNIA & HERZEGOVINA

1900 Arms Issue: Tyler, comp. ref. 13, pp. 12–13.

1912 Pictorials: Spying Eye, *S.P.A. Journal* 8:669–70 (1946); Tyler, V.E., *Linn's Stamp News,* February 7, p. 6; February 21, p. 6; March 7, p. 6 (1994).

1913 Newspaper Stamps: Spying Eye, *S.P.A. Journal* 8:66 (1945); Tyler, V.E., *Linn's Stamp News,* January 10, 1994, p. 6.

BRAZIL

1843 Bull's Eyes: *Rose, S., *Bull's Eyes* 18(2):11–25 (1987); Kigar, P.D., *Philatelic Magazine* 80:509, 511 (1972).

1844–46 Snake's Eyes: Emerson, J.F., *The American Philatelist* 52:623–27 (1939).

1850 Goat's Eyes: Bynof-Smith, comp. ref. 2B, pp. 28–31.

1861 Cat's Eyes: *Rose, S., *Bull's Eyes* 19(1):10–19 (1988).

1866 Perforate Issue: Marque, G., *The American Philatelist* 97:1085–86 (1983).

1889 100r. Postage Due: Tyler, comp. ref. 13.

1931–34 Varig Airmails: Ahrens, W., *Aero Philatelist Annals* 3:59–73 (1956).

1932 Revolutionary Issue (high values): Barros Pimentel, J.L.de, *Philatelic Journal of Great Britain* 65:57 (1955); Prant, C., *Pan American Philatelist* 2:44 (1955).

BREMEN

Broad Coverage: *Bohne, Germany ref. 1; Schloss, Germany ref. 2, pp. 25–32; *Stiedl-Billig, comp. ref. 12, Bremen.

BRITISH CENTRAL AFRICA (NYASALAND PROTECTORATE)

1895 2sh6p., 5sh., and £10 Stamps: Lowe, R., *Philatelist* 39:72–73 (1972).

BRITISH COLUMBIA AND VANCOUVER ISLAND

1860–69 Broad Coverage: *Pugh, BNA ref. 1; Smythies, BNA ref. 2, pp. 26–31.

1860 2^1/$_2$p.: Johnson, comp. ref. 6 II, p. 4.

1865 3p: Johnson, comp. ref. 6 II, p. 5.

BRITISH EAST AFRICA

1890–94 Regular Issue: Aretz, comp. ref. 1, p. 9; Johnson, comp. ref. 6 I, p. 3; Bynof-Smith, comp. ref. 3C, pp. 22–23.

BRITISH GUIANA

1853–90 Colonial Seal: Bynof-Smith, comp. ref. 3C, pp. 24–27.

1863–75 Colonial Seal: Aretz, comp. ref. 1, p. 9.

BRITISH HONDURAS

1866–87 First Design: Johnson, comp. ref. 6 II; Bynof-Smith, comp. ref. 3C, pp. 28–29.

BRITISH NORTH AMERICA (BNA)

1. Broad Coverage: *Pugh, K.W., *Reference Manual of BNA Fakes, Forgeries and Counterfeits,* 3 vols. (10 releases), published by the author, Brandon, Manitoba, Canada, 1977–81, unpaged.

2. Broad Coverage: *Smythies, E.A., *B.N.A. Fakes and Forgeries,* British North America Philatelic Society, Raleigh, North Carolina, no date, 101 pp.

BRUNSWICK

Broad Coverage: Bohne, Germany ref. 1; Schloss, Germany ref. 2, pp. 33–36; Stiedl-Billig, comp. ref. 12, Braunschweig.

BULGARIA

1879–1915 Classic Issues: *Stiedl-Billig, comp. ref. 12 (part 34).

1879–84 Classic Issues: Zagorsky, D., *Linn's Stamp News,* March 29, 1993, p. 10.

1901 War of Independence Issue: Tyler, V.E., *Linn's Stamp News,* September 5, 1994, p. 6.

1902 Shipka Pass Commemoratives: Tyler,

V.E., *Linn's Stamp News*, January 24, 1994, p. 8.

1931 Airmails: Arkhanguelsky, E.M., *Aero Philatelist Annals* **2**:49–50 (1954).

1932 Airmails: Newall, comp. ref. 8, pp. 14–17; Goodkind, H.M., *Aero Philatelist Annals* **5**:23–28 (1957).

BURMA — JAPANESE OCCUPATION

1942 Peacock o/p's — General: *Pilcher, J., and D. Filby, *Burma Peacock* **4**:35–42 (1982).

1942 Henzada Type I o/p: Pilcher, J., *Burma Peacock* **2**:22–26 (1980).

1942 Henzada Type II o/p's: Pilcher, J., *Burma Peacock* **2**:41–46 (1980).

1942 Myaungmya o/p's: Pilcher, J., *Burma Peacock* **2**:70–77 (1980).

1942 Yano Seal: *Ito, K., *Japanese Philately* **34**:59–85 (1979).

1943 Farmer Plowing: Tyler, comp. ref. 13, p. 15.

1943 Water Carrier: Tyler, comp. ref. 13, p. 16.

1943 Elephant Carrying Teak: Tyler, V.E., *Linn's Stamp News*, November 1, 1993, p. 6.

1943 Mandalay Watchtower: Tyler, V.E., *Linn's Stamp News*, November 15, 1993, p. 6.

CANADA

Broad Coverage: Pugh, BNA ref. 1; Smythies, BNA ref. 2; Cowman, A.R., *Record of Philately* **1**:70–71, 76–78.

1897 Diamond Jubilee Issue: Cheavin, W.H.S., *Philately* (London) **2**:90–92 (1949).

1897 $3 Diamond Jubilee: Cheavin, W.H.S., and E.W. Irving, *Philately* (London) **2**:43–45 (1948).

1990 February 8 39c. Flag Coil: Youngblood, W.L., *Linn's Stamp News*, November 18, 1991, pp. 12–13; January 20, 1992, p. 28; July 20, 1992, p. 31.

1992 December 30 43c. Flag Coil: Anon., *Linn's Stamp News*, June 28, 1993, p. 14.

CANAL ZONE

1904 First Series: Eckhardt, W.J., *The American Philatelist* **62**:438–49 (1949).

1904–6 Third Series: DeVoss, J.T., *American Philatelic Congress Book* **18**:35–42 (1952).

1905 8c. Overprint (Scott 15): DeVoss, J.T., *The American Philatelist* **79**:180–81 (1965).

All Above Overprints: Chemi, Beal, and DeVoss, comp. ref. 4, pp. 54–60.

1925–27 Overprint Errors: Reno, G. E., *The American Philatelist* **98**: 997 (1984).

CAPE OF GOOD HOPE

Broad Coverage: Cowman, A.R., *Stamp Lover* **25**:275–76, 313 (1933); **26**:8–9 (1933).

1899 Vryburg Issue: Rich, S.G., *Stamps* **36**:57–59 (1941).

Cancellations, Early: Roth, D., *Philately*

(London) **2**:131–34 (1949); Jurgens, A.A., *Philately* (London) **2**:193–94 (1950).

CENTRAL AMERICAN STEAMSHIP CO.

1892 Bogus Issue: Tyler, V.E., *The American Philatelist* **99**:919–21 (1985).

CENTRAL LITHUANIA

Broad Coverage: *Pacholczyk, A.G., *Central Lithuania: Specialized Stamp Catalogue*, Stochastic Press, Tucson, Arizona, 1990, 207 pp.

1920 November 23 Overprints: Kronenberg, S., *The American Philatelist* **99**:522–26 (1985).

CEYLON

1857–1906 Broad Coverage: Cowman, A.R., *Stamp Lover* **26**:259–63 (1934).

1879 2.50r. Definitive: Johnson, comp. ref. 6 II.

1940 November 5 3c. Overprint: Johnson, comp. ref. 6 II.

CHILE

Broad Coverage: *Bonilla Lara, A., *Un Estudio Sobre las Falsificaciónes de Sellos de Chile*, Santiago (supplement to *Chile Filatelico*), 1971, 46 pp., in Spanish.

1853–65 First Design (Hahn Reprints): Davis, R.W., *West-End Philatelist* **42**:71 (1952).

1867 Colombus Issue: Tyler, comp. ref. 13, p. 19.

1894 Postage Dues: Andresini, P., *Filatelia* **10**:326–27 (1926), in Italian.

1895–96 Postage Dues: Tyler, V.E., *Linn's Stamp News*, May 16, 1994, p. 6.

1896 Postage Dues: Todd, J.D., *Stamp Collecting* **103**:891 (1965).

1907 Official Overprint: Soley, L.C., *The American Philatelist* **97**:349–51 (1983).

1934–39 20 and 50p. Airmails: Bonilla Lara, A., *Aero Philatelist Annals* **8**:68–74 (1961); Fletcher, comp. ref. 5 (50 pp. only).

CHINA

Broad Coverage (especially strong on recent issues): *Practical Stamp Illustration for Identifying Forged Stamps of China*, Geography Publishing House, Beijing, 1994, 184 pp. (in Chinese but well-illustrated).

1878 Large Dragons: Negus, J., Forgeries of China's "Large Dragons" 1878, Cinderella Stamp Club, London, 1978, 14 pp.; Gray, R.E., *Counterfeits of Chinese Postage Stamps*, published by the author, Enfield, New Hampshire, 1979, 10 pp.

1903 Foochow Bisect: Johnson, comp. ref. 6 II; Sousa, J.M., and M. Rogers, *The Vexatious Foochow Bisect*, Michael Rogers, Winter Park, Florida, no date, 8 pp.

1912–23 Postal Forgeries: Fletcher, comp. ref. 5, pp. 24–27; Sousa, J.M., and M. Rogers, *Chinese Postal Forgeries*, Michael Rogers,

Winter Park, Florida, no date, 8 pp.

1913–15 10c. Junk Regular Issue: Tyler, V.E., *Linn's Stamp News*, April 29, 1996, p. 6.

1914 $1.00 Peking Print: Bowker, H.F., *Collectors Club Philatelist* **8**:19–20 (1929).

1949–52 Reprints (Official Imitations): Wetterling, J.G., *Reprints of Mainland Chinese Issues of 1949* [sic], published by the author, no location given, 1971, 18 pp.; Scott Catalogue.

CHUNKING

1893–94 2 cand. Red Issue: Tyler, V.E., *Linn's Stamp News*, May 13, 1995, p. 6.

CILICIA

Broad Coverage: *Mayo, M.M., *Cilicie: Occupation Militaire Française*, published by the author, New York, 1984, 194 pp.

COLOMBIA

1859 First Issue: Cross, J.M., *Copacarta* **8**:61–63 (1991).

1860 Second Issue: Cross, J.M., *Copacarta* **8**:87 (1991).

1861 Third Issue: Lowe, R., *Philatelist* **46**:41–43 (1979).

1862 Fourth Issue: Cross, J.M., *Copacarta* **9**:18 (1991); Lowe, R., *Philatelist* **46**:43–44 (1979).

1865 Regular Issue: Cross, J.M., *Copacarta* **4**:54–56 (1987).

1865 Registration Stamps: Cross, J.M., *Copacarta* **4**:54–56 (1987); **11**:39–41 (1993).

1865 Sobreporte Stamps: Cross, J.M., *Copacarta* **9**:54–55 (1991); Lowe, R., *Philatelist* **46**:44–45 (1979).

1865 Cubiertas: Cross, J.M., *Copacarta* **11**:64 (1994); Walton, B., *Copacarta* **12**:26–33 (1994).

1868–74 Michelsen "Reprints": *Meyr, J.N., *The American Philatelist* **51**:337–42, 635–42, 1038–44 (1938); **52**:41–48, 158–67, 226–29, 1060–67 (1938–39); **53**:30–32 (1939); Cross, J.M., *Copacarta* **2**:8–11 (1984).

1902–3 Issues: Tyler, V.E., *American Philatelic Congress Book* **58**:41–50 (1992); Cross, J.M., *Copacarta* **10**:63 (1993); Tyler, comp. ref. 13, pp. 23–24.

1919 Airmail Overprint: Rendon, A., *Colombia Filatelica* Nos. 7–9: 12–13 (1989), in Spanish.

1919–50 Airmail Issues: Newall, comp. ref. 8, pp. 34–49.

Cancellations, Forged: Cross, J.M., *Copacarta* **12**:42 (1994).

COLOMBIA — ANTIOQUIA

1868 First Issue: Lowe, R., *Philatelist* **46**:45 (1979).

1868 5c. First Issue: Phillips, C.J., *Stanley Gibbon's Monthly Journal* **15**:165 and facing plate (1905).

1875–85 Issues (Illustrations of Genuine): Palmer, M.G., *Gibbons' Stamp Monthly* **2**:166–68 (1929).

1867 1c. Regular Issue: Tyler, comp. ref. 13, p. 25.

1888 Medellin Issue (Plating Genuine): Myer, J.N., *The American Philatelist* **53**:387–90 (1940).

1899 Issue (Remainders, Reprints, etc.): Van den Berg, G., *Stamps,* August 26, 1950, p. 320.

COLOMBIA — BOLIVAR

1863 10c. Regular Issue: BPA Sperati, comp. ref. 2, p. 191 and plate 127.

1863 and 1866 10c. Stamps: Lowe, R., *Philatelist* **46**:45–46 (1979).

1879 and 1880 Issues: Hatfield, A., Jr., and B.W.H. Poole, *Philatelic Gazette* **5**:140–42, 183–84 (1915); Tyler, V.E., *Linn's Stamp News,* January 9, 1995, p. 6.

1879–85 Issues (Calman's Fake Cancels): Negus, J., *Philatelic Magazine* **66**:493–94 (1958); Mueses, D., *Seebeck: Hero or Villain?,* Michael P. Birks, no address, no date, p. 53.

COLOMBIA — CUNDINAMARCA

1870 Michelsen Forgeries: Myer, J.N., *The American Philatelist* **52**:38–41 (1938).

COLOMBIA — TOLIMA

1870 First Issue: *Wickersham, C.W., *Collectors Club Philatelist* **46**:17–27 (1927); Lowe, R., *Philatelist* **46**:46 (1979).

1870 Bogus Cubierta: Blell, W., *Copacarta* **3**:48–49 (1986).

1884 Regular Issue: Tyler, comp. ref. 13, p. 26.

1886 Two Flagpole Stamps: *Tyler, V.E., *American Philatelic Congress Book* **57**:51–58 (1991).

CONFEDERATE STATES

(General Issues)

1861–62 Broad Coverage: *Skinner, H.C., E.R. Gunter, and W.H. Sanders, *The* New *Dietz Confederate States Catalog and Handbook,* Bogg & Laurence Publishing Co., Miami, Florida, 1986, pp. 155–57; Dietz, A., *The Confederate Bulletin* No. 14:4 (1946); No. 15:4 (1946); No. 16:4 (1947); No. 17:4 (1947); No. 18:4 (1948); No. 19:4 (1948); No. 20:4 (1948); No. 21:4 (1949); No. 22:4 (1949).

1861 5c. Stamp: Green, B.M., *The Confederate States Five-Cent Green Lithograph,* Philatelic Foundation, New York, 1977, pp. 8–12.

1861 10c. Stamp: Green, B.M., *The Confederate States Ten-Cent Blue Lithograph,* see above, 1977, pp. 10–16.

1862 2c. Stamp: Green, B.M., *The Confederate States Two-Cent Green Lithograph,* see above, 1977, pp. 11–19.

1862 5c. Stamp: Green, B.M., *The Confederate States Five-Cent Blue Lithograph,* see above, 1978, pp. 7–15.

1862 10c. Stamp: BPA Sperati, comp. ref. 2, p. 197 and plate 132.

1862 5c. Typograph: Tyler, comp. ref. 1,3 p. 27.

1863 Ten c. Stamp: BPA Sperati, comp. ref. 2, p. 197 and plate 132.

Unissued 10c. Stamp: Bennett, L.F. and G.C., *S.P.A. Journal* **34**:651–55 (1972).

(Provisional Issues)

1861 Broad Coverage: *The* New *Dietz Confederate States Catalog and Handbook,* etc., see above, pp. 158–63, 169.

5c. Charleston Envelope: Calhoun, R.L., *Confederate Philatelist* **28**:95–100 (1983).

10c. Knoxville: Graham, R.B., *Confederate Philatelist* **34**:103–26, 143–72 (1989); **35**:9–30, 171–205 (1990); **36**:39–64, 159–94 (1991); *The American Philatelist* **108**:332–43 (1994).

5c. Lynchburg: Hartman, L., *Confederate Philatelist* **15**:33–43 (1970).

2c. and 5c. Memphis: *Pratt, T.H., *The Postmaster's Provisionals of Memphis, Tennessee,* Dietz Printing Company, Richmond, Virginia, 1929, 39 pp.

2c. and 5c. Mobile: Perry, E., *Pat Paragraphs* No. 54:1818–21 (1950).

2c. and 5c. New Orleans: Hartmann, L.H., *The American Philatelist* **77**:660–62 (1964).

(Phantoms)

Broad Coverage: *The* New *Dietz Confederate States Catalog and Handbook,* etc., see above, pp. 161–63.

Broad Coverage: *Rooke, H.F., *Confederate Philatelist* **13**(7):1–31 (1969); **14**(3):65–71 (1969).

10c. Stonewall Jackson "Essay": Rooke, H.F., *S.P.A. Journal* **35**:463–74 (1973).

(Postal Markings)

Broad Coverage: *The* New *Dietz Confederate States Catalog and Handbook,* etc., see above, pp. 163–68.

COSTA RICA

1862–1923 Broad Coverage: *Moya, A., *Costa Rica Filatelica* no. 6:1–4 (1934); no. 7:1–3 (1934); no. 8:1–3 (1934); no. 9:1–3 (1935); no. 10:17–19 (1935); no. 11:46–48 (1935); no. 12:70–73 (1935); no. 15:46–47 (1936); nos. 16 & 17:23–25 (1937); no. 19:22–24 (1937).

1881–82 Overprints: *Sauber, J.W., *Oxcart* **25**:98–120 (1985); **26**:6–27 (1986).

1883 Ross Overprints Fantasies: Bonilla Lara, A., *Pan American Philatelist* **3**:21–30 (1955).

1917–20 Official Overprints: Saenz Mata, C., *Oxcart* **15**:40–41 (1975).

1922 Coffee Bag Overprints: Mitchell, H.D., *Pan American Philatelist* **1**:156–58 (1955); Rodriguez, Gil, F., *Pan American Philatelist* **2**:84–85 (1956); Saenz Mata, C., *Oxcart* **12**:37–42 (1972).

1928 Lindbergh 10c. Surcharge: Tyler, V.C., *Linn's Stamp News,* May 30, 1994, p. 8.

Cancellations, Forged, etc.: Gordon, D.L. *Mainsheet* **4**, whole no. 15:89 (1976).

CRETE

Broad Coverage: *Feenstra, R.M., W. Leimenstoll, and K. Mostert, *Crete, A Handbook Catalogue About Its Philately and Postal History,* Postzegelvereniging

Griekenland Ridderkerk, The Netherlands, 1986, 198 pp.; *Feenstra, R.M., *Greece: A Collection of Forgeries,* Postzegelvereniging Griekenland, Ridderkert, The Netherlands, 1993, pp. 94–109.

1898–99 First Six Issues: Thompson, C.S., *American Philatelic Congress Book* **8**:17–26 (1942).

1898 First Issue: Liberman, W.R., *The American Philatelist* **91**:368–70 (1977).

1899 Cancellations, Forged: Liberman, W.R., *The American Philatelist* **91**:458–60 (1977).

CUBA

1855–73 Broad Coverage: Preston, R.B., *Billig's Philatelic Handbook* **5**:179–94 (1945).

1857–98 Broad Coverage: *Graus, F., Spain ref. 1.

1857 ¹/₂ and 1r. Stamps: Fletcher, comp. ref. 5, pp. 30–31.

1878 1p. King Alfonso XII: Tyler, comp. ref. 13, p. 30.

1898 King Alfonso XIII: Ragatz, comp. ref. 9, p. 36; Tyler, comp. ref. 13, p. 31.

1902–60 Broad Coverage: Jones, W.M., and R.J. Roy, Jr., *A Handbook of the Stamps of Cuba,* Pt. III, published by the authors, 1988, pp. 261–65.

1928 Lindbergh Overprint: Spying Eye, *Weekly Philatelic Gossip* March 9, 1946, p. 19.

Phantom Stamps: Rooke, H.F., *S.P.A. Journal* **36**:403–6 (1974).

CZECHOSLOVAKIA

1918–39 Broad Coverage: *Karasek, J., Z. Kvasnicka, and B. Paulicek., *Badelky Ceskoslovenskych Postovnich Znamek 1918-1939,* Nakladatelstvi Dopravy A Spotju, Prague, 1963, 367 pp., in Czech. (English translation by Chicagoland Chapter, Czechoslovak Philatelic Society, 1964).

1919 Semipostal Overprints: *Dehn, R., *The Posta Ceskoslovenska Overprints,* Czechoslovak Philatelic Society of Great Britain Monograph No. 3, Norwich, 1985, 47 pp.

1934 Music Sheets: Spying Eye, comp. ref. 11, pp. 13–19.

(Bohemia and Moravia)

1943 Theresienstadt Stamps: Anon., *Holy Land Philatelist* **5**:1107 (1959); Bohne, Germany ref. 1.

DANISH WEST INDIES

1856–1916 Broad Coverage: *Engstrom, V.E., ed., *Danish West Indies Mails, 1754-1917,* vol. 3, Scandinavian Philatelic Printing and Publishing Company, Washington, D.C., 1982, pp.20-1-20-22.

1902 Postage Dues: Spying Eye, comp. ref. 11, pp. 20–21; Tyler, V.E., *Linn's Stamp News,* June 12, 1995, p. 6.

1905–13 Postage Dues: Johnson, comp. ref. 6 I, p. 11; Tyler, V.E., *Linn's Stamp News,* Aug. 7, 1995, p. 6.

1915 Fake Cancellations on Christian X Issue: Engstrom, V.E., *The American Philatelist* **97**:805–7, 856 (1983).

DANUBE AND BLACK SEA RAILWAY

(Kustendje and Czernawoda Local Post)
1867–71 Broad Coverage: *Kelly, D.N., *London Philatelist* **60**:81–86 (1951); Ringström, S., and H.E. Tester, *The Private Ship Letter Stamps of the World,* part 2, *Australia – Europe – South America,* published by the authors, no place specified, no date, pp. 130–42.

DANUBE STEAM NAVIGATION COMPANY (D.D.S.G.)

1866–80 Broad Coverage: *Hurt, E.F., and D.N. Kelly, *The Danube Steam Navigation Company,* American Philatelic Society, State College, Pennsylvania, 1950, 64 pp.; Barefoot, J., *Forgery and Reprint Guide* Nos. 7–8, J. Barefoot Investments, York, England, 1983, 32 pp.

DANZIG

1920–24 Selected Coverage: Bohne, Germany ref. 1.
1920 First Issue Overprints: Kayssner, comp. ref. 7, vol. 1, p. 22, in German; *ibid.,* vol. 4, p. 178.
1920 "Mark" Overprints: Kayssner, comp. ref. 7, vol. 4, pp. 178–80.
1920 Slanting Overprints: Holtz, K., *Die Danzig Schragdrucke und ihre Fälschungen,* Kurt Kayssner Verlag, Buckow, Germany, 1939, 28 pp., in German; *Schuler, G., *Danzig: Die Schragdrucke und ihre Fälschungen,* INFLA-BERLIN, Berlin, 1960, 29 pp., in German.
1920 Airmail Overprints: Kayssner, comp. ref. 7, vol. 5, pp. 3–4.
1924–25 Official Overprints: Johnson, comp. ref. 6 I, p. 12; Kayssner, comp. ref. 7, vol. 3, p. 112.
1930 "15 November" Overprints: Kayssner, comp. ref. 7, vol. 1, p. 2.
1934 Winter Welfare Overprint: Kayssner, comp ref. 7, vol. 5, p. 4.

DENMARK

1851–1950 Broad Coverage: Heie, O., *Frimaerkesamleren* **8**:22, 33–34, 53, 69, 85–86, 104–5, 143–44, 173–74, 193 (1950); **9**:30–31, 50, 86, 98–99 (1951), in Danish.
1951–63 Early Issues: Schloss, comp. ref. 10, pp. 12–15.
1851 2rs. First Issue: Tester, H.E., in *Denmark: 2 Rigsbank-Skilling 1851–52,* S. Christensen, Trelleborg Philatelic Society, Trelleborg, Sweden, 1980, pp. 135–41.
1918 Overprints: Johnson, comp. ref. 6 I, p. 12.
1919–41 Parcel Post Stamps: Johnson, comp. ref. 6 I, p. 12.
1921 Postage Due Stamps: Johnson, comp. ref. 6 I, p. 12.

1925–29 First Airmails: Tyler, V.E., *Linn's Stamp News,* October 31, 1994, p. 6.

DOMINICAN REPUBLIC

1865–1933 Broad Coverage: *Smith, J.W., *The American Philatelist* **83**:237–42 (1969); **85**:143–49, 170–74 (1971); **89**:339–42 (1975).
1867 Bogus Issue: Thomen, L.F., *London Philatelist* **66**:90–92 and unnumbered plate (1957); Rooke, H.F., *Philatelist* **27**:96–97 (1961).
1879 1r. Stamp: Tyler, comp. ref. 13, p. 33.
1900 Map Issue: Tyler, comp. ref. 13, p. 34.
1902 Fake Cancels: Fournier, F., *Le Fac-Simile,* No. 4, 50 (1910), in German; Smith, J., *Mainsheet* **11**, whole no. 43:61–62 (1986).
1931–33 Sundial Airmails: Tyler, V.E., *Linn's Stamp News,* July 11, 1994, p. 6.

EASTERN RUMELIA (SOUTH BULGARIA)

1880 R.O. Overprints: *Woodward, H.P., *Collectors Club Philatelist* **39**:55–59, 103 (1960).
1885 Lion Overprints: *Woodward, H.P., *Collectors Club Philatelist* **38**:211–28 (1959).

ECUADOR

1865–72 First Issue: Funkhouser, J.W., *Pan American Philatelist* **1**:5–12, 38–46, 52–60, 83–88, 102–8, 125–31 (1954); **2**:167–68 (1955).
1865–72 First Issue: Pastor Campana, J., *Chile Filatelico* **14**:329–41 (1971), in Spanish.
1866 4r. Stamp: D'Elia, R.A., *Mainsheet* **6**, whole no. 21:3–7 (1980); **7**, whole no. 40:6–16 (1985); **15**, whole no. 59:47–48 (1990).
1872 Second Issue: Harris, L.J., *American Philatelic Congress Book* **35**:111–22 (1969).
1872 ¹/₂r. and 1p. Second Issue: Tyler, V.E., *Linn's Stamp News,* October 18, 1993, p. 6.
1881 5C. Regular Issue: Harris, L.J., *The American Philatelist* **106**:62–63 (1992).
1883–1905 Various Overprints: Chemi, Beal, and DeVoss, comp. ref. 4, pp. 71–77.
1892–96 Seebeck Reprints: Glickstein, D., *The American Philatelist* **99**:914–18 (1985).
1896 Liberal Party Commemoratives: Tyler, comp. ref. 13, pp. 35–36.
1929 May 5 10s. Airmail: Levi-Castillo, R., *Aero Philatelist Annals* **13**:75–76 (1966).
1955 1 SUCRE Fake Overprints: Levi-Castillo, R., *Airpost Journal* **34**:169–70 (1963).

EGYPT

1866 First Issue: *Byam, W., *London Philatelist* **40**:66–69, 76–84, 98–195 (1931); Kehr, E.A., *S.P.A. Journal* **25**:361–65 (1963); *Chafter, I., *L'Orient Philatélique* No. 125:105–17 (1972) and No. 126:206–22 (1973).

1867 Second Issue: *Byam, W.E., *London Philatelist* **47**:4–9, 43–46, 60–67 (1938); Vervisch, R., *Balasse Magazine* No. 287:196–97 (1986), in French.
1871 Jaffa Interpostal Seal: Kerr, E.A., *S.P.A. Journal* **17**:493–94 (1955). Caution! The item described here as a forgery has since been determined by specialists to be genuine.
1872 Third Issue: Vervisch, R., *Balasse Magazine* No. 288:250–51 (1986), in French.
1879 Inverted Overprints: Lowe, H.F., *Stamp Collectors' Fortnightly* **31**:86–87 (1925).
1884 and 1886 Postage Dues: Vervisch, R., *Balasse Magazine* No. 289:306–7 (1986), in French.
1888 Postage Dues: Tyler, comp. ref. 13, p. 37.
1922 100 and 200m. Overprints (Wmkd. Crescent and Star): Moutran, A., *Stamp Collecting* **39**:209 (1932).
1922 O.H.H.S. Official Overprint on 3m Orange Stamp: Eid, M., *L'Orient Philatélique* No. 106: 30–31 (1962).
1926 December 21 PORT FOUAD Overprints: Eid, M., *L'Orient Philatélique* No. 106:29–30 (1962).
1953 Bar Overprints: Stephan, M.S., *Linn's Weekly Stamp News,* May 16, 1955, p. 4.
Phantoms-Bicolored 1867 Issue: Smith, P.A.S., *Egyptian Topics* **3**(2):35 (1971).

EPIRUS

1914 Chimarra Issue: *Liberman, W.R., ed., *H.P.S.A. News Bulletin* **6**(5 & 6):1–17 (1968); *Vlastos, O.G., *Comparisons of Hellenic Postal Stamps 1861–1912,* O. Vlastos Ltd., Halandri, Greece, 1992, pp. 174–77; *Feenstra, R.M., *Greece: A Collection of Forgeries,* Postzergel Vereniging Griekenland, Ridderkerk, The Netherlands, 1993, pp. 73–77.
1914 Marksman Design: Vlastos, O.G., *op. cit.,* pp. 178–82.
1914 Chimarra Overprints: Feenstra, R.M., *op. cit.,* p. 78.
1914 Erseka Local Issue: Tyler, V.E., *The American Philatelist* **100**:954–55 (1986); Vlastos, O.G., *op. cit.,* pp. 183–86.
1914 Moschopolis Local Issue: Tyler, comp. ref. 13, p. 38.
1914–15 Greek Occupation Overprints: Feenstra, R.M. *op. cit.,* p. 79–80.
1916 Greek Occupation Overprints: Feenstra, R.M., *op. cit.,* p. 81.

ESTONIA

1918–24 Broad Coverage (Jaan Lubi Forgeries): Sjogren, E., *Eesti Filatelist* No. 28:3–32 (1982); No. 29:1–37 (1983); No. 31:3–27 (1987); Kayssner, comp. ref. vol. 4, pp. 185–87, in German.
1919 "Eesti Post" Overprints: Alver, H., *Eesti Filatelist* No. 26:37–64 (1980).
1920 Viking Ship Stamps: *McDonald, D., and J.R.W. Purves, *London Philatelist* **85**:76–80 (1976).
1920 35 + 10p. Aid to Wounded Issue: Tyler, comp. ref. 13, p. 39.
1920–23 Airmails: *Gleason, P., *The*

American Philatelist **89**:823–26 (1975); **92**:756–58 (1978).

1921 Nurse and Soldier Issue: Stiedl, O.E., *Postmarke* No. 260:72–73 (1932), in German.

1924 and 1925 Airmails: Kayssner, vol. 5, comp. ref. 7, pp. 9–10, in German.

Tallinn Cancellations: Alver, H., *Eesti Filatelist* No. 26:131–41 (1980).

ETHIOPIA

1894–1936 Broad Coverage: *Payne E., *Ethiopia,* Cockrill Series Booklets, no. 13, (1894–1903) 28 pp.; no. 14 (1903–5) 36 pp.; no. 15 (1905–13) 32 pp.; no. 16 (1917–36) 48 pp.; no. 17 (postmarks & cancellations) 48 pp.; no. 18 (fiscals and Fournier forgeries) 28 pp.; Philip Cockrill, Newbury England, 1981.

1894–1906 Broad Coverage: Ragatz, comp. ref. 9, pp. 54–61; Lines, A.F., *Stamp Collecting* **116**:1021–25 (1971).

1894 First Issue: Cowman, A.R., *Stamp Lover* **18**:17 (1925); Weigand, J.F., *Weekly Philatelic Gossip,* May 22, 1943, p. 248; Plumlee, K., *Weekly Philatelic Gossip,* Nov. 14, 1953, pp. 336–37.

FIJI

1870–96 Broad Coverage: *Barnett, E.A., *Gibbons' Stamp Monthly* **16**:74–76 (1943); Hicks, J.S., *Gibbons' Stamp Monthly* **15**:100–101, 108–9 (1941).

1871 Regular Issue: Spying Eye, comp. ref. 11, p. 22; Johnson, comp. ref. 6 I, p. 14.

1881–90 1 sh. and 5 sh. Stamps: Tyler, V.E., *The American Philatelist* **98**:887–88 (1984).

1903 £1 Stamp: Bynof-Smith, comp. ref. 3C, pp. 52–53.

Forged Rural Cancellations: Forrest, J., *Philatelist* **22**:214–15 (1956).

FINLAND

1850–71 Selected Issues: Bynof-Smith, comp. ref. 3D vol. 1, pp. 48–51.

1856–1932 Broad Coverage: *Ossa, M., *Forgeries of Finnish Postage Stamps,* Lauri Peltonen Ky, Hanko, Finland, 1977, 107 pp.

1866 Local Issue: Rooke, H.F., *Stamps,* September 24, 1966, pp. 592–93, 606.

1867 1m. Stamp: BPA Sperati, comp. ref. 2, p. 163 and plate 110.

1871 10p. Color Error on Wove Paper: Plander, C.E., *Collectors Club Philatelist* **18**:255–62 (1939).

1875–81 20p. Stamp: Tyler, comp. ref. 13, p. 40.

1885 5m and 10m Stamps: Aretz, comp. ref. 1, p. 18.

1930 Airmail Overprint: Rompay, R. van, *Stamps,* January 1, 1955, p. 16.

FIUME

1600–1924 Very Broad Coverage: *Dehn, R., *The Stamps and Postal History of Fiume: 1600–1924,* published by the author, Norwich, England, 1998, 120 pp.

1918–24 Broad Coverage: *Dehn, R.,

Gibbons' Stamp Monthly **38**: 21–25 (1964).

1919 First Definitive Issue: Tyler, V.E., *The American Philatelist* **98**: 995–96 (1984); Tyler, comp. ref. 13, p. 41; Tyler, V.E., *Linn's Stamp News,* May 15, 1995, p. 6.

1919 January "FRANCO" Overprints: Dehn, R. *Fil-Italia* **16**:223–28 (1990).

1920 Annunzio Portrait Designs: Aretz, comp. ref. 1, pp. 18–19; Tyler, comp. ref. 13, p. 42.

1920 Occupation Anniversary Issue: Aretz, comp. ref. 1, p. 19; Johnson, comp. ref. 6 I, pp. 14–15.

1923 "Venetian Ship" Stamps: Tyler, comp. ref. 13, p. 43.

FORGERS AND THEIR WORKS

Fournier, François: Ragatz, comp. ref. 9; Ragatz, L., ed., *Fournier's 1914 Price-List of Philatelic Forgeries,* H. Garratt-Adams, Nr. Birmingham, England, 1949, 64 pp.

Frodel, André: Kraemer, J.E., in *Oposculum I,* Forand, M., ed., RPSC Philatelic Research Foundation, Ottawa, Ontario, Canada, 1995, pp. 93–114.

Gee, David Allan: Lowe, R., *The Gee-Ma Forgeries,* Robson Lowe, Ltd., London, 1980, 12 pp.

Joseph, Madame: Worboys, D. (and R.B. West, ed.), *Madame Joseph Forged Postmarks,* Royal Philatelic Society, London and British Philatelic Trust, London, 1994, 122 pp.

Krippner, Emil Reinhard: Friebe, H., *Emil Reinhard Krippner und Seine Falsifikate,* Philatelistenverband im Kulturbund der DDR, Freiberg, Germany, 1989, 68 pp., in German.

Oneglia, Erasmo: Lowe, R., and C. Walske, *The Oneglia Engraved Forgeries: Commonly Attributed to Angelo Panelli,* James Bendon, Limassol, Cyprus, 1996, 101 pp.

Schroder, Oswald: Lowe, R., *The Oswald Schroder Forgeries,* Robson Lowe, Ltd., London, 1981, 16 pp.

Seebeck, Nicholas F: Mueses, D., *Seebeck: Hero or Villain?,* Michael P. Birks, no location given, no date, 89 pp. (Seebeck was a notorious reprinter, not a forger.)

Senf, Louis and Richard: Tyler, V.E., *American Congress Book* **34**:187–98 (1968).

Sperati, Jean de: BPA-Sperati, comp. ref. 2; *La Philatélie sans experts?,* Dees, Paris, 1946, 128 pp., in French.

Taylor, S. Allan: Kindler, J., *Philatelic Literature Review* **15**:59–89 (1966).

Thuin, Raoul Ch. de: Chemi, Beal, and De Voss, comp. ref. 4.

Various: *Tyler, V.E., *Philatelic Forgers: Their Lives and Works,* rev. ed., *Linn's Stamp News,* Sidney, Ohio, 1991, 165 pp.; *Vervisch, R., *Les Faussaires,* Ed. Groupe d'Étude des falsifications, Brussels, 1994, 258 pp., in French; Herst, H., Jr., ed., *Forensic Philately,* Herman Herst, Jr., Lake Oswego, Oregon, 1986, 133 pp.

Zareski, Michel: *Oblitérations & Marques*

Postales des États-Unis du 19ᵉ Siècle (introduction in English), published by the author, Paris, 1947, 229 pp., in French. (Many of the scarcer markings illustrated are Zareski forgeries.)

FORGERY AND FAKERY (GENERAL CONSIDERATIONS)

Anon., *The Dealers' Guide to Chemical Restoration of Postage Stamps,* 3rd ed., National Stamp Service, Quincy, Mass., 1976, 41 pp.

Arbeiter, C., and W. Rascke, *Briefmarken sachgerecht reparieren und Fälschungen erkennen,* PHILATEK-Verlag, Königsbronn, Germany, 1996, 116 pp., in German.

Brady, S., *Doctor of Millions: the Rise and Fall of Stamp King Dr. Paul Singer,* Anvil Books, Tralee, Ireland, 1965, 176 pp.

Brun, J.-F., *Out-Foxing the Fakers,* American Philatelic Society, State College, Pennsylvania, 1993, 123 pp.

Cheavin, W.H.S., Philately and X-Rays: Repairs and Fakes, *Philately* (London) **1**:190–91, 200, 208–9, 218 (1948); **2**:28–30 (1948); **2**:143–46 (1949).

Eastwood, H., *Philately Under the Lamp,* reprinted. HMJR Co., Miami Beach, 1929, 107 pp.

Künstler, G., and E.L. Martner, *Falsch oder Echt?,* Philatelia GMBH, Leverkusen, Germany, 1981, 90 pp., in German.

Milbury, C.E., *So You Want to Invest in Stamps,* Paul Bluss, New York, 1946, 136 pp.

Milbury, C.E., *What Price Philately,* The Neptune Company, New York, 1946, 110 pp.

Mueses, D.A., *De Falsificaciónes y Falsificadores,* no publisher or place listed, 1992, 249 pp., in Spanish.

Pope, E.C., ed., *Opinions: Philatelic Expertizing — An Inside View,* vol. I–V, Philatelic Foundation, New York, 1983–88, 141, 229, 198, 244, 252 pp., respectively; Odenweller, R.P., ed., vol. VI, 1992, 226 pp. (Primarily discussions of problem items examined by The Philatelic Foundation Expert Committee.)

Schmid, P.W., *How to Detect Damaged, Altered, and Repaired Stamps,* Palm Press, Huntington, New York, 1979, 105 pp.

Sefi, A.J., *Forgeries and Fakes,* Sefi, Pemberton & Co., London, 1929, 28 pp.

Singer, S., *"The People with the Callumny,"* published by the author, New York, 1908, 40 pp., bilingual, in English and French. (An exposé of the extensive repair work carried out by the author for the firm of Stanley Gibbons in London.)

Sperati, J. de, *La Philatélie sans experts?,* Dees, Paris, 1946, 124 pp. plus appendix, in French.

Toaspern, H., *Philatelic Frauds, Fakes, & Fakers,* published by the author, New York, 1936, 16 pp.

Ton, M., *Wie alte Marken kunstvoll repariert und gefälscht werden,* Kricheldorf Verlag, Freiburg, i.B., Germany, 1949, 109 pp., in German.

FORMOSA (LOCAL ISSUES)

1887–95 Broad Coverage: *Hurt, E.F., and L.N. & M. Williams, eds., *Handbook of the Private Local Posts*, Fritz Billig, Jamaica, New York, 1950, pp. 53–56.

1887–88 First "Officials": Hurt, E.F., *The American Philatelist* 62:353–59 (1949); Wong, J.N., *Collectors Club Philatelist* 28:136–37 (1949); McCleave, F., *Stamp Magazine* 17:302–4, 323 (1951).

1895 Black Flag Issues: Tung, C., *Philatelic Magazine* 64:607–9 (1956); 84:606–7 (1976).

FRANCE

1849–50 First Issue: *Vervisch, R., *La Revue Postale* Nos. 97-98: 5–26 (1976), in French; Spying Eye, comp. ref. 11, pp. 23–26.

1853–60 Empire Issue: Spying Eye, comp. ref. 11, pp. 26–27.

1853–1949 Broad Coverage Postal Forgeries: Fletcher, comp. ref. 5, pp. 34–46.

1862–73 Tête-Bêche Fakes: Cheavin, W.H.S., *Philately* (London) 2:211–13 (1950).

1869 5f Stamp: Cotin, R., *France & Colonies Philatelist* 12:25–27 (1953).

1870–71 2c. and 4c. Bordeaux Issue: Vervisch, R., *Balasse Magazine* No. 266:26–27 (1983), in French.

1870–71 Paris Balloon Mail Covers: Buckland, H.D., *The American Philatelist* 54:169–70 (1940); Pemberton, P.L., *Philatelic Journal of Great Britain* 52:21–22 (1942).

1882 5f. Postage Due Stamp: Dentelure, *The American Philatelist* 63:598–99 (1950).

1882–92 Postage Due Issue: Sousa, J.M., *Mount Nittany Philatelic Society Newsletter* 2(1):5 (1969).

1914 Red Cross Semipostals: Spying Eye, comp. ref. 11, p. 30.

1927–31 Sinking Fund Overprints: Jervis, H., and R.H.L. Jervis, *The American Philatelist* 62:532–36 (1949).

1927 First Airmail Overprints: Spying Eye, comp. ref. 11, p. 31.

1927 American Legion Errors: Cheavin, W.H.S., *Philately* (London) 3:7–9 (1950).

1928 Isle de France Airmail Overprints: Spying Eye, comp. ref. 11, p. 32.

1929 Philatelic Exposition Overprints: Spying Eye, comp. ref. 11, pp. 28–29.

1938–43 Espionage and Propaganda Stamps: Williams, E. & P. ref. 1, pp. 15–19, 31; Friedman, H., E. & P. ref. 2G, 2J, 2L.

1941 1.50f Red-Orange Iris Design: Watermark, *The American Philatelist* 53:936–37 (1950).

1943 15f. Fiscal Stamp: Friedman, H.A., *S.P.A. Journal* 39:493–99 (1977).

(Local Issues)

1871 "Office Moreau" Paris (Bogus): Spying Eye, *S.P.A. Journal* 9:227 (1946).

1914 10c. Valenciennes: Schloss, H., *Stamps*, June 4, 1949, pp. 406–7.

1945, St. Nazaire Issue: Eaton, L., *Stamps*, August 9, 1958, p. 202.

FRENCH OFFICES AND COLONIES (GENERAL TYPES)

1859–1930 Broad Coverage: *Vaurie, A.J.C., *France & Colonies Philatelist* 2:6–7, 10–11, 14–16, 18–19, 23–24 (1942–43); 3:3, 8, 11–12, 14 (1943–44).

1859–65 Eagle and Crown Type: Billig, F., *Billig's Philatelic Handbook* 3:141 (1943).

1877–80 Sage (Peace and Commerce) Type: Vaurie, A.J.C., *Weekly Philatelic Gossip*, November 27, 1943, p. 279.

1881–86 Dubois (Commerce) Type: Johnson, comp. ref. 6 I, pp. 15–16; Vaurie, A.J.C., *op. cit.*, 1942, p. 7.

1884–1906 Postage Dues: Stone, R.G., *Collectors Club Philatelist* 25:115–22 (1946).

1892–1913 Groupe (Navigation and Commerce) Type: Tyler, comp. ref. 13, p. 44; Vaurie, A.J.C., *op. cit.*, 1942, p. 7.

1902–3 Merson (Liberty and Peace) Type: Boxsius, F.H., *Philatelic Circular* No. 58:807 (1915); Wood, R.L., *France & Colonies Philatelist* 8:14 (1949); A. Brun, *France & Colonies Philatelist* 8:23 (1949).

1906 Ballay Type: Aretz, comp. ref. 1, pp. 22–23.

1942 Forged Cancellations on Vichy Airmails: Eckhardt, W.J., *The American Philatelist* 62:386–88 (1949).

GAMBIA

1869–87 Cameos: Johnson, comp. ref. 6 II, p. 15; Tyler, comp. ref. 13, p. 45.

GEORGIA (SOVIET ISSUES)

1922–23 Broad Coverage: Barefoot, J., and A. Hall, *Georgia*, J. Barefoot (Investments) Ltd., 1983, pp. 52–55.

GERMAN COLONIES (GENERAL TYPES)

1893–1919 Broad Coverage: *Bohne, Germany ref. 1.

1900–1919 Small Ship Types: Spying Eye, comp. ref. 11, pp. 34–36; Sousa, J.M., *Stamps*, February 28, 1970, pp. 484–85; Tyler, comp. ref. 13, p. 46.

1914–18 Occupation Issues (Characteristics of Genuine): Gibbs, R.M., *G.R.I.: The Postage Stamps of the German Colonies Occupied by the British 1914–1918*, Christie's-Robson Lowe, London, 1988, 280 pp.

Cancellations, Forged: Thompson, C.S., *Counterfeits: German Colonies, Postmarks*, Weekly Philatelic Gossip, Holton, Kansas, 1943 pp. 12–16.

GERMAN STATES

Nineteenth Century Broad Coverage: *Stiedl-Billig, comp. ref. 12; * Bohne, Germany ref. 1; Schloss, Germany ref. 2; BPA-Sperati, comp. ref. 2; Ragatz, comp. ref. 9.

Peter Winter Forgeries — Broad Coverage: Lowe, R., *Philatelist and PJGB* 14:85–87 (1994); 14:4–9 (1995).

GERMANY

1872–1993 Broad Coverage: *Bohne, Germany ref. 1.

1872–1953 Broad Coverage: Bynof-Smith, comp. ref. 3D, vol. 1, pp. 116–41.

1872–1950 Broad Coverage: Blizil, G.A., ed., *Fakes and Forgeries of Germany & Colonies*, Germany Philatelic Society, Valparaiso, Indiana, 1966, 150 pp.

1905–43 Espionage and Propaganda Stamps: Williams, E. & P. ref. 1, pp. 5–9, 31–40; Friedman, H., E. & P. ref. 2A–2E, 2H–2I, 2K.

1919–23 Fake Cancellations on Inflation Series: Jaffe, M.J., *The American Philatelist* 97:595–98 (1983).

1943 "Spitler" Parody: Friedman, B., *Linn's Weekly Stamp News*, August 30, 1965, p. 10; Czyl, J., *Linn's Stamp News*, January 23, 1984, p. 68.

1944 Witzleben Propaganda Stamp: Friedman, H.A., *S.P.A. Journal* 38:629–33 (1976).

1945 Ravensburg 28.4.45 Fake Overprints: Thielsch, H., *The American Philatelist* 62:450 (1949).

1948 June 21–Sept. 19 Band Type Overprints on Control Council Issues: Thielke, G., *German Postal Specialist* 46:516–20 (1995).

1977–79 200pf. and 230pf. Castle Types: Anon., *Linn's Stamp News*, September 5, 1983, p. 41.

1988–93 Significant Sights Issue: Anders, R.E.H., *German Postal Specialist* 45:498 (1994); 46:18–19 (1995); Baumann, F.W., *Linn's Stamp News*, December 5, 1994, pp. 38–39.

1990 Dusseldorf Youth Philatelic Exhibition: Baumann, F.W., *Linn's Stamp News*, December 6, 1993, p. 16.

1992 100pf. Coat of Arms (Hamburg; Berlin): Baumann, F.W., *Linn's Stamp News*, December 6, 1993, p. 16.

How to Detect German Forgeries: Bohne, W.M., *The American Philatelist* 96:1097–1103 (1982).

Cancellations, Various: Wolff, W., *600 falsche Stempel*, Arbeitsgemeinschaft Neues Handbuch der Briefmarkenkunde, Berlin, no date, 27 pp.

(French Occupation: Baden)

1947 Pictorial Definitive Issue: Tyler, V.E., *Linn's Stamp News*, August 21, 1995, p. 6.

(Berlin)

1948–49 Double Red Overprint on 60 pf. Stamp: Esrati, S.G., *The American Philatelist* 96:439–43, 467 (1982).

(Russian Occupation: Mecklenburg-Vorpommern)

1945 Oct. 21, Dec. 8, and Dec. 31 Semipostals: Marton, J.H., *Philately* (London) 3:131–32 (1951).

(German Democratic Republic)

1950–57 Propaganda Stamps: Halle, H.L., *The American Philatelist* 100:943–51 (1986).

GREAT BRITAIN

1840–1944 Broad Coverage: Bynof-Smith, comp. ref. 3C, pp. 60–77.

1840–1912 Broad Coverage: Cowman, A.R., *Stamp Lover* 24:152–55; 187–89 (1931).

1840–1911 Broad Coverage: Williams, L.N. & M. *Philatelist* 11:232–36 (1945).

1867–80 1sh. Stock Exchange Forgery: *Walske, C., *Philatelic Journal of Great Britain* 76:10–18 (1966); Fletcher, comp. ref. 5, pp. 62–63; Melville, F.J., *The Mystery of the Shilling Green,* Chas. Nissen & Co., Ltd., London, 1926, 34 pp.

1878–88 Various Issues: Lowe, R., *Philately* (London) 7:46–49 (1958).

1880 2 sh. Pale Brown Stamp: Johnson, comp. ref. 6 II, pp. 15–16; BPA-Sperati, comp. ref. 2, pp. 47–48 and plate 10.

1883–92 Govt. Parcels Officials: Hilckes, H., *Stamp Collectors' Fortnightly* 1:174 (1895).

1888 £1 Violet Brown Stamp: Irving, W., *Philately* (London) 2:63–64 (1949); Anon., 2:108 (1949).

1902 £1 Green Stamp: Anon., *Stamp Collecting* 1:107–8 (1913); Vallancey, F.H., *Stamp Collecting* 28:25 (1927).

1902–4 Board of Education Overprints: Johnson, comp. ref. 6 II, p. 16.

1923 De La Rue 1p. Airmail Essay: Tyler, V.E., *Linn's Stamp News,* December 11, 1995, p. 8.

1935–44 Propaganda Issues: Williams, E. & P. ref. 1, pp. 27–30; Friedman, H.A., *S.P.A. Journal* 36:337–47 (1974).

1991 24p. Postal Forgery: Alderfer, D., *Linn's Stamp News,* September 12, 1994, pp. 12–13; Rittmeier, W., *Deutsche Briefmarken Zeitung* 69:1488–89 (1994), in German; Youngblood, W.L., *Scott Stamp Monthly* 13(4):14–16 (1995).

(British Offices Abroad — Morocco)

1935 May 8 Silver Jubilee Overprinted Issue: Vanderwarker, R.N., *Stamps,* April 3, 1937, p. 9; de Tartas, D., *Stamps,* August 14, 1937.

GREECE AND RELATED AREAS

1861–1947 Broad Coverage: *Feenstra, R.M., *Greece — A Collection of Forgeries,* 2nd ed., Postzegel Vereniging Griekenland, Ridderkerk, The Netherlands, 1993, 136 pp.

1861–1933 Broad Coverage: Stiedl-Billig, comp. ref. 12, Griechenland I & II.

1851–1923 Broad Coverage: *Vlastos, O.M., *Comparisons of Hellenic Postal Stamps 1861–1923,* O. Vlastos, Ltd., 1992, 275 pp.

1861–82 Hermes Heads: Schloss, comp. ref. 10, pp. 35–41; Vervisch, R., *Balasse Magazine* No. 279: 76–77 (1985), in French; *Ure, B., *Bulletin of the Hellenic P.S. of G.B.* No. 96:2–12; No. 97:44–48 (1995); No. 99:42–45 (1996).

1896 5 and 10d. Olympic Stamps: Rogers, S.E., *The American Philatelist* 84:608 (1984); Vervisch, R., *Balasse Magazine* No. 261: 86–89; No. 262: 130–33 (1982), in French.

1918 5 l. Wounded Soldier Postal Tax: Tyler, V.E., *Linn's Stamp News,* December 12, 1994, p. 6.

GUATEMALA

1867 Bogus Issue: Eckhardt, W.J., *Stamps,* February 21, 1948, pp. 319–23; Rooke, H.F., *Philatelist* 27:97 (1961); Kane, C.E., *Philatelist* 30:69 (1963).

1871–1971 Broad Coverage: * Goodman, R.A., ed., *Guatemala; The Postal History and Philately,* vols. 1 and 2, Robson Lowe, Ltd., London and Bournemouth, 1969 and 1974, 643 pp.

1873 Coat of Arms Issue: Johnson, A.C., *Emco Monthly Journal* No. 327:80 (1946).

1875 Liberty Heads: Tyler, comp. ref. 13, p. 49.

1878 Indian Woman Issue: Tyler, comp. ref. 13, p. 50.

1902 Officials: Tyler, comp. ref. 13, p. 51.

GUERNSEY (GERMAN OCCUPATION)

1941–44 Coat of Arms Issue: Tyler, comp. ref. 13, p. 52; Bohne, German ref. 1.

HAITI

1881–87 Liberty Head Stamps: *Sellers, F.B., *American Philatelic Congress Book* 52:35–50 (1986); Purves, J.R.W., *Collectors Club Philatelist* 52:281–93 (1973).

1892–96 Drooping Palms Issues: Tyler, comp. ref. 13, p. 53.

1902–20 Various Overprints: Chemi, Beal, and DeVoss, comp. ref. 4, pp. 97–102.

1902 Provisional Overprints: *Jeannopoulos, P., *Haiti Philately* 17:22–36 (1991).

1904 Domestic Centenary Independence Issue: Anon., *L'Écho de la Timbrologie* 23:735 (1909).

1904 Nord Alexis Issue: *Jeannopoulos, P., *Haiti Philately* 18:101–60 (1992); Tyler, comp. ref. 13, pp. 54–55.

1906 Gold Currency Overprints: Moorhouse, B., *Mainsheet* 15 (Whole No. 57):4–5 (1990); Sellers, F.B., *American Philatelic Congress Book* 24:25–37 (1958).

1914 50c. Overprints (Scott 176): Sellers, F.B., *American Philatelic Congress Book* 40:25–42 (1974).

HAMBURG

1859–67 Broad Coverage: *Patton, D.S., *Hamburg,* Robson Lowe Ltd., London, 1963, 56 pp.; Stiedl-Billig, comp. ref. 12, Hamburg; Schloss, Germany ref. 2, pp. 37–50; Bohne, Germany ref. 1.

1861–63 Boten (Messenger) Locals: Eckhardt, W.J., *The American Philatelist* 62:346–53 (1949); *Rooke, H.F., *Philatelist* 28: 152–54, 165–68, 188–92, 210, 237, 262–63 (1962); 29:5 (1962); 30:69 (1963); 31:277 (1965); Bles, R.E., *Philatelist* 28:209 (1962); Jackson, H.T., *Philatelist* 28:209–10 (1962); Stirling, D.M., *Philatelist* 29:167 (1963); Jackson, H.T., *Cinderella Philatelist* 7:15–17

(1967); **8**:47–51 (1968); **9**:30–34 (1969); Rooke, H.F., *Cinderella Philatelist* 8:4–9, 26 (1968).

1866 1¹/₂ s. Rose Stamp: Gilgis, Germany ref. 3, vol. 2–3, pp. 1–4.

HANOVER

1850–64 Broad Coverage: *Stiedl-Billig, comp. ref. 12, Hannover; Schloss, Germany ref. 2, pp. 51–60; *Bohne, Germany ref. 1.

1850–57 First Two Designs: Vervisch, R., *Balasse Magazine* No. 278: 28–29 (1985), in French.

1853–64 3p. Red Stamps: Gilgis, Germany ref. 3, vol. 1–4, pp. 5–8.

1858–64 Clover/Horse Cut Squares: Gilgis, Germany ref. 3, vol. 2–2, pp. 8–12.

HAWAII

1851–93 Broad Coverage: *Cowman, A.R., *Stamp Collecting* 24:18–19, 135–36, 140, 244, 263–64, 287–88, 364–65 (1925); Meyer, N.A., F.R. Harris, W.J. Davey, J.K. Bash, et al., *Hawaii: Its Stamps and Postal History,* Philatelic Foundation, New York, 1948, pp. 375–98; Hogan, P., *The American Philatelist* 92:249–54 (1978).

1851–52 Missionaries: Melville, F.J., *Stamp Lover* 24:277 (1932).

1851–52 "Grinnell" Missionaries: Lindquist, H.L., *Collectors Club Philatelist* 1:88–91 (1922); Sloane, G.B., *Collectors Club Philatelist* 1:91–99 (1922); Anon., *The American Philatelist* 37:255–59 (1924); Lemann, J.A., *The American Philatelist* 38:63–74 (1924); Linn, G.W., numerous articles and editorials appearing in *Linn's Weekly Stamp News* from August 1951 to December 1952, culminating in a final report, December 8, 1952, p. 4, which stated his belief that the stamps "are just as genuine as any other of the known Missionary stamps."; Ashbrook, S., *Stamps,* October 5, 1957, pp. 36–38, concluded they were forgeries because some copies were canceled with a counterfeit Honolulu postmark that was not identical to a similar postmark on a genuine stamp in the Caspary collection; Tyler, V.E., *Linn's Stamp News,* April 29, 1996, p. 68.

1853–68 King Kamehemeha III Stamps: Eckhardt, W.J., *Stamps,* February 21, 1948, pp. 319–23.

1859–65 Numerals: *Estberg, J.F., *Plating the Hawaiian Numerals,* Mission Press, Honolulu, 1968, 88 pp. (loose-leaf); Davey, J.W., *Stamps,* November 8, 1941, pp. 189–90.

HELIGOLAND

1867–79 Broad Coverage: *Pollard, R.T., *The American Philatelist* 101:1041–53 (1987); Hardwicke, G.I., *The American Philatelist* 62:854–64, 948–54 (1949); 63:27–33 (1949); Stiedl-Billig, comp. ref. 12, Heligoland; Schloss, comp. ref. 10, pp. 43–47.

1879 1m. Stamp (Scott 22): Spying Eye, *S.P.A. Journal* **10**:527–30 (1948).

HERM ISLAND

1953 Coronation Overprints: Anon., *Stamps,* January 18, 1958, p. 83.

HONDURAS

1865 First Issue: *Green, I.I., *Collectors Club Philatelist* **46**:32–35 (1967).

1877–1933 Various Overprints and Cancels: Chemi, Beal, and DeVoss, comp. ref. 4, pp. 104–31.

1877 Overprints: Holmes, H.R., *London Philatelist* **64**:86–93 (1955); Schaff, H.H., *Weekly Philatelic Gossip,* March 14, 1942, pp. 17–18; March 28, 1942, pp. 58, 63, 67.

1895–1903 PERMITASE Handstamps: Moorhouse, B., *Mainsheet* **7** (Whole no. 24):14–15 (1981).

1895 Arias Issue: Moorhouse, B., *Mainsheet* **5**(Whole no. 17):27–29 (1979); Watchorn, H., *The American Philatelist* **79**:868–69 (1966).

1898 Railroad Train Issue: Anon., *Philately* (St. Louis) **2**:276 (1946).

1911 Independence Anniversary Overprint: Green, I.I., *Stamps,* March 20, 1943, p. 420.

1925 Baraona Issue: Green, I.I., *Stamps,* October 30, 1943, pp. 154–55.

1925 Airmail Overprints: Newall, comp. ref. 8, pp. 125–27.

1930 February Airmail Overprints: Newall, comp. ref. 8, p. 128.

HONG KONG

1862–1945 Broad Coverage: *Tsang, M., *Hong Kong Forgeries,* published by the author, Glenside, Pennsylvania, 1994, 143 pp.

1862 First Issue: Aretz, comp. ref. 1, p. 31; Weigand, J.F., *Weekly Philatelic Gossip,* June 12, 1943, p. 330.

1865 96c. Bister Stamp: BPA-Sperati, comp. ref. 2, p. 48 and plate 9.

1903 and 1904–11 $10 Stamps: Melville, F.J., *Stamp Collectors' Fortnightly* **28**:279 (1922).

1904–11 20c. Orange Brown and Black Stamp: Fletcher, comp. ref. 5, p. 65.

1942–45 da Luz Japanese Occupation Covers: *Evans, L.M., *The American Philatelist* **97**:506–10 (1983); *Spaulding, R.M., *Japanese Philately* **49**:241,252–68 (1994), **50**: 145, 179–88, 193, 216–20. 250–54 (1995); **51**:222–29 (1996), **52**:221–24 (1997), **53**:32–33, 66–67 (1998); Tsang, M., *Hong Kong Japanese Occupation and Mr. H. da Luz,* published by the author, Glenside, Pennsylvania, 1995, 116 pp. (In asserting that all da Luz covers "were found with genuine cancellations," this author ignores a preponderance of evidence proving most or all of them to be fakes or forgeries.); Tyler, V.E., *Linn's Stamp News,* May 4, 1998, pp. 10–11.

HUNGARY

1871–72 First and Second Issue: Schloss, comp. ref. 10, pp. 41–43.

1871 Lithographed First Issue: Redey, N., *Philatelic Journal of Great Britain* **31**:148–49 (1921); Ragatz, comp. ref. 9, p. 4.

1913–16 60f. Green Sideways Watermark: Aretz, comp. ref. 1, p. 32.

1918 First Airmail Overprints: Aretz, comp. ref. 1, p. 32; Gazda, I., and F. Nagy, *The American Philatelist* **101**:638 (1987).

1920 Sheaf of Wheat Overprints: Aretz, comp. ref. 1, p. 32.

1926–27 Postal Forgeries (Scott 408, 410, 413, and 414): Fletcher, comp. ref. 5, pp. 66–67.

(Romanian Occupation)

1919 First Debrecen Overprints: Noska, G., *Romanian Philatelic Studies* **3**(2):1 (1979); Kayssner, comp. ref. 7, vol. 2, pp. 70–71.

1919 Transylvania Issues (Kolozsvar and Nagyvarad): *Szalay, A.B., *Hohere Philatelie: die Philatelie der Zunkunt,* vols. 1 and 2, N.-Szeben, Sibiu — Hermannstadt, Transylvania, 1935, 1046 pp., in German; *Catalogul Marcilor Postale Romanesti '74,* p. 181, in Romanian; Aretz, comp. ref. 1, p. 33; Illyefalvi, K. V., *Baltimore Philatelist* **21** (whole no. 170):48–53 (1968).

(Overprinted Stamps)

1919 Various Occupation and Local Issues; 1944–45 and 1956 Local Issues: Miles, D., *Reference Book of Overprints on Hungarian Stamps,* published by the author, St. Ives., Huntingdon, England, 1993, 274 pp. (This volumes does not provide definitive information on the forgeries of most series covered. It does present some useful hints on the characteristics of the genuine overprints of many difficult issues.)

INDIA

A large number of references to the forgeries of the states of India and various Indian States, primarily to articles in Indian stamp journals, will be found in *Bibliography — Indian Philately,* published by the Philatelic Congress of India, Calcutta, 1988, 426 pp.

1852–1905 Broad Coverage: Cowman, A.R., *Stamp Lover* **28**:206–7 (1935); **28**:230–32 (1936).

1866 Postage (Scott 30) and Official (Scott O12–O14) Overprints: Stoney, R.F., *Philatelic Journal of India* **54**:122–24 (1950).

1882–87 1r. Stamp: Fletcher, comp. ref. 5, pp. 68–69; Johnson, comp. ref. 6 II, p. 20.

1899 Official Overprint: Johnson, comp. ref. 6 II, p. 21.

1937–40 1r. King George VI Stamp: Fletcher, comp. ref. 5, p. 70.

1949 8a. Temple Design: Fletcher, comp. ref. 5, p. 70.

IONIAN ISLANDS

1859 Broad Coverage: See following references under Greece and Related Issues: Vlastos, O.M., pp. 197–210; Feenstra, R. M., pp. 88–91.

IRAN

1868–1938 Broad Coverage: Ultee, A.J., *The American Philatelist* **97**:132–34 (1983).

1868–1935 Broad Coverage: Lewis, H.L., *The Stamps of Persia,* published by the author, Hampton, Middlesex, England, no date, pp. 105–21.

1868–1927 Broad Coverage: *Hartmann, B., *Handbuch Iran,* 2 parts, published by the author, Bayerisch Gmain, Germany, 1987 and 1990, 230 and 242 pp., in German.

1868–1908 Broad Coverage: Cowman, A.R., *Stamp Collectors' Fortnightly* **31**:152–54 (1925).

1868–76 Lion Issues: *Sadri, M., *The Lion Forgeries,* Persiphila, Glendora, California, 1984, 23 pp.

1882 Sun Regular Issue: Tyler, comp. ref. 13, p. 60.

1882 5f. Shah Nasr-ed-Din Issue: Tyler, comp. ref. 13, p. 61.

1882 10f. Shah Nasr-ed-Din Issue: Tyler, V.E., *Linn's Stamp News,* August 8, 1994, p. 6.

1891–1915 Reprints: *Douglas, R.H., *Philatelic Journal of Great Britain* **42**:95–98, 134–36 (1932); **43**:34–36 (1933).

1919 March–April Provisional Issue: Tyler, comp. ref. 13, p. 62.

1927 Airmail Overprints: Aretz, comp. ref. 1, p. 57.

IRELAND

1982 £1 Cahir Castle Definitive: Tyler, V.E., *Linn's Stamp News,* April 15, 1996, p. 6.

ISRAEL

1948 May 4 Sefad Provisional: Steinberg, K., *Stamps,* January 5, 1952, pp. 14–16; Sella (Steinberg), J.K., *Holy Land Philatelist* **6**:1304–5, 1311 (1960).

1948 May 16 Doar Ivre Issue (All Values): Hands, S.E., *London Philatelist* **68**:49 (1959); Tolkowsky, E., *Linn's Weekly Stamp News,* October 26, 1959, p. 13.

1948 May 16 Doar Ivre Issue (High Values): Walters, L., *Linn's Weekly Stamp News,* August 23, 1965, pp. 20–21; Minkus Publications, *Weekly Philatelic Gossip,* March 2, 1957, pp. 13–14; *Stamps,* March 30, 1957, p. 470; *Holy Land Philatelist* **3**:708–9 (1957).

ITALY

1861–1924 Broad Coverage: *Stiedl-Billig, comp. ref. 12, Italien and Neapel.

1862–1951 Broad Coverage: *Dehn, R., *Italian Stamps,* Heinemann, London, 1973, pp. 191–215.

1863–1946 Postal Forgeries: *Fletcher, comp. ref. 12, pp. 72–74.

1870–1925 Postage Dues: Tyler, comp. ref. 13, p. 63, Spying Eye, comp. ref. 11, pp. 39–40.

1922 Philatelic Congress Overprints: Carson, W., *Linn's Stamp News,*

December 18, 1972, p. 27; Lana, R.E., *Linn's Stamp News*, December 13, 1993, p. 14.

1924 1 l. Overprints: Aretz, comp. ref. 1, p. 36.

1924 Cruise Overprints: Lana, R.E., *Linn's Stamp News*, March 9, 1992, p. 64.

1930s Cancels on High Values: Carson, W., *Linn's Stamp News*, January 20, 1975, p. 44.

1943 Hitler–Mussolini Propaganda Stamps: Friedman, H.A., *S.P.A. Journal* **38**:633–36 (1976); Friedman, H., E. & P. ref. 2F.

1946 100 l. Postal Forgery: Dehn, R.A., *Gibbons Stamp Monthly* **41**:153–55 (1968).

1961 205 l. Withdrawn Stamp: Dehn, R.A., *Stamp Lover* **57**:110 (1965).

1964 October 15 500 l. European Town Congress Commemorative: Bello, A., *Western Stamp Collector*, July 3, 1971, p. 3.

JAMMU & KASHMIR

1866–94 Comprehensive Coverage: *Staal, F., *The Stamps of Jammu & Kashmir*, The Collectors Club, New York, 1983, 286 pp.

JAPAN

1871–79 Broad Coverage: *Wilhelmsen, K., *Japans klassiske Forfalskninger*, Tromso Filatelistiklubb, Tromso, Norway, 1981, 363 pp., in Norwegian, German, and English.

1871–72 Dragon Stamps: *Metzelaar, W., and V.E. Tyler, Forgeries & Imitations of the Dragon Stamps of Japan, I.S.J.P. Monograph 4, *Japanese Philately* **26**:(1) Part 2:1–24 (1971); *Ichida, S., *The Dragon Stamps of Japan 1871–72*, Ikeda Publishing Co., Tokyo, 1959, 221 p.

1872–76 Cherry Blossom Stamps: *Tyler, V.E., *Characteristics of Genuine Japanese Stamps: Cherry Blossom Issues of 1872–76*, Society of Philatelic Americans, Cincinnati, no date, 38 pp; *Ichida, S., *The Cherry Blossom Issues of Japan 1872–1876*, All Japan Philatelic Federation, Tokyo, 1965, 335 pp; *Tyler, V.E., and M.T. Montgomery, The Wada Cherry Blossom Forgeries, I.S.J.P. Monograph 6, *Japanese Philately* **29**(4) Supplement:1–92 (1974).

1876–79 Koban Stamps: *Wilhelmsen, K., and V.E. Tyler, The Koban Forgeries of Japan, I.S.J.P. Monograph 8, *Japanese Philately* **34**(2) Supplement:1–63 (1979).

1910–28 Military Franchise Overprints: Tyler, V.E., *Japanese Philately* **33**:33–40 (1978).

1916 10s. Heir Apparent Stamp: Bertalanffy, F.D., *Japanese Philately* **30**:33–34 (1975).

1919 First Airmail Overprints: *Fisher, G.A., Jr., and R.M. Spaulding Jr., *Japanese Philately* **14**:229–36 (1959).

1945–47 Third Showa and First New Showa Series: Peterman, S., *Japanese Philately* **35**:232–35 (1980); Tyler, comp. ref. 13, pp. 64–65; Tyler, V.E., *Linn's Stamp News*, April 4, 1994, p. 6.

1947–50 2nd to 5th National Athletic Meet Issues: Tyler, V.E., *Japanese Philately* **25**:208 (1970).

1948 and 1949 Philatelic Week Issues: Spaulding, R.M., Jr., *Japanese Philately* **20**:154–55 (1965).

(Offices in China)

1913 Overprints: Spaulding, R.M., *Japanese Philately* **49**:51 (1994).

(Offices in Korea)

1900 Overprints: Fisher, G.A., Jr., *Japanese Philately* **19**:196–97 (1964).

(Local Issue)

1868 Sutherland Locals: Spaulding, R.M., Jr., *Japanese Philately* **11**:153–54 (1956).

JORDAN-TRANSJORDAN

1942 Definitives and Dues; 1948 Occupation Definitives and Dues: Anon., *Philatelist* **24**:261 (1958); Anon., *Philatelic Journal of Great Britain* **68**:43 (1958).

KARELIA

1922 Total Coverage: Tyler, comp. ref. 13, p. 66; Tyler, V.E., *The American Philatelist* **98**:794 (1984).

KOREA

1884–1905 Broad Coverage: Zirkle, H.K., ed., *Philatelic Handbook for Korea, 1884–1905*, The Collectors Club, New York, 1970, pp. 77–80; *Mizuhara, M., *The Korean Postal History 1884–1905*, Japan Philatelic Society, Foundation, Tokyo, 1993, pp. 6–7, 253–55, 295–96, in Japanese; *Kim, J.-S., *The Facts of Korean Classic Stamps*, Inje University Press, Kimhae, Korea, 1998, 406 pp.

1884–1902 Broad Coverage: *Brady, L.R., and V.E. Tyler Jr., *Handbook of Philatelic Forgeries — Korean Empire*, Conk-Singleton Co., Seattle, Washington, 1962, 20 pp.

1884 10m. Stamp: Tyler, comp. ref. 13, p. 67.

1884 Cancellations on 5m. and 10m. Stamps: *Tyler, V.E., *Korean Philately* **17**:82–88 (1968); *Kim, J.-S., *Study on the First Korean Stamps Used in 1884*, Busan Philatelic Club, Busan, 1994, 339 pp., in Korean.

1895 50p. Yin Yang Regular Issue: Tyler, V.E., *Linn's Stamp News*, February 6, 1995, p. 6.

1897–1900 Tae Han (Tai Han) Overprints: Hyun, J., *The American Philatelist* **93**:1115–22 (1979); Klein, H.L., *The American Philatelist* **94**:1089–96 (1980). (The two previous references express opposite opinions on the genuineness of certain of these overprints. Interested collectors should read both articles.); Zirkle, H.K., *Korean Philately* **16**:94 (1967).

1949 15w. U.P.U. Stamp: Heath, W.L., *Korean Philately* **11**:90–93 (1962).

1964–66 Granite Paper Regular Issues: Phillips, D.G., *Korean Philately* **16**:69–75, 111–14 (1967); Hofheimer, H., *Korean Philately* **16**:115–16 (1967); Tyler,

V.E., *Linn's Stamp News*, July 24, 1995, p. 6; December 25, 1995, p. 6.

LABUAN

1894 Lithographed First Design: *Price, R., *London Philatelist* **91**:42–45 (1982); Shipman, L.H., *The Stamps and Postal History of North Borneo*, part 2 — *1894–1908*, The Sarawak Specialists' Society, no location given, 1979, pp. 569–77; Selsor, C.J., *London Philatelist* **85**:134–38 (1976).

LATVIA

1918–33 Broad Coverage: *Hofmann, H. von, ed., *Lettland: Handbuch Philatelie und Postgeschichte*, parts 1 and 2/3-*Die Briefmarken*, Harry V. Hofmann Verlag, Hamburg, 1988, 191 and 260 pp., in German; Tirums, M., *Latvian Collector* **8**:37–40 (1975).

1918 December 18 First Issue: Veveris, A., *S.P.A. Journal* **21**:300–301, 529 (1959).

1919 Redrawn Sun Issue (Wrong Paper): Tyler, comp. ref. 13, p. 69; Kayssner, comp. ref. 7, pp. 12–13.

1919 3k., 25k., and 75k. Arms on Pelure Paper, Imperf.: Kayssner, comp. ref. 7, vol. 1, pp. 25–27.

1919 25k. Arms on Pelure Paper: Aretz, comp. ref. 1, pp. 41–42.

1919 Liberation of Riga Issue on Pelure Paper: Kayssner, comp. ref. 7, vol. 3, p. 136.

1919–20 Liberation of Kurland Issue: Tyler, comp. ref. 13, p. 70.

1920 50k. and 1r. First National Assembly Stamps: Aretz, comp. ref. 1, p. 43.

1920 September 1 Overprints: Kayssner, comp. ref. 7, vol. 1, p. 6.

1920–21 2r. Overprint on 10k. Stamp (Scott 86): Kayssner, comp. ref. 7, vol. 1, p. 23; vol. 2, p. 85.

1921 May 31 Ruble Overprints on Latgale Relief Issue: Kayssner, comp. ref. 7, vol. 1, pp. 33–35.

1921 2r. Semipostal Overprints: Kayssner, comp. ref. 7, vol. 1, p. 14.

1923 War Invalids and 1933 Airmail Overprints on Fake Covers: Engel, A., *The American Philatelist* **97**:992–94 (1983).

1927 1 l. Surcharge on 3r. Stamp: Kayssner, comp. ref. 7, vol. 1, p. 17.

1928–32 Triangle Airmails: Tyler, comp. ref. 13, p. 71; Kayssner, comp. ref. 7, pp. 13–14.

1931 December 5 Airmail Semipostal Overprints: Kayssner, comp. ref. 7, vol. 1, p. 5.

1933 May 26 Airmail Overprints: Kayssner, comp. ref. 7, vol. 2, pp. 87–88.

1933 June 15 Airmail Semipostals: Kayssner, comp. ref. 7, vol. 5, pp. 14–15.

(German Occupation)

1919 Fake Cancels on LIBAU Overprints: Aretz, comp. ref. 1, p. 43.

(Russian Occupation)

1919 First, Second, and Third Issue Overprints: Ceresa, Russia ref. 1, vol. 3, pts. 16–18, pp. 83–110.

1919 Western Army Eagles: Ceresa, Russia ref. 1, vol. 3, pts. 16–18, pp. 110–24; Hall, A., *Western Army Eagles* (Forgery and Reprint Guide 16), J. Barefoot Ltd., York, England, 1984, 18 pp.; Tyler, V.E., *The American Philatelist* 97:416–18, 660–62 (1983); 98:433–34 (1984).

LEBANON

Most of the lithographed stamps issued between 1925 and 1957, including airmails and postage dues, have been forged to supply inexpensive items for the packet trade. Counterfeits usually were produced by typography (letterpress), so the printing method alone is sufficient to differentiate the forgeries from the lithographed originals. No detailed study, or even a comprehensive listing, of the forgeries has ever been published.

1948 September 1 Lebanese Village Airmail: Tyler, V.E., *Linn's Stamp News*, June 27, 1994, p. 6.

1952 Beirut Airport Airmails: Tyler, V.E., *Linn's Stamp News*, March 4, 1996, p. 6.

1953 Lockheed Constellation Airmails: Tyler, V.E., *Linn's Stamp News*, July 10, 1995, p. 8.

LEEWARD ISLANDS

1897 Sexagenary Overprints: *Farmer, J.A.C., *Leeward Islands: 1897 Sexagenary Overprint and its Forgeries*, published by the author, Crookham Village, Aldershot, England, 1988, 11 pp. plus plates.

LIBERIA

1860–92 Broad Coverage: Cowman, A.R., *Stamp Lover* 18:140–41 (1925).

1860–80 First Design Stamps: *Cockrill, P., *Liberia: Forgeries of the First Issues: 1860–1880* (Series Booklet No. 4), published by the author, Newburg, Berkshire, England, no date, 44 pp.; Aretz, comp. ref. 1, p. 44.

1897 3c. Bicolor Stamp: Rogers, H.H., *A Century of Liberian Philately*, K. Bileski, Winnipeg, no date, p. 19.

1938 Fake Cancels on Reprinted Airmails: Linn, G.W., *Linn's Weekly Stamp News*, March 28, 1955, p. 11.

LITHUANIA

1918–41 Broad Coverage: Grigaliunas, J., *et al.*, eds., *Postage Stamps of Lithuania*, The Collectors Club, New York, 1978, 237 pp.

1919 Kaunas Typeset Issues: Norton, W.E., *S.P.A. Journal* 39:19–33 (1976).

1922 July 22 Gediminas Castle Airmails: Newall, comp. ref. 8, pp. 174–75.

1924 January 28 60c. Airmail: Johnson, comp. ref. 6 II, p. 35; Newall, comp. ref. 8, p. 176.

1932 November 28 Anniversary of Independence Airmails: Kayssner, comp. ref. 7, vol. 5, pp. 16–18; Newall, comp. ref. 8, pp. 177–79.

1933 May 6 Kestutis Airmails: Newall, comp. ref. 8, pp. 180–82.

1935 F. Vaitkus Airmail Overprint: Newall, comp. ref. 8, p. 183.

LÜBECK

1859–64 Broad Coverage: *Stiedl-Billig, comp. ref. 12, Lübeck; Schloss, Germany ref. 2, pp. 61–66.

1859–62 First Design Stamps: Bohne, Germany ref. 1; Gilgis, Germany ref. 3, vol. 1–4, pp. 1–3.

LUNDY ISLAND

1942 Tighearna Sheet Cut-Outs: Tyler, V.E., *Linn's Stamp News*, (1/2 p.) October 30, 1995, p. 6; (2 p.) November 13, 1995, p. 6; (9 p.) November 27, 1995, p. 6.

LUXEMBOURG

1852–1908 Broad Coverage: *Stiedl-Billig, comp. ref. 12, Luxemburg.

1852–80 Broad Coverage: Schloss, comp. ref. 10, pp. 61–65.

1859–95 Broad Coverage: Ragatz, comp. ref. 9, pp. 88–98.

1859–81 Second Issue: Schon, A., *Luxembourg Philatelist* 13:40–43, 53–55 (1963); Vervisch, R., *Balasse Magazine* No. 270: 224–25 (1983), in French.

1859–60 2c. and 37 1/2 c. Stamps: BPA-Sperati, comp. ref. 2, p. 166 and plate 112.

1882 Industry and Commerce Issue: Bertrand, G., *Mémorial Philatélique*, vol. 3, Librairie L. Cros, Montpellier, 1934, p. 26, in French.

1908–26 Official Overprints: Bertrand, G., *opus cit.*, p. 27; Duffy, T.P., *Luxembourg Philatelist* 4(11):74 (1954).

1923 View of Luxembourg Souvenir Sheet: Martin, R.C., *The American Philatelist* 65:608–10 (1952); Billig, F., *Stamps*, December 14, 1940, p. 375.

1923 March 10fr. Black View of Luxembourg: Hughes, R., *West-End Philatelist* 40:3 (1950).

MALTA

1860 1/2 p. Stamp: BPA-Sperati, comp. ref. 2, p. 52 and plate 12.

1902 1p. on 2 1/2 p. Overprint: Marriner, T.F., *Philatelic Magazine*, No. 169:100 (1922).

1926 POSTAGE Overprints: Forbes-Bentley, R., *Stamp Collecting* 26:329 (1926).

MAN, ISLE OF

1973 First Postage Dues Fakes: Anon., *Philatelic Magazine* 82:445 (1974).

MANCHOUKUO

1934 February 15f. Stamp: Plowman, F.T., *Stamps*, September 27, 1941, p. 454.

MARIENWERDER

1920 Overprints: *Klein, U.E., *Marienwerderaufdrucke, echt oder falsch?* published by the author, Siegen, Germany, 1991, 29 pp. plus 23 illustrations, in German.

MAURITIUS

1847–99 Broad Coverage: Cowman, A.R., *Stamp Lover* 24:363–64 (1932); 25:6–10 (1932).

1847–59 Post Office and Post Paid Issues: Mueller, B., *Essay-Proof Journal* 39:170–72 (1982); *Linn's Stamp News*, January 24, 1994, p. 46.

1847 Post Office Stamps: Spying Eye, *S.P.A. Journal* 9:495–500 (1947).

1848 Post Paid Issue: Brunel, G., *Stamp Collector's Monthly Circular* 48:126–29, 156–58, 195–98 (1921); Anon., *Collectors Club Philatelist* 3:96–97 (1924); BPA Sperati, comp. ref. 2, p. 53 and plate 13.

1860 9p. Stamp: BPA-Sperati, comp. ref. 2, p. 53 and plate 13.

1876–77 CANCELLED Remainders: Anon., *Stamp Collectors' Fortnightly* 19:202 (1913).

1879 13p. and 38p. Stamps: BPA-Sperati, comp. ref. 2, p. 54 and plate 13.

1902–22 Fake Cancels: Aretz, comp. ref. 1, p. 45.

1902 12c. on 36c. Overprint: Anon., *South African Philatelist* 48:4 (1973).

MECKLENBURG-SCHWERIN AND MECHLENBURG-STRELITZ

1856–1867 Broad Coverage: *Stiedl-Billig, comp. ref. 12, Mecklenburg-Schwerin und Strelitz; *Bohne, Germany ref. 1; Schloss, Germany ref. 2, pp. 67–71.

MEMEL

1921 July 6 First Airmail Overprints: Kayssner, comp. ref. 7, vol. 1, p. 3; Kayssner, comp. ref. 7, vol. 4, p. 184; Aretz, comp. ref. 1, p. 47; Johnson, comp. ref. 6 I, pp. 17–18; Newall, comp. ref. 8, pp. 184–85.

1922 May 12 Second Airmail Overprints: Kayssner, comp. ref. 7, vol. 5, p. 18; Newall, comp. ref. 8, p. 186.

(Lithuanian Occupation)

1923 Harbor Issue and Overprints: Algmin, V.A., and C.E. Kane, *The American Philatelist* 96:234–35, 284 (1982); Kayssner, comp. ref. 7, vol. 2, pp. 65–67.

1923 Ship Design Harbor Issue: Tyler, comp. ref. 13, p. 73.

1923 25c. Overprints on Vytis Stamps (Scott N96-N99): Kayssner, comp. ref. 7, vol. 2, p. 65.

MEXICO

1856–1914 Overprints, Postal Markings, and Provisionals: Chemi, Beal, and DeVoss, eds., comp. ref. 4, pp. 146–286.

1856–95 Selected Coverage: Cossio, J.L., *Mexicana* 9:172–76, 182–84, 186–89 (1960).

1856–72 Broad Coverage: Schloss, H., *Stamps*, January 3, 1953, pp. 14–16.

1856–61 First Two Issues: *Smith, P. de, and M. de Fayolle, *Mexicana* 3:40–62 (1954); Pulver, D., *Linn's Stamp News*, March 11, 1991, pp. 14–15.

1856–61 Forged Cancellations on First Two Issues: Beal, J.H., *American Philatelic Congress Book* 21:99–107 (1955).

1864 Hidalgo Issue: Tyler, comp. ref. 13, p. 74.

1864 1r. with ¹/₂r. Bogus Overprint: Bloss, A.W., *Stamps*, November 7, 1953, p. 199.

1864–66 Imperial Eagles Issue: Corbett, L.V., *Imperial Eagles of Maximilian's Mexico*, Mexico Philatelic Library Association, Stanton, California, 1993, pp. 52–58; Aretz, comp. ref. 1, p. 46.

1866 Maximilian Issue: Bynof-Smith, comp. ref. 3B, pp. 90–91.

1868 Hidalgo Issue: Liera G., R., *Mexicana* 26:808–11 (1977); BPA-Sperati, comp. ref. 2, p. 193 and plate 129; Tyler, V.E., *Linn's Stamp News*, February 20, 1995, p. 6.

1872 Hidalgo Issue: Barron, J.H., *Stamp Collectors' Fortnightly* 21:178 (1915); Vannotti, F., *Mexicana* 17:466–72 (1968).

1874–95 Fake Cancels on Issues of: Pulver, D., *Linn's Stamp News*, May 23, 1994, p. 40; June 27, 1994, p. 22.

1875–79 Porte De Mar Issues: *Schimmer, K.H., *Porte De Mar*, Mexico Elmhurst Philatelic Society, International, Tucson, Arizona, 1987, pp. 111–24.

1879 Unissued Stamps: Tyler, comp. ref. 13, p. 75.

1886–88 Vale 1 cvo Bogus Overprints on 2c. Stamps: Bloss, A.W., *Stamps*, November 7, 1953, p. 199.

1887 Blue-Lined Paper Issues: Fager, E.W., and D.G. Ferguson, *Linn's Weekly Stamp News*, June 26, 1967, p. 11.

1895 5p. and 10p. Stamps: BPA-Sperati, comp. ref. 2, p. 193 and plate 129.

1913–20 Various Issues: Hopkins, H.C., *Mexicana* 5:76–82 (1956).

1913–16 Various Overprints: Love, T.R., *S.P.A. Journal* 19:239–46 (1957).

1913–14 Sonora White and Green Seals: South Texas MEPSI Chapter, *White and Green Seal Stamps of Sonora*, Mexico-Elmhurst Philatelic Society International, no location given, 1979, 6 pp.

1914 Victory at Torreon Overprint: Havemeyer, J.T., *Mexicana* 12:280–81 (1963).

1914 Large GCM Handstamp: Follansbee, N., *Mexicana* 36:80–85 (1987).

1914 ES Overprint (Non-Scott): Follansbee, N., *Mexicana* 36:202–4 (1987).

1914 Unissued Madero Head Stamps (Non-Scott): Brock, C.W., Jr., *The American Philatelist* 55:598–99 (1942).

1915 Ysla Fake Overprints (Non-Scott): Ingham, F.G., *Mexicana* 26:816–18 (1977).

1915 5c. Oaxaca Coat of Arms, Type I: Wahlberg, H., *Mexicana* 21:643–44 (1972).

1917–20 Forged Perforations on Regular Issue: Hopkins, H.C., *Mexicana* 12:261 (1963).

1935 Amelia Earhart Airmail Overprints: Ingham, F.G., *Mexicana* 23:705 (1974); Ingham, F.G., *Mexicana* 16:443 (1967); Anon., *Mexicana* 17:463 (1968).

MODENA

1852–59 Broad Coverage: *Stiedl-Billig, comp. ref. 12, Modena; Schloss, comp. ref. 10, pp. 67–72.

1852–57 First Design: Vervisch, R., *Balasse Magazine* No. 275:180–81; No. 276:232–33 (1984), in French.

MOLDOVA

1992 Aug. 31 Inverted Overprints: Tyler, V.E., and C. Dan, *Linn's Stamp News*, January 16, 1995, p. 12.

MONACO

1885 First Issue: Spying Eye *Philately* (St. Louis) 1:93 (1946); Cowman, A.R., *Stamp Lover* 17:317 (1925); Schloss, H., *Stamps*, May 24, 1947, pp. 380–81; BPA-Sperati, comp. ref. 2, p. 167 and plate 112; Ragatz, comp. ref. 9, p. 105; Aretz, comp. ref. 1, p. 49.

1920 Semipostal Overprints: Williams, T.B.C., *Stamp Lover* 19:333 (1927).

MONTENEGRO

1874–1906 Broad Coverage: *Stiedl-Billig, comp. ref. 12, Montenegro.

1874–1893 Broad Coverage: Schloss, comp. ref. 10, pp. 77–79.

1896 Cetinje Monastery Issue: Tyler, comp. ref. 13, p. 76; Johnson, comp. ref. 6 I, p. 18.

1920–21 Bogus Series: Eisenstein, H.A., *Stamps*, August 8, 1953, pp. 200–201.

1941–42 Various Occupational Airmail Overprints: Newall, comp. ref. 8, pp. 187–92.

NEPAL

1881–1935 Selected Coverage: Haverbeck, H.D.S., *The Postage Stamps of Nepal*, The Collectors Club, New York, no date [1962], pp. 109–11.

NETHERLANDS AND FORMER COLONIES

1852–1953 Broad Coverage: *Loo, P.F.A. van de, *Forgeries of Netherlands Stamps and Former Colonies* (Netherlands Indies, Netherlands New Guinea, Netherlands Antilles, and Surinam), English language edition and 1982 Supplement, Netherlands Philatelic Society of Chicago, 1978, 1982, unpaged (looseleaf).

(Netherlands)

1894 5c. Orange Color Error: O'Keefe, D., *Linn's Stamp News*, November 10, 1986, p. 39.

1913 10g. Queen Wilhelmina Stamp: Aretz, comp. ref. 1, pp. 49–50.

1913 First Issue Official Overprints: Rang, C.P., *Gibbons' Stamp Monthly* 12:52–53 (1938).

1921 First Issue Airmails: Newall, comp. ref. 8, pp. 196–97.

1924 5c. on 1c. Inverted Overprint: Aretz, comp. ref. 1, p. 51.

1928, Aug. 20 Airmails: Newall, comp. ref. 8, pp. 198–99.

(Netherlands Indies)

1908 Buiten Bezit and Java Overprints on 2¹/₂g. Stamp: Aretz, comp. ref. 1, p. 16.

1928 Sept. 20 Airmail Star Overprints: Tyler, comp. ref. 13, p. 78.

1928 Dec. 1 and 1930–32 Airmails: Newall, comp. ref. 8, pp. 200–201; van Reyen, P.E., *Linn's Stamp News*, October 12, 1981, p. 84.

NEVIS

1861–78 Engraved and Lithographed Issues: Balley, S.G., *West-End Philatelist* 45:2–5 (1955); Bynof-Smith, comp. ref. 3C, pp. 98–99.

NEW BRITAIN

1914–15 G.R.I. Overprints: Bynof-Smith, comp. ref. 3C, pp. 110–11.

NEW BRUNSWICK

1851–63 Broad Coverage: Pugh, BNA ref. 1; Smythies, BNA ref. 2, pp. 12–15, 63–64, 82–85; Mitchell, R.B., *Fakes & Forgeries of New Brunswick & Prince Edward Island*, Scotia Stamp Studio, Ltd., Halifax, 1979, pp. 1–28; *Gratton, R., *Les Cahiers de l'Académie Québécoise d'Études Philatéliques*, Opus VII, 1989, pp. H1–H27, in French.

1860 1c. Regular Issue: Tyler, V.E., *Linn's Stamp News*, May 27, 1996, p. 6.

1860 5c. Regular Issue: Tyler, V.E., *Linn's Stamp News*, April 1, 1996, p. 6.

1860 12¹/₂c. Regular Issue: Tyler, V.E., *Linn's Stamp News*, June 10, 1996, p. 6.

1860 17c. Regular Issue: Tyler, V.E., *Linn's Stamp News*, June 24, 1996, p. 6.

1863 2c. Regular Issue: Tyler, V.E., *Linn's Stamp News*, January 8, 1996, p. 6.

NEWFOUNDLAND

1857–1933 Broad Coverage: *The Encyclopaedia of British Empire Postage Stamps*, vol. 5, *The Empire in North America*, Robson Lowe Ltd., London, 1973, pp. 425–546.

1857–1932 Broad Coverage: *Pugh, BNA ref. 1.

1857–1919 Broad Coverage: Cowman, A.R., *Stamp Lover* 26:148–50, 186–87 (1933).

1857–76 Broad Coverage: Smythies, BNA ref. 2, pp. 7–11, 52–62, 76–82.

1900 Bogus Pictorial Issue: Williams, L.N., *Linn's Stamp News*, April 20, 1987, p. 24–25.

1919 June 9 $1 Alcock-Brown Fake Airmail Covers: Goodkind, H.M., *Aero Philatelist Annals* 5:55–58 (1957).

1927 May 21 De Pinedo Airmail: Bentham, L.W., *Stamp Collector*, March 8, 1982, pp. 16–17.

1930 Sept. 25 Columbia Airmail: Johnson, comp. ref. 6 I, p. 20.

1932 May 20 Dornier Airmail: Newall, comp. ref. 8, pp. 202–3.

1933 June 9 Airmail Issue Imperfs: Newall, comp. ref. 8, p. 203.

1933 July 24 Balbo Airmail: Harmer, C.H.C., *The American Philatelist* 93:435–36, 480 (1979); Newall, comp. ref. 8, pp. 204–6.

NEW GUINEA

1882-95 Faked New Guinea Cancels on Queensland Stamps: Bagnall, C.L., *Stamp Collecting* 3:78–79 (1914).

1925-28 £1 Native Village Stamp: Bynof-Smith, comp. ref. 3C, pp. 112–13; Expert Committee's Chairman, *Philately* (London) 6:191, 222 (1956).

1935 £2 and £5 Airmails: Newall, comp. ref. 8, pp. 209–11.

1939 £1 Airmail Stamp: Newall, comp. ref. 8, pp. 209–10; Expert Committee's Chairman, *Philately* (London) 6:190, 222 (1956).

NEW SOUTH WALES

1850-94 Broad Coverage: *Pope, M., *Stamp Forgeries of New South Wales*, 2nd ed., published by the author, Birmingham Gardens, New South Wales, Australia, 1995, 110 pp.

1850-92 Broad Coverage: Cowman, A.R., *Record of Philately* 1:128–29, 139–42 (1936).

1850 Jeffryes' Sidney Views: Tyler, V.E., *The American Philatelist* 99:413–14, 473 (1985).

1852-1894 Broad Coverage of Reprints: Hull, A.F.B., *Stamp Collectors' Fortnightly* 5:143, 151 (1899).

1855 5p. Diadem Issue: Tyler, V.E., *Linn's Stamp News*, April 17, 1995, p. 6.

1888-89 Emu Postal Forgery: Purves, J.R.W., *London Philatelist* 76:169–71 (1967); 79:7–15, 17 (1970).

NEW ZEALAND

1855 1sh. Yellow Green Stamp: Haworth, W., *Philatelist* 25:171–72 (1959).

1855-56 Forged Cancels (De Thuin): Lowe, R., *Philatelist* 33:131 (1967).

1871 2p. Vermilion Stamp (Faked Perfs.): Campbell, A.F., *Philatelist* 20:185 (1954).

1898-1900 Part-Perf. Fakes from Proofs: Iremonger, W.G., *Stamp Lover* 36:2 (1943); Hamilton, C., *Stamp News* 23(1):9 (1976).

1913 Auckland Exhibition Overprints: Cowell, E.G., *Weekly Philatelic Gossip*, December 28, 1946, p. 534.

1958 Jan. 15 2p. on 1¹/₂p. (Scott 290) Overprint: Hamilton, C., *Stamp News* 21(7):14 (1974).

(Locals)

1898 Great Barrier Island Pigeon Post First Issue: Sefi, A.J., *Philatelic Journal of Great Britain* 41:214–19 (1931); Newall, comp. ref. 8, p. 212; Kilgour, L.J., and T.L. Belknap, *The American Philatelist* 94:117–211 (1980).

1899 Triangle Stamp: Kilgour, L.J., *The American Philatelist* 98:350–51 (1984).

NICARAGUA

1862-80 First Designs: Bynof-Smith, comp. ref. 3B, pp. 96–97; Maxwell, C.R., *Nicarao* 5(3):10 (1995).

1862-1899: Maxwell, C.R., *Nicarao* 5(4): 13–15; 6(1):19–21 (1995).

1869-1931 Selected Overprints and Cancels: Chemi, Beal, and De Voss, eds., comp. ref. 4, pp. 287–301.

1869-80 First Designs (Reprints): Maxwell, C.R., *Nicarao* 1(1):2 (1990); Birks, M.P., *Nicarao* 1(3):13 (1991); Leavy, J.B., *Gibbons Stamp Weekly* 10:7–8 (1909).

1890-99 Seebeck Reprints: Glickstein, D., *The American Philatelist* 99:914–18 (1985).

1890-99 Faked Cancellations: Sousa, J., *Mt. Nittany Philatelic Society Newsletter* 1:50–51 (1969); *The American Philatelist* 77:138–39 (1963).

1932-33 Various Issues: Cone, R.N., *Aero Philatelist Annals* 1:39–59 (1953). This detailed article and previous ones by the same author listed in it describe certain unauthorized reprints as "counterfeits." All must be read with caution because of the unorthodox nomenclature employed.

1932 Earthquake Commemoration Issue (Reprints): Maxwell, C.R., *Nicarao* 3(3):18–19 (1993).

1932 September 11 Airmail Overprint: Newall, comp. ref. 8, pp. 215–16.

1932 Rivas and Leon-Sauce Railway Issues: A.K., *Mainsheet* 4(whole no. 15):77 (1976).

1933 Airpost Week Issue: Tyler, comp. ref. 13, p. 79; Newall, comp. ref. 8, pp. 213–14.

1941 10c. Overprint on 1c. Bright Green: Anon., *Linn's Stamp News*, August 22, 1983, p. 7.

(Province of Zelaya — Bluefields)

1904-7 Overprints: Leavy, J.B., *Gibbons Stamp Weekly* 11:175–76 (1910).

(Cabo Gracias A Dios)

1904-7 Overprints: Leavy, J.B., *Gibbons Stamp Weekly* 11:176, 221–22 (1910). Many unanswered questions still remain about the validity of certain overprints of both of the above regions. See, for example, Davies, B., *London Philatelist* 88:130–35 (1979).

NORTH BORNEO

1883-99 Broad Coverage: *Shipman, L.H., *The Stamps and Postal History of North Borneo*, parts 1 and 2, The Sarawak Specialists' Society, no location given, no date, 724 pp.

1887-92 Regular Issue: Price, R., *Sarawak Journal* 35:164–70 (1982).

1887 ¹/₂c. Rose Stamp: Selsor, C.J., *The American Philatelist* 91:703–4 (1977).

1887 2c. Brown Stamp: Selsor, C.J., *London Philatelist* 85:134–38 (1976).

1894 50c. and $1 Stamps: Price, R., *Sarawak Journal* 39:6–7 (1985).

NORTH INGERMANLAND

1920 March 21–August 2 Broad Coverage: *Ceresa, Russia comp. ref., vol. 3, parts 16–18, pp. 159–64.

1920 August 2 Issue: Anon., *Stamp Collecting* 93:35 (1959).

1920 August 2 10p. and 30p. Pictorials: Tyler, comp. ref. 13, pp. 81–82.

NORTH WEST PACIFIC ISLANDS

1915-22 Broad Coverage — Overprints: Carriker, C., *The American Philatelist* 99:234–36, 267 (1985).

NORWAY

1855-57 First Designs: Brofos, F.A., *Posthorn* 15:25–27, 70 (1958).

1863 Regular Issue: Johnson, comp. ref. 6 I, p. 21.

1924-34 10ö. and 20ö. Stamps: Larson, G., translator, *Weekly Philatelic Gossip*, August 1, 1931, p. 603.

1941 V Overprints: King-Farlow, R., *London Philatelist* 58:151–52 plus plate (1949); Berntsen, A., *Stamp Collecting* 73:305 (1949); Jahr, K., *Scandinavian Newsletter* No. 37:1–3 (1957).

NOVA SCOTIA

1851-63 Broad Coverage: Pugh, BNA ref. 1; Smythies, BNA ref. 2, pp. 16–17, 65–72, 84–89; Mitchell, R.B., *Nova Scotia Fakes & Forgeries*, Scotia Stamp Studio, Halifax, 1976, 51 pp.; *Gratton, R., *Les Cahiers de l'Académie québécoise d'Études Philatéliques*, Opus V, 1987, pp. H1–H47, in French.

1851 Regular Issue: Johnson, comp. ref. 6 I, p. 19.

1860-63 Broad Coverage: Richardson, E., *Stamps*, June 14, 1958, p. 412.

1860-63 A.A. Bartlett Letterhead Reproductions: Osterhoff, R.J., *Stamp Collector*, February 7, 1983, p. 27.

1860-63 2c. Stamp: Aretz, comp. ref. 1, p. 55.

1860-63 5c. Stamp: Eckhardt, W.J., *The American Philatelist* 62:389 (1949).

NYASSA

1895 Unissued (Bogus) Series: George, C., *Stamp Collectors' Fortnightly* 1:74 (1895); Czyl, J., *Linn's Stamp News*, August 20, 1984, p. 61.

1903 Overprints (Scott 44–48): Huggins, B., *Portu-Info* 4(1):30 (1965).

OBOCK

1892 Regular Issue and Postage Due Overprints: Aretz, comp. ref. 1, p. 56.

OLDENBURG

1852-61 Broad Coverage: *Stiedl-Billig, comp. ref. 12, Oldenburg; Bohne, Germany ref. 1; Schloss, Germany ref. 2, pp. 72–81; Paulo (Paul Ohrt?), *Mitteldeutsche Philatelisten-Zeitung* 3:112 plus plate, 128–29 (1894), in German.

1855-61 Broad Coverage: BPA-Sperati, comp. ref. 2, pp. 90–93 and plates 49–52.

ORANGE RIVER COLONY

1900 3p. on 4p. V.R.I. Bogus Stamp: Brinkman, J.H., *Weekly Philatelic Gossip*, January 7, 1933, p. 1350; February 4, 1933, pp. 1460–61.

PALESTINE

1918 5pi. E.E.F. Stamp: Buetow, G., *Holy Land Philatelist* 1:25 (1954); 2:362 (1955).

Various Forged Postmarks: Pollack, F.W., *Holy Land Philatelist* 1:228-29 (1955).

1948 ER RAMLE Postmarks: Dorfman, D., *The American Philatelist* 98:429-30 (1984).

PANAMA

1878 First Issue: Thomas, E.B., Jr., *The American Philatelist* 92:144-46 (1978).

1878 First Issue (Reprints): Myer, J.A., *The American Philatelist* 63:266-70 (1950).

1887-88 Michelsen-Curtis Favor Printings: *Helme, J.B., *Collectors Club Philatelist* 67:364-87 (1988).

1888 50c. Map Stamp: Tyler, comp. ref. 13, p. 83.

1894-1936 Overprints and Cancels: Chemi, Beal, and De Voss, eds., comp. ref. 4, pp. 302-30.

PARAGUAY

1870 2r. First Issue (Reprint): Krassa, A., *Stamps*, October 8, 1932, p. 127.

1878 Large 5 Overprints: Sandford, V.H., *London Philatelist* 81:50-52 (1972); Chemi, Beal, and De Voss, eds., comp. ref. 4, p. 332.

1878 Small 5 Overprints: Chemi, Beal, and De Voss, eds., comp. ref. 4, p. 333.

1879-81 Regular Issue (Reprints): Krassa, A., *Stamps*, October 8, 1932, p. 127.

Miscellaneous Cancels: Chemi, Beal, and De Voss, eds., comp. ref. 4, p. 331.

1886 First Official Issue: Phillips, C.J., *Stanley Gibbons Monthly Journal* 19:314-18 (1911). The modified designs of this issue characterized by Phillips and by the current *Scott Catalogue* as reprints are believed by the following authorities to be forgeries: Barron, J.H., *London Philatelist* 39:34-36 (1930); Sandford, V.H., *London Philatelist* 81:53-54 (1972). They are definitely not reprints because both the overprints and underprints are lithographed; in the originals these were applied by typography (letter press).

1890 OFICIAL Overprints: Chemi, Beal, and De Voss, eds., comp. ref. 4, p. 322.

1890 5p. and 10p. Phantoms: Branston, A.J., *London Philatelist* 87:7-8 (1978); Tyler, V.E., *Philatelic Forgers: Their Lives and Works*, rev. ed., Linn's Stamp News, Sidney, Ohio, 1991, pp. 60-63.

1923 Phantom Pictorial Series: Tyler, V.E., *Philatelic Forgers: Their Lives and Works*, rev. ed., Linn's Stamp News, Sidney, Ohio, 1991, pp. 52-53; Williams, L.N., *Linn's Stamp News*, November 21, 1988, p. 57.

1929-31 First Definitive Airmails: Newall, comp. ref. 8, p. 221.

1930 95c. Airplane and Arms Airmails: Tyler, comp. ref. 13, p. 84; Sousa, J.M., *The American Philatelist* 79:117 (1965); Newall, comp. ref. 8, pp. 222-23.

1930 1.90c. Asuncion Cathedral Airmails: Tyler, comp. ref. 13, p. 85; Watchorn, H., *The American Philatelist* 82:325-26 (1968); Newall, comp. ref. 8, pp. 222-23.

1931-39 Gunboat Airmails: Tyler, V.E., *Linn's Stamp News*, July 25, 1994, p. 8; Watchorn, H., *The American Philatelist* 79:625-26 (1966); Newall, comp. ref. 8, pp. 224-25.

1931-36 Airmail Issue: Newall, comp. ref. 8, pp. 226-27.

1931-36 10c. Airmails: Tyler, V.E., comp. ref. 13, p. 86.

1934 May 26 Zeppelin Airmail Overprints: Tyler, comp. ref. 13, p. 87.

1935 Zeppelin Airmail Overprints: Goodkind, H.M., *Aero Philatelist Annals* 6:113 (1959).

1935-39 Tobacco Triangle Airmails: Tyler, V.E., *Linn's Stamp News*, October 17, 1994, p. 6; Newall, comp. ref. 8, p. 228.

1935-38 Church of the Incarnation Airmails: Tyler, V.E., *Linn's Stamp News*, August 22, 1994, p. 6.

PARMA

1852-59 Broad Coverage: *Stiedl-Billig, comp. ref. 12, Parma; Schloss, comp. ref. 10, pp. 98-104; Weigand, J.F., *Weekly Philatelic Gossip*, September 11, 1943, pp. 8, 18-19; Cowman, A.R., *Filatelia* 10:327-31 (1926).

PERU

1857 Pacific Steam Navigation Co. Issue: Danielski, M., *Philatelist* 39:199-202 (1973).

1857-73 Broad Coverage Including Cancels: Lamy, G., and J.-A. Rinck, *Peru Postal Cancellations 1857-1873*, Andin et Cie, Lyon, France, 1964, pp. 85-95 and plate 7. The forgeries of the 1d. red 1862-63 issue discussed in this work are actually private reprints with various fake cancels.

1858 First Two Definitive Issues: Fentonia, *Philatelist* 8:12-14 (1874).

1858 March 1½ Peso Orange-Yellow Stamp: BPA-Sperati, comp. ref. 2, pp. 195-96 and plate 131.

1863 1p. Brown Stamp: Moll, H.H., *Collectors Club Philatelist* 48:364 (1969); Phillips, C.J., *Gibbons Stamp Weekly* 11:539 (1910); Gastelumendi Velarde, R., *Chile Filatelico* 37:39-41 (1964).

1866-67 10c. Llamas Stamp: Tyler, V.E., *Linn's Stamp News*, October 4, 1993, p. 6.

1868 1p. Green Stamp: Moll, H.H., *Collectors Club Philatelist* 48:362 (1969).

1872 1p. Orange Stamp: Same references as 1863 1p. brown stamp.

1873 March 2c. Llamita Stamp: *Moll, H.H., *Collectors Club Philatelist* 43:285-94 (1964).

1876 10c. Coat of Arms Stamp: Tyler, comp. ref. 13, p. 88.

1883 Triangular Overprints: *Dixon, M., *Mainsheet* 4 (whole no. 14):53-65 (1975-76); Howland, W.G., *The American Philatelist* 88:659-60 (1974).

1894 October 23 Morales Bermúdez Overprints: Bonilla Lara, A., *Chile Filatelico* 40:327-32 (1967), in Spanish.

1927 December 10 Airmail Overprint: Matthaeis, A. de., *Filigrana* 6:14-17 (1940-41), in Spanish.

1931-32 Regular Issue (Clandestine Printing): Cabello, C., *Stamp Lover* 21:340 (1933); Pemberton, P.L., *Philatelic Journal of Great Britain* 51:18-19 (1941).

1932 July 28 Piura Arms Stamps: Spying Eye, *S.P.A. Journal* 11:142-43 (1948).

(Chilean Occupation)

1881-82 Overprints: Huber, N.F., *Chile Filatelico* 41:140-41 (1968), in Spanish.

(Provisional Stamps and Overprints)

1881-84 Broad Coverage: *Howland, W.G., *The American Philatelist* 78:656-69, 672, 742-55 (1965).

1881 January 10c. and 25c. Arequipa Stamps: Vierordt, L., *American Journal of Philately* 3:262-64 (1890).

1881 January 25c. Arequipa Stamp: Brown, C.B., *Stamp Lover* 21:373-75 (1929).

(Miscellaneous)

1857-1915 Selected Postal Markings and Overprints: Chemi, Beal, and De Voss, eds., comp. ref. 4, pp. 337-54.

PHILIPPINES

1854-1897 Broad Coverage: Graus, Spain ref. 1.

1863 5c. Stamp: Eckhardt, W.J., *The American Philatelist* 62:289 (1949).

1899-1904 PHILIPPINES Overprints: Aretz, comp. ref. 1, p. 56.

1925 August 26 De Pinedo Flight Covers: Jandrue, G.E., Jr., *Weekly Philatelic Gossip*, February 25, 1928, p. 1475.

1945-46 Fake Victory Overprints: Garrett, E.A., *Stamp Collector*, August 27, 1977, pp. 26-27.

1961 Jose Rizal Bogus Souvenir Sheet: Lindquist, H.L., *Stamps*, August 26, 1961, pp. 294-95.

1980-87 Various Postal Forgeries: Stanfield, L., *Linn's Stamp News*, June 27, 1988, pp. 10-11.

1986 5.50p. Saligang Batas Stamp (Scott 1905): Sandler, S.R., *The American Philatelist* 105:808-10 (1991).

(Japanese Occupation)

1942 March 4 First Day Covers: Garrett, E.A., *The American Philatelist* 97:716-17 (1983).

1943 First Day Covers: Garrett, E.A., *Japanese Philately* 30:158-68 (1975); *Linn's Stamp News*, May 12, 1975, pp. 56-57; *A Postal History of the Japanese Occupation of the Philippines, 1942-1945*, published by the author and the United States Possessions Philatelic Society, Freeman, South Dakota, 1992, pp. 125-28, see also pp. 157-59 for fake censor marks.

(Filipino Revolutionary Government)

1898-99 2c. Postage Stamp: Sheldon, R., *Stamps*, April 7, 1945, p. 18.

1898-99 8c. Registration Stamp: Sloane, G.B., *Sloane's Column*, Bureau Issues

Association, Inc., West Somerville, Massachusetts, 1961, p. 212.

1898–99 1m. Newspaper Stamp: Sloane, G.B., as above, p. 214; Tyler, comp. ref. 13, p. 89.

1898–99 2c. Telegraph Stamp: Sloane, G.B., as above, p. 216–17.

1898–99 50c. Telegraph Stamp: Sloane, G.B., as above, p. 217; Tyler, comp. ref. 13, p. 90.

POLAND

1860–1936 Broad Coverage: Domanski, V., Jr., *Stamps*, February 9, 1946, pp. 244–45; Blunt, A., *Poland? Forgery?* Alnis Guide No. 11, Glass Slipper, York, England, 1990, not paged consecutively.

1860 First Issue: Domanski, V., Jr., and S.G. Rich, *Stamp Specialist Blue Book:*158–59 (1941); Palmer, D., *Bulletin of the Polonus Philatelic Society*, no. 54:1 (1947).

1914–19 Locals and World War I Related Issues: *Hall, A., *Poland Locals*, J. Barefoot (Investments) Ltd., York, England, 1981, 123 pp; Larking, R.N.W., *Gibbons' Stamp Monthly* 3:4–6, 24–27, 42–44, 68–71, 82–85 (1930).

1917 December 18 Przedborz Locals First Issue: Uznanski, M.E., *Stamps*, July 14, 1956, pp. 50–54.

1919 Cracow Overprints: Wolosewick, F.E., and J. Gapinski, *Stamps*, March 4, 1950, pp. 345–47; Gapinski, J., *Stamps*, February 25, 1961, pp. 298–99; March 3, 1962, pp. 368–69.

1918–19 3pf. Brown Warsaw Issue Overprints (Scott 15): Schroeder, A., *Bulletin of the Polonus Philatelic Society* No. 114:1 (1953).

1918–19 20pf. Blue Overprints (Scott 21): Kronenberg, S., *The American Philatelist* 96:898, 936 (1982).

1918–19 Lublin Overprints: Stallberg, H., *Stamps*, March 3, 1951, pp. 308–9.

1919 September 15 Gniezno Provisionals: Stallberg, H., *Stamps*, May 3, 1951, p. 306; Kronenberg, S., *Linn's Stamp News*, March 15, 1976, pp. 55–56.

1919 November Skalat Local Overprints: Kronenberg, S. and E., *The American Philatelist* 88:739–41 (1974).

1921 March 5 Semipostal Overprints: Johnson, comp. ref. 6 I, pp. 21–22; Schroeder, A., *op. cit*. No. 114:2 (1953).

1921 May 29 Semiofficial Airmails: Hall, A., *Forgery & Reprint Guide 15: Poland Airmails*, J. Barefoot Ltd., York, England 1983, pp. 3–7; Newall, comp. ref. 8, pp. 230–33.

1923 Inflation Overprints: Kronenberg, S., *The American Philatelist* 97:919 (1983).

1924 2,000,000m. Stamp: Tyler, comp. ref. 13, p. 91; Schroeder, A., *op. cit.*, No.114:1–2 (1953).

1925–27 20g. Dull Red Stamp: Schroeder, A., *op. cit.*, No.114:2–3 (1953).

1925 First Airmail Issue: Tyler, comp. ref. 13, p. 92; Newall, comp. ref. 8, pp. 234–35.

1928 May 3 Warsaw Souvenir Sheet: Spying Eye, *S.P.A. Journal* 12:346–49 (1949).

1934 May 5 Philatelic Exhibition Overprints: Spying Eye, comp. ref. 11, pp. 41–43; Schroeder A., *op. cit.*, No. 114:3 (1953).

1936 Gordon Bennett Overprints: Spying Eye, comp ref. 11, p. 43; Bialy , J.J., *The American Philatelist* 90:174 (1976).

1943 April 15 Sikorski Woldenberg P.O.W. Camp Stamp (Non-Scott): Kalawski, M., *Stamps*, November 27, 1976, pp. 614–15.

1945 September 1 1.50z. Overprint: Bialy, J.J., *Stamps*, January 27, 1979, p. 204.

1954 May 23 5z. Souvenir Sheet: Kronenberg, S., *The American Philatelist* 93:246–47 (1979).

1989 1000z. Blue Cornflower: Hines, T., *Linn's Stamp News*, March 8, 1993, p. 10.

(Postal Markings)

Various: Stulberg, F., ed., *Canadian Philatelist* 25:248–53 (1974).

(Offices in Russia)

1919 November ODESA Overprints (Non-Scott): Kronenberg, S., *The American Philatelist* 105:140–43 (1991).

PORTUGUESE COLONIES

1869–1905 Crown Issues and Reprints: *Pernes, R.R., *Crown Stamps of the Portuguese Colonies*, J.-B. Publishing Co., Crete, Nebr., 1976, 35 pp.; Quinn, T.B., *The American Philatelist* 79:841–48 (1966).

1914–26 Ceres-Design Issue: Gaylord III, H.H., *Portu-Info* 11(2):26–32 (1975).

1939–40 New York World's Fair Phantom Airmail Overprint: Myer, J.N., *The American Philatelist* 56:645–47 (1943).

PRINCE EDWARD ISLAND

1868 4p. Victoria Design: Tyler, V.E., *Linn's Stamp News*, April 3, 1995, p. 6.

1872 6c. Victoria Design: Tyler, V.E., *Linn's Stamp News*, May 1, 1995, p. 6.

PRUSSIA

1850–67 Broad Coverage (Reprints): Schloss, Germany ref. 2, pp. 82–85.

1858 and 1866 Selected Issues: Bohne, Germany ref. 1.

QUEENSLAND

1860–81 Broad Coverage: *Pope, M., *Stamp Forgeries of Queensland; South Australia, Tasmania*, published by the author, Birmingham Gardens, New South Wales, 1992, pp. 1–42.

RHODESIA

1966 January 17 INDEPENDENCE Overprints: Anon., *Linn's Weekly Stamp News*, January 15, 1968, p. 18; Robertson, J., *Stamp Collecting* 111:893–95 (1968); *Rudman, T., *South African Philatelist* 47:287–90, 310–12 (1971).

ROMAGNA

1859 Regular Issue: * Patton, D.S., *The Romagna*, The Philatelist and Postal Historian, London, 1953, 32 pp; *Philatelist* 30:92–95, 112–16 (1964); Kane, C.E., *Philatelist* 32:140 (1966); Stiedl-Billig, comp. ref. 12, Romagna; Schloss, H., *Stamps*, March 22, 1947, pp. 538–39; Weigand, J.F., *Weekly Philatelist Gossip*, September 25, 1943, pp. 57–58.

ROMANIA

1858–1930 Broad Coverage: *Stiedl-Billig, comp. ref. 12, Rümanien, parts I–III.

1858–96 Forged Cancellations: Pataki, G., *Romanian Philatelic Studies* 1(1):5–8 (1977).

1858–71 Broad Coverage: Schloss, H., comp. ref. 10, pp. 112–25.

1858–64 Fake Cancels: Pataki, G., *The American Philatelist* 99:320–21 (1985).

1858–62 First Two Issues: *Heimbüchler, F., *Romania: The Bull's Heads Issues of Moldavia: 1852-1862*, published by the author, Munich, 1994, 418 pp.

1862 and 1864 Differentiation of Two Issues: Bobeica, V., *Romanian Philatelic Studies* 6(1):14–16 (1982).

1864 Sheets Printed on Both Sides: Bobeica, V., *Romanian Philatelic Studies* 6(2):8–10 (1982).

1872 10b. Paris Printing: Tyler, comp. ref. 13, p. 94.

1881–1911 First Design Postage Dues: Tyler, comp. ref. 13, p. 100.

1890 and 1891 Numerals in 4 Corners Issue: Chitu, B.P., *Romanian Philatelic Studies* 8(2):4–5 (1984).

1893–98 1 l. and 2 l. Stamps: Johnson, comp. ref. 6 II, p. 39.

1903 Mail Coach Issue: Tyler, comp. ref. 13, p. 95; Laptev, P.C., *Romanian Philatelic Studies* 4(1):6–7 (1980).

1906–26 Forged Postal Markings: Dragomir, S., *Romanian Philatelic Studies* 7(2):1–3 (1983).

1906 General Exposition High Values: Tyler, V.E., *Linn's Stamp News*, September 19, 1994, p. 6; October 3, 1994, p. 6.

1906 First Design Semipostals: Laptev, P.C., *Romanian Philatelic Studies* 7(4):1–2 (1983).

1906 First Three Designs Semipostals: Tyler, comp. ref. 13, pp. 97–99.

1913 Scutit Franchise Stamp (Non-Scott): Noska, G. *Romanian Philatelic Studies* 3(3):1 (1979).

1918 5b. and 10b. 1918 Overprints: Tyler, comp. ref. 13, p. 96.

1927 March 15 Semipostals: Pataki, G., *Romanian Philatelic Studies* 4(1):4–5 (1980); Kayssner, comp. ref. 7, vol. 5, pp. 21–22.

1928–29 5 l. Regular Issue (Scott 326): Pataki, G., *Romanian Philatelic Studies* 7(1):8 (1983).

1928 April 29 20 l. Bessarabia Stamp: Noska, G., *Romanian Philatelic Studies* 3(1):1 (1979).

1932 November 20 Stamp Anniversary Issue: Pataki, G., *Linn's Stamp News*, April 14, 1980, pp. 62–63; *Romanian Philatelic Studies* **8**(1):11 (1984).

1945 Oradea 1 Overprints (Non-Scott): Ratai, G., *Romanian Philatelic Studies* **6**(4):1–4 (1982).

ROMAN STATES

1852–68 Broad Coverage: *Stiedl-Billig, comp. ref. 12, Kirchenstaatmarken.

1852 First Issue: *Levitsky, F.J., ed., *Roman States Forgeries: The Issue of 1852*, Triad Publications, Weston, Massachusetts, 1986, 230 pp.; Levitsky, F.J., ed., Supplement to foregoing work, same publisher, 1990, 13 pp.

1852 50b. Regular Issue: Vervisch, R., *Balasse Magazine* No. 257: 190–93 (1981), in French.

1867–70 Second Designs: *Jenkins, F.A., *Roman States Essays and Reprints: The Issues of 1867–1870*, Triad Publications, Weston, Massachusetts, 1997, 98 pp.

1867–68 Second Designs: *Levitsky, F.J., and F.A. Jenkins, *Roman States Forgeries: The Issue of 1867–1868*, Triad Publications, Weston, Massachusetts, 1990, 98 pp.; Tyler, V.E., and G.E. Peck, *The American Philatelist* **92**:580–87 (1978).

RUSSIA

1857–1917 Broad Coverage: Prigara, S.V., *Stamps*, July 11, 1942, p. 65.

1857–63 Broad Coverage: Schloss, comp. ref. 10, pp. 133–35.

1884–1924 Broad Coverage: *Stiedl-Billig, comp. ref. 12, Russland: Kaiserreich und Levant and Sowjet-Russland.

1884–1921 Broad Coverage: Redgrove, H.S., *Stamp Review* **2**(3): 5, 31, 41 (1938).

1917 10c. Blue Regular Issue: Johnson, comp. ref. 6 I, p. 23.

1918 35 and 70k. Kerensky Chainbreakers: Ceresa, Russia ref. 1E, pp. 112–14; 70 k. only, Johnson, comp. ref. 6 I, p. 24.

1921 1r. and 2r. Symbols of Agriculture: Tyler, comp. ref. 13, p. 101.

1921 20r. Agriculture and Industry: Tyler, comp. ref. 13, p. 102.

1921 100r. Regular Issue (Scott 188): Tyler, comp. ref. 13, p. 103.

1921 Volga Relief Semipostals: Johnson, comp. ref. 6 I, pp. 26–27.

1921 2250r. Semipostal: Johnson, comp. ref. 6 I, p. 27.

1922–55 Airmails: Shalimoff, G.V., *The American Philatelist* **106**:1024–29 (1992).

1922 First Airmail Issue: Aretz, comp. ref. 1, p. 61.

1922 Agriculture Semipostals: Johnson, comp. ref. 6 I, pp. 27–29.

1922 Transportation Design Semipostals: Tyler, comp. ref. 13, pp. 105–8.

1924 Lenin Mourning Issue: Tyler, comp. ref. 13, p. 104; Sousa, J.M., Jr., *The American Philatelist* **78**:683–84 (1965).

1933 Anniversary Airmail Issue: Tyler, comp. ref. 13, p. 109.

1937 February 1 Pushkin Sheet: Johnson, comp. ref. 6 I, pp. 25–26; Billig, F.,

Stamps, January 25, 1941, p. 115.

1992 25r. Dolgoruky Definitive: Baumann, F.W., *Linn's Stamp News*, August 9, 1993, p. 2.

1992 St. Petersburg Provisional Overprints: Tereshko, M., *Linn's Stamp News*, August 29, 1994, pp. 8–9.

(Finnish Occupation — Aunus)

1919 Overprints: Turunen, S., *The American Philatelist* **106**:32–33 (1992).

(The Armies)

1919 Comprehensive Coverage: *Ceresa, Russia ref. 1C.

1919 September Army of the North Issue: Tyler, comp. ref. 13, pp. 110–14; Johnson, comp. ref. 6 I, pp. 24–25.

(Offices in China)

1899–1917 Overprints: Rosselevich, A., *Journal of the Rossica Society of Russian Philately* No. 45: 40–43 (1955); Nos. 46/47: 52–55 (1955); Sklarveski, R., *Weekly Philatelic Gossip*, April 21, 1934, pp. 131–32.

(Offices in the Turkish Empire)

1863–79 Broad Coverage: *Stiedl-Billig, comp. ref. 12, Russland; Kaiserreich und Levant.

RYUKYU ISLANDS

1945–46 Kumeshima Provisional Stamp: *Spaulding, R.M., Jr., *Japanese Philately* **33**:199–205 (1978).

1946–48 Provisional Overprints on Japanese Stamps: Schoberlin, M., *Japanese Philately* **22**:122–23 (1967).

1952 10y. Overprint on 50s. Stamp: *Weiner, R.P., *The American Philatelist* **98**:998–1010 (1984); Thomas, N.S., and F.B. Thomas, *Japanese Philately* **19**:104–5 (1964).

1958 Shureimon Gate Stamp: Tyler, V.E., *Linn's Stamp News*, November 28, 1994, p. 6.

1964–66 Specimen Overprints on Karate and Turtle Series: Kamiyama, R., *Japanese Philately* **22**:179 (1967).

1971 May 10 and May 20 First Day Cancels: Kamiyama, R., *Japanese Philately* **26**:171–73 (1971).

SAAR

1920–59 Broad Coverage: Bohne, Germany ref. 1.

ST. HELENA

1856–94 First Design Stamps: Cowman, A.R., *Stamp Collecting* **24**:518 (1925).

ST. LUCIA

1860–94 Selected Issues: Cowman, A.R., *Stamp Collecting* **24**:342 (1925).

1860–82 Selected Issues: Weigand, J.F., *Weekly Philatelic Gossip*, November 20, 1943, pp. 249–50, 256.

SAINT THOMAS–LA GUAIRA–PUERTO CABELLO

1864–70 Local Issues: *Ringström, S., and H.E. Tester, *The Private Ship Letter Stamps of the World*, Part 1, *The*

Caribbean, published by the authors, no location given, no date [1976], pp. 12–109; Engstrom, V.E., ed., *Danish West Indies Mail, 1754–1917*, vol. 3, Scandinavian Philatelic Printing and Publishing Company, Washington, D.C., 1982, pp. 15-1 – 15-33.

1865 Ship Local Issue: Tyler, comp. ref. 13, p. 115.

ST. THOMAS AND PRINCE ISLANDS

1869–85 Crown Issues: Johnson, comp. ref. 6 II, p. 42; see also Portuguese Colonies.

ST. VINCENT

1861–90 First Design Types: *Lowe, R., *Philatelist* **36**:398–403 (1970); **37**:16–19 (1970); Weigand, J.F., *Weekly Philatelic Gossip*, June 3, 1944, pp. 303–4.

1880–81 1sh. Vermilion Stamp: Johnson, comp. ref. 6 II, p. 40.

1881 4p. on 1sh. Fake DeThuin Cover: Lowe, R., *Philatelist* **33**:169 (1967).

EL SALVADOR

1867–79 First Issue and 5c. Second Issue: Weigand, J.F., *Weekly Philatelic Gossip*, October 16, 1943, p. 138.

1867–74 First Issue and Overprints: Spying Eye, *Weekly Philatelic Gossip*, December 9, 1944, pp. 323–24; Werner, D.J., *Pan American Philatelist* **3**:4–11 (1956).

1867 $^{1}/_{2}$r. Stamp: Tyler, comp. ref. 13, p. 116.

1874–1980 Overprints and Cancellations: Chemi, Beal, and DeVoss, eds., comp. ref. 4, pp. 78–94.

1889 1 centavo and "1889" Handstamped Overprints: Negus, J., *Philatelic Magazine* **73**:721, 723, 767 (1965).

1890–98 Seebeck Reprints: Glickstein, D., *The American Philatelist* **99**:914–18 (1985).

1895–99 First Design Postage Dues: Tyler, comp. ref. 13, p. 117.

1900–1906 Various Overprints: Berthold, V.M., *Philatelic Gazette* **7**:208–13 (1917); **8**:4–11 (1918).

1930 Bolivar Centenary Airmails: Johnson, comp. ref. 6 I, p. 29; Tyler, V.E., *Linn's Stamp News*, October 2, 1995, p. 6.

1933 October 12, Columbus Anniversary Airmails: Newall, comp. ref. 8, pp. 68–69.

SAMOA

1877–82 Express Issue: *Hurt, E.F., *West-End Philatelist* **37**:31–33 (1947); Cowman, A.R., *Stamp Collecting* **24**:379 (1925); Aretz, comp. ref. 1, pp. 61–62.

SAN MARINO

1877–99 Coat of Arms Issue: Tyler, comp. ref. 13, p. 118; Schloss, comp. ref. 10, p. 136.

1933 April 28 Zeppelin Overprints: Aretz, B., *The American Philatelist* **48**: 540 (1935); Newall, comp. ref. 8, pp. 242–45.

1936 April 14 Overprints: Newall, comp. ref. 8, pp. 246–47.

1948–50 100 l. Overprint on 50 l. Parcel Post Stamp: Anon., *Berner Briefmarken Zeitung* 67:91 (1975), in German.

SARAWAK

1869 March 1 First Stamp: French, R.D., and P.W. Savage, *The American Philatelist* 43:160 (1930).

1871 January 3c. Stamp: Tyler, comp. ref. 13, p. 119; Johnson, comp. ref. 6 II, p. 41; French, R.D., and P.W. Savage,, *The American Philatelist* 43:223–24 (1930).

1874 2c. on 3c. Provisional: *Selsor, C.J., *S.P.A. Journal* 41:381–86 (1979); Shipman, L.H., *Sarawak Journal* 33:134–35 (1980).

This overprint is currently described as bogus in the Scott Catalogue, but many Sarawak specialists believe that the stamp does exist as a genuine issue. About 20 different forgeries are known.

Date Unknown, Sailing Ship Phantoms: Melville, F.J., *Stamp Lover* 19:37, 85 (1926).

SARDINIA

1819–20 Cavallini Stamped Letter Sheets: Lowe, R., *Philatelist* 9:113–15 (1943).

1851–63 Broad Coverage: *Stiedl-Billig, comp. ref. 12, Sardinien; Schloss, comp. ref. 10, pp. 137–40.

1855–63 5c., 20c., and 40c., Values: Tyler, comp. ref. 13, pp. 120–22; Lana, R.E., *Linn's Stamp News*, June 13, 1994, p. 30.

SAUDI ARABIA

1921–25 Various Overprints: *Graham, D., *Simplified Guide to Saudi Arabia Forgeries*, Filatco, Appleton, Wisconsin, 1986, 12 pp.

1945 Royal Meeting Commemoratives: Graham, D., *The American Philatelist* 101:527 (1987).

1982–86 1r. Definitive (Scott 882): Graham, D., *ibid.*

SAXONY

1850–57 Broad Coverage: *Stiedl-Billig, comp. ref. 12, Sachsen; Schloss, German ref. 2, pp. 86–91; BPA-Sperati, comp. ref. 2, pp. 94–95 and plates 53–55.

1850 3pf. Red Stamp: *Bohne, German ref. 1; Schloss, H., *Stamps*, January 25, 1947, pp. 142–43.

1856 10ng. Blue Stamp: Aretz, comp. ref. 1, p. 62.

SCHLESWIG-HOLSTEIN

1850–65 Broad Coverage: *Stiedl-Billig, comp. ref. 12, Schleswig-Holstein; Schloss, Germany ref. 2, pp. 92–95.

1850–65 Selected Cancellations: Bohne, Germany ref. 1.

SEDANG

1888 Local Issue: Tyler, comp. ref. 13, p. 123.

SERBIA

1866–1914 Broad Coverage: *Stiedl-Billig, comp. ref. 12, Serbien.

1866–69 Classic Issues: Schloss, comp. ref. 10, pp. 141–45; Johnson, comp. ref. 6 I, pp. 30–31.

1869–78 Prince Milan Design: Tyler, comp. ref. 13, p. 124; Johnson, comp. ref. 6 I, p. 30.

1901–3 Para Values, King Alexander Issue: Tyler, comp. ref. 13, p. 125.

1901–3 1d. King Alexander Stamp: Tyler, comp. ref. 13, p. 126.

1904 Coronation Issue: Tyler, comp. ref. 13, p. 127; Pugh, K., *Linn's Stamp News*, May 30, 1977, p. 58; Olofsson, G., *Stamps*, May 3, 1941, p. 154.

1905 King Peter Definitive Issue: Tyler, comp. ref. 13, p. 128.

1911–14 King Peter with Cap Issue: Tyler, comp. ref. 13, p. 129; Pugh, K., *Linn's Stamp News*, June 13, 1977, p. 33.

SHANGHAI

1865–66 Large Dragons: *Benzinger, H., *Journal of Chinese Philately* 27:102–3, plates I–II, 104–5, 132–38, plates 2(i)–2(ii) (1980); 28:11–18, plates 2 (ii cont.)–3(1980); 28:65–69, 2 plates (1981); Sousa, J.M., and M. Rogers, *The Shanghai Large Dragons*, Parts I–II, Michael Rogers, Winter Park, Florida, 1984 and 1985, 8 pp. each; Fletcher, H.G.L., *London Philatelist* 78:196–201 (1969).

1866 1 cand. Small Dragon: Tyler, V.E., *Linn's Stamp News*, September 4, 1995, p. 6.

1866 8c. Small Dragon: Tyler, V.E., *Linn's Stamp News*, September 18, 1995, p. 6.

1877–88 20 cash Small Dragons: Tyler, V.E., *Linn's Stamp News*, February 5, 1996, p. 6.

1877–88 60 cash Small Dragons: Tyler, V.E., *Linn's Stamp News*, February 19, 1996, p. 6.

1877–89 60 cash and 80 cash Small Dragons: Johnson, comp. ref. 6 I, pp. 31–32.

SIERRA LEONE

1859–93 First and Second Designs: Weigand, J.F., *Weekly Philatelic Gossip*, October 2, 1943, pp. 81, 95.

1859 First Stamp: BPA-Sperati, comp. ref. 2, p. 61 and plate 18.

SINGAPORE

1948 50c. and $2 Definitives: Editors, *Stamp Lover* 41:197 (1949); Fletcher, comp. ref. 5, p. 89.

1948 $1 and $2 Definitives: Jordan, A.F., *Stamp Collecting* 82:555 (1954).

SOLOMON ISLANDS

1907 Large War Canoe Issue: Tyler, V.E., *Linn's Stamp News*, March 20, 1995, p. 6; Gisburn, H.G.D., *Philately* (London) 2:152 (1949) — unauthorized imperforate reprints.

SOUTH AFRICA

1925 First Airmail Issue: *Sheffield, W.N., *South African Philatelist* 29:197 (1953); Newall, comp. ref. 8, pp. 287–88.

SOUTH AUSTRALIA

1855–1904 Broad Coverage: *Pope, M., *Stamp Forgeries of Queensland; South Australia, Tasmania*, published by the author, Birmingham Gardens, New South Wales, 1992, pp. 43–85.

SOUTHERN NIGERIA

1901–7 High Values: Porter, H.G., *Stamp Collectors' Fortnightly* 50:9–10 (1944).

SPAIN

1850–1950 Broad Coverage: *Graus, Spain ref. 1.

1850–1946 Broad Coverage (Postal Forgeries): *Graus, F., and E. Soro, *Postal Forgeries of Spain*, Filatelia Pedro Monge, Barcelona, 1977, 601 pp.

1850–1938 Broad Coverage: *Monné, A.M., *Las Falsificaciones Del Sello Español*, Estudios Filatelicos "La Corneta," Barcelona, 1966, 196 pp. and 172 plates, in Spanish.

1853–1946 Broad Coverage (Postal Forgeries): *Graus, Spain ref. 2.

1853 Regular Issue: Vervisch, R., *Balasse Magazine* No. 281:180–81 (1985), in French.

1854 Regular Issue: Vervisch, R., *Balasse Magazine* No. 282: 244–45 (1985), in French.

1856 April 11 4c. Isabella II Stamp: Tyler, comp. ref. 13, p. 130.

1876 June 10c. Alfonso XII: Tyler, comp. ref. 13, p. 131.

1907 Madrid Industrial Exposition Issue (Non-Scott): Tyler, comp. ref. 13, p. 135.

1920 First Airmail Overprints: Newall, comp. ref. 8, pp. 248–49.

1930 Railway Congress Airmails: Tyler, comp. ref. 13, p. 132.

1930 June 15 Fake Cancels on Goya First Day Covers: Nathan, S., *Stamp Collector*, June 13, 1981, p. 10.

1930 October 10 Spanish-American Union Issue: Nathan, S., *Stamp Collector*, November 10, 1979, p. 34.

1930 October 10 Lindbergh Airmail Stamp "Errors": Jones, B., *Linn's Stamp News*, April 6, 1970, p. 42.

1931 December 9 10p. Montserrat Stamp: Lenze, C., *Stamps*, November 19, 1955, p. 286.

1936–39 Fake Civil War Issues: Van Dam, T., *The American Philatelist* 96:43–50, 123–28 (1982).

1936–37 Burgos Provisional Airmail Overprints: Newall, comp. ref. 8, pp. 252–59.

1938–1950 Selected Airmail Overprints: Newall, comp. ref. 8, pp. 260–63.

1938 Republic Design Definitives: Tyler, V.E., *Linn's Stamp News*, October 16, 1995, p. 6.

(Carlist Stamps)
1873–75 Complete Coverage: *Vervisch, R., *Espagne: Les Emissions Carlistes, Groupe d'Étude des Falsifications*, no location given [Brussels], no date [ca. 1990], 20 pp.

1874 1r. and 16m. Stamps: Tyler, comp. ref. 13, pp. 133–34.

STELLALAND

1884 February First Issue: *Poole, B.W.H., *Stanley Gibbons Monthly Journal* 18: 206–8, 249–52 (1908); Aretz, comp. ref. 1, p. 65.

STRAITS SETTLEMENTS

1867–1907 Broad Coverage: Cowman, A.R., *Record of Philately* 1:45–46, 52–54 (1935).

1945–48 50c. BMA Malaya Overprint: Editors, *Stamp Lover* 41:197 (1949); Fletcher, comp. ref. 5, p. 89.

1945–48 $5 BMA Malaya Overprint: Anon., *Gibbons Stamp Monthly* 21:50 (1948).

(Japanese Occupation Overprints)
1942–43 Broad Coverage: Gallatly, J.M., *Philatelist* 25:270–72 (1959).

1942 March 16 Double Line Chop: Gallatly, J.M., *Philatelist* 26:220–21 (1960).

1942 April 3 Single-Lined Chops: Gallatly, J.M., *Philatelist* 23:147–51, 235–38 (1957).

SUDAN

1897–1911 Broad Coverage: *Stagg, E.C.W., *Sudan: The Stamps and Postal Stationery of 1867 [sic] to 1970*, Harry Hayes, Batley, West Yorkshire, England, 1977, 144 pp.; Gisburn, H.G.D., and G.S. Thompson, *Stamps and Posts of the Anglo-Egyptian Sudan*, Stanley Gibbons, Ltd., London, 1947, 120 pp.

1897 First Issue Overprints: Thompson, G.S., *Stamp Collecting* 74:397, 407, 409 (1950).

1898–1921 Camel Stamps: Gisburn, H.G.D., *Gibbons Stamp Monthly* 26:68 (1953); Brown, C.B., *Gibbons Stamp Monthly* 26:81 (1953).

SUEZ CANAL

1868 July 8 or 9 to August 15 Local Issue: *d'Humières, J.B., S. Ringström, and H.E. Tester, *The Private Ship Letter Stamps of the World*, Part 3, *The Suez Canal Company*, Leonard H. Hartmann, Louisville, Kentucky, 1985, 285 pp.; Hall, A., *Forgery & Reprint Guide*, no. 14, *Suez Canal*, J. Barefoot Ltd., York, England, 20 pp.

SURINAM

1873–1942 Broad Coverage: *Loo, P.F.A., van de, *Forgeries of Netherlands Stamps and Former Colonies*, English language edition and 1982 Supplement, Netherlands Philatelic Society of Chicago, 1978, 1982, unpaged (looseleaf).

1873 2½¢ King William III Regular Issue: Tyler, V.E., *Linn's Stamp News*, January 22, 1996, p. 8.

1892–93 Queen Wilhelmina Issue: Tyler, comp. ref. 13, p. 136.

1941 First Type Airmails (Perforated 13): Newall, comp. ref. 8, pp. 266–67.

SWAZILAND

1889–94 First Issue Overprints: Pirie, J.H.H., *South African Philatelist* 29:41–44 (1953); 35:109 (1959); Pirie, J.H.H., *Stamps and Postal History of Swaziland and of the New Republic*, Philatelic Federation of South Africa, Johannesburg, no date, pp. 18–26; Pirie, J.H.H., *London Philatelist* 59:54–56 (1950).

SWEDEN

1855–89 Selected Coverage: BPA-Sperati, comp. ref. 2, pp. 172–74 and plates 116–17.

1855–62 Broad Coverage (Reprints): Schloss, comp. ref. 10, pp. 166–67.

1855 3s. First Issue: Menzinsky, G., P. Sjöman, and S. Arerstedt, *London Philatelist* 74:165–66 (1965).

1855 3s. Errors of Color: *Åhman, S., *Den gula treskillingen*, R.M. Skogs Förlags AB, Malmö, 1975, 143 pp., in Swedish with 40 pp. English summary; Färnström, N., *Philatelist* 41:198–99 (1975); Hahn, C.M., *Scott's Monthly Stamp Journal* 62(9):4–9 (1981).

1879 Tretio Ore Error: Färnström, N., *The American Philatelist* 93:521–23 (1979); *Philatelist* 44:234–35 (1978); Tyler, V.E., *Philatelist* 44:302–3 (1978).

1920 First Airmail Overprint Inverts: Newall, comp. ref. 8, pp. 268–69.

SWITZERLAND

1843–81 Broad Coverage: Schloss, comp. ref. 10, pp. 168–190; Ragatz, comp. ref. 9, pp. 132–39.

1843–52 Selected Coverage: BPA-Sperati, comp. ref. 2, pp. 140–56 and plates 96–106.

1843–45 Cantonal Issues: *Reuterskiöld, A. de, *Philatelic Record* 29:29–33, 58–62, 77–79, 93–99, 111–15, 152–55, 176–78, 197–201 (1907). This ancient work still provides the most complete descriptions available of the various types of Cantonal forgeries.

1850–52 Federal Issues: *Kofranek, A., *The American Philatelist* 96:626–31 (1982).

1862–63 1 fr. Bronze Seated Helvetia: Kofranek, A., *The American Philatelist* 99:613–14 (1985).

1882–1907 Standing Helvetias: Caldwell, G.W., *S.P.A. Journal* 28:861–69 (1966).

1913 June 8 Lugano Flight Vignettes (non-Scott): Newall, comp. ref. 8, pp. 270–75.

1919–20 First Airmail Overprints: Newall, comp. ref. 8, pp. 276–77; Aretz, comp. ref. 1, p. 67.

1938 PRO AERO Overprint: Newall, comp. ref. 8, pp. 278–79.

(League of Nations and International Labor Bureau)
1922–43 Broad Coverage: Ganz, F., *The American Philatelist* 97:699–701, 761 (1983); Lesser, R.F., *The American Philatelist* 98:157 (1984).

(United Nations — European Office)
1950 First Issue Overprints: Tuchman, W.W., *Stamps*, June 13, 1970, p. 575.

TASMANIA

1853–99 Broad Coverage: *Pope, M., *Stamp Forgeries of Queensland; South Australia, Tasmania*, published by the author, Birmingham Gardens, New South Wales, 1992, pp. 87–120.

THAILAND

1883 August 4 First Issue: Blair, A., *Stamp Collectors' Fortnightly* 46:28 (1940).

1885 July 1 1 t. Overprints: Pears, W., *Stanley Gibbons Monthly Circular* No. 38:37–47 (1922).

1907 April 24 Provisional Overprints: Rogers, S.E., *Stamps*, May 10, 1975, p. 351; Collins, P., *Linn's Stamp News*, October 22, 1984, p. 46.

1918 Red Cross Semipostal Overprints: Smith, E.W., *Stamp Lover* 24:124 (1931).

1918 December 2 Victory Overprints: Zerner, L.W., *Stamp Lover* 27:181–84 (1934); Woodward, P.B., *Thai Philately* 1(4):66 (1978).

1939 June 24 10s. Constitution Stamp: Anon. *Philatelic Magazine* 82:499, 503 (1974).

THRACE

1913 Overprints (Scott 16–33): Aretz, comp. ref. 1, p. 68.

THURN AND TAXIS

1852–67 Broad Coverage: *Stiedl-Billig, comp. ref. 12, Thurn und Taxis; Schloss, Germany ref. 2, pp. 96–103.

1852–67 Reprints: Gilgis, Germany ref. 3, vol. 3–4, pp. 42–44.

1852–67 Selected Cancellations: Bohne, Germany ref. 1.

TIBET

Because of the crude nature of the original stamps and the numerous forgeries of them, the most useful works on counterfeit detection are those that permit plating of the genuine. The following starred references are most useful for this purpose.

1912–50 First Issue: *Bibbins, F., *Tibet: First Series, 1912: Plating Notebook*, Geoffrey Flack, Vancouver, B.C., Canada, 1992, 42 pp.; Waterfall, A.C., *The Postal History of Tibet*, 2nd ed., Pall Mall Stamp Company Ltd., 1981, pp. 146–54.

1933 Third Issue: *Bibbins, F., and G. Flack, *Tibet: Third Series, 1933-60: Plating Study*, Geoffrey Flack, Vancouver, British Columbia, Canada, 1993, 63 pp.; Waterfall, A.C., *op. cit.*, pp. 85–118, 155–59.

TRANSVAAL

1869–1903 Broad Coverage: *Mathews, I.B., et. al., *Transvaal Philately*, Reijger Publishers (Pty) Limited, Cape Town, 1986, 292 pp.

1869–79 First Republic Issues: Meisel, N., *The Transvaal Handbook*, vol. 1, published by the author, Brackendowns, South Africa, 1985, 118 pp.

1869–76 First Two Designs: Luff, J.N., *Otto's Printings of the Transvaal Stamps*, The Philatelic Record, London, 1913, 40 pp. This old reference still provides the most detailed information available on these issues.

1885–1902 Broad Coverage: McKee, H.J.A., *Philatelist* 10:2–5 (1942); Tyler, V.E., *The Congress Book* 37:173–79 (1971).

1885–93 Overprints: Pemberton, P.L., *Philatelic Journal of Great Britain* 52:77–79 (1942).

1900 £5 V.R.I. Overprint: Holmes, H.R., *London Philatelist* 95:210–11 (1986); Mathews, I.B., *London Philatelist* 96:55–56 (1987).

1902–3 £5 King Edward Design: Melville, F.J., *Stamp Collectors' Fortnightly* 28:367 (1922).

TURKEY

1863–1917 Broad Coverage: *Stiedl-Billig, comp. ref. 12, Türkei, 2 parts.

1863 First Issue: Schloss, comp. ref. 1, pp. 191–94.

1876, January Overprints: Tyler, comp. ref. 13, p. 137.

1876, September 50p. Stamp: Tyler, comp. ref. 13, p. 138.

1879–92 Various Issues: Higlett, G.A., *Philatelic Magazine* 15:227, 294 (1925).

1886–1909 Selected Issues: BPA-Sperati, comp. ref. 2, pp. 174–77 and plates 117–18.

1901–5 Printed Matter Overprints: Pugh, K.W., *Linn's Stamp News*, April 4, 1977, p. 36; April 18, 1977, p. 66.

(Occupation of Thessaly)
1898 Octagonal Military Stamps: Sousa, J.M., *The American Philatelist* 79: 337 (1966); Bentley, G.W., *Philatelic Journal of Great Britain* 51:63–65, 83 (1941); Ure, B., *Bulletin of the Hellenic P.S. of G.B.* No. 98:5–7 (1996).

(Constantinople Local Post)
1865 Liannos Issue: Tyler, comp. ref. 13, p.139.

TURKEY IN ASIA (ANATOLIA)

1920–22 Comprehensive Coverage: *Mayo, M. M., *Anatolia*, published by the author, Ivy, Virginia, 1990, 392 pp. and unpaged *Concordance & Inventory*.

TURKS ISLANDS

1867–79 First Two Issues: Spying Eye, comp. ref. 11, p. 45.

TUSCANY

1851–60 Broad Coverage: *Stiedl-Billig,

---

comp. ref. 12, Toskana; Schloss, comp. ref. 10, pp. 195–99.

1851 2 s. and 1857 1 s. Stamps: BPA-Sperati, comp. ref. 2, p. 107 and plate 66.

TWO SICILIES

(Naples)
1858–60 Broad Coverage: *Stiedl-Billig, comp. ref. 12, Neapel; Schloss, comp. ref. 10, pp. 80–90.

(Sicily)
1859 Bomba Heads: *Stiedl-Billig, comp. ref. 12, Sizilien; Schloss, comp. ref. 10, pp. 146–49.

(Neopolitan Provinces)
1861 King Victor Emmanuel II Issue: *Stiedl-Billig, comp. ref. 12, Italien and Neapel; Schloss, comp. ref. 10, pp. 55–57.

UKRAINE

1918–20 Comprehensive Coverage: *Ceresa, Russia ref. 1B, Ukraine, 26 parts.

UNITED NATIONS

1951–1957 Fake SPECIMEN Overprints on Selected Issues: Corrinet, M.S., *Linn's Stamp News*, August 5, 1991, p. 12.

1951 1¹/₂ c. Stamp Precancelled: Linn, G.W., *Linn's Weekly Stamp News*, February 9, 1959, pp. 1, 20, 22. (The figure in this article is incorrectly labeled. Be sure to use it with the corrections noted in the February 23, 1959, issue, p. 20); March 16, 1959, p. 4; March 23, 1959, pp. 4, 26; April 6, 1959, p. 4; Lawrence, K., *Scott Stamp Monthly* 13(4): 38–40 (1995); Gaines, A., *Linn's Stamp News*, January 1, 1996, p. 34.

1951 December 14 15c. Prussian Blue Airmail Error: Conway, H.E., *Linn's Stamp News*, September 26, 1977, p. 50.

1954 October 25 3c. United Nations Day Stamp: Anon., *The American Philatelist* 94:298 (1980).

UNITED STATES

(Postage Stamps)
Nineteenth Century Issues — Fakes: Mooz, W.E., *The American Philatelist* 98:791–93 (1984); Christian, C.W.B., *The American Philatelist* 98:635–36 (1984); Christian, C.W.B., *The American Philatelist* 98:219–21, 278 (1984).

1847 5c. Franklin Stamp: Brookman, L.G., *The United States Postage Stamps of the 19th Century*, vol. 1, H.L. Lindquist Publications, Inc., New York, 1966, p. 26, 98–102.

1847 10c. Washington: Brookman, L.G., *op. cit.* pp. 86–89, 98–102; BPA-Sperati, comp. ref. 2, p. 196 and plate 132.

1860 90c. Blue Washington: Ragatz, L., ed., *The Spud Papers*, Emile Bertrand, Lucerne, no date, p. 77; Brookman, L.G., *op. cit.* p. 267.

1863 2c. Black Jack: Johnson, comp. ref. 6 I, pp. 35–36.

1865 Newspaper Stamps: Braceland, J.F., Jr., *United States Specialist* 38:68–69 (1967);

---

*Mooz, W.E., *The American Philatelist* 98:424–28 (1984).

1867–71 Various Grills: *Christian, C.W.B., *The American Philatelist* 97:412–14, 599–601, 808–10 (1983).

1869 12c. S.S. Adriatic: Laurence, M., *Linn's Stamp News*, July 27, 1992, p. 3; August 10, 1992, p. 3.

1869 90 c. Lincoln: Brookman, L.G., *op. cit.*, vol. 2, p. 186.

1873 Dollar Values State Department Officials: *Mooz, W.E., *The American Philatelist* 101:155–58 (1987).

1873 Cancels on SPECIMEN Overprinted Officials: Mooz, W.E., *The American Philatelist* 98:888–91 (1984).

1875 First Issue Official Imitations: Rose, J., *Linn's Stamp News*, September 24, 1984, p. 3.

1875–85 Newspaper Stamps: *Braceland, J.F., Jr., *United States Specialist* 40:30–32, 62–65, 156–61, 248–51 (1969); Mooz, W.E., *The American Philatelist* 98:609–14 (1984).

1875–83 Department SPECIMEN Stamps: Mooz, W.E., *The American Philatelist* 98:307–12 (1984).

1883, October 1 2c. Washington: Herst, H., Jr., *Stamp Collector*, July 29, 1985, p. 15.

1893 Columbian Issue: Tyler, V.E., *Philatelic Forgers: Their Lives and Works*, rev. ed., Linn's Stamp News, Sidney, Ohio, 1991, pp. 65–66, 69–70.

1894 2c. Type I Washington, Unwatermarked: Collins, P., *Philatelist* 43:353–54 (1977); Petschel, H.K., *The American Philatelist* 97:62–64 (1983); Diehl, K., *United States Specialist* 66:204–11, 345–46 (1995).

1895 2c. Type III Washington, Watermarked: Diehl, K., *United States Specialist* 66:278–79 (1995).

1895–1978 Postal Forgeries: *Petschel, H.K., *Spurious Stamps: A History of U.S. Postal Counterfeits,* American Philatelic Society, State College, Pennsylvania, 1997, 265 pp.

1908–23 Washington-Franklin Issue Fakes: *Schmid, Paul W., *The Expert's Book*, Palm Press, Huntington, New York, 1990, 210 pp.

1909 2c. Lincoln First Day Covers: Sine, R.L., *The American Philatelist* 98:1207 (1984).

1907 1c. Jamestown Commemorative: Rowe, M., *The American Philatelist* 109:332–33 (1995).

1918–20 2c. Washington, Type VI (Scott 528A): Collins, P., *Philatelist* 43:354–55 (1977); Bennett, D.M., *United States Specialist* 49:55–57 (1978).

1918 24c. Airmail Invert: Cheavin, W.H.S., *Philately* (London) 3:54–55 (1950).

1922–25 Regular Issue First Day Covers: Griffith, G., *Stamp Collector*, May 27, 1996, pp. 1, 12.

1923–38 2c. Washington, (Scott Design Type A157): Collins, P., *Philatelist* 43:355 (1977); Hartmann, L.H., *The American Philatelist* 77:903 (1964); Tyler, comp. ref. 13, p. 141.

1928 Roessler GRAF ZEPPELIN Overprints: Couter, W.T. *The American Philatelist* 98:527-28 (1984).

1929 Kansas-Nebraska Overprints: *Schoen, R.H., *The American Philatelist* 86:303-10 (1972); DeVoss, J.T., *The American Philatelist* 86:310-12 (1972); Huntington, O., *How Are Your Kansas-Nebraskas?*, Western Stamp Collector, Albany, Oregon, 1948, 15 pp; Lawrence, K., *Linn's Stamp News*, August 20, 1990, pp. 1, 20; Anon., *Linn's Stamp News*, December 5, 1994, p. 10.

1930 April 19 $2.60 Zeppelin Stamp: Boggs, W., *Collectors Club Philatelist* 32:98, 106 (1953); Sloane, G.B., *Stamps*, May 16, 1953; Boughner, F., *Linn's Stamp News*, April 14, 1975, p. 58.

1938-54 3c. Washington Presidential: DeVoss, J.T., *The American Philatelist* 91:969-70 (1977); Tyler, V.E., *Linn's Stamp News*, March 18, 1996, p. 6.

1954-74 Various Issues: Petschel, H.K., *The American Philatelist* 96:227-29, 284 (1982).

1954-68 4c. Lincoln Liberty Issue: Faries, B., *Western Stamp Collector*, November 11, 1961, p. 5; Anon., *Stamps*, November 18, 1961, p. 334; Lawrence, K., *The American Philatelist* 106:1003-5 (1992).

1954-68 1/2c. Franklin and 30c. Lee Liberty Stamps: Faries, B., *S.P.A. Journal* 28:428-30 (1966); Lawrence, K., *The American Philatelist* 106:1003-5 (1992).

1954-68 10c. Independence Hall Liberty Issue: Youngblood, W.L., *Linn's Stamp News*, October 15, 1990, p. 24; November 16, 1992, p. 42.

1954-68 $1 Patrick Henry Liberty Issue: Youngblood, W.L., *Linn's Stamp News*, October 15, 1990, p. 24; Lawrence, K., *The American Philatelist* 108:148 (1994).

1965-78 13c. Kennedy Prominent Americans (Scott 1287): Petschel, H.K., *Stamps*, July 23, 1977, p. 195.

1965-78 15c. Holmes Prominent Americans: Youngblood, W.L., *Linn's Stamp News*, September 16, 1991, p. 24.

1970-74 6c. Eisenhower Regular Issue: Anon., *The American Philatelist* 85:692-93 (1971); Tyler, V.E., *Linn's Stamp News*, June 26, 1995, p. 6.

1970-74 8c. Multicolored Eisenhower Regular Issue: Anon., *The American Philatelist* 88:307-9 (1974).

1973-74 10c. Crossed Flags (Scott 1509): Petschel, H.K., *Stamps*, July 23, 1977, pp. 194-95.

1973-74 10c. Jefferson Memorial: DeVoss, James T., *The American Philatelist* 95:34 (1981).

1975-81 Liberty Bell Americana Issue: Youngblood, W.L., *Linn's Stamp News*, July 15, 1991, p. 24.

1975-81 13c. Liberty Bell Coil: Anon., *Stamp Collector*, August 28, 1976, p. 1; Petschel, H.K., *Linn's Stamp News*, March 16, 1981, p. 78.

1981 December 17 20c. Flag Over Supreme Court Building (Scott 1894): Youngblood, W., *Linn's Stamp News*, May 20, 1991, p. 26.

1984-91 Leonard Coleman's Photocopy Forgeries (20c. Truman, 5c. Milk Wagon, 19c. Fawn, and 19c. Balloon): Anon., *Linn's Stamp News*, June 28, 1993, p. 20; Schreiber, M., *Linn's Stamp News*, July 19, 1993, pp. 1 and 10.

1986-91 Jack London Great American Issue: Youngblood, W.L., *Linn's Stamp News*, November 16, 1992, p. 42.

(Offices in China)

1913 Unauthorized SHANGHAI CHINA Overprints: Sicker, J., *Linn's Stamp News*, September 15, 1986, p. 10.

1919 2c. Overprint on 1c. Stamp: Anon., *The American Philatelist* 107:1147 (1993).

(Carriers and Locals)

There are literally hundreds of references in the literature dealing with forgeries of the stamps of the scores of Carriers and Independent Local Posts that existed in the United States during the mid- to late-nineteenth century. To list them individually would be a formidable and lengthy task. Consequently, only a few general references and indications of the location of more specific information are included here.

Chapier, G., *et al.*, *Les Timbres de Fantaisie*, vol. 2, privately published, no location given, no date, pp. 128-43, in French.

*Lyons, L., *The Identifier for Carriers, Locals, Fakes, Forgeries and Bogus Posts of the United States*, vols. 1&2, published by the author, Westport, Connecticut, 1998, 909 pp.

*Patton, D.S., *Philatelist*, 74 articles, vols. 23 to 31: (1957-1965), see Index 31:208-209 (1965).

*Patton, D. S., *The Private Local Posts of the United States*, vol. 1, *New York State*, Robson Lowe Ltd., London, 1967, 350 pp.

Penny Post, all issues, vol. 1, January 1991 to date.

Perry, E., ed., *Byways of Philately: Privately-Owned Posts and Early Locals*, Mrs. H.W.K. Hale, no location given, 1966, 271 pp.

*Perry, E., *Pat Paragraphs*, Bureau Issues Association, Takoma Park, Maryland, 1981, various pp., especially 347-490.

Springer, S., ed., *Springer's Handbook of North American Cinderella Stamps*, 9th ed., Sherwood Springer, Hawthorne, California, 1980, pp. 25-48.

(Postal Stationery)

1853-76 Envelope Cut-Squares Broad Coverage: *Wells, L.E., *Stamps*, December 29, 1945, pp. 524-25; Sloane, G.B., *Sloane's Column*, Bureau Issues Association, West Somerville, Massachusetts, 1961, pp. 123-24.

1860-61 1c. and 10c. Star Die Cut-Squares: Youngblood, W.L., *Linn's Stamp News*, December 17, 1990, p. 44.

1876 Centennial Issue: Maisel, W., *Baltimore Philatelist* 20(1):4-5 (1967).

1894-97 Jefferson Postal Cards: Stratton, F.B., *The American Philatelist* 98:121-29, 182 (1984); Youngblood, W., *Linn's Stamp News*, March 18, 1991, p. 38.

1899-1920 Various Envelope Fakes: Slawson, G.C., *Postal Stationery* No. 136:246-55 (1969).

1902 McKinley Full Face Postal Card: Fricke, C.A., *The American Philatelist* 96:824-25 (1982); O'Keefe, D., *Linn's Stamp News*, July 29, 1985, p. 50.

1945 6c. Airmail Overprints: O'Keefe, D., *Linn's Stamp News*, October 22, 1979, p. 28.

(War Savings Stamps)

1919 $5 Franklin: Anon., *The American Philatelist* 33:59 (1919); 33:323, 383 (1920).

URUGUAY

1856-1931 Broad Coverage: *Hoffmann, R., *Estudio de las Falsificaciones de los Sellos Postales del Uruguay*, Club Filatelico del Uruguay, Montevideo, 1948, 115 pp., in Spanish.

1866-67 1c. Numeral Issue: Tyler, comp. ref. 13, p. 143.

1859 80c. Thin Numerals Stamp: Pack, C.L., *Philatelic Gazette* 2:81-82 (1911).

1882 2c. Regular Issue: Tyler, V.E., *Linn's Stamp News*, March 21, 1994, p. 6.

1908 Gunboat Issue: Kerst, H., *The American Philatelist* 98:699-700, 764 (1984); Paulos, F.D., *The American Philatelist* 101:841-48 (1987).

1925 August 25 Airmails: Newall, comp. ref. 8, pp. 293-94; Watchorn, H., *Mekeel's Weekly Stamp News* 95:76 (1960).

1926 Albatross Airmail Issue: Tyler, comp. ref. 13, p. 145.

1929-30 Punched Official Airmails: Kerst, H., *The American Philatelist* 100:146-49 (1986).

1935 Albatross Airmails: Anon., *Sanabria Airpost News*, No. 30:24-25 (1945).

1939-44 Plane and Oxcart Airmails: Tyler, comp. ref. 13, p. 146; Watchorn, H., *The American Philatelist* 83:696 (1969).

1990 1000p. Artigas Portrait Stamp (Scott 1339): Baumann, F., *Linn's Stamp News*, September 6, 1993, p. 9.

1947-49 High Value National Airport Airmails: Newall, comp. ref. 8, p. 295.

VENEZUELA

1859-70 Broad Coverage: Collyer, A.E., translator, *Stamp Lover* 16:77-78 (1923).

1863 1r. Regular Issue: Tyler, comp. ref. 13, p. 147.

1880 Bolivar Regular Issue: Aretz, comp. ref. 1, pp. 70-71; Tyler, comp. ref. 13, p. 148.

1892 Resolucion Overprints: MacPeek, D. L., *Pan-American Philatelist* 1:143-51 (1955); 2:59 (1955).

1893 25c. Discovery Commemorative: Tyler, V.E., *Linn's Stamp News*, January 23, 1995, p. 6.

1893 Bolivar Instruccion Issue: Spying Eye, *Philately* (St. Louis) 2:210 (1946).

1896 Miranda (Map) Issue: *Hall, T.W., and L.W. Fulcher, *London Philatelist* 29:282-84 (1920), 30:2-3, 30-31, 191-95, 218-22 (1921); 5c. value, Tyler, comp. ref. 13, p. 149.

1900 25c. and 50c. 1900 Overprints: De Lozada, J.S., *The American Philatelist* **58**:444-48 (1945).

1930 Airmail Issue: The so-called forgeries described by Spying Eye, comp. ref. 11, pp. 46-47, now are believed to be genuine copies of additional printings of this series. See Anon. *ASDA Bulletin*, March 1952, p. 4.

(Guyana Locals)

1903 Small Guyanas: *Wickersham, C.W., *Collectors Club Philatelist* **30**:25-38 (1951).

1903 Large Guyanas: *Wickersham, C.W., *Collectors Club Philatelist* **31**:47-55 (1952).

VICTORIA

1850-94 Broad Coverage: Cowman, A.R., *Stamp Lover* **27**:177-80 (1934).

1850-59 Jeffry's Half-Lengths, Enthroned, and Octagonal Forgeries: Purves, J.R.W., *Philatelist* **42**:295-99 (1976); Branston, A.J., *Philatelist* **43**:23 (1976).

1852-54 Victoria Enthroned Stamps: Johnson, comp. ref. 6 II, p.46.

WADHWAN

1888-89 Definitive Stamp: *Benns, R.J., *The Stamps of Wadhwan*, The India Study Circle for Philately, Eastleigh, Hampshire, United Kingdom, 1990, 55 pp.

WESTERN AUSTRALIA

1854-1912 Comprehensive Coverage: *Pope, M., *Stamps Forgeries of Western Australia*, published by the author, Birmingham Gardens, New South Wales, Australia, 1993, 108 pp.

1854-93 Broad Coverage: Cowman, A.R., *Stamp Lover* **27**:228, 264, 285-86 (1935).

WESTERN UKRAINE

1918-19 Broad Coverage: Bulat, J., *Illustrated Postage Stamp History of Western Ukranian Republic 1918-1919*, Philatelic Publications, Yonkers, New York, 1973, 96 pp.

(Romanian Occupation of Pokutia)

1919 C.M.T. Overprints: Kronenberg, S., *Romanian Philatelic Studies* **8**(1):12-13 (1984).

WHITE RUSSIA

1920 Young Couple Series: *Ceresa, R.J., Russia ref. 1C, parts 16-18, pp. 67-82; Sutton, R.J., *Philatelic Magazine* **67**:14-15 (1959); Spying Eye, comp. ref. 11, pp. 47-48.

WUHU

1894 1c. Regular Issue: Tyler, comp. ref. 13, p. 150.

WURTTEMBERG

1851-1906 Broad Coverage: *Stiedl-Billig, comp. ref. 12, Württemberg.

1851-73 Broad Coverage: Schloss, Germany ref. 2, pp. 104-8.

1851-52 First Issue Reprints: Gilgis, Germany ref. 3, vol. 3-4, pp. 39-41.

1851 1kr. Stamp: Aretz, comp. ref. 1, p. 72.

1852 18kr. Stamp: Bohne, Germany ref. 1; BPA-Sperati, comp. ref. 2, pp. 96-97 and plate 56.

1875 2m. Yellow Stamp: BPA-Sperati, comp. ref. 2, p. 97 and plate 56.

YEMEN

1926 First Issue: Conde, B., *Linn's Weekly Stamp News*, August 25, 1958, p. 14.

Index to *The Serrane Guide*

This index lists countries, colonies, states, and other entities as they originally appeared in the two-volume *Vade-Mecum*.